Children's
Literature
Review

Guide to Gale Literary Criticism Series

For criticism on	Consult these Gale series
Authors now living or who died after December 31, 1959	*CONTEMPORARY LITERARY CRITICISM (CLC)*
Authors who died between 1900 and 1959	*TWENTIETH-CENTURY LITERARY CRITICISM (TCLC)*
Authors who died between 1800 and 1899	*NINETEENTH-CENTURY LITERATURE CRITICISM (NCLC)*
Authors who died between 1400 and 1799	*LITERATURE CRITICISM FROM 1400 TO 1800 (LC)* *SHAKESPEAREAN CRITICISM (SC)*
Authors who died before 1400	*CLASSICAL AND MEDIEVAL LITERATURE CRITICISM (CMLC)*
Authors of books for children and young adults	*CHILDREN'S LITERATURE REVIEW (CLR)*
Dramatists	*DRAMA CRITICISM (DC)*
Poets	*POETRY CRITICISM (PC)*
Short story writers	*SHORT STORY CRITICISM (SSC)*
Black writers of the past two hundred years	*BLACK LITERATURE CRITICISM (BLC)*
Hispanic writers of the late nineteenth and twentieth centuries	*HISPANIC LITERATURE CRITICISM (HLC)*
Native North American writers and orators of the eighteenth, nineteenth, and twentieth centuries	*NATIVE NORTH AMERICAN LITERATURE (NNAL)*
Major authors from the Renaissance to the present	*WORLD LITERATURE CRITICISM, 1500 TO THE PRESENT (WLC)*

ISSN 0362-4145

volume 54

Children's Literature Review

Excerpts from Reviews,
Criticism, and Commentary
on Books for Children
and Young People

Deborah J. Morad
Editor

The Gale Group

DETROIT • SAN FRANCISCO • LONDON • BOSTON • WOODBRIDGE, CT

STAFF

Deborah J. Morad, *Editor*

Deborah Conn, Sara Constantakis, Catherine Goldstein, Sharon Gunton, Alan Hedblad, Motoko Fujishiro
Huthwaite, Arlene Johnson, Paul Loeber, Thomas McMahon, Malinda Mayer, Gerard J. Senick, Diane Telgen,
Stephen Tschirhart, Kathleen Witman, *Contributing Editors*

Karen Uchic, *Technical Training Specialist*

Joyce Nakamura, *Managing Editor*

Maria Franklin, *Permissions Manager*
Sarah Chesney, Edna Hedblad, Michele Lonoconus, *Permissions Associates*

Victoria B. Cariappa, *Research Manager*
Corrine A. Stocker, *Project Coordinator*
Tracie A. Richardson, Cheryl D. Warnock, *Research Associates*
Patricia Tsune Ballard, Phyllis P. Blackman, Wendy K. Festerling *Research Assistants*

Mary Beth Trimper, *Production Director*
Deborah Milliken, *Production Assistant*

Gary Leach, *Graphic Artist*
Randy Bassett, *Image Database Supervisor*
Robert Duncan, Michael Logusz, *Imaging Specialists*
Pamela A. Reed, *Imaging Coordinator*

Library of Congress Catalog Card Number 76-643301
ISBN 0-7876-2082-3
ISSN 0362-4145
Printed in the United States of America

10 9 8 7 6 5 4 3 2 1

Contents

Preface   vii
Acknowledgements   xi

Nathan Aaseng 1953- 1
  (Also writes as Nate Aaseng) American author of nonfiction and fiction; major works include the series "You Are the Coach" *(1983-86) and* "Nobel Prize Winners" *(1987).*

Karen Hesse 1952- 26
  American author of fiction, picture books, and poetry; major works include Letters from Rifka *(1992) and* Out of the Dust *(1997).*

Colin McNaughton 1951- 43
  English illustrator and author of picture books; major works include Jolly Roger and the Pirates of Abdul the Skinhead *(1988) and* Have You Seen Who's Just Moved in Next Door to Us? *(1991).*

Sheldon Oberman 1949- 69
  Canadian author of fiction and plays; major works include The Always Prayer Shawl *(1994) and* The White Stone in the Castle Wall *(1995).*

Gary Paulsen 1939- 80
  American author of fiction and nonfiction; major works include The Winter Room *(1989) and* Soldier's Heart *(1998).*

(Jerry) Brian Pinkney 1961- 127
  (Also known as J. Brian Pinkney) African-American illustrator and author of picture books; major works include Sukey and the Mermaid *(1992) and* The Adventures of Sparrowboy *(1997).*

Laura E(lizabeth Howe) Richards 1850-1943 150
  American author of fiction, nonfiction, poetry, biography, autobiography, and plays; major works include Captain January *(1891) and* Tirra Lirra: Rhymes Old and New *(1932).*

Laurence Michael Yep 1948- 175
  Chinese-American author of fiction, nonfiction, picture books, plays, and retellings; major works include The Rainbow People *(1989) and* Dragon's Gate *(1993).*

Cumulative Index to Authors   207
Cumulative Index to Nationalities   223
Cumulative Index to Titles   229

Preface

Literature for children and young adults has evolved into both a respected branch of creative writing and a successful industry. Currently, books for young readers are considered among the most popular segments of publishing. Criticism of juvenile literature is instrumental in recording the literary or artistic development of the creators of children's books as well as the trends and controversies that result from changing values or attitudes about young people and their literature. Designed to provide a permanent, accessible record of this ongoing scholarship, *Children's Literature Review (CLR)* presents parents, teachers, and librarians—those responsible for bringing children and books together—with the opportunity to make informed choices when selecting reading materials for the young. In addition, *CLR* provides researchers of children's literature with easy access to a wide variety of critical information from English-language sources in the field. Users will find balanced overviews of the careers of the authors and illustrators of the books that children and young adults are reading; these entries, which contain excerpts from published criticism in books and periodicals, assist users by sparking ideas for papers and assignments and suggesting supplementary and classroom reading. Ann L. Kalkhoff, president and editor of *Children's Book Review Service Inc.,* writes that "*CLR* has filled a gap in the field of children's books, and it is one series that will never lose its validity or importance."

Scope of the Series

Each volume of *CLR* profiles the careers of a selection of authors and illustrators of books for children and young adults from preschool through high school. Author lists in each volume reflect:

- an international scope.

- representation of authors of all eras.

- the variety of genres covered by children's and/or YA literature: picture books, fiction, nonfiction, poetry, folklore, and drama.

Although the focus of the series is on authors new to *CLR*, entries will be updated as the need arises.

Organization of This Book

An entry consists of the following elements: author heading, author portrait, author introduction, excerpts of criticism (each preceded by a bibliographical citation), and illustrations, when available.

- The **Author Heading** consists of the author's name followed by birth and death dates. The portion of the name outside the parentheses denotes the form under which the author is most frequently published. If the majority of the author's works for children were written under a pseudonym, the pseudonym will be listed in the author heading and the real name given on the first line of the author introduction. Also located at the beginning of the introduction are any other pseudonyms used by the author in writing for children and any name variations, including transliterated forms for authors whose languages use nonroman alphabets. Uncertainty as to a birth or death date is indicated by question marks.

- An **Author Portrait** is included when available.

- The **Author Introduction** contains information designed to introduce an author to *CLR* users by presenting an overview of the author's themes and styles, biographical facts that relate to the author's literary career or critical responses to the author's works, and information about major awards and prizes the author has received. The introduction begins by identifying the nationality of the author and by listing the genres in which s/he has written for children and young adults. Introductions also list a group of representative titles for which the author or illustrator being profiled is best known; this section, which begins with the words "major works include," follows the genre line of the introduction. For seminal figures, a listing of major works about the author follows when appropriate, highlighting important biographies about the author or illustrator that are not excerpted in the entry. The centered heading "Introduction" announces the body of the text.

- **Criticism** is located in three sections: **Author's Commentary** (when available), **General Commentary** (when available), and **Title Commentary** (commentary on specific titles).

  - The **Author's Commentary** presents background material written by the author or by an interviewer. This commentary may cover a specific work or several works. Author's commentary on more than one work appears after the author introduction, while commentary on an individual book follows the title entry heading.

  - The **General Commentary** consists of critical excerpts that consider more than one work by the author or illustrator being profiled. General commentary is preceded by the critic's name in boldface type or, in the case of unsigned criticism, by the title of the journal. *CLR* also features entries that emphasize general criticism on the oeuvre of an author or illustrator. When appropriate, a selection of reviews is included to supplement the general commentary.

  - The **Title Commentary** begins with the title entry headings, which precede the criticism on a title and cite publication information on the work being reviewed. Title headings list the title of the work as it appeared in its first English-language edition. The first English-language publication date of each work (unless otherwise noted) is listed in parentheses following the title. Differing U.S. and British titles follow the publication date within the parentheses. When a work is written by an individual other than the one being profiled, as is the case when illustrators are featured, the parenthetical material following the title cites the author of the work before listing its publication date.

    Entries in each title commentary section consist of critical excerpts on the author's individual works, arranged chronologically by publication date. The entries generally contain two to seven reviews per title, depending on the stature of the book and the amount of criticism it has generated. The editors select titles that reflect the entire scope of the author's literary contribution, covering each genre and subject. An effort is made to reprint criticism that represents the full range of each title's reception, from the year of its initial publication to current assessments. Thus, the reader is provided with a record of the author's critical history. Publication information (such as publisher names and book prices) and parenthetical numerical references (such as footnotes or page and line references to specific editions of works) have been deleted at the discretion of the editors to provide smoother reading of the text.

- Centered headings introduce each section, in which criticism is arranged chronologically; beginning with Volume 35, each excerpt is preceded by a boldface source heading for easier access by readers. Within the text, titles by authors being profiled are also highlighted in boldface type.

- Selected excerpts are preceded by **Explanatory Annotations,** which provide information on the critic or work of criticism to enhance the reader's understanding of the excerpt.

- A complete **Bibliographical Citation** designed to facilitate the location of the original book or article precedes each piece of criticism.

- Numerous **Illustrations** are featured in *CLR*. For entries on illustrators, an effort has been made to include illustrations that reflect the characteristics discussed in the criticism. Entries on authors who do not illustrate their own works may also include photographs and other illustrative material pertinent to their careers.

Special Features: Entries on Illustrators

Entries on authors who are also illustrators will occasionally feature commentary on selected works illustrated but not written by the author being profiled. These works are strongly associated with the illustrator and have received critical acclaim for their art. By including critical comment on works of this type, the editors wish to provide a more complete representation of the artist's career. Criticism on these works has been chosen to stress artistic, rather than literary, contributions. Title entry headings for works illustrated by the author being profiled are arranged chronologically within the entry by date of publication and include notes identifying the author of the illustrated work. In order to provide easier access for users, all titles illustrated by the subject of the entry are boldfaced.

CLR also includes entries on prominent illustrators who have contributed to the field of children's literature. These entries are designed to represent the development of the illustrator as an artist rather than as a literary stylist. The illustrator's section is organized like that of an author, with two exceptions: the introduction presents an overview of the illustrator's styles and techniques rather than outlining his or her literary background, and the commentary written by the illustrator on his or her works is called "illustrator's commentary" rather than "author's commentary." All titles of books containing illustrations by the artist being profiled are highlighted in boldface type.

Other Features: Acknowledgments, Indexes

- The **Acknowledgments** section, which immediately follows the preface, lists the sources from which material has been reprinted in the volume. It does not, however, list every book or periodical consulted for the volume.

- The **Cumulative Index to Authors** lists all of the authors who have appeared in *CLR* with cross-references to the biographical, autobiographical, and literary criticism series published by The Gale Group. A full listing of the series titles appears before the first page of the indexes of this volume.

- The **Cumulative Index to Nationalities** lists authors alphabetically under their respective nationalities. Author names are followed by the volume number(s) in which they appear.

- The **Cumulative Index to Titles** lists titles covered in *CLR* followed by the volume and page number where criticism begins.

A Note to the Reader

CLR is one of several critical references sources in the Literature Criticism Series published by The Gale Group. When writing papers, students who quote directly from any volume in the Literature Criticism Series may use the following general forms to footnote reprinted criticism. The first example pertains to material drawn from periodicals, the second to material reprinted from books.

[1]T. S. Eliot, "John Donne," *The Nation and the Athenaeum,* 33 (9 June 1923), 321-32; excerpted and reprinted in *Literature Criticism from 1400 to 1800,* Vol. 10, ed. James E. Person, Jr. (Detroit: Gale Research, 1989), pp. 28-9.

[1]Henry Brooke, *Leslie Brooke and Johnny Crow* (Frederick Warne, 1982); excerpted and reprinted in *Children's Literature Review,* Vol. 20, ed. Gerard J. Senick (Detroit: Gale Research, 1990), p. 47.

Suggestions Are Welcome

In response to various suggestions, several features have been added to *CLR* since the beginning of the series, including author entries on retellers of traditional literature as well as those who have been the first to record oral tales and other folklore; entries on prominent illustrators featuring commentary on their styles and techniques; entries on authors whose works are considered controversial; occasional entries devoted to criticism on a single work or a series of works; sections in author introductions that list major works by and about the author or illustrator being profiled; explanatory notes that provide information on the critic or work of criticism to enhance the usefulness of the excerpt; more extensive illustrative material, such as holographs of manuscript pages and photographs of people and places pertinent to the careers of the authors and artists; a cumulative nationality index for easy access to authors by nationality; and occasional guest essays written specifically for *CLR* by prominent critics on subjects of their choice.

Readers who wish to suggest authors to appear in future volumes, or who have other suggestions, are cordially invited to contact the editor. By mail: Editor, *Children's Literature Review,* The Gale Group, 27500 Drake Road, Farmington Hills, MI 48331-3535; by telephone: (800) 347-GALE; by fax: (248) 699-8065.

Acknowledgments

The editors wish to thank the copyright holders of the excerpted criticism included in this volume and the permissions managers of many book and magazine publishing companies for assisting us in securing reproduction rights. We are also grateful to the staffs of the Detroit Public Library, the Library of Congress, the University of Detroit Mercy Library, Wayne State University Purdy/Kresge Library Complex, and the University of Michigan Libraries for making their resources available to us. Following is a list of the copyright holders who have granted us permission to reproduce material in this volume of *CLR*. Every effort has been made to trace copyright, but if omissions have been made, please let us know.

COPYRIGHTED EXCERPTS IN *CLR*, VOLUME 54, WERE REPRODUCED FROM THE FOLLOWING PERIODICALS:

The ALAN Review, v. 19, Spring, 1992; v. 22, Fall, 1994; v. 25, Spring, 1998. All reproduced by permission. —*Appraisal: Science Books for Young People*, v. 22, Winter-Spring, 1989. Copyright © 1989 by the Children's Science Book Review Committee. Reproduced by permission.—*Booklist*, v. 77, September 1, 1980; v. 77, January 1, 1981; v. 77, July 15-August, 1981; v. 78, December 1, 1981; v. 79, October 1, 1982; v. 89, July, 1983; v. 80, October 1, 1983; v. 80, April 1, 1984; v. 81, October 1, 1984; v. 81, July, 1985; v. 82, October 1, 1985; v. 82, July, 1986; v. 83, September 15, 1986; v. 83, March 1, 1987; v. 84, September 15, 1987; v. 84, January 1, 1988; v. 84, February 1, 1988; v. 84, March 15, 1988; v. 85, February 1, 1989; v. 85, April 1, 1989; v. 85, May 1, 1989; v. 85, July, 1989; v. 86, October 1, 1989; v. 86, November 1, 1989; v. 86, December 15, 1989; v. 86, March 1, 1990; v. 86, May 15, 1990; v. 86, August, 1990; v. 87, October 1, 1990; v. 87, January 15, 1991; v. 87, March 15, 1991; v. 87, May 15, 1991; v. 87, July, 1991; v. 87, August, 1991; v. 88, October 15, 1991; v. 88, December 15, 1991; v. 88, July, 1992; v. 88, August, 1992; v. 89, September 1, 1992; v. 89, December 1, 1992; v. 89; December 15, 1992; v. 89, March 15, 1993; v. 89, May 15, 1993; v. 89, June 1 & 15, 1993; v. 89, July, 1993; v. 89, August, 1993; v. 90, November 15, 1993; v. 90, December 15, 1993; v. 90, January 1, 1994; v. 90, April 1, 1994; v. 90, May 15, 1994; v. 90, July, 1994; v. 90, August, 1994; v. 91, September 15, 1994; v. 91, October 1, 1994; v. 91, November 1, 1994; v. 91, March 15, 1995; v. 91, May 15, 1995; v. 91, July, 1995; v. 92, September 1, 1995; v. 92, October 15, 1995; v. 92, November 15, 1995; v. 92, December 15, 1995; v. 92, January 1, 1996; v. 92, May 1, 1996; v. 92, August, 1996; v. 93, November 15, 1996; v. 93, February 1, 1997; v. 93, May 1, 1997; v. 93, June 1 & 15, 1997; v. 93, July, 1997; v. 94, Septemeber 1, 1997; v. 94, October 1, 1997; v. 94, December 15, 1997; v. 94, January 1, 1998; v. 94, January 1 & 15, 1998. All reproduced by permission.—*Books for Keeps*, July, 1983, March, 1986; November, 1990; May, 1992; September, 1993, November, 1994; January, 1996; July, 1996. © School Bookshop Association 1983, 1986, 1990, 1992, 1993, 1994, 1996. All reproduced by permission.—*Books for Your Children*, v. 15, Winter, 1979; v. 16, Spring, 1981; v. 19, Autumn-Winter, 1984; Autumn-Winter, 1987; v. 25, Summer, 1990; v. 27, Spring, 1992. © *Books for Your Children* 1979, 1981, 1984, 1987, 1990, 1992. All reproduced by permission.—*Bulletin of the Center for Children's Books*, v. 34, April, 1981; v. 34, July-August, 1981; v. 36, January, 1983; v. 37, March, 1984; v. 39, November, 1985; v. 40, February, 1987; v. 41, September, 1987; v. 41, April, 1988; v. 42, January, 1989; v. 43, September, 1989; v. 44, December, 1990; v. 45, October, 1991; v. 45, November, 1991; v. 45, December, 1991; v. 45, March, 1992; v. 45, May, 1992; v. 46, October, 1992; v. 46, December, 1992; v. 46, February, 1993; v. 46, June, 1993; v. 46, August, 1993; v. 47, October, 1993; v. 47, November, 1993; v. 47, December, 1993; v. 47, January, 1994; v. 47, March, 1994; April, 1994; v. 47, May, 1994; v. 47, June, 1994; v. 47, July-August, 1994; v. 48, November, 1994; v. 48, December, 1994; v. 48, April, 1995; v. 48, June, 1995; v. 48, July-August, 1995; v. 49, September, 1995; v. 49, October, 1995; v. 49, January, 1996; v. 49, February, 1996; v. 49, March, 1996; v. 50, October, 1996; v. 50, November, 1996; v. 50, December, 1996; v. 50, May, 1997; v. 51, October, 1997. Copyright © 1981, 1983, 1984, 1985, 1987, 1988, 1989, 1990, 1991, 1992, 1993, 1994, 1995, 1996, 1997 by The Board of Trustees of the University of Illinois. All reproduced by permission.—*Canadian Book Review Annual*, 1994, 1995. Both reproduced by permission.—*The Canadian Bookman*, v. IV, December, 1922; v. VIII, January, 1926. Both reprinted by permission of Canadian Authors Assoc.—*Canadian Children's Literature*, v. 20:4, Winter, 1994; v. 23:3, Fall, 1997. Copyright © 1994, 1997 Canadian Children's Press. Both reproduced by permission.—*Carousel*, Autumn-Winter, 1998. Reproduced by permission.—*Children's Book Review Service Inc.*, v. 8, August, 1980. Copyright © 1980 Children's Book Review Service Inc. Reproduced by permission.—*CM: A Reviewing Journal of Canadian Materials for Young People*, v. 22, January, 1994; v. 22, May, 1994. Copyright 1994 The Canadian Library Association. Both reproduced by permission of the Manitoba Library Association.—*English Journal*, v. 78, March, 1989 for a review of "The Island" by Jerri K. Norris. Copyright © 1989 by the National Council of Teachers of English. Reproduced by permission of the publisher.—*The Five Owls*, v. V, November, 1990; v. V, May, 1991; v. IX, March-April, 1995; v. X, November-December, 1995. All reproduced by permission.—*Growing Point*, v. 15, January, 1977 for a review of "ABC and Things" and "123 and Things"; v. 17, July, 1978 for a review of "The Rat Race"; v. 21, September, 1982 for a review of "At Playschool," "At the Park," and "At the Party"; v.

Children's
Literature
Review

Nathan Aaseng

1953-

(Also writes as Nate Aaseng) American author of non-fiction and fiction.

Major works include the series "Sports Achievers" (1979-89), "You Are the Coach" (1983-86), "Sports Talk" (1986-90), "Nobel Prize Winners" (1987), and "Inside Business" (1989-90).

INTRODUCTION

Aaseng is recognized as a prolific writer of nonfiction books that lead primary- and middle-graders through an impressive collection of some of the twentieth century's greatest sports, business, and political personalities. While much of his writing career has been steeped in sports topics—from his first book about Bruce Jenner, to titles later in his career covering Michael Jordan, Barry Sanders, and Pete Rose—Aaseng also has branched out into a broad range of subjects that include science, biography, business innovation, Nobel Prize winners, and religion. Distilling great lives and accomplishments into reader-friendly prose, he welcomes his readers to his topics in such a manner that even the lives and feats of his less-celebrated, non-sports-oriented subjects, including the Navajo code talkers of World War II and Buckminster Fuller, appeal to the juvenile set. In most of his works, Aaseng characterizes personal achievement as a conscious decision by his subjects, despite whatever difficulties they face: witness titles such as *Winners Never Quit: Athletes Who Beat the Odds* (1980), *The Problem Solvers: People Who Turned Problems into Products* (1989), *and The Rejects: People and Products That Outsmarted the Experts* (1989). In addition, he has also drawn readers into his texts in a more literal sense, introducing a participant's-eye-view of coaching and presidential decision-making in his "You Are the Coach" and "You Are the President" series, respectively. In these series, readers are presented with a real-life dilemma requiring staunch decision-making. After they select from a variety of possibilities, they can turn the page and compare their decision with the choice that the coaches or presidents made. Such series reflect the challenges faced by many of Aaseng's subjects struggling to achieve their goals. "Readers will watch their favorite sport more intelligently and certainly with more sympathy for the individuals who call the shots," Karen Stang Hanley commented. Aaseng's ability to generate that sympathy—perhaps more of an appreciation for the risks people take when faced with an important decision—makes him the ideal writer to transcribe these struggles. Richard Luzer noted of *Bruce Jenner: Decathlon Winner* (1979), "Any youngster who reads this book will have a much greater appreciation of the skill and sacrifice involved in this grueling test." Of *Better Mousetraps:*

Product Improvements That Led to Success (1989), Phillis Wilson wrote, "Aaseng brings out how frustration with drudgery, hassle, or inefficiency propelled . . . individuals not to gripe, but to turn the lemon into lemonade. . . ."

Though Aaseng has been criticized for merely "adequate" prose, he is also widely acknowledged as a solid writer with a wry sense of humor and "smooth, easy style." In *Something about the Author* (*SATA*), he expressed the limitations and frustrations that writing for young people can present. "Words are my tools," he noted, "and the younger the reader, the fewer tools (words) I can use. I have to say something within their vocabulary. On the other hand, I have felt comfortable writing for young people because I do not believe in trying to impress people with huge words or intimidating style. I always thought the idea in writing was to communicate, not to show off."

Biographical Information

Aaseng, the third of five children, was born in Park

Rapids, Minnesota, which he believed throughout much of his youth to be "Park Rabbits," Minnesota. His father was a Lutheran minister, noted for a quiet nature that bordered on the taciturn—a trait Aaseng claims to have inherited, and which also led to his bare-bones writing approach, one well-fitted to younger readers. Living in a world not far removed from that described by Garrison Keillor in his humorous Lake Wobegon tales, Aaseng's family eventually moved to New Jersey for a year marked by general discomfort in their new urban surroundings before returning to Minnesota, this time St. Louis Park. A small child during elementary and junior high school, Aaseng also had a stutter, two features that set him apart from other children and made for somewhat lonely schooling. Aaseng developed an early interest in reading via the outdoor books of Jim Kjelgaard and the fantasy work of C. S. Lewis: both authors foreshadowed his later academic interest in biology and ecology and his desire to write a Tolkienish fantasy. Infusing humor into his school writing assignments, Aaseng was acknowledged by his teachers to be a "clever" writer, which also bolstered his desire to write. His experience as a cross-country runner, however, provided him with greater connectivity to his nonfiction subjects. After failing his Little League tryout, Aaseng spent years observing rather than participating in competitive sports. In high school he developed an interest in track and distance running, and finally made an impact at his first cross-country race, finishing second among his teammates. Further success in the sport developed his confidence and self-respect, two components of athletic endeavor that he brings to the sports books he continues to write.

After college, Aaseng married and worked first as a production-line worker in a canning factory and later as a microbiologist, a job he left in part to make a sincere effort at becoming a writer. While trying to find work as an editor or reporter—all the better to work his way up the writing ladder—a senior editor at Lerner Publications approached him about doing a short biography on Bruce Jenner, the 1976 Olympic decathlon champ. Lerner had a number of photographs of Jenner but no text for publication. Aaseng accepted the assignment, and the result was *Bruce Jenner: Decathlon Winner*, published in 1979.

Aaseng rarely strayed from sports-oriented nonfiction during the many years that followed—a departure from the Tolkien-flavored fantasy and humor writing he originally set out to do. Despite the benefits he derived from his successful high school sports career, though, Aaseng is careful to maintain proper perspective on the role athletes play in today's society: "It seemed as though the implicit message lingered—that success is the measure of a person's worth. My research demonstrated that, in many cases, people achieve success not because of superiority of their character, but because of a character flaw." Aaseng has tempered his many sports-related success stories with titles on the "worst" baseball teams ever and athletes who, like Aaseng early in life, could not fulfill their promising athletic career.

Major Works

Aaseng's writing career, replete with sports-centered books, began with the first volume in the "Sports Achievers" series, *Bruce Jenner: Decathalon Champ*. "Many youngsters may be unaware that the familiar cereal salesman participated in one of the most dramatic moments in recent Olympic history;" Richard Luzar noted, "[H]is story is told here simply and smoothly with a minimum of fictionalizing and a good feel for the tension and excitement of athletic competition." Many of the other books in the "Sports Achiever" series, which also includes titles on such stars as Pete Rose, Carl Lewis, and Florence Griffith Joyner, deliver similarly well-regarded storytelling to readers. They provide biographical information on each athlete's early years and recount the events that set them apart from other athletes. Aaseng's "You Are the Coach" series offers readers an opportunity to role-play as the boss in a variety of professional sports venues, including baseball, football, and hockey. Scenarios on matters ranging from salary negotiation to play calling are presented, with the outcomes and their analyses on the following pages. Aaseng guides his audience through each play of a game until the climactic moment, then offers readers the opportunity to call the play that will decide the game's outcome. A "simple but clever formula," according to Robert E. Unsworth. "It's something of a gimmick but it works well." "Sports Talk," a series Aaseng worked on following the "Sports Achievers" and "You Are the Coach" series, offers wider-ranging looks at sports, not limited to specific individuals and typically dealing with teams or general views of sports. Titles include *Baseball's Greatest Teams* (1986), *Football's Most Shocking Upsets* (1986), and *Ultramarathons: The World's Most Punishing Races* (1987). In her review of the "Sports Talk" entries *Baseball's Greatest Teams* and *Baseball's Worst Teams* (1986), Linda Ward Callaghan wrote, "While avid fans will challenge his choices, Aaseng captures baseball history from an interesting perspective that will educate and delight young readers."

Aaseng's writing success is not limited to sports, as his "Inside Business" series also generated positive feedback from reviewers. With titles such as *Better Mousetraps: Product Improvements That Led to Success* (1989) and *Midstream Changes: People Who Started Over and Made It Work* (1990), the "Inside Business" series covers the efforts and risks involved in generating success in the business world. *Mousetraps* includes information on such innovations as shavers, film, and elevators, and was considered by a *Kirkus Reviews* critic as a "delightful exploration." *Midstream Changes* introduces readers to the initial failures of such modern-day marketing icons as Colonel Sanders, who faced poverty after early business failures, Mary Kay Ash, whose distinctive pink Cadillacs may be as memorable as her cosmetics line, and Milton Bradley, a failed lithographer-turned-board-game king. Other titles in the series include *The Fortunate Fortunes: Business Successes That Began with a Lucky Break* (1989), *The Rejects: People and Products That Outsmarted the Experts*, and *Close Call: From the*

Brink of Ruin to Business Success (1990). Aaseng produced several general science titles, as well, drawing on his earlier science experience in *The Common Cold and the Flu* (1992) and *Genetics: Unlocking the Secret Code* (1996). Aaseng's 1987 "Nobel Prize Winners" series also includes two science-related titles, *The Disease Fighters: The Nobel Prize in Medicine* and *The Inventors: Nobel Prizes in Chemistry, Physics, and Medicine*, as well as a third title about Nobel Peace Prize winners. Steve Matthews wrote of the winners showcased in *The Disease Fighters*, "These eight vignettes seem more like mystery stories than factual narratives" which result in "brisk engaging reading. . . . "

Awards

In 1984, Aaseng won a Children's Choice award from the International Reading Association/Children's Book Council (CBC) for *Baseball: You Are the Manager* and *Football: You Are the Coach*. In 1985, Aaseng received a Children's Books of the Year citation from the Child Study Association of America, for *Carl Lewis: Legend Chaser*. For *The Disease Fighters: The Nobel Prize in Medicine* and *The Inventors: Nobel Prizes in Chemistry, Physics, and Medicine,* he was awarded an Outstanding Science Trade Book citation from *Children and Science* in 1987. He was awarded another Children's Choice award from the International Reading Association/CBC for *Baseball: It's Your Team* and *Football: It's Your Team,* in 1986. He was also awarded citations for Notable Children's Trade Book in the Field of Social Studies from the Children's Book Council of the National Council for the Social Studies for *Better Mousetraps: Product Improvements That Led to Success, The Fortunate Fortunes: Business Successes That Began with a Lucky Break, The Problem Solvers: People Who Turned Problems into Products, The Rejects: People and Products That Outsmarted the Experts,* and *The Unsung Heroes: Unheralded People Who Invented Famous Products*, all in 1989. *Navajo Code Talkers* was recognized as an International Reading Association/CBC Young Adult Choices selection in 1994. *Ben Carson* was a Christian Publishers Association Gold Medallion Award finalist in 1993, as was *Billy Graham* in 1994.

GENERAL COMMENTARY

Chris Hatten

SOURCE: A review of *Football's Steadiest Kickers, Football's Toughest Tight Ends,* and *Winning Women of Tennis,* in *School Library Journal,* Vol. 28, No. 7, March, 1982, p. 142.

The formula beat goes on with three new entries in this ["Sports Heroes Library"] series. **Winning Women** will prove to be a loser for most collections, as the author brings little new information to the well-publicized stories of Althea Gibson, Billie Jean King, Chris Evert Lloyd, etc. **Kickers** and **Tight Ends,** however, put the spotlight on several key NFL athletes who seldom garner the headlines and magazine cover shots that players in more glamorous positions in the game enjoy. The careers of outstanding performers such as John Mackey, Dave Casper, Ozzie Newsome, Lou Groza, Garo Yepremian and Tony Franklin are covered in a brief but very readable fashion with plenty of clear black-and-white photos ably illustrating the action-filled narrative.

Joe McKenzie

SOURCE: A review of *Football's Crushing Blockers, Superstars Stopped Short,* and *World-Class Marathoners,* in *School Library Journal,* Vol. 28, No. 9, May, 1982, p. 88.

Nathan Aaseng's three titles from Lerner's "Sports Heroes Library" won't sit on the shelves long or often. Aaseng brings back the forgotten heroes of the gridiron, the linemen, in **Football's Crushing Blockers,** which truly includes the cream of the crop: John Hannah, Marvin Powell, Leon Gray. Though several of the eight are past their prime and will be unknowns in a few years, the highlights of their careers make interesting reading. **Superstars Stopped Short** are all promising athletes whose careers were halted because of injury or death: baseball pro Lyman Bostock was accidently shot; Darryl Stingley was paralyzed by a crushing tackle at age 27. Aaseng handles these and six other stories with compassion. **World-Class Marathoners** does a solid job of making distance running come alive by telling stories of the great moments in the careers of its subjects. The runners are Frank Shorter, Grete Waitz, Bill Rodgers, Emil Zatopek, Abebe Bikila, Waldemar Cierpinski and Alberto Salazar. The photographs that accompany each text are an asset.

Joe McKenzie

SOURCE: A review of *Basketball: You Are the Coach,* and *Football: You Are the Coach,* in *School Library Journal,* Vol. 29, No. 9, May, 1983, p. 95.

A marvelous concept: put readers in the shoes of professional coaches and let them make the decisions that will lead to a win or a loss. Aaseng provides pertinent factual information including a close-up of each team, then gives readers a choice of decisions that confront the coach. Each book contains ten situations, all taken from important NBA or NFL games. The books are well written and should be as popular as the "Choose Your Own Adventure" books. They would also make good read-alouds. Photos vary in quality from poor to excellent.

Karen Stang Hanley

SOURCE: A review of *Baseball: You Are the Manager, Basketball: You Are the Coach, Football: You Are the Coach,* and *Hockey: You Are the Coach,* in *Booklist,* Vol. 79, No. 21, July, 1983, p. 1405.

Sports buffs will find themselves handing down decisions to Roger Staubach, Kareem Abdul-Jabbar, and Sandy Koufax in a new ["You Are the Coach"] series that is a winning twist on the "solve-it-yourself" genre. Each volume contains 10 case studies, all taken from professional play-off and championship games between 1958 and 1981. Aaseng sets up the situation with background on the season and the players' recent performance. Then, outlining two or more solutions to a problem at hand, he demands: "What's your decision?" On the following page the choice made at the time is discussed, along with its implications for the rest of the game. Stressing that few decisions are obviously right or wrong, Aaseng notes that debate after the match has often favored a different course of action. The text requires concentration in order to get all the facts in place but offers a rewarding look at the intricacies of sports strategy. Readers will watch their favorite sport more intelligently and certainly with more sympathy for the individuals who call the shots.

Ilene Cooper

SOURCE: A review of *Baseball's Hottest Hitters, Baseball's Power Hitters, Supersubs of Pro Sports, Basketball's Sharpshooters, Basketball's Playmakers,* and *Comeback Stars of Pro Sports,* in *Booklist,* Vol. 80, No. 3, October 1, 1983, p. 302.

All of these books in the Sports Heroes series are distinguished by clear writing, good-size type, clean layout, and numerous black-and-white photographs. This makes them a good choice for middle-graders as well as high-low readers. The books' titles simply define their subject matter. *Baseball's Hottest Hitters* offers biographies of eight batters with high averages (including Rod Carew, Pete Rose, Steve Garvey). *Baseball's Power Hitters* takes a slightly different tack, profiling batters such as Reggie Jackson known for hitting the long ball. *Supersubs* looks at utility players in baseball, football, and basketball. *Basketball's Sharpshooters* contains eight biographies of NBA stars, while *Basketball's Playmakers* takes a look at pro basketball guards whose contributions are often underrated by the public. Perhaps the most interesting book in the crop is *Comeback Stars.* It contains stories of men like Jim Plunkett and Steve Stone and one woman, Virginia Wade, who thought their careers were over but made it back to the top.

Perry Forehand

SOURCE: A review of *Baseball's Hottest Hitters, Baseball's Power Hitters, Basketball's Sharpshooters,* and *Comeback Stars of Pro Sports,* in *School Library Journal,* Vol. 30, No. 7, March, 1984, pp. 152-53.

These sports books are similar in their high interest/low vocabulary format and numerous but of average quality black-and-white photographs. *Baseball's Hottest Hitters* centers on players who maintain high batting averages. *Baseball's Power Hitters* highlights players who continually achieve the thrill of home runs. The men in *Basketball's Sharpshooters* have all perfected the exciting long range jump shot. *Comeback Stars of Pro Sports* is the only book in which players—both male and female—are noted particularly for their determination to survive disaster and disappointment and to return to their original level of success. At first glance, these books appear to be the average run of sports books, but they do have the added attraction of an introductory explanation of the theme and its importance.

Robert E. Unsworth

SOURCE: A review of *Football's Daring Defensive Backs, Football's Hard-Hitting Linebackers,* and *Football's Punishing Pass Rushers,* in *School Library Journal,* Vol. 30, No. 9, May, 1984, p. 104.

The defensive back, the last man between the ball carrier and the goal, receives little popular attention because a good one seldom receives the ball. In this addition to Lerner's large (and expanding) Sports Heroes Library, Aaseng spotlights eight *Daring Defensive Backs* in the game today, including Mel Blount of Pittsburgh, Ronnie Lott of San Francisco and Pat Thomas of the Los Angeles Rams. An opening chapter goes over the elements of the position. The profiles focus almost solely on the career highlights and statistics of the players, giving only a few facts about their private lives. The linebacker is a relatively new position in pro football. If he's good, and the eight profiled in *Hard-Hitting Linebackers* are among the best, he can knock down passes and punts. He can also make a bundle of money. Each of these biographies is similar: a little on the players' early years and college careers and then some highlights of their professional careers (all are active). Lawrence Taylor of the New York Giants, Tom Cousineau of Cleveland and Jack Ham of Pittsburgh are a representative sample. The pass rusher is a lineman or linebacker who is especially adept at getting to the quarterback. Joe Klecko of the New York Jets, Bubba Baker of Detroit and "Big Hands" Johnson of San Diego are among the eight written up in *Punishing Pass Rushers.* The profiles are short and easy-to-read, concentrating on descriptions of how well these men perform their jobs. The black-and-white photos accompanying the text in all three titles are well chosen. Aaseng respects his readers—never talks down to them—and does this sort of thing—short, eye-catching, easy-to-read profiles—as well as anyone.

Linda Ward Callaghan

SOURCE: A review of *College Basketball: You Are the Coach* and *College Football: You Are the Coach,* in *Booklist,* Vol. 81, No. 3, October 1, 1984, p. 253.

Fans of the popular reader participation series novels will welcome Aaseng's newest books [in his "You Are the Coach" series] that challenge readers to use their decision skills in choosing one of several coaching options from actual NCAA basketball championships and football bowl games. The background of both teams is given along with information on significant players, statistics, and team strengths and weaknesses. The coach's choice and outcome of the game are revealed after the reader makes a decision, and Aaseng provides discussion of each option, strategy, and the reason some options fail. Black-and-white photographs from the actual games discussed are sprinkled throughout for additional interest. A sure bet for any sports shelf.

Robert E. Unsworth

SOURCE: A review of *College Basketball: You Are the Coach* and *College Football: You Are the Coach,* in *School Library Journal,* Vol. 31, No. 4, December, 1984, p. 103.

Aaseng reworks a simple but clever formula that he has successfully used for baseball, hockey and pro football. He recounts, in some detail, the story of actual games that took place over the past 30 years or so—post-season bowl games in football and post-season tournament games in basketball. When the reader has reached the climactic moment, Aaseng stops the action and "you," the reader, become the coach, deciding the play or the strategy that will make or break the game. You then read on to find out what the coach decided and how the game ended. It's something of a gimmick but it works well. Aaseng is a good writer with great knowledge of his sports. The amount of detail that is included might be too much for slower readers, but for many browsers these books will be winners.

Linda Ward Callaghan

SOURCE: A review of *Baseball's Greatest Teams* and *Baseball's Worst Teams,* in *Booklist,* Vol. 83, No. 13, March 1, 1987, p. 1010.

With these new titles in the "Sports Talk" series, Aaseng goes out on a limb to rank the eight best and worst teams in baseball. Mixing statistics and anecdotes with archive photographs and Hall of Fame citations, the author blends history and humor with a casual friendly style to analyze the factors among players, managers, and owners that make or break a team. While Aaseng states his criteria for choosing the greatest teams, no standards are given for his worst list. The books complement each other with teams ranking among the worst contributing

to the success of the best. Because their owner sold Herb Pennock, Waite Hoyt, and Babe Ruth to the Yankees, the 1932 Red Sox rank as "7th worst." Among the best are the 1906 Cubs, 1931 Philadelphia A's, and the 1955 Brooklyn Dodgers; Aaseng's choices for the worst teams include the 1961 Kansas City A's, 1962 Mets, and, as all-time worst, the 1899 Cleveland Spiders with a 20-134 record. While avid fans will challenge his choices, Aaseng captures baseball history from an interesting perspective that will educate and delight young readers.

Tom S. Hurlburt

SOURCE: A review of *Baseball's Greatest Teams* and *Baseball's Worst Teams,* in *School Library Journal,* Vol. 33, No. 11, August, 1987, p. 78.

Considering that trying to pick the best or the worst teams from professional baseball's long history is no small task, Aaseng's books [from the "Sports Talk" series] are quite commendable. He established a criteria for selecting the teams: rather than judging solely by records, he also gave consideration to other extraneous circumstances, such as strength of competition. Eight teams from various years are ranked and featured in each book; each has an accompanying page of statistics that includes overall record, league standings, and key player's performances. Black-and-white photographs, some from the early days of professional baseball, are liberally interspersed within the text. A number of little known teams are featured along with some interesting anecdotes relating to both on- and off-field activities. While the writing style is quite ordinary, and each book does contain its share of standard sports clichés, these titles are a welcome relief from the idolatrous sports biographies that flood the juvenile market and are of interest for only a short period of time.

Phillis Wilson

SOURCE: A review of *Animal Specialists, Horned Animals, Meat-Eating Animals,* and *Prey Animals,* in *Booklist,* Vol. 84, No. 9, January 1, 1988, p. 779.

All animals compete for food, water, and space: the winners survive, the losers become extinct. Some animals have been helped in the fierce competition by an unusual twist of nature that gives them an advantage. Working from this unique perspective, Aaseng, in *Animal Specialists,* describes 10 animals with unusual skills or physical features: the world-class-commuter award goes to the arctic tern who flies round trip from the North Pole to the South Pole every year. Among the horned animals in the ungulate family that the author discusses are the familiar white-tailed deer and bighorn sheep, but readers will also be intrigued by the gemsbok, easily mistaken for the mythical unicorn. In *Meat-Eating Animals,* Aaseng's scope is evidenced by descriptions ranging from the polar bear and arctic fox on the tundra, to the caracal in the North African desert, and the familiar raccoon seen at local campsites. Rounding out the series is *Prey Animals,* which focuses on 10 herbivores, "meals-on-legs" for the carnivores, though their great speed and early-warning systems allow the strongest to survive. Statistics given include length, weight, habitat, food, number of young, and life span. With large print and consistently fine illustrations [by A. C. Dornisch], this ["Early Nature Picturebook"] series will be a welcome addition to natural-history resources.

Elizabeth LeBris

SOURCE: A review of *Animal Specialists, Horned Animals, Meat-Eating Animals,* and *Prey Animals,* in *School Library Journal,* Vol. 34, No. 6, February, 1988, p. 67.

Each book [in the "Early Nature Picturebook" series] concentrates on ten animals with the titled common characteristic. Each chapter presents an animal's habits and behaviors. A small map and fact list (height, weight, habitat, food, young, lifespan) finish each chapter. The last page of each book shows the animals drawn to scale in silhouette, with an adult woman and a boy included for comparison. *Animal Specialists* are all animals with some unique characteristic in terms of size, food needs, hunting technique, migration, etc. *Horned Animals* discusses the reasons animals have horns, how in some species both male and female sport a pair, and how horns are different from antlers. *Meat-Eating Animals* introduces the basic needs of carnivores and explains how they have adapted to become excellent hunters. *Prey Animals* looks at the flip side of carnivores. The illustrations are limited to one color portrait of each animal—full page and nicely detailed—and a map of the animal's range. An inherent problem with grouping animals in these narrow categories, though, is that many children will find the group style of book fragmented and difficult to understand.

Carolyn Phelan

SOURCE: A review of *The Disease Fighters: The Nobel Prize in Medicine, The Inventors: Nobel Prizes in Chemistry, Physics, and Medicine,* and *The Peace Seekers: The Nobel Peace Prize,* in *Booklist,* Vol. 84, No. 11, February 1, 1988, p. 929.

From Lerner's new ["Nobel Prize Winners"] series, these volumes describe some of the people awarded Nobel Prizes for their accomplishments. As the titles suggest, Aaseng focuses on the award winners rather than the award process. There's no list of medalists here or explanations of the dynamics of selection, but rather accounts of the conditions, discoveries, and events that led to the honors. *Disease Fighters* relates the work of many researchers, some well known, others unfamiliar, who have made significant progress to prevent, control, or cure diseases such as tuberculosis, diphtheria, tetanus, syphilis, polio, and diabetes. *Inventors* focuses on eight inventions or discoveries (X-ray, transistor, laser)

that resulted in Nobel recognition. In *Peace Seekers,* Aaseng devotes each chapter to the relevant issue and actions of individuals such as Jane Addams, Linus Pauling, Martin Luther King, Jr., Lech Walesa, Andrei Sakharov, and Desmond Tutu. In each book the narrative style carries the reader into a series of dramatic stories linked by common themes. Three interesting and useful collective biographies.

Steve Matthews

SOURCE: A review of *The Disease Fighters: The Nobel Prize in Medicine* and *The Peace Seekers: The Nobel Peace Prize,* in *School Library Journal,* Vol. 34, No. 7, March, 1988, p. 202.

Two entertaining and informative books. In *The Disease Fighters,* great medical research discoveries are outlined. These eight vignettes seem more like mystery stories than factual narratives. Beginning with Robert Kock and his work to cure tuberculosis (1905 Nobel Prize) through Enders, Weller, and Robbins and their experiments leading to the development of a polio vaccine (1954), Aaseng reveals the brilliant schemes, lost opportunities, and strange turns of fate which have yielded the miracles of 20th-Century medicine. The approach is anecdotal and not chronological. In *The Peace Seekers,* Aaseng gives a better overview of the prize's history. With portraits of such diverse figures as Jane Addams, Martin Luther King, Lech Walesa, and Bishop Tutu, Aaseng points out that peace advocates are often unpopular, persecuted, or even killed for their beliefs. Eight peace prize recipients are sketched; chapters are illustrated with well-chosen and provocative black-and-white photos. Both books should spark further reading whether to explore the incredible chain of events which produced the wonder drug penicillin or to understand the tragic dilemma of the Soviet Union's Andrei Sakharov. These volumes make for brisk engaging reading as they reveal the wonder and the horror of modern life. They also draw a clear picture of the nature and the importance of these prizes.

Linda Ward Callaghan

SOURCE: A review of *College Football's Hottest Rivalries, Football's Incredible Bulks, Record Breakers of Pro Sports,* and *Ultramarathons: The World's Most Punishing Races,* in *Booklist,* Vol. 84, No. 14, March 15, 1988, p. 1251.

Aaseng's new additions to the "Sports Talk" series focus on varied sports personalities and events. *Hottest Rivalries* recaps the history of six traditional contests (Yale/Harvard, Notre Dame/Southern Cal, Michigan/Ohio State, Army/Navy, Alabama/Auburn, Oklahoma/Texas), citing, in each case, team statistics in a handy chart. *Bulks* profiles ten players from the 1950s Les Bingaman to today's William Perry, whose size is matched by skill. *Record Breakers* cites outstanding baseball, hockey, football, and basketball records that set new goals for future players. *Ultramarathons* focuses on eight challenging races where courses combine difficult terrain with the challenge of adverse weather or extreme temperatures as runners test their physical endurance. Aaseng's lively prose is accompanied by black-and-white photographs (and maps in *Ultramarathons*) as well as statistical summaries that provide brief but basic facts, keeping readers informed about current sports trends and personalities.

Zena Sutherland

SOURCE: A review of *The Disease Fighters: The Nobel Prize in Medicine, The Inventors: Nobel Prizes in Chemistry, Physics, and Medicine,* and *The Peace Seekers: The Nobel Peace Prize,* in *Bulletin of the Center for Children's Books,* Vol. 41, No. 8, April, 1988, p. 149.

In a series of books that give interesting information about men and women whose signal contributions have been recognized by their winning of a Nobel Prize, the subtitles may be doubling misleading: first, there is no attempt to include—or even to list—all winners in the category the book covers, and second, some of the material in each book, while relevant, is not about the winners of Nobel prizes. In each volume, Aaseng gives background history and discusses the work of eight or nine Nobel Prize winners (not always chronologically arranged) in adequate style, not too dry, not too exclamatory.

Maria Salvadore

SOURCE: A review of *Animal Specialists, Horned Animals, Meat-Eating Animals,* and *Prey Animals,* in *Appraisal: Science Books for Young People,* Vol. 22, Nos. 1 & 2, Winter-Spring, 1989, pp. 99-100.

The polar bear gives new meaning to the term "great white hunter." They can measure up to 10 feet (300 cm) in length and weigh 1000 pounds (450 kg). Because they live on the "tundra, the northern plains where it is too cold for trees to live," the polar bear hunts other animals to survive. The polar bear and other meat-eating animals (among them the grizzly, bear, raccoon, ocelot and caracal) are discussed in brief, readable articles in one of four books by Nathan Aaseng, author of innumerable sports books. The style is both informative and interesting and should appeal to young readers.

Each of the "Early Nature Picture Book" series opens with an informative, almost chatty introduction which broadly groups animals from around the world into basic categories (meat-eating, animals with specialties, horned animals, and animals which are prey). A short article about an individual animal is accompanied by a full-color, highly detailed, realistic illustration. A small, shaded map of where the animal is found, as well as brief facts (animal size, habitat, food, young and life

span), are found at the end of each chapter. Though not clearly marked, these map segments could be used in conjunction with a globe or an atlas to clarify location and put it into geographical perspective.

These introductory books have much to commend them to younger children. An open format and thin size make them attractive for browsing as well as report writing.

Jim Maland

SOURCE: A review of *Animal Specialists, Horned Animals, Meat-Eating Animals,* and *Prey Animals,* in *Appraisal: Science Books for Young People,* Vol. 22, Nos. 1 & 2, Winter-Spring, 1989, pp. 99-100.

Delightful! In *Animal Specialists* Aaseng and [A.C.] Dornisch capture and describe some unique features of ten animals. If the emerald tree boa has such poor eyesight, why is it that it survives in great numbers? Belly up and sleeping most of the time, one would think the two-toed sloth became extinct long ago. Why not? It's a bit easier to explain the success of the elephant, the walrus and the giraffe, but what about the little koala, which can feed only on one plant? And consider the giant anteater—toothless, homeless and with an incredible tongue—even the vicious jaguar will think twice before attacking this rare creature. Why? In his clever and concise way, Aaseng presents another simple but substantive little book, one his reader will not forget.

I like all of Nathan Aaseng's books but I find *Horned Animals* particularly interesting, perhaps endearing, and I think my younger counterparts will find the same. The author uses the uniqueness of horns and antlers to describe the lives of ten animals from various niches on this earth. How does the majestic gemsbok find water in the desert? Why does the blackbuck leap straight into the air? And what about those mammoth moose antlers? Finally, what two-day-old North American animal can outrun a horse? A fascinating look at some horney creatures!

Meat-Eating Animals is really quite informative. Aaseng briefly discusses the lives of ten carnivores, some very familiar such as the raccoon, the red fox and the lion . . . and some not so familiar such as the ocelot and caracal. For each animal the author looks at how certain external features, habits and reproductive patterns lead to its success in the wild. The style is light and humorous, really quite engaging. This book will provoke a youngster to find out more about these creatures.

Reality hurts! In *Prey Animals* Aaseng gives the reader a taste of what it's like to be a gentle herbivore, constantly on the menu of some prowling predator. Whether it is the "suicidal" lemming, the flying squirrel, the nosey tapir or the poking porcupine, each has its unique defenses. However, the herbivore's real defense is its capacity to reproduce. Were it not to produce young faster than its predators, prey animals would have become extinct long ago. The author gives a good and accurate glimpse into the lives of ten interesting animals from around the world. A generally good series.

Kirkus Reviews

SOURCE: A review of *The Fortunate Fortunes: Business Successes That Began with a Lucky Break, The Problem Solvers: People Who Turned Problems into Products, The Rejects: People and Products That Outsmarted the Experts,* and *The Unsung Heroes: Unheralded People Who Invented Famous Products,* in *Kirkus Reviews,* Vol. LVII, No. 4, February 15, 1989, p. 288.

An author who has published dozens of useful books on sports initiates a series on business ["Inside Business" series]: brief sketches of inventors, innovators, and entrepreneurs associated with familiar products.

The information here is exceptionally well organized to entertain and instruct beyond the immediate facts. Subtitles neatly summarize the theme of each volume: *Business Successes That Began with a Lucky Break* covers products ranging from Kellogg's cornflakes, resulting from a batch of dough that was left to stand too long, to *Encyclopedia Britannica,* which became an unexpected money-maker after being forced on the University of Chicago as a tax write-off for the donor. *People Who Turned Problems into Products* include a wealthy woman who invented the dishwasher to minimize breakage, a poor boy who grew up to introduce insurance to ameliorate childhoods like his own, and John Deere's plow. One of the *People and Products That Outsmarted the Experts* tells about the man who started Federal Express to answer a professor who had given him a low grade on a paper suggesting such a venture; *Monopoly* was initially rejected by Parker Brothers as "everything you don't want in a game"; it took Birdseye decades to win market acceptance for his frozen foods. And the *Unheralded People Who Invented Famous Products* range from the originators of Superman to the man who sold the Coca-Cola formula for $1750 and include the unsung men behind General Motors.

The seven or eight topics in each book have plenty of variety, all skillfully employed to demonstrate the principles and practice of business as an activity and as social history. Aaseng tells his stories well; they are fascinating to read, as addictive as peanuts. Meanwhile, marginal definitions expand on the many concepts introduced (patent, profit, trademark, etc.), with context giving them extra interest. These are also accessible through boldface index entries. Good period photos and reproductions of ads enliven the format while contributing to the information presented. An excellent quartet.

Phillis Wilson

SOURCE: A review of *The Fortunate Fortunes, The Problem Solvers, The Rejects,* and *The Unsung Heroes,* in *Booklist,* Vol. 85, No. 17, May 1, 1989, p. 1543.

Aaseng gives captivating examples of exceptional marketing techniques in this quartet of titles [in the "Inside Business" series], hyped by their own outstanding dust jackets—naturals for display. Grouping his examples of entrepreneurs, inventors, tinkerers, unsung originators, and the genuinely curious by topic gives additional relevance. While Aaseng talks of "luck" in *Fortunate Fortunes,* it is obvious that perception and recognition of opportunity undergird the chance involved. Pithy quotes abound; in *Problem Solvers,* for example, Edwin Land (who invented the Polaroid camera) defines creativity as the "sudden cessation of stupidity." Youngsters will be pleased to note that some of these extraordinary role models were hardly docile as children. For example, Aaseng notes in *Rejects* that young Bill Lear (who developed the Lear jet) would often skip school and bike along highways in search of stalled cars to fix. And while the golden arches have achieved global recognition, the author relates the real story of McDonald's in *Unsung Heroes,* telling of the two brothers who, in 1948, developed the idea of fast-food restaurants. Wide margins provide space for definition of relevant corporate and industrial concepts, and period photos and reproductions of ads expand this lively account.

Janet E. Gelfand

SOURCE: A review of *The Fortunate Fortunes, The Problem Solvers, The Rejects,* and *The Unsung Heroes,* in *School Library Journal,* Vol. 35, No. 10, June, 1989, p. 110.

The concept that success of a product is attributable to the creativity, luck, and persistence of its originators is well supported by short chapters about various people and the products that they created. The companies and people behind the famous products are highlighted with particular emphasis paid to what made its creation and its acceptance by the public or by manufacturers interesting. Some of the products described are Kleenex tissues, graham crackers, Jell-O, bingo, Polaroid instant film development, and Xerox document copying. The texts are interesting, short, and to the point and are appropriately illustrated with plentiful (almost one for every two pages) black-and-white photographs of the factories, advertisements, and people related to the product being discussed. While these volumes will make interesting leisure reading, they will be particularly useful for research for careers and technology and social studies reports. However, it is unfortunate that they are published in four volumes instead of one.

Margaret A. Bush

SOURCE: A review of *The Fortunate Fortunes, The Problem Solvers, The Rejects,* and *The Unsung Heroes,* in *The Horn Book Magazine,* Vol. LXV, No. 4, July, 1989, pp. 497-98.

What a fascinating array of human history lies behind

the invention of games, beverages, machines, comic strips, and numerous other well-known products. Each of these collections includes eight or nine accounts organized around a theme: business successes that began with a "lucky break," people who turned problems into products, products once scorned as failures, people who lost out on the fame and fortune their inventions garnered for others. Maurice and Richard McDonald started the fast-food enterprise that made Ray Kroc enormously wealthy; although they were not exploited, others were, such as the two men who created Superman. From "the cracker that was banned in Boston"—the invention of health food fanatic Sylvester Graham—to the Monsanto Company's use of a Ford Foundation grant to develop Astro Turf, these stories are an irresistible collection of Americana. Informative sketches describe the origins of Bingo, Monopoly, Coca-Cola, Kleenex, and many more widely known items. The portraits and other historical photographs are likewise a felicitous source of information. A porous paper dulls the picture quality, and a slim column of extra text inserted into the wide margins to explain selected terms does so in pedestrian tones. Aside from the poor design, the volumes offer a lively history of the commonplace.

Marilyn Long Graham

SOURCE: A review of *Close Calls: From the Brink of Ruin to Business Success* and *From Rags to Riches: People Who Started Businesses from Scratch,* in *School Library Journal,* Vol. 36, No. 10, October, 1990, p. 124.

Two books [in the "Inside Business" series] about American business success that are right on target. Both are divided into chapters, each on a particular business or entrepreneur. The chapters are long enough to give an honest glimpse of each subject, but brief enough to hold interest. The writing is smooth and readable, with the terms clearly defined on the pages on which they are first used. Black-and-white photos include some interesting shots that reflect the eras in which these various companies were founded. *Close Calls* describes the difficult beginnings of the H. J. Heinz Corporation, Hallmark Cards Inc., Chrysler Corporation, and six other companies, with biographical information on their founders. *From Rags to Riches* includes brief biographies of Richard W. Sears, Milton Hershey, and J. C. Penney, among others. Those looking for information on businesses founded by minorities or women will have to look elsewhere. However, the accounts included here are fair, accurate, and interesting.

Ruth S. Vose

SOURCE: A review of *Great Summer Olympic Moments* and *Great Winter Olympic Moments,* in *School Library Journal,* Vol. 36, No. 12, December, 1990, p. 125.

A balanced look at a variety of champions in the Summer and Winter Olympics. An introduction to each book explains the beginnings of the modern games, and then discusses 13-14 champions, from runner Paavo Nurmi in the 1924 Summer Olympics through diver Greg Louganis, and from skater Sonja Henie in the 1936 Winter Olympics through ski jumpers Matti Nykänen and Eddie Edwards in 1988. Champions fade quickly from memory, but Aaseng includes such well-known stars as Jesse Owens, Jean-Claude Killy, and Nadia Comaneci. Black-and-white photos throughout help put faces on many unfamiliar names. While these are useful resources for reports on the Olympic games, the fact that most chapters deal with competitors unknown to most young people will limit the popularity of the books for general use.

Carolyn Phelan

SOURCE: A review of *Great Summer Olympic Moments* and *Great Winter Olympic Moments,* in *Booklist,* Vol. 87, No. 10, January 15, 1991, p. 1055.

With emphasis on the last three decades, each of these books recounts the feats of over a dozen modern Olympic champions from the 1920s and 1930s to 1988. While many of the athletes are no longer well known, some readers will recognize names and teams, for example, Jesse Owens, Nadia Comaneci, Greg Louganis, Sonja Henie, the 1980 U.S. hockey team, and ice dancers Torvill and Dean. Aaseng provides enough background information to set the stage for dramatic moments, writing clearly and without hype. While the many black-and-white photographs are uneven in quality, they add to each book's appeal. Neither book is indexed, and the table of contents gives no indication of who is being profiled. *Summer,* however, includes an appendix listing the athletes and their Olympic achievements.

TITLE COMMENTARY

📖 *BRUCE JENNER: DECATHLON WINNER* ("Sports Achievers" series, 1979)

Richard Luzer

SOURCE: A review of *Bruce Jenner: Decathlon Winner,* in *School Library Journal,* Vol. 26, No. 8, April, 1980, p. 102.

A good deal of background information is incorporated into this account of Jenner's triumph in the 1976 Olympics. Many youngsters may be unaware that the familiar cereal salesman participated in one of the most dramatic moments in recent Olympic history; his story is told here simply and smoothly with a minimum of fictionalizing and a good feel for the tension and excitement of athletic competition. Perhaps even more important, as we approach the 1980 Olympics, is the wealth of inside information the author manages to convey concerning the decathlon event. Any youngster who reads this book will have a much greater appreciation of the skill and sacrifice involved in this grueling test. A well-written and timely book.

ERIC HEIDEN: WINNER IN GOLD ("Sports Achievers" series, 1980)

Barbara Elleman

SOURCE: A review of *Eric Heiden: Winner in Gold* in *Booklist,* Vol. 77, No. 9, January 1, 1981, p. 627

Highlights from Eric Heiden's life and career as a speed skater are presented here in easy text and numerous black-and-white photographs. Comments about his training, family life, workouts with sister Beth, and triumphs as the 1980 five-gold-medalist are included. Glimpses of his personality are revealed, though they are somewhat dimmed by the author's overdramatic approach. How-ever, fans of the young Wisconsin star and those interested in speed skating will be interested.

Joseph Bearden

SOURCE: A review of *Eric Heiden: Winner in Gold,* in *School Library Journal,* Vol. 28, No. 1, September, 1981, p. 117.

Aaseng comes through with a well-paced account of Eric Heiden's experience in capturing a record five individual gold medals for speed skating in the 1980 Lake Placid Winter Olympics. He balances the narrative of the events in which Heiden set his records with flashbacks to his earlier years and training and includes many black-and-white photos to achieve an honest and likable profile of this young star.

PETE ROSE: BASEBALL'S CHARLIE HUSTLE ("Sports Achievers" series, 1981)

Barbara Elleman

SOURCE: A review of *Pete Rose: Baseball's Charlie Hustle,* in *Booklist,* Vol. 77, Nos. 22-23, July-August, 1981, p. 1451.

Highlights of this popular baseball player's life and career, with numerous action photographs, are the mainstay of a brief biography about the man who has earned the nickname Charlie Hustle. The story of his rise to fame, as well as some of his problems, and how he became one of a select group to have made more than 3,000 hits is told in a spirited, unsensationalized man-

ner. Fans will delight in the statistics and play-by-play scenes that Aaseng includes throughout.

Zena Sutherland

SOURCE: A review of *Pete Rose: Baseball's Charlie Hustle,* in *Bulletin of the Center for Children's Books,* Vol. 34, No. 11, July-August, 1981, p. 205.

Like most biographies of sports figures, this is a medley of boyhood interest in sports, experiences as a rookie player, the ups and downs of a professional career, and action sequences or establishment of records. This hasn't the hyperbole that weakens many books about sports heroes, although it has a fair share of admiration, both for Rose's ability as a baseball player and for the aggressiveness that won him the nickname of "Charlie Hustle." The text is continuous, with neither table of contents nor index to give access to facts; there are no statistical tables included, but the book ends with photographs and statistics for each of the fifteen players who have had three thousand hits.

Joseph Bearden

SOURCE: A review of *Pete Rose: Baseball's Charlie Hustle,* in *School Library Journal,* Vol. 28, No. 2, October, 1981, p. 137.

Emphasizing his technique and personal style, Aaseng looks at the record of the Philadelphia Phillie's star: a total of 10 seasons of more than 200 hits with over 3,000 hits through the 1979 season. While little space is devoted to Rose's off-the-field life, there is plenty of slickly laid out information about his 16 years with the Cincinnati Reds and the last 2 years with the Phillies. An entertaining read for Rose fans, with lots of black-and-white photos.

CARL LEWIS: LEGEND CHASER ("Sports Achievers" series, 1985)

Linda Ward Callaghan

SOURCE: A review of *Carl Lewis: Legend Chaser,* in *Booklist,* Vol. 81, No. 21, July, 1985, p. 1562.

Following the formula of the Lerner Achievers series, Aaseng's biography of the Olympic track star covers his childhood, early training, collegiate competition, and four-medal performance at the 1984 Olympics. Aaseng's clear, straightforward approach cites the praise and criticism that have been focused on Lewis' attempt to beat Bob Beamon's long jump record and match Jesse Owens' performance. Black-and-white photos of good to high quality illustrate the text, and a chart of statistics is appended. Young readers whose interest in track was piqued during the Los Angeles games will be pleased with this portrayal of Lewis' life.

Kathleen L. Birtciel

SOURCE: A review of *Carl Lewis: Legend Chaser,* in *School Library Journal,* Vol. 31, No. 10, August, 1985, p. 59.

Aaseng describes the physical development and sports career of the 1984 Olympic track star Carl Lewis. He emphasizes the 1984 Games and the tremendous pressure Lewis faced in his effort to win four gold medals. He also deals with the athlete's sometimes abrasive personality and frequent bad press. The coherent, easy-to-read text includes enough background material to help even students with no knowledge of field and track to appreciate Lewis' accomplishments.

Zena Sutherland

SOURCE: A review of *Carl Lewis: Legend Chaser,* in *Bulletin of the Center for Children's Books,* Vol. 39, No. 3, November, 1985, p. 41.

Although this provides some biographical material, it is less a biography than an account of the athletic career of the winner of four gold medals in the 1984 Olympics. That was the goal Carl Lewis had hoped to reach, primarily to match the record set by Jesse Owens. (The replicated catalog card erroneously states that Lewis broke Owens' record.) This does not have the adulatory tone that mars many sports books about individual athletes, but it is weakened somewhat by the writing style: the continuous text is dry, perhaps because it is so packed with small details. Statistics on Lewis in comparison to other stars of track and field are provided.

BASEBALL: IT'S YOUR TEAM ("You Are the Coach" series, 1985; also published as *It's Your Team: Baseball*)

Linda Ward Callaghan

SOURCE: A review of *Baseball: It's Your Team,* in *Booklist,* Vol. 82, No. 3, October 1, 1985, p. 273.

In the same vein as his previous books (*Baseball: You Are the Manager, Basketball: You Are the Coach,* etc.), Aaseng offers readers the opportunity to role-play as baseball team owners in 10 situations. The strategies of salary negotiation, trading players, and choosing managers are all tested as options are outlined, the owner's decision is revealed, and the outcome is analyzed. Aaseng capitalizes on the popularity of the reader-participation format by giving young fans the background data and options necessary for decision-making fun.

Margaret Montgomery

SOURCE: A review of *Baseball: It's Your Team,* in *School Library Journal,* Vol. 32, No. 3, November, 1985, pp. 93-4.

Similar to Aaseng's *You Are the Manager* books, this one asks readers to choose their own ending—from the point of view of the owner of a professional team. Aaseng sets up ten situations from baseball history (including teams, players and owners from 1961 through 1982); in each, readers are given the information about the problem, such as whether or not the 1982 Yankees should sign Reggie Jackson. Aaseng gives the pros and cons, asks readers to decide which of three alternatives they choose and tells what really happened. The style is an easy-to-read "sports-page prose." There are plenty of colorful sports idioms: "axe the manager," "fence-busters." For avid fans of pro baseball.

FOOTBALL'S MOST CONTROVERSIAL CALLS ("Sports Talk" series, 1986)

Linda Ward Callaghan

SOURCE: A review of *Football's Most Controversial Calls,* in *Booklist,* Vol. 82, No. 21, July, 1986, p. 1618.

In this fresh approach to the rules of football, Aaseng examines controversial calls to illustrate how difficult a referee's job can be. His lively, colorful narrative captures the action of ten crucial games and focuses on how rule violations affected division, conference, and Super Bowl titles and resulted in clarification of the NFL's *Official Rules for Professional Football.* While some black-and-white photographs only decorate the text, others capture the moment in question, challenging the reader to make the call. For any football fan who has disagreed with the judgment of a referee.

Todd Morning

SOURCE: A review of *Football's Most Controversial Calls,* in *School Library Journal,* Vol. 33, No. 5, January, 1987, pp. 69-70.

Few sports have as complex rules or as many chances for officials to make mistakes as professional football. Each chapter in this book covers the events leading up to a controversial call by N.F.L. officials in ten crucial games. In some cases, the controversy arose because of mistakes made by the officials; in others, the officials were correct but the rules obscure or seemingly unfair; and, in a few examples, there are still arguments as to what the correct call should have been. This is an interesting angle for a sports book. Readers are reminded that the rules are the groundwork for any game, but that the interpretation of those rules is often difficult. The writing is adequate; it is clear and easy to read, but never rises above sports reporting clichés. The black-and-white action photos add some excitement, however. Young football fans should find this an enjoyable look at the game through an unusual and important approach.

MORE WITH LESS: THE FUTURE WORLD OF BUCKMINSTER FULLER (1986)

Ilene Cooper

SOURCE: A review of *More With Less: The Future World of Buckminster Fuller,* in *Booklist,* Vol. 83, No. 2, September 15, 1986, p. 121.

Although the format and writing style are problematic and, at times, Aaseng overwrites, this biography will serve students doing units on the future. Readers will be able to get insights into the man who was called both a genius and a crackpot for his ideas such as the geodesic dome. This book not only looks at Fuller's professional career but also at his personal life. Fuller despaired many times over his career and even considered suicide; such information humanizes the man who, for many young people, will be known mainly for his works. Pages are oddly designed—the text, arranged in a column, takes up the outer half of each page and is set off with a black vertical line, often leaving the center of the book empty, except when black-and-white captioned photos or illustrations are used. Presumably it was chosen for its modern look; instead, it appears awkward. Very little is available on Fuller, and schools needing material will find this functional.

Margaret M. Hagel

SOURCE: A review of *More With Less: The Future World of Buckminster Fuller,* in *School Library Journal,* Vol. 33, No. 2, October, 1986, p. 168.

The focus of this biography is Fuller's originality, his antipathy to being compelled to think along established paths, and his love of reasoning things out for himself. His character and personal life are presented to show how they affected his later contributions to science, architecture, and invention. The black-and-white photographs and drawings help readers to understand the ideas presented in the text. . . . *More With Less* is written in a . . . straightforward style, omitting wordy detail. Younger readers and those who want to get to the essence of the man quickly will appreciate this book.

BASEBALL'S GREATEST TEAMS ("Sports Talk" series, 1986)

Zena Sutherland

SOURCE: A review of *Baseball's Greatest Teams,* in *Bulletin of the Center for Children's Books,* Vol. 40, No. 6, February, 1987, p. 101.

Aaseng, a seasoned if not profound sports writer, has chosen eight major league teams (on admittedly flexible criteria) using a four-part test. Has a team clearly stood out from its rivals? Was the team consistent in its performance? Did they win when under pressure? Did they

"earn their honors," that is, not achieve victory by playing weaker teams? Aaseng's choices are discussed on the basis of individual athletes' performances as well as team records, and while all of the material is available elsewhere, it hasn't been assembled in quite the same way, and the sweet nostalgia of names and games will appeal to most baseball buffs.

BOB DYLAN: SPELLBINDING SONG-WRITER (1987)

Betsy Hearne

SOURCE: A review of *Bob Dylan: Spellbinding Songwriter,* in *Bulletin of the Center for Children's Books,* Vol. 41, No. 1, September, 1987, p. 1.

It is true that Dylan has been secretive and often deliberately misleading about his life, but he has been the subject of enough research and writing to avoid the kinds of empty phrases that pop up in this biography ("Although he enjoyed many kinds of music, including rock 'n' roll, Bob became a folksinger. It was an easy style for a young man like Dylan, because a person did not have to be rich to be a folksinger"). Some of the statements are actually misleading: "In a lazy sort of way, he has picked and chosen some of what he has seen and put it to music," for instance, conveys nothing of the intensity of Dylan's vision and performance. Sometimes the writing is simply odd ("he is protective of his father, who has passed away"). There is some easy-to-read information to be gotten here and a six-page "timeline" of Dylan's life, along with black-and-white photographs, but the audience that is old enough to appreciate Dylan's music deserves a more complex look at his life.

Ilene Cooper

SOURCE: A review of *Bob Dylan: Spellbinding Songwriter,* in *Booklist,* Vol. 84, No. 2, September 15, 1987, p. 139.

Aaseng makes the point in this short biography that Dylan is a difficult subject to understand. The author then briefly examines the singer's varied life and career with emphasis on how Dylan's words and music spoke for a generation of young people. Black-and-white photographs appear on almost every page; the most interesting are the pictures of Dylan's hometown—Hibbing, Minnesota—and those of Dylan as a teenager. Although this will serve as an introduction to Dylan and his music, the uninitiated will need more than this slim volume to understand the mercurial singer.

Jack Forman

SOURCE: A review of *Bob Dylan: Spellbinding Songwriter,* in *School Library Journal,* Vol. 34, No. 5, January, 1988, p. 78.

This short, easy-to-read sketch provides an accurate skeleton of Dylan's shrouded life and influential music career (although calling Bob Dylan "the most important writer of popular songs of the past three decades" is debatable). Aaseng leads readers quickly through Dylan's uneventful middle class childhood to his adolescent awakening to the murmurs of social change in the late 1950s and early 1960s. He shows how Dylan as a folk musician and songwriter-poet was helped by Joan Baez and Peter, Paul, and Mary and how he has progressed to folk rock, religious soft rock, western music, and finally returned to his folk music roots. Aaseng depicts Dylan as a man who has refused to cater to his fans and the media—and through all the changes in his personal and musical life, has maintained a social awareness. Black-and-white photos offer glimpses of Dylan at different points of his career, and a helpful "timeline" of his life appears at the end of the book, although there is no index. Many questions remain about Dylan's heavily guarded private life, but this book will whet young readers' appetites.

THE INVENTORS: NOBEL PRIZES IN CHEMISTRY, PHYSICS, AND MEDICINE ("Nobel Prize Winners" series, 1987)

Margaret M. Hagel

SOURCE: A review of *The Inventors: Nobel Prizes in Chemistry, Physics, and Medicine,* in *School Library Journal,* Vol. 34, No. 11, August, 1988, p. 107.

The eight inventions in this book span the time period in which individual inventions gave way to team inventions, financed by corporate or government money. Aaseng describes the science behind X-ray photography, radio, the electrocardiograph, the phase contrast microscope, the transistor, radiocarbon dating, the LASER, and the CT scanner. Black-and-white photographs show mostly the inventor and the invention; black-and-white drawings are used to clarify the "how it works" discussions, which are clear and brief. Some of these inventions are rarely discussed in books for this age level, so this book will supply new information for school and public libraries.

John E. Christ

SOURCE: A review of *The Inventors: Nobel Prizes in Chemistry, Physics, and Medicine,* in *Science Books & Films,* Vol. 24, No. 2, November-December, 1988, p. 86.

The twentieth century is one of the most exciting epics in the history of man, in part due to the numerous inventions that have changed the way we live. *The Inventors* presents eight advances in technology that have revolutionized the modern era, with each chapter focusing on a Noble Prize winner involved in invention within those advances. Coverage includes the discovery of x-ray photography, transmission of messages by radio, the

electrocardiogram, the phase contrast microscope, the transistor, radiocarbon dating, the laser, and the CT scanner. The book is complete with well-written, interesting text and clear, illustrative photographs and illustrations that could be enjoyed even by general adult audiences. I strongly recommend this book for young adults and the parents of those young adults so they can share this adventure of discovery.

JOSE CANSECO: BASEBALL'S FORTY-FORTY MAN ("Sports Achievers" series, 1989)

Phillis Wilson

SOURCE: A review of *Jose Canseco: Baseball's Forty-Forty Man,* in *Booklist,* Vol. 85, No. 21, July, 1989, p. 1898.

When the star outfielder of the Oakland Athletics announced his 1988 goals—hit 40 home runs and steal 40 bases—he was stunned to learn, according to Aaseng, that this feat had never been accomplished during a single season. Writing in his typically crisp, accessible style, Aaseng, while complimentary, doesn't duck rumors of the ballplayer's use of steroids (untrue) or his less-than-auspicious early performance as an Oakland fifteenth-round draft choice. The author details Canseco's personal ups and downs and relates his success on the field as he wows the fans and media. Baseball enthusiasts will scoop up this readable account of the American League's Most Valuable Player for 1988 and enjoy the black-and-white photos of Canseco and other notable players.

Zena Sutherland

SOURCE: A review of *Jose Canseco: Baseball's Forty-Forty Man,* in *Bulletin of the Center for Children's Books,* Vol. 43, No. 1, September, 1989, p. 1.

It is inevitable that there should be similarities among baseball biographies, but Aaseng gets through the saga of rookie problems, batting slumps, and moments of triumph on the diamond without either adulatory descriptions or choppy game sequences. Canseco emerges as a pleasant young man and a capable outfielder who set a new mark in baseball history by winning 42 games and stealing 40 bases in the same (1988) season. Photographs of Canseco and other players may interest fans but add little to the information provided by the text.

FLORENCE GRIFFITH JOYNER: DAZZLING OLYMPIAN ("Sports Achievers" series, 1989)

Denise Wilms

SOURCE: A review of *Florence Griffith Joyner: Dazzling Olympian,* in *Booklist,* Vol. 86, No. 8, December 15, 1989, p. 827.

Griffith Joyner was a gold medalist in the 1988 Summer Olympics. While her victories made her an undisputed champion, it was her flamboyant track fashions as well as her athletic conquests that caught the eye of the media and the public. Aaseng's profile briefly describes Griffith Joyner's impoverished childhood (seventh of eleven children raised without a father in the Watts section of Los Angeles); her high school years, where track became a ticket to college; and the top-notch coaching that led to her first Olympic participation in 1984. Negative publicity such as the accusation that Griffith Joyner took steroids is not mentioned; Aaseng's emphasis is all positive. Illustrated with frequent black-and-white photographs, this will be a handy introduction to the striking Olympic star.

Janice C. Hayes

SOURCE: A review of *Florence Griffith Joyner: Dazzling Olympian,* in *School Library Journal,* Vol. 36, No. 3, March, 1990, p. 222.

Aaseng's smooth, easy style accurately captures the development of this star athlete's quest to break world records in the women's sprints. Griffith Joyner, the seventh of 11 children, began her running career chasing rabbits in the Mojave Desert. Two decades of racing—from the desert to seven world records in the women's 100 meters—are described along with her capture of three gold medals and one silver medal in the 1988 Seoul Olympics. Her hard work and flamboyant style are chronicled in both the text and in black-and-white photographs (which can't entirely do justice to her unique running costumes and highly decorated fingernails). Any reader interested in track and field, the Olympics, or women in sports will find the biography informative.

BETTER MOUSETRAPS: PRODUCT IMPROVEMENTS THAT LED TO SUCCESS ("Inside Business" series, 1989)

Kirkus Reviews

SOURCE: A review of *Better Mousetraps: Product Improvements That Led to Success,* in *Kirkus Reviews,* Vol. LVIII, No. 1, January 1, 1990, p. 43.

Don't look for trailblazers here: these innovators triumphed by refining existing inventions.

Each of these eight contagiously exciting chapters demonstrates the achievement and entrepreneurial flair of a product polisher. Eastman, a former bottle-cap salesman, traveled with dogged determination to England to learn more about developing film. King Gillette, whose grandiose ideas matched his name, wanted to reorganize the world as a single corporation but settled for revolutionizing shaving habits. Members of the Otis family invented 50 patented features for their elevators; the Tupper story reflects marketing innovations; while the

Caterpillar production demonstrates that necessity is the mother of invention: their new machinery was essential to the vast western expanses. Margaret Rudkin made a success of Pepperidge Farm with a nostalgic appeal to earlier values and stone-ground flour.

Patent charts, old ads, and fascinating trivia add to the fun; glossary-like sidebars amplify concepts like "sole proprietorship." A delightful exploration of the idiosyncratic and various ways in which individuals have shaped technology and technology in its turn has influenced society.

Phillis Wilson

SOURCE: A review of *Better Mousetraps: Product Improvements That Led to Success,* in *Booklist,* Vol. 86, No. 13, March 1, 1990, p. 1279.

Just as a savvy entrepreneur follows on the heels of his own success, so does a savvy author. *Mousetraps,* Aaseng's candid account of people who ingeniously improved, refined, or polished a product already in existence, will have readers beating a path to the bookshelves housing this and the other excellent titles in his Inside Business series. Fascinating anecdotes abound as Aaseng discusses Gillette's razor and the disposable society it launched, Pepperidge Farm products and the Tupperware™ to store them in, and diverse machinery such as the Caterpillar tractor, Rolls Royce, Zamboni ice-resurfacing machines, Otis elevators, and George Eastman's Brownie camera. Aaseng brings out how frustration with drudgery, hassle, or inefficiency propelled these individuals, not to gripe, but to turn the lemon into lemonade—a good philosophy for children to be exposed to. Period photographs, reproductions of ads, and relevant definitions placed appropriately in the margins expand this quality offering.

Margaret M. Hagel

SOURCE: A review of *Better Mousetraps: Product Improvements that Led to Success,* in *School Library Journal,* Vol. 36, No. 4, April, 1990, p. 146.

Aaseng's thesis is that it is not necessarily the inventor of an item, but the person who markets the most improved version of it who gets the most customers. Eight success stories detail the evolution of products from heavy machinery to Tupperware™, from elevators to razors. These product improvements, like their original inventions, came about because someone recognized their need and had the creative mind to design them. These individuals persevered until their improvement was a success while others failed. Each story is a piece of Americana, illustrated with black-and-white photographs and patent drawings, which, for the most part, depict the product and its designer, and occasionally how the product works. This is a book for aspiring inventors and can serve as a supplement to American history collections.

Young people who feel that everything has been invented will learn that there is a need for their creativity.

MIDSTREAM CHANGES: PEOPLE WHO STARTED OVER AND MADE IT WORK ("Inside Business" series, 1990)

Phillis Wilson

SOURCE: A review of *Midstream Changes: People Who Started Over and Made It Work,* in *Booklist,* Vol. 86, No. 18, May 15, 1990, p. 1794.

With today's prevalence of corporate mergers, takeovers, and buyouts, along with the culling of personnel that often results, Aaseng's work is timely. Young readers may be exposed to "midstream changes" within their own families, and these eight accounts are proof that creativity, risk-taking, and stamina can turn catastrophe around. In contrast to **Better Mousetraps,** more contemporary people are profiled: Conrad Hilton (of the hotel empire), Mary Kay Ash (whose pink cadillac incentives are synonymous with her cosmetics line), and Colonel Sanders of Kentucky Fried Chicken fame. Throughout, Aaseng provides a compelling account as he shows how an unlikely chain of events turned fortuitous for men like Milton Bradley, Levi Strauss, and William Coleman; period photographs and definitions of business terms expand this fascinating work.

Joan McGrath

SOURCE: A review of *Midstream Changes: People Who Started Over and Made It Work,* in *School Library Journal,* Vol. 36, No. 8, August, 1990, p. 166.

These mini-biographies of seven men and one woman who started out in one career and found themselves in another provide proof that changes are always possible, and not necessarily bad, even when they arrive unexpectedly. Included are Milton Bradley, who became the czar of the board game when his lithography business was ruined by an odd quirk of fate; Colonel Harland Sanders, who was facing a retirement in poverty after his businesses failed, and whose recipe for fried chicken made him world famous; and Mary Kay Ash, who built her own cosmetic empire. The stories are inspirational and encouraging. The problem is that young readers—including most teenagers—seldom imagine themselves as working adults, let alone as adults retooling for a second or third career. They will most likely think these success stories interesting but irrelevant to their concerns. Thus, this undemanding, thought-provoking book may be of more interest in vocational guidance, business, and adult education courses, or in literacy programs in which adult students with some knowledge of the complexity of the working world would better understand the enormous achievements and courage of these individuals. Black-and-white photographs suggest the humble beginnings that launched these amazing careers.

OVERPOPULATION: CRISIS OR CHALLENGE? (1991)

Kirkus Reviews

SOURCE: A review of *Overpopulation: Crisis or Challenge?,* in *Kirkus Reviews,* Vol. LIX, No. 7, April 1, 1991, p. 467.

In the "Science/Technology/Society" series, a dry but focused introduction to demographics-related issues. After describing the causes and deleterious effects of the population explosion, Aaseng discusses possible solutions and their moral ramifications and provides several case studies of societies that are attempting to solve the problem, delineating the reasons for their successes as well as failures. A final chapter redefines an approach to overpopulation in terms of the information provided.

Routine writing, but a clear, carefully reasoned, well-researched guide to an important issue.

Kaye Grabbe

SOURCE: A review of *Overpopulation: Crisis or Challenge?,* in *Voice of Youth Advocates,* Vol. 14, No. 3, August, 1991, p. 185.

This useful book for school reports, with Source Notes and a bibliography, presents the challenge of the world's attempts to deal with overpopulation and the abuse of limited resources. Half of the chapters deal with the ecological problems and the other half deal with problems of controlling the birth and death rates. There is a good balance in the discussions of the roles of science, society, and various moralities. The chapter "Moral Restraints on Population Technology" discusses abortion, RU486, eugenics, and politics. Aaseng looks at what different countries, i.e., Kenya, Hungary, China, are doing with regard to their population problems. In the chapter on alternatives, seven possible ways to deal with overpopulation are described: no action, production increase, voluntary family planning, government promotion, government incentives and disincentives, coercion, and social and economic change. Recommended as current, balanced material on the subject.

ROBERT E. LEE (1991)

Carolyn Phelan

SOURCE: A review of *Robert E. Lee,* in *Booklist,* Vol. 87, No. 21, July, 1991, p. 2043.

Neither debunking nor glorifying Lee's legend, Aaseng offers a balanced biography of the man who, though opposed to slavery and secession, chose to lead the Confederate army rather than Union troops in the Civil War. Illustrated with many black-and-white photographs and maps as well as reproductions of portrait paintings, the book provides a lively, interesting account of the life, times, and character of a much admired man.

Elizabeth M. Reardon

SOURCE: A review of *Robert E. Lee,* in *School Library Journal,* Vol. 37, No. 7, July, 1991, p. 92.

An adequate biography of one of the South's most revered figures. Aaseng covers Lee's difficult childhood, his early military career (during which he displayed none of his later brilliance), and his career as Commander of the Army of Northern Virginia. Although this portrait is not always adulatory—as when Aaseng covers Lee's domineering relationship with his daughters—he does repeat many of the typical compliments of the general. A better biography for the same age level is Manfred Weidhorn's *Robert E. Lee,* which Aaseng includes in his recommended reading list. An average book that doesn't cover any new territory.

📖 *ENDING WORLD HUNGER* (1991)

Jonathon Betz-Zall

SOURCE: A review of *Ending World Hunger,* in *School Library Journal,* Vol. 37, No. 8, August, 1991, p. 196.

A useful, comprehensive summary of a complex problem, and one that is well documented and well balanced. Aaseng covers all the basic points: the clinical definition of hunger, its causes and physical effects on people, a case study of Ethiopia, hunger in history, past and future technological efforts, and prospects for solutions. Rather than concentrating on any one factor, he shows how they aggravate each other and affect other problems. Aaseng also makes it clear that overpopulation is just as much a result of as it is a cause of hunger; children are the only "old age insurance" the poor can afford, and since many die, they must give birth to more to assure that some will survive. Most effectively of all, he shows how the values a society holds determine its actions. Arguments for all sides are presented fairly, although no individual is quoted anywhere. Instead, Aaseng gives over 175 footnotes, plus an up-to-date bibliography that covers both technical and moral issues. . . . Thus, this book can fill an important need for a timely, balanced, comprehensive treatment of a critical subject.

Debbie Earl

SOURCE: A review of *Ending World Hunger,* in *Voice of Youth Advocates,* Vol. 14, No. 3, August, 1991, p. 185.

Aaseng begins with an overview of the current world situation. He shows how production of food is limited by several factors: soil fertility, adequate water supply, and

methods of farming. When these factors are satisfactory, famine can still spread due to natural causes (droughts, or flooding), economic decisions (growing coffee instead of wheat, for instance), or political factors (one country declaring war on another). The situation in Ethiopia in the mid-eighties is explained in detail to show readers one scenario from recent history.

Aaseng then describes ways humans have worked throughout history to combat hunger. Mechanization of farming has changed the number of people one farmer can feed: a century ago, one farmer could grow enough food to support an average of five people, but by 1970, an average farmer was providing food for 65 others! Bioengineering, changes in irrigation techniques, fertilizer production, and weed and pest control are also covered. Even future techniques, like hydroponics are explored.

Instead of producing a simple solution to world hunger at the end of the book, Aaseng presents several likely scenarios along with their pros and cons. Ultimately, in a world that still has enough resources to feed all people, hunger is another word for injustice. Both individuals and groups of people will have to work hard and cooperate if the planet's wealth is to be redistributed to the point where all may be fed adequately.

📖 *CEREBRAL PALSY* (1991)

Constance A. Mellon

SOURCE: A review of *Cerebral Palsy,* in *School Library Journal,* Vol. 38, No. 2, February, 1992, p. 111.

A history and definition of the condition, its causes, detection, treatment, and prevention. Aaseng then presents contrasting case studies of two youngsters growing up with cerebral palsy and profiles individuals who have triumphed over their disabilities. His style is simple without being simplistic; his narrative is informative and upbeat. Even when describing some of the most debilitating aspects, he helps readers to see those with cerebral palsy as people. The design contributes greatly to the book's success; good quality black-and-white photographs feature poses of children that emphasize their personalities rather than their disabilities. A number of well-drafted, anatomical diagrams clarify relevant parts of the text.

Dorothy Furches

SOURCE: A review of *Cerebral Palsy,* in *Voice of Youth Advocates,* Vol. 15, No. 1, April, 1992, pp. 49-50.

Before reading this I had very limited knowledge of cerebral palsy. The neuromuscular system of the sometimes imperfect human body machine does allow us "independence to determine a great deal of our own destiny." But an estimated three quarters of a million people in the United States do not have neuromuscular control because they have cerebral palsy.

What is cerebral palsy? What are the causes and what prevents the condition? How is it detected and what is the treatment? In this text the answers to these questions are so interesting that once I began reading I didn't stop until I ran into the last page. I didn't need to reread any sentences or reread a previous paragraph to keep my train of thought.

The explanation of experimental treatments is easily understood: (1) Biofeedback uses an electronic sound device that tells CP exercisers whether their actions are achieving the desired results; (2) Implanted electrodes in the brain are used to trigger activity in damaged nerves; (3) The biochemistry process allows drug treatment to restore the chemical balance needed for proper muscle control. As with all experimental treatments more time and money are needed.

This is an encouraging book. Any library would serve their patrons well by including it.

📖 *NAVAJO CODE TALKERS* (1992)

Kirkus Reviews

SOURCE: A review of *Navajo Code Talkers,* in *Kirkus Reviews,* Vol. LX, No. 22, November 15, 1992, p. 1437.

The gripping story of the Native American volunteers who provided a unique military service during WW II to the very government that had oppressed their people. Using their own language, specially trained Navajo transmitted messages that the enemy could neither read nor falsify, greatly facilitating military operations in the Pacific. The background information here is particularly effective; few books so concisely summarize the Japanese advance and the American response to it, while none provides the same depth of insight into the conditions faced by these Navajo. Particularly interesting are how hard it was for them to convince other Americans that they weren't Japanese, and how some of the talkers attributed their safe return to blessing ceremonies conducted on their behalf by Navajo healers. Aaseng also shows the importance of coded communications to military operations, giving examples of how the early cracking of Japanese codes led directly to some crucial victories. After the war came white ignorance and neglect: the talkers were not officially thanked until 25 years later. An important story, compellingly told.

Roger Sutton

SOURCE: A review of *Navajo Code Talkers,* in *Bulletin of the Center for Children's Books,* Vol. 46, No. 4, December, 1992, p. 104.

With a real-guy focus that's a refreshing respite from the ecological wonder-tales that constitute many children's books about Native Americans, the versatile Aaseng here recounts the brave exploits of the "code talkers," Navajo Marines who, through their unique and complicated language, developed and employed an unbreakable code for WWII's Pacific Theater. The book includes details of the code-making and -sending with the soldier-stories of the Navajos, and the discrimination they faced from other Marines, who, uninformed of the secret code network, could be deeply suspicious of the Asian-looking Navajos among them speaking an incomprehensible tongue into the radio. The military history is exciting and easy to follow; the discussion of the Navajo codes (as well as codes used by the Japanese) is cogent and intriguing: The bombs delivered from these airplanes resembled the eggs delivered from birds, so the code word for bombs was *a-ye-shi,* which meant eggs. A good choice for an offbeat "war book," this would also make an unusual complement for both history and language arts classes. Historical photos of the code-talkers in action are included.

Chris Sherman

SOURCE: A review of *Navajo Code Talkers,* in *Booklist,* Vol. 89, No. 7, December 1, 1992, p. 657.

Aaseng's account of the Navajo code talkers who worked as part of the American military during World War II is sure to attract war buffs and students researching native American accomplishments. The author provides background on the military's use of cryptography, then describes how the Navajos were recruited to create an unbreakable code that allowed the marines to transmit information quickly and accurately. In addition to learning about Navajo participation in the war, readers will acquire a surprising amount of information about Indian culture and lore, living conditions on reservations, and how the Navajos were accepted by the military. Students enjoy Aaseng's books because they are interesting and easy to read, and this book is no different. In fact, it may even earn the author new fans.

Kathy Elmore

SOURCE: A review of *Navajo Code Talkers,* in *Voice of Youth Advocates,* Vol. 15, No. 6, February, 1993, pp. 362-63.

Navajo Code Talkers covers an interesting and relatively unknown aspect of World War II history—that Navajo Indians were recruited to confuse the Japanese code breakers during operations in the Pacific. Fast communication was important to win the war, but both Japan and the United States had broken each other's codes, so each knew their enemy's moves ahead of time. Each new code was easily decoded, until Philip Johnston, a civil engineer from Los Angeles, came up with the idea to use the Navajos. Since his parents were missionaries,

Johnston had grown up on a reservation, and was one of the few white people who could speak the language. The Navajo language is very difficult for an adult to learn. Each syllable means something specific and must be pronounced exactly. Four different tones of voice—low, high, rising, and falling—can change the meanings of words. Since the Navajo people on the reservations were so isolated, fewer than 20 people outside the tribe knew their language, and the language was flexible enough to make a code that the Japanese could never decipher.

Johnston went to the Marines with his idea, and they agreed to a pilot program and so the 382nd platoon of the U.S. marines was organized. The book goes on to describe the creation of the code, the problems of implementing the code, and the way that the Navajo Code Talkers helped in crucial battles such as Guadalcanal, Tarawa, Iwo Jima, and Okinawa. Although this book will be classified as World War II history, it is also useful for background information on the Navajo people, such as their treatment by the white man, and their religious beliefs. At the end of the war, a veil of secrecy covered the whole operation, presumably in case the code would be needed again. Twenty-five years after the war, the Navajos received belated recognition for their contribution to the war effort. Aaseng's book could be used for the nonfiction reader looking for a short, interesting read. Because of its unique subject, this book is recommended for most libraries.

THE COMMON COLD AND THE FLU (1992)

Kirkus Reviews

SOURCE: A review of *The Common Cold and the Flu,* in *Kirkus Reviews,* Vol. LX, No. 23, December 1, 1992, p. 1499.

By a frequent and well-regarded author of nonfiction on a wide variety of subjects, a cogent survey of the facts and issues surrounding the most prevalent ills still with us despite medicine's many advances. Beginning with a deftly crafted scene summing up the superstitions, beliefs, and arguments that typically attend the onset of a cold ("It's no wonder, the way you walk around after a shower . . . you can't go anywhere feeling like this . . . chicken soup for lunch," insists Mom, while Dad counters, "It's just a cold . . . you just have to tough it out. Here . . . Vitamin C"), Aaseng summarizes the history of knowledge and treatment, clarifies what's known about how these viral diseases are contracted and what may help alleviate symptoms, discusses what actually happens to the body and within cells during colds or flu, and concludes with an overview of ongoing research. . . . Sensible, thorough, and useful.

Chris Sherman

SOURCE: A review of *The Common Cold and the Flu,* in *Booklist,* Vol. 89, No. 14, March 15, 1993, p. 1309.

Aaseng examines two seasonal banes of existence, the common cold and the flu, in a readable book that reveals some exasperating facts. We learn, for example, that it may be better to tolerate a runny nose than treat it; that cold medicines using a "shotgun" approach to treatment (one product attacks a variety of symptoms) are not recommended; and that experts disagree on what causes viruses, how they're spread, and even how to treat them. But it's comforting to know that even though scientists don't know how it works, chicken soup is an effective decongestant. Aaseng provides clear explanations of how viruses attack and how our immune system responds, and he offers several theories about virus transmission. The history of virus research and promising current studies are also discussed.

THE LOCKER ROOM MIRROR: HOW SPORTS REFLECT SOCIETY (1993)

Kirkus Reviews

SOURCE: A review of *The Locker Room Mirror: How Sports Reflect Society,* in *Kirkus Reviews,* Vol. LXI, No. 5, March 1, 1993, p. 295.

Aaseng contends that the substance abuse, racism, violence, cheating, and sexism that have tarnished the image of professional and Olympic sports simply mirror blemishes of our culture as a whole. In his view, many athletes are driven to well-publicized excesses by market forces and fan expectations, while others are, or have been, held back by (generally) unadmitted, but tenacious, prejudice. He cites a host of examples: promising careers cut short; black and female athletes who bucked misconceptions; corrupt, ruthless college athletic programs; temptingly vast sums lavished by corporations and TV networks. Are things getting better? Aaseng notes that sports are becoming more governable, since rules are easier to enforce than laws, and that football, at least, is less deadly than it used to be (18 college players were killed in the 1905 season); even so, women's sports still get relatively little airtime, while the audience for wrestling's faux brutality grows apace. This able look at the impact of commercialism and the "win at any cost" philosophy makes it easier to see the less visible challenges that talented athletes face.

Jack Forman

SOURCE: A review of *The Locker Room Mirror: How Sports Reflect Society,* in *School Library Journal,* Vol. 39, No. 5, May, 1993, p. 130.

Aaseng raises questions that beg to be asked: when viewing the problems in sports today, "Are we looking through a window on a corrupt sports world? Or are we looking into a mirror that simply reflects the condition of our society?" After examining many unfortunate situations in amateur and professional athletics, he concludes that the latter question is the key. From the alcoholism of star pitcher Grover Cleveland Alexander in the 1920s to the substance abuses of Bob Welch and Len Bias, Aaseng illustrates how these stars grew up in environments that sanctioned alcohol and drug use to deal with the daily stresses of life. He claims that routine violence in ice hockey, football, and boxing are allowed to continue because society wants such behavior in its games. Similarly, he says that other ills—dishonesty, racism, sexism, and the obsession with money—are reflections of the values and behavior patterns of the larger society. He makes clear that such patterns in athletics are particularly dangerous because sports figures are seen as role models for the young. Because this provocative overview sets the issues it discusses in a context of how all Americans live, readers will be able to empathize with the problems that afflict many of their heroes and relate them to their own lives.

Roger Sutton

SOURCE: A review of *The Locker Room Mirror: How Sports Reflect Society,* in *Bulletin of the Center for Children's Books,* Vol. 46, No. 10, June, 1993, p. 306.

As his title suggests, Aaseng views the myriad problems of amateur and professional sports as reflections of the same problems in American culture as a whole. He devotes chapters to drug use, violence, cheating, race discrimination, sex discrimination, and money, generally concluding that social pressures and expectations from without are what cause the problems within: "Violence in sports is nothing more than a reflection of our society. Our games will continue to be as violent as we want them to be." (The second sentence does not necessarily follow the first, a conundrum Aaseng does not explore.) . . . Aaseng's book has broad coverage, is simply written, and is geared to a younger reading level.

Chris Sherman

SOURCE: A review of *The Locker Room Mirror: How Sports Reflect Society,* in *Booklist,* Vol. 89, Nos. 19-20, June 1 & 15, 1993, p. 1801.

Aaseng argues that the problems proliferating in professional sports today—cheating, drug abuse, violence, commercialization of sports, and racial and sexual discrimination—are not merely something new but reflections of problems prevalent in society at large. He believes, among other things, that our expectation that sports stars be exemplary citizens and role models may be unrealistic, that sports are only as violent as we want them to be, and that discrimination in sports will not end until it ends in society as a whole. In short, he views athletes as the same as other human beings and sees sports as a perfect mirror of American society. He gives readers lots to think about, and students will find many topics for papers, persuasive speeches, and debates. Aaseng notes that he consulted "hundreds" of newspaper clip-

pings and articles in preparing his book, and he provides a list of sources for each chapter.

📖 *TRUE CHAMPIONS: GREAT ATHLETES AND THEIR OFF-THE-FIELD HEROICS* (1993)

George Delalis

SOURCE: A review of *True Champions: Great Athletes and Their Off-the-Field Heroics,* in *School Library Journal,* Vol. 39, No. 6, June, 1993, pp. 112-13.

In an effort to counteract the highly publicized negative aspects of the sports world, such as drug abuse and arrogant behavior, Aaseng has compiled a book documenting the heroic efforts of a number of athletes. Some are well-known stories, such as the relationship between the Chicago Bears' Gale Sayers and Brian Piccolo, which inspired William Blinn's *Brian's Song* and Jeannie Morris's *Brian Piccolo*. Others are lesser known, such as the time Green Bay Packers head coach Bart Starr helped a stranded motorist who ran out of gas. While a nice gesture, this is hardly an act of heroism. However, the other accounts feature acts of charity, good sportsmanship, sacrifice, and personal struggle. The short, simply told passages average from two to four pages, with a few lengthier offerings, including the story of Dave Dravecky, the courageous pitcher who came back after a battle with cancer. For kids interested in pursuing these stories further, Aaseng supplies a useful list of books and articles. Interesting, inspirational, and easy to read, this book is a winner.

Mary Romano Marks

SOURCE: A review of *True Champions: Great Athletes and Their Off-the-Field Heroics,* in *Booklist,* Vol. 89, No. 22, August, 1993, p. 2044.

Many sports stars feel a responsibility to their sport and to society. Aaseng features some of these "true champions"—athletes who reflect personal courage, compassion, and heroism—in a readable, inspiring collection of profiles for sports fans. He briefly relates familiar tales about such legendary athletes as Babe Ruth and Pee Wee Reese as well as little-known stories about others who demonstrated heroism and self-sacrifice. The book is a good bet for reluctant readers, and sports enthusiasts can use the handy source-reading list to start them on the road toward learning more about the athletes who pique their interest.

📖 *YOU ARE THE GENERAL* ("Great Decisions" series, 1994)

Kirkus Reviews

SOURCE: A review of *You Are the General,* in *Kirkus Reviews,* Vol. LXII, No. 4, February 15, 1994, p. 221.

Aaseng applies to military history his highly successful "You Are . . . " format (used previously for accounts of political history and sports), allowing readers to choose among options available to commanders in seven 20th-century battles. Playing no favorites among nations, he sympathetically presents the German campaigns against France in 1914 and Britain in 1940, the 1942 Japanese attack on Midway, the D-Day invasion, the U.N. defense of South Korea in 1950, the 1968 Vietnamese Tet Offensive, and Desert Storm. Each chapter provides sufficient background information followed by the likely prospects for three or four different courses of action and, finally, the real-life choice and its result. Aaseng makes it fun to practice making such far-reaching decisions without having to face real losses of life.

📖 *YOU ARE THE PRESIDENT* ("Great Decisions" series, 1994)

Merri Monks

SOURCE: A review of *You Are the President,* in *Booklist,* Vol. 90, No. 15, April 1, 1994, p. 1430.

Aaseng devotes a chapter a piece to a crisis faced by each of eight twentieth-century U.S. presidents, among them, Theodore Roosevelt, Dwight Eisenhower, and Richard Nixon. The stated problems are accompanied by three to five possible presidential responses, putting the reader right into the Oval Office to weigh evidence and choose solutions to complex situations. The information in each chapter is basic and succinct, with a clear format: the statement of the conflict, the possible alternative solutions, a list summarizing those alternatives, the president's choice, and a description of the aftermath of the choice made by each of the presidents.

Mary Mueller

SOURCE: A review of *You Are the President,* in *School Library Journal,* Vol. 40, No. 7, July, 1994, p. 120.

Aaseng looks at eight situations during this century that have demanded decisive presidential action. He describes them in detail, presents the options that were available, and encourages readers to make their own choices. They can then turn a page and find out who the president was and what he did. There is also a "hindsight" section that details the results and long-term effects of these decisions. The Pennsylvania coal strike of 1902, the decision to drop the atomic bomb, the race riots in Little Rock, the Cuban Missile Crisis, and the Watergate burglary are included. From them, readers can see that our leaders are often faced with less-than-perfect options, and that what may be best for the country may not be politically feasible, such as Wilson's attempt to force the U.S. into joining the League of Nations. All of the presidents are pictured, as are the major players and appropriate scenes from each event. This format will help YAs understand both the scope and limitations of the power the president wields and the ways in which the office has evolved.

Laura L. Lent

SOURCE: A review of *You Are the President,* in *Voice of Youth Advocates,* Vol. 17, No. 3, August, 1994, pp. 161-62.

In this Great Decisions book, the reader assumes an active role as President of the United States. As president, the readers must make decisions on eight of the toughest crises—both foreign and domestic—to occur in the twentieth century. In order to make intelligent decisions, the reader must absorb the background information on each crisis and review the options available. As readers study each situation, they must remember that the choice they make will affect many peoples' lives; therefore, the pressure is on to choose wisely. After reviewing the options available, Aaseng reveals both the decision made by the president at that time and the results of that decision. In this way, readers can determine if their decision was better, worse or the same as the one made by the president at that time.

All eight crises differ in complexity and type so readers gain a real understanding of the various situations that twentieth century presidents face. First, Aaseng discusses how animosity between the employers and the employees in the Pennsylvania Coal Strike is diffused by Theodore Roosevelt. Then, readers step into Woodrow Wilson's shoes and try to get the United States Senate to accept the League of Nations. Late in 1940, Franklin Roosevelt has to avert entangling alliances and war to please the isolationists, yet provide aid to America's allies who desperately need our help. After being at war for four years, Harry Truman agonizes over whether or not the atomic bomb should be used to end the war with Japan.

After World War II, integration becomes a hot issue again. Thus, readers can determine whether or not Dwight Eisenhower takes the appropriate action to integrate one of Little Rock, Arkansas' high schools. Although domestic problems are brewing in the early sixties, the biggest crisis that John F. Kennedy faces is how to get rid of the missiles that the Soviets have placed in Cuba. Five years later, and in an equally ominous situation, Lyndon Johnson reviews the facts before him. South Vietnam is losing the war, and American troops are at risk. He must decide what action to take.

The last crisis that the author has selected is the break-in at the Democratic Party's National Headquarters. Richard Nixon is in trouble—especially since one of the burglars is James McCord, chief of security for Nixon's Committee to Re-elect the President. This last crisis is really interesting because readers get a chance to help President Nixon. Yet, one question remains "Can anyone help him?" This final crisis epitomizes the fun and the learning that can be obtained from this book when readers assume our nation's top position of power—the presidency.

I see this as a fantastic resource book for the teaching of American history, which can be extremely important in a classroom setting. I do not feel that it is the type of book that will be used for recreational reading by adolescents. I would, however, highly recommend that all social science teachers have copies of all of the "Great Decisions" titles in their classroom to enliven discussions and improve the students' understanding of major historical events. Aaseng's interactive approach to teaching history to American teenagers is innovative, invigorating, and informative.

SCIENCE VERSUS PSEUDOSCIENCE (1994)

Roger Sutton

SOURCE: A review of *Science Versus Pseudoscience,* in *Bulletin of the Center for Children's Books,* Vol. 47, No. 11, July-August, 1994, pp. 348-49.

Useful to both science and current events classrooms, Aaseng's debunking survey of such timely phenomena as creationism, astrology, and biorhythms will fuel debate, and force advocates on all sides to define their terms. He proceeds from a ten-point outline of the scientific method ("Ten important criteria for determining what is science") and cautions readers to recognize the distinction between science and pseudoscience, which is not necessarily the same thing as "truth" versus "non-truth," given that there are many concerns in our lives (evaluating the relative quality of literature is one example he names) which science cannot measure. While the book is sensible, it's also a bit sweeping, particularly in Aaseng's first criterion, "science is logical and rational." That's not as value-free a statement as Aaseng believes it to be; many scientific discoveries (Barbara McClintock's work with "jumping" genes, for example) come from what many believed to be illogical premises. Aaseng does acknowledge the importance of recognizing "new-frontier science," but that's a term he uses without defining. Additionally, Aaseng's argument is weakened by a reliance on secondary sources: if you want to debunk the predictions of Jeane Dixon, you should really quote her directly, not from a book that's already dedicated to your way of seeing things. While Aaseng's take on creationism fails to give quality time to its adherents and will convince only those who already accept evolutionary theory, his analysis of biorhythmic theory is a model of sustained argument, and will teach students to look closely at "scientific" claims.

Patricia Braun

SOURCE: A review of *Science Versus Pseudoscience,* in *Booklist,* Vol. 90, No. 22, August, 1994, p. 2035.

In another high-quality book that is both fast and inter-esting reading. Aaseng educates readers in recognizing what constitutes true science and makes clear the importance of recognizing erroneous theory. After establishing language as one of the keys in evaluating information, he explores areas of scientific controversy, touching on a wide variety of topics—from ESP, near-death experiences, and biorhythms to cold fusion and creation science. A short quiz designed to help readers separate truth from falsity follows, and source notes and a short bibliography contribute to the book's value.

Carolyn Angus

SOURCE: A review of *Science Versus Pseudoscience,* in *School Library Journal,* Vol. 40, No. 9, September, 1994, pp. 243-44.

Aaseng offers a great deal of information in this title that's written in an easily accessible and engaging style. He establishes the importance of recognizing pseudoscience, exploring issues on four "battlegrounds": mind and spirit, the human body, planet Earth, and the cosmos. He discusses near-death experiences, ESP, miracle cures, earthquake predictions, "creation science," UFOs, astrology, and other pseudoscientific belief systems and evaluates them against 10 criteria for determining what is science. A few captioned black-and-white photographs add interest. The source notes and suggestions for further reading are useful additions for those interested in pursuing the controversies further.

AMERICA'S THIRD-PARTY PRESIDENTIAL CANDIDATES (1995)

Mary Mueller

SOURCE: A review of *America's Third-Party Presidential Candidates,* in *School Library Journal,* Vol. 41, No. 6, June, 1995, p. 134.

Aaseng tells the stories of some of our country's most fascinating political figures, the individuals who have run for the presidency outside of the traditional party structure during this century. They cover a wide political spectrum, from the Socialist Eugene V. Debs to the Dixiecrat Strom Thurmond. Theodore Roosevelt, Robert La Follette, Henry Wallace, George Wallace, John Anderson, and Ross Perot are also included. Throughout the book, it is made clear that these men have revitalized the political system by infusing it with new ideas and new groups of voters. Each one is profiled in a similar format, with a short biographical introduction followed by an examination of his political career. The author emphasizes the ways each campaign changed some aspect of the political landscape, and explains why the issues were so important. He is positive about all of the candidates, but also describes some of their weaknesses and condemns those actions that were racist or divisive to the country. This book is attractive, with a clean layout and numerous black-and-white photos. Each chapter has a map that shows the election results. Traditional examinations of presidential campaigns, such as Diana Reische's *Electing a U. S. President,* often ignore or give limited attention to third-party candidates. Aaseng does a fine job of correcting that oversight; thus, this book fills a gap that occurs in most collections, and is a good choice for any library.

Raymond E. Houser

SOURCE: A review of *America's Third-Party Presidential Candidates,* in *Voice of Youth Advocates,* Vol. 18, No. 3, August, 1995, pp. 175-76.

Beginning with Theodore Roosevelt, eight men form third parties because they are unhappy with business as usual. Theodore Roosevelt, unhappy with the way his successor has handled the presidency, forms his "Bull Moose" party, the most successful third party movement in U.S. history. Eugene V. Debs, the perpetual Socialist party candidate, is possessed with ideas for improving the lot of common laboring folks. Robert LaFollette the Wisconsin Progressive wants to make democracy more democratic. Henry Wallance, a former vice-president, has radical ideas about farm programs and world peace. Strom Thrumond and the Dixiecrat movement protest against the Democratic stand on equal rights and states' rights. George Wallace, at first a lightning rod against black rights, is later fighting to improve the lot of the common man. John Anderson, the intellectual, who at the end of his congressional career, opens the debate on a wide range of subjects including gun control, women's rights, an energy tax, and reducing spending on defense. Finally, Ross Perot, the Texas billionaire, campaigns on, off, and on again for balancing the federal budget and making government more responsible to the needs of the people.

These men, though unsuccessful in obtaining the presidency, have provided the country the opportunity to expand the exchange of political ideas far beyond the limits of the two major parties. Further, and more importantly, many of these ideas fell on fertile soil, and though radical at first, have sprouted and become law.

This little volume provides excellent summaries of the lives and causes of the eight men mentioned above. It is very readable and would make an excellent research tool for young adult readers.

AUTOIMMUNE DISEASES (1995)

Jeanne Triner

SOURCE: A review of *Autoimmune Diseases,* in *Booklist,* Vol. 92, No. 1, September 1, 1995, p. 52.

In a clear, informative, and engaging style, Aaseng tackles the frightening yet fascinating topic of those mysterious diseases in which the body essentially attacks itself. The dramatic first chapter, detailing his son's battle with an autoimmune attack, will grab readers, and the following scientific explanation is concise and easy to understand, covering what is both known and unknown about the immune system—how it works and rebels. The summary discussions of several of the most common of the more than 40 autoimmune diseases provide enough information for short reports and can serve as a good starting point for longer projects. Teens researching the topic for personal reasons will be encouraged by the no-nonsense yet upbeat approach. These diseases can be debilitating and they cannot yet be cured, but many of their victims live full, productive lives. The black-and-white photos, helpful illustrations, and celebrity anecdotes serve to break up the scientific text, create immediacy, and maintain reader interest.

Marilyn Fairbanks

SOURCE: A review of *Autoimmune Diseases,* in *School Library Journal,* Vol. 41, No. 10, October, 1995, p. 142.

Aaseng defines the term and goes into detail about 9 of the more than 40 diseases now categorized or suspected to be autoimmune. He explains how the immune system works and outlines current theories, research, and efforts to find prevention and cures. The book begins with the author telling of his own son's battle with hemolytic anemia and concludes with biographical sketches of famous individuals who suffer from and have learned to cope with various autoimmune diseases. The conversational style makes for easy reading and the human-interest stories will grab the attention of casual readers. The terminology is simple, with words in the glossary italicized in the text. . . . The only fault is that the other 31 diseases are never named. Nonetheless, this is a solid introduction to this class of disease.

Marcia Pentz

SOURCE: A review of *Autoimmune Diseases,* in *Voice of Youth Advocates,* Vol. 18, No. 4, October, 1995, pp. 239-40.

This fine resource on autoimmune diseases combines human-interest stories of actual cases with a clear presentation of essential facts on how the immune system works and on ensuing problems when it fails to work properly. Some of the case studies are of recognized people like George and Barbara Bush and hockey player Bobby Clark. The information is enhanced by well-chosen photographs, diagrams, and drawings. There is an especially arresting photograph of a white blood cell eating rod-shaped bacteria. The language and paragraph structure are economical without sacrificing either clarity or comprehensiveness. Such diseases as multiple sclerosis, rheumatoid arthritis, and lupus are discussed, along with other topics like what is being done to effect a cure and how to live with an autoimmune disease. . . . Historical perspective is given early on in the book by a succinct but fascinating account of early discoveries about the immune system. Although students won't be flocking to read this title, those who need to know about the subject will find it clearly explained and what's more, will find it more appealing than they expected.

YOU ARE THE GENERAL II: 1800-1899 ("Great Decisions" series, 1995)

L. R. Little

SOURCE: A review of *You Are the General II: 1800-1899,* in *School Library Journal,* Vol. 42, No. 2, February, 1996, pp. 115-16.

Unlike most nonfiction presentations, this one encourages readers to participate—to become field marshals and to interact with history. Young commanders must utilize the background data provided, develop a strategy, and make a decision. Aaseng covers the British at New Orleans, 1815; the Prussians at Waterloo; the U.S. in Mexico, 1847; the Allied Army in Crimea, 1854; the Army of Northern Virginia at Gettysburg; Custer's demise at Little Bighorn; and the Boer Army in the Natal, 1899. At the end of each chapter, questions are posed with possible options. The actual battle plans are provided along with the results. This easy-to-use, provocative study features maps and black-and-white reproductions.

THE O. J. SIMPSON TRIAL: WHAT IT SHOWS US ABOUT OUR LEGAL SYSTEM (1995)

Claudia Morrow

SOURCE: A review of *The O. J. Simpson Trial: What It Shows Us about Our Legal System,* in *School Library Journal,* Vol. 42, No. 4, April, 1996, p. 160.

With an aim to show "how the legal system works," Aaseng looks briefly at each stage of the O. J. Simpson trial and attempts to convey some of what is common to all such proceedings. The truth is that this case was highly unusual, and is therefore of limited use as a guide to those unfamiliar with the legal system. Nevertheless, the book does successfully shape the headlines or sound bites that most Americans were bombarded with into a coherent and low-key account of that particular case, keeping its sensational aspects in perspective. The final chapter is a thoughtful discussion of widely held perceptions that the media, money, and racism have corrupted our administration of justice. The book's brevity and high-interest level recommends it to reluctant readers.

Ilene Cooper

SOURCE: A review of *The O. J. Simpson Trial: What It Shows Us about Our Legal System,* in *Booklist,* Vol. 92, No. 17, May 1, 1996, p. 1496.

Aaseng uses the O. J. Simpson trial as a jumping-off point to inform young people about the American criminal justice system. Among the many topics covered are investigations, the arrest process, the grand jury system, and the trial itself. Crisply incorporated and evenly handled are discussions of the roles of the defense, the prosecution, the media, jury consultation, new technologies such as DNA, and constitutional rights and responsibilities. The book is well organized and readable, and although children may not be as caught by the O. J. hook as adults, the case works well as a vehicle for showing how the system works—and sometimes doesn't.

HEAD INJURIES (1996)

Christine A. Moesch

SOURCE: A review of *Head Injuries,* in *School Library Journal,* Vol. 42, No. 7, July, 1996, p. 87.

Nathan Aaseng recalls finding out that his 13-year-old son Jay "banged up his head in a sledding accident" and the young man gives his own poignant recollections of the events as a lead-in to the detailed discussion of traumatic brain injuries, their symptoms, and possible consequences. The writing is well organized and very complete; the author describes the parts of the brain and their functions and addresses the different types of head injuries, diagnosis, treatment, long-term behavior disorders, and rehabilitation. Special emphasis is placed on prevention (seat belts, helmets, etc.) and on developing awareness that head injuries are often underestimated in their severity. The diagrams are clear and descriptive, and the black-and-white photos, especially of CT scans, are instructive. A well-done and sensitive treatment of a little-discussed topic.

Laura Tillotson

SOURCE: A review of *Head Injuries,* in *Booklist,* Vol. 92, No. 22, August, 1996, p. 1892.

The tone falls on the dry side, and the organization of information is somewhat haphazard, but this title may be worth purchasing because very few books cover this subject for children. Nathan Aaseng's experience with his son Jay, who suffered a head injury at the age of 13, serves as a jumping-off point for a discussion of what happens when brain injuries occur, what scientists know and don't know about the effects of such accidents, and the emotional and behavioral problems that may develop.

GENETICS: UNLOCKING THE SECRET CODE (1996)

Deborah Stevenson

SOURCE: A review of *Genetics: Unlocking the Secrets of Life,* in *Bulletin of the Center for Children's Books,* Vol. 50, No. 2, October, 1996, pp. 46-7.

This is not, as the title might suggest, an introduction to the principles of genetics but rather a history of major genetic discoveries and the scientists who made them. Starting with Charles Darwin and the theory of natural selection, proceeding through Thomas Hunt Morgan and his discovery of the chromosome, and ending with Har Gobind Khorana's creation of a synthetic gene, the book examines the significant genetic ideas they and four others introduced to the world. Genetics can be a fascinating field, and this clearly explains several key concepts as well as demonstrating how much progress has been made in understanding this field in such a short time; nor does Aaseng shy away from discussion of scientific politics and prejudice. The biographical information, however, often slows the narrative pace to a crawl, and strange extraneous tidbits appear in the marginal glosses (why do we need to hear about the birth of Abraham Lincoln just because he shared a natal day with Charles Darwin?); occasionally those marginal explanations, which also appear in the glossary, are misleadingly phrased.

Voice of Youth Advocates

SOURCE: A review of *Genetics: Unlocking the Secrets of Life,* in *Voice of Youth Advocates,* Vol. 20, No. 3, August, 1997, pp. 162-63.

Aaseng conveys the excitement of discovery in this collective biography of the men and women who, through careful observation and brilliant leaps of imagination, have cracked the genetic code. From Darwin and Mendel to Khorana, scientists have progressed perilously or wondrously close to creating life. There is a lot to stimulate discussion here, given current events.

AMERICAN DINOSAUR HUNTERS (1996)

Ilene Cooper

SOURCE: A review of *American Dinosaur Hunters,* in *Booklist,* Vol. 93, No. 6, November 15, 1996, p. 577.

Aaseng's writing style is lively, and he covers territory not so well traveled for kids. He begins with a brief history of paleontology and dinosaur discoveries and then goes on to profile such people as Edward Hitchock, a fossil-footprint expert; O. C. Marsh and Edward Cope, who were on opposite sides of the Bone Wars, competing for dinosaur finds; and Roy Chapman Andrews, whom Aaseng calls "the original Indiana Jones"—a photo shows him complete with wide-brimmed hat.

Susan F. Marcus

SOURCE: A review of *American Dinosaur Hunters,* in *School Library Journal,* Vol. 42, No. 12, December, 1996, pp. 125-26.

This informative and entertaining collective biography

promises to lure not only students already fascinated with the search for buried clues to the existence of prehistoric creatures, but also those who scarcely know what paleontology is. It provides concise portraits of 10 Americans who, for a variety of reasons, devoted their lives to uncovering prehistoric artifacts. Paleontologists included range from Edward Hitchcock in the 1830s, who was the first American to study and describe the remains of dinosaurs in the U.S., through Jack Horner, consultant for *Jurassic Park.* The book's appeal lies in the simplicity of the scientific explication, in the analyses of its human subjects, and in the clarity of the accompanying black-and-white photos. Among the intriguing subjects covered are the ongoing positive influence of the American Museum of Natural History; the drama of the Bone Wars, a feud between two men who jealously vied to accumulate the larger cache of fossils; and the public's fascination with fossil hunter Roy Chapman Andrews, "the original Indiana Jones."

YOU ARE THE SENATOR ("Great Decisions" series, 1997)

Jonathon Betz-Zall

SOURCE: A review of *You Are the Senator,* in *School Library Journal,* Vol. 43, No. 8, August, 1997, p. 160.

Members of the United States Senate often have to tackle major public-policy issues at times of great public debate and division. Here Aaseng discusses eight major decisions made by the Senate in the 20th century: Prohibition, the Social Security Act, the Taft-Hartley bill, the Civil Rights Act of 1964, direct election of the President, the War Powers resolution, the Gramm-Rudman bill, and the Brady bill. As he has done in his books about decision-making by presidents, generals, and Supreme Court justices, the author provides just enough background information for readers to consider three options in each situation. He then reveals the Senate's vote and the historical consequences. The format balances the interests of those on all sides of each question, and effectively portrays the emotions of the public and the decision makers. Much of this material will be new to this audience, as history textbooks ordinarily do not provide this depth of information. Period photographs and portraits of key players break up the text. A brief description of how a bill becomes law and a couple of web sites (already superseded by others) round out the presentation.

Ann Welton

SOURCE: A review of *You Are the Senator,* in *Voice of Youth Advocates,* Vol. 20, No. 3, August, 1997, p. 198.

In dry, but readable, prose, this book uses eight landmark decisions of the United States Senate (Prohibition, Social Security, the Taft-Hartley Act, the Civil Rights Act of 1964, direct election of the president, the War

Powers Act, the Gramm-Rudman bill, and the Brady bill), to illustrate how legislation is first introduced, then considered and voted into law. Each chapter gives background information on the issue under consideration. Options to either support or oppose, with arguments in support of each viewpoint, are clearly set out, and the actual decision of the Senate is given, with an analysis of the implications. This format provides clear, accurate historical information, allows readers to think, and clarifies the legislative process. The pro and con approach resembles voter pamphlets, with their presentation of arguments for and against legislation. This is a useful research tool that could be well used in civics classrooms. Liberally used, well-placed black-and-white reproductions, photographs, and maps put faces on the names and the issues. Good source notes, an exemplary bibliography, and an accurate index flesh the volume out.

📖 *YOU ARE THE JUROR* ("Great Decisions" series, 1997)

Jonathon Betz-Zall

SOURCE: A review of *You Are the Juror,* in *School Library Journal,* Vol. 44, No. 1, January, 1998, pp. 116-17.

Aaseng continues his useful series on decision making with incisive coverage of eight famous criminal trials of the 20th century. Beginning with the Lindbergh kidnapping case, he also covers the *New York Times* libel case (the state of Alabama's attempt to stifle accusations of racism), the Chicago Seven (antiwar conspiracy), Patty Hearst as outlaw, Dan White's "Twinkie defense," the Ford Motor Company's Pinto explosion, "Subway Vigilante" Bernhard Goetz, and O. J. Simpson's acquittal of murder. For each case, the author presents just enough information for readers to assume the role of juror, with three options from which to choose. He then reveals the actual results and analyzes the consequences. This format balances the passions of those on all sides of these cases and allows Aaseng to present controversial views in a palatable way. This is particularly effective when dealing with opinions that would be difficult to defend today (such as those of the Alabama officials) but that are necessary for historical understanding. An outline of how a jury is chosen is included, as is an introduction to the place of the jury in our legal system. Black-and-white photos show some relevant scenes (Chicago demonstrations), and courtroom sketches as well as portraits of famous figures are included. Other books on famous trials focus on the constitutional issues to the exclusion of the passions of the time, so this one makes a unique contribution.

Additional coverage of Aaseng's life and career is contained in the following sources published by The Gale Group: *Authors and Artists for Young Adults,* Vol. 27; *Contemporary Authors,* Vol. 106; *Junior DISCovering Authors; Major Authors and Illustrators for Children and Young Adults; Something about the Author Autobiography Series,* Vol. 12; and *Something about the Author,* Vols. 51, 88.

Karen Hesse

1952-

American author of fiction, picture books, and poetry.

Major works include *Wish on a Unicorn* (1991), *Letters from Rifka* (1992), *Phoenix Rising* (1994), *The Music of Dolphins* (1996), and *Out of the Dust* (1997).

INTRODUCTION

Hesse is perhaps best known for her Newbery Award-winning novel, *Out of the Dust,* written entirely in a lyrical, free-verse format. While she primarily writes novels for middle graders, Hesse has also experimented with other genres, including picture books and chapter books for elementary graders. She is recognized for her fresh, gentle, and unassuming approach to works for younger children and for the engaging themes and mastery of language she exhibits in her narratives for older readers. The "sense of place" in her novels has earned accolades from *Horn Book* critic Brenda Bowen, who regarded this quality "as most memorable about Karen Hesse's writing." This "sense of place" encompasses not only landscape—including diverse physical locations, from Russia to Vermont to Oklahoma—but also spaces in the heart and mind. Hesse has received further praise for her measured character development. Her novels typically feature young female protagonists who find ways to overcome significant adversity. Through their triumphs and tragedies, Hesse explores human emotions and relationships in an attempt to show what the human spirit must often endure. "I never make up any of the bad things that happen to my characters," she said in her Newbery acceptance speech. "I love my characters too much to hurt them deliberately. . . . It just so happens that in life, there's pain; sorrow lives in the shadow of joy, joy in the shadow of sorrow. The question is, do we let pain reign triumphant, or do we find a way to grow, to transform, and ultimately transcend our pain?"

Reviewers have enthusiastically described Hesse's writing as "vivid," "clear," and "colorful" and applaud her meticulous and detailed research. *Letters from Rifka* benefited in both character development and research thanks to its real-life inspiration, Hesse's Great-Aunt Lucy. Moreover, young Rifka, a girl initially intimidated by the "engulfing engine of reality" who finds solace both in writing unsent letters to her cousin Tovah and reading a collection of Alexander Pushkin poetry, sounds herself a lot like a young Hesse. "Thin and pasty," Hesse says of her youth, "I looked like I'd drifted in from another world and never quite belonged to this one. I had friends, but always I felt separate, unable to blend, not free enough to trust anyone with my core secrets." Similar sensations of detachment and loneliness drive many of the characters in her other novels, as well. In *Phoenix*

Rising, a young girl must deal with the dire consequences a nuclear power plant accident has had on her life and the lives of those around her, including a boy she gradually learns to love. In *The Music of Dolphins,* a girl raised by dolphins since the age of four tries to cope with her introduction to the human world; and in *Wish on a Unicorn,* a girl on the periphery of her school's social strata must cope with a mentally-disabled sister who believes she is the special recipient of a magical toy unicorn. *Out of the Dust*—featuring another protagonist with a harsh existence in the Oklahoma Dust Bowl of the mid-1930s—solidified Hesse's standing as a writer of both historical and issue-driven tales. "Hesse's ever-growing skill as a writer willing to take chances with her form shines through superbly in her ability to take historical facts and weave them into the fictional story of a character young people will readily embrace," wrote Carrie Schadle in *School Library Journal.* Whether raising questions about death and hope in *Phoenix Rising,* the meaning of being human and its relationship to language in *The Music of Dolphins,* the plight of refugees in *Letters from Rifka,* or the tenacity of the human spirit in *Out of the Dust,* Hesse explores her chosen emotional terrain with a deft hand and a poet's eye for relating detail.

Biographical Information

Hesse was born in Baltimore, Maryland, and grew up in a row house "surrounded by people, sights, and sounds," she once commented. Despite such an environment, feelings of isolation drove her to reading. In an essay for *Something about the Author Autobiography Series* (*SAAS*), she recalled that her "childhood home provided few places for private retreat." To find privacy she would go out the back door and climb into an apple tree. "There, cradled in the boughs of the tree, I spent hours reading. Often my bony bottom would go numb, but I loved it up there so much, I ignored the discomfort." She read one book after another, frequently forgetting what she had read and rereading it months later. John Hersey's *Hiroshima,* however, was different: "His book . . . had a profound effect on me," she stated. "If more books for children had existed at that time with real issues, if I'd seen characters survive the engulfing engine of reality, I don't think I would have felt so lonely, so isolated." Reading provided an alternate world for the shy Hesse; an active imagination provided yet another. As a young girl she believed she could fly and once had to be restrained by her mother from jumping out of an upstairs window. Angels, too, were part of her childhood experiences. "I saw the sky open late one night when I was not older than ten or twelve," she commented in *SAAS*. "As I watched, angels descended earthward." These, and other events of her childhood were filed away, to be used later in her fiction.

When Hesse's mother remarried, the new domestic package included not only a stepfather, with whom Hesse became very close, but also a stepsister who was exotic, beautiful, and a professional dancer. Hesse jealously began to compete for attention, joining amateur dramatics in high school. "I loved being on the stage, being someone else, she wrote in *SAAS*. "I definitely got noticed . . . I lost myself in my character to the point that I'd forget I was on stage. Suddenly I sort of 'woke' up and noticed people were crying." With the help of an enthusiastic drama teacher, Hesse was admitted to Towson State College, where she met her future husband. She eventually gave up theater, and the young couple eloped in 1971. "I never regretted my decision," she admitted. Soon after, Hesse's husband was shipped to Vietnam with the navy, and Hesse lived in Norfolk, Virginia, while she waited for his return. She also finished her undergraduate work, transferring to the University of Maryland. During this time, she began writing and giving readings, gaining a reputation as a poet. But before settling into her career as a novelist, she worked variously as a teacher, librarian, advertising secretary, typesetter, and proofreader. She would later credit those jobs, as well as her acting and parenting, with furthering her development as a writer. She and her husband eventually settled in Vermont, where they had two children, in 1979 and 1982. Motherhood put Hesse's poetry on hold, but soon she was experimenting with writing books. An early effort—about a family's encounter with Bigfoot—went unpublished. A subsequent short story collection, however, contained a four-page tale that a New York assistant editor with Scholastic asked Hesse to revise. What followed became Hesse's first novel, *Wish on a Unicorn*. Although Hesse is renowned as a novelist, with seven works to her credit, she began her literary career as a poet: impending motherhood and the requisite demands on her time altered her writing goals. "When I was expecting my first child, my ability to focus on the creation of poetry diminished as my need to focus on the creation of human life increased." As her children grew into greater independence, however, Hesse discovered that she could again concentrate on poetry. Her return to poetry resulted in not only her most critically lauded book, but a Newbery Medal, as well. *Out of the Dust* is written entirely in free verse. "I never attempted to write [*Out of the Dust*] any other way than in free verse. The frugality of the life, the hypnotically hard work of farming, the grimness of conditions during the dust bowl demanded an economy of words. Daddy and Ma and Billie Jo's rawboned life translated into poetry. . . ."

Major Works

In *Wish on a Unicorn*, the discovery of a toy unicorn by her learning-disabled younger sister seems to bring magic into Maggie's life. Suddenly, her pursuit of the acceptance and friendship of a small clique of girls at her school—a pursuit complicated by her sister, overworked single mother, and needy younger brother—seems to come to a successful end. Despite Maggie's apparent social improvement and a smattering of other granted wishes, though, there is more to her life and family than even a magic toy unicorn can correct. While its ending is upbeat, *Wish on a Unicorn* uncovers feelings of isolation and detachment that recur in Hesse's later novels. Nancy Vasilakis noted that "Hesse has written a compassionate story of a family who have little in the way of worldly goods but who are rich in solidarity and spirit."

Letters from Rifka drew its inspiration from Hesse's own family history. Based on the experiences of her great aunt, the book finds a young Jewish girl, Rifka, and her family fleeing persecution in the wake of the Bolshevik Revolution in Russia. Rifka writes letters to her cousin Tovah in the margins and blank pages of a treasured book of Alexander Pushkin's poetry. As the family makes their way toward the United States, illness seems to trip them up at the most inopportune times. They are stricken by typhus, and a few moments of fixing a peasant girl's hair on a train ride inflects Rifka with the girl's ringworm, preventing her from sailing across the Atlantic with the rest of her family. Upon arriving at Ellis Island, Rifka is further detained by immigration officials who suspect that the disease is not completely gone, thus preventing Rifka from joining her family. In the meantime, however, Rifka overpowers her fear of separation and makes the best she can out of the situation. After initially relying upon the kindness of strangers to help see her through the rest of her journey, she returns the favor by caring for a sickly baby and quiet boy while they are all detained at an Ellis Island holding facility.

Ellen G. Fader wrote, "Countering the misery and uncertainty are the main character's courage, determination, and sense of hope. . . ." Hanna B. Zeiger concluded that "this moving account from of a brave young girl's story brings to life the day-to-day trials and horrors experienced by many immigrants, as well as the resourcefulness and strength they found within themselves."

Phoenix Rising, a futuristic tale about a nuclear power plant accident and its horrific aftermath, features Nyle and Ezra, two youths caught in the accident's path. Thirteen-year-old Nyle and her grandmother continue tending their sheep on a Vermont farm, wearing protective masks and praying that the winds keep the contamination away. Two evacuees arrive from Boston: fifteen-year-old Ezra, who is stricken with radiation poisoning, and his mother; the two are taken in by Nyle and her grandmother. Nyle, like Rifka, experiences substantial personal growth in rising above her own difficult situation to care for the deathly ill Ezra. In doing so, she goes beyond her fear and self-protectiveness and comes to love the youth, becoming more grounded in the world around her. A critic for *Kirkus Reviews* wrote, "In the hands of a less gifted author this scenario might signal an issue-driven story, but Hesse transcends the specific to illuminate universal questions of responsibility, care, and love."

A *Publishers* Weekly reviewer called Hesse's fifth novel "as moving as a sonnet, as eloquently structured as a bell curve," and a work that "poignantly explores the most profound of themes—what it means to be human." The *Music of Dolphins* tells the story of a girl raised by dolphins who is reintroduced to a human world that she has difficulty understanding. Stranded on an island off the coast of Cuba after a plane crash, the four-year-old girl is nurtured by dolphins for ten years until she is discovered by the Coast Guard and becomes the subject of government study. She is named Mila, Spanish for miracle, because of her seemingly miraculous survival without human interaction. Despite her extraordinary ability to adapt to the island, Mila has difficulty adjusting to her new, human-populated environment. She begins to learn English and develop relationships with a few of the doctors examining her, a young man, and a similar "feral" girl who also grew up without human interaction. But all the while, the call of the wild continues to echo in Mila's head, and she longs to return to her island. When the compassionate doctors finally understand this, they disregard government orders and return her to her dolphin family. "This is a smoothly told story following the classic parameters of feral-child fiction, where the stranger in a strange land allows readers to examine their own world afresh," wrote Deborah Stevenson.

With *Out of the Dust*, Hesse returned to an historical milieu: this time, it is Oklahoma's Dust Bowl of the 1930s. Hesse worked on the novel for several years, drawing inspiration from a car trip to Colorado in 1993. Awestruck by the beauty and subtle varieties of color that she saw, she eventually internalized these feelings and assimilated them into her novel, melding them with a historical look at Dust Bowl events. After saturating herself in research, she developed the characters, Billie Jo and her family, and the format, free verse. Providing a glimpse of a bygone way of life, Hesse created a family that barely scrapes together a living by farming wheat, which is destroyed by the winds and the dust time after time. Dust is everywhere, in the sills, on the piano keys, in the body. Young Billie Jo, who loses her mother in a kitchen fire that burns her own hands, faces not only the difficulties of her grief and immediate surroundings, but an emotionally distant father, as well. The girl becomes an outcast until finally she and her father build hope out of utter desolation, and redefine what it means to be a family. "Readers may find their own feelings swaying in beat with the heroine's shifting moods as she approaches her coming of age and a state of self-acceptance," commented a reviewer for *Publisher's Weekly*. Susan Dove Lempke noted that although the story was bleak, "Hesse's writing transcends the gloom and transforms it into a powerfully compelling tale of a girl with enormous strength, courage, and love." Writing in *The Five Owls*, Thomas S. Owens concluded that *Out of the Dust* "gives a face to history" and "seems destined to become [Hesse's] signature work, a literary groundbreaker as stunning as Oklahoma's dust bowl recovery."

Awards

Wish on a Unicorn received a Children's Book of Distinction award from the *Hungry Mind Review* in 1992. *Letters from Rifka* received a Christopher Award in 1993 and was listed as a *School Library Journal* Best Book, an American Library Association (ALA) Best Book for Young Adults, and an ALA Notable Book, all in 1992. *The Music of Dolphins* received a Best Book designation by *Publishers Weekly*, was shortlisted for the Golden Kite Award by the Society of Children's Book Writers and Illustrators, and was designated one of the Best Books for Young Adults by the American Library Association, all in 1996. For *Phoenix Rising*, Hesse received the Heartland Award for Excellence in Young Adult Literature in 1998. *Out of the Dust* won the Scott O'Dell Award for Historical Fiction, a Jefferson Cup Honor Book designation from Virginia Library Association, and the Newbery Medal, all in 1998.

AUTHOR'S COMMENTARY

Karen Hesse

SOURCE: "Newbery Medal Acceptance," in *The Horn Book Magazine,* Vol. LXXIV, No. 4, July-August, 1998, pp. 422-27.

[*The following excerpt is Karen Hesse's acceptance*

speech for the 1998 Newbery Medal for **Out of the Dust,** *which she delivered at the annual conference of the American Library Association in Washington, D.C., on June 28, 1998.*]

Let me begin by extending my heartfelt congratulations to my fellow Newbery and Caldecott winners, past and present. And to all the hardworking, dedicated authors, illustrators, and librarians among us, please know, you are all winners, we are all winners. Because your work makes a difference. I celebrate every one of you.

For those of you who are wondering, here is the truth. Winning the Newbery could give a person heart failure. Even now, months after Ellen Fader phoned my once-so-quiet apartment overlooking the Connecticut River, even now my heart thunders when I think of that phone call.

I can't tell you how many hours of my childhood I spent tucked in a corner of the Enoch Pratt Free Library, devouring books, particularly Newberys. And look at me now. Members of the ALA, members of the Newbery committee, do you have any idea how extraordinary it is for me to be standing here, on this occasion?

There are so many to thank. My zayde, who sold his ticket on the *Titanic* and took the next boat over; my bubbe, Sara; my mom, Fran; my aunts, Esther and Bernice; my whole delicious family. A legion of dedicated teachers and librarians. My writing groups. My prince of a husband, Randy. Kate and Rachel, my extraordinary daughters. Katherine Paterson, my unwitting mentor. Brenda Bowen, my dazzling editor. My dear friends at Henry Holt and Puffin Books. The terrific team at Scholastic, led by Dick Robinson, Barbara Marcus, and Jean Feiwel. And my inspiration for **Out of the Dust,** Lucille Burroughs, who stared out at me from the pages of *Let Us Now Praise Famous Men,* imploring me to tell her story, even if I had to make it up.

I was told once that writing historical fiction was a bad idea. No market for it. I didn't listen. I love research, love dipping into another time and place, and asking the tough questions in a way that helps me see both question and answer with a clearer perspective. **Out of the Dust** is my third historical novel. In the first two, Rifka Nebrot and Hannah Gold brought me back to my Jewish roots. But Billie Jo Kelby brought me even deeper. She brought me back to my human roots.

I can't think about roots of any sort without thinking of my husband, Randy. We have had nearly thirty years together, to listen to each other, to learn from each other. Among his many gifts, Randy has a marvelously green thumb. I, unfortunately, do not.

Once, accidentally, I watered one of Randy's favorite house plants with vinegar. The plant looked thirsty. I thought I was doing my husband a favor. I didn't know the bottle held vinegar until I had soaked the soil, until the sharp acid filtered down through the rich dirt toward the roots. The plant died. It couldn't have done otherwise.

The innocent substitution of one liquid for another . . . it happens. In *Out of the Dust,* when Billie Jo's mother reaches for the pail, she thinks she, too, is reaching for water, pouring water to make coffee. She doesn't realize her mistake, that she is pouring kerosene, until the flames rise up from the stove.

Readers ask, could such a terrible mistake really happen? Yes. It happened often. I based the accident on a series of articles appearing in the 1934 *Boise City News.* That particular family tragedy planted the seed for **Out of the Dust,** as much as the dust storms did.

Let me tell you. I never make up any of the bad things that happen to my characters. I love my characters too much to hurt them deliberately, even the prickly ones. It just so happens that in life, there's pain; sorrow lives in the shadow of joy, joy in the shadow of sorrow. The question is, do we let the pain reign triumphant, or do we find a way to grow, to transform, and ultimately transcend our pain?

The first traceable roots for **Out of the Dust** reach back to 1993 when I took a car trip out to Colorado with fellow author Liza Ketchum. When we entered Kansas, something extraordinary happened. I fell in love. I had never been in the interior of the country before. Our first day in Kansas, we experienced a tornado. I watched, awestruck, as the sky turned green as a bruise and the air swelled with explosive energy. The second day in Kansas, we walked in a town so small it didn't have a name. It grew up beside a railroad track and never fully pulled itself from the earth. The wind never stopped blowing there. It caressed our faces, it whispered in our ears. The grass moved like a corps of dancers. The colors were unlike any I had ever encountered on the east coast or the west. And the sky and land went on to the horizon and beyond.

It took me three years to internalize that experience enough to write about it. I had been working on a picture book in which a young inner-city child longs for rain. My writing group loved the language but had problems with the main character's motivation. The question came, as it usually does, from Eileen Christelow. She asked, "Where's the emotional line here? Why does this child want it to rain so much?" I later captured the motivation, the emotional line of that picture book, even to Eileen's satisfaction, but at that moment, instead, my mind slid precipitously back sixty years to a time when people desperately wanted rain, to the dirty thirties.

A week or two later, Brenda Bowen, during a phone conversation, asked what I was working on. Either she should stop asking or I should stop answering. I know it's not good for either of us. When I replied I was researching agricultural practices on the Great Plains, the silence on the other end of the line was deadly.

"Oh," Brenda said at last. But then she said "oh" again, and this time it had a decidedly up side to the end of it. Not "oh," like "oh, no." "Oh," like "oh, yes." Brenda trusted me. She had faith that if I was excited by dust, there was a good chance that she—and, ultimately, young readers—would be, too.

But how could I re-create the dust bowl? I was born in 1952, in Baltimore, Maryland. What did I know from dust? I knew alley dust, I knew gutter dust, but what did I know of dust so extensive it blew from one state to another, across an entire nation, and out over the ocean where it rained down on the decks of ships hundreds of miles out to sea?

I phoned the Oklahoma Historical Society and asked for help. I'd found, in one of the very dry treatises on Plains agricultural practices, a reference to the *Boise City News,* a daily paper published in the Oklahoma Panhandle during the period in which I was most interested. The Oklahoma Historical Society allowed as how there had been such a paper. I asked if I might get copies of it. Yes, they said, it was available on microfilm. So off went my check to purchase the film, and when the package arrived, with giddy excitement, I rushed to my local library, and took possession of the microfilm machine, proclaiming it my exclusive property for weeks, while I dug in and lived through day after day, month after month, year after year of life in the heart of the Depression, in the heart of the dust bowl. I saturated myself with those dusty, dirty desperate times, and what I discovered thrilled me. I had thought it never rained during that period. In fact it did. Only rarely did the rain do any good. But it did rain. And through that grim time, when men jumped to their deaths from tall buildings and farmers shot themselves behind barns, I discovered there was still life going on, talent shows, dances, movies. Daily acts of generosity and kindness. Living through those dirty years, article by article, in the pages of the *Boise City News,* supplied the balance of what I needed to re-create credibly that extraordinary time and place.

I gave the manuscript to my daughters first. A novel in free verse, I didn't know if anyone would understand what I was trying to do. But both Kate and Rachel handed the limp pages back, hours later, their eyes welled with tears. Okay, I thought. They must have understood a little bit. I revised the manuscript based on Kate and Rachel's comments, and gave it next to Liza and Eileen. They asked a lot of questions, but for once they didn't ask about emotional line. I revised the manuscript again, according to Liza and Eileen's comments. The next time I sent it to Brenda Bowen. She phoned after reading it. "Agricultural practices on the Great Plains?" she asked. And then she laughed. And I felt that first flush of joy. But still there was shadow. I knew how much Brenda had loved *The Music of Dolphins.* "Could you love this as much?" I asked. "When it's all finished, could you love it as much?" And Brenda never hesitated. "It'll be great," she said. That's my Brenda. "It'll be great."

"But I want you to think," she said. "What is it about, really. What is going on with Billie Jo and Daddy, what is going on with Billie Jo and Ma. And what is going on with Billie Jo herself?"

And I knew. It was about forgiveness. The whole book. Every relationship. Not only the relationships between people, but the relationship between the people and the land itself. It was all about forgiveness.

I began my literary life as a poet. When I was expecting my first child, my ability to focus on the creation of poetry diminished as my need to focus on the creation of human life increased. For seventeen years, my brain continued to place the nurturing of my daughters above all other creative endeavors, and I forsook poetry. Not that prose is easy to write. But for me, at least, it required a different commitment of brain cells, a different commitment of energy and emotion. Part of my mind always listened for my children during those years. And that listening rendered me incapable of writing poetry. But something inexplicably wonderful happened. My daughters grew up. They reached an age of independence and self-possession that for the first time in seventeen years permitted my brain to let go of them for minutes, hours at a time, and in those minutes and hours, poetry was allowed to return and *Out of the Dust* to be born. I never attempted to write this book any other way than in free verse. The frugality of the life, the hypnotically hard work of farming, the grimness of conditions during the dust bowl demanded an economy of words. Daddy and Ma and Billie Jo's rawboned life translated into poetry, and bless Scholastic for honoring that translation and producing *Out of the Dust* with the spare understatement I sought when writing it.

I have so much respect for these people, these survivors of the dust, the Arley and Vera Wanderdales, the Mad Dog Craddocks, the Joe De La Flors. I discovered Joe in WPA material on the Internet and wove him in, a Mexican-American cowboy, hardworking, unacknowledged. I put him up high in the saddle where he belonged, where Billie Jo could look up to him.

Occasionally, adult readers grimace at the events documented in *Out of the Dust.* They ask, how can this book be for young readers? I ask, how can it not? The children I have met during my travels around the country have astounded me with their perception, their intelligence, their capacity to take in information and apply it to a greater picture, or take in the greater picture and distill it down to what they need from it.

Young readers are asking for substance. They are asking for respect. They are asking for books that challenge, and confirm, and console. They are asking for us to listen to their questions and to help them find their own answers. If we cannot attend always to those questions, to that quest for answers, whether our work is that of librarian, writer, teacher, publisher, or parent, how can they forgive us? And yet they do, every day. Just as Billie Jo forgave Ma. Just as Billie Jo forgave Daddy.

Just as Billie Jo forgave herself. And with that forgiveness Billie Jo finally set her roots and turned toward her future.

Often, our lives are so crowded, we need to hold to what is essential and weed out what is not. Reading historical fiction gives us perspective. It gives us respite from the tempest of our present day lives. It gives us a safe place in which we can grow, transform, transcend. It helps us understand that sometimes the questions are too hard, that sometimes there are no answers, that sometimes there is only forgiveness.

Hodding Carter said, "There are only two lasting bequests we can hope to give our children. One of these is roots, the other wings." Ellen Fader, members of the Newbery committee, members of ALA, from the girl who devoured Newberys in a corner of the Enoch Pratt Free Library, thank you.

GENERAL COMMENTARY

Brenda Bowen

SOURCE: "Karen Hesse," in *The Horn Book Magazine,* Vol. LXXIV, No. 4, July-August, 1998, pp. 428-32.

A profound and visceral sense of place is one of the qualities that is most memorable about Karen Hesse's writing. As I think about my relationship with Karen Hesse, I think not about *what* things happened, but *where* they happened. The sense of place in Karen's books is so strong that, as her friend and editor, when I think of Karen, I think of places.

My first experience of Karen was in a small, crowded cubicle at Scholastic, where I worked as an assistant editor. It must have been early in the day (I was on the east side of the building), and it must have been summer, because I remember light pouring in from the window. There was light; there was a plain brown envelope, and there was an address that made me want to read on. What kind of author lived on "Star Route" in a small town in Vermont?

Alas, this was an author who had written a story about a family's encounter with Bigfoot. It was impossible to believe the plot, and the Yeti angle was just plain weird. I didn't believe in that monster for a second. I very nearly packaged the manuscript up and sent it back to the author with a polite form rejection letter, but something in it made me keep reading. I could *see* that family, crowded into an old green station-wagon, hopes high, driving through the Vermont hills. I can still recall it clearly. The story was not credible, but the time and place were palpable. The voice was something to remember. I thought: This is a writer.

I wrote an encouraging letter, but declined to publish the manuscript, and I invited the author to send me more when she was next ready to submit.

I didn't see any more from her for many years.

In a different office, at a different publisher, with more oblique sun (facing east again, probably late winter), another package arrived at my desk. This one was from an agent, with four or five slender stories inside. I looked at the place from which the manuscript had been sent. There, on the title page, was Karen's name, which I didn't remember, and Star Route, which I did.

Could this be the Bigfoot lady?

One of the slender stories—just four pages long—was called "Wish on a Unicorn." "Hannie and I were walking home from school when we saw a unicorn in Newell's field." Now there's a sentence to get a story going. But at only four pages in length, there was no room for the author to explore the characters, the situation, the magic of the story. Could she revise? I asked the agent. Oh yes, she could.

That four-page picture book became Karen's first novel, which held in it so many seeds of her later work: an underprivileged family; a child who has had to shoulder more responsibility than she should; a longing to fix things for people who can't fix them for themselves. And that strong sense of place.

Where do those seeds come from? Karen—typical writer—unfailingly uncovers more about her interlocutors than she reveals about herself. I've known her fifteen years, and my sense of her childhood is sketchy at best. She was born and raised in Baltimore, Maryland; she has an older brother who fought in Vietnam; she dearly loves her mother, her aunt, her sister, her stepfather; and when she was nineteen she married her husband, Randy, and they took off to find a home for themselves, stopping only when they got to Vermont.

But though the names and dates are sketchy, here are the things I know for sure about Karen Hesse: as quiet as she appears, she's a born performer, and once she's on stage—whether on a panel at IRA, or in a cafeteria crowded with a hundred and fifty Long Island fifth-graders—she shines.

She's empathic to an extent I have never before witnessed—no nuance is too subtle for her to pick up and feel herself.

She makes everyone feel cherished—from the taxi drivers in New York who are startled by such unprovoked kindness; to her family, her publishers, her friends.

And, lest she sound like a complete Girl Scout, she has a backbone of steel.

Her books give her away, too. *Phoenix Rising* reveals

that she loves the land, and has a profound respect for it. She is unafraid of taking chances—witness *The Music of Dolphins*. She values independence—look at the wonderful Rifka, who makes that long, long journey all alone. *Sable* and *Lavender* show that family is important. Her Jewish heritage has shaped her greatly—Rifka again, and Hannah, from *A Time of Angels*. She knows that death is a part of life from being a hospice volunteer—that's in nearly all of her books. She has an ear for language, and is meticulous about word choice—*Out of the Dust*. Plus, she loves chocolate, though that book has yet to be written.

Two years after Holt published *Wish on a Unicorn,* when the manuscript from *Letters from Rifka* had been delivered, I met Karen Hesse in New York City for the first time. I took her and Barbara Kouts, her agent at the time, to a fashionable Italian restaurant on 18th Street, because I wanted to impress Karen with my taste. Another warm, sunny day—we were seated outside, and bees hovered menacingly above our food. As I looked at Karen's stricken face when the oversized *carta del giorno* was presented—her discomfort at being at such a pretentious place on such a lovely day, her dismay that a meal for three people could cost so unreasonably much—I learned something about her that I should have understood through her writing: with Karen, I couldn't fake it.

Bertolt Brecht has some words that, for me, sum up Karen's emotional honesty:

> And I always thought: the very simplest words
> Must be enough. When I say what things are like
> Everyone's heart must be torn to shreds.
> That you'll go down if you don't stand up for
>   yourself
> Surely you see that.

A cold memory this time: up in Vermont, late fall, past peak, at her home. My husband and I were up there, visiting with Karen and Randy and their two wonderful daughters, Kate and Rachel. We saw where Karen wrote, spent some time where she lived, got a sense of the texture of her life. I'd say we were in the garage when Karen told me the subject of her next book, but I don't think that's true, because I'm not even sure there is a garage up there.

But I felt as if I were in a garage—cold and hollowed out—when Karen said that her next book was going to be about a nuclear accident. I pictured a story with screaming headlines; desperate teens trapped in bomb shelters; a *Lord of the Flies* post-apocalyptic over-the-top nightmare of a book. We had just published, at Holt, Karen's two beautiful chapter books, *Sable* and *Lavender*, to excellent reviews. They were gentle, sweet, satisfying family stories. What's wrong with more of the same? the publisher inside me cried.

Of course, Karen saw right through me, but she didn't let it stop her. *Phoenix Rising,* or "Forever, Ezra," as it was called at the time, was to be the next book. I

edited *Phoenix Rising* with the manuscript propped up on my pregnant stomach that next spring. It was a difficult book, and I drew on my colleague, Donna Bray, to help me help Karen sort it out. This was not the sensationalized story I had anticipated, not in the least. Karen had reached very deep inside herself for Nyle's story, and to me it marked a maturity in her writing that we are all now privileged to witness with each new book she writes.

Phoenix turned out so well that I can't recall where I was when Karen told me she was writing a book about speech development (*The Music of Dolphins*) or, of all things, soil erosion (*Out of the Dust*). I guess I trusted her by then.

But I do remember reading *Out of the Dust* for the first time. And I know where I was. I may have appeared to be sitting at my desk at Scholastic Press, turning the pages of a typewritten manuscript, tuning out the office noise. But I was in Oklahoma in 1934. I was tasting the grit in my mouth. I was burying the dead. I was hopping a train and running away (to Hollywood, in that first draft!), out of the dust with Billie Jo.

I chose that powerful photograph by Walker Evans of Lucille Burroughs for the jacket of the book to evoke and reinforce the time and place of *Out of the Dust.* (It was only later that I discovered that Karen was looking at the exact same photograph as she was writing the manuscript.) The jacket was originally slated to be a more conventional painting, commissioned from a commercial illustrator. But such an approach would not have done the book justice. The jacket needed to show someone who had witnessed that terrible time, that arid place—just as Karen had, just as we all do when we read her unforgettable book.

A last Karen place-memory: her first ALA, in Chicago, in an airless, beige, convention hotel room. We were going to the Newbery-Caldecott banquet, and she didn't know what would be appropriate to wear. I came up to her room, and she tried on an emerald-green, princess-style dress she had bought for the occasion. It was lovely, but Karen looked in it the way she had looked at that Italian restaurant—desperately uncomfortable, trying to be something she just is not. "Wear that when you win," said I, the ever-optimistic editor, and she changed into an outfit I don't remember now, and went down to her first Newbery banquet looking plainer, but feeling just fine.

I am grateful to Karen Hesse for many things, not least for how she has given me a sense of place in publishing. Her first submission was my first "find." Her first published book was my first "discovery." And her first Newbery—well, I've always hoped that a book I'd edited would win the Newbery, too.

I don't believe Karen will wear an emerald-green princess dress at the Newbery-Caldecott banquet this year. She doesn't need to dress the part. She's found her place now.

TITLE COMMENTARY

📖 *WISH ON A UNICORN* (1991)

Hazel Rochman

SOURCE: A review of *Wish on a Unicorn,* in *Booklist,* Vol. 87, No. 14, March 15, 1991, p. 1493.

Maggie loves her younger brother, Mooch, and her brain-injured sister, Hannie, but sometimes it's just too hard caring for them while their single-parent mother works nights at the mill. At school Hannie's a drag—she even wets herself on the playground—and it's difficult for Maggie to make friends when the kids sneer at her family as trash. The plot's contrived, the folksy idiom of the first-person narrative is overdone, a stuffed unicorn is dragged in as metaphor, and the depiction of the minor characters is shallow (you can recognize the bad kid because his eyes are too close together). Yet the dogged struggle of the family in their trailer rings true—the poverty is palpable; Mooch steals food because he's hungry—and no easy solution is offered. Kids will be moved by the burdens on the oldest girl, who resents adult responsibility and yet finds the loving strength to reach beyond her years.

Publishers Weekly

SOURCE: A review of *Wish on a Unicorn,* in *Publishers Weekly,* Vol. 238, No. 17, April 12, 1991, p. 58.

Mags lives in a trailer with her overworked mother, her perpetually hungry little brother Mooch and her retarded sister Hannie. As the oldest, Mags is the responsible one, but when Hannie finds a ratty old stuffed unicorn and says it's magic, Mags almost believes her. The wishes that come true aren't spectacular: Mooch gets a sandwich after wanting something to eat, and Mags gets new clothes—hand-me-downs from her aunt, but there *is* some kind of magic. The unicorn acts as a catalyst, letting Mags see beyond the humdrum of everyday life and realize how important her family is to her. With colorful regional language (Hannie is "stubborn as an elbow,") and clear psychological insight, Hesse's debut ranks with Betsy Byars's *Pinballs* and Cynthia Voight's *Homecoming* in describing families surviving as best they can under economic privation.

Tatiana Castleton

SOURCE: A review of *Wish on a Unicorn,* in *School Library Journal,* Vol. 37, No. 5, May, 1991, p. 92.

Margaret Wade's family lives on the edge of poverty. Her mother is a single parent who works at night, and Mags feels beset by responsibilities and worries far beyond those of other 12-year-olds. Hannie, her retarded half-sister, finds a stuffed unicorn and is sure that it can grant wishes; Mags, too, almost comes to believe in the toy's power. There is no magic, but the events the unicorn's discovery precipitates lead Mags to a new realization of the depth of her love for her family. Hesse is sensitive to the youngster's mixed feelings of duty, caring, and frustration. Her plot moves satisfactorily, and she is successful in depicting the family's everyday environment; her description of the dinner Mags fixes for her brother and sister speaks volumes. The narrative is not always smooth, and the overuse of similes is distracting, but Hesse does capture the spirits of a stalwart young heroine and her family.

Nancy Vasilakis

SOURCE: A review of *Wish on a Unicorn,* in *The Horn Book Magazine,* Vol. LXVII, No. 4, July, 1991, pp. 457-58.

In her debut as a children's book writer, Karen Hesse has written a compassionate story of a family who have little in the way of worldly goods but who are rich in solidarity and spirit. As the eldest child, Mags must care for her younger brother and her brain-damaged sister, Hannie, while their mother is at work. These responsibilities weigh heavily upon a sixth grader who longs for freedom and time to develop friendships and for money to afford clothes that aren't bought at yard sales. The younger children, however, need constant watching. Six-year-old Moochie has developed the habit of sneaking into houses and taking food, and Hannie presents a special problem when she finds a dirty stuffed unicorn that she believes has magical powers to grant each person one wish. The author's use of the unicorn as a symbol of this family's essential strength is understated and effective. Despite their grumblings, both Mags and her mother rush to the defense of the younger children—Mama when Moochie is falsely accused by the neighborhood bully, Brody Lawson, of stealing a carton of Twinkies from the Lawsons' kitchen; Mags when Hannie and her unicorn disappear. The book's underlying theme is conveyed best by Hannie when, lost and alone, she at last makes her one wish upon the stuffed toy. "She'd wished for all of us. Hannie understood better than I did that we were all important. We were family." A rudimentary message that bears repeating, delivered with the force of conviction.

📖 *LETTERS FROM RIFKA* (1992)

Publishers Weekly

SOURCE: A review of *Letters from Rifka,* in *Publishers Weekly,* Vol. 239, No. 29, June 29, 1992, p. 64.

Twelve-year-old Rifka's journey from a Jewish community in the Ukraine to Ellis Island is anything but smooth sailing. Modeled on the author's great-aunt, Rifka surmounts one obstacle after another in this riveting novel. First she outwits a band of Russian soldiers, enabling her family to escape to Poland. There the family is struck with typhus. Everyone recovers, but Rifka catches ringworm on the next stage of the journey—and is denied passage to America ("If the child arrives . . . with this disease," explains the steamship's doctor, "the Americans will turn her around and send her right back to Poland"). Rifka's family must leave without her, and she is billeted in Belgium for an agreeable if lengthy recovery. Further trials, including a deadly storm at sea and a quarantine, do not faze this resourceful girl. Told in the form of "letters" written by Rifka in the margins of a volume of Pushkin's verse and addressed to a Russian relative, Hesse's vivacious tale colorfully and convincingly refreshes the immigrant experience.

Hazel Rochman

SOURCE: A review of *Letters from Rifka,* in *Booklist,* Vol. 88, No. 21, July, 1992, p. 1931.

In letters to her cousin back "home" in Russia, 12-year-old Rifka tells of her journey to America in 1919, from the dangerous escape over the border to the journey through Europe and across the sea to the new country. Rifka gets ringworm and has to stay behind in Belgium for nearly a year while her parents and brothers go on to America. The best part of the book is about her time on Ellis Island, in limbo, waiting to see if the authorities will declare her infection-free. The letters format is occasionally contrived, and few kids will care for the inflated poetry that heads each letter, though it is moving to discover that she's writing everything in the margins of her beloved book of Pushkin. The letters do allow her to bring in memories of what she has left behind, including the fierce racist persecution. Based on the experience of Hesse's great-aunt, the narrative flashes occasionally with lively Yiddish idiom ("You are bored?" her mother says to Rifka, "So I'll hire you a band"). What especially raises it above docu-novel is the emerging sense of Rifka's personality. Bald from the ringworm, poor and needy, she proves she's no greenhorn; she has a gift for languages, she's brave and clever, and if she talks too much, so be it.

Ellen G. Fader

SOURCE: A review of *Letters from Rifka,* in *School Library Journal,* Vol. 38, No. 8, August, 1992, pp. 154, 156.

In 1919, Rifka's family flees from the persecution inflicted upon them as Jews in Russia for what they hope will be a better life in America. However, the steamship company refuses to allow 12-year-old Rifka passage because she has ringworm. After more than six months of treatment in Antwerp, she is finally cured and nearly reunited with her family, only to be detained at Ellis Island. Officials there feel she could become a burden to society because her disease has left her bald; without hair she is considered less attractive and therefore may never get married. Ultimately, Rifka and a young peasant boy, who is also in danger of being refused entry, help each other gain admittance to the country of their dreams. The story is told through her letters to her Russian cousin and squeezed onto the blank pages of a book of Alexander Pushkin's poetry; appropriate quotes from the poet precede and presage the events described in the letters, which detail the embarrassment of a medical examination by a drunken and prying doctor; battles with typhus, hunger and loneliness; and a disastrous ocean crossing. Countering the misery and uncertainty are the main character's courage, determination, and sense of hope as well as the happy ending. Based largely on the memories of the author's great-aunt, this historical novel has a plot, characters, and style that will make it an often-requested choice from young readers. A vivid, memorable, and involving reading experience, in spite of the somewhat morose and bleak cover.

Betsy Hearne

SOURCE: A review of *Letters from Rifka,* in *Bulletin of the Center for Children's Books,* Vol. 46, No. 2, October, 1992, p. 44.

This epistolary novel chronicles twelve-year-old Rifka's journey from Russia to America, interrupted in Poland when she almost dies of typhus and in Belgium when the ringworm she has contracted on a freight train prevents her from boarding the ship with her family. From then on and through her stay on Ellis Island, she is alone except for the letters she writes to her cousin in the blank pages of a book of Pushkin's poetry. This device seems a little unbelievable, since Rifka's letters run to 145 pages, but the story itself is credibly developed and the voice convincing. Rifka's detainment leaves her realistically disillusioned about the immigrant experience: "You have to be perfect to come to America. I have this bald head and you, you have a crooked back. . . . We are not welcome." A number of novels have focused on the experience of Jews in Russia or new arrivals to the U.S.; this one is vivid in detailing the physical and emotional toll exacted for passage.

POPPY'S CHAIR (1993)

Kirkus Reviews

SOURCE: A review of *Poppy's Chair,* in *Kirkus Reviews,* Vol. LXI, No. 4, February 15, 1993, p. 227.

At Gramm's house for her first long visit since "Poppy" died, Leah is sad and uneasy: she's afraid to look at his picture, unwilling to sing the song they shared, and conscious of the familiar chair that, in unspoken agreement, she and Gramm are both avoiding. Hesse skillfully chooses details that reveal her characters' feelings while epitomizing their loss. Leah remains aloof during a day's shopping; that night, concerned for Gramm, she finds her sleeping in Poppy's chair. In a comforting dialogue that is both believable and wise, Gramm tells Leah how terrible, even angry, she felt when Poppy died—as Leah will when Gramm eventually dies too; still, like Gramm, Leah will be "all right." Gramm is especially well individualized, the kind of white-haired lady whose hat, gloves, and shoes all match; [Kay] Life, who uses pastels to depict the pair in an accessible, realistic style, brings a commendable subtlety to both sympathetic characterizations. Thoughtful and well crafted.

Kathryn Broderick

SOURCE: A review of *Poppy's Chair* in *Booklist,* Vol. 89, No. 14, March 15, 1993, p. 1359.

Leah usually spends two weeks every summer with Gramm and Poppy. This year, however, Poppy is gone, and Leah learns from her grandmother how to accept her grandfather's death. The story starts slowly, and this, in conjunction with the beige background and pastel illustrations, lends an appropriate slow-motion effect to the book. Then, in a very touching manner, Hesse's writing grows stronger, successfully handling the delicate subject. At the start, the young child is attracted and, at the same time, repelled by a few of Poppy's possessions—his chair, the charms he had picked out for her bracelet, a photo. But as the book closes, she has embraced these things and the memories they evoke. Finally, it is the memory of Poppy's smile, a shared song, and the warmth of Gramm's arms that comfort her most.

📖 *LESTER'S DOG* (1993)

Publishers Weekly

SOURCE: A review of *Lester's Dog,* in *Publishers Weekly,* Vol. 240, No. 35, August 30, 1993, p. 95.

This atmospheric picture book memorably evokes the long summer evenings of a bygone era, then broadens in scope to convey a boy's sudden courage and the warmth of friendship. The young narrator peppers his story with the inflections and observations of youth ("We walk down the hill on our toes to keep from going too fast") in this vivid, vibrant text, full of unexpected word choices ("Mama scoots me out of the house." "My legs feel like they're dragging bricks"). Soft pictures [by Nancy Carpenter] are dreamily nostalgic yet their vision is acutely realistic. Thus they capture fear, a ferocious dog, movement in the still heat and shadows beyond the reaches of the sun, all the while complementing the good-hearted tone of the text. The story line is spare—the boy and Corey, his hearing-impaired friend, must pass by a vicious dog on, a quest to rescue a trapped kitten. The narrator overcomes his horror of the dog and brightens a widower's day with his gift of the kitten. This unassuming tale shimmers with wisdom and persuasive intelligence.

Ruth Semrau

SOURCE: A review of *Lester's Dog,* in *School Library Journal,* Vol. 39, No. 10, October, 1993, p. 100.

A sensitive story about a boy who, with the help of a deaf friend, conquers his fear of a neighbor's dog that bit him years earlier. In the process, he saves a kitten and befriends an elderly, recently widowed man. Carpenter's pictures give vivid life to Hesse's gripping story, set in a 1940s neighborhood. The prose reverberates with powerful words—the dog "lunges," "swaggers," and "hunkers"; the kitten is a "tiny fist of fur, knotted up"; the child's legs "feel like loose Jell-O." The old man's lonely look focuses into one of loving concern when he sees and holds the homeless kitten. And the young hero, with a little help from his friend, knows he has faced down a demon. Children will beg to tell their own stories after hearing this one.

Kirkus Reviews

SOURCE: A review of *Lester's Dog,* in *Kirkus Reviews,* Vol. LXI, No. 19, October 1, 1993, p. 1275.

The unnamed narrator shivers as he watches Lester's dog light out after a car—he's had his own run-ins with the big creature and knows better than to tangle with him. Then friend Corey drags the boy on a rescue mission; he locates a small, needy kitten, summons up the courage to bark back at Lester's fierce dog, and finally makes a welcome gift of the kitten to a lonely elderly neighbor. "Garrison Avenue" comes to life in Hesse's words and Carpenter's pictures, which reveal what the carefully framed text leaves to judicious understatement: Corey wears a hearing aid. Plotting is sharp and tight; radiant painterly vistas add such details as cracked sidewalks and broken latticework, and readers are left with the satisfying feeling that this is no idyll but a real neighborhood of the not-so-distant past—one where heroic efforts and happy endings are still possible.

Betsy Hearne

SOURCE: A review of *Lester's Dog,* in *Bulletin of the Center for Children's Books,* Vol. 47, No. 3, November, 1993, p. 84.

Set in what appears to be a rural 1940s neighborhood, this is a story that will reach out to children who have been fearful of animals—or human bullies, for that matter—that they find threatening. At the age of six, the young narrator was bitten by Lester's dog. Now he can pass Lester's house only with the help of his friend Corey, who leads him up the street to the spot where Corey's found an abandoned kitten. On the way back, Lester's dog charges ferociously, and the narrator finds himself less scared than angry as he protects the kitten, yells the dog down, and deposits the kitten in the care of a lonely widower. Corey's hearing impairment is subtly incorporated into the story not as a problem but as a fact; the real problem is clearly the narrator's fear, and the fact that it is well-founded gives the story more depth than if Hesse had set out to show such fears are all in a child's mind. (Who Lester is, and why people tolerate his vicious dog, are questions rightly left peripheral to the main conflict.) The full-color illustrations are tensely textured and dramatically composed, with softly blended hues and an occasional stylistic touch reminiscent of Norman Rockwell. There's a bit of bibliotherapy here, but the storytelling and pictures are strong enough to support the message.

LAVENDER (1993)

Kirkus Reviews

SOURCE: A review of *Lavender*, in *Kirkus Reviews*, Vol. LXI, No. 19, October 1, 1993, p. 1274.

Codie has a special relationship with her aunt Alix, who lives up the block; though Alix's first child is due in two weeks, she welcomes the little girl for her usual Saturday night sleepover and assures her that, despite the big belly where Codie can see the baby move, "There will always be room" for her. Secretly, Codie is making the baby a patchwork quilt—a perfect gift for a seamstress like her aunt. When Alix is rushed to the hospital the night of the sleepover, she's concerned: she knows that "Aunt Alix has tried having a baby lots of times. This is the closest she's come to a baby fully done." The quilt is two weeks short of completion, and so, perhaps, is the baby. Working through the night, Codie finishes her gift with a border of lavender, Aunt Alix's favorite color; morning brings news that the baby's fine, and that "Lavender" is her name. This simple, easily read little story is a gem. Each telling detail—Alix's dogs comfortably settled on a lumpy sofa, licking cookie crumbs from each other's whiskers; Codie's joyous powdered sugar fight with her aunt and uncle the night before the baby is born, echoed in Alix's tone ("sweet and light, like powdered sugar"), when she finds the patchwork neatly tucked among the baby's clothes—is a gentle brushstroke in this tender, but never sentimental, portrait of a particularly nice family welcoming its newest member.

Rita Soltan

SOURCE: A review of *Lavender*, in *School Library Journal*, Vol. 39, No. 12, December, 1993, p. 89.

In this beginning chapter book, Codie is about to become a cousin. Her favorite aunt is two weeks away from giving birth and, though she's been pregnant before, "This is the closet she's come to a baby full done." This overnight visit at Aunt Alix's is different from the numerous others, because in the middle of the night the woman goes into labor. The child's anxiety over the birth and her worries about losing her special place in Alix's life are handled sensitively and realistically. Hesse incorporates a touch of symbolism with the blanket that the girl is sewing for the infant Lavender—a finished blanket will insure a full-term, healthy baby. The simple language allows for easy reading, and the full-page pencil illustrations [by Andrew Glass] break up the text nicely. Codie is a caring youngster eager to please, even when experiencing some doubts about the arrival of her first cousin. A fresh, gentle approach to a standard theme.

PHOENIX RISING (1994)

Kirkus Reviews

SOURCE: A review of *Phoenix Rising*, in *Kirkus Reviews*, Vol. LXII, No. 7, April 1, 1994, p. 480.

A massive nuclear accident has just occurred in southern Vermont. The first scene in this compelling novel parallels the kind of negligence that caused it: Eighth-grader Nyle and her friend Muncie confront a vicious neighbor whose dog has slaughtered sheep on Nyle's grandmother's farm. The young people are masked, even though a west wind has mitigated most of the fallout from the nearby plant. But Boston has been evacuated; an uncle has had to destroy his cattle; and though rain clears the air, much farmland is poisoned, death's full toll is yet to come, and the prevailing, often irrational fear will soon drive a wedge between the girls. When Gran takes in two survivors from the plant, Nyle is stricken: Ezra, 15, now lies deathly ill in the room where her mother and grandfather died. Conquering her memories and her dread, Nyle brings all her imagination to helping Ezra heal both his body and a deeply troubled spirit. In time, he starts school and begins to ponder how people, like sheep, can be led to foolishly accept a known danger; Ezra hopes to live to do better. In the hands of a less gifted author this scenario might signal an issue-driven story, but Hesse transcends the specific to illuminate universal questions of responsibility, care, and love. When Nyle compares Ezra's courage to Anne Frank's he cries out, "Do I have to die in the end too so people won't forget what I died for?" The answer is almost inevitable; yet Hesse portrays her characters' anguish and their growing tenderness with such unwavering clarity and grace that she sustains the tension of her lyrical, understated narrative right to her stunning, beautifully wrought conclusion.

Merri Monks

SOURCE: A review of *Phoenix Rising*, in *Booklist*, Vol. 90, No. 18, May 15, 1994, p. 1674.

A leak at the Cookshire nuclear plant spreads radiation contamination throughout New England, leaving death and ruination in its wake. Thirteen-year-old Nyle and her grandmother continue tending sheep on their Vermont farm, wearing protective masks and hoping the wind continues blowing east. When Ezra and his mother, evacuees from Boston, come to stay at the farm, Nyle's fear of intimacy keeps her away from Ezra, but as she comes to know him, and cares for him during a period of acute radiation sickness, she finds a way through her fear, comes to love him, and is able, in the end, to let him go. Nyle's friendship with her classmate Muncie, a dwarf, is well drawn, as is Nyle's emotional growth throughout the novel. Both the rural New England setting and the details of Nyle's day-to-day life are convincingly described. Hesse introduces important issues—environmental disaster, friendship, first love, loss, and death—in a novel that is reasonably accessible; however, the book will require effort from its intended audience, as its focus is on character growth and development, and the plot moves rather slowly.

Betsy Hearne

SOURCE: A review of *Phoenix Rising,* in *Bulletin of the Center for Children's Books,* Vol. 47, No. 10, June, 1994, pp. 321-22.

Nyle, who helps run her grandmother's Vermont sheep farm, still has painful memories of her mother's and grandfather's deaths and father's desertion. In fact, she has experienced too many losses in her own life to welcome ailing refugees from a nearby nuclear power plant disaster that has just devastated the countryside and killed an untold number of citizens. Yet when Gran takes in young Ezra and his mother, Nyle's drawn to the boy, who is weakened from radiation poisoning and struggling with the sudden destruction of everything he's loved. It's a credit to Hesse that she concentrates on character dynamics instead of exploiting situational dramatics. The love between teenaged Nyle and Ezra is delicately developed, as is the prickly friendship between Nyle and a girlfriend who's a dwarf. In fact, the generally complex scenes and personalities render unnecessary the occasional over-statements ("It scared me, thinking about a world polluted by radiation"), repetitions ("people always leaving"), and political reflections ("If people really understood how big this was, how far it went, how deep, something would be done. Now. To change things. So this could never happen again"). The story speaks for itself, as "Ezra and his mother huddled together, alone in the dark country of his illness." The friends, family, and loyal dogs that personalize this tragedy will move kids to their own thoughts about social action.

Nancy Vasilakis

SOURCE: A review of *Phoenix Rising,* in *The Horn Book Magazine,* Vol. 70, No. 5, September-October, 1994, p. 599.

Author of the widely-acclaimed historical novel **Letters from Rikfa,** Karen Hesse has turned her attention from the past to the future in this coming-of-age story set on a Vermont sheep farm shortly after a nuclear accident.

Thirteen-year-old Nyle, who has never reconciled herself to the deaths of her mother and her grandfather from cancer, is dismayed when her grandmother announces that she will be boarding two evacuees from the nuclear plant, one of whom is suffering from radiation sickness. The fifteen-year-old boy and his mother will stay in the back bedroom of their old house, the same room occupied by Nyle's mother and grandfather when they were dying. At first, the boy Ezra is barely conscious, and Nyle's attention is taken up by her prickly friendship with Muncie, whose dwarf-like stature makes her an object of ridicule and suspicion to many of the local people. As Nyle is drafted for nursing duties, however, she begins to let her defenses down and gradually falls in love with Ezra. When he finally succumbs to the disease, Nyle's emotional growth allows her to face his death with newfound strength. The story is told in measured, laconic tones, relieved by Hesse's obvious affection for her characters. In spite of their fear, neighbors and friends care for each other. The will to survive and persevere is strong. And by focusing on the love story between her two main characters, Hesse has made this story essentially one of hope and determination.

SABLE (1994)

Publishers Weekly

SOURCE: A review of *Sable,* in *Publishers Weekly,* Vol. 241, No. 17, April 25, 1994, p. 78.

Hesse turns out an exemplary chapter book with this superbly structured work about a girl and her dog. Tate's greatest wish is to keep the mutt that has strayed into her family's yard: "Mam and Pap hadn't said I could keep her," confides Tate, the narrator. "But they hadn't said I couldn't, either." The plot is familiar—Mam doesn't like dogs, Pap is sympathetic but stern, and when neighbors start complaining about the dog, Mam and Pap find it a new home, far away. Hesse, however, makes the story seem fresh. A few deft references evoke the setting, rural New England in the indeterminate past, and skillful use of easy-to-read language supplies the color (Mam, for example, doesn't simply bake bread; instead, "The muscles worked in her long back as her fist kneaded dough"). Tate herself is appealingly resourceful and determined, and the obstacles in her path are neither entirely predictable nor too neatly hurdled. Each chapter swings the reader through a spectrum of emotions and a comfortable surge of expectation.

Betsy Hearne

SOURCE: A review of *Sable,* in *Bulletin of the Center for Children's Books,* Vol. 47, No. 9, May, 1994, p. 289.

Easy to read and as basic in appeal as an animal story can be, this is young Tate's account of how she got a dog her mother didn't want, and how she got to do the woodworking her father didn't want her to try. The dog comes first, wandering into the yard as a starved stray that Tate feeds, then names Sable and adopts despite the protests of her mother, who was badly bitten as a child. Sable is gentle but has the bad habit of wandering off and returning with neighbors' belongings. Tate is forced to give away the dog to someone with a fenced yard, which gives independent Tate the idea of fencing a dog run herself. She's too late—by the time she finishes the project, Sable has run away from the new owner. Tate experiences an agonizing sense of loss, but the dog reappears, starving again and this time injured as well. The reunion coincides with Tate's parents' recognition of her responsibility; yet none of this seems pat. The protagonist's anxiety is convincing and contagious to readers, her voice carries a direct authenticity, and even the stock device of a climactic storm seems freshened by the taut pace and simple writing. The rural hard-times New England setting, reinforced by [Marcia] Sewall's homespun pencil drawings, has a sharp but unlabored presence of its own. Practicing readers will recognize this as an early chapter-book of the first order.

Elizabeth S. Watson

SOURCE: A review of *Sable,* in *The Horn Book Magazine,* Vol. 70, No. 4, July-August, 1994, p. 452.

In a clear country voice, the author relates a dog tale sweet and scary enough for any budding pet lover. Ten-year-old Tate feels like she really needs a friend. Pap doesn't seem to realize how capable she is and how much she would like to help him in the woodshop; Mam is tired and worried, and she doesn't like dogs. "I had no hope of getting a dog when Sable wandered down off the mountain last October," says Tate as she begins to tell the story of the miracle of the "scrawny mutt" she names Sable. Sable is allowed to stay for a time, until it seems that she can't be kept from wandering and bothering the neighbors; then she is given to a family friend. Tate adjusts to her loss and begins to show her growing maturity—so that she is ready to take full responsibility for Sable when she returns. A perfect theme and text for an early chapter book full of warmth and reassurance.

📖 *A TIME OF ANGELS* (1995)

Kirkus Reviews

SOURCE: A review of *A Time of Angels,* in *Kirkus Reviews,* Vol. LXIII, No. 19, October 1, 1995, p. 1429.

An intense, vivid tale of the devastating influenza epidemic of 1918. Hannah Gold's already unhappy life in Boston—both parents are trapped in Europe by the war, leaving her with two quarrelsome sisters on one hand and critical, humorless Vashti, a permanent houseguest, on the other—suddenly becomes a nightmare when people begin dying all around her, including her beloved

Tanta Rose. When the sisters show flu symptoms, Vashti orders Hannah to flee, but it's too late; feverish and semiconscious, she's taken off the train and, after a long bout that leaves her weak and voiceless, ends up convalescing with Klaus Gerhard, a kindly widower. As in *Phoenix Rising,* Hesse effectively captures the physical and emotional effects of deadly illness and makes wise observations about judging people too hastily: Reluctant to admit she eats only kosher food, Hannah nearly starves, but the worst discrimination falls on Klaus, for being German. In a strange, haunting subplot, Hannah has periodic visions of angels. An absorbing story with strongly drawn characters and a convincing sense of time and place.

Publishers Weekly

SOURCE: A review of *A Time of Angels,* in *Publishers Weekly,* Vol. 242, No. 43, October 23, 1995, p. 70.

WW I has separated Hannah Gold and her two younger sisters from their parents—their mother is trapped in Russia, where she'd gone four years earlier to visit her own mother, and their father has left for war, leaving his children at home in Boston with their Tanta Rose. The outbreak of the worldwide influenza epidemic of 1918 isolates Hannah even more, killing her aunt Rose and attacking her sisters. Rose's companion, a folk healer with little apparent affection for Hannah, insists that she cannot nurse the two sick girls with Hannah underfoot, and she belatedly honors Rose's wish to send Hannah out of Boston to healthier surroundings. Hesse intensifies the apocalyptic mood of her *Phoenix Rising,* palpably recreating the terror in the streets as the influenza spreads. An unusually nimble stylist, she is also a gifted researcher and makes superb use of period details (despite a few slip-ups in describing customs of Hannah's Jewish home). Less successfully, she overlays the historical matter with otherworldly elements. Hannah sees angels out her window at night, and when she faces crises, a violet-eyed angel saves her. The angel shepherds her to Vermont, succors her when she succumbs to influenza and watches over her as kind strangers restore her to health. The mix of realism and mysticism, to some degree compelling, is also disconcerting—it's as if Chagall's angels had been painted into a photograph by Jacob Riis.

Betsy Hearne

SOURCE: A review of *A Time of Angels,* in *Bulletin of the Center for Children's Books,* Vol. 49, No. 5, January, 1996, p. 161.

Hesse has taken on a lot here and managed to do justice to it all. This is a story about being Jewish, being abandoned, being alone with a life-threatening illness, and being able to survive through adjustment to sudden new circumstances. And these story elements, including a mystical vision that borders on fantasy, take the form of a first-person narrative set during three months of the influenza epidemic in 1918. Living in Boston with Tanta Rose and an herbalist named Vashti, Hannah Gold feels deeply responsible for her two younger sisters while her mother, who returned to Russia to care for their grandmother, is detained there by the war in which her father is fighting. When Tanta Rose dies of influenza and Hannah's sisters sicken too, Vashti sends Hannah to relatives, but the girl is already ill. She takes the wrong train, ends up in Vermont, and is saved by the Red Cross, by an old German farmer who nurses her back to health, and by a mysterious presence that seems to appear when Hannah most needs help. In spite of the large cast and canvas of events, Hesse has taken care to develop secondary characters to a complex degree: Vashti the healer is kind to patients but cruel to the children thrust upon her; the farmer holds to his pacifist views despite unpopularity with a community already alienated by his German heritage; and the scholar whom Hannah so disliked at the book's beginning and whom she reaches out to at the end goes mad with grief over the death of his own siblings. Perhaps the resolution, when Hannah finds her sisters alive and in the charge of her boyfriend's mother, is a little too good to be true, but this is the kind of fluke that sometimes happens in chaotic situations, and the groundwork has been well laid with period details that never intrude on the fiction.

THE MUSIC OF DOLPHINS (1996)

Publishers Weekly

SOURCE: A review of The Music of Dolphins, in Publishers Weekly, Vol. 243, No. 36, September 2, 1996, p. 131.

As moving as a sonnet, as eloquently structured as a bell curve, this book poignantly explores the most profound of themes—what it means to be human. The narrator, Mila, is discovered by the Coast Guard on a deserted island, where she has been living with dolphins. The so-called feral child becomes the subject of government study—pried at and poked, taught language and music. Her amazing progress contrasts with that of another "wild child," Shay, who is being studied by the same team of experts. While Shay remains locked in silence, Mila's hands can fly over the computer keyboard or the holes of a recorder, and she even tries to explain dolphin language to the eager doctors who become her family. But Mila feels the call of the wild growing stronger and doubts about the sparkling lures of civilization growing louder. Finally the longing for her island consumes her entirely. It's a difficult plot to pull off, but Hesse succeeds. While she insists on simplicity in framing the story, she also employs a high-wire writing technique, having Mila tell the story first in halting, little words (in big type), then in more complex, fluid words (in small type), so that the language and themes become increasingly sophisticated. All together, a frequently dazzling novel.

Kate McClelland

SOURCE: A review of The Music of the Dolphins, in School Library Journal, Vol. 42, No. 11, November, 1996, pp. 120, 123.

After a plane crash off the coast of Cuba, a four-year-old survives, nurtured by dolphins. At adolescence, the girl is "rescued" by the Coast Guard and turned over to a scientist who has a government grant to study the part language acquisition plays in socialization. Mila, the otherworldly "dolphin girl," is enthusiastic to please, learning to speak words and write her thoughts on a computer, but gradually she understands that she is a prisoner "in the net of humans." She begins to lose ground, regressing physically, begging to be returned to the sea. Hesse's skill is in making readers believe in this wise, intuitive feral child. Mila's longing for the sea and her dolphin family is so achingly palpable that her return is equally believable. Her story is told in her own perfectly sustained voice: the clear and simple, but profound and poetic language of a "foreigner" with a keen mind and resonant spirit but limited vocabulary. Readers, engrossed, will follow the intriguing device of changing typeface that indicates Mila's evolution-flowing script, to chunky bold, to standard size, and back—reflecting changes within her character. Deceptively easy in format, this is a complex and demanding book. Evoking a Selkie myth, it is a reminder that the link between humankind and nature is mysterious and ignored at our peril. This powerful exploration of how we become human and how the soul endures is a song of beauty and sorrow, haunting and unforgettable.

Deborah Stevenson

SOURCE: A review of The Music of Dolphins, in Bulletin of the Center for Children's Books, Vol. 50, No. 4, December, 1996, pp. 137-38.

A modern-day Mowgli, Mila has lived with the dolphins for something like a decade since, as a toddler, she was lost at sea in a plane crash. Now she's been found and "rescued"; researchers are helping her adjust to life as a human and trying to learn from her at the same time. Mila misses the water and her dolphin family, but her curiosity and openness make her receptive to new information; her love of music and her interest in another feral girl, Shay, even provide her with joy in her new home. Soon, however, the coldness of her position as research animal begins to take its toll, and her longing for return to the loving life she had known overcomes the small pleasures found on dry land. This is a smoothly told story following the classic parameters of feral-child fiction, where the stranger in a strange land allows readers to examine their own world afresh. Like many such fictions, however, this displays a deep and unquestioning romanticism and falls predictably into the clichéd dichotomy of utopian animal society and dystopic human culture. Still, the poetic evocation of Mila's life among the waves and her longing for same compels and will entrance many a reader: . . .

Mary Arnold

SOURCE: A review of *The Music of the Dolphins,* in *Voice of Youth Advocates,* Vol. 19, No. 6, February, 1997, p. 328.

Following her rescue by the Coast Guard, researchers discover that Mila has been raised by dolphins, and attempt to rehabilitate her to the human world. But in their zeal to study and learn from her, they imprison and threaten to destroy the special connection to another world that makes her unique.

A profound study of being human and the ways in which communication unites and separates living beings, Hesse's prose poem combines an intriguing format and typeface that reflects Mila's development and growing sociability, as it contrasts with the isolation and fear of another feral child, Shay. With an almost dreamlike style, Mila ponders the differences between her island home and dolphin family and the house she shares with her doctors. Even while she rapidly grasps the use of computers and becomes enthralled with making music, Mila finds herself drawn back to the sea and a more elemental way of life than civilization can offer.

Mila's rich inner voice makes her a lovely, lyrical character. The idea of a "wild child" with an adolescent's questions and yearnings is appealing; the seeming simplicity of the story line belies the complex technique. But with the *in medias res* opening, the preponderance of interior monologue and sophisticated styles, this will probably not be a first choice for reluctant readers.

📖 *OUT OF THE DUST* (1997)

Publishers Weekly

SOURCE: A review of *Out of the Dust,* in *Publishers Weekly,* Vol. 244, No. 35, August 25, 1997, p. 72.

This intimate novel, written in stanza form, poetically conveys the heat, dust and wind of Oklahoma along with the discontent of narrator Billy Jo, a talented pianist growing up during the Depression. Unlike her father, who refuses to abandon his failing farm ("He and the land have a hold on each other"), Billy Jo is eager to "walk my way West/ and make myself to home in that distant place/ of green vines and promise." She wants to become a professional musician and travel across the country. But those dreams end with a tragic fire that takes her mother's life and reduces her own hands to useless, "swollen lumps." Hesse's (*The Music of Dolphins*) spare prose adroitly traces Billy Jo's journey in and out of darkness. Hesse organizes the book like entries in a diary, chronologically by season. With each meticulously arranged entry she paints a vivid picture of

Billy Jo's emotions, ranging from desolation ("I look at Joe and know our future is drying up/ and blowing away with the dust") to longing ("I have a hunger,/ for more than food./ I have a hunger/ bigger than Joyce City") to hope (the farmers, surveying their fields,/ nod their heads as/ the frail stalks revive,/ everyone, everything, grateful for this moment,/ free of the/weight of dust"). Readers may find their own feelings swaying in beat with the heroine's shifting moods as she approaches her coming-of-age and a state of self-acceptance.

Carrie Sehadle

SOURCE: A review of *Out of the Dust,* in *School Library Journal,* Vol. 43, No. 9, September, 1997, p. 217.

In the midst of the Dust Bowl, 13-year-old Billie Jo loses her mother and unborn brother in an accident that she is partly responsible for and burns her own hands so badly that she may never again find solace in her only pleasure—playing the piano. Growing ever more distant from her brooding father, she hops on a train going west, and discovers that there is no escaping the dust of her Oklahoma home—she is part of it and it is part of her. Hesse uses free-verse poems to advance the plot, allowing the narrator to speak for herself much more eloquently than would be possible in standard prose. The author's astute and careful descriptions of life during the dust storms of the 1930s are grounded in harsh reality, yet are decidedly poetic; they will fascinate as well as horrify today's readers. Hesse deals with questions of loss, forgiveness, home, and even ecology by exposing and exploring Billie Jo's feelings of pain, longing, and occasional joy. Readers may at first balk at a work of fiction written as poetry, but the language, imagery, and rhythms are so immediate that after only a few pages it will seem natural to have the story related in verse. This book is a wonderful choice for classrooms involved in journal-writing assignments, since the poems often read like diary entries. It could also be performed effectively as readers' theater. Hesse's ever-growing skill as a writer willing to take chances with her form shines through superbly in her ability to take historical facts and weave them into the fictional story of a character young people will readily embrace.

Susan Dove Lempke

SOURCE: A review of *Out of the Dust,* in *Booklist,* Vol. 94, No. 3, October 1, 1997, p. 330.

"Daddy came in, / he sat across from Ma and blew his nose. / Mud streamed out. / He coughed and spit out / mud. / If he had cried, / his tears would have been mud too, / but he didn't cry. / And neither did Ma." This is life in the Oklahoma dust bowl in the mid-1930s. Billie Jo and her parents barely eke out a living from the land, as her father refuses to plant anything but wheat, and the winds and dust destroy the crop time after time. Playing the piano provides some solace, but there is no comfort to be had once Billie Jo's pregnant mother mistakes a bucket of kerosene for a bucket of water and dies, leaving a husband who withdraws even further and an adolescent daughter with terribly burned hands. The story is bleak, but Hesse's writing transcends the gloom and transforms it into a powerfully compelling tale of a girl with enormous strength, courage, and love. The entire novel is written in very readable blank verse, a superb choice for bringing out the exquisite agony and delight to be found in such a difficult period lived by such a vibrant character. It also spares the reader the trouble of wading through pages of distressing text, distilling all the experiences into brief, acutely observed phrases. This is an excellent book for discussion, and many of the poems stand alone sufficiently to be used as powerful supplements to a history lesson.

Peter D. Sieruta

SOURCE: A review of *Out of the Dust,* in *The Horn Book Magazine,* Vol. 74, No. 1, January-February, 1998, p. 73.

Prairie winds dark with dust blow through this novel—turning suppers gritty, burying tractors, and scouring lungs. Even the pages of the book, composed solely of first-person, free-verse poems, have a windswept appearance as fourteen-year-old Billie Jo Kelby relates her Depression-era experiences in the Oklahoma panhandle: "We haven't had a good crop in three years,/ not since the bounty of '31,/ and we're all whittled down to the bone these days." Billie Jo's world is further devastated when a kitchen fire causes the deaths of her mother and newborn brother and severely injures her hands, stalling the fledgling pianist's dream of a music career. A few of the poems are pretentious in tone or facile in execution, and some of the longer, narrative-driven pieces strain at the free verse structure, but the distinctive writing style is nonetheless remarkably successful. Filled with memorable images—such as Billie Jo's glimpse of her pregnant mother bathing outdoors in a drizzle—the spare verses showcase the poetry of everyday language; the pauses between line breaks speak eloquently, if sometimes melodramatically. The focus of the entire book is not quite as concise. As tragedies pile up over the two-year timeline (a plague of grasshoppers descends, starving cattle need to be shot, Billie Jo's father develops skin cancer), the pace becomes slightly numbing. Billie Jo's aborted escape from the dust bowl almost gets lost in the procession of bleak events, instead of serving as the book's climax. Yet her voice, nearly every word informed by longing, provides an immediacy that expressively depicts both a grim historical era and one family's healing.

Ted Hipple

SOURCE: A review of *Out of the Dust,* in *The Alan Review,* Vol. 25, No. 3, Spring, 1998, p. 113.

Set in the drought-stricken dust bowl of Oklahoma of the '30s, written in free verse, told by as memorable a heroine as you will meet in YA literature, *Out of the Dust* will wrench your gut. You will meet fifteen-year-old Billie Jo, not yet defeated by the *Grapes of Wrath* kind of poverty that grinds families to the very dust that ruins them; she is helped in her resolve by her mother. But then in a bizarre accident, one Billie Jo played an innocent but deadly part in, her mother is killed. Her father cannot cope, and Billie Jo is left with just her own personal resources. These, however, are considerable.

Please read this book. You will agree with me (and with the committee which selected it for the 1997 Newbery Medal) that it is a distinguished novel, richly meriting as wide a readership as possible among teens, among adults. It is very good.

JUST JUICE (1998)

Publishers Weekly

SOURCE: A review of *Just Juice,* in *Publishers Weekly,* Vol. 245, No. 38, September 21, 1998, p. 85.

Like her Newbery Award-winning *Out of the Dust,* Hesse once again celebrates a child's ability to extract beauty, pleasure and even signs of hope from her harsh surroundings. The opening image of Ma "spreading grape jelly so thin on the sliced white bread you can hardly find the purple" gives readers an immediate, vivid impression of the Faulstich family's poverty level. The simple, honest narrative of nine-year-old Justus ("Juice") Faulstich matter-of-factly expresses her plethora of concerns: Pa is out of work again; Ma is pregnant and keeps having dizzy spells; and she herself has to repeat third grade because no matter how hard she tries, she simply can't learn to read. On top of that, the family must come up with back taxes amounting to $1000. The outside world may be cold and cruel ("Poor as Job's turkey, that's what the church ladies say we are"), but Juice doesn't let it overshadow the warmth of her home: "We might not belong to anyone else in this whole world. But us Faulstiches, we belong to each other." Hesse's poignant story [illustrated by Robert Andrew Parker] of a family faced with seemingly insurmountable hurdles is filled with small triumphs and momentary insights. Juice's resourcefulness and faith in her father set him onto a vocational path, but also lead her to the realization that, as she learns to read, she may have to leave him behind: "Pa and me, we've been careful tiptoeing around this particular secret. But I can't let Pa's half of the secret keep me from doing something about mine." This brave heroine will pass the torch to readers everywhere; her courage is infectious.

Faith Brautigam

SOURCE: A review of *Just Juice,* in *School Library Journal,* Vol. 44, No. 10, October, 1998, pp. 100, 102.

Times are hard for the Faulstich family. Pa is out of work, Ma's pregnancy isn't progressing quite right, and the truant officer is after nine-year-old Juice. Although she is bright, letters and numbers behave differently for her than for other people, leaving her repeating the third grade and unable to read. The threat of losing their house to back taxes is the catalyst that leads Pa to open his own machine shop and Ma to make the children's schooling a priority. This is a timely event for Juice, who is just beginning to crack the reading code. Despite the absence of welfare, food stamps, and unemployment benefits, this is a contemporary story. The setting is Appalachia and the narrative is flavored with hill speech. Though the locale may seem foreign to urban or suburban children, the unity of the Faulstich family and the dignity with which they approach their poverty are absorbing and convincing. Juice's narration, for the most part, is both believable and lyrical, despite her life being " . . . as rough as a cob." In both pace and setting, the novel is reminiscent of *Sable*. All in all, a trim package with pared-down prose, a memorable main character, and enough complexities to provide ample food for thought.

Kirkus Reviews

SOURCE: A review of *Just Juice*, in *Kirkus Reviews*, Vol. LXVI, No. 21, November 1, 1998, p. 1600.

Down-to-earth, resourceful heroine Justus "Juice" Faulstich doesn't like going to school. She'd rather spend the day with her out-of-work father, or helping her mother, who's expecting her sixth child. Even though she's only nine, Juice believes she is more useful at home; secretly, she's afraid that someone will find out that she can hardly read. When Pa receives a letter explaining that they may lose their house because of past-due taxes, and Juice's older sister has to read it, Juice realizes that she's not the only one in the family with a secret. The struggling Faulstich family's strength and the atmospheric details of rural life lend the story a timeless, sturdy quality. This poignant story of love and endurance has a lot to say; fittingly, it never shouts.

COME ON, RAIN (1999)

Publishers Weekly

SOURCE: A review of *Come On, Rain*, in *Publisher's Weekly*, Vol. 245, No. 48, November 30, 1998, p. 70.

"Up and down the block,/ cats pant,/ heat wavers off tar patches in the broiling alleyway./ Miz Grace and Miz Vera bend, tending beds of drooping lupines," as a whole neighborhood waits for rain. The narrator, Tessie, is the first one to see the "clouds rolling in,/ gray clouds, bunched and bulging under a purple sky," and she engineers a joyful rain dance with her three friends, Jackie-Joyce, Liz and Rosemary. The long-sought rain "freckles our feet, glazes our toes./ We turn in circles,/ glistening in our rain skin." According to Hesse's bio on the jacket flap, this text contains her initial exploration of motifs used first in her Newbery Medal-winning novel, *Out of the Dust*. With poetic and immediate language, she again captures the cleansing experience of rainfall after a long dry spell. In an auspicious debut, [John] Muth's illustrations showcase an impressive range of perspectives, from the opening urban skyline to the subtle indication of the oncoming storm in the ruffling of a curtain to the girls' view looking up at their mothers from where they're dancing in the street. His inventive design sense and use of watercolors—smudges of shadow, glistening sidewalks and foggy city-scapes—are remarkable. This is an impressive tribute to those experiences that leave us "purely soothed,/ fresh as dew,/ turning toward the first sweet rays of the sun."

Additional coverage of Hesse's life and career is contained in the following sources published by The Gale Group: *Authors and Artists for Young Adults*, Vol. 27 and *Something about the Author*, Vols. 74, 103.

Colin McNaughton

1951-

English illustrator and author of picture books.

Major works include "Red Nose Readers" series (1985-95), *Jolly Roger and the Pirates of Abdul the Skinhead* (1988), *Have You Seen Who's Just Moved in Next Door to Us?* (1991; published in the U.S. as *Guess Who's Just Moved in Next Door?*), *Making Friends with Frankenstein: A Book of Monstrous Poems and Pictures* (1994), *Suddenly!* (1994; U.S. edition, 1995).

INTRODUCTION

A prolific illustrator and author of picture books for preschoolers and elementary graders, McNaughton is best known for his offbeat sense of humor and eclectic cartoon-like drawings. His picture books are reminiscent of the comic-book style, with outrageous, anthropomorphic animals and creatures exchanging witticisms in cartoon bubbles and labels. Celebrated for their creative and repetitive text, vivid and comic detail, and for the author's amazing ability to understand his young audience, McNaughton's books capture the ten-year-old's fascination with things that are gross, absurd, and silly. The monsters, dinosaurs, ghouls, aliens, giants, and pirates that he enjoyed drawing as a boy have become trademark characters of McNaughton's art, and his daffy situations typically fly in the face of convention. McNaughton's cartoonish personalities have much to say for themselves, reinforcing the simple text for early readers, adding an extra dollop of humor to the general ridiculousness, and adding motility to the pictures. Reviewers applaud McNaughton's gift for using silliness not only to encourage reading, but also to present some serious ideas. *Have You Seen Who's Just Moved in Next Door to Us?*, for example, is an absolute orgy of absurdity—"a diverse multitude of freaks and oddballs from all areas of literature, popular culture and the communal unconscious," declared reviewer George Hunt; yet, the book makes a strong point about tolerating differences among people. A sweeter side to McNaughton's humor can be seen in his books for very young children, such as those he has illustrated for other writers, including Allan Ahlberg and James Reeves. These easy-to-read books evoke calmer, simpler images of children and anthropomorphic animals engaged in everyday activities, such as enjoying a warm towel after a bath, splashing in a rain puddle, or discovering the seasons. Whether he is making pictures and stories for babies or engaging in weird and wild poetic preteen imaginings, McNaughton is praised for creating worlds where anything is possible, and almost everything is funny. As a critic in *Junior Bookshelf* explained in a review of *Have You Seen Who's Just Moved in Next Door to Us?*, McNaughton has a "sure feel of what children enjoy."

Biographical Information

McNaughton was born in the northern country town of Wallsend-upon-Tyne, England. His boyhood home contained no books, but plenty of comics and illustrated papers filled with slapstick humor and daffy situations. This was his formative literature, and its characteristics eventually entered his own work, with characters speaking bits of text in comic balloons and labels. McNaughton once explained in *Something about the Author* (*SATA*): "[The comic book format has] been rejected, looked down on, scorned, thought of as being cheap—and now the case has been proved, with more and more work of that kind being commissioned. France has had a fantastic tradition of comic strips—not only is it a wonderful way of telling stories, but it's the modern way for today's children: it's about movement, the step between film and book." When he was sixteen McNaughton left home and eventually made his way to London, where he studied graphic design at the Central School of Art and Design. In 1970 he married, and later went on to specialize in illustration at the Royal College of Art. His first book was published while he was still a student, and his degree show consisted entirely of published work.

After some time spent as a commercial artist and teaching at the Cambridge School of Art, McNaughton found his niche illustrating children's books for a variety of authors, most prominently Allan Ahlberg, with whom he has successfully collaborated for over ten years. McNaughton's affinity for things grotesque and silly really began to emerge when he started writing his own text to accompany his illustrations, creating a varied catalogue of over sixty books. He is married, with two sons, and lives in London.

Major Works

In collaboration with Allan Ahlberg, McNaughton produced eighteen titles for the "Red Nose Readers" series between 1985 and 1995, including *Help!* (1985), *Me and My Friend* (1986), and *Who Stole the Pie!* (1995). Called "absurd and amusing" by reviewers, the books in this series help beginning readers understand simple words and concepts. Included are illustrations of opposites—big and little, in and out—and cause-and-effect statements—rain + sun = rainbow, balloon + pin = bang. *Help!*, for example, tries to teach children to overcome their fears. In this work, a small boy is frightened by the monsters, burglars, and other hideous creatures that invade his bedroom. Gathering his courage, the boy devises a clever plan to scare away all the uninvited guests. McNaughton's characteristic comic balloons and labels are significant features of these early readers. In a review of *Help!* and other books in the series, Louise L. Sherman commented, "The simple use of words and the clear comic illustrations make these books both appealing and useful, even in special education or English as a second language classes for older students, as they are such fun that even teenagers would enjoy them."

McNaughton's childhood enthusiasm for pirates is evident in many of his self-illustrated works. *Jolly Roger and the Pirates of Abdul the Skinhead* is a pirate-adventure story about a fatherless boy named Roger, nicknamed "Jolly" by his fellow townspeople because he always looks so miserable. Tired of the chores imposed upon him by his cleaning-fanatic mother, Roger desires to run away to sea. His intentions are thwarted when a hairy, dirty, and villainous bunch of pirates, revolted by the smell of soap emanating from Roger, press-gang him. Roger's stories of being forced to wash, scrub, and tidy up enrage the pirates so much that they decide to teach his mother a lesson. Of course they are no match for her, and end up combed and scrubbed and doing the chores. Roger rescues them, and during their escape, an amnesiac pirate named Cookie is bonked on the head, recovers his memory, and reveals himself to be Roger's long-lost father. The family is happily reunited, and the pirates return to their nefarious life. McNaughton uses his lively cartoon format throughout this book. The characters dance around rowdily, spouting dialogue in balloons and constantly drawing attention to the illustrations, making them an integral part of the story. Recognizing the universal appeal of McNaughton's comic approach, Roger Sutton observed, "The illustrations combine boisterous double-paged spreads with smaller cartoon panels, all reeking with wit and stubble and a satiric edge that will be enjoyed by kids who think they are too old for picture books."

Many of McNaughton's books are written in verse or are collections of silly poems. *Have You Seen Who's Just Moved in Next Door to Us?* is a story told in verse, with the title repeating in every refrain. News of a new family joining the neighborhood spreads quickly from house to house. As readers follow the message being passed through the street, they cannot help but notice the peculiar denizens of the neighborhood: a family of eggs who all make egg puns, a house full of very domestic bikers, Mr. Thing "squirting, squelching, slithering" around his house, a school that teaches birds to say rude words, ghosts, witches, pigs, and a host of other odd and repulsive characters. The entire neighborhood is horrified by the appearance of the new neighbors, who turn out in the end to be a normal human family. The detailed illustrations and clever verse make this book delightful, as a reviewer for *Publishers Weekly* commented, "McNaughton's rollicking verse will make reading aloud a zany treat. His intricately detailed, never-ending procession of neighbors is rich with sight gags and jokes within jokes. This unique artistry displays a sense of humor that is both cheeky and camp."

Making Friends with Frankenstein is a book of silly verses with lots of horrible monsters and suitably gross themes illustrated with an array of weird and funny characters. Every monster imaginable is represented here, from Quasimodo and extraterrestrial beings, to a schoolyard bully and a kid who ate too many gummy bears. The verses range from the contemplation of a cockroach sandwich ("Hate the taste/ But love the crunch") to a "Farewell to Dracula" ("So long/Sucker!"), with lots of silliness in between. Roger Sutton observed, "Large-scaled, literal-minded, and highly funny pen-and-watercolor portraits that accompany the burlesque with competitive vigor and that have plenty of shut-the-book-here-comes-teacher vulgarity. . . . Best of all is the generous sense of personality that bounces through the book, . . . a rounded joviality that shows how a single sense of humor can wander down many paths. Kids will enjoy the stroll. So will you."

The first of McNaughton's "Preston the Pig" books, *Suddenly!* takes readers on a walk with Preston as he heads home from school. Lurking behind him is the Big Bad Wolf, and every time Preston "suddenly" changes his course, the wolf ends up the victim of his own evil plot. McNaughton uses very few words, instead letting the pictures tell most of the story. Preston eventually arrives home to his mother's welcoming arms, although at first readers think she might be the wolf. *Suddenly!* has three sequels: *Boo!* (1995), in which Preston sneaks around scaring everyone until his father sets him straight; *Oops!* (1996), which follows the same plot as *Suddenly!*, but with a "Little Red Riding Hood" theme; and *Preston's Goal* (1998), in which Preston unwittingly foils the wolf with his soccer ball.

Awards

In 1978, McNaughton won First Prize for Didactic Literature from the Cultural Activities Board of the city of Trento, Italy, for the Italian edition of combined volumes *Colin McNaughton's ABC and Things* and *Colin McNaughton's 1,2,3, and Things.* He won the British Book Design and Production Award three times: in 1989 for *Jolly Roger and the Pirates of Abdul the Skinhead,* in 1993 for *Who's That Banging on the Ceiling?,* and in 1994 for *Making Friends with Frankenstein. Jolly Roger and the Pirates of Abdul the Skinhead* also made two short lists in 1988, for the Kurt Maschler Award and the Smarties Prize for Children's Books. *Have You Seen Who's Just Moved in Next Door to Us?* won the Kurt Maschler Award, and *Watch Out for the Giant Killers!* was shortlisted for the Earthworm Award, both in 1991. *Suddenly!* was shortlisted for the Smarties Prize in 1994, and received the Book Award from the United Kingdom Reading Association and the Nottinghamshire Children's Acorn Award, both in 1995. *Here Come the Aliens!* was shortlisted for the Kate Greenaway Medal in 1995, and *Oops!* won the Smarties Prize for Children's Books, both in 1996.

AUTHOR'S COMMENTARY

Colin McNaughton

SOURCE: "Authorgraph No. 37," in *Books for Keeps,* No. 37, March, 1986, pp. 12-13.

'The older I get the more I realise that my sense of humour is exactly the same as it was when I was four years old—it hasn't changed at all!'

Which may explain how Colin McNaughton is right there with his young readers—it was kids themselves who so quickly made *Football Crazy* a standard classic of humour and wish-fulfilment. He is admired and well-reviewed, but he has never been a fashionable darling of the critics, and he notes, somewhat ruefully, that his books are not 'award' books. On the Mother Goose panel for his fourth and last year, he has never won an award himself, yet there can be scarcely a child in the land who hasn't identified with his tumbling anthropomorphic animals and boisterous, chubby humans. And for someone who says drawing has never been easy ('always honing, honing, till eventually it comes right—I'm so jealous of people who can just pick up a pen and draw'), he's done an awful lot of books.

Most of them are in colour, 'I love black and white work, but it's difficult to make a living out of it—you're expected to do a book for £100. Till recently artists have had a raw deal, and often been expected to do a picture book for £500: you're patted on the head and told to run away, sonny, for six months and live on £500. That's

what it was like for me till five years ago, when I met Sebastian Walker. What it means is you do things very quickly—and end up with not very good books. Then someone will come along who's spent the last five years on a book, and of course it's wonderful, and it sweeps the awards and everybody says what a wonderful illustrator this person is—and you've done eight books that year because you *have* to. It can be a terribly frustrating business in that way: you knew all the time you weren't doing the kind of work you were capable of simply because you had to make a living, you had a family to keep (it's different if you're on your own).

'The result is there,' pointing to his shelves, 'stacks and stacks of books with nice bits in them but . . . Ten years and 40 or 50 books—crazy!—should have been ten or 15 books to do the quality I'd like. This is the first year I've been able to sit down and do a picture book to the best of my ability without a deadline. It'll probably be awful, but—!'

Although there were no books at all at home as he grew up ('I never read *The Iliad* at four or was weaned on Dickens'), there were always comics, and the Christmas annuals like *Beano* and *Dandy:* they were his formative literature and their knockabout slapstick has been a lasting influence. He was among the first to weld words and images on one page.

'I've been talking about the comic format for years, along with people like Shirley Hughes and Jan Pienkowski. It's been rejected, looked down on, scorned, thought of as being cheap—and now the case has been proved, with more and more work of that kind being commissioned. France has had a fantastic tradition of comic strips—not only is it a wonderful way of telling stories but it's the modern way for today's children: it's about movement, the step between film and the book.'

He speaks in the Geordie accent of his native Wallsend-upon-Tyne, though softened by 15 years of making allowances for Londoners. He was born in 1951, one of three children of a pattern maker, a highly skilled craftsman in the shipyards: the other two were normal people, he says, and there's an extra spice to his present success because he used to be the black sheep of the family.

'I left home at 16—my mother has it that she threw me out; I have it that I walked out—either way I must have been pretty obnoxious. But I took care to stay close by in Newcastle, and went home with my dirty washing for Sunday lunch.

'Up there, if you had five O levels, it was art school or teachers' training, otherwise your main chance of work was the shipyards, or 'The Ministry' as it's called at Newcastle. I opted for technical college because it offered more freedom than the sixth form, but I even made a mess of getting in there—I'd applied wrongly and when I turned up for registration they'd never heard of me! I must have looked a real cartoon character, walking away, head down, weeping. . . . So I got different jobs for a year, including six months as a sign writer before they realised I was left-handed—you're not supposed to be able to write signs if you're left-handed. It was in a high-class gentleman's tailors, Isaak Walton's—we used to get these elegant tuck boxes to paint boys' names on.

'How *do* you drift into certain areas? I was introduced at school to a Youth Theatre by one marvellous teacher (it was the only good thing about school—I *detested* school, hated it so much I've only recently been able to talk about it) and this led me into areas of artistic expression that were totally alien to my working class background and friends. Acting, costumes . . . Marvellous, absolutely marvellous if you've never known that kind of ability to express feelings before. It enabled me to break out of the scheme of things that had seemed set for me—when you follow your father into the shipyards and so on.'

After a year's foundation art course in Newcastle, he studied graphic design for three years at the Central School in London ('Michael Foreman persuaded them to take me, and was my first real tutor—I've never forgiven him—no, I still love him, he's a lovely man'), going on to specialise in illustration for three years at the Royal College. He sees the benefit of art schools solely as places to make contacts, plus the inevitable influence of fellow students: he himself taught part-time for six years in Cambridge and found it enormously frustrating ('full-time might be better, for then you can keep track of people').

His first books were published while he was still at college, after Timothy Benn saw his second-year exhibition, and his degree show was made up entirely of published work. 'Publishers now tend to hang around the major colleges, scared they'll miss some new talent ever since Tom Maschler discovered Nicola Bayley!'

He tried working in all sorts of advertising and editorial areas but didn't like any of them, finding, like so many others, that the people in children's books—publishers, writers—are somehow more agreeable. 'The money in advertising is better, but you have to change everything eight times, go through 15 committees and an awful pecking order. In children's books they give you some money and leave you alone to do the book, and at the end of it there it is, a book on the shelf, not like a newspaper in the gutter. In fact, once you start thinking about it, it's a smashing job!'

He married at 19, and Francoise—an older woman at 21—supported him through college and still handles his financial affairs. They met in a pub: she and her cousin, escaping small-town France together, had met a friend of Colin's in London and hitched to Newcastle—*and* her cousin married his friend. The McNaughtons have . . . shunted through ten different London flats in 15 years, the last seven around Covent Garden. Ever since it was built four years ago, they've lived at the top of an award-winning block whose little private yards and giant balconies are alive, even in mid-winter, with greenery and worm-hunting blackbirds, with Ben, who's eight, and Timothy, six. The boys' main feeling about their dad, far from pride or surprise when his name pops up at school, seems to be one of embarrassment at his continuing to wear jeans . . . .

His present ebulliently successful partnership with Allan Ahlberg in the little "Red Nose Readers" stems from Ahlberg's choice of McNaughton as one of his "Happy Families" illustrators for Kestrel. Is it true that the wildly funny Ahlberg is in fact quite a melancholy bloke?

'That's a good description actually—we often sit together over a drink getting depressed about life! To me he's one of the best picture-book writers in the world, a wonderful communicator, with drawerfuls of ideas—anything you think of, he's thought of it already. A partnership is much easier than working on your own, it takes a lot of responsibility off your shoulders—you're only the piano player, you're not writing the piece—and we do spark each other off, even on the phone when we're not meant to be working.'

The future? He doesn't look more than a couple of years ahead, but his horizons are widening. A '50s rock'n'roll musical for children based on his story and illustrations for *Fat Pig*, 'The Story of the Pig who Wanted to Marry Cochonette' (Miss Piggy?), is in its third year in Paris, is showing in Vienna and all over Germany and Sweden, and is coming soon to England, while there are also plans afoot for an English production of his *Rat Race.*

And he wants to write—even though he finds it as hard as drawing and is cursed just as much by his inability to be satisfied: 'That really *isn't* very pleasant. Even now, after all the hundreds of drawings I've done, looking back I can only see the mistakes.' He's been spurred on by his two verses in *The Children's Book* for the famine appeal. 'I got more of a buzz out of seeing those in print than out of all my books: it's a different pleasure, and words always have a pathetic appeal to artists of awful respectability which pictures never have. I'm writing a book of poems now for Walker—well, not *poems,* humorous doggerel—it's a kind of reward for doing so many books for them in the last five years' (16 Readers in the last two years, and a joke on every page).

He gazes dreamily at something far away. 'I wrote a poem yesterday about a little girl I was at school with called Pauline Crawford . . . '

John Cohen

SOURCE: An interview with Colin McNaughton, in *Reading Time,* Vol. 38, No. 3, August, 1994, pp. 20-21.

JC Well Colin! Why 'pirates'?

CM I've been doing pirate books for a long time now

and it's something to do with the idea of sailing away, getting away from reality and not being in contact, not having to grow up either. Pirates seem to me never to grow up, going off into the seas and sunset and just playing little boys' games when you're a big boy. Someone once said that little girls grow up into women and little boys grow up into big boys, I've never really grown up and the pirate thing has it all. It's very much a boy's thing, I think, although little girls like it as well.

JC Well you've obviously got some girls in this current one, *Pirate's School.*

CM The book very much reflects my own kids' school in London. Interestingly, when they were at preschool there were 18 to 20 different nationalities in their class. I come from a predominately white, working-class background, from an area where there were very few black faces, so drawing on my own childhood is alien to me. I've had to learn because in the place where I live it is very multicultural. The characters are not there for politically correct reasons. They're reflecting the kind of schools I go into and talk to.

JC *Have You Seen Who's Just Moved in Next Door?*, [which] was the first book that I consciously registered was yours and which I thought was just wonderful, has a multicultural sort of background.

CM Yes, I'm an urban kid really; I love the countryside but I've lived in the inner cities of London for the last 25 years and it is very much a mixed multicultural society, Asians, Bangladeshis, Italians, French, Chinese, Japanese, which is fantastic, a very exciting sort of culture. I live in Covent Garden. People think no one lives there, but there's four or five thousand people [who] live there, strange people.

As far as doing books, I was still at college when I published my first book 17 or 18 years ago. I was going to be a painter, at first but couldn't see how I could make a living being a painter so I gradually drifted into doing illustration, editorial and advertising work. Gradually getting rid of all that, I ended up doing children's books. It's one of the few jobs where people say they'll give you some money to go away for six months. There are not many jobs you can get which do that. I quite like that; it suits my nature.

The writing side came later, simply because I needed some text and I needed stories. I could do the pictures, but I didn't know any writers, so at college I just started writing myself, simple things to start with, and I got published straight away with my own text so it was never a problem. Most often illustrators, when they start off, will get jobs illustrating other people's texts. It was never a question with me. Although I have illustrated other people's texts, I don't do it any more.

I probably have 60, 70, 75 books out there in the market-place at the moment and over the last 17 years. Some of them have five words in them, some of them are little board books, some of them series books but picture books I don't know, probably 25, 30 maybe.

I've just done a book for Andersen Press called *Suddenly!,* which will be out in the autumn, I've got big hopes for it. Also I'm doing a book called *Here Come the Aliens.* It's about the invasion of Earth by aliens. They never actually reach Earth. I kind of like the journeys rather than the getting there.

I've done two or three pirate books. *Pirate's School* is the second one in the series and it's three or four years since I did the last one. I really just do them when I feel like doing them. You can't do one every year because otherwise you are competing against yourself and books are expensive so people can't be buying every book. I do a poetry book every two or three years and a pirate book every two or three years and then an original one. I try and keep it circulating rather than doing the same books over and over again. I'll only do it if I come up with a reasonable idea.

Actually my work is getting younger now; it used to be 6- to 11-year-olds which is an area I really thought was neglected for picture books simply because the parents, and the kids don't buy the books at that age. The teachers and the librarians buy books, but the majority of books are bought for the younger age group by parents so it's sensible to work for that age group if you want to make a better living. However, 6 to 10-12 has always been a much more interesting age group for me, but I'm battling against heavier and heavier odds really with competition from television and the rest of it. Kids are reading less and less picture books. They are getting progressively younger when they stop reading picture books. A lot of my stuff is getting younger and simpler, maybe because I'm just getting better at it. I've always felt it's harder to write a simple picture book than it is to write complicated picture books. Complicated picture books you just throw everything in and the kitchen sink and it's impressive in that way, but to write a good, simple text with a good, simple idea with good, simple pictures is very, very difficult. Maybe I've had to go through all the complicated books to get to the simple ones so that I've learned what to leave out. I always remember someone telling me at college about drawing. You have to take the drawing so far that you destroy the drawing so that you know when to stop. If you keep stopping when it looks pretty and just nice you never know how far you can take that drawing. It's a bit like that really.

Pirate's School is getting simpler. The theme is very simple, the way it's told is very simple and the device of using a diary makes the text a lot simpler. The illustrations look very complex but actually are very simple. It's a journey. They do go somewhere in the end. It's really the journey that's interesting. I read it to kids a lot and they get a lot out of it. I relate each lesson they do in the *Pirate's School* to each lesson they do at school and I bring the teachers in and try to embarrass them. This is part of the fun of the session.

The US is a difficult market to crack. All my books bar one or two have been published in the US but none of them have been run-away successes. They all get a US edition. It's a different kind of humour I think. It's an old cliche, we assume because the Americans speak English that they are English but they are not, they're very different, completely different.

Pirate's School certainly comes across well in Australia, but a lot of Australians have a British sense of humour. A lot of the references are common to the two cultures but to the Americans they're not, so it will be interesting to see how *Pirate's School* does there because it's historical. Historical things tend to bypass those problems. The Germans and the French like me; I get the odd Italian editions but the Scandinavians, Denmark, Sweden and Norway love me. Every time I do a book we get three editions; they don't take many, they take a couple of thousand, four thousand maybe because they are tiny markets, but they like it.

Advances used to be terrible when I started out. I suppose out of the 17 years I've been writing the last 15 years I've lived solely off that and supported a family. It gets better and better all the time which is very satisfying professionally because not many people can make a living at writing.

Lots and lots of people have influenced my style, but I think the strongest influences have been people like Rollinson and Gilray, the older English engravers of the 17th and 18th century. The technique that was used in the engraving was used a lot and has been copied through line work ever since. It's where people like Sendak get their technique. Most of the good drawers if you like are heavily influenced by people like Gilray. Gilray is probably my favourite. Rollinson—Sendak would probably be influenced by him because his line is more fluid and more romantic, more flowing. I'm influenced by peoples' attitudes rather than by their styles, people who are very professional about the way they do things and have obviously thought about what they are doing.

JC Have you seen anything of the work of Australian illustrators?

CM What I've seen has been briefly when I've been in bookstores or in libraries and I've just been really very impressed because we don't get these books in England. We get the best of them, the very, very best of them or the ones which they think will sell in the UK. I know a few Australian illustrators, I know Ron Brooks and a few others, but I didn't know what to expect and what I find is that there is some great stuff over here but unfortunately the publishing in the UK is so over produced, there are so many books being produced that I see very little likelihood of it getting into the UK. It's a shame. In the agricultural world in Europe farmers are paid not to produce one year; maybe we should do that with books.

TITLE COMMENTARY

📖 *COLIN McNAUGHTON'S ABC AND THINGS; COLIN McNAUGHTON'S 1,2,3 AND THINGS* **(1976, 2 vol.; reprinted as *ABC and Things* and *1, 2, 3 and Things; 1989;* U.S. edition as *Colin McNaughton's ABC and 1,2,3: A Book for All Ages for Reading Alone or Together,* 1976)**

Margery Fisher

SOURCE: A review of *ABC and Things* and *1,2,3 and Things,* in *Growing Point,* Vol. 15, No. 7, January, 1977, p. 3050.

Not for the youngest but for children old enough to appreciate the droll originality of these compact little books. The ABC illustrates fossilised figures of speech (crime wave, elbow room, jumping the queue) in vivaciously literal scenes, while the counting book shows a fantasy-sequence from one to twenty ("Four in awe of a dinosaur," "Seventeen pigs in various wigs") with a final picture of a football team arranged like sardines within the goalpost and "50,084 Fifty thousand and eighty four could not believe just what they saw". For a learner-reader to pore over, perhaps.

J. Russell

SOURCE: A review of *ABC and Things,* in *The Junior Bookshelf,* Vol. 41, No. 3, June, 1977, pp. 159-60.

ABC and Things is a small book using the robust human figures familiar from Helen Oxenbury's work and setting them in ridiculous situations. F for 'Flying off the handle' shows miniature figures attempting aerial acrobatics from the handle of the milk jug into a bowl of sugar—complete with batman outfit and giant salt and pepper pots. A charming, sophisticated book well designed for older children to dig and delve into the detail of words and pictures. There is also a companion "1, 2, 3" counting book.

Kirkus Reviews

SOURCE: A review of *ABC and Things* and *1, 2, 3 and Things,* in *Kirkus Reviews,* Vol. XLV, No. 17, September 1, 1977, p. 928.

First printed in Britain as two separate titles—***ABC and Things*** and ***1, 2, 3 and Things,*** this starts with an alphabet of cliches, or commonplace metaphors, which are literally interpreted in the pictures. Thus "C is for Crime wave" (a surfing burglar), "S is for Storm in a teacup" (obvious), "V is for Visiting card" (the ace of spades comes to call), etc. The counting portion abandons the gimmick but remains stylishly outré: "Three ski off a giant's knee," "Ten young men in a lion's den" (their heads are mounted as trophies, the lion lolls on a Victorian couch), "Thirteen rats in old men's hats" (from stovepipe to deerstalker). Illustrated with derivative eccentricity, it's ingenious but decidedly out of the way—and sometimes prohibitively British in content.

Quentin Blake

SOURCE: A review of *ABC and Things* and *1,2,3 and Things* in *Times Educational Supplement,* No. 3848, March 30, 1990, p. B9.

"Eight, late, await their fate" reads one of the caption verses in Colin McNaughton's *1,2,3 and Things.* They're an unprepossessing bunch of juveniles, but real enough. You can tell they'll have grubby knees and things in their pockets—all except perhaps the smirking youth at the back holding up his excuse note. And we can't see all of the master on late duty, but enough to discern the sort of boring, brown-suited authority-figure he'll be. It's the pipe in the top pocket that clinches it.

1,2,3 and Things and its companion *ABC and Things* were McNaughton's first two books. Now reissued by Macmillan, 14 years on, they wear well. Probably there are passages that their author/illustrator would carry off now with more fluency; but the characteristic elements are already present: an instinctive child's-eye view of humour and sedulously observed characters, often in far-fetched verbal situations (I is for In the Soup, and the children are actually diving into it—it's green).

I like the *and Things* in McNaughton's titles. The constant renewal of the ABC and the counting book depend not only on the renewal of young readers, but also the possibility of the form as a way of bringing together ideas, situations, *things.*

WALK, RABBIT, WALK (with Elizabeth Attenborough, 1977)

E. Colwell

SOURCE: A review of *Walk, Rabbit, Walk,* in *The Junior Bookshelf,* Vol. 41, No. 6, December, 1977, p. 329.

An "easy reading" book with a picture opposite each page. The text extols the pleasures and advantages of walking as opposed to modern means of transport. Rabbit chooses to walk to the party—and gets there. His friends in a balloon, a sports car, a motorbike and a helicopter come to grief. The illustrations in subdued colour supplement the story pleasantly; the text is brief and to the point.

Merrie Lou Cohen

SOURCE: A review of *Walk, Rabbit, Walk,* in *School Library Journal,* Vol. 24, No. 8, April, 1978, p. 73.

A morality tale about self-reliance with a refreshing text and nice homey illustrations. Rabbit accepts an invitation to tea at Eagle's house and manages to enjoy nature and escape catastrophe by walking all the way instead of accepting rides from friends who zip along via a variety of mechanical devices—a hot air balloon, a sports car, a motorbike, a helicopter, roller skates. The story is funny, imaginative, and full of rollicking action. Rabbit and his pals are all lovingly portrayed, with especially engaging facial expressions.

Kirkus Reviews

SOURCE: A review of *Walk, Rabbit, Walk,* in *Kirkus Reviews,* Vol. LX, No. 21, November 1, 1992, p. 1381.

Invited to tea with Eagle, Rabbit prefers to walk: "It's a lovely day." The five other guests, each with different transportation, would gladly give him a lift, but he cheerfully turns them down: "I like to look at the flowers and the butterflies as I walk along," he explains when Fox urges that "It's perfect weather for ballooning." In the end, after the others' vehicles fortuitously fail, Rabbit gets to Eagle's house first: "Sometimes it's quicker to walk." Reviews of modes of transportation are always popular, and McNaughton's fantastical illustrations of auto and helicopter are especially amusing; the wholesome theme and its ecological subtext add an aura of good sense to this cheery tale.

THE AUTUMN BOOK: A COLLECTION OF PROSE AND POETRY (compiled by James Reeves, 1977)

M. Hobbs

SOURCE: A review of *The Autumn Book: A Collection of Prose and Poetry,* in *The Junior Bookshelf,* Vol. 42, No. 2, April, 1978, p. 108.

As befits Autumn, James Reeves has a particularly rich mixture for his latest seasonal anthology of prose and verse. There are detailed visual evocations of the season of mists and mellow fruitfulness by Keats and Clare, and less conscious accounts in diarists. There are forgotten customs and delights of Harvest Home from folklorists and also those who remember them in villages like Lark Rise. There are witches and Guy Fawkes and the pagan predecessors of his feast. There is Gerard the herbalist on Michaelmas daisies, and seasonal recipes in quaint old English. There is the mystical meaning of the season in poets such as Hopkins and Rilke. There is Leacock for humour and Rosemary Sutcliff for traditional narrative well-retold, passages "for" and "against" football from other periods, less-known areas of well-known writers like Dickens and Wordsworth, a whole short story by Walter de la Mare and much more. In fact a remarkable balance between old and new, prose and poetry, fact and fiction, with length and weight carefully considered. Am I alone in finding the slight impishness of Colin McNaughton's style not wholly in keeping with the contents of the book? Those range so far; the illustrations limit us so firmly to here and now.

THE RAT RACE: THE AMAZING ADVENTURES OF ANTON B. STANTON (1978; British edition, 1988)

Elaine Moss

SOURCE: A review of *The Rat Race: The Amazing Adventures of Anton B. Stanton,* in *Times Literary Supplement,* No. 3966, April 7, 1978, p. 385.

Colin McNaughton's *The Rat Race* will draw its stoutest fans from nine and over, for it is as sophisticated in its ideas and wordplay as it is full of visual humour. Anton B. Stanton, the hero, is a Tom Thumb. Wandering through a hole in the skirting board he enters the kingdom of the rats, is arrested as a spy and sentenced to 496 years in prison; "one year for spying and 495 for being so ugly". But he is allowed to compete in the Rat Race ("1st Prize: King for a Day") and as winner authorizes his own release. Colin McNaughton's pictures of rats falling about laughing, rats in running shorts, rats in regal regalia are fun for all, but the jokes ("2nd Prize: marriage to one of the King's daughters. 3rd Prize: marriage to two of the King's daughters") are for the Asterix age.

Margery Fisher

SOURCE: A review of *The Rat Race: The Amazing Adventures of Anton B. Stanton,* in *Growing Point,* Vol. 17, No. 2, July, 1978, p. 3371.

"The amazing adventures of Anton B. Stanton" begin when this Tom Thumb-sized son of two amiably rustic castle-dwellers finds his way down a rat-hole into an attic city of converted trunks and cupboards. Here the lad, sentenced by the King as a spy, is allowed to bid for freedom in a race; his chief opponent cheats, Anton is declared the winner and returns home to incredulous parents. This gay bit of nonsense, with its touch of satire, is illustrated in a caricature style in muted colours; the long page is well used, especially in the extended view of the race with all its vicissitudes.

Kirkus Reviews

SOURCE: A review of *The Rat Race: The Amazing Stories of Anton B. Stanton,* in *Kirkus Reviews,* Vol. XLVI, No. 14, July 15, 1978, p. 748.

One of those far-fetched but matter-of-fact little stories from England, this tells of a tiny Tom Thumb type named Anton B. Stanton, who, out of mere curiosity, follows a rat through his hole and into a rat city, where the king has him imprisoned for a spy. But a race is

approaching; the winner will be king for a day; Anton gets permission to enter and starts training in his cell. During the event a rat cheat named Gruffaw beats him out but is disqualified; Anton is declared the winner and ends his "lovely day as king of the rats" by pardoning himself and setting off for home. An inconsequential pleasantry, in period costume.

THE GREAT ZOO ESCAPE (1978; U.S. edition, 1979; reprinted, 1990)

Carol Chatfield

SOURCE: A review of *The Great Zoo Escape,* in *School Library Journal,* Vol. 26, No. 1, September, 1979, pp. 116-17.

Ruffles, a bird raconteur, lives on an isolated island in the middle of the ocean. His tall tales amuse the flock so much that no one notices the approach of a very proper, plaid-suited, bearded gentleman wielding a net until Ruffles finds himself crated and en route to a faraway zoo. Sea gulls learn of his sad plight and go for help; three feathered friends come to the rescue and release Ruffles and all the other animals from their cages. Back home Ruffles continues to tell stories to all who will listen; now, however, his favorite is true. Slightly British in tone and style, this colorfully illustrated title has a predictable outcome and fails to reach any heights of wisdom or humor along the way.

Jill Bennett

SOURCE: A review of *The Great Zoo Escape,* in *Books for Keeps,* No. 65, November, 1990, p. 7.

This is a reissue of one of Colin McNaughton's early picture books. It relates how a storytelling bird, Ruffles, is captured, taken from his island home, put in a zoo and finally escapes, thanks to the seagull telegraph system and three brave friends from the island.

The story, which comes down firmly on the side of free animals, raises the whole question of the pros and cons of zoos.

THE PIRATS: THE AMAZING ADVENTURES OF ANTON B. STANTON (1979; U.S. edition as *Anton B. Stanton and the Pirats*)

Books for Your Children

SOURCE: A review of *The Pirats: The Amazing Adventures of Anton B. Stanton,* in *Books for Your Children,* Vol. 15, No. 1, Winter, 1979, p. 12.

"Anton B. Stanton was a very small boy, just about as small as an ordinary tea cup. He lived with his Mother,

Father and two Brothers, in a large stone castle." Colin McNaughton brings a wonderfully inventive touch to the Tom Thumb theme. Being so small Anton notices other things that no one else can see. This beautifully produced romp tells how he discovers a tiny ship in the castle moat. It is manned by rats—Pirats. Splendid for children's own reading.

Children's Book Review Service

SOURCE: A review of *Anton B. Stanton and the Pirats,* in *Children's Book Review Service Inc.,* Vol. 8, No. 14, August, 1980, p. 133.

This book is a wonderful new addition to the Benn Collection. The story and illustrations blend together to present an exciting story. Anton, "a very small boy, just about as tall as a tea cup," engages in a battle with the pirates to rescue the water rats' princess. The book will fill a gap for those young people who love the excitement of pirates, as well as those who love the charm of the "little people."

Marilyn Payne Phillips

SOURCE: A review of *Anton B. Stanton and the Pirats,* in *School Library Journal,* Vol. 27, No. 1, September, 1980, p. 61.

Anton, the six-inch boy, returns from *The Rat Race* for another adventure with a different group of rats, the nefarious "Pirats." Discovered hiding on their ship and forced to walk the plank, Anton is saved from certain death by friendly Water Rats. Anton then leads the rescue mission to save the kidnapped Water Rat princess from the clutches of the Pirats and returns to humble home sweet castle in time for dinner. Bold, colorful illustrations that are sometimes out of proportion seem a bit wasted on this all bluster, no treasure yarn.

Booklist

SOURCE: A review of *Anton B. Stanton and the Pirats,* in *Booklist,* Vol. 77, No. 1, September 1, 1980, p. 45.

There is always one more good pirate story left to tell. This one combines with Tom Thumb—in the form of tiny Anton B. Stanton—and further peoples itself with rats, or "pirats," to be exact. The story line uses classic swashbuckling maneuvers: eavesdropping Anton is forced to walk the plank but is saved by water rats. He in turn helps them gather courage to storm the "pirat" ship and rescue their kidnapped princess. But it is McNaughton's easy writing style and his colorful, swashbuckling illustrations that carry the day. A freshness of ideas comes through in many little touches that he lavishes on his work. A good example is the plank-walking scene, depicted in a long, sideways-turned picture showing a dozen "still shots" of Anton's descent. It's all fast-paced fun

that will make readers wonder what Anton will get into next.

FOOTBALL CRAZY (1980; U.S. edition as Soccer Crazy, 1981)

Books for Your Children

SOURCE: A review of *Football Crazy,* in *Books for Your Children,* Vol. 16, No. 1, Spring, 1981, p. 11.

Colin McNaughton is one of the cleverest picture book artists we have. His great gift for showing action is used to tremendous effect in this simple story. Bruno (a bear), new to the town, is accepted as a substitute by the local football team and ends by becoming the greatest goalkeeper ever and saving the match from disaster.

Zena Sutherland

SOURCE: A review of *Soccer Crazy,* in *Bulletin of the Center for Children's Books,* Vol. 34, No. 8, April, 1981, p. 157.

Bright paintings of animal characters, some in strip form, tell as much of the story as does the rather pedestrian text. Bruno, new in the neighborhood, yearns to join the local soccer team, Tex's Tigers. He gets taken on as substitute, and—after another player is injured—is called into the game. He kicks badly, but then he's put in goal and Bruno saves the day with a remarkable catch and follows it with a remarkable kick, winning the game for his team by one point. Lots of action and the appeal of animal characters compensate for the slight and unoriginal plot.

D. A. Young

SOURCE: A review of *Football Crazy,* in *The Junior Bookshelf,* Vol. 45, No. 3, June, 1981, p. 107.

A book about bears AND football must surely win the hearts of small boys. Bruno is picked somewhat reluctantly for Tex's Tigers and naturally enough after a disaster or two saves the game and all is well. There are more pictures than text and the variety of picture presentation adds to their attraction. This might be a useful volume in the struggle to get the unwilling reader engaged in the process of reading.

K. Johnson

SOURCE: A review of *Football Crazy,* in *Books for Your Children,* Vol. 25, No. 2, Summer, 1990, p. 13.

Bruno (a bear) is new to the neighbourhood and hasn't any friends. From his window he can see "Tex's Tigers" practising football, and he longs to join in. With a bit of encouragement from his mum and dad he approaches the gang . . . .

From then on we follow Bruno as he sets about with enthusiasm to prove his worth to Tex and his friends. He has some mishaps along the way and he makes some near-disastrous mistakes. But in the end, Bruno triumphs with a winning goal in the big match between Tex's Tigers and Leroy's Lions. This may be a traditional story-line, but *Football Crazy* is a very appealing and captivating book which has a real sense of build-up and tension. A mixture of comic-strip with the usual picture-book style is helpful too in varying the pace, and both the text and the illustrations are excellent.

This book in our household has been one that gets requested night after night—and is enjoyed afresh on every re-reading (by the adult readers too!).

MR. AND MRS. HAY THE HORSE (written by Allen Ahlberg, 1981)

M. Hobbs

SOURCE: A review of *Mr. and Mrs. Hay the Horse,* in *The Junior Bookshelf,* Vol. 45, No. 5, October, 1981, p. 185.

Allan Ahlberg's new illustrating partners combine joyfully with him in clothing two all-too-familiar present-day situations in fantastic and colourful garb. Mrs. Lather the Washerwoman rebels against her weekly repetitious round of work, and her sudden brief moves into other fields and final decision not to work are good-humouredly supported by the rest of the family in a neat cumulative story which just may leave the young reader wondering why she was the breadwinner in the first place and what the future will bring! André Amstutz's people are delightfully solid and curvaceous. Miss and Master Hay, on the other hand, suffer agonies from having out-of-the-ordinary parents until the situation arises where circus parents can save the day at school. There is a Dickensian other-worldliness about Colin McNaughton's characterisation and colours which sorts well with the oddity of the conception. Certainly this little series is for reading without tears.

FAT PIG (1981; U.S. edition, 1987)

Ruth Hawthorn

SOURCE: A review of *Fat Pig,* in *Times Literary Supplement,* No. 4103, November 20, 1981, p. 1359.

I do . . . have misgivings about *Fat Pig* by Colin McNaughton, a more elaborate story with pictures along more red-blooded comic-book lines. The title role is not a happy one. If he eats a lot, as the farmer and Fat Pig's degenerate wild cousins urge him to do, he will grow fat enough to go to market; but this, as his barnyard friends point out, means ending his days as pork chops. Only if he *slims* can he survive. Which should he trust, his own instincts and the encouragement of his benign patron, or the raucous crowd of practical jokers, who in fact do win what can only be the first round? The pig theme has honorable precedents, but at least Pigling Bland was able to effect a getaway, and Wilbur could shelter behind the eloquence of Charlotte's web: Fat Pig is stuck with his awful dilemma. I am not against scary children's books, but this is likely to echo those anorexic anxieties of parents and older sisters, and four year olds should not be burdened with such things.

Books for Your Children

SOURCE: A review of *Fat Pig,* in *Books for Your Children,* Autumn-Winter, 1987, p. 19.

As he walks round the farmyard one morning Fat Pig overhears Farmer Pyjama say that he will be fat enough to go to the butcher in two weeks' time. Fat Pig's friends decide that his only hope is to lose weight fast, and a crash programme of dieting and exercise is drawn up for him. However he cannot resist eating on the sly, and on the eve of market day he is fatter than ever. Luckily for him, his friends have not given up, and by means of a trick they send him on the ultimate cross-country run, from which he returns utterly exhausted and thin as a rake. Regrettably, he celebrates his temporary reprieve from market by eating more than ever—some pigs never learn! Very amusing and good value.

IF DINOSAURS WERE CATS AND DOGS (adapted by Alice Low, 1981; revised with verses by McNaughton, 1991)

Ilene Cooper

SOURCE: A review of *If Dinosaurs Were Cats and Dogs,* in *Booklist,* Vol. 78, No. 7, December 1, 1981, pp. 499-500.

A man sets off to a land where everyday animals are gargantuan and have dinosauresque features. Needless to say this produces problems for the human inhabitants, who find themselves going boating in giant goldfish bowls or postponing picnics disrupted by enormous moles. The short rhyming text has childlike appeal and the oversize color illustrations provide the vast feeling the story requires. Especially agreeable is a prodigious parrot that forces the reader to turn the book vertically to take in its size. Some of the pictures work better than others, but such unevenness won't stop preschoolers from responding with chuckles at the absurdity of it all.

Christine A. Moesch

SOURCE: A review of *If Dinosaurs Were Cats and Dogs,* in *School Library Journal,* Vol. 38, No. 1, January, 1992, p. 93.

This updated version is more than revised; it contains a completely different text and new or reworked art. In the earlier book, each illustration was accompanied by a four-line poem that described how silly it would be if the world were inhabited by dinosaur-sized hens, cats, frogs, etc. McNaughton has given each animal a name (pigplodicus, chickasaur, snakeydon), but much of the humor has been lost. The appeal of the original version adapted by Alice Low was in reading about eggs winding up scrambled when laid from the height of a giant hen or in people skiing down the shell of a giant tortoise. Here the chickasaurs "let fly" with their eggs and "The Tortosaur's a carnivore—/ He'll have your guts for starters!" The text, previously succinct and gentle, now goes for meaningless action—the animals want to fight or eat the humans; while it's hardly harmful and is intended to be funny, it's just unnecessary. The exaggerated cartoons are sketchy and in some instances clever, but since most of them were in the original version, it's a mystery why McNaughton decided to revise an old favorite. This giant disappointment lands with a colossal thud.

George Hunt

SOURCE: A review of *If Dinosaurs Were Cats and Dogs,* in *Books for Keeps,* No. 82, September, 1993, p. 10.

A group of Year 5 children thought this book was brilliant. The idea is simple: take any common or garden pet, wild or domestic animal, and cross it with a dinosaur, then depict the consequences in rollicking verse and huge, vibrant, ridiculous paintings. The children delighted in the Snakeydon undulating across an entire landscape, stiltlegged Chickasauri dropping skull-crushing eggs, and a hulking Parrodactyl with a pirate on its shoulder. An excellent book for demonstrating some of the sheer enjoyment to be had from the play of words, pictures and ideas.

 KING NONN THE WISER (1981)

Marcus Crouch

SOURCE: A review of *King Nonn the Wiser,* in *The Junior Bookshelf,* Vol. 45, No. 6, December, 1981, p. 242.

King Nonn was very happy in his library, reading all day and getting always more short-sighted. But his subjects wanted him to fight dragons and right wrongs, so sadly he and his short-sighted horse went off in quest of adventure. It was all around him—giants, haunted forests, distressed maidens, dragons—but he saw none of them. After unhorsing, by accident, his warlike neighbour King Blagard of Rong, he returns home to find himself a hero. Thankfully he returns to his library. Neat drawing and an understated text tell the story admirably.

 "BOOKS OF OPPOSITES" SERIES (*Long-Short: At Home,* **U.S. edition as** *At Home; Over-Under: At Playschool,* **U.S. edition as** *At Playschool; Hide-Seek: At the Party,* **U.S. edition as** *At the Party; In-Out: At the Park,* **U.S. edition as** *At the Park; Fat-Thin: At the Shops,* **U.S. edition as** *At the Stores;* **all published in 1982)**

Margery Fisher

SOURCE: A review of *At Playschool, At the Park,* and *At the Party,* in *Growing Point,* Vol. 21, No. 3, September, 1982, pp. 3949-50.

The staid assertion that Colin McNaughton's board books are designed 'to expand a toddler's awareness of basic concepts' gives no idea of the jolly ingenuity of these delectable studies of opposites. *At Playschool* chubby twins demonstrate with blocks, models, and play-dough. *At the Park* they take risks on go-kart and slide, and queue with varying success for ice-cream. *At the Party* they enjoy themselves with balloons, cake and donkey-puzzle. These and three other books show opposites with total clarity and with an illustrative brio which cannot fail to entertain children and their attendant adults with their shrewd observation of the pleasures and pains of those years when energy is bursting and uncontrollable.

Denise M. Wilms

SOURCE: A review of *At Home, At Playschool, At the Park, At the Party,* and *At the Stores,* in *Booklist,* Vol. 79, No. 3, October 1, 1982, p. 247.

A chubby little boy is the wry star of five board books that present a wide variety of opposite situations. The visual effectiveness in getting the concepts across varies. The pair of pictures for "asleep" and "awake" is very clear-cut and quite humorous as the child bounces wildly on his bed for the "awake" scene. Much less obvious is a picture for "hit" / "miss," which shows a boy first pinning the tail on the donkey and then pinning it on the wall. Most toddlers understand "hit" in the sense of a blow rather than its meaning of striking a target, and they may not catch the sense of "miss" unless they're familiar with pin the tail on the donkey or a game like it. There are enough on-target depictions to make these worthwhile, however, and youngsters will enjoy the humorous mood, even if they may need a clarification or two.

Zena Sutherland

SOURCE: A review of *At Home,* in *Bulletin of the Center for Children's Books,* Vol. 36, No. 5, January, 1983, p. 93.

One of a set of five books that cite opposite terms, with the meanings clarified by illustrations, this is small and square, with board pages that bear no text save for the terms. The illustrations make meanings quite clear, they're funny, and they are child-oriented; for example "wet" shows a child happily, messily splashing bath water, and "dry" shows him just as happily beaming from the enveloping folds of an enormous towel, while "full" shows the boy carrying a basket of eggs and in "empty" all the eggs are broken and the boy's leaning on the empty basket. The other four books in the series, which achieves its goal of conveying concepts of opposites effectively, are set at playschool, at a party, at the park, and at stores. There's no background clutter to distract the eye from the indefatigable plump boy who appears on every page.

Merrie Lou Cohen

SOURCE: A review of *At Home, At Playschool, At the Park, At the Party,* and *At the Stores,* in *School Library Journal,* Vol. 29, No. 5, January, 1983, p. 62.

These books are attractively illustrated in full color with amusing pictures, showing many common words in opposition. They would be particularly useful for home reading, day-care centers and public libraries serving toddlers. While the pictures can be enjoyed for their lively action, explanations by the adult reader are necessary to "expand a toddler's awareness of basic concepts" as promised by the publisher. These are heavy board books, and while they will undoubtedly wear well, they are somewhat difficult for small fingers to manipulate.

THE FLIGHT OF BEMBEL RUDZUK; THE BATTLE OF ZORMLA (written by Russell Hoban, 1982)

Marcus Crouch

SOURCE: A review of *The Flight of Bembel Rudzuk* and *The Battle of Zormla,* in *The Junior Bookshelf,* Vol. 46, No. 6, December, 1982, p. 220.

By Russell Hoban's standards these little—and modestly priced—books are lightweight stuff, but they show his originality and his clear understanding of what makes small children tick. They show the serious make-believe of everyday games, seen consistently from the child's standpoint. In the first, *The Battle of Zormla,* Zormla challenges the rest to battle, and it is waged horribly with the aid of clementines, wet sponges, marmalade and other weapons readily to hand. The Empress of Zurm, despairing of peace, goes away and makes pizza, and the war reaches a most timely end as the pizza comes out of the oven. '"Three chairs for pizza" said Zormla and the warlords of Troon.' In *The Flight of Bembel Rudzuk* the wizard puts together the squidgerino squelcher, a revolting, slobbering, moaning two-boy-power monster. Bembel Rudzuk takes refuge in Gar Denshed, where the princess has been unwise enough to leave a cheesecake. With the aid of a saw Bembel and the two halves of the squelcher damage its symmetry beyond repair. Can it be mice? the princess wonders when she brings in the sorry remains for the boys' treat. All good stuff. Colin McNaughton's illustrations are also done at child level, and his boys are suitably revolting.

Zena Sutherland

SOURCE: A review of *The Flight of Bembel Rudzuk,* in *Bulletin of the Center for Children's Books,* Vol. 36, No. 5, January, 1983, p. 90.

The three lively boys who enjoyed an imaginative play session in *They Came From Aargh!* are at it again. This time [in *The Flight of Bembel Rudzuk*] two of them make a wet mess as they crawl about under a piece of cloth, their flippered feet protruding as they attack the princess (mother) in her high tower (footstool). They go hunting for their brother, and the three make inroads on a newly made cake; mother comes back from an errand, sees the cake, wonders pointedly if mice have been at it. "Squeak!" say Bembel Rudzuk and his brothers. The illustrations are fresh, funny, and vigorous, and the story is ebullient and original. Like the other book, this can be enjoyed as a read-aloud book for younger children, but the nuances of the humor and the words used within illustrations indicate a primary grades audience.

Margery Fisher

SOURCE: A review of *The Flight of Bembel Rudzuk* and *The Battle of Zormla,* in *Growing Point,* Vol. 21, No. 5, January, 1983, p. 4015.

Riddling words transform the everyday world of authoritative mother and rampageous children through their role-playing in Gar Denshed or Wendi Husa, as they gather under a rug as a Squidgerino Squelcher, anticipate the cheesecake elevenses or fight with teddy bears, while the Empress dispenses snacks and justice. In the exuberant pictures, alive with colour and implied movement, the children are slightly distorted to suggest the way imagination takes them in and out of reality.

Carolyn Noah

SOURCE: A review of *The Flight of Bembel Rudzuk* and *The Battle of Zormla,* in *School Library Journal,* Vol. 29, No. 5, January, 1983, p. 60.

In two energetic fantasy adventures, the "Hungry Three" make their return. In *The Battle* [of Zormla] three siblings attack and counterattack with wonderfully imaginative artillery constructed from household items. Peace is made when the pizza is ready. In *The Flight of Bembel Rudzuk,* two of the children form the squidgerino squelcher, a slobbersome creature made of sponges and bedclothes. The good humor, childlike perspective and imaginative portrayal of this gang of three combines here with animated full-color drawings full of expression and detail. The books' small size and word plays closely tied to illustrations make them most appropriate for children reading independently or in very small groups, by whom the "Hungry Three" will be enthusiastically welcomed.

CRAZY BEAR: FOUR STORIES IN ONE BIG BOOK (1983)

Peggy Forehand

SOURCE: A review of *Crazy Bear: Four Crazy Stories in One Big Book,* in *School Library Journal,* Vol. 30, No. 3, November, 1983, p. 66.

McNaughton has created a series of colorful cartoon drawings about Bruno, a young bear, and his wild imagination. In four short adventures, **"Cowboy Crazy," "Snow Crazy," "Pirate Crazy"** and **"Rock and Roll Crazy,"** Bruno acts out his fantasies. In **"Cowboy Crazy,"** Bruno draws his pistols to shoot an Indian, in reality a woman wearing a hat with a feather in it; he then imagines he is being chased by "hordes of furious Indians." This stereotype is an unfortunate inclusion. Humor and cartoon format are typically British. The lively illustrations are far superior to the text. Most children would find *Crazy Bear* fairly amusing but not particularly original.

"VERY FIRST BOOKS" SERIES (*Spring, Summer, Autumn, Winter,* 1983; U.S. editions, 1984)

Zena Sutherland

SOURCE: A review of *Spring, Summer, Autumn,* and *Winter,* in *Bulletin of the Center for Children's Books,* Vol. 37, No. 7, March, 1984, p. 131.

Four hardbound books introduce the year's seasons to young children. This sprightly quartet focuses on activities appropriate to the season rather than on the season itself, so that the pages for *Autumn,* for example, show blowing leaves, bonfire meals, harvest time, and falling apples. The captions are just that simple: "Fallen apples," "Fallen leaves," and the colorful pictures fill but do not strain the page space with their action and humor.

R. Baines

SOURCE: A review of *Autumn,* in *The Junior Bookshelf,* Vol. 48, No. 2, April, 1984, p. 61.

How lovely to see a board book once again, particularly one produced at such a reasonable price. Is it too much to hope that a revival of rag books for the youngest of all may be just around the corner?

The ten tough pages we have here show a small boy, attired in changing items of colourful clothing, coping with the seasonal features of autumn. In duffle coat, pom-pom hat, muffler and gloves he strides out in a gale; muffled to the eyeballs he peers through fog. Although he wears orange wellies, splashing in puddles makes his socks wet, and falling red apples crash on to his head. Finally our hero discovers the fun of torchlight and bonfires on dark nights.

This board book is one of a series of four depicting the seasons.

Barbara Elleman

SOURCE: A review of *Spring, Summer, Autumn,* and *Winter,* in *Booklist,* Vol. 80, No. 15, April 1, 1984, p. 1118.

Vivacious children enjoy the seasons in these brightly illustrated, simple board books with rounded corners and sturdy bindings. McNaughton shows the expected (falling leaves, butterflies, camping, and sledding) as well as the humorously unexpected (apples falling on the head, a child slipping into a puddle, wildlife visitors at a picnic, and a bedridden tot suffering from a cold). Words, usually one per page, bring familiar images to life, and children will enjoy thinking about the experiences that the pictures encourage.

Susan Denniston

SOURCE: A review of *Spring, Summer, Autumn,* and *Winter,* in *School Library Journal,* Vol. 30, No. 9, May, 1984, p. 68.

McNaughton's addition to the Dial "Very First Books" collection is a set of four large, delightful, toddler-resistant cardboard books which provide a tangible introduction to the seasons for preschoolers. The brightly colored, humorous illustrations portray chunky children in busy, eventful pictures. Each book has large-print one or two word descriptions and a scene involving a child in an activity related to the appropriate season. In *Autumn,* a child romps through a "puddle" resulting in the same youngster removing "wet socks." In *Spring,* a "jumping" lamb is followed by a "jumping" cherubic child. Children from snowless environments will look with bewilderment and longing at the abundant snow scenes in *Winter.* The vibrant illustrations and minimal text admirably conceptualize the changing seasons.

"FOLDAWAY" SERIES (written by Allan Ahlberg, *Circus, Zoo, Families, Monsters,* 1984)

Martyn Chesworth

SOURCE: A review of *Foldaway Families,* in *Books for Your Children,* Vol. 19, No. 3, Autumn/Winter, 1984, p. 6.

Happy exuberant books with the same element of surprise. Each page can be pulled out to reveal another dimension to the picture. There's a seaside post-card look about Colin McNaughton's illustrations: mother and father with one child on a bike pull out to a whole Victorian size family in between: a normal street suddenly reveals a large house fit for giants. They are witty and effortless and will ensure that *"looking at books together time"* will be a riotous event.

📖 **"RED NOSE READERS" SERIES (written by Allan Ahlberg, *Help!* 1985; *Jumping,* 1985; *Make a Face,* 1985; *Big Bad Pig,* 1985; *Fee Fi Fo Fum,* 1985; *Happy Worm,* 1985; *Bear's Birthday,* 1985; British edition, 1986; *So Can I,* 1985; *Shirley's Shops,* 1986; *Push the Dog,* 1986; *Crash, Bang, Wallop,* 1986; *Me and My Friend,* 1986; *Blow Me Down,* 1986; *Look Out for the Seals,* 1986; *One Two Flea,* 1986; *Tell Us a Story,* 1986; *Put on a Show!* 1995; *Who Stole the Pie?,* 1995)**

Publishers Weekly

SOURCE: A review of *Help!,* in *Publishers Weekly,* Vol. 228, No. 25, December 20, 1985, p. 66.

Those two British funny men outdo themselves at inventing visual and verbal nonsense in their series, "Red Nose Readers." Screaming-loud colors suit the furious actions described in the minimal texts of three stories. A boy (identified by a tag on his wrist) awakens and yells "Help!" when a robber (also wearing a tag) sneaks into the bedroom. The robber yells for help when a gorilla appears to threaten him, then a monster scares the gorilla, etc., until the boy gets an idea that routs the whole gang. The following two entries are equally absurd and amusing. The other three little board books Ahlberg and McNaughton invite beginners to enjoy and learn from are *Happy Worm, Fee Fi Fo Fum,* and *Big Bad Pig.*

Books for Keeps

SOURCE: A review of "Red Nose Readers," in *Books for Keeps,* No. 37, March, 1986, p. 21.

This sensibly priced series of eight hardback books, all at the same readability level, presents reading to beginners as the problem-solving activity it actually is. Each book includes three or four zany sequences which are sometimes picture/caption stories and sometimes 'word sums' like 'balloon + pin = bang'. Apart from their light touch the greatest strength of these books is the close match between text and illustration—a feature which encourages children to accurately predict words from the company they keep.

Louise L. Sherman

SOURCE: A review of *Big Bad Pig, Fee Fi Fo Fum, Happy Worm,* and *Help!,* in *School Library Journal,* Vol. 32, No. 8, April, 1986, p. 67.

A quartet of zany word and concept books whose bright droll illustrations and amusing situations will tickle the funnybones of children just beginning to read. Each contains three or four short sections, each of which explores a concept. *Big Bad Pig* illustrates the concepts big and little, in and out, [slow] and fast, square and spotty. Included in *Fee Fi Fo Fum* are cause and effect addition statements such as "rain + sun = rainbow." Opposite pairs are depicted in *Happy Worm.* In the title story of *Help!* successively larger and more gruesome creatures (each clearly labeled) enter a little boy's bedroom, scaring one another until they all flee when the boy stands up with his sheet around him and says, "Boo!" The simple use of words and the clear comic illustrations make these books both appealing and useful, even in special education or English as a second language classes for older students, as they are such fun that even teenagers would enjoy them. Although the books are small, the illustrations are large enough for the books to be used in a story hour.

Frances Ball

SOURCE: A review of *Who Stole the Pie?* and *Put On A Show!,* in *The Junior Bookshelf,* Vol. 60, No. 2, April, 1996, pp. 64-65.

These two titles from the 'Red Nose Collection' supplement Walker's "Red Nose Readers." Many familiar characters appear, including Big Bad Pig, Happy Worm, and the Seals. They are shown in a wide range of situations, on pages with designs varied to display the words in many forms and sizes: in speech bubbles, as labels, as headings and titles, as part of a few lines of text, and as questions and answers.

In *Who Stole the Pie?* some words (with their pictures) are shown in the form of small, amusing sums: cat + fish = bones, and pig + dinner = big pig. A stolen pie is seen in the hands of a masked burglar followed by a policewoman—who eats the pie. Burglar Bert then loses his football shirt, and there are other disappearances. Several pages then show words and pictures in a range of combinations which can be used for picture-word matching. The book closes with some brief stories of bizarre and amusing events.

In *Put on a Show!,* a boy discovers monsters lurking in his house but after his initial surprise it is the boy who finds a way to frighten *them.* Several unusual word combinations are given imaginative illustrations, for example, fast house and square car. As the pages turn, the characters come together for a circus performance.

Both books present words in imaginative ways likely to

amuse children of infant age. They show how words can be combined, separated, put back together in different ways—mixed with pictures or used alone. The illustrations create some delightful images, including a cat which has to mend its split fur with a zip! Although the material would be particularly useful for children using the "Red Nose Readers," the books could also be used independently.

📖 ***THERE'S AN AWFUL LOT OF WEIRDOS IN OUR NEIGHBORHOOD: A BOOK OF RATHER SILLY VERSE AND PICTURES* (U.S. edition as *"There's an Awful Lot of Weirdos in Our Neighborhood" and Other Wickedly Funny Verse*, 1987)**

Margaret Carter

SOURCE: A review of *There's An Awful Lot of Weirdos in Our Neighborhood: A Book of Rather Silly Verse and Pictures,* in *Books for Your Children,* Vol. 22, No. 3, Autumn-Winter, 1987 p. 9.

Where have all the weirdos gone?

You'll find a lot of them in Colin McNaughton's latest book, and we defy anyone not to enjoy the encounters to be made in *There's An Awful Lot of Weirdos in Our Neighbourhood.*

> My cousin Davey
> Eats anything with gravy:
> Chocolate cake, ice-cream or peas!
> But I prefer tripe
> When it's lukewarm and ripe
> And it slobbers all over your knees!

'*Poems,*' says Colin McNaughton, author-illustrator of the book featured on our front cover, 'aren't dead words on a page. They are meant to be read aloud, chanted. It's their rhythm that counts.'

Read over the verse for yourself and judge if he's succeeded. No prizes for the answer.

He calls his poems in *There's An Awful Lot of Weirdos in Our Neighbourhood* 'verses' because, as he says 'poems suggest clever kids and exams.

These are meant to be entertainment.'

He also confesses that, as an artist, 'the pleasure of words is rather awesome to me.'

That certainly comes over too because, for all their apparent ease, his verses are most skilfully crafted and the pace of their arrangement throughout the book has been monitored by ear as well as eye. So we'll go from the sing-song of

> My dad's bigger than your dad

> Got more money too

to the ruminative

> I planted some seeds
> In my garden today.
> They haven't come up yet
> I hope they're okay.

But look at that page and you'll discover a clue as to why the seeds might not have come up: an uneasy looking bird studying a series of holes in the ground . . .

Which again is a pointer to this successful marriage of writer/illustrator . . . 'You can leave words out in the verse, or not say something because you know it will be filled in by the illustration. The illustration will complete the verse—the verse means nothing without the picture.'

Weirdos is the product of a year's sabbatical taken after 'ten years practically killing myself producing about fifty books, some fifteen or sixteen of which I've written myself.'

Originally the book was intended to be a thirty-two pager, with linking illustrations for about fifteen or sixteen verses . . . Some three of four months later having written a stock of about a hundred verses he called to a halt . . .

Allan Ahlberg, Colin McNaughton's collaborator in the much-acclaimed "Red Nose Readers" series has called the verses 'Beano verses' and there's certainly in these pages all the zest and bulging life of that long-lasting classic. As Allan Ahlberg says in his foreword 'kids will love it!'

It would seem they also love the Red Noses, a series of fun-packed graded 'first readers', illustrated by Collin McNaughton and written by Allan Ahlberg, who is, says the artist, 'one of the easiest persons to work with. He has a clear idea of what he wants and he may put just ten words on a page but a dozen lines of explanation as to how he sees them illustrated.'

It's a tribute indeed from someone who considers himself not an illustrator, nor a great stylist, and whose prime aim is not to make pretty pictures but to marry ideas, words and pictures.

He reads his own work aloud to his two sons, aged eight and ten, and vets their reactions although [McNaughton stated] 'it's dangerous to listen too much to children's reactions: they may be influenced by all sorts of things other than the verses—who's their favourite friend at the moment for instance! You can't lean too much on other people: no one is ever as strict as one is with onself.' McNaughton admirers are in for another treat this Christmas—a dramatisation of his book *Fat Pig,* to be produced at the Leicester Haymarket with musical direction by no less a luminary than the producer of *42nd Street.*

So what better way to end than with the end of *Weirdos?*

The water's deep
The sharks are thin,
The current's strong
So come on in!

But as Lewis Carroll said, 'Is it really the end—or just the beginning?'

If you have any sense it will be the beginning—of your enjoyment of this collection.

E. Colwell

SOURCE: A review of *There's an Awful Lot of Weirdos in Our Neighborhood: A Book of Rather Silly Verse and Pictures,* in *The Junior Bookshelf,* Vol. 52, No. 1, February, 1988, p. 33.

'A book of rather silly verse and pictures', says the author himself. And so it is. The anthology (with its clumsy title) includes verses about all kinds of odd people and creatures that will appeal to boys and girls as exciting and fun—giants, dinosaurs, robbers, witches, dragons—all shown in garish, sometimes crude, illustrations. Some pages are in comic strip format.

Into the midst of this noise and clamour, creeps an occasional quiet poem as, for example, 'I have an oasis', surely a welcome relief, even to noise-loving children.

The Ahlbergs contribute a preface for their friend the author and illustrator. Colin McNaughton has worked with Allan Ahlberg on various projects.

Publishers Weekly

SOURCE: A review of *There's an Awful Lot of Weirdos in Our Neighborhood: And Other Wickedly Funny Verse,* in *Publishers Weekly,* Vol. 244, No. 41, October 6, 1997, p. 85.

Much of the light verse of *There's an Awful Lot of Weirdos in Our Neighborhood: And Other Wickedly Funny Verse* by Colin McNaughton, first published in 1987, exploits the joys of absurdity and bad taste. Kids are likely to be delighted by such unapologetically puerile offerings as "Monday's child is red and spotty,/Tuesday's child won't use the potty" and other goofy verses.

JOLLY ROGER AND THE PIRATES OF ABDUL THE SKINHEAD (1988)

Roger Sutton

SOURCE: A review of *Jolly Roger and the Pirates of Abdul the Skinhead,* in *Bulletin of the Center for Children's Books,* Vol. 42, No. 5, January, 1989, pp. 129-30.

Called "Jolly" because he looks so miserable all the time, Roger decides to live up to his nickname and joins up with pirates, escaping his mad-for-cleaning Mum and hoping to find his Dad, last seen in an inn on the Barbary Coast. Abdul the Skinhead and the other pirates of The Golden Behind are a smelly, stupid lot, even allowing themselves to be captured (and cleaned up) by Mum, until they're saved by Roger and the pirates' cook, who has suffered amnesia since a [bonk] on the head. Guess who? While weakened by too many annoying asides by the author, the flip tone suits the spoof, and if one leaves out the parenthetical cuteness, this will be a lot of fun to read aloud. "I'm Abdul 'the skinhead'—Hiphip!/The 'Golden Behind' is my ship. . . . " The illustrations combine boisterous double-page spreads with smaller cartoon panels, all reeking with wit and stubble and a satiric edge that will be enjoyed by kids who think they're too old for picture books.

Carolyn Phelan

SOURCE: A review of *Jolly Roger and the Pirates of Abdul the Skinhead,* in *Booklist,* Vol. 85, No. 11, February 1, 1989, p. 940.

Roger, a lad whose father was lost at sea, so resents the many chores his shrewish mother assigns that he joins a pirate band. When the brigands hear of his heavily embroidered tales of woe and mistreatment, they vow revenge, attack his mother, and end up (no match for her) doing the chores themselves. Befriending the amnesiac ship's Cookee, Roger frees his pirate chums. Cookee, bonked on the head in the fray, regains his memory and proclaims himself (surprise!) Roger's long-lost father. Reminiscent of a Gilbert and Sullivan operetta, this picture book combines a melodramatic plot with witty, irreverent dialogue, and a well-foreshadowed ending that neatly ties loose ends together. McNaughton's lively, full-color artwork suits the story well, using crosshatching and dialogue balloons in the manner of Ardizzone, but with a harried, hairy, warts-and-all approach to drawing the pirates that kids may appreciate more than their parents. Although preschoolers might enjoy the artwork and the action, much of the wordplay-based comedy may pass them by. For older children and adults, however, here's a chance to revel in wild, improbable adventures and a generous portion of "shiver me timbers" talk that's slightly off the wall.

Jill Bennett

SOURCE: A review of *Jolly Roger and the Pirates of Abdul the Skinhead,* in *The School Librarian,* Vol. 37, No. 2, May, 1989, p. 61.

Colin McNaughton's pirates are disgustingly dirty, horribly hairy and generally vilely villainous in appearance, but they prove no match for Jolly Roger's mum. Roger, nicknamed 'jolly' because he always looks so miserable, is press-ganged by the pirates before he can apply for the job of pirate cabin boy. The pong of the cursed soap he brings aboard the ship, and his tales of how neat and tidy he has to be at home, provoke Captain Abdul into leading his crew on a trip ashore to teach Roger's mum a lesson. But for all their fearsome appearance, the likes of 'Bully Boy McCoy' and 'Khan the Really Nasty' present no problem for her and she soon has them working the farm. The story does not end there and Roger manages to effect their escape and find his long-lost father.

Despite its outward appearances, this is not an easy-to-read picture book, but a longish picture-story complete with chapters, bubble talk, songs and sings. However, the considerable demands made upon the reader are well rewarded. A splendidly swashbuckling yarn with plenty of 'Oooh-aarghs,' for the over eights.

Gill Roberts

SOURCE: A review of *Jolly Roger and the Pirates of Abdul the Skinhead,* in *Books for Keeps,* No. 89, November, 1994, p. 12.

You can't read this without laughing aloud. Miserable 'Jolly' Roger is miserably engrossed in 'pretending to slice up his (equally miserable) Mum like a salami' when he's kidnapped by Captain Abdul the Skinhead and his crew of pirates. However, they're sympathetic to their 'soap-stinking,' 'scab' of a captive for 'it ain't right for a lad to be brought up so clean' and all but Roger and 'Cookee' set out at speed to teach his Mum a lesson. Things take a different turn and Cookee's 'bang on the nut' leads to a reunion and an unexpected smile. Brilliant! 9- and 10-year-olds loved it.

WHO'S BEEN SLEEPING IN MY PORRIDGE?: A BOOK OF SILLY POEMS AND PICTURES (1990; reprinted, 1998)

Marcus Crouch

SOURCE: A review of *Who's Been Sleeping In My Porridge?: A Book of Silly Poems and Pictures,* in *The Junior Bookshelf,* Vol. 54, No. 5, October, 1990, p. 234.

'Daft poems and pictures' they may be, as the author/artist proclaims in his secondary title, but both poems and pictures are performed with much dexterity. The range is remarkably wide too. All the poems are brief—at most a double page including the illustration. All are pointed. Most are witty, or filled with a relaxed good-humour. Mr. McNaughton knows his kids, their ways of thought, their traditional and contemporary games, their approach to the everyday crises of their lives. It is all here, with coloured drawings making just the right comment on the words. Dinosaurs, vampires, spacemen, giants—here they all are, and interpreted without any adult grimaces or nods and winks to the parent behind the child. Just one example:

Robot's dead,
Lack of grease.
Parson said:
"Rust in peace."

Ann Stell

SOURCE: A review of *Who's Been Sleeping in My Porridge?: A Book of Silly Poems and Pictures,* in *School Library Journal,* Vol. 37, No. 2, February, 1991, p. 73.

So everyone can't do light verse like Shel Silverstein. Or even Jack Prelutsky. At least they can try. McNaughton tries hard and his heart is in the right place—with grubby little kids. He understands their preoccupation with eating and being eaten, with smelly babies, with being small and at the mercy of boring, unfair adults, "If I were a bird/ My wings I would spread,/ I'd swoop over you/ And plop on your head!" accompanies a picture of a small boy grimly led by a large, cross father. As the author himself says: "I'd love to write nice poetry;/ I'd like to be serious once in a while./ But I yam what I yam—I'm juvenile!/ It must be the devil in me." Some of the poems are too long; others are eminently forgettable. On the other hand, eight-year-old kids don't care if all the lines scan or not, and they'll like McNaughton's colorful illustrations, done in the same broad humor as the verses they accompany.

Maurice Saxby

SOURCE: A review of *Who's Been Sleeping in My Porridge?: A Book of Silly Poems and Pictures,* in *Magpies,* Vol. 6, No. 1, March, 1991, p. 36.

Here, thankfully, is a superior addition to the putrid and petrifying poems syndrome. Superior because the verse scans properly and has some imagery and poetic artifice to it. There are literary and social allusions; the vocabulary is rich and tangy; there is a gallery of way-out characters like Sir Percy Brocklehurst and Davy Duff; true wit abounds; the yuk is controlled (**"Don't Shove that Marble Up Your Nose"**) and the illustrations are examples of genuine comic art. There are moments of zany humour here in the Lear and Nash tradition. But these pieces are contemporary and of today's world, albeit British. Look out for **"The Human Beanpole," "That Little Monster Frankenstein"** and **"I'm Gargling in the Rain."** On second thoughts, you just have to read and enjoy the entire collection.

Jane Marino

SOURCE: A review of *Who's Been Sleeping in My Porridge?: A Book of Silly Poems and Pictures,* in *School Library Journal,* Vol. 44, No. 10, October, 1998, p. 126.

A collection of poetry that has all of the same broad, slapstick humor found in McNaughton's three picture books, *Suddenly!* (1995); *Boo!* (1996); and *Oops!* (1997). Four-line jokes; longer odes filled with words of Mc-Naughton's own creation; and profiles of monsters, headgear, and an assortment of other topics fill the pages. Plays on words abound, along with longer ballads about such characters as "Doris the Pirate" and "Davy Duff" and the story of a most unusual soccer game played in the Himalayas called "Firtilstern United." The humor ranges from guffaws to a sly wink, so there's something here to tickle any funny bone. A small alien craft that lands on a bald head and a two-headed, seven-handed monster who is unhappy at school are a sampling of the amusing watercolor creatures that inhabit the pages along with kids and grownups of every size and description. Childlike humor is always in evidence in this treat for sharing or reading alone.

📖 WATCH OUT FOR THE GIANT-KILLERS! (1991)

Marcus Crouch

SOURCE: A review of *Watch Out For The Giant-Killers!*, in *The Junior Bookshelf,* Vol. 55, No. 3, June, 1991, p. 95.

Colin McNaughton's contribution to the environmental debate has been given a suitably gigantic format, 12 ³/₄ by 10¹/₄ inches. Even so his green giant can sometimes be accommodated only by putting him across a double-spread. "You're very big", said the boy.' But as the giant demonstrates, size is relative. He is a cheerful giant, capable of a practical joke, and has kept up his spirits in spite of a life of danger and sorrow. Now, after centuries of peace in the Amazonian jungle the forest is contracting, and the green giant is once more in danger from giant-killers. The little boy is left with something to think about. The story is told almost entirely in dialogue, beautifully and economically composed. It relates directly to the author's powerful and exuberant pictures, which are sure to speak to the child in all of us. Mr. McNaughton proves that an important message can also be fun, but the fun never obscures the message. He brings the splendour, luxuriance and vulnerability of the jungle vividly before our eyes. The story is prefaced by a motto which says it all: 'We have not inherited the earth from our parents. We have borrowed it from our children.'

Margery Fisher

SOURCE: A review of *Watch Out for the Giant-Killers!*, in *Growing Point,* Vol. 30, No. 2, July, 1991, p. 5557.

This fable about forests is set in Brazil, where a huge tree-giant explains to a small boy how he was forced to leave Britain when the forests were felled and when King Arthur and Jack the Giantkiller waged war against ogres turned to cannibalism. As the boy sees the thin-

ning of the rainforest from high on the giant's shoulders, the point is made visually which has already come out in stately dialogue between the two characters. Lavish, semi-grotesque jungle scenes, with inset comic portraits of knight and giants and thematic maps of threatened parts of the world, make a formidable whole in a picture-book of generous size in which idiosyncratic artwork is vigorously used for a worthy purpose.

Jennifer Taylor

SOURCE: A review of *Watch Out For the Giant-Killers!*, in *The School Librarian,* Vol. 39, No. 3, August, 1991, p. 105.

A small brown boy walking in the jungle meets a 'green huge and terrible something' who turns out to be a jolly green giant some 1,900 years old. The whole book consists of a conversation between the two; the boy asks all the usual small-boy questions ('What is your favourite food?'), and the giant settles down to tell him his story. Born on an island called Britain at a time when it was covered in trees, he had to flee when men started cutting down the trees and killing the giants, and he travelled across the oceans on the back of a whale. Now the rain forest is shrinking fast . . . There is a message here of course, but unlike some picture books on an ecological theme which run into rather earnest waters, *Watch Out for the Giant-Killers* is packed with child appeal, with plenty of puns and jokes, and larger than life illustrations to suit the epic themes.

Jill Bennett

SOURCE: A review of *Watch Out for the Giant-Killers!*, in *Books for Keeps,* No. 99, July, 1996, p. 12.

Colin McNaughton takes the Green Man of folk legend as his inspiration for this giant tale wherein the spirit of the forest in the shape of a leaf-covered giant encounters a small Indian boy deep in the Amazon forest. Their conversation together is highly entertaining and full of jokes and wordplay, but behind the banter—giant's in bold print, boy's in standard—and the lush cartoon-style illustrations is a more serious message about human nature and its impact on the planet. Readers will need to bring some knowledge of fairy tales as well as geography and history to this, and be able to tackle a longish text, if they are to reap maximum enjoyment.

📖 HAVE YOU SEEN WHO'S JUST MOVED IN NEXT DOOR TO US? (U.S. edition as *Guess Who's Just Moved in Next Door?*, 1991)

Publishers Weekly

SOURCE: A review of *Guess Who's Just Moved In Next Door?*, in *Publishers Weekly,* Vol. 238, No. 36, August 9, 1991, p. 56.

From Guess Who's Just Moved in Next Door?, *written and illustrated by Colin McNaughton.*

The word is out on the street: new neighbors have just moved in and they are strange. As the panic spreads up and down the block, the narrator embellishes the cumulative tale with droll descriptions of the neighborhood's eccentric denizens. The tension builds almost to the point of hysteria as the reader wonders what kind of new neighbor could frighten this odd lot. The terrible secret is revealed in a spectacular fold-out spread at the end, and the narrator gathers his family for a hasty retreat— "I think we'll leave this miscellanea / And return to Transylvania." With its frequent repetitions ("Have they seen who's just moved in / Next door to us?"), McNaughton's (*Jolly Roger*) rollicking verse will make reading aloud a zany treat. His intricately detailed, never-ending procession of neighbors is rich with sight gags and jokes within jokes. This unique artistry displays a sense of humor that is both cheeky and camp— and a true test of any Welcome Wagon.

Nancy Menaldi-Scanlan

SOURCE: A review of *Guess Who's Just Moved in Next Door?*, in *School Library Journal*, Vol. 37, No. 10, October, 1991, p. 101.

From its delightfully ghoulish cover to its fold-out panorama of outlandish characters, this visual feast combines the detail of Base's *The Eleventh Hour* and the cleverness of Handford's *Where's Waldo?* McNaughton's

watercolor cartoons abound with puns, sight gags, and touches of whimsy. With few exceptions, everything mentioned in the text—and more—appears in these delightful illustrations. Presented in serviceable rhyme (which is a bit forced at times), McNaughton's story tells of a group of neighbors who are horrified when outsiders buy a house on their street. The newcomers, of course, turn out to be normal humans—parents, kids, and pets—who seem incredibly strange to the longtime residents. The neighborhood denizens are a mixed bag, ranging from nursery-rhyme favorites (the Dumptys) to superheroes (Superman), from legendary characters (Santa Claus) to historical figures (Michelangelo, not the Ninja Turtle), from Hell's Angels to movie monsters. The theme of fearing those who are different in some way seems particularly relevant in our multicultural society, and it is unfortunate that the ending spoils the message of tolerance by having the vampires flee to Transylvania rather than face the newcomers. Nevertheless, the book is cleverly designed, and its often-sophisticated humor will allow it to be appreciated on several levels.

K. Johnson

SOURCE: A review of *Have You Seen Who's Just Moved In Next Door To Us?*, in *Books for Your Children*, Vol. 27, No. 1, Spring, 1992, p. 19.

There are new neighbours moving into the street, but

how will they fit in with all the other residents? Colin McNaughton takes the reader on a (longish) journey down the street to meet the locals who inevitably turn out to be more than a little peculiar, if not down-right monstrous. Take Mr Thing—'squirting, squelching, slithering' round his house. There's also the school which 'teaches birds to say rude and silly words'—no prizes for guessing which words!

This is a highly entertaining book, which is packed with visual and verbal detail, with the author playing with words and sounds, cracking jokes, turning our expectations upside down, as well as bringing in all sorts of well-known literary and other figures. It's a book which can be re-read countless times by a wide age-range, and there will always be something more to discover within its pages.

George Hunt

SOURCE: A review of *Have You Seen Who's Just Moved In Next Door To Us?*, in *Books for Keeps*, No. 81, July, 1993, p. 14.

With a verse form that goes rollicking along similar lines to the popular *There's an Awful Lot of Weirdos in Our Neighbourhood,* this book takes us on a colourful tour of a street inhabited by a diverse multitude of freaks and oddballs from all areas of literature, popular culture and the communal unconscious. Monsters, ghosts, ghouls and aliens are all horrified by the arrival of the mysterious new neighbours, whose truly disturbing identity is at last revealed on the final panoramic fold-out spread. The pages are rich with pictorial and verbal jokes, the latter carried in a subtext of speech balloons.

This book will be an instant favourite with all ages, if the reactions of the children I showed it to are anything to go by. Its message condemning prejudice just about manages to emerge from the sumptuous narrative through which it's expressed.

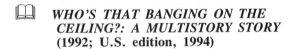

WHO'S THAT BANGING ON THE CEILING?: A MULTISTORY STORY (1992; U.S. edition, 1994)

Kirkus Reviews

SOURCE: A review of *Who's That Banging on the Ceiling?: A Multistory Story*, in *Kirkus Reviews*, Vol. LX, No. 20, October 15, 1992, p. 1314.

A vertically-opening, one-idea book with sure child appeal: working from the ground up, each high-rise tenant imagines what could be making the racket immediately above ("It sounds like elephants on pogo sticks!" "It sound like a dinosaur dancing the fandango!"); both imagined and real activities (revealed with a page turn—in this case, kids bouncing on the bed) are depicted in lively cartoon style. It's all topped off when imagination

meets reality in King Kong himself—who's tap-dancing on the roof in a spectacular foldout. "Now that really [*is*] silly."

David Lewis

SOURCE: A review of *Who's That Banging On the Ceiling?: A Multistory Story,* in *The School Librarian,* Vol. 41, No. 1, February, 1993, p. 22.

I never cease to be amazed at the ingenuity displayed by picture-book makers when it comes to exploiting the possibilities inherent in what is, in one sense, simply a set of rectangular hinged flaps. Colin McNaughton turns his new book through ninety degrees so that readers must start with the spine facing them. Thus the story unfolds as the book is opened *downwards* towards the reader. What one sees at the top of the first page-opening is a picture of a tall block of flats and then, as we turn down the pages, each double-page spread reveals two rooms, one above the other. On the lower page, the occupant wonders what is causing the noise in the room above ('What's that clack, clack, clacking on the ceiling . . . ?') and in the picture above we see what she imagines it to be ('It sounds like a dinosaur dancing the fandango!'). The next page turn reveals the truth—it's not *really* a dinosaur of course—but also presents the next puzzle ('What's that boing, boing, boinging . . . ?'). We are thus pulled irresistibly through the book, ascending the floors and solving the riddles of the noisy neighbours. Until we reach the roof, where a clever twist and a big surprise lie in wait. The book is highly successful as a page-turner—if a little awkward to handle—and beautifully unites several venerable traditions: the grotesque and the nonsensical between the covers of what turns out in the end to be a kind of 'movable'.

Kathy Piehl

SOURCE: A review of *Who's That Banging on the Ceiling?: A Multistory Story,* in *School Library Journal,* Vol. 39, No. 3, March, 1993, p. 182.

Inhabitants of a 12-story apartment building speculate about what could possibly be producing the racket above them. A turn of the page replaces fantasy with reality. For example, the pigs at a feeding trough that Mrs. Gowk envisions above her head turn out to be a group of unmannerly young men stuffing themselves at a dining-room table. McNaughton's high rise is occupied by his usual bug-eyed, plump humans, many of them scruffy and ill-mannered. The humor lies in the contrast between speculation and actuality, and part of its interest derives from the unusual format: the book is read from bottom to top rather than left to right. The final four-page foldout of King Kong is a knockout. Children may enjoy guessing what really is happening before a page turn reveals the truth, and they'll enjoy trying to spot the cat in each scene. This clever novelty book is not an essential purchase, but it will amuse young audiences.

Don Pemberton

SOURCE: A review of *Who's That Banging on the Ceiling?: A Multistory Story,* in *Magpies,* Vol. 8, No. 5, November, 1993, p. 25.

When you hear a strange sound in the ceiling but can't see its source, you imagine the sound-maker. Is it a monster? In Colin McNaughton's latest unconventional picture book, there is an apartment block reaching up 12 levels to the low-lying clouds. When a family on one level hears noises from above, they imagine something grotesque going on in the rooms on the next floor.

There's much aural verve, cartoonish mayhem and sheer surprise as the book carries you up from floor to floor into the clouds. Then on the ultimate roof there is an outcome to outdo them all.

I was delighted by the way the mental expectations of the characters (confined as they are in their rooms) are played off against what the readers see as they ride up in the freedom of their imaginary elevator. Then, too, there is a witty reversal created at the end in a double-fold-out page. On the way up, wild imaginings keep getting pinched back by reality; but when you reach the roof . . . Well, you should read it and see.

MAKING FRIENDS WITH FRANKENSTEIN: A BOOK OF MONSTROUS POEMS AND PICTURES (1993; U.S. edition, 1994)

Roger Sutton

SOURCE: A review of *Making Friends with Frankenstein: A Book of Monstrous Poems and Pictures,* in *Bulletin of the Center for Children's Books,* Vol. 47, No. 8, April, 1994, pp. 247-48.

Contemporary poetry for children is fortunate in its many voices: the lyricism of Myra Cohn Livingston and Constance Levy, the zest of Jack Prelutsky and Dennis Lee, the rhythmic snap of J. Patrick Lewis. That's just a few among the many—but is there any room left for the enthusiastically disgusting?

> Cockroach sandwich
> For my lunch,
> Hate the taste
> But love the crunch!

"Cockroach Sandwich," the opening quatrain of McNaughton's new collection, certainly sets the tone, and visually, the portrait of the grizzled old man with cockroaches running out of his mouth adds a certain statement of its own.

Cheerfully gross and often witty, the poems in *Making Friends with Frankenstein* often sound a folkloric ring akin to those playground and afterschool rhymes kids make up for themselves. *Making Friends with Franken-stein,* though not from the oral tradition and written by a single poet, keeps alive the rude delight children often bring to language, whether in playground insults ("Airhead, doughbrain, pizza face,/ Reject from the human race"—from **"Another Poem to Send to Your Worst Enemy"**), stupid puns ("Sons and daughters,/ Nephews and nieces,/ The monster is dead—/May he rest in pieces"—**"Frankenstein's Monster Is Finally Dead!"**) or gross-out noises ("Slobber, chomp, slurp, gulp! BLE-ARRGGHHOOOWOURGHH!!!"—**"A Pound of Gummy Babies"**).

The illustration for the last shows a greedy pig-child vomiting gummy bits and a barrage of yellow mucus; not your thing or my thing, certainly, but kids will, all right, eat it up (as they will the poem about the bogeyman, who "gets right up my nose"). Unlike many children's books which pander to juvenile tastes, all the while barely concealing their adult authority, this one feels unmediated and unrepentant, with the last poem being a haiku-short **"Farewell to Dracula"**: "So long,/ Sucker!" The book isn't afraid of anything and, along with its ego-puffing putdowns, offers kids their own chants to be brave, particularly spells against bullies. **"Yah, Boo, Hiss,"** finds for kids a friend ("Yah, boo, hiss/ To all of you!/ My best friend/ Is nine foot two!") and throughout, various cyclopses, the Frankenstein monster, Quasimodo, and aliens from space face defeat. Strong measures require strong words, and McNaughton doesn't hesitate to say them.

But what do kids get here that they won't get on the playground? Pictures, for one thing, large-scaled, literal-minded, and highly funny pen-and water-color portraits that accompany the burlesque with competitive vigor and that have plenty of shut-the-book-here-comes-teacher vulgarity. There are also plenty of readaloud possibilities—for them, not you. Best of all is the generous sense of personality that bounces through the book. While not all of the poems quite succeed (although McNaughton's **"The Forth Worst Pome Wot I Ever Ritted"** is actually a deconstructionist's masterpiece), taken together they have a rounded joviality that shows how a single sense of humor can wander down many paths. Kids will enjoy the stroll. So will you.

Publishers Weekly

SOURCE: A review of *Making Friends with Frankenstein: A Book of Monstrous Poems and Pictures,* in *Publishers Weekly,* Vol. 241, No. 19, May 9, 1994, p. 73.

With a dash of Monty Python and a whiff of Jack Prelutsky, McNaughton's (*Who's That Banging on the Ceiling*) deliciously outrageous poems are filled with wacky cartoon characters, nimble puns and clever spoofs. Three blue ghosts perform a "phantomine"; "in the sandbox, making trouble" are "seven witches, hubble, bubble./ (Sandwitches!)." An **"Ode to the Invisible Man"** is featured on an otherwise blank page, while an **"Abominable Verse"** about a yeti (which "rhymes so neatly with spaghetti") is illustrated by a view of the preposterous beast guzzling wine and gobbling pasta. Both poems and art are wickedly comic rather than horribly offensive, though there is plenty of noise ("slobber, chomp, slurp, gulp!") and an abundance of gross mischievousness. Frankenstein's monster is chopped to bits to the refrain "May he rest in pieces," and a thug eats a cockroach sandwich ("Hate the taste / But love the crunch!"). From the Dracula endpapers to the romp through Jekyll and Hyde Park, McNaughton's saucy good fun contains enough comic-strip verve and zany comedy to liven up even the "biggest monster party / That there's ever monster been!"

Kirkus Reviews

SOURCE: A review of *Making Friends With Frankenstein: A Book of Monstrous Poems and Pictures,* in *Kirkus Reviews,* Vol. LXII, No. 10, May 15, 1994, p. 703.

McNaughton's grimacing, pop-eyed cartoon figures are the perfect accompaniment for his uninhibited rhymes and free verse. Even though it can descend into indelicacy or tedium ("Widdly, waddly, kink-a-joo/Sing the monster SONG!/Diddly, doddly, stinkypoo/Bang the monster GONG!") the clever title poem ("When I am feeling lonely,/For Igor I will send./We'll go to my laboratory/And we will make a friend!") is more characteristic; some of the wordplay here recalls Jack Prelutsky's. Most selections feature monsters or ghoulish events ("A Cyclops Can Never Be Friends With Another": "They never see eye to eye"), while unpleasant surprises await visitors to "Jekyll and Hyde Park." But some contemporary concerns are addressed: "Georgie Porgie's been so bad—/Kissed the girls and make them mad," and "a caged bird isn't singing out of joy." Page layouts, as varied as the poetry, add visual interest to a robust collection whose humor, while occasionally gross, is sure to appeal to the target audience.

Russ Merrin

SOURCE: A review of *Making Friends with Frankenstein: A Book of Monstrous Poems and Pictures,* in *Magpies,* Vol. 9, No. 3, July, 1994, p. 39.

Horror and giggles. It's an unlikely combination but it is just what you get with McNaughton's **Making Friends with Frankenstein.** The monstrous cartoon silhouettes which haunt the endpapers in blood-red and bilious-green are bold, eye-catching and utterly delightful. Readers unfamiliar with McNaughton's other volumes of verse need look no further than the first poem to get a feel for the contents:

> Cockroach sandwich
> For my lunch
> Hate the taste
> But love the crunch!

Poems feature ogres, monsters, vampires, ghosts, crocodiles, Cyclops, headless apparitions, zombies, etc. and are accompanied by McNaughton's inimitable, wacky cartoon style artwork. This book contains over 50 humorous poems, ranging from two lines in length to two pages, and these are indexed by title for easy retrieval. With its puns, visceral humour and zany artwork, this book is fun from first page to last and is sure to appeal to pupils across the full range of primary grades.

CAPTAIN ABDUL'S PIRATE SCHOOL (1994)

Mandy Cheetham

SOURCE: A review of *Captain Abdul's Pirate School,* in *Magpies,* Vol. 9, No. 5, November, 1994, p. 25.

Readers of the **Jolly Roger** will remember Abdul the Skinhead and his band of thieving buccaneers. This time the wily Captain Abdul has opened a pirate school. The students, led by the resourceful Pickles, foil the pirate's plot to ransom their unsuspecting parents, and neatly turn the table of events to suit themselves and the Machiavellian captain.

This rumbustious piece of extravaganza incorporates all the best traditions of the pirate tale. The villains are suitably roguish. They are dressed in proper gear, some have lost bits of their bodies, they speak the right lingo and, of course, they are outwitted by a clever young protagonist. And in deference to the times there is no gender bias, the student pirates being equally divided between male and female. Action-packed illustrations which literally seem to spill over the pages minutely describe and document the progression of the story. There is a perennial demand for pirate stories, and this loud, jolly tale will delight enthusiasts of the genre.

Teresa Scragg

SOURCE: A review of *Captain Abdul's Pirate School,* in *The School Librarian,* Vol. 42, No. 4, November, 1994, p. 152.

Anarchy rules in Colin McNaughton's new picture book featuring characters who first appeared in **Jolly Roger.** This time, Captain Abdul is running a school for pirates, where spitting is allowed, brushing your teeth is frowned upon, and cheating sends you to the top of the class. The pirate pupils learn how to read treasure maps and put model ships into rum bottles, before Pickles, one of the pirate pupils, discovers Abdul's dastardly plan to kidnap them all and hold them to ransom. They hijack the ship and sail away in *The Golden Behind* to an idyllic life in the West Indies, swimming all day, stealing only from other pirates, and sending lots of treasure home to their parents. Even Captain Abdul is happy because news of the mutiny has been good publicity for the pirate school, and pirates from all over the world now send their children there!

This is a hilarious picture book for older readers. The familiar, cartoon style illustrations are full of visual jokes, and there are more jokes and puns in the dialogue and in characters' names, which will require many rereadings to understand them all. It's a wonderful fantasy, designed to appeal directly to children, though there is a lot for adults to enjoy too. My only slight criticism is that the style of the drawings lends itself to caricature, which gives some of the characters, particularly the Chinese pupil Ching Yih, a stereotyped appearance. On a more positive note, the fact that one of the pirate pupils unexpectedly turns out to be a girl is a wonderful twist at the end.

Joanne Schott

SOURCE: A review of *Captain Abdul's Pirate School,* in *Quill and Quire,* Vol. 61, No. 1, January, 1995, p. 43.

Maisy Pickles prefers painting or poetry but has been sent to Pirate School by a father who thinks such things too soft. In fact, no one in the entering class looks confident, but they soon learn to speak Pirate, to be untidy, and to rampage around town. One night Pickles overhears the teachers plotting to kidnap the students and hold them for ransom. Having learned their lessons well, the pupils tie up the pirates, dump them out on the wharf, then sail the ship to a tropical island where they lead an idyllic life, robbing only other pirates. Captain Pickles writes and paints to her heart's content.

Captain Abdul's Pirate School is riotous and rude, with as much subtlety as the pirates' cannon blasts. Headmaster Abdul has it all—peg leg, hook, rotten teeth, eye patch—and the teachers almost equal his piratical glory. Veteran author/illustrator Colin McNaughton has created a distinctive and consistent personality for each of the students, who form a crowd of all sorts, even in school uniform. Translation of standard school subjects into pirate equivalents, word play in the dialogue, and every sort of play in the pictures suggest that the author had as much fun with this as his readers will.

Kate McClelland

SOURCE: A review of *Captain Abdul's Pirate School,* in *School Library Journal,* Vol. 41, No. 1, January, 1995, p. 90.

Maisie Pickles's parents hustle her off to Captain Abdul's Pirate School to toughen her up because she likes writing poems and painting pictures. She learns her lessons so well that when she overhears a plot to kidnap the students and hold them for ransom, she deftly organizes a mutiny. After subduing the teaching staff, the youngsters set sail for the West Indies and live a boisterously adventurous life, stealing from pirates and sending the treasure home. Captain Abdul reckons his school a success to have graduated such a crew, and Maisie herself

is free to pursue her artistic interests. McNaughton's bold cartoons are well suited to the subject. His pirates convey just the right robust exaggeration; bold lines express exuberant movement and attitude. The text, written in the form of Maisie's diary, gives the impression of hand lettering on parchment and is spiced with lusty dialogue. The book is rife with broad humor. The student body, while multiethnic, is definitely not P.C. While the characters' stereotypical identities play no real part in the story, librarians should be alerted to the fact that there are visual and verbal jokes and plays on words at the expense of everyone. Chop is a "person of size," Ching Yih has slanted eyes and large white teeth, and Rosemary Lavender is crudely masculine.

📖 *SUDDENLY!* (1994; U.S. edition, 1995)

Mandy Cheetham

SOURCE: A review of *Suddenly!,* in *Magpies,* Vol. 10, No. 1, March, 1995, p. 22.

In the spirit of the fox in that enduring favourite, *Rosie's Walk,* a wolf stalks a plump young pig as he walks home from school. An excellent choice for preschool storytime programmes as the audience can follow the wolf's progress as he prepares to leap on his prey, each time with dire consequences to his person. Finally the little pig arrives home safely to a reassuring cuddle from his mum. The endpapers show the wolf being carried away to a hospital accompanied by a rude refrain.

A nice lean text and clever sequencing of the characters in each double page spread underlines the dramatic impact of the story.

Children aged between two and two and a half and four years will enjoy participating in this story, and older preschoolers will appreciate the tongue in cheek humour.

Annie Ayres

SOURCE: A review of *Suddenly!,* in *Booklist,* Vol. 91, No. 18, May 15, 1995, p. 1652.

Every time Preston "suddenly!" deviates from his path, he just misses being gobbled up by the big, bad wolf stalking the pink, plump pig. Clueless, Preston safely negotiates the walk home from school, going to the grocery store, returning to school to collect his grocery money, stopping at the park to play, collecting the groceries at the store, and coming home to his mother's arms. The incompetent wolf ends up being carried off to Wolf Hospital. The humor is visual, the mayhem is of the "Coyote and Roadrunner" cartoon variety, and the soft and sunny pastel-colored pencil-and-watercolor illustrations keep the mood light and jolly. This one-joke picture book, from the author-illustrator of *Making Friends with Frankenstein: A Book of Monstrous Poems and*

Pictures, is deftly executed and designed to amuse a young audience that will appreciate being in on the joke.

Deborah Stevenson

SOURCE: A review of *Suddenly!*, in *Bulletin of the Center for Children's Books,* Vol. 48, No. 11, July-August, 1995, pp. 388-89.

Reminiscent of Pat Hutchins' *Rosie's Walk,* this is the story of Preston, an amiable young pig who remains completely oblivious to the wolf that lingers around every corner, waiting to gobble him up. The recurring joke is one of suspense suspended as pictures show the wolf looming threateningly while the text describes Preston embarking on some innocuous activity "when SUDDEN-LY!"—and a turn of the page demonstrates that Preston has suddenly changed his path (for his own innocent reasons) and the wolf has come to violent and slapstick grief. Line-and-watercolor art in tastefully moderated colors depicts the creatures' cheerfully exaggerated actions (check out the frustrated wolf bearing down on Preston in a steamroller), keeping the lupine threat distant enough to be safely humorous for young listeners. Cartoon fans will appreciate the Road-Runnerish plot here as the predator wreaks more damage on himself (he's carried off to the Wolf Hospital at the end) than on his prey; many a young piglet will enjoy both the joke and the ironic justice.

📖 *HERE COME THE ALIENS!* (1995)

Frances Ball

SOURCE: A review of *Here Come The Aliens!*, in *The Junior Bookshelf,* Vol. 59, No. 5, October, 1995, p. 171.

Colin McNaughton's aliens are far from beautiful. They speak only a few words and those are from strange languages. Their behaviour leaves much to be desired, but they are very likable. Their peculiarities, and imaginative technology should fascinate children aged about four to seven, and they manage to do many things children are warned against. They have no table manners, they fight, they take a very relaxed view of their appearance, but as they head for earth and a battle, a frightening piece of paper drifts towards them. It shows something so worrying, so awful, that they decide to return to their own planet. It shows a class of children as they looked when aged four!

This is a pleasant story which puts into perspective some of the stories children may have heard about aliens. They may be different—but how do *we* look to *them.* It might also encourage children to think about other differences and groups, and their views. The story is told in rhyme, with lightly-coloured text set against the darkness of space. It gives an amusing, imaginative view of aliens, creating some memorable images.

From Suddenly!, *written and illustrated by Colin McNaughton.*

Margaret Clark

SOURCE: A review of *Here Come the Aliens!,* in *Books for Keeps,* No. 96, January, 1996, p. 28.

Definitely not for the end of the day is Colin McNaughton's *Here Come the Aliens!* a picture book guaranteed to excite the most reluctant of readers or listeners. The insistent beat of the verse text accompanies ever more frenzied pictures of the monstrous aliens slobbering, dribbling, grunting and burping, who keep on coming until stopped in their galactic tracks by the faces of a class of four-year-olds. A book that may alienate adults because it will arouse much chanting, jumping and shrieking at the final joke, it also inspires a relish for words.

Mary Crawford

SOURCE: A review of *Here Come the Aliens!,* in *The School Librarian,* Vol. 44, No. 1, February, 1996, p. 16.

The aliens are coming and who will save the human race? Colin McNaughton's latest book is a brilliant combination of verse and illustration. The aliens zoom towards earth through blackest night. So the verse and illustrations are set on black pages highlighting the lurid nature of the subject material which is printed in gruesome shades of pink and yellow and blue and green. Both poet and illustrator have had great fun with the aliens: this one is a typical example:

The first mate looks like wobbly jelly,
　He's sort of gaseous and smelly;
　He has an eyeball in his belly!

This book will be a winner with children of all ages and with Colin McNaughton fans everywhere. I have found that pupils who can scarcely read have memorised McNaughton's poems.

BOO! (1995; U.S. edition, 1996)

Karen Yeomans

SOURCE: A review of *Boo!*, in *The School Librarian,* Vol. 44, No. 1, February, 1996, p. 16.

This amusing new story about Preston the Pig from Colin McNaughton has all the elements of a true picture book. The illustrations are bright and colourful. Anticipation is created throughout the text, keeping the child's interest, and the repetition of 'Boo!' encourages child interaction and makes the book fun to read and ideal to be read out loud at story times. In addition the humorous twist at the conclusion of the story will delight young children. I am sure that this new picture book will become a firm favourite with all 3- to 6-year-olds.

Elisabeth Palmer Abarbanel

SOURCE: A review of *Boo!*, in *School Library Journal,* Vol. 42, No. 9, September, 1996, pp. 184-85.

Add this humorous tale to the many stellar books starring pigs. Preston the Masked Avenger sneaks, spies, and slides through the night; yells "Boo!" at his victims; and disappears into the darkness. Finally, he sneaks up on the "greatest villain in the universe," his father. Before the young porker can disappear into the night, however, his dad catches him and sends him to his room. Dad then sneaks up on Preston to teach him a lesson, but it ultimately backfires when Preston surprises his parent in the bathtub. The grown-up pig is just as playful as his son, giving the story a sense of warmth. The repetition and simplicity of the text, coupled with the familiar theme, make this book a sure hit for group sharing. The cartoonlike illustrations add delightful details to the story. Both adults and children will find new and funny pictures with each reading, such as the black cat that appears in almost every scene, pig silhouettes in the windows, and even a pig-shaped topiary.

OOPS! (1996; U.S. edition, 1997)

David Lewis

SOURCE: A review of *Oops!*, in *The School Librarian,* Vol. 44, No. 4, November, 1996, p. 147.

Colin McNaughton goes from strength to strength. This is his third Preston pig story, and the invention shows no sign of flagging. In this tale Preston is charged with delivering a basket of food to Granny's house and sets off in his red coat and hood hotly pursued by the dim wolf who cannot quite remember which story the colourful outfit reminds him of. Big bad wolf takes the short cut through the wood (a painful experience) but fails to gain any advantage, and arrives at Granny's house after Preston, still unable to recall which story he seems to be in. When he overhears Preston remarking on the dimensions of Granny's eyes, ears and teeth (the latter in a glass by the bed) he realises that they are supposed to be his lines and he then knows what to do. Of course he fails to remember the outcome of the story and the book ends very satisfactorily with Mister Wolf pursued through the wood by Preston, Granny, and Preston's dad bearing a sharp axe.

The illustrations are a delight—big and bold and very funny (McNaughton does a particularly mean wolf)—and the visual narrative is so designed that it wraps around the whole book, beginning with the front endpapers and including the front and back covers. In addition, McNaughton has a great sense of comic timing in his use of language and is able to shift effortlessly from one register to another, moving from the banalities of family conversation to the argot of the comic book to parodies of traditional tale telling. This book is a gem and deserves to become a classic.

Publishers Weekly

SOURCE: A review of *Oops!*, in *Publishers Weekly,* Vol. 244, No. 25, June 23, 1997, p. 91.

A child doesn't have to be schooled in post-modernism to get a kick out of a self-reflexive narrative. "These stories would be pretty boring if I was good, wouldn't they?" asks the lanky, bad Mr. Wolf in McNaughton's latest Preston Pig story, a fairly faithful version of "Little Red Riding Hood" with Preston cast in the title role. The central joke is that Mr. Wolf can't recall his own role: "Hmm . . . red hood, basket of food, Granny's house? That reminds me of a story, but which one?" While he racks his brain, he must suffer through the havoc wreaked by the always unwitting Preston (for example, while Mr. Wolf is trying to trap Preston with "The old 'Dig-A-Deep-Pit' dodge," the pig blithely skips across his head). Older children especially should appreciate McNaughton's smart-aleck humor (Mr. Wolf has been banned from the school grounds for "snacking on the students"), while the younger members of the target audience are just as likely to enjoy his over-the-top cartoon style emphasizing Mr. Wolf's snarly snout, buggy eyes and various physical travails.

Deborah Stevenson

SOURCE: A review of *Oops!*, in *Bulletin of the Center for Children's Books,* Vol. 51, No. 2, October, 1997, p. 59.

"It was the same old story," the text begins, but it's selling itself short—it's actually a variant on two of them, "Little Red Riding Hood" and "The Three Little Pigs." The hungry wolf slavering around is familiar, of course, but this time it's Preston the pig who sets off for Granny's house, and it's Preston telling the real Granny what big eyes, ears, and teeth *she* has that finally reminds the wolf of his role in the proceedings. The wiseacre narration is reminiscent of smart cartoons, and listeners will appreciate the humor of the wolf's repeated attempts to figure out what story he's in and the relentless fairy-tale momentum that brings him to his fate. Watercolor and colored pencil art show a pop-eyed, top-hatted wolf boinging around the pages in pursuit of the goodhearted but clumsy Preston Pig; between the running, the chaos, and the elaborate villainy, the atmosphere is strongly and happily Mack Sennett (there's even a banana-peel gag on the cover and in the book). It's cheeky, unsubtle, and often groaningly (yet enjoyably) obvious, and youngsters will wolf it down.

Cathryn M. Mercier

SOURCE: A review of *Oops!,* in *The Horn Book Magazine,* Vol. 74, No. 1, January-February, 1998, p. 66.

Preston the pig returns in this jaunty sequel to **Suddenly!** and **Boo!** in which he is again targeted by the wily, if unlucky, wolf in search of a pork dinner. The tale starts off with a third-person narrator who alerts readers to the wolf's hunger and recounts the wolf's prior failures to capture Preston. In an effective interruption, the Big Bad Wolf shrugs his shoulders in defense and speaks directly to readers about his true nature. The gesture and confidential tone may not wholly win readers to the wolf's side, but they provide an empathetic understanding of the wolf for anyone who wants one. Colin McNaughton combines light pencil sketches with vivid watercolors in primary hues to animate further this witty integration of "The Three Little Pigs" and "Little Red Riding Hood." Preston's bumbling nature amuses because it allows him to dodge all the cunning wolf-tricks; the wolf's inability to capture the pig tickles even more because it stems from his confusion about just which story he is in. Even young readers will enjoy this metafictional play as they eagerly try to predict the ending and appreciate its twist. McNaughton's merging of these two particular stories, along with his energetic yet clear graphic (and typographical) design, point to an intended audience of early readers—old enough to get the jokes and young enough to delight in them again and again.

📖 *PRESTON'S GOAL!* (1998)

Kirkus Reviews

SOURCE: A review of *Preston's Goal!,* in *Kirkus Reviews,* Vol. LXVI, No. 12, June 15, 1998, p. 897.

Intrepid, single-minded Preston Pig foils a stalking wolf through a series of unintended actions. Preston is out fiddling with his soccer ball one morning when his mother asks him to go to the store for a loaf of bread. As Preston heads out, the wolf awaits his chance. Preston traipses through another pig's garden; the gardener takes the wolf for the suspect and conks him. Then, displaying less-than-acute ball-handling skills, an oblivious Preston beans the neighborhood bully and then a policeman, both of whom mistake the wolf for the culprit and give him a licking. The wolf, thoroughly vexed, jumps his quarry, but winds up with a soccer ball for dinner. This is an ideal picture book for soccer enthusiasts; the story is not original, but it has moments of high slapstick to keep children involved.

📖 *DRACULA'S TOMB* (1998)

Mike Simkin

SOURCE: A review of *Dracula's Tomb,* in *Carousel,* No. 10, Autumn-Winter, 1998.

Despite all the warnings to Keep Out! Do Not Disturb! and Do Not Open!, Colin McNaughton has drawn together a very imaginative journal about the Count's lifestyle, fanciful obsessions, background facts and intimate possessions. This is a unique visual record of Dracula's ancestral relations followed by his school report, personal correspondence and a matchless collection of personal pets including a ghoulfish, frankenswine and ratula. This shaped book provides lots of fun, thrills and food for thought and is almost impossible to keep your hands off.

Additional coverage of McNaughton's life and career is contained in the following sources published by The Gale Group: *Contemporary Authors New Revision Series,* Vol. 47 and *Something about the Author,* Vols. 39, 92.

Sheldon Oberman

1949-

Canadian author of fiction, plays, and short stories; lyricist.

Major works include *TV Sal and the Game Show from Outer Space* (1993), *This Business with Elijah* (1993), *The Always Prayer Shawl* (1994, published in Great Britain as *Always Adam*, 1995), *The White Stone in the Castle Wall* (1995), and *By the Hanukkah Light* (1997).

INTRODUCTION

Best known for his award-winning book *The Always Prayer Shawl,* Oberman has explored his Jewish heritage and shared both traditional and personal stories which embrace the universal elements of intergenerational relationships. His earlier books, though fantasy, drew heavily on the traditions of storytelling. His other books, written for elementary graders, are very personal accounts with much autobiographical influence from his own childhood and the life stories of others, not only of his own family and heritage, but extending to the traditional tales of an Inuit storyteller. Praised for his masterful use of symbolism to represent such concepts as perpetuity and change, Oberman succeeds in maintaining simplicity and clarity in his narrative. He is recognized for his versatility, ranging from the gentle spoof of contemporary TV addicts in *TV Sal and the Game Show from Outer Space* to the poignant tales of family love, tradition, and piety as exemplified in *The Always Prayer Shawl* and *By the Hanukkah Light*. Above all, as a storyteller, Oberman weaves together a personal and family history to produce, as Stephanie Zvirin noted, "a beautifully evocative sense of continuity across generations."

Biographical Information

Oberman was born in Winnipeg, Manitoba, Canada, in 1949. With a father who was a champion weight lifter and a mother who was a psychic counselor, his childhood was bound to be out of the ordinary. His parents owned a coffee shop, working long, hard hours, and Oberman was left on his own to wander the neighborhood, meeting interesting people, observing the human condition, and eventually discovering the library where a world of heroes and adventure opened to him. He learned the art of public speaking from the local Kosher butcher, and applied it on his first job as a door-to-door salesman. Although he liked the money he made, he was dissatisfied with the requisite hypocrisy and began searching for work to define himself, taking a job as a pantry-man on a railroad dining car. He attributes his leap into adulthood to a serious accident that occurred on an early morning run. He reacted to the accident by beginning to

focus more clearly on how he wanted to live and what he wanted to do with his life.

After high school, he attended the University of Winnipeg and spent several summers traveling in Europe, North Africa, and Israel, where he did his graduate study at the University of Jerusalem. When he returned home he settled down, married, and started teaching English and drama and telling stories, the work he continues to do in various forms. In an interview with *Something about the Author (SATA)* Oberman said, "I'm moved by two impulses—teaching and writing. I give half my working day to each—mornings as a high school teacher, afternoons as a writer. Teaching offers me a secure, orderly life while being a writer keeps me hungry and spontaneous. It's an effective though precarious balance."

During his colorful career, Oberman has been a songwriter, film director, storyteller, playwright, journalist, editor, and actor. He enjoys explorations of the creative and communication impulses in himself and in his students. In *Something about the Author Autobiography Series (SAAS),* Oberman wrote, "I continued to teach at the same high school, and I still teach there part-time, over twenty years later. Teaching keeps me sharp and lets me share the literature that I love and the energy of the young who are still questioning and learning. . . ." Earlier, he told *SATA,* "I like variety and I've found it in different types of creativity; acting, directing, creating my own eccentric art out of found objects. . . . However, I'm always drawn back to the 'hardest' copy of all—the book."

Major Works

Oberman wrote *TV Sal and the Game Show from Outer Space* as a spoof on his daughter's summertime obsession with television. Sal is glued to the TV and rejects her family's invitation to go out with them. After they leave, a game show comes on in which an alien from outer space offers to trade Sal a Universal Channel Changer for a part he needs for his space ship. When Sal makes the trade, she is swept into the TV where she surfs from one bizarre alien game show to another, trapped in the outer space network. She finally manages to win a trip home, rewinding time so that her family doesn't miss her, and astounds her family by telling them that she's had enough TV. In *Quill and Quire* Joanne Findon commented, "This is a clever book that manages to critique with humor and to embrace today's video culture."

This Business with Elijah is as much for adults as it is for children. It is a collection of short stories that previously appeared in a variety of small magazines, many of them about a young boy named Danny who is trying to come to terms with his parents, his Jewish heritage, and the world around him. He is guided by an elderly neighbor, a survivor of World War II, who imparts both history and wisdom by telling Danny stories, "ancient mystical tales of their people and his own thrilling stories of his life in the Old Country and in this New Country." Oberman commented, "The old man and the boy form a special friendship that serves them both. Danny is hungry to learn about heroes and the ways of the world, tales to prepare him for his future. Old Werner needs to tell his stories so he can gather the precious moments of his past and make some final sense of his long life."

Oberman received the most attention for *The Always Prayer Shawl,* which won several awards. He wrote it as a bar mitzvah gift to his eldest son, a history of the family prayer shawl and the family name. Grandfather Adam tells his grandson the story of his life, how different life was for the peasants living in Czarist Russia. When the family flees from the soldiers to come to America, they must leave behind Grandfather Adam's beloved grandfather, too old to make the journey. Grandfather's grandfather, whose name is also Adam, gives his grandson his prayer shawl as a memento. As Grandfather Adam grows and changes, the prayer shawl changes too, with alterations and replacements as parts wear out. As the book ends, Grandfather Adam, now an old man,

passes the prayer shawl, and all it represents, to *his* grandson Adam. "Now I can teach you something that my grandfather taught me," he says. "[S]ome things change and some things don't. It is just like me. I have changed . . . but I am still Adam." Jane Robinson commented in *CM Magazine,* "This is a comforting story about the importance of tradition and the certainty of change."

On a visit to Sir Henry Pellatt's Victorian castle, Casa Loma, in Toronto, Oberman noticed one white quartz stone in a wall containing thousands of gray ones. *The White Stone in the Castle Wall* is his idea of how this might have come to be. Tommy Fiddich, a poor boy living in the slums of Toronto, considers himself "the luckiest boy of all" because his vegetable garden provides him with a decent means of support. When bad weather ruins his crops and insects destroy the rest leaving nothing but a big dirty rock, Tommy laments that he is the "unluckiest boy of all." Then he hears that Sir Henry is offering one dollar a piece for large stones for his castle wall. Tommy digs up his rock and, with tremendous labor, hauls it uphill to the castle through a rain storm that washes the rock clean. The master of the wall says he cannot buy Tommy's rock, because he has been instructed to buy only gray ones, and Tommy's is pure white quartz. Tommy turns around, dejected, but an old gardener working nearby hears Tommy's story, and revealing himself to be none other than Sir Henry, not only buys his rock, but gives him a job tending the castle gardens, so that once again Tommy is the luckiest boy of all. Berna Clark called this "a very charming tale of a very appealing young boy and a very kindly leading citizen."

In *By the Hanukkah Light,* Oberman once again brings together grandparents and grandchildren with stories of personal memories and family traditions. Every year Grandpa and Rachel polish the old silver menorah for the Hanukkah celebration, and every year Grandpa tells Rachel and Jacob the Hanukkah story of the Maccabees' defeat of the invading army. This year Grandpa adds his own Hanukkah story—how, when he was a child in Europe, his family was afraid to show the Hanukkah lights; how the family fled from war; how Grandpa fought to defeat the evil war maker; and how, when he returned to the ashes of his old home, he found the old family menorah, the same that he and Rachel have just prepared for the holiday. Ellen Mandel noted, "Oberman weaves a memorable story around a religious artifact that has survived brutalities and hazards to be lovingly handed down through generations."

Awards

In 1987, Oberman won the Canadian Authors Association Short Story Award for *The Lion in the Lake/Le Lion dans le Lac.* In 1990, after the story became a book, it won the International Silver Medal at the Leipzig Book Fair. In 1991, he won the Journey Prize nomination for Best Canadian Short Story of the Year for *This Business with Elijah,* which became the title story for a book of short stories that received a nomination for the McNally Robinson Book of the Year in 1994. *The Always Prayer Shawl* won the National Jewish Book Award and the Sydney Taylor American Librarians Award. It also received *A Child's Magazine* Best Book of the Year citation and the International Reading Association Choice citation.

AUTHOR'S COMMENTARY

Sheldon Oberman

SOURCE: "Wandering and Wondering," in *Something about the Author Autobiography Series,* Vol. 26, Gale Research, 1998, pp. 169-88.

The creative spirit loves to wander and wonder. Yet it also has a goal: to create something wonderful. That's how it is with the creative people I have known: writers, actors, artists, designers, architects, directors. That's how it's been with me, writing books, plays, and songs, directing theater and film, and performing as a storyteller. I feel most alive when my imagination is at play or at work, when I can experience something in a new way or I can create something new and interesting.

I feel lucky to be able to do this. I've known many people with great talent and determination, but for one reason or another, things didn't work out.

Luck is peculiar, and sometimes you don't know when you are lucky or unlucky. When I was young, I would not have thought there was anything fortunate about being poor or being in a minority group or being alone so much of the time. Yet those very things that seemed to be disadvantages turned out to be great assets; they helped to shape me as a writer. . . .

Many things that might seem like disadvantages turned out to be a great help in making me a writer. Being alone taught me how to use my imagination and it made me a friend who will be with me as long as I live: my own true self. What I learned from being poor is worth more than money can buy. And when I did accept my heritage, I realized the greatness of my own people, not only of the famous like King Solomon, Elijah, and the wonder-working Ba'al Shem Tov, but also the greatness of ordinary people with extraordinary hearts and spirits, an inspiration for endless stories. . . .

One of my greatest teachers was not a teacher at all, at least not a schoolteacher. And I was probably the only student he ever had.

Mr. Freedman was a butcher at Omnitsky's Kosher Meats, down the street from our store. He was a short, stout, and homely man. He had a bad lisp and glasses as thick as Coke bottles. Yet he could walk confidently into a room, face an audience, and hold their attention with a convincing and entertaining speech.

My mother decided that if Mr. Freedman could overcome his obvious handicaps, he could certainly teach me how to overcome mine. I was merely awkward, self-conscious, and lacking basic social skills, typical afflictions of a thirteen-year-old, especially a "loner."

Mr. Freedman had me write and memorize a five-minute speech and present it to him in his living room. He was tremendously impressed. He then showed me how to speak, how to pause, and how to use my hands. The next week I returned with a better speech and a better presentation. Again, he was tremendously impressed and taught me with even more techniques. I did about fifteen speeches before he judged me ready for the next level. He took me downtown to the Toastmasters Club, his public speaking group. He had me speak before a group of professionals and business people. All of them were tremendously unimpressed. After all, I was just a kid. Mr. Freedman kept training me until even those grouchy Toastmasters accepted me with their grudging applause. My parents taught me a love of creativity. Books inspired me with exciting stories and ideas. Mr. Freedman gave me my voice. . . .

I was working as a second cook in the day-coach diner. The train was snaking up a mountain pass in the Canadian Rockies. At 7 A.M. I made my way through the day coaches calling out that breakfast was being served. Most people were awake waiting for the call, and as I returned to the kitchen they crowded into the diner and began to order. Suddenly the whole train jolted. We just managed to steady the tall urn of hot coffee before it spilled over us. A couple more jolts and the train ground to a halt. The chef and I figured the engine had hit a moose, but it was far worse.

A six-ton boulder had rolled off the mountain. It hit the train, derailing six of the train cars. A day coach took the hardest blow—it was unrecognizable, a gaping wreck of metal and glass with half the seats torn away. When the boulder hit, the engineer had sped up and manoeuvered so the cars derailed against the mountain wall. Otherwise they would have fallen over the edge into the river six hundred feet below and would have pulled the entire train down with them.

We rushed about getting first-aid supplies for the injured. Luckily most people had left the day coach when I made the call for breakfast, except for a university student who had stayed behind to sleep a little longer. They found her body far down the tracks. I had walked through that coach only minutes before the boulder hit. As my shock wore off, I realized how close I had been to death.

Helicopters came for the injured, and the passengers were evacuated by a relief train. As we waited our turn, I sat at a counter in the diner writing to a friend, describing the events and my feelings as fully as I could.

It was my first truly serious writing. I had written letters to amuse some friends and assignments to please my teachers, but this was different. I was writing to express what I could not say aloud, feelings and thoughts that grew and deepened as I set them on the page. I never mailed it, and to this day I have never felt the need to read it. The important thing was that I had found the heart to write it. . . .

I began to write a journal, not a diary of events as much as a record of my thoughts and feelings. I wrote it in a black notebook that I carried in my back pocket. I still keep it these thirty years later, though now I type it into a notebook computer that I carry in my satchel. . . .

To my surprise, I was led back to childhood by my own children. My son, Adam, and my daughter, Mira, would ask me to tell them stories, especially stories about me as a child. They loved that, of course. It put me on their level. Soon I began making up stories and songs at bedtime, and we were sharing the same childlike sense of delight at a good tale.

One of their favourites was a rhyming story about a boy who rode out late at night and was surprised by a fearful creature:

> "I'm a witch, John R. W., a horrible witch!
> Cackle and hackle and snaffley snitch!
> Watch my face turn all green and my ugly nose twitch!
>
> Cackle and hackle and snaffley snitch!
> I can turn to a toad and make your skin itch!
> Cackle and hackle and snaffley snitch!"
> Said John Russell Watkins, "Why you don't scare me.
> You're as little and silly and sad as can be.
> And I've seen all those tricks while watching TV."
> And rode off, clipidy clop, clop clop.

A ghost and troll have no better luck scaring John. Finally all three creatures burst into tears as they beg him . . .

> "Please pretend to be scared. Please could you try?"
> "No!" said John R. W., "That would be a lie!"
> And he rode off, clipidy clop, clipidy clop
> He rode off, clipidy clop, clipidy clop.

I gave a copy to my friend Fred Penner, whom I had met when we were both acting in plays. He was starting out as a children's entertainer, so I hoped he could give me tips about writing for children and a bit of encouragement. Instead he told me he was planning a children's album and asked if he could use my poem. What an encouragement! Fred Penner and I went on to create many poems and songs for his albums and then for his national TV show.

I also began to write for adults. Something creative had been released; I no longer felt "bewitched" by the demands of adulthood. In fact, I could use my adult discipline and maturity to write. Without it I might keep on dreaming, but I'd produce little.

I took a year off teaching in 1978 and freelanced for Winnipeg's main paper. I wrote about whatever interested me: "The Pinball Prince of Portage Avenue," "Emergency Ward—the Fight for Life," "The Naked Zoo—Private Lives of Animals behind Bars," "Step Right Up—Working on the Midway." I was astonished by the power of being a reporter. I only had to say I was from the Free Press and suddenly I could enter almost anywhere and ask anybody almost anything. I'd then write up a story, get it published immediately, and be paid to boot.

One of my first books came through my training in journalism. *The Folk Festival Book* was written during six intense weeks as I interviewed hundreds of people from famous performers and folk festival staff to volunteers and members of the audience—all the folk who make up a folk festival. Most of my other books, even storybooks, take more than six years.

The other breakthrough of that year occurred on a trip to Toronto. I had a day and a half alone without distractions, only the Ontario wilderness outside my window and the comforting rattle and roll of the train. My mind drifted back to my childhood on Main Street, and I wrote my first significant short story. It took another twenty drafts, but it became a published work.

I returned to teaching and kept writing whenever I could. I loved writing, but I didn't know if I should dedicate myself to it. I needed to know if I had what it takes. The Banff School of Fine Arts in Alberta gave me the answer. I was accepted into its summer writing program, directed by W. O. Mitchell, a great Canadian writer. His method was perfect for my improvisational nature. For six weeks twenty of us put aside all previous writing. We began practising "Free Fall," a directed form of stream of consciousness writing to uncover fresh images, characters, settings—the raw material of our imagination. Formal writing was not accepted. No rewriting either. Free Fall was an exercise in discovery. Each morning, interesting work from the previous day was read aloud and discussed by the group without any negative criticism. The rest of the afternoon and evening was spent in writing.

Most of my earlier writing had imitated other writers. Here, I was going deeply into my own experiences and emerging with my own distinctive expression. I've been in many workshops, courses, and various writing groups. They all had particular skills to teach, but W. O. Mitchell showed me how to find my creative sources and how to believe in myself as a writer.

I continued seeking out interesting experiences. I did a couple fire walks across a path of hot coals. I collected "found" objects to create collage art which I still do as my "hobby." I took workshops in everything from massage and I Ching readings to group therapy and neurolinguistic programming. I'd rent out my house each summer and travel through Canada and the States in an old Econoline van that I set up for sleeping, eating, and, of course, writing. It was a gypsy life that delighted my kids as much as me. Lee Anne and I were no longer married, but the children were with me half the time. My eccentric interests didn't bother my kids; in fact they tell me that our best times together were when I was the most "far out."

I became a member of a commune in southern Manitoba. I bought an old caboose, moved it onto the land, and converted it into a rustic retreat. I'd drive out whenever I had a break, with the kids or on my own, light some candles, toss logs into the stove, and set the water boiling for my coffee. I would jump into my writing with the same delight as jumping into the creek outside my door. . . .

I began speaking at conferences and performing my works as well as telling traditional Jewish tales across Canada and the States. I developed workshops for teachers, writers, and communities on personal and family storytelling, even a website. One good story leads to another, and soon everyone in the workshops would be sharing stories. I also had my students record family stories and do video interviews of an elder relative. When Boyds Mills Press asked me for another book, I wanted to write one that had that intimate sense of personal and family stories. I recalled some of the stories that had moved me most.

One of my students shared the story of his grandfather Samuel, who had survived the Buchenwald concentration camp. Samuel was walking out of Germany, confused and in despair, when he stopped at a house to ask for water. There he saw a prayer shawl being used as a tablecloth. He managed to barter something for the shawl, and by rescuing it, he was changed. He felt that somehow he had rescued himself and restored his identity.

Another person told of visiting a Spanish immigrant woman and discovering an old menorah, a Jewish ritual candleholder. It had been in the woman's family for centuries, but she had not known what it was or that her ancestors were possibly Marranos, secret Jews who had hidden their religion since the Spanish Inquisition's edict of expulsion of 1492. When the Spanish woman learned more about Jewish traditions, she made sense of her grandparents' odd rituals and secretive ways. More than that, she began to make sense of her past and how it had shaped her.

Another story was about a chaplain during World War Two. He had dedicated himself to rescuing pieces of stained glass from bombed out churches. It was dangerous work, often near the front lines, and during one mission he was killed. A soldier kept up his work, and the glass later was assembled into a commemorative window in the chaplain's hometown church.

These stories were defining moments for the people who told them. At a personal level, they were like the great moments in history that shape a nation's identity. I began to think of the stories that the Jewish people recall on holidays such as Passover and Hanukkah. This all

coalesced as I wrote *By the Hanukkah Light*. Rachel hears two tales from her grandfather: a tale of their people and a tale of their own family, both miraculous tales of the Hanukkah light.

The tale of Hanukkah recounts how the light of the Temple, the Jewish symbol of spirit and faith, was almost lost but then rescued and miraculously restored. The grandfather's second story is in some ways parallel to the ancient one. He recalls being a child in Europe and his family being afraid because they were Jews, how they could not celebrate Hanukkah openly and finally fled, leaving behind their hanukkiah, the lamp of Hanukkah. He told how he returned later as an Allied soldier and fought "like the old Maccabees." Miraculously, at the end of the war, he recovered his hanukkiah in the ruins of his house, the same hanukkiah that he and the grandchildren have just cleaned and lighted.

The two stories become equally moving and meaningful. Rachel promises her grandfather, "When I grow up and have children, I will tell them these stories, the story of our people and the story of our family as we gather by the Hanukkah light." For me, stories of our past are heirlooms to treasure and to pass on to the next generation.

The White Stone in the Castle Wall is an heirloom story of an entire city. It takes place at Casa Loma, Toronto's famous "castle," which was built in 1912 by Sir Henry Pellatt. I took a tour of the old castle and became fascinated by the tour guide's talk of Sir Henry, a sort of benevolent capitalist who didn't mind spreading a bit of his wealth. When he was building his outer wall, he offered the people of Toronto a dollar for each large field stone they brought him, a full day's wages at the time. The stone rush was on, and Sir Henry bought 250,000 stones.

As I looked at the grand stone walls I noticed a single brilliantly white quartz stone. I then realized that it was the only white stone in the entire wall. My writer's "spider sense" tingled. Why only one white stone? Who brought it and how?

I turned local history into historical fiction by writing a story of John Tommy Fiddich, a poor immigrant lad who had a garden "where he worked hard every day." His harvest would earn him a silver dollar, making him "the luckiest boy of all!"

> Then the hail beat everything down
> the insects ate everything up
> and the wind blew the rest away
> except for a dirty, grey stone.

John's luck hits bottom but shoots up again when Sir Henry Pellatt calls for stones. He heaves the stone into a cart, hauls it through Old Toronto during a heavy storm, and struggles up the hill to Casa Loma. But the rain washes the grey dirt from the stone, and the master of the wall has to reject it. Sir Henry asked for only dull-colored stones:

"Your stone is all bright white. Sir Henry will not
want it. I cannot buy it from you for his wall."
John told him, "Sir Henry owns this great castle.
He owns all the lights in the streets of the city.
All that I own is this one white stone and I hauled
it up the hill for him."
The builders of the wall,
the drivers of the wagons,
the servants of the castle all said:
    "John Tommy Fiddich,
    your white stone is worthless.
    You're the unluckiest boy of all."

In the spirit of the Horatio Alger fantasies that inspired
our grandparents' generation, John's hard work and sincerity are rewarded. He fatefully meets and impresses
Sir Henry, who buys the white stone for his wall and
gives John a job working in his English flower garden. Is
John once again the luckiest boy of all, as everybody says?

    "I've been lucky and unlucky,"
    answers John Tommy Fiddich,
    "but I earned a silver dollar all the same.
    And I brought Sir Henry Pellatt
    a great white stone for Casa Loma,
    a stone that's worth a lot to him and to me."

John has created something he feels good about. That's
been my goal as well. I've looked at factors in my
childhood: being poor, being alone, being from a minority, and I've seen how they shaped me as a person and a
writer. I've looked at my adulthood, and I've made some
sense of what I've achieved and what I haven't. I suppose I
could have charted all my "ups and downs," deciding
where and how I've been lucky or unlucky, but like most
of us, I've learned that luck is not the point. Lucky and
unlucky, we do what we can with what we've got.

I've been doing what I can, trying to stay true to the
people that I love and to that creative impulse that has
given me such joy.

TITLE COMMENTARY

📖 *TV SAL AND THE GAME SHOW FROM
OUTER SPACE* (1993)

Joanne Findon

SOURCE: A review of *TV Sal and the Game Show from
Outer Space,* in *Quill and Quire,* Vol. 59, No. 10,
October, 1993, p. 40.

Sal is at the cottage and her family tries to lure her
outside, but she just wants to watch TV. One day, while
her family is out, Sal's favourite program is replaced by
a strange game show. The host (who is really a ma-

rooned space alien) promises to make Sal the next big
winner, and sucks her right inside the television set.
When she refuses to play the game, Sal is offered the
Universal Channel Changer, a device that enables her to
travel the intergalactic airwaves. She bounces from station to station, and from planet to planet, finally making
her way back home. But with the Universal Channel
Changer, life will never be quite the same again.

This is a crazy story that will delight young and old.
Sheldon Oberman's witty text is peppered with subtle
adult jokes, yet it also captures the TV-obsessed child's
view of other activities, such as Sal's mother's enticing
offer of a walk: "Come out with us to look at the fog."
Craig Terlson's exuberant illustrations are reminiscent
of both cartoons and children's own artwork. They ex-
plode across the pages, interacting energetically with the
text. TV Sal is a resourceful character who manages to
cope with her interplanetary adventures and still maintain connections with her family. She remains in control
to the last moment, when we realize that, next time, she
plans to take her family with her into Outer Space. This
is a clever book that manages to critique with humour
and to embrace today's video culture.

Catherine Sheldrick Ross

SOURCE: A review of *TV Sal and the Game Show from
Outer Space,* in *Canadian Children's Literature,* Vol.
20:4, No. 76, Winter, 1994, p. 82.

TV Sal capitalizes on the fact that children have a sub-
versive streak by taking a possible message and turning
it inside out with bounce and humour. In a beginning
that parodies discourse on the evils of TV, we learn that
Sal had been watching TV all week long at her summer
cottage: "Her father said, 'That TV will suck your brain
as empty as an old grapefruit.' Her brother said, 'Your
eyes will be as square as that TV screen.' Her mother
asked, 'Would you like to do something different, dear?
Come with us to look at the fog.'" But Sal stays home
to watch the *Pretty Piggy Supersweet Special* and ends
up making a trade with space aliens: parts to fix their
spaceship in exchange for a Universal Channel Changer
that "puts you on any TV show in the universe." As Sal
surfs from channel to channel, the intertextuality in-
voked is not to fairy tales but to game show motifs:
"'DON'T TOUCH THAT DIAL.' 'YOU'VE GOT A
TRADE!' The audience went wild." The insistent and
attention-grabbing text finds its appropriate counterpart
in Craig Terlson's high-intensity, cartoon-like illustrations.

Anna Santarossa

SOURCE: A review of *TV Sal and the Game Show
from Outer Space,* in *CM Magazine,* Vol. 22, No. 1,
January, 1994, p. 23.

TV Sal and the Game Show from Outer Space is a zany
story about a girl who watches too much TV.

Sal is at the cottage, where she has been watching TV all week long. Her family invites her to go for a walk with them, but she declines because she wants to watch more TV. After her family leaves she notices that there is something wrong with channel 2. The game show host of "Let's Make a Trade" hands her a list and tells her to go and get whatever is on that list so she can make a trade. Sal proceeds to do this and then jumps into the TV. Sal makes her trade and wins the "Universal Channel Changer," which allows her to participate in any TV show in the universe.

Sal is trapped in bizarre, alien TV shows until the next day, when "Let's Make a Trade" is on again. She wins a trip back home again and rewinds the time so that she doesn't get into trouble for being away from home.

At the end of the story her family is astounded when Sal says she doesn't want to watch any more TV.

I enjoyed this story. It was funny and cleverly written with subtle satire. All children can relate to this story, not only because most children watch far too much TV but also because all children would comprehend the anxiety of being in a foreign location and not being able to return home at will.

This book would be a welcome addition to any library.

THIS BUSINESS WITH ELIJAH (1993)

Norman Ravvin

SOURCE: A review of *This Business with Elijah,* in *Canadian Book Review Annual,* edited by Joyce M. Wilson, 1994, p. 192.

These stories appeared in a variety of little magazines, and the title piece was nominated for the prestigious Journey Prize. To expand upon this adult audience, the author and publisher have produced a teacher's guide designed to make the collection accessible to younger readers. Canadian history, Jewish customs, and everyday family pressures are the most common subjects dealt with in the guide's questions and activities for students.

Young readers may be able to relate to Oberman's favorite character, a youngster named Danny, who is often at odds with his parents and peers, and who learns the ways of the world from an elderly neighbor who is a storyteller, a natural wit, and the keeper of information about Europe before World War II.

The best stories are those that focus most directly on Danny's frustration as the adult world proves impenetrable and tantalizingly out of reach. Oberman has a knack for the initiation story, in which the child finds himself in an embarrassing or challenging situation but comes through it bearing a nugget of wisdom. Danny's world is small—just a few blocks of a Winnipeg neighbor-hood—but his adventures point toward a wider, more complicated world yet to be grasped.

THE ALWAYS PRAYER SHAWL (1994, British edition as *Always Adam*, 1995)

Publishers Weekly

SOURCE: A review of *The Always Prayer Shawl,* in *Publishers Weekly,* Vol. 240, No. 48, November 29, 1993, p. 65.

Oberman's (*Lion in the Lake*) simply told and moving story invokes the power of tradition. Adam is a Jewish boy growing up in Czarist Russia, where his grandfather, also named Adam, teaches him the importance of Jewish beliefs and customs, stressing that "some things change and some things don't." Without distancing the reader, comparisons crystallize the differences between Adam's time and the present: "When Adam went for eggs, he did not get them from a store. He got them from a chicken. When Adam felt cold, he did not turn a dial for heat. He chopped wood for a fire." When Adam and his parents emigrate, Adam's grandfather gives his prayer shawl to the boy, who responds with a promise: "I am always Adam and this is my always prayer shawl. That won't change." In America, Adam learns to live, dress and speak differently. The prayer shawl changes, too—first the fringe is replaced, then the collar and finally the cloth. But, as Adam is to explain to his own grandson, "It is still my Always Prayer Shawl." As a tender conclusion brings Adam's spiritual life full circle, Lewin underscores the cyclical theme by picturing the grandson as very like the young Adam. His realistic watercolors dynamically depict the Old World in black and white, changing to color as Adam grows up, and his affecting portraits match the quiet passion of Oberman's prose.

Stephanie Zvirin

SOURCE: A review of *The Always Prayer Shawl,* in *Booklist,* Vol. 90, No. 8, December 15, 1993, p. 750.

In a quiet story with just the right touch of sentimentality, Oberman beautifully evokes a sense of continuity across generations. Enhancing his third-person narrative with a smattering of dialogue, he tells of the Jewish boy Adam, growing up in a shtetl, whose life drastically changes when famine and chaos in old Russia force his parents to immigrate to America. At parting, Adam's beloved grandfather gives the boy a gift, a prayer shawl ("my always prayer shawl"), which was presented to the grandfather by *his* grandfather, for whom Adam was named. Lewin's first paintings, in black and white, show the white-bearded grandfather in the shtetl, the soldiers with their guns, the tall buildings in America dramatically dwarfing Adam and his parents. Then, in one double-page spread that telescopes Adam's growing into manhood, the artwork leaps into glorious color. While

Oberman's controlled text capsulizes the passage of time in words, the color paintings show Adam the man proudly wearing his Russian grandfather's shawl, then Adam the grandfather, passing the shawl and what it represents on to his own young grandson. As good as any of [Ted] Lewin's best work, the watercolors are abundantly detailed and wonderfully expressive (the grandfathers and grandsons are at once different and the same). The pictures enrich the tranquil telling, which harks back to the biblical Adam, as it movingly depicts how memory and tradition add texture and richness to our lives—even as other things around us change.

Kirkus Reviews

SOURCE: A review of *The Always Prayer Shawl,* in *Kirkus Reviews,* Vol. LXI, No. 24, December 15, 1993, p. 1595.

"Now I can teach you something that my grandfather taught me," says Adam to his grandson at the end of this generational story, " . . . some things change and some things don't." As a boy in rural Russia, the man who's now a suburban American got eggs direct from chickens and chopped wood to keep warm, but—as Adam is doing now, in their synagogue—his grandfather told him about the Jewish people and his own family: Adam was named for his grandfather's grandfather. When Adam and his parents set out for America, his grandfather gave him the earlier Adam's prayer shawl. While Adam grows up and has a family of his own, the shawl wears thin and he replaces the fringes, then the collar, at last even the cloth. But as he explains as an old man, "It is just like me. I have changed . . . But I am still Adam." The idea is simple yet resonant, and well supported in Lewin's watercolors, rendered in the black and white of old photos until Adam's middle age in what might be the 50s; as always, his subtle, warm characterizations steal the show, though the composition and detail in the b&w section are also especially fine. An engaging book, sure to find many uses.

Annette Goldsmith

SOURCE: A review of *The Always Prayer Shawl,* in *Quill and Quire,* Vol. 60, No. 1, January, 1994, p. 36.

From the rather sombre cover showing a contemplative Jewish boy wearing a prayer shawl, it is clear that this is a picture book for older readers. In simple, direct sentences, Winnipeg author, songwriter, and teacher Sheldon Oberman recounts how young Adam and his parents flee the terror of Czarist Russia. Adam's beloved grandfather stays behind, giving Adam his prayer shawl and some advice—"Some things change. And some things don't."—as parting gifts. The rest of the book demonstrates that one can retain one's identity in a new country, amid constant change, by keeping faith with tradition. The story ends as Adam, now a grandfather, passes on the same advice to his grandson.

This collaboration between author and artist is a happy one: distinguished American illustrator Ted Lewin's paintings lend depth and dignity to Oberman's story. In the first half, the illustrations are realistic black-and-white watercolours. They switch to colour when Adam grows up. The transition is disconcerting, since it happens on the second page of a double-page spread, but that is not a bad thing in itself. The book is beautifully designed, with spacious double-page spreads, elegant typography, and *à propos* endpapers. The design lends Adam's black-and-white family photos an immediacy that is in keeping with the book's theme.

Students in grades 3 or 4 and older will appreciate reading this versatile book. Pair it with Russell Freedman's *Immigrant Kids* for a fascinating look at European immigrant children in America, or with the charming *Something from Nothing,* Phoebe Gilman's Jewish folktale about a prized piece of clothing cut down until nothing is left but a story. Jewish readers will recognize the particulars of *The Always Prayer Shawl,* but the experiences it describes are universal.

Jane Robinson

SOURCE: A review of *The Always Prayer Shawl,* in *CM Magazine,* Vol. 22, No. 3, May, 1994, p. 82.

This is a comforting story about the importance of tradition and the certainty of change. At the beginning, Adam is a young Jewish boy growing up in Russia in the early 1900s. When the revolution forces his parents to seek a better life in North America, Adam must leave his grandfather, whose name is also Adam, and all that is familiar and dear. The prayer shawl his grandfather gives him takes on tremendous significance and, as Adam grows up, marries and becomes a grandfather himself, the prayer shawl remains a constant in his life. Events come full circle all those years later when Adam's grandson assures him that their "always prayer shawl" and their name "Adam" will continue through the next generations.

The text is clear, simply written and concise. Sheldon Oberman, who has written for both children and adults, keeps the story on track and enables the reader to understand even complexities like the Russian Revolution and the passing of time. While it is obviously a story of great personal importance to Oberman, audience appreciation need not be limited to a study of Jewish culture. It will easily appeal to a wide range of readers and can be applied to many situations.

The watercolor illustrations are an effective mix— a soft black and white to portray the past and muted colors to denote the present. Ted Lewin uses a realistic, portrait-like style, focusing on the main characters and their relationships. A gentle, pleasing rhythm, played out through both the words and the pictures in the story, reflects the cyclical nature of life.

Balerie Zatzman

SOURCE: A review of *The Always Prayer Shawl,* in *Canadian Children's Literature,* Vol. 23:3, No. 87, Fall, 1997, pp. 80-81.

The Always Prayer Shawl makes precious the relationship between grandparents and grandchildren. Framing ideas about continuity, this story was not only conceived for this volume, but was also produced professionally in a play version by the Winnipeg Jewish Theatre in 1995. The history of the prayer shawl in Oberman's book is also the history of its central character, Adam. We accompany him on a journey from revolutionary Russia to modern day North America, and from young boy to grandfather. A skilled storyteller, Oberman allows for different kinds of readers to enter his story, and at many levels—so that as Adam matures we are able to find our experience as child, parent or elder reflected in the narrative.

At each stage in his life, Adam is confronted by challenges: moving to a new land, a new home and school, or taking on new responsibilities; and in each instance, we discover something about how to cope with change. In their wisdom, the grandfathers distinguish between what's really important in life and what is not—teaching us that "some things change and some things don't." For, amidst all the uncertainties and challenges, there are two constants: the presence of the prayer shawl—symbolizing commitment to Jewish life—and the love of family, mirrored in the experience of the story's three generations. It is these constants that provide Adam with a foundation from which to embrace change, to value his culture and identity; to proclaim loudly "I am always Adam and this is my Always Prayer Shawl."

The thresholds in Adam's life, both as grandson and grandfather, are translated into paintings which capture the immediacy of events and emotions. We want to linger over these brief glimpses into the poignant and intimate moments between the boy and the old man, and are compelled to look for evidence of such moments in our own lives. One such encounter is found at the end of the book when Adam and his grandson sit talking together in the synagogue. The little boy is wrapped in his grandfather Adam's Always Prayer Shawl while "they shut their eyes and feel the warm sun shining on their faces." As such, even the prayer shawl presents an invitation to reflect on our own special objects of importance—that which carries with it family history and memory.

Visually, it is the prayer shawl which first greets us—a fabulous representation that lines the inside of the book as you open its covers. Ted Lewin paints with such delicate and sensitive use of light and shadow, that the soft background allows the audience to focus on the detail in the faces themselves, almost imperceptibly drawing us to the characters. It is truly as if we experience the passing of a lifetime with each turn of the page of this beautifully illustrated picture book.

If I have any reservation about *The Always Prayer Shawl,* it lies in its absolute focus on boys and their grandfathers. While I know that it was written in celebration of the author's own son's bar mitzvah, it need not omit young women from its circle, given that in much of contemporary Judaism, girls are invited to wear a "tallit" or prayer shawl, as well. However, I make reference to the issue of inclusion since Oberman's touchstone for writing was his participation in the creation of a ceremony in which *both* mother and father of the bar mitzvah might share in the event. They solved the dilemma of whose prayer shawl their son would wear by agreeing to use *his* grandfather's tallit, but with the fringes of *her* new tallit sewn on! The real-life backdrop to the tale reminds us that we can extend the fictional context by discussing ideas about the cultural recognition of gender difference, and by asking kids to explore their own legacy—the background of their name, family memories, the discovery of their own special objects or treasured relationships. All the more reason why *The Always Prayer Shawl* stands as a book to be shared at home and in the classroom. Ultimately, as the best stories do, this one impels you to tell other stories, allowing children an opportunity to bring their personal histories to their learning and writing.

THE WHITE STONE IN THE CASTLE WALL (1995)

Steve Pitt

SOURCE: A review of *The White Stone in the Castle Wall,* in *Canadian Book Review Annual,* edited by Joyce M. Wilson, 1995, p. 482.

Young Tommy is a poor lad living in the Toronto slum called Cabbagetown. When he hears that Sir Henry Pellat, a man "who owns all the lights in the city," is paying a silver dollar for every large field stone delivered to his property, Tommy hauls a huge rock to Sir Henry's house. Alas, Tommy's stone is white and the contractor has orders to buy only grey stones. Disheartened, Tommy takes refuge in Sir Henry's garden where he is befriended by a kindly old gardener. The gardener turns out to be Sir Henry himself who not only buys the stone but also gives Tommy a full-time job as a gardener.

Sheldon Oberman's yarn about how one mysterious white stone came to be included in the famous Casa Loma is charming and believable. Les Tait's beautiful drawings, each based on a real Toronto building, complement Oberman's tale perfectly.

Ironically, this story is a medieval fairy tale set in the context of Edwardian Toronto. Less than a hundred years ago, Cabbagetown kids like Tommy survived (or didn't) on the whim of robber barons like Sir Henry Pellat. The harsh reality of the era is accurately reproduced in Tait's illustrations. Tommy's tarpaper shack stands in sharp contrast to Sir Henry's palatial horse stables. The result is a pretty book that invites deeper discussion.

Sally R. Dow

SOURCE: A review of *The White Stone in the Castle Wall,* in *School Library Journal,* Vol. 42, No. 3, March, 1996, pp. 179-80.

Speculation as to how a singular white stone came to be among the 250,000 dull-colored ones in the wall surrounding Toronto's Casa Loma prompted the telling of this story. Built over 80 years ago by industrialist Sir Henry Pellatt, the medieval-style castle is surrounded by an immense wall made of stones purchased from poor citizens of Toronto. The saga of John Tommy Fiddich, a lucky boy who offers Pellatt a white stone representing hours of hard labor, is told in short, static phrases. Far better than the narration are the full-page watercolor paintings that depict the poverty of the shantytown beneath the castle, which contrasts with the splendor of its gardens and magnificent construction. A book that's of limited interest, except possibly to collectors of Toronto history.

Berna Clark

SOURCE: A review of *The White Stone in the Castle Wall,* in *The Junior Bookshelf,* Vol. 60, No. 2, April, 1996, p. 62.

There was only one white stone in the castle wall which surrounded Toronto's Casa Loma—the largest castle in north America when it was built. This very heart-warming story is the author's idea of how it might have arrived there.

John Tommy Fildich grew many vegetables in his garden and sold them at the market. He said he was the luckiest boy of all. Then a storm ruined his crops and the insects ate up everything that the storm had left except one dirty grey stone. John Tommy Fildich told everyone that his garden was totally destroyed, and said he was the unluckiest boy of all.

Then Sir Henry Pellatt who owned Casa Loma said he was about to build a wall around it and he would pay for big stones all coloured. So John Tommy Fildich rolled his stone into a cart and worked very hard to pull his cart to the castle. On the way a storm of rain washed all the dark grey colour of the stone away, so the master of the wall would not accept it as it was too clean. John was heartbroken.

Then he saw a man working in the garden, and told him that he could use his stone as he was too tired to push it back down the hill. The man John spoke to was Sir Henry Pellatt himself and he promised to buy John's

stone "because your work has made it worth a lot to me". Sir Henry gave John a job in his garden, so John Tommy Fildich became once more the luckiest boy of all.

A very charming tale of a very appealing young boy and a very kindly leading citizen.

Marvellous period illustrations by Les Tait of how people lived in old Toronto. The endpapers are maps showing the route of the white stone.

Griselda Greaves

SOURCE: A review of *The White Stone in the Castle Wall,* in *The School Librarian,* Vol. 44, No. 2, May, 1996, p. 57.

A poor boy struggles up the hill with a large grey stone in his cart. He hopes to claim the dollar that Sir Henry Pellat is paying for every dull stone brought for the wall that he is building around his modern castle. By the time the boy delivers the stone, the rain has revealed its true quartz whiteness. The boy is a friendly optimist and, true to the American dream, does indeed end up, as he claims to be, 'the luckiest boy of all'.

The text has a light touch but, apart from one illustration showing a long shaded path that John Tommy Fiddich must travel, the paintings are uninspiring in their factual accuracy. The difference between the expectations of the rich and the poor of the early nineteenth century defines the course of the story, giving this picture book, which is accessible to a child of 6, a relevance to all primary school children.

BY THE HANUKKAH LIGHT (1997)

Ellen Mandel

SOURCE: A review of *By the Hanukkah Light,* in *Booklist,* Vol. 94, No. 1, September 1, 1997, p. 139.

As they do every year, Grandpa and Rachel polish the aged silver menorah before gathering with the rest of the family to light the first candles of the Hanukkah celebration. Then, as usual, Grandpa tells the story of the Festival of Lights, recalling the ancient battle between the Jews and an invading army. This year, Grandpa extends the history, recalling Hanukkah when he was a boy in Europe. Then, "another man came with an army of soldiers" to destroy synagogues, schools, homes, and Jews. Grandpa fled Europe but returned as a modern-day Maccabee in the army that finally defeated the evil war maker. When Grandpa, the soldier, revisited his childhood home, he found the family's silver menorah—the same one he and his family now light each Hanukkah—in the ashes. Oberman has masterfully capsulized the history of Hanukkah, then overlaid the ancient events with veiled references to the Holocaust persecutions, showing how the bonds of intergenerational traditions transcend the terrors that have afflicted the Jewish people. As he did so eloquently in *The Always Prayer Shawl* (1994), Oberman weaves a memorable story around a religious artifact that has survived brutalities and hazards to be lovingly handed down through generations. On richly marbled papers, [Neil] Waldman paints with dots of color, which, like jeweled mosaics, create luminescent images of historical landscapes and loving family celebrations. A treasure for Jewish holiday collections.

Publishers Weekly

SOURCE: A review of *By the Hanukkah Light,* in *Publishers Weekly,* Vol. 244, No. 41, October 6, 1997, p. 52.

Hanukkah and WWII share the spotlight here. First Grandpa tells Rachel and Jacob the story of Hanukkah; then he describes his family's inability to fully celebrate the holiday during his childhood in Europe ("We were afraid—afraid to put our Hanukkiah in the window/ . . . afraid someone would see it and say we were Jews"). Grandpa's family flees Europe in time, and Grandpa serves as a soldier in a war that brings "all people of all nations peace once again." The dovetailing of the two stories is more neat than believable, but the message (Grandpa returns after the war to find a hanukkiah in his town's ashes) is uplifting. Waldman softens the allusions to war and persecution with his trademark pointillist-like paintings, which downplay violence in favor of family scenes and soothing palettes. Historical notes and definitions are appended.

Additional coverage of Oberman's life and career is contained in the following sources published by The Gale Group: *Something about the Author,* Vol. 85 and *Something about the Author Autobiography Series,* Vol. 26.

Gary Paulsen

1939-

American author of fiction and nonfiction.

Major works include *Hatchet* (1987), *The Winter Room* (1989), *Nightjohn* (1993), *Harris and Me: A Summer Remembered* (1993), *Soldier's Heart* (1998).

For information on Paulsen's works prior to 1988, see *CLR,* Vol. 19.

INTRODUCTION

With works grounded in his own experiences in the Minnesota wilderness, the versatile Paulsen has established himself as one of America's most popular and critically acclaimed children's writers. While he has written picture books for elementary- and middle-graders, Paulsen is best known for his work for young adults, with books that appeal to reluctant readers seeking adventure or mature teens looking for examinations of moral issues. Critics praise his true-to-life, often introspective characters, his brief yet lyrical writing style, his wry humor, and his ability to craft a compelling, readable tale. At times, his work has been compared to that of such literary giants as Ernest Hemingway, John Steinbeck, Henry David Thoreau, Mark Twain, and Jack London. The theme of survival figures most strongly in Paulsen's work—predominantly in his wilderness adventures, but also in the challenges life presents his characters. These trials range from the extraordinary to the everyday, from the horrors of slavery and war to the problems of dysfunctional families to the embarrassments of adolescence. An intimate knowledge of and respect for nature also runs throughout Paulsen's work, as his protagonists often gain understanding of their inner character while interacting with the natural world. "Paulsen's writing works because he creates books that show teen protagonists living life as a challenge," James A. Schmitz noted, adding that "Paulsen's ability to evoke powerful imagery and visualize life in both its comic and tragic forms places him alongside other craftsmen whose words will last."

Biographical Information

Paulsen was born in Minneapolis, Minnesota, in 1939. Like many of his protagonists, he did not have an easy time growing up. His parents were troubled by alcoholism and divorce, and he spent a great deal of time with family in the farms and wilds of Minnesota. By fourteen he had flunked out of ninth grade, run away from home, and joined a carnival. After taking shelter from the cold in a library, however, he discovered books—a discovery the largely self-educated author says saved his life. Fol-

lowing a stint in the army and a job as an electronics engineer, Paulsen decided to move to California to start a career as a writer. While he worked for a magazine publisher, he also wrote his own stories, until fear of "turning Hollywood" led him to move back to Minnesota. There he rented a cabin and lived off the land as he worked on his first novel, *Mr. Tucket* (1969). His career did not take off as he had hoped, however, and he failed to sell any of his work for the next few years.

Throughout the 1970s Paulsen continued to write at night as he worked various day jobs to support his family. He published several nonfiction works and a few more novels, but it was not until the 1983 publication of *Dancing Carl* that his writing career began to flourish. That year was also the first time Paulsen ran the Iditarod Race, the famous dogsled run that covers over eleven hundred miles of Alaskan tundra. He ran the race again in 1985, before giving up racing because of his health. Since then, Paulsen has devoted himself to his writing, producing almost one hundred books, from adult westerns to autobiographical reminiscences to humorous novels and picture books for younger readers. Paulsen sees his job as offering honest portrayals of life so that his readers can consider solutions to society's problems. As he once remarked, "I think art is a tool that can be used to help these things no matter who does it."

Major Works

Paulsen is perhaps best known for his tales of survival in the wilderness, and his quartet of novels about teenager Brian Robeson forms an interesting portrayal of one individual's personal growth. In *Hatchet,* thirteen-year-old Brian is the sole survivor of a plane crash, which leaves him stranded in the Canadian wilds with just a hatchet and a belt for tools. Throughout the course of the novel, he is transformed from a scared city boy into a self-sufficient young man capable of surviving until his rescue. The sequel *The River* (1991) was not quite as successful, as several critics found Brian's rescue of the psychologist sent to observe his survival skills contrived. In *Brian's Winter* (1996), Paulsen proposes an alternate ending to *Hatchet,* one in which Brian is not rescued and has to survive the winter alone. While not much different from other survival stories, the novel still earned praise for its characterization and beautiful descriptions of nature. Brian's story concludes in *Brian's Return* (1998), in which the teen finds that he is not suited to everyday life in civilization, and so returns to the wild. While not as dramatic as its predecessors, the novel convincingly communicates both the protagonist's and Paulsen's love for the sublime in nature.

The wilderness plays a similar role in *The Island* (1988), an introspective work about a teen who explores his own self through his observations of an island in a remote part of Wisconsin. Critics noted similarities between this work and Thoreau's *Walden,* and observed that its combination of humor and soul-searching made it very readable. Other Paulsen adventure stories that also contain elements of self-discovery include *Voyage of the Frog* (1989), in which a lone teen is caught in a storm on the open sea; *Canyons* (1990), where the stories of a murdered Apache brave and the young man who finds his skull one hundred years later are intertwined; and *The Car* (1994), in which an abandoned teen builds a car and takes off on a cross-country journey. Paulsen has also created numerous popular works containing more action-oriented adventure, including several volumes in the "Gary Paulsen World of Adventure" series; *The Haymeadow* (1992), in which a fourteen-year-old spends the summer alone in the mountains guarding his family's sheep; and *Call Me Francis Tucket* (1995) and *Tucket's Ride* (1997), two sequels to Paulsen's first novel that relate the further adventures of a boy separated from his parents on the American frontier.

Paulsen has more directly explored his love of the outdoors in several nonfiction accounts of his experiences in the wilderness. *Woodsong* (1990) is a memoir of time spent training his dog team in the Minnesota woods, and earned praise for its compelling and unflinching portrayal of the harsh realities of nature. Several critics compared it to the work of Jack London, as did Nancy

Vasilakis: "The lure of the wilderness is always a potent draw, and Paulsen evokes its mysteries as well as anyone since Jack London." *Father Water, Mother Woods* (1994) is a similarly engaging collection of essays on hunting and fishing in the North American woods, while *Puppies, Dogs, and Blue Northers* (1996) and *My Life in Dog Years* (1998) entertain with stories of the sled dogs the author has known and loved. Paulsen has also created picture books on similar themes, combining his prose poems with the artwork of his wife, Ruth Wright Paulsen. *Dogteam* (1993) captures the beauty of a nighttime sled-run, while *The Tortilla Factory* (1995) and *Worksong* (1997) celebrate the dignity to be found in tilling the earth or working everyday jobs.

Paulsen's ability to render true-to-life portraits of everyday, simple beauty has served him well in several novels set in the 1940s and 1950s that eschew the action of his other works. His Newbery Honor book *The Winter Room* is a peaceful, reflective portrayal of farming life in Minnesota and the stories a family shares during the quiet of winter. *The Cookcamp* (1991) is a similarly quiet yet powerful story of a young boy sent to live with his grandmother in the woods during World War II, while *A Christmas Sonata* (1992) is a moving, unsentimental portrayal of a family dealing with a terminally ill boy's last holiday. While *Harris and Me: A Summer Remembered* is also set on a farm in the 1950s, this novel showcases Paulsen's skill at humor. As the unnamed narrator and his cousin Harris move from one escapade to the next, Paulsen uses his storytelling skill and wit to reveal his characters' personalities. Humor is also the focus of several other works, from tales of losers-turned-winners, such as *The Boy Who Owned the School: A Comedy of Love* (1990) and *The Schnernoff Discoveries* (1997), to the "Culpepper Adventures" series about the amateur sleuthing efforts of glib Duncan Culpepper and his clutzy friend Amos Binder.

As apt at communicating a serious message as the absurdity of growing up or the beauty of the wilderness, Paulsen has also written several issue-oriented novels for his young adult audience. *Nightjohn* is a searing look at the brutality of slavery, told from the viewpoint of twelve-year-old Sarny, a slave girl who risks serious punishment when she learns to read. While the work earned some criticism for its graphic violence, the majority of reviewers recommended it and agreed with Frances Bradburn that "fortunately for all of us, Gary Paulsen has had the courage to risk censure in order to tell a powerful story in a style only he is capable of." The sequel *Sarny, a Life Remembered* (1997), which traces young Sarny's life during and after the Civil War, similarly earned high marks for its characterization and epic portrayal of history. Critics were less in accord over *Sisters/Hermanas* (1993), which shows the similarities between the lives of two teenage girls, a Hispanic immigrant and a middle-class Anglo cheerleader. Some reviewers found the characters stereotyped and the message obvious, while others called the characters well-developed and the story powerful and understated. Storytelling and characterization are also the strong points of *The Tent: A Tale in One Sitting* (1995), about a boy in conflict over his con-artist father's faith-healing scam, and *The Rifle* (1995), which traces the history of a hand-built firearm from its creation to its role in a modern-day tragedy. In *Soldier's Heart,* Paulsen was inspired by a real case history to craft the tale of a Minnesota youth who fights in the Civil War. Drawing on his skill at characterization and flair for description, Paulsen creates a picture of the psychological and physical costs that war exacts on soldiers. The result, according to Henry Mayer, is a "stark, utterly persuasive novel of combat life in the Civil War that may well challenge generations of middle-school readers."

Awards

Paulsen has earned three Newbery Honor Book citations: one in 1986 for *Dogsong,* one in 1988 for *Hatchet,* and another in 1990 for *The Winter Room.* The Catholic Library Association awarded him the Regina Medal in 1995 for his "continuous distinguished contribution" to children's literature, while the American Library Association similarly lauded him in 1997 with their Margaret A. Edwards Award for lifetime achievement. Three Paulsen titles were recognized as YALSA/ALA Best Books for Young Adults: *Puppies, Dogs and Blue Northers* in 1996, the *Schernoff Discoveries* in 1998, and *Soldiers Heart* in 1999.

AUTHOR'S COMMENTARY

Gary Paulsen

SOURCE: "Joys, Fears, and Changes," in *Magpies,* Vol. 4, No. 5, November, 1989, pp. 5-10.

I have a sixteen year old son. I have two children by a previous marriage who are grown and I am a grandfather—twice. My son came to me a year and a half ago and said he was scared.

I said, "What are you scared of?"

He said, "The nuclear thing."

I said, "OK, well we got to do something about it."

That was very hard for me to hear. I have raced from Anchorage to Nome, across Alaska. It is very hard to do. The end result of running that thing is that you don't recognize obstacles as such, you just know objectives. You go to Nome, no matter what. 60°-70° below, three mountain ranges, two hundred miles up the Yukon River, you get to Nome. That's what happens in that race. After that it affects your whole life. When somebody says "Fix this thing, it hurts me" I just say

"Well I'll fix it" and I don't recognize that there are obstacles to this. But how can I stop nuclear war?

So I sat down with him and I decided I would write a letter to Russia, and I did. He and I sat there and we wrote this letter to Russia, the generic letter. *Dear Russia, we don't want to kill you and we don't want you to kill us. Gary Paulsen and his son Jim do not want to blow you up and we don't want you to blow us up.* I was living in Minnesota and I called New York, the Russian Mission to the UN, and I got the address for the Russian Writers' Union in Moscow, and I mailed it. The end result of that was that a little after that there were twenty Soviet authors and educators in Minneapolis and we are trying to do something that would break down the barriers.

That's on one level. On another level I decided that I would write a book about the problem—not answers, the problem. And I wrote a book called **Sentries.** That was one of the offshoots of this thing.

The third thing that happened was that I realized that there has to be a change in what is given to young people. There are some really intelligent people out there now who say my son has no chance of making forty. That really angers me. They are going to kill my kid. They are going to kill your kids. Think of that. That's what they are doing. They resumed testing. Why? You don't sharpen a sabre not to use it. You've got to get real about this. Both countries Russia and the US have resumed testing of nuclear weapons. That is just on one level. The other level is the pollution; it is worse now than it has ever been. It is out of hand. They have blown the ozone thing away. We'll all get skin cancer. I mean there is one problem after another. Devastating problems. And what do we tell the kids: Bambi gets out of the fire.

It doesn't work any more. None of the stuff that has been written for kids works any more and there has to be a change. There has to be a radical change in what is given to young people to give them the tools required to live in the world that we have given them, the incredible mess that we are handing these guys. How do I tell my kid, "Here, you are not going to be able to eat the food I am leaving, you are not going to be able to drink the water I am leaving you, or breathe the air I am leaving you, and we are probably going to blow you all up." Go for it. Bambi gets out of the fire. Billy wins a basketball game, and is accepted by his peers. Come on! What has to be done? . . .

I can ask the questions, I don't have the solutions. I decided one thing was to give children fundamental knowledge, to give as much knowledge on all things as possible in as short a possible time. It is critical now, not even next week. I mean right now it is critical. And one of the ways I know to do this, and I think the best way, is through reading. It really is. But it is going to require a change. It is going to require that books be more than they have ever been. It is not good enough for my son to be as good as me. That sucks. Look what I did. Look at the nuclear thing that I am leaving my son. If he is just as good as me, no way. If your children are only as good as you, they are going to die. The planet will probably die. Imagine killing the planet. The only thing that is good enough now, is they have to be better than us. That means the questions that have to be asked of them are not questions that we know the answers to, so that they can begin to deal with the true problems. . . .

One thing I'm going to try and do with writing for young people is to not waste any more time on conventional stuff, because I don't think there's time for it, I don't honestly. The Chinese have a saying that a man with a toothache cannot be in love, and we as a race, as a species, the human race has evolved into such a critical condition that there has to be something done very soon, and that is what I'm going to shoot for. I think if I didn't work on it I couldn't face my son later—or ever. . . .

I think we need honesty on all levels for all things: from picture books to chapter books, to young adult novels, everything, to the weekly reader. Everything they read from now has to be true—and fast. I don't necessarily mean truths that are ugly. I mean joy and beauty too. Rambo uses beauty to sell ugliness, goes inside people's minds with glitsy, stunning beauty and sells filth. I think that beauty should be used to sell beauty.

I don't have the answers; I'm not even sure I've got the question, but I know it hasn't been done, and somebody's got to do something, and pretty soon. That's the main thing. To me one possible solution is this knowledge, to have fundamental knowledge, honesty on all levels. Don't tell the kids Bambi gets out of the forest. He doesn't. Most of them die in forest fires and it is sad. It's better not to have a fire than to figure Bambi getting out of it. . . .

You can find another way to right the whole thing so that it is not necessary to show Bambi either getting burned or not getting burned and still have the beauty of Bambi in there. It is not necessary to destroy faith. I just use Bambi as an analogy because it is deadly incorrect. To tell them that when something is really bad and is looming that there is no problem, that you will be saved always is a mistake right now. But there are other ways that that story could have been written and have all of the beauty and all the joy and everything in it and all the tension and all the conflict and all those things without having that incorrect situation involved. I believe in faith too, it's in my writing, and joy is in my writing.

I have two books coming out next fall. One is ***The Crossing*** which is about a Mexican kid in Juarez and a drunk army sergeant and the kid wants to get into America and the army sergeant tries to help him. I was the drunk sergeant and the kid really existed. I named him Manny Gustos in the story. All he wanted was to get a silver belt buckle and a big hat and live in America and get a green card. I was stationed at Fort Bliss, Texas, and I used to go to Juarez to drink because it was cheap. Two shots of tequila for a nickel. That's some awful stuff.

But in a way I tried to help him get into this country. It's kind of a bleak story, you know, but it is a true story. Most of the young adults in the world are minorities, a great many of them live in Mexico where they face real problems.

At the same time next fall I have a book called ***Hatchet*** coming out which is a book about hope. It is about a kid who lives in the woods, and lives alone for fifty-four days and survives. That urban kid makes it.

The following spring I've got a book coming out called ***The Island*** which is a complete book devoted to joy. It is about my son actually, and he'll probably sue me. It's about a boy who finds a small island in the lake near his home and starts going out there for an hour at a time, two hours at a time, and seeing things on the island. Trying to understand the ant hills, and pretty soon the island becomes a microcosm of life and he stays there. He stays on the island; he just quits coming back. He stays there because everything he needs is on the island. And his father tries to understand this, I mean, like, Is he rebelling against home? And in the end the father goes to the island, and that's what *I've* done. My son is a wonderful, intelligent, sensitive big kid. Six-two and a hundred and eighty pounds. He holds me when I get tired. Holds me, holds me down and tickles me. It is a wonderful feeling. Anyway, I went to his island and I decided he's right and I'm wrong.

There's a given here: All kids are smarter than all adults. Right? We used to say all dogs are smarter than all people, and all young people are smarter than all old people because young people and dogs have not yet designed a thermonuclear warhead.

We kept the truths from kids for years with the proviso that we wouldn't let them happen. We have lied to children for centuries. We said go ahead and be sweet and innocent and wonderful and we'll protect you. We won't let the bad things come. Well, they're here. We lied. I did the same thing with my son. That's why he's scared. Don't you worry. I'll protect you. Fourteen years of I'll protect you, and on the fourteenth year he came up to me and says, "OK, I've got this problem Hank. There's a forest fire coming. My name is Bambi and I need help." And I said, "I can't help you. Sorry." That's a heavy thing to have happen to you, to not be able to help your child when he asks you for help. But I can't. I can't because I don't have the tools to stop this madness. What I am saying is we have got to do something with them, so that they have the tools. I agree that it is sad. It is sad that their innocence is gone; it's going to be a lot sadder if we kill them.

To change my tack. The primary thing I have noticed when I travel and talk to kids is that a lot of them seem to lack the link between the book and the world. . . .

It was like the book was some mythical thing and they could not relate to the books being part of the author and the author a part of the world. It was like they had been engineered for entertainment or engineered so that they were ethereal and looked away from what the kids' real world was like. And I think that that is maybe a mistake. I think it is better if they don't elevate writers, to make writers special people. I don't think that we are. I think it is maybe better to say here is a book that relates to normal life, the normal world, and there can be that same beauty in your life, the normal life, as there is in the book. I don't know that it is a bad thing, but the links are dissolving. The writer and the book and the world are not linked together and I think that it is better that they are linked.

Cheryl Bartky

SOURCE: An interview with Gary Paulsen, in *Writer's Digest,* Vol. 74, No. 7, July, 1994, pp. 42-4, 65.

CHERYL BARTKY: How did you find, or develop, your unique voice?

GARY PAULSEN: I don't think it's something that I looked for and achieved. And it's a completely changing thing all the time. I worked really hard, and I still do. I've written for 25 years or more, and I've studied most of that time. And I still study every night, and I think the voice changes all the time. I hope it does.

CB: It changes with each story?

PAULSEN: It changes as I learn more about the language. There are rhythms, pulses in the language that allow one's voice to grow. I'm just now starting to discover some of those.

CB: What is your process of discovery?

PAULSEN: As I said, I study other writers. And then it's the combination of study and practice.

Dogsong is a good example because it was based on the fact that I had traveled 22,000 miles on sleds in the Arctic. So I started with that basic fact, and I tried to find the rhythm that came from the dogs, that came from that primitive state. I wrote it first as poems almost; then I brought it back as prose—some of it was just short little vignettes—and then later finally as a novel. I used other parts of it still later as *Woodsong,* a nonfiction book. And I'm not done with it yet. I'd like to do another book for adults. And I still call *Dogsong* up. I work on parts of that.

And I still do a lot of writing that's not published, a lot of experimental stuff. And, like with *Dogsong,* sometimes I rewrite books that are published. I'll call them up on the computer screen and work on them and see if they could have been better in a certain way.

CB: Talk more about the rhythms and pulses you've discovered in the language.

PAULSEN: It really is ancient. It isn't that it's in writing, it's that it's in life, I think, and it perhaps goes back to putting bloody skins on and dancing at the fire and telling what the hunt was like.

Three things have to be brought into the same focus: the way a reader perceives something, the way the language can be used, and the subject you're trying to write about. They must all be in conjunction and all work together to make that rhythm work, to make that bloody skin on the back thing happen. It's hard for me to do all that; it requires a lot of effort.

CB: An example of your rhythm-making in *Dogsong* reads:

It was a home.

The sled, the dogs, the food, and more food to eat when he awakened.

It was a home.

It was as much of a home as his people had had for thousands of years, and he was content. He closed his eyes and heard the wind gently sighing outside past the hides that kept him warm and snug.

It was a home, and he let his mind circle and go down, the same way a dog will circle before taking the right bed.

What a thing, he thought—what a thing it is to have meat and be warm and have a full belly. What a thing of joy.

And he slept.

And while he slept he had a dream.

How do you find the style that mirrors the essence of your stories?

PAULSEN: Again, it changes with the subject. *Dogsong* is about a primitive thing, so it's written in a primitive way. It's more of a concept-driven book, so that the rhythms, the essences, are more important than they would be in *Hatchet,* which is more of a standard story. *Hatchet* is a story-driven book (to use a Hollywood term, which I hate to do), in which the story is as important as the concept. *Hatchet* is action and more action, and lots of things going on. It requires a more technical form of writing, whereas *Dogsong* is the smell of the wind. It's a different feel that I was after, so the two books are written differently. And *Clabbered Dirt, Sweet Grass* was written again differently. I wasn't trying to describe farming. I was trying to describe farm*ers* and what their life was like, and so it would be more like *Dogsong,* requiring earthy rhythms and more earth tones.

CB: The segment about thrashing grain in *Clabbered*

Dirt, Sweet Grass is one example of those earth tones:

> Gold.
>
> Rich, pouring, a river of gold as grand as the cream that comes from the separator is the wheat or barley or oats, and the dust and noise and itching and red eyes are forgotten in that river of richness. . . .
>
> And each man and woman will find some way to come and touch it. . . . And many will do it more than once, come and feel the gold, watch the gold, and each time they do it, feel it and watch it, each and every time they will smile.

What went into your process of creating the beauty of this moment, of each detail in this book, all of which are so typical of your writing?

PAULSEN: It's [based in] how one perceives. If you turn it just slightly, a lot of the stuff on the farm would be ugly. But if you dwelled on that and looked at it from that angle, it would ruin the book, the beauty that you're trying to see. So what you do is you hold up each thing and you say, I wish to write about working with the thrashing machine and thrashing grain—which I've done and know how hard it is, and I know the dangers of it, with that goddamn belt humming right next to your face. But if I wrote that sense of it, it would change what I was trying to say. And so I looked for the beauty in that: the gold coming out of the thrashing machine, that rich grain that just runs and is the most incredible thing. I chose the perception, the view that I took of the diamond. But those still are things that happened; I didn't make them up. I just decided how they'd be used, from what angle to look at them.

CB: In *Dogsong* you wrote:

> The light was a soft blue-purple during the day, a gentle color that goes into the eyes and becomes part of the mind and goes still deeper and deeper to enter the soul. Soul color is the daylight.

How do you create a passage like that?

PAULSEN: The light *is* that way. It isn't that I'm making the light be that way, it's that the light is making the language be that way. It *does* go into your soul, it *is* that soft light, it *is* incredible.

CB: And the words just pour out that way?

PAULSEN: It isn't that they pour out. I tried to find that word, that phrase that would describe that particular light at that particular time in the North country. The *thing* decides how you will write about it, not the language. I think Dylan Thomas did that—he allowed the subject to stipulate the kind of language that he would use to talk about it. And so I study him.

CB: Your writing is structured at times like a prose poem. Another example from *Dogsong* reads:

> Out.
>
> Into the sweeps, into the great places where the land runs to the sky and into the sky until there is no land and there is no sky.
>
> Out.
>
> Into the distance where all lines end and all lines begin. Into the white line of the ice-blink where the mother of wind lives to send down the white death of the northern storms.
>
> Out.
>
> Into the mother of wind and the father of blue ice.
>
> Russel went out where there is nothing, into the wide center of everything there is.
>
> Into the north.

What goes into your choices of how to set up the words visually on the page?

PAULSEN: You know, it's interesting. I tried at one time writing with a tape recorder and having it transcribed—and I couldn't. I couldn't because I have to see it. Even the type of word processor I use makes the screen look like a page of typing. I have to see how it will look on a typewritten page. Exactly the same. I have to see how it will look for the drama of it and the way that it will go into the reader. And I don't do it grammatically. I'm not concerned with grammar as much as I am with artistic effect.

I sometimes have really long sentences because I want the reader to just come with me: Let's do this run, let's go down this hill together, and just roar down the son of a bitch, and right at the bottom. . . .

Whoop.

We'll just get up one time, just one little nudge there, because it's something I want to go into the reader a certain way. The way it looks on the page fits into what the prose says and how it says it.

CB: What's gone into your desire to write more for adults?

PAULSEN: I kept running into walls, barriers. I'd be writing on the subject that I wanted to do, and I'd hit this wall, and the wall would say if you want to write for young people, you have to stay on this side of the wall. But if you want to cover this subject the way you want to cover it, you're going to have to go through the wall.

One wall involves a kind of tacit censorship that exists

in books for young people. It's built into the system. The other kind of wall is an artistic wall. When you write for young people, you work in primary colors and concepts. It's very difficult to work with subtlety or different shades that are based on a more mature view of things, though I've tried.

CB: You can see this artistic wall you're talking about when you compare *The Winter Room* to *Clabbered Dirt, Sweet Grass.* Both deal with farm life, and thus share some scenes in common, such as the killing of animals for food. The scene from *The Winter Room*, a young adult novel, reads:

> When Father kills a pig, he doesn't shoot it like he does with a steer because he says pigs have to bleed out better.
>
> He uses the curved knife, and the men put the pig in the same pen they used for the steer. Then they flip the pig on his back, and Nels and Uncle David hold him while Father sticks the curved knife into the pig's throat. And the throat seems to jump at it, seems to pull the knife in and up in a curve to cut its big vein. And the pig screams and screams while it dies and bleeds out. The smell, the smell of the blood and the screams and the throat bleeding out is so much, so thick that I can't stand it.

A companion scene to this one appears in *Clabbered Dirt, Sweet Grass,* a book for adults:

> The pig stands, watching, waiting, its head down and cocked sideways, waiting perhaps to be fed, to be doctored, to be scratched behind the ear, waiting for all the things pigs wait for but the one thing that is coming. Must come.
>
> It is fast and takes years, all at the same time. Two men are needed. They both enter the pen, one with the knife hidden behind his leg. They push the pig into a corner with their legs, push him and hold him and then in one motion they reach down and turn him on his back and he knows, he knows and the scream starts but now there is speed, rolling speed in what is happening and when the pig is on his back one man kneels on him and spreads his front legs and the other kneels in front and slides the knife, curve side down, point first, up beneath the sternum on the pig and cuts the top artery of the heart, twists the knife a bit and the pig bleeds out.
>
> That's how they say it.
>
> The pig bleeds out.

PAULSEN: Yes. *The Winter Room* can have a little of the poetry-dance that's in *Clabbered Dirt.* But in *Winter Room* it's necessary to appeal to a lower level of understanding of what killing's about. In a weird way it means being more graphic and less subtle. In *Clabbered Dirt* I got to use more shading, to explore the concept on a wider and deeper level.

CB: Let's talk about your character portrayals. In *The Crossing* your description of the sergeant is harrowing:

> The man in the mirror showed only one scar, the one from the tiny bit of shrapnel in Vietnam that had cut white-sizzling across his left temple and missed ending him by less than a quarter-inch. The reflection showed none of the true scars—the scars that covered other parts of his body and all of his mind and thoughts, the scars that were part of the drinking.
>
> The man in the mirror looked, stood, acted, smelled and thought like a recruiting poster and was, above all things, a sergeant.

CB: Where do your characters come from? Are they based on real people?

PAULSEN: Always. The sergeant is a combination of me and another sergeant who was a friend of mine. When we were stationed at Fort Bliss, we used to go to Juarez and drink. This same friend was also in *Sentries;* he was the one who had to shoot children, and he could never be sober. I never saw him sober, because the memory of shooting the children drove him insane. I used him several times. I used what he was. I used the feeling of him in some of *The Monument;* I used thinking of him to drive me when I wrote parts of it.

CB: So your characters are the essence of yourself and other people?

PAULSEN: Yes, and people you meet, and people you know, and things you see and understand.

CB: And how do you create them on the page?

PAULSEN: Again, the character you are describing delineates the style you use to write about him. I would write differently about the sergeant than I would about Russel in *Dogsong* or Brian in *Hatchet.* They would require different kinds of writing.

CB: So ultimately it's knowing your characters? Feeling them?

PAULSEN: Almost being them.

CB: How did you develop your ability to see into the essence of people, places and things?

PAULSEN: Personal inspection at zero altitude. I mean I get in it. When I was a kid, I had a rough childhood, and I kind of self-fostered. I went to the woods—I would skip whole weeks of school and be in the woods. And I went and worked and lived on my uncle's farm to get away from my home. This allowed me to see those essences because I would do them.

It's one thing to talk about running a dog team and something else to do it. And I don't think people who haven't done it should try writing about it. I don't think they can be authentic about it. And I have never learned a substitute for that, so if I write about being drunk, it's because I drank a lot. I'm a recovered drunk. And things like that. If I have that ability that you talk about, it's because of going inside the diamond, of actually going and being there and doing those things and living that way.

CB: So it's important to write what you know?

PAULSEN: That's one way, but it's even more than that. It's kind of like write what you *are*.

David Gale

SOURCE: An interview with Gary Paulsen, in *School Library Journal*, Vol. 43, No. 6, June, 1997, pp. 24, 26-9.

David Gale: *You're best known for the adventure and survival books, but you also express a deep interest in the arts, in books like* **The Monument** *and* **Dancing Carl** *and a true concern for social justice, in books like* **The Crossing** *and* **Sentries.** *On the surface, these genres seem worlds apart. What is common to all of them, in your mind?*

Paulsen: What is common is that I don't think there is a political solution to the problems of man; I don't think there is a social solution. I think any solution is artistic. And I think art can be bent to perform. This sounds really arrogant, and I don't mean it that way at all. I don't mean *my* art. It doesn't mean that I think *I'm* helping mankind. It just means that I think art is a tool that can be used to help these things no matter who does it. Judy Blume's books are the same. And that is a commonality in all books, I think—not just mine, but all books in which an attempt has been made to be artistic with them. I think that's an attempt to use art as a tool. I think that's the only possible solution for a lot of the problems we have.

All of the books for which you are being honored are on very different topics—dogs, survival, farm life—but the one thing that stands out about each of these books, to me, is the value of life. They're very life affirming. In all of your books, the reader comes away with an overriding sense of respect: respect for animals and the natural world; respect for the individual; and respect for the reader. Tell me about that.

Paulsen: That's kind of funny, because a couple of times I have taken criticism because I write so much about death. I've had young people ask me why do I have animals die. I agree with what you're saying—it's all we've got, life. I mean it really is all we've got. As you get older—certainly as I get older—I can smell hot breath on my neck, and I feel like I'm becoming something predators look at, where I'm starting to go out to the edge of the herd and limp a little. I know very well that it's a very finite time and I think the life that we get is a wonderful thing. It appalls me how people waste it, absolutely appalls me. . . .

Your books are on such diverse topics, yet they are all based, in part, on your own remarkable experiences. How important is it for you to experience everything?

Paulsen: I think that's because of my lack of education. I tried to figure it out at one time. I don't think I lack education now because I have had 30 years of reading intensely, but at one time I did, and I believed in the concept that personal inspection at zero altitude is the only way to learn something. And I lived that way, and it's been very hard—I mean I've broken my bones—and I've been in trouble physically and mentally and all those things doing it. But I would not recommend it. And also I think that it might not work for a lot of people, to do it. I mean some of it's fun— running the Iditarod was really fun—but I've had two friends die in the last year and a half running dogs. I mean, there's an enormous danger with some of the stuff I've done. Laying a Harley over three, four times going to Alaska. I mean I talk about it as if it's light, but the truth is, people die every day on those things, so it's not necessarily a good way to learn to be a writer at all. It's just my way; I think my lack of education caused it.

I remember you saying that you even ate raw turtle eggs before writing about Brian eating them in **Hatchet.** *Can you write about things you haven't experienced?*

Paulsen: I was in a sense as ignorant of reading as Sarny was in *Nightjohn,* so I can relate to that level of it, in the sense of learning what a joy it is to know how to spell a word or to read a word and to understand it. But of course I've never been a slave, and I'm not African American, so I don't understand all of that. In that sense I had to do research and study, and it took me five years. I mean, it took a long time to learn all the things I needed to learn for a 75-page book.

One of the things that sets you apart as a writer is that your writing appeals to boys. Do you consciously try to develop a male readership?

Paulsen: No, not any more. I didn't think of boys at first. At one point, I actually toyed with the idea of writing *Hatchet* with a girl protagonist. I don't know that I even think of it at all now. But at one point I was horrified that there was so little being done for boys, and when I asked somebody why this was—and this was somebody in the publishing business—he said that boys don't read. I asked why boys don't read, and he said because there are no books for them. I mean, you just can't defeat logic like that. So I just assumed if you did something that appealed to boys, there would be boy readers.

You have written in the female voice, too, in **Nightjohn,** *and in* **The Monument,** *for instance. In books like these are you making an effort to bring in female readers, or does it all just come the way it comes?*

Paulsen: It kind of comes the way it comes. The truth is those are stories that exist. *Nightjohn* is based on real people who did real things. The reason I made it a girl is because typically young boys would have been pretty much worked to death. In slavery they literally used to try to work a man to death by the time he was 26. By 26, they thought they had all the useful work they'd get out of him, and they would work him and starve him until he died. It was a horrible thing. A young boy would not have had the opportunity to learn letters, so Sarny became the natural vehicle for that. *The Monument*—again, a young girl would be more affected artistically, I think, by a visiting artist than a young boy would. . . .

You've said to me that with one idea, you can write a sentence, a paragraph, a short story, a novel, or a series. Throughout your works, you have taken the same incidents and shaped them differently. Is this reshaping rewarding to you?

Paulsen: Years ago, when I was working in Hollywood, I wrote for men's magazines like *Argosy*—not dirty ones, but weapons magazines or cars. I did seven articles on Baron von Richthofen, the WWI fighter pilot, and in each article I proved a different thing. In one I proved that he was a pathological killer; in one I proved that he was a coward—and he was all of those things, he was every one of them, he was a hunter, he was a coward, he was physically ill, he was mentally deranged, he was brilliant. And it was possible to take one aspect of his life and prove that by writing about it. And I sold all seven articles to seven different magazines, under different names. I did that as kind of a test, and I still think that concept is there. It's possible to write about anything from all angles.

I just love the idea of doing a whole book that would show that. A really good example would be Jefferson, who was a brilliant, diseased, wonderful, evil, humorous, humorless, cowardly, courageous man. I mean I couldn't stand him if I knew him. On the other hand he was a great man. And so if you wrote about him, you should be able to get that across. And there should be some way in fiction to do the same thing. To say here is this gem, and it looks different whichever way you turn it, but it is the same gem. . . .

You've written more than 130 books now, including several dozen young adult books. Which are your personal favorites?

Paulsen: *Hatchet* is in the sense that it struck some nerve that I still don't understand, and that has made it one of my favorite books. It was not when I wrote it. I suppose maybe *Dogsong* in a sense because it's so much about running dogs, and it was when my career just exploded. I think the best thing I've ever done is *Clabbered Dirt, Sweet Grass*, which is an adult book. I think the writing, artistically, was the best thing I've ever done.

GENERAL COMMENTARY

James A. Schmitz

SOURCE: "Gary Paulsen: A Writer of His Time," in *The Alan Review,* Vol. 22, No. 1, Fall, 1994, pp. 15-18.

Between 1967 and 1976 three books were published that focused on a search for meaning and a system of values based on the author's personal relationship with the harsh yet ultimately comic natural world. Richard Brautigan's *Trout Fishing in America* (1967), Robert Pirsig's *Zen and the Art of Motorcycle Maintenance* (1974), and Norman Maclean's *A River Runs Through It and Other Stories* (1976) combined autobiography with fiction as the authors reexamined moments of their pasts.

Gary Paulsen, beginning his writing career in the same era, addressed the same concerns in his eighteen young adult books, beginning with *Mr. Tucket* (1968) and continuing on through *Canyons* (1990) and *Woodsong* (1990), a nonfictional account of his racing a dog-sled team in the Alaskan Iditarod. Paulsen's books share common characteristics that stem from his personal experiences. Enclosed in the universal coming-of-age package used by other young adult novelists are rural Midwestern settings, usually in Minnesota, Paulsen's native state; a reminiscence of the character's youthful past, often the 1950s, when Paulsen was growing up; relationships with sympathetic adults, some related, some not (Paulsen was raised by his grandmother and spent significant time with aunts and uncles); alcoholic parents (Paulsen's father was); adults who have suffered lasting physical or psychological damage from a war experience (again, Paulsen's father, and the subject of Paulsen's first nonfiction book, *The Special War*); and boys who face a direct struggle with nature while they learn about the interrelationships between man, animals, and death, a longtime Paulsen fascination.

Not all of these characteristics appear in each novel. To gain a greater insight into Paulsen's craft, it is helpful to separate his books by point of view. The first-person narratives, *Winterkill* (1976), *The Foxman* (1977), *Tiltawhirl John* (1977), *Popcorn Days and Buttermilk Nights* (1983), *Dancing Carl* (1983), and *The Winter Room* (1989) are in many ways Paulsen's best because in each novel the reader is drawn immediately into the protagonist's life.

Winterkill, Paulsen's first successful young adult novel, contains many of the elements found throughout his work. It is such a personal story that it provoked a libel suit that went all the way to the Minnesota Supreme Court before being decided in the author's favor. This situation caused Paulsen so much anxiety that he gave up writing for almost two years. It was during this period that he took up trapping and dog sledding, two activities that influenced his later writing.

In *Winterkill,* the narrator, who goes unnamed, looks

back on his troubled teen years and tells the story of the police officer Duda, who guided him toward manhood. Duda, as we find out, is no ordinary cop-on-the-beat. He is an explosive and frequently violent man, a victim, like the town drunk, Carl, of a war he cannot forget. He openly accepts bribes, has a nickname of "Nuts," and spends much of his shift sleeping with the town madam, Bonnie, the proverbial hooker-with-a-heart-of-gold. He refers to the boy and some of the other young miscreants as "puke kids," but it is obvious the author wants us to see that underneath his tough exterior is a soft-hearted sentimentalist.

When the court takes the kid away from his drunken abusive parents and sends him to work for a religious fanatic farmer determined to beat the fear of God into the boy, Duda rescues him and brings him back home. He talks the kid out of marrying a girl impregnated by someone else and stops him from robbing a garage.

Then, as the book moves toward its violent conclusion, the author introduces a technique of overt foreshadowing similar to that used by Maclean in *A River Runs Through It*. He tells us Duda will die but leaves us wondering when and how. His sympathy for this character is such that it is as if even he wished things could turn out otherwise.

> And I would like to stop the story of Duda here and tell how he got his divorce and married Bonnie and they adopted me and we bought a farm. . . . That's how it would end in a movie, with Rock Hudson playing Duda and Doris Day playing Bonnie, and that's how it *should* end, and that's how I dream of it ending almost every night, until I wake up sweating and remember that it isn't a movie and it doesn't end that way.

It is clear Paulsen envisioned his work as a tragedy. After Duda guns down two on-the-run bank robbers in cold blood, he escapes being shot by a quarreling husband and wife only to be killed by a run-away minister's son with a deer rifle.

Winterkill is in many respects a prototype for ensuing Paulsen novels. It is more episodic than plotted (a trait more true of the first-person neo-autobiographies than the more distant third-person narratives), and focuses on character—both the developing character of the confused protagonist, and, perhaps more importantly, that of the adult role model destined to become the victim of his flawed personality and own poor choices.

The Foxman is a logical extension of *Winterkill* because it uses several of the same components. The narrator is an unhappy fifteen-year-old boy (again, unnamed) sent to northern Minnesota by a judge to live with an aunt and uncle when the boy's alcoholic parents become too abusive. On the farm the boy adapts to a slower-paced life than what he was used to in the city. He and his cousin Carl become close, and one day while skiing in the backwoods they meet the mysterious Foxman.

The Foxman, so called because of the fox pelts that hang on the inside of his hut, wears a mask and lives alone because of the physical (and spiritual) disfigurement he suffered during World War II. The boy returns to the woods many times and learns from the Foxman the art of wilderness survival and the man's Thoreauean-style philosophy that emphasizes the pleasures of the mind and the ennoblement of the spirit. Then, during a sudden blizzard, the boy loses his way and suffers snow blindness. The Foxman saves him, but it is obvious to the boy now that the Foxman's cough is serious and he will not live much longer. The Foxman dies, a common characteristic found in initiation myths, but the boy has learned enough to pursue the beauty and love the Foxman knew but lost in the war.

Popcorn Days and Buttermilk Nights introduces yet another disturbed youth, this one named Carley, who comes to small-town Norsten from Minneapolis, where he was fast becoming a juvenile delinquent. Here he stays with Uncle David, a huge man with a Norwegian accent who is both a farmer and a blacksmith. Though he initially has trouble adjusting to a bucolic life-style and thinks David and his large family are a bit backward, he comes to love them and see the beauty in the golden popcorn days and buttermilk nights of fall.

The family's poverty becomes apparent, especially to Uncle David, when he can't afford to take them to a circus forty miles away. Here the author interjects epiphany and metaphor to get to the heart of the novel's theme. While drinking beer at the hole-in-the-wall bar adjacent to his blacksmith's shop, Uncle David hits on the idea of building his own circus. "To hell with them," he tells Carley defiantly. "I'm going to make my own." Uncle David utilizes his blacksmith skills to make what he can't buy—the same way he has forged Carley into a caring human being who realizes material wealth is no measure of a man's worth.

Tiltawhirl John draws also on events from Paulsen's life to demonstrate how a young boy changes and grows after spending the summer touring with a vagabond group of carnival performers. The nameless narrator leaves his northeastern North Dakota farm during his sixteenth summer and travels west where he accepts work hoeing sugar beets. He hoes alongside illegal Mexican immigrants and learns just how cruel a man his employer, Karl Elsner, is. After Elsner brutally beats him when the boy complains about being cheated of his wages, the boy runs away and is discovered stumbling along the highway by a trio of carnies: Tiltawhirl John, a con man with a secret past; Billy the Geek, John's twin brother; and Wanda, John's lover and a stripper with a heart-of-gold.

Initially the men don't want to take the boy along, but Wanda convinces them, and soon the boy is a member of their itinerant troupe. Right away he finds that carnies live by rules of their own. Their creed is simple. There are only two kinds of people, fellow carnies and what Billy calls "turkeys and toads," the customers the carnies cynically dupe as a matter of survival.

The boy enjoys the remainder of the summer as the carnival travels through the Dakotas, Wyoming, and Nebraska. He falls in love and has his first sexual experience with a fellow traveler, Janet, and thinks he might continue with his new-found way of life. But then the past catches up with Tiltawhirl John. Wanda's old lover Tucker shows up, and he and John engage in a ritualistic knife fight that leaves Tucker dead. The life that looked so good before has now been darkened by its seamy underside.

> Even Janet and the money couldn't make up for the way Tucker was sliding down and down as T-John's knife carved him up, and when he finally hit the ground and was dead I knew I wasn't a carny.

Dancing Carl is a drama that shows how a man can lift himself out of a deep-rooted depression through acts of courage and beauty. *Dancing Carl,* true to its name, was later set to dance and aired over Minnesota Public Television.

Marsh, the narrator, and his friend Willy spend their winters skating at the local rink. This particular winter they meet Carl, an enigmatic older man who takes care of the rink for the small northern Minnesota town. Carl is a World War II veteran, mentally unbalanced, who drinks regularly from a flask. He earns his name from the magical way he dances around the rink with his hands extended. The boys wonder about Carl's strange ice dance and decide to approach him to find out his secret. Marsh makes the mistake of bringing along his B-17 model. When Carl sees the plane, he smashes it to the ground and lapses into a trance in which he spits out his secret story. During the war, the plane he was flying in crashed, and Carl watched in horror as his plane and the nine other soldiers burned to death.

The boys feel awful about what they have done. Marsh, in particular, sees some secrets are best left buried.

> Halfway home I threw the model in a garbage can, threw the work away, and maybe I cried some and I thought how awful it was that you could mean well and do so much damage to someone.

Then when Carl appears to have sunk into a deeper depression, Helen comes to town and begins to skate regularly at the rink. Like Carl she is mentally ill, but Carl, through his dancing, is able to convey a special love to her that only she can understand. As the book ends, we learn from Marsh that Carl and Helen, despite some temporary happiness together, have met with tragic ends. As in the previous novels, the teenage narrator learns about life's cruel realities through the tragedy of an older person's life.

The Winter Room, too, is a tragedy in which the young narrator Eldon and his older brother Wayne learn painful lessons from their older Uncle David's apparent deceit. On their farm in the middle of a frigid Minnesota winter, the boys sit around the wood stove with their par-

ents and Uncle David and listen to his stories about Vikings and wood elves. One night David tells a story that is seemingly more real. He speaks of how he can make two axes meet in the center of a log and split it in two by swinging the two axes simultaneously at the log's opposite ends. Wayne is skeptical and grows angry and complains to his father and Eldon. Unbeknownst to Wayne, Uncle David hears his accusations.

> They looked like the pig's eyes just after Father cut its throat and it knew it was going to die. All pain and confused . . . Uncle David's eyes were, so hurt and ripped that it seemed he would crumble, and I could not shut Wayne up.

The night-time fireside stories stop; the family is broken apart until Uncle David, thinking he is alone, attempts the log-splitting feat. He succeeds as Eldon and Wayne watch—both cognizant now that myth and reality often mesh in a magical mixture of their own.

Of the twelve other Paulsen novels, this article will examine only five, all presented from the third-person point of view. These novels include *Tracker* (1984), *Dogsong* (1985), *Sentries* (1986), *The Crossing* (1987), and *The Island* (1988).

Dogsong, Tracker, and *The Island* should be considered together because all fuse the basic conflicts of man versus nature with man versus himself in an exciting interplay of the mystical and the real.

Dogsong, inspired by Paulsen's experience with dog sledding, features Russel Susskit, a fourteen-year-old Eskimo boy living outside of civilization in his Alaskan village. Despite their isolation, the natives have been corrupted by the white man's culture symbolized by the fast-paced snowmobiles. Only the old man Oogruk still retains his dog-sled team, and he is fast losing both his eyesight and his health.

Oogruk and Russel become friends, and Oogruk teaches the boy about the dogs and about the songs and journeys of his and his people's real and mythical pasts. Then, as in all heroic myths, Russel must complete the rites of passage from boy to man and embark on his own journey—one in which he will incorporate Oogruk's legacy unto himself while meeting the harsh realities of nature head on.

Russel and the dog team travel north into the remote Alaskan interior on their way toward the Bering Sea. Here the boy masters the intricacies of wilderness survival—overcoming the hardships of hunger, fear, and being lost before meeting his greatest challenge: coming face-to-face with his vision of Russel the mammoth hunter, a part-real, part-mythic ancestor of another time, and another dimension of Russel's undiscovered self:

> The dream had folded into his life and his life had folded back into the dream so many times that it was

not possible for him to find which was real and which was dream.

As both the dream and the reality unfold, Russel meets a pregnant Eskimo girl, Nancy, and together they complete the journey that forever changes them.

Tracker, too, revolves around a boy's search for his spiritual essence amidst the hardships of nature. In this sense both *Dogsong* and *Tracker* are similar to the religious quest story lines of much of contemporary Native American literature. Paulsen, talking about this aspect of his writing, has said that "spiritual progress has nothing to do with organized religion; it's a personal thing."

In *Tracker,* John Borne, thirteen, lives with his grandparents on their northern Minnesota farm. Each winter John and his grandfather hunt the nearby woods for deer meat that will feed them throughout the long hard months. But this winter John's grandfather cannot hunt; he is dying of cancer, and it is up to John to bring home the needed meat. Like Russel in *Dogsong,* John must remember everything the older man has taught him, and must figure out why a doe he spots outside the barn doesn't run when he comes upon her.

On the hunt John sees the doe again and follows her, thinking he must kill her, but then realizing he can't.

> In the night he changed from following the deer to becoming the deer. A part of him went out to the deer and a part of the deer went out of her into him, across the white light and he wasn't the same. He would never be the same again.

He follows the deer farther into the woods, wanting now only to touch her, thinking that by doing so he will capture the essence of life that he will transfer to his grandfather to save him from death. After touching the deer, John returns home, but finds that death is inevitable for both his grandfather and all living things. His ultimate discovery is that life is neither tragic nor comic, but woven together, or to use Paulsen's words, "just simply is."

> What I'm exploring is that almost mystical relationship that develops between the hunter and the hunted. It's a relationship with its own integrity, not to be violated.

The Island is in some ways Paulsen's best effort because it brings together the neo-spiritualism of *Dogsong* and *Tracker* with the fully rounded characterization of *Winterkill* and *The Winter Room.* Wil Neuton, fourteen, has lived all his life in the safe confines of Madison, Wisconsin, where, like most teenagers, he has been suffocated by shopping malls and the mass media. Then his father suddenly announces he has been transferred by the state highway department to the northern part of the state where they will live in a small cabin in the woods.

Wil thinks his life is over until they move and he dis-

covers Sucker Lake and its special uninhabited little island. Soon Wil is spending his days there—mostly alone, sometimes joined by Susan, a new-found love. Like Thoreau in *Walden* and Pirsig in *Zen and the Art of Motorcycle Maintenance* (a *New York Times* reviewer called *The Island* "Zen and the Art of Boyhood"), Wil uncovers some fundamental truths about himself and his world. The path he takes is similar to that followed by Huck Finn in *The Adventures of Huckleberry Finn* and Brautigan in *Trout Fishing in America.*

And as with Huck's Jackson's Island, evil lurks around—first in the form of the village bully, Ray, whom Wil fights and defeats, and then as Wil's father, who thinks his boy has gone crazy and needs help. The news media learns of Wil's experiment and attempts to turn him into a cliché, but Wil stays on his island, a metaphor for the magical circle he has drawn around his unlocked soul.

> Alone. He was somehow more apart from his parents than he had ever been because they were so against what he was doing. Alone from his family. Alone from his parents. Alone from what he knew.

In the end Wil returns, but he, like Paulsen's other individualistic protagonists, has irrevocably changed.

The Crossing and *Sentries* are both worth mentioning because of their strong themes and absorbing stories. *The Crossing* exhibits a strong Hemingway influence in a poignant story of Manuel Bustos. Manny is fourteen, and as long as he can remember he has been an orphan living day-to-day as a beggar in the poverty and squalor of Ciudad Juarez, Mexico. His dream is to cross the border to find the paradisiacal life in Los Estados Unidos. His plans are thwarted; his dreams appear doomed until he meets American Army Sergeant Robert Locke, a Vietnam veteran stationed at Fort Bliss, north of El Paso, Texas.

Locke, like Paulsen's other veterans, cannot forget the war and crosses the border each night to drown himself in drink. In the tragic ending Hemingway would have loved, Locke dies in a knife fight to save Manny and give him the opportunity to cross the border and find that better world Locke has lost.

Sentries is Paulsen's most ambitious work. In it he interweaves the stories of four teenagers with the lives of three mentally and physically scarred war veterans. While it seems their lives will never touch, their interdependency is driven home by the obvious conclusion that suggests the nuclear holocaust, the ultimate tragedy for which Paulsen feels adults are totally responsible.

> You know adults stink, we really do. We've polluted the earth, we've probably managed to destroy the human earth. And kids haven't done that. In that sense I think they are a lot smarter than we. I kind of wish I weren't an adult.

Paulsen's other works, while not lacking appeal, do not

match the high standards set down in these eleven novels. Still, throughout them are Paulsen's neo-Hemingway style, his Steinbeck characterization, and Melville themes that make him one of today's best young adult novelists. Paulsen's writing works because he creates books that show teen protagonists living life as a challenge—a wonderful contrast to the spiritually deadening existences forced on all too many contemporary teens stuck in the mentally lifeless urban morass. Paulsen, like his talented contemporaries Paul Zindel, Robert Cormier, M. E. Kerr, and Cynthia Voigt, need not be confined to the adolescent literature genre. Despite some occasional problems with character development, Paulsen's ability to evoke powerful imagery and visualize life in both its comic and tragic forms places him alongside other craftsmen whose words will last.

TITLE COMMENTARY

📖 *HATCHET* (1987)

Patty Campell

SOURCE: A review of *Hatchet,* in *Wilson Library Bulletin,* Vol. 62, No. 5, January, 1988, pp. 75-6.

The survival story is an extreme version of the "outsider" theme, and has long been a minor staple of young adult literature. *Robinson Crusoe* and *The Swiss Family Robinson,* of course, are the prototypes, now read by older children but beloved by teens in less-sophisticated times. These two books set the formula: a person or persons are cast out, stranded, or marooned and cut off from all civilized comforts and necessities.

In *Hatchet* Gary Paulsen has written a survival story that is quite pure in its adherence to the formula. Thirteen-year-old Brian is being flown in a private plane to visit his divorced father in the Canadian wilds. The pilot has a heart attack, and the boy manages to crash-land the plane in a lake, where it sinks. He swims to shore and, after a period of shock and self-pity, begins to cope.

An element of the formula that makes the survival story a puzzle is that the protagonist is allowed a very few pieces of technology left from the crash or found on the island. He or she must figure out how to use these tools in new ways to interact with nature for food and shelter. Paulsen has been very strict with his survivor—he has only the hatchet in the belt around his waist, a present given to him by his mother just before his departure. With it he cuts branches for a lean-to, carves spears and a bow and arrow, and figures out how to make fire by striking the heft against flint to produce sparks. Only when he loses it in the lake does Brian realize how central it is to his survival.

The heart of a good survival story, the thing that gives it meaning, is the transformation of the castaway from a soft, helpless creature into someone strong and self-reliant. Perhaps the best example is the metamorphosis of the fat, whiney girl in Harry Mazer's *The Island Keeper.* In *Hatchet,* Brian grows in strength and confidence, but the achievement is not as striking because he is not as weak and unpleasant as Mazer's character to begin with.

Near the end of the story, the formula calls for a violent upheaval of nature that wipes away most of the survivor's little contrivances, but not his (or her) newfound ability and courage. Here the cataclysm is a tornado, which destroys Brian's shelter and tools but brings the plane to the surface so that with much difficulty he can retrieve the survival kit that he knows is in the back seat.

After the problems have been solved and the survivor is living in relative comfort, the story is over and he can then be rescued, a resolution not without a small tinge of regret for the hard-won comforts now to be left behind. Paulsen has written a particularly nice rescue scene. Brian is preparing a feast from the precious freeze-dried food he has just found in the plane. As the pilot from the rescue plane steps ashore the boy waves him toward the hearth and asks graciously, "Would you like something to eat?"

Evie Wilson

SOURCE: A review of *Hatchet,* in *Voice of Youth Advocates,* Vol. 10, No. 6, February, 1988, p. 283.

Horrified passenger Brian Robeson watches as the pilot sitting next to him in the small plane has a heart attack and dies at the controls. The plane miraculously comes to rest in a small lake, but immediately sinks, leaving Brian wet and in shock. His desperate survival attempts begin, and the only obvious asset he carries is the hatchet his mother gave him on the way to the airport. Through his many ordeals, Brian learns by trial and error that, in truth, the most valuable asset he possesses is his own ability to assimilate his environment into life-saving methodology. Paulsen's knowledge of our national wilderness is obvious and beautifully shared. Beyond that Paulsen grips Brian (and the reader) by the throat, shaking him into enlightenment and self-confidence after having endured several life-threatening events. YA readers will surely identify with Brian's anger at his parents' divorce; they also will draw encouragement from his awakening self-assurance and pride.

Margery Fisher

SOURCE: A review of *Hatchet,* in *Growing Point,* Vol. 28, No. 4, November, 1989, pp. 5234-39.

Survival may be a matter of coping with severe natural

conditions or with unexpectedly heavy emotional demands, but whatever the situation the point which writers need to make most clearly is the degree of responsibility the young central character takes alone. *Hatchet* states a simple case in active terms. Brian Robeson, who is thirteen, is a passenger in a private plane on his way to visit his father, an engineer in a Canadian oil field, when the pilot dies of a heart attack. The boy, who has had a little elementary instruction in flying, manages to bring the plane down on the edge of a lake in the wilderness where he must use his wits to stay alive until (though this seems to him unlikely) he is located. The theme has been used before, most notably by Ivan Southall, but the book stands well on its own for firm concrete detail and an equally firm pattern of the boy's moods and reactions to danger. A sheltered middle class urban life hardly offers the chance to learn how to make fire without matches, to catch fish and hunt birds without suitable equipment and to build a shelter out of inadequate materials. All these things the boy achieves after painful trial and error, only to have most of his laborious contrivances blown to bits by a storm; this proves a blessing in fact for the sunk plane is brought to the surface and is noticed by a persistent pilot still searching months after the disaster. The boy has just won his greatest practical triumph, paddling to the plane in a clumsy raft to salvage anything useful, and the book ends memorably with his offhand invitation to his rescuer 'Would you like something to eat?' Behind the carefully described action, flashbacks give further insight into the boy's circumstances, his feelings about his parents' divorce and about his own plight, and the hatchet which he slung on his waist to please his mother when he said goodbye serves as a simple symbol of the energy with which a mere lad tackles a testing situation.

Audrey Laski

SOURCE: A review of *Hatchet,* in *The School Librarian,* Vol. 37, No. 4, November, 1989, pp. 161, 163.

Lord of the Flies described a large group of boys trying to survive in the wilderness, *Walkabout*, a girl and a little boy: each had much to say about issues other than survival. *Hatchet* puts a thirteen-year-old boy entirely on his own in the Canadian forests and its topic is, essentially, what it means to be a survivor. At the beginning of the book Brian is a soft city boy, acutely distressed by his parents' recent divorce; and the way his thoughts constantly return to this in the earlier pages suggests that family break-up is an important theme. But by the end, when the rescue he has long ceased to expect finally happens, obliquely triggered by what had looked like another disaster, Brian does not even think of his parents; he has become entirely his own person, an identity, a host: "My name is Brian Robeson . . . Would you like something to eat?" The passionate, repetitive rhythms of the writing, though sometimes a little overdone, powerfully communicate his terrors and triumphs, and could well make this Crusoe-story acces-

sible to slow or reluctant readers, without disturbing others.

A. R. Williams

SOURCE: A review of *Hatchet,* in *The Junior Bookshelf,* Vol. 54, No. 1, February, 1990, p. 51.

Hatchet has a strong opening situation. Thirteen-year-old Brian Robeson is a passenger in a small aircraft that crashes in the wastes of Canada, his only personal equipment a brand-new hatchet thrust on him (almost literally) by his estranged mother at parting. His pilot has died of a heart attack. The plane is mostly submerged. The radio is no longer serviceable. Once shock and fatigue have been eased Brian has to concern himself with survival which, realistically, turns out to be not as easy as tuition and reading might suggest; things do not go absolutely right first time. He perseveres, learns from errors, guards against recurrence, fights off fears. His dreams are strange, puzzling, reinforcing the basic tension of the tale. Disappointment is a constant element in the boy's lad.

Gary Paulsen's young hero is no Crusoe, no Family Robinson moving facilely from one project to the next. He has no kind climate or fertile land to assist his self-sufficiency. He must outwit the fish and the birds—and the elements—be patient and—brave. There is talk nowadays of "grace under pressure" as a cardinal virtue. Perhaps this is where Brian scores.

THE ISLAND (1988)

Stephanie Zvirin

SOURCE: A review of *The Island,* in *Booklist,* Vol. 84, No. 14, March 15, 1988, pp. 1242-44.

An appreciation of the raw beauty of wilderness, so much a part of Paulsen's writing, is particularly evident in his latest novel, a gentle, ruminative book in which 15-year-old Wil Neuton finds a "private island," where he looks deeply into reality and begins to unlock the essence of himself. On that first day, after the chaos of moving, the island provides a quiet refuge. Soon it becomes more—a place where observation, thought, and memory coalesce with a sharpness that makes life off the island somehow less real and less important. Lyrical passages intermingle with precise descriptions of the natural world as Paulsen evokes Wil's attempts to understand how he fits into the scheme of things—painting, writing about, and acting out what he feels and sees—and to explain what he is doing to his puzzled, loving parents, to his friend Susan, and to those who would label him crazy or turn his self-imposed stay on the island into a media event. At times Paulsen's prose mimics the cadence of nature; and wonderfully wry humor, more prevalent early in the novel, provides a fine counterpoint to Wil's contemplations: an encounter with a local plumber who spits tobacco ("You could have told me . . . we'd have to boil the whole house"), a talk with an idiotic psychiatrist sent to the island to evaluate Wil ("I've never had this situation before . . . you're reacting to there being nothing wrong with your life"), and snatches of Wil's own introspective wit in "Neutonian" ruminations that head each chapter. It's an unusual mix, far more dependent on description than on plot. Teenagers in search of the adventure of *Dogsong* or tension of *Tracker* won't find it here. Instead what they will glean from Wil's meandering experiences are a sense of peace and order and a keen understanding of what it means to look beyond oneself to "learn all we can about all we are."

Kirkus Reviews

SOURCE: A review of *The Island,* in *Kirkus Reviews,* Vol. LVI, No. 6, March 15, 1988, pp. 457-58.

In a milder variation on the theme of self-discovery through experience sounded in *Hatchet* (1988), Wil spends a few solitary days on an island near his home, tuning into nature and his own creativity.

Wil has just moved from Madison, Wisconsin, to a decrepit country house near his father's new highway job. Feeling dislocated but not rebellious, Wil suddenly decides to camp out on the island that he has just discovered; he sends new friend Susan to tell his parents he won't be coming home for a while. He is engrossed in trying to re-create his experiences (what his grandmother was like, a turtle capturing and eating a sunfish) in words and in paint; he observes wildlife and takes up meditation. Meanwhile, his parents don't understand and are upset; they even send a psychologist to check him out, but not before the media have descended on this odd story.

Wil is a fully developed character and—as Susan's mother suggests—gifted ("one of the thirsty people who need to know"); it's easy to imagine Paulsen as such an unusual boy. But there are some implausibilities in his story, including why a boy of 15 deciding to camp out a short distance from his home, in June, should cause such a fuss; and how such apparently limited and unimaginative parents could have produced such a son. And although there are some tautly written scenes (a fight with the local bully; Wil trying to imitate the loon's cry in order to understand the meaning of the loon), much of the book moves slowly. Fuller development of the parents would have made a stronger book; still, Wil's realization that they too are worthy of understanding makes a poignant conclusion to a novel that will appeal most to the unusual reader.

Ethel R. Twichel

SOURCE: A review of *The Island,* in *The Horn Book Magazine,* Vol. LXIV, No. 3, May-June, 1988, p. 361.

A move to northern Wisconsin leads Wil to the discovery of a small island set in a nearby lake. Rowing over in an abandoned minnow boat, he finds himself increasingly drawn to the island's isolation and to the animals and birds that share its quiet. That first day he observes the behavior of a loon and tries to absorb the very essence of the bird into himself. Finding the experience to be of profound importance to his mental and emotional growth, he leaves home to camp out on the island and briefly enjoys the opportunity for meditation and inner investigation as well as the chance to study the lives of the surrounding wildlife. Although the narrative is told in the third person, Wil's thoughts and memories are the fiber of the book. The reader is asked to enter the core of Wil's mind and to look beyond the fins and feathers of the animals he watches, a difficult and slow journey for those looking for the action of the author's *Hatchet* and *The Crossing.* As Wil's inner life is enriched, the ordinary world intrudes on his physical well being. His worried parents seek him out as does a newspaper reporter, who sees a good story in his unusual behavior. His growing attachment for a girl is a distraction, but it is the town bully's blatant attempt to terrorize him that reveals the darker side of Wil's nature. Only his encounter with a self-important psychiatrist offers some humorous moments. While the book is an admirable attempt to explore a young man's inner development, the pace is slow, and the invasion of visitors, each seeming more a stage in the plot than a truly evolved personality, makes the story seem contrived and lessens the potentially powerful impact of Wil's spiritual odyssey.

Jerri K. Norris

SOURCE: A review of *The Island,* in *English Journal,* Vol. 78, No. 3, March, 1989, p. 82.

Thoreau. Just the utterance of this two-syllable proper name makes the juniors shift in their seats, but it doesn't have to. *The Island* by Gary Paulsen presents Wil Neuton, a teenager who gets fed up with society, as a modern-day Thoreau whom most teenagers can identify with. Prompted by the thought that his "whole life is going down the toilet" because of his family's recent move to the isolated woods of northern Wisconsin from his Madison home in the city, Wil retreats to a small island in the middle of a remote pond. Soon he begins to notice his natural surroundings the beauty of a deer's reddish fur, a great blue heron's grey feathers, and the reflection of the morning sun across the pond's surface. His new interest in nature makes him realize that there is more to life than seeing who has the neatest skateboard. Turning inward, he keeps a journal of his thoughts and observations while camping on the island.

Each chapter of *The Island* begins with a notation from Wil's spiral notebook, and as the novel progresses, Wil grows from an anxious teenager whose behaviors people are beginning to classify as "weird" into a considerably more mature young man. Like Thoreau, who once said, "If a man does not keep pace with his companions, perhaps it is because he hears a different drummer," Wil comments that he "wanted to run" so that he "could get faster than some people but not as fast as some other people." Hearing the beat of the metaphorical drummer emanating from the island in the pond, Wil abandons his fiercely competitive attitude for a self-directed journey through the rest of his adolescence. Having accepted the fact that he is now in control of his life, he returns to Mom, Dad, and the house with a cooperative, humanistic attitude reminiscent of Thoreau's return from Walden Pond after his realization that in the many lives contained within a lifetime, "he could not spare any more for that one."

Paulsen, author of two Newbery Honor Books (*Dogsong* and *Hatchet*) and numerous other titles, models journal keeping and enters a new area of writing by noting the reflections of a fourteen-year-old on his relation to his surroundings. His viewpoints clash with those of his parents and friends, as Thoreau's did; hence, the novel serves wonderfully as a prelude to either *Civil Disobedience* or *Walden*. The parallels are easily traced, and the book reads fast. Besides its potential as an introduction to Thoreau's work, *The Island* realistically portrays a teenager who successfully battles the restlessness of growing up in modern society.

📖 *THE VOYAGE OF THE FROG* (1989)

Kirkus Reviews

SOURCE: A review of *The Voyage of the Frog,* in *Kirkus Reviews,* Vol. LVI, No. 24, December 15, 1988, pp. 1814-15.

Another tautly written survival story, much like *Hatchet* in design, though not in incident.

David, 14, has just inherited *Frog,* a 22-foot sailboat, from his well-loved uncle and companion, Owen, dead of a cruelly swift cancer. Mourning, David is scattering Owen's ashes, alone and out of sight of the southern California coast (Owen's last request) when he is caught by a sudden storm and knocked out by the boom. After a series of adventures that gradually makes him more competent and confident—a becalming, a shark, an oil tanker that nearly collides with him, looming but friendly whales, another storm—he encounters a research ship and accepts some supplies, but decides to make his way home alone (350 miles against wind and current) rather than abandon the untowable *Frog.*

Though David encounters plenty of life-threatening situations, there's never real doubt that he will survive; what holds attention here is the way he applies his ability to reason in coping with physical challenges and his own fear. As he acquires Owen's intimacy with *Frog* and sea, David also begins to assume Owen's best traits: his thirst for knowledge, his respect for the natural world. Like the adults in *Hatchet,* David's parents and Owen remain shadowy figures, within the range of the possible

(though few parents would willingly allow a boy to undertake such a journey), but that is beside the point: *this* story is about the voyage of the *Frog*—an epic, often lyrical journey of self-discovery, perhaps less gripping than *Hatchet* but with a subtler, more penetrating delineation of its protagonist.

Ethel R. Twichel

SOURCE: A review of *The Voyage of the Frog,* in *The Horn Book Magazine,* Vol. LXV, No. 2, March-April, 1989, p. 219.

David Alspeth's assignment from his late and much beloved uncle is truly heartbreaking; he has been asked to sail out into the Pacific, beyond the sight of land, and scatter Owen's ashes. Now, boarding the *Frog,* a twenty-two-foot sloop on which they had shared some glorious moments, fourteen-year-old David is overwhelmed by memories but hoists sail and departs for an unexpected odyssey of trial and endurance. Thinking he will be on board for only a short while, the boy is unprepared for the sudden and violent storm which almost destroys his boat and equipment and, injured and frightened, finds he must draw on all the sailing skills Owen taught him over the years. The author explains the purpose of each winch and cleat aboard the *Frog* and translates such nautical and esoteric terms as *luffing* so that they mesh unobtrusively with the story's action. And action abounds. Terrifying storms, a near miss by an oil tanker, and encounters with whales and sharks provide plenty of excitement and opportunities for David to test his seamanship and his ability to survive loneliness and fear, physical pain and hardship. As is usual in Paulsen's books, David's inner voyage is as important as the outer one. His growing identity with his boat, which Owen has bequeathed to him; his confidence in his own capabilities; and his wonderment and joy in the terrors and beauty of the ocean lift the story above a log of adventure and heroics. The author, knowledgeable in sailing lore and lyrical and powerful in descriptions of either silken seas or crashing breakers, has made the ocean both a background and a protagonist in David's transition from boy to young man.

George Hunt

SOURCE: A review of *The Voyage of the Frog,* in *Books for Keeps,* No. 74, May, 1992, p. 20.

After seeing his beloved uncle shrivel up and die of cancer, David inherits the man's sailboat and a boxful of ashes to scatter into the Pacific. On completing this ceremony, he's swept into his own rite of passage when a tempest seizes his boat and brings him face to face with the murderous splendour of the open ocean. This is an almost traditional nautical yarn, a thumping good read drenched in lashings of adrenalin and testosterone, but its more contemplative passages provide a reflective strand which should deservedly broaden its appeal.

Judith Higgins

SOURCE: A review of *The Voyage of the Frog,* in *School Library Journal,* Vol. 38, No. 8, August, 1992, p. 90.

A 14-year-old California boy obeys his dying uncle's wishes to throw his ashes into the sea from his small sailboat, *The Frog.* Without realizing it, David is blown miles off the coast; he is becalmed, nearly run down by a tanker, and slammed by a shark. In this story, too, the boy, fearful in the early pages, learns by the last chapter to face what comes his way. Another storm hits, but this time he is ready for it. This is an author who reassures readers that they can learn from mistakes, learn to live with nature, learn to survive. The first-person narrative, in Paulsen's hands, comes alive. There's no need for pages and pages of unrelenting dialogue with no exposition to hold YAs' interest.

📖 *THE WINTER ROOM* (1989)

Katharine Bruner

SOURCE: A review of *The Winter Room,* in *School Library Journal,* Vol. 35, No. 14, October, 1989, p. 136.

Of the four rooms downstairs in the northern Minnesota farmhouse, the one that might be called a living room is where Wayne and Eldon, their parents and great-uncle, and old Norwegian Nels spend their winters. There the family sits near the corner wood stove and listens, uninterrupting, as Uncle David tells stories—of the old country, of old times, of a semi-mythical lumberjack. Eldon, the younger son, begins his own story, in spring, when everything is soft. While he describes for readers the farm activities of each season and narrates memorable pranks and milestones of his boyhood, it is the palpable awareness of place and character that is unforgettable. Paulsen, with a simple intensity, brings to consciousness the texture, the smells, the light and shadows of each distinct season. He has penned a mood poem in prose. Uncle David's final story precipitates within the brothers a fuller understanding of personal identity and integrity. For those special readers who find delight in *The Winter Room,* it will become a part of their own identity and understanding. Teachers who seek to illuminate the use of ordinary English words with extraordinary descriptive power will find the introductory chapter, in particular, to be a godsend.

Kirkus Reviews

SOURCE: A review of *The Winter Room,* in *Kirkus Reviews,* Vol. LVII, No. 20, October 15, 1989, pp. 1534-35.

More a prose poem than a novel, this beautifully written evocation of a Minnesota farm perhaps 40 years ago consists of portraits of each of the four seasons, along with four brief stories told by old Uncle David in the room the family calls "The Winter Room." And, in its way most revealing, there is also an introduction ("Tuning") so skillfully written that it ironically belies its own message: that books cannot have smells, or sound, or light, since these must be supplied by the reader in response to the author's words. With his authentic descriptions, Paulsen makes it easy for the reader to comply.

It's not clear to whom Eldon, the 11-year-old narrator, speaks—mostly he describes, rather than explains, though the explanatory creeps in: "Each cow has to have a calf or it won't . . . give milk." Unlike the novels of Laura Ingalls Wilder and Jean George, which also conjure life in a particular setting through the accumulation of detail, this presentation of the marvelous minutiae of farm life supports only a gossamer plot hinging on the relationship between story and reality. As carefully structured as cobweb, the idea is there, almost invisible, from early on, when emulating a feat in a Zane Grey novel results in a dangerous prank; it resurfaces in the character of Father, who doesn't answer questions but enjoys speaking in simile; and climaxes when Eldon's brother challenges the fragile illusion of Uncle David's stories by calling them lies, causing a moving philosophical crisis in this taciturn family.

Readers will be rare, but this is too fine to be ignored as a shelf-sitter.

Frances Bradburn

SOURCE: A review of *The Winter Room,* in *Wilson Library Bulletin,* Vol. 64, No. 3, November, 1989, pp. 94-5.

In *The Winter Room,* Gary Paulsen paints a pastoral picture of growing up on a northern Minnesota farm in the midst of family: "My mother and father and my brother Wayne and my Uncle David, who isn't really my uncle but sort of my great-uncle who is very old, and Nels, who is old like David." The days extend, like the family, through the seasons, as spring with its promise of new life and awakening—an "awakening of smells . . . soft and stinky . . . ," as young Elton says—moves to summer when the ground is "cutting like butter" and wheat, oats, barley, corn, and potatoes are planted and harvested, "and the days don't stop." When fall with its killing—"Nobody says anything for a time while the animals or chickens are dying. Nothing. No sound and I hate fall."—segues into winter with its first snow and short days, the long nights are spent in the winter room, the living room. It is here during this magical time in this room used only on cold winter evenings that Elton and his older brother, Wayne, listen to Uncle David's stories. And it is here in the quietness of their mother's knitting and their father's carving and Uncle David's stories that the boys begin to realize a larger world beyond a cold Minnesota farm that extends across America, to Norway, to years and lives past and strengths both physical and emotional to which their young bodies and minds can only aspire.

Rarely is a book of such peace and sparse beauty written for middle readers. Paulsen does not pander to the young adolescent's need for action, humor, and adventure. While all these elements are a part of *The Winter Room,* they are merely a portion of the sights, smells, and sounds of a family's way of life.

Barbara Elleman

SOURCE: A review of *The Winter Room,* in *Booklist,* Vol. 86, No. 5, November 1, 1989, p. 556.

In a change of pace from his recent survival stories, *Hatchet* and *The Voyage of the Frog,* Paulsen shapes a narrative that is more a reminiscence than a story. Eldon, an 11-year-old boy, uses the evolving seasons to describe growing up on a northern Minnesota farm. The evocative prologue (which rates with Babbitt's *Tuck Everlasting* and Lowry's *Autumn Street*) entitled "Tuning," says that "if books could be more, give more, show more, own more . . . they would have smells . . . sounds . . . light." Paulsen then supplies the foundations for those elements as Eldon recounts the softness of spring when the land thaws and frozen manure begins to stink, the back-breaking work of summer thrashing and the sweetness of juicy-tasting pies, the hated autumn slaughter of pigs and chickens, and the first softly camouflaging snows of winter. Woven into the spare, crisp, and sometimes graphically written descriptions are vignettes about the pranks of Eldon and his brother and vivid profiles of Father and Great Uncle David (Mother, however, remains a shadowy figure). The book concludes with three tales told by Uncle David of his days in Norway as a younger man; one of which gives the boys new insights into the man, his stories, and the process of growing old. Meditative and provocative.

Ethel R. Twichel

SOURCE: A review of *The Winter Room,* in *The Horn Book Magazine,* Vol. LXVI, No. 2, March-April, 1990, p. 209.

Although set in the thirties, a sensitive yet unsentimental view of life on a remote northern Minnesota farm bears the flavor of a much older era because of the folk tales and memories shared by the two elderly men who live and work with young Eldon and his family. Eldon describes his farm as it passes through the four seasons, plunging the reader into the sights, sounds, smells, tastes, and textures of his rural experience. The awakening of the earth in the spring means shoving reluctant cattle through the winter's accumulation of muck, while the fall, although providing a respite from the endless labor of harvesting, is shadowed by the butchering of animals for winter provisions. On Eldon's farm there is no ques-

tion of naming a pig or raising a calf as a pet; hard work is a given, beyond complaint or resistance. Yet moments of delight and humor touch the pages. Eldon breathes the heady smell of freshly turned earth as his father plows his fields and wickedly enjoys his brother's nearly disastrous second-story leap onto the iron-hard back of a farm horse while enacting a fantasy of escape and rescue. Eldon and his older brother, Wayne, his mother and father, and the two old men, Uncle David and Nels, are brought vividly to life through Eldon's eyes. Each piece of furniture, the stubborn personality of the ancient tractor, the fields, the food—all are described in loving recollection and with total recall. An introduction, titled "Tuning," seems overwritten and overly earnest in its attempt to prepare the reader for all aspects of the author's task, and the three concluding stories Uncle David tells, while part of the family's Scandinavian background, barely escape seeming tacked on. Yet the extraordinary visualization of Eldon's boyhood surmounts these flaws; the book is another fine example of Paulsen's writing gifts.

THE BOY WHO OWNED THE SCHOOL: A COMEDY OF LOVE (1990)

Publishers Weekly

SOURCE: A review of *The Boy Who Owned the School: A Comedy of Love,* in *Publishers Weekly,* Vol. 237, No. 6, February 9, 1990, p. 63.

Most of the action of this farcical novel takes place at the high school where Jacob Freisten's primary goal is to remain unnoticed. All too often this classic loser finds himself cornered by some bully. When he is not being stuffed inside a locker or a trash can, Jacob suffers other forms of humiliation that are relayed in a string of colorful anecdotes. While running laps around the gym, he accidentally tramples Maria Tresser, the most beautiful girl in the school. Cupid's arrow strikes, and Jacob's seemingly hopeless infatuation leads to one disaster after another; but he finally wins a date with the girl of his dreams. Although Paulsen's pace may leave some readers breathless, most will relish the sharp wit and incredible energy of this ironic glimpse of high school life and young romance.

Kirkus Reviews

SOURCE: A review of *The Boy Who Owned the School: A Comedy of Love,* in *Kirkus Reviews,* Vol. LVIII, No. 5, March 1, 1990, p. 345.

A total surprise from the award-winning author of, most recently, *The Winter Room:* a comic, accessible novel about a classic 15-year-old klutz.

Slight, quiet, and much brighter than his dismal grades imply, Jacob has focused his talents on the art of being invisible and thus avoiding the jocks, of whom he is the quintessential victim. Despite his efforts, though, he's noticed by a teacher who drafts him to run the fog machine for a production of *The Wizard of Oz*. Hopelessly enamored of Maria, the popular, genuinely nice girl who plays the witch, Jacob panics at the chance of getting to know her, manages (like the Phantom of the Opera) to keep out of sight as usual, fouls up completely (and hilariously) in his not-so-simple theatrical task—and discovers, finally, that Maria likes him, too.

Since this is a Paulsen book, there's another level here. Jacob is so self-involved that he's oblivious to the subtleties of others' motives and assumes that he's the lowest in every pecking order—which is only partly true, and true in that part because he himself perpetuates it. The book is deftly constructed, the brief chapters like the brush strokes of a master painter, with remarkably apt sketches of minor characters (Uncle Frank, "tough as nails," looks "like a spark plug"). A perceptive portrait of a kid on the verge of getting out of his self-set trap of imagining any change as a threat—even change for the better: a memorably funny yet touching farce.

Leda Schubert

SOURCE: A review of *The Boy Who Owned the School: A Comedy of Love,* in *School Library Journal,* Vol. 36, No. 4, April, 1990, pp. 144-45.

Jacob Freisten, thin and freckled, the "ugliest boy in history except for one," according to his own assessment, and a total clod to boot, has perfected the art of near invisibility, of being "there but not there." He leads the kind of exaggeratedly painful life that requires careful timing and planning so he can avoid attracting attention; if people notice him, there's always a comic disaster. He even goofs up in his daydreams. His parents drink too much, his mother is devoted to his sister's blossoming career as a beauty contest winner, and he's close to failing English. His English teacher ropes him into working on the school production of *The Wizard of Oz* for extra credit, appropriately enough as the understage controller of the fog machine. This gives him an opportunity to work with Maria Tressor, the most perfect girl in the school, on whom he has a rapidly intensifying crush. But it's a mixed blessing. When it's time to fog, Jacob, the consummate timing expert, flubs it badly, and in the confusion he blurts his feelings out to Maria. She says an astonishing yes to his feeble invitation for a date, and romance blooms because, she tells him, he's a winner. This brief, humorous look at adolescent life, complete with distorted self-concept, is a departure from the intensity of much of Paulsen's work, but is no less of a survival story in its own way. The novel is told mostly through a third-person narrative with little conversation until the end, which has the effect of distancing readers; it becomes a gently ironic fable of transformation and first love, in which many readers will find themselves.

Elizabeth S. Watson

SOURCE: A review of *The Boy Who Owned the School: A Comedy of Love,* in *The Horn Book Magazine,* Vol. LXVI, No. 4, July-August, 1990, p. 458.

The author, who is well known for his adventure and outdoor survival stories, has turned his hand to a survival story of a different kind in this screamingly funny piece of writing. The hero, Jacob, is a self-styled loser, a wimp, a nobody whose constant attempts to avoid notice at all costs are foiled when his English teacher, Mrs. Hilsak, ropes him into helping with the class play. In this brief, slice-of-life story that most resembles a fairy tale for the budding adolescent, the witch appears in the guise of Mrs. Hilsak, and the beautiful but nasty princess is his older sister. Jacob is the ugly duckling who doesn't even have to turn into a swan to win his fair lady—she literally falls into his lap! While the plot is minimal—a cross between the aforementioned "Ugly Duckling" and "Cinderella"—the writing is wonderfully constructed and beautifully paced. One of the funniest scenes describes Jacob's bout with a fog machine. The laughs are plentiful in this brief, funny foray into the world of adolescence.

WOODSONG (1990)

Kirkus Reviews

SOURCE: A review of *Woodsong,* in *Kirkus Reviews,* Vol. LVIII, No. 13, July 1, 1990, pp. 933-34.

A three-time Newbery Honor winner tells—in a memoir that is even more immediate and compelling than his novels—about his intimate relationship with Minnesota's north woods and the dog team he trained for Alaska's Iditarod.

Beginning with a violent natural incident (a doe killed by wolves) that spurred his own conversion from hunter and trapper to observing habitant of the forest, Paulsen draws a vivid picture of his wilderness life—where bears routinely help themselves to his dog's food and where his fiercely protective bantam adopts a nestful of quail chicks and then terrorizes the household for an entire summer. The incidents he recounts are marvelous. Built of concrete detail, often with a subtext of irony or mystery, they unite in a modest but telling self-portrait of a man who has learned by opening himself to nature—not to idyllic, sentimental nature, but to the harsh, bloody, life-giving real thing. Like nature, the dogs are uncontrollable: independent, wildly individual, yet loyal and dedicated to their task. It takes extraordinary flexibility, courage, and generosity to accept their difficult strengths and make them a team; Paulsen sees humor in their mischief and has learned (almost at the cost of his life) that rigid discipline is irrelevant, even dangerous.

This wonderful book concludes with a mesmerizing, day-by-day account of Paulsen's first Iditarod—a thrilling, dangerous journey he was so reluctant to end that he almost turned back within sight of his goal. It's almost as hard to come to the end of his journal. This may be Paulsen's best book yet: it should delight and enthrall almost any reader.

Hazel Rochman

SOURCE: A review of *Woodsong,* in *Booklist,* Vol. 86, No. 22, August, 1990, p. 2164.

Paulsen writes about his fierce, beautiful experience with sleds and dogs, first in northern Minnesota where he lives and then in 17 grueling days with his 15-dog team in the Iditarod race. Despite occasional inflated messages about "life" and about "blood," the stories ring with truth. The language is stark as he describes big, near-mystical experiences in the snow and wind; he also shows a lightness of touch, a self-deprecating humor (even about his great vision quest); in fact, there are episodes of outright farce, both in his domestic barnyard and the Alaskan tundra. He's candid about the boredom and mundane detail (including "gastric distress" from gorging on moose chili) and about the wild hallucinations that come with sleep deprivation. The nature lore woven into the narrative is like a celebration of the "woods" (Paulsen's word for the environment): the grouse's eggs that lie cuddled in the nest; the bears hungry beyond caution; the goats whiffing and blowing snot; the high keening wail and whoop of the loon. And always there's the image of Paulsen sleeping in a tent at 35 below, warmed by the dogs jamming into the sides of his sleeping bag. The ending is subtle: not wanting to finish the race, barely able to speak to people anymore, he nearly turns the sled around to go back into the tundra; only his wife's shout breaks the spell. Like Jack London, Paulsen combines wild adventure and precise observation with intensely private discovery. We're moved by the story of the individual with his dogs and the elements—solitary, connected.

Susan Schuller

SOURCE: A review of *Woodsong,* in *School Library Journal,* Vol. 36, No. 10, October, 1990, p. 148.

An autobiographical book that gives through spare but vivid language a look at a man who thought, because he was a hunter and a trapper, that he knew about the outdoors. Instead, he discovered he knew very little until he opened himself to the realities of predators and prey, and to the lessons taught to him by the animals he encountered and the sled dogs he trained and raced. This is not a life story, with dates and names and achievements, but rather Paulsen's reflections on the peculiarities and surprises of nature. Some of the lessons are violent and painful, brought on by the natural instincts of wild animals or Paulsen's own mistakes; others are touching or humorous, and convey a sharp sense of observation and awareness of the various personality traits

of the dogs he has raised and run. And some are unexplainable—mysteries of nature that would seem incredible if written in a work of fiction. The anecdotal style and rhythmic, sometimes abrupt sentence structure demand close attention, and the switch in the last third of the book to Paulsen's day-by-day account of the Iditarod is sudden, though expected. The Iditarod story is intensely personal, focusing on Paulsen's thoughts, actions, and hallucinations during those 17 days rather than presenting a comprehensive view of the race and the competitors. Both segments of the book generate wonder at the abilities of animals and should introduce fans of Paulsen's fiction to a different type of writing.

Nancy Vasilakis

SOURCE: A review of *Woodsong,* in *The Horn Book Magazine,* Vol. LXVI, No. 6, November, 1990, p. 762.

Aficionados of Paulsen's novels will relish this autobiographical account of his life in Minnesota and Alaska, where he steeps himself in knowledge of the wild as he prepares his dogs and himself to race the grueling Iditarod, 1,180 miles across the Alaskan tundra. Clearly, the background for his outdoor and survival stories has been drawn from the details of his own life in the woods. An initial gruesome observation of a pack of wolves devouring a doe leads him to question the easy assumptions he has always held as a hunter. He acquires a few sled dogs and begins to go on solitary runs, learning the skill of dog-sledding through trial and error. The dogs are frequently his teachers. When he attempts to guide the team in the wrong direction during a blinding snowstorm, the lead dog purposely drives the sled over a ridge to teach him a lesson. One of the dogs uses a stick to communicate with him, picking it up in her mouth to show approval, dropping it when she disapproves of something he is doing. Other animals enter into the narrative, too. With disarming humility, he writes of a life-threatening confrontation with a bear, who could easily have mauled him but decides otherwise, or of a "summer of terror" when he and his family are at the mercy of a tiny bantam hen who stalks the yard in defense of her brood. The anecdotes are candid, often humorous. They are also fascinating, inexplicable, inspiring, and chilling. Lapses into overblown language or sloppy grammar—"we became accustomed to him hanging around" or "there gets to be a too relaxed attitude"—strike the occasional false note; nevertheless, the material is undeniably compelling. The lure of the wilderness is always a potent draw, and Paulsen evokes its mysteries as well as anyone since Jack London.

Stephen Fraser

SOURCE: A review of *Woodsong,* in *The Five Owls,* Vol. V, No. 2, November-December, 1990, p. 35.

With three Newbery Honor Books to his credit and the kudos of the press and review journals nationwide, Gary

Paulsen has established himself as a writer of the highest caliber: bold, lyrical, profound. His books are not easily forgotten, and his dramatic sense of story, natural images, and clean, descriptive language display a fine-honed craft and compelling immediacy that make a survival-in-the-wilderness story (**Hatchet**) a work of art.

The connection between Paulsen's art and his life are not easily separated. We learn from reading **Woodsong** that he is a survivor in the wilderness himself. This book recounts his adventures first in the wilds near his home in northern Minnesota and then in the famous Alaskan dog-sled race, the Iditarod. He makes us feel what it is like to be alone in the vast snow-covered wilderness with only his dogs as companions; through describing the threat of bears and wolves, he shares both the beauty and the violence of the natural world (he doesn't spare us any frightening details); and he takes us day by day on the grueling yet exciting seventeen-day dogsled race.

The first two thirds of the book consist of random episodes about the author's experiences outdoors, chronicling his growing respect for wildlife. It is a frightening yet awe-inspiring education, yet there are moments of pure lyricism. One of my favorite episodes describes a young boy, along with his father and the author, reaching out from a canoe to touch a three-week-old fawn as both parents—animal and human—look on nervously and wonderingly. There is humor in the book. Paulsen recounts how one of his dogs deliberately hides his hat in the snow when he isn't looking. When he finds the hat and puts it on, Paulsen insists that the dog was smiling. There is information: we learn that dogs run best at night; that dogs are customarily silent when they run; that their average speed is seven miles per hour. There is danger and tragedy. There is life, in all its beauty, power, and primal simplicity.

This is an outstanding book, one that will interest avid readers of Paulsen's other books. Yet this book will also be enjoyed by adult readers. It answers the need in all of us for pure adventure, free from the fax machines, telephones, and daily reminder books of civilization.

Joel Shoemaker

SOURCE: A review of *Woodsong,* in *Voice of Youth Advocates,* Vol. 13, No. 5, December, 1990, p. 318.

Fans will revel in this autobiographical account of the understandings Paulsen has gained by living and working with sled dog teams in the woods. The first eight chapters are anecdotal reflections, arranged thematically to tell, with great conviction and good humor, stories Paulsen has used before only in fiction such as **Dogsong:** the stink of fear and the amoral brutality of wolves hunting; the blood of deer and dogs and man; quirky encounters with a forgiving bear and a carnivorous squirrel. Equally enthralling are tales of the dogs' sense of humor, the beauty of being pulled through the full-moon

night by a "steam ghost" and the experience of "becoming a true human . . . Like going inside and becoming a cave painting." Referring to himself several times as "a piece of meat," Paulsen understands that he is "nothing more and nothing less than any other animal in the woods," an elemental, but not elementary, insight. Paulsen's conviction that mankind's control of fire is what really separates us from the other animals recalls London's classic short story *To Build a Fire.*

Paulsen's characteristic eccentricities of style—repetition and reduction of phrases—are held mostly in check. His mystical accounts of hallucinations leave one properly confused about reality—such as the old Eskimo man who repeatedly appears to rescue Paulsen and his team when they are in direst straits.

The second part of the book is a day-by-day account of Paulsen's first participation in the 1100+ mile Iditarod race in Alaska, recounting the madness, hallucinations, beauty, and dangers that lead finally to an incredible sense of peace and affirmation. The book is packed with vignettes that range among various shades of terror and lyrical beauty that beg for a booktalking introduction to lure students into reading the entire work.

CANYONS (1990)

Kirkus Reviews

SOURCE: A review of *Canyons,* in *Kirkus Reviews,* Vol. LVIII, No. 15, August 1, 1990, p. 1090.

An Apache boy on the verge of manhood is brutally executed by Army patrols; over 100 years later a contemporary 15-year-old finds his shattered skull and—responding to a compelling inner voice emanating from the skull—begins a journey to vindicate and give rest to its troubled spirit, somehow knowing that he must carry out this task in order to regain his own peace.

The phrase "I am to be a man," reiterated in the first chapter, induces some poetic and semantic resonance but is also an example of the uncurtailed writing that nearly dims this tale. Still, readers patient enough to survive the repetitive ruminations, the too-deliberate epicycles, and the unlikely details (especially a library that, as a friendly gesture, ships seven large boxes of photocopied data—and a boy who can find the crucial bit therein in one night) will be rewarded with an insightful, sympathetic vignette of the tragic end of a life, plus an intriguing glimpse of the contrast between what really happens and the clues that are left behind.

Marjorie Lewis

SOURCE: A review of *Canyons,* in *School Library Journal,* Vol. 36, No. 9, September, 1990, p. 256.

Cornered in a canyon during his first coming-of-age

horse raid, a young Apache brave, Coyote Runs, is shot execution-style by soldiers from Fort Bliss. One hundred years later, Brennan Cole discovers a skull with a hole through its forehead in a canyon where he's been camping and becomes obsessed by the need to find out the who, what, and why of the skull. With the help of a pathologist, his high-school biology teacher, and someone from the Western Historical Archives in Denver, Brennan pieces the story together. The bond between the two boys, a century apart in time but so close in age and spirit, grows stronger as Brennan now searches for the final answer: why is Coyote Runs' spirit so restless, and what does it want of him? Brennan's realization that only when Coyote Runs' haunting and haunted soul is at peace will his own disturbed self find peace climaxes in his own coming-of-age challenge. Paulsen involves readers so deeply in the lives of both characters, telling the story in alternating chapters marked by the cadence and language distinctive to each boy and his time and place, that the whole becomes a compelling and dramatic experience that is powerful stuff. Although this is, at times, over-written and affected—almost a parody of Hemingway—it will be new and unforgettable to today's readers.

Leone McDermott

SOURCE: A review of *Canyons,* in *Booklist,* Vol. 87, No. 3, October 1, 1990, pp. 326-27.

Two coming-of-age stories are interwoven and finally merged in this deft and thought-provoking adventure novel. In 1884, a young Apache named Coyote Runs embarks on the grueling horse raid that will be his test of manhood. Though he triumphs, Coyote Runs' life is cut brutally short by a band of U.S. soldiers. A century later, 14-year-old Brennan Cole finds Coyote Runs' skull on a camping trip and becomes mystically joined with the Apache boy's spirit. By returning the skull to the Apache holy ground in spite of adult opposition, Brennan succeeds in completing a personal rite of passage. Paulsen writes with an austerity appropriate to the novel's desert setting, yet he is sensitive to both cultural differences and human commonalities. The boys' lives contrast in many ways, but they are united by their need to prove themselves. Paulsen fuses this insight with exciting action to produce a work meaningful on several levels.

Edith S. Tyson

SOURCE: A review of *Canyons,* in *Voice of Youth Advocates,* Vol. 13, No. 6, February, 1991, p. 355.

About 125 years ago, in the Rio Grande country around what is now El Paso, Texas, an Apache boy of 14 named Coyote Runs, rides with the tribe on a horse-stealing raid across the Mexican border. This is his first raid, a rite of passage that will make him a "man."

In our own time, Brennan Cole, an almost 15 year old

of El Paso, is camping out, rather unwillingly, in one of the Rio Grande canyons with his divorced mother; his mother's latest boyfriend, Bill; and eight demonic little boys from Bill's church youth group. Brennan senses a strangeness in the night and finds an odd-shaped rock under his sleeping bag. The rock is a skull of a 14-year-old Apache boy with a close-range bullet hole in it.

Coyote Runs's story and Brennan's are told in alternating chapters, with a contrasting typeface. This technique may remind some of *A Nugget of Gold* by Maureen Pople; however, this is a *very* different kind of story. The grimness *is* the story, and is not relieved. Also, Pople's story has no mystical dimension. Here, Brennan is not just driven by curiosity; the last, unspoken words of Coyote Runs, thought while the U.S. trooper's gun was pressed against his head, keep repeating themselves in Brennan's mind. As Brennan drives himself to find out about the skull and to fulfill its last wish, directions and instructions suggest themselves in his mind.

Brennan is helped in his quest, appropriately, by Vietnam veterans, one of whom observes wryly that "things never change." A research librarian, also a Viet vet, is phenomenally helpful, sending crates of paper copies relating to the U.S. military and the Apaches. At the end, Brennan is back in the canyon, pursued by Mountain Rescue, who has been told only that a young boy who has been acting strangely and obsessed lately has rushed off into the canyon alone. Brennan must elude them, much as Coyote Runs had tried to elude his killers, long enough to place the skull in what had been the sacred Apache medicine place.

All of Paulsen's brilliance is here: humans with and against nature as in *Hatchet,* humans with and against each other as in *The Crossing,* and the sense of time and place and the fine-tuned suspense found in nearly all of his work. But, the tale is too grim to appeal to everyone.

THE COOKCAMP (1991)

Publishers Weekly

SOURCE: A review of *The Cookcamp,* in *Publishers Weekly,* Vol. 237, No. 50, December 14, 1990, p. 67.

This short, lyrical novel concerns a five-year-old boy who is sent to the north woods of Minnesota to live with his grandmother, a cook for a rough-and-tumble road-building crew, because his father is off fighting in World War II and his mother has taken a job in a factory. Paulsen's simply told story strikes extraordinary emotional chords, from the boy's wide-eyed wonder at the giant men and their giant machines, to his searing rage at his mother's new boyfriend (the real reason he's been packed off to the woods), to his profound love for his grandmother, to his aching loneliness for his mother. Paulsen expertly balances sensitive probing of the boy's mental and emotional life with superb descriptions of the boy helping the men build the road, making Paulsen's unnamed hero one of the most fully realized characters in recent memory. Those hungry for adventure stories, as well as more introspective readers, will be spellbound by this stirring novel, which is every bit the equal of *The Winter Room* and Paulsen's other works.

Kirkus Reviews

SOURCE: A review of *The Cookcamp,* in *Kirkus Reviews,* Vol. LIX, No. 1, January 1, 1991, p. 50.

Sent, at five, to live with his grandmother in the wilds of northern Minnesota—where she is cook for nine rough men who are building a road from nowhere to nowhere (in case the vicissitudes of WWII should make it useful)—"the boy" experiences a brief, idyllic interlude tempered by longing for his mother, as well as by other carefully selected intrusions of reality. His grandmother is quintessentially accepting and, better yet, sensible and imaginative: she gives him real work to do helping her prepare meals, tells him how to make friends with the chipmunks, makes a game of exploring her sewing box. The men, whose awesome size Paulsen astutely describes from a small boy's point of view, adopt him wholeheartedly—take him aboard the bulldozer; buy him a real knife; care for him while his grandmother takes an injured man to the hospital. But, in the long run, these treats are not enough. The boy lets slip that he's been sent from Chicago because his mother is involved with another man while his father is in the army; the grandmother promptly writes some deeply felt letters that result in his going home. A poignant final chapter provides context by summarizing the grandmother's long life.

The audience for this spare, beautifully written vignette is a question; it may take some introduction, but is well worth creative experimentation: a readaloud for good listeners in the early grades? adults? Meanwhile, like *The Winter Room* (1989), a memorable evocation of a special time and place, grounded in authentic insight into deeper truths.

Susan M. Harding

SOURCE: A review of *The Cookcamp,* in *School Library Journal,* Vol. 37, No. 2, February, 1991, p. 82.

In its simplicity of story line but depth of imagery and emotion, Paulsen's latest work is very much like MacLachlan's *Sarah, Plain and Tall.* During World War II, the father is in the army and the mother has to work, so a five-year-old boy is sent to stay with his grandmother who works as a cook for a road-building crew in northern Minnesota. At first his day consists of long stretches of quiet as he tries to amuse himself, only to have the peace invaded by the crew of large, loud, good-natured men who inhale great amounts of food, ruffle the boy's

hair, and then get back to work. The boy ultimately gets over his shyness when they take him out to work with them and let him ride in the big trucks. But still, he misses his mother, and soon he is sent back to her. Paulsen does an excellent job of portraying the lightning-quick changes of a young child's emotions, from the upheaval of being sent away to the wonder of coaxing a chipmunk to accept food from his finger, from the exhilaration of being in the large trucks to the quiet security of being sung a Norwegian lullaby. In the boy's eyes, the men are so much larger than life that they seem almost mythic, as if he had been suddenly transported to Paul Bunyan's camp. But he's not so dazzled by their size that he misses the small things: he is equally enthralled by the tiny detailed painting on his grandmother's thimble or the colors in her apple pie. While the boy is very young, his experiences are universal, making this a superb book for readers just old enough to look back and remember their childhoods and grandparents with a feeling of nostalgia.

Patty Campbell

SOURCE: A review of *The Cookcamp,* in *The New York Times Book Review,* May 5, 1991, p. 22.

Ernest Hemingway would have liked Gary Paulsen. At first.

They would have had lots to talk about together: the best way to sail a boat against a storm off Mexico, how to make a shelter in the north woods, why you should never throw a stick at a bear or turn your back on a moose. And—eventually—how a man can test himself against the wilderness. They would have agreed that the words of stories written about these things should be simple and clean and good and true. But when the talk got around to the joys of trapping and shooting, the evening would be over.

Gary Paulsen, a man who earned his way through college by trapping animals for the state of Minnesota, long ago decided that he would never kill things again. His books reveal a passionate belief in the cleansing power of a return to living in harmony with nature, especially if that means difficulty and danger. But the motivating force in his writing is compassion, not machismo. His young adult novels often focus on a young person's transformation through conquering despair and hardship—often, although not always, in the wilds.

The writer has lived his own themes. He has worked as a rancher, trapper, sailor and migrant farm laborer, and for several years he raised huskies and ran them in the Iditarod, that insanely grueling and dangerous dogsled race over 1,200 miles of Alaskan snow and ice (the subject of *Dogsong*). Although his settings are often the forests of Canada or his native Minnesota, he has also used places as disparate as a Mexican border town, a Montana sheep ranch and a North Dakota sugar-beet field. He understands serious cold and hunger and fear and fatigue—far beyond what most of us have ever experienced—and it shows in his fiction.

Yet it is an oversimplification to categorize him as a writer of survival stories for older children and teen-agers. An amazingly prolific writer, he has more than 60 books to his credit, including both adult and juvenile fiction and nonfiction. But it is 11 extraordinary novels for younger teen-agers, beginning with *Dancing Carl* in 1983, that earned both his literary and popular reputation. *Dogsong, Hatchet* and *The Winter Room* were Newbery Honor Books, and many of his novels have appeared on the American Library Association's list of best books for young adults.

In *The Cookcamp,* a book for readers in the middle grades, Mr. Paulsen has gone back to what appears to be an episode from his own childhood, the story of a 5-year-old boy's journey to a safe place in the woods. He uses the timeless, smooth-worn cadences of a folk tale. The prologue begins simply: "For a long time during a war his father was in the army and had to be away to fight, and the boy had to go live with his grandmother." The boy's mother, who has taken a job and a lover, cries, but pins a note on his jacket and puts him on the train. After a long and scary trip he arrives at a place in the forest where his grandmother is working as a cook for a rough crew of men building a road up into Canada.

From the first moment the boy's grandmother surrounds him with love and safety at the "cookcamp." She calls him her "little thimble" and gives him wonderful things to eat. He helps her serve platters of biscuits and pancakes to the huge men who come stomping into the dining room, spitting their wads of snuff into a can by the door and stuffing their dusty caps into the pockets of their bib overalls. They remind him of "big, polite bears" in the way they speak to his grandmother.

The boy has wonderful adventures at the cook camp. A chipmunk eats out of his hand; the men let him ride with them on their bulldozers and dump trucks and handle the controls; he learns to spit, and falls asleep on their big kindly laps while they play whist in the evening. Everything is as all right as it can possibly be—except that he misses his mother. So the last evening comes, the night before the day when he will go home. And all through that night his grandmother tells him stories from her life, sensing that she will never see this child as a boy again. In an epilogue Mr. Paulsen speaks in a different voice about a Norwegian-American matriarch, perhaps about his own grandmother—but it is clear that she is the woman in the story.

Told from the perspective of a very little boy, with utter simplicity and a grave humor, this short novel has an almost unbearable poignancy. "I'm here," says the grandmother. "I'll always be here." But she won't. We adults know it, and so do older children, the intended readers. Nevertheless, what sweet comfort it is to look back on that time of innocent safety before the struggle for survival began.

THE RIVER (1991)

Hazel Rochman

SOURCE: A review of *The River,* in *Booklist,* Vol. 87, No. 18, May 15, 1991, p. 1792.

In this sequel to *Hatchet,* one of the best and most popular books of the 1980s, Paulsen takes the wilderness adventure beyond self-preservation and makes teenager Brian Robeson responsible for saving someone else. It's a year later, and Brian, now 15, is persuaded to repeat what he did in *Hatchet*—survive for a period in the Canadian wilderness. This time, though, he won't be alone; Derek, a government psychologist, will take notes so that others can learn from Brian's experience. Everything goes well, in fact, too well; it's like a pleasant camping trip, until Derek is hit by lightning and lies in a coma. With no tools except a knife, Brian has to build a raft, navigate the river and the wild rapids, and haul Derek to the trading post about 100 miles downstream.

It's all very well for Paulsen to insist that luck is part of survival, but there's luck and then there's wild coincidence—are we really supposed to believe that Brian would find all the logs for the raft conveniently cut for him right there in a beavers' clearing? As usual, Paulsen overdoes the Hemingway-type cadences and sonorous repetitions, especially when he's talking about Life. But at its best, the terse, almost monosyllabic writing perfectly expresses the basic struggle in the woods. There's candor not only in the dark scene where Brian is tempted to ditch Derek and make it alone, but also in the undramatic final admission that Derek would probably have been all right even if Brian had not made the run. Young people (including the most reluctant readers) will find the survival detail as gripping as ever, and when rooted in physical fact—in what the final chapter title calls "Measurements"—the plain words tell a great story of rebirth and connection.

Publishers Weekly

SOURCE: A review of *The River,* in *Publishers Weekly,* Vol. 238, No. 24, May 31, 1991, p. 76.

Nearly two years after being marooned in the wilderness—the experience recounted in *Hatchet*—Brian agrees to go back, accompanied by Derek, a psychologist who wants to study the strategies and especially the mental toughness that brought Brian through. At first he chafes at the relative comforts, the lack of true challenge, this second time around. All that changes when Derek is struck by lightning and falls into a coma—Brian must raft Derek to the nearest outpost, 100 miles downriver.

In attempting this sequel Paulsen has set himself a difficult task, which he meets superbly. The new adventure is as riveting as its predecessor and yet, because of significant differences in the nature of its dramatic tension, is not merely a clone. The experiences of *Hatchet,* distilled by time, inform Brian's character throughout, so that the psychological terrain of the sequel is fresh and distinct. The older Brian is more reflective and accepting, and these qualities add new dimensions to his interactions with nature. And returning to the north effects a subtle but startling change: instantly, almost unconsciously, Brian finds himself absorbing every detail of the scene around him—taking the scent of the wind, reading the shape of each cloud—and in the process turning inward, finding words superfluous in the face of the wild. There is no dearth of action and physical suspense here, rendered in terse, heart-stopping prose. Paulsen, as always, pulls no punches: a scene in which Brian fantasizes about cutting Derek loose from the raft is as powerful as they come.

Hanna B. Zeiger

SOURCE: A review of *The River,* in *The Horn Book Magazine,* Vol. LXVII, No. 4, July-August, 1991, p. 459.

The images on the book jacket and the phrase "the sequel to *Hatchet*" will attract readers who loved the earlier book for the qualities of courage and resourcefulness that Brian showed in the face of life-threatening danger. These same readers deserve something better than the poorly conceived premise that begins this second book. A government survival school asks Brian to re-create his experiences in the wilderness so they can study his psychological processes. "'We teach what you did, or we try to. But the truth is, we have never done it and we don't know anybody who has ever done it. Not for real.'" Doesn't the government read newspapers, magazines, or books? Brian is drawn by this chance to test himself again, and, incredibly, his parents grant permission. In no time, he and Derek, a government psychologist, arrive at the chosen site. Because Brian has insisted that they send back all their gear and supplies for authenticity, they have nothing but a briefcase, a radio transmitter, and two knives. At this point, the fallacy in the premise is again apparent as Brian, now experienced and skilled at survival, goes about getting tools, food, and shelter organized while the psychologist makes notes and complains that Brian is not sharing his thoughts with him. When a sudden storm hits their camp, Derek is struck by lightning and thrown into a coma, and their transmitter is destroyed. Brian feels he must get Derek downriver to a trading post and medical help. Needing to make a raft—with no hatchet at hand, this time—he discovers logs of just the right size and shape left by beavers, lashes them into a raft, maneuvers Derek's dead weight onto the raft, and starts down the river. The short segment on the river rushes along with the vigor of Paulsen's best adventure writing. Brian fights the hallucinations of exhaustion and the real danger of rapids and rocks, surviving somehow to reach help. At this point, the author suddenly switches to a brief, third-person statistical account of the events and their outcome, and we never hear anything more of Brian's thoughts or feelings about his experiences. Fans of the author's work will have to wait for another Paulsen book for a better-written adventure story.

Mary Ann Capan

SOURCE: A review of *The River,* in *Voice of Youth Advocates,* Vol. 14, No. 3, August, 1991, p. 174.

Can you believe it? They want him to do it again. This time on purpose. Two years ago Brian had been stranded alone in the wilderness with nothing but a hatchet. For 54 days he relied on his own survival instincts, and there were many times when he wasn't sure he'd make it, wasn't sure he wanted to make it. Now, just when he is settled into a somewhat normal life, they want him to go back.

Government people who teach survival courses to astronauts and those in the military want to learn from Brian, really learn, how he survived. Derek, a psychologist, will go with Brian to watch, listen, and observe so that the government can do to a better job of training its people.

Brian agrees and after two weeks of planning, Derek and Brian are dropped off near a lake in the wilderness about 100 miles east of the lake where Brian's plane had previously crashed. The surroundings are similar to those from before except for a river flowing out of the lake to the south and east. On the third night out a violent thunderstorm hits. Derek is struck by a tremendous bolt of lightning when he reaches for the radio transmitter which serves as their only link with the outside world. He survives, but in a coma. The radio is dead. Brian, alone, must ensure their survival. He knows that he must get medical help for Derek soon or Derek will most likely die of dehydration. So Brian builds a raft, planning to float the two of them down river to the trading post he saw on their map.

Readers will not be disappointed with this satisfying sequel to *Hatchet* where we first met Brian. We already know Brian's capacity for survival. But this time, someone else's life depends upon Brian's ability to overcome nature. Readers vicariously ride with Brian in his race against time as he paddles down river. Paulsen encourages an over-the-shoulder view of this dangerous trip by describing with fine detail both the beauty and the power of the river. The rhythmic style that characterizes Paulsen's writing is found in the sounds of the river, in Derek's steady heartbeat, and in Brian's paddling. Paulsen is to be congratulated for constructing a sequel that is believable, not contrived. *Hatchet* is a coming-of-age story. *The River* tests Brian's mettle as an adult because he is responsible for a life other than his own. . . . Readable and tense, this story reveals another dimension of Brian and answers many of our questions about his life after "The Time."

📖 *THE MONUMENT* (1991)

Publishers Weekly

SOURCE: A review of *The Monument,* in *Publishers Weekly,* Vol. 238, No. 41, September 13, 1991, p. 81.

Rocky, an adopted, partly lame teenage girl, tells how a memorial to her small Kansas town's war dead came to be built and how her vision and those of the other residents were altered by the monument's artist. When Rocky first encounters Mick Strum, he is filthy and disheveled, sleeping off a drinking binge in his dilapidated car. But she is magnetically drawn to this unlikely seer and from him learns to observe freshly and to develop an artist's eye. In contrast to Paulsen's customary action-packed adventures, this novel is chiefly about ideas—featuring characters whose primary function seems to be expressing concepts about art and the artistic process. As such, the story has an over-intellectualized, sometimes pedantic air and may disappoint readers hoping for the gritty realism, veracity and raw power of Paulsen's best works.

Susan Knorr

SOURCE: A review of *The Monument,* in *School Library Journal,* Vol. 37, No. 10, October, 1991, pp. 146, 148.

Figuring she'll never get adopted because of her caramel-colored skin and crippled leg, Rocky finds herself chosen by Emma and Fred, a kind, indulgent, alcoholic couple from Bolton, Kansas. It's in Bolton that she finds her devoted dog, Python, who leads her to Mick, the rumpled artist hired to design a monument to the town's war dead and the person who changes Rocky's view of life, art, and the world. Through the drawings he makes in order to get a feel for the town's people and history, the citizens of Bolton see themselves and their surroundings in a new light, although they're not sure they like it. As Mick does with his sketches, Paulsen tells the story in quick, deft strokes. The gossip at the grain elevator on a summer day, Rocky's insecurities and toughness, and the varied characters are vividly yet succinctly conveyed. In just three days, Mick breezes into town, turns Rocky on to the power of art, and convinces the people of Bolton that a grove of trees will be an appropriate monument as well as an artistic statement. Avoiding a lot of artistic jargon, Paulsen carries readers along with his (and Mick's) strong images and enthusiasm. A powerful, affecting story with its comments on art and homage.

Roger Sutton

SOURCE: A review of *The Monument,* in *Bulletin of the Center for Children's Books,* Vol. 45, No. 4, December, 1991, p. 102.

Rocky had basically given up hope of being adopted ("it was my color and my left leg"), and she is pleasantly surprised by Fred and Emma, the middle-aged couple who take her in: "I think they love me and are very good to me and are completely drunk by nine o'clock every morning so that the world is just one, long alcohol haze for them, but it isn't so bad." Rocky's only real friend is a stray dog, Python, which she rescues from the sheriff, and there is little excitement in her small Kansas town until an artist, Mick, comes to design a memorial to the local boys killed in the Vietnam War. Mick is a drunk and a dreamer, and he shows Rocky that she is an artist. "Draw," he says. "It's what you do—draw." Paulsen's writing is clean and spare, etching, like Mick, the lines of the small town in precise and telling strokes. The characterization of Mick, though, is romanticized: despite his drinking and dishevelment, he is too much the Untamed Artist in a community of philistines, and the frenzied rage he unleashes in the townspeople who see, through his portraits, who they really are, is not convincing. Better are the smaller moments ("Mick went through town like a chalk storm, the little colored bits in one hand and the tablet in another"), in which Paulsen gives a solid sense to the work of creation.

Kathryn L. Havris

SOURCE: A review of *The Monument,* in *Voice of Youth Advocates,* Vol. 14, No. 5, December, 1991, p. 317.

In sparse, sensitive, moving prose, Paulsen illuminates a small town and its inhabitants' beautiful and ugly sides to create a tribute to art. Narrated by Rocky, a long-unwanted orphan adopted by unusual parents, and adopter of Python, an undesirable, mangy dog, this tale examines her awakening to the art all around, and to seeing things as they are or could be. She is a loner until the town decides it needs a monument to honor its war dead and commissions Mick Strum to create this memorial. Mick drinks a bit but his artistic ability allows him to see the soul of the town and sketch it for them, even when it is not as pretty as some of them think. He is a magical kind of person—Rocky sees him as a leprechaun—who brings to the surface what it is the town really wants for a monument. He " . . . knew that she had the hot worm in her . . . " from the moment she first walked up to him with his bottom sticking out of the station wagon window after his drunken arrival in town. Rocky wants to be an artist but doesn't know technique, and he can teach her. His guidance is to draw everything and anything. It is what Mick does because it is the only way for him to understand the town. But when he exhibits all his sketches on the night of the decision-making, there is great anger from the people. He has captured them in a way that only they are supposed to know themselves, a side not to be shown to the public even if it is common knowledge. From this anger he shows them what a monument could be, gives them the monument he wants to make, and the kind that they " . . . truly wanted and just needed to be shown." War is an ugly, disgusting business, but nations will wage it and the mothers and fathers whose children do come back from it will want help remembering them.

This book is not so much about war, or about Rocky and who and what she is, but impressions of how art creates and is created. It is life reflected in art or art reflected in life. Not art that you think is good for you, but that you need to be exposed to. Art that is all around that you only have to open your eyes and see, really see. This is a wonderful book that will make you feel special. It will also be a book to recommend for cross-curriculum education—both literature and art teachers will find joy in this. It is full of impressions, like *The Winter Room* and *The Cook Camp,* and full of the spirit of art that is yours for the looking.

THE HAYMEADOW (1992)

Betsy Hearne

SOURCE: A review of *The Haymeadow,* in *Bulletin of the Center for Children's Books,* Vol. 45, No. 9, May, 1992, p. 246.

Fourteen-year-old John's rite of passage is a summer alone in the mountains with six thousand sheep and four border collies to help out. The action is nonstop, as a rattlesnake, dog injury, stampede, flash flood, coyote pack, marauding bear, and various accidents follow in quick succession. John rises to each occasion, earning the respect he has long coveted from his taciturn father, who shows up a month into the summer and stays up all night talking—for the first time—about John's birth, his beautiful mother killed by a horse, and his grandfather, a cruel man whom John has idolized as heroic. This is in many respects formula fiction, but it's a successful formula that will have readers plunging over each cliffhanger into the next crisis until they finish the book. The protagonist is clearly imagined; the style is both consciously simple and dramatic; the dogs are appealing. There's even a touch of humor: "I don't know why it is, but if you have fifteen horses, twenty cows, and some sheep standing on a hill and a thunderstorm comes, lightning will hit the sheep. Every time. Things just happen to sheep." Not to mention their herders.

Joanne Schott

SOURCE: A review of *The Haymeadow,* in *Quill and Quire,* Vol. 58, No. 6, June, 1992, p. 39.

John hates sheep and is apprehensive when a ranch hand falls ill, leaving him the only one available to watch his father's sheep in their summer pasture. He longs to measure up to his legendary great-grandfather but confronts only his own inadequacy as one calamity follows another and a flash flood finally sweeps his camp wagon downstream. After restoring order, a period of peace allows John time to reflect. He begins to accept and

even enjoy the routine and discipline needed to keep things running. A bear later attacks the herd and John copes with the attack and its results with assurance. When his father comes to replenish supplies, he realizes John is ready to hear the unpleasant truth about the great-grandfather he had idolized, and their own father-son relationship begins to flourish.

Paulsen, three times a Newbery honour author, follows his frequent pattern of placing an adolescent boy in a situation in which survival depends on his own courage, strength, and intelligence, then creating a series of threats so he will have to use those resources. The disasters here seem almost too numerous, though none is unlikely in the setting of the Wyoming mountains. The action and drama make an exciting story and the characterization has depth. Since John's life has always included work and responsibility, he does not so much change as affirm and claim what has always been part of him.

Publishers Weekly

SOURCE: A review of *The Haymeadow,* in *Publishers Weekly,* Vol. 239, No. 25, June 1, 1992, pp. 63-4.

When John is 14, a shortage of hired hands compels him to spend the summer caring for several thousand sheep in a high-country meadow. Several days' ride from the ranch, John has only himself to rely on when disasters strike, and he learns that he is more resourceful and resilient than he'd guessed. The Newbery Honor-winning author writes with power and at times grace of the relationships between man and animal—whether examining John's custodianship of the sheep, his complex interdependence with his dogs and horses or his view of the creatures that prey on the flock. And, as in earlier novels, Paulsen describes taut scenes of physical drama and suspense. But the book's pacing is skewed—the first third is devoted to setting up the scene, after which the action is numbingly relentless—and a subplot concerning John's idealization of his great-grandfather and sudden intimacy with his father is forced and unconvincing.

Kirkus Reviews

SOURCE: A review of *The Haymeadow,* in *Kirkus Reviews,* Vol. LX, No. 12, June 15, 1992, p. 783.

Left in a remote mountain pasture to care for 6000 sheep, a Wyoming rancher's 14-year-old son has a typical Paulsen series of adventures. Tink, the loyal hand who usually watches the herd, is dying of cancer, and John's widowed dad is with him; the ranch's taciturn other hand helps get the sheep to the haymeadow and leaves John with little instruction. But the boy is capable and courageous; in just two days, he has to deal with a skunk, a rattlesnake, a wounded dog, a stampede, a flash flood, a pack of voracious coyotes, and an injury that nearly kills him; remarkably, he recovers with the loss of a few sheep and the labels off his canned goods—

only to confront a vicious bear. After 47 days, his dad comes to report that Tink, miraculously, is recovering; he plans to leave next morning but—after the first real talk father and son have ever had—decides to stay on for the summer's last weeks.

Good enough as an adventure; Paulsen's trademark run-on sentences keep it moving, and he certainly understands coping with the wild, though the perils here are so unbelievably many that they become laughable. Meanwhile, John's fixation on the self-reliant great-grandfather who founded the ranch is not well enough integrated with either the action or the present-day relationships to serve its ostensible purpose of motivating John's character and behavior. An entertaining yarn, but a minor literary effort.

A CHRISTMAS SONATA (1992)

Deborah Abbott

SOURCE: A review of *A Christmas Sonata,* in *Booklist,* Vol. 89, No. 1, September 1, 1992, p. 54.

Once again, as he did in **The Cookcamp,** Paulsen envisions a specific time through the eyes of an unnamed boy. As Christmas, 1943, approaches, the preschool child inadvertently makes two weighty discoveries, and this short novel intricately weaves them into a poignant emotional experience. First, an unpleasant neighbor of the boy, who dislikes children in general and the boy in particular, claims to be Santa Claus when caught dressed up as the holiday figure. Second, the boy's slightly older cousin Matthew, who doesn't believe in Santa, is dying. Because the boy's father is in Europe fighting the war, the boy and his mother travel to northern Minnesota to spend the holiday with Uncle Ben, Aunt Marilyn, and Matthew. While the boys savor the season as best they can, it is the adults who champion the theme that a willingness to believe can work miracles. Paulsen is a master of characterization and point of view. His ability to get inside the mind of a child and communicate his perceptions starkly, precisely and realistically is a powerful literary tool, and the descriptive first-person narrative paints a picture so vivid, no reader remains unmoved.

Publishers Weekly

SOURCE: A review of *Christmas Sonata,* in *Publishers Weekly,* Vol. 239, No. 40, September 7, 1992, pp. 69-70.

Paulsen renders an adult's reminiscence of a long-ago Christmas, introducing an unnamed narrator whose father is overseas, fighting in WWII. He and his mother spend the holiday with relatives, among them a young cousin who is dying. Christmas seems even less festive when the boy learns that Santa doesn't exist after all. Paulsen's style here is in sharp contrast to the terse

prose of his adventure novels—long, incantatory sentences, built on intentional repetition, convey the boy's turmoil and his wonder. The well-cushioned phrasing offsets the book's slightly adult sensibility, and the conclusion is rich enough to satisfy readers of all ages.

Kirkus Reviews

SOURCE: A review of *A Christmas Sonata,* in *Kirkus Reviews,* Vol. LX, No. 18, September 15, 1992, p. 1192.

Tapping his sources for **The Cookcamp** (1991) once again, Paulsen tells another evocative story about a small boy alone with his mother during WWII. It could be the same boy, perhaps a year later, who describes their long train journey to northern Minnesota to visit an aunt and uncle who live behind their country store. The boy is troubled by doubts: Before they left Chicago, he glimpsed a mean old neighbor, Mr. Henderson, dressed in a Santa suit. Is it still worth trying to be good if Mr. Henderson *is* Santa, or if Santa doesn't exist at all? Also, the boy's slightly older cousin Matthew—bedridden and known to be dying—is a subduing source of puzzlement: The boy's father might die in Europe, meaning that he would never come home—but Matthew is already home. What, then, can dying mean?

Skillfully and unsentimentally, Paulsen depicts the adults' grief as they prepare for Matthew's last Christmas through the perceptions of a narrator who is so young that he can't really comprehend, but is already a thoughtful and caring individual. The boys' friendly interaction—Matthew contrives games they can share and they worry together about Santa's existence—ring especially true. In the end, a Santa in whom the boys can believe does turn up; it's up to the reader to judge whether he's Uncle Ben's doing, or Paulsen's. A holiday heartwarmer that will appeal to a wide audience.

Jane Marino

SOURCE: A review of *A Christmas Sonata,* in *School Library Journal,* Vol. 38, No. 10, October, 1992, p. 43.

A tightly woven tale that builds quickly and imperceptibly to a quietly powerful climax. During World War II, the young narrator and his mother go out to rural Minnesota to spend Christmas with relatives, including his terminally ill cousin. The boy has many worries: his father's safety on the European front, Matthew's impending death, but most of all, his recently shattered belief in Santa Claus. His concern over that, plus the feeling that he should be good just in case, nag at him throughout his trip. He confides in Matthew, who at first seems to dismiss the issue but then seems distressed and then becomes obsessed by it. When both boys' anxieties are solved in a way neither imagined, it restores the narrator's faith in the magic of Christmas forever after. Paulsen's spare, disciplined prose transforms a seemingly slight incident into a moment strong in its impact. His child's-eye view of the world renders the denouement even more powerful with its stark, unvarnished, yet innocent, telling of events.

NIGHTJOHN (1993)

Hazel Rochman

SOURCE: A review of *Nightjohn,* in *Booklist,* Vol. 89, No. 8, December 15, 1992, pp. 727-28.

In this story Paulsen exposes two popular lies about slavery: that slaves were really content, well cared for, ignorant, and childlike, happily singing on the old plantation, and that brave, resourceful slaves escaped all the time and it was easy. He tells the story in the voice of 12-year-old Sarny, born a slave, the property of Clel Waller, whom Sarny and the other slaves are forced to call "master." Sarny's mother had been sold when the child was four "because she was a good breeder, and Waller he needed the money." In quiet, simple words, Sarny tells of daily atrocity: public whippings, unbroken labor, animal-like living conditions, and, for a woman, constant rape. Sarny tries to keep secret the fact that she's started menstruating, because it means she will be sent to the breeding shed. The conditions are historically accurate, but the question arises—as with books about the Holocaust—How do you write about such cruelty and suffering? Paulsen uses no rhetoric, but some of the gruesome scenes of dismemberment and the close-ups of beatings given nude slaves sensationalize the violence. What gives the story transcendence is the character Nightjohn, who fires Sarny with hope. He once escaped north to freedom, and now he's come back to teach slaves what is fiercely forbidden them—reading. When he's caught showing Sarny the alphabet, two of his toes are cut off, but he escapes again. A final nighttime scene of Sarny with a group of slaves in a secret underground pit school is lit with the courage of the human spirit.

Frances Bradburn

SOURCE: A review of *Nightjohn,* in *Wilson Library Bulletin,* Vol. 67, No. 5, January, 1993, pp. 87-8.

Paulsen is best known for two styles of writing: compact adventure novels and shorter, lyrical books almost tone-poem in nature. *Nightjohn* is neither of these. The story itself is told by twelve-year-old Sarny, Nightjohn's first pupil when he returns to slavery after having escaped north to freedom. Nightjohn returns to the Waller plantation and to the life of a slave in order to teach other slaves to read, "Cause to know things, for us to know things is bad for them. We get to wanting and when we get to wanting it's bad for them. They thinks we want what they got." He first teaches Sarny the letter *A* and its sounds *ayyy* and *ahhh;* then *B,* all the while admonishing the young girl to carefully hide her knowledge.

Reading meant dismemberment. A slave would lose a thumb—or a toe or a foot—if he or she was found reading or teaching another slave to read.

The inevitable occurs. In her excitement at learning to spell, write, and read the word *BAG,* Sarny fails to notice Waller's approach—and the torture begins. The white slave owner hangs Mammy from the tree until the end of the day, when he hitches the naked woman to his buggy and orders her to take him for a ride. When Nightjohn can no longer bear to see the older woman's struggle under the buggy whip, he confesses that he has been the one teaching Sarny to read. Waller orders a toe from each of the slave's feet hacked off. Dismemberment is the price extracted for the light of learning.

With *Nightjohn,* Paulsen has opened himself to several avenues of criticism. The most obvious is the amount of graphic violence throughout the book. Paulsen pulls no punches. In the kind of graphic detail for which he is famous, he exposes the evil plantation owner's excessive cruelty—the dogs starved and trained to crave human flesh, the merciless beatings of men and women alike while they hung from chains and stocks, the amputation of limbs, the "breeding" of young slave women. By the time the book is completed—and it can be read easily in one sitting—the revulsion, the horror, the awe, and the triumph are complete. Even as Nightjohn is recuperating from his trauma, he teaches Sarny the letter *H*—slavery is one letter closer to extinction. While the story is based on historical research, it is still horrifyingly violent. Reading magnifies this violence—the printed word is far more effective than television or movies, for it triggers the imagination. And the imagination is hard to control in *Nightjohn.* Many adults and adolescents alike will question the need for the novel's extensive, graphic violence.

A second, more subtle risk for Paulsen is that he is a white western author writing from the southern slave's perspective in what he perceives to be an African-American dialect. The potential exists for him to alienate both blacks and southerners. African Americans might resent him for telling a story that they feel may be more appropriately told by one of their own; southerners might resent and be embarrassed by the subtle "guilt by association" syndrome: the assumption that all southerners come from a long line of evil, cruel plantation owners who tortured slaves.

There is little doubt that *Nightjohn* will make all who read it uncomfortable. It cannot do otherwise. But, it is a story that must be told if middle readers are to begin to understand racially where we are as a nation today, the lengths we all have traveled, and the distance we have yet to go. Fortunately for all of us, Gary Paulsen has had the courage to risk censure in order to tell a powerful story in a style only he is capable of. May the adults who choose middle reader materials and suggest books to early adolescents have the courage to overlook their own fears and biases and provide this book for their patrons. It is worth the risk.

Kirkus Reviews

SOURCE: A review of *Nightjohn,* in *Kirkus Reviews,* Vol. LXI, No. 1, January 1, 1993, p. 67.

A searing picture of slavery, sometime in the 19th century at an unspecified place in the South. Sarny, young enough not to have experienced the rape that will come inexorably with child-bearing age, tells how she learned to read, and at what cost. Nightjohn has escaped more than once, but courageously returns to share his knowledge with those who have no way of knowing the world beyond their plantation. Caught, he arrives as a slave driven by the viciously cruel master, Clel Waller. Sarny has been warned of the dangers of learning to read, and knows the terrible punishments are not empty threats but realities; still, Nightjohn easily persuades her to learn—which seems more plausible than Sarny's careless writing of letters with her toe in the dirt, so that Waller catches her. Fiendishly, he chooses to punish her adopted "mammy," thus impelling a confession from Nightjohn—who survives his own brutal penalty to escape and return to teach again. The compelling events are ineradicably memorable. Paulsen begins by saying that, "Except for variations in time and character identification and placement, [they] are true and actually happened." But like that last phrase, some of the violence here is redundant: it's not necessary to describe *three* different but equally terrible deaths suffered by runaways set upon by dogs to make the point. Still, the anguish is all too real in this brief, unbearably vivid book.

Susan L. Rogers

SOURCE: A review of *Nightjohn,* in *School Library Journal,* Vol. 39, No. 3, March, 1993, p. 223.

Sarny is a slave girl, 12 years old according to Mammy's notched stick, but not yet cursed with the "trouble"—the onset of menstruation that will mark her as a breeder—so she is still allowed by the cruel owner "to be as a child." Sarny learns about the world furtively, knowing that any open display of curiosity or intelligence could mean torture or death. She overhears whispers about a new field hand recently purchased; he comes soon after, shackled and naked, covered with scars. This is Nightjohn. Secretly, he teaches Sarny to read, one letter at a time, and she carries this gift like the rarest jewels, until the day the master catches her writing one precious word in the dirt. She is beaten, Mammy is harnessed and whipped, and the master uses a hammer and chisel to take off John's middle toes. More determined than ever, they continue the lessons, until the day John escapes for good, only to return under cover of night, showing her the way to his hidden school in the forest and knowledge. Clearly, this is strong stuff. These matter-of-fact descriptions of human misery and senseless torture are probably unlike anything this age group has read or heard about. Few history classes cover this aspect of African-American slavery, and few novels or movies cut to the heart of the matter so elegantly and so

eloquently. In just 92 pages of fairly large print and simple phrases, Paulsen exposes the horrors of slavery, along with pointing out the lengths some have taken to acquire the skills that most people take for granted. The stunning impact of this novel is similar to that of Toni Morrison's *Beloved. Nightjohn* should be required reading (and discussing) for all middle grade and high school students.

DOGTEAM (1993)

Publishers Weekly

SOURCE: A review of *Dogteam,* in *Publishers Weekly,* Vol. 240, No. 35, August 30, 1993, p. 94.

The distinguished author of **Dogsong** and **Hatchet** somewhat strains for effect in this prose poem describing a night run with a team of dogs. Each stanza begins with a kind of chapter heading ("The dance," "Into the night," etc.) that signals the oncoming sights and sounds amid the eerie glacial expanses. Gary Paulsen's rhythms mimic the panting, brisk pace of the running dogs, as in the description of the wolves they encounter: "they run with us, pace the dogs, pace our hearts and our lives and then turn, turn away in the blue dark." The technique, however, is easily overdone: "Away from camp, away from people, away from houses and light and noise and into only the one thing, into only winter-night they fly away and away and away." Ruth Wright Paulsen's dogs look illuminated from within, rendered as they are in bright grays and yellows with detailed pen and ink, contrasting sharply with the soft, spare background. The landscape, on the other hand, remains impenetrable, no more likely to envelop the reader than is the highly personal text. Only in the crisp, poetic prose of an endnote does Paulsen—who has twice raced in the Iditarod—finally convey his exhilaration.

Carla Kozak

SOURCE: A review of *Dogteam,* in *School Library Journal,* Vol. 39, No. 10, October, 1993, p. 120.

There are few things more beautiful than a moonlit winter night, and Paulsen has captured that, plus the thrill of speeding across the snow via dogsled, in a text as crisp, clean, and magical as such evenings. It is the dogs' emotions, as much as the narrator's, that are evoked: the animals strain at their harnesses, singing in anticipation of the run. Ruth Wright Paulsen's illustrations show the nuances of canine behavior in the positions of ears, tails, lolling tongues, and flashing paws. The swift, strong, smiling creatures are one with the white and blue-black night; on one double-page spread, the aurora borealis in ghostly greens is their background. *Dogteam* reads aloud beautifully, but its poetry will be best understood through one-on-one sharing with an adult. All who see and hear it will, for a few moments, join in the winter run. Children who live in areas without snow will experience the wonder of its season through this book. For those living in cold climates, it may inspire a night-time ski, or skate, or at least a moonlit walk, and they will understand the dogs' dilemma: although it is comforting to come home to warmth and firelight, something in them yearns to run forever.

Carolyn Phelan

SOURCE: A review of *Dogteam,* in *Booklist,* Vol. 90, No. 6, November 15, 1993, p. 633.

As Paulsen takes his dog sled for a run on a winter's night, he carries readers along through the moonlit landscape. Immediacy and brevity mark each part of the poetic telling of the adventure—harnessing the exuberant dogs, riding through the woods and across a frozen lake, watching the wolves silently appear and disappear, and returning home. The illustrations include pen-and-ink drawings of the dogs, the sled, and sometimes the driver, tinted with watercolor and set against watercolor backgrounds. The painting is more effective than the pen-and-ink work, and the two art styles don't always blend well. As a whole, however, the book re-creates an experience unusual in picture books. Teachers might try reading it to children who consider themselves too old for picture books, particularly those who know Paulsen's other work.

DUNC AND AMOS AND THE RED TATTOOS; DUNC AND THE SCAM ARTISTS ("Culpepper Adventures" series, 1993)

Eunice Weech

SOURCE: A review of *Dunc and Amos and the Red Tattoos* and *Dunc and the Scam Artists,* in *School Library Journal,* Vol. 39, No. 10, October, 1993, pp. 126-27.

Glib Duncan Culpepper and accident-prone Amos Binder, who is infatuated with the indifferent Melissa Hansen, continue their bumbling amateur sleuthing in these two additions to the series. In *Red Tattoos,* the boys are at Camp Gitchie Goomie where they overhear a plot to get rid of the camp director. After a series of mishaps, they lead the police to a band of black marketeers. The funnier and more plausible of the two stories is *Scam Artists.* Dunc and Amos befriend a woman who they fear will be the next victim of a scam artist who has been bilking elderly citizens out of their life savings by pretending to be a long-lost relative. In a plot twist, the nice old lady turns out to be an accomplice to the crook. Both stories follow the series pattern: Amos ends up battered and bruised, a victim of his own clumsiness, and Dunc is always able to talk his friend into trying his schemes by mentioning the possibility of impressing the beloved Melissa. Paulsen moves the action along by presenting some scenes in after-the-fact dialogue. These fast-paced, humorous stories with snappy dialogue and

likable characters will appeal to reluctant middle-school readers.

SISTERS/HERMANAS (1993)

Roger Sutton

SOURCE: A review of *Sister/Hermanas,* in *Bulletin of the Center for Children's Books,* Vol. 47, No. 3, November, 1993, p. 94.

In this tidy little fable, two fourteen-year-old girls in Houston, one an illegal immigrant who works as a streetwalker, the other a frosted-blonde beauty who works at her looks, are equally manipulated by a culture that values nothing in women but their sex. Ironically, they're also manipulated by their author, who never gets beyond the stereotypes of a devout Mexican girl (Rosa) who lights a candle to Baby Jesus and then hits the streets, and a privileged Anglo girl (Traci) driven by her mother to be the perfect cheerleader and beauty pageant winner. Rosa and Traci's stories alternate in brief but portentously written chapters; their worlds collide when the Traci finds Rosa hiding from the police behind a rack of clothes in a fancy dress shop. In a flash of gratuitous epiphany, Traci realizes that "we are the same," but Rosa goes off with the cops while Traci, enlightened if not empowered, picks out a new red dress. While the book might have possibilities as an elementary exercise in consciousness raising, its lessons come too easily. The girls *are* the same: both cardboard victims of a preachy story. The book will be published in a flip/flop English/Spanish edition—two for the price of one.

Delia A. Culberson

SOURCE: A review of *Sisters/Hermanas,* in *Voice of Youth Advocates,* Vol. 16, No. 5, December, 1993, pp. 297-98.

Award-winning writer Paulsen has crafted a sensitive tale of two teenage girls from totally different social and economic backgrounds but whose lives run along strangely parallel lines. Rosa, a fourteen-year-old illegal immigrant from Mexico who lives in Houston, is illiterate, speaks no English and lives in fear of being caught by the police and deported. She makes her living as a prostitute, and although streetwise and clever, she retains a child-like purity of heart, has a simple but deep religious faith, and is devoted to her mother in Mexico to whom she sends money regularly and for whom she prays and lights candles in church. Rosa's dreams of leaving this type of life and becoming a glamorous and famous fashion model help her endure her grim circumstances and the harsh treatment she often receives at the hands of her clients. She is keenly aware how important good looks and appearance are in her business and takes great care to look sexy and provocative when she goes out to work in the evenings.

Traci, also fourteen-years-old and a middle-grade school student, comes from a wealthy family, lives in a Houston suburb, and when the story opens, she is carefully grooming herself in preparation for high school cheerleading tryouts where she will be competing against nineteen other contestants. In Traci's world, and according to her shallow mother, beauty and popularity are the most important things in life, the real keys to success, and to be a cheerleader is definitely a sign of success. Her mother started her early on various types of pageants, pretty child shows, modeling shows, etc. and since the age of five, Traci has been conscious of her appearance and has worked constantly on her looks. Now her mother pays a professional dance arranger to teach Traci a unique cheerleading routine, different and better than all the others, and, naturally, expects her daughter to put on a topnotch performance and be chosen as the very best cheerleader.

Traci's privileged lifestyle and Rosa's rough world collide when Rosa changes the usual route to her work one evening in order to avoid a cruising police car, and walks into a shopping mall. When a mall security guard notices her flashy appearance, becomes suspicious and moves towards her, Rosa runs into the fancy department store where Traci and her mother are shopping for new clothes after the cheerleading tryouts and hides under a rack of dresses. Traci discovers Rosa, and the startled girls come face to face with each other. Although the meeting lasts only a few seconds and no words are exchanged, there is an instantaneous empathy, an instinctive feeling of recognition, of sisterhood, between the two girls with the intuitive knowledge that in many ways they are the same. Traci's immediate reaction is to help Rosa avoid detection; however, Traci's mother also sees the Mexican girl, pulls Traci away and frantically calls for the security guard.

Rosa and Traci's stories are told in alternate chapters, and Paulsen has done a masterful job of creating two well-developed, believable characters trapped in environments where the elements of beauty, youth and popularity have the highest value, and are deemed essential to survival. This is an absorbing tale that rings all too true with real-life pressures and stressful situations that present no easy choices.

Ann Welton

SOURCE: A review of *Sisters/Hermanas,* in *School Library Journal,* Vol. 40, No. 1, January, 1994, p. 132.

Rosa is 14. She lives in Houston, Texas. She has dreams and aspirations. She is an illegal alien, and a prostitute. Traci is also 14. She, as well, lives in Houston, the privileged child of wealthy parents. With her huge wardrobe, social graces, and continual coaching from her mother, she is headed for success. Indeed, she has no option. She, too, is subjected to a form of prostitution that denies her any real determination of her own. The narrative engineers a brief meeting between the two girls

as Rosa flees the police in a mall. In the space of a few seconds, Traci realizes her kinship with this unknown Hispanic girl, a kinship that is quickly denied and buried by her mother as Rosa is dragged away by security guards. Alternating chapters tell the story of each adolescent in an authoritative third-person voice. Certainly a good discussion starter, the book is nonetheless didactic. The English prose is spare, and the message apparent from the opening of the second chapter, in which Traci is introduced. The parallels drawn between the two girls are too emphatic for the slight story to carry without stress. The Spanish version is a direct, workmanlike translation of the English. It tells the same story, but with little grace. Given the sociological nature of the text, this might be a better choice for high school social-studies classes than for literature study or pleasure reading.

Mandy Cheetham

SOURCE: A review of *Sisters/Hermanas,* in *Magpies,* Vol. 9, No. 5, November, 1994, p. 33.

In a dramatic conclusion to this powerful but understated short novel, two 14-year-old girls from seemingly vastly different backgrounds briefly recognise the unholy bond which exists between them. But are they so different? Rosa, an illegal immigrant from Mexico City, supports herself and her mother by selling her body on the streets. Traci, spoilt and pampered, and driven by her mother's unfulfilled ambitions, is preparing her body to become a top beauty queen.

The denouement to this compelling novel is the realisation that the future of both girls is dependent on the exploitation of their bodies. Told in Spanish and English, the stark episodic style of the text may not appeal to young adults who prefer a straightforward and conclusive narrative. The novel reflects changing social conditions in the United States caused by the influx of immigrants from Hispanic countries and in the manner of a short story, illuminates and provokes the reader.

HARRIS AND ME: A SUMMER REMEMBERED (1993)

Carol Fox

SOURCE: A review of *Harris and Me: A Summer Remembered,* in *Bulletin of the Center for Children's Books,* Vol. 47, No. 5, January, 1994, pp. 164-65.

The story begins as the unnamed hero, a friendless victim of alcoholic and abusive parents, bounces along in a 1949 pickup that's taking him to live on his uncle's farm. There, he meets the dirtiest farmhand he has ever seen and a family that eats, works, and sleeps with the unrefined intensity of backwoods heathens. This place has the pig poop, cowpies, muck, and acrid smells of which farms are really made. More than that, it has

Harris, a fearless, foolish boy who lures our thoughtful but still unschooled hero into entanglements with the environment that more often than not send the boys flying into the air while a bemused and unperturbed nature waits patiently for them to learn the rules. The boys turn pig pens into games of "GI Joe," play Tarzan from the hayloft, and emulate Gene Autry in an incident that leaves Harris with the breath knocked out of him and the reader breathless with laughter. Through it all, the lonely hero imperceptibly learns about belonging. Twain wrote ironically about a veneer of civility that covered a thoughtless and evil society of humans; Paulsen has created an opposite world. The farm life here is cruel, crude, and harsh with no nuances. There are bleating animals, profane expletives, and descriptions that will turn your stomach. But there is also hilarity, untamed confidence, genuine concern for others, and a belief in goodness—one of the most optimistic fictional worlds to invite young visitors in a long while.

Lee Bock

SOURCE: A review of *Harris and Me: A Summer Remembered,* in *School Library Journal,* Vol. 40, No. 1, January, 1994, p. 132.

A nostalgic journey through a boy's breakneck summer. Told by a narrator recalling his experiences the summer he was 11, the stories begin with his being dropped by a deputy at the farm home of a distant relative. "We heard your folks was puke drunks, is that right?" asks the beguiling and reckless nine-year-old Harris almost immediately. Of course they are, but that dismal fact of life is forgotten nearly at once as Harris leads the two of them off on one wild adventure after another. As one might suspect from Paulsen, there are no ordinary characters residing on this backwoods farm: there's Vivian, the ornery, kicking cow; 300 pound pigs who don't look kindly on wrestling matches with boys; Ernie, the attack-rooster; Louie, the hired hand with strange table manners and an artistic streak; Buzzer, his pet lynx; and Harris's older sister, Glennis, who is constantly whacking him for swearing. (At times the language does get a little salty.) The plot is a loosely constructed romp with each chapter an episode that's fast paced, highly descriptive, and funny. Using headings such as "In which war is declared and honor established," Paulsen raises readers' expectations and sets the tone for the action to follow. Some stories push beyond believability and edge into tall-tale territory, but it doesn't matter, for this is storytelling in the tradition of Twain and Harte, memorable and humorous and very telling of human nature.

Joanne Schott

SOURCE: A review of *Harris and Me: A Summer Remembered,* in *Quill and Quire,* Vol. 60, No. 3, March, 1994, p. 83.

The narrator of this memoir has been sent away from

his alcoholic parents yet again and is spending the summer on a farm with his cousin Harris, who works hard, plays hard, and swears hard, for which he is cuffed hard by his sister, Glennis.

Harris introduces his city cousin to farm work and play with generally disastrous results. Harris is a great admirer of Gene Autry, who is featured in the only available local entertainment, and his scheme to imitate his hero's flying leaps onto the back of a running horse "to save the rustlers" is almost the last thing the boys ever do. Despite trick-playing on both sides and a painful revenge exacted for a lie Harris told, a strong bond grows between the boys.

Gary Paulsen's rich and original prose creates a hilarious and sometimes touching drama of boyhood played out during a mythic summer that is self-contained and perfect, one that even the principal actors could never revisit.

Women's roles are confined mostly to cooking, and the identity the boys assign to the pigs when they act out World War II battles in the pigsty is not pretty. And remember, Harris swears. But those who have smiled all through the book in the company of the two primary characters will value the authenticity of Paulsen's voice. It is not political correctness that makes literature.

Karen Jameyson

SOURCE: A review of *Harris and Me: A Summer Remembered,* in *Magpies,* Vol. 9, No. 3, July, 1994, p. 31.

Harris and Me? "Hilarity and Me" is more likely a title for Gary Paulsen's knee-slapping nostalgic romp.

The eleven-year-old narrator, who remains nameless throughout, has been sent away from his alcoholic parents to spend a summer with some distant relatives on their farm. Little does he suspect the episodes in store once he makes the acquaintance of his nine-year-old cousin. Whether Harris is more like Huck Finn, Booth Tarkington's Penrod, or even a male version of Ramona is uncertain. But there is no doubt about his capacity for spectacular mischief. Spectacular.

We watch their pursuit of mice with the resident farm bobcat, for instance; their attack on the "commie japs"—the three-hundred-pound pigs (who win, by the way); the urinating on the electric fence episode; and a fair number of others. But most of all we become well acquainted with Harris, his remarkably coarse language, determination and indomitable spirit.

Set in American farmland in the 1950, the novel reverberates with a feeling of the era, the farm and the eccentric characters themselves. Paulsen's prose remains as controlled and taut as it is in *Hatchet* and much of his other work, his voice as vivid and authentic as can be—with the added bonus of explosive humour.

📖 *THE CAR* (1994)

Kay Weisman

SOURCE: A review of *The Car,* in *Booklist,* Vol. 90, No. 15, April 1, 1994, pp. 1436-37.

Abandoned by both his parents, 14-year-old Terry Anders decides to assemble the pieces of a car kit—a Blakely Bearcat—and take off on his own. Then he meets Waylon Jackson, a 45-year-old Vietnam veteran who has spent most of the past 20 years trucking around the U.S., and the two decide to join forces. Their cross-country odyssey has great impact on Terry: They visit an old man who recites history as if he were a participant, dine at a religious commune, and tour the site of the Battle of Little Big Horn. Waylon is a well-developed, if somewhat enigmatic, character, given to violent and sometimes unpredictable outbreaks of temper. Flashback memories interspersed between early chapters reveal that a traumatic incident in Vietnam has left him mentally unstable, and references to government checks suggest some kind of permanent disability. Although the trip works well as a metaphor for Terry's journey toward maturity, not all the story's elements are as well developed. Terry's parents seem to exist mostly as a convenient plot device rather than a source of real conflict, and Waylon's homosexuality is mentioned but never explored. Despite these flaws, *The Car* is a well-written, thoughtful coming-of-age novel.

Kirkus Reviews

SOURCE: A review of *The Car,* in *Kirkus Reviews,* Vol. LXII, No. 7, April 1, 1994, p. 483.

Paulsen's latest comes close to a classic teenage male fantasy of fleeing from home to seek independence and self. Both Terry's parents leave the same day; each phones asking him to tell the other. Since their quarrels have always obliterated any urge to parent it's no loss, especially since Terry has $1,000 and a kit to build a car. After handily putting it together and teaching himself to drive, the 14-year-old heads west. He picks up Waylon, an aging, footloose vet whose psychic wounds date to carrying out termination orders against civilians in 'Nam (as depicted in vignettes entitled "Memories," early on); Waylon takes Terry to Wayne, a war buddy who tries to temper Waylon's sporadic rages against injustice. Hoping to kindle the boy's curiosity, the two take him on a journey that includes meeting an ancient man who tells tales from US history and a madam who explains that another friend (also a prostitute) has died of AIDS; a poker game; a fundamentalist commune where women are rigidly oppressed; and the site of Custer's defeat. Scenes and camaraderie are vivid, the narrative pungent. Kids will be enthralled by Terry's freedom and his friends' aura of mystery and loyalty; they may also sympathize with Waylon's violent, though righteous, anger without understanding its terrible consequences. In an inconclusive ending, Terry heads back into a conflict with some local toughs that may well end like Custer's. What can he look forward to if he survives? Paulsen doesn't offer much. There's a strong conscience propelling this novel, but it's buried so deep that YAs caught up in the action may miss it.

Betsy Hearne

SOURCE: A review of *The Car,* in *Bulletin of the Center for Children's Books,* Vol. 47, No. 9, May, 1994, pp. 297-98.

"He was alone. His name was Terry Anders. He was fourteen years old, living in Cleveland, Ohio, and his parents had left him." This is vintage Paulsen, with the isolated boy undertaking a journey not with a boat (*The Voyage of the Frog*), dogs (*The Haymeadow,*) or implement (*Hatchet,*) but with a car he's built from a sophisticated kit with and a middle-aged Shakespeare-quoting hippy he's picked up who's also a Vietnam-vet fighting machine and student-of-life ("I am learning" is a favorite phrase). The two of them—three, since the car's an important character—pick up the veteran's buddy, who owns a super-souped Harley Davidson and who summarizes the two men's friendship, which verges on telepathic, with a kind of tough, offhand casualness that the author often uses to take readers by surprise. "Oh, we go back a long ways. Did a little war, a little peace together. There was a time when he thought he was in love with me. . . . Yeah. He's gay. You didn't know?" The point is that Waylon's homosexuality isn't important (that's all we ever hear about it), and it's Terry's job to figure out what is important about the characters or situations that highlight their odyssey, including a wise old Native American living alone on the prairie, a religious commune that oppresses women, an archetypal poker game that brings in some of the money they travel on, the brothel of a prostitute who had a heart of gold before she died of AIDS, the site of Custer's last stand ("The soldiers were the losers. And the Indians, of course"), and a series of drunken rednecks and/or cowboys who threaten the voyagers and end up bloody and bruised at the hands of the two martial arts experts. A lot of posing goes on here, but macho kids, to whom there are not enough young adult books directed in this world, will soak it up.

Catherine M. Dwyer

SOURCE: A review of *The Car,* in *Voice of Youth Advocates,* Vol. 17, No. 2, June, 1994, p. 89.

In *The Car,* Paulsen has written another coming of age novel for YAs. Fourteen-year-old Terry Anders's relationship with his parents is so bad it takes him a few days to realize he has been abandoned. When he is finally contacted by each parent, both assume that he is with the other and Terry does nothing to correct this assumption. Instead he goes out to the garage and begins to build a Blakely Bearcat. The "Cat" is a kit car which was given to Terry's father. Once the car is assembled Terry sets off from Cleveland to locate his uncle in Portland. Along the way Terry picks up a hitchhiker, Waylon Jackson, who is a Vietnam vet. Together they travel west eventually picking up a friend of Waylon's, Wayne. The three of them continue the journey attempting to learn about people, America, and themselves.

When I first started this novel I thought it would be similar to *In Country* by Bobbie Ann Mason or *The Wall* by Eve Bunting. But this story is more about growing up and learning than it is about Vietnam or even about being abandoned. Waylon and Wayne never discuss their Vietnam experiences with Terry. Wayne tells Terry that Waylon is gay but that story line is not expanded upon. One of the high points of Paulsen's earlier books like *Hatchet* and *The Voyage of the Frog* was the exploration of how the character felt: fear, loss, frustration. Terry just takes everything in stride. Despite this drawback the story is told with Paulsen's usual grace and detail and YAs will enjoy the adventures that the three companions experience. YAs will also be drawn to the precise description of building a car. . . .

📖 FATHER WATER, MOTHER WOODS: ESSAYS ON FISHING AND HUNTING IN THE NORTH WOODS (1994)

Frances Bradburn

SOURCE: A review of *Father Water, Mother Woods: Essays on Fishing and Hunting in the North Woods,* in *Booklist,* Vol. 90, No. 21, July, 1994, p. 1935.

In his introduction, Paulsen confesses that numerous inquiries about the germination of *Hatchet* (1987) became the seed of this book. Yet, as you read the graphic descriptions of hunting, camping, fishing, and the natural life of Paulsen's childhood in general, you realize that this seed has been in all of Paulsen's books, in all of Paulsen's life. The woods, the water, are the nurturing forces behind the man he has become. The most obvious correlation is the erstwhile boyhood summer camping trip, a fiasco in which five boys board one rickety boat with almost enough food and gear to swamp it. Far down the river, the boat hits a submerged log, sinking immediately and the boys are left struggling for shore. Once on land, they are engulfed in mosquitoes and indecision. How do they get home? But all sections are vintage Paulsen—the seasonal fishing trips, each portion of the year highlighted by a different fish, from sucker and "bull" to rock bass and walleye; the low-key humor of the incidents of the missed shot and the South American foreign exchange student; and the sensitive grief over the killed duck and bow-and-arrow-slain doe. This book is obviously a feast for the outdoor lover—the hunter, fisher, or camper—but it will also draw those who love the beauty of the carefully crafted description, so detailed and vivid that the reader can feel the warming of spring days and taste the bullhead skin "crackling and tasting of butter." Above all, *Father Water, Mother*

Woods is the essence of Paulsen, the revelation of the author himself and why he writes as he does.

Joel Shoemaker

SOURCE: A review of *Father Water, Mother Woods: Essays on Fishing and Hunting in the North Woods,* in *School Library Journal,* Vol. 40, No. 8, August, 1994, pp. 178-79.

Paulsen begins this collection of compelling memoirs with a foreword that reflects on the genesis of his novel *Hatchet*. He concludes by poignantly expressing doubts about the moral correctness of hunting. In between, he pares away the layers of his life, revealing a lost kid who sought sanctuary in friends and the outdoors. In half of the selections, he relates the joys of fishing. There's one essay on camping as comic disaster during high summer; the rest are about hunting. All are intensely personal and steeped in a bygone time of handset pins in a bowling alley, lack of equal rights for African Americans, corporal punishment, dress codes, and ducktail haircuts. Readers of the author's earlier works will hear echoes as old as *Winterkill* in Paulsen's description of snagging fish by the hydropower dam. The metaphor of life as a dance; his characteristic good humor; and the frequent references to blood, madness, prostitution, farts, and beer will strike a familiar chord, as will the seasonal structure through which the essays cycle. The pieces are rooted in the details of a youth spent in search of perfection: the perfect cast, perfect catch, perfect shot. Equally on target are descriptions of the pain of feeling the outsider, of being a failure at school, and of being ashamed of his parents' drunkenness. This book will appeal to Paulsen's many fans, to lovers of the outdoors, and to students of the essay.

Kirkus Reviews

SOURCE: A review of *Father Water, Mother Woods: Essays on Fishing and Hunting in the North Woods,* in *Kirkus Reviews,* Vol. LXII, No. 16, August 15, 1994, p. 1137.

Like the adolescent boys that are their target audience, these reminiscences of boyhood hunting and fishing are awkward and intense. Paulsen (*Harris and Me: A Summer Remembered,* 1993) portrays the Minnesota rivers and forests where he and his friends sought adventure in the late 1940s as more than sites to snag fish or bag grouse: They were settings in which the boys both escaped and confronted life. Paulsen, the neglected son of alcoholic parents, identifies himself as "one of the wasted ones." Showing how he and his companions sought salvation in the wilderness, "where our lives didn't hurt," Paulsen's most powerful moment comes in an essay about shooting his first deer: "He wasn't sure what he expected if he actually hit a deer. . . . When he missed he swore and made up an excuse. . . . But he had no excuse for hitting a deer. And he wanted one badly."

This is the same sense of shock and of the dreadful burden of freedom in the wild that we encounter reading Frost or Twain, and it's exquisite. Otherwise this book lurches between rambling recollection and vivid recreation of the past and is often marred by stiff writing and passive constructions.

Like much of the hunting it describes, this book has one hit among numerous misses.

Mary Ann Capan

SOURCE: A review of *Father Water, Mother Woods: Essays on Fishing and Hunting in the North Woods,* in *Voice of Youth Advocates,* Vol. 17, No. 4, October, 1994, p. 234.

This is a collection of memorable stories from the author's childhood years in northern Minnesota. This master storyteller relates incidents of fishing: along the Ninth Street bridge, on the frozen river, as well as camping and fishing expeditions downstream. He also recounts hunting stories: using a cheap single-shot .22 rifle or a bow and arrow for duck, deer, rabbit, and grouse. He elaborates on descriptions of equipment, bait, and preparations for the hunt while relating stories of hunting exploits with childhood friends. The writing style is vintage Paulsen—strings of lyrical sentences punctuated with short, choppy sentences as well as long sentences that meander like the river itself. Interspersed among the essays are line drawings by his wife, Ruth Wright Paulsen, that provide intricate details of nature and evoke the peaceful feelings that humans find in nature. Similar to *Woodsong, The Winter Room* and *Clabbered Dirt, Sweet Grass,* this quiet book speaks of cycles of time: the calendar year, the seasons, and life. As Paulsen has said before in his writings (and it doesn't matter if he's talking about fishing, hunting, farming or running the dogs) " . . . the reason for hunting is not the deer, never has been the deer, never would be the deer: the reason for hunting is just that: to hunt. To hunt the sun, the winds, the trees—to hunt the beauty. In time, in memory, it all becomes more important than the deer, than the quarry. Than the kill."

THE TENT: A PARABLE IN ONE SITTING (1995)

Merri Monks

SOURCE: A review of *The Tent: A Parable in One Sitting,* in *Booklist,* Vol. 91, No. 14, March 15, 1995, p. 1323.

Fourteen-year-old Steven's impoverished father, Corey, concocts a get-rich-quick scam. Masquerading as an itinerant preacher, he accepts the help of three con artists, who pose as sick and crippled audience members in their traveling tent show. In an unlikely rush of guilt one evening, Corey renounces the bushel baskets of money and declares his intention to return to a poor but honest lifestyle. The plot bears a strong resemblance to that of "Leap of Faith," a Steve Martin film about a con artist who fakes healings and is shaken by his encounters with the faithful. Paulsen's gift for conveying story and character in spare language is evident here, and Steven is an appealing character. The father-son role reversal is well portrayed—as Corey's moral decline progresses, Steven struggles to retain his ideals. Centering on the development of Christian ethics, the story begins with a retelling of the life of Jesus, and Bible quotes begin subsequent chapters. The resolution is trite; however, the rural Texas setting, the characterizations, and the portrayal of a self-ordained preacher are well written, and the book will find an audience, both among confirmed Paulsen fans and among reluctant readers.

Kirkus Reviews

SOURCE: A review of *The Tent: A Parable in One Sitting,* in *Kirkus Reviews,* Vol. LXIII, No. 7, April 1, 1995, p. 474.

A formulaic rags-to-riches tale about learning a skill and becoming a success, with an odd twist: The skill in question is preaching at religious revivals. Steven's father gets tired of working for minimum wage and decides to try his luck at evangelism, about which he knows nothing. Steven, 14, is initially skeptical, but comes around once the business takes off. Readers watch them gradually learn how things are done, from their uncertain first steps (about something as basic as setting up a tent), to a more confident position (they win over a hostile audience), to their eventual rise to success (they incorporate "healing" into the act). Their progress is measured by the increasing sums of money in the collection: $28, $150, $300, and much more, until Steven has run out of hiding places for it. The fake cripples who orchestrate the healings are genuinely colorful characters, full of insight: "Ever wonder why profits and prophets sound so much alike?" But as soon as he reaches the top, Steven's father has a revelation and, reforming in the last ten pages of the novel, decides to give away all the money and spend the rest of the summer preaching for real.

This has a slightly manipulative plot—the kind that overwhelms the protagonists, and makes readers willing to swallow any details as long as the characters reach their goal—accompanied by some light moralizing by Steven (the narration remains gracefully nonjudgmental), which is always peripheral to the action and takes center stage only at the end. As with all stories of success, the most enjoyable thing about this book is how quickly it reads.

Tom S. Hurlburt

SOURCE: A review of *The Tent: A Parable in One Sitting,* in *School Library Journal,* Vol. 41, No. 5, May, 1995, p. 122.

"Thirty-four years old and we don't have a pot to pee in or a window to throw it out of to call our own," is how 14-year-old Steven's dad Corey describes their existence. The boy's mother has taken off, and he and his father live in an old rented trailer and drive a broken-down truck. All of this changes in a hurry when Corey commandeers a tent, steals a Gideon Bible from a hotel room, and hits the back roads of Texas in his new occupation as a preacher. Learning the tricks of the trade as they go, Steven and Corey are soon joined by two drifters whose act of being miraculously healed by Corey helps to draw larger crowds and bigger offerings. Soon their new enterprise is earning hundreds of dollars a night and both father and son have all the riches they could ever imagine. At the height of their success, both Corey, who actually has begun to read the Bible for the first time, and Steven are consumed by guilt and they set off in an effort to right their wrongdoings. While the setting and subject matter are atypical of Paulsen, the author's unique ability to pen a story is again demonstrated. While the decision to abandon the lucrative endeavor may seem somewhat abrupt, readers will feel the main characters' dilemma in having to choose between material wealth and doing the right thing. *The Tent* may surprise Paulsen's many fans, but it will not disappoint them.

Deborah Stevenson

SOURCE: A review of *The Tent: A Parable in One Sitting,* in *Bulletin of the Center for Children's Books,* Vol. 48, No. 10, June, 1995, pp. 356-57.

Steven's father, oppressed by grinding poverty despite his labor, decides that the way to riches is to become a traveling preacher, so father and son, assisted by a stolen Bible and a few audience shills, make their way through Texas healing and saving souls. Steven is at first embarrassed, then gradually comes to despise the flocks he and his father fleece; finally, however, both he and his father hear a different message in the gospel, see their false evangelism as wrong, and decide to visit towns simply to "talk about God and maybe read some more about Jesus." There's little mainstream fiction for youth that takes Christianity, particularly fundamentalism, seriously, so it's good to see the subject tackled; Paulsen is also good at evoking a flat and dusty world of small southwestern towns, where a visiting preacher is a welcome relief from everyday life. Unfortunately his treatment of the subject often lacks subtlety, making the book seem—well—preachy and the evil more appealing than the good. Steven's father's corruption manifests itself in predictable forms, there's no exploration of what difference the audience finds between Steven's father the charlatan and Steven's father the genuine believer, and while a more dramatic ending might have been theologically unsatisfying, the final scene here is abrupt and anticlimactic. This is still a sincere and thoughtful story of spiritual growth, however, that could prompt some serious discussion.

THE TORTILLA FACTORY (1995)

Mary Bahr Fritts

SOURCE: A review of *The Tortilla Factory,* in *The Five Owls,* Vol. IX, No. 4, March-April, 1995, p. 84.

In this collaboration between husband and wife, the rendering of "seed to corn to dough to tortilla to manos morenas" is like a burrito with too few beans—very tasty, but the rich language wrapped in brushstrokes of gold, adobe, wheat, and cornstalk green leaves one craving more. Yet Paulsen does gift the reader with a way to extend the pleasure—another plateful, if you will. The book's last and unfinished sentence unleashes the never-ending cycle of which he writes, allowing reader to turn back the pages and taste Paulsen's "earth-dance" again and again.

Given the title, **The Tortilla Factory,** first sentence ("The black earth sleeps in winter") and invocation ("we have this bread to offer") initially it seems that earth and its life bread are Paulsen's subject. But reading the second sentence that winds its way to the very last page, it becomes clear that this is a hymn to the brown hands that till, plant, pick, mix, squeeze, flatten and bake. The fluid text (to be wrapped around juicy beans and eaten by white teeth, to fill a round stomach) puts the reader in mind of Paulsen's other prose-poem, **Clabbered Dirt, Sweet Grass,** which also honors those who work the land.

Everything about Ruth Wright Paulsen's art is earthy. Even the rugged linen canvas underneath the soya-based inks complements the author's words; text and illustrations work together to create a mood, filling the reader with learning, enchantment and hunger for a second helping.

The Spanish edition, translated by Gloria de Aragon Andujar, is being released simultaneously.

Ruth Semrau

SOURCE: A review of *The Tortilla Factory,* in *School Library Journal,* Vol. 41, No. 7, July, 1995, p. 74.

The Paulsens again combine their talents to produce a lovely book. A series of rich, full- and double-page oil-on-linen paintings is joined by brief, unwasteful text. Words and pictures make a song of thanksgiving for the food that springs from the earth, and the bread that it becomes through the work of human hands. Black earth, brown hands, yellow seed, green plants, and finally golden corn give way to the dim interiors of the tortilla factory. Again, brown hands are seen transforming the food from corn to bread. In the book's most evocative illustration, earthenware bowls hold beans, peppers, garlic, and onions, and hands hold a tortilla, ready to fill and eat. Paint is thickly, impressionistically applied and linen is used as background for the text. This title is beautiful to look at, and will also fit nicely into units on food, regional culture, art, and many other topics.

📖 *CALL ME FRANCIS TUCKET* (1995)

Gerry Larson

SOURCE: A review of *Call Me Francis Tucket,* in *School Library Journal,* Vol. 41, No. 6, June, 1995, pp. 112-13.

In this spirited sequel to *Mr. Tucket,* Paulsen recounts the continuing frontier adventures of Francis Tuckett, 15. Heading west by wagon train with his family a year before, Francis had been captured by the Pawnees and rescued by a savvy, one-armed mountain man. Now on his own, he is determined to return to civilization. Armed with a rifle and knowledge of the wilderness, he hunts deer and buffalo, survives a stampede, and outwits a pair of outlaws. When an abandoned wagon reveals two orphans, he takes charge, taking the children to a trading post and hesitantly leaving them with the cold, calculating owner. Traveling 10 miles, the young man is haunted by his own loss of family and returns to find Lottie and Billy beaten and burdened with chores. With fierce determination, he reclaims them and together they continue their westward journey. Francis is an understated, appealing character. His remarkable independence, resourcefulness, and perseverance are tempered by bouts of adolescent insecurity and an emotional need for family. Sharply etched characters, vivid scenery, and dramatic encounters make this book an entertaining read for young adventurers.

Helen Turner

SOURCE: A review of *Call Me Francis Tucket,* in *Voice of Youth Advocates,* Vol. 18, No. 2, June, 1995, p. 98.

Paulsen's *Mr. Tucket* introduced Francis Tucket, heading to Oregon in a wagon train with his family, told of his capture by the Pawnees and of his rescue from the tribe by trapper/trader Mr. Grimes. Francis and Mr. Grimes have gone their separate ways, and now Francis is determined to resume his search for his parents. Stampeding buffalo, murderous drifters, and a seemingly endless prairie are some of the challenges teenage Francis faces as he makes his way West. Not the least of the challenges is the discovery of two children. Lottie and Billy, whose journey West with their father has ended tragically with their father's death. Francis thinks he has found a home for the children when the owners of a trading post agree to keep them, but he realizes they will be exploited by the foster parents, so he feels he has no choice but to resume his responsibility for Lottie and Billy. Francis and his two charges ride off from the trading post, heading ever westward, and probably also heading into a third book about Francis Tucket's search for Oregon and his parents. Paulsen spins an engrossing

tale of the dangers, thrills, and hardships faced by pioneers in the mid-1800s, and peoples the story with a spirited cast.

Kirkus Reviews

SOURCE: A review of *Call Me Francis Tucket,* in *Kirkus Reviews,* Vol. LXIII, No. 11, June 1, 1995, p. 784.

Francis, 14, is alone on the frontier. In *Mr. Tucket* (1969) he was captured by Indians, rescued by the mountain man Mr. Grimes, and learned to survive. He continues his journey westward across the endless prairie, hoping to find his parents in a wagon train headed for Oregon. Along the way he is beset by thieves, caught in a buffalo stampede, and adopted by two young children whose father has died of cholera and who have been abandoned by the fearful adults in their wagon train.

Characteristic of all Paulsen's works, the narrative flow is smooth and uncluttered, the action gritty and realistic, the story thrilling. This one reads like the second book of a trilogy; it starts in the middle and doesn't go anywhere, and familiarity with the first book is mandatory. But if *Call Me Francis Tucket* is unsatisfying on its own, like good serial fiction, it will make readers eager to find out what happens next, and hope a third book is in the offing.

D. A. Young

SOURCE: A review of *Call Me Francis Tucket,* in *The Junior Bookshelf,* Vol. 60, No. 3, June, 1996, p. 123.

It is 1848 in the foothills of the Rocky Mountains where we meet Francis Alphonse Tucket who has just celebrated his fourteenth birthday with the present of a .40 calibre rifle and a magnificent cake. He and his family are in a long wagon train on its way to Oregon making its way West through hostile Indian country. That was yesterday. Now he is captive in the hands of a Pawnee hunting party. He escapes with the help of Mr. Jason Grimes, a one-armed white trader who takes him under his wing and initiates him in the skills of staying alive in the wild and inhospitable American Middle West. He learns to ride, shoot, hunt, trap and fight off attacks from Indians. He can hold his own against villains of any kind. In short he has grown into manhood in the true traditions of How The West Was Won.

Gary Paulsen likes to write about a youngster facing up to a difficult environment and so learning to persevere against odds and gain independence. The theme of Cowboys and Indians gives him an excellent background for the testing of Francis Tucket. It is a theme which may have become hackneyed but Gary Paulsen's sensitive writing guarantees that it will be accepted as genuine and real.

📖 *ESCAPE FROM FIRE MOUNTAIN* ("Gary Paulsen World of Adventure" series, 1995)

Susan F. Marcus

SOURCE: A review of *Escape from Fire Mountain,* in *School Library Journal,* Vol. 41, No. 7, July, 1995, p. 80.

Once readers accept that a girl of 13, home alone, could answer a call for help on her CB by heading into the nearby mountains by canoe and on foot; rescue two lost children; escape tree-tall flames; foil dangerous poachers; evade death in the rapids at Deadman's drop; *and* keep her head in every instance; they can relax and enjoy the constant challenges that Nikki must overcome. The book certainly delivers the adventure that the series title ["Gary Paulsen World of Adventure" series] promises. Its brevity doesn't provide for character development, but the story does trigger the same kind of thrill people get from watching a Harrison Ford movie, and it will certainly attract reluctant readers. And the fact that there's hardly an adult around, with the exception of the villainous poachers, will satisfy readers looking for a little escapist fun.

📖 *THE RIFLE* (1995)

Publishers Weekly

SOURCE: A review of *The Rifle,* in *Publishers Weekly,* Vol. 242, No. 33, August 14, 1995, pp. 85-6.

A gifted storyteller, Paulsen could have plucked this plot straight from any newspaper—an accidental shooting with a loaded gun. This tragedy doesn't occur until the final pages, however; with consummate skill, Paulsen slowly sets the stage by focusing on the weapon itself, a rifle made in 1768 and subsequently used in the Revolutionary War. He documents the painstaking, labor-intensive process of crafting a rifle by hand. And not just any rifle, but one that is "sweet"—a weapon of both beauty and deadly accuracy. He tracks its history, from the attic in which it languishes for centuries to the hands of an ultra-conservative gun freak (whose small-mindedness Paulsen exposes in withering detail), to the home of a mechanic who accepts it in trade for an auto repair. Only then do readers meet the boy Richard and sense impending doom. The remaining pages unfold with nervewracking leisure as readers squirm, awaiting the inevitable explosion. Although he sometimes uses his novel as a bully pulpit to fight the argument that "guns don't kill people, people kill people," his magnificent prose is as "sweet" as the rifle about which he writes. A truly mesmerizing tale, from beginning to end.

Kirkus Reviews

SOURCE: A review of *The Rifle,* in *Kirkus Reviews,* Vol. LXIII, No. 17, September 1, 1995, p. 1286.

Once again Paulsen proves that less is more in a short but extremely powerful cautionary tale. Four sections limn the elements of the story: the creation of the gun and its path through history, the life of a boy, the moment when the boy and the gun are "joined," and the rifle's fate after that event. This is Hitchcock's bomb under the bed: The suspense is nearly killing, yet from the 1768 scenes of the crafting of this "sweet" rifle, Paulsen forges descriptions to rival any he has written, and readers—on any side of the gun-control issue—must linger over each phrase.

Gunsmith Cornish McManus's rifle shoots farther and truer, maybe, than any firearm ever created. The rifle's next owner, woodsman John Byam, depends on the gun for his livelihood; his skill picking off British officers during the Revolution becomes legendary. Upon his death the rifle falls into the hands of a woman who hides it in her attic, where it lies undetected for more than two centuries. In 1993 it is discovered and changes hands several times before finding a place over the fireplace in the home of Harv Kline, a decent man. When Harv and his wife light the decorative candles on their mantel for Christmas Eve, the stage is set for a horrifying sequence of events that results in the death of a neighbor's 14-year-old son. Paulsen is at the peak of his powers in a book that is as shattering as the awful events it depicts. Unforgettable.

Elizabeth Bush

SOURCE: A review of *The Rifle,* in *Bulletin of the Center for Children's Books,* Vol. 49, No. 2, October, 1995, pp. 64-5.

Lovingly, almost obsessively crafted by a colonial gunsmith, the titular rifle sees service in the Revolutionary War and then passes through a series of hands and dusty attics until, some two hundred years later, it hangs decoratively over Harv Kline's fireplace. On Christmas Eve a stray spark from the cheery hearth causes the loaded rifle to discharge, sending a centuries-old ball of lead through the temple of Richard Mesington, the teenager next door. Paulsen's tale is, at heart, an argument for gun restriction. Tim Harrow, the interim owner who cons Harv into trading automotive services for the antique rifle, is effectively if unoriginally depicted as a dishonest, beer-swilling, muddled-thinking NRA zealot, while victim Richard is the archetypal American boy, the essence of innocence and promise. But Paulsen overplays his hand, offering a protracted description of the weapon's artistry and "sweetness" reverential enough to send a pacifist off to an antique-gun dealer, and turning Richard's tragedy into a freak accident rather than the inevitable outcome of civilian gun ownership. If the novella misses its mark as a gun-control polemic, however, it may serve YA readers as a provocative neo-Hellenic examination of Fate, or as an intriguing lesson in chaos theory.

Carol A. Edwards

SOURCE: A review of *The Rifle,* in *School Library Journal,* Vol. 41, No. 10, October, 1995, p. 139.

This novella focuses on a specific weapon crafted during the Revolutionary War. At the book's conclusion, set in 1994, this rifle still functions and performs as it was designed to do. Paulsen, who can create vivid portraits of individuals in relation to specific places, takes the focus off the people here, although they remain distinct characters, and puts this object—a rifle—at the core of the story. Although he seems to be saying that people don't kill people, guns do, this message is not sustained. The circumstances seem so unique and the love of weaponry so strong that the anti-gun theme is fatally weakened. For anyone whose mind is made up on this issue, this book will probably not change it. However, it could lead to intense discussion and exploration of how our society has evolved into its present gun-loving culture and into the intense anguish and human cost we collectively ignore as we continue our love affair with weaponry. For readers willing to think about this issue, for those looking for ways to introduce the debate, there is no better vehicle than this short, engagingly written story of one rifle and its fatal impact on one modern boy.

📖 *BRIAN'S WINTER* **(1996; British edition as** *Hatchet: Winter,* **1996)**

Hazel Rochman

SOURCE: A review of *Brian's Winter,* in *Booklist,* Vol. 92, No. 8, December 15, 1995, p. 700.

Writing with simplicity, Paulsen is at his best in an elemental story of wilderness survival. In this sequel to his widely popular *Hatchet* (1987), he spells out an alternative ending many readers have tried to imagine: What if 13-year-old Brian hadn't been rescued before winter came? What if he had had to face the cold months alone in the Canadian north? This time Brian has a survival kit he found in the crashed plane including two butane lighters, a rifle, a fishing line, and a sleeping bag), but otherwise he has to find food, shelter, and clothing from the world around him. He sees himself like the first Americans, learning to make arrowheads and snowshoes, getting to know the sounds and tracks and weather of his place in the wild. Of course, Brian is extraordinarily resourceful and inventive. What's more, he somehow recovers from everything without injury, even after being knocked unconscious by a 700-pound moose. There's no suspense; we know he'll make it. Yet, as in the autobiographical *Woodsong* (1990), Paulsen writes with the authoritative particularity of someone who knows the woods. This docu-novel is for outdoors lovers and also for all of those adventurers snug at home in a centrally heated high-rise. The facts are the drama.

Tim Rausch

SOURCE: A review of *Brian's Winter,* in *School Library Journal,* Vol. 42, No. 2, February, 1996, p. 102.

At the conclusion of *Hatchet,* Brian Robeson is rescued after surviving a plane crash and summer alone in the north Canadian woods. Now, in this second sequel, Paulsen shows what would have happened if the 13-year-old boy had been forced to endure the harsh winter. For a brief time, Brian lives in relative luxury, living off the contents of the recently recovered survival pack, which included a gun for hunting. Then, his freeze-dried food runs out and his rifle fails, and he realizes how careless and complacent he has become. Suddenly aware of the changing seasons, he works frantically to winterize his shelter, fashion warmer clothes from animal skins, and construct a more powerful bow and arrow. About the time he has mastered winter survival, he discovers a dog-sled trail that leads him to a trapper and final rescue. The same formula that worked before is successful here: the driving pace of the narration, the breathtaking descriptions of nature, and the boy who triumphs on the merits of efficient problem solving. The author's ability to cast a spell, mesmerize his audience, and provide a clinic in winter survival is reason enough to buy this novel. Although the plot is both familiar and predictable, Paulsen fans will not be disappointed.

Marcus Crouch

SOURCE: A review of *Hatchet: Winter,* in *The Junior Bookshelf,* Vol. 60, No. 2, April, 1996, p. 82.

This is not so much a sequel as an alternative to *Hatchet.* Suppose, the author asks, that Brian, the young teenager from a Canadian city, had not been rescued when the plane crashed in the wilds. How would he have coped with the rigours of winter? Here is the answer, and fairly convincing it is. He hunts for his food, and when ammunition for his gun runs out he replaces it with improvised weapons. Before long he has become a twentieth-century Stone Age man, with flint-tipped arrows and spear. Gary Paulsen, who knows the terrain and the problems, does not make matters easy for his young hero. Brian has a bruising encounter with a bear who initially has no animosity for the human; he merely wants Brian's food. When rabbit and foolbird cease to be enough for a diet, Brian hunts elk and is lucky to survive, luckier too because he is left with rations for a month or two. His rescue seems a little tame after all the excitements.

The novel is normally an account of people and personalities. It is difficult to write one in which there is a single character. No conversation, no conflict. The author copes well with this problem, keeping the reader at stress over a long period and not forfeiting a sense of involvement. There is a fundamental improbability—what happened to the rescue which would surely have followed the disappearance of a child?—but it is not a matter which will detract from the excitement for a young reader. An urban child might just become resistant to the text-book survival detail which gives the story its authenticity, sometimes at the expense of action.

Helen Turner

SOURCE: A review of *Brian's Winter,* in *Voice of Youth Advocates,* Vol. 19, No. 6, February, 1997, p. 332.

Brian Robeson is stranded in the Canadian wilderness following the crash of a small plane which kills the pilot, the only other person aboard. After about two months, he is rescued. The riveting account of the teenager's struggle to survive was vividly portrayed in Paulsen's *Hatchet.* Here is an alternative ending, in which Brian is not rescued at the end of the summer but instead is forced to spend the fall and part of a bitter winter in the woods. Adapting the skill he has already learned, Brian is able to fortify his cave shelter, find ways to kill larger game and protect himself against new dangers. As he ranges further from his camp, he encounters a toboggan track that leads him to the home of a Cree family of trappers. Brian stays with the Cree family until their supply plane makes its scheduled stop, leaving the wilderness on the plane.

This is more than a relating of Brian's adventures with bears, moose, blizzards and skunks. It is about animals and weather and survival, of course, but there is a beauty and a compelling depth to the writing. As Brian sometimes fails and sometimes succeeds, his characterization is consistent and believable. The descriptions of the wilderness and Brian's thoughts and interactions with all of his surroundings are woven into the narrative. There are a few references to incidents in *Hatchet,* but this story will stand alone. Pick either ending—a summer rescue or a winter rescue—and you have a great adventure story.

PUPPIES, DOGS, AND BLUE NORTHERS: REFLECTIONS ON BEING RAISED BY A PACK OF SLED DOGS (1996)

Kirkus Reviews

SOURCE: A review of *Puppies, Dogs, and Blue Northers: Reflections on Being Raised by a Pack of Sled Dogs,* in *Kirkus Reviews,* Vol. LXIV, No. 15, August 1, 1996, pp. 1156-57.

Readers who aren't misled by the New Age subtitle—*Reflections on Being Raised by a Pack of Sled Dogs*—will find themselves along on a wonderful ride.

Paulsen is not known for writing love stories, but that's exactly what this lyrical, tender account is, showcasing Cookie, his primary lead dog for some 14,000 miles (including the path of the Iditarod), who saved Paulsen's life more than once. It's also the story of one of Cook-ie's litters of pups and the joy and inspiration Paulsen found in watching them learn and grow. He has fascinating tales to tell about how Cookie and the other adult dogs trained them. All wasn't work for the pups; the fun they had when Paulsen broke one of the cardinal rules for raising pups and let them into his house makes for a sidesplitting tale. The story remains, always, Cookie's, and when the day comes that she can no longer run because of arthritis, it nearly breaks her heart—and Paulsen's too. Upon learning that his health will no longer permit him to run either, man and dog settle into a different life, one of domestic companionship, until Cookie's blessedly peaceful death (there will be, as they say, no dry eyes in the house). "Such a bond, such a love I had with Cookie"—and such a book he wrote to share that love with others.

Mollie Bynum

SOURCE: A review of *Puppies, Dogs, and Blue Northers: Reflections on Being Raised by a Pack of Sled Dogs,* in *School Library Journal,* Vol. 42, No. 11, November, 1996, p. 130.

In seven vignettes, Paulsen recounts the story of his lead dog, Cookie, as she mates and gives birth, and her puppies mature toward their destiny—to race and pull sleds. Readers are drawn into that special bond between driver and lead dog through Paulsen's real-life experiences racing in Minnesota. (Keep a tissue handy for the last chapter, "Last Run.") Ruth Wright Paulsen's occasional paintings add warmth and charm to the book. The audience for this title is a problem, due to Paulsen's direct and often nostalgic writing style, although interested teens will read it. Those who loved the author's *Woodsong* will find this new, "slimmer" volume to be a welcome addition.

Alice Johns

SOURCE: A review of *Puppies, Dogs, and Blue Northers: Reflections on Being Raised by a Pack of Sled Dogs,* in *Voice of Youth Advocates,* Vol. 19, No. 6, February, 1997, pp. 352-53.

Stories from the life of "Cookie" dominate this book about the lives and training of sled dogs. Cookie was eminent YA novelist Paulsen's "primary lead dog for something close to fourteen thousand miles—trapline, training, and one full Iditarod." She was mother of exceptional pups, a life saver of the author more than once, and trainer of other dogs and her owner.

Paulsen portrays the relationship of dogs and owners as a joyful communication of fellow beings on the earth. Sled dogs' lives from conception to birth and from dog adolescence to adulthood are lovingly described. The final chapter portrays another part of life for these beings, the illness and retirement of Cookie and Paulsen, and Cookie's death on a cold winter's night.

All readers who are dog lovers, and those involved with nature, particularly dogsled driving and living in a cold northern climate, will enjoy this book.

📖 *TUCKET'S RIDE* (1997)

Kirkus Reviews

SOURCE: A review of *Tucket's Ride,* in *Kirkus Reviews,* Vol. LXIV, No. 22, November 15, 1996, p. 1673.

Another entry in the ongoing saga of young Francis Tucket (*Call Me Francis Tucket,* 1995) and his adventures after being separated from his parents' wagon train. He is still saddled with two young children he rescued after their parents died of cholera. Francis protects a Mexican woman from an attack by an American soldier, nearly gets hung by the soldier's commander, and is captured by the brutal Comancheros during the war between the US and Mexico. Like its predecessors, this novel wanders all over the map, but it's nicely crammed with nonstop adventure. The serialized publication, sheer number of Dickensian coincidences, characters, and incidents, as well as the innocence of the main character, makes this read like *Nicholas Nickleby,* set in the Old West. Still, Paulsen proves himself nothing if not reliable—the pacing is flawless, the prose seemingly effortless, and the pages just fly by.

Ruth Semrau

SOURCE: A review of *Tucket's Ride,* in *School Library Journal,* Vol. 43, No. 3, March, 1997, p. 190.

Paulsen's saga of the (often) lone boy on the American frontier in the 1840s continues here at a breakneck pace. It is now two years after Francis was abducted by the Wicked Pawnee and then saved by the Wily Mountain Man Jason Grimes in *Mr. Tucket.* He and the two orphans he picked up in *Call Me Francis Tucket* are now trying to get to Oregon via Mexico and accidentally get tangled with armies pursuing the Mexican War. No sooner does Francis escape execution for killing a soldier than the three youngsters fall into the hands of the dreaded Comancheros. No disaster lasts long for Francis, though. Grimes, his savior from the first book, suddenly appears out of nowhere and saves him again with the same plot device. (Hey, it worked the first time.) Readers leave Francis and the two orphans hiding from their vengeful pursuers. What happens then? Wait for the next book. Chapters consist of three or four short pages with cliffhanger endings. Characters and scenes change almost from page to page. People are introduced with a line or two of explanation only to disappear a few paragraphs later. As a result, character development is necessarily sacrificed and stereotypes abound. Many readers will love these books for their exciting, nonstop action. Classroom use for social studies, however, would require careful and critical analysis by teachers and students.

📖 *WORKSONG* (1997)

Kirkus Reviews

SOURCE: A review of *Worksong,* in *Kirkus Reviews,* Vol. LXV, No. 4, February 15, 1997, p. 304.

The Paulsens create a song—really a lyric verse—in praise of ordinary workers, a refreshing slant for a culture mired in the worship of celebrity. "It is keening noise and jolting sights,/and houses up and trees in sun,/and trucks on one more midnight run." The text doesn't always name the job or worker, but refers to an aspect of it—the mentions of "flat, clean sidewalks" and "towering buildings" force readers to think about the sweepers and construction teams pictured in the illustrations. The artwork serves a dual purpose: The oil paintings gorgeously convey a tangible sense of the work environment while also ennobling its humble inhabitants. Among those shown: the woman who toils in the canteen kitchen ("making things for all to share"), workers at computer terminals ("offices filled with glowing screens"), a new mother and nurse ("gentle arms that lift and hold"). Last and surely not least, the text acknowledges why people work: "It's mother, father in a chair,/with tired eyes and loosened hair./Resting short but loving long,/resting for the next day's song."

Publishers Weekly

SOURCE: A review of *Worksong,* in *Publishers Weekly,* Vol. 244, No. 13, March 31, 1997, p. 74.

From truck driver to cafeteria cook, from nurse to deep-sea diver—"All the things there are to be" gather together in this gentle rhyming hymn to the dignity of work. Here, work is the common tie that binds, rather than the distinction that sets individuals apart. In both words and pictures, the efforts of people who spend themselves in everyday work muster a communal force—whether it is a group of office workers at their "glowing screens," the truck-farming duo of father and daughter arranging their produce, or the solitary roofer. Gary Paulsen's couplets sometimes strike a whimsical note ("ice cream cones to lick and wear"), but more often touch the heart ("gentle arms that lift and hold,/and all the soldiers brave and bold"). Ruth Wright Paulsen's textured, slightly muted oil paintings enrich the text and set off an emotional reverberation. Throughout, the subtlety of gestures (rather than facial expressions) and of concrete words (rather than feelings) keeps sentimentality at bay.

Barbara Kiefer

SOURCE: A review of *Worksong,* in *School Library Journal,* Vol. 43, No. 5, May, 1997, p. 123.

As they did in *The Tortilla Factory,* the Paulsens have once again collaborated to celebrate the labors of common people. Gary Paulsen's brief rhyming text evokes the rhythm and sounds of a musical score as he pays homage to the "keening noises and jolting sights" of a carpenter at work on a new house or truckers on "one more nighttime run." Although the author mentions "offices filled with glowing screens," the occupations celebrated within these covers are not to be found in financial houses on Wall Street or among the corporate giants. Instead, he has looked to the streets outside the skyscrapers, into the small shops, classrooms, and factories that fill our cities and into the fields, highways, and markets that extend across the countryside. Here are the mothers and fathers of the majority of America's children. Ruth Wright Paulsen's impressionistic oil paintings extend the brief text into many worlds—an ice-cream shop, a hairdressing salon, a library, and even under the sea. Individuals from many cultures carry on their daily work with great dignity, returning home to their families at the end of the day to rest and prepare to carry on the same refrain in the morning. Although the gender depictions are fairly traditional, the soft colors, spare text, and overall design of the book provide a song of praise to the unsung heroes in every child's world and to the simple satisfaction of a job well done.

Susan Dove Lempke

SOURCE: A review of *Worksong,* in *Booklist,* Vol. 93, No. 17, May 1, 1997, p. 1502.

The Paulsens collaborate here on a picture book that celebrates the world of work. "It is keening noise and jolting sights, and hammers flashing in the light, and houses up and trees in sun, and trucks on one more nighttime run" reads the rhythmic, rhyming text. A diverse selection of workers, including blue-collar laborers, professionals at computers, soldiers, and clerks, is shown at work, then coming home at the end of the day to tuck in children and prepare for "the next day's song." Children will be fascinated by the rich oil paintings showing such interesting activities as pouring red-hot steel and deep-sea diving. Occasional stumbles in the rhythm and the ultra-traditional division of labor (women shown as nurses, librarians, and hairdressers) are the downsides of this very handsome, otherwise engaging book.

AMOS BINDER, SECRET AGENT ("Culpepper Adventures" series, 1997)

Linda Bindner

SOURCE: A review of *Amos Binder, Secret Agent,* in *School Library Journal,* Vol. 43, No. 4, April, 1997, p. 114.

Through a mishap with the mail service, Amos Binder is sent an envelope addressed to A. Bender. When he and his friend Dunc open the letter to find airline tickets, cryptic orders to fly to Arizona, and a key, they enthusiastically depart on an adventure. One mishap leads to another as the boys become involved in protecting Fatima, the daughter of a Middle Eastern goodwill ambassador, and catching a jewel thief. Friends become agents, who turn into double agents, and everything erupts when the real A. Bender shows up. The adventures here, as well as the powerful roles the young characters take on, will appeal to children. Much of the plot is highly unrealistic (the boys' parents simply don't exist), and the hazards of their jobs as secret agents come from Amos's unexplained clumsiness. Still, this type of James Bond thriller that puts kids in charge of national security should prove to be popular reading.

THE SCHERNOFF DISCOVERIES (1997)

Kirkus Reviews

SOURCE: A review of *The Schernoff Discoveries,* in *Kirkus Reviews,* Vol. LXV, No. 10, May 15, 1997, p. 805.

A rollicking tale that's dressed up like a novel but reads more like a memoir, from the new comedian on the block, Paulsen.

The never-named narrator, whom readers are led to believe is Paulsen himself, is a nerd just like his friend, Harold Schernoff; together they are "easily the most unpopular boys" in their junior high. But if Harold is a brainy geek, with theories about everything from girls to fishing to bullies, the narrator operates under a somewhat dimmer star, willing to help Harold test his theories and come up with results that are just short of disastrous. Under Harold's leadership they find a sure-fire way to meet girls—by enrolling in home economics—until the football team finds out and Harold has a bigger problem to solve. Other adventures involve skiing and fishing—spectacular failures; the job they get as pinsetters in a local bowling alley results in one of the funniest episodes in the book and, incidentally, leads to the narrator's small triumph over the bully Dick Chimmer. It's all flat-out goofy and great fun, as well as an inspiring story of shared experiences that, weird as they are, form the basis of a strong and affectionate friendship.

Publishers Weekly

SOURCE: A review of *The Schernoff Discoveries,* in *Publishers Weekly,* Vol. 244, No. 20, May 19, 1997, p. 77.

Two things make this book stand out from the crowd of school-based comedies. First, there's Paulsen's joyfully unconventional thinking and quirky writing. Second, this book is told in an unusual but effective way, narrated by an unnamed 14-year-old boy about his best friend, Harold Schernoff. The two buddies are plagued with uncool reputations, but it doesn't hamstring Harold. Among many developments, Harold learns to fish (and gets yanked into the river by his would-be catch). Harold skis. Harold joins home economics class ("'It's simply chemistry' he said one morning while handing me a delicious apple tart that he'd just finished baking"). Harold kisses a girl, plays golf and works as a not-very-competent pinsetter at the bowling alley (the setting, lightly sketched, is northern Minnesota in the '50s). Harold even foils the football team thugs, dragging his best friend into respectability along the way. As in many of his novels, Paulsen matter-of-factly states the narrator's lousy home situation—indifferent, alcoholic parents—but brushes it off as a minor nuisance, something unfortunate but not central to his life. Instead, he focuses on the funny side of junior high. The humor is luminous in contrast to the faintly but deftly drawn shadows in the background. It's also a welcome boost to those who secretly fear that junior high uncoolness is a permanent state.

Carolyn Phelan

SOURCE: A review of *The Schernoff Discoveries,* in *Booklist,* Vol. 93, Nos. 19 & 20, June 1 & 15, 1997, p. 1705.

Paulsen's humorous novel, narrated by a 14-year-old, self-confessed geek, focuses on the narrator's friend, Harold. Equally geeky and brainy as well, Harold takes the lead in an episodic series of adventures ranging from the unusual but pragmatic (enrolling in home economics to meet girls) to the sneaky and possibly suicidal (taking revenge on the football players who broke his slide rule by giving them a cake flavored with 43 boxes of chocolate laxatives). The novel's late-1950s setting may limit its appeal somewhat, but Paulsen taps into two factors that haven't become outdated in the last four decades: adolescent angst over popularity with the opposite sex and the broad humor that appeals to some pre-teen and teenage boys.

Connie Tyrrell Burns

SOURCE: A review of *The Schernoff Discoveries,* in *School Library Journal,* Vol. 43, No. 7, July, 1997, pp. 96-7.

A slapstick novel about friendship set in Minnesota. The book includes autobiographical elements from Paulsen's own life (alcoholic parents, a stint in the army, running the Iditarod). Both the first-person narrator and his best (and only) friend, Harold Schernoff, are 14-year-old social outcasts. Harold also is a science whiz, complete with slide rule, who devises theories to solve all sorts of problems, from dating to dealing with bullies and learning to ski. The chapter on his solutions to first-date awkwardness is hilarious. Perhaps the best chapter is the one in which the boys, although underage, buy their very first car and drive it for a glorious eight miles before the engine explodes. Paulsen captures adolescent feelings perfectly; indeed, the novel becomes a survival story with a twist—survival of adolescence. Asides are

interjected parenthetically comparing then and now. An afterword lets readers know what happens to the characters so memorably drawn in the story. Simplicity of style, humor, and great characterization make this another winner from a popular author.

📖 *SARNY: A LIFE REMEMBERED* (1997)

Kirkus Reviews

SOURCE: A review of *Sarny: A Life Remembered,* in *Kirkus Reviews,* Vol. LXV, No. 13, July 1, 1997, pp. 1033-34.

The slave child who learned to read in *Nightjohn* (1993) looks back from the age of 94 on her life during and after the Civil War. It's a moving tale, made more so by Sarny's clipped, matter-of-fact voice—utterly distinct, with strength and determination shining through every line. Paulsen moves away both from the first book's mystic language and explicit brutality; Sarny watches hated slaveowner Waller die of a bayonet wound, and later sits with four gut-shot soldiers (whose names she still remembers so many decades later), but both scenes are virtually bloodless. When it comes to describing the occupation of Laura Harris, Sarny is all but oblique: "She lived in a fancy house in New Orleans where men came and went," and "I don't think too much on her morals. Just think on her as a friend." A friend indeed: Miss Laura, passing as white, not only pays generous wages, but gives Sarny a house and a building for her first school, and makes her heir to a huge fortune. Sarny leaves it all in her daughter Delie's hands and sets out for Texas to start more schools. The next 50 years pass in a few paragraphs, the ending seems abrupt, and, ultimately, the plot takes too many convenient turns; still, Sarny's indomitability will win over skeptics, and the way her ability to read frees more than her body will not be lost on thoughtful readers.

Bruce Anne Shook

SOURCE: A review of *Sarny: A Life Remembered,* in *School Library Journal,* Vol. 43, No. 9, September, 1997, p. 224.

Sarny, a child in Paulsen's *Nightjohn,* narrates the story of her life from girlhood until 1930, when she is 94 years old. Born into slavery and taught to read by the slave Nightjohn, she marries, bears two babies, and sees her husband worked to death. Her children are sold just as the Civil War ends. Accompanied by another freed slave, Sarny journeys toward New Orleans looking for her children, and meets Miss Laura, a light-skinned black woman with a shadowy occupation and lots of money. In New Orleans, Sarny finds her children and lives comfortably in Miss Laura's employ. She remarries, teaches black children to read, and sees her husband lynched. As the story ends, Sarny, a very rich woman, is living in Texas and waiting to die. Sarny's strong narrative voice is striking, as she remembers events in her own distinct way. It is as though readers are sitting at the feet of a real person, listening as her story spins out. Those unfamiliar with *Nightjohn* will not understand the numerous references to it, but this detracts little from the story. While Sarny suffers many terrible tragedies, her life after the war is probably far more comfortable and sheltered than the lives of the vast majority of former slaves. However, this is not meant to be a sweeping overview of history, but the highly individualized account of one woman's experiences. Just how much of the book is based on historical facts remains fuzzy, but Sarny is a wonderful, believable character. Her story makes absorbing reading.

GraceAnne A. DeCandido

SOURCE: A review of *Sarny: A Life Remembered,* in *Booklist,* Vol. 94, No. 3, October 1, 1997, p. 331.

Although it lacks the simplicity and heartbreaking beauty of *Nightjohn* (1993), this is a satisfying sequel for those who wonder what happened to the slave Sarny after Nightjohn taught her to read. When she was 24 and shortly after her two children were sold off, the Civil War came through Georgia and set her free to track down her son and daughter. This is an epic story on a delicate, human scale: Sarny and another freed slave, Lucy, hold the hands of four dying soldiers left on a field after a skirmish; rescue a small, silent white boy from a ravaged plantation; and are hired by the mysterious Miss Laura to work for her in her glittering New Orleans home. Through the rest of her long life, through sorrow, loss, and homely triumph, Sarny teaches other black people how to read and write. An afterword states that everything in the novel did indeed happen to someone: the small vignettes, such as that of Sarny reading Shakespeare to her children as they sit on a riverbank, have the ring and shapeliness of an oft-told family story. It is a great read, with characters both to hate and to cherish, and a rich sense of what it really was like then.

Janette Perkins

SOURCE: A review of *Sarny: A Life Remembered,* in *The School Librarian,* Vol. 46, No. 3, Autumn, 1998, p. 159.

This wonderful little book is a fictional narrative written in deep Southern States of America slave-speak by Sarny, an old lady of 'ninety and exactly four'. It is set just before the outbreak of the American Civil War, and portrays the epic journey of Sarny to find her children who, like her, have been sent into slavery. Sarny was taught to read and write by Nightjohn (from Gary Paulsen's previous novel) and began to teach some of the other slaves. We get an insight into the harsh realities of slavery, and when the plantation owner, a very cruel man, is killed, the slaves are set free and Sarny and her companion, Lucy, set out on the road to a war-torn New

Orleans to find her children. Along the way, they encounter the ravages of war, witness murder and plunder, and have to plunder themselves in order to survive. Sarny eventually finds her children, marries again, and opens a school for black children; but we encounter quite a lot of racial prejudice against the fact that black people were being educated.

The book is easy to read and fast moving, and stirs up the emotions; . . . The language would suit a good 12-plus reader, but some of the issues and emotions dealt with are more suitable for the 14-plus age group. This is truly a wonderful little epic novel.

MY LIFE IN DOG YEARS (1998)

Kirkus Reviews

SOURCE: A review of *My Life in Dog Years,* in *Kirkus Reviews,* Vol. LXV, No. 22, November 15, 1997, p. 1711.

Paulsen paid loving tribute to the sled dogs in his life in *Puppies, Dogs, and Blue Northers* (1996) so gives eight more canine companions equal time: Snowball, who saved his life when he was seven, to Caesar, an enthusiastic Great Dane who "overwhelmed the furniture" but was gentle with children, to Fred, who did battle with an electric fence, to Quincy, who did battle with a bear that attacked the author's wife. Thoughtful, ironic, often hilarious, these vivid character portraits not only make winning stories, but convey a deep respect for all dogs: "They are wonderful and, I think, mandatory for decent human life."

Stephanie Zvirin

SOURCE: A review of *My Life in Dog Years,* in *Booklist,* Vol. 94, Nos. 9 & 10, January 1 & 15, 1998, p. 799.

Paulsen's style has been smoother, but this honest, unpretentious celebration of dogs further entrenches his reputation as an author who is as successful at writing nonfiction as he is at writing novels. In roughly chronological chapters, he introduces eight memorable canines he has known and loved over the years. Some were pets, others he knew as trusted partners or protectors—from Snowball, the first, to Josh, who "if possible . . . is always with me." Although the chapters are linked by small details and references (often easy to recognize from his previous books), each can stand alone, with several, including a wildly funny one devoted to an adopted Great Dane named Caesar, promising good read-aloud material. Paulsen differentiates his canine friends beautifully, as only a keen observer and lover of dogs can. At the same time, he presents an intimate glimpse of himself, a lonely child of alcoholic parents, who drew strength and solace from his four-legged companions and a love of the great outdoors. Poignant but never saccharine, honest, and open, these engaging canine character studies are guaranteed to charm animal lovers and Paulsen's fans, especially those who know *Woodsong* (1990) or *Father Water, Mother Woods* (1994). There's something to please at every turn of the page.

📖 SOLDIER'S HEART (1998)

Kirkus Reviews

SOURCE: A review of *Soldier's Heart,* in *Kirkus Reviews,* Vol. LXVI, No. 13, July 1, 1998, p. 970.

The nightmare of the Civil War comes to the page in this novel from Paulsen (*The Transall Saga*), based on the real-life experiences of a young enlistee.

Charley Goddard, a hard-working, sweet-tempered Minnesota farm boy, can't wait to sign up when the call comes for men to defend the Union. But the devoted son and brother who looks forward to sending home the $11 a month he earns for his soldiering is not prepared for the inedible food, ill-fitting uniform, or the dysentery he experiences just while training. The passages on the battles of Bull Run and Gettysburg are—as they should be—disconcerting, even upsetting, in the unflinching portrayal of the bloodshed and savagery of war. What is truly remarkable is Paulsen's portrayal of Charley, who is transformed from an innocent boy into a seasoned—but not hardened or embittered—soldier. Most haunting of all, more than the fiery skirmishes themselves, is the final picture of Charley, so shaken and drained from the experience that the only peace he can envision lies within suicide. An author's note tells of Charley's true fate—dead at 23 from the psychological and physical ravages of war.

Publishers Weekly

SOURCE: A review of *Soldier's Heart,* in *Publishers Weekly,* Vol. 245, No. 29, July 20, 1998, p. 221.

Addressing the most fundamental themes of life and death, the versatile Paulsen produces a searing antiwar story. He bases his protagonist, Charley Goddard, on an actual Civil War soldier, a 15-year-old from Minnesota who lied about his age and ended up participating in most of the war's major battles. At first Paulsen's Charley is fired up by patriotic slogans and his own naïve excitement; in a rare intrusion into the narrative, the author makes it clear that ending slavery was not the impetus: "Never did they speak of slavery. Just about the wrongheadedness of the Southern 'crackers' and how they had to teach Johnny Reb a lesson." But Charley's first battle—Bull Run—immediately disabuses him of his notions about honor and glory. A few sparely written passages describe the terror of the gunfire and the smoke from the cannons. Interwoven with these descriptions, a brilliant, fast-moving evocation of Charley's thoughts shows the boy's shocked realization of the price of war, his absolute certainty that he will die and his sudden

understanding of the complex forces that prevent him from fleeing.

Details from the historical record scorch the reader's memory: congressmen bring their families to picnic and watch the fighting that first day at Bull Run; soldiers pile the bodies of the dead into a five-foot-high wall to protect themselves from a winter wind. By the time Charley is finally struck down, at Gettysburg, he has seen it all: "At last he was right, at last he was done, at last he was dead." He is not in fact dead, but a victim of "soldier's heart," defined in an eloquent foreword as a contemporaneous term for what is now called post-traumatic stress disorder.

Paulsen wages his own campaign for the audience's hearts and minds strategically and with great success. Elsewhere, as in *The Rifle,* he has told stories in service to a message; here the message follows from the story ineluctably. Charley comes across fully human, both his vulnerabilities and strengths becoming more pronounced as the novel progresses. Warfare, too, emerges complexly—while a lesser writer might attempt to teach readers to shun war by dint of the protagonist's profound disgust, Paulsen compounds the horrors of the battlefield by demonstrating how they trigger Charley's own bloodlust.

Charley cannot recover from his years of war; in a smaller but more hopeful way, neither may the audience. Paulsen's storytelling is so psychologically true that readers will feel they have lived through Charley's experiences.

Henry Mayer

SOURCE: "The Boys of War," in *The New York Times Book Review,* November 15, 1998, p. 15.

Gary Paulsen's *Soldier's Heart* is a stark, utterly persuasive novel of combat life in the Civil War that may well challenge generations of middle-school readers. . . .

Paulsen has written many successful books *(Hatchet, Nightjohn, The Island)* that explore the intersection of physical and moral challenges. *Soldier's Heart* is a notable continuation that traces the fate of a 15-year-old farm boy, Charley Goddard, from his 1861 enlistment in a volunteer Minnesota regiment through the discipline and boredom of camp life to the carnage of Bull Run and Gettysburg. Goddard was a real person (his daguerreotype graces the frontispiece), but Paulsen has worked up from archival sources and a scholarly study of the regiment a composite fictional account that draws its power from a perfectly pitched narrative voice and authentic detail.

The reader feels the young soldier's awe as he rides a plush train toward the eastern front and understands his bewilderment as he sees the first poor farms and subjected black people in the South. The horrors of combat—the noise, the fear, the drinking from a creek stained pink with blood, the piling up of corpses to make a windbreak for a field surgeon's operating theater—gradually drive away all thoughts of nationalism or abolition and force Charley to concentrate on the imperatives of survival.

📖 *THE TRANSALL SAGA* (1998)

Libby Bergstrom

SOURCE: A review of *The Transall Saga,* in *Voice of Youth Advocates,* Vol. 21, No. 4, October, 1998, p. 286.

On his first solo backpacking trip, Mark Harrison discovers a mysterious blue light, falling through it and landing in a strange land. From there, in episodes of non-stop action, he learns to survive on his own with little more than his pocketknife and a few broken matches. As days become years, Mark meets the inhabitants of this world called Transall, suffers as a slave, proves himself a noble warrior, and fights violent raids. He learns that he entered Transall through a time warp, and is on a radically different Earth changed by nuclear war and viral epidemics. Transall eventually becomes home to Mark. He falls in love and plans to get married, until he again finds the blue light and winds up back in his own time.

Paulsen touches on the serious issues of racism, slavery, and human rights, but the breakneck speed of the plot allows little time for the exploration of these themes. The characterization is shallow, and Mark comes across as almost too good to be true—for example, he is able to fluently speak the language of the Tsook, the people who have enslaved him, after only a few months with them. Readers caught up in the excitement of the plot won't notice these weaknesses, however. Mark lives out the dreams of many YAs—to be independent, respected, and powerful. Paulsen has once again done what he does

best, delivering a riveting tale of adventure and action. Expect this to be popular with Paulsen fans.

📖 *BRIAN'S RETURN* (1998)

Paula Rohrlick

SOURCE: A review of *Brian's Return,* in *Kliatt,* Vol. 32, No. 6, November, 1998, p. 8.

In this conclusion to the story that began with the classic survival tale *Hatchet* and continued in *The River* and *Brian's Winter,* Brian Robeson has returned to civilization—and he hates it. Back home and in high school, he tries to fit in, but the noise and the lack of solitude trouble him, and he misses the woods desperately. Events come to a head when a jealous football player attacks him and Brian fights back as instinctively and viciously as if he were back in the wild. The police refer him to a sympathetic counselor, who appreciates Brian's longing for the woods and supports his need to return.

Brian makes a careful list of what he needs to bring with him to survive alone in the north woods, from a canoe to the right kind of arrowheads—and the complete works of Shakespeare. But nature is unpredictable, as Brian is reminded when a deer leaps into his canoe and capsizes it, a storm collapses his tent, and he pokes his leg with an arrow. The beauty and the joy of being in the wild help Brian rise above the challenges he faces, and an encounter with a stranger reaffirms his dedication to life in the woods. An afterword by Paulsen explains that Brian's experiences are based on Paulsen's own, and that he also prefers to live in the midst of nature and away from civilization. In spare and evocative prose, the novel conveys his love of the wild. Readers will be intrigued by Brian's list and his survival skills, and enjoy his adventures, though they are not quite as dramatic as those in the other novels. This quick read will appeal to reluctant readers as well as to the many fans of *Hatchet* and its sequels.

Additional coverage of Paulsen's life and career is contained in the following sources published by The Gale Group: *Authors and Artists for Young Adults,* Vols. 2, 7; *Contemporary Authors New Revision Series,* Vol. 30; *Junior DISCovering Authors; Major Authors and Illustrators for Children and Young Adults;* and *Something about the Author,* Vols. 22, 50, 54, 79.

(Jerry) Brian Pinkney

1961-

(Also known as J. Brian Pinkney) African-American illustrator and author of picture books.

Major works include *Where Does the Trail Lead?* (written by Burton Albert, 1991), *Sukey and the Mermaid* (retold by Robert D. San Souci, 1992), *The Faithful Friend* (retold by Robert D. San Souci, 1995), *JoJo's Flying Side Kick* (1995), *The Adventures of Sparrowboy* (1997).

INTRODUCTION

Pinkney's unique and striking illustrations have garnered him consistent praise from reviewers as one of the most original and dynamic illustrators of contemporary picture books for preschoolers and primary graders. His signature medium is scratchboard, created using a technique similar to engraving in which the artist scratches away the board's black coating to reveal the white clay underneath. To give the pictures depth and dimension, Pinkney adds color by painting over the stratchboard with oils. He once commented in *Something about the Author* (*SATA*), "I like working in scratchboard because it allows me to sculpt the image. When I etch the drawing out of the board, I get a rhythm going with my lines that feels like sculpture to me." With illustrations that embrace a wide range of subjects, Pinkney is celebrated for his ability to capture the time, place, emotions, and drama of the text, while underscoring the most notable characteristics of the protagonists. His scratchboard creations have been described enthusiastically by reviewers as "distinctive," "handsome," "dignified," and "filled with motion." The vigorous yet warm movement of the lines at once animates and humanizes the characters, making them both fascinating and familiar. Reviewing *The Ballad of Belle Dorcas* (1990), Christine Behrmann noted that Pinkney's "[s]wirling scratched lines swoop through the images, bringing an aspect of eerie movement throughout." A *Publishers Weekly* reviewer commented that Pinkney's stirring images in *Alvin Ailey* (1993) "convey stateliness as well as quickness, and culminate in a vivid, motion-filled spread featuring dancers in Ailey's company reeling across the stage—and seemingly right off the pages."

Pinkney is particularly noted for his artistic renderings of African-American heritage. Initially working as an illustrator for other writers, he has provided dimension and color to reconstructed African-American folktales. To these works he added a series of biographies of famous African Americans, created in collaboration with his wife, children's author Andrea Davis Pinkney. In their collaborations, as well as individual projects, the

Pinkneys select subjects that enable them to share little-known facets of African-American history and culture with young readers. Pinkney told *Publishers Weekly*, "I feel somewhat accountable to the images I make. I want to make sure I'm doing the right thing, as Spike Lee would say. I want to put forth a positive image of blacks, in portraits that are truthful and not stereotypical." His portraits of black people—real, as in *Alvin Ailey*, fanciful, as in *Sukey and the Mermaid*, and reminiscent, as in *Where Does the Trail Lead?*—depict the black experience as noble, dignified, curious, intelligent, energetic, full of integrity, and altogether human. In a similar vein, Pinkney's self-written and self-illustrated stories based on his own personal experiences have drawn positive feedback from reviewers. Betsy Hearne applauded Pinkney's progression from an illustrator to an author/illustrator with her energetic praise of *The Adventures of Sparrowboy*, an award-winning picture book that was, for Pinkney, a culmination of much of his work. "It takes a lot of energy to fly, and this book has got it," Hearne noted. "With red and blue zooming off white, and green lines swirling from lawn to sky, and foreground figures hurling left to right or right off the page, and perspectives swooping from low to high, and images fast-forwarding in rhythmic frames, and rounded shapes rolling into angular explosions, we are *moving*. . . . *The Adventures of Sparrowboy* shows just how much a gifted illustrator can grow in originality, skill, humor, and artistic effects."

Biographical Information

Son of renowned illustrator Jerry Pinkney and author Gloria Jean Pinkney, Brian Pinkney was born in Boston in 1961. Growing up in an atmosphere of so much creativity, young Brian naturally began to draw at an early age. Both his parents encouraged their son's passions, as Gloria told *Horn Book*, "There has always been creative activity in the household." Jerry added, "When the children were growing up, one of the things Gloria and I wanted for them was to be able to make decisions about what would make them happy in terms of careers. . . . So we provided them . . . with materials and working space, but we never put any form of pressure on them." While his mother would instill in all her children a love of reading, his father served as a mentor to young Brian. "I did everything he did," Pinkney recalled in *Major Authors and Illustrators for Children and Young Adults.* "My desk was a miniature version of his desk."

Pinkney later attended the Philadelphia College of Art, where he gained exposure to different artistic mediums, including pen and ink, watercolors, oils, and acrylics. Printmaking would prove to be one of his favorite courses of study, because he enjoyed three-dimensional aspects of etching and lithography techniques. He received a bachelor of fine arts degree in 1983, and worked as a freelance illustrator for several years before returning to school for his graduate degree. During this time he began illustrating picture books by authors such as Robert D. San Souci—a collaboration that would produce three award-winning titles, including *The Boy and the Ghost* (1989). For his first few books, Pinkney adopted the familiar medium that his father used, telling *Horn Book,* "I felt most secure in watercolor, probably because I was certain what the finished artwork would look like, because of my father." Reviewers and readers, however, frequently mistook the younger Pinkney for his father, an occurrence common enough that Brian eventually dropped the "J." from his name. In an interesting sidelight, he found out after he had completed the illustrations for *The Boy and the Ghost,* that his father had declined to illustrate it because he was unable to visualize a way to portray the ghost. "When I read it," Brian told *Horn Book,* "of course, I saw the ghost perfectly, and it was [my father]." Pinkney's illustration depicts his father sporting red hair and a red beard.

While doing graduate work at the School of Visual Arts, Pinkney began experimenting with scratchboard, a three-dimensional medium that would become his favorite. "Working in scratchboard was an important turning point in my career . . . ," he explained in *SATA.* "I went back

to school because I was looking for something. I wanted the next step in my artistic vision. Working in scratchboard became what I found." Pinkney received a master of fine arts degree in 1990 and was immediately in demand for his work. He was working as an illustrator for a magazine art department when he met Andrea Davis, a magazine editor and writer. The two were married in 1991. Andrea was introduced to the world of children's books partially by modeling for her husband, first for Belle in *The Ballad of Belle Dorcas,* and later for *Sukey and the Mermaid.* The couple searched for several years for a subject on which they could collaborate when the idea came for *Alvin Ailey.* "Brian and I had wanted to work on a project together," Andrea told Susan Stan in *Five Owls,* "and we have always gone to see the Alvin Ailey American Dance Theater. At one point I said to Brian, 'I just wish there was a subject we were both interested in working on, like Alvin Ailey.'" Since then, the Pinkneys have worked together to produce *Seven Candles for Kwanzaa* (1989), *Dear Benjamin Banneker* (1994), *The Amazing Fortune Telling Book* (1995), *Bill Pickett: Rodeo Ridin' Cowboy* (1996), *I Smell Honey* (1997), *Pretty Brown Face* (1997), *Duke Ellington* (1997), and *Watch Me Dance* (1997). Brian also began to branch out into creating his own text based on his own personal experiences. He told *SATA:* "When I illustrate stories, I like to be personally involved. I like illustrating stories about African-American subject matter because I learn about my culture and heritage. I also like stories I can get involved with, like *Where Does the Trail Lead?* I illustrated my experiences growing up on Cape Cod during the summer when I was young. When I illustrated the book *Alvin* . . . I got to act out Alvin's life as a dancer. My wife and I took dance lessons, which was a lot of fun."

Major Works

Where Does the Trail Lead? features a little African-American boy exploring a seaside trail on an uninhabited island. The trail leads him past the lighthouse, over the dunes, and along the shore, where he sees rabbits and geese, and all the other pleasures of the beach. He eventually arrives at his family's campfire site where he shares his adventures with them. Phyllis G. Sidorsky commented that Pinkney "effectively captures the remoteness, the abandonment of the setting, and the boy's spirit of untrammeled discovery," while a reviewer for *Publishers Weekly* praised Pinkney's "textured illustrations," which "admirably conjure up the movement of the wind, waves, seagulls in flight and the running, leaping boy, making this seaside world very real indeed." Carolyn Phelan noted the "striking and unusual" artwork as the "most effective part of the book."

According to an author's note, *Sukey and the Mermaid* is based on "one of the relatively few authenticated African American folk tales involving mermaids." Sukey is a young girl whose stepfather exploits her cruelly as his slave. When she goes to the seashore for respite, she unintentionally calls up a beautiful mermaid who comforts and refreshes her. When Sukey's life becomes unbearable, the mermaid, now her friend, takes her to live under the sea. Though grateful for her rescue and fond of the mermaid, Sukey eventually begins to long for the world above water. The mermaid sends her home with gold for her dowry and the promise of a husband, but Sukey's greedy stepfather steals the gold, kills Sukey's intended, and then tries to capture the mermaid for himself. In the end, the stepfather receives his just reward, Sukey's lover is returned to life, and all is well. A *Kirkus Reviews* contributor found Pinkney's illustrations "his best yet," praising *Sukey and the Mermaid* as "an unusually handsome presentation of an appealing tale." Mary M. Burns lauded the work's skillfully crafted and powerful artistic dimension: "Pinkney has captured Sukey's innate dignity and strength through the demanding scratchboard medium. The figures are given sculptural dimension; the undulating waves from which the elegant mermaid emerges suggest a magical world without becoming fey; the color is commanding—mysterious, deep, almost hypnotic."

Reviewers further hailed Pinkney's sophisticated scratchboard illustrations for Robert D. San Souci's adaptation of another African-American folktale, *The Faithful Friend*. This tale from Martinique tells of two young men, one black and one white, who grew up together in the same house. When one falls in love with a beautiful girl, the other sacrifices himself for his friend's happiness. The story's suspense is "enhanced by Pinkney's brooding illustrations," Betsy Hearne commented, concluding that the tension of the "ghostly white linework against backgrounds of dark forest or dim interiors exposes a twilight side to characteristically brilliant Caribbean colors." In a similar vein, the Pinkneys introduce young readers to the African-American family celebration of Kwanzaa, in *Seven Candles for Kwanzaa*. The origin, philosophy, and terminology of the holiday are described, as are the activities and themes for each of the seven days. Jane Marino commented, "It is Brian Pinkney's distinctive illustrations that set this [book] apart from other recent nonfiction books about the holiday. The scratchboard and pastels combine for a singular and striking effect."

Pinkney has written several texts drawn from his own personal experiences, including *Max Found Two Sticks* (1994), based on his enjoyment playing the drums, and *JoJo's Flying Side Kick*, a tribute to his commitment to the martial art of Tae Kwon Do, in which he holds a black belt. When JoJo's Tae Kwon Do master tells her that tomorrow she will take her first advancement test to earn her yellow belt, she is understandably nervous. JoJo consults her friends and family, who all give her helpful advice: Granddaddy shows her his boxing shuffle, P. J. tells her to yell from her center, and Mamma suggests visualization. To add to her anxiety, a tree in JoJo's yard looks like a bandit and frightens her every time she passes it. When it is time for JoJo's test, she utilizes all the good advice, and even her fear of the bandit tree, to break a board with a flying sidekick and win her belt. Linda Ward-Callaghan praised Pinkney's carefully selected scratchboard renderings of "JoJo's turbulent emotions," and his evocative use of color to enhance each mood of the story. "His tranquil blues and warm yellows," Ward-Callaghan noted, "evoke the loving community of family and friends that surrounds JoJo, while touches of violet, added to the bandit tree and swirled through JoJo's bedroom, reflect the unsettling fears in JoJo's mind. Anyone who has faced a similar sleepless night will appreciate Pinkney's empowering story and cheer as JoJo finds her own way to channel her fears."

With its comic-book style and humor, *The Adventures of Sparrowboy* recounts the adventures of Henry who, in the midst of delivering newspapers one morning, finds himself suddenly flying. In the spirit of the superhero, Henry does what he can to put the world to right—ties up a mean dog, foils the neighborhood bullies, rescues a cat and subsequently, the cat's intended dinner: the sparrow whose powers Henry has borrowed. *The Adventures of Sparrowboy* embraces Pinkney's childhood love of comics and superheroes. In his acceptance speech for the *Boston Globe-Horn Book* Award, he recalled: "When I was twelve years old, I loved looking at comic books, and spent all my spare time drawing superheroes in the margins of my notebooks at home and at school." *The Adventures of Sparrowboy* also draws on Pinkney's reading of *Jonathan Livingston Seagull* and his own adventures as a paperboy. "I had my share of dogs chasing me, and near-collisions on my bike, . . ." he commented. "The idea for *The Adventures of Sparrowboy* grew out of these experiences— drawing superheroes, my fascination with flight, and my paper route."

Awards

In 1990 *The Boy and the Ghost* won the National Arts Club Award of Distinction and *The Ballad of Belle Dorcas* was recognized as a Notable Book in the Field of Social Studies from the National Council on the Social Studies and the Children's Book Council. Pinkney also received the latter award for *Cut from the Same Cloth, Dear Benjamin Banneker, The Dark Thirty,* and *Bill Pickett: Rodeo Ridin' Cowboy*. In 1991 *Where Does the Trail Lead?* won the Golden Kite Honor Award for illustration. *Sukey and the Mermaid* won the Coretta Scott King Honor Book Award for illustration and was named a Notable Book by the American Library Association, both in 1993. *The Dark Thirty* was designated a Newbery Honor Book and received the Coretta Scott King Honor Book Award in 1993. *The Faithful Friend* was designated a Caldecott Honor Book and received the Coretta Scott King Honor Book Award, both in 1996. *The Adventures of Sparrowboy* won the *Boston Globe-Horn Book* Award for Picture Book in 1997. *Duke Ellington: The Piano Prince and His Orchestra* was designated a Caldecott Honor Book in and a Coretta Scott King Illustrator Honor Book in 1998.

ILLUSTRATOR'S COMMENTARY

Richard Donahue

SOURCE: "Flying Starts: New Faces of 1989," in *Publishers Weekly,* December 22, 1989, pp. 26-7.

In talking about growing up and following in the footsteps of an illustrious father, Brian Pinkney says, "I got a lot of validation from him, then and now." The son of the noted illustrator Jerry Pinkney, the young Pinkney never actually received art lessons from him. Instead, the son's artistic skills were refined in a process "more like osmosis," for, as he admits, "I probably wouldn't have listened to him. To a kid, 'pick up your room' and 'paint that nose differently' sound the same." When asked whether his father offered criticism of his son's early efforts, Pinkney replied, "When I was younger he loved everything. The critique came when I got into college." And, together with talent and hard work, the critique has paid off: in September Simon & Schuster published Robert D. San Souci's *The Boy and the Ghost,* illustrated by J. Brian Pinkney.

Coincidentally, San Souci is also the author of this season's *The Talking Eggs,* which was illustrated by Pinkney *père.* And carrying coincidence a step further, Pinkney *fils,* for his next book, will be working with Denise Cronin at Knopf, the same art director who guided his father's paintings for *Mirandy and Brother Wind* to a Caldecott Honor. That new book is William Hooks's *The Ballad of Belle Dorcas,* an African-American folktale set in the 1800s. Pinkney is also illustrating Polly Carter's biography of Harriet Tubman, to be published by Silver Burdett & Ginn. Regarding the considerable research involved in these projects, Pinkney comments, "Being strictly accurate was very important to me, both from a historical and a racial standpoint."

Reaching the black community—responsibly—is one of Pinkney's major concerns. "I feel somewhat accountable to the images I make," he says. "I want to make sure I'm doing the right thing, as Spike Lee would say. I want to put forth a positive image of blacks, in portraits that are truthful and not stereotypical."

Pinkney is enrolled in the M.F.A. Program in Illustration at Manhattan's School of Visual Arts, where an exhibit of his original art (for *The Boy and the Ghost* and his two forthcoming books) is running through January. Currently he is working in scratchboard, a process in which images are etched onto a surface in reverse by scraping away a black coating on a board.

Pinkney has been careful not to trade on his father's reputation. Having abbreviated his own first name, "Jerry," to "J." (for *The Boy and the Ghost*), he's now planning to drop the initial altogether to avoid further confusion—apparently when a group of students recently asked Pinkney senior to autograph books following a lecture, he was handed copies of *The Boy and the Ghost.*

Though there's no competition brewing within the family ranks, Pinkney comments, "I'm always comparing myself to him—what he was doing at my age." But the 28-year-old is quick to add, "I'm not just chasing him, I'm forging my own way."

Brian Pinkney

SOURCE: "The Adventures of Sparrowboy," in *The Horn Book Magazine,* Vol. LXXIV, No. 1, January, 1998, pp. 49-52.

[*The following is Brian Pinkney's acceptance speech for the* Boston Globe-Horn Book *Award for picture book, which he delivered at the annual meeting of the New England Library Association in Sturbridge, Massachusetts on October 6, 1997.*]

Good morning! It's an honor to be here. My father, Jerry Pinkney, was honored with the *Boston Globe-Horn Book* Award two years ago for his illustrations in the book *John Henry* by Julius Lester. Today, I can truly say that I am following in my father's footsteps.

When I was twelve years old, I loved looking at comic books, and spent all my spare time drawing superheroes in the margins of my notebooks at home and at school. I was really growing as an artist, but my grades suffered, because I wasn't giving enough time to my schoolwork.

My parents validated me as a young artist, but they were quick to get me a tutor to help me bring up my grades. My tutor's name was Mr. Cousins, and to this day I still schedule my time the way Mr. Cousins taught me to so that I can have enough time to draw superheroes *and* take care of business. Mr. Cousins also introduced me to an unforgettable book—*Jonathan Livingston Seagull* by Richard Bach, an allegorical tale about flight and pushing past one's limitations. Mr. Cousins was an insightful man. He knew what it would take—a book about flying—to get my attention.

The next school year, I wanted a drum set more than anything. Since I wanted this so badly, my parents agreed to meet me halfway on the cost. So I went to work as a paperboy in my neighborhood. Being a paperboy was quite an adventure. I had my share of dogs chasing me, and near-collisions on my bike. But I stuck with it, and eventually I had enough money to buy my drum set. I also learned the satisfaction of earning my own money, and feeling empowered by the independence I gained from holding down a steady job.

The idea for *The Adventures of Sparrowboy* grew out of these experiences—drawing superheroes, my fascination with flight, and my paper route.

One day, while I was nodding off on the subway—which is how I get some of my best book ideas—all these elements came together, and *The Adventures of Sparrowboy* began to take shape.

The first scene that came to my thoughts was that of a paperboy falling off his bike, and instead of hitting the ground, he flies into the air. From there, I saw this boy saving people with his new-found power of flight. I realized right then that this child was a mini-superhero. And it wasn't long before I gave him the name Henry/Sparrowboy.

Next came the hard part. I knew I wanted Henry to get his power of flight from a sparrow, but I had to figure out how, exactly, this was to happen. So I went home and started sketching. I sketched for months, trying to resolve several aspects of the story—how, like a true superhero, Henry saved people in his neighborhood; how Henry became empowered by his adventure; and how he returned the power of flight back to the sparrow.

I grew obsessed with every detail of the story. That's when my wife, Andrea, began to notice that I was waking up a lot in the middle of the night to write things down. Andrea knows that when this happens, I'm falling into what we call "the abyss"—the mire of creative thought. Soon I had a dummy book to show, and Andrea, as always, was my first reader.

Then I showed the story to my editor at Simon & Schuster, Virginia Duncan, and to art director Paul Zakris. I just knew that after months of subway daydreams and night-hour sketching, Virginia and Paul would be blown away. Yes, they liked what I'd done, but suggested that I go all-out to make the story really big and fantastical. As the three of us talked about the potential *The Adventures of Sparrowboy* could have, the chain of events with all the neighbors in the story began to unfold in my mind.

Another theme that I wanted to bring to the story was that of how a child can make sense of newspaper headlines that glamorize the problems of our world. I resolved this theme by showing that young Henry can't change what happens in the news, but he *can* make a difference in his neighborhood.

Because *The Adventures of Sparrowboy* is so visually driven, the final piece of inspiration that brought the book together for me came from looking at my favorite old comic books, and from studying their color palette, language, and design.

I'd like to thank the *Boston Globe-Horn Book* Award committee for honoring *The Adventures of Sparrowboy,* and for acknowledging a book that steps beyond the traditional.

I thank my editor Virginia Duncan and art director Paul Zakris for pushing me further than I could see. And I thank Rick Richter and Stephanie Lurie and all the other folks at Simon & Schuster for their contributions in making the book a success. I thank my agent Sheldon Fogelman for his insightful guidance. I thank my parents, Jerry and Gloria Pinkney, for their insightful wisdom and years of encouragement and validation. And

finally, I'd like to thank my wife, Andrea, who, during the creation of *The Adventures of Sparrowboy,* was expecting our daughter, Chloe, and was still able to show me the patience and understanding that only a fellow writer could.

GENERAL COMMENTARY

Rudine Sims Bishop

SOURCE: "The Pinkney Family: In the Tradition," in *The Horn Book Magazine,* Vol. LXXII, No. 1, January-February, 1996, pp. 42-49.

Jerry and Gloria. Brian and Andrea. The Pinkney family is unique in African-American children's literature, perhaps in all of American children's literature: four members of the family—two generations, two couples, two artists (one an author-illustrator), two writers—all currently producing award-winning children's literature. And other family members are in the wings. How has this come about? What is there about this family that led to children's books becoming the family business? . . .

[Brian's mother] Gloria begins, "Jerry has been working at home for a very long time, over twenty-five years, and the studio is in the house. So the children have always been exposed to art. I'm a milliner and a silversmith, and I worked at home, too, so there has always been creative activity in the household. And we always supplied the children with materials. They all had their own space, so they started working at an early age."

Brian confirms his parents' account. "The main cause is my father. When we were growing up and went to museums or dance concerts or things like that, we always came home and made pictures. It was a family activity. We'd pull out the paper, and we'd all start drawing. It got to the point that it was just natural for me to draw. My mother would find me in the corner drawing and would say, 'Wow, that's beautiful. Go show your father.' And he was in his studio, which was in the house, so that's when I got to see his world."

Brian is an illustrator whose books include *Sukey and the Mermaid* by Robert San Souci, an ALA Notable and Coretta Scott King Honor Book, and three nonfiction picture books created in collaboration with his wife, Andrea Davis Pinkney. Brian has recently begun to write, and as author-illustrator, he has created *Max Found Two Sticks* and *JoJo's Flying Side Kick.*

Jerry elaborates on the children's artistic upbringing: "When the children were growing up, one of the things Gloria and I wanted for them was to be able to make decisions about what would make them happy in terms of careers. We recognized very early that they were all very talented. So we provided them, as Gloria said, with materials and working space, but we never put any form of pressure on them toward going into the arts. The first reason was that we wanted *them* to choose what they wanted to do. Secondly, because Gloria and I have a love for art, music, and literature, we wanted them to have—even if they didn't pursue it as a career—something else in their life that would give them that kind of joy. The key was that they made the decision for themselves."

Asked about art lessons, Jerry replies that they never provided formal art lessons or critiqued their work when Brian and his siblings were children. Both he and Gloria assert, and Brian concurs, that what they offered was mainly encouragement. Gloria notes that some of the children's early paintings still hang—framed—in the kitchen. . . .

Brian is Jerry and Gloria's second child. Not only is he an illustrator, but he also is a drummer and an aficionado of *tae kwan do,* a Korean martial arts form. His parents remember him as being creative from the very beginning. Brian himself recalls finding, when he was in second or third grade, a library book that told how to make figures out of pipe cleaners. He started working with pipe cleaners and eventually took the concept in his own direction, creating superheroes, cowboys, and space ships from colored wire, then taking them apart to make something new. He came to prefer his handmade original toys to store-bought ones.

Brian explored other media as well. His mother recently gave him a horse that he had sewn together when he was a child. But Brian says that he always wanted to be like his father. For his tenth birthday, he was given a miniature drafting table and paints like the ones Jerry used, and his mother set up his first studio, a converted walk-in closet.

Brian continues to follow his own direction, however. His first picture book was illustrated, like his father's work, in watercolors, but by the time he came to his second picture book, he had found his own medium, scratchboard, a technique in which the picture is scratched through an inked surface. In many of Brian's works, oil paints are then added. Jerry admires Brian's ability to deal with the pressures of working in the same field as a successful father. He sees Brian as "an incredibly courageous young man, able to handle the opening of the door, and the responsibility once the door was opened. Where I find him most courageous is what he has done with his own space. Changing from watercolor to scratchboard to oil; using what I was able to provide, then finding his own space."

Andrea Davis Pinkney, Brian's wife, is a children's book editor for Simon and Schuster and the author of three picture books—*Alvin Ailey, Seven Candles for Kwanzaa,* and *Dear Benjamin Banneker,* all illustrated by Brian. . . .

After graduation, Andrea went off to New York City, where she met Brian; they were married in 1991. Her in-laws are delighted to welcome her to the family and to the Pinkney tradition.

The first of their collaborations, *Alvin Ailey,* came after several years of looking for a way to work together. Andrea was writing for various publications and reading the manuscripts that Brian was receiving, acquiring a good sense of the kinds of picture books that were being written and of the kinds of texts Brian liked to illustrate. Brian kept encouraging Andrea to try her hand at writing children's books, and she kept holding out for a joint project, until one day she said, "I just wish we could find something we could do together—like Alvin Ailey." And their first collaborative book project was born.

When asked to describe the way they work together on a book, Brian states, "It has to be something we're both excited about. Usually that means there is some aspect that adds something for me in terms of the visuals. Then we bounce it back and forth in terms of the direction it may go in. Sometimes Andrea may do a rough draft first, and I'll read that and have some comments on it. Other times we'll sit down and maybe I'll lay out some thumbnail sketches of the way I see images going. And then Andrea has that as a structure for the story."

Andrea adds, "I like to call the books nonfiction with a twist. Oftentimes the idea will come from a very small bit of information. With the Benjamin Banneker book, my editor at Harcourt, Elizabeth Van Doren, worked with me on developing it around Banneker's correspondence with Thomas Jefferson. We get a little tidbit like that, and these projects, especially the biographies, become all-encompassing." For the Alvin Ailey book, for instance, they both took dance lessons from Ella Thompson Moore, who had been a dancer in Ailey's company. Andrea's mother had been right, after all.

Part of Andrea's introduction to the world of children's books came through modeling for Brian. Among the characters she posed for are the mermaid in *Sukey and the Mermaid* and Belle Dorcas in *The Ballad of Belle Dorcas* by William Hooks. "I had no idea that some illustrators photograph models and do research . . . I developed a whole new appreciation for the art form." Brian recollects, too, that one of the ways he entered into the world of children's books was as a model for his father. Brian remembers modeling "at about age eight or nine, and dressing up with my mother for a book about a little boy in Africa who plays the flute.". . .

When Brian illustrated his first picture book, *The Boy and the Ghost,* he too was working in watercolors. He had been assisting his father in his work, so it was a familiar medium. "I felt most secure in watercolor, probably because I was certain what the finished artwork would look like, because of my father." After Brian had completed the book, he learned that Jerry had actually declined to illustrate it because he was unable to visualize a way to portray the ghost. "When I read it, of course, I saw the ghost perfectly, and it was him."

Readers familiar with *The Boy and the Ghost* will spot Jerry sporting red hair and a red beard. It was a turn of the tables—Brian as illustrator, Jerry as model. . . .

As time passes, roles change, but the tradition continues. Jerry has done some college teaching and is now acting as mentor to some younger illustrators outside the family. And the family remains close. Brian still shows his work to his father, and Jerry is sensitive enough to provide only the kind of feedback he feels Brian wants. Father and son spend hours on the telephone weekly. Brian is pleased that his mother has now begun to read her stories to him. Andrea notes, "There's hardly a holiday or barbecue where we all don't talk about ideas and publishing and, 'What are you doing?' Usually we end up in Jerry's studio to see what he's working on, and talking about what Brian is working on. Gloria and I will ask each other, 'Have you read this book?' or, 'Do you know this writer?' It's great, and there are times when we say, 'Do you know we just spent the last *four hours* talking about books?'"

Sharing is the word that comes first to Andrea when she thinks of the family. "It's an open exchange of ideas. It's just a very rich experience, and I think we're all very fortunate." So is the field of American children's literature.

TITLE COMMENTARY

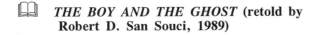 *THE BOY AND THE GHOST* (retold by Robert D. San Souci, 1989)

Kirkus Reviews

SOURCE: A review of *The Boy and the Ghost,* in *Kirkus Reviews,* Vol. LVII, No. 15, August 15, 1989, p. 1250.

Derived from two "negro ghost stories" published in 1898, a variant on the story of a traveler who stays overnight in a deserted house and is visited by a ghost who arrives in pieces. Here, the story is extended by describing Thomas as the middle child in a large, poor family, off to look for work; since he survives his fearful experience, the ghost gives him his treasure—on the condition that he share it with others who are also poor. Though not especially spooky, the story reads well. In his first picture book, Pinkney—whose style resembles that of the well-known illustrator of that name—makes a promising debut, especially in his pictures of sturdy, self-reliant Thomas.

Publishers Weekly

SOURCE: A review of *The Boy and the Ghost,* in *Publishers Weekly,* Vol. 236, No. 10, September 8, 1989, p. 68.

Children love nothing better than a good ghost story, and this wonderful version of a black American tale from the turn of the century won't disappoint. As the middle child of seven, Thomas decides he is the best one to venture to the city to earn money for the family. His parents tell him to be polite, generous, brave and honest, no matter what. On the way, he shares some soup with a stranger, who repays him by directing him to a haunted house full of treasure. As the guileless Thomas goes about preparing his supper, he is undaunted by the ghost who appears bit by bit. When the ghost roars at Thomas, he politely offers some soup. Because the boy is the first to stay long enough for the ghost to reassemble himself, he is led to the treasure behind the house. San Souci's version retains all the folksy charm of the original story of this sincere, spunky young man. An additional note traces the Old and New World roots of this folktale. Pinkney exhibits great style in his debut, depicting Thomas and the ghost in evocative, lovely watercolors. This story will delight long after the last embers have died down.

Denise Wilms

SOURCE: A review of *The Boy and the Ghost,* in *Booklist,* Vol. 86, No. 3, October 1, 1989, p. 355.

This tale's story line will be familiar to readers of *Esteban and the Ghost,* though the locale is different. Here, the adventure is set in the South and features a self-possessed black boy who braves a night in a haunted house and effectively deals with a ghost that tumbles down the chimney in pieces. Details are also changed. Thomas, the middle child in a poor family of seven, wants to earn some money to help his parents. On his way to look for a job in town, he meets a stranger who tells him about a haunted house with a hidden treasure. Thomas decides to try his luck at staying all night in the place, and later that evening discovers the ghost's mission—to show the treasure to someone who will give half of it to the poor, allowing the ghost to rest in peace. Thomas, of course, is happy to carry out the specter's wishes, and returns home to improve his family's fortunes. Pinkney's line-and-water-color drawings show deft composition and a flair for the dramatic. Scenes of shanty, family, and hot fields are quiet and restrained, but those involving the ghost are considerably more dynamic. A handy pick for story hours, especially around Halloween.

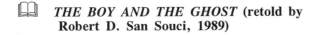 *THE BALLAD OF BELLE DORCAS* (retold by William H. Hooks, 1990)

Kirkus Reviews

SOURCE: A review of *The Ballad of Belle Dorcas,* in *Kirkus Reviews,* Vol. LVIII, No. 15, August 1, 1990, p. 1087.

Based on a Carolina conjure tale, the story of a woman

who was "free issue, her daddy being a white master, her mama being his house slave." An author's note explains that such people, "neither slaves nor full-fledged citizens," tended to intermarry; but Belle Dorcas sets her heart on Joshua and marries him even though he's a slave. When a new master threatens to sell Joshua, Belle Dorcas gets a spell from a conjure woman who warns that she must "give up Joshua to keep him": a "cunger bag" that—to Belle Dorcas' horror—changes Joshua into a tree. He can still be a man at night, however, even after the tree is used to shingle a smokehouse.

The telling here is undistinguished, but the story is poignant, intriguing, and of historical significance. In his third book, the younger Pinkney's illustrations—black scratchboard touched with subtle color—are his best to date, with sturdy, almost heroic figures set dramatically against the dark woods and cabins of the slaves' private night world. A brief "chapter book" suitable for sharing aloud.

Christine Behrmann

SOURCE: A review of *The Ballad of Belle Dorcas,* in *School Library Journal,* Vol. 36, No. 10, October, 1990, pp. 116-17.

A conjure tale from the Carolina coast. Belle Dorcas is "free issue"; that is, born of an African-American mother and a white father during the slavery period and free since birth. When it comes time to marry, she chooses no one but Joshua, the best fiddle player in the county—and a slave. She lives, as a free person, in the slave quarters with Joshua, but the plans of a new owner of the plantation to sell her husband inspire the first of several visits by Belle to Granny Lizard, the local "cunger" (conjure) woman. After asking Belle if she can bear to lose Joshua to keep him, she turns him into a giant cedar, explaining that he and Belle can be together as man and woman by night. Belle survives even the cutting of the wood of the "Joshua tree" for a smokehouse, always finding a way to be with Joshua at night. Upon her natural death, the smokehouse vanishes, replaced by two young cedars. Hook's retelling is smooth and powerful, limning the events of the plot with incisively concrete language. Pinkney's illustrations are the best element here, though; the scenes are skillfully rendered in a scratchboard style that evokes time and place while giving vivid life to characters and incident. Swirling scratched lines swoop through the images, bringing an aspect of eerie movement throughout. An entertaining ghost story with a satisfying conclusion and a memorable interpretation.

Susan Patron

SOURCE: A review of *The Ballad of Belle Dorcas,* in *The Five Owls,* Vol. V, No. 2, November, 1990, pp. 30-1.

Belle Dorcas is the daughter of a white master and his house slave. Her mama wants Belle, who was given her freedom at birth, to marry "a fine young man from the free-issue settlement," but Belle falls in love with a slave, Joshua. "Dear Mama," says Belle, "I'm breaking your heart but you are crushing mine." So the lovers are permitted to marry; they live in the slave quarters. But then the master dies unexpectedly. A new master arrives and decides to sell Joshua.

In despair and desperation, Belle Dorcas goes to the conjure woman, Granny Lizard, and exchanges her gold wedding earrings for a spell in which Belle must agree to give up Joshua to keep him. Not fully understanding the trade-off, Belle enchants Joshua as instructed. In a dramatic wordless double-page illustration, we see Joshua turn into a cedar tree.

Joshua remains a tree by day but returns to his human form by night. Even after the master orders the tree cut down and made into a smokehouse roof, the magic of the spell is sustained. Belle's consuming love, juxtaposed as it is with the terrifying force of slavery, has its own enormous and enduring power. It sustains her when she has nothing, is powerless, and even when she is half mad. The magic of the conjure woman may be seen as a metaphor for the power of love.

This conjure tale, the author explains in a prefatory note, is based on one he heard as a child growing up in the tidewater area of rural North Carolina, where conjurers were both feared and respected. Hooks explains that the term *free issue* "refers to the offspring of slave masters and slave women, children who were given their freedom at birth. Free issue people found themselves in a nether world, for they were neither slaves nor full-fledged citizens."

Brian Pinkney's illustrations are well-suited to the dramatic tension and mystery of the story. Using a fluid white crosshatched line against a black background, with soft colors sparingly added, Pinkney evokes a feeling of haunting beauty. The white line gives each picture a glowing, mysterious quality in keeping with the tone of the ballad-story. This book is a handsome production that children will want to return to often.

Betsy Hearne

SOURCE: A review of *The Ballad of Belle Dorcas,* in *Bulletin of the Center for Children's Books,* Vol. 44, No. 4, December, 1990, p. 87.

"Belle Dorcas was free issue, her daddy being a white master, her mama being his house slave." But though Belle has papers, she falls in love with a slave named Joshua, whom a new master plans to sell. Granny Lizard's conjure bag turns Joshua into a cedar tree by day, a man by night; even when the tree is chopped down to make a smokehouse, Joshua is resurrected from the cedar shingles nightly until Belle Dorcas ages and dies, leaving "two young cedar trees . . . growing side by side." An episodic legend depending on magic to resolve each threat, this combines the haunting motif of a lover transformed with a tragic historical drama. The author's note cites an oral tale from his Carolina coast childhood as the only source and gives information on Gullah conjure tales as well as on the "free" offspring of slave masters and slave women. Pinkney's full-color scratchboard illustrations swirl white lines against black backgrounds in a contrast that naturally highlights the secrecy and danger of the action. The visual effect is one of muted suspense, a tone especially appropriate for the misty past recreated here. Although this is a picture book in appearance, it's actually better suited for reading aloud to elementary students who have some historical sense in which to fit the complex elements of fantasy and reality.

Ethel L. Heins

SOURCE: A review of *The Ballad of Belle Dorcas,* in *The Horn Book Magazine,* Vol. LXVII, No. 2, March-April, 1991, pp. 208-09.

Conjure tales—stories of sorcery and magic—proliferated before the Civil War among the Gullah people of the coastal regions of the Carolinas and the Sea Islands. A tenacious holdover from African voodoo, conjuring was practiced by men and women believed to have supernatural powers. In 1899 Charles Chesnutt, an early African-American writer, published a collection of these tales; much later they were retold for children by Ray Anthony Shepard in *Conjure Tales;* its initial story, "Poor Sandy," is a version of *The Ballad of Belle Dorcas.* In William Hooks's imaginative narrative expanded from childhood memories, Belle Dorcas is as "pretty as her name, and no slave either," for she was born of a white master and his domestic slave and is legally free. Contrary to her mother's dream for her to marry a free man and live in dignity, the girl falls in love with Joshua, a talented, highly prized slave. Then a heartless new master arrives and is determined to sell the valuable Joshua and send him away; in her anguish Belle Dorcas seeks help from an old conjure woman. Desperately agreeing to an enigmatic bargain—she must give Joshua up in order to keep him—Belle, with horror, sees her husband transformed into a great cedar tree by a magic spell from which she can release him only for a few secret hours each night. The effect of the fluent, dramatic storytelling is immeasurably enhanced by the striking artwork, which casts its own spell. Emphasizing characterization through remarkable portraiture, the talented young artist has produced illustrations of emotional force; moreover, an abundance of pale swirling lines, as in scratchboard work, overlies the dark coloration and adds both beauty and atmosphere to the eerie tale of cruelty, tragedy, transfiguration, and steadfast love.

HARRIET TUBMAN AND BLACK HISTORY MONTH (written by Polly Carter, 1990)

Kirkus Reviews

SOURCE: A review of *Harriet Tubman and Black History Month,* in *Kirkus Reviews,* Vol. LVIII, No. 16, August 15, 1990, pp. 1175-76.

Tubman's story is conveyed in a lean, readable text that provides vibrant glimpses of a near-legendary figure—all through accessible dialogue comprised of Tubman's later comments about her slave years and fight for freedom—while Pinkney's scratchboard-like paintings resonate: a book guaranteed to kindle interest.

A WAVE IN HER POCKET: STORIES FROM TRINIDAD (retold by Lynn Joseph, 1991)

Kirkus Reviews

SOURCE: A review of *A Wave in Her Pocket: Stories from Trinidad,* in *Kirkus Reviews,* Vol. LIX, No. 8, April 15, 1991, p. 536.

The author of *Coconut Kind of Day* (1990) returns to the Caribbean to present a series of six vignettes featuring traditional folklore. The storyteller is Tantie, a great-aunt who is larger-than-life to narrator Amber and her cousins. Tantie has a tale for every occasion: one about the witch-like soucouyant for a picnic; one featuring Ligahoo, a powerful shape-changer, for the rainy season; or one about graveyard jumbies to explain the absence of neighbors. The most affecting narratives are the title story, concerning Tantie's lost love, and another about her encounter with papa Bois, a beloved figure in Trinidad.

Less formal folktales than flavorful slices of life, all shaped into a continuous narrative uniting the family with stories. An afterword tells more about the legends. Pinkney's skillfully evocative b&w scratchboard illustrations nicely match the spirit of the text. An entertaining introduction to a relatively unfamiliar folk tradition.

Leone McDermott

SOURCE: A review of *A Wave in Her Pocket: Stories from Trinidad,* in *Booklist,* Vol. 87, No. 18, May 15, 1991, p. 1794.

Fresh and warm as an island breeze, these six stories combine Trinidad's traditional folklore with a child's view of island life. Joseph skillfully employs a tale-within-a-tale structure: Amber, a little girl, tells of her wonderful, mysterious Tantie (or grandaunt), who has a story for every occasion. Tantie knows how to kill a soucouyant (a fiery vampire), how to handle the mischievous, ghostly jumbies, and how to put down an ordinary boor. She throws a great party, makes sweet

From A Wave in Her Pocket: Stories from Trinidad, *retold by Lynn Joseph. Illustrated by Brian Pinkney.*

mango pies, and nobody can ever get the better of her. Joseph's language sparkles, whether Amber is describing nature ("The waves were smacking the rocks with big kisses and then ducking back into the sea") or her own reactions ("Every year starting in May, the rainy season comes and sits like a heavy bushel basket on my head"). Especially nice is the understated tenderness between grandaunt and grandniece. In the title story, Tantie tells Amber of losing her childhood sweetheart, who drowned while fishing, and Amber unlocks for Tantie the true meaning of an old ocean song. Pinkney's distinctive drawings in white crosshatch on a black background echo the mysterious side of island life. This wonderful addition to the folklore shelf is spiced with magic and suspense.

Ruth Semrau

SOURCE: A review of *A Wave in Her Pocket: Stories from Trinidad,* in *School Library Journal,* Vol. 37, No. 7, July, 1991, pp. 69-70.

Tantie Delphine's stories liven all family gatherings, and serve the equally profound purpose of passing the culture to a new generation. She tells scary stories about the ball-of-fire vampire and the Ligahoo, who brings floods; tender stories of Tantie's lost lover; trickster

stories of talking monkeys; or curious stories of enchanted beads and knowledge of the future. Joseph recreates moments from her own childhood on the island of Trinidad for a wider audience without sacrificing any of the unique flavor and immediacy of some new/old legends. Graceful prose and enthralling use of the island vernacular will make delightful story times. What lucky children to have such a storytelling tantie, and how lucky readers are to have Joseph to pass the tales on to them. Pinkney's expressive scratchboard drawings complement each story with a portrait of the protagonist or the action from his own point of view.

WHERE DOES THE TRAIL LEAD? (written by Burton Albert, 1991)

Publishers Weekly

SOURCE: A review of *Where Does the Trail Lead?,* in *Publishers Weekly,* Vol. 238, No. 25, June 7, 1991, p. 65.

On Summertime Island, a boy discovers that all trails lead down "to the edge of the sea." Yet each holds its own mystery, and before the wild waves loom into view there is plenty for the boy to see and explore. Albert's evocative prose poem captures the anticipation of summer vacation, the thrill of new surroundings combined with the security of knowing that the family is near. His format is simple: a question—"Where does the trail lead?"—is eloquently answered by a variety of responses, e.g., "to a boat's bow of cattails at the edge of the sea." Finally the trail guides the boy back to "the crackle of campfires and the smell of fresh-caught fish" and a homey scene with his parents and little sister. Pinkney's (*The Ballad of Belle Dorcas; The Boy and the Ghost*) textured illustrations admirably conjure up the movement of the wind, waves, seagulls in flight and the running, leaping boy, making this seaside world very real indeed.

Kirkus Reviews

SOURCE: A review of *Where Does the Trail Lead?,* in *Kirkus Reviews,* Vol. LIX, No. 12, June 15, 1991, p. 795.

The trail in question is the route of a boy exploring "Summertime Island," where he finds a lighthouse, various creatures, "a ghost town of shanties at the edge of the sea," and a derelict boat, then returns to picnic with his parents on the beach at twilight. Pinkney's handsome scratchboard illustrations depict an inquisitive, self-reliant black boy, with the medium's rather somber tones reflecting the narrative's introspective quality. Quiet, but nice.

Phyllis G. Sidorsky

SOURCE: A review of *Where Does the Trail Lead?,* in *School Library Journal,* Vol. 37, No. 7, July, 1991, p. 52.

A poetic evocation of a boy's solitary exploration of an uninhabited island. One summer's day a black youngster dashes along a seaside trail, past a lighthouse, over dunes, along wave-whipped shores, catching glimpses of rabbits scampering into bushes and geese flying overhead. "Where does the trail lead?" is the question posed throughout the brief narrative. There is a sense of loneliness, and yet readers will catch the boy's excitement as he strikes out along the trail, absorbing all of its sights and sounds. He enthusiastically shares his adventures at story's end with his family gathered around a campfire on the beach. Using a palette of muted violet, sienna, ochre, cobalt, and spruce green in his scratchboard illustrations, Pinkney enlivens his paintings with flicks of bright color. He effectively captures the remoteness, the abandonment of the setting, and the boy's spirit of untrammeled discovery.

Carolyn Phelan

SOURCE: A review of *Where Does the Trail Lead?*, in *Booklist*, Vol. 87, No. 22, August, 1991, p. 2152.

In this picture book, the text creates a mood. By following a trail through a coastal island and past a lighthouse, tide pools, trees, dunes, railroad tracks, and so on, it lulls the listener into the quiet pace of the setting and the wonders that await discovery there. Pinkney's illustrations put a black boy at the center of the story, leading him through an active exploration of the island and bringing him home at twilight to his family's campfire by the sea. Striking and unusual, the artwork is the most effective part of the book. As he did in Hooks' *Ballad of Belle Dorcas,* Pinkney uses scratchboard for the linear elements, then tints each illustration with delicate strokes of muted color. A good change of pace for story hours with a seaside theme.

📖 SUKEY AND THE MERMAID (retold by Robert D. San Souci, 1992)

Kirkus Reviews

SOURCE: A review of *Sukey and the Mermaid,* in *Kirkus Reviews,* Vol. LX, No. 4, February 15, 1992, p. 260.

Weary of the unreasonable demands of Mister Jones, her new stepfather, Sukey escapes to the water's edge, where she meets "a beautiful, brown-skinned, black-eyed mermaid"—Mama Jo—who befriends and comforts her and each day gives her a gold coin. Mister Jones drinks up most of the money; eventually, he tries to capture the mermaid, who escapes and takes Sukey to her undersea kingdom. Homesick, Sukey bargains for a chance to go home and is also given a dowry and the promise of a fine husband, to be named Dembo. Wicked Mister Jones steals the dowry and kills Dembo; but Mama Jo appears one last time to bring him back to life.

A careful note explains that this eventful, richly com-

plex story was based on a folktale from the Sea Islands of South Carolina, as well as on Caribbean and West African sources. Pinkney's delicately tinted scratchboard illustrations are his best yet; the many fine lines swirl through the dramatic black ground, catching the sea's luminous glow and softening the sturdy figures with diaphanous garments. An unusually handsome presentation of an appealing tale.

Betsy Hearne

SOURCE: A review of *Sukey and the Mermaid*, in *Bulletin of the Center for Children's Books,* Vol. 45, No. 7, March, 1992, p. 192.

An organic blend of fantasy and South Carolina island folklore, this exemplifies the best ongoing tradition of storytelling in picture book format. The heroine is young Sukey, who, to escape from her oppressive stepfather, goes daily to the seashore for a visit with a brown-skinned mermaid: "Thee, thee, down below,/ Come to me, Mama Jo." After trying to capture the mermaid with Sukey's summons, the angry stepfather works the girl nearly to death. She escapes underwater and returns with a dowry of gold, only to have her true love struck down; twice more the mermaid intervenes, once to revive Sukey's betrothed and once to drown the villain. It's a long story, but one supported with strong writing and some of Brian Pinkney's most expansive illustration. His compositions are broadly conceived, his white hatch over dark colors richly textured, and his characters skillfully drawn in both face and figure. From her black eyes to her deep-green tail, the mermaid is a natural extension of the wild seascapes. However tenuous the narrative connection with West African sources—and San Souci cites some research in a brief author's note—the language and art together take on rich African-American hues in this newly imagined version.

Mary M. Burns

SOURCE: A review of *Sukey and the Mermaid,* in *The Horn Book Magazine,* Vol. LXVIII, No. 5, September, 1992, pp. 593-94.

Many familiar motifs can be identified in this tale of a child, abused by her stepfather, who finds succor through the magical intervention of a beautiful African-American mermaid. Yet, the diction of the narrator sets it in a specific locale and gives it a unique flavor. The central character is Sukey, who, one hot afternoon, sings a snatch of half-remembered song: "Thee, thee, down below, / Come to me, Mama Jo." The mermaid thus summoned listens to her woes, gives her a coin to appease her parents, and becomes her friend. As Sukey's lot fails to improve, the mermaid offers her the endless comfort of the kingdom beneath the sea—which refuge Sukey accepts until longing for the world becomes too strong and she wins the right to return by posing a riddle to her protector. Although grieved by the outcome, the mermaid lives up to her side of the bargain and generously provides for Sukey's future. But, in the last analysis, it is not the mermaid's gifts but Sukey's own integrity which wins Sukey freedom and love. Pinkney has captured Sukey's innate dignity and strength through the demanding scratchboard medium. The figures are given sculptural dimension; the undulating waves from which the elegant mermaid emerges suggest a magical world without becoming fey; the color is commanding—mysterious, deep, almost hypnotic. The combination of text and illustrations is indeed as powerful as it is appealing. According to the appended author's note, this captivating retelling of a South Carolina story is "one of the relatively few authenticated African-American folktales involving mermaids." In fleshing out the brief narrative that was his original inspiration, San Souci did considerable research and concluded that the earliest version was, in all probability, African. It is this documented attention to detail that gives the story additional credibility and value for folklore collections—a fine blending of scholarship and the storyteller's art, complemented by an outstanding visual interpretation.

THE ELEPHANT'S WRESTLING MATCH (written by Judy Sierra, 1992)

Janice Del Negro

SOURCE: A review of *The Elephant's Wrestling Match,* in *Booklist,* Vol. 88, No. 22, August, 1992, p. 2019.

Using his talking drum, the monkey sends the boastful mighty elephant's challenge to a wrestling match throughout the savannah. One by one, the she-leopard, the crocodile, and the rhinoceros are overpowered by the powerful beast. Then the tiny bat challenges the mighty elephant. At first, the elephant refuses to wrestle with the bat because she is too small and weak. But when the elephant is accused of being afraid, he finally agrees to the match—only to be defeated when the quick and clever bat flies into his ear. When the monkey beats news on his talking drum of the bat's victory, the angry elephant crushes the instrument, and "That is why nowadays you don't see monkeys playing the talking drum." Pinkney's scratchboard illustrations are involving and powerful, and Sierra's retelling of this folktale, derived from the Bulu people of Cameroon, Africa, is smooth and lively—the rhythmic, repetitive language makes the text not only eminently "tellable" but also ultimately memorable.

Linda Greengrass

SOURCE: A review of *The Elephant's Wrestling Match,* in *School Library Journal,* Vol. 38, No. 9, September, 1992, p. 211.

When mighty elephant challenges all the animals, great and small, to a wrestling match, monkey announces the challenge on his talking drum. The leopard, crocodile, and rhinoceros all respond, only to be easily thwarted by

the mighty beast. Each time, monkey beats out the results on the drum. Finally, the bat, small but clever, defeats him. When monkey beats out the news, the enraged elephant smashes his drum. That is why to this day, the story tells readers, "you don't see monkeys playing the talking drum." Although the themes in this folktale from Cameroon are familiar, what makes this fine version unusual is that it offers many of the best elements of storytelling. Young listeners will certainly anticipate elephant's imminent downfall the moment the tiny bat arrives on the scene, yet this enhances rather than detracts from the enjoyment of the tale. Through simple, rhythmic language, Sierra creates an effect that is quite sophisticated. Listeners can almost hear the beating of the drum. Furthermore, the text's repetitive and cumulative nature invites audiences to join in. In his splendid scratchboard drawings, Pinkney brings just enough expression to the faces of the animals to add texture to the tale without distracting from the overall feeling of oral tradition at work. The illustrations are large and brightly evocative of the African savannah, making this book a fine choice for group sharing.

THE DARK THIRTY: SOUTHERN TALES OF THE SUPERNATURAL (written by Patricia C. McKissack, 1992)

Publishers Weekly

SOURCE: A review of *The Dark Thirty: Southern Tales of the Supernatural,* in *Publishers Weekly,* Vol. 239, No. 40, September 7, 1992, p. 96.

"When I was growing up in the South," writes McKissack, "we called the half hour just before nightfall the dark-thirty." Her nine stories and one poem, however, are far too good to be reserved for "that special time when it is neither day nor night and when shapes and shadows play tricks on the mind." These short works—haunting in both senses of the word—explore aspects of the African American experience in the South, from slavery to the Underground Railroad and emancipation, from the era of Pullman cars to the desegregation of buses, from the terror of the Ku Klux Klan to '60s activism. Here, African Americans' historical lack of political power finds its counterbalance in a display of supernatural power: ghosts exact vengeance for lynchings; slaves use ancient magic to enforce their master's promise of emancipation. As carefully executed as McKissack's writings, Pinkney's black-and-white scratchboard illustrations enhance the book's atmosphere, at once clearly regional in setting and otherworldly in tone.

HAPPY BIRTHDAY, MARTIN LUTHER KING (written by Jean Marzollo, 1993)

Ilene Cooper

SOURCE: A review of *Happy Birthday, Martin Luther King,* in *Booklist,* Vol. 89, No. 8, December 15, 1992, p. 740.

Marzollo and Pinkney offer a simple yet effective look at King's life, focusing on his ability to affect change and bring people together. Beginning with the birth of King ("His parents loved him very much"), Marzollo describes his education, his life as a pastor, and his involvement in the civil rights movement. The book is at its best when it describes the qualities that made King so special: "He asked people not to fight with each other. He said there were peaceful ways to solve problems. . . . When he spoke, people listened." But there are also some noticeable lapses: though King and his father are shown in several spreads, King's wife, Coretta, and their children are never mentioned. King's death is dealt with in one brief sentence. Nevertheless, in her foreword Marzollo advises parents that they may find the words "shot and killed" inappropriate for preschoolers, though discussing his death could help them understand the grieving process. Pinkney's scratchboard art is outstanding. From the warm dust jacket picture, showing King surrounded by children, to the final spread, set at King's grave, the bold pictures with their changing perspectives are immediate and moving. Libraries will have calls for this on King's birthday and throughout the year.

Kirkus Reviews

SOURCE: A review of *Happy Birthday, Martin Luther King,* in *Kirkus Reviews,* Vol. LX, No. 24, December 15, 1992, p. 1575.

In a thoughtful note, Marzollo suggests that adults may wish to change the words "shot and killed" to "died" when sharing this book with preschoolers, but goes on to advise that "if we handle the subject sensitively, we will find that children, like ourselves, can look at truth and cope with death." Narrating King's life and accomplishments with a dignity and simplicity that is equally appropriate for young children or less accomplished older readers, the author concludes with a graceful summary of the reasons he is honored with a special day. Pinkney has created powerful, rather dark and somber illustrations using his trademark scratchboard technique with minimal color added, eloquently conveying the continuing grief for the our loss while dramatizing King's gentler strengths as well as his more heroic moments. A quiet, poignantly telling book.

Roger Sutton

SOURCE: A review of *Happy Birthday, Martin Luther King,* in *Bulletin of the Center for Children's Books,* Vol. 46, No. 6, February, 1993, p. 185.

[S]imple and direct . . . this very easy biography of Martin Luther King is distinguished by its succinct explanations of King's achievements: "Once there was a law in some places that said that black children and white children couldn't go to school together. Martin Luther King and other people, including many very brave children, had this law changed, too. Now black children and white children can go to school together." Occasionally, there's a tone of talking down to children ("His dream was that people everywhere would learn to live together without being mean to one another") but the narrative of King's life is smooth and accessible. Pinkney's scratchboard paintings are fluidly drawn, warm, and dignified, the restless lines of the scratchboarding animating and humanizing what could have been a daunting canonization.

CUT FROM THE SAME CLOTH: AMERICAN WOMEN OF MYTH, LEGEND, AND TALL TALE (retold by Robert D. San Souci, 1993)

Kirkus Reviews

SOURCE: A review of *Cut From the Same Cloth: American Women of Myth, Legend, and Tall Tale,* in *Kirkus Reviews,* Vol. LXI, No. 7, April 1, 1993, p. 464.

A frequent author retells old stories and, in effect, fashions new ones to fill a void that—he says in his preface—he deplores. Arranged geographically from northeast to west (including Alaska and Hawaii), these 15 tales of clever, strong-willed, or larger-than-life women represent several cultures—Anglo-, Native-, African-, and Mexican-American. Introductory remarks discuss locale or culture or note parallels in world folklore. The results are entertaining and often tellable. Yet San Souci alters stories to suit his purpose: e.g., the woman he calls "Old Sally Cato" is unnamed in his Missouri source, while the male giant she kills was "Bally Sally Cato"; even the African-American connection seems tenuous. Compared to one cited source, "Annie Christmas" is cleaned up almost beyond recognition. Neither is the subtitle quite accurate: two protagonists are sisters under the fur. And while the animal tales enhance ethnicity ("Sister Fox . . . " is the only Mexican American tale), they have a mean-spirited tone not found in the others. Detailed notes give clues to how much San Souci has embellished, rather than "collected," here; Pinkney's handsome b&w scratchboard illustrations and a spacious layout give the book a distinguished look. As they stand, the stories are useful; but it would be more honest to explain the rationale for the substantial revisions.

Publishers Weekly

SOURCE: A review of *Cut from the Same Cloth: American Women of Myth, Legend, and Tall Tale,* in *Publishers Weekly,* Vol. 240, No. 17, April 26, 1993, p. 81.

Stories culled from the melting pot of American culture (Hawaiian, Eskimo and Native American, among others) unite a league of female folk heroes as courageous, irascible and noble as any of their more famous male counterparts. This intriguing collection is the culmination of extensive research by folklorist San Souci (*The*

Talking Eggs; The Tsar's Promise), who invests each tale with the flavor and vigor of its individual subculture—the twangy Southern slang of longshoreman Annie Christmas, for example, contrasts vividly with the quiet strength of "Otoonah, an Eskimo Huntress." Not surprisingly, several stories feature the added challenge of overcoming the disrespect of males unwilling to accept a strong-willed female. The somewhat academic-sounding title seems to invite comparisons between male and female figures, diverting attention from the anthology's recreational and literary value. Pinkney's characteristically fine-lined scratchboard illustrations capture each woman's strength, often accentuating a tale's preposterous humor. In a succinct introduction, Jane Yolen credits the author with "rescuing the silent women, giving them back their tongues," for which many readers will be grateful.

Betsy Hearne

SOURCE: A review of *Cut From the Same Cloth: American Women of Myth, Legend, and Tall Tale,* in *Bulletin of the Center for Children's Books,* Vol. 46, No. 10, June, 1993, pp. 328-29.

Grouped by region—Northeast, South, Midwest, Southwest, and West—these fifteen stories offer a satisfying balance to the male-dominated tall tale figures. There's also a good ethnic mix here: six of the heroines are Native American, four African American, two Anglo American, one Mexican American, and one Hawaiian. If any particular characteristic seems to distinguish these superhumans from their male counterparts, it's the fact that the women's deeds tend to be less staggering than haunting. The Miwok legend of Hekeke, for instance, in which Hekeke is kidnapped by a cannibalistic giant and must watch him consume his victims until she destroys him, has a tone more reminiscent of Odysseus' experience in the cave of the Cyclops than of any Paul Bunyan-type feats. Otoonah's determined survival after being abandoned on an island by her brothers during a period of starvation is as adventurous a quest as you'll find anywhere. Others, such as "Molly Cottontail," are lighter-hearted or, like "Sweet Betsey from Pike," sharp-edged. San Souci has varied his retellings to suit the style of each story, and his introductions, source notes, and bibliography are commendably thorough. Brian Pinkney's signature scratchboard illustrations, one of which introduces each tale, are particularly well tuned to the heroic mode. This is a first-class resource for school media centers where students work with tall tales, or for public libraries where parents and professionals read folklore aloud and do storytelling.

Elizabeth S. Watson

SOURCE: A review of *Cut From the Same Cloth: American Women of Myth, Legend, and Tall Tale,* in *The Horn Book Magazine,* Vol. LXIX, No. 5, September, 1993, p. 612.

A strong collection of tales—Native-American, African-American, Anglo-American, Eskimo, and Hawaiian—from all sections of the United States feature female counterparts of Mike Fink and Paul Bunyan. Some of the heroines are familiar, but many are not. Jane Yolen states in her introduction, "These are truly women of wonder, women of power." Pinkney's illustrations underscore the strength of the heroines. The essence of each tale is captured in a full-page drawing, rendered in the style of a woodcut, which perfectly fits the sense of rough-and-ready early Americana that is basic to the stories. The humor, strength, and charisma of the women flow from the pictures. All the tales are thoroughly documented.

📖 *SEVEN CANDLES FOR KWANZAA* (written by Andrea Davis Pinkney, 1993)

Janice Del Negro

SOURCE: A review of *Seven Candles for Kwanzaa,* in *Booklist,* Vol. 89, No. 21, July, 1993, p. 1962.

This beautifully designed, attractive picture book describes the origin and traditions of the seven-day African American holiday of Kwanzaa. In clear, direct language, [Andrea] Pinkney talks about the importance of the harvest, the family togetherness, and the cultural pride that Kwanzaa celebrates. Her descriptions include a day-by-day account of the holiday that embraces the seven principles of Kwanzaa and the rituals recognizing them. Her joyful text is accompanied by equally joyful scratchboard illustrations [by Brian Pinkney] set within colorful textile-like borders, depicting a family preparing for and celebrating the holiday. A congenial combination of text and pictures that can be used by older children as well as picture book readers, this is a multiple-copy choice for school and public libraries.

Publishers Weekly

SOURCE: A review of *Seven Candles for Kwanzaa,* in *Publishers Weekly,* Vol. 240, No. 38, September 20, 1993, p. 33.

A seven-day-long holiday that begins December 26, Kwanzaa was invented in 1966 by an African American scholar. If Kwanzaa gains in popularity (not to mention name recognition), it will be in no small part due to efforts like the Pinkneys' (*Alvin Ailey*). Brian Pinkney's distinctive scratchboard art lures in the reader; his scenes of family life are as homey and recognizable as Kwanzaa is exotic, and his exquisite borders pay tribute to the African heritage which the holiday honors. Andrea Davis Pinkney, for her part, doesn't try to tell a story, since the illustrations do that. Rather, she approaches the holiday in child-friendly language, describing it "like a family day in the park and Thanksgiving and a birthday, all rolled into one!" She outlines the individual principles that inform each of the holiday's seven days (e.g, the sixth day celebrates Kuumba, or creativity) and she describes various festivities (for Kuumba, making up dances, planting seedlings and so on). A literal cause for celebration.

Kirkus Reviews

SOURCE: A review of *Seven Candles for Kwanzaa,* in *Kirkus Reviews,* Vol. LXI, No. 19, October 1, 1993, p. 1278.

An introduction to the history, symbols, and customary celebration of this African-American holiday. Scratchboard illustrations stress the importance of Kwanzaa as a family event with warmly colored, harmoniously composed domestic scenes. Cultural cross-connections are drawn in the first two pictures (an American family exchanges gifts, including a length of kente cloth; then identically posed figures are transposed to a traditional African village) and enhanced by borders in African motifs. The author briefly discusses the Seven Principles, suggesting activities for Kwanzaa and through the year. Similar in information to Chocolate's *Kwanzaa* (1990) and *My First Kwanzaa Book* (1992), but the visual riches and less didactic tone here are superior.

Jane Marino

SOURCE: A review of *Seven Candles for Kwanzaa,* in *School Library Journal,* Vol. 39, No. 10, October, 1993, p. 47.

Another book about the African-American holiday that introduces its origin, philosophy, and terminology. After an opening background note, Kwanzaa is described in an upbeat tone, and in an accessible style. Each day's activities and themes are described in a personal voice, using such phrases as "For ujamaa we save up our coins . . . " The use of pronouns is not consistent, however, and when they appear, it's not clear who is speaking. It is Brian Pinkney's distinctive illustrations that set this apart from other recent nonfiction books about the holiday, such as Deborah M. Newton Chocolate's *Kwanzaa* and Dianne M. MacMillan's *Kwanzaa.* The scratchboard and pastels combine for a singular and striking effect. Each double-page spread has text on one side and illustration on the other, bordered with an African pattern. As each day of the holiday passes, one more candle is shown lit on the seven-candle *kinara.* With its readable text and appealing artwork, this one's a welcome addition

📖 ALVIN AILEY (written by Andrea Davis Pinkney, 1993)

Publishers Weekly

SOURCE: A review of *Alvin Ailey,* in *Publishers Weekly,* Vol. 240, No. 35, August 30, 1993, p. 96.

In their first children's book collaboration, this markedly talented husband-and-wife team offers a warm profile of dancer and choreographer Alvin Ailey (1931-1989), whose dance company lives on today. The author deftly combines elements of fiction and biography, intertwining Ailey's alleged thoughts and conversations with facts about his childhood, his introduction to the world of dance in Los Angeles during the mid-1940s and his founding of the Alvin Ailey American Dance Theater in New York City in 1958. This effective amalgam of genres easily draws the reader into Ailey's life, lending it appeal for those previously unacquainted with the legendary artist as well as for young fans eager to learn how Ailey launched his impressive career. Matching the finesse of the writing are Brian Pinkney's signature scratchboard renderings handpainted with oil pastels, which manage to convey stateliness as well as quickness, and which culminate in a vivid, motion-filled spread featuring dancers in Ailey's company reeling across the stage—and seemingly right off the pages.

Jim Naughton

SOURCE: "Young Bookshelf," in *Washington Post Book World,* Vol. XXIII, No. 37, September 12, 1993, p. 8.

Andrea Davis Pinkney's text is a bit monotonous because she seldom varies her sentence patterns and a bit vague for she tells rather than shows. Still, she conveys both the joy Ailey found in dancing as well as the importance of his artistic innovation. Brian Pinkney's illustrations have a static muscularity which, in this case, is a mixed blessing. The style captures Ailey's boldness and his vitality, but is ill-suited for portraying the fluid movements of his choreography. The book, nonetheless, is invigorating and informative, a worthy introduction to the work of a major American artist.

Carol Jones Collins

SOURCE: A review of *Alvin Ailey,* in *School Library Journal,* Vol. 39, No. 12, December, 1993, pp. 107-08.

An accessible picture-book biography that recounts Ailey's boyhood in Texas and his roots in the black church, moves with him and his mother to Los Angeles where he begins to dance, and then proceeds on to New York where he hones his talents and forms his own troupe. Brian Pinkney's marvelously detailed scratchboard drawings are tinted with pastels to show the sweep and flow of dancers caught in the act of leaping, twirling, and soaring through the air. His figures are large and bold, reflecting the spiritual and creative energy of Ailey himself and the performance artists who brought his choreography to life. As such, the book is both informative and inspiring and will make an excellent addition to most collections.

Hanna B. Zeiger

SOURCE: A review of *Alvin Ailey,* in *The Horn Book Magazine,* Vol. LXX, No. 2, March, 1994, pp. 221-22.

In a simply told but inspiring story of a pioneer in American modern dance, the author focuses on four periods in Alvin Ailey's life. The book opens with a glimpse of Ailey as a young boy stomping his feet and clapping his hands to the music in the True Vine Baptist Church in Navasota, Texas, where he was born. It then follows Ailey as he and his mother move to Los Angeles, where he sees Katherine Dunham and her dancers and is swept away by the sight of black people performing their own dances. In the third part, Ailey studies dance at the Lester Horton Dance Theater School, where he begins to develop his own highly individual style of dance. In the last section, Ailey comes to New York to continue his studies and, gathering a group of nine young black dancers, founds the Alvin Ailey American Dance Theater; the company will ultimately perform such dances as *Blues Suite, Revelations,* and *Cry* to acclaim all over the world. A brief additional section gives details about Ailey's life, his work, and honors. The scratchboard drawings hand-colored with oil pastels give life and vibrancy to the dancers' movements. The picture of golden "high-stepping ladies . . . sweeping their skirts" in fact seems to dance off the page. Brian Pinkney's illustrations convey Alvin Ailey's grace as a dancer as well as his strength and pride in his art.

THE DREAM KEEPER, AND OTHER POEMS (written by Langston Hughes, 1994)

Henrietta Smith

SOURCE: A review of *The Dream Keeper, and Other Poems,* in *The Horn Book Magazine,* Vol. LXX, No. 5, September, 1994, pp. 603-04.

Langston Hughes's poems range from the romantic to the poignant, from the spiritual to the challenging. His lyrical voice asks for recognition of the Negro, offers encouragement, and reminds his African-American brothers of their glorious past. Although the pieces in *The Dream Keeper* were written over a half-century ago—the original edition was first published in 1932—the words have the same strength of meaning and power as if they had been written today. In remembering his heritage, the African American still "speaks of rivers." The words of "Minstrel Man"—"Because my feet are gay from dancing / You do not know I die?"—still ring true for those African Americans who are striving for equality in the world of drama and the theater. The African-American mother still reminds her offspring that "life for me ain't been no crystal stair." Brian Pinkney has brought a vigorous contemporary look to the pictures that accompany each of the selections in this new edition of *The Dream Keeper.* In contrast to Helen Sewell's quiet, almost idyllic, sketches for the 1932 edition, Pinkney's scratchboard illustrations are alive with mo-

tion. There is a definition in the physical features of the people that show that they are undeniably of African-American descent; the figures of the "Negro Dancers" simply exude joy; the realism given to the tattooed "Sailor" lets one see the mermaid on his arm and the bluebird on his back. Details like the clothing of the dapper dandy and signs of modern architecture move the book into the 1990s without diminishing the message of the poems. This edition, enhanced by the inclusion of seven additional selections, is a splendid combination of timeless words and timely illustrations. As Lee Bennett Hopkins says in his introduction, "Via the words of Langston Hughes—the dreamer—his gift to us of his strong voice will long and long live on."

DAY OF DELIGHT: A JEWISH SABBATH IN ETHIOPIA (written by Maxine Rose Schur, 1994)

Publishers Weekly

SOURCE: A review of *Day of Delight: A Jewish Sabbath in Ethiopia,* in *Publishers Weekly,* Vol. 241, No. 36, September 5, 1994, p. 110.

Laden with information, this picture book introduces a fascinating, little-known population of black Jews who live in the mountains of Ethiopia. Schur takes readers through the various rituals performed by each segment of the community to prepare for the Sabbath. In meticulous detail, she describes food, chores, clothing, customs and activities, peppering the text with Ethiopian words and phrases. The sheer volume of information overwhelms and occasionally supplants traditional narrative; the value of this work lies in its economical evocation of an entire way of life, not in the telling of a specific tale. An author's note at the end explains the history and status of this small group, whose members call themselves *Beta Israel,* "Those of the House of Israel," but who are known as strangers ("falashas") to other Ethiopians. A glossary and pronunciation guide is also included. Pinkney's signature scratchboard illustrations celebrate the African roots of the *Beta Israel* with affecting visual images that are startlingly at odds with more familiar depictions of more familiar Jewry.

Loretta Kreider Andrews

SOURCE: A review of *Day of Delight: A Jewish Sabbath in Ethiopia,* in *School Library Journal,* Vol. 40, No. 10, October, 1994, p. 103.

Fascinating in its detail about one ethnic/religious group in Africa, this story also tells about one of the many ways in which Jews have traditionally lived. The book is visually appealing, with scratchboard illustrations that convey the beauty of the green and brown Ethiopian highlands and the Amharic-speaking people who live there. Facing pages are outlined in bright colors reminiscent of the borders of the *Shamma* (cloth) they weave and wear. The story is simple and tenderly told. Menelik, 10, narrates the events and activities in his family on one day before a Sabbath and the observance that follows. As daily routines and conversations are recounted, readers learn about what the family eat, the crafts they engage in, their language, the difficulties of farming there, and above all, the importance of the Sabbath to them. The Africanness of Menelik's people is emphasized. They are richly brown in color; vigorous drums remind them that the Sabbath is about to arrive; their houses (unfortunately referred to as "huts") look like those throughout many parts of Africa. At the same time, the Sabbath theme and the service inside the *mequrab* (synagogue) discusses the *Beta Israel,* or "Those of the House of Israel" as the Ethiopian Jews call themselves, and their loyalty to their faith. The story is unique for this age group in its effective and empathetic portrayal of an endangered African culture. It is a gem.

Stephanie Zvirin

SOURCE: A review of *Day of Delight: A Jewish Sabbath in Ethiopia,* in *Booklist,* Vol. 91, No. 3, October 1, 1994, p. 334.

Set in Ethiopia, this book not only explores how the Jewish Sabbath is celebrated in a far-flung land, but also gives us a glimpse of a vanishing cultural group, the Falasha, and their way of life. In a quiet, yet joyful story, Menelik, the son of a blacksmith, talks about the black Jews in his small community as they earn their living weaving, farming, and shaping iron tools and as they prepare for their Sabbath. Pinkney's sturdy, attractive painted scratchboard illustrations catch the reverence and the everyday detail without a hint of sentimentality. A fine choice for the multicultural shelf, this will also have children who celebrate Shabbat in the U.S. eagerly comparing their own holiday with Menelik's. A glossary and pronunciation guide are included, as is an author's note explaining Ethiopia's black Jewish population.

📖 *DEAR BENJAMIN BANNEKER* (written by Andrea Davis Pinkney, 1994)

Carolyn Phelan

SOURCE: A review of *Dear Benjamin Banneker,* in *Booklist,* Vol. 91, No. 2, September 15, 1994, p. 138.

Born to free black parents in 1731, Benjamin Banneker grew up on their Maryland tobacco farm. He, too, became a farmer until, in his late fifties, he taught himself astronomy and wrote his own almanac, the first by an African American. He sent a copy of the almanac to Secretary of State Thomas Jefferson, along with a letter taking Jefferson to task for slaveholding. Excerpts from his letter and Jefferson's reply appear in the book. Since the eighteenth-century language requires some interpretation, the author summarizes the general meaning of each quoted passage. The book's conclusion ("But his almanacs and the letter he wrote to Thomas Jefferson showed everybody that all men are indeed created equal") is a rather flabby ending to an otherwise well-thought-out text. The artwork, subtle shades of oil paints over scratchboard pictures, is handsome as well as distinctive. Varied in composition and tone, the illustrations include landscapes, portraits, and scenes from Banneker's life. Sweeping lines and repeated contours give the illustrations a feeling of energy and life. A most attractive introduction to Banneker.

Kirkus Reviews

SOURCE: A review of *Dear Benjamin Banneker,* in *Kirkus Reviews,* Vol. LXII, No. 20, October 15, 1994, p. 1414.

This outline of the accomplishments of the distinguished African-American astronomer and mathematician focuses on the landmark publication of his first almanac and an eloquent 1791 letter to Thomas Jefferson. Banneker protested "the almost general prejudice and prepossession which is so previlent [sic] in the world against those of my complexion" and criticized Jefferson for holding slaves, detained "by fraud and violence," despite his claim, in the Declaration of Independence, that "all men are created equal." The letter and Jefferson's reply were printed in Banneker's popular second almanac. Compared to the gracefully phrased excerpts of Banneker's and Jefferson's letters (Why not append the entire texts?), Andrea Pinkney's (*Seven Candles for Kwanzaa*) determinedly simple narrative seems choppy.

Still, the text is serviceable; and Brian Pinkney's glowing paint-and-scratchboard illustrations vibrate with dignity and purpose.

Deborah Stevenson

SOURCE: A review of *Dear Benjamin Banneker,* in *Bulletin of the Center for Children's Books,* Vol. 48, No. 3, November, 1994, p. 100.

Benjamin Banneker is one of the African-American heroes of the republic, a tobacco farmer gifted with an inventive and scientific mind that led him to assist in the surveying of Washington, D.C. and to become the first black man to create an almanac. The Pinkneys chronicle Banneker's work on his almanac and, most particularly, his letter to Thomas Jefferson, then secretary of state, protesting the country's—and Jefferson's—involvement in slavery. This is the account of a particular aspect of Banneker's life rather than a biography—we don't know when he died or whether he had a wife and children, the main text of the book doesn't discuss his surveying, and no source notes are included—but it's a compact evocation of the integrity and talent of a man who rose above the constraints of his era. Brian Pinkney's scratchboard art is at its most luminous in this book, with shimmering landscapes (including a starry night reminiscent of Van Gogh) and portraits of strong and thoughtful men. This is a useful complement to picture-book biographies of Thomas Jefferson and to more general surveys of early American life.

THE FAITHFUL FRIEND (retold by Robert D. San Souci, 1995)

Betsy Hearne

SOURCE: A review of *The Faithful Friend,* in *Bulletin of the Center for Children's Books,* Vol. 49, No. 1, September, 1995, pp. 28-9.

[This story] celebrates a friendship threatened by forces of evil: when the Caribbean plantation owner's son, Clement, falls in love with beautiful Pauline, his white friend Hippolyte protects them from her guardian's zombies, first by turning the couple away from poisoned water and mangoes, then by hiding in their bridal chamber to kill a deadly serpent. Alas, the snake disappears. Hippolyte is accused of planning to kill his friend out of jealousy, and, just as the zombies have threatened, he turns to stone when he explains the black magic. Fortunately, he's brought back to life by an old beggar resurrected, just for this purpose, from the grave where Clement and Hippolyte had paused in their travels to give him a decent burial. If it sounds complicated, it is, but San Souci has a gift for adaptations that read smoothly without cheating their folkloric sources. His informed note discusses the tale type, placing this West Indian variant from Martinique in a broader cross-cultural context and describing changes he's made along with the reasons for them. Older picture-book audiences will relish the story's suspense, which is enhanced by Pinkney's brooding illustrations. The tension of his sophisticated ghostly white linework against backgrounds of dark forest or dim interiors exposes a twilight side to characteristically brilliant Caribbean colors.

JOJO'S FLYING SIDE KICK (1995)

Maria B. Salvadore

SOURCE: A review of *JoJo's Flying Side Kick,* in *The Horn Book Magazine,* Vol. LXXI, No. 4, September, 1995, p. 591.

Tae Kwon Do Master Kim tells JoJo that she is ready for the final test for her promotion to a yellow belt. "To earn the yellow belt, you must break a board with a flying side kick. You'll be tested tomorrow." That night, JoJo cannot sleep for her fear of the test and of the "creepy bandit tree" in front of her house, which seems to lunge at JoJo when she walks past it and tries to climb into her window at night. In class the next day, however, JoJo adapts the advice given to her by Granddaddy, her mother, and her friend, P. J., to deliver a perfect flying side kick. By visualizing the bandit tree,

she smashes both the board and her fears simultaneously. The movement and texture of Pinkney's signature scratchboard-and-oil illustrations augment mood and tension, effectively depicting JoJo's worry, giving a face to her fear in the form of the sinister bandit tree, and celebrating her ultimate triumph. The author-illustrator, who holds a black belt in Tae Kwon Do, describes the ancient Korean martial art form in a brief note.

Kate McClelland

SOURCE: A review of *JoJo's Flying Side Kick,* in *School Library Journal,* Vol. 41, No. 9, September, 1995, p. 184.

In order for JoJo to advance from a white to a yellow belt in Tae Kwon Do, she must break a board with a flying side kick. Little wonder she worries! Everyone offers support and advice. Granddaddy recommends that she do a little fancy footwork "to chase away the jitters," the way he did before his boxing matches. Her friend advises her that, when she yells "KIAH," she should make it come from deep in her stomach for greater power. Her mother advocates a winning visualization technique. When the big test comes, JoJo does all three. She dances a bit on her feet, shouts from deep inside, and visualizes a "creepy" tree in her own yard that has always frightened her. She successfully calls upon her own inner resources to overcome more than one fear and earns the coveted yellow belt. Pinkney's art lifts this story above the narrow realm of self-help bibliotherapy. His illustrations, executed in scratchboard and oil, excel at the depiction of movement—whether it is the movement of a scary tree (archetype for any number of childhood fears) or the movement of a flying side kick. Children will be fascinated by the sport, by the refreshing female protagonist, and by the thrill of her accomplishment. An author's note gives more information about Tae Kwon Do. This will not be a shelf-sitter.

Publishers Weekly

SOURCE: A review of *JoJo's Flying Side Kick,* in *Publishers Weekly,* Vol. 242, No. 37, September 11, 1995, p. 85.

JoJo, a Tae Kwon Do white belt student, must break a board with a flying side kick in order to earn her yellow belt. She adds her worry about the test to her ever-present fear of the tree that looms "like a creepy bandit" in her front yard, but confides her nervousness to Granddaddy, her friend P. J. and her mother. All three offer advice drawn from their own experiences ("Visualize your technique. . . . That's what I do before a tennis match," says Mom). JoJo utilizes their suggestions as well as her own resources: visualizing the board as the creepy tree, she leaps into the air and smashes it. Energetic scratchboard and oil illustrations swirl with movement in a vivid palette of deep blues, greens and white. Pinkney renders the tree as reasonably ominous;

accordingly, the late addition of a spooky face and hands to illustrate JoJo's terror is somewhat over the top. As in Pinkney's *Max Found Two Sticks,* the action plays out within a compressed time span, concentrating the tension. While the prose is not as taut this time, the author/artist again gets effortlessly into the mind of his protagonist.

In addition to his career in children's books, Pinkney holds a black belt in Tae Kwan Do and has competed nationally and internationally.

Linda Ward-Callaghan

SOURCE: A review of *JoJo's Flying Side Kick,* in *Booklist,* Vol. 92, No. 4, October 15, 1995, p. 412.

To earn her Tae Kwon Do yellow belt, JoJo must break a board with a flying side kick, and she is less than confident. Family and friends offer advice to ease her anxiety over the upcoming test. Grandaddy shows her a little shuffle step he used in boxing, P. J. advises a yell from the diaphragm, and Mama explains how to visualize. But how can JoJo succeed when she's even afraid of the creepy bandit tree in her yard? Pinkney's distinctive scratchboard technique employs swirls of oil color, mirroring JoJo's turbulent emotions, carefully etched with detail. His tranquil blues and warm yellows evoke the loving community of family and friends that surrounds JoJo, while touches of violet, added to the bandit tree and swirled through JoJo's bedroom, reflect the unsettling fears in JoJo's mind. Anyone who has faced a similar sleepless night will appreciate Pinkney's empowering story and cheer as JoJo finds her own way to channel her fears.

WILEY AND THE HAIRY MAN (retold by Judy Sierra, 1996)

Publishers Weekly

SOURCE: A review of *Wiley and the Hairy Man,* in *Publishers Weekly,* Vol. 242, No. 50, December 11, 1995, p. 70.

In her author's note, Sierra, a puppeteer and storyteller who has for two decades relayed this Alabama folktale to children, explains that hers is "an oral rather than a literary adaptation." And with its catchy dialect, droll dialogue and split-second timing, her story makes an exemplary read-aloud. After Wiley's daddy disappears from a ferryboat, folks blame the Hairy Man who roams a nearby swamp, and Wiley's mama cautions him that the Hairy Man "will get you, too, if you don't watch out." But with her help, the boy manages to best the villain, tricking him into using his "conjure man" powers to Wiley's own advantage. Outwitted for a third and final time, the Hairy Man is banished "for good and forever," which makes for a comforting ending for youngsters who may have been a bit frightened. For, at

Pinkney's able hands, the red-eyed, furry, drooling, hooved Hairy Man cuts quite a villainous figure indeed. The intricate, swirling lines of the artist's skillfully composed oil paintings on scratchboard convey the story's superb dynamism—as well as its inherent humor. Another worthy collaboration by the creators of *The Elephant's Wrestling Match.*

Kirkus Reviews

SOURCE: A review of *Wiley and the Hairy Man,* in *Kirkus Reviews,* Vol. LXIII, No. 24, December 15, 1995, p. 1776.

Wiley and his mother fool the powerful Hairy Man once, twice, three times, sending him fleeing back into the swamp. Since Molly Bang's 1976 rendition (bearing the same title), this deliciously scary Alabama folktale has become a storyteller favorite—but it has yet to find illustrations that do it justice. Bang's had plenty of character but were small, busy, and pale gray; Pinkney's swirling scratchboard scenes glow with color, but the paint is smeared, the figures static, and the drawing rough to the point of looking unfinished. The creature seems more comical than menacing, a big, cloven-hoofed ogre with hair like rusty steel wool, snaggly teeth, and physical proportions that change from scene to scene. Sierra and Bang drew from the same original source, and their texts are very similar; use the new as a replacement or alternative to the old—better yet, learn the story and tell it!

Betsy Hearne

SOURCE: A review of *Wiley and the Hairy Man,* in *Bulletin of the Center for Children's Books,* Vol. 49, No. 7, March, 1996, p. 242.

Based on an African-American story collected for the Federal Writers' Project in Alabama, this tale has a wealth of tellings . . . as well as oral interpretations by noted storytellers such as Jackie Torrance and Judy Sierra herself. It's a spooky story however it's told, and that's its prime attraction. Wiley is being stalked by the same wicked creature that carried off his daddy, but with the help of his mama, who's a powerful conjure woman in her own right (and smart, to boot), Wiley tricks the Hairy Man three times and drives him howling into the swamp. While colors and lines sometimes compete with each other for attention, Brian Pinkney's oil paintings on scratchboard are definitely the scariest yet. This Hairy Man is awfully human except, of course, for his cow hoofs. His red eyes, pointy teeth, and wild hair add considerable tension to the brooding swirls that characterize Pinkney's compositions. The eerie-green swamp scenes and generous amount of text per page suggest an older picture-book audience that will eat this up at Halloween or just any old time there's a place for ghosts, goblins, and things that go bump in the night.

Mary M. Burns

SOURCE: A review of *Wiley and the Hairy Man,* in *The Horn Book Magazine,* Vol. LXXII, No. 3, May, 1996, p. 344.

"The Hairy Man got your daddy," Wiley's mother tells him, "and he'll get you, too, if you don't watch out." If Wiley and his mama can fool the Hairy Man three times, then that ugly, drooling conjure man with the feet of a cow must leave them alone forever. By himself, Wiley first tricks the Hairy Man into making all the rope in the county disappear, thus releasing Wiley's hound dogs. Next, with his mother's help, Wiley has the haughty Hairy Man change into a tiny possum, small enough to fit into his own croaker sack, which Wiley tosses into the river. Finally Wiley's mama allows the Hairy Man to take her baby—really one of her baby pigs—fooling that mean man for the third time. The retelling of this Southern folktale is fluid and accessible. Through use of dialogue without dialect and a lissome narration, Sierra captures the cadence of the oral language of Alabama. Pinkney's signature illustrations, oil paintings on scratchboard, effectively portray the isolated rural setting and depict a truly ugly, unswervingly mean, and altogether unappealing Hairy Man. Muted color, broad and fine lines, and varied, carefully placed paintings create a fresh and appropriately nefarious look for an ever-popular, appealing folktale.

📖 **WHEN I LEFT MY VILLAGE (written by Maxine Rose Schur, 1996)**

Kirkus Reviews

SOURCE: A review of *When I Left My Village,* in *Kirkus Reviews,* Vol. LXIII, No. 24, December 15, 1995, p. 1775.

From the team behind *Day of Delight* (1994), a fictionalized account of one of the Falasha airlifts from Ethiopia to Israel, narrated in an elevated, almost epic style by 12-year-old Menelik. His father—caught between famine and oppression—decides to leave Ethiopia. Menelik describes their adventures in the mountains and deserts, their passage to Sudan, their flight to Israel, and the modern wonders found there.

The narrative is both dramatic and lyrical; evocative images fill the book: "We ate sunset-colored yogurt. And we drank tea made from tiny paper tents dipped in hot water." With great artistry, Schur weaves disparate strands of the story—history, adventure, family drama, etc.—into a polished narrative. The subjects of Pickney's scratchboard illustrations—mainly people—are vividly delineated by fine white curves and hatch marks on the black background. The effect is quite striking: The pictures look like negatives of etchings. A handsome work.

Publishers Weekly

SOURCE: A review of *When I Left My Village,* in *Publishers Weekly,* Vol. 243, No. 2, January 8, 1996, p. 70.

In their trenchant sequel to the acclaimed *Day of Delight,* Schur and Pinkney recount the perilous journey of 12-year-old Menelik and his family as they brave overwhelming odds to make their way from Ethiopia to Israel. As Ethiopian Jews, or Beta Israel, they have faced religious persecution since the Marxist military government's rise to power in 1978 (a concluding note supplies background information). Although conditions are insupportable, the Beta Israel have been forbidden to leave the country for Israel, and so Menelik, his younger brother and their parents steal away from their home one night with just a few possessions and a scant supply of food. They can travel only at night, and on foot; Menelik's father estimates that they will need two weeks. Writing with pathos deepened by memorable imagery, Schur casts Menelik as the narrator of this arduous, ultimately triumphant flight. Pinkney's fittingly stark, accomplished scratchboard art gracefully reflects the family's movement from darkness into light.

Susan Scheps

SOURCE: A review of *When I Left My Village,* in *School Library Journal,* Vol. 42, No. 3, March, 1996, p. 198.

From The Faithful Friend, *retold by Robert D. San Souci. Illustrated by Brian Pinkney.*

This companion to Schur's *Day of Delight* (1994) follows a family of Ethiopian Jews (the Beta Israel) in their escape from drought and persecution. Traveling at night on foot through mountains, plains, and desert, 12-year-old Menelik, his parents, and younger brother head for a Sudanese refugee camp. From there, the people are airlifted to Israel; given homes, clothing, and food; and assimilated into a culture that offers them freedom, safety, and equality. The boy tells the story of the perilous journey—of days filled with hunger, fear of discovery, and death; of a furtive border crossing; of weeks of unsanitary living in the crowded camp; and, finally, of resettlement in a small white hut in the hills near Jerusalem. The book reads like a true adventure story. Pinkney's full-page, black-and-white scratchboard illustrations add reality to this fictionalized account of the recent rescue mission that saved the remnants of a little-known civilization. A map of the Middle East shows the family's escape route, and an author's note adds historical information.

📖 BILL PICKETT: RODEO RIDIN' COWBOY
(written by Andrea Davis Pinkney, 1996)

Publishers Weekly

SOURCE: A review of *Bill Pickett: Rodeo-Ridin' Cowboy*, in *Publishers Weekly*, Vol. 243, No. 35, August 26, 1996, p. 97.

The husband-and-wife team behind *Dear Benjamin Banneker* and *Alvin Ailey* continue their superb profiles of noteworthy African Americans with this rip-roarin' salute to a legendary cowboy. Andrea Pinkney's informed, colorful text, peppered with cowboy slang ("Hot-diggity-dewlap!"), provides a lively foil for Brian Pinkney's distinctive scratchboard illustrations. His medium, with its old-fashioned woodcut flavor, works well for biography in general and this one in particular; the fluid lines and energetic cross-hatchings create a sense of motion that reinforce the depictions of the cowhand's active life. Readers will follow with interest the tale of the "feistiest boy south of Abilene" who grew up to become a famous rodeo performer, renowned for his "bulldogging" stunt (which he invented as a child, after watching a bulldog subdue a restless cow by biting its sensitive upper lip). The author gives Pickett's (ca. 1860-1932) life story ample context, too, bolstering it with information about the role of African Americans in settling the West; an afterword discusses black cowboys in general. As Pickett's fans might have said, "Hooeee!"

Deborah Stevenson

SOURCE: A review of *Bill Pickett: Rodeo-Ridin' Cowboy*, in *Bulletin of the Center for Children's Books*, Vol. 50, No. 3, November, 1996, p. 110.

Bill Pickett is a rodeo legend, famed for pioneering bulldogging (now formally known as "steer wrestling") and thrilling turn-of-the-century audiences in Wild West shows. The Pinkneys here trace his life from his birth into slavery to his days as a Texas cowhand to his increasing fame, describing en route his family life and his struggles with racism. The text's tone is pleasantly folksy and Pickett's exciting adventures simply explained (though it seems unlikely that the cowboy's nickname of "The Dusky Demon" came, as the text maintains, from "the dusty dirt cloud that billowed behind him whenever he performed his fearless riding," and there's surprisingly no mention of the Bill Pickett postage stamp). Brian Pinkney's scratchboard illustrations use white highlights to give a shimmer of heat and glamour to the proceedings as snorting bulls and thundering horses gallop through the pages. A note about black cowboys and a bibliography are included.

Lauren Adams

SOURCE: A review of *Bill Pickett: Rodeo-Ridin' Cowboy*, in *The Horn Book Magazine*, Vol. LXXII, No. 6, November, 1996, pp. 761-62.

The author and illustrator team up for another picture book biography, once again choosing an extraordinary black American who has not been widely written about for children. The introductory verse ("Folks been tellin' the tale / since way back when. / They been talkin' bout that Pickett boy. / Growed up to be a rodeo-ridin' man"), next to a 1908 photo of Pickett, sets the tone for the folksy turns of phrase woven throughout the narrative. The story begins with Pickett's father, who was born into slavery on a wagon train journey from South Carolina to Texas. Freed after the Civil War, he and his wife raise crops on a small plot of land, but their second of thirteen children, Bill, is drawn immediately to the cowboys driving cattle. Young Bill goes to work as a cowhand all over Texas until he is discovered by the rodeo for his unique bulldogging style—holding down a cow by biting its lower lip—which brings him fame on the circuit. Pinkney points out that while "many rodeo owners believed black cowboys should ride with their own kind . . . the newspapers didn't seem to care if Bill was black or white—Bill's *bulldogging* was news!" Pinkney provides the historical background of pioneering farmers and ranchers of the late nineteenth century but focuses on one boy's dream of becoming a real American cowboy. The afterword tells more about the rodeo and about the settling of Texas during Reconstruction that included many newly freed blacks. Acknowledgments on the copyright page indicate extensive research. The swirling strokes of Brian Pinkney's hand-colored scratchboards capture the young boy's enthusiasm and the excitement of the rodeo.

J. D. Biersdorfer

SOURCE: "Ever Punched a Cow?," in *The New York Times Book Review*, November 10, 1996, p. 42.

One of the most popular rodeo performers in history was the African-American cowpuncher Bill Pickett, whose memory has survived and flourished despite the attempts of the United States Postal Service to immortalize him on a 1994 stamp (a likeness of his brother, Ben, was mistakenly used instead). *Bill Pickett: Rodeo-Ridin' Cowboy,* written by Andrea D. Pinkney and illustrated by Brian Pinkney, is a far more fitting tribute to the renowned bulldogger, who would wrestle steers up close and personally by chomping down on their upper lips with his own teeth. This storybook biography traces Pickett's early life and eventual rise to the upper ranks of professional rodeo fame, and also provides two pages of historical information on black cowboys as well as a 10-book bibliography. The textured scratchboard illustrations are rendered in a somber color palette that's reminiscent of the Frederic Remington and Charles Russell paintings of the Old West back when it was new.

📖 *THE ADVENTURES OF SPARROWBOY* (1997)

Publishers Weekly

SOURCE: A review of *The Adventures of Sparrowboy,* in *Publishers Weekly,* Vol. 244, No. 10, March 10, 1997, p. 66.

Though sobering front-page headlines worry a young paperboy, the comics—especially a strip called Falconman—lift him up. Quite literally, in fact. After Henry peruses a Falconman strip in which a magical falcon converts a police trooper into a superman by lending him the power to fly, the boy's bike collides with a similarly gifted sparrow. Suddenly airborne, the boy delivers his newspapers in flight while saving innocent neighbors from a menacing bully and his growling pooch. For the course of Henry's transformation, the book adopts a comic-strip format, accenting the boxed, action-filled pictures with brief, punchy text and a chorus of sound effects like "CHIRP!" "WHOOSH!" and "THONK!"

In a final, satisfying coup, Henry comes to the rescue of the benevolent sparrow, vulnerable because it has temporarily relinquished its powers of flight to Henry, a development that readers will delight in discovering before the boy does. The plot unravels chiefly through Pinkney's airy, motion-filled art, expertly rendered in scratchboard, transparent dyes and gouaches in creamy colors never before seen in a comic book. Clever quips and asides add humor and playful melodrama. Pinkney clearly had a blast creating this soaring story, and his high spirits are transferable to the reader—ZAP!

John Peters

SOURCE: A review of *The Adventures of Sparrowboy,* in *School Library Journal,* Vol. 43, No. 4, April, 1997, p. 115.

Fretting over headlines in the newspapers he's delivering, Henry almost runs over a sparrow on the sidewalk.

There's a flash of light, and suddenly, like his comic-strip hero Falconman, the boy is swooping through the skies fighting evil—or, at least, collaring a scary dog, rescuing a cat from a bully's clutches, and repeatedly snatching the temporarily flightless sparrow out of danger in the nick of time. Like newspaper comics, Pinkney's full-color scratchboard scenes are done in page-sized panels, with a minimum of text but maximum action, dramatized by swirling lines, wide gestures, and "THONK!" "ZAP!" sound effects. Henry's heroics will win readers over instantly; he may not save the world, but before he returns to Earth, he does make his suburban neighborhood "just a little better." That's a plausible goal for any actual or would-be superhero.

Roger Sutton

SOURCE: A review of *The Adventures of Sparrowboy,* in *The Horn Book Magazine,* Vol. LXXIII, No. 4, July, 1997, pp. 445-46.

Henry the paperboy enjoys the heroic exploits of comic hero Falconman, whose superpowers are bestowed on him by a generous falcon. So when a little bird along his route gifts Henry similarly, he's soon saving the neighborhood—and a suddenly flightless little sparrow—from marauding bullies, menacing dogs, troublesome twins, and a hungry cat. The rescues slyly overlap and dovetail, giving coherence to the fantasy contrivance, and in fine comic-strip style, Pinkney lets the pictures do the talking, limiting text to brief action markers ("Meanwhile . . . Bruno was still up to no good"), dialogue ("Let's catch that little birdie . . . "), and sound effects ("ZAP!"). Pinkney's signature scratchboard paintings are here loosened by humor and movement, and the balance of double-page spreads, single-page paintings, and panels is adroit in framing and pacing the story. Design, subject, and speed make this picture book ideal for almost-readers ready to try their own wings.

Betsy Hearne

SOURCE: A review of *The Adventures of Sparrowboy,* in *The Horn Book Magazine,* Vol. LXXIV, No. 1, January, 1998, pp. 49-52.

It takes a lot of energy to fly, and this book has got it. With red and blue zooming off white, and green lines swirling from lawn to sky, and foregrounded figures hurling left to right or right off the page, and perspectives swooping from low to high, and images fast-forwarding in rhythmic frames, and rounded shapes rolling into angular explosions, we are *moving*. We are moving right along with Henry the paper boy, because when things go wrong, Henry flies on borrowed power: he hogties a roughneck dog, arrests a runaway wagon, saves a threatened cat, and then saves the sparrow the cat's after. All by bird lift, otherwise known as imagination. Kids will go soaring in this picture book . . . or is it a comic book? Or is it the best of both? Whatever you call it, *The Adventures of Sparrowboy* shows just how much a gifted illustrator can grow in originality, skill, humor, and artistic effects. And I can promise you that when you and your listener finish Henry's paper route, you will feel, like Henry, just a little bit better about all the stuff the news headlines dump on you every day.

I SMELL HONEY; PRETTY BROWN FACE (written by Andrea Davis Pinkney, 1997)

Publishers Weekly

SOURCE: A review of *I Smell Honey* and *Pretty Brown Face,* in *Publishers Weekly,* Vol. 244, No. 10, March 10, 1997, p. 65.

The Pinkneys (*Alvin Ailey*) celebrate African American family life in this pair of board books. *I Smell Honey,* a toddler watches her mother prepare a meal of sweet potato pie, fried catfish, red beans and collards; in *Pretty Brown Face,* a father and son, with the help of a mirror, enumerate the charms of the toddler's face. Andrea Pinkney's text for the more enjoyable Honey has a cheerful lilt—"We boil the greens./Stir the beans./Flip the fish./Slice the pie"—and captures much of the simple ritual satisfaction of preparing a meal, as when the child narrator says, "Feel wet leaves/of collard greens." But while the books convey palpable, affectionate warmth between child and parent, overall they may disappoint the Pinkney's fans. The plain, literal illustrations are a departure from Brian Pinkney's more usual strong, dynamic work. In striving for a simpler style, he produces relatively monotonous settings and somewhat inexpressive faces. Ironically, the characters' features in *Face* are unattractively askew; and the wavy "mirror" in the back cover distorts readers' faces as much as in any funhouse.

DUKE ELLINGTON: THE PIANO PRINCE AND HIS ORCHESTRA (written by Andrea Davis Pinkney, 1997)

Publishers Weekly

SOURCE: A review of *Duke Ellington: The Piano Prince and His Orchestra,* in *Publishers Weekly,* Vol. 245, No. 9, March 2, 1998, p. 68.

Dig out a recording of "Take the 'A' Train" and prepare to cut the rug as the Pinkneys strut their stuff. A tantalizing combination of sassy prose and swinging artistry, this electrifying picture-book biography of one of the biggest stars in the musical constellation jumps and jives to a palpable beat. Andrea Davis Pinkney's smooth prose slides off the tongue, and the pages crackle with the energy of her fresh and original descriptions (she describes Ellington as a musician with "fine-as-pie good looks" who plays compositions "smoother than a hairdo sleeked with pomade"; and Carnegie Hall as "a symphony hall so grand that even the seats wore velvet"). The story traces Ellington's life, from his luke-

warm beginnings as a musician (a reluctant pianist, he "kissed the piano a fast good-bye" as a child, deeming it an "umpy-dump sound that was headed nowhere worth following"), through his surrender to the siren song of ragtime and eventual success as a legendary composer and band leader. Brian Pinkney's signature scratchboard illustrations create a shimmering backdrop of colors and lines that swoop in tandem with the words; the arcing lines and swirls draw the eye effortlessly across the pages in a surge of motion. His swanky palette is pure delight, a jazzy Art Deco blend that segues from sunny yellow to shades of cerise, chartreuse, mauve and peacock blue. This husband-and-wife team captures the spirit of an individual, an era and a musical style. The uninitiated may well be inspired to open their ears to the world of jazz, and for enthusiasts, this is a worthy homage to an American-born music and one of its great leaders.

CENDRILLON: A CREOLE CINDERELLA (written by Robert D. San Souci, 1998)

Publishers Weekly

SOURCE: A review of *Cendrillon: a Creole Cinderella,* in *Publishers Weekly,* Vol. 245, No. 28, July 13, 1998, p. 76.

"You may think you know this story I am going to tell you, but you have not heard it for true," begins the washerwoman and unlikely godmother who narrates this spirited retelling. From the team behind *The Faithful Friend* comes an adaptation of a Creole tale that recasts familiar elements into the fashions and customs of the colonial West Indies. There is the haughty stepmother Prosperine, "puffed-up proud because her grandfather had come from France," the godmother who taps a breadfruit with a mahogany wand and transforms it into a carriage, and Cendrillon, who escapes at midnight with one pink slipper embroidered with roses. Pinkney's oil and scratchboard illustrations burst with vigorous movement as he captures the exotic palette and the lush textures of the "green-green island in the so-blue Mer des Antilles." The lyrical cadences of the text spattered with French and Creole words combine with the sensuous paintings to bring the tropics to life. However, the story's charm lies not in the well-matched Caribbean bride and groom or in the (rather predictable) happy ending, but in the authentic voice of the godmother. Her affection for the kind Cendrillon inspires her bold and selfless acts to ensure the happiness of another (and her quirky foibles prove equally appealing as she indulges in bowl after bowl of chocolate sherbet while proudly watching the couple's nuptials). Through this colorful and deeply human godmother, readers witness the enduring power of love.

Additional coverage of Pinkney's life and career is contained in the following sources published by The Gale Group: *Major Authors and Illustrators for Children and Young Adults* and *Something about the Author,* Vol. 74.

Laura E(lizabeth Howe) Richards

1850-1943

American author of fiction, nonfiction, poetry, biography, autobiography, and plays.

Major works include *Sketches and Scraps* (1881), *Queen Hildegarde: A Story for Girls* (1889), *Captain January* (1891), *The Golden Windows: A Book of Fables for Young and Old* (1903), *Tirra Lirra: Rhymes Old and New* (collected and printed, 1932).

INTRODUCTION

A prolific and successful author during the late nineteenth and early twentieth centuries, a time known as the "Golden Age" of children's literature, Richards produced an immense catalogue of books in a variety of genres—from romantic novels and biographies of famous women for young adults, particularly girls, to nursery rhymes for infants and toddlers. She is best known to contemporary readers for the nonsense verse that she initially made up for her own children and later published, and for her novel *Captain January,* made famous, in part, by a motion picture starring Shirley Temple in 1936. While *Captain January* remains her most recognized work of fiction today, several of Richards's stories for young girls were widely popular in her day, including *Queen Hildegarde*, which spun off four additional titles about the same character, and a series of five books about a girl named Margaret. Romantic in style and simplistic in plot, these stories are about "typical" girls of the late nineteenth century, filled with literary and historical allusions that sent readers off to the library on research expeditions. Though none of her "girls' stories" are in print today, as they contain overly sentimental prose and an idealized view of society that dates them, they did, however, have a profound effect on the girls who read them. Ruth Hill Viguers recounted, "Anne Parrish [spoke] of the 'peace' that the Hildegarde stories still brought her, and expressed surprise over the impression made on contemporaries by the wallpaper in Hildegarde's room. After forty years Kathleen Norris, whose childhood ambition had been to possess such a room, could still describe the wallpaper. . . . Along with the charm of atmosphere to be found in all (the girls' books) and the incidents, situations, and people that grew out of her memories, they are full of fundamental values. . . ." In a similar vein, Richards's biographies for young adults, mostly about women, employ a romantic writing style filled with as much imagination as fact. At the time, these biographies fulfilled a need for inspirational nonfiction for girls, and included such heroines as Florence Nightingale, Abigail Adams, and Laura Bridgman, a blind and deaf girl who learned to communicate. Reviewers, however, have regarded these biographies as outdated, melodramatic, and

trite, as Anne Scott Mac-Leod, writing in *Twentieth-Century Children's Writers,* stated, "Though she strengthened her accounts with excerpts from diaries, letters, and journals, Richards also greatly oversimplified both the characters of her subjects and the historical context of their lives. This, together with an old-fashioned style, has dated the biographies."

In contrast, Richards's verse has established her reputation in children's literature. Recognized as a competent versifier and humorist, Richards has the distinction of being the "first prominent American writer of nonsense verse for children," noted Malcolm Usrey in *Dictionary of Literary Biography,* and, until the late twentieth century, "the only woman to have written this kind of verse." Although occasionally criticized for lacking the skill and intricacy of rhymers such as A. A. Milne, Edward Lear, and Lewis Carroll, Richards's nonsense poems have commanded more respect from recent critics than her fiction. *Tirra Lirra,* her best collection, is one of the few books by Richards still in print today, and has been prized by readers well into adulthood. Celebrated for its absurd incongruities, invented words, use of sound, and exaggerated rhythms, *Tirra Lirra*'s light-hearted, cheerful verses were a welcome change from the sentimentality of many works for children at the time. In *Children's Writers*, Anne Scott MacLeod regarded Richards to be "a good deal less sentimental in her approach to children and poetry than were many of her contemporaries. . . ." While the world changed around her, Richards maintained the same humor, fun, and easygoing writing style throughout her career that won her a wide audience since she spun her first verses for her own babies. Praising Richards's "hurdy-gurdy," a term Richards coined to describe her own affinity for rhyming, Anne Scott McLeod remarked, "She used a variety of rhyme schemes, mostly strong, unsubtle tetrameters, ballad forms, and limericks. . . . And while her made-up words were neither as witty as Carroll's nor as unselfconscious as Lear's, such inventions as the wigglewasticus and the ichthyosnortoryx gave her poems a nice sense of freedom. 'Eletelephony' . . . is a truly funny play on tangled words, and 'An elderly lady named Mackintosh / [who] set out to ride in a hackintosh' anticipates Ogden Nash. . . . Laura E. Richards deserves her niche in children's literature. If she was never highly original, still she was humorous, irreverent, and pleasant to the ear. Unlike her prose, her verse is surprisingly undated."

Biographical Information

Born in Boston, Massachusetts, Richards was the fourth of six children of Samuel Gridley and Julia Ward Howe. Greatly admired by all their children, Mr. and Mrs. Howe substantially influenced every aspect of Laura's life, both as a child and an adult. Her mother, the author of "The Battle Hymn of the Republic," was a daunting Victorian social activist and philosopher with a strong devotion to her family, a wild, unpredictable sense of humor, and firm opinions about good literature and music, all of which Laura absorbed into her own life. Her father, also a social activist, was an educator who for many years directed the Perkins Institute and Massachusetts School for the Blind, and was the first person to teach a blind and deaf person how to communicate. Richards was named after this student, Laura Bridgman, and later wrote a biography of her for children. In Richards's two volumes of autobiography, *When I Was Your Age* (1894), for children, and *Stepping Westward* (1931), for adults, she recalls an idyllic childhood filled with singing, games of imagination, and wonderful books, a legacy which she passed on to her own children. Tutored at home during her early childhood, Richards later attended Massachusetts schools, including Miss Caroline Wilby's School in Boston. In 1871 she married architect Henry Richards, who had been the Howes' neighbor in Boston, and the couple settled in Green Peace, Laura's childhood home. Shortly after the birth of her first child, Richards began writing. Her earliest publications were spun from tales and verses she made up for her own children. As she recounts in her autobiography *Stepping Westward*, "I had always rhymed easily; now, with the coming of the babies, and the consequent weeks and months of quiet, came a prodigious welling up of rhymes. . . . I wrote, and sang, and wrote, and could not stop. The first baby was plump and placid, with a broad, smooth back which made an excellent writing desk. She lay on her front, across my lap; I wrote on her back, the writing pad quite as steady as the writing of jingles required." Richards published some of these first verses in *St. Nicholas* magazine, a publication for children.

When Henry was asked to take over the family paper mill in Maine, the Richards moved to Gardiner where Laura raised their children and became an active and involved member of the community, a life very much reflective of her mother's. Her first book, *Five Mice in a Mouse-Trap*, a series of anecdotes told by the Man in the Moon, was published in 1880. She subsequently published over ninety volumes of work, consisting of nonsense verse, poetry, fiction for young adults, biographies for adults and children, plays, and fables. She did this while raising five children—one who died during infancy, inspiring the two books *The Joyous Story of Toto* (1885) and *Toto's Merry Winter* (1887)—and pouring energy into her community work. Instrumental in founding the Women's Philanthropic Union and the Gardiner Library Association, Richards also founded a social club for working girls and a History Class—later the Current Events Club—for adult discussion on winter evenings. She provided entertainment for children after school, sang in the church choir and the Choral Society, and generally had a hand in everything going on in Gardiner. In 1886 she invited some of her ten-year-old son's friends over to make their acquaintance. That evening, the Howe Club, named for her father, was formed—meeting every Saturday for an hour and a half with the purpose of giving "the boys something that school in its crowded curriculum could not give; to enlarge first their vocabulary and then their horizon; to show them the fair face of poetry; first and last to give them a good time. . . ." The Howe Club continued for twenty-five years, and included on its membership rolls were the names of future congressmen, a state governor, and many other successful professional men.

In 1893 the Richards's paper mill burned to the ground. Although a new mill was built, it had trouble competing with the large mills, and in 1900 it was permanently closed. The Richards, after considering the possibility of opening a school, decided instead to run a summer camp for boys. This was a relatively new idea at the time, and Camp Merryweather, named after a family in one of Richards's books, became the first camp for boys in Maine. There, under the trees, Richards wrote many of her novels for young girls. She continued to write for her entire life. In *Junior Book of Authors* she once said of her work, "No one can possibly imagine how I have enjoyed my writing. It was work, but it was also the most delightful play. . . . I have had a very long and very happy life. I hope you will all live as long and be as happy." She published her last volume of verse for adults, *The Hottentot and Other Ditties*, in 1939. She died in Gardiner in 1941 at the age of 93.

Major Works

During her lifetime, Richards was well known for several different types of writing. It was her nonsense verses, written primarily for her children and tuned to a child's ear, that brought her first, and last, to the attention of the reading public. *Sketches and Scraps* was the first book of nonsense verse by an American published in the United States, and the only one of her books illustrated by her husband, Henry Richards. Many of Richards's verses were published in *St. Nicholas* magazine. Eventually she collected these and other verses into the book *Sketches and Scraps*, something she was to do more than once during her writing career. Many of its initial readers, in later years, remembered this book with great affection. In an article in *Horn Book*, Ruth Hill Viguers noted that "Edmund Pearson . . . said [that he] would not part with his copy of *Sketches and Scraps* for the rarest of literary treasures, including three Gutenberg Bibles." Richards also became well known to an entire generation of American women because of her "girls' stories." The first of these was *Queen Hildegarde*, in which a rich fifteen-year-old girl is sent to live on a farm for the summer. Although she is shocked by the simple life of the farm families, she eventually adjusts and makes friends with the local children. She ends up arranging an operation for a disabled girl and an education for an ambitious boy. *Queen Hildegarde* was followed by four sequels—*Hildegarde's Holiday* (1891), *Hildegarde's Home* (1892), *Hildegarde's Neighbors* (1895), and *Hildegarde's Harvest* (1897). The popularity of this new genre of books, with a "typical" young female as the central character, encouraged Richards to write many more books for girls in a similar, romantic style with comparable central characters.

Captain January is widely recognized today for its adaptation to film—first in 1924, starring Baby Peggy, then again in 1936, starring Shirley Temple. Set in Maine, it is the sentimental story of an old lighthouse keeper who, ten years before the story begins, rescued a baby in a storm, and has raised her as his own child, naming her Star Bright. When Star's aunt comes to the island on an excursion, she recognizes her dead sister's lost child and wants to take the child back with her. But Star refuses to go, staying with the Captain until he dies. *Captain January* was Richards's most popular book during her lifetime. First published in 1891, it was still a best-seller in 1931. Its sequel, *Star Bright* (1927), was a crashing failure, however, with a central character too childish and improbable, even for sentimental tastes. Despite the success of *Captain January*, Richards personally favored her moralistic tales and fables for children, *The Golden Windows: A Book of Fables for Young and Old* and *The Silver Crown: Another Book of Fables* (1906). Of these books, Ruth Hill Viguers commented, "They are brief allegories, some subtle, a few baffling, many simple, many touched with humor, most of them tender."

Yet of all her many published works, the one which has garnered her the most praise from reviewers of children's literature is *Tirra Lirra: Rhymes Old and New*, her best collection of nonsense verse. Since its first printing in 1932, *Tirra Lirra* has remained in circulation and claims an enduring place among treasuries of poetry for children. In it, Richards combined many of the verses published earlier, some as early as 1902, in *St. Nicholas* and other children's magazines with brand new flights of silliness and "hurdy-gurdy." Some of these verses are so familiar, that each generation has taken them as its own. The verse most often anthologized, and regarded as one of her finest and funniest rhymes, is "Eletelephony": "Once there was a elephant, / Who tried to use the telephant—/ No! no! I mean an elephone / Who tried to use the telephone—/ (Dear me! I am not certain quite / That even now I've got it right.)/ Howe'er it was, he got his trunk / Entangled in the telephunk." Other verses, however, that contain comic scenes of beheadings, hangings, and drownings may now be considered too violent, while poems such as "The Buffalo" have been criticized for engendering racial stereotypes. While David McCord criticized the "poor rhyming" and "nonsense thrown for a loss" of some of the poems, he also regarded *Tirra Lirra* as predecessor to later nonsense verse: "[O]n rereading *Tirra Lirra* I am haunted now and then by a vagary of voices that were to follow [Richards]," voices such as A. A. Milne, James Thurber, and Ogden Nash. In 1932, Letha M. Davidson wrote, "When really good nonsense rhymes that seem funny to children are as scarce as they are, a book like this is an event," while in 1985, Malcolm Usrey stated in the *Dictionary of Literary Biography*, "*Tirra Lirra* is one of the best books of nonsense verse for children. . . . "

Awards

Richards, with her sister, Maude Howe Elliot, received the first Pulitzer Prize awarded in biography for *Julia Ward Howe*, a biography of their mother, written for adults, in 1917. *Tirra Lirra: Rhymes Old and New* was a Junior Literary Guild selection in 1932 and received the Lewis Carroll Shelf Award in 1959. Richards was honored with a D.H.L. from the University of Maine in Orono in 1936. In 1937, *Harry in England* was regarded as a younger honor book at the Spring Book Festival.

AUTHOR'S COMMENTARY

Laura Elizabeth Richards

SOURCE: In *Stepping Westward*, D. Appleton and Company, 1931, 397 p.

[Green Peace] was the original house round which my earliest recollections centre. Some time in the Fifties my father found it insufficient for his growing family, and built the New Part; it remained the New Part until a

Street Commission swept house and garden and all out of existence. . . .

In [the dining] room my mother sang to us. My first memory of her is at the piano, in black velvet, singing in her golden voice. Here, too, she played for us to dance. . . .

My mother's singing formed an important part in our education. She had a beautiful high soprano voice, which had been carefully trained by Cardini, a pupil of Manuel Garcia. Musical to her finger tips, she knew (I firmly believed) all the songs in the world; she certainly knew a great many of them. Language was no barrier to her; French, German and Italian were at her familiar command, and any other language was accessible if required. In Rome, she studied Hebrew with a learned Rabbi; in the West Indies. . . .

"Julia knows three words of Spanish," wrote my father, "and talks it all day long!"

Latin was her intimate friend through life; at fifty she took up Greek, which she called her diamond necklace, and cherished and enjoyed through the remaining forty years.

When we gathered delightedly round the piano, at Green Peace and in all the other houses we came to know and love, we soon began to sing with her. German songs, many of them brought back from Heidelberg by Uncle Sam Ward, who was a student there; gay student choruses of *"Juch hei"* and *"Vivallera-lera,"* in which we joined as lustily as if we were Burschen ourselves; sparkling French songs whose gaiety was enchanting, whatever their moral might be. . . .

Italian songs that flowed like water under moonlight; to say nothing of English and Scottish ballads without end.

We never knew that we were studying French, German, Italian; that we were acquiring a vocabulary; that ear and voice were being trained by a past mistress in the management of both. When we went to school, our teachers realized it; so, I have been given to understand, did those of our children in their turn. . . .

I linger about Green Peace, loth to leave it. I have been describing it ever since I began to write, first in *Five Mice in a Mouse-Trap,* again in *When I Was Your Age.*

As to my birthplace, I can only paraphrase Thomas Hood:

> I quite forget, I quite forget
> The house where I was born; . . .

My mother has often told me that one day, when I was about four years old, she found me lying on the floor with a book before me, turning the pages carefully, and reciting the Ballad of "Fair Annie of Lochroyan." On being interrogated, I said I was "reading." I have been reading ever since. . . .

Ballads, old and new, have always been among the "chief of my diet." I could never get enough of them; so was it when I was a babe, so is it now I am a grandame. My mother began it, I suspect, as she began most of my reading for me (except what I owe to my father, of which anon). It was she, of course, who repeated "Fair Annie" to me till it was my own; and "Lord Thomas and Fair Elinor," sung by her to a quaint old lilting tune, antedated even that. I may or may not be forgiven for quoting Andrew Fletcher of Saltoun's "very wise man" who said that "could he make the ballads of a nation, he would not care who made the laws." The sentiment can never, to me, become hackneyed; I know so much more about ballads than about laws.

In the Fifties we were not smothered, as we are today, in Children's Books. I had *Aunt Effie's Rhymes,* that clear, delicious little spring, from which anthologists have been dipping crystal draughts ever since. If I ever knew who "Aunt Effie" was, I forget now, but the blessings of a whole generation of children must attend her.

I had Grimm, of course, and Hans Andersen, and knew them by heart; and *Merry Tales for Little Folks;* a notable volume, edited by Madame de Chatelain; and *The King of the Golden River,* a lifelong joy, one of the most precious of all children's books. Then there were *The Rose and the Ring,* and *The London Doll* and *The Country Doll,* and Miss Alcott's dear *Flower Fables,* of which she was ashamed, she told me, in later life, but which I loved dearly. And there was *Tales from Catland,* greatly beloved; and *Holiday House,* ever delightful, and reprinted, I am happy to say, of late years; and, oh! *Rainbows for Children!* and Mayne Reid. . . .

Of course we had the *Wonder Book* and *Tanglewood Tales;* I cannot remember when we did not have them; but I did not stop there with Hawthorne. I delighted in *Twice-Told Tales* and *Mosses from an Old Manse.* These I read over and over, till I knew them almost by heart. "Howe's Masquerade," "Rappaccini's Daughter" (most terrible of all), "Lady Eleanor's Mantle," "The Great Carbuncle"; these were strong enchantments, never to be forgotten.

And these bring me to Irving, to the *Tales of the Alhambra,* and *Wolfert's Roost,* and *The Sketch-book.* "The love of lovely words" has always been strong in me; the very title, "The Adelantado of the Seven Cities," brings a thrill even today.

I cannot tell when I began upon Scott and Dickens; they, with the Bible and Shakespeare, seem in memory a kind of foundation for everything else. I fancy my parents read them aloud to us all, beginning with my elder sisters; I probably listened and assimilated more than I knew at the time. There is a kind of deep familiarity that seems to come from the beginning of things, as with *Mother Goose* and Lear's *Nonsense Book.* My father was our chief exponent of Scott and Dickens. He read, in half hours snatched from the service of humanity, and we listened, never supposing he had anything more important to do. No "simplified editions" (*"horresco referens!"*) for the Howe children. The splendid sentences rolled out as they were written, in the deep, melodious, unforgettable voice. If we did not understand every word, what did it matter? We heard the sound, the glory of them; the meaning could wait. . . .

Other book-sanctuaries I did in some sort penetrate, owing to their illustrations. My first glimpse of Homer was not through Chapman (*pace* John Keats!), but through Flaxman's illustrations, which brought Homer alive to me at an early age. The same kindly hand led me through Dante, with horrified fascination. I know exactly what the Seventh Hell looks like. These volumes, splendid quartos rich in vellum and gilding, with superb print and margins, were stolen by a drunken gardener, and sold, one supposed, for drink. It seems a pity; I have seen no Dantes like them.

Perhaps Shakespeare, too, may have come to me in this way. Certainly among my earliest memories are those of the great folio copy of Boydell's *Scenes from Shakespeare,* bound in diamond calf, over which I would hang—it seems now—for hours together. I am very sure that I was intimate with Jack Falstaff before I ever read a word about him, and with Sir Joshua Reynolds's exquisite Puck, and with all that goodly company.

Hogarth's terrible folios, too, were painfully familiar; and there was a dreadful volume on smallpox, with life-size colored plates showing every stage of the disease. Horrid, morbid little girl! I would open it and shut it, and run away and come back.

The big purple morocco Bible had no pictures, which had in some ways its advantages. I somehow think of my father reading that; but it was my mother who sang the hymns.

In the same way I made friends with Thackeray. His own and Richard Doyle's delightful pictures introduced me to the Newcomes and Pendennis and the rest, but I have Mr. Doyle alone to thank for *Brown, Jones and Robinson,* a precious volume which taught me much about foreign parts.

The first novel I read to myself was *John Halifax.* I am sorry to say I find John dull now, but then I enjoyed him greatly. And there was *Jane Eyre,* which some of my schoolmates were not allowed to read.

But all this written, and little or nothing said about poetry, other than ballads! I would rather read poetry than eat my dinner any day. It has been so all my life. Coventry Patmore's admirable *Children's Garland* and *Thalatta* were my first anthologies; Mrs. Browning, Whittier, and Tennyson, my first individual poets. I cannot have been more than eight or ten when, as I have described [in **When I Was Your Age**], it was my delight to go and read to an old blind woman in the workshop of the Perkins Institution, the "Rhyme of the Duchess May," and other highly romantic ballads of the Lady of

Casa Guidi. Poor old Margaret! I have often wondered what she made of it.

Mrs. Browning is little read to-day. I am glad to have Mrs. Woolf say a good word for "Aurora Leigh," which I read with ardor at fifteen or so; I wish she had had a word for the ballads as well. "The Lay of the Brown Rosary" used to enthral as much as it terrified me; and "The Rhyme of the Duchess May" still brings its own thrill, and makes me ten years old once more.

> Oh, the little birds sang east,
> And the little birds sang west,
>   Toll slowly!
> And I thought me how God's greatness
> Flows around our incompleteness,
> Round our restlessness, His rest.

If that says nothing to you, it is perhaps because you do not hear my mother sing it to its own tune, composed by her.

I was about thirteen when I came to Shelley and Coleridge, and new worlds opened about me. A friend of my father's, Mr. Horatio Woodman, read "Christabel" to me. I can remember jumping up in my excitement, and walking up and down the room, as the magic lines sang in my ears. I was a great girl of sixteen before I discovered Browning, and for some years I walked hand in hand with him and Rossetti—and always Shelley. I was late with Keats, I cannot imagine why.

As for Wordsworth, I was woman grown before I really came to him. As a child, I resented, half-consciously, the "simple" poems with which the now-beloved Great One took such infinite pains. I did not want my poetry simple. I wanted it to flash and ring and roll; bells and trumpets for Laura Elizabeth!

> The Assyrian came down like the wolf on the fold.

Those ten words meant more to me than the whole of the "Pet Lamb," with "We Are Seven" thrown in.

But what says Captain Corcoran?

> "Though I'm anything but clever,
> I could talk like that forever!"

My general idea, as I look back through the long years, seems to have been, "If you see a book, read it, especially if it is poetry!" My education would seem to stand on a solid (!) foundation of fairy stories, romance, and poetry, with more or less history tucked in here and there by way of mortar.

Pondering these things, I seem to hear the kind voice of my good brother-in-law, the learned Professor.

"My dear Laura," he says, "Mathematics, Chemistry and Physics are the tripod on which modern education stands."

Alas! But what a good time I had! . . .

[At Green Peace] begins a whole library of volumes, bound for the most part in lively colors; how condense them? Four years saw the birth of the first three of my seven children, Alice, Rosalind, and Henry Howe; saw, contemporary with these births, the acquisition of my hurdy gurdy. Ballads and songs and the like, early assimilated, had given me a good ear for metre and rhythm (say *jingle,* woman, and have done with it!). I had always rhymed easily; now, with the coming of the babies, and the consequent weeks and months of quiet, came a prodigious welling up of rhymes, mostly bringing their tunes (or what passed for tunes; the baby, bless it, knew no better!) with them. I wrote, and sang, and wrote, and could not stop. The first baby was plump and placid, with a broad, smooth back which made an excellent writing desk. She lay on her front, across my lap; I wrote on her back, the writing pad quite as steady as the writing of jingles required.

"Little John Bottlejohn," "The Shark," "The Queen of the Orkney Islands," etc., etc., all had their own tunes, to which, once they were written down, the baby was trotted. (Yes, we trotted our babies; they liked it; I never saw that they got any harm by it. I never trotted my grandchildren!)

I mean to be a model of reticence about my published works. . . . I may, however, be allowed one little item about the first-named jingle. It was written in the late Seventies. In April, 1885, the *Scottish-American Journal* of Montreal printed a letter from Mr. J. Clark Murray, asking for information about

> a song I heard lately sung for the amusement of my children by a young lady who came recently to this country from Aberdeenshire, and who kindly, at my request, wrote out the accompanying copy. The song deals with an ancient theme which has been frequently treated, not only in older Scottish ballads, but in the earlier literature of all European nations. The song itself bears all the impress of a very modern composition, for it strikes me as treating the mermaid myth in a spirit of fun, which implies that the myth is no longer the object of that simple credulity which gives a charm to the veritable legendary ballad. The lady, however, who furnished me with this copy of the song, could tell me nothing about it, except that, when a child, she had heard it sung by an old woman who used to come about her father's house. I shall, therefore, be obliged to any of your readers who can give me any information about the history of the song.

I gave the desired information.

This is perhaps the highest compliment I ever received, unless it were the unconscious tribute of the five-year-old child, who, when called upon in Sunday school to give her Christmas verse, forgot the hymn, and recited instead:

> The owl and the eel and the warming pan,

> They went to call on the soap-fat man.
> The soap-fat man, he was not within,
> He'd gone for a ride on his rolling pin.
> So they all came back by way of the town
> And turned the meeting-house upside down!

It is a pity she could not sing it; the tune was a rather pretty one. . . .

It was in the office of Ware and Van Brunt that my husband came to know John Ames Mitchell, familiarly known as Johnny. The two young men took to each other at once, and Johnny became a frequent and always welcome visitor at Green Peace. He was a merry, witty, delightful little man, overflowing with fun and life. He could no more keep his hand from making pictures than I could keep mine from making nonsense rhymes. My husband assumed the role of *deus ex machina,* which has since become so familiar to him. "Papa" attended to everything, from the broken doll to the shattered bicycle, from the column of figures that would not add right to the sewing machine that would not take a stitch, and the furnace that "behaved so strangely"; one and all and everything, "Papa" must and did correct.

"Why," said he, "don't you and Johnny join forces; let him make pictures for your rhymes, send them to a magazine and get them published?"

We took fire at once, or rather we combined the little flames that were already burning on our separate hearths. I have some of the drawings now, framed and hanging up, reminders of a pleasant time. We tied them up with thrills of delightful anticipation, sent them to *St. Nicholas,* then in its early days, and waited. It was hard to wait. We did not see why people were so slow. Never mind! when the answer came it was most kindly-favorable, accepting both verses and pictures, and asking for more; and we made our bow together, Johnny Mitchell and I, in those friendly pages. In the early bound volumes of the magazine you will find them all, **"John Bottlejohn"** and the rest. When the rhymes came to be published in book form, it was with other illustrations. Why this was, I cannot remember, but no others could be like Johnny's to me. . . .

My first book was published in 1880, *Five Little Mice in a Mouse Trap,* a book which I am glad to find children still reading. The children in it were for the most part as imaginary as the Man in the Moon, who in his own fantastic way (I was nothing if not fantastic in those days) tells the story; yet there may be traces here and there of my own children's words and ways, possibly of those of myself and Brother Harry, twenty-odd years before.

This was followed in 1881 by *Sketches and Scraps,* the only one in which H[enry] R[ichards] and I worked together, he illustrating the rhymes as I wrote them. In a moment of folly, now hardly credible to me, I consented, some years later, to the destruction of the plates of this book, and have regretted it ever since. The pictures were in bright colors, and had a quality of their own which endeared them to children.

Next came, in 1885, the editing and largely the writing, of *Four Feet, Two Feet, and No Feet,* a venture into the realm of natural history, where I did not really belong. In the same year I wrote *The Joyous Story of Toto;* and the year after, *Toto's Merry Winter.* These books, which I count among the best I have written, have a special little sad interest for me.

Not long before that, my baby died, my little Maud, a creature so bright and sweet that her sudden departure— less than two days from rosy health to the last breath drawn in my arms—left a blank that at first nothing could fill. H. R., my tower of strength, did not fail me; the other children were dearer than ever; sweet Myra Sawyer helped them and me through the first days and weeks. All would not do; I must have work. So I wrote— I hardly know how—these two little merry tales. It was a great relief and a great help.

It was in 1889 that I began upon the series of so-called "girls' books," which were to occupy a good deal of my time for the next fifteen years. The "Hildegarde" books, the "Margaret" books; I do not know that I have anything special to say about these. The later ones are better written than the earlier ones; if I were twenty years younger, I would write *Queen Hildegarde* over again.

Meanwhile the "hurdy gurdy" was usually ready at my call, and poured forth any quantity of nursery rhymes. When rhyming is in the blood, anything may bring on the fit. Witness a day when I sat cowering over the fire, shivering through the first stage of Influenza. In sheer misery I rocked to and fro in my seat; and so rocking, began to croon, words and tune coming together.

> A poor unfortunate Hottentot,
> He was not content with his Lottentot;
> Quoth he, "for my dinner,
> As I am a sinner,
> There's nothing to put in the Pottentot!"

The actions and the fate of my Hottentot unrolled before me. I finished with a moral:

> This poor unfortunate Hottentot,
> Had better have borne with his Lottentot:
> A simple banana
> Had staved off Nirvana,
> But what had become of my plottentot?

and felt better for the exercise.

In 1890, these rhymes, together with the early ones from *St. Nicholas* and those contained in *Sketches and Scraps,* were collected and published under the title of *In My Nursery.* This book, dedicated to my dear mother, has always been one of my favorites.

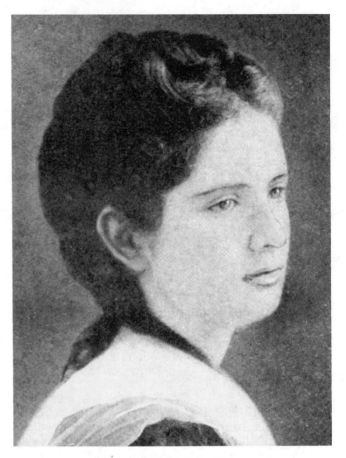

Laura E. Richards in 1870.

1890 was to see yet another book, in speaking of which I must pause a little.

When we came to Maine, H. R. did not entirely give up architecture, the profession of his heart. He built a number of houses in the first ten years of our life in Maine, among them one for Mrs. Charles H. Dorr, at Bar Harbor. Mrs. Dorr was an old and intimate friend of my mother's, having been engaged in early life to my mother's brother. She was always a kind friend to us both. When the house was finished, she asked me to make her a visit. I well remember how one day during this visit, sitting on the rocks below the house, and looking out to sea, I saw a distant lighthouse, and began dreaming and wondering as to what life might be in such a place.

So, up out of the sea, as it were, came to me the little story called *Captain January.* I wrote it quickly, and was rather pleased with it, but when I took it to my publishers, they would have nothing to say to it. It was too short for a long story, too long for a short story; very sorry, but not in their line. I think this story went to every reputable publisher, or to all that I knew about, in this country, and to several in England. No one would have it. Instructed, and rather sorrowful, I put the little manuscript away in a drawer, still feeling that it had some elements of possible success. A year or two later, I chanced to meet Mr. Dana Estes, Sr., with whom I had a pleasant personal acquaintance. He asked me what I had been writing.

"Nothing," I said, "except the little story that you refused."

And then, perhaps seeing some interest or sympathy in his kind face, I said,

"Mr. Estes, would you be willing to read that little story yourself, and give me your personal opinion of it?"

It was much to ask of a publisher, but he kindly consented. That was forty years ago, and *Captain January* still heads my list of sales.

I tell this for the encouragement of young writers whose manuscripts come fluttering home to them, unwelcome fledglings, not wanted in the nest.

Not long ago I went to see the film version of *Captain January*. I was displeased at the interpolations and adaptations, but the child actress, Baby Peggy, won my heart. At one point, sitting alone in the friendly darkness, I laughed aloud. It was where, after a truly beautiful representation of the storm, the lighthouse, the old seaman with the rescued child in his arms, the scene suddenly changed, and showed the lighthouse in broad sunlight, the sea at its feet calm and sparkling and covered with—pelicans! The scene, which in tempest might perfectly well have been the coast of Maine, had had its fair weather rehearsals, at least, in Florida.

I wrote not only jingles, but short stories, for *St. Nicholas* and for my good friend of many years, the *Youth's Companion*. In 1891, these little stories, together with all the rhymes written after the publication of *In My Nursery*, were published under the title of *Five Minute Stories;* this to be followed in due course of years by *More Five Minute Stories,* and *Three Minute Stories.* These, like the jingles, were all for little children.

My next venture, in 1893, was *Melody,* a highly sentimental little tale; and that same year, *When I Was Your Age,* a book of reminiscences of my childhood and that of my brothers and sisters. Stories of the *Captain January* length having seemed to justify themselves, I wrote a number of others, *Marie, Nautilus,* etc., all of which appeared sometime in the Nineties.

Before I leave this period, I must relate a little episode that always amused me greatly. A friend of my daughter Betty's, living in a neighboring town, came by invitation to spend the week-end with us. A sweet, well-mannered child, she seemed to enjoy her brief visit, and left us with smiles and cheerful words; but when her mother asked her how she enjoyed the days at the Yellow House, her face fell.

"I had a nice time," she said, "but, oh, Mother, Mrs. Richards didn't have *one grand moment* while I was there." I have often wondered what this dear child expected me

to do; whether she expected me, like Miss Havisham in Pip's vivid imagination, to sit in a black velvet coach, and wave a flag out of a window. . . .

During later years, I have written several little novels. When I first "commenced author," I thought I could not possibly do anything of this sort; I could write for children or for girls, but the tender passion was beyond me. Well, I have accomplished even that after a fashion. I hardly know how it came about; partly, no doubt, because life was growing always fuller and richer. I overflowed my banks!

For another thing, I was learning *to see.* The rhymes and jingles, the nursery tales, even the girls' books, were cobwebs spun more or less out of my own brain. But here, all around me, were people living and moving and having their being; New England people, strong and humorous and kind, all living lives of intense interest, all with stories to tell. Here was a speech so vigorous and racy, so full of quaint and delightful idiom, that every linguistic fibre in me cried out to preserve it, to write down the words that sounded all day in my delighted ears.

I could not walk along the street, but incident and anecdote jostled me.

A farmer, in town for the day, standing beside his horse, who shakes a disapproving head over his nose bag.

"Wal!" says the man, "I can't wag your jaws for ye!"

The neighbor—long dead—who told of a stranger wooing and winning his daughter Ida.

"What gits me," he said, "is what he see in Idy!"

That went straight into *Mrs. Tree,* the second of the little novels above mentioned. The first was *Geoffrey Strong,* the story of a young physician in a New England village. In the course of it I described a village tea party, and among the guests an old lady with twinkling eyes and a cap suggesting the Corinthian Order. This was Mrs. Marcia Tree. She appeared suddenly, unexpectedly; I see her as clearly as I see the friend I met yesterday. *Geoffrey Strong* disposed of, she intimated that she too had a story to tell; there must be another book, about her.

I wrote *Mrs. Tree* mostly at Camp, sitting about under trees, with the Boys running all about me. Nothing mattered; it was really she who wrote the story; I merely held and guided the pen.

I had never known any one in the least like Mrs. Tree; but no sooner did she appear in print than I began to receive letters asking how and when I had known the writers' grandmothers or great-aunts. One lady, after kindly praising my life-like portrait of her husband's great-aunt, Mme. Du Chêne, commented on my skilful adaptation of her name: "Chêne—Oak—Tree!"

Again, driving through Hankerson's Woods (they went into a story too, be sure!) my friend the Neighborhood Nurse—not to be confounded with District or Hospital Nurse—pointed out to me the farmhouse where she had nursed one of twin brothers, who, living under one roof, were not on speaking terms with each other. I never saw these gentlemen, but they took instant shape for me in Samuel and Simeon Sill, and I had great fun in combining their story with that of Calvin Parks, master mariner and candy-peddler.

Then, I took to writing fables, two volumes of them, *The Golden Windows* and *The Silver Crown.* These, like *Mrs. Tree* and *Pippin* and *The Squire* and all the rest, must speak for themselves. I count them my best work. Later still, at the request of a friendly publisher, I began to write short biographies of famous women. There are five of these, beginning with *Florence Nightingale* and ending with *Laura Bridgman.*

In the years following my mother's death in 1910, her *Life and Letters,* written in collaboration with my sister, Maud Howe Elliott, occupied much of my time; a labor of love, if ever there was one. I did not know how to stop! . . .

It was not far from 37 Brimmer Street round the corner to 148 Charles Street, to Mrs. James T. Fields and Sarah Orne Jewett. . . .

[Sarah Jewett's] reputation was established, and much of her beautiful work accomplished, before the days of our friendship. I was just beginning to emerge from the "juvenile" stage of writing, and her criticism and advice were invaluable to me. I can never forget her kind and faithful criticism of *Queen Hildegarde,* my first stumbling essay in books for girls. One brief sentence of hers has been worth more than gold and silver to me. In those years I was writing a great deal of verse, ballads, lyrics, even essays in French forms, enjoying myself immensely. I knew that my hurdy gurdy was not a lyre, but I found it extremely amusing and even inspiring to try for lyric tones on it.

"Don't scatter your fire!" said Sarah Jewett. "You are a prose writer: stick to your own tool!"

I laid the words to heart, and have kept to them as well as I could ever since. The hurdy gurdy still holds out. Broken once or twice, it has been mended, and still grinds out its little tunes on occasion. But my gratitude to my dear friend has never grown old. . . .

Green Peace, childhood home of Laura E. Richards in Boston, Masachusetts. After her marriage, Laura and her husband, Henry, resided at Green Peace before moving with their children to Gardiner, Maine.

GENERAL COMMENTARY

Ruth Hill Viguers

SOURCE: "Laura E. Richards, Joyous Companion: Part III, in *The Horn Book Magazine,* Vol. XXXII, No. 5, October, 1956, pp. 376-88.

In *Stepping Westward* Laura Richards says, "My education would seem to stand on a solid (!) foundation of fairy stories, romance, and poetry, with more or less history tucked in here and there by way of mortar."

"Pondering these things, I seem to hear the kind voice of my good brother-in-law, the learned Professor.

"'My dear Laura,' he says, 'Mathematics, Chemistry and Physics are the tripod on which modern education stands.'

"Alas! But what a good time I had!"

It would be difficult to convince the true lover of literature that there is any other reason for books than the good times they give—the good times that become better and better as the reader grows toward appreciation of the best. Mrs. Richards gives not only her readers a good time but herself as well. Indeed, what could be more fun than to be the first person to think of "Eletelephony" and to see for the first time the surprise and delight on her listeners' faces?

> Once there was an elephant,
> Who tried to use the telephant—
> No! no! I mean an elephone
> Who tried to use the telephone—
> (Dear me! I am not certain quite
> That even now I've got it right.)
>
> Howe'er it was, he got his trunk
> Entangled in the telephunk;
> The more he tried to get it free,
> The louder buzzed the telephee—
> (I fear I'd better stop this song
> Of elephop and telephong!)

She has spoken of the "welling up" of nursery rhymes and jingles as she cared for her babies. Her early books also were a natural part of her fun with her children. Her first one, *Five Mice in a Mouse-Trap,* published in 1880, is made up of the kind of stories children will beg their mothers for if they have any suspicion that their mothers are capable of making stories. Surely they were inspired by her own children's demands just as the children of the book, while imaginary, yet show "traces here and there of my own children's words and ways, possibly of those of myself and Brother Harry, twenty-odd years before." The Man in the Moon tells the stories and, because he can see everywhere, they have great variety of scenes and subjects. Lucky the young children who had this book before the days of limiting

their printed material to "the familiar"! There are nonsense stories of Eskimos and polar bears and wolves, fantastic flights to China and adventures under the sea. May Lamberton Becker speaks of reading *Five Mice in a Mouse-Trap* over and over, as a child.

Handling this book today with its thick, dark red covers, its profusion of pictures—some of them by Kate Greenaway—its variety of stories and its appealing children, I regret that it has been unavailable to little children for so long. To them it would not seem dated, even today.

Other collections of stories for little children, though published later, after the phenomenal success of *Captain January,* and including stories and rhymes which had appeared in *St. Nicholas* and *The Youth's Companion,* certainly derived from experiences with her own children. *Five Minute Stories, Three Minute Stories, A Happy Little Time,* and the rest, are simple little tales of the kind a mother makes up on the spur of the moment for her waiting children, but, having been made by such a mother as Laura Richards, can give pleasure to many besides her own children. The last named, written for a child sick in bed, and dedicated to her youngest, must have made Betty's convalescence a thing to remember with happiness all her life.

The Joyous Story of Toto and *Toto's Merry Winter,* with their background of the forest, and Toto's forest friends and his love for his dear grandmother, are extravagant nonsense tales, some so jolly it is difficult indeed to realize that they were written just after the death of her fifth child, Maud, in infancy. " . . . I must have work. So I wrote—I hardly know how—these two little merry tales. It was a great relief and a great help."

Sketches and Scraps is the only book on which she and her husband worked together, he illustrating the rhymes as she wrote them. The plates for this were early destroyed, to her lasting regret, for she believed these brightly colored pictures had a unique quality especially endearing to children. There are many to whom mention of this book brings intense remembered pleasure. One is Anne Eaton; another Edmund Pearson who, in a letter to May Lamberton Becker, said he would not part with his copy of *Sketches and Scraps* for the rarest of literary treasures, including three Gutenberg Bibles. Bernard Darwin, grandson of the great scientist, in an article in the London *Times Literary Supplement* in 1941, regretted the loss of "the great book" and quoted rhymes from it which he and his wife both remembered from childhood. Later, when he had again obtained a copy, he wrote to Mrs. Richards thanking her for the "intense pleasure" she had given them and assuring her that pictures as well as rhymes had come up to their expectations.

In *Four Feet, Two Feet, and No Feet* she learned the lesson that in her writing she should keep to those things with which she was really at home. This was "a venture into the realm of natural history, where I did not really belong." Her pleasure in nature was in its beauty; it was her husband who knew how to make the children respond to its wonders and mysteries. She was the minstrel and the storyteller, he the scientist.

In 1889 she began to write her "girls' books" and in the next fifteen years eleven in the Hildegarde and Three Margarets series were published. " . . . I do not know that I have anything special to say about these. The later ones are better written than the earlier ones; if I were twenty years younger, I would write *Queen Hildegarde* over again."

A girl growing up in the first thirty years of the twentieth century would not dismiss them so briefly. I doubt if Mrs. Richards realized how widely these books were read and how generally loved. A paragraph from any of them, or even mention of the titles, brings to memory a picture of five girls thirty-odd years ago and three thousand miles away from Gardiner. They are relaxed in the late afternoon sunshine on a green lawn that slopes down to the glistening waters of Puget Sound. In front of them are the wooded San Juan Islands, the snowy Olympics. But their minds are on other scenes: a secret room under a stairway where a girl of another generation had put away her dolls; a young girl dancing in the moonlight or rescuing a selfish woman's jewels from a fire; a glamorous Cuban girl's romance and adventures during the Spanish-American War; the arrival in their new home of the ingratiating Merryweather family with a mother who disciplines her children with rhymes: "The book is on the chair, / And the hat is on the stair, / And the boots are everywhere, / Children mine!"

There were the books, too, from which Hildegarde or Margaret or other characters were always quoting. Back to the library would go the five girls, not only to get another Richards book, but to find out *why* Rita called Peggy "Calibana" or who Berengaria and Saladin were. Love of books and poetry overflowed into her girls' stories and caught many another girl in its tide.

In the years that have passed, these five girls could not, probably, remember each other's names, bosom friends though they were for two long years, but I doubt if any has entirely forgotten the magic conjured up by the chronicler of Hildegarde Graham and Margaret Montfort.

Alexander Woollcott, whose long correspondence with Laura Richards brought stimulation and delight to both, mentioned Anne Parrish's speaking of the "peace" that the Hildegarde stories still brought her, and expressed surprise over the impression made on contemporaries by the wallpaper in Hildegarde's room. After forty years Kathleen Norris, whose childhood ambition had been to possess such a room, could still describe the wallpaper!

Laura Richards speaks of her girls' stories, as well as her nursery rhymes and jingles, as being "cobwebs spun more or less out of my own brain." The analogy is hard to credit, for the things which filled her head were too strong and vital to be called cobwebs. It was full of joyful childhood memories of companionship and fun in wood and fields and orchards, and in the various parts of the Institution, in nooks and stairways and hiding places of her several childhood homes. It was full of memories of associations with people of many backgrounds, friends of many ages with simulating and creative minds. It was full of family pleasures: games and plays and tableaux; dancing with "Bacchic Frenzy" to their mother's playing till they tumbled down exhausted; listening to their father read aloud from Dickens and Scott, Shakespeare and the Bible, in "his deep, melodious, unforgettable voice," and to their mother's reading of poetry and singing of ballads.

These were the "cobwebs" from which she spun her stories. *Queen Hildegarde* may seem contrived, as well as such books as *Star Bright,* which was an unfortunate concession to the repeated demands for a sequel to *Captain January,* but the later girls' books, particularly those in the Hildegarde and Margaret series, grow better and better. Along with the charm of atmosphere to be found in all of them and the incidents, situations and people that grew out of her memories, they are full of fundamental values: the virtues of kindness, wisdom, understanding, dignity and old-fashioned goodness; the love of books and appreciation of the English language; and always humor.

In the meantime her "hurdy-gurdy" was pouring forth nursery rhymes.

> When rhyming is in the blood, anything may bring on the fit. Witness a day when I sat cowering over the fire, shivering through the first stage of Influenza. In sheer misery I rocked to and fro in my seat; and so rocking, began to croon, words and tune coming together.

> "A poor unfortunate Hottentot,
> He was not content with his Lottentot;
> Quoth he, 'For my dinner,
> As I am a sinner,
> There's nothing to put in the Pottentot!'"

In 1890 a number of new rhymes with the early ones from *St. Nicholas* and those from *Sketches and Scraps* were collected and published under the title *In My Nursery.*

In the same year, while visiting Mrs. Charles H. Dorr at Bar Harbor, whose house was among those Henry Richards had built in the first ten years of life in Maine, Mrs. Richards was sitting on the rocks below the house, looking out to sea.

> I saw a distant lighthouse, and began dreaming and wondering as to what life might be in such a place. . . . So, up out of the sea, as it were, came to me the little story called *Captain January.* I wrote it quickly, and was rather pleased with it, but when I took it to my publishers, they would have nothing to say to it. It was too short for a long story, too long for a short story; very sorry, but not in their line.

The story went to and was returned from many publishers in England and the United States, and at last Laura put it away. A year or two later, when she met Mr. Estes by chance, he asked her what she had been writing. "Nothing," was her reply, "except a little story that you refused." Mr. Estes read the story himself. Forty years later it still headed the list of sales of her books. Today it is the most easily procured of all of Laura Richards's storybooks, and it has twice been made into a motion picture.

In a letter to Mrs. Richards written in March, 1932, Mr. Woollcott recounted reactions to his review of *Stepping Westward* in *The New Yorker*. Almost daily, for two months after it appeared, letters came from people all over the country telling of their own happy memories of Laura Richards's books, and thanking him for reminding them of *Captain January,* many of whom described frantic searches for mislaid copies of the well-loved story. Mr. Woollcott himself remembered recognizing, even as a boy reading omnivorously, the books he would always like: *Huckleberry Finn,* Kenneth Grahame's *The Golden Age, Little Women,* Howard Pyle's *Robin Hood,* and *Captain January.*

Stories of *Captain January* length having justified themselves, Mrs. Richards wrote a number of others, all in the nineties: *Marie, Nautilus, Isla Heron, Rosin the Beau.* They are sentimental little tales, but for all their dreamlike quality there is actuality and charm in the Maine settings. Later ones begin to show more contact with reality. In *Narcissa, Jim of Hellas* and *Some Say* she was beginning to notice and translate into her stories the people who belong to Maine as truly as do the rocky coasts. In these, as in her Hildegarde and Margaret stories, there is often continuity. While each story is separate, characters appear and reappear, or their children and grandchildren become known. Rosin the Beau is the son of Marie, the friend and benefactor of Melody, and in *Bethesda Pool,* the fiddler at the dance is his pupil. Reading all her books together, one becomes aware of the different worlds in which she was living. Never was she separated from life in the Yellow House or in the whole of Gardiner, yet her book people must have been real to her too. It is as if she were capturing but small segments of their lives in her stories, so that if one were to take the Road to Rome or to visit the village of Cyrus, or to step onto a certain rocky Maine Island, one would find the people of her books living out their natural lives.

The influences of her childhood are evident in her characters. The stories of the blind child, Marie, the deaf-mute boy, Jacob of *Isla Heron*—and there are others—show not only an understanding of the problems of handicapped people, but a recognition of the possible richness of any life despite physical infirmities.

From these stories, the step to her novel writing was a gentle one. When she first began to write she did not think she could ever write a novel.

. . . the tender passion was beyond me. Well, I have

accomplished even that after a fashion. I hardly know how it came about; partly, no doubt, because life was growing always fuller and richer. I overflowed my banks!

For another thing, I was learning *to see* . . . here, all around me, were people living and moving and having their being; New England people, strong and humorous and kind, all living lives of intense interest, all with stories to tell. Here was a speech so vigorous and racy, so full of quaint and delightful idiom, that every linguistic fibre in me cried out to preserve it, to write down the words that sounded all day in my delighted ears.

I could not walk down the street, but incident and anecdote jostled me. . . .

While Mrs. Richards was writing of a village tea party in *Geoffrey Strong,* Mrs. Marcia Tree appeared and became so alive she had to have her own book. "I wrote *Mrs. Tree* mostly at Camp, sitting about under trees, with the Boys running all about me. Nothing mattered; it was really she who wrote the story; I merely held and guided the pen."

Probably *A Daughter of Jehu,* the first of her stories laid in the town of Cyrus, shows more of herself than any of her other novels: her philosophy, her relationships with young and old, as well as the intrepid horsewoman she was—a true daughter of the "Chevalier"—until an illness in late girlhood. The Cyrus stories, too, would seem to have been written easily, as if she were merely reporting events of a well-known and well-loved town. She indulged her love of nonsense in the names of her characters, and while she might seem to laugh a little at them, it is because laughter is easy, even at herself. Always she loved and understood them. If at times her characters seem exaggerated it is probably because they are true. The novelist who would be convincing must deal in understatement. Laura Richards did not attempt to make her characters believable; she painted them as her delighted eyes saw them.

Said someone to Laura, "But in a place like Gardiner there must be many 'characters'; people who are really individual and quaint?"

"There are; many of them," replied Laura. "I am beginning to realize that at eighty-odd I am one of them."

Her childlike pleasure in imaginative things slips even into her novels. Trap doors, hidden rooms and secret passages abound in her girls' stories. In *The Squire* there is a secret room off the library where the old scholar's Greek books are kept. In *The Squire,* too, the romantic memories of her father's tales of his Greek experiences come again into play.

Her novels belong to the period between 1901 and 1923. *Geoffrey Strong* was the first, *The Squire* the last, but in the years between she had not stopped turning her hurdy-gurdy or writing her girls' stories. And in that time she had also begun writing fables and biographies for young people, and all this time she was doing what was to her the great work of her life: the work of editing the letters and journals of her father. She had begun to prepare for this the year after his death in 1876. The first volume appeared in 1906, the second in 1909 when she gave it to her mother on her ninetieth birthday.

In the years following her mother's death in 1910 *The Life and Letters of Julia Ward Howe,* written in collaboration with her sister Maud Howe Elliott, occupied much time, " . . . a labor of love, if ever there was one. I did not know how to stop!"

Her biographies reflect the nature of the people who were important to her in her own growth. Florence Nightingale had received advice from her father but they had more in common than the giving and accepting of advice, and the second Howe child had been named after her. Here was a subject for a biography whose life was familiar and understood.

Laura Bridgman had been important to her from her birth, for she herself was named after the blind-deaf-mute child whom Samuel Gridley Howe had taken at the age of eight and brought into communication with the world.

Elizabeth Fry—how like Laura's father in her multitude of good works! The name of anyone who had not only brought about prison reform but had improved conditions in hospitals and asylums must certainly have been a household word in the Howe family, one more family tradition to influence the children's growing personalities.

Much as she appreciated and carefully as she recorded the work of her subjects, she could always look at them with balance and objectivity. After one entry in Elizabeth Fry's diary, humorless and full of self-condemnation, Laura interposes, "Poor Betsy! if only she would shut up her journal, and go and read a story to the children, or take the dogs for a walk, how much happier she would be!" Late in Mrs. Fry's life, the indomitable woman returned exhausted and ill after a journey to Ireland to help in prison reform, and Laura, understanding so well the forces that drive great philanthropists, cannot resist commenting, "I only hope her devoted children refrained from saying, 'Dear mother, we told you so!'"

Elizabeth Fry, and Abigail Adams too, had much in common with Laura's mother, and Joan of Arc was the kind of heroine Laura's romantic and idealistic soul must have adored from earliest childhood. Next to literature, history was her forte, and French history seems always to have been of particular interest to her. How delightful must have been the papers she presented to the History Class! Her *Glimpses of a French Court* give a sampling of the charm of her informal excursions into history. While her story of Joan of Arc may not bring the heroine herself completely to life, Laura was definitely

moved by the heroic drama of Joan's life and inspired by the victory of the First World War to present it against faithful historical background.

Though her young people's biographies were written at the request of her publishers, her subjects were all people whom she "knew," for whom she was the natural biographer.

Two Noble Lives is drawn from her definitive biographies of her parents, and *When I Was Your Age* does for her children what every child would have from his mother, preserving the years of the young Laura and her family. The memories of one's childhood are never more clear than during the childhood of one's own children. *Stepping Westward,* written after she was eighty, is wise and beautiful in its balance and perspective, but *When I Was Your Age* could have been written only during the growing years of her own boys and girls.

Her fables have been quoted so often that many of them are as familiar as folk tales, their authorship not even recognized. (In them we see, perhaps, more than in any of her writings, the influence of the metaphysical poets and of Stevenson's philosophy as shown in his fables.) Two volumes contain the bulk of Mrs. Richards's fables: *Golden Windows* and *The Silver Crown.* The title story of the first is perhaps best known of all, and the idea of it captured her imagination and held it through the years. It is repeated in her last novel when the Squire is gazing at his last sunset "touching the eastern hills with unimaginable glory, lighting the humble farmhouse windows to dazzling splendor." They are brief allegories, some subtle, a few baffling, many simple, many touched with humor, most of them tender. In one of them, **"Theology,"** the Angel who understands things, asks,

> "What are you quarreling about, children?"
> "About our God!" said the children.
> "Oh!" said the Angel. "The God of Strife, I presume?"
> "No!" cried one. "He is the God of Peace!"
> "He is the God of Wisdom!" said another.
> "He is the God of Love!" said a third.
> "Indeed!" said the Angel, "I never should have thought it."

Though they are stories in the fable pattern, presenting ideals and moral percepts, the children who appear in them are inevitably real. She knew children so well she could not, even in an allegory, cover them with veils of sentimentality.

Ruth Hill Viguers

SOURCE: "Laura E. Richards, Joyous Companion: Part IV, in *The Horn Book Magazine,* Vol. XXXII, No. 6, December, 1956, pp. 467-76.

Writing was as natural as breathing to Laura Richards.

And it was as necessary to her. So had it been to her mother, who could turn off a nonsense rhyme with the same dexterity as her daughter, but did not consider nonsense consequential, and who took her actual writing with such seriousness as to achieve even her children's respect for her "precious time" set aside each day for uninterrupted writing or study. One difference between these two extraordinary women was in their attitude toward their work. To Julia Ward Howe her writing was an answer to the demands of the spirit, a fulfillment. To Laura it was a part of living, important, as breathing is important, but not to be wondered about. It had its economic value at certain times, and the kind of writing she did at those times may have been dictated, somewhat, by the need to help with the family budget or the school expenses. But when these times of stress were over her writing did not taper off. While work published under her name ran to well over eighty volumes, these do not represent all her writing. She was always writing: songs for the Gardiner Centennial, greetings to the Current Events Club, tributes to friends, letters and articles to the paper, often in rhyme, verses and articles about books, the library, the children. Unpublished poems sent to friends for one reason or another—a tribute to a boy killed in the First World War, a congratulatory rhyme, a message of appreciation—continually come to light. She wrote for publication. And she wrote! Her family remember her as always writing on her lap; her friends remember the bit of paper and pencil that her pocket inevitably held.

Early in the writing of her girls' stories she went to her friend Sarah Orne Jewett, whose reputation as an author was already established, for help and criticism on her own work. "In those years I was writing a great deal of verse, ballads, lyrics, even essays in French forms, enjoying myself immensely. I knew that my hurdy gurdy was not a lyre, but I found it extremely amusing and even inspiring to try for lyric tones on it.

"*'Don't scatter your fire!'* said Sarah Jewett. 'You are a prose writer: stick to your own tool!'"

She "laid her friend's words to heart" but through her life her attitude toward her writing did not greatly change. She knew her limitations but she also recognized the importance of her special genius, knew that writing was something to enjoy, as were books and reading, even as were all the good things of life—to enjoy and to share.

Because of this her hurdy-gurdy could never run down. When her last collections of nonsense verse and nursery rhymes, *Tirra Lirra, Merry-Go-Round* and *I Have a Song to Sing You,* were published, they included rhymes written in her eighties which were as good as her earlier work, *"and in just the same way,"* said May Lamberton Becker.

> Once I longed to be a poet;
>   Longed to touch the lovely lyre;
> Joy celestial, I would know it,

> Holy rage and tragic fire.
> So I twanged amain, while swelled
>   Loud my carol, wild and wordy;
> Till, glancing at the thing I held,—
>   Lo! it was a hurdy-gurdy!

> Turn, my hurdy-gurdy turn!
>   Sing, whatever skies be dreary,
> Let no child in sadness yearn,
>   Keep the babies bright and cheery!
> Every day be glad and gay,
>   Rosy, cosy, cream and curdy;
> Dancing, glancing down the way,
>   Turn, still turn, my hurdy-gurdy!

In the preface to *Merry-Go-Round,* published in 1935, Margaret Widdemer says, "She writes with the nearly lost background of wide, lightly carried Victorian culture, in the vein of the great Victorian nonsense writers for children. And children do not change. It is good to feel that in this book they will be given a sound grounding in lively, brilliant nonsense of a sort which our wearier, less-educated age finds hard to produce." . . .

Alliteration, good vital English and nonsensical words, funny situations, meticulous rhythms, fantastic animals, strange grown-ups, jolly children, music and tenderness are all here, and much more. These are the classics of the nursery. Among future generations of children it will be for her gaily singing music box that Laura Richards will be remembered.

In 1896 Laura came to know Edwin Arlington Robinson. Because he was an acquaintance of her elder son, she had heard of him for some time before she met him. When they did meet, shortly after the death of his mother, he was to experience the healing of such rare friendship as Laura could give. There was bound to be profit on both sides in the friendship between this rather shy young man, whom his boyhood contemporaries could never entirely understand, and the "Veteran Scribbler," as she called herself—outgoing, friendly, so quick to see humor in a situation, yet with sharp, sensitive understanding as well. Laura speaks warmly and with pride of E. A. R. but she makes no mention of the great practical help which she gave the young poet. His first volume, *The Torrent and the Night Before,* convinced her of his genius and, with friends of like conviction, she gave him letters of introduction, wrote to editors, gave readings from the poems, and did everything possible to further the recognition of his second book, *The Children of the Night.* He came twice to the Richards's family camp at Lake Cobbosseecontee, meeting there Hays Gardiner, Dr. George Hodges, Lawrence Joseph Henderson, and others who were to become his lifelong friends. Her small book, *E. A. R.,* published shortly after Mr. Robinson's death, tells the story of the early years of the poet, the beauty of his home relationships, and her association with him. " . . . among the friends of my later life, he has been one of the most highly valued." Even after he left Gardiner their friendship did not lessen. They never failed to meet yearly or oftener, for "a handclasp and an hour of golden talk," and their regular and happy correspondence lasted until the poet's death.

The First World War came, the second of the three major wars which affected Laura closely and deeply. She saw her younger son enter the army a private and come out a first lieutenant with the *Croix de Guerre.* The intensity of her feeling found relief in a book of songs and marching rhymes, *To Arms!* and her biography of Joan of Arc. Yet she was not deflected from work that must go on in Gardiner, and between 1917 and 1919 the campaign for a new high school enlisted her devotion and talents.

The Henry Richards's golden wedding anniversary was celebrated on June 17, 1921, with four of the original wedding guests present. There was dancing on the lawn, with Laura and Henry leading the Virginia Reel. The music was made by Horace Hildreth (the present United States Ambassador to Pakistan) and his brother Charles, both of them Howe Club Boys.

In March of the next year came great sorrow in the death from pneumonia of the Richards's first born, Alice, but they were comforted by the knowledge of the great contribution she had made as a teacher for twenty-seven years in the Gardiner High School; by the tributes paid to her by her associates and the whole town of Gardiner; and by the founding by her friends of the Alice M. Richards Memorial Library in the High School.

The other children were also doing significant work in educational and literary fields: Henry at Groton, John at St. Paul's School in Concord, Julia and Betty both married to schoolmasters, and Rosalind writing her own stories. Merryweather Camp was continuing and growing, giving them each year the chance to drink "once more the deep draught of young life which always strengthens and heartens us." And the thirteen adoring grandchildren, to whom she was "Gumidy," brought Laura deep happiness. Her dedication in *Tirra Lirra,* "To John Richards II, my youngest grandchild, and William Davis Ticknor III, my eldest great-grandchild: Two Very Young Gentlemen," with the rhyme that follows, shows that her path to childhood was as direct and gay as always.

While the last two decades of Laura's life saw the publication of only ten books—in contrast to the period when two or three were often published in a single year—those ten include some of her finest: *Harry in England,* based on her husband's actual experiences as a little boy visiting his grandmother, in whose home Laura had visited as a bride; her autobiography, *Stepping Westward;* her biography of her father; her account of the youth of Edwin Arlington Robinson; three volumes of verse which include the best of earlier collections no longer in print, verses published before only in periodicals, and some new pourings forth from her hurdy-gurdy; and finally, *What Shall the Children Read?*—a distillation of her thoughts on children's reading and her experiences with children and books for three-quarters of a century. This last is dedicated "To the Merryweath-

er Boys who are now planning the reading of the Merryweather Grandchildren."

In a letter to Laura in 1939, Theodore Roosevelt, Jr., recalls his father's and mother's delightful habit of reciting rhymes and poetry to their children, and the special pleasure they all had in the work of a certain writer, many of whose rhymes he could still recite. He upbraids Mrs. Richards for one "scandalous omission" in *What Shall the Children Read?*—the omission of Laura E. Richards herself.

Alexander Woollcott, whose friendship with Laura Richards began in her eighties, considered "that all the years I never knew Mrs. Richards were just years wasted by one of destiny's monstrous mismanagements " "If there was one person," said Samuel Hopkins Adams, "whom Aleck held in affectionate reverence, it was the lovely and gentle Laura E. Richards." On one series of the Town Crier's special radio broadcasts Woollcott serenaded his "ten favorite Americans" of whom she was one. Their friendship continued until her death, his letters often being signed "Old Faithful." The last letter he wrote, as far as anyone knows—six days after Mrs. Richards's death and three days before his own—was to Miss Rosalind Richards. In it he told of his private "village" of people important to him. "Well, of course Laura Richards dwelt in my village. What a delight, what a refreshment, what a nourishment it was to see her and to hear her and to think about her I have no words to tell even you. Now I can only think about her. I do that a great deal. I always shall. . . . What a triumphant life!"

When Laura was eighty-six the University of Maine recognized the state's adopted daughter by giving her the honorary degree of Doctor of Letters. On her ninetieth birthday the Gardiner Public Library Association published a volume in her honor, called *Laura E. Richards and Gardiner,* in which were printed articles, letters and poems which had previously appeared in local newspapers, dedicatory verses, and some of her fables. While few people during her life ever realized how much she did for Gardiner, hers was a personality which brought response even as it drew people to her.

Less than two years before her death, two new poems were published in the "Conning Tower" of the New York *Post.* The intensity of feeling in the first, **"Dunkirk,"** is reminiscent of that shown by her mother during an earlier war in "Mine eyes have seen the glory of the coming of the Lord." In the second, **"A Toast,"** her love for Greece—planted in childhood by her father's romantic stories of his youth, nourished by a lifetime of reading and study, and growing with the years—found expression once more:

> Hellas a rouse to you!
> No heart but bows to you,
> No voice but cheers.
> Stand, as your fathers stood!
> 'Tis their heroic blood

Flows in immortal flood
Down through the years.

All hearts that claim the free
Guerdon of liberty,
Strong hearts and true,
All eyes that seek the light
Turn where your beacon bright
Shatters the whelming night.
Hellas, to you!

Elizabeth Coatsworth was present at the Richards's seventieth wedding anniversary held in the secluded garden of the Yellow House. She speaks of the gaiety of the occasion, the witty talk "and a warm kindness to brighten it," of the two whose laughter still came spontaneously and frankly though they had each lived more than ninety years: "old age seemed a delightful thing." Letters to Anne Carroll Moore, written in Laura's eighties and nineties, show this same spontaneity and lively interest in everything. In 1941 Anne Eaton in *The Horn Book* voiced what so many felt, "that there is no one today younger in spirit than Laura E. Richards." As late as October 27th, before Mrs. Richards's death in January, 1943, Elizabeth Coatsworth received a characteristic gay little note and rhyme. "Neither the war, which she felt very deeply," said Miss Coatsworth, "nor the weight of years, nor sickness had succeeded in subduing her brave gaiety of heart." "Joyful" is the word that appears again and again in her writing, and because hers was a life of joyful giving, it brought her almost ninety-three years of love and honor.

At ninety Julia Ward Howe was asked to "express the aim of life." Her answer was: "To learn; to teach; to serve; to enjoy!"

At eighty her daughter added, "This utterance comes more deeply home to me with every year; I realize more and more how these four aspects of life are linked together: how, whenever I have tried to teach, I have been the chief learner; and whenever I have tried to serve, the chief pleasure has been mine." Not the tinkling of a hurdy-gurdy, these words, but music of the symphony that was her life.

TITLE COMMENTARY

📖 *GLIMPSES OF THE FRENCH COURT: SKETCHES FROM FRENCH HISTORY* (1893)

The Dial

SOURCE: A review of *Glimpses of the French Court: Sketches from French History,* in *The Dial,* Vol. XV, No. 179, December 1, 1893, p. 347.

Mrs. Laura E. Richards's volume of *Glimpses of the French Court* comprises a series of sketches from French history—"**The Story of Jean Baptiste,**" "**Turenne,**" "**A Corsair of France,**" etc. The author writes in a brisk, chirping, fairy-tale sort of style, that is at times oddly at variance with the gravity of her topic. But the book is wholesome and spirited, and it should prove a welcome and useful gift to younger readers. There are a number of portraits, one or two of them exceedingly well done.

📖 *MELODY: THE STORY OF A CHILD* (1893)

The Dial

SOURCE: A review of *Melody: the Story of a Child,* in *The Dial,* Vol. XV, No. 179, December 1, 1893, p. 349.

Melody, the Story of a Child will doubtless be very successful, if for no other reason than because it is written by Mrs. Laura E. Richards, the author of *Captain January.* It is a sweet and simple story of a blind girl, who is gifted with a remarkable voice. The adopted child of two maiden ladies in a little New England village, she is stolen from them by an ambitious musician; and the tale of her unhappiness, ending finally in a joyous return to her home, is prettily told. The subordinate characters are well handled and have much individuality; and in the little heroine, Mrs. Richards has really created a starry soul.

📖 *NAUTILUS* (1895)

The Nation

SOURCE: A review of *Nautilus,* in *The Nation,* Vol. 61, No. 1587, November 28, 1895, p. 393.

The excessive exuberance which has marked some of Mrs. Laura E. Richards's former stories seems to have broken out on the cover of her latest book, *Nautilus.* Here a black and white square-rigged "schooner" sails with jibboom pointing skyward across a white and yellow sea, driven by a wind as violent as the brilliant chrome sky. Such a remarkable design may be imagined to have absorbed a good deal of superfluous color from the pages. Whatever the cause of improvement, we have, this time, a fairly straightforward tale of a boy, unspoiled by much ill-treatment, who was rescued from a miserable life by a good, undreamt of uncle. Perhaps to children, used as they are to believe "six impossible things before breakfast," it will not seem too unlikely that a foreign uncle should first have made known his existence by sailing up the river and, with little ceremony, carrying off the boy in his schooner *Nautilus.*

The Dial

SOURCE: A review of *Nautilus,* in *The Dial,* Vol. XIX, No. 228, December 16, 1895, p. 393.

A new book by the author of **Captain January** and **Melody** is welcome, and though this one lacks a little of their fine simplicity, it has still the power to charm. Mrs. Laura E. Richards's style is easy and graceful, and her character-drawing, though on broad lines, is good. **Nautilus,** with its gay decorative cover, is the story of a Spanish ship, laden with treasure of shells and sea-products, which sails up a New England river to the amazement of a quiet little town. The contrasts are effective, and the plot developed by them is interesting. The cuts by Mr. W. L. Taylor are capital.

FIVE MINUTE STORIES (1895; reprinted, 1924; British edition, 1906)

Bookman

SOURCE: A review of *Five Minute Stories,* in *Bookman,* Vol. LXVII, December, 1924, p. 120.

This is the sixth edition of a book of one hundred and one short stories and rhymes which has made many friends on both sides of the Atlantic. Mrs. Richards is grave, gay, matter-of-fact, fanciful, all in turn. Even the slightest of the tales has its ethical note, seldom obtrusive but still there. It is a little difficult to say what the subjects of the stories are, because these are so varied and the smallest of incidents often suggests a story to the writer. Two of the tales are called **"Buttercup Gold"** and **"Mathematics."** The first tells how a little girl wanted to get the gold from the buttercups for her tired mother. She patiently picked hundreds of them, boiled them, and with the help of a kind old gentleman took out some gold pieces from the bottom of the pan. **"Mathematics"** tells in verse of a nightmare which came to a little boy who had been doing arithmetic just before he went to bed. These stories are what they claim to be—five minute stories, and they ought to replenish very usefully many a grown-up armoury whose stock is getting low.

THREE MARGARETS (1897)

The Dial

SOURCE: A review of *Three Margarets,* in *The Dial,* Vol. XXIII, No. 276, December 16, 1897, p. 401.

Three Margarets, by Mrs. Laura E. Richards, is conceived on a new plan. The Margarets are three cousins of the same name,—one from the East, one from a ranch in the West, and one from a Cuban plantation,—who come together for a summer's visit to an uncle whom they have never seen. There is here an opportunity for contrast in character, which Mrs. Richards skillfully, but somewhat melodramatically, improves. It is on the whole a charming little story, with a good deal of human nature in it; but it has not the beauty which the author herself achieved in **Captain January.** The pictures, by Miss Ethelred B. Barry, are pretty, though a trifle insipid, and the cover is clever.

FLORENCE NIGHTINGALE, ANGEL OF THE CRIMEA: A STORY FOR YOUNG PEOPLE (1909)

A. L. A. Booklist

SOURCE: A review of *Florence Nightingale: The Angel of the Crimea,* in *A. L. A. Booklist,* Vol. 6, No. 6, February, 1910, p. 223.

The story of this noble woman told in very attractive style, showing marked sympathy and emphasizing the great and womanly qualities that make its subject one of the most honored of the world's helpers. Gives an excellent picture of hospital nursing and of the horrors of war. A welcome addition to the inspirational biographies for older children; well printed and bound.

THE NAUGHTY COMET AND OTHER FABLES AND STORIES (1910; revised edition, 1925)

Bookman

SOURCE: A review of *The Naughty Comet,* in *Bookman,* Vol. LXVII, December, 1924, p. 206.

Stories and verses make up this pleasing little book for children. The stories are in that gay, whimsical vein that specially appeals to the fancifulness of a child, and the verses go with a good swing and often tell a story. All lovers of Grimm will find here something to their taste, for there is a touch of Grimm in many of the tales—that fantastic ruthlessness which is melodrama in the nursery. The little old man who lived at the bottom of a well and kept a cook who lived on the ground above, and who, not recognising him when at last he crept out of his home, cooked him for his own dinner in mistake for a radish, might almost have been a Grimm creation. So too might have been the ambitious rockinghorse. Miss Laura E. Richards has already proved her popularity with the younger generation, and this revised edition of one of her most successful books will be widely welcomed.

TWO NOBLE LIVES: SAMUEL GRID-LEY HOWE, JULIA WARD HOWE (1911)

The Outlook

SOURCE: A review of *Two Noble Lives,* in *The Outlook,* Vol. XCIX, October 14, 1911, p. 390.

Two Noble Lives, by Laura E. Richards, is a beautiful tribute to her father and mother, Samuel Gridley Howe and Julia Ward Howe, names known all over our land and still held in reverent memory across the sea. The little book is adapted from an earlier volume and is especially designed for use in schools. It has the genuine simplicity so often an inherent part of the great personalities portrayed. Dr. Howe began his work for his fellows as long ago as the time when Greece fought for her independence, in 1824. He lived in Greece for six years, soldier and surgeon and the best kind of social worker, solving problems that now require elaborate conventions even to discuss, and raising money himself to carry out his helpful schemes. Of his work for the blind in Boston it is needless to speak. The name of his pupil Laura Bridgman is as well known as that of Helen Keller. The abuses common in the treatment of the insane roused his efforts, and his spirit was apparently undaunted. He often said, "Obstacles are things to overcome." Truly he followed the Master, and in his wake the blind received their sight, the dumb spake, and the poor heard good tidings. His life is still an inspiration to those who work for their fellow-men. His wife, so recently gone away from a devoted circle of friends, lived to a beautiful old age. Indefatigable at home among her children, she entered sympathetically into Dr. Howe's philanthropies, and yet made a distinct place for herself by her own public activities and with her busy pen. The story of her "Battle Hymn of the Republic" is told with great effect, and will influence children of our day to reverence the patriotism of their ancestors. No better book nor more interesting book could be given to school-children to read than this simple story of the magnificent victories of these true heroes of peace.

The New York Times

SOURCE: A review of *Two Noble Lives,* in *The New York Times,* October 22, 1911, p. 637.

Mrs. Laura E. Richards has prepared for young readers an adaptation of an earlier volume memorial of her distinguished parents, Dr. Samuel Gridley Howe and Julia Ward Howe, and it is published in a pretty booklet entitled *Two Noble Lives.* The brief biographical sketches are written in a very pleasing way and contain matter that will greatly interest children. The story of Dr. Howe's life includes a very good account of his romantic and perilous experiences while helping the Greeks in their fight for independence and while, a little later, he was ministering to suffering Polish troops who, driven from home by the Russians, had taken refuge in Prussia.

☐ FAIRY OPERETTAS (1916)

The Literary Digest

SOURCE: A review of *Fairy Operettas,* in *The Literary Digest,* Vol. LIII, No. 24, December 9, 1916, p. 1567.

Mrs. Richards has taken hold of the famous nursery legends like "Cinderella," "Babes in the Wood," "Puss in Boots," and has turned them into easy little plays for school presentation. They can either be used as plays or given as little operettas, inasmuch as they are set to such familiar tunes as "My Heart's in the Highlands," "When Johnny Comes Marching Home," "The Campbells Are Coming," "There'll Be a Hot Time in the Old Town To-night," and "The Old Gray Bonnet." This combination of new words with old tunes—a method employed in the Salvation Army—is a rather good idea, although there may be some musical esthetes who will doubt whether "There'll Be a Hot Time in the Old Town To-night" is an advisable melody for children to learn. Mrs. Richards has discovered a very pleasant way of combining a musical love with the dramatic instinct.

☐ ELIZABETH FRY: THE ANGEL OF THE PRISONS (1916)

The Survey

SOURCE: A review of *Elizabeth Fry: The Angel of the Prisons,* in *The Survey,* Vol. XXXVIII, No. 1, April 21, 1917, p. 76.

From Geoffrey Strong, *written by Laura E. Richards. Illustrated by Henry Richards.*

The utter inability of the reader to tell how much of this book is fact and how much is Mrs. Richards's (witness the scholarly letter written by the "screaming, swearing" women prisoners at Newgate, which is presented with no question as to its having actually beenwritten by them) is its chief defect. My guess is that it will entrance many a child and tell him absorbing things that he will not learn in his school history.

The book is largely composed of extracts from the journals of Elizabeth Fry and her sisters, which account for the vividness of the picture it gives. Imagine the shock to one's reverence for the tradition that Elizabeth Fry has become, to read in her diary, written when she was seventeen: "Company to dinner. I must beware of not being a flirt, it is an abominable character; I hope I shall never be one, and yet I fear I am one now a little." And again: "I must not mump when my sisters are liked and I am not."

In the days of her fame, when the king and queen of France paid homage to her good works, this Quaker woman uttered one maxim in the course of a report on French prisons that might well be hung on the walls of our modern prison commission offices: "When thee builds a prison, thee had better build with the thought ever in thy mind that thee and thy children may occupy the cells."

📖 ABIGAIL ADAMS AND HER TIMES (1917)

The Outlook

SOURCE: A review of *Abigail Adams and Her Times,* in *The Outlook,* Vol. 117, December 12, 1917, p. 614.

A fascinating story of colonial times; fascinating to those who are interested in the details which make up the major part of all human lives, but are absent from most histories. Abigail Adams was the wife of John Adams, second President of the United States. The author has shown both skill and discretion in keeping herself in the background and composing her story mostly of the diary of the husband and the letters of the wife. The biography is almost an autobiography.

The American Review of Reviews

SOURCE: A review of *Abigail Adams and Her Times,* in *The American Review of Reviews,* Vol. LVII, No. 1, January, 1918, p. 100.

Abigail Adams was the wife of John Adams, and hence the first mistress of the White House. But even if she had never had a part in official life, she was one of the most interesting women of her time and well deserves a biography. Mrs. Richards tells the story of her childhood and later life from the diaries and letters that were

written by her, and which deal with much of the real history of the period.

The Literary Digest

SOURCE: A review of *Abigail Adams and Her Times,* in *The Literary Digest,* Vol. 56, No. 4, January 26, 1918, p. 38.

So few are the biographies for children this season that the new one from the pen of Mrs. Richards stands out as particularly welcome. The subject, too, is one that lends itself to full historical treatment. Interesting, indeed, in these days of conservation, are the prices given by the practical Abigail. Potatoes at ten dollars a bushel and butter at twelve dollars a pound for the Revolution make us feel that we are living in reasonable days, despite the "high cost of living."

📖 HONOR BRIGHT: A STORY FOR GIRLS (1920)

The Canadian Bookman

SOURCE: "Recent Fiction for Girls," in *The Canadian Bookman,* Vol. 4, No. 12, December, 1922, p. 324.

More insistent and persistent than any other demand from girl readers is that for school stories. There are, fortunately, two of fairly recent date that the children's librarian can welcome: *Mehitable,* by Katherine Adams and *Honor Bright* by Laura Richards. . . .

Honor Bright, in Laura Richards's book, is also a nice and not faultless little girl, and the slight story gives not only a good picture of school days in Switzerland and of Alpine peasant life, but conveys an impression of the grandeur and beauty of the mountains and a sense of true values in life. It compares favorably with Laura Richards's earlier stories and as in them books are frequently mentioned in such a way as to interest readers in them—often an effective means of opening out paths of more advanced reading to girls.

📖 HONOR BRIGHT'S NEW ADVENTURE (1925)

The Canadian Bookman

SOURCE: A review of *Honor Bright's New Adventure,* in *The Canadian Bookman,* Vol. VIII, No. 1, January, 1926, p. 55.

This is a sequel to *Honor Bright,* and like each of the long list of Laura Richards's books, is a story well told. The heroine enters a new world with her notable journey to Switzerland with which this tale begins. But most of the action and scene of the story is on the island of

Bermuda. It is interesting in plot and full of color, with humor to add spice.

📖 *TIRRA LIRRA: RHYMES OLD AND NEW*
　　(1932)

The New York Times Book Review

SOURCE: A review of *Tirra Lirra: Rhymes Old and New,* in *The New York Times Book Review,* October 23, 1932, p. 13.

Readers of an older generation stand ready to bless Mrs. Becker and the publishers for conceiving and carrying out the idea of this book of Mrs. Richards's poems and nonsense verses, old and new—an omnibus volume, in short, of this charming author, whose first books were published some fifty years ago.

It is an event of note in the world of children's books to find poems written, some of them in 1881, as fresh and appealing to children today as then. Some of the poems are new, but only from memory of the contents of the older volumes could the reader tell which are reprinted, for the new ones are as fresh and lively, as perfect in versification and rhythm as the earlier ones. Since no reader can make a perfect anthology for another, each individual will find gaps; but if we must forego **"The Palace"** of coral and pearl and the wistful **"Day Dream,"** have we not **"The Seven Little Tigers and the Aged Cook," "Bobbily Boo and Wallypotump"** and **"Skinny Mrs. Snipkin and Fat Mrs. Wobblechin,"** who seem in a fair way to attain the immortality they deserve? It is to be hoped that this new volume will call to children's attention others of Mrs. Richards's books. No story of the doings of boys and girls could be more enchanting than Mrs. Richards's account of her own lively childhood, told in **When I Was Your Age.** The Queen Hildegarde stories still hold 13 and 14 year olds with their very real girl characters against a background of good breeding.

It seems ungrateful to say it, but one feels the volume is worthy of a more distinguished format and illustrations. For readers from 6 to 60.

Louis Untermeyer

SOURCE: A review of *Tirra Lirra: Rhymes Old and New,* in *The Saturday Review of Literature,* Vol. IX, No. 15, October 29, 1932, p. 210.

Of course I had first learned my letters and wormed my way through Mother Goose conveniently hyphenated into single syllables, but literature began for me with *St. Nicholas* and music with "The *St. Nicholas* Song-Book." My first toy-theatre was used to present "Chris and the Wonderful Lamp" and I collected cigarette pictures to the tune of "Punkydoodle and Jollapin." Little did I care that the author of that insistent jingle was the daughter

of Julia Ward Howe—children think no more of the names of authors than does the average reader—I could not even tell you that the words of "Punkydoodle and Jollapin" and that unforgettable refrain beginning "And every little wave had its nightcap on" were written by Laura E. Richards. But I treasured the syllables to the last inflection until high school made me ashamed of them. Then the years blurred the outlines, the details were confused, and I forgot what happened to the frog who lived in a bog on the banks of Lake Okeefinokee; I could not recall anything about the sad little Cossack except that he lived by the river Don; I even ceased to remember the names, as well as the legend, of Mrs. Snipkin and Mrs. Wobblechin.

Now someone—evidently May Lamberton Becker, who furnishes this volume with a charming and intimate introduction—has urged Mrs. Richards to put into one volume the verses written more than forty years ago and several written the day before yesterday. Mrs. Richards, they tell me, is eighty-one years old. I do not believe it. Mrs. Richards is much older—as old, I would say, as Edward Lear—or much younger, younger even than Christopher Robin. One of her hands turns a moonstruck hurdy-gurdy; the other fingers the pipes of Peter Pan. This ought to be obvious to anyone who reads the timeless nonsense-verses I have already mentioned; or the more reasonable tale of Prince Tatters who, in rousing succession, lost his cap, coat, and ball; or that neatly disguised lesson in agronomy and domestic science, called **"Alice's Supper";** or that harrowing and magnificently condensed drama which I insist on quoting in full:

> As Jeremi' and Josephine
> Were walky-talking on the green,
> They met a man who bore a dish
> Of (anything you like to wish!)
>
> They stared to see the man so bold;
> They really thought he must be cold,
> For he was clad, though chill the day,
> In (anything you choose to say!)
>
> The man returned their stare again;
> But now the story gives me pain,
> For he remarked in scornful tone,
> (I'll let you manage this alone!)
>
> And there is even worse to come;
> The man (I've been informed by some)
> Inflicted on the blameless two
> (I leave the punishment to you!)
>
> This simple tale is thus, you see,
> Divided fair 'twixt you and me,
> And nothing more I've heard or seen
> Of Jeremi' or Josephine.

If there is anything to regret in this volume, it is an occasional omission. Such regret is sharpened because someone has advised the author to include **"From New York to Boston"** which, with its burden "Riding the resonant rail," is not only too sophisticated but too reminiscent of John Godfrey Saxe's famous "Riding on the rail." Yet, even as I write, I am conscious that this is carping. It is sufficient to say that *Tirra Lirra* contains all the old Laura Richards favorites and thirty new ones, that there are one hundred and ninety richly illustrated pages [by Marguerite Davis], more than one hundred lively verses about everything under the sun and several things that grow under an especially mad moon. Unhappy—and rare—is the child to whom the book will not be fernseed and open sesame.

Letha M. Davidson

SOURCE: A review of *Tirra Lirra: Rhymes Old and New,* in *Library Journal,* Vol. 57, No. 20, November 15, 1932, p. 971.

When really good nonsense rhymes that seem funny to children are as scarce as they are, a book like this is an event. It is a collection of the best of Mrs. Richards's contributions to *St. Nicholas* thirty years ago, together with some new ones whose inclusion May Lamberton Becker delightfully explains in her introduction. The pictures are full of humor, and fit the text perfectly. This book is scheduled for a long life, for it contains the essence of true fun.

David McCord

SOURCE: "A Second Look: 'Tirra Lirra'," in *The Horn Book Magazine,* Vol. LV, No. 6, December, 1979, pp. 690-94.

The classic children's story in book form, if absolutely genuine, keeps pace with age by doing one of five things. It persists, like *The Railway Children* and *The Wizard of Oz;* it gradually fades, like *Uncle Remus;* it continues to grow, like *Treasure Island, The Wind in the Willows,* and Edward Lear's *Book of Nonsense;* it gives early and substantial promise of growth, like *Charlotte's Web;* or—but here in splendid isolation—it simply dominates, like *Alice.* In all these examples, merit alone remains intrinsic as the algebraic constant in an equation where x equals time, and y equals public taste.

Not so at all with any classic anthology of verse—Palgrave's *Golden Treasury,* for example. For in this case x and y will reflect the changing values of time and taste, quite severely and separately, with respect to each and every poem included. And this holds true for all collections (self-made or not) of the work of an individual poet: collected poems, that is; or (to a somewhat lesser extent) selected poems. Now the book here under consideration is the quite famous *Tirra Lirra* by Laura E. Richards; many of the poems were first published in 1902 by Dana Estes and Company of Boston. This congenial ragbag of nonsense verse—*Rhymes Old and New*—stands poised at present in its seventeenth Little, Brown printing: still friendly, healthy, out of breath; full of

grace and gusto; but also full of too much careless and uncrafted writing and, of course, of melted sugar. This venerable edition (with the still charming illustrations by Marguerite Davis) is highly praised in an overly enthusiastic and insufficiently stern introduction by Laura Richards's friend, May Hill Arbuthnot. Another friend and admirer, May Lamberton Becker, introduced in a similar manner the original *Tirra Lirra* some forty-seven years ago.

Now, when one renovates a fine old New England house of say 1810, the owner's basic change is apt to be the addition of a wing or a breezeway and garage. But with a collection—a proven collection—of poems like these for the young, nothing can be altered, nothing can be replaced. One can only guess at where the roof leaks, so to speak, and at what items may be beneficially removed from the attic. In other words, I think even the veteran admirer of *Tirra Lirra* would agree that a smaller and carefully reselected volume might give the old lady new life. One of the strengths of Elizabeth Madox Roberts's *Under the Tree* is bare-bones brevity. Immortality will claim it because (beyond quality itself) it is spare and tidy and virtually flawless from beginning to end. *Tirra Lirra* will not prove an easy task if someone cares to try to cut it; but at least the obvious poems—those with poor rhyming, nonsense thrown for a loss, and those that "bubbled up within her" to boil over on the stove—could be quickly discarded.

To say so much is not to overlook the charm, the gusto, and the sheer ingenuity of the very best of *Tirra Lirra*'s treasures. Some of these poems first appeared in that dearly remembered *St. Nicholas* magazine of my youth, where brightness of perception in prose, verse, and illustration was what counted. And that, quite clearly, is what counted in the mind of Mrs. Richards, daughter of Julia Ward Howe. But Julia Ward Howe was the aphoristic craftsman: "grapes of wrath," "His terrible swift sword." She wrote her poetry within a shrine; her daughter wrote (symbolically) while on the run. Laura Richards obviously never sweated over the music that her hurdy-gurdy, as she called her Muse, delivered. And certainly unfortunate flaws enter into such poems as **"The Outlandishman," "The Strange Beast,"** and **"Dog-gerel"**—as unhappy as its appalling title and thick with the kind of baby talk which Morris Bishop could and did dismantle and destroy. Flaws enter into **"Some Families of My Acquaintance," "The Gargoyle and the Griffin," "Mrs. Snipkin and Mrs. Wobblechin."** And there is disenchantment, too, in **"An Indian Ballad"** in spite of the really good idea behind it and Mr. Longfellow obligingly in the background. The Wahwah-bocky, Peeksy Wiggin, Michiky Moo topteepee language is what puts this space-child down. Mind, I am not just poking fun: I am simply suggesting where and how the garden—to shift the metaphor—needs weeding.

It is certain that Laura Richards loved nonsense. She obviously loved the nonsense of Edward Lear, who died in 1888, when the author of *Tirra Lirra* was producing books for children as one might thread a string of beads.

Said the boy to the brook that was rippling away,
"Oh! little brook, pretty brook, will you not stay?
Oh stay with me! play with me! all the day long,
And sing in my ears your sweet murmuring song."
Said the brook to the boy as it hurried away,
"And is't for my music you ask me to stay?
I was silent until from the hillside I gushed.
Should I pause for an instant, my song would
                                    be hushed."

From Sketches and Scraps, *written by Laura E. Richards.*
Illustrated by Frank T. Merrill.

But Laura Richards treated nonsense as a commodity. It is not that easily come by. The masters of memorable nonsense in English and American literature are very few: among them, Swift, Lear, Lewis Carroll, Thackeray, W. S. Gilbert, L. Frank Baum, de la Mare, Joyce, Don Marquis, Thurber, and Bill Pratt, the sawbuck philosopher of Williamstown, Massachusetts. For immortal Bill Pratt, in his skilled ignorance, was one of the very best. Even Ogden Nash, a master of wit and the abstruse art of distorting and twisting common words, could not create *pure* nonsense words in the manner of Lear, Carroll, Joyce, and Thurber. Mrs. Richards often wavers on the edge of cuteness.

Let us look, then, at a few examples of pure nonsense words (original words, that is) of Edward Lear, L. Frank Baum, James Thurber, and Laura Richards. Here they are:

Lear: *pomsidilious, borascible, Quangle Wangle, Chankly Bore, Pobble, Gromboolian, Jumblies, Coast of Coromandel, sparry in the pilderpips, scroobious, Willaby-wat.*

Baum: *Scoodlers, Munchkins, Skeezers, Ozma, Quadlings, Inga, gump, Kalidahs, Zixie of Ix.*

Thurber: *Tocko, Thag, Hunder, Golux, Zorn, Todal, Mok-Mok, Xingu, St. Nillin's Day.*

Richards: *Tirra lirra, Ptoodlecumtumpsydyl, pugly wugly, Wah-wah-bocky, Viddipocks, foodle fish, Orung-outung-tung, Wiggledywasticus, Bobbily Boo, Poskos, Punkydoodle, Crumpet Cat, Phrisky Phrog.*

I have deliberately *not* chosen Mrs. Richards's poorest examples; but it should be clear that while she owes something to Lear, her nearest contemporary, she comes nowhere close to matching his slippery magic or even the magic of Baum and the more severe and staccato Thurber.

All these weaknesses I have pointed out solely because *Tirra Lirra* contains so many good and spontaneous things which would be better observed in a new curtailed collection to be called, perhaps, *The Best of Tirra Lirra.* Such a lovely poem as **"Song of the Mother Whose Children are Fond of Drawing"**—

Oh, make me a floppy
Great poppy to copy—

should never be lost. Nor that humble little gem of four-foot revelation, whose title is simply **"The Mouse."** Nor **"Phil's Secret"**; nor **"Drinking Vessels"**; nor one of the classic rhythm poems in all of children's literature, **"The Baby Goes to Boston."** If the very memory of the joy of riding in a train pulled by some great throbbing 4-6-2 (steam locomotive language) on a long straight stretch of track over beautiful ballast doesn't send the spiders up and down your spine, you were born too late to have lived. But here is Laura Richards with the sound of it; and just as truly and metrically stated as that other wondrous music in Stephen Spender's "The Express."

Ting! ting! the bells ring,
  Jiggle joggle, jiggle joggle!
Ting! ting! the bells ring,
  Jiggle joggle jee!
Ring for joy because we go
Riding with the locomo,
Loky moky poky stoky
  Smoky choky chee!

In conclusion, may I more than suggest that Laura Richards's verse has had some specific influence on two or three writers of our time? Indeed, on rereading *Tirra Lirra* I am haunted now and then by a vaguery of voices that were to follow her. Perhaps she did not give an actual name to that open-air intercom known as a walkie-talkie, but consider as out of a pretransistor past the couplet:

As Jeremi' and Josephine
Were walky-talking on the green.

And even a casual reader will sense the future echo of A. A. Milne's *When We Were Very Young* in such as

"Trifles are trifles!" says little Prince Tatters.

In simple truth, almost all of **"Prince Tatters"** antici-pates the voice of Christopher Robin. Furthermore, the very name of Robin brings me to Mrs. Richards's **"Robin a Bobbin"** written far in advance of a popular song of (at a guess) some fifty years ago:

> When the red red robin
> Comes bob bob bobbin' along.

And, so help me, here is some genuine James Thurber of *The 13 Clocks*—not just the words but the *accent:*

> The Wizard of Wogg
> Did various things
> With his Glimmering Glog.

It seems to me impossible that Thurber did not know *Tirra Lirra.* For Laura Richards is, among other things, the only poet I am aware of who can combine baby talk and violent deaths. You will remember that no blood is ever spilled throughout some blood-curdling adventures in Baum's Land of Oz. But in no fewer than twelve poems in *Tirra Lirra* does death overtake (and under-take) certain characters:

> And so they made corned beef of him
> And ate him then and there.

> But I'm happy to say
> He was drowned the next day.

> The monster struck her full on the head,
> And with pain and with terror she fell down dead.

As to Ogden Nash: As a boy he went to the famous Camp Merryweather—on Great Pond, largest of the Belgrade Lakes down in Maine—which was run by Mr. and Mrs. Richards. Mrs. Richards read aloud to the boys each day. I know for a fact that Ogden shone at word games while there; and surely the *Tirra Lirra* influence was early on him in that brief (and her most anthologized) poem called **"Eletelephony"**:

> Once there was an elephant,
> Who tried to use the telephant.

Or take **"The Mameluke and the Hospodar,"** which sounds as though Nash invented it:

> "If your name were Hosporus,
> *That* would rhyme with Bosporus."
> "Yes, but it is n't, and so it does n't.
> You make my brain reel, and you muzz n't."

Well, Laura Richards, for all her cheerful gusto and bravura doesn't make me laugh; Ogden Nash does. But then in that descending chain of Mark Twain to Stephen Leacock to Robert Benchley, all three make me laugh. Well, as a Greek Stephen-Leacock herald says some-where in a Leacock parody: "I have other avocations." So did one gracious and triumphant lady with her hurdy-gurdy.

HARRY IN ENGLAND, BEING THE PARTLY-TRUE ADVENTURES OF H. R. IN THE YEAR 1857 (1937)

Anne T. Eaton

SOURCE: A review of *Harry in England,* in *The New York Times Book Review,* May 2, 1937, p. 10.

In *Harry in England,* the "partly true adventures" of the author's husband when, as a little boy of 9, he went, in 1857, to visit his grandmother, Mrs. Richards has written a companion piece to her charming picture of mid-nineteenth century American childhood, *When I Was Your Age.* Both books are written with the same quiet humor and imaginative understanding of children. Though *Harry in England* is more definitely a story, what is done and said bears all the earmarks of truth. Harry himself, his pets, Henry the Hedgehog and Tom the Dormouse, Carter the gardener, Jim Marriott, Harry's cousin, whose liking for a fight promoted many a good-natured contest, Mr. Dakyn, the tutor, are all very much alive.

The beauty of the English country, long peaceful after-noons spent in fields and woods, visits to stately country houses of an older, quieter day, are all in the pages of Mrs. Richards's book, and Reginald Birch's attractive drawings reproduce the same atmosphere. Mrs. Rich-ards's style has the ease and pleasant simplicity of a tale told to a group of listeners. Harry's English adventures will have a real interest for boys and girls from 9 to 12, and the author has preserved for us a true and charming picture of child life eighty years ago.

New York Herald Tribune

SOURCE: A review of *Harry in England,* in *New York Herald Tribune,* Vol. 13, No. 36, May 9, 1937, p. 14.

It is hard for any one old enough to have been brought up on Laura E. Richards and Reginald Birch to approach their brand-new collaboration in anything like a reason-able spirit. You want to cheer, and having to stop to say why seems rather a loss of time. Here is a story precise-ly like those you loved when you were little by that very woman who writes now, believe it or not, just exactly as she did then, and here are the same sort of pictures that you loved, drawn by the same man today, in the same way exactly. It's uncanny. Even more uncanny is their effect on your grandchildren, supposing you have any; they will like them as well as you did.

The story is based on what Mrs. Richards has been told about her husband's visit to England alone as a little boy in the year 1857. Around these transferred memories her fancy freely plays. The grown-ups in the book come out of—or would be at home in—Cranford or the coun-try seat of the Fauntleroys, but its children, although true to the '50s, are also true to English child life in the privileged classes today. For parents in English society are still determined, even at some cost to themselves, to preserve for their children the more serene and less competitive surroundings of the childhood of an earlier day, and in this they are still to a certain degree successful. This doubles the book's attraction to children, who find themselves rather than the past in its pages.

The Horn Book Magazine

SOURCE: A review of *Harry in England,* in *The Horn Book Magazine,* Vol. XIII, No. 3, May-June, 1937, p. 152.

The story is based upon a real journey which Dr. Richards, the author's husband, took as a boy to visit his grandmother in England. It tells of his good time on the sailing ship and the special friend he made in Captain Barnaby Buncle; his friends, pets and good times at his grandmother's home, and the wonderful surprise she planned for him when he went away to school. Written with a mellow charm and simplicity by an able and experienced writer, this book is a gem.

Times Literary Supplement

SOURCE: A review of *Harry in England,* in *Times Literary Supplement,* No. 1847, June 26, 1937, p. 481.

This book carries one back in a delightful way to bygone days. The author is the daughter of Dr. Ward Howe, the American philanthropist who influenced Florence Nightingale in the days of her youth and of Julia Ward Howe, who wrote the "Battle Hymn of the Republic." The story is based on the adventures of the author's own husband, who really was a little boy in the year 1857. The illustrations are by Reginald Birch, whose pictures of long-haired, velvet-suited, early-to-die little Lord Fauntleroy delighted English children in the eighties and nineties of last century. Though not so long-haired, the Harry of the illustrations has a certain look of Lord Fauntleroy about him. But the quiet, serious child presented in the frontispiece, which is no doubt taken from a very old photograph or daguerreotype, belongs to an earlier period. And it is this Harry whom Mrs. Richards presents in her story. It is a pleasant, simple tale which takes things for granted in the Edgeworthian manner, and does not indulge in sentimentality, either over childish feelings or over the lordly homes of England. Modern children, who are on the whole not sentimental or snobbish, will probably like it.

I HAVE A SONG TO SING YOU: STILL MORE RHYMES (1938)

The Booklist

SOURCE: A review of *I Have A Song to Sing You: Still More Rhymes,* in *The Booklist,* Vol. 35, No. 3, October 1, 1938, p. 52.

A collection of over eighty poems, some of which have appeared in *Child Life, Saint Nicholas,* and *Story Parade,* and in other periodicals. This book is designed for the child fond of rollicking humor in poetry, and the black-and-white drawings suit the verses. A companion volume to *Tirra Lirra.*

Anne T. Eaton

SOURCE: A review of *I Have A Song to Sing You: Still More Rhymes,* in *The New York Times Book Review,* October 2, 1938, p. 12.

All young children respond, as all children should, to nonsense, and if boys and girls make the acquaintance of genuine nonsense early, they acquire a taste which they will keep all their lives to their infinite enjoyment.

Since Mrs. Richards published, in 1881, her **Sketches and Scraps** with delightful pictures in color by her husband, she has never stopped writing verses, and those which come from her pen today are as spontaneous, as deliciously absurd, as musical as those written many years ago. They have a story element which for little children ranges them with Mother Goose; what 5 or 6 year old for example will not thrill to Tom the Pigman who

> was so tall
> Folks used him for a ladder,
> Whenever they wanted to climb
> a wall,
> For Tom the Pigman they
> would call,
> And up and over him they
> would crawl,
> Which made him all the madder,

or the little old woman who wanted to go to the Barbary Main and so

> She bought her a washtub and
> set up a mast;
> Said she, "'Twill be safe,
> though it may not be fast."

There are many other absurd adventures, there are toads and kangaroos and gorillas, and here and there a little lyric describing the brown seaweed, or the birds in the garden. Mrs. Richards is past master at inventing new, delightful words, and concocting proper names, as in the case of the goblin with the squillywinks, and the rhyme of the Befum of Boggily.

It was a happy thought to combine with Mrs. Richards's verses the work of such an accomplished artist as Reginald Birch. His drawings will delight young and old with their combination of humor and charm, their spirit of fun and lively action.

Mary R. Lucas

SOURCE: A review of *I Have a Song to Sing You: Still More Rhymes,* in *The Library Journal,* Vol. 63, No. 19, November 1, 1938, p. 848.

Humorous and fanciful poems, both, long and short. This is a companion volume to **Tirra Lirra** and **Merry-Go-Round.** The subject range is wide and the nonsensical as well as the lyrical types are represented in good proportion. As is natural, Mrs. Richards's verse reminds us of our own early *St. Nicholas* experience and yet one would not call it old fashioned.

Additional coverage of Richards's life and career is contained in the following sources published by The Gale Group: *Contemporary Authors,* Vol. 137; *Dictionary of Literary Biography,* Vol. 42; *Major Authors and Illustrators for Children and Young Adults;* and *Yesterday's Authors of Books for Children,* Vol. 1.

Laurence Michael Yep
1948-

Chinese-American author of fiction, nonfiction, picture books, plays, and retellings; editor.

Major works include *Sweetwater* (1973), *Dragonwings* (1975), *Child of the Owl* (1977), *The Rainbow People* (adapted, 1989), *Dragon's Gate* (1993).

Major works about the author include *Presenting Laurence Yep* by Dianne Johnson-Feelings (1995).

For information on Yep's career prior to 1989, see *CLR*, Vols. 3, 17.

INTRODUCTION

Considered a distinguished contributor to both multicultural literature and literature for young people, Yep is credited with exposing his readers to a realistic, non-stereotypical view of Chinese and Chinese-American people and culture. Directing his works to primary graders, middle schoolers, and young adults, he creates books in a number of genres: fantasy, science fiction, historical fiction, realistic fiction, humorous fiction, mysteries, retellings, and picture books; in addition, he has written science fiction and plays for adults and has compiled and edited an anthology of short stories by Chinese-American writers. Yep is considered a prolific author of range and depth whose perceptive, moving accounts of people of Asian descent, both historical and contemporary, treat universal themes while drawing on native history, folklore, philosophy, and experience. His protagonists, Chinese or Chinese-American boys and girls who struggle to develop personal identities while honoring their heritage and traditions, learn to accept themselves and—in the cases of the immigrant and American-born characters—to survive in two cultures simultaneously.

Praised for his understanding of children and young adults, Yep is also acknowledged for creating solid characterizations of parents, grandparents, and other grown-ups. One of his most consistent themes is the establishment of close family relationships; his works often emphasize loyalty to both family and community. He also addresses larger issues such as racism, the battle between good and evil, and the interdependence and sacredness of life, as well as personal issues such as dealing with a changing body, establishing independence from parents, and celebrating the power of the imagination. As a literary stylist, Yep is often lauded for the beauty of his writing; his prose is commended for its smooth pace, figurative language, and expressive use of symbolism and metaphor. Although he is occasionally criticized for weakening his books with forced dialogue

and plots that lose momentum, Yep is generally regarded as a writer whose works have helped to broaden the scope of juvenile literature in a sensitive and thoughtful manner. Called a "literary bridge builder" by Karen Ferris Morgan in *Twentieth-Century Young Adult Writers,* Yep promises, in the words of Joe Stines in *Dictionary of Literary Biography,* "to be an important influence on the continued development of children's literature." In *Through the Eyes of a Child,* Donna E. Norton commented, "The widest range of Asian-American experience in children's literature is found in the works of Laurence Yep," while Dianne Johnson-Feelings, writing in *Presenting Laurence Yep,* concluded, "The garden of children's literature is richer and more inviting because of the mutations of the seeds planted and nurtured by Laurence Yep."

Biographical Information

Yep has noted that his writing is a vehicle for exploring his identity as a Chinese American. Drawing on his own search for cultural identification, he often takes the perspective of an outsider. Writing in *Literature for To-*

day's Young Adults, Yep commented, "Probably the reason that much of my writing has found its way to a teenage audience is that I'm always pursuing the theme of being an outsider—an alien—and many teenagers feel they're aliens." He added that writing about himself "requires me to take a razor blade and cut through my defenses. I'm bleeding when I finish. . . ." He told *Something about the Author,* "In a sense I have no one culture to call my own since I exist peripherally in several. However, in my writing I can create my own." Born in San Francisco, Yep is the son of a father who came to the United States from China at the age of eight, and a mother who was born in Ohio and raised in West Virginia before moving to California. Yep grew up in an African-American neighborhood, where, he wrote in *Literature for Today's Young Adults,* "I was the all-purpose Asian. When we played war, I was the Japanese who got killed; then, when the Korean War came along, I was a North Korean Communist. This sense of being the odd-one-out is probably what made me relate to the Narnia and the Oz books. They were about loneliness and kids in alien societies learning to adjust to foreign cultures." While attending a bilingual parochial grade school in San Francisco's Chinatown, Yep worked in the family grocery store, which, he wrote in his autobiography *The Lost Garden,* was "my version of one of Mark Twain's steamboats, giving me my first schooling as a writer." He also lived among an extended family who told him stories about China and helped him to understand his Chinese heritage. While still a boy, Yep began to keep a file of family stories, a resource that would later provide him with a wealth of material. In high school, a mostly white institution, Yep discovered science fiction; at this point, he wrote, "I really began to feel like an outsider. I lost my grammar school friends because they went into basketball while I went into science fiction." Yep began to write short stories in the genre and, while a freshman at Marquette University in Milwaukee, published his first tale in a magazine. He later transferred to the University of California at Santa Cruz, and completed his education at the State University of New York at Buffalo, where he earned a doctorate in English.

After completing his degree, Yep became a part-time English teacher at the university level while continuing to publish science fiction stories in such publications as *Galaxy* and *Worlds of If;* several of his stories have been anthologized. When a friend in publishing—later to become his wife—suggested that he write a science fiction novel for children, Yep wrote his first book, *Sweetwater.* Published in 1973, the novel is set in a half-submerged city on the planet Harmony and features both the Silkies, descendants of early colonists from Earth, and the native Argans, a spider-like people segregated in an old section of the city. After the book's publication, Yep realized that the experience of the Argans was similar to that of the Chinese in America. Out of *Sweetwater* grew *Drangonwings,* a historical novel about a Chinese-American aviator and his son. In a publicity release, Yep described *Dragonwings* as the work "in which I finally confronted my own Chinese-American

identity." His novels and stories began to reflect his heritage, his personal experience, and his family background. For example, Yep used his father's kite-flying in *Dragonwings;* his maternal grandmother as the inspiration for a character in *Child of the Owl* and its sequel *Thief of Hearts* (1995); his own experiences and those of his father and uncles in *Sea Glass* (1979); and his mother's early life in *The Star Fisher* (1991). He also has extensively researched Chinese history and folktales and has published a number of retellings both in collections and as individual volumes. Yep continues to teach while pursuing his literary career and has been a professor of literature and creative writing at several California universities, including the University of California at Berkeley, where he has also been a visiting lecturer in Asian-American studies and a writer-in-residence. Having come to terms with himself as an American of Chinese descent, Yep recalled in *The Lost Garden,* "[W]hen I was a child, I didn't want to be Chinese. It took me years to realize that I was Chinese whether I wanted to be or not." Now, he concluded, being Chinese "is something that is a part of me from the deepest levels of my soul to my most everyday actions."

Major Works

In *Sweetwater,* Yep describes how thirteen-year-old Tyree, a musically talented Silkie, goes against his father's wishes to establish a musical bond with old Amadeus, a respected Argan; this bond allows Tyree and his family to survive bloodthirsty attacks by a greedy Argan and a huge sea dragon. William H. Green of *Children's Literature* called *Sweetwater* "a rich piece of imagination and a well-constructed story," while Brian Stableford of *Vector 78* commented, "*Sweetwater* has one powerful thing going for it, and that is the fact that its writing is, in every sense of the word, beautiful. . . . [T]his is prose of a quality far too rarely seen in science fiction." Yep's first historical novel, *Dragonwings,* is often considered his best-known work. Written after six years of research, the novel tells the fictionalized story of Fung Joe Guey, an immigrant who flew a biplane of his own construction over Oakland, California, in 1909. Based in fact but fleshed out with Chinese folklore and the author's invention, *Dragonwings* describes how the pilot Windrider and his eight-year-old son Moon Shadow deal with prejudice and the vagaries of a new land as they work toward fulfilling Windrider's dream of flying. Aided by Windrider's Uncle Bright Star and two white women, Miss Whitelaw and her niece Robin, Windrider and Moon Shadow successfully launch their airplane, Dragonwings. Writing in *The New York Times Book Review,* Ruth H. Pelmas noted that "as an exquisitely written poem of praise to the courage and industry of the Chinese-American people, [*Dragonwings*] is a triumph," while Frank Chin of *Interracial Books for Children Bulletin* predicted, "Yep has written an Asian American myth that will someday be as deeply rooted in American folklore as Paul Bunyan and Johnny Appleseed." Yep's next book, *Child of the Owl,* is a novel set in San Francisco during the late 1960s. It is narrated by

Casey, a motherless twelve-year-old girl of Chinese-American descent who is sent to stay with her paternal grandmother Paw-Paw. Confused by her dual heritage, Casey gains strength and wisdom from her grandmother's stories and from life in Chinatown; in addition, she learns to place the dreams of her father, a compulsive gambler, in perspective. Writing in *Book World—The Washington Post,* Maxine Hong Kingston noted, "There are scenes in *Child of the Owl* . . . that will make every Chinese-American child gasp with recognition," while a critic in *Kirkus Reviews* called *Child of the Owl* a "beautifully transmuted Chinatown legend and an odds-on popular favorite as well." In *Thief of Hearts,* which is set thirty years after *Child of the Owl,* Yep introduces Casey's daughter Stacy, who is half Chinese and half Caucasian. Shocked when a schoolmate calls her "half-breed" for defending Hong Ch'un, a Chinese girl accused of theft at their school, Stacy accompanies her mother and great-grandmother to Chinatown to search for Hong Ch'un after she runs away. In the process, Stacy gains self-knowledge as she learns about her culture. Hazel Rochman wrote of *Thief of Hearts,* "Any kid caught between cultures will relate to Stacy's search for home," while Margaret A. Chang noted that the book's "warm depiction of a mixed-race child in a changing world, combined with a page-turning mystery, should guarantee a wide audience."

As a writer of historical fiction, Yep is acknowledged for the ambition of his "Serpent's Children" trilogy, works that encompass both Chinese and American history. These books—*The Serpent's Children* (1984), *Mountain Light* (1985), and *Dragon's Gate* (1993)—are set in nineteenth-century China during the Taiping Rebellion, when Chinese peasants aided the ruling Manchus in pushing the British out of the Middle Kingdom, and in California, where immigrant Chinese men toiled to build the transcontinental railroad. The third volume of the series, perhaps the most well-received, describes how young Otter travels to the "Golden Mountain" to be with his uncle, a worker on the railroad in the Sierra Nevada mountains. Otter struggles to survive prejudice, starvation, beatings, and disillusionment as he learns to find his place in this new land. Betsy Hearne noted that "the carefully researched details will move students to thought and discussion about a powerful piece of American history," while Margaret A. Chang wrote, "Yep convinces readers that the Chinese railroad workers were indeed men to match the towering mountains of the west." As a fantasist, Yep is well known for his "Dragon" quartet; the series, which includes *Dragon of the Lost Sea* (1982), *Dragon Steel* (1985), *Dragon Cauldron* (1991), and *Dragon War* (1992), features Shimmer, an exiled dragon princess with magical powers who tries to restore her lost homeland. Aided by the children Thorn and Indigo, the witch Civet, and the trickster-hero Monkey, Shimmer regains her rightful heritage through perilous battles, heroic sacrifices, and amazing escapes; in addition, Thorn, who is revealed to be the lost prince of the kingdom, is restored to his throne. The series, which blends fantasy and humor with Chinese folklore, is noted for being more substantial than usual quest fantasies of its type. In her review of the third volume, Margaret A. Chang commented, "Yep draws from Chinese folk tradition to paint landscapes and situations with an 'Arabian Nights' extravagance," while a critic in *Kirkus Reviews,* assessing the final volume, noted, "Yep's vivid—and occasionally bizarre—characters and images are powerfully imaginative, a welcome respite from sword-and-sorcery stereotypes."

As a reteller, Yep is perhaps best known for *The Rainbow People,* a collection of twenty Chinese folktales based on stories collected from Chinese immigrants in California for a World Protection Agency project in the 1930s. Including horror tales, moral tales, trickster tales, and love stories, the volume, according to Ethel R. Twichell, is "a valuable addition to any folk and fairy tale collection"; Ilene Cooper added that it is "a powerful compilation that will be read for its own magic." During the 1990s, Yep authored several volumes of retellings from China; in addition, he created an informational book and a novella on Hiroshima for young adults and wrote several volumes of middle grade fiction, including realistic and humorous stories as well as mysteries.

Awards

Dragonwings won the International Reading Association Children's Book Award, the Carter G. Woodson Book Award, and the American Library Association Children's Book Award in 1976; in the same year, it was named a Newbery Medal Honor Book, a *Boston Globe-Horn Book* Award Honor Book, and a Jane Addams Children's Book Award Honor Book. In 1979, *Dragonwings* won the Lewis Carroll Shelf Award and in 1984, the Friends of Children and Literature Award; in 1995, it also won the Children's Literature Association Phoenix Award for a book published twenty years previously with lasting value. *Child of the Owl* won the *Boston Globe-Horn Book* Award in 1977 and the Jane Addams Children's Book Award in 1978. In 1979, *Sea Glass* won a silver medal from the Commonwealth Club of California. *The Rainbow People* was named a *Boston Globe-Horn Book* Award Honor Book in 1989. In 1992, *The Star Fisher* won the Christopher Award. *Dragon's Gate* was named a Newbery Medal Honor Book in 1994.

AUTHOR'S COMMENTARY

Laurence Yep

SOURCE: "Green Cord," in *The Horn Book Magazine,* Vol. LXV, No. 3, May-June, 1989, pp. 318-22.

There are two sources of history for anyone who writes historical fiction for children. The first source is the adult version of history with facts and dates and statistics; the second source is a child's version of history.

Had I only read the first type, I probably would never have written *Dragonwings, Serpent's Children,* or *Mountain Light*. But I grew up with stories about China. However, it was not the China of the travelogues; it was not the China of vast, ancient monuments. It was the China my father knew before he came to America at the age of eight. So it was China as perceived by a child and colored by memory over the years.

My father has never seen the Great Wall or the Forbidden City. His China was small villages; each village had its own distinctive architecture, depending on which country its men had found employment in. After working in that country, the men would return to their villages in China, and there they would build a home that imitated the houses of the prosperous in the country they had left—though in some places, these transplanted houses might also have gun ports to defend against bandits.

But the difference between my father's China and the China of the travelogues is the difference between a child's version of history and an adult's. Adult history thunders on a grand scale like a movie in cinemascope; but for all of its size, it is still flat, and its actors are like ants except for a few close-ups of the stars. But a child's history is like a hologram that can be held in the palm, quiet and small but three-dimensional. It treats its subjects with an immediateness that makes them seem to live and breathe.

Adult history is full of dry discussions of abstractions, such as runaway inflation. But that was just a concept to me until I heard about how my paternal grandmother in China would have to pack a small suitcase full of paper currency just to buy a box of matches. When one hears such anecdotes, the theoretical becomes all too real.

The drawback in using a child's history is that it is based on a child's egocentric perceptions, which are limited by the very nature of the observer. However, what these perceptions may lose in scope, they gain in concreteness and intimacy with which other people can identify. If this is true of a child's history, it is even truer of historical fiction written for children. While the facts of adult history are necessary for background material, they have as much to do with the creation of a novel as a backdrop has to do with the creation of a play.

Dragonwings could not discuss the rise of the labor movement in California, but it could show a child's view when a group of angry white workers, who blamed the Chinese labor for their troubles, riot in Chinatown. Nor was there room to discuss psychological traits of the obsessive-compulsive; but I could write about a man intent upon building an airplane.

I first began thinking of the difference between a child's

version of history and an adult's when I finally made a pilgrimage to West Virginia.

In our family's own personal story West Virginia is as much a mythical homeland as China, for my mother was born in Ohio and then raised in West Virginia, where my paternal grandfather started a Chinese laundry in Clarksburg. Subsequently, my mother's family moved to the nearby town of Bridgeport, where they spent most of their childhood. Since my mother, my uncle, and my aunts had left West Virginia for California when they were all children, West Virginia, too, was a homeland constructed from children's histories.

West Virginia was always a semimythical place of green, wooded hills that rolled on endlessly. It was a place of four seasons—a strange thing for someone like myself, since my own homeland of San Francisco has only two seasons, wet and dry. Bridgeport was also a little town full of houses with big porches which were perfect for children to jump from—even if that was forbidden. In fact, a good deal of what my mother and my aunts and uncle did was forbidden to children. Their mischief was a year-round activity. Winter meant sneaking into the back hills where grownups could not observe my mother doing unladylike bellywhops on a sled. Spring was trying to avoid drinking those awful spring tonics. Summer was escaping the heat by wading in the "crick" in your underwear while you looked for arrowheads.

Though I haven't been to China yet, I did decide to go to the second of my mythical homelands, West Virginia. When I did my research for the trip, it was strange to go from a child's history in which everything is brighter, bigger, and lovelier to the history of adults. The houses, the "cricks," the cellars vanish. Instead, I found the bare facts buried in books like bones in the dirt: wedding licenses, birth certificates, and wills full of dates and lifeless statistics.

Above all, I was dealing with the process of acculturation—a topic in which the new wave of Asian immigrants have generated interest. So it is useful to see what happened some sixty years ago to other Asian children. But acculturation is yet another abstraction spawned by adult history; and as I found when I taught creative writing in the Asian American Studies program at Berkeley, abstractions are useful for theoretical discussions but not for writing stories that other people will want to read.

Both my parents faced problems of acculturation. But my father, who lived in a white neighborhood of San Francisco, was always within walking and—sometimes of necessity—running distance of Chinatown. However, my mother and her family were the only Chinese in the area until another Chinese laundry opened up in competition.

Of course, my mother's family would not have been the first group of immigrants to face the burden of having two cultures. But most would have solved the problem by clinging only to their old ways and language and pretending that they were on a little island that was supposed to be a part of China. Or, as so many other American families have done, they could have thrown off their ancestral heritage and severed their roots to the past—a simple enough thing for my mother and her brother and sisters since the white children of the town quickly came to accept the laundryman's children on an equal basis.

However, my mother's family solution was to juggle elements of both cultures. Though they stayed Chinese in some central core, they also developed a curiosity and open-mindedness about the larger white culture around them. My grandmother not only learned how to speak English but how to cook and bake American dishes. Though it may sound odd nowadays, back then my grandmother's specialty was apple pies. In fact, my grandmother once bragged to me that her pies always fetched the best price at church auctions—Methodist or Baptist. I think my grandmother's ecumenicism helped win acceptance in that small white community. Even in her later years, my grandmother displayed a remarkable adaptability. She listened equally to traditional Chinese music and to American rock-and-roll. In fact, she actually liked the Beatles before I did, and she once told me that the Everly Brothers' "Wake Up, Little Susie" was one of the funniest songs she had ever heard.

In general my mother's family carried out their various adventures and misadventures with a good will and a sense of humor—whether it was facing up to bullies in playgrounds or to real bulls in snowy pastures. Whenever I want to picture what it means for a "face to shine," I have only to remember my mother and my surviving aunt when they describe West Virginia.

More than ever, I think their solution is particularly germane to modern times. It isn't only immigrant children who must face the problem of adapting. With modern mobility, the flood of information through various media, and the rapid pace of change, we must all perform a similar balancing act each day.

So I find it useful to keep in mind a visit that my aunt made to West Virginia back in 1951. Neither she nor my mother—with their children's memories—could remember the address of their house in Bridgeport. Yet once there in the town, my aunt was able to trace her way back to the house. Unfortunately, she had not written down the address, nor was she able to give me directions on how to find it. To find the house, or the spot where it had been, she had to be there physically again. Since her visit, an interstate freeway had been built in the area so that new housing developments and shopping malls had sprung up where there had once been farms; and there was even an airport from which one could fly to New York.

Through the kindness of the historical society, I was able to find the laundry, which had been replaced by a bank. I seemed to have perplexed the congregation of the church across the street as I took photos of the parking lot. However, I was unable to find the house in Bridgeport, which was a disappointment because I had wanted to check on something. On my aunt's visit she had knocked at the door of their old house and introduced herself. The present occupants had then asked her about this tenacious weed that they could not get rid of. They had chopped it with hoes, dosed it with herbicide, and dug up its roots with spades. But the plant kept growing back as if it were determined to stay.

It turned out to be a Chinese vegetable that my grandparents had planted so long ago. It had transplanted well from China to America. One purpose of my trip to West Virginia was to see if our Chinese vegetable was still prospering—and perhaps exasperating a subsequent generation of American gardeners. Though I can't be sure, I like to think that it is.

It may be something as simple and yet as indestructible as a weed that links us to our past and binds us to our dreams. Seed, cast into strange soil, may thrive and grow—just like children and just like their history. In fact, a child's history is about growth itself, not only in terms of the body but also in terms of consciousness. Despite all of its limitations, a child's version of history is more useful for writing than adult history.

Far too often, adult history reads like an autopsy report. Writers spew out statistics like a coroner examining a corpse. Or they array the facts and dates like bones upon a table and consider their job done. But a person is not just a skeleton, and history is not just statistics. So writers of historical fiction must be like necromancers summoning up the spirits of the past. Their stories must be inspired in the original sense of the word, for these writers must breathe their own spirits into their tales before their books can come to life. For these acts of magic they have children's history.

A child's history, like magic, never quite goes away. It is there, only hidden, like the laughter of unseen children in a garden. Magic and children's history can be cemented over but never buried. Adults can put up steel and lay asphalt, but their buildings and streets can never outlast magic and memory. Memory pays no rent and is assessed no taxes, yet its value is infinite. It is like the sound of a "crick" heard on a dusty summer afternoon decades ago in West Virginia. It is all the sweeter for never being seen, only heard about.

Laurence Yep

SOURCE: "A Garden of Dragons," in *The ALAN Review,* Vol. 19, No. 3, Spring, 1992, pp. 7-8.

I once asked a friend how many hours of maintenance her English-style garden required. She simply laughed and said that I was no gardener if I had to ask that. I think, perhaps, that I understand now—except my garden has grown green-scaled dragons instead of greenpetalled snapdragons. For the last twelve years I have had those beasts romping not only in the garden of my imagination but wearing out a manual Hermes, an electric Olivetti, an Osborne computer and now a Macintosh.

When I sold my first science-fiction story at 18, I had always intended to use Chinese mythology in science-fiction as well as in fantasy. Almost five thousands years have created layer upon layer of myth and a history just as deep. I thought it would be easy to use what I wanted.

However, at the same time, I wanted to respect the culture that had produced that rich, mythical heritage. I didn't want to plunder odd bits willy-nilly the way less scrupulous writers had. For me, it was the difference between archaeology and grave-robbing.

To my surprise, I found it difficult to understand a set of myths where there was no ultimate evil. Instead, the creations of light balance the creations of darkness; and a legendary villain can wind up in Heaven as a bureaucrat.

More importantly, it was hard to reset my mental gyroscopes to enter that Chinese universe. In our western cosmos, the supernatural and the natural are opposing and even antagonistic forces. The fantastical is synonymous with illusion and has no existence in the real world.

However, in a Chinese universe, the supernatural and the natural are simply the different ends of the same spectrum. In fact, Chinese fantasy stories developed not from fiction but from early historical writing. In order to explain historical events, such as rebellions and changes in dynasties, writers recorded strange omens. At first, they were short, prose narratives—as bland as a police report. When it came time for later generations of writers to write down the strange occurrences of their time, they began to embellish their own accounts with imagery and dialogue. In subsequent centuries, writers began to make up stories that imitated the earlier factual narratives.

I enjoyed doing the research, delving as carefully as an archaeologist. By 1980, I had re-calibrated my intellectual instruments and was ready to make the leap. I thought the perfect vehicle was a folktale that I had found in which the Monkey King captures a river spirit who has flooded an entire city.

It seemed fairly straightforward, so I tried to put it down on paper as a picture book. However, I kept asking myself: who was this river spirit, whom I had renamed Civet, and why was she doing such terrible things? Trying to answer my question made the story swell from 8 pages into an outline for 800 pages. It became obvious to me that I would have to do it as a series beginning with a novel called The Green Darkness—which was the name of Civet's forest home.

The story became a conventional fantasy novel in which children from our world find themselves in an alternate world based on Chinese myth. The Monkey King pursues Civet to our reality and during the battle several normal children from our universe are drawn back to theirs. After a half-dozen drafts, I thought the story was almost ready to send in. However, towards the end of the novel, I introduced two new characters, a dragon and her pet boy. They were such lively characters that they stole whatever scene they were in; and I realized that I had to tear up almost everything and rebuild the story around that dragon called Shimmer and her pet boy.

In the process of rewriting the story, I asked myself what was the source of the water that Civet used to destroy the city, and the answer came to me easily. I had just finished reading Sir Aurel Stein's own account of a journey across a dazzling white, slaty desert that had been the former bed of a sea. During that trip, slabs of salt cut through men's boots and the ankles of the camels as they traveled among the ancient ruins—details that went into the novel. It seemed natural to have Civet steal a sea. Furthermore, there might be a clan of dragons living in that sea. With that as a starting premise, the story metamorphosed into *Dragon of the Lost Sea.* Once they were homeless, the clan would become refugees until one day one of them encounters Civet once again. In that manner, Shimmer the Dragon acquired not only the title of princess but a history as well.

There is a point in writing when I feel as if I have reached the crest of hill. The journey's end may still lie a long distance away, but it is now all downhill. As part of that momentum, it almost seems as if the characters have a life of their own and begin telling me what they would do. However, a creature with a pedigree as long as a royal dragon's thinks she knows her story better than the writer. I have never written about a character quite so independent, even demanding, as Shimmer. She was tired of always having the human view and insisted on having her turn—down to the tiny, puny snouts with which we humans are cursed.

By now, I had been rubbing shoulders with Shimmer for a while and had begun to sense her flaws as well as her comical quirks. When it came to write the sequel, *Dragon Steel,* I decided to expand on her dilemma. Though she was old by human years, she was relatively young as a dragon. Since Shimmer had been exiled at a relatively young age, she had only a rudimentary—and highly romanticized—knowledge of governing.

It not only fit what I knew of her character but let me root my fantasy firmly in history—for the best fantasy is nurtured by the past. After having read about the rulers of several continents, I realized that a title did not magically imbue a person with wisdom. Quite the opposite in fact. Some of the worst rulers had been no more experienced than Shimmer. However, the history provided examples of men and women who had risen to the expectations of their people, and how Shimmer meets her challenge is the heart of the novel.

Since I had tried to take an unconventional view of dragons, I also wanted to do the same with their homes under the sea. What could a dragon garden or palace look like? As an undergraduate at U.C. Santa Cruz, I had taken marine biology and oceanography courses and had been enchanted by the real undersea world. It would be difficult to come up with anything more grotesque than a hagfish or more charmingly comic than a sea hare. To make the undersea dragon kingdom seem strange and exotic to the reader, I only had to go as far as the real ocean.

By now I hope that I have shown that fantasy and reality are intertwined rather than forces antagonistic to one another. Just because fantasy places natural laws in abeyance, reason does not have to follow physics out the window.

Instead, the reverse is true. Obtaining a magical object should be as challenging to the mind as it is to the body. For instance, how would you protect a great treasure in a vault warded by magic as well as by armies? The answer lay in numbers: to multiply it many times over. That then raised the question of how to find that treasure in case of an emergency. To find the true treasure, one must use a solitary object that was so simple and ordinary-looking that a thief would overlook it. That puzzle became the climax of the second novel.

Up to this point, I had been writing the novels based upon an outline and a fairly elaborate chronology of events that I had written for myself while creating *Dragon of the Lost Sea.*

However, I knew that an outline was not the skeleton of a story. It was a scaffolding inside of which the true stories could be fashioned. Since events or characters had moved in a different direction from the outline, I would revise the outline instead of making them conform to the outline.

It became clear to me when I began the third novel of the series, *Dragon Cauldron,* that I would have to rewrite the outline because it was necessary to kill off at least one if not two of the main characters. If Shimmer and her friends keep escaping from trouble unscathed, there was no jeopardy. Without jeopardy, there would be no drama and little emotional truth.

By now I knew Shimmer and her friends were capable of great sacrifices, but I found it difficult to write about it—though I tried for six years. Nothing worked until I shifted voices, letting the Monkey King take over the narration. As an immortal, the Monkey King is naturally cheerful even in the most dire of situations. Tough and yet funny, his consciousness provided the right platform from which I could observe a world in crisis.

I also needed to change the outline because I wanted to incorporate some new Chinese folklore I had found. I have to confess that it took me three years to learn how to use the U.C. Berkeley library system, but when I did,

I found a treasure trove of Chinese folklore, including flying mountains that appeared when the sun rose at midnight and the unforgettable, creepy Boneless King, who was born from an egg dropped by a snow-white dog.

Finally, I thought I understood dragons better. In the first three books, I had tried to capture their quirkiness and strength, but I had not caught their beauty or their gallantry. It was something I had glimpsed the more I read about them in Chinese folklore; and it was something I tried especially to put into the final novel, *Dragon War,* in which Shimmer's wit as much as her courage brings victory to her and her clan.

After four books, I know that there is a certain point in creating a world where you stop being the owner and become an observer instead. It's rather like having the title deed to a garden. That scrap of paper is significant only to the lawyers; the garden's occupants, the flora and fauna, could not care less what I call myself; and I feel lucky when they show themselves to me. As Mr. Collins in Jane Austen's *Pride and Prejudice* would gush, "Such condescension!"

When they have deigned to appear, the dragons have taught me that there is more than one way to reach the truth and more than one way to portray it. There is more than one way to discover a heritage and more than one way to explore it. Fantasy may be the longer path, but its rewards are far more satisfying.

GENERAL COMMENTARY

Dianne Johnson-Feelings

SOURCE: In *Presenting Laurence Yep,* Twayne Publishers, 1995, 135 p.

The spirit of the Dragon series is Laurence Yep's spirit—the spirit of a man who is concerned about those of varying backgrounds finding a common ground, but who is concerned, too, with more individual issues such as personal identity and the meaning of home. San Francisco is Laurence Yep's home, by way of a somewhat circuitous family history. His father, Yep Gim Lew, was born in China and joined his own father, a railroad worker in the United States, at the age of ten. Yep's mother, Franche Yep, was born in Lima, Ohio, and reared in Clarksburg, West Virginia, before moving to California, where she met her future husband through their involvement in sports. Their first son is Spike, whose given name is Thomas. Laurence is their only other child.

It was Spike who gave Laurence his name, after "a saint he had been studying in school—a saint that had died a particularly gruesome death by being roasted on a grill like a leg of lamb." Perhaps this circumstance prefigures Yep's interest in adventure, conflict, and warfare of the sort that is so much a part of the Dragon series. When he and his father flew kites, for instance: "The sparrow kites interested me the most since they were used for duels." He talks about visiting San Francisco's De Young Museum, "which in those days had a marvelous collection of weapons, from small little tankettes . . . to strange spears with three twisting corkscrew-like blades." He talks, too, about his collection of toy soldiers: "In time, I went from individual battles to entire campaigns and even wars; and often the background became as important as the warfare." Very easily, the same statement can be applied to his writing. . . . Just as revealing is the context in which Yep places this discussion about war toys: He created these wars and worlds because, often, he had to rely on his own imagination for diversion and entertainment.

Even more than diversion and entertainment, however, Yep's imagination was a survival mechanism. One of the earliest points in the autobiography [*The Lost Garden*] where he mentions his imagination is when his neighborhood was going through changes with old residents and friends moving away and housing projects being built. He felt "isolated and alone" as he tried to make sense of the changes: "Had I done something wrong? Was this a punishment? I wound up falling back upon my own imagination, learning to value games that I could play by myself."

His games with his imagination have become, too, his livelihood. One of the most ironic anecdotes in the autobiography occurs during his college years at Marquette University in Milwaukee, Wisconsin. Majoring in journalism, he was told by one of his professors that he "had more of a talent for fiction than for fact." A bit disillusioned with his studies and feeling as though he were wasting his parents' modest resources by pursuing his education (though they were completely supportive): "I found myself turning inward. Stuck physically in Milwaukee, I could only go back to San Francisco in my imagination." It was at this point that he wrote his first science fiction story, **"The Selchey Kids,"** for which he was paid a penny a word, and which went on to be included in the *World's Best Science Fiction of 1969.* Yep had learned one of the major themes that he explores in *Dragon Steel:* "the mind can go any place it wants."

There are many facets of the mind of the man called Laurence Yep. Speaking about characterization and narrative voice, he explains how he "settles into" whatever character acts as a focus for a book's viewpoint. He goes on to mention the effect that this has on his personal life: "[My wife] particularly disliked it when I was writing about Shimmer the dragon because the 'dragon' in me would also come out."

In light of his science fiction and fantasy worlds, it comes as no surprise to Yep's fans that there is also a scientist in him; at one point, he was torn between majoring in chemistry and English in college. While contemplating this dilemma, he recalls: "I realized that I enjoyed making stories even more than making bombs. It was more of an impulse at that point in my life; but that is the way many self-truths reveal themselves—like a sprout germinating from a seed that has to work its way up through the dark soil and find a path that will lead it up from underneath a rock." Of course, he became a writer. And the garden imagery in this passage undergirds *The Lost Garden,* Yep's autobiography, which chronicles his development as both an individual and a writer.

The garden of the title refers specifically to his father's garden, and writing the autobiography served as a kind of therapy after his father's death. But other members of his extended family are important as well. When his imagination takes him home to San Francisco from Milwaukee, it is a home populated with his brother, mother, grandparents, nieces, aunts, uncles, and cousins. It is largely based on their stories and histories, in concert with his imagination and his own experience, that he nurtures his "garden of dragons" and his other books. His Dragon series is a major achievement, set as it is in magical worlds. But often, the site of Yep's garden is San Francisco, the place he will always call home: "I couldn't live anywhere else."

Laurence Yep experienced at least two different San Franciscos—inside and outside of Chinatown. He lived outside of Chinatown in an apartment above his parents' grocery store. The hard work and the daily routine of operating the store taught him many things: "[My chores] gave a rhythm to my day to which I became accustomed—a habit which still proves useful." One of the writers he discusses in the autobiography is Mark Twain, whose experiences inspired *The Tom Sawyer Fires* and *The Mark Twain Murders.* He notes in particular Twain's contention that "he learned everything he needed to know about human nature" aboard the boats he rode up and down the Mississippi River. And making an unexpected but appropriate connection, Yep sees the store as "my version of one of Mark Twain's steamboats, giving me my first schooling as a writer."

In his neighborhood were a few Chinese people (it was not until the relaxation of housing discrimination in the 1960s that Chinese began to move outside of Chinatown in large numbers), a large proportion of black people, some white people, and a few "beatnik filmmakers" (because rents were inexpensive). He attended St. Mary's Grammar School, near Chinatown, which had been a mission to convert Chinese Americans. The older members of his family were not Christians, and the only connection Laurence had with their traditional and sacred New Year celebration was the firecrackers that he was allowed to shoot off. His immediate family did not speak Chinese at home, and so when St. Mary's was transformed from a "regular" school into a Chinese school, Laurence "resented being put into the dummies' class and forced to learn a foreign language."

There are two especially revealing passages in Yep's autobiography. The first incident takes place as he stands on the sidewalk, overseeing groceries that must be taken into the store: "I remember a group of children who came down the block, both black and white. They were pretending they were soldiers in World War II. Suddenly they began making me a target, assuming that I was Japanese. Saul came along and chased them off; but I realized that I was the neighborhood's all-purpose Asian." The second takes place in his home while he watches a cartoon show in which the protagonist enters into a conflict with Chinese laundrymen. To Yep, these caricatured characters did not seem real, "and I remember putting my fingers up by the sides of my eyes to slant them like the characters in the cartoon and running around making high, sing-song noises. My horrified mother said to me, 'You're Chinese. Stop that.'" These passages are fascinating for several reasons. First, they demonstrate how complicated it is for people to work through the issue of ethnic and personal identity. On the one hand, the young Yep is ostracized because he is Asian, though, as in his language class anecdote, he thinks of that which is Chinese as foreign to some extent. Those who taunt him are not educated enough to know, or care, that there are various Asian cultures. On the other hand, he is so much a part of American mainstream culture that he does not readily recognize images, though distorted, of his own ethnic community.

These passages say just as much, however, about American society as they say about Laurence Yep. He recognizes this by putting his own feelings of not wanting to be Chinese into a larger context of the importance of conformity in America of the 1950s and earlier. For example, Harry Truman once wrote to his wife, "I think one man is just as good as another so long as he's honest and decent and not a nigger or a Chinaman." He continued, "[Uncle Will] does hate Chinese and Japs. So do I. It is race prejudice, I guess. But I am strongly of the opinion Negroes ought to be in Africa, yellow men in Asia and white men in Europe and America." Laurence Yep contrasts this kind of attitude to the present, "when so many children are now proud of their ethnic heritages." His literature, certainly, contributes to the current climate to which he alludes. To Laurence Yep, multiculturalism is an honorable concept—more than a fad, he says, and more like a tide. His willingness to confront what he calls his Chineseness, through his books, helps Chinese- and Asian-American young people confront this issue themselves. Author and critic Maxine Hong Kingston expresses her own enthusiasm about Yep's writing this way: "There are scenes in *Child of the Owl* . . . that will make every Chinese-American child gasp with recognition. 'Hey! That happened to me. I did that. I saw that,' the young reader will say, and be glad that a writer set it down, and feel comforted, less eccentric, less alone." At the same time, Yep's writing has the potential to help non-Asians to understand the issue vicariously. Depending on the specific cast of characters, the identification is direct.

The person who most helped Laurence Yep to confront his Chinese heritage was his maternal grandmother, Marie Lee. Because she did not speak English, they could not communicate verbally as much as they would have liked. "Instead, what I learned, I picked up in a subtle fashion, soaking up things like a sponge so that years later I was able to use it in a book." These things included ways of dressing, smells, tastes, and a feel for the "right" way to do things such as the preparation of rice, and most significant, a respect for history and experience. It was largely because of her influence that Yep began when he was still young to keep a file of family stories that he would use later in *Child of the Owl,* which is largely connected to his grandmother's experience; *Sea Glass,* which is his favorite because it is in many ways about his father and uncles; and *Dragonwings,* in which one of the main characters, Windrider, is inspired by the kite-flying of Yep's own father.

This concern is reflected even in his fantasy books. When Shimmer is reunited with a former teacher in *Dragon Steel,* she introduces herself this way: "A very stubborn young dragon once told you that she didn't want to learn history because it was boring. And you told her that history was like a great beast that one either learned how to ride or got trampled by." It is this same teacher, Lady Francolin, who, even in her old age, is trying to put together an oral history of her clan. Yep's work is a beautiful translation, blending, and transformation of the oral into the written. And just as Yep constructs family histories starting with the stories of individuals, he knows that even larger histories, those of countries and societies, are often best told through the stories of ordinary people.

Laurence Yep, the writer, is and has been always a reader himself. In particular, he enjoyed the fantasy books of Andre Norton, whose appeal for him was "the exotic worlds she created with their mysterious, half-ruined cities." But more revealing and significant is his response to L. Frank Baum's Oz series: "In the Oz books, you usually have some child taken out of his or her everyday world and taken to a new land where he or she must learn new customs and adjust to new people. There was no time for being stunned or for complaining. The children took in the situation and adapted. . . . The Oz books talked about survival. They dealt with the real mysteries of life—like finding yourself and your place in the world. And that was something I tried to do every day I got on and off the bus."

At this point in his life, Laurence Yep has gotten on and off the bus not only to go to school in Chinatown and then return home, but in many other places over several decades. After studying at Marquette University, he transferred to the University of California at Santa Cruz, where he completed his bachelor's degree in 1970. He earned a doctorate in English from the State University of New York at Buffalo in 1975, where he wrote his dissertation on Faulkner, another writer, as Yep notes, who could not escape his home. Since that time, Yep has been a professor of literature and of creative writing at various universities, including Foothill College in

Mountain View, California, San Jose City College in San Jose, California, and the University of California at Berkeley. . . .

[Charlotte] Zolotow, a well-respected children's book editor, was Laurence Yep's first editor at Harper and Row. Her assistant was Joanne Ryder, Yep's college friend who would become his wife. It was she who showed his work to Zolotow, and his career in the world of children's literature began with the publication of *Sweetwater* in 1973. Zolotow recognized Yep's gift for depicting interpersonal relationships and his sense of humor. Further, she contends that he is one of the most intellectual of American children's authors. She recalls that his manuscripts required little editing on her part or revision on his part; they were submitted in nearly perfect shape. Zolotow felt strongly that Yep would be good at writing realistic work, in addition to science fiction, and encouraged him to write *Dragonwings.* *Dragon's Gate* was begun during the same period, and the two books are linked with at least one common character and some of the same issues. Zolotow is touched that the book was dedicated to her but is not surprised that it is an award-winning story. The complete list of Yep's work is so extensive that it demands an entire appendix. Part of what is significant, in any case, is that Yep has won recognition and praise for books in several different genres: historical fiction, fantasy, contemporary realism, and folklore. One of his . . . books is *American Dragons: Twenty-Five Asian American Voices* [1993], of which he is the editor. Several reviewers were partially critical. Hazel Rochman, for example, notes that not all of the pieces are equally polished, an observation shared by others. But everyone would, I think, agree with Margaret A. Chang that "the collection is valuable for its new voices and for the old ones drawn from hard-to-find sources." She goes on to say that *American Dragons* is "a kaleidoscopic, occasionally brilliant, illumination of the Asian-American experience." This kind of praise attests to Yep's accomplishment as an editor/anthologist, yet another genre to add to his impressive, inclusive list.

Laurence Yep can be called an extraordinary, ordinary person, whose autobiography employs the metaphors of puzzles and gardens to make sense of the memories that are his life. Memories are, he says, "like apple trees" in that they do not always grow "true"; it is possible for one kind of seed to produce a different variety of apple. Yep makes sense of this in a writer's terms, contending that what might be negative for the planter can be positive for an author: "Memories fall like so many seeds into the imagination where they germinate in their own rhythm and timing; and it doesn't matter if they do not grow exactly as the original. In fact, if the harvest is to be special, it's sometimes better if they don't grow 'true.'" The garden of children's literature is richer and more inviting because of the mutations of the seeds planted and nurtured by Laurence Yep. His **"Garden of Dragons,"** along with his many other books, are just as tenacious as the tenacious Chinese vegetable garden still growing where it was planted by his grandparents in West Virginia. They are just as powerful as the memory of his father's garden, which really is not lost at all. . . .

[In 1993, Laurence Yep] released four picture books, enlarging his artistic range. For the creation of an illustrated picture book is, indeed, a different kind of project, in many respects, from the writing of a novel. Often, the pacing of an illustrated story is very quick; the characterizations are not always full but rely heavily on a specific trait; the author must take into consideration the interplay betweens words and images. Yep explains it this way: "You know, I had a hard time doing a picture book (be)cause I, I keep wanting to put in scenes and expand moments like I would in a novel, you know, but a picture book has to be stripped down." Further, as a writer of picture book texts, Yep has concerns about the illustrations that accompany his words. He points out to me the political maneuvering involved in finding the illustrators one might want because of the way that publishing house loyalties work. With some artists, even skilled ones, he sometimes worries that Chinese characters will be drawn with queues, which are stereotyped in his opinion, or with slanted eyes. But Yep is happy with the way that his publishers have approached the issue of illustration and how the art in the various books has come out. He has joined the ranks of picture book authors with mastery and grace.

Part of the gracefulness of Yep's craftsmanship stems from its roots in Chinese folklore, a major underpinning of all his work. In *The Shell Woman and the King,* for instance, he gives the reader some background information on the original tale that he is now retelling. His major point is that the kings in the era of the Southern Han were known for being extravagant and cruel. The king in Yep's story lives up to this image. Because he desires the Shell Woman for himself, he captures her husband, threatens to torture and kill him, and demands that the Shell Woman perform three wonders in order to save him. In the end, the Shell Woman prevails, and the king is destroyed, by the forceful use of her intelligence.

The Boy Who Swallowed Snakes, created by Yep as opposed to being based on a Chinese tale, is also about the triumph of those with good qualities over those with evil qualities. . . . [The story] deals with an aristocrat whose fate becomes intertwined with that of a young boy after the boy finds that which the man is trying to rid himself of—a snake that is capable of amassing wealth but that is also potentially evil. When the snake does not prove harmful for Little Chou, and in fact multiplies in number, the man thinks, "If one snake could make me wealthy, how much could ten thousand snakes steal?" The moral of the story revolves around the narrator's observation that "the rich man's heart was greedy where Little Chou's heart had been pure." The snake, like an idea or money or effort, can be used to good or evil purposes. It is always imperative to consider context.

A part of putting anything in context involves having information and perspective. *The Ghost Fox,* Yep's most recent chapter book (for intermediate readers), explores exactly that problem. While Little Lee's father is away on his travels as a merchant, a ghost fox inhabits and attempts to conquer the soul of Little Lee's mother. While the fox, in the body of the mother, exhibits evil behavior in Little Lee's presence, he does not do so before the eyes of the extended family and community. Not being open to the full story or to perspectives other than their own, they question Little Lee's actions and attitudes instead of trying to understand him or believe in him. Thus, "He knew that everything depended on him. Up until now, the grown-ups had only made mistakes."

Little Lee does find a way to rid his mother's body and soul of the Ghost Fox. And one of the neighbors who was most doubtful about him declares that she knew that he was a saint all along. But he pays no attention to her, focusing instead on what is important—enjoying a normal life again with his mother and his returning father. What Yep has focused on here, as in many of his books, is the capacity of young people to think, to feel, to solve problems, to create, and more. Just as the adults in *The Ghost Fox* fail to give Little Lee credit for his insight into and understanding of the events happening around them, such is often the case with writers of children's and young adult books and other real-life adults. Yep never makes that mistake. He believes in both the power of children's literature and the energy, potential, and intelligence of his readers.

Several of Yep's most recent books are picture books, too—*The Man Who Tricked a Ghost* (illustrated by Isadore Seltzer) and *The Butterfly Boy* (illustrated by Jeanne M. Lee). The former is a Chinese ghost story first recorded in the third century. The latter is based on the writings of Chuang Tzu, a fourth-century B.C. philosopher. It is this story that relates to the foregoing discussion. The butterfly boy, in essence, is not very different from the owl/woman or the star fisher; he is butterfly and boy, and both and neither: "There once was a boy who dreamed he was a butterfly, and, as a butterfly, he always dreamed he was a boy, and he was never sure which he liked better." More important, this butterfly/boy is a reader; he observes, reads all that surrounds him, all that makes up the natural world:

> The world was like a book to him,
> and the fields and hills,
> the rivers and lakes,
>   were like pages full of words
>   —words that he understood as a butterfly
>   but not as a boy.

Unlike the butterfly/boy, Yep's readers can understand the words as young men and women. Yep's stories will help his more mature, sophisticated readers as they begin, too, to read human interaction. The butterfly/boy is in some ways totally ignorant of the rules and mores of society, and he does not seem to care. That is one kind of freedom. But another kind of freedom is to know the place of tradition, respect that tradition, and yet find a

way to transform it and make it useful and meaningful in one's life. This is the accomplishment of so many of Laurence Yep's characters, across time and place. Finally, like the butterfly/boy, some of Yep's readers will read not just as people but as butterflies, reading and understanding from a place that is not tangible, that is spiritual yet real.

The Butterfly Boy serves as reminder that there is not always a clear or evident separation between children's or young adult literature and "adult" literature. *The Butterfly Boy* is in its own way as powerful and poetic as Yep's longer fiction. It is a gift to all readers and will, undoubtedly, cultivate an already established audience into a whole new audience for his writing: a young audience who will "graduate" to his earlier titles as they grow older.

This same universality is accomplished in his collections of Chinese folklore, whose audience cannot be defined by age. Neither is his audience defined by socioeconomic class. If anything, Yep writes about and for "common" people. . . .

The stories in *The Rainbow People* are retellings of tales collected by Jon Lee in Oakland, California's, Chinatown during the 1930s as part of a Works Progress Administration project. Yep retells Lee's collected tales also in *Tongues of Jade,* along with some gathered later in San Francisco's Chinatown by Wolfram Eberhard. Yep's introduction to each book and each unit is short but useful, compelling readers to think about questions that most of them have probably never considered, even in this age of multiculturalism. In the introduction to *The Rainbow People* he stresses the point that there are layers and more layers to any culture; that Chinese culture is not monolithic—some aspects of Chinese culture can be viewed in a generalized way, but others are specific to a certain region or subculture. He informs readers that most American collections of Chinese folktales are taken from many different regions and explains that "trying to understand Chinese-Americans from these tales is like trying to comprehend Mississippian ancestors by reading a collection of Vermont folktales."

What matters, though, is that the stories be told. This is the significance of the title of *Tongues of Jade.* It refers to the practice in ancient China of cutting pieces of jade—which was believed to have the ability to preserve the body—to fit parts of the bodies of the deceased. The tongue was one of the parts of the body that was sometimes covered in jade, "perhaps in the hope that [the deceased] would speak again." Yep thinks of the Chinese-American experience as "a poem whose rhymes are still unfinished," and that can be finished only by writers such as himself, who speak for those who no longer can. . . .

Moreover, he feels that it is imperative that not only the Chinese-American experience be recorded and told, but the larger Asian-American experience as well. Toward that end, one of his most recent efforts is *American*

Dragons: Twenty-Five Asian American Voices, a collection of short stories edited by Yep. The writers whose pieces he includes are Chinese, Japanese, Indian, Filipino, Korean, Tibetan, Cambodian, and Vietnamese. Some of the writers are former students of Yep's. His current editor, Antonia Markiet, who has worked with him in some capacity since 1973, cites this fact as just one example of his enormous generosity as a mentor. It is her observation that part of his strength as an editor is that he does not allow his voice to intrude upon the voices of the contributors to the anthology. He respects the feelings and the integrity of the writers. . . .

Their writings, regardless of the author's ethnicity, are arranged into groupings labeled Identity, In the Shadow of Giants, The Wise Child, World War Two, Love, and Guides. They address numerous topics that echo many of the concerns in Yep's own work. These include explorations of ideals of beauty, children serving as translators for their parents here in America, assimilation, historical information, the myth of the model minority, persecution in American society, interracial relationships, respect for elders and tradition, stereotyping, and being of mixed blood. All of the stories deal with Asian-American experiences from the perspective of young people.

Significantly, in the afterword to *American Dragons,* Yep speaks not just of Chinese-American literature for young people or Asian-American literature but of African-American, Latino-American, and Native-American literature—literature reflecting all people of color, and ultimately, "a common humanity" He sees writing in the same way as the characters in *Dragon War* view what is called the world mirror: "It reflects the many worlds of which ours is only one possibility." To Yep, literature is the world mirror through which all people, all writers can tell their stories and all readers can see theirs reflected; it is the mirror through which all readers have access to the realities, fantasies, and visions of others. It is entirely appropriate, then, that the Children's Literature Association recognized Yep's contribution to the field by awarding him the 1995 Phoenix Award for *Dragonwings.* The award is presented each year to an author for a title published 20 years earlier that has lasting value and resonance across time and across readerships. This is a description that applies to Yep's body of work as a whole.

TITLE COMMENTARY

📖 *THE RAINBOW PEOPLE* (adapted, 1989)

Illene Cooper

SOURCE: A review of *The Rainbow People,* in *Booklist,* Vol. 85, No. 15, April 1, 1989, pp. 1393-394.

In his introduction to this collection of 20 Chinese folktales, Yep tells readers how his father and the other fruit pickers in the orchards near Sacramento would gather after work to tell stories. But, Yep says, these tales served as more than entertainment; they were also "strategies for living," a necessity for immigrants far from home and family. Basing his book on stories collected for a 1940s WPA project, Yep provides tellings that are dynamic and involving. He starts with a horror tale that is sure to catch readers. **"Bedtime Snacks"** recounts how a timid boy named Shakey confronts his own worst fears when a horrible monster, Dagger Claws, devours his auntie and his brother and wants him for dessert. Yep provides introductions for each of the sections— "Tricksters," "Fools," "Virtue and Vices," "In Chinese America," and "Love"—and though thoughtful, they mean even more after the stories have been digested. While this will be useful as a curriculum supplement, the book needs no classroom link; it is a powerful compilation that will be read for its own magic.

Constance A. Mellon

SOURCE: A review of *The Rainbow People,* in *School Library Journal,* Vol. 35, No. 9, May, 1989, p. 123.

Twenty Chinese folktales, selected and retold by Yep from those collected in the 1930s in the Oakland Chinatown as part of a WPA project. His introduction helps children to see the Chinese workers, gathered in a shack after their day of "hot, grueling work," telling stories to pass the time before sleep comes. Each section is prefaced by a short explanation of how the tales might relate to the Chinese-American experience. Yep retells the stories simply and directly, attempting to use his own voice while preserving the "spirit and spare beauty" of the original tales. He does this by weaving bits of rich description into short, clear telling. The tales, while drawn from and depicting Chinese culture, present a variety of familiar motifs and types: wizards and saints, shape changing and magical objects, pourquoi tales and lessons. An "Afterword" provides suggestions for further reading on Chinese folktales. This is an excellent introduction to Chinese and Chinese-American folklore that reads aloud well, that will provide little-known tales for telling, and that is simple enough for older children to read by themselves.

Kirkus Reviews

SOURCE: A review of *The Rainbow People,* in *Kirkus Reviews,* Vol. LVII, No. 10, May 15, 1989, p. 774.

Here, the author of such sensitive depictions of the Chinese-American experience as *Dragonwings* anthologizes 20 folk tales told by Chinese immigrants in California.

Culled from 69 stories collected in a 30's WPA project, the tales are organized into sections with themes like

"Tricksters" or "Virtues and Vices," each with a thoughtful introduction placing the individual stories in the context of the feelings and background of the original tellers (most of them living in Oakland). Yep's telling is vigorous, often poetic, imbued with earthy humor and realism touched with fatalism. Most moving are a Rip Van Winkle-like tale of a man who gambles with the gods and comes home thousands of years later (**"Homecoming"**); and the title story, about a wanderer who sets the rainbow people free only to lose the one among them whom he's beginning to love.

In his introduction, Yep mentions Kenneth Burke's description of folk tales as "strategies for living," a theme he has integrated effectively here in this trenchant tribute to the resonance of storytelling in a particular culture—a richly entertaining collection for readers and storytellers. A handsomely designed collection—[illustrator David] Wiesner's understated b&w chapter openers are beautifully composed, counterpointing rather than competing with the stories.

Ethel R. Twichell

SOURCE: A review of *The Rainbow People,* in *The Horn Book Magazine,* Vol. LXV, No. 3, May-June, 1989, p. 382.

A selection of folk tales stems from the author's interest in stories told by workers during the time his father picked fruit in the Chinese orchards near Sacramento. Yep has chosen and rewritten stories from a collection gathered and translated by Jon Lee from people in Oakland's Chinatown in the 1930s. The tales often express the loneliness and isolation felt by the so-called old-timers—men living without wives and family in the land they called the Golden Mountain—and perhaps helped them preserve a sense of tradition in their harsh new surroundings. The stories are arranged by theme—tricksters, fools, virtues and vices, for example—and vary from the brutal tale **"Bedtime Snack,"** which recalls some of the grisly quality of the Grimms, to the story of a wayward woodcutter whose experience watching two chess players resembles that of Rip Van Winkle. Ghosts, spirits, and monsters abound. Old people are ignored or persecuted but get their revenge. Loyal young people perform great acts of bravery and sacrifice, often amid the jeers of siblings and neighbors. Retold in the author's own words, the stories maintain the flavor and pungency of their origins and provide a valuable addition to any folk and fairy tale collection.

DRAGON CAULDRON (1991)

Kirkus Reviews

SOURCE: A review of *Dragon Cauldron,* in *Kirkus Reviews,* Vol. LIX, No. 8, April 15, 1991, p. 541.

The further adventures of dragon Princess Shimmer

(*Dragon of the Lost Sea,* 1982; *Dragon Steel,* 1985), who is still attempting to restore her lost home.

Shimmer, the Monkey wizard, the witch Civet, and two human children (Thorn and Indigo) are all seeking the Smith and his wife Snail Woman in their fabulous flying mountain: only their old magic is strong enough to repair the fabulous Dragon Cauldron so that it can once again hold the sea and pour it back to form the dragons' home. They succeed, but only after loosing a terrible evil—the Nameless One, strongest of the wicked Kings from the past—and only after Thorn loses his human life and becomes bound in the Cauldron as its soul.

Writing and images here are powerful enough for this to stand on its own; Yep's strong, earthy characters are notable as individuals even when a reader coming into the middle of the sequence doesn't know their history. Meanwhile, characters from Chinese folklore—the Monkey trickster, the dragon—continue to give this ripsnorting fantasy a special flavor. More to come.

Margaret A. Chang

SOURCE: A review of *Dragon Cauldron,* in *School Library Journal,* Vol. 37, No. 6, June, 1991, pp. 113-14.

Shimmer, the dragon princess, pursues the quest she began in *Dragon of the Lost Sea* (1988) and continued in *Dragon Steel* (1985). Although she possesses the magic cauldron capable of reclaiming her clan's lost sea home, it is damaged. With her loyal companions, the children Thorn and Indigo; her former enemy Civet; and the trickster-hero Monkey, Shimmer now seeks the only being capable of repairing the cauldron. Monkey recounts their headlong flight from one adventure to another, with ever-higher stakes, until at last they inadvertently release the evil Nameless One, who threatens the entire world. Cementing their friendship with insulting wisecracks, heroic rescues, and enormous sacrifice, these companions clearly value group loyalty above personal honor. Yep draws from Chinese folk tradition to paint landscapes and situations with an "Arabian Nights" extravagance. The characters in this action-adventure are sketched in broad strokes, without the subtle shading found in his realistic stories, *Dragonwings* (1975) and *Child of the Owl* (1977). Readers with a taste for dragons will want to join Shimmer on her quest, which is far from complete.

THE STAR FISHER (1991)

Anne Lundin

SOURCE: A review of *The Star Fisher,* in *The Five Owls,* Vol. V, No. 5, May, 1991, pp. 100-01.

Is America more of a "melting pot" or a "tossed salad"? Does the immigrant to our shores mingle in the great national gumbo or divide in a common bowl of distinct textures and tastes?

Books about the immigrant experience in America often make us wonder about the experience of the outsider among us. *The Star Fisher* is the author's mythic experience of becoming American. Lawrence Yep, born and raised in San Francisco, grew up with stories about West Virginia, where his grandparents, mother, aunts, and uncle once settled, seeking a home away from the Chinatowns on the two coasts. With generations of storytelling, West Virginia becomes a towering family tree, worth climbing and re-creating as fiction.

Through the eyes of Joan Lee, the author's mother, Laurence Yep tells of his grandparents' laundry business in a converted school in Clarksburg, West Virginia. A Chinese family moving to the mountains is uncommon enough in the 1920s to stir passions within this small community. "Darn monkeys" are the first words of greeting, followed by other inhospitable words scrawled on fences. But there is also Miss Lucy, a retired schoolteacher, "a little bird of a woman" whose house smells like a museum, filled with her grandfather's stuffed animals and other inherited collections, whose own hobby is simply "people."

Her persistence with this hobby makes all the difference. Miss Lucy "follows her bliss," as Joseph Campbell would say, by the graceful arts of taking tea and making award-winning apple pies as well as the martial art of standing tall before bullies, once convinced that "This is not to be borne." While Miss Lucy is clearly a minor character, though based on a true person from the family legion of stories, she stands out as extraordinary, with all the ponderous heart of a Eudora Welty character, a generous storyteller and guardian angel.

Perhaps the author embroiders this character so fully because the ordeal of the family, his own flesh and blood, is freighted with feeling. The poignancy of family roots, their making and breaking, is suggested in an image introduced in the title and continued throughout the story: the star fisher. This mysterious name becomes clear in a bedtime story told by one sister to another, a familiar folktale about the capture and escape of a kingfisher bird, disguised as a beautiful woman, who belongs in the sky catching stars. She becomes a symbol of the dispossessed belonging, or not, to two worlds.

Mary M. Burns

SOURCE: A review of *The Star Fisher,* in *The Horn Book Magazine,* Vol. LXVII, No. 3, May, 1991, p. 334.

The lovely Chinese legend of the star fisher, similar in many ways to stories of the seal wife, serves as an analogy to the plight of the Lee family, who in 1927 move from Ohio to West Virginia in search of a better life. Like the central character of that legend, the nar-

rator, fifteen-year-old Joan, feels out of place—caught between the necessity of adapting to American ways and the traditions of her Chinese heritage as maintained by her parents. Although their new landlord, the iconoclastic Miss Lucy Bradshaw, extends a welcoming hand, the majority of the townspeople exhibit their prejudice in a variety of ways—from outright threats to calculated ostracism. Papa Lee, trained as a scholar in China, had hoped to found a substantial laundry business; stubborn Mama, unwilling to accept Miss Lucy's kindly proffered assistance in managing the household, ruins nearly every meal she prepares. Nothing seems to work. And, as her parents are not fluent in English, Joan becomes their liaison with the outside world and the supervisor of her siblings. Finally, at school, she meets an unusual girl who, like herself, is ignored by the other students. Through this friendship and the persistence of Miss Lucy, the Lee family's fortunes change, beginning with Mama's efforts to bake an edible apple pie—surely one of the most memorable sequences in recent fiction for children. Based on experiences from Laurence Yep's own family history, the story offers unique insight into the plight of ethnic minorities. It is disturbing but never depressing, poignant but not melancholy, for the principal characters—particularly Mama, who almost steals the show—are individuals with a strong sense of their own worth, facing difficulties with humor, determination, and pride. As in his earlier *Dragonwings*, the author uses italics when recording conversations in English, a device that distinguishes the differences in narrative tone without becoming intrusive. Indeed, nothing seems intrusive in this finely crafted novel: the message is a strong one but it is integrated into the development of plot and personalities. Thus, the book is a pleasure to read, entertaining its audience even as it educates their hearts.

Carla Kozak

SOURCE: A review of *The Star Fisher,* in *School Library Journal,* Vol. 37, No. 5, May, 1991, p. 113.

On the first night in their new home in a small West Virginia town, 15-year-old Joan Lee lulls her little sister to sleep with the story of a magical kingfisher who is held captive in human form by her mortal husband, but who is later helped by her daughter. She soon joins her mother in the stars, but is sometimes seen, comet-like, attempting to bridge heaven and Earth. Joan, the oldest daughter of the only Chinese family in 1927 Clarksburg, at first sees only herself in the story's symbols: caught between two worlds. As she braves the curiosity and prejudice of the townspeople, helps bridge a friendship between her mother and an elderly neighbor, and gets acquainted with an enigmatic classmate, she realizes that she is not the only one struggling to find a niche. Joan's story will appeal to any reader who has ever felt excluded, but she and her family seem to hold many more stories begging to be shared. Based on tales Yep gleaned from his mother and her family, whose resilience and humor shine through, *The Star Fisher* offers tantalizing glimpses of interesting characters, but abruptly shifts focus from a family story with the younger sister as a strong character to a relationship between mother and daughter. Basically, there is too much depth and complexity here to be confined to one book.

Kirkus Reviews

SOURCE: A review of *The Star Fisher,* in *Kirkus Reviews,* Vol. LIX, No. 10, May 15, 1991, p. 677.

The author of **Dragonwings** draws on his mother's childhood to depict a Chinese family's experiences when they arrive from Ohio to open a West Virginia laundry in 1927.

Eldest child Joan Lee is 15; unlike their parents, she and her siblings were born in the US and speak English. Their first two encounters set up the difficulties they will face and how they will be countered: when they step off the train in Clarksburg, ne'er-do-well bigots greet them with cruel taunts; but their landlady, a retired schoolmistress, warmly welcomes and befriends them. Still, "The Star Fisher," a Chinese folk tale Joan shares with her little sister, symbolizes Joan's position even after she gains acceptance: like the child of the selkie-like bird-wife in the story, she sees through two sets of eyes.

Yep has shaped his family's stories into a rather old-fashioned novel of small-town prejudice bowing to good will and some humorously applied ingenuity. Joan is provided with another spunky outcast as a friend; pungent family interaction and abundant period details help to complete a vivid picture. While learning to cook, Mrs. Lee bakes a series of inedible apple pies that strain credulity, but they do serve the plot well when she finally bakes a good one and makes a hit at a church social. A likable, thoughtful story about a young woman learning to value her own differences.

📖 THE LOST GARDEN (1991)

John Philbrook

SOURCE: A review of *The Lost Garden,* in *School Library Journal,* Vol. 37, No. 8, August, 1991, p. 208.

Although this memoir takes readers through Yep's college years, the focus is clearly on his childhood. Born and raised in San Francisco, he gives a vivid account of life in that city in the '50s and '60s and his own quest for personal identity. Raised largely in the mainstream culture, yet influenced also by his Chinese heritage, Yep's piecing together of his own puzzle provides fascinating insights into the whole American mosaic. Readers of his novels will be intrigued by references to their gestation and what people and episodes from life were transformed into now classic fiction. Whether musing on his inventive parents; growing up Asian in a black, Hispanic, and white neighborhood; or enduring the drudgery in the family store, Yep always offers something of value for readers to enjoy and mull over. Family photographs add to the immediacy and illustrate the text to a greater degree than in most biographies. The writing is warm, wry, and humorous—right to the dryly droll colophon. *The Lost Garden* will be welcomed as a literary autobiography for children and, more, a thoughtful probing into what it means to be an American.

Zena Sutherland

SOURCE: A review of *The Lost Garden,* in *Bulletin of the Center for Children's Books,* Vol. 45, No. 2, October, 1991, p. 52.

Whether his books are science fiction or realistic fiction, Laurence Yep writes with a sure sense of what to emphasize and what's tangential. To achieve the same kind of discernment in writing of his own life is even more impressive, for Yep's sense of story is such that he never dwells on what is personal-but-dull. A quiet humor pervades his writing, and some of the anecdotes of this life story are made memorable by that wry humor. The book is permeated with affection for members of Yep's family, but it is never cloying, and he writes with perceptive retrospection of the ambivalence of belonging to two cultures and with candor about the problems that entailed.

Hazel Rochman

SOURCE: A review of *The Lost Garden,* in *Booklist,* Vol. 88, No. 4, October 15, 1991, p. 427.

Yep's autobiography lacks the liveliness and grace of his best fiction. For the most part, Yep keeps the personal at a distance, the organization has little shape or focus, and the good stuff is nearly buried in nostalgic anecdotes about family, neighborhood, and school. However, there is inherent drama in the story of the ambivalent immigrant boy ("I was the Chinese American raised in a black neighborhood, a child who had been too American to fit into Chinatown and too Chinese to fit in elsewhere"), and readers will enjoy his account of how his memories of being an outsider are transformed into his stories. This is a natural choice for curriculum units on immigration and multiculturalism and as a lead-in to some of the outstanding adult writing on growing up Chinese American.

📖 TONGUES OF JADE (adapted, 1991)

Roger Sutton

SOURCE: A review of *Tongues of Jade,* in *Bulletin of the Center for Children's Books,* Vol. 45, No. 3, November, 1991, p. 80.

Like Yep's *The Rainbow People,* these Chinese-American folktales are vividly retold from a 1930s WPA collection and are introduced in sections that set the stories into cultural context. And, like its companion volume, this is full of electrifying demons and ghosts, as well as humans of memorable strength or frailty. Striking images—cats' eyes of yellow jade placed over the eyes of a corpse, for instance—enrich the crisp action. The tonal range is generous: from scary to humorous (or both, as when a scholar's ghost returns for the ending of a rhyme he can't remember); from explanatory (**"The Tiger Cat"** is a pourquoi tale) to moral (justice is served in spades to the greedy rich). These will not only enliven a study of immigrant history or ethnic minorities in the U.S., but will also serve as a dynamic source for storytellers seeking material for older elementary, junior high, and high school audiences.

John Philbrook

SOURCE: A review of *Tongues of Jade,* in *School Library Journal,* Vol. 37, No. 12, December, 1991, p. 132.

Drawing on the same WPA project that provided the bare bones for his *Rainbow People* (1989), Yep has crafted a fine collection of short stories based in the oral Chinese-American tradition. *Tongues of Jade* has a distinctly more Chinese feeling than the previous title, and supernatural tales predominate. Organized under headings like "Roots," "Family Ties," etc., the stories are sometimes thoughtful, always effective, and usually point to some moral. The writing is replete with lush descriptions, witty asides, and crackling dialogue. Each story is a world of its own; each is successful and satisfying. All open with an attractive ink-and-wash illustration. The selections range from tragic to touching to richly humorous. The only peculiarities are the mini-essays that introduce the sections. While earnest in intent, they are not substantial enough to supply meaningful context and tie the pieces together by the slenderest of threads. This aside, Yep has gathered an excellent compilation of folktales that will be enjoyed by a wide audience of readers—and listeners.

Illene Cooper

SOURCE: A review of *Tongues of Jade,* in *Booklist,* Vol. 88, No. 8, December 15, 1991, pp. 757-58.

Retold by Yep, here are 17 stories that come from a variety of Chinese-American communities. Filled with wonder and magic, the tales present, among others, talking animals, helpful spirits who live in a melon, and a fisherman who dispenses advice as well as wizardry. This is a companion volume to *The Rainbow People,* which contains stories that Yep found in WPA collections. Though not quite as captivating as the stories in the previous book, this assortment displays the same kind of earthy charm, and Yep's appealing retellings add verve to the more enigmatic tales.

DRAGON WAR (1992)

Publishers Weekly

SOURCE: A review of *Dragon War,* in *Publishers Weekly,* Vol. 239, No. 23, May 18, 1992, p. 71.

Monkey opens this narration—part of the saga of the dragons' efforts to reclaim their home—where the events of *Dragon Cauldron* left off: he and his companions are captives of the Boneless King and the traitorous dragon Pomfret. After several escapes and skirmishes, they gather an army of dragons, defeat the King and reclaim the lost prince, their friend Thorn. Like its predecessors, this fantasy contains numerous inventive touches: the protagonists' changes of form—into horses and even fleas—enable them to elude the evil King; creatures such as the King's animate stone statues, and the fire-rats that scamper among them and heat the stone to breaking-point. The final battle, once joined, combines heart-stopping valor and fiendishly clever contests of wit. But the action to that point is overly drawn out, with a surfeit of near-climactic encounters and a few too many reversals of fortune. Further, readers new to the series may be confused by the characters' sketchy introductions and the complexity of past events alluded to but never clarified.

Margaret A. Chang

SOURCE: A review of *Dragon War,* in *School Library Journal,* Vol. 38, No. 6, June, 1992, p. 144.

The evil, immortal, Boneless King, inhabiting the body of the human tyrant, Butcher, has declared all-out war on dragonkind. In this concluding volume in the series, Shimmer, the dragon princess, and her friends join her beleaguered kin as they fight for their lives. Monkey, an ebullient trickster-hero from Chinese folklore, recounts harrowing captures; hairsbreadth escapes; clever ruses; vast battles on air, land, and sea; heroic sacrifices; and dizzying, sometimes confusing, shape changes. Thorn, the human boy who has been Shimmer's companion since *Dragon of the Lost Sea* (1982), who helped her regain the magic cauldron in *Dragon Steel* (1985), and who sacrificed his body to reforge the cauldron in *Dragon Cauldron* (1991), spends most of this book as the soul of the cauldron, an object of enormous power. With the help of some potent immortals, both Thorn and Shimmer regain their rightful heritage. While the swirl of inventive details may obscure the emotional trajectory, the story provides a rare glimpse of Chinese mythic patterns. Shimmer's adventures continue to emphasize group loyalty over personal honor, and conclude with an audacious scene portraying the "many worlds of which ours is only one possibility," a concept rooted in Taoist and Buddhist thought. Because it would be hard to follow events and character changes without reading the earlier books, this one is recommended where the others have been enjoyed.

Kirkus Reviews

SOURCE: A review of *Dragon War,* in *Kirkus Reviews,* Vol. LX, No. 11, June 1, 1992, p. 725.

Fourth (and last?) in the saga of dragon princess Shimmer's struggle to restore her lost home: At the end of **Dragon Cauldron** (1991), Shimmer, the Monkey wizard, and human child Indigo were captured by the evil Boneless King, while selfless human Thorn became part of the Cauldron so that it could restore Shimmer's Inland Sea. Now they escape to help the dragons overcome the Boneless King, who's borne to the beginning of time by Shimmer's suddenly repentant renegade brother. Thorn, restored, is revealed as the throne's lost heir; Indigo becomes a dragon; and the Monkey cartwheels away on new mischief.

Yep's vivid—and occasionally bizarre—characters and images are powerfully imaginative, a welcome respite from sword-and-sorcery stereotypes. Watching them bicker while snatching defeat from the jaws of victory is entertaining, while the breakneck pacing never lags. Not for every reader, but destined to be a special favorite for a few.

AMERICAN DRAGONS: TWENTY-FIVE ASIAN AMERICAN VOICES (edited by Yep 1993)

Hazel Rochman

SOURCE: A review of *American Dragons: Twenty-Five Asian American Voices,* in *Booklist,* Vol. 89, No. 18, May 15, 1993, p. 1684.

The universal search for a way home underlies these strongly autobiographical stories, poems, and essays about kids whose parents come from a wide diversity of places and cultures, including China, Japan, Korea, and Tibet. The pieces are loosely organized by theme ("The Wise Child," "Guides," etc.), and Yep's unpretentious brief introductions to each section and each writer focus on issues of identity, on what he calls the "war zone" in school and neighborhood and also at the dinner table. In Wakako Yamauchi's exquisite story. "And the Soul Shall Dance," a woman remembers her Japanese American childhood in the California desert and the neighbor Mrs. Oka, whom everyone labeled "strange": only now does the narrator realize Mrs. Oka's suffering, an immigrant trapped in a loveless marriage far from home. Some of the best pieces are about kids across generations: the teenager who bonds with her tyrannical grandmother; the gifted student who gives up the boy she loves because of her parents' expectations ("His brown was different from mine. . . . Those pigments keep us apart"). Not all the pieces are as polished: several writers overdramatize the conflict and repeat their message many times. But that message is ambiguous, and the characters aren't sentimentalized or stereotyped. These writers are frank about self-hatred and family pressure, about the confines of tradition—in all its rich variety—

and the lure of the mainstream. Of course, Asian Americans will recognize themselves in many of these pieces; so will immigrants everywhere. In fact, all teens will see something of themselves in the struggle to find "an identity that isn't generic."

Deborah Stevenson

SOURCE: A review of *American Dragons: Twenty-Five Asian American Voices,* in *Bulletin of the Center for Children's Books,* Vol. 46, No. 11, July-August, 1993, p. 362.

Yep breaks this collection of poems, stories, and one short play into thematic sections—Identity, World War II, In the Shadow of Giants, The Wise Child, Love, and Guides—which helps to focus the varied voices contained here. He includes work from the old and the young, the known (Maxine Hong Kingston and Jeanne Wakatsuki Houston) and the unknown (ten of these stories, according to the copyright page, are making their first appearance). Viewpoints represented are those of Asian Americans with differing ethnic origins: Tibetan Americans, Vietnamese Americans, Chinese Americans, Korean Americans, Japanese Americans, Thai Americans all speak about fitting in, growing up, and relating to previous generations. Young readers probably won't mind the tendency of some stories to be overexplanatory and a little amateurish, since the thematic focus and sincerity of emotion keeps the book together, providing a look across worlds and generations through stories and poems such as Longhang Nguyen's "Rain Music," Lensey Namioka's "Who's Hu," and Janice Mirikitani's "For My Father." Yep also includes a futuristic sci-fi story, William F. Wu's "Black Powder," which suggests that our relationship to our origins and ancestors will remain even when we live in space. Varied yet controlled, this is an East-meets-West collection that kids will enjoy.

THE SHELL WOMAN AND THE KING: A CHINESE FOLKTALE (1993)

Hazel Rochman

SOURCE: A review of *The Shell Woman and the King: A Chinese Folktale,* in *Booklist,* Vol. 89, No. 21, July, 1993, p. 1973.

A woman as strong as she is beautiful is the hero of this Chinese folktale of transformation. Uncle Wu marries Shell, a magical woman with the power to change herself into a seashell. But the greedy ruler of the kingdom wants her, so he sets her three increasingly difficult tasks to make her submit to his will. Like scenes under water or in the moonlit sky, [Yang Ming-Yi's] framed ink-and-watercolor paintings contrast Shell's delicacy and shifting, dancing movement with the stiff, flamboyant palace of the greedy king. Yep has adapted the story from an eighteenth-century collection of Chinese folktales, and he retells it in a direct, contemporary style in which people "visit" and "chat" and feel "terribly embarrassed." In the end, Shell defeats the king by transforming his wish into a curse that burns up his palace with flames like birds and flowers, and she and Uncle Wu race home together. The pictures express the shape changing that is the very heart of the story.

Kirkus Reviews

SOURCE: A review of *The Shell Woman and the King: A Chinese Folktale,* in *Kirkus Reviews,* Vol. LXI, No. 16, August 15, 1993, p. 1082.

A beautiful woman with the power to transform herself into a seashell outwits the evil king who commands her to abandon her husband and marry him instead. When Shell refuses, the king imprisons her husband and demands that Shell obtain for him three wonders as ransom, including luck by the bushel. Fortunately, he neglects to specify what sort of luck; and when Shell brings him a large, fire-eating dog, the king and his magnificent palace are destroyed. Thus evil is unequivocally punished, but—in contrast to most Western fairy tales—the heroine reaps no extraordinary reward for her courage and conjugal loyalty; presumably, defying a rapacious monarch and surviving are enough. Yang's watercolor-and-ink paintings capture the tale's beauty and violence in tones ranging from misty gray-blue and shell pink to fiery coral, crimson, and jade. An unusual touch is the subtle, gray damask patterning providing a textured background for the type.

Betsy Hearne

SOURCE: A review of *The Shell Woman and the King: A Chinese Folktale,* in *Bulletin of the Center for Children's Books,* Vol. 47, No. 2, October, 1993, p. 63.

When likable Uncle Wu marries a magical woman from the sea, he's proud enough to boast of her accomplishments, which quickly reach the ears of a greedy king. Shell must then fulfill three seemingly impossible requests or lose her beloved Wu and become the king's wife: first, she must provide the hair of a toad; second, the arm of a ghost; and third, a bushel of luck. Each of these Shell accomplishes, but the king has not stipulated what kind of luck she must provide. Needless to say, what he gets is not what he wanted. With the practiced confidence that made *The Rainbow People* such a successful collection, Yep narrates this eighteenth-century tale without diluting its life-and-death elements or intruding on its inherently strong form. Yang Ming-Yi's illustrations move gracefully from a shell-pink motif to a fiery red that finally consumes the villain; similarly, his compositions include both serene seascapes and the amputation of a clawed arm. It's a mark of respect for folklore when re-creators encompass both its beauty and

its terror, something this author-artist team has accomplished with finesse.

📖 *THE MAN WHO TRICKED A GHOST* (1993)

Kirkus Reviews

SOURCE: A review of *The Man Who Tricked a Ghost,* in *Kirkus Reviews,* Vol. LXI, No. 15, August 1, 1993, p. 1010.

Sung is a man so brave that he thinks nothing of walking home at night, despite his friend's warning. Accosted by a ghost (none of your flimsy European wraiths—this huge, solid-looking warrior has a fiercely craggy visage and "antique armor made of rhinoceros hide with metal scales"), Sung boldly claims to be a ghost, too. Undaunted by the ghost's mission—to scare or kill the overcourageous Sung, whom he doesn't recognize—Sung tricks him at every turn, even getting the ghost to confide that "once we are spat upon we cannot change our shape"—a useful bit of information that in the end not only saves Sung but enriches him. Yep's simple, lively narrative perfectly suits an entertaining trickster tale that, he notes, dates in written form to the third century; [Isadore] Seltzer matches its energy and humor in vibrant, freely rendered paintings that will enthrall listeners as much as the spooky, funny story. A winner.

Linda Boyles

SOURCE: A review of *The Man Who Tricked a Ghost,* in *School Library Journal,* Vol. 39, No. 9, September, 1993, p. 227.

Sung is an unusually brave man. So when a friend warns him not to travel a dark and dangerous road home, he sets out happily. On his way he meets a ghost—a fierce warrior dressed in antique armor who, it turns out, has been looking for him, determined to either teach him a lesson in fear, or kill him. Concealing his true identity, quick-witted Sung says that he too is a ghost, a novice. They travel along companionably, the true ghost giving him "tips about ghosting" and transforming himself into numerous hideous shapes, trying for the one that will scare a fearless human. In the process, Sung learns the apparition's deepest secret, which he uses to defeat him and to make himself rich. Yep's retelling of this ancient Chinese tale is zesty and exuberant, matching his hero's clever, cocky style. The story moves along at a good clip, fleshing out the characters and building anticipation of the trick at the end. The language is relaxed, with a conversational flow that reads aloud well. Seltzer's illustrations are as robust as the telling, offering a dramatic visual interpretation of the text that further enhances the book's suitability for group sharing. His strong compositions and rich, vibrant palette command the eye and create a sense of drama and dimension. A stunning addition to any collection.

THE BUTTERFLY BOY (adapted from the writings of Chuang Tzu, 1993)

Publishers Weekly

SOURCE: A review of *The Butterfly Boy,* in *Publishers Weekly,* Vol. 240, No. 35, August 30, 1993, p. 96.

Drawn from the writings of Chuang Tzu, the fourth-century B.C. thinker sometimes called the Butterfly Philosopher, this delicate prose poem tells of "a boy who dreamed he was a butterfly and, as a butterfly, he always dreamed he was a boy." Though the boy endures the laughter of others as he tries to suck nectar from flowers and finds beauty in stagnant water, he is heaped with praise after he fails to bow before a marauding warlord (who reminds the boy of a beetle on its back). Yet the dreamy boy cares little for the world's opinion, for he is happy as he is. Yep's simple language is exquisite in its clarity and, like a pebble thrown into water, creates ripples of meaning. A similar ethereal sensibility graces [Jeanne M.] Lee's paintings. Mottled backgrounds capture the story's ephemeral essence while the somewhat stylized figures are drawn with the care of a calligrapher. Details of the boy's butterfly visions are highlighted in sumptuously colored boxes superimposed, cartouche-like, upon the page, like patterns on a kimono. Quiet strength and inner serenity pervade this masterly combination of text, artwork and design.

Kirkus Reviews

SOURCE: A review of *The Butterfly Boy,* in *Kirkus Reviews,* Vol. LXI, No. 17, September 1, 1993, p. 1154.

"Drawn from the writings of Chuang Tzu [fourth century B.C.], . . . the Butterfly Philosopher," a tale that explicates the idea that wisdom may lie in an altogether fresh point of view. The first part of the story is somewhat confusing: "a boy . . . dreamed he was a butterfly, and, as a butterfly, he always dreamed he was a boy." His literally acting like a butterfly causes "trouble"—when he tries to fly above a buffalo, he lands on its back and is carried off; when he's hungry, he astonishes bystanders by sucking a flower's nectar. However, like a butterfly, he doesn't mind derisive laughter, and he has a special understanding of natural beauty—and also of an invading army (he imagines it to be a centipede) and its warlord, whom he sees as a beetle on its back (the insulted lord lets him go as "either madman or a prophet"). When lord and army perish, the Butterfly Boy is suddenly revered, "but praise meant no more to him than insults." In Lee's spare, carefully constructed paintings, figures are stylized and the butterfly's alternate visions appear in insets. Not easy or entirely successful but, still, a philosophic tale with worthy and venerable roots, certainly worthy of discussion.

Lauralyn Persson

SOURCE: A review of *The Butterfly Boy,* in *School Library Journal,* Vol. 40, No. 2, February, 1994, p. 99.

The Butterfly Boy " . . . dreamed he was a butterfly, and, as a butterfly, he always dreamed he was a boy." He often acts like one, dancing on the flowers on a lady's robe and riding on a buffalo's back. He is unconcerned with the opinions of those who laugh at him, even when he mocks an invading army and is brought before the commander (a scene that briefly provides some dramatic action). Yep's skill as a writer shows in his elegant language and his ability to express ideas gracefully and specifically that might otherwise be vague. One of the themes of this story (which is based on writings of an ancient Chinese philosopher) is reverence for nature and joy in its cycles. This is undoubtedly a worthy message, but, unfortunately, this book has too little plot and too much philosophy, and many youngsters are sure to find parts of it confusing. The attractive paintings, glowing double-paged spreads, are as poetic as the unrhymed text. The images are full of emotion and entirely appropriate to the culture depicted. Overall, Lee's artwork is a considerable asset to this collaboration. However, the story has limited child appeal.

DRAGON'S GATE (1993)

Betsy Hearne

SOURCE: A review of *Dragon's Gate,* in *Bulletin of the Center for Children's Books,* Vol. 47, No. 4, December, 1993, pp. 136-37.

An ambitious sequel to *The Serpent's Children* and *Mountain Light,* this tracks young Otter from his home in Kwangtung Province, China, to the Sierra Mountain range, where he joins his adoptive father and uncle to build a tunnel through solid rock for the transcontinental railroad. To establish a large cast, two diametrically diverse settings, and events from the years 1865 through 1867 is a tall order for one novel. Yep has succeeded in realizing the primary characters and the irrepressibly dramatic story of what amounted to slave labor for Chinese immigrants at the hands of ruthless bosses. In the process, however, secondary characters are flattened, the sense of time is foreshortened, the action piles up too fast, and explanation of motives sometimes replaces or repeats actual development. One key incident, for instance, involves a musician whose instrument is stolen, whereupon Otter inspires his crew of outcasts to chip in for another because "his music had become part of my life," something that will surprise readers who have only heard about this music once or twice before. The very same morning, the musician's fingers freeze and must be chopped off with a kitchen knife, an explosion blinds Otter's father, and Otter is publicly whipped for defying orders—all of this shortly followed by an avalanche. While such a sequence may very likely have occurred, it has the effect of crowding a work of fiction.

Where the pace and focus are controlled, as in Otter and his uncle's scaling a peak to save their snowed-in camp, the writing becomes more credibly layered; and even when the story surfaces to a shallower level, the carefully researched details will move students to thought and discussion about a powerful piece of American history.

Margaret A. Chang

SOURCE: A review of *Dragon's Gate,* in *School Library Journal,* Vol. 40, No. 1, January, 1994, p. 135.

Yep uses the lively storytelling techniques of his "Dragon" fantasy-adventure novels to re-create a stirring historical event—here, the construction of the transcontinental railroad. *Serpent's Children* (1984) and *Mountain Light* (1985) described the political and natural disasters that led to widespread famine in 19th-century southern China. Cassia and Foxfire, the "Serpent's Children," came from a long line of revolutionaries. Foxfire followed his dreams across the sea to the "Golden Mountain," California, where he earned enough money to revitalize his village. *Dragon's Gate* opens in China with Foxfire making a triumphant visit home. Otter, Cassia's adopted son, who tells the story, worships his uncle and longs to follow him back to the Golden Mountain. Granted his wish at last, Otter finds Foxfire working on "Snow Tiger," a mountain in the Sierra Nevada range, where Chinese laborers strive to hew a tunnel through solid rock. Appalled by the living conditions and disillusioned with his uncle, Otter must struggle to survive racial prejudice, cold, starvation, the foreman's whip, and the dangers of frostbite and avalanche while trying to reconcile his ideals and dreams with harsh reality, and to find his place in a strange land. Combining believable characters with thrilling adventure, Yep convinces readers that the Chinese railroad workers were indeed men to match the towering mountains of the west. Because the first few chapters, set in China, may be a bit confusing to children who have not read the previous two books, this will likely need booktalking.

Julie Corsaro

SOURCE: A review of *Dragon's Gate,* in *Booklist,* Vol. 90, No. 9, January 1, 1994, p. 817.

This is an engaging survival-adventure story, a social history, a heroic quest. The story opens in rural China in 1865 as 14-year-old Otter, the privileged son of wealthy land owners, eagerly sails to California to join his father and legendary uncle on the transcontinental railroad. On a freezing, snow-filled mountain in the Sierras, Otter begins his harrowing journey toward self-knowledge as a member of a crew of outcasts headed by Uncle Foxfire, a dreamer who seems to have been defeated as much by western racism as by the fears of his Chinese companions. While the long tale brings together the many hardships known to have been suffered by Chinese la-

borers—cold and hunger, poverty and exhaustion, maimings and death—it is leavened by some humor. The language has an appealing naturalism, and the concerns (equality, identity, family loyalty, ethnic conflict) are universally human. While the cast is large, the characterization is balanced; Yep shows that even the Irish overseer who viciously whips Otter is an idealist. This dovetails nicely with Yep's *The Serpent's Children* and *Mountain Light.*

THE GHOST FOX (1994)

Hazel Rochman

SOURCE: A review of *The Ghost Fox,* in *Booklist,* Vol. 90, No. 6, November 15, 1993, pp. 626-27.

In a chapter-book fantasy based on an old Chinese story, Little Lee must save his mother from a dangerous ghost fox that is stealing her soul. The evil fox disguises itself as a human in the daytime, but in the dark comes scratching at the door of the house and enters the mother's dreams. Each morning she acts more and more disoriented, first sad and then mean and ugly. Through the long, harsh winter, Little Lee's father is away trading on the river, and the villagers ignore the trouble. The boy must set things right himself. The comic chapters about the defeat of the ghost fox are not as tightly written as the family scenes, but kids will enjoy the clever reversal when Little Lee defeats the trickster fox with his own disguise and trickery. [Jean and Mou-Sien] Tseng's full-page black-and-white illustrations in seventeenth-century Chinese style have depth and drama, combining authentic details of dress and architecture with a strong sense of narrative. What haunts you about this story is the elemental terror of the strong, loving parent who turns into a stranger.

Kirkus Reviews

SOURCE: A review of *The Ghost Fox,* in *Kirkus Reviews,* Vol. LXI, No. 24, December 15, 1993, p. 1598.

Familial relationships are exquisitely rendered in this supernatural story drawn from a 17th-century collection by Chinese scholar Pu Sung-ling. After Little Lee accidentally bumps a stranger on a street while carrying cargo to his father Big Lee's ship, Big Lee sails away, promising to return by the New Year. Tension builds as the stranger, a "young gentleman in a red robe," follows Little Lee and his mother to their home. Scratching sounds are heard in the night; the shadow of a fox passes before Little Lee's bedroom window; but as long as the doors stay bolted, the boy and his mother are safe. But one night after the two, exhausted, have forgotten to lock the doors, the ghost fox enters, hungry for souls. The Tsengs' pen-and-ink illustrations evocatively capture 17th-century Chinese dress and architecture, while Yep's narrative depicts the dauntless triumph of good over evil with eerie grace and humor.

Betsy Hearne

SOURCE: A review of *The Ghost Fox,* in *Bulletin of the Center for Children's Books,* Vol. 47, No. 7, March, 1994, p. 240.

Clean writing and a suspenseful plot make this small novel, adapted from a traditional Chinese story, especially well suited for kids who are ready to exercise their skills and interests on chapter books but who are not yet ready for longer fiction. With practice born of his excellent folklore collection (*The Rainbow People,*) Yep keeps his style simple and respects the narrative elements enough to keep them scary. While his father is away on a merchant ship, Little Lee must fend off a ghost fox that threatens to steal his mother's soul: "Later that night, a scrabbling sound woke Little Lee. It sounded as if an animal was outside their house. It sounded as if claws were scraping the hard dirt outside." After the creature breaks in, Little Lee's mother changes from sweet-tempered to terrible and the townspeople blame Little Lee. It is only through his own wit and bravery that he saves the situation, to the accolades of everyone. What more could young heroes ask? The Tsengs' pen-and-ink drawings, too, are action-packed and have been researched to reflect accurately the seventeenth-century period during which the story was first collected.

THE BOY WHO SWALLOWED SNAKES (1994)

Publishers Weekly

SOURCE: A review of *The Boy Who Swallowed Snakes,* in *Publishers Weekly,* Vol. 240, No. 50, December 13, 1993, p. 70.

Little Chou leads a poor but honest life with his widowed mother. When he comes across a basket of silver, he tries to return it, but the owner refuses, knowing that the silver is tainted by the curse of an evil ku snake. Determined not to inflict the snake on others, Little Chou bravely swallows it. But more snakes spring from him, lighting up the sky like meteors— followed by more eating and still more snakes. Finally the reptiles visit their judgment on their greedy previous owner, while Little Chou and his mother reap the fruits of his unselfishness and courage. Yep's original folktale neatly balances magic and mystery with sprightly humor: as Little Chou dutifully gathers the multiplying snakes for consumption one evening, his mother hands him a rice bowl and chopsticks, commenting tartly, "Evil or not, you might as well eat them like a civilized person." [Illustrators Jean and Mousien Tseng] follow suit: their expressive watercolors capture both the spooky iridescence of the slithery creatures and the comic aspects of the boy's matter-of-fact determination to eat as many of them as he must. For the reader, as for Little Chou, this proves rewarding fare indeed.

Kirkus Reviews

SOURCE: A review of *The Boy Who Swallowed Snakes,* in *Kirkus Reviews,* Vol. LXII, No. 1, January 1, 1994, p. 76.

Puzzlingly described as an "original folktale," the bizarre story of Little Chou, a poor Chinese boy who finds, hidden in a basket of silver, an evil *ku* snake that kills people and takes their money to its master. When the snake proves indestructible, Little Chou swallows it in hopes of being rid of its evil, but that night a mysterious light emanating from his stomach becomes two *ku* snakes, which he also resolutely eats. The next night there are fifty dancing, luminous snakes, then a hundred, and finally so many that it appears that "the stars had fallen from the sky and emptied into the courtyard." When the greedy master of the original *ku* snake comes to reclaim his abandoned "pet," Little Chou tricks him into eating it and the man dies horribly. Good and evil receive their just deserts in this cautionary tale, but the snakes are a grotesquely ambiguous symbol, described as lethal yet also beautiful and almost innocently playful (in the end, Little Chou actually misses the creatures he's been at such pains to destroy). Further, the story's logic collapses at a crucial juncture: why, if the rich man was so fearful of the *ku* snake that he tried to get rid of it, would he wish to reclaim it when it had multiplied a thousandfold? The Tsengs' watercolors range from exotically colorful to murkily mysterious, with the characters' expressions and poses dramatically exaggerated.

John Philbrook

SOURCE: A review of *The Boy Who Swallowed Snakes,* in *School Library Journal,* Vol. 40, No. 4, April, 1994, p. 123.

Honest Little Chou sees a rich man leave a basket of silver in the forest, but when he tries to return it, the man denies ownership. Taking possession of the silver, the boy finds a small snake wound around his leg. After failed attempts to get rid of it, he and his mother learn that it is a *ku* snake, which, they are told, will bring treasure but also death. Little Chou reacts by eating the reptile. The snake, however, keeps duplicating itself until there are thousands. Yep resolves this situation in an ingenious way with the good ending happily and the bad getting their just deserts. Highly entertaining, morally relevant, told with gusto, wry wit, and a social conscience, this original story (CIP classification notwithstanding) is one of Yep's finest books. The Tsengs match his prose, page by page, with verve and insight in their ink and watercolor paintings that exhibit great beauty and cleverness. Especially notable are Little Chou's facial expressions, which faithfully and insouciantly mirror every nuance of the text. Not to be missed.

THE JUNIOR THUNDER LORD (1994)

Kirkus Reviews

SOURCE: A review of *The Junior Thunder Lord,* in *Kirkus Reviews,* Vol. LXII, No. 20, October 15, 1994, p. 1419.

A three-year drought is upon the land. The merchant Yue heads south to sell his goods. He encounters an ogre who stirs a memory for Yue: that once he was advised to help those in need. Yue buys the man a meal, then five more helpings. Needless to say, the ogre turns out to be a junior thunder lord and repays his debt to Yue in spades. Yep's tale is fun, the action swift, illustrated with a highly stylized, bold hand, but it stumbles on an important point: Without the ogre/lord's payback, the narrative would have little bite, so the idea of 'goodness for goodness' sake goes begging. Kept at the level of one good turn deserves another, however, things clip merrily along, and everyone's happy in the end.

Julie Yates Walton

SOURCE: A review of *The Junior Thunder Lord,* in *Booklist,* Vol. 91, No. 5, November 1, 1994, p. 504.

As a struggling student, Yue is helped by a friend who remarks, "Those at the top should help those at the bottom." Years later, as a merchant traveling far from his drought-stricken home, Yue generously buys a meal for Bear Face, a hungry, comically gauche stranger. Bear Face gratefully follows Yue everywhere, saving his life during a storm at sea and finally returning with him to Yue's parched village. Citing the proverb that began the story, Bear Face reveals his true identity—Junior Thunder Lord—and beckons the sky dragons to rain upon his friend's land. From then on, the "village always had all the rain it needed. And when it was pouring the hardest, Yue and his wife would go outside to wave up at their friend as he drove his storm clouds overhead." Yep's spare, crisp language gracefully defers to the dynamic story line, and Van Nutt's striking illustrations. Using the smooth, round lines of caricature and a palette of deep jewel colors, Van Nutt evokes both modernity and antiquity—a fine balance for a seventeenth-century tale with a twentieth-century message.

Elizabeth Bush

SOURCE: A review of *The Junior Thunder Lord,* in *Bulletin of the Center for Children's Books,* Vol. 48, No. 4, December, 1994, p. 149.

"Those at the top should help those at the bottom." The axiom's first occurrence sets the theme; its second appearance could be considered reinforcement; but by the third iteration it is clear this tale of a generous merchant's encounter with a huge brute has a Big Message. When he was a young and not-so-bright student, Yue had been tutored by a clever classmate; now Yue's

conscience urges him to befriend the uncouth Bear Face, whom he meets at an inn during a period of drought. The grateful lout follows Yue around, saves him from drowning at sea, and then lifts him into the sky to squeeze rain from the clouds. Bear Face is actually a minor thunder dragon, exiled by his dragon brothers for bad behavior; now he promises Yue's village will always have enough rainfall because "when I was at my lowest, you lifted me up." Yep's tale, taken from a seventeenth-century Chinese collection, tends to ramble; comically intended idioms such as "What a botch-up!" and "I go away for a little while and you let things slide" break the fairy-tale tone. Van Nutt's paintings neatly capture Yue's good-natured innocence and Bear Face's appalling manners, but despite an abundance of detail, they lack texture and depth. Many children may empathize with Yue's early school problems and chuckle at Bear Face's breach of etiquette; they certainly will get the moral.

TIGER WOMAN (1994)

Donna L. Scanlon

SOURCE: A review of *Tiger Woman,* in *School Library Journal,* Vol. 42, No. 2, February, 1996, p. 99.

In this picture-book version of a Shantung folk song, a selfish old woman refuses to share her bean curd with a beggar, warning him that she is " . . . a tiger when famished." He replies that she will be what she says she is and departs. Soon after, she is transformed into a tiger. Pursued by a mob of soldiers, she undergoes subsequent transformations each time she encounters food. Finally, while in the form of a pig and about to be slaughtered, she spies a cube of bean curd and repents her greediness, thus returning to her human form. Yep's rollicking narrative, interspersed with couplets and verse, is smooth and crisp. He has an ear for rhythm and adds just enough detail to enhance the tale. Roth's watercolors mesh with the text, sprawling across each double-page spread. The paintings are full of motion, humor, and accurate detail. The expression on the old woman's face when she is restored is priceless: sorrowful and repentant, but a bit offended as well. Although the tale reads aloud well, it is a little too long for preschool story time. Read it one-on-one with younger listeners; older groups will love it.

TREE OF DREAMS: TEN TALES FROM THE GARDEN OF NIGHT (retold, 1995)

Margaret A. Chang.

SOURCE: A review of *Tree of Dreams: Ten Tales from the Garden of Night,* in *School Library Journal,* Vol. 41, No. 3, March, 1995, p. 221.

Drawing on sources acknowledged at the end of the book, Yep retells 10 stories from Japan, India, China, Greece, Brazil, and Senegal in lively prose, shaping plot and point of view to emphasize each tale's dream aspect. In one selection, Badger guardians speak to their generous benefactor in his dream. In another, a prince braves distance and danger to find the princess of his dreams. In a third, a boy's dream spirit enters the body of a cricket, while a warrior dreams a lifetime as an ant, and learns humility. In yet another, a boy gains wisdom from the tree of dreams growing deep in the rain forest, only to incur murderous jealousy from other members of his tribe. A preface reminds readers that "dreaming is a bond that unites us," while an afterword briefly touches on the literary, scientific, and Freudian views on dreams. [Isadore] Seltzer offers one illustration per tale in a brash, deliberately rough-hewn style emphasizing the tales' strangeness. A collection to read for pure enjoyment, or to ponder the connection between dreams and folklore.

Betsy Hearne

SOURCE: A review of *Tree of Dreams: Ten Tales from the Garden of Night,* in *Bulletin of the Center for Children's Books,* Vol. 48, No. 8, April, 1995, pp. 289-90.

As ineffable as dreams may seem, these ten stories about them are surprisingly solid, coherent, and invariably involving. From Japan, India, China, Greece, Brazil, and Senegal, Yep has drawn a choice selection: the first is a magical tale of badgers rewarding a couple for their kindness; the last is a riddle story with remarkable resemblances to the Biblical Joseph and his dreams. In between comes a varied parade of active plots and unusual characters, highlighted by smooth but never pretentious narrative and a natural incorporation of dialogue. In addition to a poetic preface and an informative afterword, the stories are each introduced by a densely hued oil painting, populated with figures of drolly undreamy solidity, and a brief comment. Except for two specific acknowledgments, however, the bibliography does not match specific stories with their sources. We must trust that the clarity and grace of Yep's adaptations bear witness to his care in authentically reflecting earlier versions.

Nancy Vasilakis

SOURCE: A review of *Tree of Dreams: Ten Tales from the Garden of Night,* in *The Horn Book Magazine,* Vol. LXXI, No. 6, November, 1995, p. 752.

In prefatory and concluding remarks, Yep discusses many aspects of dreams, delving into some current research on their physiology and pointing to their timelessness as well as to the various interpretations of dreams among different peoples. Yep sees dreams as a bond to unite all cultures and to aid creativity. He includes ten stories in which dreams play a prominent part, from a variety of nations throughout the world—China, India, Japan, Greece, Brazil, and Senegal. On occasion, animals are the bridge between the daytime and the nocturnal worlds. For example, in **"The Helpful Badger,"** a Japanese tale

that honors generosity of spirit, a man's kindness to a family of badgers is rewarded when they come to his aid after robbers attack his home. In another story of Chinese origin, a boy makes up for his clumsiness in killing his father's prized cricket when he takes on the form of that fighting insect in a dream and reaps great honors for his courage and wit. The heroes in these tales discover that dreams can grant their wishes or predict the future. Even true love can be found through the medium of dreams, as readers discover in the Indian story **"Dream Girl."** Yep provides contemporary readers and storytellers with some tales that are not widely available and presents them in the lively, evocative prose which readers of his other collections of folktales will recognize.

📖 *HIROSHIMA: A NOVELLA* (1995)

Hazel Rochman

SOURCE: A review of *Hiroshima: A Novella,* in *Booklist,* Vol. 91, No. 14, March 15, 1995, p. 1329.

In quiet, simple prose, Yep tells what happens when the atomic bomb is dropped on Hiroshima in 1945. He tells it in short chapters in the present tense, switching from crewmen on the Enola Gay to children in a Hiroshima classroom; then he describes the attack, the mushroom cloud, and the destruction of the city; finally, he talks about the aftermath, immediate and long term, including the arms race and the movement for peace. One chapter explains the physics of the explosion and of radiation. The facts are so dramatic and told with such controlled intensity that we barely need the spare fictionalization about a young Hiroshima child who is there when the bomb falls and who later comes to the U.S. for treatment (Yep says in an afterword that she's a composite of several children). The account is fair, non-hectoring, and totally devastating. Though accessible to middle-grade readers, this will also interest older readers, who will find nothing condescending in content or format. Fifty years later, the event is still the focus of furious controversy (even the numbers are in dispute), and this novella will start classroom discussion across the curriculum.

Kirkus Reviews

SOURCE: A review of *Hiroshima: A Novella,* in *Kirkus Reviews,* Vol. LXIII, No. 9, May 1, 1995, p. 642.

Though deeply felt, a choppy, confusing account of Hiroshima's destruction that reads like a set of preliminary notes.

Mixing tenses and cutting back and forth between the Enola Gay's flight and the activities of two Hiroshima teenagers, Riko and Sachi, Yep sets the scene in very general terms, describes the bomb's immediate and lingering devastation, then closes with quick looks at the Cold War, Sadako Sasaki's story, a 1985 peace march, and related topics. Yep has done his homework, appending four pages of adult sources, but he barrages readers with raw numbers; the significance of repeated references to an unnamed Japanese colonel exercising his horse on the day of the bomb remains unclear; Sachi (who doesn't leave her home for three years after the bomb and eventually becomes a "Hiroshima maiden," one of a group of disfigured survivors sent to the US for restorative surgery) is a composite character with only a rudimentary background or personality.

Publishers Weekly

SOURCE: A review of *Hiroshima: A Novella,* in *Publishers Weekly,* Vol. 242, No. 19, May 8, 1995, p. 297.

Yep's account of the bombing of Hiroshima and its devastating aftermath is at once chilling and searing, hushed and thundering. Within a factual framework, the author sets the fictional story of a girl named Sachi, allegedly a composite of several young residents of the bombed city. On the morning of August 6, 1945, 12-year-old Sachi and her classmates pull on their pitifully inadequate air-raid hoods when an alarm sounds, signifying the approach of an American bomber. They and others feel, ironically, a deep sense of relief when the aircraft passes by—the plane's mission, in fact, is to scout out the weather over Hiroshima; if there are clouds, the Enola Gay will be directed to drop its atom bomb on another city. But a single gap opens in the clouds directly over the target site, and "the sunlight pours through the hole on to the city." This is the last bit of brightness in Yep's story, which with haunting simplicity describes the actual bombing: "There is a blinding light like a sun. There is a boom like a giant drum. There is a terrible wind. Houses collapse like boxes. Windows break everywhere. Broken glass swirls like angry insects."

Though Yep's spare, deliberate description of the bomb's consequences delivers a brutal emotional punch—and though it is on the whole extremely well suited to the target audience—his novella has some jarring stylistic elements, Broken into brief chapters ("The Bomb," "The City," "The Attack," "Destruction," "Peace?"), the narrative is choppy. The text, for example, makes a hasty chronological jump from the announcement that WW II is over to Sachi's experience as one of 25 "Hiroshima Maidens"; who in 1955 traveled to the United States for plastic surgery to correct disfiguring burns. And although expressing an opinion is clearly the novelist's prerogative, it should be noted that the story Yep relays is hardly balanced; witness the two simple sentences about the Japanese bombing of Pearl Harbor, which make no mention of the resulting human casualties: "Four years before, on December 7, 1941, Japanese planes attacked American ships in Hawaii without warning. Caught by surprise, many ships and planes were wrecked at the naval base, Pearl Harbor."

Yet in what is one of his tale's most haunting moments, Yep interjects the resonant words of an American—the Enola Gay's copilot—who, surveying the destruction just after the bomb has hit Hiroshima, scribbles a note to himself: "What have we done?" This powerful chronicle ensures that what was done on that awful day will remain in readers' memories for a very long time.

LATER, GATOR (1995)

Kirkus Reviews

SOURCE: A review of *Later, Gator,* in *Kirkus Reviews,* Vol. LXIII, No. 8, April 15, 1995, p. 564.

Teddy's younger brother, Bobby, is kind, helpful, and loving; Teddy therefore does what he must to make Bobby's life miserable. But all that trusting innocence has a way of taking the fun out of the meanest pranks. When Teddy buys his brother an alligator for his birthday, Bobby loves his new pet and is infuriatingly grateful. All too aware of Teddy's real motives, the boys' parents are determined to get rid of the alligator. For once, the brothers are on the same side, and Teddy comes to recognize his real affection for his young sibling.

This amusing, occasionally didactic, story is good fun for younger readers. While most of the peripheral characters are ciphers, Bobby is affectingly genuine; Teddy, though initially detestable, becomes more likable as the story progresses. An entertaining ending is marred by an afterword expounding the villainy of mistreating pets, but this remains an interesting slice-of-life portrait based in San Francisco's Chinatown.

Publishers Weekly

SOURCE: A review of *Later, Gator,* in *Publishers Weekly,* Vol. 242, No. 19, May 8, 1995, p. 296.

Adopting a light tone far removed from the solemnity of *Hiroshima,* Yep trains his attention on a close-knit family in San Francisco's Chinatown. Teddy's mother, insisting that he put some effort into choosing a birthday present for his practically perfect younger brother, sends him to the pet shop to buy a turtle. But Teddy, no paragon, picks out a baby alligator instead, hoping to horrify little Bobby. (A note tacked onto the end of the novel advises readers on more humane approaches to choosing a pet.) Bobby, however, is thrilled, and Teddy finds himself working with Bobby to persuade their parents to let the alligator stay. Yep's portrayal of the family is warm, wise and humorous. In examining classic issues like sibling rivalry, he adds the special filter of the Chinese American experience: just after Teddy complains to his mother that everyone likes Bobby better than him, Teddy tells the reader, "Right about now I could have really used a hug. My parents, though, never showed their affection like the white parents on television. I wanted a hug so bad that it almost hurt." The story may be a slender one, but the insights here are generous.

John Philbrook

SOURCE: A review of *Later, Gator,* in *School Library Journal,* Vol. 41, No. 7, July, 1995, p. 83.

Overly wise Teddy decides to disobey his mother's orders and get his eight-year-old brother, Bobby, a baby alligator for his birthday. He rationalizes this as part of a campaign to toughen up his goody-goody sibling. Of course, it backfires, but in unexpected ways that bring Teddy to a real appreciation of his younger brother. The boys' warm and eccentric extended family of aunts, uncles, cousins, and grandmother, not to mention a slightly demented landlord, adds depth and counterpoint to a delightfully funny yet touching narrative. Except for a short, trite scene on a bus, plotting is inventive and involving. A Catch-22 episode involving begging restaurant scraps to feed the alligator has hilarious consequences. Universal themes of sibling rivalry and the death of a pet are handled in a subtle, masterful way. There are also a few dashes of wry social commentary on Chinese American and white attitudes toward one another. Refreshing reading and another winner from Yep.

THIEF OF HEARTS (1995)

Hazel Rochman

SOURCE: A review of *Thief of Hearts,* in *Booklist,* Vol. 91, No. 21, July, 1995, p. 1880.

Stacy has always felt comfortable in her suburban middle school, but when someone calls her a "half-breed," she's shocked into realizing that she's not "just like everyone else"; she finds herself caught between the worlds of her mixed Chinese and American heritage. The story is set 30 years after Yep's acclaimed *Child of the Owl* (1977), which was about Stacy's mother and great-grandmother in the 1960s. Now the three women go on a journey back to San Francisco's Chinatown, where Stacy learns about their immigrant past in all its richness and struggle. The characters are well drawn, but the plot is full of contrivances (including a newly arrived Chinese classmate who is suspected of being a thief), and Stacy has an irritating habit of discussing every conversation and incident and family embrace in relation to her search for identity. Yet her comments are eloquent, much more interesting than the plot, with its slight detective story and sudden awakenings. Any kid caught between cultures will relate to Stacy's search for home: "When one world ends, you find another . . . Maybe you even make your own."

Margaret A. Chang

SOURCE: A review of *Thief of Hearts,* in *School Library Journal,* Vol. 41, No. 8, August, 1995, p. 145.

Yep's sequel to his superb *Child of the Owl* (1977)

touches lightly, and with gentle humor, on issues of identity, communication among generations, racial stereotyping, and cross-cultural understanding. Stacy, who lives with her Caucasian father and Chinese mother and great-grandmother in a suburb of San Francisco, tells the story. Her mother, Casey, was the streetwise protagonist of the previous title, and the frail, ancient woman Stacy calls Tai-Paw was the grandmother who gave Casey a home and roots. Stacy has never thought of herself as anything but American—until the day her parents ask her to befriend a Chinese immigrant, Hong Ch'un. The two girls take an instant dislike to one another. When items stolen from people around the school are found in Hong Ch'un's backpack, a schoolmate calls Stacy "half-breed" for defending her. Disgraced, Hong Ch'un runs away, and Stacy, her mother, and Tai-Paw search through Chinatown for her. Their three-generation journey, intertwining memories and revelations with present action, forms the emotional heart of the narrative. Stacy's understanding of herself and others seems at times too facile, and explanations of history and cultural differences occasionally intrude on the plot. The new book is short and fast-moving, but lacks the sass and bite of its predecessor, and some of the writing is imprecise. Still, its warm depiction of a mixed-race child in a changing world, combined with a page-turning mystery, should guarantee a wide audience.

Roger Sutton

SOURCE: A review of *Thief of Hearts,* in *Bulletin of the Center for Children's Books,* Vol. 49, No. 1, September, 1995, pp. 34-5.

Stacy is not pleased that she's been elected by her parents to show a new girl from China around school, particularly when it turns out that Hong Ch'un is snotty and difficult, even calling Stacy *t'ung chung,* "mixed seed." Stacy's mother (whose story was told in *Child of the Owl,* is of Chinese descent, and her father Caucasian, and when Hong Ch'un is accused by the other kids of stealing, Stacy feels torn between parental instruction, ethnic loyalty, and peer acceptance. This bicultural dilemma is somewhat forced into a formulaic school-story (and is ludicrously concluded via a mad-scientist prank Stacy's father cooks up to find out the real thief), but in between set-up and denouement comes a marvelously rendered plot sequence that takes Stacy, her mother, and great-grandmother ("Tai-Paw") to San Francisco's Chinatown, where Hong Ch'un has run to escape her torment and homesickness. There, Mom and Tai-Paw find remnants of family and memories, and Stacy begins to see more of her own cultural and personal history. As she did in *Child of the Owl,* Tai-Paw tells an old and resonant Chinese story that gives the novel its title, but the relevance here of the Thief of Hearts story to Stacy's various dilemmas is not readily apparent. While unevenly paced and textured, the book at heart is a strong portrait of a child finding her present in the past.

📖 *THE CITY OF DRAGONS* (1995)

Publishers Weekly

SOURCE: A review of *The City of Dragons,* in *Publishers Weekly,* Vol. 242, No. 40, October 2, 1995, p. 74.

"Once there was a boy with the saddest face in the world. Even when he was happy, everyone who saw him thought he must be sad, and they became sad, too." Embellishing the memory of a disfigured, outcast boy of his childhood with folklore from southern China, Yep deftly crafts an imaginative moral tale. Shunned because of his disturbing appearance although he is both polite and good, the boy runs away with a band of giants that hunts for pearls—the tears of dragons. The jaded dragons are impervious to the saddest of the giants' tales; but when they see the boy's sorrowful face, they weep bowlfuls and the boy, returning home with the gems, receives a hero's welcome. Just as the author does with his dialogue, [Jean and Mou-Sien Tseng] spike their exotic, mystical watercolors with just enough humor to leaven a potentially heavy theme—the value and power of one's uniqueness. Fresh, unusual and impressive, this is a worthy addition to the ever-expanding Yep collection.

Kay Weisman

SOURCE: A review of *The City of Dragons,* in *Booklist,* Vol. 92, No. 6, November 15, 1995, p. 566.

A young boy with the saddest face in the world feels bad about the pain his appearance causes his parents. Donning a wide-brimmed hat, he runs away and meets a caravan of giants on their annual trek to the City of Dragons. Impressed because they think he must be very brave to deal with such sadness, the giants hire him to help gather treasure. The boy's face moves the dragons to tears, enabling them to cry pearls for the giants to collect. This tale's folkloric style meshes nicely with the Tsengs' fanciful watercolor illustrations, resulting in an appealing and thoughtful story. A good choice for primary read-alouds, this may spark discussions about disabilities and appreciation for everyone's true worth.

📖 *RIBBONS* (1996)

Hazel Rochman

SOURCE: A review of *Ribbons,* in *Booklist,* Vol. 92, No. 9 & 10, January 1, 1996, p. 836.

Robin, 11, is a gifted dancer, and she bitterly resents having to give up her ballet classes to help her parents pay for her lame grandmother to come from Hong Kong to live with them in San Francisco. To make things worse, Grandmother treats Robin with contempt. But when Robin discovers Grandmother's terrible secret— her grotesquely mangled broken feet—their relationship suddenly changes. Chinese foot-binding is dramatic so-

cial history, but the contemporary fiction is contrived, with purposive dialogue and coincidences and heavy metaphors. Robin's feet begin to hurt because she practices ballet on concrete floors with too-tight shoes; and, in case we still don't get the parallel, she reads the story of the brave little mermaid who wanted to walk even though it hurt. Yep has written novels with considerable depth and subtlety about the Chinese American experience, but here we get only glimpses of Robin's interracial family and her neighborhood friends; they never quite come together as people in a story. As in Yep's *Hiroshima* (1995), it's the fact that's compelling.

Deborah Stevenson

SOURCE: A review of *Ribbons,* in *Bulletin of the Center for Children's Books,* Vol. 49, No. 6, February, 1996, p. 210.

Robin lives for ballet, adoring her stern teacher, Madame Oblamov, and anticipating a glorious career. She's therefore devastated when her parents call a halt to her ballet on financial grounds: they're devoting every penny they've got to bringing her mother's mother over from Hong Kong and getting her settled—in Robin's old room, while Robin shares with her little brother, Ian. The unfairness of Robin's predicament is accentuated by her grandmother's obvious preference for Ian and her parents' reluctance to intercede when the old lady's favoritism makes Robin's life difficult. The Little Princess aspect of the story, with poor put-upon Robin beset at every turn, isn't especially believable but will be very gratifying to readers, particularly when they realize, along with Robin's parents, that Robin's year of deprivation has led to permanent physical consequences (Robin's constant home practicing of ballet in ill-fitting shoes has led to deformation of her feet) and that her parents are wracked with guilt. The rapprochement between Robin and her grandmother is a bit sudden but is warm and engaging, and the family dynamics here are soapishly absorbing. Most memorable is Robin's cranky but strong-minded grandmother whose granddaughter definitely takes after her; kids who appreciate a story about fighting for one's dreams will enjoy Robin's saga.

Margaret A. Chang

SOURCE: A review of *Ribbons,* in *School Library Journal,* Vol. 42, No. 2, February, 1996, p. 104.

Yep once again explores the hazardous terrain that separates a Eurasian girl from her Chinese mother and grandmother. At 11, Robin has found her life's passion: ballet. Then she learns that her high-minded, impecunious parents can no longer afford lessons, now that they are bringing Grandmother over from Hong Kong. Refusing to give up the world she loves, Robin continues to practice in the garage on a cement floor, wearing toe shoes she rapidly outgrows. Meanwhile, Grandmother arrives, limping painfully with the aid of two canes. Though Mother forbids any mention of her disability, Robin's ignorance about bound feet strains credibility. The girl's wary hostility toward the old woman who so disrupts her life turns to active dislike, and then to understanding when she sees her uncovered damaged feet. Andersen's story "The Little Mermaid," awkwardly patched into the narrative, symbolizes the determination to transcend pain shared by Robin and her grandmother. The parent's inattention to their daughter's damaging practice sessions seems contrived to further the plot, and the murkier depths of mutilation in the cause of beauty are never sounded. If Robin's self-knowledge seems unnaturally mature, it is because she is telling about her emotions rather than letting readers feel them. This said, Robin's final epiphany, using the book's symbolic title to great effect, is genuinely felt, and genuinely moving. An appealing story that draws readers into the world of ballet while offering an authentic and sometimes amusing look at the dynamics of Chinese-American family life.

THE CASE OF THE GOBLIN PEARLS (1997)

Publishers Weekly

SOURCE: A review of *The Case of the Goblin Pearls,* in *Publishers Weekly,* Vol. 243, No. 51, December 16, 1996, pp. 59-60.

Yep is off to a roaring start with this launch to a mystery series set in San Francisco's Chinatown. As it begins, 12-year-old Lily's glamorous great-aunt ("Tiger Lil") comes to visit from Hollywood. A whirlwind of energy, the 60-something former film star ropes Lily and her family and friends into helping with a float she's been hired to organize for the Chinese New Year parade. In the process, Lily learns a great deal about her personal and cultural heritage, and she and her "auntie" help unravel an insurance scam involving a stolen pearl necklace, as well as uncover a sweatshop operation at which the mother of one of Lily's school friends is haplessly employed. Snappy dialogue, realistic characterizations and a plot with lots of action keep the pages turning, and the layers of social relevance (the sweatshop story line; Lily's growing realization of the complexities of her Chinese heritage) add substance. Readers will look forward to more installments featuring this spunky heroine—not to mention her wisecracking auntie.

Carol A. Edwards

SOURCE: A review of *The Case of the Goblin Pearls,* in *School Library Journal,* Vol. 43, No. 3, March, 1997, pp. 194-95.

Lily's Auntie Tiger Lil comes to stay with the girl's family while organizing a float for the Chinese New Year's parade in San Francisco. A street gang called the Powell Street Boys threatens to disrupt the parade and steal the "Goblin Pearls" worn by Miss Lion Salve, and so sets the scene for the suspense. Although too many characters are

introduced and not fully developed, this first title in a new series has real possibilities. The two heroines, Tiger Lil, a fading Hollywood star, and her niece and name-sake, Lily, carry the story. The mystery involves the pearls, Chinatown, and a local sweatshop called "Happy Fortune." The bad guys aren't obvious right off the bat, but clue follows clue as events unfold and even though Lily doesn't intend to get involved, she is the one who pieces the truth together. There is a lot of culturally specific material nicely introduced as Lily discovers her heritage and makes connections at the same time that readers do. Some of the unfairness of the sweatshop seems overly dramatized, especially when the workers are so kind as to share their nearly nonexistent wages with a stranger. But there are some nice touches, such as tidbits left hanging in the air for youngsters to puzzle over before being explained. With enough fun and intrigue to keep the pages turning, this is a worthwhile series title.

Elizabeth Bush

SOURCE: A review of *The Case of the Goblin Pearls,* in *Bulletin of the Center for Children's Books,* Vol. 50, No. 9, May, 1997, p. 339.

Heists by the Powell Street Boys are escalating in San Francisco's Chinatown, and there has even been talk among politicians of canceling the Chinese New Year parade. The influential Wong family is determined to flaunt the safety of their community by allowing daughter Tiffany to wear the priceless "Goblin Pearls" necklace on Mr. Soo's Lion Salve parade float. When the pearls are swiped right off Tiffany's neck during the festivities, "Tiger Lil" Leung, erstwhile screen star and current promoter for Lion Salve, steps in to investigate, with the bungling assistance of her great-niece (and our narrator), Lily Lew. There's precious little mystery here; even novice crime-crackers won't have much trouble fingering the culprits, and Officer Quan's shoddy investigative technique will appall whodunit diehards. Yep does scratch beneath Chinatown's gaudy veneer to reveal prejudices within San Francisco's Chinese community, where children of immigrants who have moved "up the hill" look down literally and figuratively on the J.O.J.'s (Just Off the Jet), many of whom struggle for low wages in deplorable sweatshops. But the social commentary, however apt, cannot rescue the floundering plot, and mystery fans won't consider this much of a gem.

THE KHAN'S DAUGHTER: A MONGOLIAN FOLKTALE (adapted, 1997)

Carol Ann Wilson

SOURCE: A review of *The Khan's Daughter: A Mongolian Folktale,* in *School Library Journal,* Vol. 43, No. 2, February, 1997, p. 99.

In order to fulfill a prophecy and win the hand of the

Khan's daughter in marriage, Möngke, a shepherd, must succeed in three trials. His mother-in-law-to-be sets the first two. To prove his strength, he must steal the wealth of seven demons. To demonstrate his bravery, he must vanquish the enemy. The third trial, however, is imposed by the Khan's daughter herself, after which a humbled but determined Möngke does indeed become a wise and beloved husband. While this retelling of a Mongolian folktale adheres to the predictable and traditional quest motif, Yep succeeds in endowing his characters with multidimensional personalities. Möngke is brave, foolish, boastful, then finally contrite. Women are not simply trophies but actively determine their destiny. The well-paced story effortlessly balances humor and adventure, fantasy and reality, and is wonderfully enhanced by the artwork. From their ravishing cover with its acrylic portrait of the Khan's daughter (and a dashing but much smaller Möngke) superimposed on luminous gold leaf, through the gold-framed watercolors that add a wealth of detail and atmosphere, [Jean and Mou-Sien Tseng] once again capture a faraway place and time and make it eminently accessible to children—just as they did in Margaret Mahy's *The Seven Chinese Brothers* (1990). As a sprightly read-aloud or an opportunity for independent readers to lose themselves in an unfamiliar and fascinating culture, this is a solid addition to folklore collections.

Karen Morgan

SOURCE: A review of *The Khan's Daughter: A Mongolian Folktale,* in *Booklist,* Vol. 93, No. 11, February 1, 1997, p. 940.

Yep begins this retelling of a Mongolian folktale by introducing Mongke, a confident, likable young shepherd who believes that his destiny includes both marriage to the khan's daughter and the ability to meet every challenge placed before him. Although he bests some tremendous opponents, his most difficult match proves to be the khan's daughter herself. Yep's strong folkloric narrative is amplified by splendid watercolor illustrations: some children will like the liveliness of the horses; others will relish the gruesome demon spirits, pore over the battle scenes, or enjoy the finely detailed costumes. With engaging human characters, frightful monsters, dramatic tension within a warrior-based society, powerful illustrations, and plenty of action, this is the sort of book that will appeal to diverse ages and sensibilities.

Maeve Visser Knoth

SOURCE: A review of *The Khan's Daughter: A Mongolian Folktale,* in *The Horn Book Magazine,* Vol. LXXIII, No. 2, March, 1997, pp. 208-09.

Möngke's father, a poor man, tells the boy that he is to become rich and marry the Khan's daughter. After many years of waiting for the prophecy to come true, the penniless young man decides to travel to the city of the Khan to assert his claim. Incredulous, the royal family sets Möngke three impossible tasks. After accomplishing the first two out of sheer luck, Möngke fails in his attempt to conquer Bagatur the Clever and Mighty—only to find that his foe is really the Khan's daughter in disguise. She is delighted to marry a "prudent husband who won't get himself killed at the first opportunity," and they live as equals "for the rest of their lives." Yep's retelling of the Mongolian tale is fluid and engaging. The story is humorous and quite modern, with an independent heroine and a moral that touts the value of reason and equality. The text is enhanced by the Tsengs' detailed double-page watercolor paintings, which provide a rich cultural and geographical setting to the story without sacrificing its humor. Many of the illustrations are panoramic views of the Khan's court or of the countryside, with the hapless antihero Möngke at center stage.

📖 ***THE DRAGON PRINCE: A CHINESE BEAUTY AND THE BEAST TALE*** (adapted, 1997)

Karen Morgan

SOURCE: A review of *The Dragon Prince: A Chinese Beauty and the Beast Tale,* in *Booklist,* Vol. 93, No. 21, July, 1997, p. 1817.

A small, harmless water serpent that is saved from death by a young teen changes into an immense dragon and threatens a poor farmer's life. The farmer's only chance lies in convincing one of his seven daughters to marry the dragon. Readers familiar with fairy tales may guess that the youngest and prettiest daughter, who was the serpent's savior, will agree to the marriage to save her father. In this Chinese variant of "Beauty and the Beast," dragon and girl soar into the night sky and then plunge into a deep sea, where the girl's courage and character are tested again before she discovers that her future husband is a handsome human and ruler of the sea kingdom. After spending some time in her husband's kingdom, she visits her family's home, where both her inner and her outward strength are further tested. [Kam] Mak's illustrations dramatically combine realism and fantasy. The suspense of the story and the charm of its language should appeal to readers of different ages. A good choice for reading aloud.

Kirkus Reviews

SOURCE: A review of *The Dragon Prince: A Chinese Beauty and the Beast Tale,* in *Kirkus Reviews,* Vol. LXV, No. 16, August 15, 1997, p. 1316.

The subtitle says all: A dragon ambushes a poor farmer and promises to eat the unfortunate man unless one of the farmer's seven daughters marries him. Six daughters run away in fear, but Seven can't bear to see her father suffer and consents to marry the dragon. Seven is not afraid of the dragon; she finds him beautiful and tells him so. At that the dragon transforms into a handsome prince and the two are very happy together until Seven begins to grow homesick. During a visit to her family, her real troubles begin—one of her sisters is jealous of Seven's match. She gets rid of Seven and returns to the prince in her sister's place, but the prince's heart is not fooled. Yep tells the tale with colorful descriptions and repeated refrains, while Mak's splendid, realistic paintings, in dark jewel tones bordered with white, extend the text elegantly—the scene of the dragon flying over Chinese tile roofs is especially beautiful.

Publishers Weekly

SOURCE: A review of *The Dragon Prince: A Chinese Beauty and the Beast Tale,* in *Publishers Weekly,* Vol. 244, No. 35, August 25, 1997, p. 71.

For aficionados of the "Beauty and the Beast" theme, this southern Chinese adaptation of a traditional Chinese tale gains notability through Yep's elegant, carefully crafted storytelling. Seven, the seventh and youngest daughter of a poor farmer, consents to marry a dragon in order to save her father's life. The courageous girl soon perceives a strange beauty beneath the dragon's ferocity. Touching his cheek, she says, "I know the loom and stove and many ordinary things, but my hand has never touched wonder." The dragon then dances, "curling his powerful body as easily as a giant golden ribbon" and spins until he becomes "a column of light, and from the light stepped a handsome prince" An original twist involves an attempt by Seven's vindictive sister, Three, to usurp her riches and position. In contrast to Yep's fluent prose, Mak's visual imagery appears disjointed. Incongruously lifelike representations of the characters tend to chafe against the narrative's fantasy elements rather than ushering readers through the magical journey.

THE IMP THAT ATE MY HOMEWORK (1998)

Publishers Weekly

SOURCE: A review of *The Imp That Ate My Homework,* in *Publishers Weekly,* Vol. 244, No. 48, November 24, 1997, pp. 74-5.

Jim's Grandpop is widely known as the meanest man in Chinatown, and Jim is afraid of him. But then he meets the Imp, a truly nasty Chinese genie who has escaped from a dug-up vase. The Imp is out to wreck Jim and his family with his destructive tricks and capers—and who is going to believe Jim when he tells his teacher that the Imp ate his homework for a snack? Only cranky old Grandpop has the key to defeating their magical opponent. Yep deftly draws a picture of a family tiptoeing around a volatile patriarch. But the point is well made that sometimes children don't know everything about their grandparents—especially Jim, who doesn't know that Grandpop is secretly the supernatural warrior Chung Kuei, who defeated the Imp hundreds of years ago. Some readers may wish for an explanation of exactly what the Imp is and what it represents in Chinese culture; [Benrei] Huang's drawings, at least, give readers a clear picture of an ugly demon with four arms, horns and leering grin, stirring up mischief for his own wicked pleasure. Readers will be cheering as Grandpop makes the Imp so mad it throws a tantrum and yells, "I'm going to sue for slander." Good-natured fun.

Kirkus Reviews

SOURCE: A review of *The Imp That Ate My Homework,* in *Kirkus Reviews,* Vol. LXV, No. 23, December 1, 1997, p. 1782.

It sounds like a flimsy excuse, but for young Jim it's literally true: An imp really does eat his homework, as well as gets him into further trouble with his mother, his father, and his teacher in Chinese school. Why? Because Jim's ever-crabby grandfather is the reincarnation of legendary imp-fighter Chung Kuei, and the newly escaped imp—with four arms and red eyes, and invisible to everyone else—is bent on avenging centuries of persecution. Once Jim overcomes his reluctance to ask "Grandpop" for help, a wild chase through San Francisco's Chinatown ensues, marked by pratfalls, chaos, and transformations. At last Grandpop corners the imp, drives it into a frenzy with a barrage of corny jokes and insults, then stuffs it into a silk pillow. Yep telescopes the plot severely; he occasionally checks the pace long enough for a peek into a sweatshop, or a conversation about the younger generation's drift away from traditional culture. Still, readers will not be able to put this light, funny fantasy down.

Kay Weisman

SOURCE: A review of *The Imp That Ate My Homework,* in *Booklist,* Vol. 94, No. 8, December 15, 1997, p. 698.

Jim, growing up with his parents in a Chinese neighborhood in San Francisco, has always had trouble relating to Grandpop, aka the meanest man in Chinatown. But when a six-foot-tall, four-armed, furry green imp enters Jim's life, hilariously wreaking havoc on his school and home life, it seems Grandpop may be Jim's most valuable ally. The two join forces against this ancient, magical creature, and in the process, Jim comes to understand and appreciate his grandfather's many talents. Writing in a lighter vein and for a younger audience than usual, Yep is only partially successful. The concept of a demonic personality controlling the daily activities of a modern child will draw readers into the story, but Yep's strength is his attention to details of real life and places in Chinatown. Still, this book and the recent *Later, Gator* (1995) may be a good way to entice readers to try Yep's other works.

THE COOK'S FAMILY (1998)

Stephanie Zvirin

SOURCE: A review of *The Cook's Family*, in *Booklist*, Vol. 94, No. 9 & 10, January 1, 1998, p. 817.

Although an author's note hangs the story on an actual incident, the setup of Yep's latest novel demands that we suspend our disbelief. As they pass a small restaurant in Chinatown, Robin and her grandmother are recruited by a waiter to pretend to be the family of the restaurant's Chinese cook, who is refusing to perform his duties. The fantasy is haltingly played out by all, with Robin and her grandmother returning to the restaurant the following week to pick up their roles (a real leap for Robin, who looks more like her Caucasian father than like her Chinese mother). For Grandmother, the game is a link to a homeland left behind; for Robin, it is a respite from her parents' bickering and a chance for her to understand more about her Chinese heritage. It is Robin's learning about Chinese history and custom that is the most intriguing part of the story, which also strikes at the heart of what family means in different cultures.

Additional coverage of Yep's life and career is contained in the following sources published by The Gale Group: *Authors and Artists for Young Adults*, Vol. 5; *Contemporary Authors New Revision Series*, Vol. 46; *Contemporary Literary Criticism*, Vol. 35; *Dictionary of Literary Biography*, Vol. 52; *Junior DISCovering Authors*; *Major Authors and Illustrators for Children and Young Adults*; and *Something about the Author*, Vols. 7, 69.

CUMULATIVE INDEXES

How to Use This Index

The main reference

Baum, L(yman) Frank 1856–
1919 15

list all author entries in this and previous volumes of *Children's Literature Review:*

The cross-references

See also CA 103; 108; DLB 22; JRDA
MAICYA; MTCW; SATA 18; TCLC 7

list all author entries in the following Gale biographical and literary sources:

AAYA = *Authors & Artists for Young Adults*
AITN = *Authors in the News*
BLC = *Black Literature Criticism*
BW = *Black Writers*
CA = *Contemporary Authors*
CAAS = *Contemporary Authors Autobiography Series*
CABS = *Contemporary Authors Bibliographical Series*
CANR = *Contemporary Authors New Revision Series*
CAP = *Contemporary Authors Permanent Series*
CDALB = *Concise Dictionary of American Literary Biography*
CDBLB = *Concise Dictionary of British Literary Biography*
CLC = *Contemporary Literary Criticism*
CMLC = *Classical and Medieval Literature Criticism*
DAB = *DISCovering Authors: British*
DAC = *DISCovering Authors: Canadian*
DAM = *DISCovering Authors: Modules*
       DRAM: *Dramatists Module;* *MST*: *Most-Studied Authors Module;*
       MULT: *Multicultural Authors Module;* *NOV*: *Novelists Module;*
       POET: *Poets Module;* *POP*: *Popular Fiction and Genre Authors Module*
DC = *Drama Criticism*
DLB = *Dictionary of Literary Biography*
DLBD = *Dictionary of Literary Biography Documentary Series*
DLBY = *Dictionary of Literary Biography Yearbook*
HLC = *Hispanic Literature Criticism*
HW = *Hispanic Writers*
JRDA = *Junior DISCovering Authors*
LC = *Literature Criticism from 1400 to 1800*
MAICYA = *Major Authors and Illustrators for Children and Young Adults*
MTCW = *Major 20th-Century Writers*
NCLC = *Nineteenth-Century Literature Criticism*
NNAL = *Native North American Literature*
PC = *Poetry Criticism*
SAAS = *Something about the Author Autobiography Series*
SATA = *Something about the Author*
SSC = *Short Story Criticism*
TCLC = *Twentieth-Century Literary Criticism*
WLC = *World Literature Criticism, 1500 to the Present*
YABC = *Yesterday's Authors of Books for Children*

CUMULATIVE INDEX TO AUTHORS

Aardema, Verna **17**
See also Vugteveen, Verna Aardema
See also MAICYA; SAAS 8; SATA 4, 68

Aaseng, Nate
See Aaseng, Nathan

Aaseng, Nathan 1953- **54**
See also AAYA 27; CA 106; CANR 36;
JRDA; MAICYA; SAAS 12; SATA 51,
88; SATA-Brief 38

Abbott, Sarah
See Zolotow, Charlotte S(hapiro)

Achebe, (Albert) Chinua(lumogu) 1930-.. **20**
See also AAYA 15; BLC 1; BW 2; CA 1-4R;
CANR 6, 26, 47, 73; CLC 1, 3, 5, 7, 11, 26,
51, 75; DA; DAB; DAC; DAM MST, MULT,
NOV; DLB 117; MAICYA; MTCW 1; SATA
40; SATA-Brief 38; WLC

Adams, Richard (George) 1920- **20**
See also AAYA 16; AITN 1, 2; CA 49-52; CANR
3, 35; CLC 4, 5, 18; DAM NOV; JRDA;
MAICYA; MTCW 1; SATA 7, 69

Adelberg, Doris
See Orgel, Doris

Adkins, Jan 1944- **7**
See also CA 33-36R; MAICYA; SAAS 19; SATA
8, 69

Adler, Irving 1913- **27**
See also CA 5-8R; CANR 2, 47; MAICYA; SAAS
15; SATA 1, 29

Adoff, Arnold 1935- **7**
See also AAYA 3; AITN 1; CA 41-44R; CANR
20, 37, 67; JRDA; MAICYA; SAAS 15; SATA
5, 57, 96

Aesop 620(?)B.C.-564(?)B.C. **14**
See also CMLC 24; MAICYA; SATA 64

Affabee, Eric
See Stine, R(obert) L(awrence)

Ahlberg, Allan 1938-........................... **18**
See also CA 111; 114; CANR 38, 70; MAICYA;
SATA 68; SATA-Brief 35

Ahlberg, Janet 1944-1994 .... **18**
See also CA 111; 114; 147; MAICYA; SATA 68;
SATA-Brief 32; SATA-Obit 83

Aiken, Joan (Delano) 1924- **1, 19**
See also AAYA 1, 25; CA 9-12R; CANR 4, 23,
34, 64; CLC 35; DLB 161; JRDA; MAICYA;
MTCW 1; SAAS 1; SATA 2, 30, 73

Akers, Floyd
See Baum, L(yman) Frank

Alcock, Vivien 1924-........................... **26**
See also AAYA 8; CA 110; CANR 41; JRDA;
MAICYA; SATA 45, 76; SATA-Brief 38

Alcott, Louisa May 1832-1888 .... **1, 38**
See also AAYA 20; CDALB 1865-1917; DA;
DAB; DAC; DAM MST, NOV; DLB 1, 42,
79; DLBD 14; JRDA; MAICYA; NCLC 6,
58; SATA 100; SSC 27; WLC; YABC 1

Alexander, Lloyd (Chudley) 1924-... **1, 5, 48**
See also AAYA 1, 27; CA 1-4R; CANR 1, 24,
38, 55; CLC 35; DLB 52; JRDA; MAICYA;
MTCW 1; SAAS 19; SATA 3, 49, 81

Aliki **9**
See also Brandenberg, Aliki Liacouras

Allan, Mabel Esther 1915-1998 .... **43**
See also CA 5-8R; 167; CANR 2, 18, 47;
MAICYA; SAAS 11; SATA 5, 32, 75

Allen, Adam
See Epstein, Beryl (M. Williams); Epstein, Samuel

Allen, Pamela 1934-............................ **44**
See also CA 126; CANR 53; SATA 50, 81

Andersen, Hans Christian 1805-1875 .... **6**
See also DA; DAB; DAC; DAM MST, POP;
MAICYA; NCLC 7; SATA 100; SSC 6; WLC;
YABC 1

Angeli, Marguerite (Lofft) de
See de Angeli, Marguerite (Lofft)

Angell, Judie
See Gaberman, Judie Angell

Angelou, Maya 1928- **53**
See also Johnson, Marguerite (Annie)
See also AAYA 7, 20; BLC 1; BW 2; CA 65-68;
CANR 19, 42, 65; CLC 12, 35, 64, 77; DA;
DAB; DAC; DAM MST, MULT, POET, POP;
DLB 38; MTCW 1; SATA 49; WLCS

Anglund, Joan Walsh 1926-.................... **1**
See also CA 5-8R; CANR 15; SATA 2

Anno, Mitsumasa 1926-.................... **2, 14**
See also CA 49-52; CANR 4, 44; MAICYA; SATA
5, 38, 77

Anthony, John
See Ciardi, John (Anthony)

Ardizzone, Edward (Jeffrey Irving) 1900-
1979 .... **3**
See also CA 5-8R; 89-92; CANR 8; DLB 160;
MAICYA; SATA 1, 28; SATA-Obit 21

Armstrong, William H(oward) 1914- **1**
See also AAYA 18; AITN 1; CA 17-20R; CANR
9, 69; JRDA; MAICYA; SAAS 7; SATA 4

Arnold, Emily 1939-
See McCully, Emily Arnold
See also CA 109; MAICYA; SATA 50, 76

Arnosky, James Edward 1946- **15**
See also Arnosky, Jim
See also CA 69-72; CANR 12, 32; SATA 22

Arnosky, Jim
See Arnosky, James Edward
See also MAICYA; SATA 70

Arrick, Fran
See Gaberman, Judie Angell
See also CLC 30

Aruego, Jose (Espiritu) 1932- **5**
See also CA 37-40R; CANR 42; MAICYA; SATA 6,
68

Arundel, Honor (Morfydd) 1919-1973 .... **35**
See also CA 21-22; 41-44R; CAP 2; CLC 17;
SATA 4; SATA-Obit 24

Ashabranner, Brent (Kenneth) 1921-...... **28**
See also AAYA 6; CA 5-8R; CANR 10, 27,
57; JRDA; MAICYA; SAAS 14; SATA 1,
67

Asheron, Sara
See Moore, Lilian

Ashey, Bella
See Breinburg, Petronella

Ashley, Bernard 1935-............................ **4**
See also CA 93-96; CANR 25, 44; MAICYA;
SATA 47, 79; SATA-Brief 39

Asimov, Isaac 1920-1992 .... **12**
See also AAYA 13; BEST 90:2; CA 1-4R; 137;
CANR 2, 19, 36, 60; CLC 1, 3, 9, 19, 26,
76, 92; DAM POP; DLB 8; DLBY 92; INT
CANR-19; JRDA; MAICYA; MTCW 1; SATA
1, 26, 74

Atwater, Florence (Hasseltine Carroll) 1896-
1979 .... **19**
See also CA 135; MAICYA; SATA 16, 66

Atwater, Richard (Tupper) 1892-1948..... **19**
See also CA 111; 135; MAICYA; SATA 54, 66;
SATA-Brief 27

Avi **24**
See also Wortis, Avi
See also AAYA 10; SATA 71

Awdry, Wilbert Vere 1911-1997 .... **23**
See also CA 103; 157; DLB 160; SATA 94

Aylesworth, Thomas G(ibbons) 1927-1995 ... **6**
See also CA 25-28R; 149; CANR 10, 26; SAAS
17; SATA 4, 88

Ayme, Marcel (Andre) 1902-1967 .... **25**
See also CA 89-92; CANR 67; CLC 11; DLB 72;
SATA 91

Babbitt, Natalie (Zane Moore) 1932-... **2, 53**
See also CA 49-52; CANR 2, 19, 38; DLB 52;
JRDA; MAICYA; SAAS 5; SATA 6, 68

Bacon, Martha Sherman 1917-1981 .... **3**
See also CA 85-88; 104; SATA 18; SATA-
Obit 27

Bahlke, Valerie Worth 1933-1994
See Worth, Valerie
See also CA 41-44R; 146; CANR 15, 44; SATA 81

Baillie, Allan (Stuart) 1943- **49**
See also AAYA 25; CA 118; CANR 42; SAAS
21; SATA 87

Baker, Jeannie 1950-........................... **28**
See also CA 97-100; CANR 69; SATA 23, 88

Bancroft, Laura
See Baum, L(yman) Frank

Bang, Garrett
See Bang, Molly Garrett

Bang, Molly Garrett 1943- **8**
See also CA 102; MAICYA; SATA 24, 69

Banks, Lynne Reid
See Reid Banks, Lynne
See also AAYA 6; CLC 23

Banner, Angela **24**
See also Maddison, Angela Mary

Bannerman, Helen (Brodie Cowan Watson)
1862(?)-1946 .... **21**
See also CA 111; 136; DLB 141; MAICYA;
SATA 19

Barklem, Jill 1951-............................. **31**
See also CA 161; SATA 96

Barrie, J(ames) M(atthew) 1860-1937 .... **16**
See also CA 104; 136; CDBLB 1890-1914; DAB;
DAM DRAM; DLB 10, 141, 156; MAICYA;
SATA 100; TCLC 2; YABC 1

Base, Graeme (Rowland) 1958- **22**
See also CA 134; CANR 69; MAICYA; SATA
67, 101

Bashevis, Isaac
See Singer, Isaac Bashevis

Baum, L(yman) Frank 1856-1919 .... **15**
See also CA 108; 133; DLB 22; JRDA; MAICYA;
MTCW 1; SATA 18, 100; TCLC 7

Baum, Louis F.
See Baum, L(yman) Frank

Baumann, Hans 1914-........................ **35**
See also CA 5-8R; CANR 3; SATA 2

Bawden, Nina (Mary Mabey) 1925- **2, 51**
See also Kark, Nina Mary (Mabey)
See also CA 17-20R; CANR 8, 29, 54; DAB;
DLB 14, 161; JRDA; MAICYA; SAAS 16;
SATA 72

Baylor, Byrd 1924- **3**
See also CA 81-84; MAICYA; SATA 16, 69

Beckman, Gunnel 1910- **25**
See also CA 33-36R; CANR 15; CLC 26;
MAICYA; SAAS 9; SATA 6

Bedard, Michael 1949- **35**
See also AAYA 22; CA 159; SATA 93

Belaney, Archibald Stansfeld 1888-1938
See Grey Owl
See also CA 114; DLBD 17; SATA 24

Bellairs, John (A.) 1938-1991 .... **37**
See also CA 21-24R; 133; CANR 8, 24; JRDA;
MAICYA; SATA 2, 68; SATA-Obit 66

Bemelmans, Ludwig 1898-1962 .... **6**
See also CA 73-76; DLB 22; MAICYA; SATA 15,
100

Benary, Margot
See Benary-Isbert, Margot

Benary-Isbert, Margot 1889-1979 .... **12**
See also CA 5-8R; 89-92; CANR 4, 72; CLC 12;
MAICYA; SATA 2; SATA-Obit 21

Bendick, Jeanne 1919- **5**
See also CA 5-8R; CANR 2, 48; MAICYA; SAAS
4; SATA 2, 68

Berenstain, Jan(ice) 1923-.................... **19**
See also CA 25-28R; CANR 14, 36; MAICYA;
SAAS 20; SATA 12, 64

Berenstain, Stan(ley) 1923- **19**
See also CA 25-28R; CANR 14, 36; MAICYA;
SAAS 20; SATA 12, 64

Berger, Melvin H. 1927- **32**
See also CA 5-8R; CANR 4; CLC 12; SAAS 2;
SATA 5, 88

Berna, Paul 1910-1994 .... **19**
See also CA 73-76; 143; SATA 15; SATA-Obit
78

Berry, James 1925-............................. **22**
See also CA 135; JRDA; SATA 67

Beskow, Elsa (Maartman) 1874-1953 ...... **17**
See also CA 135; MAICYA; SATA 20

Bess, Clayton 1944- **39**
See also Locke, Robert

Bethancourt, T. Ernesto **3**
See also Paisley, Tom
See also AAYA 20; SATA 11

Bianco, Margery (Williams) 1881-1944 ..... **19**
See also CA 109; 155; DLB 160; MAICYA;
SATA 15

Bickerstaff, Isaac
See Swift, Jonathan

Biegel, Paul 1925- **27**
See also CA 77-80; CANR 14, 32, 73; SAAS 18;
SATA 16, 79

Billout, Guy (Rene) 1941- **33**
See also CA 85-88; CANR 26; SATA 10

Biro, B(alint) S(tephen) 1921-
See Biro, Val
See also CA 25-28R; CANR 11, 39; MAICYA;
SATA 67

Biro, Val **28**
See also Biro, B(alint) S(tephen)
See also SAAS 13; SATA 1

Bjoerk, Christina 1938-...................... **22**
See also CA 135; SATA 67, 99

Bjork, Christina
See Bjoerk, Christina

Blades, Ann (Sager) 1947- **15**
See also CA 77-80; CANR 13, 48; JRDA;
MAICYA; SATA 16, 69

Blake, Quentin (Saxby) 1932- **31**
See also CA 25-28R; CANR 11, 37, 67; MAICYA;
SATA 9, 52, 96

Blake, William 1757-1827 .... **52**
See also CDBLB 1789-1832; DA; DAB; DAC;
DAM MST, POET; DLB 93, 163; MAICYA;
NCLC 13, 37, 57; PC 12; SATA 30; WLC

Bland, E.
See Nesbit, E(dith)

Bland, Edith Nesbit
See Nesbit, E(dith)

Bland, Fabian
See Nesbit, E(dith)

Block, Francesca (Lia) 1962- **33**
See also AAYA 13; CA 131; CANR 56; SAAS
21; SATA 80

Blos, Joan W(insor) 1928- **18**
See also CA 101; CANR 21; JRDA; MAICYA;
SAAS 11; SATA 33, 69; SATA-Brief 27

Blue, Zachary
See Stine, R(obert) L(awrence)

Blumberg, Rhoda 1917-...................... **21**
See also CA 65-68; CANR 9, 26; MAICYA;
SATA 35, 70

Blume, Judy (Sussman) 1938-............. **2, 15**
See also AAYA 3, 26; CA 29-32R; CANR 13, 37,
66; CLC 12, 30; DAM NOV, POP; DLB 52;
JRDA; MAICYA; MTCW 1; SATA 2, 31, 79

Blutig, Eduard
See Gorey, Edward (St. John)

Blyton, Enid (Mary) 1897-1968 .... **31**
See also CA 77-80; 25-28R; CANR 33; DLB 160;
MAICYA; SATA 25

Bodker, Cecil 1927- **23**
See also CA 73-76; CANR 13, 44; CLC 21;
MAICYA; SATA 14

Bolton, Elizabeth
See St. John, Nicole

Bond, (Thomas) Michael 1926- **1**
See also CA 5-8R; CANR 4, 24, 49; MAICYA;
SAAS 3; SATA 6, 58

Bond, Nancy (Barbara) 1945- **11**
See also CA 65-68; CANR 9, 36; JRDA;
MAICYA; SAAS 13; SATA 22, 82

Bontemps, Arna(ud Wendell) 1902-1973 ... **6**
See also BLC 1; BW 1; CA 1-4R; 41-44R; CANR
4, 35; CLC 1, 18; DAM MULT, NOV, POET;
DLB 48, 51; JRDA; MAICYA; MTCW 1;
SATA 2, 44; SATA-Obit 24

Bookman, Charlotte
See Zolotow, Charlotte S(hapiro)

Boston, L(ucy) M(aria Wood) 1892-1990 ..... **3**
See also CA 73-76; 131; CANR 58; DLB 161;
JRDA; MAICYA; SATA 19; SATA-Obit 64

Boutet de Monvel, (Louis) M(aurice)
1850(?)-1913 .... **32**
See also SATA 30

Bova, Ben(jamin William) 1932- **3**
See also AAYA 16; CA 5-8R; CAAS 18; CANR
11, 56; CLC 45; DLBY 81; INT CANR-11;
MAICYA; MTCW 1; SATA 6, 68

Bowler, Jan Brett
See Brett, Jan (Churchill)

Boyd, Candy Dawson 1946- **50**
See also BW 2; CA 138; JRDA; SATA 72

Brancato, Robin F(idler) 1936- **32**
See also AAYA 9; CA 69-72; CANR 11, 45; CLC
35; JRDA; SAAS 9; SATA 97

Brandenberg, Aliki Liacouras 1929-
See Aliki
See also CA 1-4R; CANR 4, 12, 30; MAICYA;
SATA 2, 35, 75

Branley, Franklyn M(ansfield) 1915- **13**
See also CA 33-36R; CANR 14, 39; CLC 21;
MAICYA; SAAS 16; SATA 4, 68

Breinburg, Petronella 1927- **31**
See also CA 53-56; CANR 4; SATA 11

Brett, Jan (Churchill) 1949- **27**
See also CA 116; CANR 41; MAICYA; SATA
42, 71

Bridgers, Sue Ellen 1942- **18**
See also AAYA 8; CA 65-68; CANR 11, 36; CLC
26; DLB 52; JRDA; MAICYA; SAAS 1; SATA
22, 90

Briggs, Raymond Redvers 1934- **10**
See also CA 73-76; CANR 70; MAICYA; SATA
23, 66

Brink, Carol Ryrie 1895-1981 .... **30**
See also CA 1-4R; 104; CANR 3, 65; JRDA;
MAICYA; SATA 1, 31, 100; SATA-Obit 27

Brinsmead, H(esba) F(ay) 1922- **47**
See also CA 21-24R; CANR 10; CLC 21;
MAICYA; SAAS 5; SATA 18, 78

Brooke, L(eonard) Leslie 1862-1940 .... **20**
See also DLB 141; MAICYA; SATA 17

Brooks, Bruce 1950- **25**
See also AAYA 8; CA 137; JRDA; MAICYA;
SATA 72; SATA-Brief 53

Brooks, George
See Baum, L(yman) Frank

Brooks, Gwendolyn 1917- **27**
See also AAYA 20; AITN 1; BLC 1; BW 2; CA
1-4R; CANR 1, 27, 52; CDALB 1941-1968;
CLC 1, 2, 4, 5, 15, 49; DA; DAC; DAM MST,
MULT, POET; DLB 5, 76, 165; MTCW 1;
PC 7; SATA 6; WLC

Brown, Marc (Tolon) 1946- **29**
See also CA 69-72; CANR 36; MAICYA; SATA
10, 53, 80

Brown, Marcia 1918- **12**
See also CA 41-44R; CANR 46; DLB 61;
MAICYA; SATA 7, 47

Brown, Margaret Wise 1910-1952 .... **10**
See also CA 108; 136; DLB 22; MAICYA; SATA
100; YABC 2

Brown, Roderick (Langmere) Haig-
See Haig-Brown, Roderick (Langmere)

Browne, Anthony (Edward Tudor) 1946-... **19**
See also CA 97-100; CANR 36; MAICYA; SATA
45, 61; SATA-Brief 44

Bruchac, Joseph III 1942- **46**
See also AAYA 19; CA 33-36R; CANR 13, 47;
DAM MULT; JRDA; NNAL; SATA 42, 89

Bruna, Dick 1927- **7**
See also CA 112; CANR 36; MAICYA; SATA
43, 76; SATA-Brief 30

Brunhoff, Jean de 1899-1937 .... **4**
See also CA 118; 137; MAICYA; SATA 24

Brunhoff, Laurent de 1925- **4**
See also CA 73-76; CANR 45; MAICYA; SATA 24,
71

Bryan, Ashley F. 1923- **18**
See also BW 2; CA 107; CANR 26, 43; MAICYA;
SATA 31, 72

Buffie, Margaret 1945- **39**
See also AAYA 23; CA 160; JRDA; SATA 71

Bunting, Anne Evelyn 1928-
See Bunting, Eve
See also AAYA 5; CA 53-56; CANR 5, 19, 59; SATA
18

Bunting, Eve **28**
See also Bunting, Anne Evelyn
See also JRDA; MAICYA; SATA 64

Burnett, Frances (Eliza) Hodgson 1849-
1924 .... **24**
See also CA 108; 136; DLB 42, 141; DLBD 13,
14; JRDA; MAICYA; SATA 100; YABC 2

Burnford, S. D.
See Burnford, Sheila (Philip Cochrane Every)

Burnford, Sheila (Philip Cochrane Every) 1918-
1984 .... **2**
See also CA 1-4R; 112; CANR 1, 49; JRDA;
MAICYA; SATA 3; SATA-Obit 38

Burningham, John (Mackintosh) 1936-..... **9**
See also CA 73-76; CANR 36; MAICYA; SATA
16, 59

Burton, Hester (Wood-Hill) 1913- **1**
See also CA 9-12R; CANR 10; DLB 161;
MAICYA; SAAS 8; SATA 7, 74

Burton, Virginia Lee 1909-1968 .... **11**
See also CA 13-14; 25-28R; CAP 1; DLB 22;
MAICYA; SATA 2, 100

Byars, Betsy (Cromer) 1928- **1, 16**
See also AAYA 19; CA 33-36R; CANR 18, 36,
57; CLC 35; DLB 52; INT CANR-18; JRDA;
MAICYA; MTCW 1; SAAS 1; SATA 4, 46,
80

Caines, Jeannette (Franklin) 1938- **24**
See also BW 2; CA 152; SATA 78; SATA-Brief
43

Caldecott, Randolph (J.) 1846-1886 .... **14**
See also DLB 163; MAICYA; SATA 17, 100

Calhoun, Mary **42**
See also Wilkins, Mary Huiskamp
See also SATA 2

Calvert, John
See Leaf, (Wilbur) Munro

Cameron, Eleanor (Frances) 1912-1996 .... **1**
See also CA 1-4R; 154; CANR 2, 22; DLB 52;
JRDA; MAICYA; MTCW 1; SAAS 10; SATA
1, 25; SATA-Obit 93

Campbell, Bruce
See Epstein, Samuel

Carigiet, Alois 1902-1985 .... **38**
See also CA 73-76; 119; SATA 24; SATA-Obit 47

Carle, Eric 1929- **10**
See also CA 25-28R; CANR 10, 25; MAICYA;
SAAS 6; SATA 4, 65

Carroll, Lewis **2, 18**
See also Dodgson, Charles Lutwidge
See also CDBLB 1832-1890; DLB 18, 163, 178;
JRDA; NCLC 2, 53; PC 18; WLC

Carter, Alden R(ichardson) 1947- **22**
See also AAYA 17; CA 135; CANR 58; SAAS
18; SATA 67

Carwell, L'Ann
See McKissack, Patricia (L'Ann) C(arwell)

Cassedy, Sylvia 1930-1989 .... **26**
See also CA 105; CANR 22; JRDA; SATA 27,
77; SATA-Obit 61

Causley, Charles (Stanley) 1917- **30**
See also CA 9-12R; CANR 5, 35; CLC 7; DLB
27; MTCW 1; SATA 3, 66

Chambers, Catherine E.
See St. John, Nicole

Chambers, Kate
See St. John, Nicole

Charles, Nicholas J.
See Kuskin, Karla (Seidman)

Charlip, Remy 1929- **8**
See also CA 33-36R; CANR 44; MAICYA; SATA
4, 68

Chase, Alice
See McHargue, Georgess

Chauncy, Nan(cen Beryl Masterman) 1900-
1970 .... **6**
See also CA 1-4R; CANR 4; MAICYA; SATA 6

Childress, Alice 1920-1994 .... **14**
See also AAYA 8; BLC 1; BW 2; CA 45-48; 146;
CANR 3, 27, 50; CLC 12, 15, 86, 96; DAM
DRAM, MULT, NOV; DC 4; DLB 7, 38;
JRDA; MAICYA; MTCW 1; SATA 7, 48, 81

Chimaera
See Farjeon, Eleanor

Choi, Sook Nyul **53**
See also SATA 73

Christie, (Ann) Philippa
See Pearce, Philippa
See also CA 5-8R; CANR 4

Christopher, John 2
See also Youd, (Christopher) Samuel
See also AAYA 22

Christopher, Matt(hew Frederick) 1917-
1997 33
See also CA 1-4R; 161; CANR 5, 36; JRDA;
MAICYA; SAAS 9; SATA 2, 47, 80; SATA-
Obit 99

Ciardi, John (Anthony) 1916-1986 19
See also CA 5-8R; 118; CAAS 2; CANR 5, 33;
CLC 10, 40, 44; DAM POET; DLB 5; DLBY
86; INT CANR-5; MAICYA; MTCW 1; SAAS
26; SATA 1, 65; SATA-Obit 46

Clark, Ann Nolan 1896-1995 16
See also CA 5-8R; 150; CANR 2, 48; DLB 52;
MAICYA; SAAS 16; SATA 4, 82; SATA-
Obit 87

Clark, M. R.
See Clark, Mavis Thorpe

Clark, Mavis Thorpe 1909- 30
See also CA 57-60; CANR 8, 37; CLC 12;
MAICYA; SAAS 5; SATA 8, 74

Clarke, Pauline 1921- 28
See also CANR 45; DLB 161; MAICYA

Cleary, Beverly (Atlee Bunn) 1916- 2, 8
See also AAYA 6; CA 1-4R; CANR 2, 19, 36,
66; DLB 52; INT CANR-19; JRDA; MAICYA;
MTCW 1; SAAS 20; SATA 2, 43, 79

Cleaver, Bill 6
See also DLB 52; SATA 22; SATA-Obit 27

Cleaver, Elizabeth (Mrazik) 1939-1985 13
See also CA 97-100; 117; SATA 23; SATA-Obit 43

Cleaver, Vera (Allen) 1919-1992 6
See also AAYA 12; CA 73-76; 161; CANR 38;
DLB 52; JRDA; MAICYA; SATA 22, 76

Clerk, N. W.
See Lewis, C(live) S(taples)

Clifton, (Thelma) Lucille 1936- 5
See also BLC 1; BW 2; CA 49-52; CANR 2, 24, 42;
CLC 19, 66; DAM MULT, POET; DLB 5, 41;
MAICYA; MTCW 1; PC 17; SATA 20, 69

Coatsworth, Elizabeth (Jane) 1893-1986 2
See also CA 5-8R; 120; CANR 4; DLB 22;
MAICYA; SATA 2, 56, 100; SATA-Obit 49

Cobalt, Martin
See Mayne, William (James Carter)

Cobb, Vicki 1938- 2
See also CA 33-36R; CANR 14; JRDA; MAICYA;
SAAS 6; SATA 8, 69

Coe, Douglas
See Epstein, Beryl (M. Williams); Epstein, Samuel

Cohen, Daniel (E.) 1936- 3, 43
See also AAYA 7; CA 45-48; CANR 1, 20, 44;
JRDA; MAICYA; SAAS 4; SATA 8, 70

Cole, Brock 1938- 18
See also AAYA 15; CA 136; JRDA; MAICYA;
SATA 72

Cole, Joanna 1944- 5, 40
See also CA 115; CANR 36, 55, 70; MAICYA;
SATA 49, 81; SATA-Brief 37

Colin, Ann
See Ure, Jean

Collier, James L(incoln) 1928- 3
See also AAYA 13; CA 9-12R; CANR 4, 33, 60;
CLC 30; DAM POP; JRDA; MAICYA; SAAS
21; SATA 8, 70

Collodi, Carlo 1826-1890 5
See also Lorenzini, Carlo
See also NCLC 54

Colt, Martin
See Epstein, Beryl (M. Williams); Epstein,
Samuel

Colum, Padraic 1881-1972 36
See also CA 73-76; 33-36R; CANR 35; CLC 28;
MAICYA; MTCW 1; SATA 15

Conford, Ellen 1942- 10
See also AAYA 10; CA 33-36R; CANR 13, 29,
54; JRDA; MAICYA; SATA 6, 68

Conly, Robert Leslie 1918(?)-1973
See O'Brien, Robert C.
See also CA 73-76; 41-44R; MAICYA; SATA 23

Conrad, Pam 1947-1996 18
See also AAYA 18; CA 121; 151; CANR 36;
JRDA; MAICYA; SAAS 19; SATA 52, 80;
SATA-Brief 49; SATA-Obit 90

Cooke, Ann
See Cole, Joanna

Cooke, John Estes
See Baum, L(yman) Frank

Cooney, Barbara 1917- 23
See also CA 5-8R; CANR 3, 37, 67; MAICYA;
SATA 6, 59, 96

Cooper, Susan (Mary) 1935- 4
See also AAYA 13; CA 29-32R; CANR 15, 37,
63; DLB 161; JRDA; MAICYA; SAAS 6;
SATA 4, 64

Corbett, Scott 1913- 1
See also CA 1-4R; CANR 1, 23; JRDA; MAICYA;
SAAS 2; SATA 2, 42

Corbett, W(illiam) J(esse) 1938- 19
See also CA 137; MAICYA; SATA 50, 102; SATA-
Brief 44

Corcoran, Barbara 1911- 50
See also AAYA 14; CA 21-24R; CAAS 2; CANR
11, 28, 48; CLC 17; DLB 52; JRDA; SAAS
20; SATA 3, 77

Cormier, Robert (Edmund) 1925- 12
See also AAYA 3, 19; CA 1-4R; CANR 5, 23;
CDALB 1968-1988; CLC 12, 30; DA; DAB;
DAC; DAM MST, NOV; DLB 52; INT CANR-
23; JRDA; MAICYA; MTCW 1; SATA 10,
45, 83

Cowles, Kathleen
See Krull, Kathleen

Cox, Palmer 1840-1924 24
See also CA 111; DLB 42; SATA 24

Creech, Sharon 1945- 42
See also AAYA 21; CA 159; SATA 94

Cresswell, Helen 1934- 18
See also AAYA 25; CA 17-20R; CANR 8, 37;
DLB 161; JRDA; MAICYA; SAAS 20; SATA
1, 48, 79

Crew, Gary 1947- 42
See also AAYA 17; CA 142; SATA 75

Crews, Donald 7
See also CA 108; MAICYA; SATA 32, 76; SATA-
Brief 30

Cross, Gillian (Clare) 1945- 28
See also AAYA 24; CA 111; CANR 38;
DLB 161; JRDA; MAICYA; SATA 38,
71

Crossley-Holland, Kevin 1941- 47
See also CA 41-44R; CANR 47; DLB 40, 161;
MAICYA; SAAS 20; SATA 5, 74

Crutcher, Chris(topher C.) 1946- 28
See also AAYA 9; CA 113; CANR 36; JRDA;
MAICYA; SATA 52, 99

Cummings, Pat (Marie) 1950- 48
See also BW 2; CA 122; CANR 44; MAICYA;
SAAS 13; SATA 42, 71

Curry, Jane L(ouise) 1932- 31
See also CA 17-20R; CANR 7, 24, 44; MAICYA;
SAAS 6; SATA 1, 52, 90

Dahl, Roald 1916-1990 .... 1, 7, 41
See also AAYA 15; CA 1-4R; 133; CANR 6,
32, 37, 62; CLC 1, 6, 18, 79; DAB; DAC;
DAM MST, NOV, POP; DLB 139; JRDA;
MAICYA; MTCW 1; SATA 1, 26, 73; SATA-
Obit 65

Dale, George E.
See Asimov, Isaac

Daly, Nicholas 1946- 41
See also Daly, Niki
See also CA 111; CANR 36; MAICYA; SATA 37,
76

Daly, Niki
See Daly, Nicholas
See also SAAS 21

Dangerfield, Balfour
See McCloskey, (John) Robert

Danziger, Paula 1944- 20
See also AAYA 4; CA 112; 115; CANR 37; CLC
21; JRDA; MAICYA; SATA 36, 63, 102;
SATA-Brief 30

Darling, Sandra
See Day, Alexandra

d'Aulaire, Edgar Parin 1898-1986 21
See also CA 49-52; 119; CANR 29; DLB 22;
MAICYA; SATA 5, 66; SATA-Obit 47

d'Aulaire, Ingri (Mortenson Parin) 1904-1980 .... **21**
See also CA 49-52; 102; CANR 29; DLB 22; MAICYA; SATA 5, 66; SATA-Obit 24

Day, Alexandra **22**
See also CA 136; SAAS 19; SATA 67, 97

de Angeli, Marguerite (Lofft) 1889-1987 ..... **1**
See also AITN 2; CA 5-8R; 122; CANR 3; DLB 22; MAICYA; SATA 1, 27, 100; SATA-Obit 51

de Brissac, Malcolm
See Dickinson, Peter (Malcolm)

de Brunhoff, Jean
See Brunhoff, Jean de

De Brunhoff, Laurent
See Brunhoff, Laurent de

DeClements, Barthe 1920-...................... **23**
See also CA 105; CANR 22, 45; JRDA; SATA 35, 71

DeJong, Meindert 1906-1991 .... **1**
See also CA 13-16R; 134; CANR 36; DLB 52; MAICYA; SATA 2; SATA-Obit 68

de la Mare, Walter (John) 1873-1956...... **23**
See also CA 163; CDBLB 1914-1945; DAB; DAC; DAM MST, POET; DLB 162; SATA 16; SSC 14; TCLC 4, 53; WLC

Delving, Michael
See Williams, Jay

Demijohn, Thom
See Disch, Thomas M(ichael)

Denslow, W(illiam) W(allace) 1856-1915 .... **15**
See also DLB 188; SATA 16

dePaola, Thomas Anthony 1934-
See dePaola, Tomie
See also CA 49-52; CANR 2, 37; MAICYA; SATA 11, 59

dePaola, Tomie **4, 24**
See also dePaola, Thomas Anthony
See also DLB 61; SAAS 15

Derry Down Derry
See Lear, Edward

Dhondy, Farrukh 1944- **41**
See also AAYA 24; CA 132; MAICYA; SATA 65

Dickinson, Peter (Malcolm) 1927-.......... **29**
See also AAYA 9; CA 41-44R; CANR 31, 58; CLC 12, 35; DLB 87, 161; JRDA; MAICYA; SATA 5, 62, 95

Dillon, Diane 1933-.......................... **44**
See also MAICYA; SATA 15, 51

Dillon, Eilis 1920-1994 .... **26**
See also CA 9-12R; 147; CAAS 3; CANR 4, 38; CLC 17; MAICYA; SATA 2, 74; SATA-Obit 83

Dillon, Leo 1933- **44**
See also MAICYA; SATA 15, 51

Disch, Thomas M(ichael) 1940-............. **18**
See also AAYA 17; CA 21-24R; CAAS 4; CANR 17, 36, 54; CLC 7, 36; DLB 8; MAICYA; MTCW 1; SAAS 15; SATA 92

Disch, Tom
See Disch, Thomas M(ichael)

Dixon, Paige
See Corcoran, Barbara

Doctor X
See Nourse, Alan E(dward)

Dodgson, Charles Lutwidge 1832-1898 ..... **2**
See also Carroll, Lewis
See also DA; DAB; DAC; DAM MST, NOV, POET; MAICYA; SATA 100; YABC 2

Dogyear, Drew
See Gorey, Edward (St. John)

Doherty, Berlie 1943-........................ **21**
See also AAYA 18; CA 131; JRDA; MAICYA; SAAS 16; SATA 72

Domanska, Janina 1913(?)-1995 .... **40**
See also AITN 1; CA 17-20R; 147; CANR 11, 45; MAICYA; SAAS 18; SATA 6, 68; SATA-Obit 84

Donovan, John 1928-1992 .... **3**
See also AAYA 20; CA 97-100; 137; CLC 35; MAICYA; SATA 72; SATA-Brief 29

Dorritt, Susan
See Schlein, Miriam

Dorros, Arthur (M.) 1950-................... **42**
See also CA 146; SAAS 20; SATA 78

Dowdy, Mrs. Regera
See Gorey, Edward (St. John)

Doyle, Brian 1935- **22**
See also AAYA 16; CA 135; CANR 55; JRDA; MAICYA; SAAS 16; SATA 67

Dr. A
See Asimov, Isaac; Silverstein, Alvin

Dr. Seuss **1, 9, 53**
See also Geisel, Theodor Seuss; LeSieg, Theo.; Seuss, Dr.; Stone, Rosetta

Drapier, M. B.
See Swift, Jonathan

Drescher, Henrik 1955- **20**
See also CA 135; MAICYA; SATA 67

Driving Hawk, Virginia
See Sneve, Virginia Driving Hawk

Dryden, Pamela
See St. John, Nicole

Duder, Tessa 1940- **43**
See also CA 147; SAAS 23; SATA 80

Duke, Kate 1956- **51**
See also SATA 90

Duncan, Lois 1934- **29**
See also AAYA 4; CA 1-4R; CANR 2, 23, 36; CLC 26; JRDA; MAICYA; SAAS 2; SATA 1, 36, 75

Dunne, Marie
See Clark, Ann Nolan

Duvoisin, Roger Antoine 1904-1980 .... **23**
See also CA 13-16R; 101; CANR 11; DLB 61; MAICYA; SATA 2, 30; SATA-Obit 23

Eager, Edward McMaken 1911-1964 ...... **43**
See also CA 73-76; DLB 22; MAICYA; SATA 17

Eckert, Horst 1931-
See Janosch
See also CA 37-40R; CANR 38; MAICYA; SATA 8, 72

Edgy, Wardore
See Gorey, Edward (St. John)

Edmund, Sean
See Pringle, Laurence (Patrick)

Edwards, Al
See Nourse, Alan E(dward)

Ehlert, Lois (Jane) 1934- **28**
See also CA 137; MAICYA; SATA 35, 69

Ellen, Jaye
See Nixon, Joan Lowery

Ellis, Sarah 1952-............................. **42**
See also CA 123; CANR 50; JRDA; SATA 68

Emberley, Barbara A(nne) 1932-............. **5**
See also CA 5-8R; CANR 5; MAICYA; SATA 8, 70

Emberley, Ed(ward Randolph) 1931-........ **5**
See also CA 5-8R; CANR 5, 36; MAICYA; SATA 8, 70

Ende, Michael (Andreas Helmuth) 1929-1995 .... **14**
See also CA 118; 124; 149; CANR 36; CLC 31; DLB 75; MAICYA; SATA 61; SATA-Brief 42; SATA-Obit 86

Engdahl, Sylvia Louise 1933-.................. **2**
See also CA 29-32R; CANR 14; JRDA; MAICYA; SAAS 5; SATA 4

Enright, Elizabeth 1909-1968.................. **4**
See also CA 61-64; 25-28R; DLB 22; MAICYA; SATA 9

Epstein, Beryl (M. Williams) 1910-........ **26**
See also CA 5-8R; CANR 2, 18, 39; SAAS 17; SATA 1, 31

Epstein, Samuel 1909-........................ **26**
See also CA 9-12R; CANR 4, 18, 39; SAAS 17; SATA 1, 31

Estes, Eleanor 1906-1988 .... **2**
See also CA 1-4R; 126; CANR 5, 20; DLB 22; JRDA; MAICYA; SATA 7, 91; SATA-Obit 56

Estoril, Jean
See Allan, Mabel Esther

Ets, Marie Hall 1893-1984 .... **33**
See also CA 1-4R; CANR 4; DLB 22; MAICYA; SATA 2

Farjeon, Eleanor 1881-1965................... **34**
See also CA 11-12; CAP 1; DLB 160; MAICYA; SATA 2

Author Index

Farmer, Penelope (Jane) 1939- **8**
See also CA 13-16R; CANR 9, 37; DLB 161;
JRDA; MAICYA; SAAS 22; SATA 40; SATA-
Brief 39

Feelings, Muriel (Grey) 1938- **5**
See also BW 1; CA 93-96; MAICYA; SAAS 8;
SATA 16

Feelings, Thomas 1933-
See Feelings, Tom
See also BW 1; CA 49-52; CANR 25; MAICYA;
SATA 8

Feelings, Tom **5**
See also Feelings, Thomas
See also AAYA 25; SAAS 19; SATA 69

Ferry, Charles 1927- **34**
See also CA 97-100; CANR 16, 57; SAAS 20;
SATA 43, 92

Field, Rachel (Lyman) 1894-1942 .... **21**
See also CA 109; 137; DLB 9, 22; MAICYA;
SATA 15

Fine, Anne 1947- **25**
See also AAYA 20; CA 105; CANR 38; JRDA;
MAICYA; SAAS 15; SATA 29, 72

Fisher, Aileen (Lucia) 1906- **49**
See also CA 5-8R; CANR 2, 17, 37; MAICYA;
SATA 1, 25, 73

Fisher, Leonard Everett 1924- **18**
See also CA 1-4R; CANR 2, 37; DLB 61;
MAICYA; SAAS 1; SATA 4, 34, 73

Fitch, John IV
See Cormier, Robert (Edmund)

Fitzgerald, Captain Hugh
See Baum, L(yman) Frank

Fitzgerald, John D(ennis) 1907(?)-1988 ..... **1**
See also CA 93-96; 126; MAICYA; SATA 20;
SATA-Obit 56

Fitzhardinge, Joan Margaret 1912-
See Phipson, Joan
See also CA 13-16R; CANR 6, 23, 36; MAICYA;
SATA 2, 73

Fitzhugh, Louise 1928-1974 .... **1**
See also AAYA 18; CA 29-32; 53-56; CANR 34;
CAP 2; DLB 52; JRDA; MAICYA; SATA 1,
45; SATA-Obit 24

Flack, Marjorie 1897-1958 .... **28**
See also CA 112; 136; MAICYA; SATA 100;
YABC 2

Fleischman, Paul 1952- **20**
See also AAYA 11; CA 113; CANR 37; JRDA;
MAICYA; SAAS 20; SATA 39, 72; SATA-
Brief 32

Fleischman, (Albert) Sid(ney) 1920- **1, 15**
See also CA 1-4R; CANR 5, 37, 67; JRDA;
MAICYA; SATA 8, 59, 96

Forbes, Esther 1891-1967 .... **27**
See also AAYA 17; CA 13-14; 25-28R; CAP 1;
CLC 12; DLB 22; JRDA; MAICYA; SATA 2,
100

Foreman, Michael 1938- **32**
See also CA 21-24R; CANR 10, 38, 68; MAICYA;
SAAS 21; SATA 2, 73

Foster, Genevieve Stump 1893-1979 .... **7**
See also CA 5-8R; 89-92; CANR 4; DLB 61;
MAICYA; SATA 2; SATA-Obit 23

Fox, J. N.
See Janeczko, Paul B(ryan)

Fox, Mem **23**
See also Fox, Merrion Frances
See also MAICYA

Fox, Merrion Frances 1946-
See Fox, Mem
See also CA 127; SATA 51

Fox, Paula 1923- **1, 44**
See also AAYA 3; CA 73-76; CANR 20, 36, 62;
CLC 2, 8; DLB 52; JRDA; MAICYA; MTCW
1; SATA 17, 60

Freedman, Russell (Bruce) 1929- **20**
See also AAYA 4, 24; CA 17-20R; CANR 7, 23,
46; JRDA; MAICYA; SATA 16, 71

Freeman, Don 1908-1978 .... **30**
See also CA 77-80; CANR 44; MAICYA; SATA 17

French, Fiona 1944- **37**
See also CA 29-32R; CANR 40; MAICYA; SAAS
21; SATA 6, 75

French, Paul
See Asimov, Isaac

Fritz, Jean (Guttery) 1915- **2, 14**
See also CA 1-4R; CANR 5, 16, 37; DLB 52;
INT CANR-16; JRDA; MAICYA; SAAS 2;
SATA 1, 29, 72

Fujikawa, Gyo 1908-1998 .... **25**
See also CA 113; CANR 46; MAICYA; SAAS
16; SATA 39, 76; SATA-Brief 30

Fuller, Maud
See Petersham, Maud (Sylvia Fuller)

Gaberman, Judie Angell 1937- **33**
See also AAYA 11; CA 77-80; CANR 49; JRDA;
SATA 22, 78

Gag, Wanda (Hazel) 1893-1946 .... **4**
See also CA 113; 137; DLB 22; MAICYA; SATA
100; YABC 1

Galdone, Paul 1907(?)-1986 .... **16**
See also CA 73-76; 121; CANR 13; MAICYA;
SATA 17, 66; SATA-Obit 49

Gallant, Roy A(rthur) 1924- **30**
See also CA 5-8R; CANR 4, 29, 54; CLC 17;
MAICYA; SATA 4, 68

Gantos, Jack **18**
See also Gantos, John (Bryan), Jr.

Gantos, John (Bryan), Jr. 1951-
See Gantos, Jack
See also CA 65-68; CANR 15, 56; SATA 20, 81

Gard, Janice
See Latham, Jean Lee

Gardam, Jane 1928- **12**
See also CA 49-52; CANR 2, 18, 33, 54; CLC
43; DLB 14, 161; MAICYA; MTCW 1; SAAS
9; SATA 39, 76; SATA-Brief 28

Garden, Nancy 1938- **51**
See also AAYA 18; CA 33-36R; CANR 13, 30;
JRDA; SAAS 8; SATA 12, 77

Garfield, Leon 1921-1996 .... **21**
See also AAYA 8; CA 17-20R; 152; CANR 38,
41; CLC 12; DLB 161; JRDA; MAICYA;
SATA 1, 32, 76; SATA-Obit 90

Garner, Alan 1934- **20**
See also AAYA 18; CA 73-76; CANR 15, 64;
CLC 17; DAB; DAM POP; DLB 161;
MAICYA; MTCW 1; SATA 18, 69

Garnet, A. H.
See Slote, Alfred

Gay, Marie-Louise 1952- **27**
See also CA 135; SAAS 21; SATA 68

Gaze, Gillian
See Barklem, Jill

Geisel, Theodor Seuss 1904-1991
See Dr. Seuss
See also CA 13-16R; 135; CANR 13, 32; DLB
61; DLBY 91; MAICYA; MTCW 1; SATA 1,
28, 75, 100; SATA-Obit 67

George, Jean Craighead 1919- **1**
See also AAYA 8; CA 5-8R; CANR 25; CLC 35;
DLB 52; JRDA; MAICYA; SATA 2, 68

Gerrard, Roy 1935-1997 .... **23**
See also CA 110; 160; CANR 57; SATA 47, 90;
SATA-Brief 45; SATA-Obit 99

Gewe, Raddory
See Gorey, Edward (St. John)

Gibbons, Gail 1944- **8**
See also CA 69-72; CANR 12; MAICYA; SAAS
12; SATA 23, 72

Giblin, James Cross 1933- **29**
See also CA 106; CANR 24; MAICYA; SAAS
12; SATA 33, 75

Ginsburg, Mirra **45**
See also CA 17-20R; CANR 11, 28, 54; SATA 6,
92

Giovanni, Nikki 1943- **6**
See also AAYA 22; AITN 1; BLC 2; BW 2; CA
29-32R; CAAS 6; CANR 18, 41, 60; CLC 2,
4, 19, 64; DA; DAB; DAC; DAM MST, MULT,
POET; DLB 5, 41; INT CANR-18; MAICYA;
MTCW 1; PC 19; SATA 24; WLCS

Glenn, Mel 1943- **51**
See also AAYA 25; CA 123; CANR 49, 68; SATA
51, 93; SATA-Brief 45

Glubok, Shirley (Astor) **1**
See also CA 5-8R; CANR 4, 43; MAICYA; SAAS
7; SATA 6, 68

Goble, Paul 1933- **21**
See also CA 93-96; CANR 16; MAICYA; SATA 25,
69

Godden, (Margaret) Rumer 1907- **20**
See also AAYA 6; CA 5-8R; CANR 4, 27, 36, 55; CLC 53; DLB 161; MAICYA; SAAS 12; SATA 3, 36

Goffstein, (Marilyn) Brooke 1940- **3**
See also CA 21-24R; CANR 9, 28; DLB 61; MAICYA; SATA 8, 70

Goodall, John Strickland 1908-1996 ...... **25**
See also CA 33-36R; 152; MAICYA; SATA 4, 66; SATA-Obit 91

Gordon, Sheila 1927- **27**
See also CA 132; SATA 88

Gorey, Edward (St. John) 1925- **36**
See also CA 5-8R; CANR 9, 30; DLB 61; INT CANR-30; MAICYA; SATA 29, 70; SATA-Brief 27

Goscinny, Rene 1926-1977 .... **37**
See also CA 117; 113; SATA 47; SATA-Brief 39

Graham, Bob 1942- **31**
See also CA 165; SATA 63, 101

Graham, Lorenz (Bell) 1902-1989 .... **10**
See also BW 1; CA 9-12R; 129; CANR 25; DLB 76; MAICYA; SAAS 5; SATA 2, 74; SATA-Obit 63

Grahame, Kenneth 1859-1932 .... **5**
See also CA 108; 136; DAB; DLB 34, 141, 178; MAICYA; SATA 100; TCLC 64; YABC 1

Gramatky, Hardie 1907-1979 .... **22**
See also AITN 1; CA 1-4R; 85-88; CANR 3; DLB 22; MAICYA; SATA 1, 30; SATA-Obit 23

Greenaway, Kate 1846-1901 .... **6**
See also CA 137; DLB 141; MAICYA; SATA 100; YABC 2

Greene, Bette 1934- **2**
See also AAYA 7; CA 53-56; CANR 4; CLC 30; JRDA; MAICYA; SAAS 16; SATA 8, 102

Greenfield, Eloise 1929- **4, 38**
See also BW 2; CA 49-52; CANR 1, 19, 43; INT CANR-19; JRDA; MAICYA; SAAS 16; SATA 19, 61

Gregory, Jean
See Ure, Jean

Grewdead, Roy
See Gorey, Edward (St. John)

Grey Owl **32**
See also Belaney, Archibald Stansfeld
See also DLB 92

Grifalconi, Ann 1929- **35**
See also CA 5-8R; CANR 9, 35; MAICYA; SAAS 16; SATA 2, 66

Grimes, Nikki 1950- **42**
See also CA 77-80; CANR 60; SATA 93

Gripe, Maria (Kristina) 1923-................. **5**
See also CA 29-32R; CANR 17, 39; MAICYA; SATA 2, 74

Grode, Redway
See Gorey, Edward (St. John)

Gruelle, John (Barton) 1880-1938
See Gruelle, Johnny
See also CA 115; SATA 35; SATA-Brief 32

Gruelle, Johnny **34**
See also Gruelle, John (Barton)
See also DLB 22

Guillot, Rene 1900-1969 .... **22**
See also CA 49-52; CANR 39; SATA 7

Guy, Rosa (Cuthbert) 1928- **13**
See also AAYA 4; BW 2; CA 17-20R; CANR 14, 34; CLC 26; DLB 33; JRDA; MAICYA; SATA 14, 62

Haar, Jaap ter **15**
See also ter Haar, Jaap

Hadley, Lee 1934-1995........................ **40**
See also Irwin, Hadley
See also CA 101; 149; CANR 19, 36; MAICYA; SATA 47, 89; SATA-Brief 38; SATA-Obit 86

Haertling, Peter 1933-
See Hartling, Peter
See also CA 101; CANR 22, 48; DLB 75; MAICYA; SATA 66

Hagon, Priscilla
See Allan, Mabel Esther

Haig-Brown, Roderick (Langmere) 1908-1976 .... **31**
See also CA 5-8R; 69-72; CANR 4, 38; CLC 21; DLB 88; MAICYA; SATA 12

Haley, Gail E(inhart) 1939- **21**
See also CA 21-24R; CANR 14, 35; MAICYA; SAAS 13; SATA 43, 78; SATA-Brief 28

Hamilton, Clive
See Lewis, C(live) S(taples)

Hamilton, Gail
See Corcoran, Barbara

Hamilton, Virginia 1936- **1, 11, 40**
See also AAYA 2, 21; BW 2; CA 25-28R; CANR 20, 37, 73; CLC 26; DAM MULT; DLB 33, 52; INT CANR-20; JRDA; MAICYA; MTCW 1; SATA 4, 56, 79

Hamley, Dennis 1935- **47**
See also CA 57-60; CANR 11, 26; SAAS 22; SATA 39, 69

Handford, Martin (John) 1956- **22**
See also CA 137; MAICYA; SATA 64

Hansen, Joyce (Viola) 1942- **21**
See also BW 2; CA 105; CANR 43; JRDA; MAICYA; SAAS 15; SATA 46, 101; SATA-Brief 39

Hargrave, Leonie
See Disch, Thomas M(ichael)

Harris, Christie (Lucy) Irwin 1907- **47**
See also CA 5-8R; CANR 6; CLC 12; DLB 88; JRDA; MAICYA; SAAS 10; SATA 6, 74

Harris, Joel Chandler 1848-1908 .... **49**
See also CA 104; 137; DLB 11, 23, 42, 78, 91; MAICYA; SATA 100; SSC 19; TCLC 2; YABC 1

Harris, Lavinia
See St. John, Nicole

Harris, Rosemary (Jeanne) **30**
See also CA 33-36R; CANR 13, 30; SAAS 7; SATA 4, 82

Hartling, Peter **29**
See also Haertling, Peter
See also DLB 75

Haskins, James S. 1941- **3, 39**
See also Haskins, Jim
See also AAYA 14; BW 2; CA 33-36R; CANR 25, 48; JRDA; MAICYA; SATA 9, 69

Haskins, Jim
See Haskins, James S.
See also SAAS 4

Haugaard, Erik Christian 1923-............ **11**
See also CA 5-8R; CANR 3, 38; JRDA; MAICYA; SAAS 12; SATA 4, 68

Hautzig, Esther Rudomin 1930- **22**
See also CA 1-4R; CANR 5, 20, 46; JRDA; MAICYA; SAAS 15; SATA 4, 68

Hay, Timothy
See Brown, Margaret Wise

Haywood, Carolyn 1898-1990 .... **22**
See also CA 5-8R; 130; CANR 5, 20; MAICYA; SATA 1, 29, 75; SATA-Obit 64

Heine, Helme 1941- **18**
See also CA 135; MAICYA; SATA 67

Henkes, Kevin 1960- **23**
See also CA 114; CANR 38; MAICYA; SATA 43, 76

Henry, Marguerite 1902-1997 .... **4**
See also CA 17-20R; 162; CANR 9; DLB 22; JRDA; MAICYA; SAAS 7; SATA 100; SATA-Obit 99

Hentoff, Nat(han Irving) 1925- **1, 52**
See also AAYA 4; CA 1-4R; CAAS 6; CANR 5, 25; CLC 26; INT CANR-25; JRDA; MAICYA; SATA 42, 69; SATA-Brief 27

Herge **6**
See also Remi, Georges

Hesse, Karen 1952-............................ **54**
See also AAYA 27; CA 168; SATA 74

Highwater, Jamake (Mamake) 1942(?)- **17**
See also AAYA 7; CA 65-68; CAAS 7; CANR 10, 34; CLC 12; DLB 52; DLBY 85; JRDA; MAICYA; SATA 32, 69; SATA-Brief 30

Hill, Eric 1927-................................. **13**
See also CA 134; MAICYA; SATA 66; SATA-Brief 53

Hilton, Margaret Lynette 1946-
See Hilton, Nette
See also CA 136; SATA 68

Hilton, Nette 25
See also Hilton, Margaret Lynette
See also SAAS 21

Hinton, S(usan) E(loise) 1950- 3, 23
See also AAYA 2; CA 81-84; CANR 32, 62; CLC 30, 111; DA; DAB; DAC; DAM MST, NOV; JRDA; MAICYA; MTCW 1; SATA 19, 58

Ho, Minfong 1951- 28
See also CA 77-80; CANR 67; SATA 15, 94

Hoban, Russell (Conwell) 1925- 3
See also CA 5-8R; CANR 23, 37, 66; CLC 7, 25; DAM NOV; DLB 52; MAICYA; MTCW 1; SATA 1, 40, 78

Hoban, Tana 13
See also CA 93-96; CANR 23; MAICYA; SAAS 12; SATA 22, 70

Hoberman, Mary Ann 1930- 22
See also CA 41-44R; MAICYA; SAAS 18; SATA 5, 72

Hogrogian, Nonny 1932- 2
See also CA 45-48; CANR 2, 49; MAICYA; SAAS 1; SATA 7, 74

Holling, Holling C(lancy) 1900-1973 50
See also CA 106; MAICYA; SATA 15; SATA-Obit 26

Holton, Leonard
See Wibberley, Leonard (Patrick O'Connor)

Hopkins, Lee Bennett 1938- 44
See also AAYA 18; CA 25-28R; CANR 29, 55; JRDA; MAICYA; SAAS 4; SATA 3, 68

Houston, James A(rchibald) 1921- 3
See also AAYA 18; CA 65-68; CANR 38, 60; DAC; DAM MST; JRDA; MAICYA; SAAS 17; SATA 13, 74

Howe, James 1946- 9
See also CA 105; CANR 22, 46, 71; JRDA; MAICYA; SATA 29, 71

Howker, Janni 1957- 14
See also AAYA 9; CA 137; JRDA; MAICYA; SAAS 13; SATA 72; SATA-Brief 46

Hudson, Jan 1954-1990 40
See also AAYA 22; CA 136; JRDA; SATA 77

Hughes, Edward James
See Hughes, Ted
See also DAM MST, POET

Hughes, (James) Langston 1902-1967 17
See also AAYA 12; BLC 2; BW 1; CA 1-4R; 25-28R; CANR 1, 34; CDALB 1929-1941; CLC 1, 5, 10, 15, 35, 44, 108; DA; DAB; DAC; DAM DRAM, MST, MULT, POET; DC 3; DLB 4, 7, 48, 51, 86; JRDA; MAICYA; MTCW 1; PC 1; SATA 4, 33; SSC 6; WLC

Hughes, Monica (Ince) 1925- 9
See also AAYA 19; CA 77-80; CANR 23, 46; JRDA; MAICYA; SAAS 11; SATA 15, 70

Hughes, Shirley 1927- 15
See also CA 85-88; CANR 24, 47; MAICYA; SATA 16, 70

Hughes, Ted 1930- 3
See also Hughes, Edward James
See also CA 1-4R; CANR 1, 33, 66; CLC 2, 4, 9, 14, 37; DAB; DAC; DLB 40, 161; MAICYA; MTCW 1; PC 7; SATA 49; SATA-Brief 27

Hungerford, Pixie
See Brinsmead, H(esba) F(ay)

Hunt, Irene 1907- 1
See also AAYA 18; CA 17-20R; CANR 8, 57; DLB 52; JRDA; MAICYA; SATA 2, 91

Hunter, Kristin (Eggleston) 1931- 3
See also AITN 1; BW 1; CA 13-16R; CANR 13; CLC 35; DLB 33; INT CANR-13; MAICYA; SAAS 10; SATA 12

Hunter, Mollie 1922- 25
See also McIlwraith, Maureen Mollie Hunter
See also AAYA 13; CANR 37; CLC 21; DLB 161; JRDA; MAICYA; SAAS 7; SATA 54

Hurd, Clement (G.) 1908-1988 49
See also CA 29-32R; 124; CANR 9, 24; MAICYA; SATA 2, 64; SATA-Obit 54

Hurd, Edith (Thacher) 1910-1997 49
See also CA 13-16R; 156; CANR 9, 24; MAICYA; SAAS 13; SATA 2, 64; SATA-Obit 95

Hurmence, Belinda 1921- 25
See also AAYA 17; CA 145; JRDA; SAAS 20; SATA 77

Hutchins, Pat 1942- 20
See also CA 81-84; CANR 15, 32, 64; MAICYA; SAAS 16; SATA 15, 70

Hyde, Margaret O(ldroyd) 1917- 23
See also CA 1-4R; CANR 1, 36; CLC 21; JRDA; MAICYA; SAAS 8; SATA 1, 42, 76

Hyman, Trina Schart 1939- 50
See also CA 49-52; CANR 2, 36, 70; DLB 61; MAICYA; SATA 7, 46, 95

Irving, Robert
See Adler, Irving

Irwin, Ann(abelle Bowen) 1915- 40
See also Irwin, Hadley
See also CA 101; CANR 19, 36; MAICYA; SATA 44, 89; SATA-Brief 38

Irwin, Hadley 40
See also Hadley, Lee; Irwin, Ann(abelle Bowen)
See also AAYA 13; SAAS 14

Isadora, Rachel 1953(?)- 7
See also CA 111; 137; MAICYA; SATA 54, 79; SATA-Brief 32

Iwamatsu, Jun Atsushi 1908-1994
See Yashima, Taro
See also CA 73-76; 146; CANR 45; MAICYA; SATA 14, 81

Iwasaki (Matsumoto), Chihiro 1918-1974 18

Jackson, Jesse 1908-1983 28
See also BW 1; CA 25-28R; 109; CANR 27; CLC 12; MAICYA; SATA 2, 29; SATA-Obit 48

Jacques, Brian 1939- 21
See also AAYA 20; CA 127; CANR 68; JRDA; SATA 62, 95

James, Dynely
See Mayne, William (James Carter)

Janeczko, Paul B(ryan) 1945- 47
See also AAYA 9; CA 104; CANR 22, 49; SAAS 18; SATA 53, 98

Janosch 26
See also Eckert, Horst

Jansson, Tove Marika 1914- 2
See also CA 17-20R; CANR 38; MAICYA; SATA 3, 41

Jarrell, Randall 1914-1965 6
See also CA 5-8R; 25-28R; CABS 2; CANR 6, 34; CDALB 1941-1968; CLC 1, 2, 6, 9, 13, 49; DAM POET; DLB 48, 52; MAICYA; MTCW 1; SATA 7

Jeffers, Susan 1942- 30
See also CA 97-100; CANR 44; MAICYA; SATA 17, 70

Jennings, Paul 1943- 40
See also SATA 88

Johnson, Angela 1961- 33
See also CA 138; SATA 69, 102

Johnson, James Weldon 1871-1938 32
See also BLC 2; BW 1; CA 104; 125; CDALB 1917-1929; DAM MULT, POET; DLB 51; MTCW 1; PC 24; SATA 31; TCLC 3, 19

Johnson, Marguerite (Annie)
See Angelou, Maya

Johnston, Julie 1941- 41
See also AAYA 27; CA 146; CANR 69; SAAS 24; SATA 78

Johnston, Norma
See St. John, Nicole
See also AAYA 12; JRDA; SATA 29

Jonas, Ann 1932- 12
See also CA 118; 136; MAICYA; SATA 50; SATA-Brief 42

Jones, Diana Wynne 1934- 23
See also AAYA 12; CA 49-52; CANR 4, 26, 56; CLC 26; DLB 161; JRDA; MAICYA; SAAS 7; SATA 9, 70

Jones, Geraldine
See McCaughrean, Geraldine

Jones, Tim(othy) Wynne
See Wynne-Jones, Tim(othy)

Jordan, June 1936- 10
See also AAYA 2; BLCS; BW 2; CA 33-36R; CANR 25, 70; CLC 5, 11, 23, 114; DAM MULT, POET; DLB 38; MAICYA; MTCW 1; SATA 4

Joyce, Bill
See Joyce, William

Joyce, William 1959(?)- 26
See also CA 124; SATA 72; SATA-Brief 46

Kaestner, Erich 1899-1974 .... **4**
See also CA 73-76; 49-52; CANR 40; DLB 56; MAICYA; SATA 14

Kalman, Maira 1949(?)- **32**
See also CA 161; SATA 96

Kark, Nina Mary (Mabey)
See Bawden, Nina (Mary Mabey)
See also SATA 4

Katz, Welwyn Wilton 1948- **45**
See also AAYA 19; CA 154; JRDA; SATA 62, 96

Keats, Ezra Jack 1916-1983 .... **1, 35**
See also AITN 1; CA 77-80; 109; DLB 61; MAICYA; SATA 14, 57; SATA-Obit 34

Keeping, Charles (William James) 1924-1988 .... **34**
See also AAYA 26; CA 21-24R; 125; CANR 11, 43; MAICYA; SATA 9, 69; SATA-Obit 56

Kelleher, Victor (Michael Kitchener) 1939- **36**
See also CA 126; CANR 56; SATA 75; SATA-Brief 52

Keller, Holly 1942- **45**
See also CA 118; SATA 76; SATA-Brief 42

Kellogg, Steven 1941- **6**
See also CA 49-52; CANR 1; DLB 61; MAICYA; SATA 8, 57

Kemp, Gene 1926- **29**
See also CA 69-72; CANR 12; MAICYA; SATA 25, 75

Kennedy, Joseph Charles 1929-
See Kennedy, X. J.
See also CA 1-4R; CANR 4, 30, 40; SATA 14, 86

Kennedy, X. J. **27**
See also Kennedy, Joseph Charles
See also CAAS 9; CLC 8, 42; DLB 5; SAAS 22

Kenny, Kathryn
See Krull, Kathleen

Kenny, Kevin
See Krull, Kathleen

Kerr, M. E. **29**
See also Meaker, Marijane (Agnes)
See also AAYA 2, 23; CLC 12, 35; SAAS 1

Kerry, Lois
See Duncan, Lois

Khalsa, Dayal Kaur 1943-1989 .... **30**
See also CA 137; MAICYA; SATA 62

Kherdian, David 1931- **24**
See also CA 21-24R; CAAS 2; CANR 39; CLC 6, 9; JRDA; MAICYA; SATA 16, 74

King-Smith, Dick 1922- **40**
See also CA 105; CANR 22, 48; MAICYA; SATA 47, 80; SATA-Brief 38

Kipling, (Joseph) Rudyard 1865-1936 .... **39**
See also CA 105; 120; CANR 33; CDBLB 1890 1914; DA; DAB; DAC; DAM MST, POET; DLB 19, 34, 141, 156; MAICYA; MTCW 1; PC 3; SATA 100; SSC 5; TCLC 8, 17; WLC; YABC 2

Klein, Norma 1938-1989 .... **2, 19**
See also AAYA 2; CA 41-44R; 128; CANR 15, 37; CLC 30; INT CANR-15; JRDA; MAICYA; SAAS 1; SATA 7, 57

Klein, Robin 1936- **21**
See also AAYA 21; CA 116; CANR 40; JRDA; MAICYA; SATA 55, 80; SATA-Brief 45

Knight, David C(arpenter) 1925- **38**
See also CA 73-76; SATA 14

Knight, Kathryn Lasky
See Lasky, Kathryn

Knye, Cassandra
See Disch, Thomas M(ichael)

Konigsburg, E(laine) L(obl) 1930- **1, 47**
See also AAYA 3; CA 21-24R; CANR 17, 39, 59; DLB 52; INT CANR-17; JRDA; MAICYA; MTCW 1; SATA 4, 48, 94

Korinets, Iurii Iosifovich
See Korinetz, Yuri (Iosifovich)

Korinetz, Yuri (Iosifovich) 1923- **4**
See also CA 61-64; CANR 11; SATA 9

Korman, Gordon (Richard) 1963- **25**
See also AAYA 10; CA 112; CANR 34, 56; JRDA; MAICYA; SATA 49, 81; SATA-Brief 41

Kotzwinkle, William 1938- **6**
See also CA 45-48; CANR 3, 44; CLC 5, 14, 35; DLB 173; MAICYA; SATA 24, 70

Kovalski, Maryann 1951- **34**
See also CA 163; SAAS 21; SATA 58, 97

Krahn, Fernando 1935- **3**
See also CA 65-68; CANR 11; SATA 49; SATA-Brief 31

Krauss, Ruth (Ida) 1911-1993 .... **42**
See also CA 1-4R; 141; CANR 1, 13, 47; DLB 52; MAICYA; SATA 1, 30; SATA-Obit 75

Krementz, Jill 1940- **5**
See also AITN 1, 2; CA 41-44R; CANR 23, 46; INT CANR-23; MAICYA; SAAS 8; SATA 17, 71

Kruess, James 1926-
See Kruss, James
See also CA 53-56; CANR 5; MAICYA; SATA 8

Krull, Kathleen 1952- **44**
See also CA 106; SATA 52, 80; SATA-Brief 39

Kruss, James **9**
See also Kruess, James

Kuklin, Susan 1941- **51**
See also AAYA 27; CA 130; CANR 67; SATA 63, 95

Kuratomi, Chizuko 1939- **32**
See also CA 21-24R; CANR 10; SATA 12

Kurelek, William 1927-1977 .... **2**
See also CA 49-52; CANR 3; JRDA; MAICYA; SATA 8; SATA-Obit 27

Kuskin, Karla (Seidman) 1932- **4**
See also CA 1-4R; CANR 4, 22, 41; MAICYA; SAAS 3; SATA 2, 68

Lagerloef, Selma (Ottiliana Lovisa) 1858-1940
See Lagerlof, Selma (Ottiliana Lovisa)
See also CA 108; SATA 15; TCLC 4, 36

Lagerlof, Selma (Ottiliana Lovisa) **7**
See also Lagerloef, Selma (Ottiliana Lovisa)
See also SATA 15

Lang, T. T.
See Taylor, Theodore

Langstaff, John (Meredith) 1920- **3**
See also CA 1-4R; CANR 4, 49; MAICYA; SATA 6, 68

Langton, Jane (Gillson) 1922- **33**
See also CA 1-4R; CANR 1, 18, 40; MAICYA; SAAS 5; SATA 3, 68

Larkin, Maia
See Wojciechowska, Maia (Teresa)

Lasky, Kathryn 1944- **11**
See also AAYA 19; CA 69-72; CANR 11; JRDA; MAICYA; SATA 13, 69

Latham, Jean Lee 1902-1995 .... **50**
See also AITN 1; CA 5-8R; CANR 7; CLC 12; MAICYA; SATA 2, 68

Latham, Mavis
See Clark, Mavis Thorpe

Lauber, Patricia (Grace) 1924- **16**
See also CA 9-12R; CANR 6, 24, 38; JRDA; MAICYA; SATA 1, 33, 75

Lavine, Sigmund Arnold 1908- **35**
See also CA 1-4R; CANR 4, 19, 41; SATA 3, 82

Lawson, Robert 1892-1957 .... **2**
See also CA 118; 137; DLB 22; MAICYA; SATA 100; YABC 2

Lea, Joan
See Neufeld, John (Arthur)

Leaf, (Wilbur) Munro 1905-1976 .... **25**
See also CA 73-76; 69-72; CANR 29; MAICYA; SATA 20

Lear, Edward 1812-1888 .... **1**
See also DLB 32, 163, 166; MAICYA; NCLC 3; SATA 18, 100

Lee, Dennis (Beynon) 1939- **3**
See also CA 25-28R; CANR 11, 31, 57, 61; DAC; DLB 53; MAICYA; SATA 14, 102

Lee, Julian
See Latham, Jean Lee

Le Guin, Ursula K(roeber) 1929- **3, 28**
See also AAYA 9, 27; AITN 1; CA 21-24R; CANR 9, 32, 52; CDALB 1968-1988; CLC 8, 13, 22, 45, 71; DAB; DAC; DAM MST, POP; DLB 8, 52; INT CANR-32; JRDA; MAICYA; MTCW 1; SATA 4, 52, 99; SSC 12

Author Index

L'Engle, Madeleine (Camp Franklin) 1918- **1, 14**
See also AAYA 1; AITN 2; CA 1-4R; CANR 3, 21, 39, 66; CLC 12; DAM POP; DLB 52; JRDA; MAICYA; MTCW 1; SAAS 15; SATA 1, 27, 75

Lenski, Lois 1893-1974 .... **26**
See also CA 13-14; 53-56; CANR 41; CAP 1; DLB 22; MAICYA; SATA 1, 26, 100

Lerner, Carol 1927- **34**
See also CA 102; CANR 70; SAAS 12; SATA 33, 86

LeShan, Eda J(oan) 1922- **6**
See also CA 13-16R; CANR 21; SATA 21

LeSieg, Theo.
See Dr. Seuss

Lester, Julius (Bernard) 1939-............ **2, 41**
See also AAYA 12; BW 2; CA 17-20R; CANR 8, 23, 43; JRDA; MAICYA; SATA 12, 74

Levitin, Sonia (Wolff) 1934-.................. **53**
See also AAYA 13; CA 29-32R; CANR 14, 32; CLC 17; JRDA; MAICYA; SAAS 2; SATA 4, 68

Lewin, Hugh 1939-............................. **9**
See also CA 113; CANR 38; MAICYA; SATA 72; SATA-Brief 40

Lewis, C(live) S(taples) 1898-1963 .... **3, 27**
See also AAYA 3; CA 81-84; CANR 33, 71; CDBLB 1945-1960; CLC 1, 3, 6, 14, 27; DA; DAB; DAC; DAM MST, NOV, POP; DLB 15, 100, 160; JRDA; MAICYA; MTCW 1; SATA 13, 100; WLC

Lindgren, Astrid (Ericsson) 1907- **1, 39**
See also CA 13-16R; CANR 39; MAICYA; SATA 2, 38

Lindgren, Barbro 1937- **20**
See also CA 149; SATA 63; SATA-Brief 46

Lindsay, Norman Alfred William 1879-1969 .... **8**
See also CA 102; SATA 67

Lionni, Leo(nard) 1910- **7**
See also CA 53-56; CANR 38; DLB 61; MAICYA; SATA 8, 72

Lipsyte, Robert (Michael) 1938-............ **23**
See also AAYA 7; CA 17-20R; CANR 8, 57; CLC 21; DA; DAC; DAM MST, NOV; JRDA; MAICYA; SATA 5, 68

Little, (Flora) Jean 1932- **4**
See also CA 21-24R; CANR 42, 66; DAC; DAM MST; JRDA; MAICYA; SAAS 17; SATA 2, 68

Lively, Penelope (Margaret) 1933- **7**
See also CA 41-44R; CANR 29, 67; CLC 32, 50; DAM NOV; DLB 14, 161; JRDA; MAICYA; MTCW 1; SATA 7, 60, 101

Livingston, Myra Cohn 1926-1996 .... **7**
See also CA 1-4R; 153; CANR 1, 33, 58; DLB 61; INT CANR-33; MAICYA; SAAS 1; SATA 5, 68; SATA-Obit 92

Lobel, Arnold (Stark) 1933-1987 .... **5**
See also AITN 1; CA 1-4R; 124; CANR 2, 33; DLB 61; MAICYA; SATA 6, 55; SATA-Obit 54

Locke, Robert 1944-
See Bess, Clayton
See also CA 129; SATA 63

Locker, Thomas 1937-......................... **14**
See also CA 128; CANR 66; MAICYA; SATA 59

Lofting, Hugh (John) 1886-1947 .... **19**
See also CA 109; 137; CANR 73; DLB 160; MAICYA; SATA 15, 100

Lorenzini, Carlo 1826-1890
See Collodi, Carlo
See also MAICYA; SATA 29, 100

Louisburgh, Sheila Burnford
See Burnford, Sheila (Philip Cochrane Every)

Lowry, Lois 1937-......................... **6, 46**
See also AAYA 5; CA 69-72; CANR 13, 43, 70; DLB 52; INT CANR-13; JRDA; MAICYA; SAAS 3; SATA 23, 70

Lunn, Janet (Louise Swoboda) 1928- **18**
See also CA 33-36R; CANR 22; JRDA; MAICYA; SAAS 12; SATA 4, 68

Macaulay, David (Alexander) 1946-..... **3, 14**
See also AAYA 21; BEST 89:2; CA 53-56; CANR 5, 34; DLB 61; INT CANR-34; MAICYA; SATA 46, 72; SATA-Brief 27

MacDonald, Golden
See Brown, Margaret Wise

Mackay, Claire 1930- **43**
See also CA 105; CANR 22, 50; SATA 40, 97

MacLachlan, Patricia 1938- **14**
See also AAYA 18; CA 118; 136; JRDA; MAICYA; SATA 62; SATA-Brief 42

Maddison, Angela Mary 1923-
See Banner, Angela
See also CA 53-56; SATA 10

Maestro, Betsy C(rippen) 1944-............. **45**
See also CA 61-64; CANR 8, 23, 37; MAICYA; SATA 59; SATA-Brief 30

Maestro, Giulio 1942- **45**
See also CA 57-60; CANR 8, 23, 37; MAICYA; SATA 8, 59

Mahy, Margaret 1936-......................... **7**
See also AAYA 8; CA 69-72; CANR 13, 30, 38; JRDA; MAICYA; SATA 14, 69

Major, Kevin (Gerald) 1949- **11**
See also AAYA 16; CA 97-100; CANR 21, 38; CLC 26; DAC; DLB 60; INT CANR-21; JRDA; MAICYA; SATA 32, 82

Manley, Seon 1921- **3**
See also CA 85-88; SAAS 2; SATA 15

March, Carl
See Fleischman, (Albert) Sid(ney)

Mark, Jan(et Marjorie) 1943-............... **11**
See also CA 93-96; CANR 17, 42; MAICYA; SATA 22, 69

Markoosie **23**
See also Markoosie, Patsauq
See also DAM MULT; NNAL

Markoosie, Patsauq 1942-
See Markoosie
See also CA 101

Marks, J
See Highwater, Jamake (Mamake)

Marks-Highwater, J
See Highwater, Jamake (Mamake)

Marrin, Albert 1936-......................... **53**
See also CA 49-52; CANR 30, 58; SATA 53, 90; SATA-Brief 43

Marsden, John 1950- **34**
See also AAYA 20; CA 135; SAAS 22; SATA 66, 97

Marshall, Edward
See Marshall, James (Edward)

Marshall, James (Edward) 1942-1992 .... **21**
See also CA 41-44R; 139; CANR 38; DLB 61; MAICYA; SATA 6, 51, 75

Martin, Ann M(atthews) 1955- **32**
See also AAYA 6; CA 111; CANR 32; INT CANR-32; JRDA; MAICYA; SATA 44, 70; SATA-Brief 41

Martin, Fredric
See Christopher, Matt(hew Frederick)

Maruki, Toshi 1912- **19**

Matas, Carol 1949-......................... **52**
See also AAYA 22; CA 158; SATA 93

Mathis, Sharon Bell 1937-...................... **3**
See also AAYA 12; BW 2; CA 41-44R; DLB 33; JRDA; MAICYA; SAAS 3; SATA 7, 58

Mattingley, Christobel (Rosemary) 1931- **24**
See also CA 97-100; CANR 20, 47; MAICYA; SAAS 18; SATA 37, 85

Mayer, Mercer 1943- **11**
See also CA 85-88; CANR 38; DLB 61; MAICYA; SATA 16, 32, 73

Mayne, William (James Carter) 1928- **25**
See also AAYA 20; CA 9-12R; CANR 37; CLC 12; JRDA; MAICYA; SAAS 11; SATA 6, 68

Mazer, Harry 1925-......................... **16**
See also AAYA 5; CA 97-100; CANR 32; INT 97-100; JRDA; MAICYA; SAAS 11; SATA 31, 67

Mazer, Norma Fox 1931- **23**
See also AAYA 5; CA 69-72; CANR 12, 32, 66; CLC 26; JRDA; MAICYA; SAAS 1; SATA 24, 67

McBratney, Sam 1943- **44**
See also CA 155; SATA 89

McCaffrey, Anne (Inez) 1926-............... **49**
See also AAYA 6; AITN 2; BEST 89:2; CA 25-28R; CANR 15, 35, 55; CLC 17; DAM NOV, POP; DLB 8; JRDA; MAICYA; MTCW 1; SAAS 11; SATA 8, 70

McCaughrean, Geraldine 1951- **38**
See also AAYA 23; CA 117; CANR 52; SATA 87

McCloskey, (John) Robert 1914-............. **7**
See also CA 9-12R; CANR 47; DLB 22;
MAICYA; SATA 2, 39, 100

McClung, Robert M(arshall) 1916- **11**
See also AITN 2; CA 13-16R; CANR 6, 21, 46;
MAICYA; SAAS 15; SATA 2, 68

McCord, David (Thompson Watson) 1897-
1997 .... **9**
See also CA 73-76; 157; CANR 38; DLB 61;
MAICYA; SATA 18; SATA-Obit 96

McCulloch, Sarah
See Ure, Jean

McCully, Emily Arnold **46**
See also Arnold, Emily
See also SAAS 7; SATA 5

McDermott, Gerald 1941-..................... **9**
See also AITN 2; CA 85-88; MAICYA; SATA 16,
74

McFadden, Kevin Christopher 1961(?)-..... **29**
See also AAYA 13; CA 136; CANR 66; JRDA;
SATA 68

McGovern, Ann 1930-........................... **50**
See also CA 49-52; CANR 2, 44; MAICYA; SAAS
17; SATA 8, 69, 70

McHargue, Georgess 1941- **2**
See also CA 25-28R; CANR 24; JRDA; SAAS 5;
SATA 4, 77

McIlwraith, Maureen Mollie Hunter
See Hunter, Mollie
See also SATA 2

McKee, David (John) 1935- **38**
See also CA 137; MAICYA; SATA 70

McKinley, (Jennifer Carolyn) Robin
1952- **10**
See also AAYA 4; CA 107; CANR 31, 64; DLB
52; JRDA; MAICYA; SATA 50, 89; SATA-
Brief 32

McKissack, Patricia (L'Ann) C(arwell)
1944- **23**
See also BW 2; CA 118; CANR 38; JRDA;
MAICYA; SATA 51, 73

McMillan, Bruce 1947- **47**
See also CA 73-76; CANR 13, 35; MAICYA;
SATA 22, 70

McMillan, Naomi
See Grimes, Nikki

McNaughton, Colin 1951- **54**
See also CA 112; CANR 47; SATA 39, 92

Meaker, Marijane (Agnes) 1927-
See Kerr, M. E.
See also CA 107; CANR 37, 63; INT 107; JRDA;
MAICYA; MTCW 1; SATA 20, 61, 99

Meltzer, Milton 1915-.......................... **13**
See also AAYA 8; CA 13-16R; CANR 38; CLC
26; DLB 61; JRDA; MAICYA; SAAS 1; SATA
1, 50, 80

Merriam, Eve 1916-1992 .... **14**
See also CA 5-8R; 137; CANR 29; DLB 61;
MAICYA; SATA 3, 40, 73

Merrill, Jean (Fairbanks) 1923- **52**
See also CA 1-4R; CANR 4, 38; MAICYA; SATA
1, 82

Metcalf, Suzanne
See Baum, L(yman) Frank

Meyer, June
See Jordan, June

Milne, A(lan) A(lexander) 1882-1956 ..... **1, 26**
See also CA 104; 133; DAB; DAC; DAM MST;
DLB 10, 77, 100, 160; MAICYA; MTCW 1;
SATA 100; TCLC 6; YABC 1

Milne, Lorus J. **22**
See also CA 33-36R; CANR 14; SAAS 18; SATA
5

Milne, Margery **22**
See also CA 33-36R; CANR 14; SAAS 18; SATA
5

Minarik, Else Holmelund 1920- **33**
See also CA 73-76; CANR 48; MAICYA; SATA
15

Mohr, Nicholasa 1938- **22**
See also AAYA 8; CA 49-52; CANR 1, 32, 64;
CLC 12; DAM MULT; DLB 145; HLC; HW;
JRDA; SAAS 8; SATA 8, 97

Molin, Charles
See Mayne, William (James Carter)

Monjo, F(erdinand) N(icholas III) 1924-
1978 .... **2**
See also CA 81-84; CANR 37; MAICYA; SATA
16

Montgomery, L(ucy) M(aud) 1874-1942 ...... **8**
See also AAYA 12; CA 108; 137; DAC; DAM
MST; DLB 92; DLBD 14; JRDA; MAICYA;
SATA 100; TCLC 51; YABC 1

Moore, Lilian 1909-............................. **15**
See also CA 103; CANR 38; MAICYA; SATA
52

Morpurgo, Michael 1943- **51**
See also CA 158; SATA 93

Moser, Barry 1940- **49**
See also MAICYA; SAAS 15; SATA 56, 79

Mowat, Farley (McGill) 1921- **20**
See also AAYA 1; CA 1-4R; CANR 4, 24, 42,
68; CLC 26; DAC; DAM MST; DLB 68; INT
CANAR-24; JRDA; MAICYA; MTCW 1;
SATA 3, 55

Mude, O.
See Gorey, Edward (St. John)

Mueller, Joerg 1942-........................... **43**
See also CA 136; SATA 67

Mukerji, Dhan Gopal 1890-1936 .... **10**
See also CA 119; 136; MAICYA; SATA 40

Muller, Jorg
See Mueller, Joerg

Mun
See Leaf, (Wilbur) Munro

Munari, Bruno 1907-........................... **9**
See also CA 73-76; CANR 38; MAICYA; SATA 15

Munsch, Robert (Norman) 1945-........... **19**
See also CA 121; CANR 37; MAICYA; SATA
50, 83; SATA-Brief 48

Murphy, Jill (Frances) 1949- **39**
See also CA 105; CANR 44, 50; MAICYA; SATA
37, 70

Murphy, Jim 1947- **53**
See also AAYA 20; CA 111; SATA 37, 77; SATA-
Brief 32

Myers, Walter Dean 1937-............. **4, 16, 35**
See also AAYA 4, 23; BLC 3; BW 2; CA 33-36R;
CANR 20, 42, 67; CLC 35; DAM MULT,
NOV; DLB 33; INT CANR-20; JRDA;
MAICYA; SAAS 2; SATA 41, 71; SATA-Brief
27

Myers, Walter M.
See Myers, Walter Dean

Naidoo, Beverley 1943- **29**
See also AAYA 23; CA 160; SATA 63

Nakatani, Chiyoko 1930-1981 .... **30**
See also CA 77-80; SATA 55; SATA-Brief 40

Namioka, Lensey 1929- **48**
See also AAYA 27; CA 69-72; CANR 11, 27, 52;
SAAS 24; SATA 27, 89

Napoli, Donna Jo 1948- **51**
See also AAYA 25; CA 156; SAAS 23; SATA 92

Naylor, Phyllis (Reynolds) 1933- **17**
See also AAYA 4; CA 21-24R; CANR 8, 24, 59;
JRDA; MAICYA; SAAS 10; SATA 12, 66,
102

Needle, Jan 1943-.............................. **43**
See also AAYA 23; CA 106; CANR 28; SAAS
23; SATA 30, 98

Nesbit, E(dith) 1858-1924 .... **3**
See also CA 118; 137; DLB 141, 153, 178;
MAICYA; SATA 100; YABC 1

Ness, Evaline (Michelow) 1911-1986 .... **6**
See also CA 5-8R; 120; CANR 5, 37; DLB 61;
MAICYA; SAAS 1; SATA 1, 26; SATA-
Obit 49

Neufeld, John (Arthur) 1938- **52**
See also AAYA 11; CA 25-28R; CANR 11, 37,
56; CLC 17; MAICYA; SAAS 3; SATA 6, 81

Nielsen, Kay (Rasmus) 1886-1957 .... **16**
See also MAICYA; SATA 16

Nimmo, Jenny 1942- **44**
See also CA 108; CANR 52; SATA 87

Nixon, Joan Lowery 1927-.................... **24**
See also AAYA 12; CA 9-12R; CANR 7, 24, 38;
JRDA; MAICYA; SAAS 9; SATA 8, 44, 78

Noestlinger, Christine 1936- **12**
See also CA 115; 123; CANR 38; MAICYA;
SATA 64; SATA-Brief 37

North, Andrew
See Norton, Andre

North, Captain George
See Stevenson, Robert Louis (Balfour)

Norton, Alice Mary
See Norton, Andre
See also MAICYA; SATA 1, 43

Norton, Andre 1912- **50**
See also Norton, Alice Mary
See also AAYA 14; CA 1-4R; CANR 68; CLC 12; DLB 8, 52; JRDA; MTCW 1; SATA 91

Norton, Mary 1903-1992 .... **6**
See also CA 97-100, 139; DLB 160; MAICYA; SATA 18, 60; SATA-Obit 72

Nourse, Alan E(dward) 1928-1992 .... **33**
See also CA 1-4R; 145; CANR 3, 21, 45; DLB 8; SATA 48

Oakley, Graham 1929- **7**
See also CA 106; CANR 38, 54; MAICYA; SATA 30, 84

Oberman, Sheldon 1949- **54**
See also CA 152; SAAS 26; SATA 85

O'Brien, Robert C. **2**
See also Conly, Robert Leslie
See also AAYA 6

O'Connor, Patrick
See Wibberley, Leonard (Patrick O'Connor)

O'Dell, Scott 1898-1989 .... **1, 16**
See also AAYA 3; CA 61-64; 129; CANR 12, 30; CLC 30; DLB 52; JRDA; MAICYA; SATA 12, 60

Ofek, Uriel 1926- **28**
See also CA 101; CANR 18; SATA 36

Ogilvy, Gavin
See Barrie, J(ames) M(atthew)

O Mude
See Gorey, Edward (St. John)

Oneal, Elizabeth 1934-
See Oneal, Zibby
See also CA 106; CANR 28; MAICYA; SATA 30, 82

Oneal, Zibby **13**
See also Oneal, Elizabeth
See also AAYA 5; CLC 30; JRDA

Orgel, Doris 1929- **48**
See also AITN 1; CA 45-48; CANR 2; SAAS 19; SATA 7, 85

Orlev, Uri 1931- **30**
See also AAYA 20; CA 101; CANR 34; SAAS 19; SATA 58

Ormerod, Jan(ette Louise) 1946- **20**
See also CA 113; CANR 35; MAICYA; SATA 55, 70; SATA-Brief 44

O'Shea, (Catherine) Pat(ricia Shiels) 1931- **18**
See also CA 145; SATA 87

Ottley, Reginald Leslie 1909-1985 .... **16**
See also CA 93-96; CANR 34; MAICYA; SATA 26

Owen, Gareth 1936- **31**
See also CA 150; SAAS 14; SATA 83

Oxenbury, Helen 1938- **22**
See also CA 25-28R; CANR 35; MAICYA; SATA 3, 68

Paisley, Tom 1932-
See Bethancourt, T. Ernesto
See also CA 61-64; CANR 15; SATA 78

Parish, Margaret Cecile 1927-1988
See Parish, Peggy
See also CA 73-76; 127; CANR 18, 38; MAICYA; SATA 73

Parish, Peggy **22**
See also Parish, Margaret Cecile
See also SATA 17; SATA-Obit 59

Park, Barbara 1947- **34**
See also CA 113; SATA 40, 78; SATA-Brief 35

Park, (Rosina) Ruth (Lucia) **51**
See also CA 105; CANR 65; SATA 25, 93

Pascal, Francine 1938- **25**
See also AAYA 1; CA 115; 123; CANR 39, 50; JRDA; MAICYA; SATA 51, 80; SATA-Brief 37

Patent, Dorothy Hinshaw 1940- **19**
See also CA 61-64; CANR 9, 24; MAICYA; SAAS 13; SATA 22, 69

Paterson, Katherine (Womeldorf) 1932- **7, 50**
See also AAYA 1; CA 21-24R; CANR 28, 59; CLC 12, 30; DLB 52; JRDA; MAICYA; MTCW 1; SATA 13, 53, 92

Paton Walsh, Gillian 1937-
See Walsh, Jill Paton
See also CANR 38; JRDA; MAICYA; SAAS 3; SATA 4, 72

Paulsen, Gary 1939- **19, 54**
See also AAYA 2, 17; CA 73-76; CANR 30, 54; JRDA; MAICYA; SATA 22, 50, 54, 79

Pearce, Philippa **9**
See also Christie, (Ann) Philippa
See also CLC 21; DLB 161; MAICYA; SATA 1, 67

Pearson, Kit 1947- **26**
See also AAYA 19; CA 145; CANR 71; JRDA; SATA 77

Peck, Richard (Wayne) 1934- **15**
See also AAYA 1, 24; CA 85-88; CANR 19, 38; CLC 21; INT CANR-19; JRDA; MAICYA; SAAS 2; SATA 18, 55, 97

Peck, Robert Newton 1928- **45**
See also AAYA 3; CA 81-84; CANR 31, 63; CLC 17; DA; DAC; DAM MST; JRDA; MAICYA; SAAS 1; SATA 21, 62

Peet, Bill **12**
See also Peet, William Bartlett

Peet, William Bartlett 1915-
See Peet, Bill
See also CA 17-20R; CANR 38; MAICYA; SATA 2, 41, 78

Pene du Bois, William (Sherman) 1916-1993 .... **1**
See also CA 5-8R; CANR 17, 41; DLB 61; MAICYA; SATA 4, 68; SATA-Obit 74

Petersham, Maud (Sylvia Fuller) 1890-1971 .... **24**
See also CA 73-76; 33-36R; CANR 29; DLB 22; MAICYA; SATA 17

Petersham, Miska 1888-1960 .... **24**
See also CA 73-76; CANR 29; DLB 22; MAICYA; SATA 17

Petry, Ann (Lane) 1908-1997 .... **12**
See also BW 1; CA 5-8R; 157; CAAS 6; CANR 4, 46; CLC 1, 7, 18; DLB 76; JRDA; MAICYA; MTCW 1; SATA 5; SATA-Obit 94

Peyton, K. M. **3**
See also Peyton, Kathleen Wendy
See also AAYA 20; DLB 161; SAAS 17

Peyton, Kathleen Wendy 1929-
See Peyton, K. M.
See also CA 69-72; CANR 32, 69; JRDA; MAICYA; SATA 15, 62

Pfeffer, Susan Beth 1948- **11**
See also AAYA 12; CA 29-32R; CANR 31, 58; JRDA; SAAS 17; SATA 4, 83

Pfister, Marcus **42**
See also SATA 83

Phipson, Joan **5**
See also Fitzhardinge, Joan Margaret
See also AAYA 14; SAAS 3

Pienkowski, Jan (Michal) 1936- **6**
See also CA 65-68; CANR 11, 38; MAICYA; SATA 6, 58

Pierce, Meredith Ann 1958- **20**
See also AAYA 13; CA 108; CANR 26, 48; JRDA; MAICYA; SATA 67; SATA-Brief 48

Pig, Edward
See Gorey, Edward (St. John)

Pike, Christopher
See McFadden, Kevin Christopher
See also CANR 66

Pilgrim, Anne
See Allan, Mabel Esther

Pilkey, Dav 1966- **48**
See also CA 136; SATA 68

Pinkney, (Jerry) Brian 1961- **54**
See also SATA 74

Pinkney, J. Brian
See Pinkney, (Jerry) Brian

Pinkney, Jerry 1939- **43**
See also MAICYA; SAAS 12; SATA 41, 71; SATA-Brief 32

Pinkwater, Daniel Manus 1941-............. **4**
See also Pinkwater, Manus
See also AAYA 1; CA 29-32R; CANR 12, 38;
CLC 35; JRDA; MAICYA; SAAS 3; SATA
46, 76

Pinkwater, Manus
See Pinkwater, Daniel Manus
See also SATA 8

Polacco, Patricia 1944-......................... **40**
See also SATA 74

Politi, Leo 1908-1996 .... **29**
See also CA 17-20R; 151; CANR 13, 47;
MAICYA; SATA 1, 47; SATA-Obit 88

Pollock, Mary
See Blyton, Enid (Mary)

Potter, (Helen) Beatrix 1866-1943 .... **1, 19**
See also CA 108; 137; DLB 141; SATA 100; YABC
1

Poulin, Stephane 1961-........................ **28**
See also CA 165; SATA 98

Prelutsky, Jack 1940-......................... **13**
See also CA 93-96; CANR 38; DLB 61;
MAICYA; SATA 22, 66

Pringle, Laurence (Patrick) 1935-............ **4**
See also CA 29-32R; CANR 14, 60; MAICYA;
SAAS 6; SATA 4, 68

Proeysen, Alf 1914-1970 .... **24**
See also Proysen, Alf
See also CA 136

Provensen, Alice 1918-......................... **11**
See also CA 53-56; CANR 5, 44; MAICYA; SATA
9, 70

Provensen, Martin (Elias) 1916-1987 ...... **11**
See also CA 53-56; 122; CANR 5, 44; MAICYA;
SATA 9, 70; SATA-Obit 51

Proysen, Alf
See Proeysen, Alf
See also SATA 67

Pullman, Philip (Nicholas) 1946-........... **20**
See also AAYA 15; CA 127; CANR 50; JRDA;
MAICYA; SAAS 17; SATA 65

Pyle, Howard 1853-1911 .... **22**
See also CA 109; 137; DLB 42, 188; DLBD 13;
MAICYA; SATA 16, 100; TCLC 81

Ramal, Walter
See de la Mare, Walter (John)

Ransome, Arthur (Michell) 1884-1967 ...... **8**
See also CA 73-76; DLB 160; MAICYA; SATA
22

Raskin, Ellen 1928-1984 .... **1, 12**
See also CA 21-24R; 113; CANR 37; DLB 52;
MAICYA; SATA 2, 38

Rau, Margaret 1913-........................... **8**
See also CA 61-64; CANR 8; SATA 9

Rayner, Mary 1933-........................... **41**
See also CA 69-72; CANR 12, 29, 52; SATA 22, 87

Reid Banks, Lynne 1929-..................... **24**
See also Banks, Lynne Reid
See also CA 1-4R; CANR 6, 22, 38; JRDA;
MAICYA; SATA 22, 75

Reiss, Johanna (de Leeuw) 1929(?)- **19**
See also CA 85-88; JRDA; SATA 18

Remi, Georges 1907-1983
See Herge
See also CA 69-72; 109; CANR 31; SATA 13;
SATA-Obit 32

Rey, H(ans) A(ugusto) 1898-1977 .... **5**
See also CA 5-8R; 73-76; CANR 6; DLB 22;
MAICYA; SATA 1, 26, 69, 100

Rey, Margret (Elisabeth) 1906-1996 .... **5**
See also CA 105; 155; CANR 38; MAICYA;
SATA 26, 86; SATA-Obit 93

Rhine, Richard
See Silverstein, Alvin

Rhue, Morton
See Strasser, Todd

Richards, Laura E(lizabeth Howe) 1850-
1943 .... **54**
See also CA 120; 137; DLB 42; MAICYA; YABC
1

Richler, Mordecai 1931-..................... **17**
See also AITN 1; CA 65-68; CANR 31, 62; CLC
3, 5, 9, 13, 18, 46, 70; DAC; DAM MST,
NOV; DLB 53; MAICYA; MTCW 1; SATA
44, 98; SATA-Brief 27

Richter, Hans Peter 1925-..................... **21**
See also CA 45-48; CANR 2; MAICYA; SAAS
11; SATA 6

Rigg, Sharon
See Creech, Sharon

Rinaldi, Ann 1934-........................... **46**
See also AAYA 15; CA 111; JRDA; SATA 51,
78; SATA-Brief 50

Ringgold, Faith 1930-......................... **30**
See also AAYA 19; CA 154; SATA 71

Riq
See Atwater, Richard (Tupper)

Robert, Adrian
See St. John, Nicole

Roberts, Charles G(eorge) D(ouglas) 1860-
1943 .... **33**
See also CA 105; DLB 92; SATA 88; SATA-Brief
29; TCLC 8

Rockwell, Thomas 1933-....................... **6**
See also CA 29-32R; CANR 44; MAICYA; SATA
7, 70

Rodari, Gianni 1920-1980 .... **24**

Rodda, Emily 1948(?)- **32**
See also CA 164; SATA 97

Rodgers, Mary 1931-......................... **20**
See also CA 49-52; CANR 8, 55; CLC 12; INT
CANR-8; JRDA; MAICYA; SATA 8

Rodman, Maia
See Wojciechowska, Maia (Teresa)

Rosen, Michael (Wayne) 1946-.............. **45**
See also CANR 52; SATA 84

Roughsey, Dick 1921(?)-1985 .... **41**
See also CA 109; SATA 35

Rubinstein, Gillian (Margaret) 1942- **35**
See also AAYA 22; CA 136; SATA 68

Rudomin, Esther
See Hautzig, Esther Rudomin

Ryder, Joanne (Rose) 1946-................. **37**
See also CA 112; 133; MAICYA; SATA 65; SATA-
Brief 34

Rylant, Cynthia 1954-......................... **15**
See also AAYA 10; CA 136; JRDA; MAICYA;
SAAS 13; SATA 50, 76; SATA-Brief 44

Sachar, Louis 1954-........................... **28**
See also CA 81-84; CANR 15, 33; JRDA; SATA
63; SATA-Brief 50

Sachs, Marilyn (Stickle) 1927-................ **2**
See also AAYA 2; CA 17-20R; CANR 13, 47; CLC
35; JRDA; MAICYA; SAAS 2; SATA 3, 68

Sage, Juniper
See Brown, Margaret Wise; Hurd, Edith (Thacher)

**Saint-Exupery, Antoine (Jean Baptiste Marie
Roger) de** 1900-1944 .... **10**
See also CA 108; 132; DAM NOV; DLB 72;
MAICYA; MTCW 1; SATA 20; TCLC 2, 56;
WLC

St. John, Nicole **46**
See also Johnston, Norma
See also CANR 32; SAAS 7; SATA 89

Salinger, J(erome) D(avid) 1919-........... **18**
See also AAYA 2; CA 5-8R; CANR 39; CDALB
1941-1968; CLC 1, 3, 8, 12, 55, 56; DA; DAB;
DAC; DAM MST, NOV, POP; DLB 2, 102,
173; MAICYA; MTCW 1; SATA 67; SSC 2,
28; WLC

Sanchez, Sonia 1934-......................... **18**
See also BLC 3; BW 2; CA 33-36R; CANR 24, 49;
CLC 5, 116; DAM MULT; DLB 41; DLBD 8;
MAICYA; MTCW 1; PC 9; SATA 22

Sanchez-Silva, Jose Maria 1911-........... **12**
See also CA 73-76; MAICYA; SATA 16

San Souci, Robert D. 1946-................. **43**
See also CA 108; CANR 46; SATA 40, 81

Sasek, Miroslav 1916-1980 .... **4**
See also CA 73-76; 101; SATA 16; SATA-Obit 23

Sattler, Helen Roney 1921-1992 .... **24**
See also CA 33-36R; CANR 14, 31; SATA 4, 74

Sawyer, Ruth 1880-1970 .... **36**
See also CA 73-76; CANR 37; DLB 22;
MAICYA; SATA 17

Say, Allen 1937-............................... **22**
See also CA 29-32R; CANR 30; JRDA; MAICYA;
SATA 28, 69

Scarlett, Susan
See Streatfeild, (Mary) Noel

Scarry, Richard (McClure) 1919-
1994 .... **3, 41**
See also CA 17-20R; 145; CANR 18, 39; DLB
61; MAICYA; SATA 2, 35, 75; SATA-Obit 90

Schlein, Miriam 1926- **41**
See also CA 1-4R; CANR 2, 52; SATA 2, 87

Schmidt, Annie M. G. 1911-1995 .... **22**
See also CA 135; 152; SATA 67; SATA-Obit 91

Schwartz, Alvin 1927-1992 .... **3**
See also CA 13-16R; 137; CANR 7, 24, 49;
MAICYA; SATA 4, 56; SATA-Obit 71

Schwartz, Amy 1954- **25**
See also CA 110; CANR 29, 57; INT CANR-29;
SAAS 18; SATA 47, 83; SATA-Brief 41

Schweitzer, Byrd Baylor
See Baylor, Byrd

Scieszka, Jon 1954- **27**
See also AAYA 21; CA 135; SATA 68

Scott, Jack Denton 1915-1995 .... **20**
See also CA 108; CANR 48; MAICYA; SAAS
14; SATA 31, 83

Sebestyen, Ouida 1924- **17**
See also AAYA 8; CA 107; CANR 40; CLC 30;
JRDA; MAICYA; SAAS 10; SATA 39

Sefton, Catherine
See Waddell, Martin

Selden, George **8**
See also Thompson, George Selden
See also DLB 52

Selsam, Millicent Ellis 1912-1996 .... **1**
See also CA 9-12R; 154; CANR 5, 38; MAICYA;
SATA 1, 29; SATA-Obit 92

Sendak, Maurice (Bernard) 1928- **1, 17**
See also CA 5-8R; CANR 11, 39; DLB 61; INT
CANR-11; MAICYA; MTCW 1; SATA 1, 27

Seredy, Kate 1899-1975 .... **10**
See also CA 5-8R; 57-60; DLB 22; MAICYA;
SATA 1; SATA-Obit 24

Serraillier, Ian (Lucien) 1912-1994 .... **2**
See also CA 1-4R; 147; CANR 1; DLB 161;
MAICYA; SAAS 3; SATA 1, 73; SATA-
Obit 83

Seuss, Dr.
See Dr. Seuss

Sewell, Anna 1820-1878 .... **17**
See also DLB 163; JRDA; MAICYA; SATA 24, 100

Sharp, Margery 1905-1991 .... **27**
See also CA 21-24R; 134; CANR 18; DLB 161;
MAICYA; SATA 1, 29; SATA-Obit 67

Shearer, John 1947- **34**
See also CA 125; SATA 43; SATA-Brief 27

Shepard, Ernest Howard 1879-1976 .... **27**
See also CA 9-12R; 65-68; CANR 23; DLB 160;
MAICYA; SATA 3, 33, 100; SATA-Obit 24

Shippen, Katherine B(inney) 1892-1980 .... **36**
See also CA 5-8R; 93-96; SATA 1; SATA-Obit
23

Showers, Paul C. 1910- **6**
See also CA 1-4R; CANR 4, 38, 59; MAICYA;
SAAS 7; SATA 21, 92

Shulevitz, Uri 1935- **5**
See also CA 9-12R; CANR 3; DLB 61; MAICYA;
SATA 3, 50

Silverstein, Alvin 1933- **25**
See also CA 49-52; CANR 2; CLC 17; JRDA;
MAICYA; SATA 8, 69

Silverstein, Shel(by) 1932- **5**
See also CA 107; CANR 47; JRDA; MAICYA;
SATA 33, 92; SATA-Brief 27

Silverstein, Virginia B(arbara Opshelor)
1937- **25**
See also CA 49-52; CANR 2; CLC 17; JRDA;
MAICYA; SATA 8, 69

Simmonds, Posy **23**

Simon, Hilda Rita 1921- **39**
See also CA 77-80; SATA 28

Simon, Seymour 1931- **9**
See also CA 25-28R; CANR 11, 29; MAICYA;
SATA 4, 73

Singer, Isaac
See Singer, Isaac Bashevis

Singer, Isaac Bashevis 1904-1991 .... **1**
See also AITN 1, 2; CA 1-4R; 134; CANR 1, 39;
CDALB 1941-1968; CLC 1, 3, 6, 9, 11, 15,
23, 38, 69, 111; DA; DAB; DAC; DAM MST,
NOV; DLB 6, 28, 52; DLBY 91; JRDA;
MAICYA; MTCW 1; SATA 3, 27; SATA-Obit
68; SSC 3; WLC

Singer, Marilyn 1948- **48**
See also CA 65-68; CANR 9, 39; JRDA;
MAICYA; SAAS 13; SATA 48, 80; SATA-
Brief 38

Sis, Peter 1949- **45**
See also CA 128; SATA 67

Sleator, William (Warner III) 1945- **29**
See also AAYA 5; CA 29-32R; CANR 46; JRDA;
MAICYA; SATA 3, 68

Slote, Alfred 1926- **4**
See also JRDA; MAICYA; SAAS 21; SATA 8,
72

Small, David 1945- **53**
See also SATA 50, 95; SATA-Brief 46

Smith, Dick King
See King-Smith, Dick

Smith, Lane 1959- **47**
See also AAYA 21; CA 143; SATA 76

Smucker, Barbara (Claassen) 1915- **10**
See also CA 106; CANR 23; JRDA; MAICYA;
SAAS 11; SATA 29, 76

Sneve, Virginia Driving Hawk 1933- **2**
See also CA 49-52; CANR 3, 68; SATA 8, 95

Snyder, Zilpha Keatley 1927- **31**
See also AAYA 15; CA 9-12R; CANR 38; CLC
17; JRDA; MAICYA; SAAS 2; SATA 1, 28,
75

Sobol, Donald J. 1924- **4**
See also CA 1-4R; CANR 1, 18, 38; JRDA;
MAICYA; SATA 1, 31, 73

Soto, Gary 1952- **38**
See also AAYA 10; CA 119; 125; CANR 50; CLC
32, 80; DAM MULT; DLB 82; HLC; HW;
INT 125; JRDA; SATA 80

Souci, Robert D. San
See San Souci, Robert D.

Southall, Ivan (Francis) 1921- **2**
See also AAYA 22; CA 9-12R; CANR 7, 47;
JRDA; MAICYA; SAAS 3; SATA 3, 68

Speare, Elizabeth George 1908-1994 .... **8**
See also CA 1-4R; 147; JRDA; MAICYA; SATA
5, 62; SATA-Obit 83

Spence, Eleanor (Rachel) 1928- **26**
See also CA 49-52; CANR 3; SATA 21

Spier, Peter (Edward) 1927- **5**
See also CA 5-8R; CANR 41; DLB 61; MAICYA;
SATA 4, 54

Spinelli, Jerry 1941- **26**
See also AAYA 11; CA 111; CANR 30, 45; JRDA;
MAICYA; SATA 39, 71

Spykman, E(lizabeth) C(hoate) 1896-
1965 .... **35**
See also CA 101; SATA 10

Spyri, Johanna (Heusser) 1827-1901 ...... **13**
See also CA 137; MAICYA; SATA 19, 100

Stanley, Diane 1943- **46**
See also CA 112; CANR 32, 64; SAAS 15; SATA
37, 80; SATA-Brief 32

Stanton, Schuyler
See Baum, L(yman) Frank

Staunton, Schuyler
See Baum, L(yman) Frank

Steig, William (H.) 1907- **2, 15**
See also AITN 1; CA 77-80; CANR 21, 44; DLB
61; INT CANR-21; MAICYA; SATA 18, 70

Steptoe, John (Lewis) 1950-1989 .... **2, 12**
See also BW 1; CA 49-52; 129; CANR 3, 26;
MAICYA; SATA 8, 63

Sterling, Dorothy 1913- **1**
See also CA 9-12R; CANR 5, 28; JRDA;
MAICYA; SAAS 2; SATA 1, 83

Stevenson, James 1929- **17**
See also CA 115; CANR 47; MAICYA; SATA
42, 71; SATA-Brief 34

Stevenson, Robert Louis (Balfour) 1850-
1894 .... **10, 11**
See also AAYA 24; CDBLB 1890-1914; DA;
DAB; DAC; DAM MST, NOV; DLB 18, 57,
141, 156, 174; DLBD 13; JRDA; MAICYA;
NCLC 5, 14, 63; SATA 100; SSC 11; WLC;
YABC 2

Stine, Jovial Bob
See Stine, R(obert) L(awrence)

Stine, R(obert) L(awrence) 1943-........... **37**
See also AAYA 13; CA 105; CANR 22, 53; JRDA;
SATA 31, 76

Stone, Rosetta
See Dr. Seuss

Strasser, Todd 1950- **11**
See also AAYA 2; CA 117; 123; CANR 47; JRDA;
MAICYA; SATA 41, 45, 71

Streatfeild, (Mary) Noel 1895(?)-1986..... **17**
See also CA 81-84; 120; CANR 31; CLC 21;
DLB 160; MAICYA; SATA 20; SATA-Obit 48

Stren, Patti 1949- **5**
See also CA 117; 124; SATA 88; SATA-Brief 41

Strong, Charles
See Epstein, Beryl (M. Williams); Epstein, Samuel

Suhl, Yuri (Menachem) 1908-1986 .... **2**
See also CA 45-48; 121; CANR 2, 38; MAICYA;
SAAS 1; SATA 8; SATA-Obit 50

Sutcliff, Rosemary 1920-1992 .... **1, 37**
See also AAYA 10; CA 5-8R; 139; CANR 37;
CLC 26; DAB; DAC; DAM MST, POP; JRDA;
MAICYA; SATA 6, 44, 78; SATA-Obit 73

Swift, Jonathan 1667-1745 .... **53**
See also CDBLB 1660-1789; DA; DAB; DAC;
DAM MST, NOV, POET; DLB 39, 95, 101;
LC 1; PC 9; SATA 19; WLC

Tarry, Ellen 1906- **26**
See also BW 1; CA 73-76; CANR 69; SAAS 16;
SATA 16

Tate, Eleanora E(laine) 1948-................ **37**
See also AAYA 25; BW 2; CA 105; CANR 25,
43; JRDA; SATA 38, 94

Taylor, Mildred D. **9**
See also AAYA 10; BW 1; CA 85-88; CANR 25;
CLC 21; DLB 52; JRDA; MAICYA; SAAS 5;
SATA 15, 70

Taylor, Theodore 1921-........................ **30**
See also AAYA 2, 19; CA 21-24R; CANR 9, 25, 38,
50; JRDA; MAICYA; SAAS 4; SATA 5, 54, 83

Tejima 1931- **20**

Tenniel, John 1820-1914 .... **18**
See also CA 111; MAICYA; SATA 74; SATA-
Brief 27

ter Haar, Jaap 1922-
See Haar, Jaap ter
See also CA 37-40R; SATA 6

Thiele, Colin (Milton) 1920- **27**
See also CA 29-32R; CANR 12, 28, 53; CLC 17;
MAICYA; SAAS 2; SATA 14, 72

Thomas, Ianthe 1951- **8**
See also SATA-Brief 42

Thomas, Joyce Carol 1938- **19**
See also AAYA 12; BW 2; CA 113; 116; CANR
48; CLC 35; DLB 33; INT 116; JRDA;
MAICYA; MTCW 1; SAAS 7; SATA 40, 78

Thompson, George Selden 1929-1989
See Selden, George
See also CA 5-8R; 130; CANR 21, 37; INT
CANR-21; MAICYA; SATA 4, 73; SATA-
Obit 63

Thompson, Julian F(rancis) 1927- **24**
See also AAYA 9; CA 111; CANR 30, 56; JRDA;
MAICYA; SAAS 13; SATA 55, 99; SATA-
Brief 40

Thompson, Kay 1912(?)-1989 .... **22**
See also CA 85-88; 169; MAICYA; SATA 16

Tobias, Tobi 1938- **4**
See also CA 29-32R; CANR 16; SATA 5, 82

Tomfool
See Farjeon, Eleanor

Totham, Mary
See Breinburg, Petronella

Townsend, John Rowe 1922- **2**
See also AAYA 11; CA 37-40R; CANR 41; JRDA;
MAICYA; SAAS 2; SATA 4, 68

Travers, P(amela) L(yndon) 1906-1996 ..... **2**
See also CA 33-36R; 152; CANR 30; DLB 160;
MAICYA; SAAS 2; SATA 4, 54, 100; SATA-
Obit 90

Trease, (Robert) Geoffrey 1909-1998 ...... **42**
See also CA 5-8R; 165; CANR 7, 22, 38;
MAICYA; SAAS 6; SATA 2, 60; SATA-
Obit 101

Treece, Henry 1912-1966 .... **2**
See also CA 1-4R; 25-28R; CANR 6, 60; DLB
160; MAICYA; SATA 2

Tresselt, Alvin 1916-........................... **30**
See also CA 49-52; CANR 1; MAICYA; SATA 7

Trezise, Percy (James) 1923-................ **41**
See also CA 132

Tudor, Tasha 1915-............................. **13**
See also CA 81-84; MAICYA; SATA 20, 69

Tunis, Edwin (Burdett) 1897-1973 .... **2**
See also CA 5-8R; 45-48; CANR 7; MAICYA;
SATA 1, 28; SATA-Obit 24

Twohill, Maggie
See Gaberman, Judie Angell

Uchida, Yoshiko 1921-1992 .... **6**
See also AAYA 16; CA 13-16R; 139; CANR 6,
22, 47, 61; JRDA; MAICYA; MTCW 1; SAAS
1; SATA 1, 53; SATA-Obit 72

Uderzo, Albert 1927- **37**

Uncle Gus
See Rey, H(ans) A(ugusto)

Uncle Shelby
See Silverstein, Shel(by)

Ungerer, Jean Thomas 1931-
See Ungerer, Tomi
See also CA 41-44R; MAICYA; SATA 5, 33

Ungerer, Tomi **3**
See also Ungerer, Jean Thomas

Unnerstad, Edith (Totterman) 1900- **36**
See also CA 5-8R; CANR 6, 72; SATA 3

Ure, Jean 1943- **34**
See also CA 125; CANR 48; JRDA; MAICYA;
SAAS 14; SATA 48, 78

Usher, Margo Scegge
See McHargue, Georgess

Van Allsburg, Chris 1949- **5, 13**
See also CA 113; 117; CANR 38; DLB 61;
MAICYA; SATA 37, 53

Van Dyne, Edith
See Baum, L(yman) Frank

Ventura, Piero (Luigi) 1937-................. **16**
See also CA 103; CANR 39; MAICYA; SATA
61; SATA-Brief 43

Vincent, Gabrielle (a pseudonym) **13**
See also CA 126; MAICYA; SATA 61

Viorst, Judith 1931-............................. **3**
See also BEST 90:1; CA 49-52; CANR 2, 26,
59; DAM POP; DLB 52; INT CANR-26;
MAICYA; SATA 7, 70

Voigt, Cynthia 1942- **13, 48**
See also AAYA 3; CA 106; CANR 18, 37, 40;
CLC 30; INT CANR-18; JRDA; MAICYA;
SATA 48, 79; SATA-Brief 33

Vugteveen, Verna Aardema 1911-
See Aardema, Verna
See also CA 5-8R; CANR 3, 18, 39

Waddell, Martin 1941- **31**
See also AAYA 23; CA 113; CANR 34, 56; SAAS
15; SATA 43, 81

Wallace, Ian 1950-............................. **37**
See also CA 107; CANR 25, 38, 50; MAICYA;
SATA 53, 56

Walsh, Jill Paton **2**
See also Paton Walsh, Gillian
See also AAYA 11; CLC 35; DLB 161; SAAS 3

Walter, Mildred Pitts 1922- **15**
See also BW 2; CA 138; JRDA; MAICYA; SAAS
12; SATA 69; SATA-Brief 45

Walter, Villiam Christian
See Andersen, Hans Christian

Ward, E. D.
See Gorey, Edward (St. John)

Warshofsky, Isaac
See Singer, Isaac Bashevis

Watanabe, Shigeo 1928-........................ **8**
See also CA 112; CANR 45; MAICYA; SATA
39; SATA-Brief 32

Watson, Clyde 1947- **3**
See also CA 49-52; CANR 4, 39; MAICYA; SATA
5, 68

Waystaff, Simon
See Swift, Jonathan

Weary, Ogdred
See Gorey, Edward (St. John)

Webb, Christopher
See Wibberley, Leonard (Patrick O'Connor)

Weiss, Harvey 1922- **4**
See also CA 5-8R; CANR 6, 38; MAICYA; SAAS
19; SATA 1, 27, 76

Weiss, Miriam
See Schlein, Miriam

Wells, Rosemary 1943- **16**
See also AAYA 13; CA 85-88; CANR 48; CLC
12; MAICYA; SAAS 1; SATA 18, 69

Wersba, Barbara 1932- **3**
See also AAYA 2; CA 29-32R; CANR 16, 38;
CLC 30; DLB 52; JRDA; MAICYA; SAAS 2;
SATA 1, 58

Westall, Robert (Atkinson) 1929-1993 .... **13**
See also AAYA 12; CA 69-72; 141; CANR 18,
68; CLC 17; JRDA; MAICYA; SAAS 2; SATA
23, 69; SATA-Obit 75

Weston, Allen
See Norton, Andre

White, E(lwyn) B(rooks) 1899-1985 .... **1, 21**
See also AITN 2; CA 13-16R; 116; CANR 16,
37; CLC 10, 34, 39; DAM POP; DLB 11, 22;
MAICYA; MTCW 1; SATA 2, 29, 100; SATA-
Obit 44

White, Robb 1909- **3**
See also CA 1-4R; CANR 1; SAAS 1; SATA 1, 83

Wibberley, Leonard (Patrick O'Connor) 1915-
1983 .... **3**
See also CA 5-8R; 111; CANR 3; SATA 2, 45;
SATA-Obit 36

Wiesner, David 1956- **43**
See also SATA 72

Wiggin, Kate Douglas (Smith) 1856-
1923 .... **52**
See also CA 137; MAICYA

Wilder, Laura (Elizabeth) Ingalls 1867-
1957 .... **2**
See also AAYA 26; CA 111; 137; DLB 22; JRDA;
MAICYA; SATA 15, 29, 100

Wildsmith, Brian 1930- **2, 52**
See also CA 85-88; CANR 35; MAICYA; SAAS
5; SATA 16, 69

Wilhelm, Hans 1945- **46**
See also CA 119; CANR 48; SAAS 21; SATA 58

Wilkins, Mary Huiskamp 1926-
See Calhoun, Mary
See also CA 5-8R; CANR 2, 18; SATA 84

Wilkinson, Brenda 1946- **20**
See also BW 2; CA 69-72; CANR 26, 51; JRDA;
SATA 14, 91

Willard, Barbara (Mary) 1909-1994 .... **2**
See also CA 81-84; 144; CANR 15; DLB 161;
MAICYA; SAAS 5; SATA 17, 74

Willard, Nancy 1936- **5**
See also CA 89-92; CANR 10, 39, 68; CLC 7,
37; DLB 5, 52; MAICYA; MTCW 1; SATA
37, 71; SATA-Brief 30

Williams, Barbara 1925- **48**
See also CA 49-52; CANR 1, 17; SAAS 16;
SATA 11

Williams, Beryl
See Epstein, Beryl (M. Williams)

Williams, Charles
See Collier, James L(incoln)

Williams, Jay 1914-1978 .... **8**
See also CA 1-4R; 81-84; CANR 2, 39; MAICYA;
SATA 3, 41; SATA-Obit 24

Williams, Kit 1946(?)- **4**
See also CA 107; SATA 44

Williams, Margery
See Bianco, Margery (Williams)

Williams, Vera B. 1927- **9**
See also CA 123; CANR 38; MAICYA; SATA
53, 102; SATA-Brief 33

Williams-Garcia, Rita **36**
See also AAYA 22; CA 159; SATA 98

Wisniewski, David 1953- **51**
See also CA 160; SATA 95

Wodge, Dreary
See Gorey, Edward (St. John)

Wojciechowska, Maia (Teresa) 1927- **1**
See also AAYA 8; CA 9-12R; CANR 4, 41; CLC
26; JRDA; MAICYA; SAAS 1; SATA 1,
28, 83

Wolff, Sonia
See Levitin, Sonia (Wolff)

Wolny, P.
See Janeczko, Paul B(ryan)

Wood, Audrey **26**
See also CA 137; MAICYA; SATA 50, 81; SATA-
Brief 44

Wood, Don 1945- **26**
See also CA 136; MAICYA; SATA 50; SATA-
Brief 44

Woodson, Jacqueline 1964- **49**
See also CA 159

Worth, Valerie **21**
See also Bahlke, Valerie Worth
See also MAICYA; SATA 8, 70

Wortis, Avi 1937-
See Avi
See also CA 69-72; CANR 12, 42; JRDA;
MAICYA; SATA 14

Wrightson, (Alice) Patricia 1921- **4, 14**
See also AAYA 5; CA 45-48; CANR 3, 19, 36;
JRDA; MAICYA; SAAS 4; SATA 8, 66

Wryde, Dogear
See Gorey, Edward (St. John)

Wynne-Jones, Tim(othy) 1948- **21**
See also CA 105; CANR 39; SATA 67, 96

Yaffe, Alan
See Yorinks, Arthur

Yarbrough, Camille 1938- **29**
See also BW 2; CA 105; 125; SATA 79

Yashima, Taro **4**
See also Iwamatsu, Jun Atsushi

Yee, Paul (R.) 1956- **44**
See also AAYA 24; CA 135; JRDA; SATA 67, 96

Yeoman, John 1934- **46**
See also CA 106; SATA 28, 80

Yep, Laurence Michael 1948- **3, 17, 54**
See also AAYA 5; CA 49-52; CANR 1, 46; CLC
35; DLB 52; JRDA; MAICYA; SATA 7, 69

Yolen, Jane (Hyatt) 1939- **4, 44**
See also AAYA 4,22; CA 13-16R; CANR 11, 29,
56; DLB 52; INT CANR-29; JRDA; MAICYA;
SAAS 1; SATA 4, 40, 75

Yorinks, Arthur 1953- **20**
See also CA 106; CANR 38; MAICYA; SATA
33, 49, 85

Youd, (Christopher) Samuel 1922-
See Christopher, John
See also CA 77-80; CANR 37; JRDA; MAICYA;
SATA 47; SATA-Brief 30

Young, Ed (Tse-chun) 1931- **27**
See also CA 116; 130; MAICYA; SATA 10, 74

Zei, Alki **6**
See also CA 77-80; SATA 24

Zim, Herbert S(pencer) 1909-1994 .... **2**
See also CA 13-16R; 147; CANR 17; JRDA;
MAICYA; SAAS 2; SATA 1, 30; SATA-
Obit 85

Zimnik, Reiner 1930- **3**
See also CA 77-80; SATA 36

Zindel, Paul 1936- **3, 45**
See also AAYA 2; CA 73-76; CANR 31, 65; CLC
6, 26; DA; DAB; DAC; DAM DRAM, MST,
NOV; DC 5; DLB 7, 52; JRDA; MAICYA;
MTCW 1; SATA 16, 58, 102

Zolotow, Charlotte S(hapiro) 1915- **2**
See also CA 5-8R; CANR 3, 18, 38; DLB 52;
MAICYA; SATA 1, 35, 78

Zuromskis, Diane
See Stanley, Diane

Zuromskis, Diane Stanley
See Stanley, Diane

Zwerger, Lisbeth 1954- **46**
See also MAICYA; SAAS 13; SATA 66

CUMULATIVE INDEX TO NATIONALITIES

AMERICAN

Aardema, Verna 17
Aaseng, Nathan 54
Adkins, Jan 7
Adler, Irving 27
Adoff, Arnold 7
Alcott, Louisa May 1, 38
Alexander, Lloyd (Chudley) 1, 5, 48
Aliki 9
Angelou, Maya 53
Anglund, Joan Walsh 1
Armstrong, William H(oward) 1
Arnosky, James Edward 15
Aruego, Jose (Espiritu) 5
Ashabranner, Brent (Kenneth) 28
Asimov, Isaac 12
Atwater, Florence (Hasseltine Carroll) 19
Atwater, Richard (Tupper) 19
Avi 24
Aylesworth, Thomas G(ibbons) 6
Babbitt, Natalie (Zane Moore) 2, 53
Bacon, Martha Sherman 3
Bang, Molly Garrett 8
Baum, L(yman) Frank 15
Baylor, Byrd 3
Bellairs, John (A.) 37
Bemelmans, Ludwig 6
Benary-Isbert, Margot 12
Bendick, Jeanne 5
Berenstain, Jan(ice) 19
Berenstain, Stan(ley) 19
Berger, Melvin H. 32
Bess, Clayton 39
Bethancourt, T. Ernesto 3
Block, Francesca (Lia) 33
Blos, Joan W(insor) 18
Blumberg, Rhoda 21
Blume, Judy (Sussman) 2, 15
Bond, Nancy (Barbara) 11
Bontemps, Arna(ud Wendell) 6

Bova, Ben(jamin William) 3
Boyd, Candy Dawson 50
Brancato, Robin F(idler) 32
Branley, Franklyn M(ansfield) 13
Brett, Jan (Churchill) 27
Bridgers, Sue Ellen 18
Brink, Carol Ryrie 30
Brooks, Bruce 25
Brooks, Gwendolyn 27
Brown, Marcia 12
Brown, Marc (Tolon) 29
Brown, Margaret Wise 10
Bruchac, Joseph III 46
Bryan, Ashley F. 18
Bunting, Eve 28
Burnett, Frances (Eliza) Hodgson 24
Burton, Virginia Lee 11
Byars, Betsy (Cromer) 1, 16
Caines, Jeannette (Franklin) 24
Calhoun, Mary 42
Cameron, Eleanor (Frances) 1
Carle, Eric 10
Carter, Alden R(ichardson) 22
Cassedy, Sylvia 26
Charlip, Remy 8
Childress, Alice 14
Choi, Sook Nyul 53
Christopher, Matt(hew Frederick) 33
Ciardi, John (Anthony) 19
Clark, Ann Nolan 16
Cleary, Beverly (Atlee Bunn) 2, 8
Cleaver, Bill 6
Cleaver, Vera (Allen) 6
Clifton, (Thelma) Lucille 5
Coatsworth, Elizabeth (Jane) 2
Cobb, Vicki 2
Cohen, Daniel (E.) 3, 43
Cole, Brock 18
Cole, Joanna 5, 40
Collier, James L(incoln) 3

Colum, Padraic 36
Conford, Ellen 10
Conrad, Pam 18
Cooney, Barbara 23
Corbett, Scott 1
Corcoran, Barbara 50
Cormier, Robert (Edmund) 12
Cox, Palmer 24
Creech, Sharon 42
Crews, Donald 7
Crutcher, Chris(topher C.) 28
Cummings, Pat (Marie) 48
Curry, Jane L(ouise) 31
Danziger, Paula 20
d'Aulaire, Edgar Parin 21
d'Aulaire, Ingri (Mortenson Parin) 21
Day, Alexandra 22
de Angeli, Marguerite (Lofft) 1
DeClements, Barthe 23
DeJong, Meindert 1
Denslow, W(illiam) W(allace) 15
dePaola, Tomie 4, 24
Dillon, Diane 44
Dillon, Leo 44
Disch, Thomas M(ichael) 18
Domanska, Janina 40
Donovan, John 3
Dorros, Arthur (M.) 42
Dr. Seuss 1, 9, 53
Duke, Kate 51
Duncan, Lois 29
Duvoisin, Roger Antoine 23
Eager, Edward McMaken 43
Ehlert, Lois (Jane) 28
Emberley, Barbara A(nne) 5
Emberley, Ed(ward Randolph) 5
Engdahl, Sylvia Louise 2
Enright, Elizabeth 4
Epstein, Beryl (M. Williams) 26
Epstein, Samuel 26

223

Estes, Eleanor 2
Ets, Marie Hall 33
Feelings, Muriel (Grey) 5
Feelings, Tom 5
Ferry, Charles 34
Field, Rachel (Lyman) 21
Fisher, Aileen (Lucia) 49
Fisher, Leonard Everett 18
Fitzgerald, John D(ennis) 1
Fitzhugh, Louise 1
Flack, Marjorie 28
Fleischman, (Albert) Sid(ney) 1, 15
Fleischman, Paul 20
Forbes, Esther 27
Foster, Genevieve Stump 7
Fox, Paula 1, 44
Freedman, Russell (Bruce) 20
Freeman, Don 30
Fritz, Jean (Guttery) 2, 14
Fujikawa, Gyo 25
Gaberman, Judie Angell 33
Gag, Wanda (Hazel) 4
Galdone, Paul 16
Gallant, Roy A(rthur) 30
Gantos, Jack 18
Garden, Nancy 51
George, Jean Craighead 1
Gibbons, Gail 8
Giblin, James Cross 29
Giovanni, Nikki 6
Glenn, Mel 51
Glubok, Shirley (Astor) 1
Goble, Paul 21
Goffstein, (Marilyn) Brooke 3
Gordon, Sheila 27
Gorey, Edward (St. John) 36
Graham, Lorenz (Bell) 10
Gramatky, Hardie 22
Greene, Bette 2
Greenfield, Eloise 4, 38
Grifalconi, Ann 35
Grimes, Nikki 42
Gruelle, Johnny 34
Guy, Rosa (Cuthbert) 13
Hadley, Lee 40
Haley, Gail E(inhart) 21
Hamilton, Virginia 1, 11, 40
Hansen, Joyce (Viola) 21
Harris, Joel Chandler 49
Haskins, James S. 3, 39
Hautzig, Esther Rudomin 22
Haywood, Carolyn 22
Henkes, Kevin 23
Henry, Marguerite 4
Hentoff, Nat(han Irving) 1, 52
Hesse, Karen 54
Highwater, Jamake (Mamake) 17
Hinton, S(usan) E(loise) 3, 23
Hoban, Russell (Conwell) 3
Hoban, Tana 13
Hoberman, Mary Ann 22
Hogrogian, Nonny 2
Holling, Holling C(lancy) 50
Hopkins, Lee Bennett 44
Howe, James 9
Hughes, (James) Langston 17
Hunt, Irene 1
Hunter, Kristin (Eggleston) 3
Hurd, Clement (G.) 49
Hurd, Edith (Thacher) 49
Hurmence, Belinda 25
Hyde, Margaret O(ldroyd) 23
Hyman, Trina Schart 50

Irwin, Ann(abelle Bowen) 40
Isadora, Rachel 7
Jackson, Jesse 28
Janeczko, Paul B(ryan) 47
Jarrell, Randall 6
Jeffers, Susan 30
Johnson, Angela 33
Johnson, James Weldon 32
Jonas, Ann 12
Jordan, June 10
Joyce, William 26
Kalman, Maira 32
Keats, Ezra Jack 1, 35
Keller, Holly 45
Kellogg, Steven 6
Kennedy, X. J. 27
Kerr, M. E. 29
Khalsa, Dayal Kaur 30
Kherdian, David 24
Klein, Norma 2, 19
Knight, David C(arpenter) 38
Konigsburg, E(laine) L(obl) 1, 47
Kotzwinkle, William 6
Krauss, Ruth (Ida) 42
Krementz, Jill 5
Krull, Kathleen 44
Kuklin, Susan 51
Kuskin, Karla (Seidman) 4
Langstaff, John (Meredith) 3
Langton, Jane (Gillson) 33
Lasky, Kathryn 11
Latham, Jean Lee 50
Lauber, Patricia (Grace) 16
Lavine, Sigmund Arnold 35
Lawson, Robert 2
Leaf, (Wilbur) Munro 25
Le Guin, Ursula K(roeber) 3, 28
L'Engle, Madeleine (Camp Franklin) 1, 14
Lenski, Lois 26
Lerner, Carol 34
LeShan, Eda J(oan) 6
Lester, Julius (Bernard) 2, 41
Levitin, Sonia (Wolff) 53
Lionni, Leo(nard) 7
Lipsyte, Robert (Michael) 23
Livingston, Myra Cohn 7
Lobel, Arnold (Stark) 5
Locker, Thomas 14
Lowry, Lois 6, 46
MacLachlan, Patricia 14
Maestro, Betsy C(rippen) 45
Maestro, Giulio 45
Manley, Seon 3
Marrin, Albert 53
Marshall, James (Edward) 21
Martin, Ann M(atthews) 32
Mathis, Sharon Bell 3
Mayer, Mercer 11
Mazer, Harry 16
Mazer, Norma Fox 23
McCaffrey, Anne (Inez) 49
McCloskey, (John) Robert 7
McClung, Robert M(arshall) 11
McCord, David (Thompson Watson) 9
McCully, Emily Arnold 46
McDermott, Gerald 9
McGovern, Ann 50
McHargue, Georgess 2
McKinley, (Jennifer Carolyn) Robin 10
McKissack, Patricia (L'Ann) C(arwell) 23
McMillan, Bruce 47
Meltzer, Milton 13
Merriam, Eve 14

Merrill, Jean (Fairbanks) 52
Milne, Lorus J. 22
Milne, Margery 22
Minarik, Else Holmelund 33
Mohr, Nicholasa 22
Monjo, F(erdinand) N(icholas III) 2
Moore, Lilian 15
Moser, Barry 49
Mukerji, Dhan Gopal 10
Munsch, Robert (Norman) 19
Murphy, Jim 53
Myers, Walter Dean 4, 16, 35
Namioka, Lensey 48
Napoli, Donna Jo 51
Naylor, Phyllis (Reynolds) 17
Ness, Evaline (Michelow) 6
Neufeld, John (Arthur) 52
Nixon, Joan Lowery 24
Norton, Andre 50
Nourse, Alan E(dward) 33
O'Brien, Robert C. 2
O'Dell, Scott 1, 16
Oneal, Zibby 13
Orgel, Doris 48
Parish, Peggy 22
Park, Barbara 34
Pascal, Francine 25
Patent, Dorothy Hinshaw 19
Paterson, Katherine (Womeldorf) 7, 50
Paulsen, Gary 19, 54
Peck, Richard (Wayne) 15
Peck, Robert Newton 45
Peet, Bill 12
Pene du Bois, William (Sherman) 1
Petersham, Maud (Sylvia Fuller) 24
Petersham, Miska 24
Petry, Ann (Lane) 12
Pfeffer, Susan Beth 11
Pierce, Meredith Ann 20
Pilkey, Dav 48
Pinkney, Jerry 43
Pinkney, (Jerry) Brian 54
Pinkwater, Daniel Manus 4
Polacco, Patricia 40
Politi, Leo 29
Prelutsky, Jack 13
Pringle, Laurence (Patrick) 4
Provensen, Alice 11
Provensen, Martin (Elias) 11
Pyle, Howard 22
Raskin, Ellen 1, 12
Rau, Margaret 8
Reiss, Johanna (de Leeuw) 19
Rey, H(ans) A(ugusto) 5
Rey, Margret (Elisabeth) 5
Richards, Laura E(lizabeth Howe) 54
Rinaldi, Ann 46
Ringgold, Faith 30
Rockwell, Thomas 6
Rodgers, Mary 20
Ryder, Joanne (Rose) 37
Rylant, Cynthia 15
Sachar, Louis 28
Sachs, Marilyn (Stickle) 2
Salinger, J(erome) D(avid) 18
Sanchez, Sonia 18
San Souci, Robert D. 43
Sattler, Helen Roney 24
Sawyer, Ruth 36
Say, Allen 22
Scarry, Richard (McClure) 3, 41
Schlein, Miriam 41
Schwartz, Alvin 3

Schwartz, Amy 25
Scieszka, Jon 27
Scott, Jack Denton 20
Sebestyen, Ouida 17
Selden, George 8
Selsam, Millicent Ellis 1
Sendak, Maurice (Bernard) 1, 17
Seredy, Kate 10
Shearer, John 34
Shippen, Katherine B(inney) 36
Showers, Paul C. 6
Silverstein, Alvin 25
Silverstein, Shel(by) 5
Silverstein, Virginia B(arbara Opshelor) 25
Simon, Hilda Rita 39
Simon, Seymour 9
Singer, Isaac Bashevis 1
Singer, Marilyn 48
Sleator, William (Warner III) 29
Slote, Alfred 4
Small, David 53
Smith, Lane 47
Smucker, Barbara (Claassen) 10
Sneve, Virginia Driving Hawk 2
Snyder, Zilpha Keatley 31
Sobol, Donald J. 4
Soto, Gary 38
Speare, Elizabeth George 8
Spier, Peter (Edward) 5
Spinelli, Jerry 26
Spykman, E(lizabeth) C(hoate) 35
Stanley, Diane 46
Steig, William (H.) 2, 15
Steptoe, John (Lewis) 2, 12
Sterling, Dorothy 1
Stevenson, James 17
Stine, R(obert) L(awrence) 37
St. John, Nicole 46
Strasser, Todd 11
Suhl, Yuri (Menachem) 2
Tarry, Ellen 26
Tate, Eleanora E(laine) 37
Taylor, Mildred D. 9
Taylor, Theodore 30
Thomas, Ianthe 8
Thomas, Joyce Carol 19
Thompson, Julian F(rancis) 24
Thompson, Kay 22
Tobias, Tobi 4
Tresselt, Alvin 30
Tudor, Tasha 13
Tunis, Edwin (Burdett) 2
Uchida, Yoshiko 6
Van Allsburg, Chris 5, 13
Viorst, Judith 3
Voigt, Cynthia 13, 48
Walter, Mildred Pitts 15
Watson, Clyde 3
Weiss, Harvey 4
Wells, Rosemary 16
Wersba, Barbara 3
White, E(lwyn) B(rooks) 1, 21
White, Robb 3
Wibberley, Leonard (Patrick O'Connor) 3
Wiesner, David 43
Wiggin, Kate Douglas (Smith) 52
Wilder, Laura (Elizabeth) Ingalls 2
Wilkinson, Brenda 20
Willard, Nancy 5
Williams, Barbara 48
Williams, Jay 8
Williams, Vera B. 9
Williams-Garcia, Rita 36

Wisniewski, David 51
Wojciechowska, Maia (Teresa) 1
Wood, Audrey 26
Wood, Don 26
Woodson, Jacqueline 49
Worth, Valerie 21
Yarbrough, Camille 29
Yashima, Taro 4
Yep, Laurence Michael 3, 17, 54
Yolen, Jane (Hyatt) 4, 44
Yorinks, Arthur 20
Young, Ed (Tse-chun) 27
Zim, Herbert S(pencer) 2
Zindel, Paul 3, 45
Zolotow, Charlotte S(hapiro) 2

AUSTRALIAN
Baillie, Allan (Stuart) 49
Baker, Jeannie 28
Base, Graeme (Rowland) 22
Brinsmead, H(esba) F(ay) 47
Chauncy, Nan(cen Beryl Masterman) 6
Clark, Mavis Thorpe 30
Crew, Gary 42
Fox, Mem 23
Graham, Bob 31
Hilton, Nette 25
Jennings, Paul 40
Kelleher, Victor (Michael Kitchener) 36
Klein, Robin 21
Lindsay, Norman Alfred William 8
Marsden, John 34
Mattingley, Christobel (Rosemary) 24
Ormerod, Jan(ette Louise) 20
Ottley, Reginald Leslie 16
Phipson, Joan 5
Rodda, Emily 32
Roughsey, Dick 41
Rubinstein, Gillian (Margaret) 35
Southall, Ivan (Francis) 2
Spence, Eleanor (Rachel) 26
Thiele, Colin (Milton) 27
Travers, P(amela) L(yndon) 2
Trezise, Percy (James) 41
Wrightson, (Alice) Patricia 4, 14

AUSTRIAN
Bemelmans, Ludwig 6
Noestlinger, Christine 12
Orgel, Doris 48
Zwerger, Lisbeth 46

BELGIAN
Herge 6
Vincent, Gabrielle (a pseudonym) 13

CANADIAN
Bedard, Michael 35
Blades, Ann (Sager) 15
Buffie, Margaret 39
Burnford, Sheila (Philip Cochrane Every) 2
Cameron, Eleanor (Frances) 1
Cleaver, Elizabeth (Mrazik) 13
Cox, Palmer 24
Doyle, Brian 22
Ellis, Sarah 42
Gay, Marie-Louise 27
Grey Owl 32
Haig-Brown, Roderick (Langmere) 31
Harris, Christie (Lucy) Irwin 47
Houston, James A(rchibald) 3
Hudson, Jan 40
Hughes, Monica (Ince) 9

Johnston, Julie 41
Katz, Welwyn Wilton 45
Khalsa, Dayal Kaur 30
Korman, Gordon (Richard) 25
Kovalski, Maryann 34
Kurelek, William 2
Lee, Dennis (Beynon) 3
Little, (Flora) Jean 4
Lunn, Janet (Louise Swoboda) 18
Mackay, Claire 43
Major, Kevin (Gerald) 11
Markoosie 23
Matas, Carol 52
Milne, Lorus J. 22
Montgomery, L(ucy) M(aud) 8
Mowat, Farley (McGill) 20
Munsch, Robert (Norman) 19
Oberman, Sheldon 54
Pearson, Kit 26
Poulin, Stephane 28
Richler, Mordecai 17
Roberts, Charles G(eorge) D(ouglas) 33
Smucker, Barbara (Claassen) 10
Stren, Patti 5
Wallace, Ian 37
Wynne-Jones, Tim(othy) 21
Yee, Paul (R.) 44

CHILEAN
Krahn, Fernando 3

CHINESE
Namioka, Lensey 48
Young, Ed (Tse-chun) 27

CZECH
Sasek, Miroslav 4
Sis, Peter 45

DANISH
Andersen, Hans Christian 6
Bodker, Cecil 23
Drescher, Henrik 20
Haugaard, Erik Christian 11
Minarik, Else Holmelund 33
Nielsen, Kay (Rasmus) 16

DUTCH
Biegel, Paul 27
Bruna, Dick 7
DeJong, Meindert 1
Haar, Jaap ter 15
Lionni, Leo(nard) 7
Reiss, Johanna (de Leeuw) 19
Schmidt, Annie M. G. 22
Spier, Peter (Edward) 5

ENGLISH
Adams, Richard (George) 20
Ahlberg, Allan 18
Ahlberg, Janet 18
Aiken, Joan (Delano) 1, 19
Alcock, Vivien 26
Allan, Mabel Esther 43
Ardizzone, Edward (Jeffrey Irving) 3
Arundel, Honor (Morfydd) 35
Ashley, Bernard 4
Awdry, Wilbert Vere 23
Baker, Jeannie 28
Banner, Angela 24
Barklem, Jill 31
Base, Graeme (Rowland) 22
Bawden, Nina (Mary Mabey) 2, 51

Bianco, Margery (Williams) **19**
Biro, Val **28**
Blake, Quentin (Saxby) **31**
Blake, William **52**
Blyton, Enid (Mary) **31**
Bond, (Thomas) Michael **1**
Boston, L(ucy) M(aria Wood) **3**
Breinburg, Petronella **31**
Briggs, Raymond Redvers **10**
Brooke, L(eonard) Leslie **20**
Browne, Anthony (Edward Tudor) **19**
Burnett, Frances (Eliza) Hodgson **24**
Burningham, John (Mackintosh) **9**
Burton, Hester (Wood-Hill) **1**
Caldecott, Randolph (J.) **14**
Carroll, Lewis **2, 18**
Causley, Charles (Stanley) **30**
Chauncy, Nan(cen Beryl Masterman) **6**
Christopher, John **2**
Clarke, Pauline **28**
Cooper, Susan (Mary) **4**
Corbett, W(illiam) J(esse) **19**
Cresswell, Helen **18**
Cross, Gillian (Clare) **28**
Crossley-Holland, Kevin **47**
Dahl, Roald **1, 7, 41**
de la Mare, Walter (John) **23**
Dhondy, Farrukh **41**
Dickinson, Peter (Malcolm) **29**
Dodgson, Charles Lutwidge **2**
Doherty, Berlie **21**
Farjeon, Eleanor **34**
Farmer, Penelope (Jane) **8**
Fine, Anne **25**
Foreman, Michael **32**
French, Fiona **37**
Gardam, Jane **12**
Garfield, Leon **21**
Garner, Alan **20**
Gerrard, Roy **23**
Goble, Paul **21**
Godden, (Margaret) Rumer **20**
Goodall, John Strickland **25**
Grahame, Kenneth **5**
Greenaway, Kate **6**
Grey Owl **32**
Haig-Brown, Roderick (Langmere) **31**
Hamley, Dennis **47**
Handford, Martin (John) **22**
Harris, Rosemary (Jeanne) **30**
Hill, Eric **13**
Howker, Janni **14**
Hughes, Monica (Ince) **9**
Hughes, Shirley **15**
Hughes, Ted **3**
Hutchins, Pat **20**
Jacques, Brian **21**
Jones, Diana Wynne **23**
Keeping, Charles (William James) **34**
Kelleher, Victor (Michael Kitchener) **36**
Kemp, Gene **29**
King-Smith, Dick **40**
Kipling, (Joseph) Rudyard **39**
Lear, Edward **1**
Lewis, C(live) S(taples) **3, 27**
Lively, Penelope (Margaret) **7**
Lofting, Hugh (John) **19**
Macaulay, David (Alexander) **3, 14**
Mark, Jan(et Marjorie) **11**
Mayne, William (James Carter) **25**
McBratney, Sam **44**
McCaughrean, Geraldine **38**
McKee, David (John) **38**

McNaughton, Colin **54**
Milne, A(lan) A(lexander) **1, 26**
Morpurgo, Michael **51**
Murphy, Jill (Frances) **39**
Naidoo, Beverley **29**
Needle, Jan **43**
Nesbit, E(dith) **3**
Nimmo, Jenny **44**
Norton, Mary **6**
Oakley, Graham **7**
Ottley, Reginald Leslie **16**
Owen, Gareth **31**
Oxenbury, Helen **22**
Pearce, Philippa **9**
Peyton, K. M. **3**
Pienkowski, Jan (Michal) **6**
Potter, (Helen) Beatrix **1, 19**
Pullman, Philip (Nicholas) **20**
Ransome, Arthur (Michell) **8**
Rayner, Mary **41**
Reid Banks, Lynne **24**
Rosen, Michael (Wayne) **45**
Serraillier, Ian (Lucien) **2**
Sewell, Anna **17**
Sharp, Margery **27**
Shepard, Ernest Howard **27**
Simmonds, Posy **23**
Streatfeild, (Mary) Noel **17**
Sutcliff, Rosemary **1, 37**
Swift, Jonathan **53**
Tenniel, John **18**
Townsend, John Rowe **2**
Travers, P(amela) L(yndon) **2**
Trease, (Robert) Geoffrey **42**
Treece, Henry **2**
Ure, Jean **34**
Walsh, Jill Paton **2**
Westall, Robert (Atkinson) **13**
Wildsmith, Brian **2, 52**
Willard, Barbara (Mary) **2**
Williams, Kit **4**
Yeoman, John **46**

FILIPINO
Aruego, Jose (Espiritu) **5**

FINNISH
Jansson, Tove Marika **2**
Unnerstad, Edith (Totterman) **36**

FRENCH
Ayme, Marcel (Andre) **25**
Berna, Paul **19**
Billout, Guy (Rene) **33**
Boutet de Monvel, (Louis) M(aurice) **32**
Brunhoff, Jean de **4**
Brunhoff, Laurent de **4**
Goscinny, Rene **37**
Guillot, Rene **22**
Saint-Exupery, Antoine (Jean Baptiste Marie Roger) de **10**
Uderzo, Albert **37**
Ungerer, Tomi **3**

GERMAN
Baumann, Hans **35**
Benary-Isbert, Margot **12**
d'Aulaire, Edgar Parin **21**
Ende, Michael (Andreas Helmuth) **14**
Hartling, Peter **29**
Heine, Helme **18**
Janosch **26**
Kaestner, Erich **4**

Kruss, James **9**
Levitin, Sonia (Wolff) **53**
Rey, H(ans) A(ugusto) **5**
Rey, Margret (Elisabeth) **5**
Richter, Hans Peter **21**
Wilhelm, Hans **46**
Zimnik, Reiner **3**

GREEK
Aesop **14**
Zei, Alki **6**

HUNGARIAN
Biro, Val **28**
Galdone, Paul **16**
Seredy, Kate **10**

INDIAN
Dhondy, Farrukh **41**
Mukerji, Dhan Gopal **10**

IRISH
Bunting, Eve **28**
Colum, Padraic **36**
Dillon, Eilis **26**
O'Shea, (Catherine) Pat(ricia Shiels) **18**
Swift, Jonathan **53**

ISRAELI
Ofek, Uriel **28**
Orlev, Uri **30**
Shulevitz, Uri **5**

ITALIAN
Collodi, Carlo **5**
Munari, Bruno **9**
Rodari, Gianni **24**
Ventura, Piero (Luigi) **16**

JAMAICAN
Berry, James **22**

JAPANESE
Anno, Mitsumasa **2, 14**
Iwasaki (Matsumoto), Chihiro **18**
Kuratomi, Chizuko **32**
Maruki, Toshi **19**
Nakatani, Chiyoko **30**
Say, Allen **22**
Tejima **20**
Watanabe, Shigeo **8**
Yashima, Taro **4**

KOREAN
Choi, Sook Nyul **53**

MYANMARI
Rayner, Mary **41**

NEW ZEALANDER
Allen, Pamela **44**
Duder, Tessa **43**
Mahy, Margaret **7**
Park, (Rosina) Ruth (Lucia) **51**

NIGERIAN
Achebe, (Albert) Chinua(lumogu) **20**

NORTHERN IRISH
Waddell, Martin **31**

NORWEGIAN
d'Aulaire, Ingri (Mortenson Parin) **21**

Proeysen, Alf **24**

POLISH
Domanska, Janina **40**
Hautzig, Esther Rudomin **22**
Janosch **26**
Orlev, Uri **30**
Pienkowski, Jan (Michal) **6**
Shulevitz, Uri **5**
Singer, Isaac Bashevis **1**
Suhl, Yuri (Menachem) **2**
Wojciechowska, Maia (Teresa) **1**

RUSSIAN
Asimov, Isaac **12**
Ginsburg, Mirra **45**
Korinetz, Yuri (Iosifovich) **4**

SCOTTISH
Baillie, Allan (Stuart) **49**
Bannerman, Helen (Brodie Cowan Watson) **21**
Barrie, J(ames) M(atthew) **16**
Burnford, Sheila (Philip Cochrane Every) **2**
Hunter, Mollie **25**
Stevenson, Robert Louis (Balfour) **10, 11**

SOUTH AFRICAN
Daly, Nicholas **41**
Gordon, Sheila **27**
Lewin, Hugh **9**
Naidoo, Beverley **29**

SPANISH
Sanchez-Silva, Jose Maria **12**

SWEDISH
Beckman, Gunnel **25**
Beskow, Elsa (Maartman) **17**
Bjoerk, Christina **22**
Gripe, Maria (Kristina) **5**
Lagerlof, Selma (Ottiliana Lovisa) **7**
Lindgren, Astrid (Ericsson) **1, 39**
Lindgren, Barbro **20**
Unnerstad, Edith (Totterman) **36**

SWISS
Carigiet, Alois **38**
Duvoisin, Roger Antoine **23**
Glenn, Mel **51**
Mueller, Joerg **43**
Pfister, Marcus **42**
Spyri, Johanna (Heusser) **13**

THAI
Ho, Minfong **28**

TRINIDADIAN
Guy, Rosa (Cuthbert) **13**

WELSH
Arundel, Honor (Morfydd) **35**
Dahl, Roald **1, 7, 41**

Nationality Index

CUMULATIVE INDEX TO TITLES

1, 2, 3 (Hoban) **13**:109
1, 2, 3 to the Zoo (Carle) **10**:71
1 Is One (Tudor) **13**:195
3 and 30 Watchbirds (Leaf) **25**:127
3 X 3: A Picture Book for All Children Who Can Count to Three (Kruss) **9**:85
3rd September 1939 (Gordon) **27**:94
4-Way Stop and Other Poems (Livingston) **7**:172
10-Nin No Yukai Na Hikkoshi (Anno) **14**:40
26 Letters and 99 Cents (Hoban) **13**:112
The 35th of May; or, Conrad's Ride to the South Seas (Kaestner) **4**:123
The 60s Reader (Haskins) **39**:57
The 100-Year-Old Cactus (Lerner) **34**:130
121 Pudding Street (Fritz) **14**:110
1,2,3 and Things (McNaughton) **54**:48
The 379th White Elephant (Guillot) **22**:56
The 500 Hats of Bartholomew Cubbins (Dr. Seuss) **9**:172
729 Animal Allsorts (Oxenbury) **22**:141
729 Curious Creatures (Oxenbury) **22**:141
729 Merry Mix-Ups (Oxenbury) **22**:141
729 Puzzle People (Oxenbury) **22**:141
1812: The War Nobody Won (Marrin) **53**:83
123456789 Benn (McKee) **38**:160
A and THE; or, William T. C. Baumgarten Comes to Town (Raskin) **1**:155
A Apple Pie (Greenaway) **6**:134
A, B, See! (Hoban) **13**:106
A Is for Always (Anglund) **1**:19
A Is for Annabelle (Tudor) **13**:194
A, My Name Is Ami (Mazer) **23**:231
AB to Zogg: A Lexicon for Science-Fiction and Fantasy Readers (Merriam) **14**:199
Abby (Caines) **24**:62
Abby, My Love (Irwin) **40**:111
ABC (Burningham) **9**:39
ABC (Cleaver) **13**:72
ABC (Lear) **1**:126

ABC (Munari) **9**:125
ABC (Pienkowski) **6**:233
ABC and Things (McNaughton) **54**:48
The ABC Bunny (Gag) **4**:90
ABC of Things (Oxenbury) **22**:138
ABC Word Book (Scarry) **41**:164
ABCDEFGHIJKLMNOPQRSTUVWXYZ (Kuskin) **4**:138
The ABC's of Astronomy: An Illustrated Dictionary (Gallant) **30**:87
The ABC's of Chemistry: An Illustrated Dictionary (Gallant) **30**:88
ABC's of Ecology (Asimov) **12**:47
ABC's of Space (Asimov) **12**:45
ABC's of the Earth (Asimov) **12**:46
ABC's of the Ocean (Asimov) **12**:45
Abdul (Wells) **16**:207
Abel's Island (Steig) **15**:193
Abigail Adams and Her Times (Richards) **54**:168
The Abominable Swamp Man (Haley) **21**:144
About David (Pfeffer) **11**:201
About Michael Jackson (Haskins) **39**:50
About the B'nai Bagels (Konigsburg) **1**:119
About the Foods You Eat (Simon) **9**:215
About the Sleeping Beauty (Travers) **2**:176
Above and Below Stairs (Goodall) **25**:53
Abraham Lincoln (d'Aulaire and d'Aulaire) **21**:43
Abraham Lincoln (Foster) **7**:94
Abraham Lincoln's World (Foster) **7**:92
Absolute Zero: Being the Second Part of the Bagthorpe Saga (Cresswell) **18**:109
Absolutely Normal Chaos (Creech) **42**:40
Abuela (Dorros) **42**:69
Ace: The Very Important Pig (King-Smith) **40**:158
The Acorn Quest (Yolen) **4**:268
Across America on an Emigrant Train (Murphy) **53**:113
Across Five Aprils (Hunt) **1**:109
Across the Sea (Goffstein) **3**:57

Across the Sea from Galway (Fisher) **18**:126
Across the Stream (Ginsburg) **45**:16
Action Replay (Rosen) **45**:146
Adam and Eve and Pinch-Me (Johnston) **41**:87
Adam and Paradise Island (Keeping) **34**:110
Adam Clayton Powell: Portrait of a Marching Black (Haskins) **3**:63
Adam's War (Levitin) **53**:74
Add-a-Line Alphabet (Freeman) **30**:76
Addictions: Gambling, Smoking, Cocaine Use, and Others (Hyde) **23**:164
Adiós, Josefina! (Sanchez-Silva) **12**:232
The Adler Book of Puzzles and Riddles: Or, Sam Loyd Up to Date (Adler) **27**:17
Adler und Taube (Kruss) **9**:86
Admission to the Feast (Beckman) **25**:12
Adrift (Baillie) **49**:6
Adventure at Black Rock Cave (Lauber) **16**:113
Adventure in Granada (Myers) **16**:142
Adventure in Legoland (Matas) **52**:85
Adventures in Making: The Romance of Crafts around the World (Manley) **3**:145
The Adventures of a Puppet (Collodi) See *The Adventures of a Puppet*
The Adventures of Aku: Or, How It Came About That We Shall Always See Okra the Cat Lying on a Velvet Cusion, While Okraman the Dog Sleeps among the Ashes (Bryan) **18**:34
The Adventures of Andy (Bianco) **19**:52
The Adventures of Charlotte and Henry (Graham) **31**:96
The Adventures of Fathead, Smallhead, and Squarehead (Sanchez) **18**:200
The Adventures of Hershel of Ostropol (Hyman) **50**:84
The Adventures of Huckleberry Finn (Moser) **49**:170
The Adventures of King Midas (Reid Banks) **24**:191
The Adventures of Lester (Blake) **31**:22

The Adventures of Lowly Worm (Scarry) **41**:171

The Adventures of Odysseus and the Tale of Troy (Colum) **36**:24

The Adventures of Paddy Pork (Goodall) **25**:43

The Adventures of Peter and Lotta (Beskow) **17**:18

The Adventures of Pinocchio (Collodi)
   See *The Adventures of Pinocchio*

The Adventures of Sparrowboy (Pinkney) **54**:148

The Adventures of Spider: West African Folk Tales (Pinkney) **43**:155

Aesopia (Aesop)
   See *Aesop's Fables*

Aesop's Fables (Aesopia) (Aesop) **14**:1-22

Aesop's Fables (Zwerger) **46**:198

Africa Dream (Greenfield) **4**:100

After a Suicide: Young People Speak Up (Kuklin) **51**:112

After the First Death (Cormier) **12**:143

After the Goat Man (Byars) **16**:53

After the Rain (Mazer) **23**:232

After the War (Matas) **52**:92

After Thursday (Ure) **34**:178

Against All Opposition: Black Explorers in America (Haskins) **39**:65

Age of Aquarius: You and Astrology (Branley) **13**:44

The Age of Giant Mammals (Cohen) **3**:37

Aging (Silverstein, Silverstein, and Silverstein) **25**:217

A-Going to the Westward (Lenski) **26**:103

The Agony of Alice (Naylor) **17**:59

Ah! Belle cité!/A Beautiful City ABC (Poulin) **28**:193

A-Haunting We Will Go: Ghostly Stories and Poems (Hopkins) **44**:89

Ah-Choo (Mayer) **11**:170

Aida (Leo and Diane Dillon) **44**:42

AIDS (Nourse) **33**:145

AIDS: Deadly Threat (Silverstein and Silverstein) **25**:223

AIDS: What Does It Mean to You? (Hyde) **23**:172

The Aimer Gate (Garner) **20**:115

Ain't Gonna Study War No More: The Story of America's Peace Seekers (Meltzer) **13**:146

Aio the Rainmaker (French) **37**:41

Air (Adler) **27**:17

Air in Fact and Fancy (Slote) **4**:199

Air Is All around You (Branley) **13**:30

The Air of Mars and Other Stories of Time and Space (Ginsburg) **45**:10

Air Raid-Pearl Harbor! The Story of December 7, 1941 (Taylor) **30**:185

Airlift for Grandee (Park) **51**:172

AK (Dickinson) **29**:60

Akai Boshi (Anno) **14**:44

Akavak: An Eskimo Journey (Houston) **3**:84

The Alamo (Fisher) **18**:137

Alan Garner's Book of British Fairy Tales (Garner) **20**:117

Alan Garner's Fairytales of Gold (Garner) **20**:116

Alan Mendelsohn, the Boy from Mars (Pinkwater) **4**:169

The Alarm Clock (Heine) **18**:149

Alban (Lindgren) **20**:155

Albatross Two (Thiele) **27**:207

Albert's Toothache (Williams) **48**:190

Albeson and the Germans (Needle) **43**:131

Album of Dogs (Henry) **4**:112

Album of Horses (Henry) **4**:112

The Alchemists: Magic into Science (Aylesworth) **6**:50

Alcohol: Drink or Drug? (Hyde) **23**:160

Alcohol: Uses and Abuses (Hyde) **23**:175

Alcoholism (Silverstein and Silverstein) **25**:213

Alesia (Greenfield) **38**:84

Alessandra: Alex in Rome (Duder) **43**:66

Alex (Duder) **43**:64

Alex in Rome (Duder) **43**:66

Alex in Winter (Duder) **43**:65

Alexander and the Terrible, Horrible, No Good, Very Bad Day (Viorst) **3**:207

Alexander and the Wind-Up Mouse (Lionni) **7**:133

Alexander Soames: His Poems (Kuskin) **4**:137

Alexander the Gander (Tudor) **13**:190

Alexander's Great March (Baumann) **35**:50

Alexandra (O'Dell) **16**:178

Alfie and the Ferryboat (Keeping) **34**:89

Alfie Finds "The Other Side of the World" (Keeping) **34**:89

Alfie Gets In First (Hughes) **15**:128

Alfie Gives a Hand (Hughes) **15**:130

Alfie's Feet (Hughes) **15**:129

The Alfred G. Graebner Memorial High School Handbook of Rules and Regulations: A Novel (Conford) **10**:94

Alias Madame Doubtfire (Fine) **25**:21

Alice the Artist (Waddell) **31**:190

Alice's Adventures in Wonderland (Carroll) **2**:31; **18**:38-80

Alice's Adventures in Wonderland (Moser) **49**:165

Alice's Adventures in Wonderland (Tenniel) **18**:201-28

Alien on the 99th Floor (Nimmo) **44**:155

All Aboard Overnight (Betsy and Giulio Maestro) **45**:85

All about Arthur (An Absolutely Absurd Ape) (Carle) **10**:78

All about Horses (Henry) **4**:114

All About Pets (Bianco) **19**:52

All about Prehistoric Cave Men (Epstein and Epstein) **26**:57

All about Sam (Lowry) **46**:37

All about the Desert (Epstein and Epstein) **26**:55

All About Whales (Patent) **19**:164

All Alone (Henkes) **23**:124

All Around You (Bendick) **5**:36

All Because I'm Older (Naylor) **17**:56

All Butterflies: An ABC (Brown) **12**:105

All Day Long: Fifty Rhymes of the Never Was and Always Is (McCord) **9**:100

All Fall Down (Oxenbury) **22**:148

All in a Day (Anno) **14**:45

All in Free but Janey (Hyman) **50**:70

All In One Piece (Murphy) **39**:173

All in the Woodland Early (Yolen) **4**:265

The All Jahdu Storybook (Hamilton) **40**:85

The All Jahdu Storybook (Moser) **49**:181

All Join In (Blake) **31**:28

All My Men (Ashley) **4**:15

All My Shoes Comes in Twos (Hoberman) **22**:108

All on a Mountain Day (Fisher) **49**:33

All Over Town (Brink) **30**:12

All Shapes and Sizes (Hughes) **15**:132

All Sizes of Noises (Kuskin) **4**:137

All the Cats in the World (Levitin) **53**:64

All the Colors of the Race: Poems (Adoff) **7**:37

All the King's Horses (Foreman) **32**:88

All the Pretty Horses (Jeffers) **30**:130

All the Small Poems (Worth) **21**:224

All the Summer Voices (Corcoran) **50**:18

All the Weyrs of Pern (McCaffrey) **49**:153

All Things Bright and Beautiful: A Hymn (Politi) **29**:192

All This Wild Land (Clark) **16**:84

All Those Secrets of the World (Yolen) **44**:194

All through the Night (Field) **21**:78

All Times, All Peoples: A World History of Slavery (Meltzer) **13**:141

All Together Now (Bridgers) **18**:23

All upon a Stone (George) **1**:89

All Us Come Cross the Water (Clifton) **5**:54

All Wet! All Wet! (Stanley) **36**:134

Allan Pinkerton: America's First Private Eye (Lavine) **35**:148

Allergies (Silverstein and Silverstein) **25**:215

The Alley (Estes) **2**:73

Alligator (Scott) **20**:201

The Alligator Case (Pene du Bois) **1**:62

Alligator Pie (Lee) **3**:115

Alligator Shoes (Dorros) **42**:65

The Alligator Under the Bed (Nixon) **24**:135

Alligators All Around (Sendak) **1**:167

Alligators and Crocodiles (Zim) **2**:225

All-of-a-Sudden Susan (Coatsworth) **2**:53

Allumette: A Fable, with Due Respect to Hans Christian Andersen, the Grimm Brothers, and the Honorable Ambrose Bierce (Ungerer) **3**:199

Almost a Hero (Neufeld) **52**:132

The Almost All-White Rabbity Cat (DeJong) **1**:55

Almost Starring Skinnybones (Park) **34**:158

Alone in the Crowd (Pascal) **25**:185

Alone in the Wild Forest (Singer) **1**:173

Aloneness (Brooks) **27**:44-56

Along a Lonely Road (Waddell) **31**:202

Along Came a Dog (DeJong) **1**:56

Along Sandy Trails (Clark) **16**:83

Along This Way: The Autobiography of James Weldon Johnson (Johnson) **32**:169

Alpha Centauri: The Nearest Star (Asimov) **12**:54

Alphabeasts (King-Smith) **40**:160

Alphabet Art: Thirteen ABC's from Around the World (Fisher) **18**:127

Alphabet Soup (Yeoman) **46**:174

The Alphabet Symphone: An ABC Book (McMillan) **47**:159

The Alphabet Tree (Lionni) **7**:133

Altogether, One at a Time (Konigsburg) **1**:119

Alvin Ailey (Pinkney) **54**:141

Always Adam (Oberman) **54**:75

The Always Prayer Shawl (Oberman) **54**:75

Always Reddy (Henry) **4**:110

Always Sebastian (Ure) **34**:193

Always to Remember: The Story of the Vietnam Veterans Memorial (Ashabranner) **28**:12

Always Wondering: Some Favorite Poems of Aileen Fisher (Fisher) **49**:60

Am I Beautiful? (Minarik) **33**:128

Amanda and the Bear (Tudor) **13**:193

Amanda, Dreaming (Wersba) **3**:215

The Amazing and Death-Defying Diary of Eugene Dingman (Zindel) **45**:197

The Amazing Bone (Steig) **15**:193

The Amazing Egg (McClung) **11**:192

The Amazing Felix (McCully) **46**:69

Amazing Grace: The Story Behind the Song (Haskins) **39**:66

The Amazing Laser (Bova) **3**:31

Amazing Mr. Pelgrew (Schlein) **41**:180

The Amazing Mr. Prothero (Arundel) **35**:12

The Amazing Pig: An Old Hungarian Tale (Galdone) **16**:103

Amazing World of Words (Wildsmith) **52**:201

Amelia Bedelia (Parish) **22**:154

Amelia Bedelia and the Baby (Parish) **22**:165

Amelia Bedelia and the Surprise Shower (Parish) **22**:156

Amelia Bedelia Goes Camping (Parish) **22**:167

Amelia Bedelia Helps Out (Parish) **22**:164

Amelia Bedelia's Family Album (Parish) **22**:168

America and Vietnam: The Elephant and the Tiger (Marrin) **53**:90

An American ABC (Petersham and Petersham) **24**:170

American Astronauts and Spacecraft: A Pictorial History from Project Mercury through Apollo 13 (Knight) **38**:110

American Astronauts and Spacecraft: A Pictorial History from Project Mercury through the Skylab Manned Missions (Knight) **38**:110

American Colonial Paper House: To Cut Out and Color (Ness) **6**:208

American Dinosaur Hunters (Aaseng) **54**:24

American Dragons: Twenty-Five Asian American Voices (Yep) **54**:191

American Heroes: In and Out of School (Hentoff) **52**:65

The American Speller: An Adaptation of Noah Webster's Blue-Backed Speller (Cooney) **23**:25

America's Endangered Birds: Programs and People Working to Save Them (McClung) **11**:191

America's Stamps: The Story of One Hundred Years of U.S. Postage Stamps (Petersham and Petersham) **24**:176

America's Third-Party Presidential Candidates (Aaseng) **54**:21

The Amethyst Ring (O'Dell) **16**:178

Amifika (Clifton) **5**:58

Amish Adventure (Smucker) **10**:191

An Amish Family (Naylor) **17**:51

Among the Dolls (Sleator) **29**:200

Amos and Boris (Steig) **2**:158

Amos Binder, Secret Agent (Paulsen) **54**:122

Amphigorey (Gorey) **36**:94

Amphigorey Also (Gorey) **36**:103

Amphigorey Too (Gorey) **36**:98

Amy and Laura (Sachs) **2**:131

Amy Elizabeth Explores Bloomingdale's (Konigsburg) **47**:145

Amy Moves In (Sachs) **2**:131

Amy Said (Waddell) **31**:196

Amzat and His Brothers (Fox) **44**:75

Anancy and Mr. Dry-Bone (French) **37**:52

Anancy-Spiderman (Berry) **22**;9

Anansi the Spider: A Tale from the Ashanti (McDermott) **9**:110

Anastasia, Absolutely (Lowry) **46**:49

Anastasia Again! (Lowry) **6**:195

Anastasia, Ask Your Analyst (Lowry) **46**:29

Anastasia at This Address (Lowry) **46**:41

Anastasia at Your Service (Lowry) **6**:196

Anastasia Has the Answers (Lowry) **46**:33

Anastasia Krupnik (Lowry) **6**:194

Anastasia on Her Own (Lowry) **46**:31

Anastasia's Chosen Career (Lowry) **46**:36

Anatole (Galdone) **16**:88

Anatole and the Cat (Galdone) **16**:89

Anatole and the Pied Piper (Galdone) **16**:102

Anchor Man (Jackson) **28**:139

Anchors Aweigh: The Story of David Glasgow Farragut (Latham) **50**:105

Ancient Civilizations (Pullman) **20**:186

Ancient Egypt (Cohen) **43**:51

An Ancient Heritage: The Arab-American Minority (Ashabranner) **28**:16

Ancient Indians: The First Americans (Gallant) **30**:104

Ancient Monuments and How They Were Built (Cohen) **3**:37

The Ancient Visitors (Cohen) **3**:38

And All Between (Snyder) **31**:163

And Condors Danced (Snyder) **31**:168

And It Rained (Raskin) **1**:155

And It Was So (Tudor) **13**:196

And Maggie Makes Three (Nixon) **24**:147

And So My Garden Grows (Spier) **5**:219

And Then What Happened, Paul Revere? (Fritz) **2**:79

And This Is Laura (Conford) **10**:94

And to Think That I Saw It on Mulberry Street (Dr. Seuss) **1**:84; **9**:172

And Twelve Chinese Acrobats (Yolen) **44**:204

Andrew Carnegie and the Age of Steel (Shippen) **36**:179

Andrew Jackson (Foster) **7**:95

Andrew Young: Man with a Mission (Haskins) **39**:35

The Andrews Raid: Or, The Great Locomotive Chase, April 12, 1862 (Epstein and Epstein) **26**:54

Androcles and the Lion (Galdone) **16**:94

Android at Arms (Norton) **50**:151

Andy All Year Round: A Picture Book of Four Seasons and Five Senses (Merriam) **14**:195

Andy Buckram's Tin Men (Brink) **30**:15

Andy (That's My Name) (dePaola) **4**:55

The Angel and the Donkey **50**:204

The Angel and the Donkey (Paterson) **50**:204

Angel and the Polar Bear (Gay) **27**:87

The Angel and the Wild Animal (Foreman) **32**:101

Angel Dust Blues: A Novel (Strasser) **11**:246

Angel Face (Klein) **19**:95

Angel Square (Doyle) **22**:32

The Angel with a Mouth Organ (Mattingley) **24**:128

Angela's Airplane (Munsch) **19**:143

Angelina and the Birds (Baumann) **35**:42

Angelo (Blake) **31**:18

Angelo, the Naughty One (Politi) **29**:185

Angels and Other Strangers: Family Christmas Stories (Paterson) **7**:237

Angel's Gate (Crew) **42**:58

Angie's First Case (Sobol) **4**:212

The Angry Moon (Sleator) **29**:199

Angus and the Cat (Flack) **28**:120

The Animal (Kherdian) **24**:114

Animal and Plant Mimicry (Patent) **19**:151

Animal Antics (Janosch) **26**:80

Animal Architects (Freedman) **20**:76

Animal Clocks and Compasses: From Animal Migration to Space Travel (Hyde) **23**:154

Animal Fact/Animal Fable (Simon) **9**:213

The Animal Fair (Provensen and Provensen) **11**:209

The Animal Family (Jarrell) **6**:162

Animal Fathers (Freedman) **20**:78

Animal Games (Freedman) **20**:78

The Animal Hedge (Fleischman) **20**:65

Animal Hospital (Berger) **32**:9

Animal Instincts (Freedman) **20**:75

The Animal Kingdom (Guillot) **22**:58

Animal Nursery Tales (Scarry) **41**:166

Animal Rights: A Handbook for Young Adults (Cohen) **43**:57

Animal Superstars (Freedman) **20**:82

Animal Superstitions (Aylesworth) **6**:56

Animal Territories (Cohen) **3**:38

The Animal, the Vegetable, and John D. Jones (Byars) **16**:58

Animal Tracks (Dorros) **42**:70

Animalia (Base) **22**:4

The Animals and the Ark (Kuskin) **4**:135

Animals and Their Babies (Carle) **10**:79

Animals and Their Niches: How Species Share Resources (Pringle) **4**:183

Animals as Parents (Selsam) **1**:159

The Animals' Carol (Causley) **30**:40

The Animals' Conference (Kaestner) **4**:125

Animals Everywhere (d'Aulaire and d'Aulaire) **21**:46

Animals for Sale (Munari) **9**:124

Animals in Field and Laboratory: Science Projects in Animal Behavior (Simon) **9**:201

Animals in Winter (Poulin) **28**:198

Animals in Your Neighborhood (Simon) **9**:211

The Animals' Lullaby (Nakatani) **30**:155

The Animals of Doctor Schweitzer (Fritz) **14**:111

Animals of the Bible (Asimov) **12**:56

Annabelle Pig and the Travellers (McKee) **38**:180

Annabelle Swift, Kindergartner (Schwartz) **25**:195

Annaluise and Anton (Kaestner) **4**:123

Anne of Avonlea (Montgomery) **8**:134

Anne of Green Gables (Montgomery) **8**:131

Anne of Ingleside (Montgomery) **8**:139

Anne of the Island (Montgomery) **8**:137

Annegret und Cara (Benary-Isbert) **12**:73

Anneli the Art Hater (Fine) **25**:21

Annerton Pit (Dickinson) **29**:46

Annie and the Wild Animals (Brett) **27**:39

The Annie Moran (Hurd and Hurd) **49**:115

Annie on My Mind (Garden) **51**:66

Annie Pat and Eddie (Haywood) **22**:98

Annie's Monster (Corcoran) **50**:38

Annie's Promise (Levitin) **53**:71

Anno Mitsumasa No Gashu (Anno) **14**:35

Anno's Alphabet: An Adventure in Imagination (Anno) **2**:1

Anno's Animals (Anno) **14**:34

Anno's Britain (Anno) **14**:39

Anno's Counting Book (Anno) **14**:32

Anno's Counting House (Anno) **14**:40

Anno's Flea Market (Anno) **14**:43

Anno's Hat Tricks (Anno) **14**:44

Anno's Italy (Anno) **14**:37

Anno's Journey (Anno) **14**:33

Anno's Magical ABC: An Anamorphic Alphabet (Anno) **14**:39

Anno's Medieval World (Anno) **14**:37

Anno's Mysterious Multiplying Jar (Anno) **14**:41

Anno's Three Little Pigs (Anno) **14**:44

Anno's U.S.A. (Anno) **14**:41

Ann's Alpine Adventure (Allan) **43**:5

Another Day (Ets) **33**:81

Another Fine Mess (Needle) **43**:137

Another Helping of Chips (Hughes) **15**:133

Anpao: An American Indian Odyssey (Highwater) **17**:23

Ant and Bee: An Alphabetical Story for Tiny Tots (Banner) **24**:18

Ant and Bee and Kind Dog: An Alphabetical Story (Banner) **24**:19

Ant and Bee and the ABC (Banner) **24**:19

Ant and Bee and the Doctor (Banner) **24**:19

Ant and Bee and the Secret (Banner) **24**:19

The Ant and Bee Big Buy Bag (Banner) **24**:19

Ant and Bee Go Shopping (Banner) **24**:20

Ant and Bee Time (Banner) **24**:19

Ant Cities (Dorros) **42**:65

Antarctica: The Great White Continent (Schlein) **41**:190

Anthony Burns: The Defeat and Triumph of a Fugitive Slave (Hamilton) **40**:76

The Anti-Muffins (L'Engle) **14**:153

Anton and Anne (Carigiet) **38**:74

Anton B. Stanton and the Pirats (McNaughton) **54**:50

Anton the Goatherd (Carigiet) **38**:72

The Ants Who Took Away Time (Kotzwinkle) **6**:183

Any Me I Want to Be: Poems (Kuskin) **4**:140

Anybody Home? (Fisher) **49**:58

Anything Can Happen on the River (Brink) **30**:6

Anything for a Friend (Conford) **10**:95

Appalachia: The Voices of Sleeping Birds (Moser) **49**:177

Appelard and Liverwurst (Mayer) **11**:173

Appelemando's Dreams (Polacco) **40**:190

The Apple and Other Fruits (Selsam) **1**:160

Apple Bough (Streatfeild) **17**:195

The Apple Tree (Bianco) **19**:52

Apples (Hogrogian) **2**:87

Apples, How They Grow (McMillan) **47**:161

The Apprentices (Garfield) **21**:113

The Apprenticeship of Duddy Kravitz (Richler) **17**:64

April and the Dragon Lady (Namioka) **48**:66

April Fools (Krahn) **3**:103

Apt. 3 (Keats) **1**:113; **35**:137

Aquarius (Mark) **11**:152

Aquatic Insects and How They Live (McClung) **11**:186

Arabel and Mortimer (Aiken) **19**:13

Arabella (Fox) **23**:114

Arabel's Raven (Aiken) **1**:2

Arabian Frights and Other Stories (Rosen) **45**:149

Arabian Horses (Patent) **19**:157

Arbor Day (Fisher) **49**:42

Archaelogists Dig for Clues (Duke) **51**:55

Die Arche Noah (Benary-Isbert) **12**:70

Archer Armadillo's Secret Room (Singer) **48**:127

Archer's Goon (Jones) **23**:193

Archimedes and the Door of Science (Bendick) **5**:40

Architect of the Moon (Wynne-Jones) **21**:231

The Architects (Fisher) **18**:123

Are All the Giants Dead? (Norton) **6**:225

Are We Almost There? (Stevenson) **17**:163

Are You in the House Alone? (Peck) **15**:156

Are You My Friend Today? (Fujikawa) **25**:41

Are You There God? It's Me, Margaret (Blume) **2**:15

Ariadne, Awake! (Moser) **49**:189

Ariadne Awake! (Orgel) **48**:94

Arilla Sun Down (Hamilton) **11**:76

Arithmetic Can Be Fun (Leaf) **25**:130

The Ark (Benary-Isbert) **12**:70

The Ark of Father Noah and Mother Noah (Petersham and Petersham) **24**:162

The Arkadians (Alexander) **48**:26

Arly (Peck) **45**:122

Arly's Run (Peck) **45**:124

Arm in Arm: A Collection of Connections, Endless Tales, Reiterations, and Other Echolalia (Charlip) **8**:28

The Arm of the Starfish (L'Engle) **1**:129

Armitage, Armitage, Fly Away Home (Aiken) **1**:2

Armored Animals (Zim) **2**:225

The Armourer's House (Sutcliff) **1**:183; **37**:149

Around Fred's Bed (Pinkwater) **4**:165

Around the Clock with Harriet: A Book about Telling Time (Betsy and Giulio Maestro) **45**:73

Around the World in Eighty Days (Burningham) **9**:44

Around the Year (Tudor) **13**:196

Arrow to the Sun: A Pueblo Indian Tale (McDermott) **9**:111

Art and Archaeology (Glubok) **1**:95

The Art and Industry of Sandcastles: Being an Illustrated Guide to Basic Constructions along with Divers Information Devised by One Jan Adkins, a Wily Fellow (Adkins) **7**:18

The Art Experience: Oil Painting, 15th-19th Centuries (Fisher) **18**:125

The Art Lesson (dePaola) **24**:102

The Art of America from Jackson to Lincoln (Glubok) **1**:95

The Art of America in the Gilded Age (Glubok) **1**:95

The Art of Ancient Mexico (Glubok) **1**:96

The Art of Ancient Peru (Glubok) **1**:96

The Art of China (Glubok) **1**:97

The Art of India (Glubok) **1**:97

The Art of Japan (Glubok) **1**:97

The Art of Lands in the Bible (Glubok) **1**:98

The Art of the Etruscans (Glubok) **1**:98

The Art of the New American Nation (Glubok) **1**:99

The Art of the North American Indian (Glubok) **1**:99

The Art of the Northwest Coast Indians (Glubok) **1**:99

The Art of the Spanish in the United States and Puerto Rico (Glubok) **1**:100

Art, You're Magic! (McBratney) **44**:126

Arthur, for the Very First Time (MacLachlan) **14**:181

Arthur Goes to Camp (Brown) **29**:8

Arthur, High King of Britain (Morpurgo) **51**:141

Arthur Meets the President (Brown) **29**:19

Arthur Mitchell (Tobias) **4**:215

Arthur's April Fool (Brown) **29**:9

Arthur's Baby (Brown) **29**:16

Arthur's Birthday (Brown) **29**:18

Arthur's Christmas (Brown) **29**:12

Arthur's Eyes (Brown) **29**:5

Arthur's Halloween (Brown) **29**:8

Arthur's Nose (Brown) **29**:3

Arthur's Pet Business (Brown) **29**:19

Arthur's Teacher Trouble (Brown) **29**:14

Arthur's Thanksgiving (Brown) **29**:10

Arthur's Tooth (Brown) **29**:12

Arthur's Valentine (Brown) **29**:6

The Artificial Heart (Berger) **32**:38

Artificial Intelligence: A Revision of Computers That Think? (Hyde) **23**:167

Arts and Crafts You Can Eat (Cobb) **2**:64

Ash Road (Southall) **2**:147

Ashanti to Zulu: African Traditions (Leo and Diane Dillon) **44**:29

Asimov's Guide to Halley's Comet: The Awesome Story of Comets (Asimov) **12**:63

Ask Mr. Bear (Flack) **28**:120

Asking about Sex and Growing Up: A Question-And-Answer Book for Boys and Girls (Cole) **40**:22

Asleep, Asleep (Ginsburg) **45**:19

Assignment: Sports (Lipsyte) **23**:205

Astercote (Lively) **7**:151

Asterix and the Banquet (Goscinny and Uderzo) **37**:82

Asterix and the Big Fight (Goscinny and Uderzo) **37**:75

Asterix and the Chieftain's Shield (Goscinny and Uderzo) **37**:81

Asterix and the Goths (Goscinny and Uderzo) **37**:76

Asterix and the Great Crossing (Goscinny and Uderzo) **37**:81

Asterix and the Laurel Wreath (Goscinny and Uderzo) **37**:77

Asterix at the Olympic Games (Goscinny and Uderzo) **37**:76

Asterix in Britain (Goscinny and Uderzo) **37**:75

Asterix in Spain (Goscinny and Uderzo) **37**:76

Asterix the Gaul (Goscinny and Uderzo) **37**:74

The Asteroids (Nourse) **33**:139

The Astonishing Stereoscope (Langton) **33**:111

Astrology and Foretelling the Future (Aylesworth) **6**:50

Astrology: Sense or Nonsense? (Gallant) **30**:92

At Home (Hill) **13**:93

At Home (McNaughton) **54**:53

At Home: A Visit in Four Languages (Hautzig) **22**:83

At Mary Bloom's (Aliki) **9**:25

At Our House (Lenski) **26**:120

At Playschool (McNaughton) **54**:53

At Swords' Points (Norton) **50**:136

At the Beach (Tobias) **4**:217

At the Forge of Liberty (Carter) **22**:23

At the Park (McNaughton) **54**:53

At the Party (McNaughton) **54**:53

At the Sign of the Dog and Rocket (Mark) **11**:156

At the Stores (McNaughton) **54**:53

At the Stroke of Midnight: Traditional Fairy Tales Retold (Cresswell) **18**:103

Athletic Shorts: Six Short Stories (Crutcher) **28**:107

Atomic Energy (Adler) **27**:24

Atoms (Berger) **32**:3

Atoms and Molecules (Adler) **27**:20

Atoms, Molecules, and Quarks (Berger) **32**:37

Atoms Today and Tomorrow (Hyde) **23**:153

Attaboy, Sam! (Lowry) **46**:42

Attack of the Killer Fishsticks (Zindel) **45**:200

Attar of the Ice Valley (Wibberley) **3**:224

Audubon Cat (Calhoun) **42**:27

August the Fourth (Farmer) **8**:86

Augustus Caesar's World, a Story of Ideas and Events from B.C. 44 to 14 A.D. (Foster) **7**:93

Auno and Tauno: A Story of Finland (Henry) **4**:109

Aunt Bernice (Gantos) **18**:141

Aunt Green, Aunt Brown, and Aunt Lavender (Beskow) **17**:16

Aunt Isabel Makes Trouble (Duke) **51**:54

Aunt Isabel Tells a Good One (Duke) **51**:52

Auntie and Celia Jane and Miki (Petersham and Petersham) **24**:164

Das Austauschkind (Noestlinger) **12**:189

The Author and Squinty Gritt (Williams) **48**:206

Autoimmune Diseases (Aaseng) **54**:22

Automobile Factory (Berger) **32**:18

Autumn (McNaughton) **54**:55

The Autumn Book: A Collection of Prose and Poetry (McNaughton) **54**:49

Autumn Harvest (Tresselt) **30**:204

Autumn Story (Barklem) **31**:2

Autumn Street (Lowry) **6**:195

Avocado Baby (Burningham) **9**:50

Le Avventure di Pinocchio (The Marvellous Adventures of Pinocchio; Pinocchio; The Story of a Puppet) (Collodi) **5**:69

Away and Ago: Rhymes of the Never Was and Always Is (McCord) **9**:102

Away from Wood Street (Allan) **43**:27

Away Went the Balloons (Haywood) **22**:102

Awful Evelina (Pfeffer) **11**:200

Axe Time, Sword Time (Corcoran) **50**:22

Axe-Age, Wolf-Age: A Selection from the Norse Myths (Crossley-Holland) **47**:42

Aztec Indians (McKissack) **23**:237

Aztecs and Spaniards: Cortes and the Conquest of Mexico (Marrin) **53**:83

B is een beer (Bruna) **7**:50

B Is for Bear: An ABC (Bruna) **7**:50

"B" Is for Betsy (Haywood) **22**:90

B, My Name Is Bunny (Mazer) **23**:231

Baaa (Macaulay) **14**:175

The Baabee Books, Series I (Khalsa)   **30**:144
The Baabee Books, Series III (Khalsa)   **30**:144
Babar and Father Christmas (Brunhoff)   **4**:32
Babar and His Children (Brunhoff)   **4**:32
Babar and the Old Lady (Brunhoff)   **4**:37
Babar and the Professor (Brunhoff)   **4**:34
Babar and the Wully-Wully (Brunhoff)   **4**:39
Babar at Home (Brunhoff)   **4**:32
Babar at the Seashore (Brunhoff)   **4**:38
Babar at the Seaside (Brunhoff)   **4**:38
Babar Comes to America (Brunhoff)   **4**:36
Babar Goes on a Picnic (Brunhoff)   **4**:38
Babar Goes Skiing (Brunhoff)   **4**:38
Babar in the Snow (Brunhoff)   **4**:38
Babar Loses His Crown (Brunhoff)   **4**:37
Babar the Gardener (Brunhoff)   **4**:38
Babar the King (Brunhoff)   **4**:31
Babar Visits Another Planet (Brunhoff)   **4**:38
Babar's Birthday Surprise (Brunhoff)   **4**:38
Babar's Castle (Brunhoff)   **4**:35
Babar's Childhood (Brunhoff)   **4**:37
Babar's Coronation (Brunhoff)   **4**:37
Babar's Cousin: That Rascal Arthur (Brunhoff)   **4**:33
Babar's Day Out (Brunhoff)   **4**:38
Babar's Fair (Brunhoff)   **4**:34
Babar's French Lessons (Brunhoff)   **4**:35
Babar's Mystery (Brunhoff)   **4**:39
Babar's Picnic (Brunhoff)   **4**:34
Babar's Trunk (Brunhoff)   **4**:38
Babar's Visit to Bird Island (Brunhoff)   **4**:34
Babe: The Gallant Pig (King-Smith)   **40**:144; **41**:124
The Babes in the Wood (Caldecott)   **14**:74
Babies! (Patent)   **19**:166
Babushka Baba Yaga (Polacco)   **40**:196
Babushka's Doll (Polacco)   **40**:188
Babushka's Mother Goose (Polacco)   **40**:200
The Baby (Burningham)   **9**:46
Baby Bear Books (Hill)   **13**:93
Baby Bear's Bedtime (Hill)   **13**:95
Baby Bunting (Caldecott)   **14**:78
Baby Dinosaurs (Sattler)   **24**:219
A Baby for Max (Lasky)   **11**:121
Baby Island (Brink)   **30**:11
The Baby Project (Ellis)   **42**:81
A Baby Sister for Frances (Hoban)   **3**:75
A Baby Starts to Grow (Showers)   **6**:244
The Baby, the Bed, and the Rose (Naylor)   **17**:61
Baby Time: A Grownup's Handbook to Use with Baby (Brown)   **29**:18
The Baby Uggs Are Watching (Prelutsky)   **13**:170
The Baby Zoo (McMillan)   **47**:180
The Baby's Catalogue (Ahlberg and Ahlberg)   **18**:9
Baby's First Christmas (dePaola)   **24**:101
The Baby-Sitter II (Stine)   **37**:116
The Baby-Sitter III (Stine)   **37**:123
Back Home (Pinkney)   **43**:168
The Back House Ghosts (*The Haunting of Ellen: A Story of Suspense*) (Waddell)   **31**:177
Back in the Beforetime: Tales of the California Indians (Curry)   **31**:86
Back to Class (Glenn)   **51**:88
Back to School with Betsy (Haywood)   **22**:92
Backbone of the King: The Story of Paka'a and His Son Ku (Brown)   **12**:102
Backstage (Isadora)   **7**:104
The Backward Day (Krauss)   **42**:114
The Backwoodsmen (Roberts)   **33**:201
The Backyard Astronomer (Nourse)   **33**:137
Backyard Bear (Murphy)   **53**:111
Backyard Bestiary (Blumberg)   **21**:25

Bacteria: How They Affect Other Living Things (Patent)   **19**:155
Bad, Badder, Baddest (Voigt)   **48**:185
Bad Boy, Good Boy (Ets)   **33**:90
Bad Girls (Voigt)   **48**:183
The Bad Guys (Baillie)   **49**:16
The Bad Island (Steig)   **2**:158
The Bad Little Duckhunter (Brown)   **10**:54
Bad Sam! (Lindgren)   **20**:157
A Bad Spell for the Worst Witch (Murphy)   **39**:171
The Bad Speller (Steig)   **2**:159
The Bad Times of Irma Baumlein (Brink)   **30**:16
Badger on the Barge and Other Stories (Howker)   **14**:127
Badger's Fate (Hamley)   **47**:64
The Bad-Tempered Ladybird (Carle)   **10**:81
A Bag of Moonshine (Garner)   **20**:118
Bagthorpes Abroad: Being the Fifth Part of the Bagthorpe Saga (Cresswell)   **18**:112
Bagthorpes Haunted: Being the Sixth Part of the Bagthorpe Saga (Cresswell)   **18**:112
Bagthorpes Unlimited: Being the Third Part of the Bagthorpe Saga (Cresswell)   **18**:110
Bagthorpes v. the World: Being the Fourth Part of the Bagthorpe Saga (Cresswell)   **18**:110
Bailey Goes Camping (Henkes)   **23**:127
Baily's Bones (Kelleher)   **36**:124
The Baker and the Basilisk (McHargue)   **2**:117
The Bakers: A Simple Book about the Pleasures of Baking Bread (Adkins)   **7**:22
The Ballad of Aucassin and Nicolette (Causley)   **30**:41
The Ballad of Belle Dorcas (Pinkney)   **54**:133
The Ballad of Benny Perhaps (Brinsmead)   **47**:14
The Ballad of Biddy Early (Moser)   **49**:174
The Ballad of St. Simeon (Serraillier)   **2**:135
The Ballad of the Pilgrim Cat (Wibberley)   **3**:224
The Ballad of the Pirate Queens (Yolen)   **44**:205
Ballet Dance for Two (Ure)   **34**:170
The Ballet Family Again (Allan)   **43**:12
Ballet Shoes: A Story of Three Children on the Stage (Streatfeild)   **17**:185
Ballet Shoes for Anna (Streatfeild)   **17**:198
The Ballet Twins (Estoril)   **43**:16
Balloon Journey (Guillot)   **22**:67
The Ballooning Adventures of Paddy Pork (Goodall)   **25**:43
Bam! Zam! Boom! A Building Book (Merriam)   **14**:197
A Band of Angels (Thompson)   **24**:229
Bang Bang You're Dead (Fitzhugh)   **1**:71
Banjo (Peck)   **45**:117
Barbara Jordan: Speaking Out (Haskins)   **39**:33
Barbara's Birthday (Stevenson)   **17**:159
Bard of Avon: The Story of William Shakespeare (Stanley)   **46**:146
Barefoot in the Grass (Armstrong)   **1**:22
A Bargain for Frances (Hoban)   **3**:75
The Barge Children (Cresswell)   **18**:100
Barishnikov's Nutcracker (Klein)   **19**:95
Baron Bruno; or, The Unbelieving Philosopher and Other Fairy Stories (Caldecott)   **14**:72
The Barque of the Brothers: A Tale of the Days of Henry the Navigator (Baumann)   **35**:40
Bartholomew and the Oobleck (Dr. Seuss)   **9**:177
Baseball Flyhawk (Christopher)   **33**:39
Baseball in April and Other Stories (Soto)   **38**:189
Baseball: It's Your Team (Aaseng)   **54**:11
Baseball Pals (Christopher)   **33**:37
The Baseball Trick (Corbett)   **1**:42
Baseball's All-Time All-Stars (Murphy)   **53**:103
Baseball's Greatest Teams (Aaseng)   **54**:12
Basil of Baker Street (Galdone)   **16**:89

The Basket Counts (Christopher)   **33**:43
Basketball Sparkplug (Christopher)   **33**:37
Bass and Billy Martin (Phipson)   **5**:182
The Bassumtyte Treasure (Curry)   **31**:82
The Bastable Children (Nesbit)   **3**:161
The Bates Family (Ottley)   **16**:186
Bath Time for John (Graham)   **31**:92
The Bathwater Gang (Spinelli)   **26**:205
Bathwater's Hot (Hughes)   **15**:131
The Bat-Poet (Jarrell)   **6**:158
Bats: Night Fliers (Betsy and Giulio Maestro)   **45**:89
Bats: Wings in the Night (Lauber)   **16**:115
Battle against the Sea: How the Dutch Made Holland (Lauber)   **16**:111
The Battle for the Atlantic (Williams)   **8**:223
Battle in the Arctic Seas: The Story of Convoy PQ 17 (Taylor)   **30**:189
Battle in the English Channel (Taylor)   **30**:192
The Battle of Bubble and Squeak (Pearce)   **9**:156
The Battle of Reuben Robin and Kite Uncle John (Calhoun)   **42**:19
The Battle of the Dinosaurs (Knight)   **38**:126
The Battle of the Galah Trees (Mattingley)   **24**:123
The Battle of Zormla (McNaughton)   **54**:54
The Battle off Midway Island (Taylor)   **30**:190
Battleground: The United States Army in World War II (Collier)   **3**:44
Bayou Suzette (Lenski)   **26**:106
Be Brave, Billy (Ormerod)   **20**:176
Be Ready at Eight (Parish)   **22**:164
Bea and Mr. Jones (Schwartz)   **25**:190
Beach Ball (Sis)   **45**:164
Beach Ball—Left, Right (McMillan)   **47**:180
Beach Day (Oxenbury)   **22**:143
A Beach for the Birds (McMillan)   **47**:183
Beach House (Stine)   **37**:120
Beach Party (Ryder)   **37**:87
Beach Party (Stine)   **37**:113
The Beachcombers (Cresswell)   **18**:105
Beady Bear (Freeman)   **30**:70
Beanpole (Park)   **34**:155
Beans: All about Them (Silverstein and Silverstein)   **25**:212
The Bear and His Brothers (Baumann)   **35**:46
The Bear and the People (Zimnik)   **3**:242
A Bear Called Paddington (Bond)   **1**:27
Bear Circus (Pene du Bois)   **1**:62
Bear Cub (Clark)   **16**:82
The Bear Detectives: The Case of the Missing Pumpkins (Berenstain and Berenstain)   **19**:29
A Bear for Christmas (Keller)   **45**:48
Bear Goes to Town (Browne)   **19**:67
Bear Hunt (Browne)   **19**:63
The Bear on the Moon (Ryder)   **37**:97
The Bear Scouts (Berenstain and Berenstain)   **19**:25
Bear Trouble (Moore)   **15**:140
The Bear Who Had No Place to Go (Stevenson)   **17**:152
The Bear Who Saw the Spring (Kuskin)   **4**:136
The Bear Who Wanted to Be a Bear (Mueller)   **43**:118
The Bear Who Wanted to Stay a Bear (Mueller)   **43**:118
Bears (Krauss)   **42**:111
Bear's Adventure (Wildsmith)   **52**:187
The Bears' Almanac: A Year in Bear Country (Berenstain and Berenstain)   **19**:28
The Bear's Autumn (Tejima)   **20**:202
Bear's Birthday (McNaughton)   **54**:56
The Bears' Christmas (Berenstain and Berenstain)   **19**:26
The Bear's House (Sachs)   **2**:131

Bears in the Night (Berenstain and Berenstain) **19**:27

The Bears' Nature Guide (Berenstain and Berenstain) **19**:29

The Bears of the Air (Lobel) **5**:164

Bears of the World (Patent) **19**:155

Bears on Wheels (Berenstain and Berenstain) **19**:26

The Bears' Picnic (Berenstain and Berenstain) **19**:25

Bear's Picture (Pinkwater) **4**:162

The Bears' Vacation (Berenstain and Berenstain) **19**:26

The Bear's Water Picnic (Yeoman) **46**:174

The Bears Will Get You! (Nimmo) **44**:148

The Bear's Winter House (Yeoman) **46**:174

Bearskin (Hyman) **50**:86

Bearymore (Freeman) **30**:80

The Beast Master (Norton) **50**:140

The Beast of Monsieur Racine (Ungerer) **3**:200

The Beast with the Magical Horn (Cameron) **1**:39

A Beastly Circus (Parish) **22**:157

Beasts and Nonsense (Ets) **33**:80

The Beasts of Never (McHargue) **2**:117

Beat of the City (Brinsmead) **47**:8

The Beat of the Drum (Waddell) **31**:194

Beat the Story-Drum, Pum-Pum (Bryan) **18**:34

Beatrice and Vanessa (Yeoman) **46**:177

Beats Me, Claude (Nixon) **24**:148

Beauty: A Retelling of the Story of Beauty and the Beast (McKinley) **10**:121

Beauty and the Beast (Brett) **27**:42

Beauty and the Beast (Harris) **30**:120

Beauty and the Beast (Moser) **49**:183

Beauty and the Beast (Pearce) **9**:154

The Beauty Queen (Pfeffer) **11**:198

The Beaver Pond (Tresselt) **30**:212

Because of a Flower (Milne and Milne) **22**:122

Because of a Tree (Milne and Milne) **22**:118

Because We Are (Walter) **15**:206

Becca Backward, Becca Frontward: A Book of Concept Pairs (McMillan) **47**:168

The Beckoning Lights (Hughes) **9**:77

Becky's Birthday (Tudor) **13**:197

Becky's Christmas (Tudor) **13**:197

Bed-knob and Broomstick (Norton) **6**:222

Bedtime (Duke) **51**:47

Bedtime for Frances (Hoban) **3**:75

The Bee Rustlers (Needle) **43**:134

The Bee Tree (Polacco) **40**:195

Bee Tree and Other Stuff (Peck) **45**:106

Been to Yesterdays: Poems of a Life (Hopkins) **44**:99

Bees Can't Fly, but They Do: Things That Are Still a Mystery to Science (Knight) **38**:119

Bees, Wasps, and Hornets, and How They Live (McClung) **11**:187

The Beethoven Medal (Peyton) **3**:171

Beetles and How They Live (Patent) **19**:151

Beetles, Lightly Toasted (Naylor) **17**:61

Beezus and Ramona (Cleary) **2**:45; **8**:47

The Befana's Toyshop: A Twelfth Night Story (Rodari) **24**:208

Before Freedom, When I Just Can Remember: Twenty-Seven Oral Histories of Former South Carolina Slaves (Hurmence) **25**:96

Before the Sun Dies: The Story of Evolution (Gallant) **30**:104

Before the War, 1908-1939: An Autobiography in Pictures (Goodall) **25**:51

Before You Came This Way (Baylor) **3**:13

Before You Were a Baby (Showers) **6**:244

The Beggar Queen (Alexander) **48**:14

Begin at the Beginning (Schwartz) **25**:191

A Beginner's Book of Vegetable Gardening (Lavine) **35**:157

Beginner's Love (Klein) **19**:94

Beginning Mobiles (Parish) **22**:165

The Beginning of the Earth (Branley) **13**:38

A Begonia for Miss Applebaum (Zindel) **45**:197

Beheaded, Survived (Williams) **48**:204

Behind the Attic Wall (Cassedy) **26**:13

Behind the Back of the Mountain: Black Folktales from Southern Africa (Aardema) **17**:4

Behind the Back of the Mountain: Black Folktales from Southern Africa (Leo and Diane Dillon) **44**:24

Behind the Bike Sheds (Needle) **43**:141

Bel the Giant and Other Stories (Clarke) **28**:75

Belinda (Allen) **44**:14

The Bell Family (Family Shoes) (Streatfeild) **17**:192

A Bell for Ursli (Carigiet) **38**:69

The Bells of Christmas (Hamilton) **40**:81

The Bells of Rome (Allan) **43**:25

Below the Root (Snyder) **31**:161

Ben Loves Anna (Hartling) **29**:103

Bend and Stretch (Ormerod) **20**:180

Beneath the Hill (Curry) **31**:70

Beneath Your Feet (Simon) **9**:211

Benjamin and the Pillow Saga (Poulin) **28**:196

Benjamin and Tulip (Wells) **16**:205

Benjamin Franklin (d'Aulaire and d'Aulaire) **21**:50

Benjamin Pig and the Apple Thieves (McKee) **38**:180

Benjamin West and His Cat Grimalkin (Henry) **4**:110

Benjamin's Barn (Jeffers) **30**:136

Ben's Baby (Foreman) **32**:101

Ben's Box (Foreman) **32**:101

Ben's Dream (Van Allsburg) **5**:240

Ben's Gingerbread Man (Daly) **41**:55

Ben's Trumpet (Isadora) **7**:104

Benson Boy (Southall) **2**:148

The Bent-Back Bridge (Crew) **42**:61

Beowulf (Crossley-Holland) **47**:39

Beowulf (Sutcliff) **1**:183; **37**:155

Beowulf the Warrior (Serraillier) **2**:135

The Berenstain Bears and the Messy Room (Berenstain and Berenstain) **19**:31

The Berenstain Bears and the Missing Dinosaur Bone (Berenstain and Berenstain) **19**:31

The Berenstain Bears and the Sitter (Berenstain and Berenstain) **19**:31

The Berenstain Bears and the Spooky Old Tree (Berenstain and Berenstain) **19**:30

The Berenstain Bears and Too Much Junk Food (Berenstain and Berenstain) **19**:32

The Berenstain Bears' Christmas Tree (Berenstain and Berenstain) **19**:31

The Berenstain Bears' Counting Book (Berenstain and Berenstain) **19**:29

The Berenstain Bears Go to the Doctor (Berenstain and Berenstain) **19**:31

The Berenstain Bears Learn about Strangers (Berenstain and Berenstain) **19**:32

The Berenstain Bears' Moving Day (Berenstain and Berenstain) **19**:31

The Berenstain Bears' Science Fair (Berenstain and Berenstain) **19**:30

The Berenstain Bears Visit the Dentist (Berenstain and Berenstain) **19**:31

The Berenstains' B Book (Berenstain and Berenstain) **19**:27

Berlin, City Split in Two (Garden) **51**:63

Bernard into Battle (Sharp) **27**:166

Bernard the Brave (Sharp) **27**:166

Berries in the Scoop: A Cape Cod Cranberry Story (Lenski) **26**:119

Bertie and May (Norton) **50**:149

Bertie and the Bear (Allen) **44**:6

Bertie Boggin and the Ghost Again! (Waddell) **31**:191

Bertie's Escapade (Grahame) **5**:135

Bess and the Sphinx (Coatsworth) **2**:53

Best Christmas Book Ever! (Scarry) **41**:170

Best Counting Book Ever (Scarry) **41**:166

Best First Book Ever! (Scarry) **41**:168

The Best Friend (Stine) **37**:119

Best Friends (Pascal) **25**:186

Best Little House (Fisher) **49**:44

Best Make-it Book Ever! (Scarry) **41**:168

The Best Mistake Ever! and Other Stories (Scarry) **41**:170

The Best New Thing (Asimov) **12**:46

The Best of Enemies (Bond) **11**:28

The Best of Michael Rosen (Rosen) **45**:150

The Best of the Bargain (Domanska) **40**:46

The Best Older Sister (Choi) **53**:49

The Best Present (Keller) **45**:52

The Best Train Set Ever (Hutchins) **20**:149

Best True Ghost Stories of the 20th Century (Knight) **38**:129

Best Witches: Poems for Halloween (Yolen) **44**:188

Best Word Book Ever (Scarry) **41**:161

The Best-Kept Secret (Rodda) **32**:211

Der Besuch (Heine) **18**:149

Betje Big gaat naar de markt (Bruna) **7**:52

The Betrayal; The Secret (Stine) **37**:122

Betrayed (Sneve) **2**:143

Betsy and Billy (Haywood) **22**:91

Betsy and Mr. Kilpatrick (Haywood) **22**:100

Betsy and the Boys (Haywood) **22**:93

Betsy and the Circus (Haywood) **22**:96

Betsy's Busy Summer (Haywood) **22**:96

Betsy's Little Star (Haywood) **22**:94

Betsy's Play School (Haywood) **22**:103

Betsy's Winterhouse (Haywood) **22**:97

Better Mousetraps: Product Improvements That Led to Success (Aaseng) **54**:14

Better Than All Right (Pfeffer) **11**:197

Betty Friedan: A Voice for Women's Rights (Meltzer) **13**:149

Between Earth and Sky: Legends of Native American Sacred Places (Bruchac) **46**:21

Between Madison and Palmetto (Woodson) **49**:203

Beware the Fish! (Korman) **25**:105

Beyond Another Door (Levitin) **53**:60

Beyond Dreamtime: The Life and Lore of the Aboriginal Australian (Cummings) **48**:43

Beyond Earth: The Search for Extraterrestrial Life (Gallant) **30**:93

Beyond the Bambassu (Guillot) **22**:63

Beyond the Burning Lands (Christopher) **2**:37

Beyond the Chocolate War (Cormier) **12**:151

Beyond the Dark River (Hughes) **9**:71

Beyond the Divide (Lasky) **11**:119

Beyond the Labyrinth (Rubinstein) **35**:211

Beyond the Rainbow Warrior: A Collection of Stories to Celebrate 25 Years of Greenpeace (Morpurgo) **51**:151

Beyond the Ridge (Goble) **21**:137

Beyond the Tomorrow Mountains (Engdahl) **2**:69

Beyond the Weir Bridge (Burton) **1**:30

Beyond Two Rivers (Kherdian) **24**:112

The BFG (Dahl) **7**:82

A Biblical Garden (Lerner) **34**:127

The Bicycle Man (Say) **22**:210

Big and Little (Krauss) **42**:131

Big and Little (Scarry) **41**:171
Big Anthony and the Magic Ring (dePaola) **4**:62
Big Bad Bertie (Waddell) **31**:183
Big Bad Bruce (Peet) **12**:203
Big Bad Pig (McNaughton) **54**:56
The Big Book of Brambly Hedge (Barklem) **31**:5
The Big Cheese (Bunting) **28**:46
The Big Cheese (Schlein) **41**:182
Big City Port (Betsy and Giulio Maestro) **45**:73
The Big Cleanup (Weiss) **4**:224
Big Dog, Little Dog (Brown) **10**:51
Big Dreams and Small Rockets: A Short History of Space Travel (Lauber) **16**:114
Big Friend, Little Friend; Daddy and I . . .; I Make Music; and My Doll, Keshia (Greenfield) **38**:92
Big Game Benn (McKee) **38**:167
Big Goof and Little Goof (Cole) **40**:27
The Big Honey Hunt (Berenstain and Berenstain) **19**:24
The Big Janosch Book of Fun and Verse (Janosch) **26**:79
The Big Joke Game (Corbett) **1**:43
Big Little Davy (Lenski) **26**:120
Big Man and the Burn-Out (Bess) **39**:4
Big Mose (Shippen) **36**:174
Big Ones, Little Ones (Hoban) **13**:104
The Big Orange Splot (Pinkwater) **4**:166
The Big Pets (Smith) **47**:199
Big Red Barn (Brown) **10**:66
The Big Red Barn (Bunting) **28**:48
Big Sister Tells Me That I'm Black (Adoff) **7**:33
The Big Six (Ransome) **8**:180
Big Sixteen (Calhoun) **42**:29
The Big Smith Snatch (Curry) **31**:87
Big Talk (Schlein) **41**:177
Big Top Benn (McKee) **38**:171
Big Tracks, Little Tracks (Branley) **13**:29
The Big Tree of Bunlahy: Stories of My Own Countryside (Colum) **36**:42
Big Wheel (Singer) **48**:142
The Big World and the Little House (Krauss) **42**:113
Bigfoot Makes a Movie (Nixon) **24**:138
The Biggest House in the World (Lionni) **7**:132
Bigmouth (Gaberman) **33**:15
The Bike Lesson (Aiken) **19**:24
Bike Trip (Betsy and Giulio Maestro) **45**:85
Bilgewater (Gardam) **12**:167
Bill and Pete (dePaola) **4**:61
Bill and Pete Go Down the Nile (dePaola) **24**:98
Bill and Stanley (Oxenbury) **22**:142
Bill Bergson and the White Rose Rescue (Lindgren) **1**:135
Bill Bergson Lives Dangerously (Lindgren) **1**:135; **39**:145
Bill Bergson, Master Detective (Lindgren) **1**:135; **39**:144
Bill Cosby: America's Most Famous Father (Haskins) **39**:56
Bill Pickett: Rodeo Ridin' Cowboy (Pinkney) **54**:147
A Billion for Boris (Rodgers) **20**:191
Billions of Bats (Schlein) **41**:192
Bill's Garage (Spier) **5**:228
Bill's New Frock (Fine) **25**:23
Bill's Service Station (Spier) **5**:228
Billy Goat and His Well-Fed Friends (Hogrogian) **2**:87
Billy Jo Jive and the Case of the Midnight Voices (Shearer) **34**:168
Billy Jo Jive and the Case of the Missing Pigeons (Shearer) **34**:167

Billy Jo Jive and the Case of the Sneaker Snatcher (Shearer) **34**:167
Billy Jo Jive and the Walkie Talkie Caper (Shearer) **34**:168
Billy Jo Jive, Super Private Eye: The Case of the Missing Ten Speed Bike (Shearer) **34**:166
Billy's Balloon Ride (Zimnik) **3**:242
Billy's Picture (Rey and Rey) **5**:196
Bimwili and the Zimwi: A Tale from Zanzibar (Aardema) **17**:7
Binary Numbers (Watson) **3**:211
Binge (Ferry) **34**:55
The Bionic Bunny Show (Brown) **29**:11
Bionics (Berger) **32**:21
Birches (Young) **27**:220
Bird and Flower Emblems of the United States (Simon) **39**:196
The Bird and the Stars (Showers) **6**:246
The Bird Began to Sing (Field) **21**:77
The Bird Smugglers (Phipson) **5**:184
Bird Watch: A Book of Poetry (Yolen) **44**:192
Birds at Home (Henry) **4**:109
A Bird's Body (Cole) **40**:4
The Birds' Christmas Carol (Wiggin) **52**:154
Birds, Frogs, and Moonlight (Cassedy) **26**:12
The Birds of Summer (Snyder) **31**:165
Birds on Your Street (Simon) **9**:208
Birds: Poems (Adoff) **7**:37
Birdsong (Haley) **21**:146
Birdsong Lullaby (Stanley) **46**:135
The Birdstones (Curry) **31**:80
Birk the Berserker (Klein) **21**:164
Birkin (Phipson) **5**:180
Birth Control (Nourse) **33**:146
Birth of a Forest (Selsam) **1**:160
Birth of an Island (Selsam) **1**:160
Birth of the Firebringer (Pierce) **20**:184
Birth of the Republic (Carter) **22**:22
The Birth of the United States (Asimov) **12**:50
Birthday (Steptoe) **2**:162
The Birthday Door (Merriam) **14**:203
The Birthday Moon (Duncan) **29**:80
The Birthday Party (Krauss) **42**:122
The Birthday Party (Oxenbury) **22**:144
The Birthday Present (Munari) **9**:125
Birthday Presents (Rylant) **15**:174
The Birthday Tree (Fleischman) **20**:63
The Birthday Visitor (Uchida) **6**:257
A Birthday Wish (Emberley) **5**:100
The Birthday Wish (Iwasaki) **18**:154
Birthdays of Freedom: America's Heritage from the Ancient World (Foster) **7**:95
Birthdays of Freedom: From the Fall of Rome to July 4, 1776, Book Two (Foster) **7**:97
The Bishop and the Devil (Serraillier) **2**:136
Bitter Rivals (Pascal) **25**:186
Bizarre Crimes (Berger) **32**:32
Bizarre Murders (Berger) **32**:28
Bizou (Klein) **19**:95
The Black Americans: A History in Their Own Words, 1619-1983 (Meltzer) **13**:145
Black and Blue Magic (Snyder) **31**:154
Black and White (Brown) **10**:52
The Black BC's (Clifton) **5**:53
Black Beauty: His Grooms and Companions. The Autobiography of a Horse (Sewell) **17**:130-47
Black Beauty: His Grooms and Companions. The Uncle Tom's Cabin of the Horse (Sewell) **17**:130-47
The Black Cauldron (Alexander) **1**:11; **5**:18
Black Dance in America: A History Through Its People (Haskins) **39**:61

The Black Death, 1347-1351 (Cohen) **3**:39
Black Dog (Allen) **44**:13
Black Dog (Mattingley) **24**:125
The Black Dog Who Went into the Woods (Hurd) **49**:130
The Black Dog Who Went into the Woods (McCully) **46**:58
Black Dolly: The Story of a Junk Cart Pony (Keeping) **34**:88
Black Duck and Water Rat (Trezise) **41**:141
Black Eagles: African Americans in Aviation (Haskins) **39**:73
Black Folktales (Lester) **2**:112
Black Forest Summer (Allan) **43**:6
Black Gold (Henry) **4**:113
Black Hearts in Battersea (Aiken) **1**:2
Black Holes, White Dwarfs, and Superstars (Branley) **13**:43
Black Horses for the King (McCaffrey) **49**:156
Black in America: A Fight for Freedom (Jackson and Landau) **28**:142
Black is Beautiful (McGovern) **50**:114
Black Is Brown Is Tan (Adoff) **7**:32
The Black Island (Herge) **6**:148
Black Jack (Garfield) **21**:98
Black Jack: Last of the Big Alligators (McClung) **11**:185
The Black Joke (Mowat) **20**:172
Black Magic: A Pictorial History of the Negro in American Entertainment (Meltzer) **13**:125; **17**:44
Black Misery (Hughes) **17**:45
Black Music in America: A History Through Its People (Haskins) **39**:52
The Black Pearl (O'Dell) **1**:145
The Black Pearl and the Ghost; or, One Mystery after Another (Myers) **16**:138
Black Pilgrimage (Feelings) **5**:106
The Black Sheep (Merrill) **52**:108
Black Ships Before Troy: The Story of the Iliad (Sutcliff) **37**:183
Black Swan (Dhondy) **41**:79
Black Theater in America (Haskins) **39**:42
Blackberry Ink (Wilhelm) **46**:160
Blackberry Ink: Poems (Merriam) **14**:202
Blackbird Singing (Bunting) **28**:49
Blackbriar (Sleator) **29**:199
Blacksmith at Blueridge (Bunting) **28**:45
The Bladerunner (Nourse) **33**:138
Blair's Nightmare (Snyder) **31**:166
The Blanket (Burningham) **9**:47
The Blanket Word (Arundel) **35**:22
Blaze: The Story of a Striped Skunk (McClung) **11**:186
A Blessing in Disguise (Tate) **37**:192
Blewcoat Boy (Garfield) **21**:122
Blind Date (Stine) **37**:108
Blinded by the Light (Brancato) **32**:72
Blodin the Beast (Morpurgo) **51**:143
The Blonk from Beneath the Sea (Bendick) **5**:38
Blood (Zim) **2**:225
Blood Feud (Sutcliff) **37**:166
Blood Line (Hamley) **47**:62
The Bloodhound Gang in the Case of Princess Tomorrow (Fleischman) **15**:111
The Bloodhound Gang in the Case of the 264-Pound Burglar (Fleischman) **15**:111
The Bloodhound Gang in the Case of the Cackling Ghost (Fleischman) **15**:111
The Bloodhound Gang in the Case of the Flying Clock (Fleischman) **15**:111
The Bloodhound Gang in the Case of the Secret Message (Fleischman) **15**:111

Title Index

The Bloody Country (Collier and Collier) **3**:44
Blossom Culp and the Sleep of Death (Peck) **15**:165
A Blossom Promise (Byars) **16**:65
The Blossoms and the Green Phantom (Byars) **16**:65
The Blossoms Meet the Vulture Lady (Byars) **16**:64
Blow Me Down (McNaughton) **54**:56
Blowfish Live in the Sea (Fox) **1**:76
Blubber (Blume) **2**:16
Blue above the Trees (Clark) **30**:57
The Blue Bird (French) **37**:35
Blue Canyon Horse (Clark) **16**:80
The Blue Day (Guillot) **22**:60
The Blue Door (Rinaldi) **46**:93
Blue Dragon Days (Allan) **43**:7
Blue Fin (Thiele) **27**:204
The Blue Hawk (Dickinson) **29**:45
The Blue Jackal (Brown) **12**:106
The Blue Misty Monsters (Waddell) **31**:184
Blue Moose (Pinkwater) **4**:163
Blue Mystery (Benary-Isbert) **12**:73
Blue Remembered Hills: A Recollection (Sutcliff) **37**:176
The Blue Sword (McKinley) **10**:123
The Blue Thing (Pinkwater) **4**:166
Blue Tights (Williams-Garcia) **36**:203
Blue Trees, Red Sky (Klein) **2**:97
Blueberries for Sal (McCloskey) **7**:205
Blueberry Corners (Lenski) **26**:105
Bluebirds Over Pit Row (Cresswell) **18**:104
A Blue-Eyed Daisy (Rylant) **15**:170
Blue's Broken Heart (Merrill) **52**:103
Bo the Constrictor That Couldn't (Stren) **5**:231
Boat Book (Gibbons) **8**:95
A Boat for Peppe (Politi) **29**:188
Boat Ride with Lillian Two Blossom (Polacco) **40**:184
The Boats on the River (Flack) **28**:128
Bob and Jilly (Schmidt) **22**:221
Bob and Jilly Are Friends (Schmidt) **22**:222
Bob and Jilly in Trouble (Schmidt) **22**:223
Bob Dylan: Spellbinding Songwriter (Aaseng) **54**:12
The Bobbin Girl (McCully) **46**:73
The Bodach (*The Walking Stones*) (Hunter) **25**:78
The Bodies in the Bessledorf Hotel (Naylor) **17**:60
The Body (Nourse) **33**:134
Body Sense/Body Nonsense (Simon) **9**:217
The Body Snatchers (Cohen) **3**:39
Boek zonder woorden (Bruna) **7**:51
Bold John Henebry (Dillon) **26**:25
Bollerbam (Janosch) **26**:74
Bon Voyage, Baabee (Khalsa) **30**:144
Bones (Zim) **2**:226
The Bonfire Party (Clarke) **28**:80
The Bongleweed (Cresswell) **18**:105
Bonhomme and the Huge Beast (Brunhoff) **4**:39
Bonnie Bess, the Weathervane Horse (Tresselt) **30**:202
Bonnie Dundee (Sutcliff) **37**:177
Bony-Legs (Cole) **40**:5
Boo! (McNaughton) **54**:67
Boo, the Boy Who Didn't Like the Dark (Leaf) **25**:130
Boo, Who Used to Be Scared of the Dark (Leaf) **25**:130
A Book about Names: In Which Custom, Tradition, Law, Myth, History, Folklore, Foolery, Legend, Fashion, Nonsense, Symbol, Taboo Help Explain How We Got Our Names and What They Mean (Meltzer) **13**:146

The Book of American Negro Poetry (Johnson) **32**:155
The Book of American Negro Spirituals (Johnson) **32**:159
A Book of Astronauts for You (Branley) **13**:31
A Book of Christmas (Tudor) **13**:201
The Book of Dragons (Nesbit) **3**:162
The Book of Eagles (Sattler) **24**:224
A Book of Flying Saucers for You (Branley) **13**:39
A Book of Goblins (Garner) **20**:108
The Book of Indians (Holling) **50**:48
A Book of Mars for You (Branley) **13**:34
A Book of Moon Rockets for You (Branley) **13**:28
The Book of Nursery and Mother Goose Rhymes (de Angeli) **1**:52
A Book of Outer Space for You (Branley) **13**:37
A Book of Planet Earth for You (Branley) **13**:42
A Book of Planets for You (Branley) **13**:29
A Book of Satellites for You (Branley) **13**:27
A Book of Scary Things (Showers) **6**:247
A Book of Seasons (Provensen and Provensen) **11**:212
A Book of Stars for You (Branley) **13**:33
The Book of the Goat (Scott) **20**:198
A Book of the Milky Way Galaxy for You (Branley) **13**:32
The Book of the Pig (Scott) **20**:199
The Book of Three (Alexander) **1**:12; **5**:18
A Book of Venus for You (Branley) **13**:36
"Books of Opposites" (McNaughton) **54**:53
Boom Town (Levitin) **53**:78
Border Hawk: August Bondi (Alexander) **5**:17
Bored with Being Bored!: How to Beat The Boredom Blahs (Stine) **37**:105
Bored—Nothing to Do! (Spier) **5**:226
Boris (Haar) **15**:115
Borka: The Adventures of a Goose with No Feathers (Burningham) **9**:38
Born of the Sun (Cross) **28**:89
Born to the Land: An American Portrait (Ashabranner) **28**:12
Born to Trot (Henry) **4**:111
The Borrowers (Norton) **6**:220
The Borrowers Afield (Norton) **6**:221
The Borrowers Afloat (Norton) **6**:222
The Borrowers Aloft (Norton) **6**:223
The Borrowers Avenged (Norton) **6**:226
The Boss (Baillie) **49**:14
Boss Cat (Hunter) **3**:97
Boss of the Pool (Klein) **21**:164
Bostock and Harris: Or, the Night of the Comet (Garfield) **21**:114
The Boston Coffee Party (McCully) **46**:61
A Bottled Cherry Angel (Ure) **34**:181
Botts, the Naughty Otter (Freeman) **30**:73
Bound for the Rio Grande: The Mexican Struggle, 1845-1850 (Meltzer) **13**:131
Bound Girl of Cobble Hill (Lenski) **26**:104
The Boundary Riders (Phipson) **5**:178
A Bouquet of Littles (Krauss) **42**:127
Bows against the Barons (Trease) **42**:173
A Box Full of Infinity (Williams) **8**:231
A Box of Nothing (Dickinson) **29**:56
The Box with Red Wheels (Petersham and Petersham) **24**:177
Boxes (Merrill) **52**:100
Boxes! Boxes! (Fisher) **18**:133
A Boy, a Dog, a Frog, and a Friend (Mayer) **11**:166
A Boy, a Dog, and a Frog (Mayer) **11**:159
Boy Alone (Ottley) **16**:183
A Boy and Fire Huskies (Guillot) **22**:59
The Boy and the Ghost (Pinkney) **54**:133

The Boy and the Ghost (San Souci) **43**:183
The Boy and the Monkey (Garfield) **21**:100
The Boy and the Whale (Sanchez-Silva) **12**:232
The Boy Apprenticed to an Enchanter (Colum) **36**:25
Boy Blue (McBratney) **44**:118
A Boy Called Slow: The True Story of Sitting Bull (Bruchac) **46**:19
The Boy from Cumeroogunga: The Story of Sir Douglas Nicholls, Aboriginal Leader (Clark) **30**:62
A Boy Had a Mother Who Bought Him a Hat (Kuskin) **4**:141
A Boy in Eirinn (Colum) **36**:22
The Boy in the Drawer (Munsch) **19**:143
A Boy of Taché (Blades) **15**:54
The Boy Pharaoh: Tutankhamen (Streatfeild) **17**:198
Boy: Tales of Childhood (Dahl) **41**:33
The Boy Who Could Find Anything (Nixon) **24**:137
The Boy Who Didn't Believe in Spring (Clifton) **5**:54
The Boy Who Had No Heart (Petersham and Petersham) **24**:178
The Boy Who Lived with the Bears (Bruchac) **46**:21
The Boy Who Lost His Face (Sacher) **28**:204
The Boy Who Owned the School: A Comedy of Love (Paulsen) **54**:97
The Boy Who Reversed Himself (Sleator) **29**:205
The Boy Who Sailed with Columbus (Foreman) **32**:107
The Boy Who Spoke Chimp (Yolen) **4**:268
The Boy Who Swallowed Snakes (Yep) **54**:195
The Boy Who Was Followed Home (Mahy) **7**:183
The Boy Who Wasn't There (Wilhelm) **46**:170
The Boy with the Helium Head (Naylor) **17**:57
Boy without a Name (Lively) **7**:159
The Boyfriend (Stine) **37**:115
The Boyhood of Grace Jones (Langton) **33**:113
Boys and Girls, Girls and Boys (Merriam) **14**:198
Boys at Work (Soto) **38**:207
The Boys' War: Confederate and Union Soldiers Talk about the Civil War (Murphy) **53**:108
A Boy's Will (Haugaard) **11**:110
Brady (Fritz) **2**:79
Brainbox Sorts It Out (Noestlinger) **12**:188
The Brains of Animals and Man (Freedman) **20**:76
Brainstorm (Myers) **4**:157
Brainwashing and Other Forms of Mind Control (Hyde) **23**:162
"Brambly Hedge Books" (Barklem) **31**:2
The Brambly Hedge Treasury (Barklem) **31**:6
A Brand-New Uncle (Seredy) **10**:181
Brats (Kennedy) **27**:101
Brave Buffalo Fighter (Waditaka Tatanka Kisisohitika) (Fitzgerald) **1**:69
The Brave Cowboy (Anglund) **1**:19
Brave Eagle's Account of the Fetterman Fight, 21 December 1866 (Goble) **21**:129
Brave Irene (Steig) **15**:201
The Brave Little Goat of Monsieur Séguin: A Picture Story from Provence (Nakatani) **30**:156
The Brave Little Toaster: A Bedtime Story for Small Appliances (Disch) **18**:114
The Brave Little Toaster Goes to Mars (Disch) **18**:116
The Bravest Thing (Napoli) **51**:160
Bravo, Ernest and Celestine! (Vincent) **13**:216
Bread and Honey (Southall) **2**:149
Bread and Jam for Frances (Hoban) **3**:76
Bread—and Roses: The Struggle of American Labor, 1865-1915 (Meltzer) **13**:124

The Breadhorse (Garner) **20**:112

Breadsticks and Blessing Places (Boyd) **50**:3

The Breadwitch (Nimmo) **44**:151

Break Dancing (Haskins) **39**:51

Break for the Basket (Christopher) **33**:38

Break in the Sun (Ashley) **4**:17

Break of Dark (Westall) **13**:257

A Break with Charity: A Story about the Salem Witch Trials (Rinaldi) **46**:84

Breakaway (Yee) **44**:165

Breakfast Time, Ernest and Celestine (Vincent) **13**:219

Breaking Up (Klein) **19**:92

Breakthrough: Women in Archaeology (Williams) **48**:199

Breakthrough: Women in Politics (Williams) **48**:198

Breakthroughs in Science (Asimov) **12**:34

The Bremen Town Musicians (Domanska) **40**:49

The Bremen Town Musicians (Wilhelm) **46**:169

Brenda and Edward (Kovalski) **34**:114

Brendan the Navigator: A History Mystery about the Discovery of America (Fritz) **14**:114

Brer Rabbit and His Tricks (Gorey) **36**:92

Brer Rabbit: Stories from Uncle Remus (Brown) **10**:50

Brian Wildsmith's 1, 2, 3s (Wildsmith) **2**:211

Brian Wildsmith's ABC (Wildsmith) **2**:208

Brian Wildsmith's Amazing World of Words (Wildsmith) **52**:201

Brian Wildsmith's Birds (Wildsmith) **2**:208

Brian Wildsmith's Circus (Wildsmith) **2**:209

Brian Wildsmith's Fishes (Wildsmith) **2**:210

Brian Wildsmith's Mother Goose: A Collection of Nursery Rhymes (Wildsmith) **2**:210

Brian Wildsmith's Puzzles (Wildsmith) **2**:211

Brian Wildsmith's The Twelve Days of Christmas (Wildsmith) **2**:212

Brian Wildsmith's Wild Animals (Wildsmith) **2**:212

Brian's Return (Paulsen) **54**:126

Brian's Winter (Paulsen) **54**:119

Brickyard Summer (Janeczko) **47**:109

The Bridge Between (St. John) **46**:99

Bridge of Friendship (Allan) **43**:26

Bridge to Terabithia (Paterson) **7**:232

Bridger: The Story of a Mountain Man (Kherdian) **24**:115

Bridges to Change: How Kids Live on a South Carolina Sea Island (Krull) **44**:109

Bridges to Cross (Janeczko) **47**:104

Bridget and William (Gardam) **12**:168

A Bridle for Pegasus (Shippen) **36**:173

Bridle the Wind (Munsch) **19**:14

Briefe an Pauline (Kruss) **9**:87

Brigham Young and Me, Clarissa (Williams) **48**:196

The Bright and Morning Star (Harris) **30**:114

The Bright Design (Shippen) **36**:170

Bright Lights Blaze Out (Owen) **31**:145

Bright Morning (Bianco) **19**:57

Bright Shadow (Avi) **24**:12

Bright Shadow (Thomas) **19**:221

Bright Stars, Red Giants, and White Dwarfs (Berger) **32**:30

Brighty of the Grand Canyon (Henry) **4**:112

Bring to a Boil and Separate (Irwin) **40**:108

Bringing the Rain to Kapiti Plain (Aardema) **17**:6

Brinsly's Dream (Breinburg) **31**:68

British Folk Tales: New Versions (Crossley-Holland) **47**:45

Broken Days (Rinaldi) **46**:91

Broken Hearts (Stine) **37**:120

The Broken Spoke (Gorey) **36**:98

Bronto's Wings (McKee) **38**:157

El Bronx Remembered: A Novella and Stories (Mohr) **22**:131

The Bronze Bow (Speare) **8**:208

The Bronze Trumpeter (Nimmo) **44**:138

Bronzeville Boys and Girls (Brooks) **27**:44-56

Brother André of Montreal (Clark) **16**:82

Brother, Can You Spare a Dime? The Great Depression, 1929-1933 (Meltzer) **13**:126

Brother Dusty-Feet (Sutcliff) **1**:184; **37**:150

Brother Eagle, Sister Sky: A Message from Chief Seattle (Jeffers) **30**:137

A Brother for Momoko (Iwasaki) **18**:153

Brother Night (Kelleher) **36**:127

Brother to the Wind (Leo and Diane Dillon) **44**:36

Brother to the Wind (Walter) **15**:207

The Brothers Grimm: Popular Folk Tales (Foreman) **32**:90

The Brothers Lionheart (Lindgren) **39**:154

Brothers of the Heart: A Story of the Old Northwest 1837-1838 (Blos) **18**:18

Brothers of the Wind (Yolen) **4**:268

Brown Angels: An Album of Pictures and Verse (Myers) **35**:204

"*The Brownie Books*" (Cox) **24**:65-83

Bruce Jenner: Decathalon Winner (Aaseng) **54**:9

Brumbie Dust: A Selection of Stories (Ottley) **16**:185

Bruno Munari's ABC (Munari) **9**:125

Bruno Munari's Zoo (Munari) **9**:127

Bub, or the Very Best Thing (Babbitt) **53**:38

Bubble, Bubble (Mayer) **11**:167

Bubbles (Cummings) **48**:43

Bubbles (Greenfield) **4**:96

Buddies (Park) **34**:156

Buddy's Adventures in the Blueberry Patch (Beskow) **17**:15

Budgerigar Blue (Mattingley) **24**:125

Buffalo Bill (d'Aulaire and d'Aulaire) **21**:51

The Buffalo Nickel Blues Band! (Gaberman) **33**:10

Buffalo: The American Bison Today (Patent) **19**:163

Buffalo Woman (Goble) **21**:134

Bufo: The Story of a Toad (McClung) **11**:179

Buford the Little Bighorn (Peet) **12**:198

The Bug That Laid the Golden Eggs (Selsam) **1**:160

Bugs for Dinner? The Eating Habits of Neighborhood Creatures (Epstein and Epstein) **26**:71

Bugs: Poems (Hoberman) **22**:112

Bugs Potter Live at Nickaninny (Korman) **25**:107

Building Blocks (Voigt) **13**:235

Building Blocks of the Universe (Asimov) **12**:32

Building Construction (Berger) **32**:21

A Building on Your Street (Simon) **9**:207

Bulbs, Corms, and Such (Selsam) **1**:161

The Bully (Needle) **43**:143

The Bumblebee Flies Anyway (Cormier) **12**:149

The Bumblebee's Secret (Schlein) **41**:181

Bummer Summer (Martin) **32**:200

The Bun: A Tale from Russia (Brown) **12**:104

The Bundle Book (Krauss) **42**:115

Bunnicula: A Rabbit-Tale of Mystery (Howe) **9**:56

Bunny, Hound, and Clown (Mukerji) **10**:135

Burglar Bill (Ahlberg and Ahlberg) **18**:4

The Burglar Next Door (Williams) **8**:235

The Buried Moon and Other Stories (Bang) **8**:19

The Burma Road (Epstein and Epstein) **26**:45

The Burning of Njal (Treece) **2**:182

The Burning Questions of Bingo Brown (Byars) **16**:66

The Burning Time (Matas) **52**:88

Burt Dow, Deep-Water Man: A Tale of the Sea in the Classic Tradition (McCloskey) **7**:210

Bury Me Deep (Pike) **29**:174

The Bus under the Leaves (Mahy) **7**:182

Busiest People Ever (Scarry) **3**:183

Busy, Busy Town (Scarry) **41**:171

Busy Day: A Book of Action Words (Betsy and Giulio Maestro) **45**:68

Busy Houses (Scarry) **41**:169

Busy Monday Morning (Domanska) **40**:52

But in the Fall I'm Leaving (Rinaldi) **46**:78

But Jasper Came Instead (Noestlinger) **12**:189

But Ostriches. . . (Fisher) **49**:53

The Butter Battle Book (Dr. Seuss) **9**:194; **53**:135

Butterfiles and Moths: How They Function (Patent) **19**:154

The Butterflies Come (Politi) **29**:190

The Butterfly Boy (Yep) **54**:193

The Butterfly Lion (Morpurgo) **51**:148

Button Soup (Orgel) **48**:96

By Camel or by Car: A Look at Transportation (Billout) **33**:21

By the Great Horn Spoon! (Fleischman) **1**:73

By the Hanukkah Light (Oberman) **54**:78

By the Sandhills of Yamboorah (Ottley) **16**:183

By the Sea: An Alphabet Book (Blades) **15**:55

By the Shores of Silver Lake (Wilder) **2**:205

C Is for City (Cummings) **48**:56

C Is for City (Grimes) **42**:92

C Is for Clown: A Circus of "C" Words (Berenstain and Berenstain) **19**:28

"*C" Is for Cupcake* (Haywood) **22**:102

The Cabin Faced West (Fritz) **14**:110

The Caboose Who Got Loose (Peet) **12**:202

Cactus (Lerner) **34**:138

Caddie Woodlawn (Brink) **30**:7

Caddie Woodlawn: A Play (Brink) **30**:13

Cakes and Custard: Children's Rhymes (Oxenbury) **22**:139

The Caldecott Aesop (Caldecott) **14**:79

Caldicott Place (The Family at Caldicott Place) (Streatfeild) **17**:197

Caleb (Crew) **42**:62

Caleb and Kate (Steig) **15**:196

The Calendar (Adler) **27**:23

Calendar Art: Thirteen Days, Weeks, Months, and Years from Around the World (Fisher) **18**:137

A Calf Is Born (Cole) **5**:64

Calico Bush (Field) **21**:76

Calico Captive (Speare) **8**:205

Calico, the Wonder Horse; or, The Saga of Stewy Slinker (Burton) **11**:45

California Demon (Singer) **48**:141

Call Me Bandicoot (Pene du Bois) **1**:63

Call Me Charley (Jackson) **28**:137

Call Me Francis Tucket (Paulsen) **54**:117

The Call of the Wolves (Murphy) **53**:107

The Callender Papers (Voigt) **13**:233

Callie's Castle (Park) **51**:175

Callie's Family (Park) **51**:182

The Callow Pit Coffer (Crossley-Holland) **47**:25

Camels Are Meaner Than Mules (Calhoun) **42**:18

Camilla (L'Engle) **1**:129

Camping Out: A Book of Action Words (Betsy and Giulio Maestro) **45**:74

Can Bears Predict Earthquake? Unsolved Mysteries of Animal Behavior (Freedman) **20**:82

Can I Keep Him? (Kellogg) **6**:170

Can You Catch Josephine? (Poulin) **28**:195

Can You Sue Your Parents for Malpractice? (Danziger) **20**:53

Canada Geese (Scott) **20**:195

Cancer in the Young: A Sense of Hope (Hyde) **23**:171

Cancer Lab (Berger) **32**:13

A Candle for St. Antony (Spence) **26**:198

Candy (White) **3**:220

Candy Floss (Godden) **20**:130

Cannonball Simp (Burningham) **9**:41

Can't Hear You Listening (Irwin) **40**:114

Can't You Make Them Behave, King George? (Fritz) **14**:113

Can't You Sleep, Little Bear? (Waddell) **31**:191

Canterbury Tales (Hyman) **50**:80

The Canterbury Tales (McCaughrean) **38**:137

The Canterville Ghost (Zwerger) **46**:197

The Cantilever Rainbow (Krauss) **42**:127

Canyons (Paulsen) **54**:100

The Capricorn Bracelet (Sutcliff) **1**:184; **37**:164

Captain Abdul's Pirate School (McNaughton) **54**:64

Captain Grey (Avi) **24**:5

Captain Kidd's Cat (Lawson) **2**:109

Captain of the Planter: The Story of Robert Smalls (Sterling) **1**:177

Captain Pottle's House (Cooney) **23**:22

Captain Whiz-Bang (Stanley) **46**:138

The Captain's Watch (Garfield) **21**:106

The Captive (O'Dell) **16**:174

Capyboppy (Peet) **12**:198

The Car (Paulsen) **54**:113

The Car Trip (Oxenbury) **22**:145

Careers in an Airport (Paulsen) **19**:172

Cargo Ships (Zim) **2**:226

Carl Goes Shopping (Day) **22**:26

Carl Lewis: Legend Chaser (Aaseng) **54**:10

Carl Linneaus: The Man Who Put the World of Life in Order (Silverstein and Silverstein) **25**:203

Carl Sagan: Superstar Scientist (Cohen) **43**:47

Carlisles All (St. John) **46**:117

Carlisle's Hope (St. John) **46**:116

Carlota (O'Dell) **16**:173

Carousel (Crews) **7**:61

Carousel (Cummings) **48**:54

Carousel (Wildsmith) **52**:193

Carrie's War (Bawden) **2**:10; **51**:20

The Carrot Seed (Krauss) **42**:109

Carry On, Mr. Bowditch (Latham) **50**:97

Cars and How They Go (Cole) **40**:5

Cars and Trucks and Things That Go (Scarry) **41**:166

Cars, Boats, Trains, and Planes of Today and Tomorrow (Aylesworth) **6**:52

Cart and Cwidder (Jones) **23**:184

The Cartoonist (Byars) **16**:55

A Case of Blue Murder (McBratney) **44**:126

The Case of the Cackling Car (Singer) **48**:127

The Case of the Dog-lover's Legacy (St. John) **46**:115

The Case of the Fixed Election (Singer) **48**:134

The Case of the Goblin Pearls (Yep) **54**:201

The Case of the Gone Goose (Corbett) **1**:43

The Case of the Sabotaged School Play (Singer) **48**:126

The Case of the Silver Skull (Corbett) **1**:43

Casey and the Great Idea (Nixon) **24**:140

Casey at the Bat: A Ballad of the Republic Sung in the Year 1888 (Polacco) **40**:184

Caspar and His Friends (Baumann) **35**:48

Cassie Binegar (MacLachlan) **14**:182

Castle (Macaulay) **14**:170

Castle in Spain (Guillot) **22**:71

The Castle in the Sea (O'Dell) **16**:178

The Castle Number Nine (Bemelmans) **6**:65

A Castle of Bone (Farmer) **8**:80

The Castle of Llyr (Alexander) **1**:12; **5**:19

The Castle of the Crested Bird (Guillot) **22**:70

The Castle of Yew (Boston) **3**:26

Castle on the Border (Benary-Isbert) **12**:75

Castors Away (Burton) **1**:30

Cat and Canary (Foreman) **32**:97

Cat and Dog (Minarik) **33**:125

The Cat and the Captain (Coatsworth) **2**:54

The Cat Ate My Gymsuit (Danziger) **20**:50

Cat Goes Fiddle-I-Fee (Galdone) **16**:106

Cat, Herself (Hunter) **25**:90

The Cat in the Hat (Dr. Seuss) **1**:84; **9**:182

The Cat in the Hat Beginner Book Dictionary, by the Cat Himself and P. D. Eastman (Dr. Seuss) **9**:188

The Cat in the Hat Comes Back! (Dr. Seuss) **9**:184

Cat Poems (Hyman) **50**:79

The Cat Who Went to Heaven (Coatsworth) **2**:54

The Cat Who Wished to Be a Man (Alexander) **1**:12; **5**:22

Catch a Little Rhyme (Merriam) **14**:194

Catch That Pass! (Christopher) **33**:44

Catch the Ball! (Carle) **10**:85

The Catcher in the Rye (Salinger) **18**:171-94

Catcher with a Glass Arm (Christopher) **33**:39

Catching the Wind (Ryder) **37**:93

Caterpillars (Sterling) **1**:178

Caterpillars and How They Live (McClung) **11**:183

The Caterpillow Fight (McBratney) **44**:132

Catfish (Hurd and Hurd) **49**:127

A Cathedral Courtship, and Penelope's English Experiences (Wiggin) **52**:157

Cathedral: The Story of Its Construction (Macaulay) **3**:140

Catrin in Wales (Allan) **43**:7

The Cats (Phipson) **5**:184

A Cat's Body (Cole) **5**:68

The Cats' Burglar (Parish) **22**:166

The Cats from Summer Island (Unnerstad) **36**:196

The Cat's Midsummer Jamboree (Kherdian) **24**:116

The Cats of Seroster (Westall) **13**:259

The Cats' Opera (Dillon) **26**:23

The Cat's Purr (Bryan) **18**:35

The Cat's Quizzer (Dr. Seuss) **9**:193

Catseye (Norton) **50**:141

Caught in the Act (Nixon) **24**:150

A Cavalcade of Goblins (Garner) **20**:108

The Cave above Delphi (Corbett) **1**:43

The Cave Painters (Trezise) **41**:141

Cave Under the City (Mazer) **16**:133

The Caves of the Great Hunters (Baumann) **35**:36

The Cay (Taylor) **30**:176

CDB! (Steig) **2**:159

CDC? (Steig) **15**:200

Cecily G. and the Nine Monkeys (Rey) **5**:192

The Celery Stalks at Midnight (Howe) **9**:59

Cells: Building Blocks of Life (Silverstein and Silverstein) **25**:203

Cells: The Basic Structure of Life (Cobb) **2**:64

Cendrillon: A Creole Cinderella (Pinkney) **54**:149

Censorship (Berger) **32**:27

Centerburg Tales (McCloskey) **7**:207

Centerfield Ballhawk (Christopher) **33**:62

Central City/Spread City: The Metropolitan Regions Where More and More of Us Spend Our Lives (Schwartz) **3**:188

The Centurion (Treece) **2**:183

Ceramics: From Clay to Kiln (Weiss) **4**:223

Cerebral Palsy (Aaseng) **54**:16

The Ceremony of Innocence (Highwater) **17**:30

A Certain Magic (Orgel) **48**:82

Chain Letter (Pike) **29**:171

Chain of Fire (Naidoo) **29**:166

Chains, Webs, and Pyramids: The Flow of Energy in Nature (Pringle) **4**:179

A Chair for My Mother (Williams) **9**:232

Chair Person (Jones) **23**:197

The Chalk Box Story (Freeman) **30**:81

Challenge at Second Base (Christopher) **33**:39

The Challenge of the Green Knight (Serraillier) **2**:136

Challenge of the Wolf Knight (Stine) **37**:107

Chameleons and Other Quick-Change Artists (Simon) **39**:191

Champion Dog, Prince Tom (Fritz) **14**:111

The Champion of Olympia, an Adventure (Guillot) **22**:70

Chance, Luck, and Destiny (Dickinson) **29**:44

Chancy and the Grand Rascal (Fleischman) **1**:73

Change for a Penny (Epstein and Epstein) **26**:56

The Change-Child (Curry) **31**:74

The Changeling (Snyder) **31**:157

The Changeling (Sutcliff) **37**:165

Changes, Changes (Hutchins) **20**:145

The Changing City (Mueller) **43**:115

The Changing Countryside (Mueller) **43**:115

The Changing Earth (Viorst) **3**:207

The Changing Maze (Snyder) **31**:167

Changing the Face of North America: The Challenge of the St. Lawrence Seaway (Lauber) **16**:113

The Changing Tools of Science: From Yardstick to Synchrotron (Adler) **27**:10

Changing Tunes (Napoli) **51**:168

Chanticleer and the Fox (Cooney) **23**:22

Chanticleer, the Real Story of the Famous Rooster (Duvoisin) **23**:92

Chapters: My Growth as a Writer (Duncan) **29**:75

Chariot in the Sky: A Story of the Jubilee Singers (Bontemps) **6**:82

Charity at Home (Willard) **2**:216

Charles Darwin: The Making of a Scientist (Gallant) **30**:90

Charles Dickens: The Man Who Had Great Expectations (Stanley) **46**:149

Charles Keeping's Book of Classic Ghost Stories (Keeping) **34**:108

Charles Keeping's Classic Tales of the Macabre (Keeping) **34**:109

Charley, Charlotte and the Golden Canary (Keeping) **34**:89

Charley Starts from Scratch (Jackson) **28**:139

Charlie and the Chocolate Factory (Dahl) **1**:49; **7**:69

Charlie and the Great Glass Elevator: The Further Adventures of Charlie Bucket and Willy Wonka, Chocolate-Maker Extraordinary (Dahl) **1**:50; **7**:73

Charlie Lewis Plays for Time (Kemp) **29**:118

Charlie Moon and the Big Bonanza Bust-Up (Hughes) **15**:129

"Charlie Needs a Cloak" (dePaola) **4**:55

Charlie Pippin (Boyd) **50**:4

Charlie's House (Daly) **41**:61

Charlie's World: A Book of Poems (Hopkins) **44**:87

Charlotte and the White Horse (Krauss) **42**:121

Charlotte Sometimes (Farmer) **8**:78

Charlotte's Web (White) **1**:193

Charmed (Singer) **48**:137

Charmed Life (Jones) **23**:187

Chartbreak (Cross) **28**:92

Chartbreaker (Cross) **28**:92

Chase Me, Catch Nobody! (Haugaard)　**11**:109
Chasing the Goblins Away (Tobias)　**4**:216
Chaucer and His World (Serraillier)　**2**:137
The Cheater (Stine)　**37**:122
The Checkup (Oxenbury)　**22**:145
The Cheerleader (Klein)　**19**:97
Cheerleaders: The First Evil (Stine)　**37**:118
Cheerleaders: The Second Evil (Stine)　**37**:118
Cheerleaders: The Third Evil (Stine)　**37**:119
The Chemicals of Life: Enzymes, Vitamins, Hormones (Asimov)　**12**:31
The Chemicals We Eat and Drink (Silverstein and Silverstein)　**25**:209
Chemistry in the Kitchen (Simon)　**9**:203
Chernowitz! (Gaberman)　**33**:8
Cherokee Bat and the Goat Guys (Block)　**33**:32
Cherokee Run (Smucker)　**10**:189
The Cherry Tree (Wildsmith)　**52**:196
The Cherry Tree Party (Unnerstad)　**36**:200
Chess-Dream in a Garden (Sutcliff)　**37**:184
Chessmen of Doom (Bellairs)　**37**:23
Chester Chipmunk's Thanksgiving (Williams)　**48**:195
Chester Cricket's New Home (Selden)　**8**:202
Chester Cricket's Pigeon Ride (Selden)　**8**:201
Chester the Out-Of-Work Dog (Singer)　**48**:140
Chester the Worldly Pig (Peet)　**12**:196
Chester's Way (Henkes)　**23**:130
The Chestnut Soldier (Nimmo)　**44**:143
The Chestry Oak (Seredy)　**10**:178
Chevrolet Saturdays (Boyd)　**50**:5
The Chewing-Gum Rescue and Other Stories (Mahy)　**7**:186
The Chichi Hoohoo Bogeyman (Sneve)　**2**:144
A Chick Hatches (Cole)　**5**:64
Chicken Soup with Rice (Sendak)　**1**:167
Chicken Sunday (Polacco)　**40**:192
Chidwick's Chimney (Thiele)　**27**:209
Chief Joseph, War Chief of the Nez Percé (Ashabranner and Davis)　**28**:4
The Chief of the Herd (Mukerji)　**10**:133
The Chief's Daughter (Sutcliff)　**37**:160
The Child Abuse Help Book (Haskins)　**39**:40
The Child in the Bamboo Grove (Harris)　**30**:114
Child of Fire (O'Dell)　**16**:169
Child of the Morning (Corcoran)　**50**:30
Child of the Owl (Yep)　**3**:235
Child O'War: The True Story of a Boy Sailor in Nelson's Navy (Garfield)　**21**:105
The Children Come Running (Coatsworth)　**2**:54
The Children Next Door (Sharp)　**27**:166
Children of Christmas: Stories for the Season (Rylant)　**15**:174
The Children of Green Knowe (Boston)　**3**:26
The Children of Noisy Village (Lindgren)　**1**:135
The Children of Odin: The Book of Northern Myths (Colum)　**36**:24
The Children of Primrose Lane (Streatfeild)　**17**:189
Children of the Blitz: Memories of Wartime Childhood (Westall)　**13**:260
Children of the Forest (Beskow)　**17**:16
Children of the Great Lake (Trezise)　**41**:144
The Children of the House (Pearce)　**9**:152
Children of the Longhouse (Bruchac)　**46**:23
Children of the Maya: A Guatemalan Indian Odyssey (Ashabranner)　**28**:9
Children of the Northlights (d'Aulaire and d'Aulaire)　**21**:42
Children of the Sun (Leo and Diane Dillon)　**44**:35
Children of the Wild West (Freedman)　**20**:84
The Children of the Wind (Guillot)　**22**:68
Children of the Wolf (Yolen)　**44**:176
Children of Winter (Doherty)　**21**:57

The Children on the Top Floor (Streatfeild)　**17**:196
The Children on Troublemaker Street (Lindgren)　**39**:151
The Children Who Followed the Piper (Colum)　**36**:26
The Children's Homer (Colum)　**36**:24
The Children's War (Taylor)　**30**:186
A Children's Zoo (Hoban)　**13**:111
A Child's Book of Poems (Fujikawa)　**25**:38
A Child's Christmas in Wales (Hyman)　**50**:78
A Child's First Picture Dictionary (Moore)　**15**:139
A Child's Garden of Verses (Stevenson)　**11**:222-43
A Child's Good Morning (Brown)　**10**:62
A Child's Good Night Book (Brown)　**10**:51
Childtimes: A Three-Generation Memoir (Greenfield)　**4**:101
A Chill in the Lane (Allan)　**43**:24
Chilly Stomach (Caines)　**24**:64
Chilly Stomach (Cummings)　**48**:47
Chimney Sweeps: Yesterday and Today (Giblin)　**29**:87
Chin Chiang and the Dragon's Dance (Wallace)　**37**:209
The China Coin (Baillie)　**49**:13
China Homecoming (Fritz)　**14**:120
The China People (Farmer)　**8**:76
Chinaman's Reef Is Ours (Southall)　**2**:149
The Chinese Americans (Meltzer)　**13**:142
Chinese Handcuffs (Crutcher)　**28**:105
The Chinese Mirror (Ginsburg)　**45**:18
Chinese Mother Goose Rhymes (Young)　**27**:217
Chip Rogers, Computer Whiz (Simon)　**9**:221
Chipmunk Song (Ryder)　**37**:89
Chipmunks on the Doorstep (Tunis)　**2**:191
Chips and Jessie (Hughes)　**15**:132
The Chocolate War (Cormier)　**12**:130
Choo Choo: The Story of a Little Engine Who Ran Away (Burton)　**11**:44
Chris & Croc (Pfister)　**42**:137
The Christ Child, as Told by Matthew and Luke (Petersham and Petersham)　**24**:163
Christian Morgenstern: Lullabies, Lyrics and Gallows Songs (Zwerger)　**46**:202
Christmas (Cooney)　**23**:27
The Christmas Anna Angel (Sawyer)　**36**:159
The Christmas Ark (San Souci)　**43**:186
Christmas at Home (*Christmas at Longtime*) (Brinsmead)　**47**:15
Christmas at Longtime (Brinsmead)
　See *Christmas at Home*
The Christmas Book (Bruna)　**7**:49
The Christmas Box (Merriam)　**14**:202
A Christmas Carol (Ryder)　**37**:95
A Christmas Carol (Zwerger)　**46**:197
The Christmas Eve Mystery (Nixon)　**24**:142
A Christmas Fantasy (Haywood)　**22**:101
The Christmas Gift (McCully)　**46**:63
Christmas in Noisy Village (Lindgren)　**1**:136
Christmas in the Barn (Brown)　**10**:62
Christmas in the Stable (Lindgren)　**1**:136
Christmas Is a Time of Giving (Anglund)　**1**:19
Christmas Manger (Rey)　**5**:194
The Christmas Sky (Branley)　**13**:33
A Christmas Sonata (Paulsen)　**54**:107
The Christmas Star (Pfister)　**42**:136
The Christmas Story (Keeping)　**34**:90
A Christmas Story (Wildsmith)　**52**:195
Christmas Time (Gibbons)　**8**:94
Christmas Time: Verses and Illustrations (Field)　**21**:79
The Christmas Tree House (Wallace)　**37**:208
The Christmas Whale (Duvoisin)　**23**:92

Christmas with Tamworth Pig (Kemp)　**29**:113
Christopher Columbus (Ventura)　**16**:193
Chronicles of Avonlea, in Which Anne Shirley of Green Gables and Avonlea Plays Some Part (Montgomery)　**8**:136
"The Chronicles of Narnia" (Lewis)　**3**:126
The Chronicles of Robin Hood (Sutcliff)　**37**:149
Chuggy and the Blue Caboose (Freeman)　**30**:68
The Church Cat Abroad (Oakley)　**7**:215
The Church Mice Adrift (Oakley)　**7**:217
The Church Mice and the Moon (Oakley)　**7**:216
The Church Mice at Bay (Oakley)　**7**:218
The Church Mice at Christmas (Oakley)　**7**:220
The Church Mice in Action (Oakley)　**7**:223
The Church Mice Spread Their Wings (Oakley)　**7**:217
The Church Mouse (Oakley)　**7**:213
El Cid (McCaughrean)　**38**:145
Les cigares du pharaon (Herge)　**6**:148
The Cigars of the Pharaoh (Herge)　**6**:148
Cinderella (French)　**37**:48
Cinderella (Galdone)　**16**:102
Cinderella (McKissack)　**23**:237
Cinderella; or, The Little Glass Slipper (Brown)　**12**:98
The Cinderella Show (Ahlberg and Ahlberg)　**18**:12
Cindy's Sad and Happy Tree (Orgel)　**48**:76
Cindy's Snowdrops (Orgel)　**48**:75
Cinnabar, the One O'Clock Fox (Henry)　**4**:113
Circle of Gold (Boyd)　**50**:3
Circle of Seasons (Clark)　**16**:83
A Circle of Seasons (Fisher)　**18**:132
A Circle of Seasons (Livingston)　**7**:174
Circles, Triangles, and Squares (Hoban)　**13**:103
A Circlet of Oak Leaves (Sutcliff)　**37**:161
Circus (McNaughton)　**54**:55
Circus (Prelutsky)　**13**:164
The Circus Baby (Petersham and Petersham)　**24**:177
The Circus in the Mist (Munari)　**9**:128
The Circus Is Coming (Streatfeild)　**17**:187
Circus Shoes (Streatfeild)　**17**:187
City: A Story of Roman Planning and Construction (Macaulay)　**3**:142
City and Suburb: Exploring an Ecosystem (Pringle)　**4**:180
City of Birds and Beasts: Behind the Scenes at the Bronx Zoo (Scott)　**20**:197
City of Darkness (Bova)　**3**:32
The City of Dragons (Yep)　**54**:200
City of Gold (French)　**37**:39
The City of Gold and Lead (Christopher)　**2**:38
City of Gold and Other Stories from the Old Testament (Dickinson)　**29**:50
City of Gold and Other Stories from the Old Testament (Foreman)　**32**:91
City Poems (Lenski)　**26**:124
City Rhythms (Grifalconi)　**35**:69
City Seen from A to Z (Isadora)　**7**:108
City Within a City: How Kids Live in New York's Chinatown (Krull)　**44**:106
The Civil Rights Movement in America from 1865 to the Present (McKissack)　**23**:238
Clams Can't Sing (Stevenson)　**17**:157
Clancy's Cabin (Mahy)　**7**:183
Clancy's Coat (Bunting)　**28**:56
Clap Hands (Oxenbury)　**22**:148
Clarence Goes to Town (Lauber)　**16**:112
Clarence, the TV Dog (Lauber)　**16**:111
The Clarinet and Saxophone Book (Berger)　**32**:14
The Clashing Rocks: The Story of Jason (Serraillier)　**2**:137

Class Dismissed! High School Poems (Glenn)
51:85
Class Dismissed II: More High School Poems
(Glenn) **51**:87
Class Three and the Beanstalk (Waddell) **31**:191
Claudia and the Phantom Phone Calls (Martin)
32:203
Claudius Bald Eagle (McBratney) **44**:122
The Clay Marble (Ho) **28**:134
*Clay, Wood, and Wire: A How-To-Do-It Book of
Sculpture* (Weiss) **4**:220
Clean As a Whistle (Fisher) **49**:51
Clean Enough (Henkes) **23**:125
Clean Your Room, Harvey Moon! (Cummings)
48:51
Clean-Up Day (Duke) **51**:47
Clear Skin, Healthy Skin (Nourse) **33**:141
Clementina's Cactus (Keats) **35**:143
Cleopatra (Stanley) **46**:152
Clever Cakes (Rosen) **45**:142
Climbing to Danger (Allan) **43**:19
Clippity Clop (Allen) **44**:16
The Cloak (Garfield) **21**:109
The Clock Struck Twelve (Biegel) **27**:33
The Clock Tower Ghost (Kemp) **29**:117
The Clock We Live On (Asimov) **12**:33
Clocks and How They Go (Gibbons) **8**:90
Clocks and More Clocks (Hutchins) **20**:145
Cloning and the New Genetics (Hyde) **23**:170
Close Enough to Touch (Peck) **15**:162
Close Your Eyes (Jeffers) **30**:132
The Clothes Horse and Other Stories (Ahlberg and
Ahlberg) **18**:12
The Cloud Book: Words and Pictures (dePaola)
4:57
The Cloud over Clarence (Brown) **29**:5
C.L.O.U.D.S. (Cummings) **48**:47
The Cloverdale Switch (Bunting) **28**:48
The Clown (Corcoran) **50**:22
The Clown of God: An Old Story (dePaola) **4**:61
The Clown-Arounds (Cole) **40**:3
The Clown-Arounds Go on Vacation (Cole) **40**:3
Cluck Baa (Burningham) **9**:51
A Clue in Code (Singer) **48**:127
The Clue of the Black Cat (Berna) **19**:38
Clues in the Woods (Parish) **22**:156
Clunie (Peck) **45**:113
Coal (Adler) **27**:20
Coal Camp Girl (Lenski) **26**:120
The Coat-Hanger Christmas Tree (Estes) **2**:73
Cockatoos (Blake) **31**:29
Cockney Ding-Dong (Keeping) **34**:100
Cockroaches (Cole) **5**:61
Cockroaches: Here, There, and Everywhere
(Pringle) **4**:176
Code Name Kris (Matas) **52**:81
Coded Signals (Hamley) **47**:63
The Coelura (McCaffrey) **49**:146
C.O.L.A.R.: A Tale of Outer Space (Slote)
4:203
A Cold Wind Blowing (Willard) **2**:216
Colin McNaughton's 1,2,3 and Things
(McNaughton) **54**:48
*Colin McNaughton's ABC and 1,2,3: A Book for
All Ages for Reading Alone or Together*
(McNaughton) **54**:48
Colin McNaughton's ABC and Things
(McNaughton) **54**:48
Coll and His White Pig (Alexander) **1**:13; **5**:19
Collage and Construction (Weiss) **4**:225
Collected Poems, 1951-1975 (Causley) **30**:37
Colly's Barn (Morpurgo) **51**:135
Colm of the Islands (Harris) **30**:125

*Colonial Craftsmen and the Beginnings of Ameri-
can Industry* (Tunis) **2**:192
Colonial Living (Tunis) **2**:192
*Colonies in Orbit: The Coming of Age of Human
Settlements in Space* (Knight) **38**:120
Colonies in Revolt (Carter) **22**:22
Color Farm (Ehlert) **28**:114
Color: From Rainbow to Lasers (Branley) **13**:43
*Color in Reproduction: Theory and Techniques for
Artists and Designers* (Simon) **39**:197
Color in Your Life (Adler) **27**:16
The Color Kittens (Brown) **10**:59
A Color of His Own (Lionni) **7**:137
The Color Wizard: Level One (Leo and Diane
Dillon) **44**:38
Color Zoo (Ehlert) **28**:111
Colors (Pienkowski) **6**:230
A Colour of His Own (Lionni) **7**:137
Colours (Hughes) **15**:132
Colours (Pienkowski) **6**:230
*Columbia and Beyond: The Story of the Space
Shuttle* (Branley) **13**:44
Columbus (d'Aulaire and d'Aulaire) **21**:51
The Columbus Story (Politi) **29**:190
Colvin and the Snake Basket (McBratney) **44**:120
Come a Stranger (Voigt) **13**:240
Come Again, Pelican (Freeman) **30**:72
Come Alive at 505 (Brancato) **32**:73
Come and Have Fun (Hurd and Hurd) **49**:124
Come Away (Livingston) **7**:170
Come Away from the Water, Shirley (Burningham)
9:47
Come Back, Amelia Bedelia (Parish) **22**:160
Come Like Shadows (Katz) **45**:37
Come Lucky April (Ure) **34**:192
Come On, Patsy (Snyder) **31**:165
Come On, Rain (Hesse) **54**:42
Come Sing, Jimmy Jo (Paterson) **50**:194
Come to Mecca, and Other Stories (Dhondy)
41:75
Com'era una volta (Ventura) **16**:197
Comet in Moominland (Jansson) **2**:93
Comets (Branley) **13**:49
Comets (Knight) **38**:107
*Comets, Meteoroids and Asteroids: Mavericks of
the Solar System* (Branley) **13**:40
Comets, Meteors, and Asteroids (Berger) **32**:25
*The Comic Adventures of Old Mother Hubbard and
Her Dog* (dePaola) **24**:88
*The Comical Tragedy or Comical Comedy of Punch
and Judy* (Brown) **10**:49
Coming Home (Waddell) **31**:201
Coming Home from the War: An Idyll (Kruss) **9**:87
The Coming of the Bear (Namioka) **48**:65
Coming-and-Going Men: Four Tales (Fleischman)
20:67
Commander Toad in Space (Yolen) **44**:174
Commercial Fishing (Zim) **2**:226
Commodore Perry in the Land of the Shogun
(Blumberg) **21**:29
The Common Cold and the Flu (Aaseng) **54**:18
Communication (Adler) **27**:22
Companions of Fortune (Guillot) **22**:54
Company's Coming (Small) **53**:151
Company's Coming (Yorinks) **20**:217
*The Complete Adventures of Charlie and Mr. Willy
Wonka* (Dahl) **7**:77
The Complete Book of Dragons (Nesbit) **3**:162
The Complete Computer Popularity Program
(Strasser) **11**:251
The Complete Story of the Three Blind Mice
(Galdone) **16**:107
The Computer Nut (Byars) **16**:60

Computer Sense, Computer Nonsense (Simon)
9:221
Computer Talk (Berger) **32**:31
Computers (Berger) **32**:8
Computers: A Question and Answer Book (Berger)
32:35
Computers in Your Life (Berger) **32**:24
*Computers That Think? The Search for Artificial
Intelligence* (Hyde) **23**:167
Comrades for the Charter (Trease) **42**:175
Comus (Hyman) **50**:84
Confessions of a Teenage Baboon (Zindel) **45**:190
Confessions of a Toe-Hanger (Harris) **47**:79
Confessions of an Only Child (Klein) **2**:97
The Confidence Man (Garfield) **21**:113
Conker (Morpurgo) **51**:126
The Conquest of the Atlantic (d'Aulaire and
d'Aulaire) **21**:40
Conrad: The Factory-Made Boy (Noestlinger)
12:187
Consider the Lilies: Plants of the Bible (Paterson)
50:195
The Constellations: How They Came to Be
(Gallant) **30**:95
Consumer Protection Labs (Berger) **32**:14
The Contender (Lipsyte) **23**:202
Continent in the Sky (Berna) **19**:36
*The Controversial Coyote: Predation, Politics, and
Ecology* (Pringle) **4**:182
The Conversation Club (Stanley) **46**:133
The Cookcamp (Paulsen) **54**:101
Cookie Craft (Williams) **48**:194
The Cookie Tree (Williams) **8**:229
The Cook's Family (Yep) **54**:204
Cool Cooking: Sixteen Recipes without a Stove
(Hautzig) **22**:84
A Cool Kid—like Me! (Wilhelm) **46**:166
The Cool Kids' Guide to Summer Camp (Stine)
37:105
Cool Simon (Ure) **34**:188
Coot Club (Ransome) **8**:176
Copernicus: Titan of Modern Astronomy (Knight)
38:101
Cops and Robbers (Ahlberg and Ahlberg) **18**:5
Corals (Zim) **2**:226
Corazon Aquino: Leader of the Philippines
(Haskins) **39**:53
Corduroy (Freeman) **30**:75
Corduroy's Christmas (Freeman) **30**:82
Corduroy's Party (Freeman) **30**:82
Corgiville Fair (Tudor) **13**:199
The Coriander (Dillon) **26**:24
Corn Is Maize: The Gift of the Indians (Aliki) **9**:24
Cornelius (Lionni) **7**:140
Cornrows (Yarbrough) **29**:209
Cornzapoppin'! (Williams) **48**:193
Costumes for Plays and Playing (Haley) **21**:146
Costumes to Make (Parish) **22**:158
The Cottage at Crescent Beach (Blades) **15**:55
A Cottage for Betsy (Sawyer) **36**:162
Cotton in My Sack (Lenski) **26**:114
"Could Be Worse!" (Stevenson) **17**:153
Could You Stop Josephine? (Poulin) **28**:195
Count and See (Hoban) **13**:101
Count Karlstein (Pullman) **20**:187
Count on Your Fingers African Style (Pinkney)
43:157
Count Up: Learning Sets (Burningham) **9**:50
Count Your Way Through China (Haskins) **39**:53
Count Your Way Through Germany (Haskins)
39:62
Count Your Way Through Italy (Haskins) **39**:62
Count Your Way Through Japan (Haskins) **39**:53

Count Your Way Through Russia (Haskins) **39**:53

Count Your Way Through the Arab World (Haskins) **39**:53

The Counterfeit African (Williams) **8**:221

The Counterfeit Man: More Science Fiction Stories (Nourse) **33**:134

The Counterfeit Tackle (Christopher) **33**:40

Counting America: The Story of the United States Census (Ashabranner and Ashabranner) **28**:14

Counting Wildflowers (McMillan) **47**:166

Country, Cat, City, Cat (Kherdian) **24**:109

Country Mouse and City Mouse (McKissack) **23**:237

Country Noisy Book (Brown) **10**:49

Country of Broken Stone (Bond) **11**:28

The Country of the Heart (Wersba) **3**:215

The Country Pancake (Fine) **25**:24

A Country Tale (Stanley) **46**:135

Country Watch (King-Smith) **40**:151

The County Fair (Tudor) **13**:190

Courage, Dana (Pfeffer) **11**:203

The Course of True Love Never Did Run Smooth (Singer) **48**:124

The Court of the Stone Children (Cameron) **1**:39

The Courtship, Merry Marriage, and Feast of Cock Robin and Jenny Wren, to Which Is Added the Doleful Death of Cock Robin (Cooney) **23**:26

The Courtship of Animals (Selsam) **1**:161

The Courtship of Birds (Simon) **39**:194

Cousins (Hamilton) **40**:82

Cowardly Clyde (Peet) **12**:205

Cowboy and His Friend (Anglund) **1**:19

Cowboy Cal and the Outlaw (Calhoun) **42**:9

Cowboy Dreams (Khalsa) **30**:151

Cowboy Small (Lenski) **26**:114

Cowboys and Cattle Ranching: Yesterday and Today (Lauber) **16**:117

The Cowboy's Christmas (Anglund) **1**:20

Cowboys, Indians, and Gunfighters: The Story of the Cattle Kingdom (Marrin) **53**:91

Cowboys of the Wild West (Freedman) **20**:85

Cowboy's Secret Life (Anglund) **1**:20

Cow's Party (Ets) **33**:85

Coyote Cry (Baylor) **3**:14

Coyote in Manhattan (George) **1**:89

The Cozy Book (Hoberman) **22**:114

The Crab that Crawled Out of the Past (Milne and Milne) **22**:119

Crabs (Zim) **2**:227

Crack in the Heart (Orgel) **48**:91

Cracker Jackson (Byars) **16**:61

Crackerjack Halfback (Christopher) **33**:39

The Craft of Sail (Adkins) **7**:20

Crafty Caspar and His Good Old Granny (Janosch) **26**:78

The Crane (Zimnik) **3**:242

The Crane Maiden (Tresselt) **30**:211

Crash! Bang! Boom! (Spier) **5**:221

Crash, Bang, Wallop (McNaughton) **54**:56

Crazy about German Shepherds (Ashabranner) **28**:14

Crazy Bear: Four Stories in One Big Book (McNaughton) **54**:55

A Crazy Flight and Other Poems (Livingston) **7**:169

The Crazy Gang Next Door (Williams) **48**:205

The Crazy Horse Electric Game (Crutcher) **28**:105

Crazy Weeekend (Soto) **38**:204

The Creation (Wildsmith) **52**:200

Creeper's Jeep (Gramatky) **22**:42

Creepy Castle (Goodall) **25**:47

The Creoles of Color of New Orleans (Haskins) **3**:63

Creta (Ventura) **16**:196

The Cricket and the Mole (Janosch) **26**:79

Cricket in a Thicket (Fisher) **49**:39

The Cricket in Times Square (Selden) **8**:196

Crinkleroot's Book of Animal Tracks and Wildlife Signs (Arnosky) **15**:4

Crisis on Conshelf Ten (Hughes) **9**:69

Crisis on Doona (McCaffrey) **49**:154

Crocodarling (Rayner) **41**:125

Crocodile Dog (Kemp) **29**:123

The Crocodile in the Tree (Duvoisin) **23**:105

Crocodile Man (Biegel) **27**:36

The Crocodile Who Wouldn't Be King (Janosch) **26**:76

A Crocodile's Tale: A Philippine Folk Tale (Aruego) **5**:30

Crocus (Duvoisin) **23**:106

Cromwell's Boy (Haugaard) **11**:108

Cromwell's Glasses (Keller) **45**:44

The Crooked Snake (Wrightson) **4**:240

Cross Your Fingers, Spit in Your Hat: Superstitions and Other Beliefs (Schwartz) **3**:188

Cross-Country Cat (Calhoun) **42**:25

The Crossing (Paulsen) **19**:176

Crossing: Australian and New Zealand Short Stories (Duder) **43**:68

Crossing the New Bridge (McCully) **46**:71

The Crossroads of Time (Norton) **50**:137

The Cross-Stitch Heart and Other Plays (Field) **21**:71

Crosstime Agent (Norton) **50**:143

The Crotchety Crocodile (Baumann) **35**:43

Crow and Hawk (Rosen) **45**:149

Crow Boy (Yashima) **4**:251

Crowds of Creatures (Clarke) **28**:80

The Crown of Violet (Trease) **42**:182

Crow's Nest (Allan) **43**:25

The Crucible Year (St. John) **46**:107

The Cruise of the Arctic Star (O'Dell) **1**:145

The Cruise of the Santa Maria (Dillon) **26**:27

Cruising to Danger (Hagon) **43**:15

Crummy Mummy and Me (Fine) **25**:22

Crusher is Coming! (Graham) **31**:97

Crutches (Hartling) **29**:101

Cry Softly! The Story of Child Abuse (Hyde) **23**:166

Crystal (Myers) **16**:143

The Crystal Gryphon (Norton) **50**:152

Crystal Singer (McCaffrey) **49**:144

The Cuckoo Child (King-Smith) **40**:162

The Cuckoo Sister (Alcock) **26**:5

The Cuckoo Tree (Aiken) **1**:3

Cuckoobush Farm (King-Smith) **40**:152

The Cucumber King: A Story with a Beginning, a Middle, and an End, in which Wolfgang Hogelmann Tells the Whole Truth (Noestlinger) **12**:184

Cue for Treason (Trease) **42**:177

Cults (Cohen) **43**:58

Culture Shock (Rosen) **45**:140

The Cupboard (Burningham) **9**:47

Curious George (Rey) **5**:193

Curious George Flies a Kite (Rey and Rey) **5**:198

Curious George Gets a Medal (Rey) **5**:198

Curious George Goes to the Hospital (Rey and Rey) **5**:199

Curious George Learns the Alphabet (Rey) **5**:199

Curious George Rides a Bike (Rey) **5**:196

Curious George Takes a Job (Rey) **5**:196

The Curious Tale of Hare and Hedgehog (Janosch) **26**:80

Curlicues: The Fortunes of Two Pug Dogs (Worth) **21**:222

The Curse of Cain (Southall) **2**:150

The Curse of the Blue Figurine (Bellairs) **37**:12

The Curse of the Egyptian Mummy (Hutchins) **20**:153

The Curse of the Squirrel (Yep) **17**:208

The Curse of the Viking Grave (Mowat) **20**:172

The Curse of the Werewolf (Biegel) **27**:35

Curses, Hexes, and Spells (Cohen) **43**:37

The Curses of Third Uncle (Yee) **44**:161

Curtain Up (Streatfeild) **17**:190

Curtains (Stine) **37**:113

Custom Car: A Nuts-and-Bolts Guide to Creating One (Murphy) **53**:106

Cut from the Same Cloth: American Women of Myth, Legend, and Tall Tale (Pinkney) **54**:139

Cut from the Same Cloth: American Women of Myth, Legend, and Tall Tale (San Souci) **43**:190

Cutlass Island (Corbett) **1**:44

Cuts, Breaks, Bruises, and Burns: How Your Body Heals (Cole) **40**:10

The Cut-Ups (Marshall) **21**:180

The Cut-Ups Cut Loose (Marshall) **21**:184

The Cybil War (Byars) **16**:57

Cyrano the Crow (Freeman) **30**:72

Cyrus the Unsinkable Sea Serpent (Peet) **12**:203

D. H. Lawrence: The Phoenix and the Flame (Trease) **42**:189

D. W. All Wet (Brown) **29**:17

D. W. Flips! (Brown) **29**:15

Da lontano era un'isola (Munari) **9**:129

Daddles: The Story of a Plain Hound Dog (Sawyer) **36**:164

Daddy (Caines) **24**:62

Daddy, Daddy, Be There (Boyd) **50**:7

Daddy Darwin's Dovecot: A Country Tale (Caldecott) **14**:82

Daddy Is a Monster...Sometimes (Steptoe) **12**:240

Daddy Jake the Runaway, and Short Stories Told after Dark by Uncle Remus (Harris) **49**:61-107

Dad's Back (Ormerod) **20**:177

Daedalus and Icarus (Farmer) **8**:79

Daggie Dogfoot (King-Smith) **40**:140

Daisy (Coatsworth) **2**:54

Daisy (Wildsmith) **52**:189

Daisy Summerfield's Style (Goffstein) **3**:58

Daisy, Tell Me! (Calhoun) **42**:17

Daisy-Head Mayzie (Dr. Seuss) **53**:141

Daisy's Christmas (Waddell) **31**:197

Damia (McCaffrey) **49**:155

Dance for Two (Ure) **34**:170

Dance in the Desert (L'Engle) **1**:130

A Dance to Still Music (Corcoran) **50**:20

The Dancers (Myers) **16**:137

Dancers in the Garden (Ryder) **37**:98

The Dancing Bear (Dickinson) **29**:42

The Dancing Bear (Morpurgo) **51**:140

The Dancing Camel (Byars) **1**:35

The Dancing Class (Oxenbury) **22**:144

The Dancing Garlands (Allan) **43**:12

Dancing Girl (Paulsen) **19**:174

The Dancing Granny (Bryan) **18**:34

The Dancing Kettle and Other Japanese Folk Tales (Uchida) **6**:250

Dancing Shoes (Streatfeild) **17**:193

Dancing Shoes (Streatfeild)
   See *Wintle's Wonders*

Dandelion (Freeman) **30**:74

Danger from Below: Earthquakes, Past, Present, and Future (Simon) **9**:213

Title Index

Danger in Dinosaur Valley (Nixon) **24**:136
Danger in the Old Fort (St. John) **46**:114
Danger on the Mountain (Haar) **15**:114
Danger Point: The Wreck of the Birkenhead (Corbett) **1**:44
Dangerous Inheritance (Allan) **43**:20
The Dangerous Life of the Sea Horse (Schlein) **41**:193
Dangerous Love (Pascal) **25**:185
Dangerous Spring (Benary-Isbert) **12**:77
Dangleboots (Hamley) **47**:60
Daniel's Story (Matas) **52**:85
Danny Dunn and the Anti-Gravity Paint (Williams and Abrashkin) **8**:222
Danny Dunn and the Automatic House (Williams and Abrashkin) **8**:227
Danny Dunn and the Fossil Cave (Williams and Abrashkin) **8**:225
Danny Dunn and the Heat Ray (Williams and Abrashkin) **8**:225
Danny Dunn and the Homework Machine (Williams and Abrashkin) **8**:223
Danny Dunn and the Smallifying Machine (Williams and Abrashkin) **8**:230
Danny Dunn and the Swamp Monster (Williams and Abrashkin) **8**:232
Danny Dunn and the Universal Glue (Williams and Abrashkin) **8**:236
Danny Dunn and the Voice from Space (Williams and Abrashkin) **8**:229
Danny Dunn and the Weather Machine (Williams and Abrashkin) **8**:223
Danny Dunn, Invisible Boy (Williams and Abrashkin) **8**:233
Danny Dunn on a Desert Island (Williams and Abrashkin) **8**:223
Danny Dunn on the Ocean Floor (Williams and Abrashkin) **8**:224
Danny Dunn, Scientific Detective (Williams and Abrashkin) **8**:234
Danny Dunn, Time Traveler (Williams and Abrashkin) **8**:226
Danny Goes to the Hospital (Collier) **3**:44
Danny: The Champion of the World (Dahl) **7**:74
The Dare (Stine) **37**:123
The Daring Game (Pearson) **26**:174
The Dark (Munsch) **19**:141
The Dark Ages (Asimov) **12**:42
The Dark and Deadly Pool (Nixon) **24**:150
The Dark at the Top of the Stairs (McBratney) **44**:130
The Dark Behind the Curtain (Cross) **28**:88
The Dark Bright Water (Wrightson) **4**:246
The Dark Canoe (O'Dell) **1**:146
Dark Harvest: Migrant Farmworkers in America (Ashabranner) **28**:8
The Dark Is Rising (Cooper) **4**:44
The Dark of the Tunnel (Naylor) **17**:59
Dark Piper (Norton) **50**:147
The Dark Secret of Weatherend (Bellairs) **37**:16
The Dark Thirty: Southern Tales of the Supernatural (Pinkney) **54**:138
The Dark Way: Stories from the Spirit World (Hamilton) **40**:84
The Dark Wood of the Golden Birds (Brown) **10**:59
The Darkangel (Pierce) **20**:182
A Darker Magic (Bedard) **35**:60
Darkest Hours (Carter) **22**:22
Darkness and the Butterfly (Grifalconi) **35**:76
Darlene (Greenfield) **4**:103
The Date Palm: Bread of the Desert (Simon) **39**:195
The Daughter of Don Saturnino (O'Dell) **16**:173

Daughter of Earth: A Roman Myth (McDermott) **9**:119
Daughters of Eve (Duncan) **29**:73
d'Aulaire's Trolls (d'Aulaire and d'Aulaire) **21**:53
David and Della (Zindel) **45**:200
David and Dog (Hughes) **15**:124
David and Jonathan (Voigt) **48**:176
David: From the Story Told in the First Book of Samuel and the First Book of Kings (Petersham and Petersham) **24**:169
David He No Fear (Graham) **10**:109
David Starr, Space Ranger (Asimov) **12**:30
David's Father (Munsch) **19**:144
David's Little Indian: A Story (Brown) **10**:66
David's Witch Doctor (Mahy) **7**:184
Davy and His Dog (Lenski) **26**:120
Davy Goes Places (Lenski) **26**:122
Dawn (Bang) **8**:23
Dawn (Shulevitz) **5**:206
Dawn and Dusk: Poems of Our Time (Causley) **30**:32
Dawn from the West: The Story of Genevieve Caulfield (Rau) **8**:185
A Dawn in the Trees: Thomas Jefferson, the Years 1776 to 1789 (Wibberley) **3**:224
Dawn Land (Bruchac) **46**:12
Dawn of Fear (Cooper) **4**:43
Dawn Rider (Hudson) **40**:97
Dawn Wind (Sutcliff) **1**:184; **37**:155
The Day Adam Got Mad (Lindgren) **39**:164
Day and Night (Duvoisin) **23**:101
The Day Chiro Was Lost (Nakatani) **30**:157
The Day Martin Luther King, Jr., was Shot: A Photo History of the Civil Rights Movement (Haskins) **39**:67
A Day No Pigs Would Die (Peck) **45**:95
Day of Delight: A Jewish Sabbath in Ethiopia (Pinkney) **54**:142
Day of Earthlings (Bunting) **28**:48
A Day of Pleasure: Stories of a Boy Growing Up in Warsaw (Singer) **1**:173
The Day of the Dinosaurs (Bunting) **28**:44
The Day the Gang Got Rich (Kotzwinkle) **6**:181
The Day the Numbers Disappeared (Bendick) **5**:40
The Day the Sun Danced (Hurd and Hurd) **49**:125
The Day the Teacher Went Bananas (Howe) **9**:59
The Day the Tide Went Out...and Out...and Out...and Out...and Out...and Out (McKee) **38**:164
The Day They Came to Arrest the Book (Hentoff) **52**:61
A Day with Daddy (Tresselt) **30**:204
A Day with Wilbur Robinson (Joyce) **26**:85
Daybreak (Norton) **50**:134
The Daybreakers (Curry) **31**:74
Daydreamers (Greenfield) **4**:103
Daylight Robbery (Williams) **8**:235
Days of Fear (Nixon) **24**:144
Days of Terror (Smucker) **10**:190
The Days of the Dragon's Seed (St. John) **46**:110
Days with Frog and Toad (Lobel) **5**:173
Dazzle the Dinosaur (Pfister) **42**:137
The Dead Bird (Brown) **10**:66
The Dead Letter Box (Mark) **11**:154
Dead Man's Light (Corbett) **1**:44
The Dead Moon and Other Tales from East Anglia and the Fen Country (Crossley-Holland) **47**:40
The Dead Tree (Tresselt) **30**:214
Deadly Ants (Simon) **9**:214
A Deadly Game of Magic (Nixon) **24**:144
Deadly Music (Hamley) **47**:66
The Deadman Tapes (Rosen) **45**:141

Deadmen's Cave (Wibberley) **3**:225
Dealing with the Devil (Cohen) **43**:38
Dear Benjamin Banneker (Pinkney) **54**:143
Dear Bill, Remember Me? and Other Stories (Mazer) **23**:224
Dear God, Help!!! Love, Earl (Park) **34**:163
Dear Lola: Or, How to Build Your Own Family (Gaberman) **33**:7
Dear Lovey Hart: I Am Desperate (Conford) **10**:93
Dear Mr. Henshaw (Cleary) **8**:59
The Dear One (Woodson) **49**:201
Dear Prosper (Fox) **44**:61
Dear Readers and Riders (Henry) **4**:115
Dear Robin: Letters to Robin Klein (Klein) **21**:165
Dear Shrink (Cresswell) **18**:110
Dear Snowman (Janosch) **26**:76
Death Is Natural (Pringle) **4**:181
Death of a Dinosaur (Bunting) **28**:44
The Death of Evening Star: The Diary of a Young New England Whaler (Fisher) **18**:124
The Death of Sleep (McCaffrey) **49**:152
Death of the Iron Horse (Goble) **21**:135
Death Penalty (Hamley) **47**:65
Death Run (Murphy) **53**:102
Deathwatch (White) **3**:221
Debbie and Her Dolls (Lenski) **26**:124
Debbie and Her Family (Lenski) **26**:124
Debbie and Her Grandma (Lenski) **26**:123
Debbie Goes to Nursery School (Lenski) **26**:124
Debbie Herself (Lenski) **26**:124
Debby and Her Pets (Lenski) **26**:124
Debutante Hill (Duncan) **29**:65
The December (Garfield) **21**:120
December Decorations: A Holiday How-To Book (Parish) **22**:162
The December Rose (Garfield) **21**:120
Deenie (Blume) **2**:16
Deer at the Brook (Arnosky) **15**:9
Deer in the Snow (Schlein) **41**:179
Deer Valley Girl (Lenski) **26**:123
Deezle Boy (Spence) **26**:199
Delbert, the Plainclothes Detective (Nixon) **24**:135
Del-Del (Kelleher) **36**:129
Delilah and the Dishwater Dogs (Nimmo) **44**:151
Delilah and the Dogspell (Nimmo) **44**:148
The Deliverers of Their Country (Zwerger) **46**:196
Delivery Van: Words for Town and Country (Betsy and Giulio Maestro) **45**:82
Delpha Green and Company (Cleaver and Cleaver) **6**:108
The Delphic Choice (St. John) **46**:121
The Demon Headmaster (Cross) **28**:88
Der Denker Greift Ein (Noestlinger) **12**:188
Department Store (Gibbons) **8**:98
Depend on Katie John (Calhoun) **42**:7
Desert Beneath the Sea (McGovern) **50**:125
Desert Dan (Coatsworth) **2**:55
Desert Hunter: The Spider Wasp (Williams) **48**:191
The Desert Is Theirs (Baylor) **3**:14
The Desert People (Clark) **16**:81
A Desert Year (Lerner) **34**:136
Desperate Search (Christopher) **33**:47
Devil by the Sea (Bawden) **51**:27
The Devil Hole (Spence) **26**:197
The Devil in Vienna (Orgel) **48**:84
Devil on My Back (Hughes) **9**:78
The Devil on the Road (Westall) **13**:253
Devil Pony (Christopher) **33**:51
The Devil Rides with Me and Other Fantastic Stories (Slote) **4**:203
Devil-in-the-Fog (Garfield) **21**:97
Devils and Demons (Blumberg) **21**:28

The Devil's Arithmetic (Yolen) **44**:184
The Devil's Children (Dickinson) **29**:39
Devil's Hill (Chauncy) **6**:90
The Devil's Other Storybook (Babbitt) **53**:35
Devil's Race (Avi) **24**:11
The Devil's Storybook (Babbitt) **2**:5
The Diamond Champs (Christopher) **33**:52
The Diamond in the Window (Langton) **33**:107
Diana Ross: Star Supreme (Haskins) **39**:49
Diary of A Goose Girl (Wiggin) **52**:161
Dicey's Song (Voigt) **13**:230
Dick Bruna's Animal Book (Bruna) **7**:51
Dick Bruna's Word Book (Bruna) **7**:53
Dick Foote and the Shark (Babbitt) **2**:5
Dick Whittington and His Cat (Brown) **12**:95
Did Adam Name the Vinegarroon? (Kennedy) **27**:98
Did I Ever Tell You How Lucky You Are? (Dr. Seuss) **1**:85
The Diddakoi (Godden) **20**:133
Dido and Pa (Aiken) **19**:17
Die Softly (Pike) **29**:174
Died on a Rainy Sunday (Aiken) **1**:3
Dierenboek (Bruna) **7**:51
Dietrich of Berne and the Dwarf-King Laurin: Hero Tales of the Austrian Tirol (Sawyer) **36**:164
A Different Beat (Boyd) **50**:8
Dig, Drill, Dump, Fill (Hoban) **13**:103
The Diggers (Brown) **10**:67
Digging Up Dinosaurs (Aliki) **9**:28
Dimitri and the False Tsars (Baumann) **35**:53
Din Dan Don, It's Christmas (Domanska) **40**:45
Dinah's Mad, Bad Wishes (McCully) **46**:63
Dinky Hocker Shoots Smack! (Kerr) **29**:143
Dinner Ladies Don't Count (Ashley) **4**:18
Dinner Time (Pienkowski) **6**:231
Dinosaur Bob and His Adventures with the Family Lazardo (Joyce) **26**:84
Dinosaur Dances (Yolen) **44**:189
Dinosaur Days (Knight) **38**:121
Dinosaur for a Day (Murphy) **53**:110
The Dinosaur Is the Biggest Animal That Ever Lived and Other Wrong Ideas You Thought Were True (Simon) **9**:220
Dinosaur Story (Cole) **5**:63
Dinosaur Time (Parish) **22**:161
The Dinosaur Trap (Bunting) **28**:44
Dinosaurs (Cohen) **43**:49
Dinosaurs (Zim) **2**:227
Dinosaurs Alive and Well! A Guide to Good Health (Brown) **29**:19
Dinosaurs and All That Rubbish (Foreman) **32**:87
Dinosaurs and People: Fossils, Facts, and Fantasies (Pringle) **4**:184
Dinosaurs and Their World (Pringle) **4**:174
Dinosaurs and Their Young (Freedman) **20**:84
Dinosaurs, Asteroids, and Superstars: Why the Dinosaurs Disappeared (Branley) **13**:47
Dinosaurs Beware! A Safety Guide (Brown) **29**:9
Dinosaurs Divorce: A Guide to Changing Families (Brown) **29**:14
Dinosaur's Housewarming Party (Klein) **19**:89
Dinosaurs of North America (Sattler) **24**:216
"Dinosaurs" That Swam and Flew (Knight) **38**:130
Dinosaurs to the Rescue: A Guide to Protecting Our Planet (Brown) **29**:20
Dinosaurs Travel: A Guide for Families on the Go (Brown) **29**:17
Dinosaurs Walked Here and Other Stories Fossils Tell (Lauber) **16**:123
Diogenes: The Story of the Greek Philosopher (Aliki) **9**:21
A Dip of the Antlers (McBratney) **44**:117
Directions and Angles (Adler) **27**:23

Dirk Lives in Holland (Lindgren) **39**:151
Dirt Bike Racer (Christopher) **33**:53
Dirt Bike Runaway (Christopher) **33**:56
Dirty Beasts (Dahl) **41**:32
Dirty Dave (Hilton) **25**:60
Dirty Dave, the Bushranger (Hilton) **25**:60
The Disappearance (Guy) **13**:83
The Disappearing Dog Trick (Corbett) **1**:44
Disaster (Sobol) **4**:211
Disastrous Floods and Tidal Waves; Disastrous Volcanoes (Berger) **32**:25
Discontinued (Thompson) **24**:229
Discovering Rocks and Minerals: A Nature and Science Guide to Their Collection and Identification (Gallant) **30**:88
Discovering the American Stork (Scott) **20**:195
Discovering the Mysterious Egret (Scott) **20**:197
Discovering the Royal Tombs at Ur (Glubok) **1**:100
Discovering What Earthworms Do (Simon) **9**:202
Discovering What Frogs Do (Simon) **9**:202
Discovering What Gerbils Do (Simon) **9**:204
Discovering What Goldfish Do (Simon) **9**:202
The Discovery of the Americas (Betsy and Giulio Maestro) **45**:83
Disease Detectives (Berger) **32**:19
Disney's James and the Giant Peach (Smith) **47**:207
The Ditch Picnic (Unnerstad) **36**:197
The Diverting History of John Gilpin (Caldecott) **14**:73
Divide and Rule (Mark) **11**:148
The Divorce Express (Danziger) **20**:54
Do Bears Have Mothers, Too? (Fisher) **49**:55
Do Like Kyla (Johnson) **33**:94
Do Lord Remember Me (Lester) **41**:102
Do Tigers Ever Bite Kings? (Wersba) **3**:216
Do You Have the Time, Lydia? (Ness) **6**:207
Do You Want to Be My Friend? (Carle) **10**:74
Doctor Change (Cole) **40**:11
Doctor De Soto (Steig) **15**:197
Doctor Dolittle (Lofting) **19**:120
Doctor Dolittle: A Treasury (Lofting) **19**:131
Doctor Dolittle and the Green Canary (Lofting) **19**:129
Doctor Dolittle and the Secret Lake (Lofting) **19**:129
Doctor Dolittle in the Moon (Lofting) **19**:126
Doctor Dolittle's Caravan (Lofting) **19**:124
Doctor Dolittle's Circus (Lofting) **19**:124
Doctor Dolittle's Garden (Lofting) **19**:125
Doctor Dolittle's Puddleby Adventures (Lofting) **19**:130
Doctor Dolittle's Return (Lofting) **19**:128
Doctor Dolittle's Zoo (Lofting) **19**:124
Doctor Sean (Doctor Shawn) (Breinburg) **31**:67
Doctor Shawn (Breinburg)
   See *Doctor Sean*
The Doctors (Fisher) **18**:123
Dodos Are Forever (King-Smith) **40**:156
Does This School Have Capital Punishment? (Hentoff) **52**:59
The Dog (Burningham) **9**:47
A Dog and a Half (Willard) **2**:217
Dog Breath: The Horrible Trouble with Hally Tosis (Pilkey) **48**:109
Dog Days and Cat Naps (Kemp) **29**:116
The Dog Days of Arthur Cane (Bethancourt) **3**:18
Dog In, Cat Out (Rubinstein) **35**:213
Dog People: Native Dog Stories (Bruchac) **46**:21
A Dog So Small (Pearce) **9**:149
The Dog That Called the Signals (Christopher) **33**:56

The Dog That Could Swim under Water: Memoirs of a Springer Spaniel (Selden) **8**:196
The Dog That Pitched a No-Hitter (Christopher) **33**:59
The Dog That Stole Football Plays (Christopher) **33**:54
The Dog Who Insisted He Wasn't (Singer) **48**:120
The Dog Who Wouldn't Be (Mowat) **20**:170
The Dog Writes on the Window with His Nose and Other Poems (Kherdian) **24**:108
Dogger (Hughes) **15**:124
Dogs and Dragons, Trees and Dreams: A Collection of Poems (Kuskin) **4**:144
A Dog's Body (Cole) **40**:12
Dogs Don't Tell Jokes (Sacher) **28**:204
Dogsbody (Jones) **23**:185
Dogsong (Paulsen) **19**:175
Dogteam (Paulsen) **54**:109
Dogzilla (Pilkey) **48**:106
The Do-It-Yourself House That Jack Built (Yeoman) **46**:186
Dollar a Share (Epstein and Epstein) **26**:43
The Dollar Man (Mazer) **16**:128
Dollars and Cents for Harriet (Betsy and Giulio Maestro) **45**:80
Dollars from Dandelions: 101 Ways to Earn Money (Sattler) **24**:215
Dollmaker: The Eyelight and the Shadow (Lasky) **11**:116
The Dolls' Christmas (Tudor) **13**:193
The Dolls' House (Godden) **20**:125
The Dolphin Crossing (Walsh) **2**:197
Dolphins and Porpoises (Patent) **19**:165
Dom and Va (Christopher) **2**:39
Domestic Arrangements (Klein) **19**:93
Dominic (Steig) **2**:159
Donald and the . . . (Gorey) **36**:93
The Dong with a Luminous Nose (Gorey) **36**:93
The Dong with the Luminous Nose (Lear) **1**:127
The Donkey That Sneezed (Biro) **28**:39
Donkey-Donkey, the Troubles of a Silly Little Donkey (Duvoisin) **23**:90
Donna Jean's Disaster (Williams) **48**:204
Donna Summer: An Unauthorized Biography (Haskins) **39**:43
Don't Call Me Slob-o (Orgel) **48**:98
Don't Care High (Korman) **25**:108
Don't Count Your Chicks (d'Aulaire and d'Aulaire) **21**:48
Don't Forget the Bacon (Hutchins) **20**:148
Don't Forget to Fly: A Cycle of Modern Poems (Janeczko) **47**:100
Don't Look and It Won't Hurt (Peck) **15**:151
Don't Look behind You (Duncan) **29**:79
Don't Make Me Smile (Park) **34**:153
Don't Play Dead before You Have To (Wojciechowska) **1**:196
Don't Put Mustard in the Custard (Rosen) **45**:134
Don't Rent My Room! (Gaberman) **33**:16
Don't Sit under the Apple Tree (Brancato) **32**:69
Don't Slam the Door When You Go (Corcoran) **50**:17
Don't Spill It Again, James (Wells) **16**:208
Don't Stand in the Soup: The World's Funniest Guide to Manners (Stine) **37**:105
Don't Tell the Whole World! (Cole) **40**:28
Don't Tell the Whole World! (Duke) **51**:51
Don't You Remember? (Clifton) **5**:55
Don't You Turn Back (Grifalconi) **35**:71
Don't You Turn Back (Hughes) **17**:47
Don't You Turn Back: Poems by Langston Hughes (Hopkins) **44**:85
Doodle Soup (Ciardi) **19**:81

Title Index

The Doom Stone (Zindel) **45**:202
The Door Between (Garden) **51**:74
The Door in the Hedge (McKinley) **10**:122
The Door in the Wall (de Angeli) **1**:53
Door to the North (Coatsworth) **2**:55
The Doorbell Rang (Hutchins) **20**:153
Dorcas Porkus (Tudor) **13**:191
Dorothea Lange: Life through the Camera (Meltzer) **13**:148
Dorrie's Book (Sachs) **2**:132
A Double Discovery (Ness) **6**:203
The Double Life of Pocahontas (Fritz) **14**:118
The Double Planet (Asimov) **12**:34
The Double Quest (Sobol) **4**:206
Double Spell (Lunn) **18**:158
Double Trouble (DeClements) **23**:36
Douglas the Drummer (Owen) **31**:147
Dove and Sword: A Novel of Joan of Arc (Garden) **51**:80
Down a Dark Hall (Duncan) **29**:70
Down from the Lonely Mountain: California Indian Tales (Curry) **31**:70
Down Half the World (Coatsworth) **2**:55
Down to Earth (Wrightson) **4**:242
Down Under, Down Under: Diving Adventures on the Great Barrier Reef (McGovern) **50**:123
Downtown (Mazer) **23**:229
Dr. Anno's Magical Midnight Circus (Anno) **2**:2
Dr. Beaumont and the Man with the Hole in His Stomach (Epstein and Epstein) **26**:67
Dr. Merlin's Magic Shop (Corbett) **1**:45
Dr. Seuss's ABC (Dr. Seuss) **1**:85; **9**:187
Dr. Seuss's Sleep Book (Dr. Seuss) **1**:85; **9**:187
Dr. Smith's Safari (Say) **22**:208
Drac and the Gremlin (Baillie) **49**:10
The Drackenberg Adventure (Alexander) **48**:19
Dracula: A Toy Theatre for All Ages (Gorey) **36**:99
Dracula's Tomb (McNaughton) **54**:68
Draft Horses (Patent) **19**:163
Dragon Boy (King-Smith) **40**:168
Dragon Cauldron (Yep) **54**:187
Dragon Gets By (Pilkey) **48**:101
The Dragon in the Ghetto Caper (Konigsburg) **47**:132
Dragon Magic (Norton) **50**:152
Dragon Night and Other Lullabies (Yolen) **4**:266
The Dragon of an Ordinary Family (Mahy) **7**:179
The Dragon of an Ordinary Family (Oxenbury) **22**:137
The Dragon of Og (Godden) **20**:136
Dragon of the Lost Sea (Yep) **17**:205
The Dragon Prince: A Chinese Beauty and the Beast Tale (Yep) **54**:202
Dragon Steel (Yep) **17**:207
The Dragon Takes a Wife (Myers) **4**:156
Dragon War (Yep) **54**:190
Dragondrums (McCaffrey) **49**:143
Dragonflies (Simon) **39**:189
Dragonflight (McCaffrey) **49**:139
Dragonfly Summer (Farmer) **8**:79
The Dragonfly Years (Hunter) **25**:88
Dragonquest (Baillie) **49**:23
Dragonquest: Being the Further Adventures of the Dragonriders of Pern (McCaffrey) **49**:140
Dragon's Blood: A Fantasy (Yolen) **44**:175
The Dragon's Eye (St. John) **46**:123
Dragon's Fat Cat (Pilkey) **48**:102
Dragon's Gate (Yep) **54**:193
Dragon's Halloween: Dragon's Fifth Tale (Pilkey) **48**:108
Dragons in the Waters (L'Engle) **14**:150
Dragon's Merry Christmas (Pilkey) **48**:102
Dragonsdawn (McCaffrey) **49**:149

Dragonsinger (McCaffrey) **49**:142
Dragonsong (McCaffrey) **49**:141
Dragonwings (Yep) **3**:236
Drag-Strip Racer (Christopher) **33**:56
Drake, The Man They Called a Pirate (Latham) **50**:102
Drawing from Nature (Arnosky) **15**:6
Drawing Life in Motion (Arnosky) **15**:8
Dread Companion (Norton) **50**:150
The Dreadful Future of Blossom Culp (Peck) **15**:163
The Dream Book: First Comes the Dream (Brown) **10**:59
Dream Catcher and Other Stories (Baillie) **49**:22
Dream Dancer (Bunting) **28**:44
Dream Days (Grahame) **5**:128
The Dream Keeper and Other Poems (Hughes) **17**:37
The Dream Keeper, and Other Poems (Pinkney) **54**:142
Dream of Dark Harbor (Kotzwinkle) **6**:183
A Dream of Hunger Moss (Allan) **43**:33
The Dream Time (Treece) **2**:183
The Dream Watcher (Wersba) **3**:216
Dream Weaver (Yolen) **4**:265
The Dream-Eater (Ende) **14**:99
The Dreamer (Moser) **49**:187
The Dream-House (Crossley-Holland) **47**:35
Dreaming of Larry (Ure) **34**:190
Dreamland Lake (Peck) **15**:153
Dreams (Keats) **1**:114; **35**:138
Dreams of a Perfect Earth (Milne and Milne) **22**:124
Dreams of Victory (Conford) **10**:90
Dreams, Visions, and Drugs: A Search for Other Realities (Cohen) **3**:39
Drei Mal Drei: An Einem Tag (Kruss) **9**:85
Dressing (Oxenbury) **22**:141
The Driftway (Lively) **7**:154
Drina Dances in Italy (Estoril) **43**:8
Drina Dances on Stage (Estoril) **43**:8
The Drinking Gourd (Monjo) **2**:120
The Drive (Oxenbury) **22**:145
A Drop of Blood (Showers) **6**:243
Drowned Ammet (Jones) **23**:188
Drug Abuse A-Z (Berger) **32**:44
Drug Wars (Hyde) **23**:176
The Drugstore Cat (Petry) **12**:210
The Drummer Boy (Garfield) **21**:100
Drummer Hoff (Emberley and Emberley) **5**:94
Dry or Wet? (McMillan) **47**:170
Dry Victories (Jordan) **10**:118
Drylongso (Hamilton) **40**:86
Drylongso (Pinkney) **43**:170
Duck Boy (Mattingley) **24**:126
Duck Dutch (Haar) **15**:114
Duck on a Pond (Willard) **2**:217
Ducks and Dragons: Poems for Children (Kemp) **29**:116
Ducky (Wisniewski) **51**:201
The Dueling Machine (Bova) **3**:32
Duke Ellington: The Piano Prince and His Orchestra (Pinkney) **54**:149
Dukes (Peck) **45**:118
The Dumb Bunnies (Pilkey) **48**:108
The Dumb Bunnies' Easter (Pilkey) **48**:110
The Dumb Cake (Garfield) **21**:109
Dumb Cane and Daffodils: Poisonous Plants in the House and Garden (Lerner) **34**:135
Dump Days (Spinelli) **26**:204
Dunc and Amos and the Red Tattoos (Paulsen) **54**:110

Dunc and the Scam Artists (Paulsen) **54**:110
The Dunkard (Selden) **8**:199
The Duplicate (Sleator) **29**:206
Dust (Adler) **27**:10
Dust Bowl: The Story of Man on the Great Plains (Lauber) **16**:112
Dust of the Earth (Cleaver and Cleaver) **6**:110
Dustland (Hamilton) **11**:80
Dusty and Smudge and the Bride (Schmidt) **22**:222
Dusty and Smudge Keep Cool (Schmidt) **22**:222
Dusty and Smudge Spill the Paint (Schmidt) **22**:211
Dwarf Long-Nose (Orgel) **48**:71
Dwarf Nose (Zwerger) **46**:200
The Dwarfs of Nosegay (Biegel) **27**:32
The Dwindling Party (Gorey) **36**:102
Dynamite's Funny Book of the Sad Facts of Life (Stine) **37**:104
Dynamo Farm (Epstein and Epstein) **26**:42
Each Peach Pear Plum (Ahlberg and Ahlberg) **18**:5
Each Peach Pear Plum: An I Spy Story (Ahlberg and Ahlberg) **18**:5
Eagle and Dove (Kruss) **9**:86
Eagle Fur (Peck) **45**:112
Eagle Island (Baillie) **49**:9
The Eagle Kite (Fox) **44**:77
Eagle Mask: A West Coast Indian Tale (Houston) **3**:85
The Eagle of the Ninth (Sutcliff) **1**:185; **37**:151
Eagle Song (Bruchac) **46**:23
Eagle's Egg (Sutcliff) **37**:174
An Early American Christmas (dePaola) **24**:99
Early Humans: A Prehistoric World (Berger) **32**:39
Early in the Morning: A Collection of New Poems (Causley) **30**:42
Early in the Morning: A Collection of New Poems (Foreman) **32**:100
Early Thunder (Fritz) **2**:80
Early Words: Color Book (Scarry) **41**:167
Ears Are for Hearing (Keller) **45**:54
The Earth in Action (Hyde) **23**:158
Earth: Our Planet in Space (Simon) **9**:220
The Earth: Planet Number Three (Branley) **13**:32
Earth Songs (Fisher) **18**:136
The Earth under Sky Bear's Feet (Bruchac) **46**:20
Earthdark (Hughes) **9**:69
The Earth-Father (Crossley-Holland) **47**:34
Earthquake (Christopher) **33**:50
Earthquakes: Nature in Motion (Nixon) **24**:142
Earthquakes: New Scientific Ideas about How and Why the Earth Shakes (Lauber) **16**:117
Earth's Changing Climate (Gallant) **30**:94
Earth's Enigmas: A Book of Animal and Nature Life (Roberts) **33**:191
Earth's Vanishing Forests (Gallant) **30**:106
"The Earthsea Quartet" (Le Guin) **28**:144-88
Earthsea Trilogy (Le Guin) **3**:118
East End at Your Feet (Dhondy) **41**:72
East of the Sun and West of the Moon (Mayer) **11**:174
East of the Sun and West of the Moon: A Play (Moser) **49**:173
East of the Sun and West of the Moon: Old Tales from the North (Nielsen) **16**:155
Easter (Fisher) **49**:48
The Easter Cat (DeJong) **1**:56
The Easter Mystery (Nixon) **24**:142
The Easter Story (Wildsmith) **52**:197
Easter Treat (Duvoisin) **23**:99
Easy Avenue (Doyle) **22**:33
An Easy Introduction to the Slide Rule (Asimov) **12**:39

Eating Fractions (McMillan) **47**:178

Eating Out (Oxenbury) **22**:144

Eating the Alphabet: Fruits and Vegetables from A to Z (Ehlert) **28**:112

Eats: Poems (Adoff) **7**:35

Eavesdropping on Space: The Quest of Radio Astronomy (Knight) **38**:116

Der Ebereschenhof (Benary-Isbert) **12**:72

Echo in the Wilderness (Brinsmead) **47**:13

Echoes of the White Giraffe (Choi) **53**:45

The Echoing Green (Rayner) **41**:128

The Eclectic Abecedarium (Gorey) **36**:105

Eclipse: Darkness in Daytime (Branley) **13**:39

Ecology (Bendick) **5**:48

Ecology: Science of Survival (Pringle) **4**:175

Ed Emberley's A B C (Emberley) **5**:100

Ed Emberley's Amazing Look Through Book (Emberley) **5**:101

Ed Emberley's Big Green Drawing Book (Emberley) **5**:102

Ed Emberley's Big Orange Drawing Book (Emberley) **5**:102

Ed Emberley's Big Purple Drawing Book (Emberley) **5**:103

Ed Emberley's Crazy Mixed-Up Face Game (Emberley) **5**:103

Ed Emberley's Drawing Book: Make a World (Emberley) **5**:98

Ed Emberley's Drawing Book of Animals (Emberley) **5**:97

Ed Emberley's Drawing Book of Faces (Emberley) **5**:99

Ed Emberley's Great Thumbprint Drawing Book (Emberley) **5**:100

Eddie and Gardenia (Haywood) **22**:95

Eddie and His Big Deals (Haywood) **22**:96

Eddie and Louella (Haywood) **22**:97

Eddie and the Fire Engine (Haywood) **22**:94

Eddie, Incorporated (Naylor) **17**:55

Eddie Makes Music (Haywood) **22**:97

Eddie the Dog Holder (Haywood) **22**:100

Eddie's Green Thumb (Haywood) **22**:99

Eddie's Happenings (Haywood) **22**:101

Eddie's Menagerie (Haywood) **22**:104

Eddie's Pay Dirt (Haywood) **22**:95

Eddie's Valuable Property (Haywood) **22**:102

Edgar Allan Crow (Tudor) **13**:194

Edgar Allen (Neufeld) **52**:121

The Edge of the Cloud (Peyton) **3**:172

Edie on the Warpath (Spykman) **35**:221

Edith Jackson (Guy) **13**:81

Edith Wilson: The Woman Who Ran the United States (Giblin) **29**:94

An Edwardian Christmas (Goodall) **25**:48

Edwardian Entertainments (Goodall) **25**:53

An Edwardian Holiday (Goodall) **25**:49

An Edwardian Season (Goodall) **25**:50

An Edwardian Summer (Goodall) **25**:47

Egg Thoughts and Other Frances Songs (Hoban) **3**:76

Egg to Chick (Selsam) **1**:161

The Eggs: A Greek Folk Tale (Aliki) **9**:20

Eggs on Your Nose (McGovern) **50**:123

Ego-Tripping and Other Poems for Young People (Giovanni) **6**:116

The Egypt Game (Snyder) **31**:154

The Egyptians (Asimov) **12**:41

Eight Days of Luke (Jones) **23**:184

Eight for a Secret (Willard) **2**:217

Eight Plus One: Stories (Cormier) **12**:148

The Eighteenth Emergency (Byars) **1**:35

Einstein Anderson Goes to Bat (Simon) **9**:218

Einstein Anderson Lights Up the Sky (Simon) **9**:219

Einstein Anderson Makes Up for Lost Time (Simon) **9**:216

Einstein Anderson, Science Sleuth (Simon) **9**:216

Einstein Anderson Sees Through the Invisible Man (Simon) **9**:219

Einstein Anderson Shocks His Friends (Simon) **9**:216

Einstein Anderson Tells a Comet's Tale (Simon) **9**:217

The El Dorado Adventure (Alexander) **48**:17

Elbert's Bad Word (Wood and Wood) **26**:224

Electricity in Your Life (Adler) **27**:19

The Electromagnetic Spectrum: Key to the Universe (Branley) **13**:44

Electromagnetic Waves (Adler) **27**:13

Electronics (Adler) **27**:14

Electronics for Boys and Girls (Bendick) **5**:34

Elegy on the Death of a Mad Dog (Caldecott) **14**:74

The Elementary Mathematics of the Atom (Adler) **27**:19

Elena (Stanley) **46**:156

Elephant Boy: A Story of the Stone Age (Kotzwinkle) **6**:180

Elephant Families (Dorros) **42**:73

Elephant in a Well (Ets) **33**:91

Elephant Road (Guillot) **22**:61

The Elephant Who Liked to Smash Small Cars (Merrill) **52**:108

The Elephants of Sargabal (Guillot) **22**:58

The Elephant's Wish (Munari) **9**:125

The Elephant's Wrestling Match (Pinkney) **54**:138

Eleven Kids, One Summer (Martin) **32**:206

The Eleventh Hour (Base) **22**:5

Elf Children of the Woods (Beskow) **17**:16

Elfwyn's Saga (Wisniewski) **51**:194

Eli (Peet) **12**:204

Elidor (Garner) **20**:101

Elidor and the Golden Ball (McHargue) **2**:117

Elijah the Slave (Singer) **1**:174

Elisabeth the Cow Ghost (Pene du Bois) **1**:63

Eliza and the Elves (Field) **21**:69

Elizabeth Blackwell, Pioneer Woman Doctor (Latham) **50**:106

Elizabeth Fry: The Angel of the Prisons (Richards) **54**:167

Elizabite: The Adventures of a Carnivorous Plant (Rey) **5**:194

Eliza's Daddy (Thomas) **8**:213

Ellen Dellen (Gripe) **5**:148

Ellen Grae (Cleaver and Cleaver) **6**:101

Ellen Tebbits (Cleary) **2**:45; **8**:45

Ellie and the Hagwitch (Cresswell) **18**:111

Ellis Island: Gateway to the New World (Fisher) **18**:136

The Elm Street Lot (Pearce) **9**:153

Elmer Again (McKee) **38**:180

Elmer: The Story of a Patchwork Elephant (McKee) **38**:159

Elmer's Colours; Elmer's Day; Elmer's Friends; Elmer's Weather (McKee) **38**:181

Eloise: A Book for Precocious Grown-Ups (Thompson) **22**:226

Eloise at Christmastime (Thompson) **22**:226

Eloise in Moscow (Thompson) **22**:227

Eloise in Paris (Thompson) **22**:226

Eloquent Crusader: Ernestine Rose (Suhl) **2**:165

The Elves and the Shoemaker (Galdone) **16**:105

Elvis and His Friends (Gripe) **5**:148

Elvis and His Secret (Gripe) **5**:148

Elvis! Elvis! (Gripe) **5**:148

Elvis Karlsson (Gripe) **5**:148

The Emergency Book (Bendick) **5**:41

Emer's Ghost (Waddell) **31**:178

Emil and Piggy Beast (Lindgren) **1**:136

Emil and the Detectives (Kaestner) **4**:121

Emil's Pranks (Lindgren) **1**:136

Emily (Bedard) **35**:65

Emily Emerson's Moon (Merrill) **52**:104

Emily of New Moon (Montgomery) **8**:138

Emily Upham's Revenge: Or, How Deadwood Dick Saved the Banker's Niece: A Massachusetts Adventure (Avi) **24**:5

Emily's Runaway Imagination (Cleary) **2**:45; **8**:50

Emlyn's Moon (Nimmo) **44**:141

Emma (Stevenson) **17**:163

The Emma Dilemma (Waddell) **31**:180

Emma in Love (Arundel) **35**:17

Emma in Winter (Farmer) **8**:78

Emma Tupper's Diary (Dickinson) **29**:41

Emma's Island (Arundel) **35**:12

Emmet (Politi) **29**:193

Emmet Otter's Jug-Band Christmas (Hoban) **3**:76

The Emperor and the Kite (Yolen) **4**:257

The Emperor and the Kite (Young) **27**:216

The Emperor's New Clothes (Burton) **11**:50

The Emperor's Winding Sheet (Walsh) **2**:197

Empires Lost and Won: The Spanish Heritage in the Southwest (Marrin) **53**:96

The Empty Sleeve (Garfield) **21**:121

The Empty Window (Bunting) **28**:51

The Enchanted: An Incredible Tale (Coatsworth) **2**:56

The Enchanted Caribou (Cleaver) **13**:73

The Enchanted Castle (Nesbit) **3**:162

The Enchanted Drum (Orgel) **48**:77

The Enchanted Horse (Harris) **30**:122

The Enchanted Island: Stories from Shakespeare (Serraillier) **2**:137

The Enchanted Schoolhouse (Sawyer) **36**:162

The Enchanted Tapestry: A Chinese Folktale (San Souci) **43**:182

Enchantress from the Stars (Engdahl) **2**:69

Encore for Eleanor (Peet) **12**:205

Encounter (Yolen) **44**:195

Encounter at Easton (Avi) **24**:6

Encounter Near Venus (Wibberley) **3**:225

Encyclopedia Brown and the Case of the Dead Eagles (Sobol) **4**:210

Encyclopedia Brown and the Case of the Midnight Visitor (Sobol) **4**:211

Encyclopedia Brown and the Case of the Secret Pitch (Sobol) **4**:207

Encyclopedia Brown, Boy Detective (Sobol) **4**:207

Encyclopedia Brown Carries On (Sobol) **4**:212

Encyclopedia Brown Finds the Clues (Sobol) **4**:208

Encyclopedia Brown Gets His Man (Sobol) **4**:208

Encyclopedia Brown Lends a Hand (Sobol) **4**:210

Encyclopedia Brown Saves the Day (Sobol) **4**:209

Encyclopedia Brown Shows the Way (Sobol) **4**:209

Encyclopedia Brown Solves Them All (Sobol) **4**:208

Encyclopedia Brown Takes the Case (Sobol) **4**:209

Encyclopedia Brown's Record Book of Weird and Wonderful Facts (Sobol) **4**:211

The Encyclopedia of Ghosts (Cohen) **43**:45

The Encyclopedia of Monsters (Cohen) **43**:41

End of Exile (Bova) **3**:32

The End of the Tale (Corbett) **19**:83

The End of the World (Branley) **13**:40

Ending World Hunger (Aaseng) **54**:16

The Endless Steppe: Growing Up in Siberia (Hautzig) **22**:77

The Endocrine System: Hormones in the Living World (Silverstein and Silverstein) **25**:205

Title Index

The Ends of the Earth: The Polar Regions of the World (Asimov) **12**:52
The Enemies (Klein) **21**:162
The Enemy (Garfield) **21**:109
An Enemy at Green Knowe (Boston) **3**:27
Energy (Adler) **27**:23
Energy (Berger) **32**:31
Energy and Power (Adler) **27**:9
Energy for the 21st Century (Branley) **13**:42
Energy from the Sun (Berger) **32**:17
Energy: Power for People (Pringle) **4**:179
Energy: The New Look (Hyde) **23**:166
Enjoying Opera (Streatfeild) **17**:196
The Ennead (Mark) **11**:147
The Enormous Crocodile (Dahl) **7**:77
Enrico Fermi: Father of Atomic Power (Epstein and Epstein) **26**:62
The Environment (Adler) **27**:26
Environments Out There (Asimov) **12**:42
Enzymes in Action (Berger) **32**:6
Epaminondas (Merriam) **14**:195
The Epics of Everest (Wibberley) **3**:226
Epilepsy (Silverstein and Silverstein) **25**:212
Eric Carle's Storybook: Seven Tales by the Brothers Grimm (Carle) **10**:80
Eric Heiden: Winner in Gold (Aaseng) **54**:10
The Erie Canal (Spier) **5**:220
Ernest and Celestine (Vincent) **13**:216
Ernest and Celestine's Patchwork Quilt (Vincent) **13**:219
Ernest and Celestine's Picnic (Vincent) **13**:217
Ernest et Célestine au Musée (Vincent) **13**:221
Ernest et Célestine Chez le Photographe (Vincent) **13**:217
Ernest et Célestine, Musiciens des Rues (Vincent) **13**:216
Ernest et Célestine Ont Perdu Siméon (Vincent) **13**:216
Ernest et Célestine Vont Pique-Niquer (Vincent) **13**:217
Ernstjan en Snabbeltje (Haar) **15**:114
Escapade (Goodall) **25**:50
Escape from Egypt (Levitin) **53**:73
Escape from Fire Mountain (Paulsen) **54**:118
Escape from Tyrannosaurus (Bunting) **28**:44
Esio Trot (Dahl) **41**:45
ESP (Aylesworth) **6**:50
ESP: The New Technology (Cohen) **43**:46
Estuaries: Where Rivers Meet the Sea (Pringle) **4**:178
E.T.! The Extra-Terrestrial (Kotzwinkle) **6**:184
E.T.! The Extra-Terrestrial Storybook (Kotzwinkle) **6**:185
Eugene the Brave (Conford) **10**:95
Eulalie and the Hopping Head (Small) **53**:147
Euphonia and the Flood (Calhoun) **42**:22
Eva (Dickinson) **29**:58
Evangeline Booth: Daughter of Salvation (Lavine) **35**:151
Eva's Ice Adventure (Wallace) **37**:213
Even Stevens F.C. (Rosen) **45**:150
An Evening at Alfie's (Hughes) **15**:131
Ever Ride a Dinosaur? (Corbett) **1**:45
Everett Anderson's 1-2-3 (Clifton) **5**:58
Everett Anderson's Christmas Coming (Clifton) **5**:54
Everett Anderson's Friend (Clifton) **5**:57
Everett Anderson's Friend (Grifalconi) **35**:72
Everett Anderson's Goodbye (Grifalconi) **35**:73
Everett Anderson's Nine Month Long (Clifton) **5**:59
Everett Anderson's Nine Month Long (Grifalconi) **35**:73

Everett Anderson's Year (Clifton) **5**:55
Everglades Country: A Question of Life or Death (Lauber) **16**:117
Ever-Ready Eddie (Haywood) **22**:100
Every Living Thing (Rylant) **15**:171
Every Man Heart Lay Down (Graham) **10**:108
Every Time I Climb a Tree (McCord) **9**:100
Everybody Needs a Rock (Baylor) **3**:15
Everyone Knows What a Dragon Looks Like (Williams) **8**:235
Everyone's Trash Problem: Nuclear Wastes (Hyde) **23**:165
Everything Grows (McMillan) **47**:174
Everything Happens to Stuey (Moore) **15**:140
Everything I Know about Writing (Marsden) **34**:150
Everything Moves (Simon) **9**:210
Everything under a Mushroom (Krauss) **42**:129
Everything You Need to Survive: Brothers and Sisters; Everything You Need to Survive: First Dates; Everything You Need to Survive: Homework; Everything You Need to Survive: Money Problems (Stine) **37**:106
Everywhere (Brooks) **25**:35
Evil Encounter (Levitin) **53**:75
The Evil Spell (McCully) **46**:65
Evolution (Adler) **27**:19
Evolution (Cole) **40**:18
Evolution Goes On Every Day (Patent) **19**:150
Exactly Alike (Ness) **6**:201
The Excretory System: How Living Creatures Get Rid of Wastes (Silverstein and Silverstein) **25**:208
Exiled from Earth (Bova) **3**:33
Exiles of the Stars (Norton) **50**:150
Exit Barney McGee (Mackay) **43**:106
Exotic Birds (Singer) **48**:138
The Expeditions of Willis Partridge (Weiss) **4**:222
Experiments in Chemistry (Branley) **13**:24
Experiments in Optical Illusion (Branley) **13**:24
Experiments in Science (Branley) **13**:23
Experiments in Sky Watching (Branley) **13**:28
Experiments in the Principles of Space Travel (Branley) **13**:25
Experiments with a Microscope (Branley) **13**:26
Experiments with Airplane Instruments (Branley) **13**:24
Experiments with Atomics (Branley) **13**:25
Experiments with Electricity (Branley) **13**:23
Experiments with Light (Branley) **13**:26
The Exploits of Moominpappa (Jansson) **2**:93
Exploration and Conquest: The Americas after Columbus: 1500-1620 (Betsy and Giulio Maestro) **45**:88
Exploration of the Moon (Branley) **13**:31
Explorers of the Atom (Gallant) **30**:91
Explorers on the Moon (Herge) **6**:148
Exploring by Astronaut: The Story of Project Mercury (Branley) **13**:30
Exploring by Satellite: The Story of Project Vanguard (Branley) **13**:26
Exploring Chemistry (Gallant) **30**:86
Exploring Fields and Lots: Easy Science Projects (Simon) **9**:212
Exploring Mars (Gallant) **30**:84
Exploring the Brain (Silverstein and Silverstein) **25**:210
Exploring the Mind and Brain (Berger) **32**:29
Exploring the Moon (Gallant) **30**:83
Exploring the Moon: A Revised Edition of the Science Classic (Gallant) **30**:83
Exploring the Planets (Gallant) **30**:86
Exploring the Sun (Gallant) **30**:86

Exploring the Universe (Gallant) **30**:84
Exploring the Weather (Gallant) **30**:85
Exploring the World of Social Insects (Simon) **39**:182
Exploring under the Earth: The Story of Geology and Geophysics (Gallant) **30**:87
Extraterrestrial Civilizations (Asimov) **12**:57
The Eye of Conscience: Photographers and Social Change, with 100 Photographs by Noted Photographers, Past and Present (Meltzer) **13**:131
Eyes in the Fishbowl (Snyder) **31**:156
Eyes of Darkness (Highwater) **17**:31
The Eyes of Karen Connors (Duncan)
    See *The Third Eye*
The Eyes of the Amaryllis (Babbitt) **53**:31
The Eyes of the Killer Robot (Bellairs) **37**:20
Eyes of the Wilderness (Roberts) **33**:207
The Faber Book of Northern Folk-Tales (Crossley-Holland) **47**:37
The Faber Book of Northern Legends (Crossley-Holland) **47**:35
Fables (Lobel) **5**:174
Fables (Scarry) **41**:161
Fables (Scarry) **41**:161
Fables from Aesop (Biro) **28**:35
A Fabulous Creature (Snyder) **31**:164
Face at the Edge of the World (Bunting) **28**:59
The Face in the Frost (Bellairs) **37**:5
Face-Off (Christopher) **33**:46
Faces in the Water (Naylor) **17**:56
Facing It (Brancato) **32**:74
Facing It (Thompson) **24**:227
The Factories (Fisher) **18**:128
Facts, Frauds, and Phantasms: A Survey of the Spiritualist Movement (McHargue) **2**:118
Fair Play (Leaf) **25**:125
Fair's Fair (Garfield) **21**:116
Fair-Weather Friends (Gantos) **18**:141
The Fairy Doll (Godden) **20**:127
Fairy Operettas (Richards) **54**:167
The Fairy Rebel (Reid Banks) **24**:196
Fairy Tales of the Brothers Grimm (Nielsen) **16**:157
The Faithful Friend (Pinkney) **54**:144
The Faithful Friend (San Souci) **43**:193
A Fall from the Sky: The Story of Daedalus (Serraillier) **2**:138
Fall Is Here! (Sterling) **1**:178
Fall Secrets (Boyd) **50**:6
Fallen Angels (Myers) **35**:191
Falling in Love: Romantic Stories for Young Adults (Duder) **43**:69
False Face (Katz) **45**:33
Families (McNaughton) **54**:55
Family (Donovan) **3**:51
Family (Oxenbury) **22**:141
The Family Album (Yeoman) **46**:184
A Family Apart (Nixon) **24**:149
The Family at Caldicott Place (Streatfeild) **17**:197
The Family at Caldicott Place (Streatfeild)
    See *Caldicott Place*
The Family Book of Mary-Claire (Spence) **26**:199
The Family Christmas Tree Book (dePaola) **4**:65
The Family Conspiracy (Phipson) **5**:179
A Family Failing (Arundel) **35**:20
Family Grandstand (Brink) **30**:13
A Family of Foxes (Dillon) **26**:24
A Family Project (Ellis) **42**:81
Family Reunion (Singer) **48**:144
Family Sabbatical (Brink) **30**:14
Family Secrets (Corcoran) **50**:40
Family Secrets (Klein) **19**:97

Family Shoes (Streatfeild)   **17**:192
Family Shoes (Streatfeild)
   See *The Bell Family*
The Family Tower (Willard)   **2**:217
Famine (Blumberg)   **21**:25
Famous American Architects (Lavine)   **35**:150
Famous American Negroes (Hughes)   **17**:39
Famous Industrialists (Lavine)   **35**:148
Famous Men of Modern Biology (Berger)   **32**:3
Famous Merchants (Lavine)   **35**:149
Famous Naturalists (Milne and Milne)   **22**:118
Famous Negro Athletes (Bontemps)   **6**:84
Famous Negro Heroes of America (Hughes)   **17**:43
Famous Negro Music Makers (Hughes)   **17**:41
The Famous Stanley Kidnapping Case (Snyder)
   31:164
*The Fanatic's Ecstatic, Aromatic Guide to Onions,
   Garlic, Shallots, and Leeks* (Singer)   **48**:123
Fancy That! (Allen)   **44**:11
Fannie Lou Hamer (Jordan)   **10**:119
Fanny and the Battle of Potter's Piece (Lively)
   7:163
Fanny's Sister (Lively)   **7**:161
The Fantastic Brother (Guillot)   **22**:64
Fantastic Mr. Fox (Dahl)   **1**:51; **7**:73
Fantasy Summer (Pfeffer)   **11**:204
*Far and Few: Rhymes of the Never Was and Always
   Is* (McCord)   **9**:98
Far Away from Anywhere Else (Le Guin)
   See *Very Far Away from Anywhere Else*
Far Beyond and Back Again (Biegel)   **27**:32
*The Far Forests: Tales of Romance, Fantasy, and
   Suspense* (Aiken)   **19**:10
Far from Home (Sebestyen)   **17**:91
Far from Shore (Major)   **11**:130
Far Out the Long Canal (DeJong)   **1**:57
The Far Side of Evil (Engdahl)   **2**:70
Far to Go (Streatfeild)   **17**:200
Far Voyager: The Story of James Cook (Latham)
   50:105
The Faraway Island (Corcoran)   **50**:23
Farewell to Shady Glade (Peet)   **12**:196
Farm Animals (Patent)   **19**:160
Farm Babies (Freedman)   **20**:82
The Farm Summer 1942 (Moser)   **49**:190
Farmer Duck (Waddell)   **31**:200
The Farmer in the Dell (Stanley)   **46**:128
Farmer Palmer's Wagon Ride (Steig)   **2**:160
Farmer Pelz's Pumpkins (Thiele)   **27**:212
Farmer Schulz's Ducks (Thiele)   **27**:210
The Farthest Shore (Le Guin)   **28**:144-88; **3**:123
The Farthest-Away Mountain (Reid Banks)   **24**:191
Fashion Is Our Business (Epstein and Epstein)
   26:44
*Fast and Slow: Poems for Advanced Children and
   Beginning Parents* (Ciardi)   **19**:80
Fast Friends: Two Stories (Stevenson)   **17**:156
Fast Is Not a Ladybug (Schlein)   **41**:175
Fast Sam, Cool Clyde, and Stuff (Myers)   **4**:156
The Fast Sooner Hound (Bontemps)   **6**:79
Fast Talk on a Slow Track (Williams-Garcia)
   36:205
Fast-Slow, High-Low: A Book of Opposites (Spier)
   5:222
Fat Chance, Claude (Nixon)   **24**:149
Fat Charlie's Circus (Gay)   **27**:88
Fat Elliot and the Gorilla (Pinkwater)   **4**:162
Fat Lollipop (Ure)   **34**:189
Fat Men from Space (Pinkwater)   **4**:168
Fat Pig (McNaughton)   **54**:52
Fat Polka-Dot Cat and Other Haiku (Betsy and
   Giulio Maestro)   **45**:66
Father Bear Comes Home (Minarik)   **33**:124

Father Christmas (Briggs)   **10**:24
Father Christmas Goes on Holiday (Briggs)   **10**:25
Father Figure (Peck)   **15**:160
Father Fox's Pennyrhymes (Watson)   **3**:211
A Father Like That (Zolotow)   **2**:233
*Father Water, Mother Woods: Essays On Fishing
   and Hunting in the North Woods* (Paulsen)
   54:114
Father's Arcane Daughter (Konigsburg)   **47**:138
Fathom Five (Westall)   **13**:254
The Fattest Dwarf of Nosegay (Biegel)   **27**:34
The Favershams (Gerrard)   **23**:119
Favor for a Ghost (Christopher)   **33**:57
Fawn (Peck)   **45**:104
FBI (Berger)   **32**:18
*The Fearless Treasure: A Story of England from
   Then to Now* (Streatfeild)   **17**:192
Fears and Phobias (Hyde)   **23**:163
The Fearsome Inn (Singer)   **1**:174
The Feast of Lanterns (Say)   **22**:209
Feast or Famine? The Energy Future (Branley)
   13:45
The Feather Star (Wrightson)   **4**:241
Featherbrains (Yeoman)   **46**:183
Feathered Ones and Furry (Fisher)   **49**:54
The Feathered Serpent (O'Dell)   **16**:176
Feathers and Fools (Fox)   **23**:117
Feathers for Lunch (Ehlert)   **28**:114
Feathers, Plain and Fancy (Simon)   **39**:184
*Feathertop: Based on the Tale by Nathaniel
   Hawthorne* (San Souci)   **43**:189
February Dragon (Thiele)   **27**:203
Fee Fi Fo Fum (McNaughton)   **54**:56
Feeding Babies (Nakatani)   **30**:161
Feel the Wind (Dorros)   **42**:66
*Feeling Mad, Feeling Sad, Feeling Bad, Feeling
   Glad* (McGovern)   **50**:120
Feelings (Aliki)   **9**:32
Feet and Other Stories (Mark)   **11**:154
The Feet of the Furtive (Roberts)   **33**:203-04
Felice (Brown)   **12**:100
Felicia the Critic (Conford)   **10**:91
Felita (Mohr)   **22**:133
Fell (Kerr)   **29**:156
Fell Back (Kerr)   **29**:157
Fell Down (Kerr)   **29**:158
Femi and Old Grandaddie (Pinkney)   **43**:155
Fenny, The Desert Fox (Baumann)   **35**:52
Fenwick's Suit (Small)   **53**:157
The Ferlie (Hunter)   **25**:77
Ferryboat (Betsy and Giulio Maestro)   **45**:78
A Few Fair Days (Gardam)   **12**:161
A Few Flies and I: Haiku By Issa (Merrill)
   52:109
Fiddle-i-fee: A Traditional American Chant
   (Stanley)   **46**:129
Fiddlestrings (de Angeli)   **1**:53
The Fido Frame-Up (Singer)   **48**:125
Fierce: The Lion (Ness)   **6**:209
Fierce-Face, the Story of a Tiger (Mukerji)   **10**:135
Fifteen (Bunting)   **28**:47
Fifteen (Cleary)   **2**:46; **8**:48
*The Fifth of March: The Story of the Boston
   Massacre* (Rinaldi)   **46**:87
Fifty Below Zero (Munsch)   **19**:145
Figgie Hobbin: Poems for Children (Causley)
   30:34
Figgs and Phantoms (Raskin)   **12**:218
Fight against Albatross Two (Thiele)   **27**:207
*Fighting Back: What Some People Are Doing about
   Aids* (Kuklin)   **51**:103
Fighting Fires (Kuklin)   **51**:111

The Fighting Ground (Avi)   **24**:11
*Fighting Men: How Men Have Fought through the
   Ages* (Treece)   **2**:184
Fighting Shirley Chisholm (Haskins)   **3**:64
Fighting Words (Small)   **53**:152
Figleafing through History: The Dynamics of Dress
   (Harris)   **47**:82
The Figure in the Shadows (Bellairs)   **37**:9
Figure of 8: Narrative Poems (Causley)   **30**:33
A Figure of Speech (Mazer)   **23**:222
The Filthy Beast (Garfield)   **21**:109
Fin M'Coul: The Giant of Knockmany Hill
   (dePaola)   **4**:66
The Final Correction (McBratney)   **44**:118
The Final Test (Owen)   **31**:142
Find a Stranger, Say Goodbye (Lowry)   **6**:193
Find Out by Touching (Showers)   **6**:241
Find the Constellations (Rey)   **5**:196
Find the Hidden Insect (Cole)   **5**:66
Find the White Horse (King-Smith)   **40**:169
Find Waldo Now (Handford)   **22**:74
Find Your ABC's (Scarry)   **41**:166
Finders Keepers (Rodda)   **32**:212
The Finding (Bawden)   **51**:33
Finding a Poem (Merriam)   **14**:196
Finding Home (Kherdian)   **24**:111
Finding Out about Jobs: TV Reporting (Bendick)
   5:48
A Fine Boy for Killing (Needle)   **43**:133
A Fine White Dust (Rylant)   **15**:172
Finestkind O'Day: Lobstering in Maine (McMillan)
   47:159
Finger Rhymes (Brown)   **29**:7
Fingers (Sleator)   **29**:203
*Finishing Becca: The Story of Peggy Shippen and
   Benedict Arnold* (Rinaldi)   **46**:89
Finn Family Moomintroll (Jansson)   **2**:93
The Finn Gang (Waddell)   **31**:179
Finn MacCool and the Small Men of Deeds
   (O'Shea)   **18**:169
Finn's Folly (Southall)   **2**:150
Finzel the Farsighted (Fleischman)   **20**:66
Fiona on the Fourteenth Floor (Allan)   **43**:12
Fire and Hemlock (Jones)   **23**:194
Fire Engine Shapes (McMillan)   **47**:170
Fire Fighters (Blumberg)   **21**:24
Fire! Fire! (Gibbons)   **8**:98
The Fire Game (Stine)   **37**:116
A Fire in My Hands: A Book of Poems (Soto)
   38:195
The Fire in the Stone (Thiele)   **27**:205
Fire in Your Life (Adler)   **27**:5
The Fire Station (Munsch)   **19**:143
The Fire Station (Spier)   **5**:228
The Fire Stealer (Cleaver)   **13**:70
The Fire-Brother (Crossley-Holland)   **47**:31
Fireflies (Ryder)   **37**:85
The Firehouse (Spier)   **5**:228
The Firemen (Kotzwinkle)   **6**:180
Fires in the Sky: The Birth and Death of Stars
   (Gallant)   **30**:93
The Firetail Cat (McBratney)   **44**:130
Fireweed (Walsh)   **2**:198
*Fireworks, Picnics, and Flags: The Story of the
   Fourth of July Symbols* (Giblin)   **29**:88
Fireworks: The Science, the Art, and the Magic
   (Kuklin)   **51**:113
The First ABC (Lear)   **1**:127
First Adventure (Coatsworth)   **2**:56
The First Book of Africa (Hughes)   **17**:43
The First Book of Airplanes (Bendick)   **5**:37
The First Book of Berlin: A Tale of a Divided City
   (Knight)   **38**:105

Title Index

The First Book of Codes and Ciphers (Epstein and Epstein) **26**:54

The First Book of Deserts: An Introduction to the Earth's Arid Lands (Knight) **38**:100

The First Book of Electricity (Epstein and Epstein) **26**:49

The First Book of England (Streatfeild) **17**:194

The First Book of Fishes (Bendick) **5**:41

The First Book of Glass (Epstein and Epstein) **26**:52

The First Book of Hawaii (Epstein and Epstein) **26**:51

The First Book of How to Fix It (Bendick) **5**:39

The First Book of Italy (Epstein and Epstein) **26**:55

The First Book of Jazz (Hughes) **17**:40

The First Book of Maps and Globes (Epstein and Epstein) **26**:56

The First Book of Mars: An Introduction to the Red Planet (Knight) **38**:102

The First Book of Measurement (Epstein and Epstein) **26**:57

The First Book of Medieval Man (Sobol) **4**:206

The First Book of Mexico (Epstein and Epstein) **26**:53

The First Book of Negroes (Hughes) **17**:38

The First Book of News (Epstein and Epstein) **26**:60

The First Book of Printing (Epstein and Epstein) **26**:52

The First Book of Rhythms (Hughes) **17**:40

The First Book of Ships (Bendick) **5**:38

The First Book of Sound: A Basic Guide to the Science of Acoustics (Knight) **38**:98

The First Book of Space Travel (Bendick) **5**:37

The First Book of Supermarkets (Bendick) **5**:37

The First Book of Teaching Machines (Epstein and Epstein) **26**:58

The First Book of the Ballet (Streatfeild) **17**:192

The First Book of the Caribbean (Hughes) **17**:42

The First Book of the Ocean (Epstein and Epstein) **26**:57

The First Book of the Opera (Streatfeild) **17**:196

The First Book of the Sun (Knight) **38**:106

The First Book of the West Indies (Hughes) **17**:42

The First Book of the World Health Organization (Epstein and Epstein) **26**:59

The First Book of Time (Bendick) **5**:40

The First Book of Washington, D. C.: The Nation's Capital (Epstein and Epstein) **26**:57

The First Book of Words: Their Family Histories (Epstein and Epstein) **26**:50

The First Child (Wells) **16**:203

The First Christmas (dePaola) **24**:95

First Dates (Stine) **37**:106

First Day of School (Oxenbury) **22**:145

The First Days of Life (Freedman) **20**:77

The First Dog (Brett) **27**:41

The First Few Friends (Singer) **48**:122

The First Four Years (Wilder) **2**:205

The First Freedom: The Tumultuous History of Free Speech in America (Hentoff) **52**:59

First Graces (Tudor) **13**:195

First Ladies (Blumberg) **21**:25

First Ladybugs; First Grade Valentines; Hello, First Grade (Ryder) **37**:99

A First Look at Birds (Selsam) **1**:162

A First Look at Leaves (Selsam) **1**:162

A First Look at Mammals (Selsam) **1**:162

The First Margaret Mahy Story Book: Stories and Poems (Mahy) **7**:181

The First Noel (Domanska) **40**:53

The First Peko-Neko Bird (Krahn) **3**:103

First Pink Light (Greenfield) **4**:99; **38**:82

First Prayers (Tudor) **13**:193

The First Seven Days: The Story of the Creation from Genesis (Galdone) **16**:91

First Snow (McCully) **46**:60

The First Story (Brown) **10**:55

The First Strawberries: A Cherokee Story (Bruchac) **46**:13

First the Good News (Gaberman) **33**:12

First There Was Frances (Graham) **31**:95

The First Time I Saw Paris (Pilgrim) **43**:9

The First Travel Guide to the Bottom of the Sea (Blumberg) **21**:28

The First Travel Guide to the Moon: What to Pack, How to Go, and What to See When You Get There (Blumberg) **21**:26

The First Travel Guide to the Moon: What to Pack, How to Go, and What You Do When You Get There (Blumberg) **21**:26

The First Two Lives of Lukas-Kasha (Alexander) **5**:24

First Words (Burningham) **9**:51

The Fish (Bruna) **7**:49

Fish and How They Reproduce (Patent) **19**:149

Fish Eyes: A Book You Can Count On (Ehlert) **28**:112

Fish Facts and Bird Brains: Animal Intelligence (Sattler) **24**:220

Fish for Supper (Goffstein) **3**:58

A Fish Hatches (Cole) **5**:65

Fish Head (Fritz) **2**:80

Fish Is Fish (Lionni) **7**:133

The Fish with the Deep Sea Smile (Brown) **10**:48

The Fisherman and the Bird (Levitin) **53**:63

Fisherman of Galilee (Fisher) **49**:35

The Fisherman under the Sea (Tresselt) **30**:212

The Fisherman's Son: Adapted from a Georgian Folktale (Ginsburg) **45**:13

"Fitting In": Animals in Their Habitats (Berger) **32**:15

Five Children and It (Nesbit) **3**:163

Five Dolls and the Duke (Clarke) **28**:80

Five Dolls and the Monkey (Clarke) **28**:75

Five Dolls and Their Friends (Clarke) **28**:80

Five Dolls in a House (Clarke) **28**:74

Five Dolls in the Snow (Clarke) **28**:76

Five Down: Numbers as Signs (Burningham) **9**:50

Five Finger Discount (DeClements) **23**:38

The Five Hundred (Dillon) **26**:31

Five Minute Stories (Richards) **54**:166

Five Minutes' Peace (Murphy) **39**:173

Flambards (Peyton) **3**:172

Flambards in Summer (Peyton) **3**:173

The Flambards Trilogy (Peyton) **3**:173

Flame-Coloured Taffeta (Sutcliff) **37**:179

The Flash Children (Allan) **43**:27

Flash, Crash, Rumble, and Roll (Branley) **13**:32

Flash Eddie and the Big Bad Wolf (McBratney) **44**:129

Flash Flood (Thiele) **27**:205

Flash the Dash (Freeman) **30**:78

Fleas (Cole) **5**:62

The Fledgling (Langton) **33**:115

Fletcher and Zenobia Save the Circus (Gorey) **36**:94

Flicks (dePaola) **4**:63

Flies in the Water, Fish in the Air: A Personal Introduction to Fly Fishing (Arnosky) **15**:9

Flight 714 (Hergé) **6**:149

The Flight of Bembel Rudzuk (McNaughton) **54**:54

The Flight of Dragons (Dickinson) **29**:49

Flight of Exiles (Bova) **3**:33

Flight to the Forest (Willard) **2**:218

Flight Today and Tomorrow (Hyde) **23**:153

Flint's Island (Wibberley) **3**:226

Flip-Flop and Tiger Snake (Thiele) **27**:205

Flip-Flop Girl (Paterson) **50**:202

Flipsville, Squaresville (Berenstain and Berenstain) **19**:25

Floating and Sinking (Branley) **13**:34

Flock of Watchbirds (Leaf) **25**:128

Flocks of Birds (Zolotow) **2**:234

The Flood at Reedsmere (Burton) **1**:31

Florence Griffith Joyner: Dazzling Olympian (Aaseng) **54**:13

Florence Nightingale, Angel of the Crimea: A Story for Young People (Richards) **54**:166

Florina and the Wild Bird (Carigiet) **38**:70

Flossie and the Fox (McKissack) **23**:237

The Flower Mother (Calhoun) **42**:18

The Flower of Sheba (Orgel) **48**:94

A Flower with Love (Munari) **9**:130

Flowers of a Woodland Spring (Lerner) **34**:123

The Flowers of Adonis (Sutcliff) **37**:161

The Flute (Achebe) **20**:8

The Flute Book (Berger) **32**:9

Fly! A Brief History of Flight (Moser) **49**:186

Fly Away Home (Bunting) **28**:65

Fly Away Home (Noestlinger) **12**:185

Fly by Night (Jarrell) **6**:165

Fly High, Fly Low (Freeman) **30**:70

Fly Homer Fly (Peet) **12**:199

Fly into Danger (Phipson) **5**:184

Flyaway Girl (Grifalconi) **35**:78

Fly-by-Night (Peyton) **3**:176

The Flying Carpet (Brown) **12**:98

The Flying Fox Warriors (Roughsey and Trezise) **41**:141

Flying Jake (Smith) **47**:198

A Flying Saucer Full of Spaghetti (Krahn) **3**:104

The Flying Ship (Harris) **30**:117

Flying with the Eagle, Racing the Great Bear: Stories from Native North America (Bruchac) **46**:13

Fofana (Guillot) **22**:64

The Fog Comes on Little Pig Feet (Wells) **16**:204

Fog Hounds, Wind Cat, Sea Mice (Aiken) **19**:15

Fog in the Meadow (Ryder) **37**:85

"Foldaway" Series (McNaughton) **54**:55

Follow a Fisher (Pringle) **4**:178

Follow My Black Plume (Trease) **42**:186

Follow That Bus! (Hutchins) **20**:148

Follow the Dream: The Story of Christopher Columbus (Sis) **45**:165

Follow the Road (Tresselt) **30**:205

Follow the Water from Brook to Ocean (Dorros) **42**:68

Follow the Wind (Tresselt) **30**:204

The Followers (Bunting) **28**:48

Fonabio and the Lion (Guillot) **22**:69

Fondai and the Leopard-Men (Guillot) **22**:71

Food (Adler) **27**:26

The Food Market (Spier) **5**:228

The Fool (Garfield) **21**:109

The Fool of the World and the Flying Ship: A Russian Tale (Ransome) **8**:184

The Fools of Chelm and Their History (Singer) **1**:174

Football Crazy (McNaughton) **54**:51

Football Fugitive (Christopher) **33**:51

Football's Most Controversial Calls (Aaseng) **54**:11

Footprints at the Window (Naylor) **17**:56

For All the Wrong Reasons (Neufeld) **52**:127

For Always (Bunting) **28**:47

For Good Measure: The Story of Modern Measurement (Berger) **32**:3

For Me to Say: Rhymes of the Never Was and Always Is (McCord) **9**:101

For Pollution Fighters Only (Hyde) **23**:159

A for the Ark (Duvoisin) **23**:97

For the Love of Venice (Napoli) **51**:168

Forbidden Frontier (Harris) **47**:80

Forbidden Paths of Thual (Kelleher) **36**:115

Forerunner Foray (Norton) **50**:153

Forest of the Night (Townsend) **2**:169

A Forest Year (Lerner) **34**:131

Forever (Blume) **2**:17; **15**:72

The Forever Christmas Tree (Uchida) **6**:253

Forever Free: The Story of the Emancipation Proclamation (Sterling) **1**:178

Forever Laughter (Freeman) **30**:77

The Forge in the Forest (Colum) **36**:35

Forgetful Fred (Williams) **8**:233

The Forgetful Wishing Well: Poems for Young People (Kennedy) **27**:100

A Formal Feeling (Oneal) **13**:157

A Formidable Enemy (Allan) **43**:23

The Fort of Gold (Dillon) **26**:22

Fortunately (Charlip) **8**:27

Fortune (Stanley) **46**:141

A Fortune for the Brave (Chauncy) **6**:89

The Fortune-Tellers (Alexander) **48**:23

The Fortune-Tellers (Hyman) **50**:82

Forward, Commandos! (Bianco) **19**:58

Fossils Tell of Long Ago (Aliki) **9**:21

Fossils: The Ice Ages (Gallant) **30**:100

Foster Care and Adoption (Hyde) **23**:168

The Foundling and Other Tales of Prydain (Alexander) **1**:13; **5**:22

The Fountain of Youth: Stories to Be Told (Colum) **36**:36

Four Ancestors (Bruchac) **46**:22

Four Brave Sailors (Ginsburg) **45**:18

The Four Corners of the World (Duvoisin) **23**:96

Four Days in the Life of Lisa (Noestlinger) **12**:187

Four Dolls (Godden) **20**:136

The Four Donkeys (Alexander) **1**:14

Four Fur Feet (Brown) **10**:67

The Four Grannies (Jones) **23**:190

Four Little Troubles (Marshall) **21**:171

Four on the Shore (Marshall) **21**:180

Four Rooms from the Metropolitan Museum of Art (Ness) **6**:208

The Four Seasons of Brambly Hedge (Barklem) **31**:6

Four Stories for Four Seasons (dePaola) **4**:59

Fours Crossing (Garden) **51**:66

The Four-Story Mistake (Enright) **4**:74

The Fourteenth Cadillac (Jackson) **28**:141

The Fourth Grade Wizards (DeClements) **23**:37

The Fourth Plane at the Flypast (Hamley) **47**:58

Fox All Week (Marshall) **21**:179

Fox and His Friends (Marshall) **21**:177

The Fox and the Cat: Animal Tales from Grimm (Crossley-Holland) **47**:44

The Fox and the Hare (Ginsburg) **45**:2

Fox at School (Marshall) **21**:177

The Fox Busters (King-Smith) **40**:139

Fox Eyes (Brown) **10**:61

The Fox Friend (Coatsworth) **2**:57

Fox Hill (Worth) **21**:223

The Fox Hole (Southall) **2**:151

Fox in Love (Marshall) **21**:177

Fox in Socks (Dr. Seuss) **1**:85; **9**:188

The Fox Jumps over the Parson's Gate (Caldecott) **14**:81

Fox on Wheels (Marshall) **21**:178

Fox Song (Bruchac) **46**:14

The Fox Steals Home (Christopher) **33**:52

The Fox Went Out on a Chilly Night: An Old Song (Spier) **5**:217

The Foxman (Paulsen) **19**:171

Fox's Dream (Tejima) **20**:203

Fractures, Dislocations, and Sprains (Nourse) **33**:142

Fragile Flag (Langton) **33**:116

Francis Fry, Private Eye (McBratney) **44**:129

Francis: The Poor Man of Assisi (dePaola) **24**:90

Frank and Ernest (Day) **22**:24

Frank and Ernest Play Ball (Day) **22**:26

Frank and Zelda (Kovalski) **34**:117

Frankie's Dad (Ure) **34**:184

Frankie's Hat (Mark) **11**:157

Frankie's Story (Waddell) **31**:189

Franklin and the Messy Pigs (Wilhelm) **46**:164

Franklin Stein (Raskin) **1**:155

Franzi and Gizi (Bianco) **19**:56

The Freak (Matas) **52**:94

Freaky Friday (Rodgers) **20**:190

Freckle Juice (Blume) **15**:72

Freckly Feet and Itchy Knees (Rosen) **45**:140

Fred (Simmonds) **23**:243

Fred the Angel (Waddell) **31**:195

Freddy's Book (Neufeld) **52**:127

Frederick (Lionni) **7**:131

Frederick Douglass: Slave-Fighter-Freeman (Bontemps) **6**:83

Frederick Douglass: The Black Lion (McKissack) **23**:239

Frederick Sanger: The Man Who Mapped Out a Chemical of Life (Silverstein and Silverstein) **25**:202

Fred's Dream (Ahlberg and Ahlberg) **18**:3

Fred's First Day (Cummings) **48**:46

Free As I Know (Naidoo) **29**:165

Free Fall (Wiesner) **43**:205

Free to Be Muhammad Ali (Lipsyte) **23**:207

Freedom Comes to Mississippi: The Story of Reconstruction (Meltzer) **13**:127

Freedom Train: The Story of Harriet Tubman (Sterling) **1**:179

Freedom's Landing (McCaffrey) **49**:156

Freight Train (Crews) **7**:56

Das fremde Kind (Zwerger) **46**:194

French Postcards (Klein) **19**:91

The Frenzied Prince, Being Heroic Stories of Ancient Ireland (Colum) **36**:45

Fresh Brats (Kennedy) **27**:102

Fresh Paint: New Poems (Merriam) **14**:203

Freshwater Fish and Fishing (Arnosky) **15**:5

Freunde (Heine) **18**:147

Friend Dog (Adoff) **7**:36

A Friend for Dragon (Pilkey) **48**:101

A Friend Is Someone Who Likes You (Anglund) **1**:20

Friend Monkey (Travers) **2**:177

Friend or Foe (Morpurgo) **51**:118

Friend: The Story of George Fox and the Quakers (Yolen) **4**:259

The Friendly Beasts: An Old English Christmas Carol (dePaola) **24**:89

The Friendly Wolf (Goble) **21**:131

The Friends (Guy) **13**:78

Friends (Heine) **18**:147

Friends (Oxenbury) **22**:141

The Friends Have a Visitor (Heine) **18**:149

The Friends' Racing Cart (Heine) **18**:149

Friends till the End: A Novel (Strasser) **11**:247

The Fright: Who's Talking? (Ure) **34**:184

Fritz and the Beautiful Horses (Brett) **27**:38

Frog and Toad All Year (Lobel) **5**:170

Frog and Toad Are Friends (Lobel) **5**:165

Frog and Toad Together (Lobel) **5**:167

Frog Goes to Dinner (Mayer) **11**:168

A Frog He Would A-Wooing Go (Caldecott) **14**:81

The Frog in the Well (Tresselt) **30**:207

The Frog Prince (Galdone) **16**:100

The Frog Prince, Continued (Scieszka) **27**:154

Frog Went A-Courtin' (Langstaff) **3**:109

Frog, Where Are You? (Mayer) **11**:165

The Frogmen (White) **3**:221

Frogs and Toads of the World (Simon) **39**:192

A Frog's Body (Cole) **5**:66

Frogs, Toads, Salamanders, and How They Reproduce (Patent) **19**:148

From a Child's Heart (Grimes) **42**:90

From Afar It Is an Island (Munari) **9**:129

From Anna (Little) **4**:151

From Flower to Flower: Animals and Pollination (Lauber) **16**:122

From Hand to Mouth: Or, How We Invented Knives, Forks, Spoons, and Chopsticks and the Table Manners to Go with Them (Giblin) **29**:90

From Head to Toe: How a Doll Is Made (Kuklin) **51**:111

From Lew Alcindor to Kareem Abdul Jabbar (Haskins) **3**:64

From Living Cells to Dinosaurs: Our Restless Earth (Gallant) **30**:101

From Log Roller to Lunar Rover: The Story of Wheels (Knight) **38**:115

From Pond to Prairie: The Changing World of a Pond and Its Life (Pringle) **4**:176

From Shore to Ocean Floor: How Life Survives in the Sea (Simon) **9**:207

From Spring to Spring: Poems and Photographs (Duncan) **29**:76

From Sputnik to Space Shuttles: Into the New Space Age (Branley) **13**:52

From the Mixed-Up Files of Mrs. Basil E. Frankweiler (Konigsburg) **1**:120

From the Notebooks of Melanin Sun (Woodson) **49**:206

From the Thorenson Dykes (McBratney) **44**:119

Front Court Hex (Christopher) **33**:48

Front Porch Stories at the One-Room School (Tate) **37**:192

Frontier Living (Tunis) **2**:192

Frontier Wolf (Sutcliff) **37**:171

Fumio and the Dolphins (Nakatani) **30**:158

Fungus the Bogeyman (Briggs) **10**:26

Fungus the Bogeyman Plop-Up Book (Briggs) **10**:33

The Funniest Dinosaur Book Ever (Wilhelm) **46**:163

Funniest Storybook Ever (Scarry) **3**:183

Funny Bananas (McHargue) **2**:118

Funny, How the Magic Starts (McBratney) **44**:123

The Funny Side of Science (Berger) **32**:9

The Funny Thing (Gag) **4**:89

Funnybones (Ahlberg and Ahlberg) **18**:8

Fur Magic (Norton) **50**:147

The Fur Seals of Pribilof (Scott) **20**:200

Furry (Keller) **45**:56

The Further Adventures of Nils (Lagerlof) **7**:110

The Further Adventures of Robinson Crusoe (Treece) **2**:184

Further Tales of Uncle Remus: The Misadventures of Brer Rabbit, Brer Fox, Brer Wolf, the Doodang and Other Creatures (Lester) **41**:108

Title Index

Further Tales of Uncle Remus: The Misadventures of Brer Rabbit, Brer Fox, Brer Wolf, the Doodang and Other Creatures (Pinkney) **43**:165

Fusion Factor (Matas) **52**:77

Future Story (French) **37**:46

FutureLife: The Biotechnology Revolution (Silverstein and Silverstein) **25**:220

Futuretrack 5 (Westall) **13**:258

Gabriel's Girl (St. John) **46**:113

Gaby and the New Money Fraud (Berna) **19**:40

Gadabouts and Stick-at-Homes: Wild Animals and Their Habitats (Milne and Milne) **22**:123

The Gadget Book (Weiss) **4**:226

A Gaggle of Geese (Merriam) **14**:192

Galactic Derelict (Norton) **50**:139

Galax-Arena (Rubinstein) **35**:213

Galaxies: Islands in Space (Knight) **38**:122

The Gales of Spring: Thomas Jefferson, the Years 1789-1801 (Wibberley) **3**:226

The Galleon from Manila (Hurd) **49**:120

The Galloping Goat and Other Stories (Naylor) **17**:49

Gambling—Who Really Wins? (Haskins) **39**:36

The Game of Baseball (Epstein and Epstein) **26**:60

A Game of Catch (Cresswell) **18**:102

Game of Danger (Duncan) **29**:66

A Game of Soldiers (Needle) **43**:141

Games (Klein) **21**:162

Games and Puzzles You Can Make Yourself (Weiss) **4**:228

The Games the Indians Played (Lavine) **35**:153

Gaps in Stone Walls (Neufeld) **52**:134

The Garden (Matas) **52**:95

The Garden of Abdul Gasazi (Van Allsburg) **5**:238

The Garden Shed (Keeping) **34**:97

The Garden under the Sea (Selden) **8**:196

The Gardener (Small) **53**:159

The Gardens of Dorr (Biegel) **27**:31

"Garfield's Apprentices" (Garfield) **21**:109

A Garland of Games and Other Diversions: An Alphabet Book (Cooney) **23**:27

Garth Pig and the Ice Cream Lady (Rayner) **41**:122

Garth Pig Steals the Show (Rayner) **41**:129

Gary and the Very Terrible Monster (Williams) **48**:189

Gases (Cobb) **2**:65

Gatalop the Wonderful Ball (Baumann) **35**:52

Gather Together in My Name (Angelou) **53**:13

The Gathering (Hamilton) **11**:82

The Gathering of Darkness (Fox) **44**:77

A Gathering of Days: A New England Girl's Journal 1830-32 (Blos) **18**:14

A Gathering of Gargoyles (Pierce) **20**:183

Gathering of Pearl (Choi) **53**:48

The Gats! (Goffstein) **3**:59

Gaudenzia, Pride of the Palio (Henry) **4**:113

Gavriel and Jemal: Two Boys of Jerusalem (Ashabranner) **28**:8

Gay-Neck, the Story of a Pigeon (Mukerji) **10**:131

General Store (Field) **21**:81

The Genetics Explosion (Silverstein and Silverstein) **25**:219

Genetics: Unlocking the Secret Code (Aaseng) **54**:23

Gengoroh and the Thunder God (Tresselt) **30**:212

The Genie of Sutton Place (Selden) **8**:200

The Gentle Desert: Exploring an Ecosystem (Pringle) **4**:183

Gentlehands (Kerr) **29**:148

The Gentleman and the Kitchen Maid (Stanley) **46**:151

Gentleman Jim (Briggs) **10**:30

Geoffrey Strangeways (Murphy) **39**:177

Geography Can Be Fun (Leaf) **25**:132

Geological Disasters: Earthquakes and Volcanoes (Aylesworth) **6**:55

(George) (Konigsburg) **1**:120

George and Martha (Marshall) **21**:168

George and Martha Encore (Marshall) **21**:169

George and Martha, One Fine Day (Marshall) **21**:173

George and Martha Rise and Shine (Marshall) **21**:171

George and Martha, Tons of Fun (Marshall) **21**:175

George and Red (Coatsworth) **2**:57

George and the Cherry Tree (Aliki) **9**:18

George Shrinks (Joyce) **26**:83

George, the Babysitter (Hughes) **15**:122

George Washington (d'Aulaire and d'Aulaire) **21**:43

George Washington (Foster) **7**:93

George Washington and the Birth of Our Nation (Meltzer) **13**:151

George Washington's Breakfast (Fritz) **2**:81

George Washington's Cows (Small) **53**:154

George Washington's World (Foster) **7**:91

George's Marvelous Medicine (Dahl) **7**:80

Georgie Has Lost His Cap (Munari) **9**:125

Geraldine First (Keller) **45**:61

Geraldine, the Music Mouse (Lionni) **7**:138

Geraldine's Baby Brother (Keller) **45**:59

Geraldine's Big Snow (Keller) **45**:51

Geraldine's Blanket (Keller) **45**:46

Gerbils: All about Them (Silverstein and Silverstein) **25**:213

Germfree Life: A New Field in Biological Research (Silverstein and Silverstein) **25**:203

Germs! (Patent) **19**:159

Germs Make Me Sick! (Berger) **32**:33

Gertrude the Goose Who Forgot (Galdone) **16**:101

De geschiedenis van Noord-America (Haar) **15**:114

Get On Board: The Story of the Underground Railroad (Haskins) **39**:70

Get Ready for Robots! (Lauber) **16**:123

Get Set! Go! Overcoming Obstacles (Watanabe) **8**:216

Get Well, Clown-Arounds! (Cole) **40**:3

Get-a-Way and Hary Janos (Petersham and Petersham) **24**:164

Getting Along in Your Family (Naylor) **17**:52

Getting Along with Your Friends (Naylor) **17**:54

Getting Along with Your Teachers (Naylor) **17**:55

Getting Born (Freedman) **20**:79

Ghastlies, Goops and Pincushions: Nonsense Verse (Kennedy) **27**:102

The Ghastly Gertie Swindle, With the Ghosts of Hungryhouse Lane (McBratney) **44**:128

Ghond, the Hunter (Mukerji) **10**:132

The Ghost and Bertie Boggin (Waddell) **31**:177

The Ghost Belonged to Me (Peck) **15**:154

The Ghost Children (Bunting) **28**:63

The Ghost Dance Caper (Hughes) **9**:70

Ghost Doll (McMillan) **47**:164

The Ghost Downstairs (Garfield) **21**:105

The Ghost Fox (Yep) **54**:194

The Ghost Girl (Waddell) **31**:183

Ghost Host (Singer) **48**:132

Ghost in a Four-Room Apartment (Raskin) **1**:156

Ghost in the House (Cohen) **43**:57

The Ghost in the Mirror (Bellairs) **37**:26

The Ghost in the Noonday Sun (Fleischman) **1**:74

Ghost Lane (Curry) **31**:83

The Ghost of Grania O'Malley (Morpurgo) **51**:147

The Ghost of Skinny Jack (Lindgren) **39**:162

Ghost of Summer (Bunting) **28**:46

The Ghost of Thomas Kempe (Lively) **7**:154

The Ghost on Saturday Night (Fleischman) **15**:107

Ghost Paddle: A Northwest Coast Indian Tale (Houston) **3**:85

Ghost Sitter (Mattingley) **24**:127

Ghostly Companions (Alcock) **26**:4

Ghostly Companions: A Feast of Chilling Tales (Alcock) **26**:4

Ghostly Haunts (Morpurgo) **51**:143

Ghostly Tales of Love and Revenge (Cohen) **43**:55

Ghost's Hour, Spook's Hour (Bunting) **28**:61

Ghosts I Have Been (Peck) **15**:159

The Ghosts of Cougar Island (Parish) **22**:168

The Ghosts of Departure Point (Bunting) **28**:54

The Ghosts of Glencoe (Hunter) **25**:76

The Ghosts of Hungryhouse Lane (McBratney) **44**:122

The Ghosts of Now (Nixon) **24**:145

The Ghosts of Stone Hollow (Snyder)
  See *The Truth about Stone Hollow*

Ghosts of the Deep (Cohen) **43**:56

The Ghosts of War (Cohen) **43**:52

The Ghosts The Indians Feared (Lavine) **35**:156

The Giant (Pene du Bois) **1**:63

Giant Cold (Dickinson) **29**:55

The Giant Colour Book of Mathematics: Exploring the World of Numbers and Space (Adler) **27**:15

The Giant Devil-Dingo (Roughsey) **41**:140

The Giant Golden Book of Cat Stories (Coatsworth) **2**:57

The Giant Golden Book of Mathematics: Exploring the World of Numbers and Space (Adler) **27**:14

Giant John (Lobel) **5**:163

The Giant Panda at Home (Rau) **8**:188

The Giant Planets (Nourse) **33**:138

The Giant Squid (Bunting) **28**:52

The Giants' Farm (Yolen) **4**:263

The Giants Go Camping (Yolen) **4**:265

The Giant's Toe (Cole) **18**:83

Gidja the Moon (Roughsey and Trezise) **41**:141

The Gift (Dickinson) **29**:43

The Gift (Nixon) **24**:143

A Gift for Mama (Hautzig) **22**:85

A Gift for Sula Sula (Ness) **6**:201

A Gift from St. Francis: The First Crèche (Cole) **40**:25

Gift from the Sky (Milne and Milne) **22**:119

The Gift of a Lamb: A Shepherd's Tale of the First Christmas Told as a Verse-Play (Causley) **30**:40

A Gift of Magic (Duncan) **29**:69

The Gift of Sarah Barker (Yolen) **4**:267

The Gift of the Magi (Zwerger) **46**:190

The Gift of the Sacred Dog (Goble) **21**:133

The Gift of the Tree (Tresselt) **30**:214

The Gift-Giver (Hansen) **21**:150

The Gigantic Balloon (Park) **51**:176

Gigi cerca il suo berretto (Munari) **9**:125

Gilberto and the Wind (Ets) **33**:88

Gimme a Kiss (Pike) **29**:172

Ginger Pye (Estes) **2**:73

The Gingerbread Boy (Galdone) **16**:100

The Gingerbread Rabbit (Jarrell) **6**:158

Giorgio's Village (dePaola) **24**:91

Gip in the Television Set (Rodari) **24**:207

A Giraffe and a Half (Silverstein) **5**:209

The Giraffe and the Pelly and Me (Dahl) **31**:25; **41**:35

The Giraffe in Pepperell Street (Klein) **21**:158
Giraffe: The Silent Giant (Schlein) **41**:187
Giraffes, the Sentinels of the Savannas (Sattler) **24**:224
The Girl and the Goatherd; or, This and That and Thus and So (Ness) **6**:205
A Girl Called Boy (Hurmence) **25**:93
The Girl Called Moses: The Story of Harriet Tubman (Petry) **12**:210
The Girl in the Golden Bower (Yolen) **44**:202
The Girl in the Opposite Bed (Arundel) **35**:15
The Girl in the Painting (Bunting) **28**:47
A Girl like Abby (Irwin) **40**:111
Girl Missing: A Novel (Noestlinger) **12**:186
The Girl of His Dreams (Mazer) **16**:133
The Girl of the Golden Gate (Garner) **20**:116
The Girl on the Outside (Walter) **15**:205
The Girl Who Cried Flowers and Other Tales (Yolen) **4**:260
The Girl Who Loved Caterpillars (Merrill) **52**:113
The Girl Who Loved the Wind (Yolen) **4**:260
The Girl Who Loved Wild Horses (Goble) **21**:131
The Girl Who Married the Moon: Stories from Native North America (Bruchac) **46**:16
The Girl Who Sat By the Ashes (Colum) **36**:24
The Girl Who Wanted a Boy (Zindel) **45**:194
The Girl Who Would Rather Climb Trees (Schlein) **41**:186
The Girl without a Name (Beckman) **25**:12
The Girlfriend (Stine) **37**:116
The Girls and Yanga Marshall (Berry) **22**:8
Girls Can Be Anything (Klein) **2**:98
Giselle (Ottley) **16**:184
Give A Dog a Bone (Wildsmith) **52**:190
Give and Take (Klein) **19**:96
Give Dad My Best (Collier) **3**:45
The Giver (Lowry) **46**:43
Giving Away Suzanne (Duncan) **29**:66
The Giving Tree (Silverstein) **5**:209
The Gizmo (Jennings) **40**:128
Glaciers: Nature's Frozen Rivers (Nixon) **24**:140
Glasblasarns Barn (Gripe) **5**:144
The Glassblower's Children (Gripe) **5**:144
Glasses and Contact Lenses: Your Guide to Eyes, Eyewear, and Eye Care (Silverstein and Silverstein) **25**:226
Glasses—Who Needs 'Em? (Smith) **47**:201
The Glassmakers (Fisher) **18**:121
Glimpses of Louisa (Alcott) **1**:9
Glimpses of the French Court: Sketches from French History (Richards) **54**:165
Gloria Chipmunk, Star! (Nixon) **24**:140
The Glorious Flight: Across the Channel with Louis Blériot July 25, 1909 (Provensen and Provensen) **11**:215
The Glory Girl (Byars) **16**:59
Glory in the Flower (St. John) **46**:100
Die Glücklichen Inseln Hinter dem Winde (Kruss) **9**:83
Die Glücklichen Inseln Hinter dem Winde Bd. 2 (Kruss) **9**:84
Glue Fingers (Christopher) **33**:49
Gluskabe and the Four Wishes (Bruchac) **46**:18
Gnasty Gnomes (Stine) **37**:105
The Gnats of Knotty Pine (Peet) **12**:203
Go and Hush the Baby (Byars) **1**:35
Go Away, Stay Away! (Haley) **21**:145
Go Fish (Cummings) **48**:51
Go Jump in the Pool! (Korman) **25**:105
Go Saddle the Sea (Aiken) **19**:11
The Goats (Cole) **18**:84
Goat's Trail (Wildsmith) **52**:192
Gobble, Growl, Grunt (Spier) **5**:220

The Goblin under the Stairs (Calhoun) **42**:13
The Goblins Giggle and Other Stories (Bang) **8**:17
The God beneath the Sea (Garfield) **21**:102
The God Beneath the Sea (Keeping) **34**:94
God Bless the Gargoyles (Pilkey) **48**:114
God is in the Mountain (Keats) **35**:131
God Wash the World and Start Again (Graham) **10**:109
Godfather Cat and Mousie (Orgel) **48**:88
God's Radar (Gaberman) **33**:11
God's Trombones: Seven Negro Sermons in Verse (Johnson) **32**:165
Goggle-Eyes (Fine) **25**:23
Goggles! (Keats) **1**:114; **35**:135
Going Back (Lively) **7**:159
Going Backwards (Klein) **19**:98
Going Barefoot (Fisher) **49**:35
Going Home (Mohr) **22**:134
Going on a Whale Watch (McMillan) **47**:181
Going Over to Your Place: Poems for Each Other (Janeczko) **47**:105
Going Solo (Dahl) **41**:37
Going to My Ballet Class (Kuklin) **51**:104
Going to My Gymnastics Class (Kuklin) **51**:107
Going to My Nursery School (Kuklin) **51**:105
Going Up!: A Color Counting Book (Sis) **45**:162
Going West (Waddell) **31**:181
Gold and Gods of Peru (Baumann) **35**:46
Gold Dust (McCaughrean) **38**:150
Gold: The Fascinating Story of the Noble Metal through the Ages (Cohen) **3**:40
The Golden Age (Grahame) **5**:126
The Golden Basket (Bemelmans) **6**:64
The Golden Brothers (Garner) **20**:116
The Golden Bunny and 17 Other Stories and Poems (Brown) **10**:63
The Golden Collar (Clarke) **28**:75
The Golden Door: The United States from 1865 to 1918 (Asimov) **12**:54
The Golden Egg Book (Brown) **10**:55
The Golden Fleece and the Heroes Who Lived Before Achilles (Colum) **36**:25
The Golden Heart of Winter (Singer) **48**:139
The Golden Hind (Hurd) **49**:124
The Golden One (Treece) **2**:185
The Golden Pasture (Thomas) **19**:221
The Golden Road (Montgomery) **8**:136
The Golden Serpent (Myers) **4**:160
The Golden Shadow (Garfield) **21**:106
The Golden Stick (Paulsen) **19**:171
The Golden Sword of Dragonwalk (Stine) **37**:107
Goldengrove (Walsh) **2**:199
Gold-Fever Trail: A Klondike Adventure (Hughes) **9**:68
Goldie, the Dollmaker (Goffstein) **3**:59
Goldilocks and the Three Bears (Brett) **27**:41
Goldilocks and the Three Bears (Marshall) **21**:184
Golem (Wisniewski) **51**:199
The Golem: A Version (Hyman) **50**:85
The Golem and the Dragon Girl (Levitin) **53**:72
Golly Gump Swallowed a Fly (Cole) **5**:68
The Golly Sisters Go West (Byars) **16**:63
A Gondola for Fun (Weiss) **4**:220
Gone A-Whaling: The Lure of the Sea and the Hunt for the Great Whale (Murphy) **53**:118
Gone Is Gone; or, The Story of a Man Who Wanted to Do Housework (Gag) **4**:90
Gone-Away Lake (Enright) **4**:75
Gonna Sing My Head Off! American Folk Songs for Children (Krull) **44**:102
Good Dog, Carl (Day) **22**:24
Good Ethan (Fox) **1**:77
The Good Friends (Bianco) **19**:54

The Good Giants and the Bad Pukwudgies (Fritz) **14**:117
Good Griselle (Yolen) **44**:203
Good Hunting, Blue Sky (Parish) **22**:154
Good Hunting, Little Indian (Parish) **22**:154
The Good Knight Ghost (Bendick) **5**:38
Good Luck Duck (DeJong) **1**:57
Good Luck to the Rider (Phipson) **5**:177
The Good Master (Seredy) **10**:171
Good Moon Rising (Garden) **51**:81
Good Morning (Bruna) **7**:53
Good Morning (Oxenbury) **22**:143
Good Morning, Baby Bear (Hill) **13**:95
Good News (Cummings) **48**:43
Good News! (Duke) **51**:51
Good News (Greenfield) **4**:96
Good Night (Oxenbury) **22**:143
Good Night, Fred (Wells) **16**:211
Good Night, Owl! (Hutchins) **20**:146
Good Night, Prof, Dear (Townsend) **2**:170
Good Night to Annie (Merriam) **14**:20
Good Old James (Donovan) **3**:51
Good Queen Bess: The Story of Elizabeth I of England (Stanley) **46**:143
Good Rhymes, Good Times (Hopkins) **44**:98
Good, Says Jerome (Clifton) **5**:55
The Good Side of My Heart (Rinaldi) **46**:80
The Good, the Bad, and the Goofy (Smith) **47**:202
Good Work, Amelia Bedelia (Parish) **22**:162
Goodbye, Charlie (Bunting) **28**:44
Good-bye, Chicken Little (Byars) **16**:56
Goodbye Max (Keller) **45**:49
Good-bye to the Jungle (Townsend) **2**:171
The Goodbye Walk (Ryder) **37**:100
The Good-Byes of Magnus Marmalade (Orgel) **48**:75
The Good-for-Nothing Prince (Williams) **8**:230
The Good-Luck Pencil (Stanley) **46**:136
Goodnight (Hoban) **3**:77
Goodnight Kiss (Stine) **37**:118
Goodnight Moon (Brown) **10**:55
Goodnight Moon (Hurd) **49**:118
Goody Hall (Babbitt) **2**:6
Goofbang Value Daze (Thompson) **24**:232
A Goose on Your Grave (Aiken) **19**:18
A Gopher in the Garden, and Other Animal Poems (Prelutsky) **13**:163
Gordon the Goat (Leaf) **25**:127
Gorey Posters (Gorey) **36**:99
The Gorgon's Head: The Story of Perseus (Serraillier) **2**:138
Gorilla (Browne) **19**:67
Gorilla (McClung) **11**:194
Gorky Rises (Steig) **15**:197
Gowie Corby Plays Chicken (Kemp) **29**:115
Graham Oakley's Magical Changes (Oakley) **7**:219
Grammar Can Be Fun (Leaf) **25**:115
Gran and Grandpa (Oxenbury) **22**:145
Un gran pequeño (Sanchez-Silva) **12**:232
Grand Constructions (Ventura) **16**:195
Grand Papa and Ellen Aroon (Monjo) **2**:121
Grandad's Magic (Graham) **31**:99
Grandfather (Baker) **28**:19
Grandfather Learns to Drive (Kruss) **9**:88
Grandfather's Dream (Keller) **45**:58
Grandfather's Trolley (McMillan) **47**:189
Le grandi costruzioni (Ventura) **16**:195
Grandma and Grandpa (Oxenbury) **22**:145
The Grandma in the Apple Tree 80 (Orgel) **48**:80
The Grandma Mixup (McCully) **46**:62
Grandma Moses: Painter of Rural America (Oneal) **13**:160

Grandmama's Joy (Greenfield) **38**:83
Grandmas at Bat (McCully) **46**:68
Grandmas at the Lake (McCully) **46**:65
Grandma's Bill (Waddell) **31**:198
Grandmother (Baker) **28**:19
Grandmother Cat and the Hermit (Coatsworth) **2**:58
Grandmother's Journey (Unnerstad) **36**:192
Grandpa and Bo (Henkes) **23**:127
Grandpa's Face (Greenfield) **38**:87
Grandpa's Great City Tour: An Alphabet Book (Stevenson) **17**:160
Grandpa's Wonderful Glass (Epstein and Epstein) **26**:58
Granny and the Desperadoes (Parish) **22**:159
Granny and the Indians (Parish) **22**:157
The Granny Project (Fine) **25**:20
Granny Reardun (Garner) **20**:113
Granny, the Baby, and the Big Gray Thing (Parish) **22**:161
Granny the Pag (Bawden) **51**:42
Granny Was a Buffer Girl (Doherty) **21**:57
Granpa (Burningham) **9**:52
Graphology: A Guide to Handwriting Analysis (Aylesworth) **6**:53
The Grass-Eaters (Paulsen) **19**:170
Grasshopper on the Road (Lobel) **5**:172
A Grateful Nation: The Story of Arlington National Cemetery (Ashabranner) **28**:15
Graven Images: 3 Stories (Fleischman) **20**:64
Gravity Is a Mystery (Branley) **13**:36
The Gray Kangaroo at Home (Rau) **8**:189
Gray Magic (Norton) **50**:144
The Great Airship Mystery: A UFO of the 1890s (Cohen) **43**:39
The Great American Crazies (Haskins) **39**:34
The Great American Gold Rush (Blumberg) **21**:30
The Great Ball Game: A Muskogee Story (Bruchac) **46**:15
The Great Ballagundi Damper Bake (Mattingley) **24**:124
Great Big Air Book (Scarry) **41**:164
The Great Big Car and Truck Book (Scarry) **41**:160
The Great Big Especially Beautiful Easter Egg (Stevenson) **17**:159
Great Big Schoolhouse (Scarry) **41**:163
The Great Blueness and Other Predicaments (Lobel) **5**:165
The Great Brain (Fitzgerald) **1**:69
The Great Brain at the Academy (Fitzgerald) **1**:69
The Great Brain Reforms (Fitzgerald) **1**:69
The Great Duffy (Krauss) **42**:110
The Great Fire (Murphy) **53**:114
The Great Flood (Spier) **5**:224
The Great Flood Mystery (Curry) **31**:84
The Great Gatenby (Marsden) **34**:149
Great Ghosts (Cohen) **43**:53
The Great Gilly Hopkins (Paterson) **7**:235
Great Gran Gorilla and the Robbers (Waddell) **31**:192
The Great Green Mouse Disaster (Waddell) **31**:179
The Great Heritage (Shippen) **36**:169
The Great Houdini: Magician Extraordinary (Epstein and Epstein) **26**:46
Great Ideas of Science: The Men and the Thinking behind Them (Asimov) **12**:45
The Great Land of the Elephants (Guillot) **22**:71
The Great Marathon Football Match (Ahlberg and Ahlberg) **18**:3
The Great Millionaire Kidnap (Mahy) **7**:184
Great Northern? (Ransome) **8**:182

Great Painters (Ventura) **16**:197
The Great Pie Robbery (Scarry) **41**:164
The Great Piratical Rumbustification & The Librarian and the Robbers (Mahy) **7**:185
The Great Quarterback Switch (Christopher) **33**:57
The Great Race of the Birds and Animals (Goble) **21**:134
The Great Rip-off (St. John) **46**:116
The Great Sleigh Robbery (Foreman) **32**:86
Great Steamboat Mystery (Scarry) **41**:167
The Great Waldo Search (Handford) **22**:75
The Great Wall of China (Fisher) **18**:134
The Great Watermelon Birthday (Williams) **9**:231
The Great Wheel (Lawson) **2**:109
The Great White Shark (Bunting) **28**:53
The Great Zoo Escape (McNaughton) **54**:50
Greater Than Angels (Matas) **52**:96
Greedy Greeny (Gantos) **18**:142
Greedy Mariani and Other Folktales of the Antilles (Hyman) **50**:72
Greek Myths (McCaughrean) **38**:148
The Greeks (Asimov) **12**:38
Green Blades Rising: The Anglo-Saxons (Crossley-Holland) **47**:32
The Green Children (Crossley-Holland) **47**:24
The Green Coat (Gripe) **5**:148
Green Darner: The Story of a Dragonfly (Lerner) **34**:124
Green Darner: The Story of a Dragonfly (McClung) **11**:180
Green Eggs and Ham (Dr. Seuss) **1**:86; **9**:185
Green Finger House (Harris) **30**:120
The Green Flash and Other Tales of Horror, Suspense, and Fantasy (Aiken) **1**:4
The Green Futures of Tycho (Sleator) **29**:202
Green Grass and White Milk (Aliki) **9**:23
Green Grows the Garden (Bianco) **19**:55
The Green Kids (McBratney) **44**:125
The Green Laurel (Spence) **26**:192
The Green Man (Haley) **21**:146
The Green Piper (Kelleher) **36**:121
Green Says Go (Emberley) **5**:96
Green Street (Arundel) **35**:9
The Greengage Summer (Godden) **20**:128
The Greentail Mouse (Lionni) **7**:135
Greenwitch (Cooper) **4**:45
Greetings from Sandy Beach (Graham) **31**:100
Gregory Griggs and Other Nursery Rhyme People (Lobel) **5**:172
The Gremlins (Dahl) **7**:68
Greta the Strong (Sobol) **4**:209
The Grey Gentlemen ("To Damon. To inquire of him if he cou'd tell me by the Style, who writ me a Copy of Verses that came to me in an unknown Hand") (Ende) **14**:97
The Grey King (Cooper) **4**:47
The Grey Lady and the Strawberry Snatcher (Bang) **8**:20
Greyling: A Picture Story from the Islands of Shetland (Yolen) **4**:257
Griffin's Castle (Nimmo) **44**:153
Grishka and the Bear (Guillot) **22**:61
The Groober (Byars) **1**:36
Grossvater Lerner auf Fahren (Kruss) **9**:88
The Grouchy Ladybug (Carle) **10**:81
The Grounding of Group 6 (Thompson) **24**:227
The Grove of Green Holly (Willard) **2**:218
Grover (Cleaver and Cleaver) **6**:104
Growin' (Grimes) **42**:89
Growing Colors (McMillan) **47**:171
Growing Pains: Diaries and Drawings for the Years 1908-1917 (Gag) **4**:91

Growing Season (Carter) **22**:17
The Growing Story (Krauss) **42**:110
The Growing Summer (Streatfeild) **17**:196
The Growing Summer (Streatfeild)
  See *The Magic Summer*
Growing Up Wild: How Young Animals Survive (Freedman) **20**:77
Growing Vegetable Soup (Ehlert) **28**:110
Gryphon in Glory (Norton) **50**:161
The Guard Mouse (Freeman) **30**:75
The Guardian Angels (Haskins) **39**:44
The Guardian Circle (Buffie) **39**:25
The Guardian of Isis (Hughes) **9**:73
The Guardians (Christopher) **2**:39
Guarneri: Story of a Genius (Wibberley) **3**:227
Guess Again: More Weird and Wacky Inventions (Murphy) **53**:104
Guess How Much I Love You (McBratney) **44**:126
Guess Who's Just Moved in Next Door? (McNaughton) **54**:60
The Guest (Marshall) **21**:171
Guests in the Promised Land (Hunter) **3**:98
Guillot's African Folk Tales (Guillot) **22**:68
Guilt and Gingerbread (Garfield) **21**:117
The Guinea Pig ABC (Duke) **51**:46
Guinea Pigs: All about Them (Silverstein and Silverstein) **25**:206
Guinea Pigs Far and Near (Duke) **51**:47
The Guizer: A Book of Fools (Garner) **20**:112
Gull Number 737 (George) **1**:89
Gulliver's Travels (Swift)
  See *Travels into Several Remote Nations of the World, in Four Parts; By Lemuel Gulliver*
The Gulls of Smuttynose Island (Scott) **20**:196
Gumdrop and the Dinosaur (Biro) **28**:39
Gumdrop and the Farmer's Friend (Biro) **28**:30
Gumdrop and the Monster (Biro) **28**:38
Gumdrop and the Pirates (Biro) **28**:40
Gumdrop and the Secret Switches (Biro) **28**:34
Gumdrop and the Steamroller (Biro) **28**:33
Gumdrop at Sea (Biro) **28**:36
Gumdrop Finds a Friend (Biro) **28**:32
Gumdrop Finds a Ghost (Biro) **28**:33
Gumdrop Gets His Wings (Biro) **28**:33
Gumdrop Goes Fishing (Biro) **28**:36
Gumdrop Goes to London (Biro) **28**:32
Gumdrop Has a Birthday (Biro) **28**:33
Gumdrop Has a Tummy Ache (Biro) **28**:36
Gumdrop Is the Best Car (Biro) **28**:36
Gumdrop on the Brighton Run (Biro) **28**:33
Gumdrop on the Farm (Biro) **28**:36
Gumdrop on the Move (Biro) **28**:31
Gumdrop Posts a Letter (Biro) **28**:33
Gumdrop: The Story of a Vintage Car (Biro) **28**:30
Gumdrop's Magic Journey (Biro) **28**:36
Guy Lenny (Mazer) **16**:128
Gyo Fujikawa's A to Z Picture Book (Fujikawa) **25**:38
Gyo Fujikawa's Come Follow Me...to the Secret World of Elves and Fairies and Gnomes and Trolls (Fujikawa) **25**:40
Gyo Fujikawa's Oh, What a Busy Day! (Fujikawa) **25**:38
Gypsy (Seredy) **10**:179
Gypsy Gold (Worth) **21**:223
Gypsy Moth: Its History in America (McClung) **11**:188
H. M. S. Hood vs. Bismarck: The Battleship Battle (Taylor) **30**:191
The Ha Ha Bonk Book (Ahlberg and Ahlberg) **18**:8
Hadassah: Esther the Orphan Queen (Armstrong) **1**:22
Haircuts for the Woolseys (dePaola) **24**:102

Hairs in the Palm of the Hand (Mark) **11**:151
Hairy Tales and Nursery Crimes (Rosen) **45**:133
Hakon of Rogen's Saga (Haugaard) **11**:102
Hakon's Saga (Haugaard) **11**:102
Half a Kingdom: An Icelandic Folktale (McGovern) **50**:119
Half a Moon and One Whole Star (Pinkney) **43**:159
Half a World Away (Chauncy) **6**:91
Half Magic (Eager) **43**:80
Half-a-Ball-of-Kenki: An Ashanti Tale Retold (Aardema) **17**:6
The Half-a-Moon Inn (Fleischman) **20**:63
Halfway Across the Galaxy and Turn Left (Klein) **21**:161
Hallapoosa (Peck) **45**:121
Halley: Comet 1986 (Branley) **13**:48
Halloween (Gibbons) **8**:99
Halloween ABC (Smith) **47**:197
Halloween Howls: Riddles That Are a Scream (Betsy and Giulio Maestro) **45**:72
Halloween Night (Stine) **37**:122
Halloween Party (Stine) **37**:114
Halloween Treats (Haywood) **22**:104
The Hallo-Wiener (Pilkey) **48**:112
Halmoni and the Picnic (Choi) **53**:47
Hamilton (Peck) **45**:109
The Hamish Hamilton Book of Goblins (Garner) **20**:108
The Hammerhead Light (Thiele) **27**:207
The Hand of Apollo (Coatsworth) **2**:58
Hand Rhymes (Brown) **29**:13
A Handful of Thieves (Bawden) **2**:11; **51**:16
A Handful of Time (Pearson) **26**:176
Handles (Mark) **11**:155
Handmade in America: The Heritage of Colonial Craftsman (Lavine) **35**:149
The Hand-Me-Down Kid (Pascal) **25**:184
Handtalk: An ABC of Finger Spelling and Sign Language (Charlip) **8**:31
Hang a Thousand Trees with Ribbons: The Story of Phillis Wheatley (Rinaldi) **46**:92
Hang for Treason (Peck) **45**:107
Hang on, Hopper! (Pfister) **42**:139
Hang Tough, Paul Mather (Slote) **4**:200
Hangin' Out with Cici (Pascal) **25**:183
Hangin' Out with Cici; or, My Mother Was Never a Kid (Pascal) **25**:183
Hanging On: How Animals Carry Their Young (Freedman) **20**:78
Hansel and Gretel (Browne) **19**:64
Hansel and Gretel (Galdone) **16**:104
Hansel and Gretel (Jeffers) **30**:134
Hansel and Gretel (Zwerger) **46**:188
Hansel and Gretel and Other Stories (Nielsen) **16**:157
Hansi (Bemelmans) **6**:63
Happy Birthday, Baabee (Khalsa) **30**:144
The Happy Birthday Letter (Flack) **28**:130
Happy Birthday, Martin Luther King (Pinkney) **54**:138
The Happy Birthday Mystery (Nixon) **24**:139
Happy Birthday, Sam (Hutchins) **20**:149
Happy Birthday to You! (Dr. Seuss) **9**:185
Happy Birthday with Ant and Bee (Banner) **24**:19
The Happy Day (Krauss) **42**:112
Happy Days at Bullerby (Lindgren) **39**:150
The Happy Funeral (Bunting) **28**:53
The Happy Hedgehog Band (Waddell) **31**:200
The Happy Hocky Family! (Smith) **47**:204
The Happy Hunter (Duvoisin) **23**:102
The Happy Islands behind the Winds (Kruss) **9**:83
The Happy Lion (Duvoisin) **23**:99

The Happy Place (Bemelmans) **6**:69
Happy Times in Noisy Village (Lindgren) **1**:137; **39**:150
Happy Valentine's Day, Emma! (Stevenson) **17**:167
Happy Worm (McNaughton) **54**:56
Happy's Christmas (Gramatky) **22**:45
Harbor (Crews) **7**:60
Harbour (Crews) **7**:60
Hard Drive to Short (Christopher) **33**:43
The Hard Life of the Teenager (Collier) **3**:45
The Hare and the Bear and Other Stories (Tresselt) **30**:214
The Hare and the Tortoise (Galdone) **16**:92
The Hare and the Tortoise (Wildsmith) **2**:212
The Hare and the Tortoise & The Tortoise and the Hare / La Liebre y la Tortuga & La Tortuga y la Liebre (Pene du Bois) **1**:63
Hare's Choice (Hamley) **47**:60
The Hare's Race (Baumann) **35**:56
Hari, the Jungle Lad (Mukerji) **10**:131
Harlequin and the Gift of Many Colors (Charlip) **8**:29
Harlequinade (Streatfeild) **17**:189
Harnessing the Sun: The Story of Solar Energy (Knight) **38**:118
Harold Thinks Big (Murphy) **53**:101
Harold Urey: The Man Who Explored from Earth to Moon (Silverstein and Silverstein) **25**:204
Harpoon of the Hunter (Markoosie) **23**:211-13
Harquin: The Fox Who Went Down to the Valley (Burningham) **9**:41
Harriet and the Crocodiles (Waddell) **31**:180
Harriet and the Flying Teachers (Waddell) **31**:189
Harriet and the Haunted School (Waddell) **31**:182
Harriet and the Robot (Waddell) **31**:185
Harriet at Play (Betsy and Giulio Maestro) **45**:74
Harriet at School (Betsy and Giulio Maestro) **45**:74
Harriet at Work (Betsy and Giulio Maestro) **45**:74
Harriet Goes to the Circus: A Number Concept Book (Betsy and Giulio Maestro) **45**:67
Harriet Reads Signs and More Signs: A Word Concept Book (Betsy and Giulio Maestro) **45**:70
Harriet: The Life and World of Harriet Beecher Stowe (St. John) **46**:125
Harriet the Spy (Fitzhugh) **1**:71
Harriet Tubman and Black History Month (Pinkney) **54**:135
Harriet Tubman, Conductor on the Underground Railroad (Petry) **12**:210
Harriet Tubman: Guide to Freedom (Epstein and Epstein) **26**:61
Harriet's Hare (King-Smith) **40**:172
Harris and Me: a Summer Remembered (Paulsen) **54**:111
Harry and Hortense at Hormone High (Zindel) **45**:195
Harry and Tuck (Keller) **45**:57
Harry Cat's Pet Puppy (Selden) **8**:200
Harry in England, Being the Partly-True Adventures of H.R. in the Year 1857 (Richards) **54**:172
Harry's Mad (King-Smith) **40**:146
Harum Scarum: The Little Hare Book (Janosch) **26**:81
Has Anyone Here Seen William? (Graham) **31**:99
The Hat (Ungerer) **3**:200
Hatchet (Paulsen) **19**:177; **54**:92
Hatchet: Winter (Paulsen) **54**:119
Hating Alison Ashley (Klein) **21**:161
The Hating Book (Zolotow) **2**:234
The Hatters (Fisher) **18**:122

Hattie and the Fox (Fox) **23**:114
Hattie the Backstage Bat (Freeman) **30**:77
Haunted House (Hughes) **15**:123
Haunted House (Parish) **22**:159
Haunted House (Pienkowski) **6**:230
Haunted Island (Nixon) **24**:149
The Haunted Mountain (Hunter) **25**:80
The Haunted Souvenir Warehouse: Eleven Tales of Unusual Hauntings (Knight) **38**:121
Haunted United (Hamley) **47**:59
The Haunters of the Silences: A Book of Animal Life (Roberts) **33**:199
The Haunting (Mahy) **7**:187
The Haunting of Cassie Palmer (Alcock) **26**:2
The Haunting of Chas McGill and Other Stories (Westall) **13**:257
The Haunting of Ellen: A Story of Suspense (Waddell)
    See *The Back House Ghosts*
The Haunting of Frances Rain (Buffie) **39**:15
The Haunting of Kildoran Abbey (Bunting) **28**:47
The Haunting of SafeKeep (Bunting) **28**:58
Have a Happy Measle, a Merry Mumps, and a Cheery Chickenpox (Bendick) **5**:38
Have You Seen Josephine? (Poulin) **28**:193
Have You Seen My Cat? (Carle) **10**:77
Have You Seen Who's Just Moved In Next Door to Us? (McNaughton) **54**:60
Havelok the Dane (Crossley-Holland) **47**:22
Havelok the Dane (Serraillier) **2**:139
Hawk, I'm Your Brother (Baylor) **3**:15
The Hawk that Dare Not Hunt by Day (O'Dell) **16**:171
Hawk's Vision (Hamley) **47**:65
The Hawkstone (Williams) **8**:231
The Haymeadow (Paulsen) **54**:106
Hazardous Substances: A Reference (Berger) **32**:37
Hazel Rye (Cleaver and Cleaver) **6**:114
Hazel's Amazing Mother (Wells) **16**:213
He Bear, She Bear (Berenstain and Berenstain) **19**:29
A Head Full of Hats (Fisher) **18**:121
Head in the Clouds (Southall) **2**:152
Head Injuries (Aaseng) **54**:23
Headaches: All about Them (Silverstein and Silverstein) **25**:222
The Headless Cupid (Snyder) **31**:158
The Headless Horseman Rides Tonight: More Poems to Trouble Your Sleep (Prelutsky) **13**:168
Healer (Dickinson) **29**:54
Health Can Be Fun (Leaf) **25**:127
Hear Your Heart (Showers) **6**:243
Heart Disease (Silverstein and Silverstein) **25**:214
Heart Disease: America's #1 Killer (Silverstein and Silverstein) **25**:214
The Heart of Stone (Orgel) **48**:74
Heartbeat (Mazer and Mazer) **23**:233
Heartbeats: Your Body, Your Heart (Silverstein and Silverstein) **25**:220
Heart's Blood (Yolen) **44**:178
Heartsease (Dickinson) **29**:38
Heat (Adler) **27**:18
Heat (Cobb) **2**:65
Heat (Graham) **31**:95
Heat and Temperature (Bendick) **5**:47
Heather, Oak, and Olive: Three Stories (Sutcliff) **1**:185; **37**:164
The Heavenly Host (Asimov) **12**:51
Heavy Equipment (Adkins) **7**:26
Heavy Is a Hippopotamus (Schlein) **41**:176
Heb jij een hobbie? (Bruna) **7**:52
Heckedy Peg (Wood and Wood) **26**:223

Hector Protector and As I Went over the Water (Sendak) **1**:167

The Hedgehog Boy: A Latvian Folktale (Langton) **33**:118

Hee Haw (McGovern) **50**:115

Heidi (Harris) **30**:123

Heidi (Spyri) **13**:174

Heiligenwald (Benary-Isbert) **12**:73

Heimkehr aus dem Kriege (Kruss) **9**:87

Heinrich Schliemann, Discoverer of Buried Treasure (Selden) **8**:198

The Helen Oxenbury Nursery Story Book (Oxenbury) **22**:146

The Helen Oxenbury Rhyme Book (Oxenbury) **22**:148

Helen Oxenbury's ABC of Things (Oxenbury) **22**:138

Helga's Dowry: A Troll Love Story (dePaola) **4**:59

H-E-L-L-L-P! The Crazy Gang Is Back! (Williams) **48**:207

Hello and Good-by (Hoberman) **22**:109

Hello, Dandelions (Williams) **48**:197

Hello, Little Pig (Janosch) **26**:81

Hello, Star (Haywood) **22**:106

Hello, Tree! (Ryder) **37**:98

Hell's Edge (Townsend) **2**:172

Help! (McNaughton) **54**:56

"Help!" Yelled Maxwell (Stevenson) **17**:153

Helpers (Hughes) **15**:122

Helpful Mr. Bear (Kuratomi) **32**:187

Helping Horse (Phipson) **5**:183

The Henchmans at Home (Burton) **1**:31

Hengest's Tale (Walsh) **2**:200

Henny Penny (Galdone) **16**:93

Henry (Bawden) **51**:35

Henry Aaron: Home-Run King (Epstein and Epstein) **26**:65

Henry and Beezus (Cleary) **8**:46

Henry and Mudge in Puddle Trouble: The Second Book of Their Adventures (Rylant) **15**:173

Henry and Mudge: The First Book of Their Adventures (Rylant) **15**:173

Henry and Ribsy (Cleary) **2**:46; **8**:47

Henry and the Clubhouse (Cleary) **8**:50

Henry and the Paper Route (Cleary) **2**:47; **8**:48

Henry Huggins (Cleary) **2**:47; **8**:44

Henry, the Hand-Painted Mouse (Merrill) **52**:99

Henry the Sailor Cat (Calhoun) **42**:34

Henry-Fisherman: A Story of the Virgin Islands (Brown) **12**:94

Henry's Fourth of July (Keller) **45**:47

Henry's Happy Birthday (Keller) **45**:55

Henry's Picnic (Keller) **45**:47

Henry's Red Sea (Smucker) **10**:188

Hepatica Hawks (Field) **21**:77

Hepzibah (Dickinson) **29**:47

Her Majesty, Aunt Essie (Schwartz) **25**:191

Her Majesty, Grace Jones (Langton) **33**:106

Her Seven Brothers (Goble) **21**:135

Her Stories: African American Folktales, Fairy Tales and True Tales (Hamilton) **40**:91

Her Stories: African American Folktales, Fairy Tales, and True Tales (Leo and Diane Dillon) **44**:48

Heracles the Strong (Serraillier) **2**:139

Herb Seasoning (Thompson) **24**:232

Herbert Hated Being Small (Kuskin) **4**:143

Herbert Rowbarge (Babbitt) **53**:32

Hercules: The Story of an Old-Fashioned Fire Engine (Gramatky) **22**:40

A Herd of Deer (Dillon) **26**:30

Here a Chick, Therea Chick (McMillan) **47**:163

Here Are the Brick Street Boys (Ahlberg and Ahlberg) **18**:3

Here Come the Aliens! (McNaughton) **54**:66

Here Comes Charlie Moon (Hughes) **15**:127

Here Comes Herb's Hurricane! (Stevenson) **17**:152

Here Comes John (Graham) **31**:92

Here Comes McBroom (Fleischman) **15**:108

Here Comes the Bus! (Haywood) **22**:98

Here Comes Theo (Graham) **31**:92

Here Comes Thursday! (Bond) **1**:27

Here I Come—Ready or Not! (Merrill) **52**:110

Here I Stay (Coatsworth) **2**:58

Here There Be Dragons (Yolen) **44**:201

Here There Be Unicorns (Yolen) **44**:203

Here There Be Witches (Yolen) **44**:207

Here We Go Round: A Career Story for Girls (Allan) **43**:3

Hereafterthis (Galdone) **16**:98

Here's a Penny (Haywood) **22**:92

Here's Baabee, Baabee's Things, Baabee Gets Dressed, Baabee's Home (Khalsa) **30**:144

The Heritage of Music (Shippen) **36**:181

Heritage of the Star (Engdahl) **2**:70

Herman the Loser (Hoban) **3**:77

The Hermit and Harry and Me (Hogrogian) **2**:88

The Hermit and the Bear (Yeoman) **46**:180

Hermit Dan (Parish) **22**:163

Hero (Baillie) **49**:12

A Hero Ain't Nothin but a Sandwich (Childress) **14**:88

The Hero and the Crown (McKinley) **10**:125

The Hero from Otherwhere (Williams) **8**:232

Hero Legends of the World (Baumann) **35**:54

The Hero of Barletta (Napoli) **51**:153

Hero of Lesser Causes (Johnston) **41**:85

Heroes and History (Sutcliff) **1**:186; **37**:160

Herpes (Nourse) **33**:144

Hershel and the Hanukkah Goblins (Hyman) **50**:80

Hetty (Willard) **2**:218

Hetty and Harriet (Oakley) **7**:221

Hey, Al (Yorinks) **20**:217

Hey, Dad! (Doyle) **22**:29

Hey Diddle Diddle (Caldecott) **14**:78

The Hey Hey Man (Fleischman) **15**:110

Hey, Kid! Does She Love Me? (Mazer) **16**:132

Hey, Lover Boy (Rockwell) **6**:240

Hey Preso! You're a Bear (Janosch) **26**:78

Hey, That's My Soul You're Stomping On (Corcoran) **50**:24

Hey, What's Wrong with This One? (Wojciechowska) **1**:196

Hey Willy, See the Pyramids (Kalman) **32**:180

Hezekiah Horton (Tarry) **26**:212

Hi, Cat! (Keats) **1**:114; **35**:136

Hi! Ho! The Rattlin' Bog and Other Folk Songs for Group Singing (Langstaff) **3**:109

Hi Johnny (Hunter) **25**:74

Hi, Mr. Robin! (Tresselt) **30**:203

Hi, Mrs. Mallory! (Thomas) **8**:214

Hi There, Supermouse! (Ure) **34**:175

Hiawatha (Jeffers) **30**:135

Hiccup (Mayer) **11**:172

Hickory Stick Rag (Watson) **3**:212

Hidden Gold (Clarke) **28**:75

The Hidden House (Brown) **10**:63

The Hidden House (Waddell) **31**:197

The Hidden Shrine (Myers) **16**:142

Hidden Treasure (Allen) **44**:9

The Hidden World: Life under a Rock (Pringle) **4**:181

Hidden Worlds: Pictures of the Invisible (Simon) **9**:220

Hide and Seek (Coatsworth) **2**:59

Hide and Seek Fog (Duvoisin) **23**:103

Hide and Seek Fog (Tresselt) **30**:208

The Hideout (Bunting) **28**:66

Hide-Seek: At the Party (McNaughton) **54**:53

The Hideway (Corcoran) **50**:35

Hiding (Klein) **19**:89

Hiding Out (Rockwell) **6**:238

Higbee's Halloween (Peck) **45**:123

Higglety Pigglety Pop! or, There Must Be More to Life (Sendak) **1**:168

Higgle-wiggle: Happy Rhymes (Wilhelm) **46**:170

High and Haunted Island (Chauncy) **6**:92

The High Deeds of Finn MacCool (Sutcliff) **1**:186; **37**:160

High Elk's Treasure (Sneve) **2**:144

The High Hills (Barklem) **31**:6

The High House (Arundel) **35**:10

The High King (Alexander) **1**:14; **5**:21

High on a Hill: A Book of Chinese Riddles (Young) **27**:218

High Sounds, Low Sounds (Branley) **13**:34

High Tide for Labrador (Bunting) **28**:44

High, Wide and Handsome and Their Three Tall Tales (Merrill) **52**:105

High Wind for Kansas (Calhoun) **42**:10

The High World (Bemelmans) **6**:72

Higher on the Door (Stevenson) **17**:166

The Highest Hit (Willard) **5**:248

The Highly Trained Dogs of Professor Petit (Brink) **30**:14

High-Rise Secret (Lenski) **26**:122

Highway to Adventure: The River Rhone of France (Lauber) **16**:112

The Highwayman (Keeping) **34**:106

High-Wire Henry (Calhoun) **42**:32

Hiking and Backpacking (Paulsen) **19**:172

Hilary's Summer on Her Own (Allan) **43**:8

Hildegarde and Maximilian (Krahn) **3**:104

Hilding's Summer (Lindgren) **20**:155

The Hill and the Rock (McKee) **38**:173

The Hill of the Fairy Calf: The Legend of Knockshogowna (Causley) **30**:39

Hills End (Southall) **2**:152

The Hills of Varna (Trease) **42**:180

Him She Loves? (Kerr) **29**:153

Hindu Fables, for Little Children (Mukerji) **10**:133

The Hippo Boat (Nakatani) **30**:157

Hiram Bingham and the Dream of Gold (Cohen) **43**:45

Hiroshima: A Novella (Yep) **54**:197

His Own Where (Jordan) **10**:116

Hisako's Mysteries (Uchida) **6**:255

The Hispanic Americans (Meltzer) **13**:142

History Can Be Fun (Leaf) **25**:131

The History of Helpless Harry: To Which Is Added a Variety of Amusing and Entertaining Adventures (Avi) **24**:8

The History of Little Tom Tucker (Galdone) **16**:96

The History of Mother Twaddle and the Marvelous Achievements of Her Son Jack (Galdone) **16**:99

The History of Simple Simon (Galdone) **16**:92

Hit and Run (Stine) **37**:120

The Hit-Away Kid (Christopher) **33**:59

The Hitchhiker (Stine) **37**:121

Hitler! (Marrin) **53**:84

Hitting, Pitching, and Running—Maybe (Paulsen) **19**:170

Hitty, Her First Hundred Years (Field) **21**:72

The Hoax on You (Singer) **48**:134

Hobby (Yolen) **44**:210

Hobo Toad and the Motorcycle Gang (Yolen) **4**:259

The Hoboken Chicken Emergency (Pinkwater) **4**:167

The Hobyahs (Biro) **28**:39

The Hobyahs (San Souci) **43**:191

The Hockey Machine (Christopher) **33**:58

Hoists, Cranes, and Derricks (Zim) **2**:227

Hold Everything (Epstein and Epstein) **26**:64

Hold Fast (Major) **11**:127

Hold on to Love (Hunter) **25**:88

Hold Zero! (George) **1**:90

Holding Me Here (Conrad) **18**:87

Holding Up the Sky: Young People in China (Rau) **8**:194

The Hole in the Hill (Park) **51**:170

A Hole Is to Dig: A First Book of First Definitions (Krauss) **42**:116

Holes and Peeks (Jonas) **12**:174

Holiday Gifts, Favors and Decorations That You Can Make (Sattler) **24**:213

The Hollow Land (Gardam) **12**:169

Holly from the Bongs: A Nativity Play (Garner) **20**:102

The Hollywood Kid (Wojciechowska) **1**:197

Home at Last! A Young Cat's Tale (Lauber) **16**:119

Home Before Dark (Bridgers) **18**:23

Home for a Bunny (Brown) **10**:66

Home Free (Lasky) **11**:121

Home from Far (Little) **4**:147

Home in the Sky (Baker) **28**:20

Home Is the Sailor (Godden) **20**:132

A Home Is to Share...and Share...and Share... (Gaberman) **33**:12

Home on the Range: Cowboy Poetry (Janeczko) **47**:119

Home Place (Pinkney) **43**:166

The Home Run Trick (Corbett) **1**:45

Home to the Island (Allan) **43**:10

Homeboy (Hansen) **21**:150

Homecoming (Voigt) **13**:226

The Homeless: Profiling the Problem (Hyde) **23**:175

Homer and the Circus Train (Gramatky) **22**:43

Homer Price (McCloskey) **7**:203

Homesick: My Own Story (Fritz) **14**:117

The Homeward Bounders (Jones) **23**:190

The Homework Machine (Williams and Abrashkin) **8**:223

Hominids: A Look Back at Our Ancestors (Sattler) **24**:222

The Honest Thief: A Hungarian Folktale (Biro) **28**:32

Honestly, Katie John! (Calhoun) **42**:9

Honey, I Love and Other Love Poems (Leo and Diane Dillon) **44**:34

A Honey of a Chimp (Klein) **19**:92

The Honeybee and the Robber: A Moving / Picture Book (Carle) **10**:84

Hongry Catch the Foolish Boy (Graham) **10**:110

Honker: The Story of a Wild Goose (McClung) **11**:183

Honkers (Yolen) **44**:201

Honor Bright: A Story for Girls (Richards) **54**:168

Honor Bright's New Adventure (Richards) **54**:168

Hoof and Claw (Roberts) **33**:204

Hoofprint on the Wind (Clark) **16**:83

Hoops (Myers) **16**:139

Hooray for Diffendoofer Day! (Dr. Seuss) **53**:143

Hooray for Me! (Charlip) **8**:31; **15**:143

Hoover's Bride (Small) **53**:156

Hop Aboard, Here We Go! (Scarry) **41**:165

Hop on Pop (Dr. Seuss) **1**:86; **9**:187

Hopper (Pfister) **42**:135

Hopper Hunts for Spring (Pfister) **42**:135

Horace (Keller) **45**:55

Horatio (Foreman) **32**:86

Hormones (Nourse) **33**:142

Horn Crown (Norton) **50**:162

The Horn of Roland (Williams) **8**:229

Horned Helmet (Treece) **2**:185

The Horns of Danger (Allan) **43**:33

Horror, Fright, and Panic: Emotions that Affect Our Lives (Hyde) **23**:163

Horse (Gardam) **12**:170

A Horse and a Hound, a Goat and a Gander (Provensen and Provensen) **11**:213

The Horse and His Boy (Lewis) **3**:134; **27**:104-51

A Horse Came Running (DeJong) **1**:57

The Horse Comes First (Calhoun) **42**:20

The Horse Hunters (Peck) **45**:121

The Horse in the Camel Suit (Pene du Bois) **1**:64

The Horse, the Fox, and the Lion (Galdone) **16**:92

Horse with Eight Hands (Phipson) **5**:183

The Horse Without a Head (Berna) **19**:33

Horsemaster (Singer) **48**:128

Horses (Brown) **10**:53

Horses and Their Wild Relatives (Patent) **19**:156

A Horse's Body (Cole) **5**:66

Horses of America (Patent) **19**:157

Horses of Dreamland (Duncan) **29**:78

The Horses The Indians Rode (Lavine) **35**:155

Horseshoe Crab (McClung) **11**:184

Horton Hatches the Egg (Dr. Seuss) **9**:174

Horton Hears a Who! (Dr. Seuss) **1**:86; **9**:179

The Hospital Book (Howe) **9**:57

The Hospitals (Fisher) **18**:129

The Hostage (Taylor) **30**:194

Hot and Cold (Adler) **27**:13

Hot-Air Henry (Calhoun) **42**:28

Hotel for Dogs (Duncan) **29**:69

Hotline (Hyde) **23**:161

The Hotshot (Slote) **4**:202

Houn' Dog (Calhoun) **42**:6

The Hound of Ulster (Sutcliff) **1**:186; **37**:158

The Hounds of the Morrigan (O'Shea) **18**:167

The House at Pooh Corner (Milne) **26**:126

A House by the Sea (Ryder) **37**:100

A House for Spinner's Grandmother (Unnerstad) **36**:200

The House Gobbaleen (Alexander) **48**:27

The House in Cornwall (Streatfeild)
  See *The Secret of the Lodge*

The House in Norham Gardens (Lively) **7**:158

The House in the Water: A Book of Animal Life (Roberts) **33**:201

A House Is a House for Me (Hoberman) **22**:113

A House like a Lotus (L'Engle) **14**:154

The House of a Hundred Windows (Brown) **10**:53

The House of a Mouse (Fisher) **49**:59

The House of Cornwall (Streatfeild)
  See *The Secret of the Lodge*

The House of Dies Drear (Hamilton) **1**:103

The House of Four Seasons (Duvoisin) **23**:100

The House of Hanover: England in the Eighteenth Century (Garfield) **21**:111

The House of Secrets (Bawden) **2**:12; **51**:13

The House of Sixty Fathers (DeJong) **1**:58

House of Stairs (Sleator) **29**:200

The House of Thirty Cats (Calhoun) **42**:10

The House of Wings (Byars) **1**:36

The House on Hackman's Hill (Nixon) **24**:147

The House on the Shore (Dillon) **26**:21

The House that Jack Built (Caldecott) **14**:73

The House that Jack Built (Galdone) **16**:90

The House that Sailed Away (Hutchins) **20**:148

The House with a Clock in its Walls (Bellairs) **37**:7

The House with Roots (Willard) **2**:218

The House You Pass on the Way (Woodson) **49**:207

Houseboat Girl (Lenski) **26**:120

The Housenapper (Curry)
  See *Mindy's Mysterious Miniature*

Houses (Adler) **27**:18

The Houses The Indians Built (Lavine) **35**:155

How a House Happens (Adkins) **7**:19

The How and Why of Growing (Milne and Milne) **22**:122

How Animals Behave (Bendick) **5**:48

How Animals Defend Their Young (Freedman) **20**:80

How Animals Learn (Freedman) **20**:75

How Animals Live Together (Selsam) **1**:162

How Animals Tell Time (Selsam) **1**:163

How Beastly! (Yolen) **4**:266

How Birds Fly (Freedman) **20**:79

How Did We Find Out about Atoms? (Asimov) **12**:53

How Did We Find Out about Black Holes? (Asimov) **12**:56

How Did We Find Out about Coal? (Asimov) **12**:58

How Did We Find Out about Comets? (Asimov) **12**:52

How Did We Find Out about Computers? (Asimov) **12**:63

How Did We Find Out about Dinosaurs? (Asimov) **12**:50

How Did We Find Out about DNA? (Asimov) **12**:64

How Did We Find Out about Earthquakes? (Asimov) **12**:56

How Did We Find Out about Electricity? (Asimov) **12**:49

How Did We Find Out about Energy? (Asimov) **12**:52

How Did We Find Out about Genes? (Asimov) **12**:62

How Did We Find Out about Life in the Deep Sea? (Asimov) **12**:60

How Did We Find Out about Nuclear Power? (Asimov) **12**:53

How Did We Find Out about Numbers? (Asimov) **12**:50

How Did We Find Out about Oil? (Asimov) **12**:58

How Did We Find Out about Our Human Roots? (Asimov) **12**:58

How Did We Find Out about Outer Space? (Asimov) **12**:55

How Did We Find Out about Solar Power? (Asimov) **12**:59

How Did We Find Out about the Atmosphere? (Asimov) **12**:64

How Did We Find Out about the Beginning of Life? (Asimov) **12**:60

How Did We Find Out about the Universe? (Asimov) **12**:61

How Did We Find Out about Vitamins? (Asimov) **12**:51

How Did We Find Out the Earth Is Round? (Asimov) **12**:48

How Do Apples Grow? (Betsy and Giulio Maestro) **45**:85

How Do I Eat It? (Watanabe) **8**:216

How Do I Go? (Hoberman) **22**:108

How Do I Put It On? Getting Dressed (Watanabe) **8**:216

How Do You Lose Those Ninth Grade Blues? (DeClements) **23**:35

How Do You Make an Elephant Float? and Other Delicious Riddles (Hopkins) **44**:93

How Droofus the Dragon Lost His Head (Peet) **12**:201

How Giraffe Got Such a Long Neck—And Why Rhino Is So Grumpy (Rosen) **45**:147

How God Fix Jonah (Graham) **10**:104

How Green You Are! (Doherty) **21**:55

How Heredity Works: Why Living Things Are as They Are (Bendick) **5**:47

How, Hippo! (Brown) **12**:104

How I Broke Up With Ernie (Stine) **37**:112

How I Came to Be a Writer (Naylor) **17**:53

How Insects Communicate (Patent) **19**:149

How It Feels When a Parent Dies (Krementz) **5**:155

How Lazy Can You Get? (Naylor) **17**:54

How Life Began (Adler) **27**:8

How Life Began (Berger) **32**:45

How Life Began: Creation versus Evolution (Gallant) **30**:92

How Many Days to America? A Thanksgiving Story (Bunting) **28**:62

How Many Kids Are Hiding on My Block? (Merrill) **52**:110

How Many Miles to Babylon? (Fox) **1**:77

How Many Spots Does a Leopard Have? And Other Tales (Lester) **41**:107

How Many Teeth? (Showers) **6**:242

How Much and How Many: The Story of Weights and Measures (Bendick) **5**:35

How My Family Lives in America (Kuklin) **51**:108

How Pizza Came to Queens (Khalsa) **30**:149

How Pizza Came to Our Town (Khalsa) **30**:149

How Puppies Grow (Selsam) **1**:163

How Rabbit Tricked His Friends (Tresselt) **30**:211

How Santa Claus Had a Long and Difficult Journey Delivering His Presents (Krahn) **3**:104

How Six Found Christmas (Hyman) **50**:71

How Summer Came to Canada (Cleaver) **13**:65

How the Animals Got Their Colours: Animal Myths from Around the World (Rosen) **45**:144

How the Doctor Knows You're Fine (Cobb) **2**:65

How the Grinch Stole Christmas (Dr. Seuss) **1**:86; **9**:184

How the Leopard Got His Skin (Achebe) **20**:8

How the Reindeer Saved Santa (Haywood) **22**:105

How the Sun Was Brought Back to the Sky: Adapted from a Slovenian Folk Tale (Ginsburg) **45**:8

How the Whale Became (Hughes) **3**:92

How to Be a Hero (Weiss) **4**:225

How to Be a Space Scientist in Your Own Home (Simon) **9**:218

How to Be an Inventor (Weiss) **4**:230

How to be Funny: An Extremely Silly Guidebook (Stine) **37**:103

How to Behave and Why (Leaf) **25**:129

How to Eat Fried Worms (Rockwell) **6**:236

How to Eat Fried Worms and Other Plays (Rockwell) **6**:239

How to Get Out of the Bath and Other Problems (Rosen) **45**:133

How to Make a Cloud (Bendick) **5**:44

How to Make an Earthquake (Krauss) **42**:118

How to Make Your Own Books (Weiss) **4**:227

How to Make Your Own Movies: An Introduction to Filmmaking (Weiss) **4**:227

How to Read a Rabbit (Fritz) **14**:112

How to Run a Railroad: Everything You Need to Know about Model Trains (Weiss) **4**:228

How Tom Beat Captain Najork and His Hired Sportsmen (Blake) **31**:19

How Tom Beat Captain Najork and His Hired Sportsmen (Hoban) **3**:78

How We Found Out about Vitamins (Asimov) **12**:51

How We Got Our First Cat (Tobias) **4**:218

How Wilka Went to Sea: And Other Tales from West of the Urals (Ginsburg) **45**:8

How You Talk (Showers) **6**:242

How You Were Born (Cole) **40**:7

How Your Mother and Father Met, and What Happened After (Tobias) **4**:217

Howard (Stevenson) **17**:156

Howliday Inn (Howe) **9**:58

Howl's Moving Castle (Jones) **23**:195

Hubert's Hair-Raising Adventure (Peet) **12**:193

Hug Me (Stren) **5**:230

Huge Harold (Peet) **12**:194

Hugo (Gripe) **5**:142

Hugo and Josephine (Gripe) **5**:143

Hugo och Josefin (Gripe) **5**:143

The Hullabaloo ABC (Cleary) **2**:47

The Human Body: How We Evolved (Cole) **40**:16

The Human Body: Its Structure and Operation (Asimov) **12**:37

Human Nature-Animal Nature: The Biology of Human Behavior (Cohen) **3**:40

The Human Rights Book (Meltzer) **13**:140

Humbert, Mister Firkin, and the Lord Mayor of London (Burningham) **9**:40

Humbug (Bawden) **51**:38

Humbug Mountain (Fleischman) **15**:109

Humphrey: One Hundred Years along the Wayside with a Box Turtle (Flack) **28**:123

Hunches in Bunches (Dr. Seuss) **9**:194

Der Hund Herr Müller (Heine) **18**:145

The Hundred Islands (Clark) **30**:61

A Hundred Million Francs (Berna) **19**:33

The Hundred Penny Box (Leo and Diane Dillon) **44**:24

The Hundred Penny Box (Mathis) **3**:149

The Hundredth Dove and Other Tales (Yolen) **4**:264

Hungarian Folk-Tales (Biro) **28**:34

Hungry Fred (Fox) **44**:61

Hungry, Hungry Sharks (Cole) **40**:13

The Hungry Leprechaun (Calhoun) **42**:9

Huni (French) **37**:34

Hunt the Thimble (French) **37**:43

Hunted in Their Own Land (Chauncy) **6**:92

Hunted Like a Wolf: The Story of the Seminole War (Meltzer) **13**:129

Hunted Mammals of the Sea (McClung) **11**:191

Hunter and His Dog (Wildsmith) **52**:185

The Hunter and the Animals: A Wordless Picture Book (dePaola) **24**:89

Hunter in the Dark (Hughes) **9**:74

Hunters and the Hunted: Surviving in the Animal World (Patent) **19**:156

The Hunting of Shadroth (Kelleher) **36**:116

The Hunting of the Snark: An Agony in Eight Fits (Carroll) **2**:34

Huon of the Horn (Norton) **50**:134

The Hurdy-Gurdy Man (Bianco) **19**:53

Hurrah, We're Outward Bound! (Spier) **5**:219

Hurray for Monty Ray! (McBratney) **44**:128

Hurricane (Wiesner) **43**:207

Hurricane Guest (Epstein and Epstein) **26**:59

Hurricane Watch (Betsy and Giulio Maestro) **45**:76

Hurricane Watch (Branley) **13**:51

Hurricanes and Twisters (Adler) **27**:6

Hurry Home, Candy (DeJong) **1**:58

Hurry Hurry: A Tale of Calamity and Woe; or a Lesson in Leisure (Hurd and Hurd) **49**:114

The Hypnotiser (Rosen) **45**:137

I, Adam (Fritz) **2**:81

I Am a Clown (Bruna) **7**:52

I Am a Hunter (Mayer) **11**:165

I Am a Man: Ode to Martin Luther King, Jr. (Merriam) **14**:197

I Am Not Going to Get Up Today! (Dr. Seuss) **53**:139

I Am Papa Snap and These Are My Favorite No Such Stories (Ungerer) **3**:201

I Am Phoenix: Poems for Two Voices (Fleischman) **20**:67

I Am Somebody! A Biography of Jesse Jackson (Haskins) **39**:67

I Am the Cheese (Cormier) **12**:139

I Am the Running Girl (Adoff) **7**:35

I Am the Universe (Corcoran) **50**:33

I Be Somebody (Irwin) **40**:110

I Can (Oxenbury) **22**:147

I Can Build a House! (Watanabe) **8**:217

I Can Count More (Bruna) **7**:51

I Can Do It! (Watanabe) **8**:217

I Can Fly (Krauss) **42**:115

I Can Read (Bruna) **7**:50

I Can Ride It! Setting Goals (Watanabe) **8**:217

I Can Take a Walk! (Watanabe) **8**:217

I Can—Can You? (Parish) **22**:165

I Can't Stand Losing You (Kemp) **29**:123

I Don't Live Here! (Conrad) **18**:86

I Don't Want to Go to Bed (Lindgren) **39**:163

I Feel a Little Jumpy around You: A Book of Her Poems and His Poems (Janeczko) **47**:117

I Feel the Same Way (Moore) **15**:141

I Go by Sea, I Go by Land (Travers) **2**:178

I grandi pittori (Ventura) **16**:197

I Had Trouble in Getting to Solla Sollew (Dr. Seuss) **9**:189

I Hadn't Meant to Tell You This (Woodson) **49**:204

I Hate My Teddy Bear (McKee) **38**:171

I Hate You, I Hate You (Leaf) **25**:135

I Have a Dream: The Life and Words of Martin Luther King, Jr. (Haskins) **39**:71

I Have a Song to Sing You: Still More Rhymes (Richards) **54**:173

I Have Four Names for My Grandfather (Lasky) **11**:114

I Have to Go! (Munsch) **19**:145

I Hear (Oxenbury) **22**:147

I, Houdini: The Autobiography of a Self-Educated Hamster (Reid Banks) **24**:193

I Klockornas Tid (Gripe) **5**:145

I Know a City: The Story of New York's Growth (Shippen) **36**:174

I Know a Policeman (Williams) **48**:188

I Know What You Did Last Summer (Duncan) **29**:70

I Know Why the Caged Bird Sings (Angelou) **53**:9

I Like Old Clothes (Hoberman) **22**:112

I Like Weather (Fisher) **49**:39

I Like Winter (Lenski) **26**:115

I Love Guinea Pigs (King-Smith) **40**:173

I Love My Mother (Zindel) **3**:248

I Love You, Stupid! (Mazer) **16**:131

I Loved Rose Ann (Hopkins) **44**:88

I Marched with Hannibal (Baumann) **35**:44

I Met a Man (Ciardi) **19**:76

I, Momolu (Graham) **10**:106

I Need a Lunch Box (Caines) **24**:64

I Need a Lunch Box (Cummings) **48**:49

I Never Asked You to Understand Me (DeClements) **23**:36

I Never Loved Your Mind (Zindel) **3**:248
I Own the Racecourse! (Wrightson) **4**:242
I Read Signs (Hoban) **13**:107
I Read Symbols (Hoban) **13**:107
I Sailed with Columbus (Schlein) **41**:197
I Saw a Ship A-Sailing (Domanska) **40**:43
I Saw the Sea Come In (Tresselt) **30**:205
I See (Oxenbury) **22**:147
I See a Song (Carle) **10**:76
I See a Voice (Rosen) **45**:131
I See the Moon: Good-Night Poems and Lullabies (Pfister) **42**:135
I See What I See! (Selden) **8**:197
I Shall Not Be Moved (Angelou) **53**:16
I Sing the Song of Myself: An Anthology of Auto-biographical Poems (Kherdian) **24**:109
I Smell Honey (Pinkney) **54**:149
I Stay Near You: One Story in Three (Kerr) **29**:155
I Stood Upon a Mountain (Fisher) **49**:56
I Thought I Heard the City (Moore) **15**:142
I Touch (Oxenbury) **22**:147
I, Trissy (Mazer) **23**:221
I, Tut: The Boy Who Became Pharaoh (Schlein) **41**:188
I Walk and Read (Hoban) **13**:108
I Want a Brother or Sister (Lindgren) **39**:159
I Want a Dog (Khalsa) **30**:146
I Want to Go Home! (Korman) **25**:106
I Want to Go to School Too (Lindgren) **39**:159
I Want to Paint My Bathroom Blue (Krauss) **42**:121
I Want to Stay Here! I Want to Go There! A Flea Story (Lionni) **7**:137
I Was Born in a Tree and Raised by Bees (Arnosky) **15**:2
I Was There (Richter) **21**:189
I Wear the Morning Star (Highwater) **17**:32
I Went for a Walk (Lenski) **26**:120
I Wish I Had a Pirate Suit (Allen) **44**:11
I Wish I Had an Afro (Shearer) **34**:166
I Wish That I Had Duck Feet (Dr. Seuss) **1**:87; **9**:189
I Wish You Love (Corcoran) **50**:22
I Wonder How, I Wonder Why (Fisher) **49**:38
I Would Rather Be a Turnip (Cleaver and Cleaver) **6**:106
I Write It (Krauss) **42**:128
The Ice Ghosts Mystery (Curry) **31**:77
The Ice Is Coming (Wrightson) **4**:245
Ice Magic (Christopher) **33**:47
If All the Seas Were One Sea (Domanska) **40**:41
If All the Swords in England (Willard) **2**:219
If Dinosaurs Were Cats and Dogs (McNaughton) **54**:52
If Dragon Flies Made Honey: Poems (Kherdian) **24**:108
If He's My Brother (Williams) **48**:193
If I Asked You, Would You Stay? (Bunting) **28**:56
If I Had... (Mayer) **11**:164
If I Had My Way (Klein) **2**:98
If I Love You, Am I Trapped Forever? (Kerr) **29**:144
If I Owned a Candy Factory (Stevenson) **17**:152
If I Ran the Circus (Dr. Seuss) **1**:87; **9**:181
If I Ran the Zoo (Dr. Seuss) **1**:87; **9**:178
If It Weren't for Sebastian (Ure) **34**:174
If It Weren't for You (Zolotow) **2**:234
If Only I Could Tell You: Poems for Young Lovers and Dreamers (Merriam) **14**:201
If the Earth Falls In (Clark) **30**:61
If This Is Love, I'll Take Spaghetti (Conford) **10**:98
If Wishes Were Horses and Other Rhymes from Mother Goose (Jeffers) **30**:133

If You Grew Up with Abraham Lincoln (McGovern) **50**:112
If You Lived in Colonial Times (McGovern) **50**:111
If You Lived on Mars (Berger) **32**:43
If You Lived with the Circus (McGovern) **50**:115
If You Lived with the Sioux Indians (McGovern) **50**:117
If You Love Me, Let Me Go (St. John) **46**:107
If You Sailed on the Mayflower (McGovern) **50**:115
If You Say So, Claude (Nixon) **24**:141
If You Walk Down This Road (Duke) **51**:53
If You Were a Writer (Nixon) **24**:151
Iggie's House (Blume) **2**:17
Ik ben een clown (Bruna) **7**:52
Ik kan lezen (Bruna) **7**:50
Iktomi and the Boulder: A Plains Indian Story (Goble) **21**:137
Il venditore di animali (Munari) **9**:124
Il viaggio di Colombo (Ventura) **16**:193
Il viaggio di Marco Polo (Ventura) **16**:194
I'll Always Love You (Wilhelm) **46**:161
I'll Be You and You Be Me (Krauss) **42**:119
I'll Get There; It Better Be Worth the Trip (Donovan) **3**:52
I'll Go My Own Way (Hunter) **25**:90
I'll Love You When You're More Like Me (Kerr) **29**:147
I'll Make You Small (Wynne-Jones) **21**:230
Illinois (Carter) **22**:22
The Illustrated Dinosaur Dictionary (Sattler) **24**:218
The Illustrated Marguerite Henry (Henry) **4**:116
The Illyrian Adventure (Alexander) **48**:15
Ilse Janda, 14 (Noestlinger) **12**:186
I'm Going to Sing: Black American Spirituals, Volume 2 (Bryan) **18**:35
I'm Gonna Make You Love Me: The Story of Diana Ross (Haskins) **39**:39
I'm Hiding (Livingston) **7**:168
I'm in the Zoo, Too! (Ashabranner) **28**:13
I'm Only Afraid of the Dark (At Night!) (Stren) **5**:235
I'm Really Dragged but Nothing Gets Me Down (Hentoff) **1**:107; **52**:54
I'm the King of the Castle! Playing Alone (Watanabe) **8**:217
I'm Trying to Tell You (Ashley) **4**:18
I'm Waiting (Livingston) **7**:169
The Image Game (St. John) **46**:126
Imagine If (Heine) **18**:146
Immigrant Kids (Freedman) **20**:81
Imogene's Antlers (Small) **53**:148
The Imp That Ate My Homework (Yep) **54**:203
The Importance of Crocus (Duvoisin) **23**:107
The Important Book (Brown) **10**:57
Important Dates in Afro-American History (Hopkins) **44**:86
The Important Visitor (Oxenbury) **22**:145
The Impossible People: A History Natural and Unnatural of Beings Terrible and Wonderful (McHargue) **2**:118
Impossible, Possum (Conford) **10**:90
The Improbable Adventures of Marvelous O'Hara Soapstone (Oneal) **13**:155
The Improbable Book of Records (Blake) See *The Puffin Book of Improbable Records*
The Improbable Book of Records (Yeoman) **46**:178
Impunity Jane: The Story of a Pocket Doll (Freedman) **20**:127
In a Beaver Valley: How Beavers Change the Land (Pringle) **4**:175
In a Blue Velvet Dress: Almost a Ghost Story (Waddell) **31**:176

In a Forgotten Place (Orgel) **48**:76
In a People House (Dr. Seuss) **9**:192
In a Place of Danger (Fox) **44**:69
In Crack Willow Wood (McBratney) **44**:131
In for Winter, Out for Spring (Pinkney) **43**:167
In Lane Three, Alex Archer (Duder) **43**:64
In My Boat (Betsy and Giulio Maestro) **45**:67
In My Father's House (Rinaldi) **46**:85
In My Garden (Zolotow) **2**:235
In My Mother's House (Clark) **16**:75
In My Own Time: Almost an Autobiography (Bawden) **51**:41
In My Tent (Singer) **48**:140
In Nueva York (Mohr) **22**:132
In One Door and Out the Other: A Book of Poems (Fisher) **49**:52
In Powder and Crinoline: Old Fairy Tales (Nielsen) **16**:155
In School: Learning in Four Languages (Hautzig) **22**:83
In Search of Ancient Crete (Ventura) **16**:196
In Search of Ghosts (Cohen) **3**:40
In Search of Pompeii (Ventura) **16**:196
In Search of Troy (Ventura) **16**:196
In Search of Tutankhamun (Ventura) **16**:196
In Spite of All Terror (Burton) **1**:32
In Summer Light (Oneal) **13**:158
In Summertime It's Tuffy (Gaberman) **33**:2
In the Beginning: Creation Stories from Around the World (Hamilton) **40**:79
In the Beginning: Creation Stories From Around the World (Moser) **49**:172
In the Company of Clowns: A Commedia (Bacon) **3**:11
In the Country of Ourselves (Hentoff) **1**:108; **52**:56
In the Face of Danger (Nixon) **24**:153
In the Flaky Frosty Morning (Kuskin) **4**:140
In the Forest (Ets) **33**:75
In the Land of Small Dragon (Clark) **16**:85
In the Land of Ur: The Discovery of Ancient Mesopotamia (Baumann) **35**:50
In the Middle of the Night (Fisher) **49**:41
In the Middle of the Trees (Kuskin) **4**:135
In the Middle of the World (Korinetz) **4**:130
In the Night Kitchen (Sendak) **1**:168; **17**:118
In the Palace of the Ocean King (Singer) **48**:146
In the Park: An Excursion in Four Languages (Hautzig) **22**:82
In the Rabbitgarden (Lionni) **7**:136
In the Time of the Bells (Gripe) **5**:145
In the Woods, In the Meadow, In the Sky (Fisher) **49**:43
In Their Own Words: A History of the American Negro, Vol. I: 1619-1865, Vol. II: 1865-1916; Vol. III: 1916-1966 (Meltzer) **13**:121
In Your Own Words: A Beginner's Guide to Writing (Cassedy) **26**:13
In-Between Miya (Uchida) **6**:255
The Inca (McKissack) **23**:237
Inca and Spaniard: Pizarro and the Conquest of Peru (Marrin) **53**:87
Inch by Inch (Lionni) **7**:128
Incident at Loring Groves (Levitin) **53**:68
The Incredible Journey (Burnford) **2**:19
The Incredible Journey of Lewis and Clark (Blumberg) **21**:30
The Incredible Television Machine (LeShan) **6**:189
Independent Voices (Merriam) **14**:195
India Under Indira and Rajiv Gandhi (Haskins) **39**:59
Indian Captive: The Story of Mary Jemison (Lenski) **26**:105
Indian Chiefs (Freedman) **20**:86

Indian Corn and Other Gifts (Lavine) **35**:153
Indian Encounters: An Anthology of Stories and Poems (Coatsworth) **2**:59
Indian Festivals (Showers) **6**:245
The Indian in the Cupboard (Reid Banks) **24**:194
Indian Mound Farm (Coatsworth) **2**:59
Indian Summer (Monjo) **2**:121
Indians (Tunis) **2**:193
The Indy 500 (Murphy) **53**:103
Ingri and Edgar Parin d'Aulaire's Book of Greek Myths (d'Aulaire and d'Aulaire) **21**:52
Inky Pinky Ponky: Children's Playground Rhymes (Rosen) **45**:132
The Inn-Keepers Apprentice (Say) **22**:209
In-Out: At the Park (McNaughton) **54**:53
Insect Masquerades (Simon) **39**:184
Insect Worlds: A Guide for Man on the Making of the Environment (Milne and Milne) **22**:123
An Insect's Body (Cole) **40**:6
Inside Jazz (Collier) **3**:45
Inside Out (Martin) **32**:200
Inside, Outside, Upside Down (Berenstain and Berenstain) **19**:26
Inside: Seeing Beneath the Surface (Adkins) **7**:21
Inside the Atom (Asimov) **12**:31
Inside Turtle's Shell, and Other Poems of the Field (Ryder) **37**:87
Inspector Peckit (Freeman) **30**:78
Integers: Positive and Negative (Adler) **27**:25
Intelligence: What Is It? (Cohen) **3**:41
Inter-City (Keeping) **34**:103
Interstellar Pig (Sleator) **29**:203
Into a Strange Land: Unaccompanied Refugee Youth in America (Ashabranner and Ashabranner) **28**:10
Into the Deep Forest with Henry David Thoreau (Murphy) **53**:114
Into the Dream (Sleator) **29**:210
Into the Woods: Exploring the Forest Ecosystem (Pringle) **4**:178
The Intruder (Townsend) **2**:172
The Invaders: Three Stories (Treece) **2**:185
The Inventors: Nobel Prizes in Chemistry, Physics, and Medicine (Aaseng) **54**:13
The Invisible Dog (King-Smith) **40**:166
The Inway Investigators; or, The Mystery at McCracken's Place (Yolen) **4**:258
IOU's (Sebestyen) **17**:91
Irma and Jerry (Selden) **8**:201
Iron Cage (Norton) **50**:154
The Iron Giant: A Story in Five Nights (Hughes) **3**:92
Iron John (Hyman) **50**:83
The Iron Lily (Willard) **2**:220
The Iron Lion (Dickinson) **29**:42
Iron Mountain (Clark) **30**:59
The Iron Ring (Alexander) **48**:29
The Iron Way (Cross) **28**:85
Irrepressible Spirit: Conversations with Human Rights Activists (Kuklin) **51**:114
Irrigations: Changing Deserts into Gardens (Adler) **27**:17
Is Anybody There? (Bunting) **28**:63
Is It Larger? Is It Smaller? (Hoban) **13**:110
Is It Red? Is It Yellow? Is It Blue? An Adventure in Color (Hoban) **13**:104
Is It Rough? Is It Smooth? Is It Shiny? (Hoban) **13**:109
Is That You, Miss Blue? (Kerr) **29**:146
Is There Life in Outer Space? (Branley) **13**:50
Is This a Baby Dinosaur? (Selsam) **1**:163
Is This Kid "Crazy"? Understanding Unusual Behavior (Hyde) **23**:169

Is This You? (Krauss) **42**:120
Isaac Campion (Howker) **14**:130
Isaac Newton: Mastermind of Modern Science (Knight) **38**:98
Isabel's Noel (Yolen) **4**:257
Isamu Noguchi: The Life of a Sculptor (Tobias) **4**:214
The Isis Pedlar (Hughes) **9**:75
Isla (Dorros) **42**:73
The Island (Paulsen) **19**:177; **54**:93
Island Baby (Keller) **45**:57
Island Boy (Cooney) **23**:32
An Island in a Green Sea (Allan) **43**:22
The Island Keeper (Mazer) **16**:130
The Island of Ghosts (Dillon) **26**:33
The Island of Horses (Dillon) **26**:22
The Island of Nose (Schmidt) **22**:222
Island of Ogres (Namioka) **48**:64
The Island of One (Bunting) **28**:48
Island of the Blue Dolphins (O'Dell) **1**:146; **16**:163
The Island of the Grass King: The Further Adventures of Anatole (Willard) **5**:248
The Island of the Skog (Kellogg) **6**:172
Island of the Strangers (Waddell) **31**:181
Island of Wild Horses (Scott) **20**:198
The Island on Bird Street (Orlev) **30**:164
L'Isle noire (Herge) **6**:148
Isle of the Sea Horse (Brinsmead) **47**:10
It Ain't All for Nothin' (Myers) **4**:158
It Can't Hurt Forever (Singer) **48**:121
It Doesn't Always Have to Rhyme (Merriam) **14**:193
It Figures!: Fun Figures of Speech (Betsy and Giulio Maestro) **45**:87
It Happened in Arles (Allan) **43**:13
It Happened in Pinsk (Yorinks) **20**:216
It Happened One Summer (Phipson) **5**:178
It Looks Like Snow: A Picture Book (Charlip) **8**:26
It Started in Madeira (Allan) **43**:16
It Started with Old Man Bean (Kherdian) **24**:110
It's a Gingerbread House: Bake It! Build It! Eat It! (Williams) **9**:230
It's a New Day: Poems for Young Brothas and Sistuhs (Sanchez) **18**:200
It's about Time (Schlein) **41**:178
It's an Aardvark-Eat-Turtle World (Danziger) **20**:55
It's Christmas (Prelutsky) **13**:169
It's Getting Beautiful Now (Calhoun) **42**:17
It's Halloween (Prelutsky) **13**:166
It's Hard to Read a Map with a Beagle on Your Lap (Singer) **48**:142
It's My Earth, Too: How I Can Help the Earth Stay Alive (Krull) **44**:103
It's Not the End of the World (Blume) **2**:17
It's Not What You Expect (Klein) **2**:98
It's OK If You Don't Love Me (Klein) **19**:89
It's Snowing! It's Snowing! (Prelutsky) **13**:171
It's Spring! (Minarik) **33**:127
It's Spring, She Said (Blos) **18**:14
It's Thanksgiving (Prelutsky) **13**:170
It's Time Now! (Tresselt) **30**:211
It's Too Frightening for Me! (Hughes) **15**:123
It's Too Noisy! (Duke) **51**:49
It's Up to Us (Matas) **52**:77
It's Valentine's Day (Prelutsky) **13**:171
It's Your Team: Baseball (Aaseng) **54**:11
Itsy-Bitsy Beasties: Poems from Around the World (Rosen) **45**:146
Izzy, Willy-Nilly (Voigt) **13**:238
Jack and Nancy (Blake) **31**:18
Jack and the Beanstalk (Biro) **28**:39

Jack and the Fire Dragon (Haley) **21**:148
Jack and the Meanstalk (Wildsmith) **52**:198
Jack and the Whoopee Wind (Calhoun) **42**:30
Jack Holborn (Garfield) **21**:95
Jack Horner's Pie: A Book of Nursery Rhymes (Lenski) **26**:98
Jack Jouett's Ride (Haley) **21**:143
Jack of Hearts (French) **37**:33
Jack the Treacle Eater (Causley) **30**:43
Jack the Treacle Eater (Keeping) **34**:110
Jack the Wise and the Cornish Cuckoos (Calhoun) **42**:24
Jackanapes (Caldecott) **14**:79
Jackaroo (Voigt) **13**:237
Jackie Robinson: Baseball's Gallant Fighter (Epstein and Epstein) **26**:65
Jackie, the Pit Pony (Baumann) **35**:41
Jackknife for a Penny (Epstein and Epstein) **26**:56
Jacko (Goodall) **25**:44
Jackpot of the Beagle Brigade (Epstein and Epstein) **26**:70
Jackrabbit Goalie (Christopher) **33**:53
Jack's Fantastic Voyage (Foreman) **32**:107
Jacob Have I Loved (Paterson) **7**:238; **50**:189
Jacob Two-Two and the Dinosaur (Richler) **17**:80
Jacob Two-Two Meets the Hooded Fang (Richler) **17**:73
Jafta (Lewin) **9**:90
Jafta—My Father (Lewin) **9**:90
Jafta—My Mother (Lewin) **9**:90
Jafta—The Journey (Lewin) **9**:92
Jafta—The Town (Lewin) **9**:92
Jafta—The Wedding (Lewin) **9**:90
Jaguarundi (Hamilton) **40**:90
Jahdu (Hamilton) **11**:82
Jahdu (Pinkney) **43**:157
Jake (Slote) **4**:199
Jamberoo Road (Spence) **26**:193
Jambo Means Hello: Swahili Alphabet Book (Feelings and Feelings) **5**:107
James (Park) **51**:183
James and the Giant Peach (Dahl) **1**:51; **7**:68
James and the Rain (Kuskin) **4**:134
James Bond in Win, Place, or Die (Stine) **37**:107
James Van Derzee: The Picture-Takin' Man (Haskins) **39**:36
Janaky and the Giant and Other Stories (Dhondy) **41**:80
Jane Martin, Dog Detective (Bunting) **28**:57
Jane, Wishing (Tobias) **4**:216
Jane Yolen's Mother Goose Songbook (Yolen) **44**:197
Janet Hamm Needs a Date for the Dance (Bunting) **28**:59
Janey (Zolotow) **2**:235
Jangle Twang (Burningham) **9**:51
Janie's Private Eyes (Snyder) **31**:168
Janni's Stork (Harris) **30**:123
Jar and Bottle Craft (Sattler) **24**:214
A Jar of Dreams (Uchida) **6**:259
The Jargoon Pard (Norton) **50**:155
Jasmine (Duvoisin) **23**:105
Jason and Marceline (Spinelli) **26**:203
Jason and the Money Tree (Levitin) **53**:59
Jason Bodger and the Priory Ghost (Kemp) **29**:120
Jay Bird (Ets) **33**:91
Jazz Country (Hentoff) **1**:108; **52**:52
The Jazz Man (Grifalconi) **35**:70
Jean and Johnny (Cleary) **2**:48; **8**:49
Jean D'Arc (Fisher) **49**:52
The Jedera Adventure (Alexander) **48**:20
Jeeter, Mason and the Magic Headset (Gaberman) **33**:14

Jeffrey Bear Cleans Up His Act (Steptoe)　**12**:241
Jeffrey Strangeways (Murphy)　**39**:177
Jellybean (Duder)　**43**:63
Jem's Island (Lasky)　**11**:117
The Jenius (King-Smith)　**40**:155
Jennie's Hat (Keats)　**1**:115; **35**:130
Jennifer and Josephine (Peet)　**12**:199
Jennifer, Hecate, Macbeth, William McKinley, and Me, Elizabeth (Konigsburg)　**1**:121
Jennifer Jean, the Cross-Eyed Queen (Naylor)　**17**:49
Jenny and Jupie to the Rescue (Fujikawa)　**25**:40
Jeremiah in the Dark Woods (Ahlberg and Ahlberg)　**18**:4
Jeremy Isn't Hungry (Williams)　**48**:196
Jesper (Matas)　**52**:81
Jesse (Soto)　**38**:206
Jesse and Abe (Isadora)　**7**:108
Jesse Jackson: A Biography (McKissack)　**23**:241
Jessica (Henkes)　**23**:130
Jethro and the Jumbie (Cooper)　**4**:49
The Jetty (Mattingley)　**24**:125
Jewelry from Junk (Sattler)　**24**:213
The Jewish Americans: A History in Their Own Words, 1650-1950 (Meltzer)　**13**:143
The Jews in America: A Picture Album (Meltzer)　**13**:150
The Jezebel Wolf (Monjo)　**2**:122
Jigger's Day Off (Morpurgo)　**51**:131
Jigsaw Continents (Berger)　**32**:18
Jim Along, Josie: A Collection of Folk Songs and Singing Games for Young Children (Langstaff)　**3**:110
Jim and the Beanstalk (Briggs)　**10**:23
Jim Bridger's Alarm Clock and Other Tall Tales (Fleischman)　**15**:110
Jim Button and Luke the Engine-Driver (Ende)　**14**:97
Jim Grey of Moonbah (Ottley)　**16**:187
Jim Knopf und Lukas der Lokomotivführer (Ende)　**14**:97
Jim: The Story of a Backwoods Police Dog (Roberts)　**33**:205
Jim-Dandy (Irwin)　**40**:115
Jimmy Has Lost His Cap: Where Can It Be? (Munari)　**9**:125
Jimmy Lee Did It (Cummings)　**48**:46
Jimmy of Cherry Valley (Rau)　**8**:186
Jimmy, the Pickpocket of the Palace (Napoli)　**51**:160
Jimmy Yellow Hawk (Sneve)　**2**:145
Jimmy Zest (McBratney)　**44**:119
The Jimmy Zest All-Stars (McBratney)　**44**:121
Jingle Bells (Kovalski)　**34**:116
Jingo Django (Fleischman)　**1**:74
Ji-Nongo-Nongo Means Riddles (Aardema)　**17**:5
Ji-Nongo-Nongo Means Riddles (Pinkney)　**43**:156
Jinx Glove (Christopher)　**33**:48
Jip: His Story (Paterson)　**50**:205
Jo in the Middle (Ure)　**34**:187
Joan of Arc (Williams)　**8**:225
Jobs in Fine Arts and Humanities (Berger)　**32**:12
Jobs That Save Our Environment (Berger)　**32**:11
Jock and Jill (Lipsyte)　**23**:208
Jock's Island (Coatsworth)　**2**:59
Jodie's Journey (Thiele)　**27**:211
Joe and the Snow (dePaola)　**4**:54
Johannes Kepler and Planetary Motion (Knight)　**38**:99
John and the Rarey (Wells)　**16**:203
John Barleycorn (French)　**37**:45
John Brown: A Cry for Freedom (Graham)　**10**:111
John Burningham's ABC (Burningham)　**9**:39

John Diamond (Garfield)　**21**:115
John Henry (Lester)　**41**:110
John Henry (Pinkney)　**43**:172
John Henry: An American Legend (Keats)　**1**:115; **35**:130
John Henry Davis (Leaf)　**25**:126
John J. Plenty and Fiddler Dan: A New Fable of the Grasshopper and the Ant (Ciardi)　**19**:78
John S. Goodall's Theatre: The Sleeping Beauty (Goodall)　**25**:50
Johnny Lion's Bad Day (Hurd and Hurd)　**49**:127
Johnny Lion's Book (Hurd and Hurd)　**49**:124
Johnny Long Legs (Christopher)　**33**:44
Johnny Maple-Leaf (Tresselt)　**30**:202
Johnny No Hit (Christopher)　**33**:52
Johnny the Clockmaker (Ardizzone)　**3**:4
Johnny Tremain: A Novel for Old and Young (Forbes)　**27**:57-74
Johnny's in the Basement (Sacher)　**28**:201
Jo-Jo the Melon Donkey (Morpurgo)　**51**:126
Jojo's Flying Side Kick (Pinkney)　**54**:144
Jokes from Black Folks (Haskins)　**3**:65
The Jolly Postman or Other People's Letters (Ahlberg and Ahlberg)　**18**:10
Jolly Roger and the Pirates of Abdul the Skinhead (McNaughton)　**54**:58
Jonah, the Fisherman (Zimnik)　**3**:243
Jonathan Cleaned Up, Then He Heard a Sound: Or, Blackberry Subway Jam (Munsch)　**19**:142
Jose Canseco: Baseball's Forty-Forty Man (Aaseng)　**44**:13
Josefin (Gripe)　**5**:142
Josefina February (Ness)　**6**:200
Joseph and His Brothers: From the Story Told in the Book of Genesis (Petersham and Petersham)　**24**:169
Josephine (Gripe)　**5**:142
Joseph's Other Red Sock (Daly)　**41**:54
Joseph's Yard (Keeping)　**34**:91
Josh (Southall)　**2**:153
The Journey (Marsden)　**34**:148
Journey (Thomas)　**19**:22
The Journey Back (Reiss)　**19**:218
Journey behind the Wind (Wrightson)　**4**:247
Journey between Worlds (Engdahl)　**2**:70
Journey by First Camel (Konigsburg) See *Journey to an 800 Number*
Journey Cake, Ho! (Sawyer)　**36**:161
Journey from Peppermint Street (DeJong)　**1**:58
Journey Home (Uchida)　**6**:258
Journey into a Black Hole (Branley)　**13**:52
Journey into Jazz (Hentoff)　**52**:56
Journey to America (Levitin)　**53**:56
Journey to an 800 Number (*Journey by First Camel*) (Konigsburg)　**47**:139
A Journey to England (Unnerstad)　**36**:194
Journey to Jericho (O'Dell)　**1**:147
Journey to Jo'burg (Naidoo)　**29**:162
Journey to the Planets (Lauber)　**16**:120
Journey to Topaz: A Story of the Japanese-American Evacuation (Uchida)　**6**:256
Journey to Untor (Wibberley)　**3**:228
The Journey with Grandmother (Unnerstad)　**36**:192
The Journey with Jonah (L'Engle)　**1**:130
Journeys of Sebastian (Krahn)　**3**:105
Joy to the World: Christmas Legends (Sawyer)　**36**:165
Joyful Noise: Poems or Two Voices (Fleischman)　**20**:68
Juan and the Asuangs (Aruego)　**5**:28
Juanita (Politi)　**29**:186

Judgment on Janus (Norton)　**50**:142
Judith Teaches (Allan)　**43**:4
Judy and the Baby Elephant (Haar)　**15**:116
Judy the Bad Fairy (Waddell)　**31**:195
Judy's Journey (Lenski)　**26**:111
Jules Verne: Portrait of a Prophet (Freedman)　**20**:74
Julian (Khalsa)　**30**:150
Julia's House (Gripe)　**5**:147
Julias Hus och Nattpappan (Gripe)　**5**:147
Julie of the Wolves (George)　**1**:90
Julie's Tree (Calhoun)　**42**:31
Julius (Pilkey)　**48**:105
Jumanji (Van Allsburg)　**5**:239
The Jumblies (Gorey)　**36**:92
Jumbo Spencer (Cresswell)　**18**:98
Jump Ball: A Basketball Season in Poems (Glenn)　**51**:94
Jump on Over! The Adventures of Brer Rabbit and His Family (Moser)　**49**:174
Jumper Goes to School (Parish)　**22**:158
Jumping (McNaughton)　**54**:56
Jumping the Nail (Bunting)　**28**:67
June 7! (Aliki)　**9**:23
June 29, 1999 (Wiesner)　**43**:213
June Anne June Spoon and Her Very Adventurous Search for the Moon (Kuskin)　**4**:139
Jungle Beasts and Men (Mukerji)　**10**:130
The Jungle Book (Kipling)　**39**:74-118
Jungle Jingles (King-Smith)　**40**:161
Junie B. Jones and a Little Monkey Business (Park)　**34**:163
Junie B. Jones and Her Big Fat Mouth (Park)　**34**:164
Junie B. Jones and the Stupid Smelly Bus (Park)　**34**:162
Junior Intern (Nourse)　**33**:130
The Junior Thunder Lord (Yep)　**54**:196
Juniper: A Mystery (Kemp)　**29**:122
The Juniper Tree and Other Tales from Grimm (Sendak)　**1**:169
Junius Over Far (Hamilton)　**11**:92
Junk Castle (Klein)　**21**:159
Junk Day on Juniper Street and Other Easy-to-Read Stories (Moore)　**15**:142
Jupiter Boots (Nimmo)　**44**:145
Jupiter: King of the Gods, Giant of the Planets (Branley)　**13**:46
Jupiter: The Largest Planet (Asimov)　**12**:49
Just a Summer Romance (Martin)　**32**:203
Just Across the Street (Field)　**21**:78
Just An Overnight Guest (Tate)　**37**:187
Just as Long as We're Together (Blume)　**15**:82
Just between Us (Pfeffer)　**11**:200
Just Cats: Learning Groups (Burningham)　**9**:50
Just Ferret (Kemp)　**29**:125
Just Juice (Hesse)　**54**:41
Just Like Archie (Daly)　**41**:58
Just Like Everyone Else (Bunting)　**28**:47
Just Like Everyone Else (Kuskin)　**4**:135
Just Like Me (Ormerod)　**20**:179
Just Like Me (Schlein)　**41**:180
Just Me (Ets)　**33**:89
Just Me and My Dad (Mayer)　**11**:172
Just Morgan (Pfeffer)　**11**:196
Just One Apple (Janosch)　**26**:74
Just Plain Fancy (Polacco)　**40**:189
Just Right (Moore)　**15**:142
Just the Thing for Geraldine (Conford)　**10**:92
Just Us Women (Caines)　**24**:63
Just Us Women (Cummings)　**48**:45
Justice and Her Brothers (Hamilton)　**11**:79
Justice Lion (Peck)　**45**:114

Title Index

Justin and the Best Biscuits in the World (Walter) **15**:208

Justin Morgan Had a Horse (Henry) **4**:109

Juvenile Justice and Injustice (Hyde) **23**:162

The Kaha Bird: Folk Tales from the Steppes of Central Asia (Ginsburg) **45**:4

Karen Kepplewhite Is the World's Best Kisser (Bunting) **28**:55

Karen's Curiosity (Provensen and Provensen) **11**:209

Karen's Opposites (Son No. 6) (Provensen and Provensen) **11**:209

Karen's Witch (Martin) **32**:204

Karlson Flies Again (Lindgren) **39**:157

Karlsson-on-the-Roof (Lindgren) **39**:153

Kasho and the Twin Flutes (Pinkney) **43**:156

Kashtanka (Moser) **49**:181

Kat Kong (Pilkey) **48**:106

Kate (Little) **4**:150

The Kate Greenaway Treasury: An Anthology of the Illustrations and Writings of Kate Greenaway (Greenaway) **6**:135

Kate Greenaway's Book of Games (Greenaway) **6**:135

Kate Greenaway's Language of Flowers (Greenaway) **6**:133

Kate Rider (Burton) **1**:32

Kate Shelley: Bound for Legend (San Souci) **43**:194

Katherine Dunham (Haskins) **39**:41

Kathleen, Please Come Home (O'Dell) **16**:173

Kati in America (Lindgren) **39**:151

Kati in Paris (Lindgren) **39**:148

Katie and Kit at the Beach (dePaola) **24**:98

Katie John (Calhoun) **42**:6

Katie John and Heathcliff (Calhoun) **42**:26

Katie, Kit, and Cousin Tom (dePaola) **24**:98

Katie's Good Idea (dePaola) **24**:98

Katy and the Big Snow (Burton) **11**:49

Kazoete Miyo (Anno) **14**:32

Keep Calm (Phipson) **5**:185

Keep Smiling Through (Rinaldi) **46**:91

Keep the Pot Boiling (Clarke) **28**:77

Keep Your Mouth Closed, Dear (Aliki) **9**:19

The Keeper (Naylor) **17**:60

The Keeper of the Isis Light (Hughes) **9**:72

Keepers of Life: Discovering Plants through Native American Stories and Earth Activities for Children (Bruchac) **46**:17

Keepers of the Animals: Native American Stories and Wildlife Activities for Children (Bruchac) **46**:7

Keepers of the Earth: Native American Stories and Environmental Activities for Children (Bruchac) **46**:7

Keepers of the Night: Native American Stories and Nocturnal Activities for Children (Bruchac) **46**:17

The Keeping Days (St. John) **46**:99

Keeping Henry (Bawden) **51**:35

The Keeping Quilt (Polacco) **40**:182

Kelly, Dot, and Esmeralda (Goodall) **25**:45

The Kellyhorns (Cooney) **23**:22

The Kelpie's Pearls (Hunter) **25**:75

Kenny's Window (Sendak) **1**:170

Kept in the Dark (Bawden) **51**:31

Kermit the Hermit (Peet) **12**:196

Kermit's Garden of Verses (Prelutsky) **13**:170

Kerstmis (Bruna) **7**:49

The Kestrel (Alexander) **5**:25

Kettering: Master Inventor (Lavine) **35**:147

A Kettle of Hawks and Other Wildlife Groups (Arnosky) **15**:4

Kevin's Grandma (Williams) **48**:191

The Key (Cresswell) **18**:107

The Key (Dillon) **26**:28

Key to the Treasure (Parish) **22**:156

The Key Word, and Other Mysteries (Asimov) **12**:55

The Khan's Daughter: A Mongolian Folktale (Yep) **54**:201

The Kid in the Red Jacket (Park) **34**:157

Kid Power (Pfeffer) **11**:199

Kid Power Strikes Back (Pfeffer) **11**:205

The Kid Who Only Hit Homers (Christopher) **33**:46

Kidnapped on Astarr (Nixon) **24**:142

The Kidnapping of Christina Lattimore (Nixon) **24**:137

The Kids' Cat Book (dePaola) **4**:63

The Kids' Code and Cipher Book (Garden) **51**:66

Kids in Court: The ACLU Defends Their Rights (Epstein and Epstein) **26**:69

Killashandra (McCaffrey) **49**:147

Killer Fish (Freedman) **20**:83

Killer Snakes (Freedman) **20**:83

Killer Whales (Simon) **9**:212

Killing Mr. Griffin (Duncan) **29**:71

Kilmeny of the Orchard (Montgomery) **8**:135

Kim/Kimi (Irwin) **40**:112

Kimako's Story (Jordan) **10**:120

Kim's Place and Other Poems (Hopkins) **44**:85

Kind Hearts and Gentle Monsters (Yep) **17**:205

A Kind of Wild Justice (Ashley) **4**:16

Kinda Blue (Grifalconi) **35**:79

A Kindle of Kittens (Godden) **20**:136

The Kindred of the Wild: A Book of Animal Life (Roberts) **33**:191

The King and His Friends (Aruego) **5**:27

King Arthur (Haar) **15**:115

The King at the Door (Cole) **18**:81

King Bidgood's in the Bathtub (Wood and Wood) **26**:222

King George's Head Was Made of Lead (Monjo) **2**:122

King Grisly-Beard (Sendak) **1**:171

King Henry's Palace (Hutchins) **20**:152

King Horn (Crossley-Holland) **47**:23

The King in the Garden (Garfield) **21**:118

King Krakus and the Dragon (Domanska) **40**:48

King Nimrod's Tower (Garfield) **21**:117

King Nonn the Wiser (McNaughton) **54**:53

King of Another Country (French) **37**:54

The King of Ireland's Son (Colum) **36**:22

King of Kazoo (Peck) **45**:109

King of Spuds; Who's for the Zoo? (Ure) **34**:186

The King of the Cats (Guillot) **22**:66

King of the Cats: A Ghost Story (Galdone) **16**:103

King of the Cloud Forests (Morpurgo) **51**:127

The King of the Copper Mountains (Biegel) **27**:28

King of the Reindeer and Other Animal Stories (Guillot) **22**:70

King of the Wind (Henry) **4**:111

King of Wreck Island (Cooney) **23**:21

King Rollo and the Birthday; King Rollo and the Bread; King Rollo and the New Shoes (McKee) **38**:167

King Rollo's Autumn; King Rollo's Spring; King Rollo's Summer; King Rollo's Winter (McKee) **38**:175

King Rollo's Letter and Other Stories (McKee) **38**:174

King Rollo's Playroom and Other Stories (McKee) **38**:173

King Stork (Hyman) **50**:71

King Tree (French) **37**:37

The King Who Saved Himself from Being Saved (Ciardi) **19**:79

The King Who Tried to Fry an Egg on His Head (Ginsburg) **45**:20

The Kingdom and the Cave (Aiken) **1**:4

A Kingdom in a Horse (Wojciechowska) **1**:197

The Kingdom of the Sun (Asimov) **12**:34

The Kingdom Under the Sea and Other Stories (Aiken) **19**:9

The Kingfisher Book of Children's Poetry (Rosen) **45**:135

The King's Beard (Wibberley) **3**:228

The King's Corsair (Guillot) **22**:56

The King's Equal (Paterson) **50**:201

The King's Falcon (Fox) **1**:78

The King's Fifth (O'Dell) **1**:148

The King's Flower (Anno) **14**:33

Kings in Exile (Roberts) **33**:202

The King's Monster (Haywood) **22**:104

The King's New Clothes (McKissack) **23**:239

The King's Room (Dillon) **26**:30

The King's Stilts (Dr. Seuss) **9**:174

The King's White Elephant (Harris) **30**:115

Kintu: A Congo Adventure (Enright) **4**:71

Kirk's Law (Peck) **45**:116

The Kissimmee Kid (Cleaver and Cleaver) **6**:113

Kit (Gardam) **12**:171

Kitchen Carton Crafts (Sattler) **24**:212

The Kitchen Knight: A Tale of King Arthur (Hyman) **50**:81

The Kitchen Madonna (Godden) **20**:132

The Kite That Braved Old Orchard Beach: Year-Round Poems for Young People (Kennedy) **27**:103

The Kite That Won the Revolution (Asimov) **12**:37

Kitten Can (McMillan) **47**:165

Kitten for a Day (Keats) **35**:139

Kitten from One to Ten (Ginsburg) **45**:15

Kiviok's Magic Journey: An Eskimo Legend (Houston) **3**:86

Klippity Klop (Emberley) **5**:98

Knave of Dreams (Norton) **50**:158

The Knee-High Man and Other Tales (Lester) **2**:112

Kneeknock Rise (Babbitt) **2**:6

The Knife (Stine) **37**:117

The Knight and the Dragon (dePaola) **4**:64

The Knight of the Golden Plain (Hunter) **25**:89

The Knight of the Lion (McDermott) **9**:117

Knight's Castle (Eager) **43**:83

Knight's Fee (Sutcliff) **1**:187; **37**:154

Knights in Armor (Glubok) **1**:100

The Knights of King Midas (Berna) **19**:37

Knights of the Crusades (Williams) **8**:225

Knights of the Kitchen Table (Scieszka) **27**:156

Knights of the Kitchen Table (Smith) **47**:200

Knock at a Star: A Child's Introduction to Poetry (Kennedy) **27**:99

Know about AIDS (Hyde) **23**:174

Know about Alcohol (Hyde) **23**:165

Know about Drugs (Hyde) **23**:159

Know about Smoking (Hyde) **23**:169

Know Your Feelings (Hyde) **23**:161

Koala Lou (Fox) **23**:115

Kodomo: Children of Japan (Kuklin) **51**:113

Kofi and His Magic (Angelou) **53**:19

Komodo! (Sis) **45**:169

König Hupf der 1 (Heine) **18**:147

Koning Arthur (Haar) **15**:115

Konrad: Oder, das Kind aus der Konservenbüchs (Noestlinger) **12**:187

Konta stis ragies (Zei) **6**:262

Koya Delaney and the Good Girl Blues (Greenfield) **38**:93

Kpo, the Leopard (Guillot) **22**:57

The Kraymer Mystery (Allan) **43**:19

Kristy and the Snobs (Martin) **32**:205

Kristy's Great Idea (Martin) **32**:202

The Kweeks of Kookatumdee (Peet) **12**:207

Labour in Vain (Garfield) **21**:109

The Labours of Herakles (Crossley-Holland) **47**:49

The Lace Snail (Byars) **16**:54

The Lad of the Gad (Garner) **20**:117

Lad With a Whistle (Brink) **30**:12

Ladder of Angels: Scenes from the Bible (L'Engle) **14**:152

Ladies of the Gothics: Tales of Romance and Terror by the Gentle Sex (Manley) **3**:145

Ladis and the Ant (Sanchez-Silva) **12**:232

Lady Daisy (King-Smith) **40**:164

Lady Ellen Grae (Cleaver and Cleaver) **6**:102

The Lady in the Box (McGovern) **50**:127

The Lady of Guadalupe (dePaola) **4**:63

The Lady Who Put Salt in Her Coffee (Schwartz) **25**:195

Ladybug (McClung) **11**:184

Lady's Girl (Bunting) **28**:44

Lafcadio, the Lion Who Shot Back (Silverstein) **5**:208

Lambs for Dinner (Betsy and Giulio Maestro) **45**:69

The Lamp From the Warlock's Tomb (Bellairs) **37**:21

The Lamplighter's Funeral (Garfield) **21**:109

The Land Beyond (Gripe) **5**:145

Land in the Sun: The Story of West Africa (Ashabranner and Davis) **28**:5

The Land of Black Gold (Hergé) **6**:148

The Land of Canaan (Asimov) **12**:46

Land of Dreams (Foreman) **32**:95

The Land of Forgotten Beasts (Wersba) **3**:217

Land under the Sea (Nixon) **24**:146

Landet Utanfor (Gripe) **5**:145

Landings (Hamley) **47**:56

Langston Hughes: A Biography (Meltzer) **13**:125

Language and Man (Adler) **27**:24

The Language of Goldfish (Oneal) **13**:156

The Lantern Bearers (Sutcliff) **1**:187; **37**:154

A Lantern in the Window (Fisher) **49**:33

Larger than Life (Lunn) **18**:158

The Lark and the Laurel (Willard) **2**:220

Lark in the Morning (Garden) **51**:77

Larry Makes Music (Unnerstad) **36**:198

Lasca and Her Pups (Trezise) **41**:142

Last Act; Spellbound (Pike) **29**:171

The Last Battle (Lewis) **3**:135; **27**:104-51

The Last Battle (Wibberley) **3**:228

The Last Dinosaur (Murphy) **53**:105

The Last Guru (Pinkwater) **4**:168

The Last Hundred Years: Household Technology (Cohen) **43**:42

The Last Hundred Years: Medicine (Cohen) **43**:40

The Last King of Cornwall (Causley) **30**:40

The Last Little Cat (DeJong) **1**:59

The Last Mission (Mazer) **16**:130

The Last Noo-Noo (Murphy) **39**:180

Last One Home is A Green Pig (Hurd and Hurd) **49**:123

The Last Planet (Norton) **50**:135

The Last Princess: The Story of Princess Ka'iulani of Hawai'i (Stanley) **46**:145

The Last Silk Dress (Rinaldi) **46**:81

The Last Slice of Rainbow and Other Stories (Aiken) **19**:16

Last Summer with Maizon (Woodson) **49**:199

Last Sunday (Peck) **45**:110

The Last Tales Of Uncle Remus (Lester) **41**:109

The Last Tales Of Uncle Remus (Pinkney) **43**:171

The Last Two Elves in Denmark (Calhoun) **42**:13

The Last Viking (Treece) **2**:186

The Late Spring (Fritz) **14**:110

Later, Gator (Yep) **54**:198

Laura's Luck (Sachs) **2**:132

Laurie Loved Me Best (Klein) **21**:164

Laurie's New Brother (Schlein) **41**:184

Lavender (Hesse) **54**:36

Lavender-Green Magic (Norton) **50**:154

Lavinia's Cottage (Goodall) **25**:53

The Lazies: Tales of the Peoples of Russia (Ginsburg) **45**:6

The Lazy Bear (Wildsmith) **2**:213

Lazy Blackbird, and Other Verses (Prelutsky) **13**:164

Lazy Tinka (Seredy) **10**:182

Lazy Tommy Pumpkinhead (Pene du Bois) **1**:64

Leaders of the Middle East (Haskins) **39**:49

Leaper: The Story of an Atlantic Salmon (McClung) **11**:181

Learning to Say Good-By: When a Parent Dies (LeShan) **6**:188

The Least One (Politi) **29**:184

The Least One (Sawyer) **36**:156

Leave the Cooking to Me (Gaberman) **33**:15

Leave Well Enough Alone (Wells) **16**:208

The Leaving Morning (Johnson) **33**:96

The Left Overs (Spence) **26**:199

The Left-Hander's World (Silverstein and Silverstein) **25**:216

The Legacy of Lucian Van Zandt (St. John) **46**:115

Legend Days (Highwater) **17**:30

The Legend of New Amsterdam (Spier) **5**:226

The Legend of Old Befana: An Italian Christmas Story (dePaola) **4**:65

The Legend of Rosepetal (Zwerger) **46**:195

The Legend of Scarface: A Blackfeet Indian Tale (San Souci) **43**:179

The Legend of Sleepy Hollow: Retold from Washington Irving (San Souci) **43**:182

The Legend of St. Columba (Colum) **36**:44

The Legend of Tarik (Myers) **16**:138

The Legend of the Bluebonnet: An Old Tale of Texas (dePaola) **24**:91

The Legend of the Indian Paintbrush (dePaola) **24**:100

The Legend of the Willow Plate (Tresselt) **30**:210

Legends of Hawaii (Colum) **36**:27

Legends of the Saints (Petry) **12**:212

Leif Eriksson: First Voyage to America (Shippen) **36**:172

Leif the Lucky (d'Aulaire and d'Aulaire) **21**:47

Leif the Unlucky (Haugaard) **11**:109

A Lemon and a Star (Spykman) **35**:216

The Lemonade Trick (Corbett) **1**:46

Lena Horne (Haskins) **39**:45

Lenny and Lola (Brown) **29**:4

Lenny Kandell, Smart Aleck (Conford) **10**:99

Lens and Shutter: An Introduction to Photography (Weiss) **4**:226

Lentil (McCloskey) **7**:200

Leonard Everett Fisher's Liberty Book (Fisher) **18**:126

Leonardo Da Vinci (Stanley) **46**:156

Leonardo da Vinci (Williams) **8**:226

Leonardo da Vinci: The Artist, Inventor, Scientist in Three-Dimensional, Movable Pictures (Provensen and Provensen) **11**:218

The Leopard (Bodker) **23**:11

Leopard's Prey (Wibberley) **3**:229

The Leopard's Tooth (Kotzwinkle) **6**:182

Leo's Christmas Surprise (Daly) **41**:55

Leroy Is Missing (Singer) **48**:126

Lester and the Unusual Pet (Blake) **31**:20

Lester at the Seaside (Blake) **31**:20

Lester's Dog (Hesse) **54**:35

Let Me Fall before I Fly (Wersba) **3**:218

Let the Balloon Go (Southall) **2**:153

Let the Circle Be Unbroken (Taylor) **9**:228

Let There Be Light: A Book about Windows (Giblin) **29**:91

Let X Be Excitement (Harris) **47**:81

Let's Be Early Settlers with Daniel Boone (Parish) **22**:156

Let's Be Friends Again! (Wilhelm) **46**:163

Let's Be Indians (Parish) **22**:154

Let's Celebrate: Holiday Decorations You Can Make (Parish) **22**:162

Let's Cook without Cooking (Hautzig) **22**:76

Let's Do Better (Leaf) **25**:128

Let's Find Out about Earth (Knight) **38**:105

Let's Find Out about Insects (Knight) **38**:105

Let's Find Out about Magnets (Knight) **38**:103

Let's Find Out about Mars (Knight) **38**:103

Let's Find Out about Rocks and Minerals (Knight) **38**:109

Let's Find Out about Sound (Knight) **38**:118

Let's Find Out about Telephones (Knight) **38**:104

Let's Find Out about the Ocean (Knight) **38**:109

Let's Find Out about Weather (Knight) **38**:104

Let's Go Dinosaur Tracking! (Duke) **51**:51

Let's Go Dinosaur Tracking! (Schlein) **41**:196

Let's Go Home, Little Bear (Waddell) **31**:199

Let's Grow a Garden (Fujikawa) **25**:39

Let's Hear It for the Queen (Childress) **14**:92

Let's Make More Presents: Easy and Inexpensive Gifts for Every Occasion (Hautzig) **22**:84

Let's Make Presents: 100 Gifts for Less than $1.00 (Hautzig) **22**:77

Let's Make Rabbits: A Fable (Lionni) **7**:139

Let's Paint a Rainbow (Carle) **10**:85

Let's Play! (Fujikawa) **25**:38

Let's Try It Out: Hot and Cold (Simon) **9**:206

A Letter for Tiger (Janosch) **26**:79

The Letter, The Witch, and the Ring (Bellairs) **37**:9

A Letter to Amy (Keats) **1**:115; **35**:135

Letterbox: The Art and History of Letters (Adkins) **7**:27

Letters from Italy (Fisher) **18**:127

Letters from Rifka (Hesse) **54**:33

Letters from the General (Biegel) **27**:33

Letters from the Inside (Marsden) **34**:150

Letters to Horseface: Being the Story of Wolfgang Amadeus Mozart's Journey to Italy, 1769-1770, When He Was a Boy of Fourteen (Monjo) **2**:123

Letters to Judy: What Your Kids Wish They Could Tell You (Blume) **15**:80

Letters to Pauline (Kruss) **9**:87

Letting Swift River Go (Yolen) **44**:198

Der Leuchtturm auf den Hummer-Klippen (Kruss) **9**:82

Liar, Liar (Yep) **17**:206

Libby on Wednesday (Snyder) **31**:169

Libby, Oscar and Me (Graham) **31**:94

The Library (Small) **53**:155

La Liebre y la Tortuga & La Tortuga y la Liebre / The Hare and the Tortoise & The Tortoise and the Hare (Pene du Bois) **1**:63

Life and Death (Zim) **2**:228

Life and Death in Nature (Simon) **9**:211

The Life and Death of a Brave Bull (Wojciechowska) **1**:198

The Life and Death of Martin Luther King, Jr. (Haskins) **3**:65
Life Doesn't Frighten Me (Angelou) **53**:17
The Life I Live: Collected Poems (Lenski) **26**:122
Life in Colonial America (Speare) **8**:210
Life in the Dark: How Animals Survive at Night (Simon) **9**:208
Life in the Middle Ages (Williams) **8**:227
Life in the Universe (Silverstein and Silverstein) **25**:200
The Life of Jack Sprat, His Wife, and His Cat (Galdone) **16**:94
The Life of Winston Churchill (Wibberley) **3**:229
Life on Ice: How Animals Survive in the Arctic (Simon) **9**:210
Life Story (Burton) **11**:51
Life with Working Parents: Practical Hints for Everyday Situations (Hautzig) **22**:84
Lift Every Voice (Sterling and Quarles) **1**:179
Lift Every Voice and Sing: Words and Music (Johnson) **32**:173
Light (Crews) **7**:58
Light and Darkness (Branley) **13**:41
The Light Beyond the Forest: The Quest for the Holy Grail (Sutcliff) **37**:170
A Light in the Attic (Silverstein) **5**:212
A Light in the Dark: The Life of Samuel Gridley Howe (Meltzer) **13**:120
The Lightey Club (Singer) **48**:131
Lightfoot: The Story of an Indian Boy (Shippen) **36**:172
Lighthouse Island (Coatsworth) **2**:60
The Lighthouse Keeper's Son (Chauncy) **6**:94
The Lighthouse on the Lobster Cliffs (Kruss) **9**:82
Lightning (Bendick) **5**:39
Lightning and Thunder (Zim) **2**:228
The Lightning Bolt (Bedard) **35**:61
Lights, Lenses, and Lasers (Berger) **32**:39
Lights Out (Stine) **37**:117
Like Nothing At All (Fisher) **49**:37
A Likely Place (Fox) **1**:78
The Lilith Summer (Irwin) **40**:105
Lillian Wald: Angel of Henry Street (Epstein and Epstein) **26**:46
Lillie of Watts: A Birthday Discovery (Walter) **15**:203
Lillie of Watts Takes a Giant Step (Walter) **15**:204
Lillypilly Hill (Spence) **26**:192
Lily and the Lost Boy (Fox) **44**:68
Limericks (Ehlert) **28**:109
Limericks by Lear (Lear) **1**:127
Lincoln: A Photobiography (Freedman) **20**:87
Lines Scribbled on an Envelope and Other Poems (L'Engle) **1**:131
Linnea in Monet's Garden (Bjork) **22**:12
Linnea's Almanac (Bjork) **22**:15
Linnea's Windowsill Garden (Bjork) **22**:15
Linsey Woolsey (Tudor) **13**:192
The Lion and the Bird's Nest (Nakatani) **30**:158
The Lion and the Mouse: An Aesop Fable (Young) **27**:218
Lion and the Ostrich Chicks and Other African Folk Tales (Bryan) **18**:36
The Lion and the Unicorn (Baumann) **35**:42
The Lion Cub (Dillon) **26**:27
A Lion for Lewis (Wells) **16**:212
Lion Gate and Labyrinth (Baumann) **35**:48
A Lion in the Meadow (Mahy) **7**:178
A Lion in the Night (Allen) **44**:7
The Lion, the Witch, and the Wardrobe (Lewis) **3**:135 **27**:104-51
The Lion's Whiskers: Tales of High Africa (Ashabranner and Davis) **28**:3

Lisa (Matas) **52**:78
Lisa and Lottie (Kaestner) **4**:124
Lisa, Bright and Dark (Neufeld) **52**:122
Lisa's War (Matas) **52**:78
Listen for the Fig Tree (Mathis) **3**:149
Listen for the Singing (Little) **4**:152
Listen, Little Girl, Before You Come to New York (Leaf) **25**:123
Listen, Rabbit (Fisher) **49**:40
Listen to a Shape (Brown) **12**:107
Listen to the Crows (Pringle) **4**:180
Listen to the Wind (Brinsmead) **47**:10
Listening (Seredy) **10**:172
The Listening Walk (Showers) **6**:242
Lito and the Clown (Politi) **29**:192
The Little Auto (Lenski) **26**:100
Little Babar Books (Brunhoff) **4**:37, 38
Little Bear (Minarik) **33**:122
Little Bear's Friend (Minarik) **33**:125
Little Bear's Visit (Minarik) **33**:125
Little Blue and Little Yellow: A Story for Pippo and Ann and Other Children (Lionni) **7**:127
Little Boat Lighter Than a Cork (Krauss) **42**:130
A Little Book of Little Beasts (Hoberman) **22**:110
Little Books (Burningham) **9**:46, 47
A Little Boy Was Drawing (Duvoisin) **23**:90
The Little Brass Band (Brown) **10**:65
Little Brother (Baillie) **23**:7
Little Brother and Little Sister (Cooney) **23**:31
The Little Brute Family (Hoban) **3**:78
The Little Captain (Biegel) **27**:29
The Little Captain and the Pirate Treasure (Biegel) **27**:34
The Little Captain and the Seven Towers (Biegel) **27**:30
The Little Carousel (Brown) **12**:93
Little Chameleon (Cassedy) **26**:11
Little Chicken (Brown) **10**:52
The Little Cow and the Turtle (DeJong) **1**:59
The Little Cowboy (Brown) **10**:56
A Little Destiny (Cleaver and Cleaver) **6**:112
Little Dog Lost (Guillot) **22**:71
The Little Dog of Fo (Harris) **30**:118
Little Dog Toby (Field) **21**:72
Little Dogs of the Prarie (Scott) **20**:196
Little Dracula at the Seashore (Waddell)
  See *Little Dracula at the Seaside*
Little Dracula at the Seaside (*Little Dracula at the Seashore*) (Waddell) **31**:189
Little Dracula Goes to School (Waddell) **31**:189
Little Dracula's Christmas (Waddell) **31**:186
Little Dracula's First Bite (Waddell) **31**:186
The Little Drummer Boy (Keats) **1**:116; **35**:134
Little Eddie (Haywood) **22**:93
The Little Farmer (Brown) **10**:56
A Little Fear (Wrightson) **14**:214
The Little Fir Tree (Brown) **10**:64
The Little Fisherman, a Fish Story (Brown) **10**:53
The Little Fishes (Haugaard) **11**:105
Little Foxes (Morpurgo) **51**:122
Little Frightened Tiger (Brown) **10**:63
Little Fur Family (Brown) **10**:53
The Little Giant Girl and the Elf Boy (Minarik) **33**:125
Little Giants (Simon) **9**:219
The Little Girl and the Dragon (Minarik) **33**:128
A Little Girl of Nineteen Hundred (Lenski) **26**:99
The Little Girl Who Lived Down the Road (Daly) **41**:52
Little Grunt and the Big Egg: A Prehistoric Fairy Tale (dePaola) **24**:103
Little Hobbin (Zwerger) **46**:202
The Little House (Burton) **11**:47

Little House in the Big Woods (Wilder) **2**:205
Little House on the Prairie (Wilder) **2**:206
Little Indian (Parish) **22**:157
The Little Indian Basket Maker (Clark) **16**:80
The Little Island (Brown) **10**:54
Little John (Orgel) **48**:81
The Little Juggler (Cooney) **23**:26
The Little King, the Little Queen, the Little Monster and Other Stories You Can Make up Yourself (Krauss) **42**:128
Little Kit: Or, the Industrious Flea Circus (McCully) **46**:71
Little Leo (Politi) **29**:188
Little Little (Kerr) **29**:150
Little Little Sister (Curry) **31**:87
Little Lost Lamb (Brown) **10**:53
A Little Love (Hamilton) **11**:91
A Little Lower than the Angels (McCaughrean) **38**:139
The Little Man (Kaestner) **4**:127
The Little Man and the Big Thief (Kaestner) **4**:127
The Little Man and the Little Miss (Kaestner) **4**:127
Little Man in the Family (Shearer) **34**:166
Little Monster at Home (Mayer) **11**:173
Little Monster at School (Mayer) **11**:173
Little Monster at Work (Mayer) **11**:173
Little Monster's Alphabet Book (Mayer) **11**:173
Little Monster's Bedtime Book (Mayer) **11**:173
Little Monster's Counting Book (Mayer) **11**:173
Little Monster's Mother Goose (Mayer) **11**:173
Little Monster's Neighborhood (Mayer) **11**:173
Little Monster's Word Book (Mayer) **11**:172
Little Navajo Bluebird (Clark) **16**:76
Little O (Unnerstad) **36**:191
Little Obie and the Flood (Waddell) **31**:198
Little Obie and the Kidnap (Waddell) **31**:201
Little Old Automobile (Ets) **33**:79
Little Old Mrs. Pepperpot and Other Stories (Proysen) **24**:181
A Little Oven (Estes) **2**:74
Little Plum (Godden) **20**:131
A Little Prayer (Cooney) **23**:27
The Little Prince (Saint-Exupery) **10**:137-61
The Little Prince (Saint-Exupery)
  See *Le petit prince*
Little Rabbit Foo Foo (Rosen) **45**:141
Little Rabbit, the High Jumper (Schlein) **41**:180
Little Raccoon and No Trouble at All (Moore) **15**:142
Little Raccoon and Poems from the Woods (Moore) **15**:144
Little Raccoon and the Outside World (Moore) **15**:140
Little Raccoon and the Thing in the Pool (Moore) **15**:140
Little Red Cap (Zwerger) **46**:191
Little Red Hen (Domanska) **40**:44
The Little Red Hen (Galdone) **16**:99
The Little Red Hen (McKissack) **23**:237
The Little Red Horse (Sawyer) **36**:160
Little Red Nose (Schlein) **41**:177
Little Red Riding Hood (Galdone) **16**:99
Little Red Riding Hood (Goodall) **25**:56
Little Red Riding Hood (Hyman) **50**:76
The Little Roaring Tiger (Zimnik) **3**:243
Little Rystu (Ginsburg) **45**:11
A Little Schubert (Goffstein) **3**:59
Little Spot Board Books (Hill) **13**:96
The Little Spotted Fish (Yolen) **4**:261
The Little Swineherd and Other Tales (Fox) **44**:61
Little Tiger, Get Well Soon! (Janosch) **26**:81

Little Tim and the Brave Sea Captain (Ardizzone) **3**:5
Little Toot (Gramatky) **22**:39
Little Toot and the Loch Ness Monster (Gramatky) **22**:46
Little Toot on the Grand Canal (Gramatky) **22**:45
Little Toot on the Mississippi (Gramatky) **22**:45
Little Toot on the Thames (Gramatky) **22**:44
Little Toot through the Golden Gate (Gramatky) **22**:46
Little Town on the Prairie (Wilder) **2**:206
The Little Train (Lenski) **26**:105
Little Tricker the Squirrel Meets Big Double the Bear (Moser) **49**:176
Little Whale (McGovern) **50**:120
The Little Witch (Mahy) **7**:180
Little Wolf (McGovern) **50**:111
Little Women; or, Meg, Jo, Beth, and Amy (Alcott) **1**:10; **38**:1-63
The Little Wood Duck (Wildsmith) **2**:213
The Little Worm Book (Ahlberg and Ahlberg) **18**:7
The Littlest One in the Family (Duncan) **29**:66
Liverwurst Is Missing (Mayer) **11**:175
Lives at Stake: The Science and Politics of Environmental Health (Pringle) **4**:185
The Lives of Christopher Chant (Jones) **23**:197
Lives of Musicians: Good Times, Bad Times (And What the Neighbors Thought) (Krull) **44**:102
The Lives of Spiders (Patent) **19**:155
Lives of the Artists: Masterpieces, Messes (And What the Neighbors Thought) (Krull) **44**:112
Lives of the Writers: Comedies, Tragedies (And What the Neighbors Thought) (Krull) **44**:105
Living in Imperial Rome (Dillon) **26**:31
Living Lanterns: Luminescence in Animals (Simon) **39**:186
Living Things (Bendick) **5**:42
Living Up the Street: Narrative Recollections (Soto) **38**:186
Liza Lou and the Yeller Belly Swamp (Mayer) **11**:170
Lizard in the Sun (Ryder) **37**:96
Lizard Music (Pinkwater) **4**:164
Lizzie Dripping (Cresswell) **18**:105
Lizzie Lights (Chauncy) **6**:93
Lizzie Silver of Sherwood Forest (Singer) **48**:129
Lizzie's Invitation (Keller) **45**:50
Lizzy's Lion (Gay) **27**:84
Loads of Codes and Secret Ciphers (Janeczko) **47**:103
The Loathsome Couple (Gorey) **36**:99
The Loathsome Dragon (Wiesner) **43**:203
Lob Lie-by-the-Fire; or, The Luck of Lingborough (Caldecott) **14**:83
Local News (Soto) **38**:200
Loch (Zindel) **45**:201
Lock, Stock, and Barrel (Sobol) **4**:207
Locked in Time (Duncan) **29**:77
The Locker Room Mirror: How Sports Reflect Society (Aaseng) **54**:18
Locks and Keys (Gibbons) **8**:91
Lodestar, Rocket Ship to Mars: The Record of the First Operation Sponsored by the Federal Commission for Interplanetary Exploration, June 1, 1971 (Branley) **13**:24
Loggerhead Turtle: Survivor From the Sea (Scott) **20**:194
Logic for Beginners: Through Games, Jokes, and Puzzles (Adler) **27**:18
Lois Lenski's Big Book of Mr. Small (Lenski) **26**:125
Lollipop: Kinderroman (Noestlinger) **12**:188

The Lollipop Princess: A Play for Paper Dolls in One Act (Estes) **2**:74
A Lollygag of Limericks (Livingston) **7**:173
Lon Po Po: A Red-Riding Hood Story from China (Young) **27**:222
London Bridge Is Falling Down (Emberley) **5**:96
London Bridge Is Falling Down! (Spier) **5**:217
Lone Bull's Horse Raid (Goble) **21**:130
The Loneliness of Mia (That Early Spring) (Beckman) **25**:15
The Lonely Hearts Club (Klein) **21**:163
Lonely Veronica (Duvoisin) **23**:103
The Loners (Garden) **51**:64
Lonesome Boy (Bontemps) **6**:83
Long Ago When I Was Young (Nesbit) **3**:164
The Long and Short of Measurement (Cobb) **2**:66
Long, Broad, and Quickeye (Ness) **6**:205
The Long Christmas (Sawyer) **36**:157
A Long Hard Journey: The Story of the Pullman Porter (McKissack) **23**:240
The Long Journey (Corcoran) **50**:13
The Long Journey from Space (Simon) **9**:219
Long Journey Home: Stories from Black History (Lester) **2**:113
The Long Lost Coelacanth and Other Living Fossils (Aliki) **9**:23
Long Neck and Thunder Foot (Foreman) **32**:96
The Long Red Scarf (Hilton) **25**:59
Long River (Bruchac) **46**:19
The Long Road to Gettysburg (Murphy) **53**:109
The Long Secret (Fitzhugh) **1**:72
Long Shot for Paul (Christopher) **33**:41
Long Stretch at First Base (Christopher) **33**:38
Long Tom and the Dead Hand (Crossley-Holland) **47**:49
The Long View into Space (Simon) **9**:214
The Long Voyage: The Life Cycle of a Green Turtle (Silverstein and Silverstein) **25**:207
The Long Walk (Mattingley) **24**:124
A Long Way from Verona (Gardam) **12**:162
The Long Way Home (Benary-Isbert) **12**:76
The Long Winter (Wilder) **2**:206
Longbeard the Wizard (Fleischman) **15**:107
The Longest Weekend (Arundel) **35**:13
Long-Short: At Home (McNaughton) **54**:53
Longtime Passing (Brinsmead) **47**:12
Look Again! (Hoban) **13**:101
Look Around! A Book About Shapes (Fisher) **18**:137
Look at Me! (Daly) **41**:58
Look at Your Eyes (Showers) **6**:242
Look in the Mirror (Epstein and Epstein) **26**:64
Look Out for the Seals (McNaughton) **54**:56
Look, There Is a Turtle Flying (Domanska) **40**:39
Look Through My Window (Little) **4**:149
Look to the Night Sky: An Introduction to Star Watching (Simon) **9**:212
Look What I Can Do (Aruego) **5**:29
Look What I've Got! (Browne) **19**:63
Look Who's Playing First Base (Christopher) **33**:45
Look-Alikes (Drescher) **20**:60
The Looking Book (Hoberman) **22**:110
Looking for Santa Claus (Drescher) **20**:60
Looking for Your Name: A Collection of Contempory Poems (Janeczko) **47**:113
Looking-for-Something: The Story of a Stray Burro of Ecuador (Clark) **16**:79
The Looking-Glass Castle (Biegel) **27**:33
The Look-It-Up Book of Mammals (Lauber) **16**:114
The Look-It-Up Book of Stars and Planets (Lauber) **16**:115

The Loon's Necklace (Cleaver) **13**:68
Loopy (Gramatky) **22**:41
The Lorax (Dr. Seuss) **1**:87; **9**:192
The Lord Is My Shepherd: The Twenty-Third Psalm (Tudor) **13**:202
Lord of Thunder (Norton) **50**:142
Lord Rex: The Lion Who Wished (McKee) **38**:163
The Lord's Prayer (d'Aulaire and d'Aulaire) **21**:41
Lordy, Aunt Hattie (Thomas) **8**:212
Lorry Driver (Munari) **9**:125
Losers Weepers (Needle) **43**:138
Losing Joe's Place (Korman) **25**:112
Lost at the Fair (Sharp) **27**:163
The Lost Boy (Fox) **44**:68
Lost Cities (Gallant) **30**:101
The Lost Diamonds of Killiecrankie (Crew) **42**:60
The Lost Dispatch: A Story of Antietam (Sobol) **4**:206
The Lost Farm (Curry) **31**:78
The Lost Garden (Yep) **54**:189
Lost in the Barrens (Mowat) **20**:168
The Lost Island (Dillon) **26**:20
The Lost Lake (Say) **22**:211
The Lost Locket (Matas) **52**:88
Lost Wild America: The Story of Our Extinct and Vanishing Wildlife (McClung) **11**:185
Lost Wild Worlds: The Story of Extinct and Vanishing Wildlife of the Eastern Hemisphere (McClung) **11**:190
The Lothian Run (Hunter) **25**:78
Lotje, de kleine olifant (Haar) **15**:116
Lotta on Troublemaker Street (Lindgren) **1**:137
Lotta's Bike (Lindgren) **39**:154
Lotta's Christmas Surprise (Lindgren) **39**:157
Lotta's Easter Surprise (Lindgren) **39**:163
Lotta's Progress (St. John) **46**:126
Lottie and Lisa (Kaestner) **4**:124
The Lotus and the Grail: Legends from East to West (Harris) **30**:116
The Lotus Caves (Christopher) **2**:40
The Lotus Cup (Curry) **31**:84
Louie (Keats) **35**:139
Louie's Search (Keats) **35**:141
Louis the Fish (Yorinks) **20**:216
Louisa May: The World and Works of Louisa May Alcott (St. John) **46**:124
Louly (Brink) **30**:17
Love and Betrayal and Hold the Mayo! (Pascal) **25**:185
Love and Tennis (Slote) **4**:202
Love and the Merry-Go-Round (Harris) **30**:125
Love Is a Special Way of Feeling (Anglund) **1**:20
Love Is One of the Choices (Klein) **19**:90
Love You Forever (Munsch) **19**:145
A Lovely Tomorrow (Allan) **43**:29
The Loyal Cat (Namioka) **48**:68
Lucie Babbidge's House (Cassedy) **26**:15
Lucifer Wilkins (Garfield) **21**:107
Lucinda's Year of Jubilo (Sawyer) **36**:155
The Luck of Pokey Bloom (Conford) **10**:93
The Luckiest Girl (Cleary) **2**:48
The Luckiest One of All (Peet) **12**:206
The Lucky Baseball Bat (Christopher) **33**:36
Lucky Chuck (Cleary) **8**:61
Lucky Little Lena (Flack) **28**:126
Lucky, Lucky White Horse (Epstein and Epstein) **26**:59
Lucky Porcupine! (Schlein) **41**:191
Lucky Seven: Sports Stories (Christopher) **33**:45
Lucky Starr and the Big Sun of Mercury (Asimov) **12**:31
Lucky Starr and the Moons of Jupiter (Asimov) **12**:32

Lucky Starr and the Oceans of Venus (Asimov) **12**:31

Lucky Starr and the Pirates of the Asteroids (Asimov) **12**:30

Lucky Starr and the Rings of Saturn (Asimov) **12**:32

The Lucky Stone (Clifton) **5**:59

Lucky You (Leaf) **25**:133

Lucretia Mott, Gentle Warrior (Sterling) **1**:179

Lucy and Tom at the Seaside (Hughes) **15**:123

Lucy and Tom Go to School (Hughes) **15**:122

Lucy and Tom's 1,2,3 (Hughes) **15**:134

Lucy and Tom's A.B.C. (Hughes) **15**:130

Lucy and Tom's Christmas (Hughes) **15**:127

Lucy and Tom's Day (Hughes) **15**:120

Lucy Brown and Mr. Grimes (Ardizzone) **3**:5

Lucy's Bay (Crew) **42**:57

Ludell (Wilkinson) **20**:207

Ludell and Willie (Wilkinson) **20**:210

Ludell's New York Time (Wilkinson) **20**:210

Luke and Angela (Noestlinger) **12**:188

Luki-Live (Noestlinger) **12**:188

Lulu and the Flying Babies (Simmonds) **23**:244

Lum Fu and the Golden Mountains (Tresselt) **30**:214

Lumberjack (Kurelek) **2**:101

Lumps, Bumps, and Rashes: A Look at Kids' Diseases (Nourse) **33**:140

Luna: The Story of a Moth (McClung) **11**:181

The Lure of the Wild: The Last Three Animal Stories (Roberts) **33**:209

Luther Tarbox (Adkins) **7**:22

Lyddie (Paterson) **50**:199

Lyme Disease: The Great Imitator (Silverstein, Silverstein, and Silverstein) **25**:226

M. C. Higgins, the Great (Hamilton) **1**:104; **11**:71

M. E. and Morton (Cassedy) **26**:14

Ma and Pa Dracula (Martin) **32**:205

MA nDA LA (Adoff) **7**:31

MA Nda La (McCully) **46**:58

Machine Tools (Zim) **2**:229

The Machine-Gunners (Westall) **13**:249

Macho Nacho and Other Rhyming Riddles (Betsy and Giulio Maestro) **45**:89

The MacLeod Place (Armstrong) **1**:22

The Macmillan Book of Astronomy (Gallant) **30**:102

Madame Doubtfire (Fine) **25**:21

Madeline (Bemelmans) **6**:66

Madeline and Ermadello (Wynne-Jones) **21**:229

Madeline and the Bad Hat (Bemelmans) **6**:73

Madeline and the Gypsies (Bemelmans) **6**:74

Madeline in London (Bemelmans) **6**:76

Madeline's Rescue (Bemelmans) **6**:69

Mademoiselle Misfortune (Brink) **30**:10

Madicken (Lindgren) **39**:149

Das Maerchen von Rosenblaettchen (Zwerger) **46**:195

Maggie: A Sheep Dog (Patent) **19**:163

Maggie and the Pirate (Keats) **35**:141

Maggie Forevermore (Nixon) **24**:149

Maggie Rose, Her Birthday Christmas (Sawyer) **36**:160

Maggie the Freak (Bunting) **28**:47

Maggie, Too (Nixon) **24**:146

"Magic": A Biography of Earvin Johnson (Haskins) **39**:40

Magic and the Night River (Bunting) **28**:46

The Magic Auto (Janosch) **26**;76

The Magic Bed-knob; or, How to Become a Witch in Ten Easy Lessons (Norton) **6**:219

Magic by the Lake (Eager) **43**:84

Magic Camera (Pinkwater) **4**:162

The Magic Change: Metamorphosis (Silverstein and Silverstein) **25**:204

The Magic Circle (Napoli) **51**:156

The Magic City (Nesbit) **3**:164

The Magic Doctor (Biro) **28**:35

The Magic Finger (Dahl) **1**:52; **7**:72

Magic for Marigold (Montgomery) **8**:139

The Magic Gate (Williams) **8**:222

The Magic Grandfather (Williams) **8**:237

The Magic Hare (Moser) **49**:185

Magic House of Numbers (Adler) **27**:8

Magic in the Alley (Calhoun) **42**:15

Magic in the Mist (Hyman) **50**:73

The Magic Listening Cap: More Folk Tales from Japan (Uchida) **6**:251

The Magic Meadow (d'Aulaire and d'Aulaire) **21**:51

Magic Money (Clark) **16**:77

The Magic Moscow (Pinkwater) **4**:171

The Magic of Color (Simon) **39**:198

Magic or Not? (Eager) **43**:86

The Magic Pawnshop: A New Year's Eve Fantasy (Field) **21**:71

The Magic Pictures: More about the Wonderful Farm (Ayme) **25**:1

The Magic Porridge Pot (Galdone) **16**:101

The Magic Pudding: Being the Adventures of Bunyip Bluegum and His Friends Bill Barnacle and Sam Sawnoff (Lindsay) **8**:101

The Magic Rug (d'Aulaire and d'Aulaire) **21**:38

The Magic Saddle (Mattingley) **24**:127

The Magic School Bus at the Waterworks (Cole) **40**:14

The Magic School Bus in the Time of the Dinosaurs (Cole) **40**:32

The Magic School Bus inside a Hurricane (Cole) **40**:34

The Magic School Bus inside the Earth (Cole) **40**:20

The Magic School Bus inside the Human Body (Cole) **40**:24

The Magic School Bus Lost in the Solar System (Cole) **40**:28

The Magic School Bus on the Ocean Floor (Cole) **40**:30

The Magic Spectacles and Other Easy to Read Stories (Moore) **15**:141

The Magic Stone (Farmer) **8**:77

The Magic Stove (Ginsburg) **45**:17

The Magic Summer (The Growing Summer) (Streatfeild) **17**:196

Magic to Burn (Fritz) **14**:112

The Magic Tree: A Tale from the Congo (McDermott) **9**:110

The Magic Vase (French) **37**:50

The Magic Well (Ventura) **16**:193

The Magical Adventures of Pretty Pearl (Hamilton) **11**:86

The Magical Cockatoo (Sharp) **27**:165

Magical Melons (Brink) **30**:12

Magician (Baillie) **49**:15

The Magician (Shulevitz) **5**:205

The Magician and Double Trouble (McKee) **38**:171

The Magician and the Balloon (McKee) **38**:166

The Magician and the Dragon (McKee) **38**:168

The Magician and the Petnapping (McKee) **38**:165

The Magician and the Sorcerer (McKee) **38**:163

The Magician Who Lost His Magic (McKee) **38**:161

The Magician's Apprentice (McKee) **38**:177

The Magician's Nephew (Lewis) **3**:135; **27**:104-51

The Magicians of Caprona (Jones) **23**:189

Magnets (Adler) **27**:21

The Magnificent Morris Mouse Clubhouse (Gibbons) **8**:92

Magnolia's Mixed-Up Magic (Nixon) **24**:143

Magnus Powermouse (King-Smith) **40**:143

Magpie Island (Thiele) **27**:206

Maho Tsukai No ABC (Anno) **14**:39

Mai contenti (Munari) **9**:125

Maid of the Wood (French) **37**:46

The Maiden on the Moor (Singer) **48**:146

Maikäfer Flieg!: Mein Vater, das Kriegsende, Cohn und Ich (Noestlinger) **12**:185

Maizon at Blue Hill (Woodson) **49**:202

The Majesty of Grace (Langton) **33**:106

Major André, Brave Enemy (Duncan) **29**:68

Major: The Story of a Black Bear (McClung) **11**:180

Make a Circle, Keep Us In: Poems for a Good Day (Adoff) **7**:32

Make a Face (McNaughton) **54**:56

Make a Joyful Noise! (Haywood) **22**:105

Make a Joyful Noise unto the Lord! The Life of Mahalia Jackson, Queen of Gospel Singers (Jackson) **28**:142

Make It Special: Cards, Decorations, and Party Favors for Holidays and Other Celebrations (Hautzig) **22**:86

Make Way for Ducklings (McCloskey) **7**:200

Make Way for Dumb Bunnies (Pilkey) **48**:113

Make Way for Sam Houston (Fritz) **14**:121

Making Friends (Ormerod) **20**:180

Making Friends with Frankenstein: A Book of Monstrous Poems and Pictures (McNaughton) **54**:63

Making It (Corcoran) **50**:28

Making Music for Money (Collier) **3**:46

The Making of an Afro-American: Martin Robison Delaney, 1812-1885 (Sterling) **1**:180

The Making of Fingers Finnigan (Doherty) **21**:56

The Making of Man: The Story of Our Ancient Ancestors (Collier) **3**:46

Making Sense of Money (Cobb) **3**:66

Making Sneakers (McMillan) **47**:162

Making the Mississippi Shout (Calhoun) **42**:4

Making the Movies (Bendick) **5**:34

Makoto, the Smallest Boy: A Story of Japan (Uchida) **6**:256

Malcolm X (Adoff) **7**:31

Malcolm X: A Force for Change (Grimes) **42**:91

Malcolm X: By Any Means Necessary (Myers) **35**:200

The Maldonado Miracle (Taylor) **30**:187

The Malibu and Other Poems (Livingston) **7**:170

Mama (Hopkins) **44**:88

Mama and Her Boys (Hopkins) **44**:91

Mama Hattie's Girl (Lenski) **26**:117

Mama, I Wish I Was Snow—Child, You'd Be Very Cold (Krauss) **42**:126

Mama One, Mama Two (MacLachlan) **14**:181

Mama, Papa and Baby Joe (Daly) **41**:58

Mammals and How They Live (McClung) **11**:182

Mammals of the Sea (Silverstein and Silverstein) **25**:205

Man and the Horse (Ventura) **16**:195

Man Changes the Weather (Bova) **3**:34

The Man from the Other Side (Orlev) **30**:165

Man from the Sky (Avi) **24**:8

Man in Space to the Moon (Branley) **13**:37

The Man in the Manhole and the Fix-It Men (Brown) **10**:54

The Man in the Manhole and the Fix-It Men (Hurd) **49**:118

The Man in the Woods (Wells) **16**:212
Man Mountain (Waddell) **31**:200
Man Must Speak: The Story of Language and How We Use It (Gallant) **30**:89
Man of the Monitor: The Story of John Ericsson (Latham) **50**:103
Man the Measurer: Our Units of Measure and How They Grew (Gallant) **30**:91
The Man Who Could Call Down Owls (Bunting) **28**:55
The Man Who Kept His Heart in a Bucket (Levitin) **53**:70
The Man Who Kept His Heart in a Bucket (Pinkney) **43**:168
The Man Who Knew Too Much: A Moral Tale from the Baila of Zambia (Lester) **41**:113
The Man Who Loved Books (Fritz) **14**:115
The Man Who Played Accordion Music (Tobias) **4**:218
The Man Who Sang the Sillies (Ciardi) **19**:77
The Man Who Sang the Sillies (Gorey) **36**:89
The Man Who Talked to a Tree (Baylor) **3**:15
The Man Who Took the Indoors Out (Lobel) **5**:168
The Man Who Tricked a Ghost (Yep) **54**:192
The Man Who Was Going to Mind the House: A Norwegian Folk-Tale (McKee) **38**:161
The Man Who Was Poe (Avi) **24**:14
The Man Whose Mother Was a Pirate (Mahy) **7**:180
The Man Whose Name Was Not Thomas (Stanley) **46**:129
Man with a Sword (Treece) **2**:186
The Man with Eyes like Windows (Owen) **31**:146
The Man with the Purple Eyes (Zolotow) **2**:235
Maniac Magee (Spinelli) **26**:205
Man-Made Moons: The Earth Satellites and What They Will Tell Us (Adler) **27**:9
Ein Mann für Mama (Noestlinger) **12**:185
Manners Can Be Fun (Leaf) **25**:116
Man's Reach for the Stars (Gallant) **30**:89
Man's Reach into Space (Gallant) **30**:87
The Mansion in the Mist (Bellairs) **37**:25
The Many Lives of Benjamin Franklin (Aliki) **9**:25
The Many Mice of Mr. Brice (Dr. Seuss) **9**:193
Many Smokes, Many Moons: A Chronology of American Indian History through Indian Art (Highwater) **17**:28
Many Thousand Gone: African Americans from Slavery to Freedom (Hamilton) **40**:88
Many Thousand Gone: African Americans from Slavery to Freedom (Leo and Diane Dillon) **44**:46
Many Waters (L'Engle) **14**:155
Mao Tse-Tung and His China (Marrin) **53**:88
A Map of Nowhere (Cross) **28**:94
The Maplin Bird (Peyton) **3**:177
Marah (Merrill) **52**:113
Marathon and Steve (Rayner) **41**:128
Marc Brown's Full House (Brown) **29**:4
Marcella's Guardian Angel (Ness) **6**:208
The March on Washington (Haskins) **39**:72
Marcia (Steptoe) **12**:238
Marco Polo (Ventura) **16**:194
Marconi: Pioneer of Radio (Epstein and Epstein) **26**:43
Mardie to the Rescue (Lindgren) **39**:160
The Mare on the Hill (Locker) **14**:158
Marek, the Little Fool (Domanska) **40**:50
Margaret and Taylor (Henkes) **23**:125
Margaret Sanger: Pioneer of Birth Control (Meltzer) **13**:127
Margaret Wise Brown's Wonderful Story Book (Brown) **10**:56

Maria: A Christmas Story (Taylor) **30**:196
Maria Molina and the Days of the Dead (Krull) **44**:109
Maria Tallchief (Tobias) **4**:213
Marian Anderson (Tobias) **4**:213
Marianna May and Nursey (dePaola) **24**:93
Maria's House (Merrill) **52**:112
Marilka (Domanska) **40**:41
Mark and the Monocycle (McKee) **38**:158
The Mark of Conte (Levitin) **53**:59
The Mark of the Horse Lord (Sutcliff) **1**:188; **37**:158
Mark Time (McBratney) **44**:116
Mark Twain: A Writer's Life (Meltzer) **13**:149
The Mark Twain Murders (Yep) **17**:205
Marked by Fire (Thomas) **19**:219
Marly the Kid (Pfeffer) **11**:198
Marra's World (Coatsworth) **2**:60
Marrying Off Mother (Noestlinger) **12**:185
Mars (Branley) **13**:25
Mars: Planet Number Four (Branley) **13**:25
Mars, the Red Planet (Asimov) **12**:55
Martha, the Movie Mouse (Lobel) **5**:164
Martha's Birthday (Wells) **16**:203
Martin de Porres: Saint of the New World (Tarry) **26**:215
Martin Luther King, Jr.: A Man to Remember (McKissack) **23**:235
Martin Luther King: The Man Who Climbed the Mountain (Paulsen) **19**:170
Martin's Hats (Blos) **18**:18
Martin's Mice (King-Smith) **40**:153
The Marvellous Adventures of Pinocchio (Collodi) See *Le Avventure di Pinocchio*
The Marvelous Misadventures of Sebastian (Alexander) **1**:16; **5**:21
Marvin K. Mooney Will You Please Go Now (Dr. Seuss) **1**:88
Mary, Come Running (Merrill) **52**:109
Mary Had a Little Lamb (McMillan) **47**:175
Mary Jane (Sterling) **1**:180
Mary Malloy and the Baby Who Wouldn't Sleep (Daly) **41**:62
Mary McLeod Bethune (Greenfield) **4**:99
Mary McLeod Bethune: A Great American Educator (McKissack) **23**:236
Mary of Mile 18 (Blades) **15**:52
Mary of Nazareth (Bodker) **23**:14
Mary Poppins (Travers) **2**:178
Mary Poppins from A to Z (Travers) **2**:179
Mary Poppins in the Park (Travers) **2**:179
The Marzipan Moon (Willard) **5**:249
The Mask (Bunting) **28**:48
Mask for My Heart (St. John) **46**:111
Masquerade (Williams) **4**:231
The Master Monkey (Mukerji) **10**:135
Master of the Elephants (Guillot) **22**:64
Master of the Grove (Kelleher) **36**:118
The Master of the Winds: And Other Tales from Siberia (Ginsburg) **45**:3
The Master Puppeteer (Paterson) **7**:231
Masters of Modern Music (Berger) **32**:5
Math Curse (Smith) **47**:206
Mathematics (Adler) **27**:26
Mathematics: The Story of Numbers, Symbols, and Space (Adler) **27**:12
Mathinna's People (Chauncy) **6**:92
Matilda (Dahl) **41**:40
Matilda Jane (Gerrard) **23**:119
De matroos (Bruna) **7**:50
Matt and Jo (Southall) **2**:155
Matt Gargan's Boy (Slote) **4**:201
Matteo (French) **37**:42

A Matter of Principle: A Novel (Pfeffer) **11**:202
The Matter with Lucy (Grifalconi) **35**:72
Matty's Midnight Monster (Kemp) **29**:126
Maude and Walter (Oneal) **13**:160
Maudie in the Middle (Naylor) **17**:62
Maura's Angel (Reid Banks) **24**:195
Maurice Maeterlinck's "Blue Bird" (Wildsmith) **52**:181
Maurice Sendak's Really Rosie: Starring the Nutshell Kids (Sendak) **17**:121
Maurice's Room (Fox) **1**:79
Max (Isadora) **7**:102
Max in Hollywood, Baby (Kalman) **32**:185
Max Makes a Million (Kalman) **32**:182
Maxie, Rosie, and Earl—Partners in Grime (Park) **34**:161
Maxine in the Middle (Keller) **45**:53
Max's Bath (Wells) **16**:213
Max's Bedtime (Wells) **16**:213
Max's Birthday (Wells) **16**:213
Max's Breakfast (Wells) **16**:213
Max's Christmas (Wells) **16**:213
Max's First Word (Wells) **16**:209
Max's New Suit (Wells) **16**:209
Max's Ride (Wells) **16**:209
Max's Toys: A Counting Book (Wells) **16**:209
The May Day Mystery (Allan) **43**:21
The Maya (McKissack) **23**:237
Maybe You Should Fly a Jet! Maybe You Should Be a Vet! (Dr. Seuss) **9**:194
Maybelle, the Cable Car (Burton) **11**:51
The Mayday Rampage (Bess) **39**:7
Mazel and Shlimazel; or, The Milk of the Lioness (Singer) **1**:175
McBroom and the Beanstalk (Fleischman) **15**:109
McBroom and the Big Wind (Fleischman) **15**:107
McBroom and the Great Race (Fleischman) **15**:110
McBroom Tells a Lie (Fleischman) **15**:108
McBroom Tells the Truth (Fleischman) **1**:75
McBroom the Rainmaker (Fleischman) **15**:107
McBroom's Almanac (Fleischman) **15**:112
McBroom's Ear (Fleischman) **15**:107
McBroom's Ghost (Fleischman) **1**:75
McBroom's Zoo (Fleischman) **1**:75
McElligot's Pool (Dr. Seuss) **9**:175
McGruer and the Goat (Mattingley) **24**:129
Me and Jeshua (Spence) **26**:199
Me and Katie (the Pest) (Martin) **32**:201
Me and My Bones (Gallant) **30**:90
Me and My Captain (Goffstein) **3**:60
Me and My Family Tree (Showers) **6**:247
Me and My Friend (McNaughton) **54**:56
Me and My Little Brain (Fleischman) **1**:70
Me and My Shadow (Dorros) **42**:66
Me and Neesie (Greenfield) **4**:99
Me and the Man on the Moon-Eyed Horse (Fleischman) **15**:109
Me and the Terrible Two (Conford) **10**:92
Me and Willie and Pa: The Story of Abraham Lincoln and His Son Tad (Monjo) **2**:124
"Me and You and a Dog Named Blue" (Corcoran) **50**:25
Me Me Me Me Me: Not a Novel (Kerr) **29**:153
Me, Mop, and the Moondance Kid (Myers) **35**:193
Me, Myself and I (Matas) **52**:81
Me, Myself, and I: A Tale of Time Travel (Curry) **31**:86
Me Too (Cleaver and Cleaver) **6**:109
The Mean Old Mean Hyena (Prelutsky) **13**:167
The Measure of the Universe (Asimov) **12**:61
Measure with Metric (Branley) **13**:41
Measuring (Bendick) **5**:45

Meatball (McCully) **46**:66

Medals for Morse, Artist and Inventor (Latham) **50**:97

Medical Center Lab (Berger) **32**:16

Medicine (Zim) **2**:229

Medicine from Microbes: The Story of Antibiotics (Epstein and Epstein) **26**:60

Medicine in Action: Today and Tomorrow (Hyde) **23**:154

Medicine Man's Daughter (Clark) **16**:82

Medicine Show: Conning People and Making Them Like It (Calhoun) **42**:23

A Medieval Feast (Aliki) **9**:30

Meet Danitra Brown (Grimes) **42**:92

Meet Me at Tamerlane's Tomb (Corcoran) **50**:21

Meet Murdock (Naylor) **17**:50

Meet My Folks! (Hughes) **3**:93

Meet the Austins (L'Engle) **1**:131

Meet the Giant Snakes (Simon) **9**:214

Meet the Monsters (Yolen) **44**:210

Meeting Death (Hyde) **23**:176

Ho megalos peripatos tou Petrou (Zei) **6**:261

Megan's Star (Baillie) **49**:9

Megastar (Ure) **34**:178

Mein Urgrossvater, die Helden und Ich (Kruss) **9**:87

Mein Urgrossvater und Ich (Kruss) **9**:83

The Mellops' Go Spelunking (Ungerer) **3**:202

Melody: The Story of a Child (Richards) **54**:165

Melric and the Balloon (McKee) **38**:166

Melric and the Dragon (McKee) **38**:168

Melusine: A Mystery (Reid Banks) **24**:199

Memory: How It Works and How to Improve It (Gallant) **30**:95

Men from the Village Deep in the Mountains and Other Japanese Folk Tales (Bang) **8**:18

Men, Microscopes, and Living Things (Shippen) **36**:176

Men of Archaeology (Shippen) **36**:182

Men of Medicine (Shippen) **36**:177

Men of the Hills (Treece) **2**:187

Menstruation: Just Plain Talk (Nourse) **33**:142

The Mercy Man (Nourse) **33**:135

Merle the High Flying Squirrel (Peet) **12**:202

Merlin and the Dragons (Yolen) **44**:208

Merlin Dreams (Dickinson) **29**:59

Merlin's Magic (Clarke) **28**:74

The Mermaid and the Whale (McHargue) **2**:119

Mermaid of Storms (Calhoun) **42**:16

The Mermaid Summer (Hunter) **25**:91

Merry Christmas (Marshall) **21**:181

Merry Christmas, Amelia Bedelia (Parish) **22**:167

Merry Christmas, Baabee (Khalsa) **30**:144

Merry Christmas, Ernest and Celestine (Vincent) **13**:220

Merry Christmas from Betsy (Haywood) **22**:101

Merry Christmas from Eddie (Haywood) **22**:106

Merry Christmas, Space Case (Marshall) **21**:181

Merry Christmas, Strega Nona (dePaola) **24**:96

Merry Merry FIBruary (Orgel) **48**:83

The Merry Pranks of Till Eulenspiegel (Zwerger) **46**:199

Merry, Rose, and Christmas-Tree June (Orgel) **48**:78

Merry-Go-Round (Heine) **18**:147

The Merrymaker (Suhl) **2**:165

Message to Hadrian (Trease) **42**:183

A Messenger for Parliament (Haugaard) **11**:107

Messy Baby (Ormerod) **20**:177

Metamorphosis: The Magic Change (Silverstein and Silverstein) **25**:204

Meteor! (Polacco) **40**:179

Meteors and Meteorites: An Introduction to Meteoritics (Knight) **38**:108

Metric Can Be Fun! (Leaf) **25**:135

Mexico (Epstein and Epstein) **26**:53

Mia (*Mia Alone*) (Beckman) **25**:14

Mia Alone (Beckman)
See *Mia*

Mia Alone (Beckman) **25**:14

Mice and Mendelson (Aiken) **19**:12

Mice, Moose, and Men: How Their Populations Rise and Fall (McClung) **11**:188

Michael and the Mitten Test (Wells) **16**:203

Michael Bird-Boy (dePaola) **4**:57

Michael Faraday: Apprentice to Science (Epstein and Epstein) **26**:63

Michael Foreman's Mother Goose (Foreman) **32**:106

Michael Foreman's World of Fairy Tales (Foreman) **32**:105

Michael Jackson, Superstar! (McKissack) **23**:236

Michael Rosen's ABC (Rosen) **45**:151

Mickey's Magnet (Branley) **13**:25

Mickie (Unnerstad) **36**:200

Microbes at Work (Selsam) **1**:163

Microscopic Animals and Plants (Patent) **19**:148

The Middle Moffat (Estes) **2**:74

The Middle of Somewhere: A Story of South Africa (Gordon) **27**:94

The Middle Sister (Duncan) **29**:66

Midnight Adventure (Briggs) **10**:23

The Midnight Adventures of Kelly, Dot, and Esmeralda (Goodall) **25**:45

A Midnight Clear: Stories for the Christmas Season (Paterson) **50**:204

The Midnight Farm (Jeffers) **30**:136

The Midnight Fox (Byars) **1**:36

The Midnight Horse (Sis) **45**:163

Midnight Hour Encores (Brooks) **25**:32

Midnight Is a Place (Aiken) **1**:4

Midnight Soup and a Witch's Hat (Orgel) **48**:90

Midstream Changes: People Who Started Over and Made it Work (Aaseng) **54**:15

Midsummer Magic (Dillon) **26**:20

Mieko (Politi) **29**:193

Miffy in the Hospital (Bruna) **7**:52

Miffy's Dream (Bruna) **7**:52

The Mighty Ones (DeJong) **1**:59

Mik and the Prowler (Uchida) **6**:253

Mike Mulligan and His Steam Shovel (Burton) **11**:44

Miki (Petersham and Petersham) **24**:161

Miki and Mary: Their Search for Treasures (Petersham and Petersham) **24**:166

Milk and Honey: A Year of Jewish Holidays (Yolen) **44**:210

Milk: The Fight for Purity (Giblin) **29**:90

The Milkmaid (Caldecott) **14**:78

Milkweed (Selsam) **1**:164

Milkweed Butterflies: Monarchs, Models, and Mimics (Simon) **39**:185

The Milky Way Galaxy: Man's Exploration of the Stars (Bova) **3**:34

The Milky Way: Galaxy Number One (Branley) **13**:34

Mill (Macaulay) **14**:173

Millicent (Baker) **28**:19

Millicent and the Wind (Munsch) **19**:144

Millie's Boy (Peck) **45**:101

Millie's Secret (Fujikawa) **25**:40

Millions of Cats (Gag) **4**:87

The Mills Down Below (Allan) **43**:31

The Mills of God (Armstrong) **1**:23

The Mimosa Tree (Cleaver and Cleaver) **6**:105

Mind Control (Berger) **32**:34

Mind Drugs (Hyde) **23**:156

Mind the Gap (Rosen) **45**:145

Mind Your Manners! (Parish) **22**:161

Mind Your Own Business (Rosen) **45**:128

Mindy's Mysterious Miniature (*The Housenapper*) (Curry) **31**:75

Mine (Mayer) **11**:166

Mine for a Year (Kuklin) **51**:98

Mine for Keeps (Little) **4**:147

The Minerva Program (Mackay) **43**:108

Minestrone: A Ruth Krauss Selection (Krauss) **42**:131

Ming Lo Moves the Mountain (Lobel) **5**:176

Mini Beasties (Rosen) **45**:144

Mini-Bike Hero (Mackay) **43**:104

Mini-Bike Racer (Mackay) **43**:104

Mini-Bike Rescue (Mackay) **43**:107

The Min-Min (Clark) **30**:56

Minn of the Mississippi (Holling) **50**:54

Minnie's Yom Kippur Birthday (Singer) **48**:133

The Minnow Family—Chubs, Dace, Minnows, and Shiners (Pringle) **4**:180

The Minnow Leads to Treasure (Pearce) **9**:143

The Minnow Leads to Treasure (Pearce)
See *Minnow on the Say*

Minnow on the Say (*The Minnow Leads to Treasure*) (Pearce) **9**:143

The Minority Peoples of China (Rau) **8**:193

The Minpins (Dahl) **41**:46

The Minstrel and the Dragon Pup (Sutcliff) **37**:182

The Minstrel and the Mountain (Yolen) **4**:257

Minty: A Story of Young Harriet Tubman (Pinkney) **43**:174

The Mintyglo Kid (Cross) **28**:89

Mio, My Son (Lindgren) **39**:146

Miracle in Motion: The Story of America's Industry (Shippen) **36**:177

Miracle on the Plate (Christopher) **33**:42

The Miracle Tree (Mattingley) **24**:129

The Miracles of Jesus (dePaola) **24**:99

The Miraculous Hind: A Hungarian Legend (Cleaver) **13**:66

Miranda the Great (Estes) **2**:74

Miranda's Pilgrims (Wells) **16**:204

Miranda's Umbrella (Biro) **28**:40

Mirandy and Brother Wind (McKissack) **23**:239

Mirandy and Brother Wind (Pinkney) **43**:162

Mirette on the High Wire (McCully) **46**:67

Mirror Magic (Simon) **9**:215

Mirror, Mirror (Garfield) **21**:109

Mirror of Her Own (Guy) **13**:84

The Mirror Planet (Bunting) **28**:48

Mischief City (Wynne-Jones) **21**:230

The Mischievous Martens (Lindgren) **39**:151

Mischievous Meg (Lindgren) **39**:149

Miss Bianca (Sharp) **27**:162

Miss Bianca and the Bridesmaid (Sharp) **27**:165

Miss Bianca in the Antarctic (Sharp) **27**:164

Miss Bianca in the Orient (Sharp) **27**:164

Miss Bianca in the Salt Mines (Sharp) **27**:163

Miss Dog's Christmas Treat (Marshall) **21**:169

Miss Emily and the Bird of Make-Believe (Keeping) **34**:105

Miss Happiness and Miss Flower (Godden) **20**:131

Miss Maggie (Rylant) **15**:169

Miss Nelson Has a Field Day (Marshall) **21**:180

Miss Nelson Is Back (Marshall) **21**:177

Miss Nelson Is Missing (Marshall) **21**:172

Miss Rumphius (Cooney) **23**:31

Miss Wirtles' Revenge (Morpurgo) **51**:119

Missee Lee (Ransome) **8**:180

Missing Children (Hyde) **23**:171*

Missing in Manhattan (Allan) **43**:17
The Missing Lollipop (McBratney) **44**:121
The Missing Maple Syrup Sap Mystery; or, How Maple Syrup Is Made (Gibbons) **8**:90
The Missing Milkman (Duvoisin) **23**:104
The Missing Piece (Silverstein) **5**:211
The Missing Piece Meets the Big O (Silverstein) **5**:212
Missing Since Monday (Martin) **32**:202
The Mission Bell (Politi) **29**:189
Mister Magnolia (Blake) **31**:23
Mister Peale's Mammoth (Epstein and Epstein) **26**:65
Mister Penny (Ets) **33**:74
Mister Penny's Circus (Ets) **33**:88
Mister Penny's Race Horse (Ets) **33**:84
Mistresses of Mystery: Two Centuries of Suspense Stories by the Gentle Sex (Manley) **3**:145
Misty of Chincoteague (Henry) **4**:110
Mitch and Amy (Cleary) **2**:48; **8**:52
The Mitten: A Ukrainian Folktale (Brett) **27**:42
The Mitten: An Old Ukrainian Folktale (Tresselt) **30**:208
Mitzi and Frederick the Great (Williams) **48**:203
Mitzi and the Terrible Tyrannosaurus Rex (Williams) **48**:201
The Mixed-Up Chameleon (Carle) **10**:79
Mixed-Up Magic (Cole) **40**:22
The Mixed-Up Twins (Haywood) **22**:95
The Mock Revolt (Cleaver and Cleaver) **6**:107
Mockingbird Morning (Ryder) **37**:90
Model Buildings and How to Make Them (Weiss) **4**:229
Model Cars and Trucks and How to Build Them (Weiss) **4**:227
Modern Ballads and Story Poems (Causley) **30**:32
Modern China (Carter) **22**:20
Modern Electronics (Carter) **22**:20
Moe Q. McGlutch, He Smoked Too Much (Raskin) **1**:156
Moe the Dog in Tropical Paradise (Stanley) **46**:148
The Moffats (Estes) **2**:75
Mog at the Zoo (Pienkowski) **6**:233
Mog's Mumps (Pienkowski) **6**:230
Moira's Birthday (Munsch) **19**:146
Moja Means One: Swahili Counting Book (Feelings and Feelings) **5**:105
Mojo and the Russians (Myers) **4**:157
Mokokambo, the Lost Land (Guillot) **22**:63
Mole Hole (Dickinson) **29**:58
Molly o' the Moors: The Story of a Pony (Keeping) **34**:88
Mom, the Wolf Man, and Me (Klein) **2**:99
Mommies at Work (Merriam) **14**:192
Momo: Oder, die Seltsame Geschichte von D. Zeitdieben U. von D. Kind, das D. Menschen D. Gestohlene Zeit Zurückbrachte; Ein Märchenroman (Ende) **14**:97
Momoko and the Pretty Bird (Iwasaki) **18**:154
Momoko's Birthday (Iwasaki) **18**:154
Momoko's Lovely Day (Iwasaki) **18**:153
Momo's Kitten (Yashima) **4**:253
Mom's Home (Ormerod) **20**:180
The Mona Lisa Mystery (Hutchins) **20**:151
The Money Tree (Small) **53**:151
The Monkey and the Crocodile: A Jataka Tale from India (Galdone) **16**:94
Monkey and the Three Wizards (Foreman) **32**:89
Monkey Business: Hoaxes in the Name of Science (Adler) **27**:9
Monkey Day (Krauss) **42**:123
Monkey in the Jungle (Hurd) **49**:126
Monkey in the Middle (Bunting) **28**:56

Monkey Island (Fox) **44**:72
Monkey See, Monkey Do (Oxenbury) **22**:143
Monkey-Monkey's Trick: Based on an African Folk Tale (McKissack) **23**:240
Monkeys (Zim) **2**:229
The Monster and the Tailor: A Ghost Story (Galdone) **16**:104
The Monster and the Teddy Bear (McKee) **38**:179
The Monster Den: Or Look What Happened at My House—And to It (Ciardi) **19**:79
The Monster Den; or, Look What Happened at My House—and to It (Gorey) **36**:91
Monster Dinosaur (Cohen) **43**:44
The Monster from Underground (Cross) **28**:95
The Monster Garden (Alcock) **26**:6
A Monster in the Mailbox (Gordon) **27**:91
Monster Night at Grandma's House (Peck) **15**:159
Monsters (Blumberg) **21**:28
Monsters (McNaughton) **54**:55
Monsters Are Like That (Daly) **41**:55
The Monsters' Ball (dePaola) **4**:54
Monsters from the Movies (Aylesworth) **6**:49
The Monster's Legacy (Norton) **50**:163
A Monstrous Story (Hilton) **25**:60
The Month Brothers: A Slavic Tale (Stanley) **46**:132
Monticello (Fisher) **18**:138
Monty (Stevenson) **17**:155
The Monument (Paulsen) **54**:105
Moominpappa at Sea (Jansson) **2**:94
Moominsummer Madness (Jansson) **2**:94
Moominvalley in November (Jansson) **2**:94
The Moon (Asimov) **12**:40
The Moon and a Star and Other Poems (Livingston) **7**:168
Moon and Me (Irwin) **40**:109
The Moon by Night (L'Engle) **1**:132
The Moon: Earth's Natural Satellite (Branley) **13**:29
The Moon in Fact and Fancy (Slote) **4**:198
The Moon in the Cloud (Harris) **30**:111
Moon Man (Ungerer) **3**:202
The Moon of Gomrath (Garner) **20**:101
A Moon or a Button: A Collection of First Picture Ideas (Krauss) **42**:124
The Moon Ribbon and Other Tales (Yolen) **4**:262
Moon, Stars, Frogs, and Friends (MacLachlan) **14**:181
The Moon Walker (Showers) **6**:247
Moonbeam on a Cat's Ear (Gay) **27**:85
Moon-Bells and Other Poems (Moon-Whales and Other Moon Poems) (Hughes) **3**:93
The Mooncusser's Daughter (Aiken) **1**:5
Moondial (Cresswell) **18**:112
Moonflute (Wood and Wood) **26**:221
The Moonglow Roll-O-Rama (Pilkey) **48**:110
Moonlight (Ormerod) **20**:175
The Moonlight Man (Fox) **44**:66
The Moons of Our Solar System (Knight) **38**:113
The Moon's Revenge (Aiken) **19**:18
Moonseed and Mistletoe: A Book of Poisonous Wild Plants (Lerner) **34**:132
Moonsong Lullaby (Highwater) **17**:29
Moon-Uncle, Moon-Uncle: Rhymes from India (Cassedy) **26**:12
Moon-Whales and Other Moon Poems (Hughes) See *Moon-Bells and Other Poems*
Moose (Foreman) **32**:87
Moose (Scott) **20**:200
Moose and Goose (Brown) **29**:4
Moose, Goose, and Little Nobody (Raskin) **12**:223
Mop, Moondance, and the Nagasaki Knights (Myers) **35**:198

Mop Top (Freeman) **30**:70
More About Animals (Bianco) **19**:53
More About Rebecca of Sunnybrook Farm (Wiggin) **52**:166
More Adventures of the Great Brain (Fitzgerald) **1**:70
More and More Ant and Bee: Another Alphabetical Story (Banner) **24**:18
More Bunny Trouble (Wilhelm) **46**:165
More Experiments in Science (Branley) **13**:23
More Minds (Matas) **52**:94
More Mr. Small (Lenski) **26**:125
More of Brer Rabbit's Tricks (Gorey) **36**:93
A More Perfect Union: The Story of Our Constitution (Betsy and Giulio Maestro) **45**:79
More Short and Shivery: Thirty Terrifying Tales (San Souci) **43**:192
More Small Poems (Worth) **21**:221
More Stories of Baseball Champions: In the Hall of Fame (Epstein and Epstein) **26**:65
More Stories to Solve: Fifteen Folktales from Around the World (Sis) **45**:164
More Surprises: An I Can Read Book (Hopkins) **44**:94
More Tales from Grimm (Gag) **4**:94
More Tales of Uncle Remus: The Further Adventures of Brer Rabbit, His Friends, Enemies, and Others (Lester) **41**:107
More Tales of Uncle Remus: The Further Adventures of Brer Rabbit, His Friends, Enemies, and Others (Pinkney) **43**:161
More Than One (Hoban) **13**:105
More with Less: The Future World of Buckminister Fuller (Aaseng) **54**:12
More Words of Science (Asimov) **12**:48
Moreta: Dragonlady of Pern (McCaffrey) **49**:145
Morgan the Magnificent (Wallace) **37**:216
Morgan's Zoo (Howe) **9**:60
Mori No Ehon (Anno) **14**:34
Morning Is a Little Child (Anglund) **1**:21
Morning Star, Black Sun: The Northern Cheyenne Indians and America's Energy Crisis (Ashabranner) **28**:5
Morris's Disappearing Bag: A Christmas Story (Wells) **16**:207
The Mortal Instruments (Bethancourt) **3**:18
Mortimer (Munsch) **19**:143
Mortimer Says Nothing (Aiken) **19**:16
Mortimer's Cross (Aiken) **19**:14
Moses (Shippen) **36**:171
Moses' Ark: Stories from the Bible (Leo and Diane Dillon) **44**:39
Moses: From the Story Told in the Old Testament (Petersham and Petersham) **24**:169
Moss and Blister (Garfield) **21**:109
Mossflower (Jacques) **21**:154
Mossop's Last Chance (Morpurgo) **51**:129
The Most Important Thing (Ure) **34**:178
The Most Wonderful Egg in the World (Heine) **18**:148
Motel of the Mysteries (Macaulay) **14**:171
The Mother Beaver (Hurd and Hurd) **49**:127
Mother Carey (Wiggin) **52**:166
Mother Carey's Chickens (Wiggin) **52**:166
The Mother Chimpanzee (Hurd and Hurd) **49**:129
Mother Crocodile (Guy) **13**:85
Mother Goose; or, The Old Nursery Rhymes (Greenaway) **6**:132
Mother Goose: Seventy-Seven Verses (Tudor) **13**:192
Mother Goose's Little Misfortunes (Schwartz) **25**:196

Mother, Mother, I Feel Sick, Send for the Doctor Quick, Quick, Quick: A Picture Book and Shadow Play (Charlip) **8**:27
The Mother Whale (Hurd and Hurd) **49**:128
The Mother's Day Mice (Bunting) **28**:59
Mother's Helper (Oxenbury) **22**:143
Moths and Butterflies and How They Live (McClung) **11**:184
Motion and Gravity (Bendick) **5**:45
Motors and Engines and How They Work (Weiss) **4**:225
Motown and Didi: A Love Story (Myers) **16**:141
The Mountain Goats of Temlaham (Cleaver) **13**:65
Mountain Light (Yep) **17**:208
Mountain Rose (Stren) **5**:234
Mountain with a Secret (Guillot) **22**:67
The Mouse and His Child (Hoban) **3**:78
The Mouse and the Motorcycle (Cleary) **2**:48; **8**:51
The Mouse Butcher (King-Smith) **40**:142
Mouse Days: A Book of Seasons (Lionni) **7**:139
Mouse House (Godden) **20**:128
Mouse Manor (Eager) **43**:79
Mouse Numbers and Letters (Arnosky) **15**:6
The Mouse Rap (Myers) **35**:194
The Mouse Sheriff (Janosch) **26**:77
Mouse Soup (Lobel) **5**:171
Mouse Tales (Lobel) **5**:168
Mouse Trouble (Yeoman) **46**:176
Mouse Views: What the Class Pet Saw (McMillan) **47**:182
Mouse Woman and the Mischief-Makers (Harris) **47**:87
Mouse Woman and the Muddleheads (Harris) **47**:88
Mouse Woman and the Vanished Princesses (Harris) **47**:84
Mouse Writing (Arnosky) **15**:6
The Mousewife (Freedman) **20**:126
The Moves Make the Man (Brooks) **25**:30
Movie Monsters (Aylesworth) **6**:51
Movie Shoes (The Painted Garden) (Streatfeild) **17**:190
Moving (Graham) **31**:95
Moving (Rosen) **45**:148
The Moving Adventures of Old Dame Trot and Her Comical Cat (Galdone) **16**:98
The Moving Coffins: Ghosts and Hauntings Around the World (Knight) **38**:128
Moving Day (Tobias) **4**:215
Moving Heavy Things (Adkins) **7**:25
Moving Molly (Hughes) **15**:124
Moy Moy (Politi) **29**:191
Mr. Adams's Mistake (Parish) **22**:166
Mr. and Mrs. Hay the Horse (McNaughton) **54**:52
Mr. and Mrs. Muddle (Hoberman) **22**:114
Mr. and Mrs. Noah (Lenski) **26**:113
Mr. and Mrs. Pig's Evening Out (Rayner) **41**:121
Mr. Archimedes' Bath (Allen) **44**:5
Mr. Bass' Planetoid (Cameron) **1**:40
Mr. Bat's Great Invention (Noestlinger) **12**:184
Mr. Bats Meisterstück; oder, die Total Verjüngte Oma (Noestlinger) **12**:184
Mr. Bear and Apple Jam (Kuratomi) **32**:190
Mr. Bear and the Robbers (Kuratomi) **32**:189
Mr. Bear Goes to Sea (Kuratomi) **32**:188
Mr. Bear in the Air (Kuratomi) **32**:189
Mr. Bear, Postman (Kuratomi) **32**:191
Mr. Bear, Station-Master (Kuratomi) **32**:190
Mr. Bear's Christmas (Kuratomi) **32**:190
Mr. Bear's Drawing (Kuratomi) **32**:190
Mr. Bear's Meal (Kuratomi) **32**:191
Mr. Bear's Trumpet (Kuratomi) **32**:189

Mr. Bear's Winter Sleep (Kuratomi) **32**:191
Mr. Bell Invents the Telephone (Shippen) **36**:174
Mr. Benn, Red Knight (McKee) **38**:157
Mr Bidery's Spidery Garden (McCord) **9**:101
Mr. Bojangles: The Biography of Bill Robinson (Haskins) **39**:54
Mr. Cat in Business (Rodari) **24**:210
Mr. Corbett's Ghost and Other Stories (Garfield) **21**:99
Mr. Fong's Toy Shop (Politi) **29**:195
Mr. Frumble's Worst Day Ever! (Scarry) **41**:171
Mr Gumpy's Motor Car (Burningham) **9**:45
Mr Gumpy's Outing (Burningham) **9**:43
Mr. Kelso's Lion (Bontemps) **6**:84
Mr. Kneebone's New Digs (Wallace) **37**:219
Mr. Little (Peck) **45**:114
Mr. Magus Is Waiting for You (Kemp) **29**:121
Mr. McFadden's Hallowe'en (Godden) **20**:134
Mr. McGee (Allen) **44**:10
Mr. McGee and the Blackberry Jam (Allen) **44**:15
Mr. Miller the Dog (Heine) **18**:145
Mr. Monkey and the Gotcha Bird: An Original Tale (Myers) **16**:142
Mr. Mysterious and Company (Fleischman) **1**:75
Mr. Mysterious's Secrets of Magic (Fleischman) **15**:108
Mr. Noah and the Second Flood (Burnford) **2**:20
Mr. Nobody's Eyes (Morpurgo) **51**:130
Mr. Plunkett's Pool (Rubinstein) **35**:213
Mr. Revere and I (Lawson) **2**:110
Mr. Skinner's Skinny House (McGovern) **50**:121
Mr. T. Anthony Woo: The Story of a Cat, a Dog, and a Mouse (Ets) **33**:79
Mr. Tucket (Paulsen) **19**:169
Mr. Wuzzel (Janosch) **26**:75
Mrs. Armitage on Wheels (Blake) **31**:27
Mrs. Beggs and the Wizard (Mayer) **11**:167
Mrs. Cockle's Cat (Pearce) **9**:149
Mrs. Discombobulous (Mahy) **7**:179
Mrs. Dog's Own House (Calhoun) **42**:19
Mrs. Fish, Ape, and Me, the Dump Queen (Mazer) **23**:226
Mrs. Frisby and the Rats of NIMH (O'Brien) **2**:127
Mrs. Katz and Tush (Polacco) **40**:193
Mrs. Moskowitz and the Sabbath Candlesticks (Schwartz) **25**:191
Mrs. Pepperpot Again and Other Stories (Proysen) **24**:182
Mrs. Pepperpot in the Magic Wood (Proysen) **24**:183
Mrs. Pepperpot to the Rescue (Proysen) **24**:182
Mrs. Pepperpot's Busy Day (Proysen) **24**:183
Mrs. Pepperpot's Christmas (Proysen) **24**:184
Mrs. Pepperpot's Outing and Other Stories (Proysen) **24**:183
Mrs. Pepperpot's Year (Proysen) **24**:185
Mrs. Pig Gets Cross and Other Stories (Rayner) **41**:125
Mrs. Pig's Bulk Buy (Rayner) **41**:123
Much Bigger than Martin (Kellogg) **6**:174
Muck and Magic: Stories from the Countryside (Morpurgo) **51**:146
Mud Puddle (Munsch) **19**:141
Mud Time and More: Nathaniel Stories (Arnosky) **15**:3
The Muddle-Headed Wombat and the Invention (Park) **51**:175
The Muddle-Headed Wombat in the Snow (Park) **51**:173
The Muddle-Headed Wombat in the Springtime (Park) **51**:174
The Muddle-Headed Wombat in the Treetops (Park) **51**:172

The Muddle-Headed Wombat on Holiday (Park) **51**:172
Muffie Mouse and the Busy Birthday (Nixon) **24**:137
The Mulberry Music (Orgel) **48**:80
The Mule on the Motorway (Berna) **19**:39
Muley-Ears, Nobody's Dog (Henry) **4**:113
Mummies (McHargue) **2**:119
Mummies Made in Egypt (Aliki) **9**:27
The Mummy, The Will, and The Crypt (Bellairs) **37**:15
Mum's Place (Ottley) **16**:188
Mum's the Word (Morpurgo) **51**:146
Mungoon-Gali the Giant Goanna (Trezise) **41**:144
The Muppet Guide to Magnificent Manners: Featuring Jim Henson's Muppets (Howe) **9**:60
Murmel, Murmel, Murmel (Munsch) **19**:143
The Muscular System: How Living Creatures Move (Silverstein and Silverstein) **25**:207
Museum: The Story of America's Treasure Houses (Schwartz) **3**:189
Mushroom in the Rain (Ginsburg) **45**:6
Music, Music for Everyone (Williams) **9**:235
The Music of Dolphins (Hesse) **54**:39
The Music of What Happens: Poems That Tell Stories (Janeczko) **47**:108
Musk Oxen: Bearded Ones of the Arctic (Rau) **8**:188
Mustang, Wild Spirit of the West (Henry) **4**:115
A Mustard Seed of Magic (St. John) **46**:105
My Ballet Class (Isadora) **7**:105
My Book about Me: By Me, Myself. I Wrote It! I Drew It! With a Little Help from My Friends Dr. Seuss and Roy McKie (Dr. Seuss) **9**:191
My Brother Fine with Me (Clifton) **5**:56
My Brother Sam Is Dead (Collier and Collier) **3**:47
My Brother Sean (Shawn Goes to School) (Breinburg) **31**:66
My Cat Has Eyes of Sapphire Blue (Fisher) **49**:55
My Cat Maisie (Allen) **44**:12
My Cousin Abe (Fisher) **49**:39
My Crazy Sister (Goffstein) **3**:60
My Darling, My Hamburger (Zindel) **3**:249
My Darling Villain (Reid Banks) **24**:192
My Day on the Farm (Nakatani) **30**:160
My Dog is Lost (Keats) **35**:121
My Dog Rinty (Ets) **33**:77
My Dog Rinty (Tarry) **26**:213
My Family Vacation (Khalsa) **30**:148
My Father, the Coach (Slote) **4**:200
My Father's Hands (Ryder) **37**:100
My Favorite Thing (Fujikawa) **25**:40
My First Chanukah (dePaola) **24**:103
My First Love and Other Disasters (Pascal) **25**:183
My First Word Book (Scarry) **41**:171
My Folks Don't Want Me to Talk about Slavery: Twenty-One Oral Histories of Former North Carolina Slaves (Hurmence) **25**:94
My Friend Has Four Parents (Hyde) **23**:167
My Friend Jacob (Clifton) **5**:60
My Friend John (Zolotow) **3**:236
My Friend Walter (Morpurgo) **51**:129
My Friend Wants to Run Away (Hyde) **23**:166
My Friend's Got This Problem, Mr. Candler: High School Poems (Glenn) **51**:91
My Gang (Waddell) **31**:182
My Grandma Lived in Gooligulch (Base) **22**:3
My Great Grandpa (Waddell) **31**:195
My Great-Grandfather and I: Useful and Amusing Occurrences and Inspirations from the Lobster Shack on Helgoland Told to the "Leathery Lisbeth" and Embellished with Verses from My Great-Grandfather and Me (Kruss) **9**:83

My Great-Grandfather, the Heroes, and I: A Brief Study of Heroes in Verse and Prose, Made Up and Told in Several Attic Rooms by My Great-Grandfather and Myself (Kruss) **9**:87
My Heart's in Greenwich Village (Manley) **3**:146
My Heart's in the Heather (Manley) **3**:146
My Island Grandma (Lasky) **11**:115
My Life as a Body (Klein) **19**:100
My Life in Dog Years (Paulsen) **54**:124
My Little Hen (Provensen and Provensen) **11**:211
My Love, My Love; or, the Peasant Girl (Guy) **13**:88
My Mama Needs Me (Cummings) **48**:45
My Mama Needs Me (Walter) **15**:206
My Mama Says There Aren't Any Zombies, Ghosts, Vampires, Creatures, Demons, Monsters, Fiends, Goblins, or Things (Viorst) **3**:208
My Many Colored Days (Dr. Seuss) **53**:142
My Mate Shofiq (Needle) **43**:131
My Mother and I (Fisher) **49**:46
My Mother Got Married (And Other Disasters) (Park) **34**:159
My Mother's Ghost (Buffie) **39**:27
My Mother's Loves: Stories and Lies from My Childhood (Poulin) **28**:197
My Name Is Paula Popowich! (Hughes) **9**:77
My New Kitten (Cole) **40**:33
My Nightingale is Singing (Lindgren) **39**:162
My Painted House, My Friendly Chicken, and Me (Angelou) **53**:18
My Parents Think I'm Sleeping (Prelutsky) **13**:173
My Pets (Hill) **13**:93
My Puppy Is Born (Cole) **5**:63
My Real Family (McCully) **46**:70
My Robot Buddy (Slote) **4**:201
My Rotten Redheaded Older Brother (Polacco) **40**:198
My School (Spier) **5**:228
My Shalom, My Peace: Paintings and Poems by Jewish and Arab Children (Ofek) **28**:190
My Side of the Mountain (George) **1**:91
My Sister Sif (Park) **51**:180
My Sister, the Vampire (Garden) **51**:79
My Spain: A Storyteller's Year of Collecting (Sawyer) **36**:165
My Special Best Words (Steptoe) **2**:163
My Street's a Morning Cool Street (Thomas) **8**:213
My Teddy Bear (Nakatani) **30**:160
My Treasures (Nakatani) **30**:161
My Trip to Alpha I (Slote) **4**:202
My Very First Book (Petersham and Petersham) **24**:177
My Very First Book of Colors (Carle) **10**:77
My Very First Book of Numbers (Carle) **10**:77
My Very First Book of Shapes (Carle) **10**:77
My Very First Book of Words (Carle) **10**:77
My Very First Library (Carle) **10**:77
My Visit to the Dinosaurs (Aliki) **9**:21
My War with Goggle-Eyes (Fine) **25**:23
My War With Mrs. Galloway (Orgel) **48**:87
My World (Brown) **10**:58
My Year (Dahl) **41**:49
Myna Bird Mystery (Berna) **19**:40
Myself and I (St. John) **46**:110
The Mysteries of Harris Burdick (Van Allsburg) **13**:209
Mysteries of Migration (McClung) **11**:194
Mysteries of Outer Space (Branley) **13**:50
Mysteries of the Satellites (Branley) **13**:53
Mysteries of the Universe (Branley) **13**:50
The Mysterious Disappearance of Leon (I Mean Noel) (Raskin) **1**:156

The Mysterious Giant of Barletta: An Italian Folktale (dePaola) **24**:95
The Mysterious Mr. Ross (Alcock) **26**:5
The Mysterious Prowler (Nixon) **24**:136
Mysterious Queen of Magic (Nixon) **24**:142
The Mysterious Red Tape Gang (Nixon) **24**:135
The Mysterious Tadpole (Kellogg) **6**:175
The Mystery at Monkey Run (Christopher) **33**:42
Mystery at the Edge of Two Worlds (Harris) **47**:88
The Mystery Beast of Ostergeest (Kellogg) **6**:170
The Mystery Began in Madeira (Allan) **43**:16
Mystery Coach (Christopher) **33**:46
Mystery in Arles (Allan) **43**:13
Mystery in Rome (Allan) **43**:25
Mystery in Wales (Allan) **43**:19
Mystery Monsters of Loch Ness (Lauber) **16**:118
The Mystery Of Drear House: The Conclusion of the Dies Drear Chronicle (Hamilton) **40**:73
Mystery of Hurricane Castle (Nixon) **24**:133
The Mystery of Saint-Salgue (Berna) **19**:38
The Mystery of Sleep (Silverstein and Silverstein) **25**:224
The Mystery of Stonehenge (Branley) **13**:35
The Mystery of the Bog Forest (Milne and Milne) **22**:125
The Mystery of the Diamond in the Wood (Kherdian) **24**:113
The Mystery of the Flying Orange Pumpkin (Kellogg) **6**:177
The Mystery of the Giant Footsteps (Krahn) **3**:105
Mystery of the Grinning Idol (Nixon) **24**:134
Mystery of the Haunted Woods (Nixon) **24**:134
Mystery of the Hidden Cockatoo (Nixon) **24**:134
The Mystery of the Loch Ness Monster (Bendick) **5**:49
The Mystery of the Magic Green Ball (Kellogg) **6**:175
Mystery of the Midnight Menace (Garden) **51**:76
The Mystery of the Missing Red Mitten (Kellogg) **6**:172
Mystery of the Night Raiders (Garden) **51**:75
Mystery of the Secret Marks (Garden) **51**:77
Mystery of the Secret Square (Hagon) **43**:20
Mystery of the Secret Stowaway (Nixon) **24**:134
Mystery of the Ski Slopes (Allan) **43**:14
The Mystery of the Stolen Blue Paint (Kellogg) **6**:178
Mystery of the Watchful Witches (Garden) **51**:79
The Mystery on Crabapple Hill (Christopher) **33**:40
Mystery on the Fourteenth Floor (Allan) **43**:12
Myths of the World (Colum) **36**:37
The Na of Wa (Aardema) **17**:3
The Name of The Tree: A Bantu Folktale (Wallace) **37**:218
Names, Sets, and Numbers (Bendick) **5**:43
Nana Upstairs and Nana Downstairs (dePaola) **4**:54
The Nanny Goat and the Fierce Dog (Keeping) **34**:98
Naomi in the Middle (Klein) **2**:100
The Nap Master (Kotzwinkle) **6**:183
Napoleon and the Napoleonic Wars (Marrin) **53**:90
Napper Goes for Goal (Waddell) **31**:178
Napper Strikes Again (Waddell) **31**:180
Napper's Golden Goals (Waddell) **31**:183
The Napping House (Wood and Wood) **26**:221
The Nargun and the Stars (Wrightson) **4**:244
Nasty! (Rosen) **45**:131
Nat King Cole (Haskins) **39**:48
Nathaniel (Arnosky) **15**:2

Nathaniel Hawthorne: Captain of the Imagination (Manley) **3**:147
Nathaniel Talking (Greenfield) **38**:89
National Geographic Picture Atlas of Our Universe (Gallant) **30**:96
The National Weather Service (Berger) **32**:7
Native American Animal Stories Told by Joseph Bruchac (Bruchac) **46**:9
Native American Stories (Bruchac) **46**:7
Nattpappan (Gripe) **5**:146
Natural Fire: Its Ecology in Forests (Pringle) **4**:184
The Nature of Animals (Milne and Milne) **22**:120
The Nature of Plants (Milne and Milne) **22**:121
The Nature of the Beast (Howker) **14**:128
Nature's Champions: The Biggest, the Fastest, the Best (Silverstein and Silverstein) **25**:219
Nature's Clean-Up Crew: The Burying Beetles (Milne and Milne) **22**:124
Nature's Great Carbon Cycle (Milne and Milne) **22**:125
Nature's Living Lights: Fireflies and Other Bioluminescent Creatures (Silverstein and Silverstein) **25**:225
Nature's Weather Forecasters (Sattler) **24**:215
The Naughty Comet and Other Fables and Stories (Richards) **54**:166
Naughty Nancy (Goodall) **25**:46
Naughty Nancy Goes to School (Goodall) **25**:55
Naughty Nancy, The Bad Bridesmaid (Goodall) **25**:46
Nautilus (Richards) **54**:165
Navajo Code Talkers (Aaseng) **54**:17
The Near East (Asimov) **12**:42
Near the Window Tree: Poems and Notes (Kuskin) **4**:142
A Near Thing for Captain Najork (Hoban) **3**:81
A Necklace of Raindrops (Aiken) **1**:6
Neighborhood Odes (Soto) **38**:196
The Neighbors (Brown) **12**:103
Neighbors Unknown (Roberts) **33**:203
Nella nebbia di Milano (Munari) **9**:128
Nellie: A Cat on Her Own (Babbitt) **53**:36
The Neon Motorcycle (Rockwell) **6**:237
Nerilka's Story: A Pern Adventure (McCaffrey) **49**:148
Nessie the Monster (Hughes) **3**:94
Nettie Jo's Friends (McKissack) **23**:240
Never Born a Hero (Naylor) **17**:58
Never Hit a Porcupine (Williams) **48**:193
Never to Forget: The Jews of the Holocaust (Meltzer) **13**:134
The Neverending Story (Ende) **14**:99
The New Air Book (Berger) **32**:12
The New Americans: Changing Patterns in U. S. Immigration (Ashabranner) **28**:6
The New Americans: Cuban Boat People (Haskins) **39**:43
New Baby (McCully) **46**:61
The New Baby at Your House (Cole) **40**:10
A New Baby Is Coming to My House (Iwasaki) **18**:153
The New Boy (Keller) **45**:56
New Broome Experiment (Epstein and Epstein) **26**:44
New Chronicles of Rebecca (Wiggin) **52**:166
The New Earth Book: Our Changing Planet (Berger) **32**:23
The New Food Book: Nutrition Diet, Consumer Tips, and Foods of the Future (Berger) **32**:20
New Found World (Shippen) **36**:168
New Friends for Susan (Uchida) **6**:251
The New Girl (Stine) **37**:110
New Guys around the Block (Guy) **13**:85

A New Home, A New Friend (Wilhelm) **46**:161
The New Kid on the Block (Prelutsky) **13**:172
New Life: New Room (Jordan) **10**:119
New Patches for Old (Mattingley) **24**:125
The New Pet (Flack) **28**:128
A New Promise (Pascal) **25**:186
New Road! (Gibbons) **8**:96
New Shoes (Streatfeild) **17**:195
New Town: A Story about the Bell Family (Streatfeild) **17**:195
The New Water Book (Berger) **32**:10
The New Wizard of Oz (Baum) **15**:42
New Year's Day (Aliki) **9**:20
The New Year's Mystery (Nixon) **24**:138
New York City Too Far from Tampa Blues (Bethancourt) **3**:19
New York for Nicola (Allan) **43**:11
New Zealand: Yesterday and Today (Mahy) **7**:184
The Newspapers (Fisher) **18**:130
Next Door To Xandau (Orgel) **48**:79
Next Time I Will: An Old English Tale (Orgel) **48**:93
Next-Door Neighbors (Ellis) **42**:82
Next-Door Neighbours (Ellis) **42**:82
Nibble, Nibble: Poems for Children (Brown) **10**:67
Nice Girl from Good Home (Gaberman) **33**:13
A Nice Girl Like You (St. John) **46**:109
The Nicest Gift (Politi) **29**:194
Nicholas and the Fast Moving Diesel (Ardizzone) **3**:6
Nicholas Bentley Stoningpot III (McGovern) **50**:122
The Nicholas Factor (Myers) **16**:140
Nicholas Knock and Other People (Lee) **3**:116
Nicky Goes to the Doctor (Scarry) **3**:184
Nicola Mimosa (Ure) **34**:178
Nicolette and the Mill (Guillot) **22**:63
Night (Keats) **35**:136
The Night After Christmas (Stevenson) **17**:158
Night Again (Kuskin) **4**:144
Night and Day (Brown) **10**:50
Night Birds on Nantucket (Aiken) **1**:6
Night Cry (Naylor) **17**:58
The Night Daddy (Gripe) **5**:146
Night Dive (McGovern) **50**:123
Night Fall (Aiken) **1**:6
The Night Flight (Ryder) **37**:89
Night in the Country (Rylant) **15**:172
The Night It Rained Pancakes: Adapted from a Russian Folktale (Ginsburg) **45**:14
The Night Journey (Hyman) **50**:74
The Night Journey (Lasky) **11**:116
Night Journeys (Avi) **24**:6
Night Kites (Kerr) **29**:155
Night Noises (Fox) **23**:117
Night of Masks (Norton) **50**:142
Night of the Gargoyles (Wiesner) **43**:216
Night of the Whale (Spinelli) **26**:203
The Night of the White Deer (Paulsen) **19**:172
Night on Neighborhood Street (Greenfield) **38**:90
Night Outside (Wrightson) **14**:216
Night Race to Kawau (Duder) **43**:62
The Night Swimmers (Byars) **16**:56
Night Terrors (Murphy) **53**:112
The Night the Lights Went Out (Freeman) **30**:71
The Night the Monster Came (Calhoun) **42**:29
Night Tree (Bunting) **28**:66
The Night Wind (Allan) **43**:24
A Night without Stars (Howe) **9**:58
The Nightingale (Bedard) **35**:64
The Nightingale (Zwerger) **46**:194
Nightjohn (Paulsen) **54**:108

Nightmares: Poems to Trouble Your Sleep (Prelutsky) **13**:165
Night's Nice (Emberley and Emberley) **5**:92
Nights of the Pufflings (McMillan) **47**:187
Nights with Uncle Remus: Myths and Legends of the Old Plantation (Harris) **49**:61-107
The Nightwalker (Hurmence) **25**:96
The Night-Watchmen (Cresswell) **18**:100
Nijntje in het ziekenhuis (Bruna) **7**:52
Nijntje's droom (Bruna) **7**:52
Nikos and the Sea God (Gramatky) **22**:43
Nilda (Mohr) **22**:130
Nils (d'Aulaire and d'Aulaire) **21**:50
Nils Holgerssons underbara resa genom Sverige (Lagerlof) **7**:110
Nine Days to Christmas (Ets) **33**:85
Nine for California (Levitin) **53**:76
Nine Lives (Alexander) **5**:18
The Nine Lives of Homer C. Cat (Calhoun) **42**:8
The Nine Lives of Montezuma (Morpurgo) **51**:118
Nine O'Clock Lullaby (Singer) **48**:139
The Nine Planets (Branley) **13**:27
Nino and His Fish (Hurd and Hurd) **49**:123
No, Agatha! (Isadora) **7**:106
No Applause, Please (Singer) **48**:120
No Arm in Left Field (Christopher) **33**:47
No Bath Tonight (Yolen) **4**:265
No Beat of Drum (Burton) **1**:32
No Boats on Bannermere (Trease) **42**:183
No Coins, Please (Korman) **25**:107
No Easy Circle (Naylor) **17**:50
No Fighting, No Biting! (Minarik) **33**:124
No Friends (Stevenson) **17**:165
No Kidding (Brooks) **25**:34
No Kiss for Mother (Ungerer) **3**:202
No Measles, No Mumps for Me (Showers) **6**:248
No More Baths (Cole) **18**:82
No More Magic (Avi) **24**:4
No More Monsters for Me! (Parish) **22**:166
No More Tomorrow (Ottley) **16**:188
No Need for Monty (Stevenson) **17**:168
No Night without Stars (Norton) **50**:157
No Pattern for Love (Epstein and Epstein) **26**:47
No Place for a Goat (Sattler) **24**:217
No Place for Me (DeClements) **23**:37
No Place Like (Kemp) **29**:117
No Promises in the Wind (Hunt) **1**:109
No Such Country (Crew) **42**:56
No Such Things (Peet) **12**:206
No Way of Knowing: Dallas Poems (Livingston) **7**:174
Noah and the Ark (dePaola) **24**:94
Noah's Ark (Haley) **21**:143
Noah's Ark (Spier) **5**:224
Noah's Ark (Wildsmith) **52**:200
Noah's Brother (King-Smith) **40**:149
Noah's Cats and the Devil's Fire (Moser) **49**:182
The Noble Doll (Coatsworth) **2**:60
Nobodies and Somebodies (Orgel) **48**:92
Nobody Knows but Me (Bunting) **28**:47
Nobody Plays with a Cabbage (DeJong) **1**:60
Nobody Stole the Pie (Levitin) **53**:63
Nobody's Family Is Going to Change (Fitzhugh) **1**:73
Noël Chez Ernest et Célestine (Vincent) **13**:220
Noisy (Hughes) **15**:131
The Noisy Bird Book (Brown) **10**:51
Noisy Book (Brown) **10**:48
Noisy Nora (Lofting) **19**:127
Noisy Nora (Wells) **16**:205
Noisy Words (Burningham) **9**:51
Nomi No Ichi (Anno) **14**:43
None of the Above (Wells) **16**:205

Nonsense Book (Lear) **1**:127
Nonstop Nonsense (Mahy) **7**:184
Noodle (Leaf) **25**:122
Noodweer op de Weisshorn (Haar) **15**:114
The Noon Balloon (Brown) **10**:62
Noonan: A Novel About Baseball, ESP, and Time Warps (Fisher) **18**:127
Norby and the Invaders (Asimov) **12**:64
Norby and the Lost Princess (Asimov) **12**:63
Norby, the Mixed-Up Robot (Asimov) **12**:62
Norby's Other Secret (Asimov) **12**:62
The No-Return Trail (Levitin) **53**:61
Norma and the Washing Machine (Rosen) **45**:138
Norma Jean, Jumping Bean (Cole) **40**:15
Norman the Doorman (Freeman) **30**:71
Norse Gods and Giants (d'Aulaire and d'Aulaire) **21**:53
The Norse Myths: A Retelling (Crossley-Holland) **47**:36
North, South, East, and West (Branley) **13**:32
North Town (Graham) **10**:105
Northern Lullaby (Leo and Diane Dillon) **44**:45
A Nose for Trouble (Singer) **48**:127
Noses Are Special (Sattler) **24**:218
Not Enough Beds for the Babies (Hoberman) **22**:109
Not Now, Bernard (McKee) **38**:170
Not Quite as Grimm (Janosch) **26**:77
Not Separate, Not Equal (Wilkinson) **20**:211
Not So Fast, Songololo (Daly) **41**:56
Not What You Expected (Aiken) **1**:7
Notes for Another Life (Bridgers) **18**:25
Notes to a Science Fiction Writer (Bova) **3**:35
Nothing at All (Gag) **4**:92
Nothing but a Pig (Cole) **18**:82
Nothing Ever Happens on My Block (Raskin) **1**:157
Nothing Like a Fresh Coat of Paint (Spier) **5**:225
Nothing to Be Afraid Of (Mark) **11**:150
The Nothing-Place (Spence) **26**:194
Nothing's Fair in Fifth Grade (DeClements) **23**:34
The Not-Just-Anybody Family (Byars) **16**:63
The Not-So-Jolly Roger (Scieszka) **27**:156
The Not-So-Jolly Roger (Smith) **47**:200
Now is Your Time! The African-American Struggle for Freedom (Myers) **35**:195
Now It's Fall (Lenski) **26**:114
Now One Foot, Now the Other (dePaola) **4**:65
Now Sheba Sings the Song (Angelou) **53**:15
Now That I Know (Klein) **19**:100
Now We Are Six (Milne) **26**:126
Now We Can Go (Jonas) **12**:177
Noy Lives in Thailand (Lindgren) **39**:152
Nuclear Power: From Physics to Politics (Pringle) **4**:185
Nuki and the Sea Serpent: A Maori Story (Park) **51**:174
Number 24 (Billout) **33**:21
Number Art: Thirteen 123s from Around the World (Fisher) **18**:132
Number Play (Burningham) **9**:50
Number the Stars (Lowry) **46**:37
Numbers of Things (Oxenbury) **22**:137
Numbers Old and New (Adler) **27**:14
Numerals: New Dresses for Old Numbers (Adler) **27**:18
Nungadin and Willijen (Trezise) **41**:143
The Nursery "Alice" (Carroll) **2**:35
Nussknacker und Mausekoenig (Zwerger) **46**:191
The Nutcracker and the Mouse King (Zwerger) **46**:191
Nuts about Nuts (Rosen) **45**:147

Nuts to You and Nuts to Me: An Alphabet Book of Poems (Hoberman) **22**:111

Nutshell Library (Sendak) **1**:171

O Jerusalem (Yolen) **44**:208

O Sliver of Liver: Together with Other Triolets, Cinquains, Haiku, Verses, and a Dash of Poems (Livingston) **7**:173

O Zebron Falls! (Ferry) **34**:52

Obedient Jack: An Old Tale (Galdone) **16**:97

Observation (Bendick) **5**:45

An Ocean World (Sis) **45**:168

Ocean-Born Mary (Lenski) **26**:104

Oceanography Lab (Berger) **32**:9

Octagon Magic (Norton) **50**:146

The October Child (Spence) **26**:197

An Octopus Is Amazing (Keller) **45**:54

The Odyssey (McCaughrean) **38**:151

The Odyssey of Ben O'Neal (Taylor) **30**:189

Odyssey of Courage: The Story of Alvar Nunez Cabeza de Vaca (Wojciechowska) **1**:198

Of Course Polly Can Do Almost Everything (Lindgren) **39**:157

Of Course Polly Can Ride a Bike (Lindgren) **1**:137; **39**:154

Of Dikes and Windmills (Spier) **5**:219

Of Man and Mouse: How House Mice Became Laboratory Mice (Lauber) **16**:116

Of Nightingales That Weep (Paterson) **7**:230

Of Time and of Seasons (St. John) **46**:102

Of Two Minds (Matas) **52**:89

Off into Space! Science for Young Space Travelers (Hyde) **23**:154

Off to Bed: Seven Stories for Wide-Awakes (Petersham and Petersham) **24**:178

Off to the Gold Fields (Fisher) **49**:32

The Ogre and His Bride (Tresselt) **30**:213

The Ogre Downstairs (Jones) **23**:183

Oh, A-Hunting We Will Go (Langstaff) **3**:110

Oh, Kojo! How Could You! An Ashanti Tale (Aardema) **17**:7

Oh, Rick! (Bunting) **28**:47

Oh, Say Can You Say? (Dr. Seuss) **9**:193

Oh, the Places You'll Go! (Dr. Seuss) **53**:139

Oh, Were They Ever Happy! (Spier) **5**:225

Oh, What A Mess (Wilhelm) **46**:164

Oh What a Noise! (Shulevitz) **5**:204

Oil and Gas: From Fossils to Fuels (Nixon) **24**:136

The O.J. Simpson Trial: What It Shows Us about Our Legal System (Aaseng) **54**:23

Okina Mono No Sukina Osama (Anno) **14**:33

Ol' Dan Tucker (Langstaff) **3**:110

Ola (d'Aulaire and d'Aulaire) **21**:39

Ola and Blakken and Line, Sine, Trine (d'Aulaire and d'Aulaire) **21**:40

Old Con and Patrick (Sawyer) **36**:160

Old Hat, New Hat (Berenstain and Berenstain) **19**:26

Old Henry (Blos) **18**:19

Old John (Hartling) **29**:102

The Old Joke Book (Ahlberg and Ahlberg) **18**:3

The Old Man and His Birds (Ginsburg) **45**:21

The Old Man and the Bear (Janosch) **26**:81

The Old Man of Mow (Garner) **20**:103

Old Man Whickutt's Donkey (Calhoun) **42**:22

Old Mother Hubbard and Her Dog (Galdone) **16**:90

Old Mother Hubbard's Dog Dresses Up (Yeoman) **46**:182

Old Mother Hubbard's Dog Learns To Play (Yeoman) **46**:182

Old Mother Hubbard's Dog Needs a Doctor (Yeoman) **46**:182

Old Mother Hubbard's Dog Takes up Sport (Yeoman) **46**:182

Old Mrs. Twindlytart and Other Rhymes (Livingston) **7**:169

Old Peter's Russian Tales (Ransome) **8**:170

Old Possum's Book of Practical Cats (Gorey) **36**:101

Old Rosie, the Horse Nobody Understood (Moore) **15**:139

Old Sadie and the Christmas Bear (Naylor) **17**:58

The Old Testament (de Angeli) **1**:53

The Old Woman and Her Pig (Galdone) **16**:90

The Old Woman Who Lived in a Vinegar Bottle (Godden) **20**:133

An Older Kind of Magic (Wrightson) **4**:244

Older Men (Klein) **19**:98

The Oldest Man, and Other Timeless Stories (Kotzwinkle) **6**:181

An Old-Fashioned Thanksgiving (Alcott) **1**:11

Oley, the Sea Monster (Ets) **33**:78

Oliver Button Is a Sissy (dePaola) **4**:62

Oliver, Clarence, and Violet (Stevenson) **17**:158

Oliver Sundew, Tooth Fairy (McBratney) **44**:131

Olle's Ski Trip (Beskow) **17**:16

Olles Skidfärd (Beskow) **17**:16

Ollie's Ski Trip (Beskow) **17**:16

The Olympians: Great Gods and Goddesses of Ancient Greece (Fisher) **18**:134

Oma (Hartling) **29**:99

Oma and Bobo (Schwartz) **25**:194

Omelette: A Chicken in Peril! (Owen) **31**:147

On a marche sur la lune (Herge) **6**:148

On a Summer Day (Lenski) **26**:117

On Beyond Zebra (Dr. Seuss) **1**:88; **9**:180

On Christmas Day in the Morning! (Langstaff) **3**:110

On Christmas Eve (Brown) **10**:68

On Fire (Sebestyen) **17**:92

On Fortune's Wheel (Voigt) **48**:173

On Guard (Napoli) **51**:165

On My Horse (Greenfield) **38**:96

"On Stage, Flory!" (Allan) **43**:8

On the Day Peter Stuyvesant Sailed into Town (Lobel) **5**:166

On the Edge (Cross) **28**:90

On the Farm (Hopkins) **44**:98

On the Forest Edge (Lerner) 122

On the Go: A Book of Adjectives (Betsy and Giulio Maestro) **45**:69

On the Other Side of the Gate (Suhl) **2**:165

On the Run (Bawden) **51**:13

On the Sand Dune (Orgel) **48**:77

On the Town: A Book of Clothing Words (Betsy and Giulio Maestro) **45**:72

On the Way Home (Murphy) **39**:171

On the Way Home (Wilder) **2**:206

On the Wing: The Life of Birds from Feathers to Flight (Brooks) **25**:35

On to Widecombe Fair (Hyman) **50**:73

Once a Mouse...A Fable Cut in Wood (Brown) **12**:101

Once Around the Block (Henkes) **23**:128

Once Around the Galaxy (Gallant) **30**:98

Once More upon a Totem (Harris) **47**:84

Once on a Time (Milne) **1**:142

Once, Said Darlene (Sleator) **29**:201

Once There Was a Swagman (Brinsmead) **47**:14

Once There Were Giants (Waddell) **31**:195

Once Under the Cherry Blossom Tree: An Old Japanese Tale (Say) **22**:209

Once upon a Holiday (Moore) **15**:139

Once upon a Time in a Pigpen and Three Other Margaret Wise Brown Books (Brown) **10**:68

Once upon a Totem (Harris) **47**:76

Once We Went on a Picnic (Fisher) **49**:55

The Once-a-Year Day (Bunting) **28**:43

The One and Only Two Heads (Ahlberg and Ahlberg) **18**:8

One at a Time: His Collected Poems for the Young (McCord) **9**:103

The One Bad Thing about Father (Monjo) **2**:124

One Big Wish (Williams) **8**:237

One by One: Garth Pig's Rain Song (Rayner) **41**:131

One by Sea (Corbett) **1**:46

One Day in Paradise (Heine) **18**:150

One Earth, Many People: The Challenge of Human Population Growth (Pringle) **4**:175

One Fat Summer (Lipsyte) **23**:205

One Fine Day (Hogrogian) **2**:88

One Fish, Two Fish, Red Fish, Blue Fish (Dr. Seuss) **1**:88; **9**:185

One Frog Too Many (Mayer) **11**:169

One Green Leaf (Ure) **34**:182

One Guinea Pig Is Not Enough (Duke) **51**:56

The One Hundredth Thing about Caroline (Lowry) **46**:28

One Hungry Spider (Baker) **28**:20

1 Hunter (Hutchins) **20**:151

One I Love, Two I Love, and Other Loving Mother Goose Rhymes (Hogrogian) **2**:88

The One in the Middle is the Green Kangaroo (Blume) **15**:72

One Monday Morning (Shulevitz) **5**:202

One Monster after Another (Mayer) **11**:168

One More Flight (Bunting) **28**:45

One More River (Reid Banks) **24**:190

One More River to Cross: The Stories of Twelve Black Americans (Haskins) **39**:64

One More Time! (Ferry) **34**:54

One Morning in Maine (McCloskey) **7**:207

One Nation, Many Tribes: How Kids Live in Milwaukee's Indian Community (Krull) **44**:109

One of Three (Johnson) **33**:95

One Order to Go (Glenn) **51**:86

The One Pig with Horns (Brunhoff) **4**:40

One Proud Summer (Mackay) **43**:107

One Saturday Morning (Duke) **51**:53

One Small Blue Bead (Baylor) **3**:16

One Small Fish (Ryder) **37**:99

One Sun: A Book of Terse Verse (McMillan) **47**:174

One Thousand and One Arabian Nights (McCaughrean) **38**:133

One Thousand Christmas Beards (Duvoisin) **23**:100

One to Grow On (Little) **4**:149

One Trick Too Many: Fox Stories from Russia (Ginsburg) **45**:5

One, Two, Buckle My Shoe: A Book of Counting Rhymes (Haley) **21**:141

One Two Flea (McNaughton) **54**:56

One, Two, One Pair! (McMillan) **47**:176

One, Two, Three: An Animal Counting Book (Brown) **29**:3

One, Two, Three with Ant and Bee: A Counting Story (Banner) **24**:18

One Was Johnny: A Counting Book (Sendak) **1**:172

One Way to Ansonia (Gaberman) **33**:14

One Wide River to Cross (Emberley and Emberley) **5**:93

One Winter Night in August and Other Nonsense Jingles (Kennedy) **27**:97

One World (Foreman) **32**:103

One-Eyed Cat (Fox) **44**:64

One-Eyed Jake (Hutchins) **20**:150

101 Questions and Answers about the Universe (Gallant) **30**:99

101 Things to Do With a Baby (Ormerod) **20**:177

The Only Earth We Have (Pringle) **4**:174

Ooh-La-La (Max in Love) (Kalman) **32**:183

Ookie-Spooky (Ginsburg) **45**:14

Oops! (McNaughton) **54**:67

Ootah's Lucky Day (Parish) **22**:158

The Opal-Eyed Fan (Norton) **50**:160

The Open Gate (Seredy) **10**:178

Open House for Butterflies (Krauss) **42**:125

Operation: Dump the Chump (Park) **34**:154

Operation Sippacik (Godden) **20**:133

Operation Time Search (Norton) **50**:145

The Optical Illusion Book (Simon) **9**:210

The Orchard Book of Greek Myths (McCaughrean) **38**:148

The Orchard Cat (Kellogg) **6**:171

Orchard of the Crescent (Nimmo) **44**:141

Ordinary Jack: Being the First Part of the Bagthorpe Saga (Cresswell) **18**:108

Orfe (Voigt) **48**:177

The Origin of Life (Silverstein and Silverstein) **25**:201

The Original Freddie Ackerman (Irwin) **40**:115

Orlando, the Brave Vulture (Ungerer) **3**:203

Orphans from the Sea (Scott) **20**:200

Orphans of the Wind (Haugaard) **11**:103

Orpheus: Myths of the World (Colum) **36**:37

Osa's Pride (Grifalconi) **35**:77

Oscar Lobster's Fair Exchange (Selden) **8**:196

Oscar Wilde's The Happy Prince (Young) **27**:223

Othello (Lester) **41**:113

The Other Bone (Young) **27**:220

The Other, Darker Ned (Fine) **25**:18

Other People's Houses (Bianco) **19**:56

The Other Side: How Kids Live in a California Latino Neighborhood (Krull) **44**:106

The Other Side of Dark (Nixon) **24**:148

The Other Side of the Fence (Ure) **34**:179

Otherwise Known as Sheila the Great (Blume) **2**:17

Otis Spofford (Cleary) **8**:46

Otto and the Magic Potatoes (Pene du Bois) **1**:64

Otto at Sea (Pene du Bois) **1**:65

Otto in Texas (Pene du Bois) **1**:65

Otus: The Story of a Screech Owl (McClung) **11**:182

Otwe (Aardema) **17**:3

Ouch! (Babbitt) **53**:39

Ouch! A Book about Cuts, Scratches, and Scrapes (Berger) **32**:45

Our Animal Friends at Maple Hill Farm (Provensen and Provensen) **11**:211

Our Atomic World (Berger) **32**:44

Our Colourful World and Its Peoples (Guillot) **22**:67

Our Dog (Oxenbury) **22**:145

Our Federal Union: The United States from 1816-1865 (Asimov) **12**:51

Our Hungry Earth: The World Food Crisis (Pringle) **4**:181

Our Man Weston (Korman) **25**:106

Our Ollie (Ormerod) **20**:179

Our Patchwork Planet: The Story of Plate Tectonics (Betsy and Giulio Maestro) **45**:91

Our Six-Legged Friends and Allies: Ecology in Your Backyard (Simon) **39**:189

Our Sixth-Grade Sugar Babies (Bunting) **28**:65

Our Veronica Goes to Petunia's Farm (Duvoisin) **23**:102

Our Village: Poems (Yeoman) **46**:181

Our Wild Weekend (Waddell) **31**:187

Our World: The People's Republic of China (Rau) **8**:187

Out from This Place (Hansen) **21**:152

Out in the Dark and Daylight (Fisher) **49**:57

Out Loud (Merriam) **14**:198

Out of the Blue (Ellis) **42**:86

Out of the Dark (Katz) **45**:40

Out of the Dust (Hesse) **54**:40

Out of Time (Marsden) **34**:149

Outcast (Sutcliff) **1**:189; **37**:151

Outdoors on Foot (Arnosky) **15**:2

The Outlanders (Cresswell) **18**:102

Outside (Norton) **50**:156

The Outside Child (Bawden) **51**:37

OUTside INside Poems (Adoff) **7**:36

Outside Over There (Sendak) **17**:123

The Outside Shot (Myers) **16**:141

The Outsiders (Hinton) **3**:70; **23**:146

Outward Dreams: Black Inventors and Their Inventions (Haskins) **39**:63

Over in the Meadow (Keats) **35**:137

Over in the Meadow: An Old Nursery Counting Rhyme (Galdone) **16**:107

Over Sea, Under Stone (Cooper) **4**:42

Over the Deep Blue Sea (Wildsmith) **52**:197

Over the Hills to Nugget (Fisher) **49**:31

Over the Moon: A Book of Sayings (Hughes) **15**:126

Over the Sea's Edge (Curry) **31**:75

Over, Under, and Through, and Other Spatial Concepts (Hoban) **13**:102

Overcoming Acne: The How and Why of Healthy Skin Care (Silverstein, Silverstein, and Silverstein) **25**:226

Overlord: D-Day and the Invasion of Europe (Marrin) **53**:81

The Overnight (Stine) **37**:111

Overnight Sensation (Nixon) **24**:154

Overpopulation: Crisis or Challange? (Aaseng) **54**:15

Over-Under: At Playschool (McNaughton) **54**:53

Owl and Billy (Waddell) **31**:186

Owl and Billy and the Space Days (Waddell) **31**:192

The Owl and the Pussycat (Lear) **1**:127

The Owl and the Woodpecker (Wildsmith) **2**:213

An Owl and Three Pussycats (Provensen and Provensen) **11**:214

Owl at Home (Lobel) **5**:169

Owl Babies (Waddell) **31**:202

Owl Lake (Tejima) **20**:202

Owl Moon (Yolen) **44**:183

The Owl Service (Garner) **20**:103

Owls in the Family (Mowat) **20**:170

The Owlstone Crown (Kennedy) **27**:100

Ownself (Calhoun) **42**:21

Oworo (Guillot) **22**:56

The Ox of the Wonderful Horns and Other African Folktales (Bryan) **18**:32

Ox-Cart Man (Cooney) **23**:28

Oxygen Keeps You Alive (Branley) **13**:37

Pacala and Tandala, and Other Rumanian Folk Tales (Ure) **34**:171

Pacific Crossing (Soto) **38**:199

A Pack of Liars (Fine) **25**:22

A Pack of Lies: Twelve Stories in One (McCaughrean) **38**:142

The Pack Rat's Day and Other Poems (Prelutsky) **13**:165

Paco's Miracle (Clark) **16**:81

Paddington Abroad (Bond) **1**:28

Paddington at Large (Bond) **1**:28

Paddington at Work (Bond) **1**:28

Paddington Bear (Bond) **1**:28

Paddington Helps Out (Bond) **1**:29

Paddington Marches On (Bond) **1**:29

Paddington Takes the Air (Bond) **1**:29

Paddiwak and Cosy (Doherty) **21**:60

Paddle-to-the-Sea (Holling) **50**:50

Paddy Finds a Job (Goodall) **25**:51

Paddy Goes Traveling (Goodall) **25**:53

Paddy Pork to the Rescue (Goodall) **25**:54

Paddy Pork—Odd Jobs (Goodall) **25**:54

Paddy Pork's Holiday (Goodall) **25**:47

Paddy the Penguin (Galdone) **16**:89

Paddy to the Rescue (Goodall) **25**:54

Paddy Under Water (Goodall) **25**:54

Paddy's Evening Out (Goodall) **25**:45

Paddy's New Hat (Goodall) **25**:50

Paddy's Payday (Day) **22**:25

Paddy's Pot of Gold (King-Smith) **40**:159

Pageants of Despair (Hamley) **47**:54

Pagoo (Holling) **50**:55

The Pain and the Great One (Blume) **15**:80

Paint, Brush, and Palette (Weiss) **4**:223

Painted Devil (Bedard) **35**:67

The Painted Fan (Singer) **48**:144

The Painted Garden (Streatfeild)
See *Movie Shoes*

The Painted Garden: A Story of a Holiday in Hollywood (Streatfeild) **17**:190

The Painter's Trick (Ventura) **16**:193

Pajamas for Kit (dePaola) **24**:98

Palmiero and the Ogre (Domanska) **40**:38

Palmistry (Aylesworth) **6**:53

Pamela Camel (Peet) **12**:206

Pampalche of the Silver Teeth (Ginsburg) **45**:9

Pancakes for Breakfast (dePaola) **4**:60

Pancakes, Pancakes! (Carle) **10**:74

Panda and the Bunyips (Foreman) **32**:97

Panda and the Bushfire (Foreman) **32**:100

Panda and the Odd Lion (Foreman) **32**:94

Panda's Puzzle, and His Voyage of Discovery (Foreman) **32**:90

Papa Albert (Moore) **15**:140

Papa Lucky's Shadow (Daly) **41**:59

Papa Small (Lenski) **26**:116

Papagayo, the Mischief Maker (McDermott) **9**:119

The Paper Airplane Book (Simon) **9**:204

The Paper Bag Princess (Munsch) **19**:142

Paper Chains (Langton) **33**:114

Paper Dolls (Pfeffer) **11**:204

Paper, Ink, and Roller: Print-Making for Beginners (Weiss) **4**:220

Paper John (Small) **53**:149

Paper, Paper Everywhere (Gibbons) **8**:95

The Paper Party (Freeman) **30**:79

The Paperboy (Pilkey) **48**:113

The Papermakers (Fisher) **18**:122

Papio: A Novel of Adventure (Kelleher) **36**:119

Pappa Pellerin's Daughter (Gripe) **5**:143

Pappa Pellerins Dotter (Gripe) **5**:143

The Parables of Jesus (dePaola) **24**:99

Parade (Crews) **7**:62

The Parade Book (Emberley) **5**:91

Pardon Me, You're Stepping on My Eyeball! (Zindel) **3**:250

Paris, Pee Wee, and Big Dog (Guy) **13**:87

The Park (Hill) **13**:93

The Park in the Dark (Waddell) **31**:192

Parker Pig, Esquire (dePaola) **4**:54

Park's Quest (Paterson) **50**:196

Parrakeets (Zim) **2**:229

Parsley (Bemelmans) **6**:72

Parsley Sage, Rosemary and Time (Curry) **31**:78

A Part of the Dream (Bunting) **28**:47
A Part of the Sky (Peck) **45**:125
Partners, Guests, and Parasites: Coexistence in Nature (Simon) **39**:186
The Party (Pike) **29**:172
Party Frock (Streatfeild) **17**:190
Party Rhymes (Brown) **29**:17
Party Shoes (Streatfeild) **17**:190
Parzival: The Quest of the Grail Knight (Paterson) **50**:207
Pascal and the Lioness (Guillot) **22**:68
Passage to America: The Story of the Great Migrations (Shippen) **36**:171
Passager (Yolen) **44**:209
Past Eight O'Clock (Aiken) **19**:17
Pastures of the Blue Crane (Brinsmead) **47**:6
Le Patchwork (Vincent) **13**:219
Patchwork Plays (Field) **21**:75
The Patchwork Quilt (Pinkney) **43**:158
Path of Hunters: Animal Struggle in a Meadow (Peck) **45**:100
Path of the Pale Horse (Fleischman) **20**:65
Patrick (Blake) **31**:18
Patrick Kentigern Keenan (Hunter) **25**:74
Patrick Kentigern Keenan (Hunter)
    See *The Smartest Man in Ireland*
A Pattern of Roses (Peyton) **3**:177
Patterson's Track (Spence) **26**:191
Paul Laurence Dunbar: A Poet to Remember (McKissack) **23**:236
Paul Robeson (Greenfield) **4**:98
Paul Robeson: The Life and Times of a Free Black Man (Hamilton) **1**:104
Pauline and the Prince of the Wind (Kruss) **9**:86
Pauline und der Prinz im Wind (Kruss) **9**:86
Paul's Horse, Herman (Weiss) **4**:221
Pavo and the Princess (Ness) **6**:202
Pay Cheques and Picket Lines: All about Unions in Canada (Mackay) **43**:109
Peabody (Wells) **16**:212
Peace at Last (Murphy) **39**:169
Peace, O River (Garden) **51**:72
The Peaceable Kingdom (Coatsworth) **2**:60
The Peacock Spring (Godden) **20**:134
Peanuts for Billy Ben (Lenski) **26**:116
The Pear Tree, The Birch Tree, and The Barberry Bush (Carigiet) **38**:74
The Pearl (Heine) **18**:148
Pearl's Place (Graham) **31**:92
Peasant Pig and the Terrible Dragon (Scarry) **41**:169
The Pedaling Man and Other Poems (Hoban) **3**:81
The Peddlers (Fisher) **18**:123
The Pedlar of Swaffham (Crossley-Holland) **47**:28
Pedro (Flack and Larsson) **28**:127
Pedro, the Angel of Olvera Street (Politi) **29**:185
Peek-a-Boo! (Ahlberg and Ahlberg) **18**:8
Peeper, First Voice of Spring (Lerner) **34**:122
Peeper: First Voice of Spring (McClung) **11**:190
The Peep-Larssons Go Sailing (Unnerstad) **36**:195
Peepo! (Ahlberg and Ahlberg) **18**:8
Pegasus in Flight (McCaffrey) **49**:153
Peggy (Duncan) **29**:68
The Pekinese Princess (Clarke) **28**:73
Pelican (Wildsmith) **52**:188
Pelle's New Suit (Beskow) **17**:16
Pelles Nya Kläder (Beskow) **17**:16
Pencil, Pen, and Brush Drawing for Beginners (Weiss) **4**:222
Penelope's English Experiences (Wiggin) **52**:157
Penelope's Experiences in Scotland (Wiggin) **52**:159
Penelope's Irish Experiences (Wiggin) **52**:160

Penelope's Postscripts: Switzerland, Venice, Wales, Devon, Home (Wiggin) **52**:167
Penelope's Progress (Wiggin) **52**:159
The Penguin Book (Rau) **8**:186
Penguin Pete (Pfister) **42**:135
Penguin Pete, Ahoy! (Pfister) **42**:137
Penguin Pete and Little Tim (Pfister) **42**:138
Penguin Pete and Pat (Pfister) **42**:134
Penguin Pete's New Friends (Pfister) **42**:134
Penguins at Home: Gentoos of Antarctica (McMillan) **47**:184
Penguins, of All People! (Freeman) **30**:77
Penguins on Parade (Lauber) **16**:112
Pennington's Heir (Peyton) **3**:178
Pennington's Last Term (Peyton) **3**:178
Penny and Peter (Haywood) **22**:93
Penny and the White Horse (Bianco) **19**:57
Penny Goes to Camp (Haywood) **22**:94
Penny Pollard in Print (Klein) **21**:163
Penny Pollard's Diary (Klein) **21**:160
Pentecost and the Chosen One (Corbett) **19**:83
Pentecost of Lickey Top (Corbett) **19**:84
People (Spier) **5**:227
People Are Our Business (Epstein and Epstein) **26**:46
The People Could Fly: American Black Folk Tales (Hamilton) **11**:93
The People Could Fly: American Black Folk Tales (Leo and Diane Dillon) **44**:37
People Might Hear You (Klein) **21**:159
The People of New China (Rau) **8**:189
The People of the Ax (Williams) **8**:234
People Who Make a Difference (Ashabranner) **28**:13
People Who Make Movies (Taylor) **30**:175
The People's Choice: The Story of Candidates, Campaigns, and Elections (Schwartz) **3**:190
The People's Republic of China (Rau) **8**:187
The Peopling of Planet Earth: Human Population Growth through the Ages (Gallant) **30**:105
The Peppermint Family (Brown) **10**:60
The Peppermint Pig (Bawden) **2**:12; **51**:26
The Peppernuts (Petersham and Petersham) **24**:179
Percy and the Five Houses (Minarik) **33**:127
A Perfect Father's Day (Bunting) **28**:66
The Perfect Pal (Gantos) **18**:141
Perfect Pigs: An Introduction to Manners (Brown) **29**:11
The Perfect Present (Foreman) **32**:85
Perilous Pilgrimage (Treece) **2**:187
Periwinkle (Duvoisin) **23**:106
Permanent Connections (Bridgers) **18**:27
The Person in the Potting Shed (Corcoran) **50**:27
Pet of the Met (Freeman) **30**:69
Pet Show! (Keats) **1**:116; **35**:138
The Pet Store (Spier) **5**:228
Pete and Roland (Graham) **31**:92
Pete Rose: Baseball's Charlie Hustle (Aaseng) **54**:10
Peter and Butch (Phipson) **5**:181
Peter and Lotta's Christmas (Beskow) **17**:18
Peter and the Wolf: A Musical Fairy Tale (Mueller) **43**:121
Peter and Veronica (Sachs) **2**:132
Peter Duck (Ransome) **8**:174
Peter Graves (Pene du Bois) **1**:65
Peter in Blueberryland (Beskow) **17**:15
Peter Pan; or, The Boy Who Would Not Grow Up (Barrie) **16**:2-40
Peter Piper's Alphabet: Peter Piper's Practical Principles of Plain and Perfect Pronunciation (Brown) **12**:100
Peter the Great (Stanley) **46**:136

Peter Treegate's War (Wibberley) **3**:229
Peter's Adventures in Blueberry Land (Beskow) **17**:15
Peter's Chair (Keats) **1**:116; **35**:132
Petey (Tobias) **4**:217
Petey Moroni's Camp Runamok Diary (Cummings) **48**:54
Petey's Bedtime Story (Small) **53**:153
Le petit prince (*The Little Prince*) (Saint-Exupery) **10**:137-61
Petroleum: Gas, Oil, and Asphalt (Adler) **27**:25
Petronella (Williams) **8**:233
Petros' War (Zei) **6**:261
Petrosinella, A Neapolitan Rapunzel (Stanley) **46**:130
Petrouchka (Cleaver) **13**:70
Pets for Keeps (King-Smith) **40**:148
Pets in a Jar: Collecting and Caring for Small Wild Animals (Simon) **9**:209
Petter och Lotta på Äventyr: Bilderbok (Beskow) **17**:18
Petters och Lottas Jul (Beskow) **17**:18
Petunia (Duvoisin) **23**:96
Petunia and the Song (Duvoisin) **23**:96
Petunia, Beware! (Duvoisin) **23**:101
Petunia, I Love You (Duvoisin) **23**:104
Petunia Takes a Trip (Duvoisin) **23**:98
Petunia the Silly Goose Stories (Duvoisin) **23**:107
Petunia's Christmas (Duvoisin) **23**:96
Petunia's Treasure (Duvoisin) **23**:106
Pezzettino (Lionni) **7**:137
Phantom Animals (Cohen) **43**:53
The Phantom Ice Cream Man: More Nonsense Verse (Kennedy) **27**:97
Phebe Fairchild: Her Book (Lenski) **26**:101
The Philadelphia Adventure (Alexander) **48**:21
Philbert the Fearful (Williams) **8**:227
Philip Hall Likes Me. I Reckon Maybe (Greene) **2**:85
Philomena (Seredy) **10**:180
Phoebe and the Prince (Orgel) **48**:78
Phoebe Danger, Detective, In the Case of the Two-Minute Cough (Fleischman) **20**:66
Phoebe's Revolt (Babbitt) **2**:6
The Phoenix and the Flame: D. H. Lawrence, a Biography (Trease) **42**:189
The Phoenix Forest (Milne and Milne) **22**:119
Phoenix Rising (Hesse) **54**:36
Phone Calls (Stine) **37**:111
The Photo Dictionary of Football (Berger) **32**:23
The Photo Dictionary of the Orchestra (Berger) **32**:24
Piccolo's Prank (Politi) **29**:193
Pick It Up (Epstein and Epstein) **26**:63
Pickle Creature (Pinkwater) **4**:169
A Pickle for a Nickel (Moore) **15**:140
Pick-Up Sticks (Ellis) **42**:84
Picnic (McCully) **46**:59
The Picnic (Unnerstad) **36**:197
Picnic at Babar's (Brunhoff) **4**:34
Picnic at Mudsock Meadow (Polacco) **40**:194
The Picnic Dog (Mattingley) **24**:122
A Picnic for Ernest and Celestine (Vincent) **13**:217
A Pictorial History of the Negro in America (Hughes and Meltzer) **17**:42
The Picts and the Martyrs; or, Not Welcome at All (Ransome) **8**:181
A Picture Book of Cows (Patent) **19**:158
Picture Book of Revolutionary War Heroes (Fisher) **18**:124
The Picture Life of Franklin Delano Roosevelt (Epstein and Epstein) **26**:61
The Picture Story of Britain (Streatfeild) **17**:192

Title Index

Picture Tales from Spain (Sawyer) **36**:150

A Pie in the Sky (Rodari) **24**:208

A Piece of Cake (Murphy) **39**:176

A Piece of Home (Levitin) **53**:76

A Piece of the Power: Four Black Mayors (Haskins) **3**:65

Pieces of Another World: The Story of Moon Rocks (Branley) **13**:39

Pieces of Land: Journeys to Eight Islands (Crossley-Holland) **47**:29

The Pied Piper of Hamelin (Biro) **28**:36

The Piemakers (Cresswell) **18**:98

Pierino and the Bell (Cassedy) **26**:11

Piero Ventura's Book of Cities (Ventura) **16**:191

Pierre: A Cautionary Tale (Sendak) **1**:172

Pig Tale (Oxenbury) **22**:139

Pigeon Post (Ransome) **8**:177

The Pigeon with the Tennis Elbow (Christopher) **33**:49

Pigeons (Schlein) **41**:194

Piggins (Yolen) **44**:179

Piggy in the Middle (Needle) **43**:138

Piggybook (Browne) **19**:70

The Pigman (Zindel) **3**:251

The Pigman and Me (Zindel) **45**:198

The Pigman's Legacy (Zindel) **45**:193

Pigs Ahoy! (Wilhelm) **46**:163

The Pigs' Book of World Records (Stine) **37**:103

Pigs Might Fly (King-Smith) **40**:140

Pigs Might Fly (Rodda) **32**:210

Pigs Plus: Learning Addition (Burningham) **9**:50

The Pigs' Wedding (Heine) **18**:145

The Pig-Tale (Carroll) **2**:35

The Pile of Junk (Schlein) **41**:184

Pilgrim's Progress (Moser) **49**:191

Pilly Soems (Rosen) **45**:150

Pilyo the Piranha (Aruego) **5**:29

The Pinballs (Byars) **16**:54

Pink and Say (Polacco) **40**:198

Pink Lemonade: Poems for Children (Schmidt) **22**:223

The Pink Motel (Brink) **30**:15

Pinkerton, Behave! (Kellogg) **6**:176

Pinky Pye (Estes) **2**:75

Pinocchio (Collodi)
  See *Le Avventure di Pinocchio*

Pinquo (Thiele) **27**:209

Pioneer Oceanographer: Alexander Agassiz (Epstein and Epstein) **26**:58

Pipes & Pearls: A Gathering of Tales (Bedard) **35**:59

Pipes and Plumbing Systems (Zim) **2**:230

The Pip-Larssons Go Sailing (Unnerstad) **36**:195

Pippa Passes (Corbett) **1**:46

Pippi Goes on Board (Lindgren) **1**:138; **39**:147

Pippi in the South Seas (Lindgren) **1**:138; **39**:147

Pippi Longstocking (Lindgren) **1**:138; **39**:133

Pippi on the Run (Lindgren) **39**:156

Pippo Gets Lost (Oxenbury) **22**:151

Pirate Island Adventure (Parish) **22**:161

The Pirate Queen (McCully) **46**:72

The Pirate Uncle (Mahy) **7**:185

Pirates Ahoy! (Wilhelm) **46**:163

Pirate's Island (Townsend) **2**:173

The Pirats: The Amazing Adventures of Anton B. Stanton (McNaughton) **54**:50

Pish, Posh, Said Hieronymus Bosch (Leo and Diane Dillon) **44**:44

The Pistachio Prescription (Danziger) **20**:52

A Pistol in Greenyards (Hunter) **25**:76

Pitcher Plants: The Elegant Insect Traps (Lerner) **34**:128

A Pitiful Place (Needle) **43**:139

The Pixy and the Lazy Housewife (Calhoun) **42**:14

Pizza for Breakfast (Kovalski) **34**:117

The Place (Coatsworth) **2**:61

A Place Apart (Fox) **44**:62

A Place Called Heartbreak: A Story of Vietnam (Myers) **35**:204

A Place Called Ugly (Avi) **24**:8

The Place My Words Are Looking For: What Poets Say about and through Their Work (Janeczko) **47**:110

A Place to Come Back To (Bond) **11**:30

A Place to Live (Bendick) **5**:43

A Place to Play (Ahlberg and Ahlberg) **18**:3

A Place to Scream (Ure) **34**:193

Plague (Ure) **34**:185

Plague 99 (Ure) **34**:185

Plague Ship (Norton) **50**:136

Plain City (Hamilton) **40**:89

Plains Warrior: Chief Quanah Parker and the Comanches (Marrin) **53**:95

The Plan for Birdsmarsh (Peyton) **3**:180

The Planet of Junior Brown (Hamilton) **1**:104

The Planet-Girded Suns: Man's View of Other Solar Systems (Engdahl) **2**:71

The Planets: Exploring the Solar System (Gallant) **30**:97

The Planets in Our Solar System (Branley) **13**:46

Planets, Stars, and Galaxies (Berger) **32**:22

Plant Explorer: David Fairchild (Epstein and Epstein) **26**:58

Plant Families (Lerner) **34**:134

Planting a Rainbow (Ehlert) **28**:110

Plants and Insects Together (Patent) **19**:149

Plants in Winter (Cole) **5**:63

Plants That Make You Sniffle and Sneeze (Lerner) **34**:138

Play Ball, Amelia Bedelia (Parish) **22**:160

Play Day: A Book of Terse Verse (McMillan) **47**:178

Play Nimrod for Him (Ure) **34**:187

Play on Words (Provensen and Provensen) **11**:210

Play Rhymes (Brown) **29**:15

A Play to the Festival (Allan) **43**:8

Play with Me (Ets) **33**:81

Play with Spot (Hill) **13**:96

Play-by-Play (Glenn) **51**:86

The Playground (Duke) **51**:47

Playing (Oxenbury) **22**:141

Playing Beatie Bow (Park) **51**:177

Playing Possum (Eager) **43**:83

Playmates (Ahlberg and Ahlberg) **18**:9

Playschool (Oxenbury) **22**:145

Please, Don't Eat My Cabin (Merrill) **52**:111

Please Don't Squeeze Your Boa, Noah (Singer) **48**:145

The Pleasure Garden (Garfield) **21**:112

Plenty of Fish (Selsam) **1**:164

Plink, Plink, Plink (Baylor) **3**:16

Pocahontas (d'Aulaire and d'Aulaire) **21**:49

A Pocket for Corduroy (Freeman) **30**:81

A Pocket Full of Seeds (Sachs) **2**:133

The Pocket Mouse (Willard) **2**:221

Pocket Poems: Selected for a Journey (Janeczko) **47**:103

Pocket-Handkerchief Park (Field) **21**:75

Poems (Field) **21**:80

Poems for Children (Field) **21**:81

Poems for the Very Young (Rosen) **45**:148

Poems Here and Now (Kherdian) **24**:107

Poems in My Luggage (Thiele) **27**:212

Poems of Lewis Carroll (Carroll) **2**:35

Poetry from A to Z: A Guide for Young Writers (Janeczko) **47**:115

Poetry Is (Hughes) **3**:94

Poetspeak: In Their Work, about Their Work (Janeczko) **47**:101

Poisonous Snakes (Simon) **9**:216

The Polar Express (Van Allsburg) **13**:211

Police Lab (Berger) **32**:15

Policeman Small (Lenski) **26**:122

The Polite Penguin (Brown) **10**:50

Pollution Lab (Berger) **32**:11

Polly Oliver's Problem: A Story for Girls (Wiggin) **52**:158

Polly Patchwork (Field) **21**:72

Polly Vaughn: A Traditional British Ballad (Moser) **49**:182

Polly's Tiger (Phipson) **5**:183

Poltergeists: Hauntings and the Haunted (Knight) **38**:111

Pompei (Ventura) **16**:196

A Pony and a Trap (Dillon) **26**:23

Pony from Tarella (Clark) **30**:56

The Pooh Story Book (Milne) **1**:142

The Pool of Fire (Christopher) **2**:41

The Pool of Knowledge: How the United Nations Share Their Skills (Shippen) **36**:175

The Pool Party (Soto) **38**:202

Poona Company (Dhondy) **41**:75

Poor Cecco: The Wonderful Story of a Wonderful Wooden Dog Who Was the Jolliest Toy in the House Until He Went Out to Explore the World (Bianco) **19**:51

Poor Richard in France (Monjo) **2**:129

Poor Stainless: A New Story about the Borrowers (Norton) **6**:224

Poor Tom's Ghost (Curry) **31**:81

The Popcorn Book (dePaola) **4**:60

Popcorn Days and Buttermilk Nights (Paulsen) **19**:174

Popinjay Stairs: A Historical Adventure about Samuel Pepys (Trease) **42**:191

Popo and Fifina, Children of Haiti (Bontemps) **6**:78; **17**:38

Popol et Virginie au pays des lapinos (Herge) **6**:149

Popol Out West (Herge) **6**:149

Poppy Pig Goes to Market (Bruna) **7**:52

Poppy's Chair (Hesse) **54**:34

The Porcelain Cat (Leo and Diane Dillon) **44**:38

Pork and Beans: Play Date (Stine) **37**:109

Porko Von Popbutton (Pene du Bois) **1**:65

Porridge Poetry: Cooked, Ornamented, and Served by Hugh Lofting (Lofting) **19**:124

Portals to the Past: The Story of Archaeology (Shippen) **36**:180

Portfolio of Horse Paintings (Henry) **4**:112

Portfolio of Horses (Henry) **4**:112

Portly McSwine (Marshall) **21**:174

The Portmanteau Book (Rockwell) **6**:237

Portrait of Ivan (Fox) **1**:79

Portrait of Mary (Grimes) **42**:94

Possum Magic (Fox) **23**:113

The Post Office Book: Mail and How It Moves (Gibbons) **8**:93

The Post Office Cat (Haley) **21**:144

Postcard Poems: A Collection of Poetry for Sharing (Janeczko) **47**:99

Postmarked the Stars (Norton) **50**:148

The Potato Kid (Corcoran) **50**:37

Potatoes: All about Them (Silverstein and Silverstein) **25**:214

The Potters' Kitchen (Isadora) **7**:103

The Potter's Wheel (St. John) **46**:119

Poverty in America (Meltzer) **13**:150

Power of Three (Jones) **23**:186

Power Play (Christopher)   **33**:51
Power Play (Pascal)   **25**:184
Practical Music Theory: How Music Is Put Together from Bach to Rock (Collier)   **3**:48
The Practical Princess (Williams)   **8**:230
The Practical Princess and Other Liberating Fairy Tales (Williams)   **8**:236
A Prairie Boy's Summer (Kurelek)   **2**:103
A Prairie Boy's Winter (Kurelek)   **2**:103
Prairie School (Lenski)   **26**:115
Prairie Songs (Conrad)   **18**:86
Prank (Lasky)   **11**:120
Prayer for a Child (Field)   **21**:80
Prehistoric Animals (Cohen)   **43**:49
Prehistoric Animals (Epstein and Epstein)   **26**:54
Prehistoric Mammals: A New World (Berger)   **32**:36
Preposterous: Poems of Youth (Janeczko)   **47**:112
Preston's Goal! (McNaughton)   **54**:68
Pretend You're a Cat (Pinkney)   **43**:166
Pretty Brown Face (Pinkney)   **54**:149
Pretty Polly (King-Smith)   **40**:165
Pretty Pretty Peggy Moffitt (Pene du Bois)   **1**:66
Pretzel (Rey and Rey)   **5**:195
Pretzel and the Puppies (Rey and Rey)   **5**:195
Pretzels (Dorros)   **42**:64
Pride of Lions: The Story of the House of Atreus (St. John)   **46**:108
The Prime Minister's Brain (Cross)   **28**:90
The Prime of Tamworth Pig (Kemp)   **29**:112
Prime Time (Pfeffer)   **11**:205
Primrose Day (Haywood)   **22**:91
The Primrose Path (Matas)   **52**:90
Prince Bertram the Bad (Lobel)   **5**:163
Prince Caspian: The Return to Narnia (Lewis)   **3**:136; **27**:104-51
The Prince in Waiting (Christopher)   **2**:41
Prince Lachlan (Hilton)   **25**:60
The Prince of the Dolomites: An Old Italian Tale (dePaola)   **4**:64
Prince of the Jungle (Guillot)   **22**:60
The Prince of the Pond: Otherwise Known As De Fawg Pin (Napoli)   **51**:154
Prince Rabbit and the Princess Who Could Not Laugh (Milne)   **1**:143
Princess Alice (Bawden)   **51**:34
The Princess and the Clown (Mahy)   **7**:180
The Princess and the Giants (Snyder)   **31**:160
The Princess and the God (Orgel)   **48**:96
The Princess and the Moon (Wildsmith)   **52**:197
The Princess and the Musician (French)   **37**:44
Princess Ashley (Peck)   **15**:166
Princess Gorilla and a New Kind of Water (Aardema)   **17**:8
The Princess of the Golden Mane (Garner)   **20**:116
The Printers (Fisher)   **18**:122
Printer's Devil (Epstein and Epstein)   **26**:42
Prisoner of Vampires (Garden)   **51**:71
The Prisoners of September (Garfield)   **21**:108
The Private Lives of Orchids (Simon)   **39**:192
Private Lives of the Stars (Gallant)   **30**:101
The Procession (Mahy)   **7**:179
Professor Noah's Spaceship (Wildsmith)   **52**:185
Professor Wormbog in Search for the Zipperump-a-Zoo (Mayer)   **11**:172
Profiles in Black Power (Haskins)   **3**:66
Project 1-2-3 (Merriam)   **14**:197
Project Boy (Lenski)   **26**:118
Project Panda Watch (Schlein)   **41**:192
Projects with Air (Simon)   **9**:209
Projects with Plants (Simon)   **9**:207
The Prom Queen (Stine)   **37**:117
A Promise for Joyce (Duncan)   **29**:66

A Promise Is a Promise (Munsch)   **19**:146
The Promised Year (Uchida)   **6**:252
Promises Are for Keeping (Rinaldi)   **46**:77
A Proper Little Lady (Hilton)   **25**:61
A Proper Little Nooryeff (Ure)   **34**:172
Prophets of Doom (Cohen)   **43**:54
The Protectors: The Petrova Twist (Stine)   **37**:109
The Proud Circus Horse (Zimnik)   **3**:244
The Proud Maiden: Tungak, and the Sun: A Russian Eskimo Tale (Ginsburg)   **45**:7
A Proud Taste for Scarlet and Miniver (Konigsburg)   **1**:122
The Proud Wooden Drummer (Kruss)   **9**:88
The Prydain Chronicles (Alexander)   **1**:16
Psi High and Others (Nourse)   **33**:135
Psst! Doggie— (Keats)   **1**:117; **35**:138
Psychology in Action (Hyde)   **23**:156
Pterosaurs, the Flying Reptiles (Sattler)   **24**:220
Puddin' Poems: Being the Best of the Verse from "The Magic Pudding" (Lindsay)   **8**:106
The Puffin Book of Improbable Records (The Improbable Book of Records) (Blake)   **31**:21
The Puffin Book of Improbable Records (Yeoman)   **46**:178
The Puffin Book of Magic Verse (Causley)   **30**:37
The Puffin Book of Salt-Sea Verse (Causley)   **30**:39
Puffins Climb, Penguins Rhyme (McMillan)   **47**:186
Pumpers, Boilers, Hooks, and Ladders: A Book of Fire Engines (Fisher)   **18**:121
Pumpkin Moonshine (Tudor)   **13**:189
Punch and Judy (Emberley)   **5**:92
Puniddles (McMillan)   **47**:163
Punography Too (McMillan)   **47**:163
Puppeteer (Lasky)   **11**:121
Puppies, Dogs, and Blue Northers: Reflections on Being Raised by a Pack of Sled Dogs (Paulsen)   **54**:120
Puppy Love (Hill)   **13**:93
Puppy Summer (DeJong)   **1**:60
Puritan Adventure (Lenski)   **26**:107
The Purple Coat (Schwartz)   **25**:192
Push (Graham)   **31**:95
Push, Pull, Empty, Full: A Book of Opposites (Hoban)   **13**:102
Push the Dog (McNaughton)   **54**:56
The Pushcart War (Merrill)   **52**:106
Puss in Boots (Brown)   **12**:96
Puss in Boots (Galdone)   **16**:101
Pussy Willow (Brown)   **10**:61
A Pussycat's Christmas (Brown)   **10**:59
Put a Saddle on the Pig (McBratney)   **44**:124
Put on a Show! (McNaughton)   **54**:56
Puttes Aventyr i Blåbärsskogen (Beskow)   **17**:15
Putting on a Show (Berger)   **32**:22
Putting the Sun to Work (Bendick)   **5**:49
Putting up with Mitchell: My Vancouver Scrapbook (Ellis)   **42**:84
Pyramid (Macaulay)   **3**:143
Pysen (Unnerstad)   **36**:190
Python's Party (Wildsmith)   **2**:214
Quag Keep (Norton)   **50**:161
The Quangle Wangle's Hat (Lear)   **1**:127
The Quangle Wangle's Hat (Oxenbury)   **22**:138
The Quarreling Book (Zolotow)   **2**:236
Quarter Horses (Patent)   **19**:161
Quasars, Pulsars, and Black Holes in Space (Berger)   **32**:17
The Queen Always Wanted to Dance (Mayer)   **11**:166
The Queen and Rosie Randall (Oxenbury)   **22**:140
The Queen Elizabeth Story (Sutcliff)   **1**:189; **37**:148

The Queen Elizabeth Story (Sutcliff)   **37**:148
The Queen of Eene (Prelutsky)   **13**:167
Queen of Hearts (Cleaver and Cleaver)   **6**:111
The Queen of the What Ifs (Klein)   **19**:93
Queen of the Wheat Castles (Mattingley)   **24**:123
Queen Victoria (Streatfeild)   **17**:194
The Queen's Nose (King-Smith)   **40**:144
Quentin Blake's ABC (Blake)   **31**:27
Quentin Blake's Nursery Rhyme Book (Blake)   **31**:24
Quest Crosstime (Norton)   **50**:143
The Quest for Artificial Intelligence (Patent)   **19**:162
A Quest for Orion (Harris)   **30**:119
The Quest of Captain Cook (Selsam)   **1**:164
The Quest of Galileo (Lauber)   **16**:113
The Question and Answer Book about the Human Body (McGovern)   **50**:112
The Question Box (Williams)   **8**:226
A Question of Survival (Thompson)   **24**:228
Questions and Answers about Ants (Selsam)   **1**:165
Questions and Answers about Horses (Selsam)   **1**:165
Questions and Answers about Sharks (McGovern)   **50**:118
Quick, Let's Get Out of Here (Rosen)   **45**:132
The Quicksand Book (dePaola)   **4**:59
A Quiet Night In (Murphy)   **39**:179
The Quiet Noisy Book (Brown)   **10**:60
The Quiet Revolution: The Struggle for the Rights of Disabled Americans (Haskins)   **39**:37
Quiet! There's a Canary in the Library (Freeman)   **30**:76
The Quilt (Jonas)   **12**:175
The Quinkins (Roughsey and Trezise)   **41**:140
Quips and Quirks (Watson)   **3**:213
Quito Express (Bemelmans)   **6**:66
The Quitting Deal (Tobias)   **4**:215
The Rabbit (Burningham)   **9**:46
Rabbit Hill (Lawson)   **2**:110
Rabbit Island (Mueller)   **43**:119
Rabbit Makes a Monkey of Lion (Pinkney)   **43**:163
The Rabbit Story (Tresselt)   **30**:206
Rabbits: All about Them (Silverstein and Silverstein)   **25**:210
Rabbits and Redcoats (Peck)   **45**:108
Rabbits, Rabbits (Fisher)   **49**:58
Rabble Starkey (Lowry)   **46**:34
Raccoons and Ripe Corn (Arnosky)   **15**:11
Raccoons, Coatimundis, and Their Family (Patent)   **19**:154
The Race (Hurd)   **49**:115
The Race (Matas)   **52**:83
The Race of the Golden Apples (Leo and Diane Dillon)   **44**:43
A Racecourse for Andy (Wrightson)   **4**:242
The Racers: Speed in the Animal World (Simon)   **39**:196
Rachel Carson: Who Loved the Sea (Latham)   **50**:106
The Rachel Field Story Book (Field)   **21**:80
Rachel Parker, Kindergarten Show-Off (Martin)   **32**:206
The Racing Cart (Heine)   **18**:149
Rackety-Bang and Other Verses (Rockwell)   **6**:235
Radio Astronomy (Nourse)   **33**:149
Radio Fifth Grade (Korman)   **25**:111
Radio: From Marconi to the Space Age (Carter)   **22**:21
Radio Man/Don Radio (Dorros)   **42**:72
Raffy and the Nine Monkeys (Rey)   **5**:192
The Raggle-Taggle Fellow (Schlein)   **41**:182
Raging Robots and Unruly Uncles (Mahy)   **7**:186

Raiders from the Rings (Nourse) **33**:133
The Railroads (Fisher) **18**:128
The Railway Children (Nesbit) **3**:164
The Railway Engine and the Hairy Brigands (Mahy) **7**:181
Railway Ghosts and Highway Horrors (Cohen) **43**:54
Railway Passage (Keeping) **34**:99
The Railway Phantoms (Hamley) **47**:65
"Railway Series" (Awdry) **23**:1-7
Rain (Spier) **5**:228
Rain and Hail (Branley) **13**:31
Rain and the Valley (Hurd and Hurd) **49**:125
The Rain Car (Janosch) **26**:76
The Rain Cloud (Rayner) **41**:123
Rain Comes to Yamboorah (Ottley) **16**:184
The Rain Door (Blake) **31**:26
Rain Drop Splash (Tresselt) **30**:201
Rain Forest Secrets (Dorros) **42**:67
Rain Player (Wisniewski) **51**:195
Rain Rain Rivers (Shulevitz) **5**:203
Rainbow and Mr. Zed (Nimmo) **44**:148
The Rainbow Fish (Pfister) **42**:136
Rainbow Fish to the Rescue! (Pfister) **42**:139
Rainbow Jordan (Childress) **14**:93
A Rainbow of My Own (Freeman) **30**:74
Rainbow Pavement (Cresswell) **18**:103
The Rainbow People (Yep) **54**:186
Rainbow Rhino (Sis) **45**:159
Rainbow Valley (Montgomery) **8**:137
Rainbow Writing (Merriam) **14**:199
Rainbows and Fireworks (Pfeffer) **11**:197
Rainbows Are Made: Poems by Carl Sandburg (Hopkins) **44**:91
Rainbows, Mirages, and Sundogs: The Sky as a Source of Wonder (Gallant) **30**:103
The Rain-Giver (Crossley-Holland) **47**:29
Raining Cats and Dogs (Yolen) **44**:200
Rainy Day Magic (Gay) **27**:86
Rainy Rainy Saturday (Prelutsky) **13**:168
Rajpur: Last of the Bengal Tigers (McClung) **11**:193
Ralph Bunche: A Most Reluctant Hero (Haskins) **3**:66
Ralph S. Mouse (Cleary) **8**:58
Rama, the Gypsy Cat (Byars) **16**:53
Rama, the Hero of India: Valmiki's "Ramayana" Done into a Short English Version for Boys and Girls (Mukerji) **10**:134
Ramona and Her Father (Cleary) **8**:55
Ramona and Her Mother (Cleary) **8**:56
Ramona Forever (Cleary) **8**:62
Ramona Quimby, Age 8 (Cleary) **8**:57
Ramona the Brave (Cleary) **2**:49; **8**:55
Ramona the Pest (Cleary) **2**:49; **8**:52
The Randolph Caldecott Picture Book (Caldecott) **14**:83
Randolph Caldecott's John Gilpin and Other Stories (Caldecott) **14**:84
Randy's Dandy Lions (Peet) **12**:195
Ransom (Duncan) **29**:67
Rapscallion Jones (Marshall) **21**:179
Rapunzel (Hyman) **50**:75
Rasmus and the Tramp (Lindgren) **39**:148
Rasmus and the Vagabond (Lindgren) **1**:139; **39**:148
Raspberry One (Ferry) **34**:54
The Rat Race: The Amazing Adventures of Anton B. Stanton (McNaughton) **54**:50
Ratbags and Rascals: Funny Stories (Klein) **21**:160
Rats and Mice: Friends and Foes of Man (Silverstein and Silverstein) **25**:200
Rat's Christmas Party (Murphy) **53**:101

Rattlesnakes (Freedman) **20**:84
The Raucous Auk: A Menagerie of Poems (Hoberman) **22**:110
Raven's Cry (Harris) **47**:78
Ray Charles (Mathis) **3**:151
Razzle-Dazzle Riddles (Betsy and Giulio Maestro) **45**:76
Reaching for Dreams: A Ballet from Rehearsal to Opening Night (Kuklin) **51**:100
Read One: Numbers as Words (Burningham) **9**:50
Reading (Ormerod) **20**:177
Reading Can Be Fun (Leaf) **25**:132
Ready or Not (St. John) **46**:98
Ready, Steady, Go! (Watanabe) **8**:216
The Real Book about Alaska (Epstein and Epstein) **26**:47
The Real Book about Amazing Birds (Merriam) **14**:191
The Real Book about Benjamin Franklin (Epstein and Epstein) **26**:48
The Real Book about Franklin D. Roosevelt (Merriam) **14**:191
The Real Book about Inventions (Epstein and Epstein) **26**:47
The Real Book about Pirates (Epstein and Epstein) **26**:48
The Real Book about Spies (Epstein and Epstein) **26**:48
The Real Book about Submarines (Epstein and Epstein) **26**:50
The Real Book about the Sea (Epstein and Epstein) **26**:51
The Real Hole (Cleary) **2**:50; **8**:49
The Real Plato Jones (Bawden) **51**:40
The Real Thief (Steig) **2**:160
Realm of Algebra (Asimov) **12**:36
Realm of Measure (Asimov) **12**:34
Realm of Numbers (Asimov) **12**:33
Rear-View Mirrors (Fleischman) **20**:68
The Reason for the Pelican (Ciardi) **19**:75
Rebecca of Sunnybrook Farm (Wiggin) **52**:162
Rebel (Baillie) **49**:16
The Rebel (Burton) **1**:33
Rebel on a Rock (Bawden) **51**:28
Rebellion Town: Williamsburg, 1776 (Taylor) **30**:187
Rebels of the Heavenly Kingdom (Paterson) **7**:242
Rechenka's Eggs (Polacco) **40**:180
Recipes for Art and Craft Materials (Sattler) **24**:214
Recycling Resources (Pringle) **4**:179
Red, Blue, Yellow Shoe (Hoban) **13**:112
The Red Bus and the Green Car (Beskow) **17**:18
Red Earth, Blue Sky: The Australian Outback (Rau) **8**:191
Red Fox: The Story of His Adventurous Career in the Ringwaak Wilds, and of His Final Triumph over the Enemies of His Kind (Roberts) **33**:195
Red Hart Magic (Norton) **50**:160
Red Hawk's Account of Custer's Last Battle: The Battle of Little Bighorn, 25 June 1876 (Goble) **21**:128
Red Head (Eager) **43**:79
Red Hot Hightops (Christopher) **33**:58
The Red King (Kelleher) **36**:125
Red Leaf, Yellow Leaf (Ehlert) **28**:115
Red Light, Green Light (Brown) **10**:52
Red Magic: A Collection of the World's Best Fairy Tales from All Countries (Nielsen) **16**:158
"Red Nose Readers" (McNaughton) **54**:56
Red Pawns (Wibberley) **3**:229
Red Riding Hood (Marshall) **21**:182

Red Riding Hood: Retold in Verse for Boys and Girls to Read Themselves (Gorey) **36**:97
The Red Room Riddle (Corbett) **1**:46
The Red Secret (Nimmo) **44**:142
Red Shift (Garner) **20**:109
The Red Towers of Granada (Trease) **42**:188
The Red Woollen Blanket (Graham)
   See *The Red Woollen Blanket*
The Red Woollen Blanket (*The Red Woolen Blanket*) (Graham) **31**:98
Redbird: The Story of a Cardinal (McClung) **11**:185
Redecorating Your Room for Practically Nothing (Hautzig) **22**:77
Redwall (Jacques) **21**:153
Redwork (Bedard) **35**:62
Regards to the Man in the Moon (Keats) **35**:142
Reigning Cats and Dogs (Levitin) **53**:61
Reilly (Rayner) **41**:127
The Relatives Came (Rylant) **15**:171
Religions (Haskins) **3**:66
The Reluctant Dragon (Grahame) **5**:135
The Reluctant Pitcher (Christopher) **33**:42
The Remarkable Journey of Prince Jen (Alexander) **48**:22
The Remarkable Plant in Apartment 4 (Betsy and Giulio Maestro) **45**:64
The Remarkable Plant in Flat No. 4 (Betsy and Giulio Maestro) **45**:64
The Remarkable Riderless Runaway Tricycle (McMillan) **47**:160
Remember Me (Pike) **29**:173
Remember Me to Harold Square (Danziger) **20**:56
Remember the Days: A Short History of the Jewish American (Meltzer) **13**:134
Remember the Ladies: The First Women's Rights Convention (St. John) **46**:126
Remembering the Good Times (Peck) **15**:164
Remove Protective Coating a Little at a Time (Donovan) **3**:53
The Renegades of Pern (McCaffrey) **49**:150
Der Rennwagen (Heine) **18**:149
The Renowned History of Little Red Riding-Hood (Hogrogian) **2**:89
Representing Super Doll (Peck) **15**:154
The Reproductive System: How Living Creatures Multiply (Silverstein and Silverstein) **25**:206
Reptiles and How They Reproduce (Patent) **19**:150
Rescue! An African Adventure (Kelleher) **36**:119
The Rescuers (Sharp) **27**:161
Rescuing Gloria (Cross) **28**:95
The Restless Dead: Ghostly Tales from around the World (Cohen) **43**:44
The Restless Robin (Flack) **28**:126
Restoree (McCaffrey) **49**:139
Retreat to Glory: The Story of Sam Houston (Latham) **50**:104
The Return (Levitin) **53**:66
Return of the Buffalo (Scott) **20**:196
The Return of the Great Brain (Fitzgerald) **1**:70
The Return of the Headless Horseman (Christopher) **33**:55
Return of the Home Run Kid (Christopher) **33**:63
Return of the Indian (Reid Banks) **24**:197
Return of the Moose (Pinkwater) **4**:169
The Return of the Twelves (Clarke) **28**:77
Return to Gone-Away (Enright) **4**:76
Return to Morocco (St. John) **46**:120
Return to Sender (Henkes) **23**:126
Return to South Town (Graham) **10**:111
Return to the Happy Islands (Kruss) **9**:84
The Revenge of Samuel Stokes (Lively) **7**:163

The Revenge of the Incredible Dr. Rancid and His Youthful Assistant, Jeffrey (Conford) **10**:97
The Revenge of the Wizard's Ghost (Bellairs) **37**:19
Revolt at Ratcliffe's Rags (Cross) **28**:86
Revolutionaries: Agents of Change (Haskins) **3**:67
The Reward Worth Having (Williams) **8**:235
Rhyme Stew (Dahl) **41**:43
Rhymes Around the Day (Ormerod) **20**:176
Ribbons (Yep) **54**:200
Ribsy (Cleary) **2**:50; **8**:51
Rice without Rain (Ho) **28**:133
Rich and Famous: The Future Adventures of George Stable (Collier) **3**:48
Richard (Keeping) **34**:99
Richard Pryor: A Man and His Madness (Haskins) **39**:46
Richard Scarry's Color Book (Scarry) **3**:185
The Richleighs of Tantamount (Cleary) **3**:221
The Riddle Book (Crossley-Holland) **47**:38
Riddle City, USA: A Book of Geography Riddles (Betsy and Giulio Maestro) **45**:88
The Riddle of the Drum: A Tale from Tizapán, Mexico (Aardema) **17**:5
The Riddle of the Rosetta Stone: Key to Ancient Egypt (Giblin) **29**:93
Ride a Purple Pelican (Prelutsky) **13**:173
Ride into Danger (Treece) **2**:188
A Ride into Morning: The Story of Tempe Wick (Rinaldi) **46**:84
Ride Off: Learning Subtraction (Burningham) **9**:50
Ride Proud, Rebel! (Norton) **50**:141
Ride When You're Ready (Bunting) **28**:44
The Rider and His Horse (Haugaard) **11**:106
Riders of the Storm (Burton) **1**:34
Riders of the Wind (Guillot) **22**:62
Riding Home (Sanders) **46**:120
The Rifle (Paulsen) **54**:118
Right Now (Kherdian) **24**:113
The Right to Remain Silent (Meltzer) **13**:129
The Righteous Revenge of Artemis Bonner (Myers) **35**:199
The Rights of the Victim (Hyde) **23**:168
Rilla of Ingleside (Montgomery) **8**:138
A Ring of Endless Light (L'Engle) **14**:152
Ring Out! A Book of Bells (Yolen) **4**:261
Ring-Rise, Ring-Set (Hughes) **9**:75
Rise & Shine (French) **37**:49
The Rise of Mammals (Gallant) **30**:103
Rising Damp (Corcoran) **50**:26
Rising Early: Story Poems and Ballads of the Twentieth Century (Causley) **30**:32
The Rising Tide (Allan) **43**:28
Risking Love (Orgel) **48**:86
Rita the Weekend Rat (Levitin) **53**:57
River (Keeping) **34**:103
The River (Paulsen) **54**:103
The River and the Forest (Korinetz) **4**:131
A River Dream (Say) **22**:211
River Winding (Zolotow) **2**:236
Riverman (Baillie) **49**:8
The River-Minded Boy (Calhoun) **42**:5
The Road Ahead (Lowry) **46**:34
A Road Down in the Sea (Graham) **10**:109
The Road from Home: The Story of an Armenian Girl (Kherdian) **24**:109
Road to Alaska: The Story of the Alaska Highway (Epstein and Epstein) **26**:44
The Road to Camlann: The Death of King Arthur (Sutcliff) **37**:175
The Road to Damietta (O'Dell) **16**:179
The Road to Dunmore (Dillon) **26**:27
The Road to Miklagard (Treece) **2**:188
The Road under the Sea (Park) **51**:171

Roald Dahl's Revolting Rhymes (Dahl) **7**:81
The Roan Colt (Ottley) **16**:183
The Roan Colt of Yamboorah (Ottley) **16**:183
Roanoke: A Novel of the Lost Colony (Levitin) **53**:57
Roar and More (Kuskin) **4**:134
The "Roaring 40" (Chauncy) **6**:92
Robber Hopsika (Biegel) **27**:32
The Robbers (Bawden) **51**:30
Robbie and the Leap Year Blues (Klein) **19**:93
Robert E. Lee (Aaseng) **54**:15
Robert Francis Weatherbee (Leaf) **25**:116
Robert Fulton, Boy Craftsman (Henry) **4**:109
Robert Koch: Father of Bacteriology (Knight) **38**:98
Robert Rows the River (Haywood) **22**:99
Robin and His Merry Men (Serraillier) **2**:139
Robin Hood of Sherwood Forest (McGovern) **50**:113
The Robin Hooders (Clarke) **28**:77
Robin in the Greenwood: Ballads of Robin Hood (Serraillier) **2**:140
Robin of Sherwood (Morpurgo) **51**:149
Robot (Pienkowski) **6**:232
The Robot and Rebecca and the Missing Owser (Yolen) **4**:268
The Robot and Rebecca: The Mystery of the Code-Carrying Kids (Yolen) **4**:266
The Robot Birthday (Bunting) **28**:51
The Robot People (Bunting) **28**:48
Robotics: Past, Present, and Future (Knight) **38**:126
The Robots Are Here (Silverstein and Silverstein) **25**:221
Robots in Fact and Fiction (Berger) **32**:23
Rock Collecting (Keller) **45**:47
Rock 'n' Roll Nights: A Novel (Strasser) **11**:249
Rock Star (Collier) **3**:48
Rocket Island (Taylor) **30**:193
The Rocket Pioneers: On the Road to Space (Epstein and Epstein) **26**:51
Rocket to Limbo (Nourse) **33**:130
Rockets and Satellites (Branley) **13**:30
The Rocking Horse Secret (Godden) **20**:135
Rocks and Minerals and the Stories They Tell (Adler) **27**:7
The Rocks of Honey (Wrightson) **4**:241
Röda Bussen och Gröna Bilen (Beskow) **17**:18
Rogue Reynard (Norton) **50**:133
Roland the Minstrel Pig (Steig) **2**:161
Roll of Thunder, Hear My Cry (Taylor) **9**:226
Roller Skates (Sawyer) **36**:150
Rolling Harvey down the Hill (Prelutsky) **13**:167
The Rolling Rice Ball (Tresselt) **30**:212
The Roman Empire (Asimov) **12**:40
The Roman Moon Mystery (Williams) **8**:221
The Roman Republic (Asimov) **12**:39
Romance in Italy (Allan) **43**:7
Romansgrove (Allan) **43**:26
Rome under the Emperors (Dillon) **26**:31
Romeo and Juliet—Together (and Alive!) at Last (Avi) **24**:13
Rondo in C (Fleischman) **20**:70
Ronia, The Robber's Daughter (Lindgren) **39**:160
Ronnie and Rosie (Gaberman) **33**:2
Ronnie and the Giant Millipede (Nimmo) **44**:154
Roof Fall! (Cresswell) **18**:104
Roofs of Gold: Poems to Read Aloud (Colum) **36**:46
Room for Randy (Jackson) **28**:139
A Room Made of Windows (Cameron) **1**:40
A Room of His Own (Beckman) **25**:13
Room with No Windows (Kemp) **29**:124

Roomrimes: Poems (Cassedy) **26**:15
Rooster Brother (Hogrogian) **2**:89
The Rooster Crows: A Book of American Rhymes and Jingles (Petersham and Petersham) **24**:171
Rooster Sets Out to See the World (Carle) **10**:76
The Rooster Who Set Out to See the World (Carle) **10**:76
The Rooster Who Understood Japanese (Uchida) **6**:258
The Rooster's Horns: A Chinese Puppet Play to Make and Perform (Young) **27**:217
The Root Cellar (Lunn) **18**:160
Root River Run (Kherdian) **24**:114
Roots Are Food Finders (Branley) **13**:41
Rosa (Politi) **29**:192
Rosa Parks (Greenfield) **4**:97
Rosata (Keller) **45**:60
Roscoe's Leap (Cross) **28**:92
A Rose for Pinkerton (Kellogg) **6**:177
Rose Meets Mr. Wintergarten (Graham) **31**:101
Rose O' the River (Wiggin) **52**:166
The Rose on My Cake (Kuskin) **4**:138
Roseberry's Great Escape (Duke) **51**:50
Rosebud (Bemelmans) **6**:67
Rosebud (Emberley) **5**:93
Roses Sing on New Snow: A Delicious Tale (Yee) **44**:164
Rosie and Michael (Viorst) **3**:208
Rosie and the Rustlers (Gerrard) **23**:122
Rosie Swanson—Fourth-Grade Geek for President (Park) **34**:161
Rosie's Babies (Waddell) **31**:197
Rosie's Walk (Hutchins) **20**:142
Rosy Starling (Garfield) **21**:109
The Rotten Book (Rodgers) **20**:190
Rotten Island (Steig) **15**:199
Rotten Ralph (Gantos) **18**:140
Rotten Ralph's Rotten Christmas (Gantos) **18**:143
Rotten Ralph's Trick or Treat (Gantos) **18**:143
The Rotten Years (Wojciechowska) **1**:198
Round and Round and Round (Hoban) **13**:106
Round behind the Ice-House (Fine) **25**:19
Round the Twist (Jennings) **40**:127
Round Trip (Jonas) **12**:173
The Roundabout on the Roof (Baumann) **35**:46
The Rowan (McCaffrey) **49**:151
Rowan Farm (Benary-Isbert) **12**:72
The Royal Raven (Wilhelm) **46**:171
Rub-a-Dub-Dub: Val Biro's 77 Favorite Nursery Rhymes (Biro) **28**:40
Ruby (Guy) **13**:79
Ruby and the Dragon (Owen) **31**:147
The Ruby in the Smoke (Pullman) **20**:187
Ruby Mae Has Something to Say (Small) **53**:152
Ruby Throat: The Story of a Humming Bird (McClung) **11**:178
Rudi and the Distelfink (Monjo) **2**:125
Rudyard Kipling: Creative Adventurer (Manley) **3**:147
Ruffles Is Lost (Wilhelm) **46**:168
Rufus M. (Estes) **2**:75
Rufus, the Fox: Adapted from the French of Samivel (Bianco) **19**:56
Rufus, the Red-Necked Hornbill (Lauber) **16**:113
Rumanian Folk Tales (Ure) **34**:171
Rumbelow's Dance (Blake) **31**:23
Rumbelow's Dance (Yeoman) **46**:180
Rumble Fish (Hinton) **3**:71; **23**:148
Rummage (Mattingley) **24**:126
Rumpelstiltskin's Daughter (Stanley) **46**:158
Rumplestiltskin (Galdone) **16**:106
Run (Sleator) **29**:199

Run, Billy, Run (Christopher) **33**:54
Run for the Money (Corbett) **1**:47
Run, Run, Run (Hurd) **49**:122
Run Softly, Go Fast (Wersba) **3**:218
The Runaway (Cross) **28**:85
The Runaway Brownie (Calhoun) **42**:12
The Runaway Bunny (Brown) **10**:50
The Runaway Bunny (Hurd) **49**:117
The Runaway Elephant (Tarry) **26**:214
Runaway James and the Night Owl (Kuratomi)
  32:188
Runaway Ralph (Cleary) **8**:54
The Runaway Sleigh Ride (Lindgren) **39**:161
Runaway Sugar: All about Diabetes (Silverstein
  and Silverstein) **25**:220
The Runaway Summer (Bawden) **51**:18
*Runaway to Freedom: A Story of the Underground
  Railway* (Smucker) **10**:189
The Runaway Train (Farmer) **8**:87
The Runner (Voigt) **13**:236
Running Loose (Crutcher) **28**:103
Runny Days, Sunny Days: Merry Verses (Fisher)
  49:34
A Russian Farewell (Fisher) **18**:129
Rusty Rings a Bell (Branley) **13**:26
Ruth: From the Story Told in the Book of Ruth
  (Petersham and Petersham) **24**:169
*Rx for Tomorrow: Tales of Science Fiction, Fan-
  tasy, and Medicine* (Nourse) **33**:136
Saber-Toothed Tiger and Other Ice Age Mammals
  (Cole) **5**:65
Sable (Hesse) **54**:37
The Sacramento: Golden River of California
  (Epstein and Epstein) **26**:61
Sacred Places (Yolen) **44**:209
The Sad Story of Veronica Who Played the Violin
  (McKee) **38**:175
Saddlebottom (King-Smith) **40**:147
Sad-Faced Boy (Bontemps) **6**:79
Safari Adventure in Legoland (Matas) **52**:87
Safety Can Be Fun (Leaf) **25**:124
The Saga of Erik the Viking (Foreman) **32**:96
Sailing: From Jibs to Jibing (Paulsen) **19**:173
The Sailing Hatrack (Coatsworth) **2**:61
Sailing Small Boats (Weiss) **4**:224
Sailing to Cythera and Other Anatole Stories
  (Willard) **5**:245
Sailing with the Wind (Locker) **14**:160
The Sailor (Bruna) **7**:50
Sailor Bear (Waddell) **31**:202
The Sailor Dog (Brown) **10**:63
Sailor Jack and the 20 Orphans (Mahy) **7**:179
Saint Francis (Wildsmith) **52**:200
Saint Francis and the Animals (Politi) **29**:191
Saint George and the Dragon (McCaughrean)
  38:144
*Saint George and the Dragon: A Golden Legend
  Adapted from Edmund Spenser's Faerie Queen*
  (Hyman) **50**:77
Saint George and the Dragon: A Mummer's Play
  (Langstaff) **3**:111
Salford Road (Owen) **31**:141
Salford Road and Other Poems (Owen) **31**:142
Sally-Ann in the Snow (Breinburg) **31**:68
Sally-Ann's Skateboard (Breinburg) **31**:68
Sally-Ann's Umbrella (Breinburg) **31**:67
Sally's Secret (Hughes) **15**:121
A Salmon for Simon (Blades) **15**:55
Salt: A Russian Folktale (Langton) **33**:119
*Saltwater City: An Illustrated History of the
  Chinese in Vancouver* (Yee) **44**:162
*Salvador and Mister Sam: A Guide to Parakeet
  Care* (Gibbons) **8**:88

Sam (Corcoran) **50**:11
Sam and the Superdroop (Leaf) **25**:129
Sam and the Tigers (Pinkney) **43**:174
Sam, Bangs, and Moonshine (Ness) **6**:203
Sam Patch: The High, Wide, and Handsome Jumper
  (Bontemps) **6**:81
Sam the Referee (Ahlberg and Ahlberg) **18**:3
Sam Vole and His Brothers (Waddell) **31**:203
Sama (Guillot) **22**:55
Sammy Streetsinger (Keeping) **34**:106
Sam's All-Wrong Day (Fujikawa) **25**:41
Sam's Ball (Lindgren) **20**:157
Sam's Biscuit (Lindgren) **20**:156
Sam's Car (Lindgren) **20**:156
Sam's Cookie (Lindgren) **20**:156
Sam's Lamp (Lindgren) **20**:157
Sam's Place: Poems from the Country (Moore)
  15:143
Sam's Potty (Lindgren) **20**:158
Sam's Teddy (Lindgren) **20**:156
Sam's Teddy Bear (Lindgren) **20**:156
Sam's Wagon (Lindgren) **20**:158
Samson: Last of the California Grizzlies (McClung)
  11:188
Samstag im Paradies (Heine) **18**:150
Samuel Todd's Book of Great Colors (Konigsburg)
  47:143
Samuel Todd's Book of Great Inventions
  (Konigsburg) **47**:144
The Samurai and the Long-Nosed Devils (Namioka)
  48:62
Samurai of Gold Hill (Uchida) **6**:257
The Samurai's Daughter: A Japanese Legend (San
  Souci) **43**:188
The Samurai's Tale (Haugaard) **11**:110
San Domingo: The Medicine Hat Stallion (Henry)
  4:116
San Francisco (Fritz) **2**:81
San Francisco Boy (Lenski) **26**:118
The San Sebastian (Dillon) **26**:21
The Sanctuary Tree (St. John) **46**:104
Sand and Snow (Kuskin) **4**:139
The Sand Forest (Brinsmead) **47**:15
The Sandman and the Turtles (Morpurgo) **51**:135
The Sandwich (Wallace) **37**:208
Sandy the Sailor (Clarke) **28**:76
Santa Claus Forever! (Haywood) **22**:105
Santiago (Clark) **16**:80
A Santo for Pasqualita (Clark) **16**:80
A Sapphire for September (Brinsmead) **47**:9
Sara Will (Bridgers) **18**:26
Sarah and After: The Matriarchs (Reid Banks)
  24:190
Sarah Bishop (O'Dell) **16**:175
Sarah, Plain and Tall (MacLachlan) **14**:184
Sarah's Room (Orgel) **48**:74
Sarny: A Life Remembered (Paulsen) **54**:123
Sasha, My Friend (Corcoran) **50**:12
Sassinak (McCaffrey) **49**:151
Satellites in Outer Space (Asimov) **12**:35
Saturday in Paradise (Heine) **18**:150
Saturday, the Twelfth of October (Mazer) **23**:223
The Saturdays (Enright) **4**:73
Saturn and Beyond (Asimov) **12**:57
Saturn: The Spectacular Planet (Branley) **13**:48
The Saucepan Journey (Unnerstad) **36**:188
Save Our School (Cross) **28**:87
Saving Electricity (Epstein and Epstein) **26**:66
Saving Grace (Owen) **31**:146
Saving Sweetness (Stanley) **46**:157
Say Goodnight (Oxenbury) **22**:148
Sayonara, Mrs. Kackleman (Kalman) **32**:181
The Scarebird (Sis) **45**:161

The Scarecrow Book (Giblin) **29**:85
The Scarecrows (Westall) **13**:255
Scaredy-Cat (Fine) **25**:21
Scarface (Norton) **50**:133
Scary, Scary Halloween (Bunting) **28**:60
Scavenger Hunt (Pike) **29**:173
Scavengers in Space (Nourse) **33**:131
The Schernoff Discoveries (Paulsen) **54**:122
Schloss an der Grenze (Benary-Isbert) **12**:75
Schnitzel Is Lost (Wilhelm) **46**:168
Schnitzel's First Christmas (Wilhelm) **46**:166
Das Schönste Ei der Welt (Heine) **18**:148
The School (Burningham) **9**:46
School (McCully) **46**:60
School for Sillies (Williams) **8**:230
The School Mouse (King-Smith) **40**:170
The Schoolbus Comes at Eight O'Clock (McKee)
  38:181
Schoolmaster Whackwell's Wonderful Sons (Orgel)
  48:73
The Schoolmasters (Fisher) **18**:122
The Schoolmouse (King-Smith) **40**:170
The Schools (Fisher) **18**:132
Science ABC (Knight) **38**:99
Science and Music: From Tom-Tom to Hi-Fi
  (Berger) **32**:2
Science at the Ball Game (Aylesworth) **6**:53
Science at Work: Projects in Oceanography (Simon)
  9:206
Science at Work: Projects in Space Science (Simon)
  9:204
The Science Book of Meteorology (Knight) **38**:100
Science Can Be Fun (Leaf) **25**:134
"Science Early Learners" (Graham) **31**:95
Science Experiments You Can Eat (Cobb) **2**:66
Science in a Vacant Lot (Simon) **9**:203
Science Looks at Mysterious Monsters (Aylesworth)
  6:56
The Science of Music (Berger) **32**:41
Science Projects in Ecology (Simon) **9**:204
Science Projects in Pollution (Simon) **9**:206
Science versus Pseudoscience (Aaseng) **54**:21
Scoop: Last of the Brown Pelicans (McClung)
  11:187
Scorpions (Myers) **35**:190
Scouting with Baden-Powell (Freedman) **20**:74
Scram, Kid! (McGovern) **50**:116
Scrambled Eggs Super! (Dr. Seuss) **9**:178
Scrappy, the Pup (Ciardi) **19**:76
Scruffy (Parish) **22**:168
A Scythe, a Rooster, and a Cat (Domanska) **40**:49
The Sea Egg (Boston) **3**:28
Sea Elf (Ryder) **37**:99
A Sea Full of Sharks (Betsy and Giulio Maestro)
  45:83
Sea Glass (Yep) **17**:204
Sea Gull (Farmer) **8**:77
The Sea Is All Around (Enright) **4**:72
The Sea King: Sir Francis Drake and His Times
  (Marrin) **53**:94
The Sea Lion and the Slick (Freeman) **30**:79
Sea Magic and Other Stories of Enchantment
  (Harris) **30**:116
The Sea of Gold and Other Tales from Japan
  (Uchida) **6**:254
Sea Otters and Seaweed (Lauber) **16**:118
Sea People (Mueller) **43**:121
The Sea Rover (Guillot) **22**:58
*The Sea Rovers: Pirates, Privateers, and Bucca-
  neers* (Marrin) **53**:82
Sea So Big, Ship So Small (Bendick) **5**:40
Sea Songs (Fisher) **18**:135
Sea Star (McClung) **11**:189

Sea Star, Orphan of Chincoteague (Henry) 4:111

The Sea Stranger (Crossley-Holland) 47:31

The Sea View Hotel (Stevenson) 17:155

The Sea Wall (Dillon) 26:26

The Sea World Book of Sharks (Bunting) 28:49

The Sea World Book of Whales (Bunting) 28:51

The Sea-Beggar's Son (Monjo) 2:125

Seabird (Holling) 50:53

Seacrow Island (Lindgren) 1:139; 39:153

The Seagull (Farmer) 8:77

The Seal and the Slick (Freeman) 30:79

A Seal upon My Heart (Conrad) 18:88

The Seals (Dillon) 26:28

The Seal-Singing (Harris) 30:113

The Seance (Nixon) 24:140

Sean's Red Bike (*Shawn's Red Bike*) (Breinburg) 31:67

Search for a Stone (Munari) 9:129

The Search for Delicious (Babbitt) 2:7; 53:24

The Search for Life (Aylesworth) 6:52

Seashore Story (Yashima) 4:254

Seashores and Shadows (Thiele) 27:209

A Season for Unicorns (Levitin) 53:66

Season of Ponies (Snyder) 31:153

Season of the Briar (Brinsmead) 47:7

Season of the Two-Heart (Duncan) 29:67

Season Songs (Hughes) 3:95

Seasons (Berger) 32:44

Seasons (Burningham) 9:43

The Seasons for Singing: American Christmas Songs and Carols (Langstaff) 3:111

Seasons of Splendour: Tales, Myths, and Legends of India (Foreman) 32:99

Seasons of the Tallgrass Prairie (Lerner) 34:125

The Sea-Thing Child (Hoban) 3:82

The Second Bend in the River (Rinaldi) 46:93

The Second Books of American Negro Spirituals (Johnson) 32:163

The Second Jungle Book (Kipling) 39:74-118

The Second Margaret Mahy Story Book: Stories and Poems (Mahy) 7:181

The Second Mrs. Giaconda (Konigsburg) 47:133

Second Summer with Ladis (Sanchez-Silva) 12:232

The Secret (Coatsworth) 2:61

Secret Agents Four (Sobol) 4:208

The Secret Bedroom (Stine) 37:115

The Secret Birthday Message (Carle) 10:75

The Secret Box (Cole) 5:61

The Secret Box Mystery (Nixon) 24:135

The Secret Clocks: Time Senses of Living Things (Simon) 9:213

The Secret Friends (Chauncy) 6:91

The Secret Garden (Burnett) 24:21-60

Secret in a Sealed Bottle: Lazarro Spallanzani's Work with Microbes (Epstein and Epstein) 26:67

Secret in the Stlalakum Wild (Harris) 47:83

The Secret Knowledge of Grown-Ups (Wisniewski) 51:202

The Secret Name (Wilkinson) 48:188

The Secret of Bone Island (McBratney) 44:123

The Secret of Gumbo Grove (Tate) 37:188

The Secret of Light (Adler) 27:4

The Secret of Sarah Revere (Rinaldi) 46:90

Secret of the Andes (Clark) 16:77

Secret of the Hawk (Wibberley) 3:230

The Secret of the Indian (Reid Banks) 24:200

The Secret of the Lodge (*The House in Cornwall*; *The House of Cornwall*) (Streatfeild) 17:188

Secret of the Maori Cave (Park) 51:170

The Secret of the Missing Boat (Berna) 19:38

The Secret of the Royal Mounds: Henry Layard and the First Cities of Assyria (Cummings) 48:44

The Secret of the Sachem's Tree (Monjo) 2:125

The Secret of the Singing Strings (St. John) 46:114

The Secret Passage (Bawden) 51:13

Secret Sea (White) 3:222

Secret Selves (Gaberman) 33:5

Secret, Silent Screams (Nixon) 24:151

The Secret Soldier: The Story of Deborah Sampson (McGovern) 50:117

The Secret Staircase (Barklem) 31:5

The Secret Trails (Roberts) 33:204

Secret Water (Ransome) 8:179

The Secret World of Polly Flint (Cresswell) 18:111

Secrets of a Wildlife Watcher (Arnosky) 15:7

Secrets of the Shopping Mall (Peck) 15:162

Secrets of the Underground Room (Bellairs) 37:24

Secrets of Walden Rising (Baillie) 49:22

The Secrets on Beacon Hill (St. John) 46:115

See My Lovely Poison Ivy and Other Verses about Witches, Ghosts, and Things (Moore) 15:143

See the Circus (Rey) 5:198

See through the Sea (Selsam) 1:165

See What I Am (Duvoisin) 23:105

See What I Found (Livingston) 7:168

See You Around, Sam! (Lowry) 46:50

See You Later (Pike) 29:173

See You Thursday (Ure) 34:171

Seeds: Pop, Stick, Glide (Lauber) 16:119

The Seeing Stick (Yolen) 4:264

Seeing the Earth from Space: What the Man-Made Moons Tell Us (Adler) 27:13

The Seekers (Dillon) 26:33

El segundo verano de Ladis (Sanchez-Silva) 12:232

The Selfish Giant (Zwerger) 46:193

The Self-Made Snowman (Krahn) 3:105

Self-Portrait: Trina Schart Hyman (Hyman) 50:74

Selina's New Family (Pilgrim) 43:17

A Semester in the Life of a Garbage Bag (Korman) 25:109

A Sending of Dragons (Yolen) 44:181

Sense of Direction: Up and Down and All Around (Cobb) 2:67

A Sense of Shame and Other Stories (Needle) 43:134

The Sense Organs: Our Link with the World (Silverstein and Silverstein) 25:205

Sense Suspense: A Guessing Game for the Five Senses (McMillan) 47:185

Senses (Graham) 31:95

Sentries (Paulsen) 19:175

Serafina the Giraffe (Brunhoff) 4:35

The Serpent Never Sleeps: A Novel of Jamestown and Pocahontas (O'Dell) 16:180

The Serpent's Children (Yep) 17:206

The Serpent's Teeth: The Story of Cadmus (Farmer) 8:80

Servants of the Devil (Aylesworth) 6:49

Sets (Adler) 27:22

Sets and Numbers for the Very Young (Adler) 27:23

Settling America: The Ethnic Expression of Fourteen Contemporary Poets (Kherdian) 24:106

Seven Candles for Kwanzaa (Pinkney) 54:140

The Seven Days of Creation (Fisher) 18:130

Seven Days to a Brand-New Me (Conford) 10:97

Seven Kisses in a Row (MacLachlan) 14:183

Seven Little Monsters (Sendak) 17:123

The Seven Ravens (Zwerger) 46:189

Seven Silly Circles (Conrad) 18:88

Seven Stories about a Cat Named Sneakers (Brown) 10:65

Seven Stories by Hans Christian Andersen (Carle) 10:82

Seven White Pebbles (Clarke) 28:77

Seven Wild Pigs: Eleven Picture Book Fantasies (Heine) 18:150

Seven-Day Magic (Eager) 43:88

Seventeen against the Dealer (Voigt) 48:172

Seventeen and In-Between (DeClements) 23:35

Seventeen Kings and Forty-Two Elephants (Mahy) 7:181

Seventeen Seconds (Southall) 2:155

The Seventh Mandarin (Yolen) 4:259

The Seventh Pebble (Spence) 26:198

The Seventh Raven (Dickinson) 29:52

The Seven-Times Search (Biegel) 27:29

Several Kinds of Silence (Singer) 48:132

Sexual Abuse: Let's Talk about It (Hyde) 23:169

Sexually Transmitted Diseases (Nourse) 33:150

Shadow (Brown) 12:107

The Shadow Cage and Other Tales of the Supernatural (Pearce) 9:155

Shadow Dancers (Curry) 31:84

The Shadow Guests (Aiken) 19:12

Shadow in Hawthorn Bay (Lunn) 18:165

Shadow in the North (Lindgren) 20:188

The Shadow in the Plate (Pullman) 20:188

Shadow Lord (Yep) 17:207

Shadow of a Bull (Wojciechowska) 1:199

Shadow of a Unicorn (St. John) 46:118

Shadow of the Hawk (Trease) 42:180

The Shadow of Vesuvius (Dillon) 26:32

The Shadow on the Hills (Thiele) 27:207

The Shadow on the Sun (Harris) 30:112

Shadow over the Back Court (Christopher) 33:38

Shadow Shark (Thiele) 27:209

Shadows (Adler) 27:15

Shadows and Light: Nine Stories by Anton Chekhov (Grifalconi) 35:70

Shadows on the Lake (Waddell) 31:188

Shadows on the Wall (Naylor) 17:55

Shadrach (DeJong) 1:60

Shadrach, Meshach and Abednego: From the Book of Daniel (Galdone) 16:92

Shadrach's Crossing (Avi) 24:10

Shag: Last of the Plains Buffalo (McClung) 11:182

Shaggy (Pfister) 42:135

Shags Finds a Kitten (Fujikawa) 25:41

Shaka: King of the Zulus (Stanley) 46:139

Shaka, King of the Zulus: A Biography (Cohen) 3:42

Shaker Paper House: To Cut Out and Color (Ness) 6:209

Shakes, Quakes, and Shifts: Earth Tectonics (Branley) 13:40

Shakespeare Stories (Foreman) 32:97

Shakespeare Stories (Garfield) 21:118

Shan's Lucky Knife: A Buremese Folk Tale (Merrill) 52:104

Shapes (Bendick) 5:42

Shapes (Schlein) 41:175

Shapes and Things (Hoban) 13:100

Shapes, Shapes, Shapes (Hoban) 13:111

The Shaping of England (Asimov) 12:43

The Shaping of North America from Earliest Times to 1763 (Asimov) 12:48

Sharelle (Neufeld) 52:131

Sharing Susan (Bunting) 28:67

Shark Lady: The True Adventures of Eugenie Clark (McGovern) 50:120

Shark Shock (Napoli) 51:159

Sharks (Blumberg) 21:24

Sharks (Freedman) 20:86

Sharks (McGovern) 50:118

Title Index

Sharks (Zim) **2**:230

Sharks in the Shadows (Thiele) **27**:209

Sharks, the Super Fish (Sattler) **24**:221

Shatterbelt (Thiele) **27**:211

Shaun and the Cart-Horse (Keeping) **34**:88

Shawn Goes to School (Breinburg)
  See *My Brother Sean*

Shawn's Red Bike (Breinburg)
  See *Sean's Red Bike*

Shaw's Fortune: The Picture Story of a Colonial Plantation (Tunis) **2**:194

She Come Bringing Me That Little Baby Girl (Greenfield) **4**:97

She Never Looked Back: Margaret Mead in Samoa (Epstein and Epstein) **26**:68

The Sheep Book (Patent) **19**:161

The Sheep-Pig (King-Smith) **40**:144; **41**:124

Sheet Magic: Games, Toys and Gifts from Old Sheets (Parish) **22**:159

Sheila Rae, the Brave (Henkes) **23**:129

Sheila's Dying (Carter) **22**:21

She'll Be Coming Around the Mountain (Orgel) **48**:95

The Shell Woman and the King: A Chinese Folktale (Yep) **54**:191

A Shepherd Watches, A Shepherd Sings (Taylor) **30**:190

The Sheriff of Rottenshot (Prelutsky) **13**:169

Shh! We're Writing the Constitution (Fritz) **14**:122

Shhhh (Henkes) **23**:131

SHHhhhh……Bang, a Whispering Book (Brown) **10**:51

The Shield Ring (Sutcliff) **1**:189; **37**:152

Shifting Sands (Sutcliff) **37**:167

The Shimmershine Queens (Yarbrough) **29**:210

Shimmy Shimmy Coke-Ca-Pop! A Collection of City Children's Street Games and Rhymes (Langstaff) **3**:112

The Shining Company (Sutcliff) **37**:181

Ship Models and How to Build Them (Weiss) **4**:227

Ship of Danger (Allan) **43**:25

The Ship That Came Down the Gutter (Kotzwinkle) **6**:181

The Ship Who Sang (McCaffrey) **49**:139

Shirley Temple Black: Actress to Ambassador (Haskins) **39**:58

Shirley's Shops (McNaughton) **54**:56

Shirlick Holmes and the Case of the Wandering Wardrobe (Yolen) **4**:267

The Shirt off a Hanged Man's Back (Hamley) **47**:57

Shivers and Goose Bumps: How We Keep Warm (Branley) **13**:49

Shoebag (Kerr) **29**:158

Shoes from Grandpa (Fox) **23**:117

The Shooting Star (Benary-Isbert) **12**:74

Shooting Stars (Keller) **45**:53

The Shopping Basket (Burningham) **9**:49

Shopping Trip (Oxenbury) **22**:143

Short and Shivery: Thirty Chilling Tales (San Souci) **43**:183

Short and Tall (Scarry) **41**:167

The Short Voyage of the 'Albert Ross' (Mark) **11**:150

Shortstop from Tokyo (Christopher) **33**:44

A Shovelful of Earth (Milne and Milne) **22**:125

The Show Must Go On (McCully) **46**:60

Show-and-Tell Frog (Duke) **51**:53

Showdown (Pascal) **25**:185

Shrewbettina Goes to Work (Goodall) **25**:51

Shrewbettina's Birthday (Goodall) **25**:44

The Shrinking of Treehorn (Gorey) **36**:94

Sia Lives on Kilimanjaro (Lindgren) **1**:140

The Sick Day (MacLachlan) **14**:180

The Sick of Being Sick Book (Stine) **37**:104

The Sickest Don't Always Die the Quickest (Jackson) **28**:140

Sid and Sol (Yorinks) **20**:214

Side by Side: Poems to Read Together (Hopkins) **44**:95

Sidewalk Story (Mathis) **3**:151

Sideways Arithmetic from Wayside School (Sacher) **28**:204

Sideways Stories from Wayside School (Sacher) **28**:200

The Siege of Babylon (Dhondy) **41**:73

Siegfried (Stanley) **46**:146

Sight and Seeing: A World of Light and Color (Simon) **39**:199

The Sign of the Beaver (Speare) **8**:210

The Sign of the Chrysanthemum (Paterson) **7**:230

The Sign of the Unicorn: A Thriller for Young People (Allan) **43**:11

The Sign on Rosie's Door (Sendak) **17**:111

The Signposters (Cresswell) **18**:99

Silas and Ben-Godik (Bodker) **23**:13

Silas and the Black Mare (Bodker) **23**:12

Silas and the Runaway Coach (Bodker) **23**:13

Silent Night (Jeffers) **30**:136

Silent Night (Stine) **37**:116

Silent Ship, Silent Sea (White) **3**:222

Silent Sound: The World of Ultrasonics (Knight) **38**:124

Silky: An Incredible Tale (Coatsworth) **2**:61

Silly Goose (Ormerod) **20**:179

Silly Mother (Duncan) **29**:66

The Silly Tail Book (Brown) **29**:10

Silver (Mazer) **23**:233

Silver Bells and Cockle Shells (Clarke) **28**:79

The Silver Branch (Sutcliff) **1**:190; **37**:153

The Silver Chair (Lewis) **3**:136; **27**:104-51

The Silver Christmas Tree (Hutchins) **20**:147

The Silver Crown (O'Brien) **2**:128

Silver Days (Levitin) **53**:69

The Silver Mace: A Story of Williamsburg (Petersham and Petersham) **24**:179

Silver on the Tree (Cooper) **4**:47

The Silver Sword (Serraillier) **2**:141

The Silver Train to Midnight (Brinsmead) **47**:16

The Silver Whistle (Williams) **8**:231

Simon (Sutcliff) **1**:190; **37**:150

The Simon and Schuster Book of Fact and Fallacies (Blumberg) **21**:28

Simon Boom Gives a Wedding (Suhl) **2**:166

Simon Pure (Thompson) **24**:230

Simon Underground (Ryder) **37**:84

Simon's Book (Drescher) **20**:59

Simon's Song (Emberley and Emberley) **5**:97

Simple Gifts: The Story of the Shakers (Yolen) **4**:263

Simple Pictures Are Best (Willard) **5**:247

The Simple Prince (Yolen) **4**:264

Sing a Song for Sixpence (Caldecott) **14**:75

Sing Down the Moon (O'Dell) **1**:148

Sing, Little Mouse (Fisher) **49**:51

Sing, Pierrot, Sing: A Picture Book in Mime (dePaola) **24**:94

Sing to the Dawn (Ho) **28**:132

The Singing Cave (Dillon) **26**:22

The Singing Hill (DeJong) **1**:61

The Singing Mountain (Levitin) **53**:78

The Singing Tortoise and Other Animal Folk Tales (Yeoman) **46**:184

The Singing Tree (Seredy) **10**:176

A Single Light (Wojciechowska) **1**:199

A Single Speckled Egg (Levitin) **53**:60

Singularity (Sleator) **29**:205

Sink It, Rusty (Christopher) **33**:39

Sir Arthur Evans, Discoverer of Knossos (Selden) **8**:198

Sir Cedric (Gerrard) **23**:120

Sir Cedric Rides Again (Gerrard) **23**:120

Sir Francis Drake: His Daring Deeds (Gerrard) **23**:121

Sirga, Queen of the African Bush (Guillot) **22**:55

Sister (Greenfield) **4**:97

Sister of the Bride (Cleary) **8**:50

Sisters/Hermanas (Paulsen) **54**:110

Six and Silver (Phipson) **5**:178

Six Men (McKee) **38**:163

The Six Swans (San Souci) **43**:183

Sixes and Sevens (Yeoman) **46**:175

A Six-Pack and a Fake I.D.: Teens Look at the Drinking Question (Cohen) **43**:47

The Sixpenny Island (Park) **51**:173

Sixth Grade Can Really Kill You (DeClements) **23**:36

Sixth Grade Secrets (Sacher) **28**:203

Sixth-Grade Sleepover (Bunting) **28**:60

The Size Spies (Needle) **43**:133

Sizes and Shapes in Nature—What They Mean (Patent) **19**:153

The Skate Patrol (Bunting) **28**:52

The Skate Patrol and the Mystery Writer (Bunting) **28**:54

Skateboard Tough (Christopher) **33**:62

Skates! (Keats) **1**:117; **35**:138

Skating Shoes (*White Boots*) (Streatfeild) **17**:191

The Skeletal System: Frameworks for Life (Silverstein and Silverstein) **25**:208

Sketching Outdoors in Spring (Arnosky) **15**:10

Ski Pup (Freeman) **30**:73

Ski Weekend (Stine) **37**:115

Skiing to Danger (Allan) **43**:14

The Skin: Coverings and Linings of Living Things (Silverstein and Silverstein) **25**:209

The Skin Horse (Bianco) **19**:52

The Skin Spinners (Aiken) **19**:9

Skinnybones (Park) **34**:155

Skip (Fisher) **49**:34

Skip Around the Year (Fisher) **49**:47

Skip Trip (Burningham) **9**:51

Skipper John's Cook (Brown) **12**:96

Skipping Village (Lenski) **26**:98

The Skirt (Soto) **38**:197

The Sknuks (Thiele) **27**:208

Skrallan and the Pirates (Lindgren) **39**:153

Sky Dogs (Moser) **49**:176

Sky Dogs (Yolen) **44**:190

A Sky Full of Poems (Merriam) **14**:203

The Sky is Falling (Corcoran) **50**:36

The Sky Is Falling (Pearson) **26**:178

The Sky Is Free (Clark) **30**:60

Sky Man on the Totem Pole? (Harris) **47**:84

Sky Songs (Fisher) **18**:133

The Sky Was Blue (Zolotow) **2**:236

Sky Words (Singer) **48**:143

The Sky-God Stories (Aardema) **17**:3

Skymaze (Rubinstein) **35**:212

The Skyscraper Book (Giblin) **29**:86

Slam Bang (Burningham) **9**:51

Slam Book (Martin) **32**:203

Slappy Hooper, the Wonderful Sign Painter (Bontemps) **6**:80

Slater's Mill (Monjo) **2**:126

The Slave Dancer (Fox) **1**:79

Slavery: From the Rise of Western Civilization to the Renaissance (Meltzer) **13**:128

Slavery, Volume II: From the Renaissance to Today (Meltzer) **13**:128

A Slave's Tale (Haugaard) **11**:103

Sledges to the Rescue (Briggs) **10**:23

Sleep and Dreams (Silverstein and Silverstein) **25**:210

Sleep Is for Everyone (Showers) **6**:246

Sleep Two, Three, Four! A Political Thriller (Neufeld) **52**:125

The Sleepers (Curry) **31**:71

Sleepers (Khalsa) **30**:148

The Sleepers on the Hill (Waddell) **31**:176

Sleeping (Ormerod) **20**:177

The Sleeping Beauty (Mayer) **11**:175

Sleeping Beauty and Other Favourite Fairy Tales (Foreman) **32**:94

Sleeping Ugly (Stanley) **46**:132

The Sleepwalker (Stine) **37**:113

Sleepy ABC (Brown) **10**:62

The Sleepy Owl (Pfister) **42**:133

Sleepy People (Goffstein) **3**:61

Sleepy Ronald (Gantos) **18**:140

Sloan and Philamina; or, How to Make Friends with Your Lunch (Stren) **5**:231

Slumber Party (Pike) **29**:170

The Sly Old Cat (Potter) **1**:153

A Small Civil War (Neufeld) **52**:130

Small Faces (Soto) **38**:187

Small Fry (Merriam) **14**:194

The Small Ones (Paulsen) **19**:171

Small Pig (Lobel) **5**:164

Small Poems (Worth) **21**:220

Small Poems Again (Worth) **21**:224

A Small Tall Tale from the Far Far North (Sis) **45**:171

The Smallest Cow in the World (Paterson) **50**:201

The Smallest Dinosaurs (Simon) **9**:218

The Smallest Elephant in the World (Tresselt) **30**:207

The Smallest Witch (Sattler) **24**:218

The Smartest Man in Ireland (Patrick Kentigern Keenan) (Hunter) **25**:74

Smeller Martin (Lawson) **2**:111

Smile, Ernest and Celestine (Vincent) **13**:217

Smile Like a Plastic Daisy (Levitin) **53**:65

Smile Please, Ernest and Celestine (Vincent) **13**:217

Smith (Garfield) **21**:97

Smith's Hoard (Clarke) **28**:75

Smoke from Cromwell's Time (Aiken) **1**:7

Smoke over Golan (Ofek) **28**:190

Smokey (Peet) **12**:195

Snail in the Woods (Ryder) **37**:86

Snail Tale: The Adventures of a Rather Small Snail (Avi) **24**:4

Snail, Where Are You? (Ungerer) **3**:203

Snails (Zim) **2**:230

Snails of Land and Sea (Simon) **39**:193

The Snail's Spell (Ryder) **37**:87

Snake Fights, Rabbit Fights & More: A Book about Animal Fighting (Schlein) **41**:189

The Snake That Went to School (Moore) **15**:139

Snakes and Ladders (Morpurgo) **51**:141

Snakes and Ladders: Poems about the Ups and Downs of Life (Klein) **21**:162

Snakes Are Hunters (Lauber) **16**:124

A Snake's Body (Cole) **5**:67

Snakes: The Facts and the Folklore (Simon) **39**:190

Snakes: Their Place in the Sun (McClung) **11**:192

Snapshots (Klein) **19**:96

Sneakers: Seven Stories about a Cat (Brown) **10**:65

The Sneetches and Other Stories (Dr. Seuss) **9**:186

Sniff Shout (Burningham) **9**:51

Sniper (Taylor) **30**:195

Snippy and Snappy (Gag) **4**:89

The Snopp on the Sidewalk, and Other Poems (Prelutsky) **13**:166

The Snow (Burningham) **9**:46

Snow before Christmas (Tudor) **13**:190

The Snow Country Prince (Wildsmith) **52**:195

Snow Day (Betsy and Giulio Maestro) **45**:81

Snow Is Falling (Branley) **13**:31

The Snow Monkey at Home (Rau) **8**:190

The Snow Spider (Nimmo) **44**:140

Snow Tracks (George) **1**:92

Snow White (Hyman) **50**:72

Snow White in New York (French) **37**:47

The Snow Wife (San Souci) **43**:190

Snow Woman (McKee) **38**:178

Snowbound (Mazer) **16**:128

Snowbound with Betsy (Haywood) **22**:98

Snow-Cat (Calhoun) **42**:25

The Snowman (Briggs) **10**:29

The Snowman (Stine) **37**:115

The Snowstorm (Carigiet) **38**:71

Snow-White and Rose-Red (Cooney) **23**:27

Snowy and Woody (Duvoisin) **23**:106

The Snowy Day (Keats) **1**:117; **35**:122

Snuff (Blake) **31**:19

Snuffie (Bruna) **7**:51

Snuffy (Bruna) **7**:51

So Can I (McNaughton) **54**:56

So Long at the Fair (Irwin) **40**:113

So Many Marvels (Shippen) **36**:176

So Much to Tell You . . . (Marsden) **34**:146

So What If I'm a Sore Loser? (Williams) **48**:200

So You Want to Be a Chemist (Nourse) **33**:134

So You Want to Be a Chemist (Nourse) **33**:134

So You Want to Be a Doctor (Nourse) **33**:131

So You Want to Be a Lawyer (Nourse) **33**:131

So You Want to Be a Scientist (Nourse) **33**:132

So You Want to Be a Surgeon (Nourse) **33**:135

So You Want to Be an Engineer (Nourse) **33**:133

So, You're Getting Braces: A Guide to Orthodontics (Silverstein and Silverstein) **25**:216

Soccer Crazy (McNaughton) **54**:51

Soccer Shock (Napoli) **51**:154

Social Welfare (Myers) **4**:157

Sock Craft: Toys, Gifts, and Other Things to Make (Sattler) **24**:213

Socks (Cleary) **2**:51; **8**:54

Socrates and the Three Little Pigs (Anno) **14**:44

Solägget (Beskow) **17**:18

Solar Energy (Branley) **13**:26

The Solar System (Asimov) **12**:53

The Soldier and Death: A Russian Folk Tale Told in English (Ransome) **8**:171

Soldier and Tsar in the Forest: A Russian Tale (Shulevitz) **5**:205

Soldier, Soldier, Won't You Marry Me? (Langstaff) **3**:112

Soldier's Heart (Paulsen) **54**:125

The Solid Gold Kid (Mazer and Mazer) **16**:129; **23**:225

Solids, Liquids, and Gases (Bendick) **5**:47

Solids, Liquids, and Gases: From Superconductors to the Ozone Layer (Berger) **32**:42

A Solitary Blue (Voigt) **13**:233

The Solomon System (Naylor) **17**:58

Solomon the Rusty Nail (Steig) **15**:200

Solomon's Child (Clark) **30**:62

Some Birthday! (Polacco) **40**:191

Some of Aesop's Fables, with Modern Instances (Caldecott) **14**:79

Some of the Days of Everett Anderson (Clifton) **5**:53

Some Swell Pup; or, Are You Sure You Want a Dog? (Sendak) **17**:122

Somebody Else's Nut Tree: And Other Tales from Children (Krauss) **42**:123

Somebody Spilled the Sky (Krauss) **42**:130

Somebody's House (Hurd and Hurd) **49**:122

Someday Angeline (Sacher) **28**:201

Someday, Said Mitchell (Williams) **48**:192

Someone Could Win a Polar Bear (Ciardi) **19**:80

Someone Else's Ghost (Buffie) **39**:27

Someone Is Hiding On Alcatraz Island (Bunting) **28**:57

Someone to Love (Mazer) **23**:229

Someplace Beautiful (Brinsmead) **47**:15

The Something (Babbitt) **2**:8

Something for Now, Something for Later (Schlein) **41**:179

Something Left to Lose (Brancato) **32**:70

Something New Begins: New and Selected Poems (Moore) **15**:144

Something on my Mind (Grimes) **42**:90

Something Special (Rodda) **32**:209

Something Special for Me (Williams) **9**:234

Something Upstairs: A Tale of Ghosts (Avi) **24**:13

Something Weird Is Going On (Harris) **47**:91

Sometimes I Dance Mountains (Baylor) **3**:16

Sometimes I Think I Hear My Name (Avi) **24**:9

Sometimes My Mom Drinks Too Much (Krull) **44**:102

Somewhere in the Darkness (Myers) **35**:197

Son No. 6 (Guillen)

  See *Karen's Opposites*

Son of a Gun (Ahlberg and Ahlberg) **18**:6

Son of Columbus (Baumann) **35**:35

Son of Interflux (Korman) **25**:109

The Son of Someone Famous (Kerr) **29**:145

Song for a Dark Queen (Sutcliff) **37**:169

Song for a Tattered Flag (Trease) **42**:192

A Song for Gar (Merrill) **52**:101

A Song for Uncle Harry (Kherdian) **24**:115

The Song in My Drum (Hoban) **3**:82

A Song in Stone: City Poems (Hopkins) **44**:92

The Song in the Walnut Grove (Kherdian) **24**:112

The Song of Pentecost (Corbett) **19**:82

Song of Sedna (San Souci) **43**:180

Song of the Boat (Graham) **10**:110

Song of the Boat (Leo and Diane Dillon) **44**:28

Song of the City (Owen) **31**:143

Song of the Gargoyle (Snyder) **31**:169

Song of the Magdalene (Napoli) **51**:163

Song of the Sea Otter (Hurd) **49**:131

Song of the Swallows (Politi) **29**:187

Song of the Trees (Taylor) **9**:225

Songbird Story (Rosen) **45**:147

Songman (Baillie) **49**:17

Songs for Alex (Duder) **43**:67

Songs for Mr. Small (Lenski) **26**:118

Songs from Dreamland: Original Lullabies (Duncan) **29**:80

Songs of Experience (Blake) **52**:1-49

Songs of Innocence (Blake) **52**:1-49

Songs of Innocence and of Experience: Shewing the Two Contrary States of the Human Soul (Blake) **52**:1-49

Songs of the Dream People: Chants and Images from the Indians and Eskimos of North America (Houston) **3**:86

Songs of the Fog Maiden (dePaola) **4**:62

Sonora Beautiful (Clifton) **5**:60

Sons from Afar (Voigt) **48**:168

Title Index

Sons of the Steppe: The Story of How the Conqueror Genghis Khan was Overcome (Baumann) 35:38
Sonsense Nongs (Rosen) 45:146
Sootface: An Ojibwa Cinderella Story (San Souci) 43:193
Sophia Scrooby Preserved (Bacon) 3:11
Sophie Hits Six (King-Smith) 40:164
Sophie in the Saddle (King-Smith) 40:170
Sophie Is Seven (King-Smith) 40:174
Sophie's Snail (King-Smith) 40:155
Sophie's Tom (King-Smith) 40:163
S.O.R. Losers (Avi) 24:12
The Sorcerer's Apprentice (Leo and Diane Dillon) 44:46
The Sorely Trying Day (Hoban) 3:82
The Soul Brothers and Sister Lou (Hunter) 3:99
Sound (Owen) 31:95
Sound and Ultrasonics (Adler) 27:12
A Sound of Chariots (Hunter) 25:81
The Sound of Coaches (Garfield) 21:107
The Sound of the Dragon's Feet (Zei) 6:262
A Sound to Remember (Levitin) 53:62
Sounder (Armstrong) 1:23
Soup (Peck) 45:103
Soup 1776 (Peck) 45:126
Soup and Me (Peck) 45:106
Soup for President (Peck) 45:111
Soup in the Saddle (Peck) 45:117
Soup on Fire (Peck) 45:120
Soup on Ice (Peck) 45:120
Soup on Wheels (Peck) 45:115
Soup's Goat (Peck) 45:119
Sour Land (Armstrong) 1:24
South Pole Station (Berger) 32:7
South Swell (Wibberley) 3:230
South Town (Graham) 10:105
Southerly Buster (Mattingley) 24:127
Southern Africa: South Africa, Namibia, Swaziland, Lesotho, and Botswana (Blumberg) 21:27
Southern Fried Rat and Other Gruesome Tales (Cohen) 43:43
Space and Time (Bendick) 5:42
Space Case (Marshall) 21:175
Space Challenger: The Story of Guion Bluford (Haskins) 39:47
Space Colony: Frontier of the 21st Century (Branley) 13:47
Space Demons (Rubinstein) 35:211
The Space People (Bunting) 28:48
Space Shots, Shuttles, and Satellites (Berger) 32:31
Space Songs (Fisher) 18:138
Space Station Seventh Grade (Spinelli) 26:201
A Space Story (Kuskin) 4:143
Space Talk (Berger) 32:32
Space Telescope (Branley) 13:51
Space Telescope: A Voyage into Space Book (Betsy and Giulio Maestro) 45:76
Space Trap (Hughes) 9:77
Space Witch (Freeman) 30:72
The Spaghetti Party (Orgel) 48:96
The Spanish Armada (Williams) 8:228
Spanish Hoof (Peck) 45:119
The Spanish Letters (Hunter) 25:75
The Spanish Smile (O'Dell) 16:177
The Spanish-American War (Marrin) 53:89
Spark of Opal (Clark) 30:58
Sparky: The Story of a Little Trolley Car (Gramatky) 22:42
Sparrow Alone (Colum) 36:40
The Sparrow Bush (Coatsworth) 2:62
Sparrow Socks (Selden) 8:198

The Sparrow's Song (Wallace) 37:214
Speak Out in Thunder Tones: Letters and Other Writings by Black Northerners, 1787-1865 (Sterling) 1:181
Speak Out on Rape! (Hyde) 23:161
Speak Up, Blanche! (McCully) 46:66
Speak Up: More Rhymes of the Never Was and Always Is (McCord) 9:104
Speaking Out: Teenagers Take on Race, Sex, and Identity (Kuklin) 51:109
The Special Present (Mattingley) 24:124
A Special Trick (Mayer) 11:165
The Specter (Nixon) 24:143
Speedboat (Marshall) 21:171
Speedy, The Hook and Ladder Truck (Hurd and Hurd) 49:117
A Spell Is Cast (Cameron) 1:41
The Spell of the Sorcerer's Skull (Bellairs) 37:18
The Spellcoats (Jones) 23:189
The Spettecake Holiday (Unnerstad) 36:192
Sphinx: The Story of a Caterpillar (Lerner) 34:126
Sphinx: The Story of a Caterpillar (McClung) 11:178
A Spider Bought a Bicycle and Other Poems (Rosen) 45:136
Spider Magic (Patent) 19:158
Spiderman-Anancy (Berry) 22:9
The Spiders Dance (Ryder) 37:86
The Spider's Web (Keeping) 34:98
Spiderweb for Two: A Melendy Maze (Enright) 4:75
Spike: The Story of a Whitetail Deer (McClung) 11:179
Spin a Soft Black Song: Poems for Children (Giovanni) 6:115
The Spirit House (Sleator) 29:207
The Spirit of the Lord: Revivalism in America (Cohen) 3:42
Spirit of the Place (Hamley) 47:66
The Spitball Gang (Paulsen) 19:173
Splash, Splash (Dorros) 42:66
The Splendor of Iridescence: Structural Colors in the Animal World (Simon) 39:187
The Splintered Sword (Serraillier) 2:188
The Spook Birds (Bunting) 28:52
The Spooky Tail of Prewitt Peacock (Peet) 12:202
Sports (Berger) 32:29
The Sports (Fisher) 18:129
Sports Great Magic Johnson (Haskins) 39:60
Sports Medicine (Berger) 32:26
Spot at Play (Hill) 13:96
Spot at the Fair (Hill) 13:96
Spot at the Farm (Hill) 13:96
Spot Goes to School (Hill) 13:95
Spot Goes to the Beach (Hill) 13:96
Spot Goes to the Circus (Hill) 13:97
Spot Looks at Colors (Hill) 13:96
Spot Looks at Shapes (Hill) 13:96
Spot on the Farm (Hill) 13:96
Spot's Birthday Party (Hill) 13:94
Spot's First Christmas (Hill) 13:94
Spot's First Walk (Hill) 13:92
Spot's First Words (Hill) 13:96
Spotted Salamander (McClung) 11:182
Spotty (Rey and Rey) 5:195
Die Sprechmachine (Kruss) 9:86
The Sprig of Broom (Willard) 2:222
Spring (McNaughton) 54:55
Spring Begins in March (Little) 4:148
Spring Comes to the Ocean (George) 1:92
Spring Holidays (Epstein and Epstein) 26:59
Spring Is (Domanska) 40:45
Spring Is a New Beginning (Anglund) 1:21

Spring Is Here (Lenski) 26:107
Spring Is Here! (Sterling) 1:181
Spring Snow (Duvoisin) 23:102
Spring Story (Barklem) 31:2
The Springs of Joy (Tudor) 13:202
Springtime in Noisy Village (Lindgren) 39:152
The Spy on Third Base (Christopher) 33:60
The Spy Who Never Was and Other True Spy Stories (Knight) 38:122
Square as a House (Kuskin) 4:136
Squawwk! (Rockwell) 6:236
Squeak Saves the Day and Other Tooley Tales (Snyder) 31:168
Squeak-a-Lot (Waddell) 31:199
Squeeze Play: A Baseball Story (Glenn) 51:90
Squib (Bawden) 2:13; 51:19
Squid and Spider: A Look at the Animal Kingdom (Billout) 33:23
Squirrel Watching (Schlein) 41:198
The Squirrel Wife (Pearce) 9:153
Squirrels (Wildsmith) 2:214
St. Francis of Assisi (Bawden) 51:32
St. George's Day in Williamsburg (Hurd and Hurd) 49:122
St. Jerome and the Lion (Godden) 20:131
St. Jerome and the Lion (Moser) 49:180
St. Patrick's Day in the Morning (Bunting) 28:50
Stable of Fear (Bunting) 28:44
Stage Fright (Martin) 32:201
The Stained Glass Window (Lively) 7:161
Stalin: Russia's Man of Steel (Marrin) 53:86
The Stalker (Nixon) 24:146
Stand in the Wind (Little) 4:151
Stanley and Rhoda (Wells) 16:209
Star Baby (Nixon) 24:153
Star Born (Norton) 50:138
Star Boy (Goble) 21:133
The Star Fisher (Yep) 54:187
A Star for the Latecomer (Zindel) 45:192
Star Gate (Norton) 50:138
Star Gazing, Comet Tracking, and Sky Mapping (Berger) 32:36
The Star in the Pail (McCord) 9:102
A Star in the Sea (Silverstein and Silverstein) 25:202
Star Man's Son: 2250 A.D. (Norton) 50:134
Star of Night: Stories for Christmas (Paterson) 7:237
Star Rangers (Norton) 50:135
Star Signs (Fisher) 18:133
The Star Spangled Banner (d'Aulaire and d'Aulaire) 21:47
Star Surgeon (Nourse) 33:132
A Star to the North (Corcoran) 50:14
Stardust otel (Janeczko) 47:114
The Starlight Cloak (Nimmo) 44:152
A Starlit Somersault Downhill (Pinkney) 43:170
Starring Peter and Leigh: A Novel (Pfeffer) 11:199
Starring Sally J. Freedman as Herself (Blume) 15:76
Starrring Becky Suslow (Orgel) 48:91
Starry Messenger: Galileo Galilei (Sis) 45:176
Starry Night (Waddell) 31:185
Stars (Berger) 32:6
The Stars Are Ours! (Norton) 50:136
The Stars: Decoding Their Messages (Adler) 27:7
The Stars: Steppingstones into Space (Adler) 27:7
The Star-Spangled Banner (Spier) 5:222
Starting with Melodie (Pfeffer) 11:203
The Statue of Liberty (Fisher) 18:134
The Statue of Liberty: America's Proud Lady (Haskins) 39:51
Stay Tuned (Corcoran) 50:39

Stay Up Late (Kalman) **32**:179
Staying Alive in Year 5 (Marsden) **34**:149
Staying Home Alone on a Rainy Day (Iwasaki) **18**:152
The Steadfast Tin Soldier (Brown) **12**:97
The Steamroller: A Fantasy (Brown) **10**:68
Steel Magic (Norton) **50**:144
Steffie Can't Come Out to Play (Gaberman) **33**:4
Steinmetz: Maker of Lightning (Lavine) **35**:146
Step by Step: All by Myself (McMillan) **47**:169
Step into the Night (Ryder) **37**:90
Stepmother (Mahy) **7**:182
The Stereo Hi-Fi Handbook (Berger) **32**:22
Steven Kellogg's Yankee Doodle (Kellogg) **6**:174
Stevie (Steptoe) **2**:163
Sticks, Spools, and Feathers (Weiss) **4**:223
Still More Small Poems (Worth) **21**:222
The Stinky Cheese Man: And Other Fairly Stupid Tales (Smith) **47**:202
Stitch in Snow (McCaffrey) **49**:147
A Stitch in Time (Lively) **7**:160
A Stitch In Time (Rinaldi) **46**:88
The Stolen Fire: Legends of Heroes and Rebels from Around the World (Baumann) **35**:54
The Stolen Lake (Aiken) **19**:13
The Stolen Oracle (Williams) **8**:221
Stone and Steel: A Look at Engineering (Billout) **33**:22
The Stone Book (Garner) **20**:113
The Stone Doll of Sister Brute (Hoban) **3**:83
Stone Giants and Flying Heads (Bruchac) **46**:6
Stone Giants and Flying Heads: More Iroquois Folk Tales (Bruchac) **46**:6
The Stone Menagerie (Fine) **25**:18
The Stone Mouse (Nimmo) **44**:151
The Stone of Victory and Other Tales (Colum) **36**:47
The Stone Silenus (Yolen) **44**:179
Stone Soup (McGovern) **50**:114
Stone Soup: An Old Tale (Brown) **12**:94
The Stonecutter: A Japanese Folk Tale (McDermott) **9**:115
The Stone-Faced Boy (Fox) **1**:81
Stoneflight (McHargue) **2**:120
Stones in Water (Napoli) **51**:166
The Stones of Green Knowe (Boston) **3**:28
The Stonewalkers (Alcock) **26**:2
Stonewall (Fritz) **14**:114
Stopping by Woods on a Snowy Evening (Jeffers) **30**:132
Storie di tre uccellini (Munari) **9**:124
Stories about Rosie (Voigt) **13**:240
Stories for Summer (Proysen) **24**:185
Stories for the Bible (Tresselt) **30**:214
Stories from Shakespeare (McCaughrean) **38**:151
Stories from the Old Testament: Joseph, Moses, Ruth, David (Petersham and Petersham) **24**:169
Stories to Solve: Folktales from Around the World (Sis) **45**:158
Storm (Crossley-Holland) **47**:43
Storm Alert: Understanding Weather Disasters (Aylesworth) **6**:55
Storm and Other Old English Riddles (Crossley-Holland) **47**:26
Storm at the Jetty (Fisher) **18**:130
Storm Boy (Thiele) **27**:202
Storm from the West (Willard) **2**:222
Storm in the Night (Cummings) **48**:48
Storm over Warlock (Norton) **50**:140
Storm Rising (Singer) **48**:135
A Storm without Rain (Adkins) **7**:28
Storms (Adler) **27**:17

Storms (Berger) **32**:5
Stormy, Misty's Foal (Henry) **4**:114
A Story, A Story: An African Tale (Haley) **21**:141
The Story about Ping (Flack) **28**:121
The Story Book of Aircraft (Petersham and Petersham) **24**:167
The Story Book of Clothes (Petersham and Petersham) **24**:165
The Story Book of Corn (Petersham and Petersham) **24**:168
The Story Book of Cotton (Petersham and Petersham) **24**:170
The Story Book of Food (Petersham and Petersham) **24**:165
The Story Book of Foods from the Field (Petersham and Petersham) **24**:168
The Story Book of Houses (Petersham and Petersham) **24**:165
The Story Book of Rayon (Petersham and Petersham) **24**:170
The Story Book of Rice (Petersham and Petersham) **24**:168
The Story Book of Ships (Petersham and Petersham) **24**:167
The Story Book of Silk (Petersham and Petersham) **24**:170
The Story Book of Sugar (Petersham and Petersham) **24**:168
The Story Book of Things We Use (Petersham and Petersham) **24**:165
The Story Book of Things We Wear (Petersham and Petersham) **24**:170
The Story Book of Trains (Petersham and Petersham) **24**:167
The Story Book of Transportation (Petersham and Petersham) **24**:165
The Story Book of Wheat (Petersham and Petersham) **24**:168
The Story Book of Wheels (Petersham and Petersham) **24**:167
The Story Book of Wheels, Ships, Trains, Aircraft (Petersham and Petersham) **24**:167
The Story Book of Wool (Petersham and Petersham) **24**:170
Story for a Black Night (Bess) **39**:2
The Story Girl (Montgomery) **8**:135
The Story of a Baby (Ets) **33**:75
The Story of a Castle (Goodall) **25**:55
The Story of a Farm (Goodall) **25**:57
The Story of a High Street (Goodall) **25**:55
The Story of a Main Street (Goodall) **25**:55
The Story of a Nail (Adler) **27**:15
The Story of a Puppet (Collodi)
    See *Le Avventure di Pinocchio*
The Story of America (Haar) **15**:114
The Story of an English Village (Goodall) **25**:48
The Story of Babar, the Little Elephant (Brunhoff) **4**:30
The Story of Chicken Licken (Ormerod) **20**:178
The Story of Christopher Columbus (McGovern) **50**:110
The Story of Doctor Dolittle, Being the History of His Peculiar Life at Home and Astonishing Adventures in Foreign Parts (Lofting) **19**:120
The Story of Dogs (Lauber) **16**:114
The Story of Easter (Fisher) **49**:48
The Story of Ferdinand (Leaf) **25**:116
The Story of Folk Music (Berger) **32**:16
The Story of George Washington Carver (Bontemps) **6**:82
The Story of Grains: Wheat, Corn, and Rice (Parish) **22**:155
The Story of Holly and Ivy (Godden) **20**:130

The Story of Johnny Appleseed (Aliki) **9**:17
The Story of Jumping Mouse: A Native American Legend (Steptoe) **12**:241
The Story of Light (Adler) **27**:25
The Story of Money (Betsy and Giulio Maestro) **45**:87
The Story of Mrs. Tubbs (Lofting) **19**:123
The Story of Numbers (Lauber) **16**:114
The Story of Paul Bunyan (Emberley and Emberley) **5**:92
The Story of Persephone (Farmer) **8**:85
The Story of Religion (Betsy and Giulio Maestro) **45**:90
The Story of Ruth (Asimov) **12**:47
The Story of Stevie Wonder (Haskins) **3**:67
The Story of the Amulet (Nesbit) **3**:165
The Story of the Dancing Frog (Blake) **31**:25
The Story of the International Red Cross (Epstein and Epstein) **26**:58
The Story of the Milky Way: A Cherokee Tale (Bruchac) **46**:20
Story of the Negro (Bontemps) **6**:80
The Story of the Presidents of the United States of America (Petersham and Petersham) **24**:178
The Story of the Seashore (Goodall) **25**:57
The Story of the Seaside (Goodall) **25**:57
The Story of the Statue of Liberty (Betsy and Giulio Maestro) **45**:77
The Story of the Three Wise Kings (dePaola) **24**:92
The Story of Vampires (Aylesworth) **6**:53
The Story of Werewolves (Aylesworth) **6**:54
The Story of William Penn (Aliki) **9**:18
The Story of William Tell (Aliki) **9**:17
The Story of Witches (Aylesworth) **6**:54
The Story of Your Foot (Silverstein and Silverstein) **25**:223
The Story of Your Mouth (Silverstein and Silverstein) **25**:221
A Story to Tell (Bruna) **7**:51
Storybook Dictionary (Scarry) **41**:162
A Storybook from Tomi Ungerer (Ungerer) **3**:203
Stotan! (Crutcher) **28**:104
The Stowaway to the Mushroom Planet (Cameron) **1**:41
Stranded (Christopher) **33**:48
The Strange Affair of Adelaide Harris (Garfield) **21**:104
The Strange Appearance of Howard Cranebill, Jr. (Drescher) **20**:58
Strange Attractors (Sleator) **29**:207
The Strange Child (Zwerger) **46**:194
Strange Creatures (Simon) **9**:217
A Strange Enchantment (Allan) **43**:32
Strange Mysteries from Around the World (Simon) **9**:215
Strange Objects (Crew) **42**:53
Strange Partners (Lavine) **35**:147
Strange Travelers (Lavine) **35**:148
The Stranger (Van Allsburg) **13**:213
A Stranger at Green Knowe (Boston) **3**:29
Stranger at the Inlet (Epstein and Epstein) **26**:45
A Stranger Came Ashore (Hunter) **25**:85
Stranger Danger? (Fine) **25**:23
The Stranger from Somewhere in Time (McBratney) **44**:129
The Stranger from the Sea (Guillot) **22**:70
The Stranger in Primrose Lane (Streatfeild) **17**:189
Stranger on the Ball Club (Slote) **4**:199
Stranger with My Face (Duncan) **29**:75
Strangers' Bread (Willard) **5**:247
Strangers Dark and Gold (St. John) **46**:101
Strangers in Africa (Ashabranner and Davis) **28**:5
Strangers in New York (Pilgrim) **43**:12

Strangers in Skye (Allan) **43**:4
Strangers in Wood Street (Allan) **43**:32
Strawberry Girl (Lenski) **26**:108
The Streamlined Pig (Brown) **10**:48
Streams to the River, River to the Sea: A Novel of Sacagawea (O'Dell) **16**:179
Street Gangs: Yesterday and Today (Haskins) **3**:68
A Street of Little Shops (Bianco) **19**:53
Strega Nona: An Old Tale (dePaola) **4**:57
Strega Nona's Magic Lessons (dePaola) **24**:91
Strictly for Laughs (Conford) **10**:100
Striding Slippers (Ginsburg) **45**:12
Strike! (Corcoran) **50**:31
A String in the Harp (Bond) **11**:26
A String of Chances (Naylor) **17**:57
Strings: A Gathering of Family Poems (Janeczko) **47**:102
Stripe: The Story of a Chipmunk (McClung) **11**:179
A Striving after Wind (St. John) **46**:103
The Strongest One of All: A Caucasian Folktale (Ginsburg) **45**:11
The Stronghold (Hunter) **25**:84
Struggle for a Continent: The French and Indian Wars, 1690-1760 (Marrin) **53**:85
Stuart Little (White) **1**:195
Studenplan: Roman (Noestlinger) **12**:187
The Stupids Die (Marshall) **21**:175
The Stupids Have a Ball (Marshall) **21**:172
The Stupids Step Out (Marshall) **21**:170
The Submarine Bird (Scott) **20**:198
The Submarine Pitch (Christopher) **33**:51
Such Nice Kids (Bunting) **28**:64
A Sudden Puff of Glittering Smoke (Fine) **25**:24
A Sudden Silence (Bunting) **28**:62
A Sudden Swirl of Icy Wind (Fine) **25**:25
Suddenly! (McNaughton) **54**:65
Suds: A New Daytime Drama (Gaberman) **33**:10
The Sugar Disease: Diabetes (Silverstein and Silverstein) **25**:218
Sugar Ray Leonard (Haskins) **39**:41
Sugaring Time (Lasky) **11**:117
Suicide: The Hidden Epidemic (Hyde) **23**:164
Sukey and the Mermaid (Pinkney) **54**:137
Sukey and the Mermaid (San Souci) **43**:186
The Sultan's Perfect Tree (Yolen) **4**:263
Sumi and the Goat and the Tokyo Express (Uchida) **6**:256
Sumi's Prize (Uchida) **6**:253
Sumi's Special Happening (Uchida) **6**:254
Summer (McNaughton) **54**:55
The Summer after the Funeral (Gardam) **12**:166
A Summer at Sea (Allan) **43**:13
The Summer Birds (Farmer) **8**:76
The Summer Book (Jansson) **2**:95
Summer Fun (Haywood) **22**:105
Summer Girls, Love Boys, and Other Short Stories (Mazer) **23**:228
Summer Ice: Life Along the Antarctic Peninsula (McMillan) **47**:188
A Summer in a Canon: A California Story (Wiggin) **52**:156
The Summer In Between (Spence) **26**:191
A Summer in Brittany (Estoril) **43**:8
A Summer in Provence (Pilgrim) **43**:10
A Summer in the South (Marshall) **21**:172
Summer Is for Growing (Clark) **16**:82
A Summer Life (Soto) **38**:192
The Summer Night (Zolotow) **2**:237
The Summer Noisy Book (Brown) **10**:60
Summer of Decision (Allan) **43**:6
Summer of Fear (Duncan) **29**:70
Summer of Little Rain (Fisher) **49**:36

The Summer of My German Soldier (Greene) **2**:86
The Summer of the Falcon (George) **1**:93
The Summer of the Swans (Byars) **1**:37
Summer on Wheels (Soto) **38**:207
The Summer People (Townsend) **2**:174
Summer Rules (Lipsyte) **23**:208
Summer Story (Barklem) **31**:2
Summer Switch (Rodgers) **20**:191
A Summer to Die (Lowry) **6**:192
The Summer with Spike (Willard) **2**:223
The Summerboy (Lipsyte) **23**:209
The Summer-House Loon (Fine) **25**:17
Summers of the Wild Rose (Harris) **30**:124
The Sun (Zim) **2**:231
The Sun and Its Family (Adler) **27**:9
Sun and Moon (Pfister) **42**:134
The Sun, Dancing: Christian Verse (Causley) **30**:41
Sun Dogs and Shooting Stars: A Skywatcher's Calendar (Branley) **13**:45
Sun Flight (McDermott) **9**:118
Sun God, Moon Witch (Katz) **45**:32
The Sun He Dies: A Novel about the End of the Aztec World (Highwater) **17**:29
Sun Horse, Moon Horse (Sutcliff) **37**:167
The Sun Looks Down (Schlein) **41**:177
The Sun: Our Nearest Star (Branley) **13**:30
The Sun: Star Number One (Branley) **13**:31
The Sun, the Wind, the Sea and the Rain (Schlein) **41**:183
Sun Up (Tresselt) **30**:203
Sun Up, Sun Down (Gibbons) **8**:97
Sunburn (Stine) **37**:122
Sunday Father (Neufeld) **52**:129
Sunday Morning (Viorst) **3**:209
The Sunday Outing (Pinkney) **43**:172
Sundiata: Lion King of Mali (Wisniewski) **51**:196
The Sun-Egg (Beskow) **17**:18
The Sun's Asleep Behind the Hill (Ginsburg) **45**:16
Sunshine (Bemelmans) **6**:68
Sunshine (Klein) **19**:88
Sunshine (Ormerod) **20**:174
Sunshine Makes the Seasons (Branley) **13**:40
The Sunshine Years (Klein) **19**:89
Super People: Who Will They Be? (Bendick) **5**:50
Super, Super, Superwords (McMillan) **47**:172
Superbowl Upset (Gaberman) **33**:17
Supercharged Infield (Christopher) **33**:57
Supercomputers (Carter) **22**;18
Superfudge (Blume) **15**:77
Supergirl (Mazer) **23**:230
Superhare (Heine) **18**:146
The Supermarket Mystery (Scarry) **41**:164
Supermouse (Ure) **34**:175
The Supernatural: From ESP to UFOs (Berger) **32**:18
Superpuppy: How to Choose, Raise, and Train the Best Possible Dog for You (Pinkwater) **4**:167
Supersuits (Cobb) **2**:67
Suppose You Met a Witch (Serraillier) **2**:142
The Supreme, Superb, Exalted and Delightful, One and Only Magic Building (Kotzwinkle) **6**:182
Surprise for Davy (Lenski) **26**:113
The Surprise Mouse (Mattingley) **24**:124
The Surprise Party (Hutchins) **20**:144
The Surprise Picnic (Goodall) **25**:48
Surprises: An I Can Read Book of Poems (Hopkins) **44**:93
Surrender (White) **3**:222
Surrogate Sister (Bunting) **28**:58
Survival Camp! (Bunting) **28**:47
The Survivor (White) **3**:223
The Survivors (Hunter) **3**:101

The Survivors: Enduring Animals of North America (Scott) **20**:194
Susan (Smucker) **10**:189
Susanna B. and William C. (Field) **21**:78
Suzuki Goodbye (McBratney) **44**:130
Swallowdale (Ransome) **8**:174
Swallows and Amazons (Ransome) **8**:171
The Swallow's Song (St. John) **46**:106
Swampy Alligator (Gantos) **18**:142
Swan Sky (Tejima) **20**:205
Swans (Scott) **20**:201
Sweeney's Ghost (Fisher) **18**:125
Sweet Baby Coming (Greenfield) **38**:96
Sweet Bells Jangled out of Tune (Brancato) **32**:73
Sweet Dreams, Spot (Hill) **13**:95
Sweet Friday Island (Taylor) **30**:193
Sweet Illusions (Myers) **16**:143
The Sweet Patootie Doll (Calhoun) **42**:5
Sweet Pea: A Black Girl Growing Up in the Rural South (Krementz) **5**:150
Sweet Whispers, Brother Rush (Hamilton) **11**:84
Sweetgrass (Hudson) **40**:94
Sweetwater (Yep) **3**:238
The Swift Deer (McClung) **11**:184
A Swiftly Tilting Planet (L'Engle) **14**:150
Swimathon! (Cross) **28**:91
Swimming with Sea Lions and Other Adventures in the Galapagos Islands (McGovern) **50**:126
Swimmy (Lionni) **7**:129
The Swineherd (Zwerger) **46**:190
The Swing in the Summerhouse (Langton) **33**:109
Swings and Roundabouts (Ure) **34**:181
Swiss Holiday (Allan) **43**:5
Switch On, Switch Off (Berger) **32**:41
Switcharound (Lowry) **46**:32
The Switherby Pilgrims (Spence) **26**:193
The Swoose (King-Smith) **40**:168
The Sword and the Circle: King Arthur and the Knights of the Round Table (Sutcliff) **37**:173
The Sword and the Scythe (Williams) **8**:221
Sword at Sunset (Sutcliff) **37**:156
The Sword is Drawn (Norton) **50**:132
The Sword of Esau (Southall) **2**:156
The Sword of King Arthur (Williams) **8**:229
The Sword of the Spirits (Christopher) **2**:42
Sword of the Wilderness (Coatsworth) **2**:62
Swords from the North (Treece) **2**:189
Sworn Enemies (Matas) **52**:86
Sylvester and the Magic Pebble (Steig) **2**:161
The Sylvia Game (Alcock) **26**:3
Sylvie and Bruno (Carroll) **2**:36
Symbiosis: A Book of Unusual Friendships (Aruego) **5**:28
Symbol Art: Thirteen Squares, Circles, Triangles from Around the World (Fisher) **18**:136
Symbols: A Silent Language (Adkins) **7**:24
Tabi No Ehon (Anno) **14**:33
Tabi No Ehon II (Anno) **14**:37
Tabi No Ehon III (Anno) **14**:39
Tabi No Ehon IV (Anno) **14**:41
The Table, the Donkey, and the Stick: Adapted from a Retelling by the Brothers Grimm (Galdone) **16**:102
Tackle without a Team (Christopher) **33**:60
Taffy and Melissa Molasses (Haywood) **22**:100
The Tail of the Trinosaur (Causley) **30**:35
The Tailor and the Giant (Kruss) **9**:88
The Tailor of Gloucester (Potter) **1**:153
Takao and Grandfather's Sword (Uchida) **6**:252
Take a Look at Snakes (Betsy and Giulio Maestro) **45**:86
Take a Number (Bendick) **5**:39
Take Another Look (Hoban) **13**:105

Take Joy! The Tasha Tudor Christmas Book (Tudor) **13**:198
Take Me Out to the Ballgame (Kovalski) **34**:119
Take My Word For It (Marsden) **34**:150
Take Sky: More Rhymes of the Never Was and Always Is (McCord) **9**:99
Take This Hammer (Epstein and Epstein) **26**:62
Take Two and...Rolling! (Pfeffer) **11**:205
Take Wing (Little) **4**:148
The Take-along Dog (McCully) **46**:64
Takedown (Christopher) **33**:61
Taking a Stand Against Racism and Racial Discrimination (McKissack) **23**:242
Taking Care of Carruthers (Marshall) **21**:176
Taking Care of Terrific (Lowry) **6**:197
Taking My Cat to the Vet (Kuklin) **51**:102
Taking My Dog to the Vet (Kuklin) **51**:102
The Taking of Mariasburg (Thompson) **24**:231
The Taking of Room 114: A Hostage Drama in Poems (Glenn) **51**:93
Taking Root: Jewish Immigrants in America (Meltzer) **13**:138
Taking Sides (Klein) **2**:100
Taking Sides (Soto) **38**:194
Taking Terri Mueller (Mazer) **23**:227
Taking the Ferry Home (Conrad) **18**:89
Taktuk, an Arctic Boy (Flack and Lomen) **28**:119
A Tale for Easter (Tudor) **13**:190
Tale of a One-Way Street and Other Stories (Aiken) **19**:12
The Tale of Dan de Lion (Disch) **18**:115
The Tale of Gockel, Hinkel and Gackeliah (Orgel) **48**:73
The Tale of the Faithful Dove (Potter) **1**:153
The Tale of the Mandarin Ducks (Leo and Diane Dillon) **44**:39
The Tale of the Mandarin Ducks (Paterson) **50**:198
The Tale of Thomas Mead (Hutchins) **20**:150
The Tale of Three Landlubbers (Serraillier) **2**:143
A Tale of Time City (Jones) **23**:196
The Tale of Tuppenny (Potter) **1**:154
Tales and Legends of Hawaii: At the Gateways of the Day (Colum) **36**:27
Tales and Legends of Hawaii: The Bright Islands (Colum) **36**:27
Tales for the Third Ear, from Equatorial Africa (Aardema) **17**:3
Tales from a Finnish Fireside (Bianco) **19**:54
Tales from a Finnish Tupa (Bianco) **19**:54
Tales from Gold Mountain: Stories of the Chinese in the New World (Yee) **44**:162
Tales from Grimm (Gag) **4**:91
Tales from The Jungle Book (McKinley) **10**:126
Tales from the Land Under My Table (Wilhelm) **46**:160
Tales from the Mabinogion (Crossley-Holland) **47**:41
Tales from the Shop That Never Shuts (Waddell) **31**:191
Tales from the Story Hat (Aardema) **17**:3
Tales Mummies Tell (Lauber) **16**:121
Tales of a Dead King (Myers) **16**:140
Tales of a Fourth Grade Nothing (Blume) **2**:18
Tales of a Gambling Grandma (Khalsa) **30**:145
Tales of Momolu (Graham) **10**:104
The Tales of Olga da Polga (Bond) **1**:29
The Tales of Uncle Remus: The Adventures of Brer Rabbit (Lester) **41**:104
The Tales of Uncle Remus: The Adventures of Brer Rabbit (Pinkney) **43**:160
Tales Told by a Machine (Rodari) **24**:210
Talk about a Family (Greenfield) **4**:101; **38**:83

The Talking Eggs: A Folktale from the American South (Pinkney) **43**:163
The Talking Eggs: A Folktale from the American South (San Souci) **43**:184
The Talking Machine: An Extraordinary Story (Kruss) **9**:86
Talking with Artists (Cummings) **48**:52
Talking with Artists, Volume Two (Cummings) **48**:55
Talking with the Animals (Cohen) **3**:42
Talking Without Words (Ets) **33**:91
Tall Man in the Pivot (Christopher) **33**:39
Tall Ships (Lasky) **11**:114
Tallyho, Pinkerton! (Kellogg) **6**:178
Tamarindo! (Brown) **12**:101
Tamar's Wager (Coatsworth) **2**:62
Taming the Star Runner (Hinton) **23**:149
Tamworth Pig and the Litter (Kemp) **29**:113
Tamworth Pig Stories (Kemp) **29**:122
Tancy (Hurmence) **25**:93
Tangara: "Let Us Set Off Again" (Chauncy) **6**:91
Tant Grön, Tant Brun och Tant Gredelin (Beskow) **17**:16
Tapping Earth's Heat (Lauber) **16**:119
Tar Beach (Ringgold) **30**:168-71
Taran Wanderer (Alexander) **1**:17; **5**:20
Tarantulas on the Brain (Singer) **48**:123
The Tar-Baby, and Other Rhymes of Uncle Remus (Harris) **49**:61-107
Taronga (Kelleher) **36**:123
The Tasha Tudor Book of Fairy Tales (Tudor) **13**:198
Tasha Tudor's Bedtime Book (Tudor) **13**:201
Tasha Tudor's Old Fashioned Gifts: Presents and Favors for All Occasions (Tudor) **13**:202
Tasha Tudor's Sampler (Tudor) **13**:199
La Tasse Cassée (Vincent) **13**:219
Taste, Touch, and Smell (Adler) **27**:21
Tatsinda (Enright) **4**:76
The Tattooed Potato and Other Clues (Raskin) **12**:223
Tatty Apple (Nimmo) **44**:139
The Tavern at the Ferry (Tunis) **2**:194
Taxi: A Book of City Words (Betsy and Giulio Maestro) **45**:81
Taxis and Toadstools: Verses and Decorations (Field) **21**:69
T-Backs, T-Shirts, Coat, and Suit (Konigsburg) **47**:147
Teach Me to Fly, Skyfighter! (Yee) **44**:160
Teach Us, Amelia Bedelia (Parish) **22**:163
Teacup Full of Roses (Mathis) **3**:151
Tea-Leaf on the Roof (Ure) **34**:183
The Team That Couldn't Lose (Christopher) **33**:42
The Team That Stopped Moving (Christopher) **33**:51
Tear Down the Walls! (Sterling) **1**:181
The Tears of the Dragon (Tresselt) **30**:210
The Teddy Bear Habit; or, How I Became a Winner (Collier) **3**:49
Teddy Bear's Scrapbook (Howe) **9**:57
Teddy's Ear (Daly) **41**:55
Teen Guide to AIDS Prevention (Nourse) **33**:149
Teen Guide to Birth Control: The Guide to Safe Sex (Nourse) **33**:147
Teen Guide to Survival (Nourse) **33**:150
Teen Sex (Hyde) **23**:175
Teen-Age Treasury of Good Humor (Manley) **3**:148
Teen-Age Treasury of Our Science World (Manley) **3**:148
Teen-Age Treasury of the Arts (Manley) **3**:148
Teenagers Who Made History (Freedman) **20**:73

Teeny Tiny Tales (Scarry) **41**:162
The Teeny-Tiny Woman: A Ghost Story (Galdone) **16**:105
TEEP and BEEP Go to Sleep (Mayer) **11**:176
The Teeth of the Gale (Aiken) **19**:19
Teetoncey (Taylor) **30**:188
Teetoncey and Ben O'Neal (Taylor) **30**:188
Tehanu: The Last Book of Earthsea (Le Guin) **28**:144-88
Telboek no. 2 (Bruna) **7**:51
Telephone Systems (Zim) **2**:231
Telephone Tales (Rodari) **24**:208
Television Works Like This (Bendick) **5**:36
Tell About the Cowbarn, Daddy (Merrill) **52**:105
Tell Me a Story, Mama (Johnson) **33**:94
Tell Me a Tale: A Book about Storytelling (Bruchac) **46**:23
Tell Me If the Lovers Are Losers (Voigt) **13**:229
Tell Tales (Rosen) **45**:139
Tell the Truth, Marly Dee (Williams) **48**:202
Tell Us a Story (McNaughton) **54**:56
Temperature and You (Betsy and Giulio Maestro) **45**:82
Ten Apples Up on Top! (Dr. Seuss) **9**:187
Ten Black Dots (Crews) **7**:56
Ten Kids, No Pets (Martin) **32**:204
Ten, Nine, Eight (Bang) **8**:22
Ten Pink Piglets: Garth Pig's Wall Song (Rayner) **41**:131
Ten Sleepy Sheep (Keller) **45**:45
Ten-Cent Island (Park) **51**:173
Tendo Setsu No Hon (Anno) **14**:37
The Tenement Tree (Seredy) **10**:180
Tennis Shoes (Streatfeild) **17**:186
The Tent: A Parable in One Sitting (Paulsen) **54**:115
The Tenth Good Thing about Barney (Viorst) **3**:209
Term Paper (Rinaldi) **46**:76
The Terrible Churnadryne (Cameron) **1**:41
Terrible, Horrible Edie (Spykman) **35**:219
The Terrible Nung Gwama: A Chinese Folktale (Young) **27**:218
The Terrible Roar (Pinkwater) **4**:161
The Terrible Tales of Happy Days School (Duncan) **29**:76
The Terrible Temptation (Arundel) **35**:19
Terrible Things (Bunting) **28**:50
The Terrible Tiger (Prelutsky) **13**:164
Terrible Troll (Mayer) **11**:165
The Terrible Troll-Bird (d'Aulaire and d'Aulaire) **21**:54
Terrorism: A Special Kind of Violence (Hyde) **23**:173
The Terrorists (Meltzer) **13**:144
Terry and the Caterpillars (Selsam) **1**:166
Terry on the Fence (Ashley) **4**:15
Tessie (Jackson) **28**:139
Tex (Hinton) **23**:148
Texas Tomboy (Lenski) **26**:115
Thaddeus Stevens and the Fight for Negro Rights (Meltzer) **13**:123
Thank You, Amelia Bedelia (Parish) **22**:155
Thank You, Dr. Martin Luther King, Jr.! (Tate) **37**:191
Thank You, Henrietta (Daly) **41**:58
Thanksgiving Day (Gibbons) **8**:97
The Thanksgiving Mystery (Nixon) **24**:141
That Dreadful Day (Stevenson) **17**:163
That Early Spring (Beckman) **25**:15
That Early Spring (Beckman)
  See *The Loneliness of Mia*
That Terrible Halloween Night (Stevenson) **17**:156

That Was Then, This Is Now (Hinton) **3**:72; **23**:147
That Wonderful Pelican (Scott) **20**:194
That'd Be Telling (Rosen) **45**:135
That's My Baby (Lindgren) **39**:158
That's Not Fair! (Fujikawa) **25**:41
That's Silly (Sleator) **29**:202
That's Why (Fisher) **49**:31
Theater Shoes; or, Other People's Shoes (Streatfeild) **17**:190
Then Again, Maybe I Won't (Blume) **2**:18
Then There Were Five (Enright) **4**:75
Theo Runs Away (Hartling) **29**:101
Theodore and the Talking Mushroom (Lionni) **7**:135
Theodore Roosevelt, an Initial Biography (Foster) **7**:97
There, Far Beyond the River (Korinetz) **4**:129
There Is No Rhyme for Silver (Merriam) **14**:193
There Once Was a Time (Ventura) **16**:197
There Was an Old Woman (Kellogg) **6**:173
There's a Bat in Bunk Five (Danziger) **20**:53
There's a Boy in the Girl's Bathroom (Sacher) **28**:202
There's a Nightmare in My Closet (Mayer) **11**:160
There's a Nightmare in My Cupboard (Mayer) **11**:160
There's a Rainbow in My Closet (Stren) **5**:232
There's Always Danny (Ure) **34**:185
There's an Awful Lot of Weirdos in Our Neighborhood: A Book of Rather Silly Verse and Pictures (McNaughton) **54**:57
"There's an Awful Lot of Weirdos in Our Neighborhood" and Other Wickedly Funny Verse (McNaughton) **54**:57
There's No Place like Home (Brown) **29**:12
There's Nothing to Do! (Stevenson) **17**:164
These Happy Golden Years (Wilder) **2**:207
They Didn't Come Back (Berna) **19**:39
They Found a Cave (Chauncy) **6**:89
They Lived with the Dinosaurs (Freedman) **20**:81
They Never Came Home (Duncan) **29**:67
They Put on Masks (Baylor) **3**:17
They Put Out to Sea: The Story of the Map (Duvoisin) **23**:91
They Walk in the Night (Coatsworth) **2**:63
They Who Walk in the Wild (Roberts) **33**:206
Thidwick, the Big-Hearted Moose (Dr. Seuss) **9**:176
The Thief (Rockwell) **6**:239
A Thief in the Village and Other Stories (Berry) **22**:7
Thief of Hearts (Yep) **54**:199
The Thieves and the Raven (Janosch) **26**:75
The Thieving Dwarfs (Calhoun) **42**:11
Thimble Summer (Enright) **4**:71
Thing (Klein) **21**:158
The Thing in the Woods (Alcock) **26**:7
Thingnapped! (Klein) **21**:161
Things in Corners (Park) **51**:183
Things That Go Bump in the Night: A Collection of Original Stories (Yolen) **44**:189
Things That Sometimes Happen: Very Short Stories for Very Young Readers (Avi) **24**:4
Things That Spin: From Tops to Atoms (Adler) **27**:13
Things to Make and Do for Columbus Day (Gibbons) **8**:89
Things to Make and Do for Halloween (Gibbons) **8**:89
Things to Make and Do for Valentine's Day (dePaola) **4**:58
Things to Make and Do for Your Birthday (Gibbons) **8**:89

Think Metric (Branley) **13**:38
Think of Shadows (Moore) **15**:144
Thinking Big: The Story of a Young Dwarf (Kuklin) **51**:98
The Third Eye (The Eyes of Karen Connors) (Duncan) **29**:77
The Third Eye (Hunter) **25**:86
The Third Magic (Katz) **45**:35
The Third Margaret Mahy Story Book: Stories and Poems (Mahy) **7**:183
The Third Road (Bacon) **3**:12
Thirteen (Charlip) **8**:32
The Thirteen Days of Yule (Hogrogian) **2**:89
The Thirteen Moons (George) **1**:93
Thirteen Moons on Turtle's Back (Bruchac) **46**:10
The Thirteenth Member: A Story of Suspense (Hunter) **25**:79
Thirty-Six Exposures (Major) **11**:132
Thirty-Two Moons: The Natural Satellites of Our Solar System (Knight) **38**:113
This Business with Elijah (Oberman) **54**:75
This Can't Be Happening at Macdonald Hall! (Korman) **25**:105
This Crowded Planet (Hyde) **23**:155
This Dear-Bought Land (Latham) **50**:100
This Delicious Day: 65 Poems (Janeczko) **47**:107
This Is a Recording (Corcoran) **50**:15
This Is a River: Exploring an Ecosystem (Pringle) **4**:176
This Is Australia (Sasek) **4**:196
This Is Cape Kennedy (Sasek) **4**:193
This Is Edinburgh (Sasek) **4**:190
This Is Greece (Sasek) **4**:194
This Is Historic Britain (Sasek) **4**:196
This Is Hong Kong (Sasek) **4**:194
This Is Ireland (Sasek) **4**:193
This Is Israel (Sasek) **4**:192
This Is London (Sasek) **4**:188
This Is Munich (Sasek) **4**:191
This Is My House (Dorros) **42**:70
This Is New York (Sasek) **4**:189
This Is Paris (Sasek) **4**:187
This Is Rome (Sasek) **4**:189
This Is San Francisco (Sasek) **4**:192
This Is Texas (Sasek) **4**:194
This is the Forest (Hurd and Hurd) **49**:126
This Is the United Nations (Sasek) **4**:195
This Is Venice (Sasek) **4**:192
This Is Washington, D.C. (Sasek) **4**:195
This Is Your Century (Trease) **42**:187
This Little Nose (Ormerod) **20**:180
This Place Has No Atmosphere (Danziger) **20**:55
This Restless Earth (Lauber) **16**:116
This School Is Driving Me Crazy (Hentoff) **52**:57
This Star Shall Abide (Engdahl) **2**:71
This Strange New Feeling (Lester) **41**:100
This Street's for Me! (Hopkins) **44**:86
This Thumbprint (Krauss) **42**:128
This Union Cause: The Growth of Organized Labor in America (Shippen) **36**:178
This Year's Garden (Rylant) **15**:170
Thistly B. (Tudor) **13**:192
Thomas and the Warlock (Hunter) **25**:77
Thomas' Snowsuit (Munsch) **19**:144
Thor: Last of the Sperm Whales (McClung) **11**:187
Thoroughbred Horses (Patent) **19**:161
Those Amazing Computers! Uses of Modern Thinking Machines (Berger) **32**:10
Those Mysterious UFOs: The Story of Unidentified Flying Objects (Knight) **38**:117
A Thousand Lights and Fireflies (Tresselt) **30**:209
Threat to the Barkers (Phipson) **5**:179
Three Aesop Fox Fables (Galdone) **16**:96

Three and One to Carry (Willard) **2**:223
The Three Bears (Galdone) **16**:97
The Three Bears Rhyme Book (Yolen) **44**:181
Three Big Hogs (Pinkwater) **4**:164
The Three Billy Goats Gruff (Brown) **12**:99
The Three Billy Goats Gruff (Galdone) **16**:97
Three Billy Goats Gruff (McKissack) **23**:239
Three by the Sea (Marshall) **21**:176
Three by Three: A Picture Book for All Children Who Can Count to Three (Kruss) **9**:85
Three Days on a River in a Red Canoe (Williams) **9**:231
Three Gay Tales from Grimm (Gag) **4**:93
Three Girls and a Secret (Guillot) **22**:65
Three Gold Pieces: A Greek Folk Tale (Aliki) **9**:20
The Three Golden Heads of the Well (Garner) **20**:116
The Three Golden Keys (Sis) **45**:172
Three Heads Made of Gold (Causley) **30**:40
The Three Jovial Huntsmen (Caldecott) **14**:75
Three Jovial Huntsmen (Jeffers) **30**:128
Three Kinds of Stubborn (Calhoun) **42**:19
Three Little Kittens (Galdone) **16**:107
The Three Little Pigs (Biro) **28**:40
The Three Little Pigs (Galdone) **16**:95
Three Margerets (Richards) **54**:166
Three on the Run (Bawden) **2**:14; **51**:13
Three Promises to You (Leaf) **25**:133
The Three Robbers (Ungerer) **3**:204
Three Rolls and One Doughnut: Fables from Russia (Ginsburg) **45**:3
Three Saxon Nobles, and Other Verses (Prelutsky) **13**:163
The Three Sillies (Galdone) **16**:103
Three Sisters (Mazer) **23**:230
The Three Sneezes and Other Swiss Tales (Duvoisin) **23**:91
Three Stalks of Corn (Politi) **29**:194
Three Terrible Trins (King-Smith) **40**:171
Three Up a Tree (Marshall) **21**:182
Three Wishes (Clifton) **5**:58
The Three Wishes (Galdone) **16**:90
The Three-Day Enchantment (Hunter) **25**:90
Threshold of the Stars (Berna) **19**:36
Through a Brief Darkness (Peck) **15**:153
Through Grandpa's Eyes (MacLachlan) **14**:180
Through the Broken Mirror with Alice (Wojciechowska) **1**:200
Through the Eyes of Wonder: Science Fiction and Science (Bova) **3**:35
Through the Hidden Door (Wells) **16**:214
Through the Looking-Glass and What Alice Found There (Carroll) **2**:36; **18**:38-80
Through the Looking-Glass, and What Alice Found There (Moser) **49**:169
Through the Looking-Glass, and What Alice Found There (Tenniel) **18**:201-28
Through the Magic Mirror (Browne) **19**:62
Through the Mickle Woods (Moser) **49**:184
Through the Window (Keeping) **34**:93
Through the Year with Harriet (Betsy and Giulio Maestro) **45**:75
Throwing Shadows (Konigsburg) **47**:138
Thumbeline (Zwerger) **46**:196
Thunder and Lightnings (Mark) **11**:145
Thunder Cake (Polacco) **40**:186
Thunder in the Sky (Peyton) **3**:180
Thunder of Valmy (Trease) **42**:184
Thunderbolt and Rainbow: A Look at Greek Mythology (Billout) **33**:22
Thurgood Marshall: A Life for Justice (Haskins) **39**:68
Thursday's Child (Streatfeild) **17**:197

Tía María's Garden (Clark) **16**:82

Tic, Tac, and Toc (Munari) **9**:124

Ticket to Freedom (Harris) **30**:126

Tickle, Tickle (Oxenbury) **22**:148

Tico and the Golden Wings (Lionni) **7**:130

A Tide Flowing (Phipson) **5**:186

Tiffky Doofky (Steig) **15**:196

Tiger by the Tail: And Other Science Fiction Stories (Nourse) **33**:133

A Tiger Called Thomas (Zolotow) **2**:237

Tiger Eyes (Blume) **15**:78

Tiger in the Bush (Chauncy) **6**:89

Tiger: The Story of a Swallowtail Butterfly (McClung) **11**:179

The Tiger Who Wore White Gloves; or, What You Are You Are (Brooks) **27**:44-56

Tiger Woman (Yep) **54**:196

The Tiger's Bones and Other Plays for Children (Hughes) **3**:96

Tiger's Milk (Mattingley) **24**:124

Tigger and Friends (Hamley) **47**:61

Tight End (Christopher) **33**:55

Tikta'liktak: An Eskimo Legend (Houston) **3**:86

Tikvah Means Hope (Polacco) **40**:200

Till the Break of Day (Wojciechowska) **1**:200

Tilly Mint and the Dodo (Doherty) **21**:60

Tilly Mint Tales (Doherty) **21**:56

Tilly Witch (Freeman) **30**:77

Tiltawhirl John (Paulsen) **19**:171

Tim All Alone (Ardizzone) **3**:6

Tim and Charlotte (Ardizzone) **3**:6

Tim and Ginger (Ardizzone) **3**:7

Tim in Danger (Ardizzone) **3**:7

Tim Tadpole and the Great Bullfrog (Flack) **28**:123

Tim to the Lighthouse (Ardizzone) **3**:7

Tim to the Rescue (Ardizzone) **3**:8

Time after Time (Berger) **32**:14

Time and Mr. Bass: A Mushroom Planet Book (Cameron) **1**:42

Time Cat: The Remarkable Journey of Jason and Gareth (Alexander) **5**:18

Time Enough for Drums (Rinaldi) **46**:79

The Time Garden (Eager) **43**:85

Time Ghost (Katz) **45**:40

Time in Your Life (Adler) **27**:5

A Time of Angels (Hesse) **54**:38

The Time of the Cranes (St. John) **46**:122

The Time of the Ghost (Jones) **23**:191

Time of the Harvest: Thomas Jefferson, the Years 1801-1826 (Wibberley) **3**:230

The Time of the Kraken (Williams) **8**:235

The Time of the Young Soldiers (Richter) **21**:189

Time of Trial (Burton) **1**:34

Time of Trial, Time of Hope: The Negro in America, 1919-1941 (Meltzer) **13**:123

Time of Wonder (McCloskey) **7**:209

Time To. . . (McMillan) **47**:173

Time to Get Out of the Bath, Shirley (Burningham) **9**:48

Time to Go Back (Allan) **43**:23

Time to Go Home (Spence) **26**:196

A Time to Keep: The Tasha Tudor Book of Holidays (Tudor) **13**:200

A Time to Love (Benary-Isbert) **12**:73

The Time Traders (Norton) **50**:139

Time-Ago Lost: More Tales of Jahdu (Hamilton) **1**:105

Time-Ago Tales of Jahdu (Hamilton) **1**:106

The Times of My Life: A Memoir (Ashabranner) **28**:15

The Times They Used to Be (Clifton) **5**:56

Timewarp Summer (St. John) **46**:112

Timm Thaler (Kruss) **9**:85

Timmy and the Tin-Can Telephone (Branley) **13**:28

Timothy Goes to School (Wells) **16**:211

Timothy Robbins Climbs the Mountain (Tresselt) **30**:208

Timothy's Quest: A Story for Anybody, Old or Young (Wiggin) **52**:157

Tim's Last Voyage (Ardizzone) **3**:8

The Tin Can Beast and Other Stories (Biegel) **27**:34

Tin Cans (Rockwell) **6**:238

Tin Lizzie (Spier) **5**:223

Tin Lizzy, and How She Ran (Epstein and Epstein) **26**:41

Tina and Nina (Baumann) **35**:48

Tina Gogo (Gaberman) **33**:3

The Tinder Box (Bedard) **35**:62

The Tinderbox (Moser) **49**:175

Tingalayo (Duke) **51**:49

TINK Goes Fishing (Mayer) **11**:176

TINKA Bakes a Cake (Mayer) **11**:176

Tinker and Tanker (Scarry) **41**:160

Tinker and Tanker and Their Space Ship (Scarry) **41**:160

Tinker and Tanker in Africa (Scarry) **41**:160

Tinker and Tanker: Knights of the Round Table (Scarry) **41**:160

Tinker Tailor: Folk Song Tales (Keeping) **34**:90

Tinker Tailor: Folk Songs (Keeping) **34**:90

The Tin-Pot Foreign General and the Old Iron Woman (Briggs) **10**:33

Tintin au pays de l'or noir (Herge) **6**:148

Tintin au Tibet (Herge) **6**:148

Tintin en Amérique (Herge) **6**:147

Tintin in America (Herge) **6**:147

Tintin in Tibet (Herge) **6**:148

The Tiny Planets: Asteroids of Our Solar System (Knight) **38**:112

The Tiny Seed (Carle) **10**:73

The Tiny Seed and the Giant Flower (Carle) **10**:73

Tiny TINK! TONK! Tales (Mayer) **11**:176

Tirra Lirra: Rhymes Old and New (Richards) **54**:169

Titanic Crossing (Williams) **48**:206

Titch (Hutchins) **20**:145

Tituba of Salem Village (Petry) **12**:211

To All My Fans, with Love, from Sylvie (Conford) **10**:98

To Be a Logger (Lenski) **26**:123

To Be a Slave (Lester) **2**:114

"To Damon. To inquire of him if he cou'd tell me by the Style, who writ me a Copy of Verses that came to me in an unknown Hand"
    See *The Grey Gentlemen*

To kaplani tis Vitrinas (Zei) **6**:260

To Live in Two Worlds: American Indian Youth Today (Ashabranner) **28**:7

To Look at Any Thing (Hopkins) **44**:89

To Make a Wee Moon (Naylor) **17**:50

To Market! To Market! (Spier) **5**:218

To Shake a Shadow (Naylor) **17**:49

To Stand against the Wind (Clark) **16**:85

To the Dark Tower (Kelleher) **36**:132

To the Ends of the Universe (Asimov) **12**:41

To the Wild Sky (Southall) **2**:156

To Walk the Sky Path (Naylor) **17**:50

Toad of Toad Hall (Milne) **1**:143

The Toby Man (King-Smith) **40**:157

Toc, toc, chi è? Apri la porta (Munari) **9**:124

Today is Saturday (Snyder) **31**:157

Today We Are Brother and Sister (Adoff) **7**:36

Told by Uncle Remus: New Stories of the Old Plantation (Harris) **49**:61-107

Tom and Pippo and the Dog (Oxenbury) **22**:151

Tom and Pippo and the Washing Machine (Oxenbury) **22**:149

Tom and Pippo Go for a Walk (Oxenbury) **22**:149

Tom and Pippo Go Shopping (Oxenbury) **22**:150

Tom and Pippo in the Garden (Oxenbury) **22**:150

Tom and Pippo in the Snow (Oxenbury) **22**:151

Tom and Pippo Make a Friend (Oxenbury) **22**:151

Tom and Pippo Make a Mess (Oxenbury) **22**:149

Tom and Pippo Read a Story (Oxenbury) **22**:149

Tom and Pippo See the Moon (Oxenbury) **22**:150

Tom and Pippo's Day (Oxenbury) **22**:150

Tom and Sam (Hutchins) **20**:144

Tom and the Two Handles (Hoban) **3**:83

Tom Fobble's Day (Garner) **20**:115

Tom Fox and the Apple Pie (Watson) **3**:213

The Tom Sawyer Fires (Yep) **17**:207

Tom Titmarsh's Devil (Garfield) **21**:109

Tom, Tom, the Piper's Son (Galdone) **16**:92

Tomboy (Klein) **19**:90

The Tombs of Atuan (Le Guin) **3**:123; **28**:144-88

Tomfoolery: Trickery and Foolery with Words (Schwartz) **3**:190

Tomie dePaola's Book of Christmas Carols (dePaola) **24**:100

Tomie dePaola's Book of Poems (dePaola) **24**:101

Tomie dePaola's Favorite Nursery Tales (dePaola) **24**:97

Tomie dePaola's Kitten Kids and the Big Camp-Out (dePaola) **24**:100

Tomie dePaola's Kitten Kids and the Haunted House (dePaola) **24**:100

Tomie dePaola's Kitten Kids and the Missing Dinosaur (dePaola) **24**:100

Tomie dePaola's Kitten Kids and the Treasure Hunt (dePaola) **24**:100

Tomie dePaola's Mother Goose (dePaola) **24**:95

Tommy Helps, Too (Rey) **5**:194

Tommy, Tilly, and Mrs. Tubbs (Lofting) **19**:128

The Tomorrow City (Hughes) **9**:70

Tomorrow Is a Lovely Day (Allan) **43**:29

Tomorrow Is Also a Day (Ure) **34**:186

Tomorrow's Wizard (MacLachlan) **14**:182

Tom's Midnight Garden (Pearce) **9**:144

Tom's Sausage Lion (Morpurgo) **51**:125

Tomtebobarnen (Beskow) **17**:16

The Tomten (Lindgren) **39**:149

Tom-Toms in Kotokro (Guillot) **22**:59

Tongue of Flame: The Life of Lydia Maria Child (Meltzer) **13**:122

Tongues of Jade (Yep) **54**:189

Tonight at Nine (Janosch) **26**:74

Tonight Is Carnaval (Dorros) **42**:68

Tono Antonio (Sawyer) **36**:150

Tonweya and the Eagles, and Other Lakota Indian Tales (Pinkney) **43**:156

Tony and Me (Slote) **4**:200

Tony the Pony (Moore) **15**:140

Tony's Bread: An Italian Folktale (dePaola) **24**:103

Too Big (d'Aulaire and d'Aulaire) **21**:49

Too Big (Keller) **45**:45

Too Hot to Handle (Christopher) **33**:41

Too Many Hopkins (dePaola) **24**:102

Too Many Rabbits (Parish) **22**:161

Too Many Tamales (Soto) **38**:203

Too Much Garbage (Lauber) **16**:118

Too Much Noise (McGovern) **50**:112

The Too-Great Bread Bake Book (Gibbons) **8**:91

Tool Book (Gibbons) **8**:92

Toolchest: A Primer of Woodcraft (Adkins) **7**:21

Toolmaker (Walsh) **2**:201

Tools in Your Life (Adler) **27**:6

Tools of Modern Biology (Berger) **32**:4

The Tools of Science: From Yardstick to Cyclotron (Adler) **27**:10
Tooth and Claw: A Look at Animal Weapons (Freedman) **20**:80
The Tooth Book (Dr. Seuss) **9**:194
The Tooth Book (Nourse) **33**:141
Tooth-Gnasher Superflash (Pinkwater) **4**:171
The Toothpaste Millionaire (Merrill) **52**:111
Toppen and I at the Croft (Unnerstad) **36**:197
The Toppling Towers (Willard) **2**:223
Topsy (Flack) **28**:123
Topsy-Turvies: Pictures to Stretch the Imagination (Anno) **2**:2
The Topsy-Turvy Emperor of China (Singer) **1**:175
The Topsy-Turvy Storybook (King-Smith) **40**:167
Tornado Alert! (Betsy and Giulio Maestro) **45**:80
Tornado! Poems (Adoff) **7**:33
Torolv the Fatherless (Clarke) **28**:76
The Toronto Story (Mackay) **43**:110
The Tortilla Factory (Paulsen) **54**:116
The Tortoise and the Tree (Domanska) **40**:47
The Tortoise's Tug of War (Betsy and Giulio Maestro) **45**:63
Toucans Two, and Other Poems (Prelutsky) **13**:164
Touch Will Tell (Brown) **12**:107
Touchdown for Tommy (Christopher) **33**:38
Touching (Neufeld) **52**:123
Touching All the Bases: Baseball for Kids of All Ages (Mackay) **43**:111
The Tough Coughs as He Ploughs the Dough (Dr. Seuss) **53**:138
Tough Luck (Doherty) **21**:59
The Tough Princess (Waddell) **31**:187
Tough Tiffany (Hurmence) **25**:92
Tough to Tackle (Christopher) **33**:45
The Tough Winter (Lawson) **2**:111
Toughy and His Trailer Truck (Hurd and Hurd) **49**:120
The Tournament of the Lions (Williams) **8**:224
The Tower of London (Fisher) **18**:138
Tower of the Stars (Harris) **30**:121
Town and Country (Provensen and Provensen) **11**:219
The Town Cats, and Other Tales (Alexander) **5**:23
The Town Mouse and the Country Mouse (Galdone) **16**:96
The Town That Forgot It Was Christmas (Proysen) **24**:183
Town Watch (King-Smith) **40**:152
The Toy Shop (Spier) **5**:228
The Toy Trumpet (Grifalconi) **35**:71
The Toymaker (Waddell) **31**:199
Tracker (Paulsen) **19**:174
Tracks (Bess) **39**:5
Tracks (Crew) **42**:58
Tractors (Zim) **2**:231
Tractors: From Yesterday's Steam Wagons to Today's Turbo-Charged Giants (Murphy) **53**:104
Traffic: A Book of Opposites (Betsy and Giulio Maestro) **45**:71
Trail Blazer of the Seas (Latham) **50**:99
Trail of Apple Blossoms (Hunt) **1**:110
Train Ride (Steptoe) **2**:164
Train Whistles: A Language in Code (Betsy and Giulio Maestro) **45**:75
Train Whistles: A Language in Code (Sattler) **24**:214
Traitor: The Case of Benedict Arnold (Fritz) **14**:116
The Transall Saga (Paulsen) **54**:126
The Transfigured Hart (Yolen) **4**:261
The Trap (Cresswell) **18**:107

The Trapp Family Book (Wilhelm) **46**:160
Trapped by the Mountain Storm (Fisher) **49**:31
Das Traumfresserchen (Ende) **14**:99
Traveling America with Today's Poets (Kherdian) **24**:107
The Traveling Ball of String (Calhoun) **42**:14
Traveling Shoes (Streatfeild) **17**:195
Travellers by Night (Alcock) **26**:3
Travels for Two: Stories and Lies from My Child-hood (Poulin) **28**:199
Travels into Several Remote Nations of the World, in Four Parts; By Lemuel Gulliver (*Gulliver's Travels*) (Swift) **53**:160-207
The Travels of Babar (Brunhoff) **4**:31
The Travels of Columbus (Ventura) **16**:193
The Travels of Marco (Merrill) **52**:100
Travels of Marco Polo (Ventura) **16**:194
The Treasure (Shulevitz) **5**:206
Treasure Island (Stevenson) **10**:193-235
The Treasure of Alpheus Winterborn (Bellairs) **37**:11
The Treasure of the Long Sault (Hughes) **9**:77
The Treasure of Topo-El-Bampo (O'Dell) **1**:148
The Treasure-Hunting Trip (Janosch) **26**:78
Tree by Leaf (Singer) **48**:170
Tree Flowers (Lerner) **34**:130
A Tree for Peter (Seredy) **10**:177
Tree House Island (Corbett) **1**:47
The Tree House of Jimmy Domino (Merrill) **52**:101
Tree in the Trail (Holling) **50**:52
Tree of Dreams: Ten Tales from the Garden of Night (Yep) **54**:196
A Tree on Your Street (Simon) **9**:208
Tree Products (Adler) **27**:22
A Treeful of Pigs (Lobel) **5**:173
The Treegate Series (Wibberley) **3**:231
Treegate's Raiders (Wibberley) **3**:231
Treehorn's Treasure (Gorey) **36**:99
Treehorn's Wish (Gorey) **36**:104
The Trek (Jonas) **12**:176
The Trial of Anna Cotman (Alcock) **26**:8
Trial Valley (Cleaver and Cleaver) **6**:111
Trick a Tracker (Foreman) **32**:93
A Trick of Light (Corcoran) **50**:16
Trig (Peck) **45**:110
The Trip (Keats) **35**:140
The Trip to Panama (Janosch) **26**:78
Trip Trap (Dhondy) **41**:77
Tristan and Iseult (Sutcliff) **1**:190; **37**:163
Triumphs of Modern Science (Berger) **32**:2
Troia (Ventura) **16**:196
Troll Country (Marshall) **21**:174
A Troll in a Hole (McKissack) **23**:241
The Trolley to Yesterday (Bellairs) **37**:22
Der Trommler und die Puppe (Kruss) **9**:88
The Troubadour (Guillot) **22**:69
Trouble Half-Way (Mark) **11**:156
Trouble in the Jungle (Townsend) **2**:175
Trouble on the Tracks (Napoli) **51**:166
Trouble on Titan (Nourse) **33**:130
Trouble River (Byars) **16**:53
The Trouble with Adventurers (Harris) **47**:90
The Trouble with Charlie (Nixon) **24**:142
The Trouble with Donovan Croft (Ashley) **4**:14
The Trouble with Jack (Hughes) **15**:121
The Trouble with Princesses (Harris) **47**:89
The Trouble with Tuck (Taylor) **30**:191
Trouble with Vanessa (Ure) **34**:185
Trouble's Child (Walter) **15**:207
Trubloff: The Mouse Who Wanted to Play the Balalaika (Burningham) **9**:39
The Truce of the Games (Sutcliff) **37**:163

Truck (Crews) **7**:57
A Truckload of Rice (Berna) **19**:39
Trucks (Gibbons) **8**:92
Trucks (Zim) **2**:232
The True Adventure of Daniel Hall (Stanley) **46**:154
The True Adventures of Grizzly Adams (McClung) **11**:194
True Champions: Great Athletes and Their Off-the-Field Heroics (Aaseng) **54**:19
The True Confessions of Charlotte Doyle (Avi) **24**:15
The True Cross (Wildsmith) **52**:182
The True Francine (Brown) **29**:7
True Sea Adventures (Sobol) **4**:210
The True Story of the Three Little Pigs (Smith) **47**:199
The True Story of the Three Little Pigs: by A. Wolf; as Told to Jon Scieszka (Scieszka) **27**:154
The Trumpet Book (Berger) **32**:19
The Trumpet of the Swan (White) **1**:195
Trumpets in the West (Trease) **42**:179
Trust a City Kid (Yolen) **4**:256
The Truth about Dragons (Blumberg) **21**:26
The Truth about Mary Rose (Sachs) **2**:133
The Truth about Santa Claus (Giblin) **29**:89
The Truth about Stone Hollow (*The Ghosts of Stone Hollow*) (Snyder) **31**:161
The Truth about the Ku Klux Klan (Meltzer) **13**:144
The Truth About the Moon (Bess) **39**:3
The Truth about Unicorns (Giblin) **29**:93
Truth or Dare (Pfeffer) **11**:204
The Truthful Harp (Alexander) **1**:18; **5**:20
Try It Again, Sam: Safety When You Walk (Viorst) **3**:210
The Tsar's Promise: A Russian Tale (San Souci) **43**:187
Tsubo No Naka (Anno) **14**:41
Tuck Everlasting (Babbitt) **2**:8; **53**:25
Tuck Triumphant (Taylor) **30**:195
Tucker Pfeffercorn: An Old Story Retold (Moser) **49**:187
Tucker's Countryside (Selden) **8**:199
Tucket's Ride (Paulsen) **54**:121
Tuesday (Wiesner) **43**:209
Tugboats Never Sleep (Lasky) **11**:114
TUK Takes a Trip (Mayer) **11**:176
Tulku (Dickinson) **29**:48
Tumbleweed (King-Smith) **40**:150
Tuned Out (Wojciechowska) **1**:200
Tunes for a Small Harmonica (Wersba) **3**:220
The Tunnel of Hugsy Goode (Estes) **2**:75
Tunnel Vision (Gaberman) **33**:6
Tunnels (Epstein and Epstein) **26**:70
Tunnels (Gibbons) **8**:98
The Turbulent Term of Tyke Tiler (Kemp) **29**:114
Turkey Brother, and Other Tales (Bruchac) **46**:6
Turkey for Christmas (de Angeli) **1**:54
Turn It Up! A Novel (Strasser) **11**:250
Turnabout (Leaf) **25**:134
The Turnabout Trick (Corbett) **1**:47
The Turnip (Domanska) **40**:40
Turramulli the Giant Quinkin (Roughsey and Trezise) **41**:141
The Turret (Sharp) **27**:163
Turtle and Snail (Oneal) **13**:155
The Turtle and the Dove (Freeman) **30**:74
The Turtle and the Monkey: A Philippine Tale (Galdone) **16**:105
Turtle in July (Pinkney) **43**:164
Turtle in July (Singer) **48**:135
Turtle Meat, and Other Stories (Bruchac) **46**:10

Tusk Tusk (McKee) **38**:165

Tut, Tut (Smith) **47**:208

Tutankhamon (Ventura) **16**:196

TV and Movie Animals (Paulsen) **19**:173

The TV Kid (Byars) **16**:54

TV Sal and the Game Show from Outer Space (Oberman) **54**:74

'Twas the Night Before Thanksgiving (Pilkey) **48**:100

The Twelve and the Genii (Clarke) **28**:77

The Twelve Clever Brothers and Other Fools: Folktales from Russia (Ginsburg) **45**:13

Twelve Dancing Princesses (Nielsen) **16**:155

The Twelve Dancing Princesses: A Fairy Story (Lunn) **18**:159

The Twelve Days of Christmas (Brett) **27**:39

The Twelve Months: A Greek Folktale (Aliki) **9**:26

The Twelve Robbers (Biegel) **27**:30

Twelve Tales from Aesop (Carle) **10**:83

The Twelve Tasks of Asterix (Goscinny and Uderzo) **37**:82

Twentieth Century Discovery (Asimov) **12**:44

Twenty Ways To Lose Your Best Friend (Singer) **48**:136

Twenty-Four and Stanley (Weiss) **4**:219

The Twenty-Four Days Before Christmas (L'Engle) **1**:132

The Twenty-One Balloons (Pene du Bois) **1**:66

The Twenty-one Mile Swim (Christopher) **33**:53

Twenty-Two, Twenty-Three (Raskin) **12**:225

The Twilight of Magic (Lofting) **19**:127

Twilight Tales (Unnerstad) **36**:198

Twin and Super-Twin (Cross) **28**:95

Twin Spell (Lunn) **18**:158

Twink (Neufeld) **52**:123

Twins: The Story of Multiple Births (Cole) **5**:62

Twist of Gold (Morpurgo) **51**:121

Twist, Wiggle, and Squirm: A Book about Earthworms (Pringle) **4**:177

Twisted (Stine) **37**:109

The Twisted Window (Duncan) **29**:78

A Twister of Twists, a Tangler of Tongues (Schwartz) **3**:190

The Twits (Dahl) **7**:78

Two Admirals (McKee) **38**:165

Two and Too Much (Cummings) **48**:50

Two and Two Are Four (Haywood) **22**:91

Two are Better than One (Brink) **30**:15

Two Bear Cubs (Jonas) **12**:173

Two Boys of Jerusalem (Ashabranner) **28**:8

Two Can Toucan (McKee) **38**:157

The Two Cars (d'Aulaire and d'Aulaire) **21**:51

Two Crows Counting (Orgel) **48**:96

Two Different Girls (Bunting) **28**:47

Two Dog Biscuits (Cleary) **8**:49

Two Fables (Dahl) **41**:39

The Two Faces of Silenus (Clarke) **28**:81

The Two Giants (Foreman) **32**:86

Two Greedy Bears (Ginsburg) **45**:10

Two Hoots (Cresswell) **18**:107

Two Hoots and the Big Bad Bird (Cresswell) **18**:107

Two Hoots and the King (Cresswell) **18**:108

Two Hoots Go to the Sea (Cresswell) **18**:107

Two Hoots in the Snow (Cresswell) **18**:108

Two Hoots Play Hide-and-Seek (Cresswell) **18**:107

The 290 (O'Dell) **16**:172

Two Hundred Years of Bicycles (Murphy) **53**:103

Two If By Sea (Fisher) **18**:123

Two Laughable Lyrics (Lear) **1**:128

Two Little Gigglers (Unnerstad) **36**:199

Two Little Trains (Brown) **10**:58

Two Lonely Ducks, a Counting Book (Duvoisin) **23**:99

Two Love Stories (Lester) **2**:115

Two Monsters (McKee) **38**:174

Two Moral Tales (Mayer) **11**:168

Two More Moral Tales (Mayer) **11**:168

Two Noble Lives: Samuel Gridley Howe, Julia Ward Howe (Richards) **54**:166

The Two of Them (Aliki) **9**:26

The Two Old Bachelors (Lear) **1**:128

Two Pairs of Shoes (Leo and Diane Dillon) **44**:35

Two Piano Tuners (Goffstein) **3**:61

Two Shoes, New Shoes (Hughes) **15**:132

The Two Sisters (Arundel) **35**:11

Two Sisters and Some Hornets (Epstein) **26**:64

Two Stories: "The Road to Dunmore" and "The Key" (Dillon) **26**:28

Two Strikes on Johnny (Christopher) **33**:37

Two Thousand Years of Space Travel (Freedman) **20**:73

Two Under Par (Henkes) **23**:128

Two Wheels, Two Heads (Ahlberg and Ahlberg) **18**:8

The Two-Thousand-Pound Goldfish (Byars) **16**:58

Tye May and the Magic Brush (Bang) **8**:21

Tyrannosaurus Rex and Its Kin: The Mesozoic Monsters (Sattler) **24**:223

Tyrone the Dirty Rotten Cheat (Wilhelm) **46**:167

Tyrone, the Double Dirty Rotten Cheater (Wilhelm) **46**:167

Tyrone, the Horrible (Wilhelm) **46**:165

Ty's One-Man Band (Walter) **15**:205

UFO (Blumberg) **21**:24

UFOs: A Pictorial History from Antiquity to the Present (Knight) **38**:123

UFOs, ETs, and Visitors from Space (Berger) **32**:40

The Ugly Duckling (Moore) **15**:145

Ultramarine (Nimmo) **44**:145

The Ultra-Violet Catastrophe! or, The Unexpected Walk with Great-Uncle Magnus Pringle (Mahy) **7**:183

Umbrella (Yashima) **4**:253

Unbuilding (Macaulay) **14**:172

Uncanny! Even More Surprising Stories (Jennings) **40**:126

Uncharted Stars (Norton) **50**:148

Unclaimed Treasures (MacLachlan) **14**:183

Uncle Charlie Weasel and the Cuckoo Bird (McBratney) **44**:121

Uncle Charlie Weasel's Winter (McBratney) **44**:122

Uncle Elephant (Lobel) **5**:175

Uncle Lemon's Spring (Yolen) **4**:267

Uncle Misha's Partisans (Suhl) **2**:166

Uncle Remus and His Friends: Old Plantation Stories, Songs and Ballads (Harris) **49**:61-107

Uncle Remus, His Songs and His Sayings: Folklore of the Old Plantation (Harris) **49**:61-107

Uncle Vova's Tree (Polacco) **40**:185

"Unconditional Surrender": U. S. Grant and the Civil War (Marrin) **53**:92

Under a Changing Moon (Benary-Isbert) **12**:78

Under the Autumn Garden (Mark) **11**:147

Under the Early Morning Trees: Poems (Adoff) **7**:35

Under the Green Willow (Coatsworth) **2**:63

Under the Lemon Tree (Hurd and Hurd) **49**:131

Under the Moon (Ryder) **37**:92

Under the Orange Grove (Dillon) **26**:29

Under the Sun and over the Moon (Crossley-Holland) **47**:48

Under the Sunday Tree (Greenfield) **38**:86

Under the Trees and through the Grass (Tresselt) **30**:208

Under the Window: Pictures and Rhymes for Children (Greenaway) **6**:131

Under Your Feet (Ryder) **37**:95

Underground (Macaulay) **3**:144

Underground Man (Meltzer) **13**:130

Underground to Canada (Smucker) **10**:189

The Undersea People (Bunting) **28**:48

The Underside of the Leaf (Goffstein) **3**:61

Understanding Body Talk (Aylesworth) **6**:54

Understanding Radioactivity (Milne and Milne) **22**:126

The Undertaker's Gone Bananas (Zindel) **45**:192

The Underwater World of the Coral Reef (McGovern) **50**:119

Undone! More Mad Endings (Jennings) **40**:128

Uneasy Money (Brancato) **32**:75

Die Unendliche Geschichte (Ende) **14**:99

Unfortunately Harriet (Wells) **16**:204

The Unfriendly Book (Zolotow) **2**:237

Unhurry Harry (Merriam) **14**:200

The Unions (Fisher) **18**:131

The Unique World of Mitsumasa Anno: Selected Works (1968-1977) (Anno) **14**:35

The Universe (Zim) **2**:232

The Universe Between (Nourse) **33**:134

The Universe: From Flat Earth to Black Holes— and Beyond (Asimov) **12**:39

The Universe: From Flat Earth to Quasar (Asimov) **12**:39

University: The Students, Faculty, and Campus Life at One University (Schwartz) **3**:191

The Unknown Paintings of Kay Nielsen (Nielsen) **16**:158

Unreal! Eight Surprising Stories (Jennings) **40**:126

Until the Celebration (Snyder) **31**:163

The Untold Tale (Haugaard) **11**:107

Unusual Partners: Symbiosis in the Living World (Silverstein and Silverstein) **25**:201

L'uomo a cavallo (Ventura) **16**:195

L'uomo del camion (Munari) **9**:125

Up a Road Slowly (Hunt) **1**:110

Up a Tree (Young) **27**:220

Up and Up (Hughes) **15**:125

Up Country (Carter) **22**:23

Up from Jericho Tel (Konigsburg) **47**:141

Up in Seth's Room: A Love Story (Mazer) **23**:226

Up in Sister Bay (Ferry) **34**:51

Up in the Air (Flack) **28**:124

Up Periscope (White) **3**:223

Up the Alley with Jack and Joe (Kotzwinkle) **6**:182

Up the Chimney Down and Other Stories (Aiken) **19**:15

Up the Pier (Cresswell) **18**:104

Up the Windy Hill: A Book of Merry Verse with Silhouettes (Fisher) **49**:32

Up There (Hill) **13**:93

Up to Low (Doyle) **22**:30

Up, Up the Mountain (Fisher) **49**:47

The Uproar (Orgel) **48**:79

Upside-Downers: More Pictures to Stretch the Imagination (Anno) **2**:2

The Upstairs Room (Reiss) **19**:217

Uptown (Steptoe) **2**:164

The Urchin (Unnerstad) **36**:190

Us and Uncle Fraud (Lowry) **46**:30

Us Boys of Westcroft (Breinburg) **31**:67

Use Your Brain (Showers) **6**:245

Use Your Head, Dear (Aliki) **9**:31

The Uses of Space (Bova) **3**:36

V Is for Victory: America Remembers World War II (Krull) **44**:110

Vacation Time: Poems for Children (Giovanni) **6**:117

Vaccination and You (Cohen) **3**:43

The Vagabonds Ashore (Berna) **19**:41

Vagabonds of the Pacific (Berna) **19**:41

The Valentine (Garfield) **21**:109

The Valentine Bears (Bunting) **28**:55

A Valentine Fantasy (Haywood) **22**:103

A Valentine for Cousin Archie (Williams) **48**:200

Valentine Frankenstein (Gaberman) **33**:18

The Valentine Mystery (Nixon) **24**:139

The Valiant Chatti-Maker (Godden) **20**:137

Valiant Scots: People of the Highlands Today (Lauber) **16**:112

The Valley Between (Thiele) **27**:209

Valley of the Broken Cherry Trees (Namioka) **48**:62

Valley of the Smallest: The Life Story of a Shrew (Fisher) **49**:45

Vampires (Garden) **51**:65

Vampires and Other Ghosts (Aylesworth) **6**:49

The Vandemark Mummy (Voigt) **48**:174

The Vanishing Border: A Photographic Journey along Our Frontier with Mexico (Ashabranner) **28**:10

Vanishing Wildlife of Latin America (McClung) **11**:192

The Vanishment of Thomas Tull (Ahlberg and Ahlberg) **18**:5

VD: The Silent Epidemic (Hyde) **23**:159

VD-STD: The Silent Epidemic (Hyde) **23**:159

Vegetables from Stems and Leaves (Selsam) **1**:166

The Velvet Room (Snyder) **31**:154

The Velveteen Rabbit; Or, How Toys Become Real (Bianco) **19**:50

The Vengeance of the Witch Finder (Bellairs) **37**:27

Venus and Mercury (Nourse) **33**:136

Venus, Near Neighbor of the Sun (Asimov) **12**:59

Veronica (Duvoisin) **23**:101

Veronica and the Birthday Present (Duvoisin) **23**:104

Veronica Ganz (Sachs) **2**:134

Veronica's Smile (Duvoisin) **23**:103

The Very Busy Spider (Carle) **10**:85

Very Far Away from Anywhere Else (*Far Away from Anywhere Else; A Very Long Way from Anywhere Else*) (Le Guin) **3**:123

Very Far from Here (Hamley) **47**:55

Very First Books (Wells) **16**:209, 213

"*Very First Books*" (McNaughton) **54**:55

The Very Hungry Caterpillar (Carle) **10**:72

Very Last First Time (Wallace) **37**:213

A Very Long Tail: A Folding Book (Carle) **10**:76

The Very Long Train: A Folding Book (Carle) **10**:76

A Very Long Way from Anywhere Else (Le Guin) See *Very Far Away from Anywhere Else*

The Very Nice Things (Merrill) **52**:102

A Very Special House (Krauss) **42**:117

A Very Touchy Subject (Strasser) **11**:251

The Very Worst Monster (Hutchins) **20**:153

A Very Young Circus Flyer (Krementz) **5**:154

A Very Young Dancer (Krementz) **5**:151

A Very Young Gymnast (Krementz) **5**:153

Very Young Poets (Brooks) **27**:44-56

A Very Young Rider (Krementz) **5**:152

A Very Young Skater (Krementz) **5**:154

The Vicar of Nibbleswicke (Dahl) **41**:49

The Vicksburg Veteran (Monjo) **2**:126

Victorians Abroad (Goodall) **25**:51

Victory at Valmy (Trease) **42**:184

Victory in the Pacific (Marrin) **53**:81

Victory on Janus (Norton) **50**:145

The View beyond My Father (Allan) **43**:29

The View from Saturday (Konigsburg) **47**:148

Viking's Dawn (Treece) **2**:189

Viking's Sunset (Treece) **2**:189

Village Books (Spier) **5**:228

The Village by the Sea (Fox) **44**:69

The Village of Round and Square Houses (Grifalconi) **35**:74

Village of the Vampire Cat (Namioka) **48**:63

The Village Tree (Yashima) **4**:250

Vim the Rag Mouse (Daly) **41**:53

Vine Clad Hill (Allan) **43**:5

The Vinegar Works: Three Volumes on Moral Instruction (Gorey) **36**:91

The Vingananee and the Tree Toad: A Liberian Tale (Aardema) **17**:7

The Violin Book (Berger) **32**:8

Violins and Shovels: The WPA Arts Projects (Meltzer) **13**:138

Virgil Nosegay and the Cake Hunt (Biegel) **27**:35

Virgil Nosegay and the Hupmobile (Biegel) **27**:36

Virgil Nosegay and the Wellington Boots (Biegel) **27**:36

Virginia's General: Robert E. Lee and the Civil War (Marrin) **53**:93

The Virus Invaders (Nourse) **33**:151

Viruses (Nourse) **33**:139

Viruses: Life's Smallest Enemies (Knight) **38**:125

De vis (Bruna) **7**:49

Visions of America, by the Poets of Our Time (Kherdian) **24**:106

A Visit to William Blake's Inn: Poems for Innocent and Experienced Travelers (Willard) **5**:250

Visiting Pamela (Klein) **19**:91

Visiting the Art Museum (Brown) **29**:13

The Visitor (Heine) **18**:149

The Visitor (Oxenbury) **22**:145

Vitamins (Nourse) **33**:141

The Voice of Liberty: The Story of Emma Lazarus (Merriam) **14**:192

The Voice of the People: American Democracy in Action (Betsy and Giulio Maestro) **45**:90

Vol 714 pour Sydney (Herge) **6**:149

Volcano: The Eruption and Healing of Mount St. Helens (Lauber) **16**:121

Volcanoes (Branley) **13**:51

Volcanoes and Earthquakes (Adler) **27**:16

Volcanoes: Nature's Fireworks (Nixon) **24**:137

The Voyage Begun (Bond) **11**:29

The Voyage of Mael Duin (Dillon) **26**:29

The Voyage of Osiris: A Myth of Ancient Egypt (McDermott) **9**:116

The Voyage of QV 66 (Lively) **7**:162

The Voyage of the Dawn Treader (Lewis) **3**:137; **27**:104-51

The Voyage of the Frog (Paulsen) **54**:95

The Voyagers, Being Legends and Romances of Atlantic Discovery (Colum) **36**:35

The Voyages of Doctor Dolittle (Lofting) **19**:122

Voyages: Poems by Walt Whitman (Hopkins) **44**:96

Vulcan: The Story of a Bald Eagle (McClung) **11**:180

W. E. B. DuBois: A Biography (Hamilton) **1**:106; **26**:149

Wagging Tails: An Album of Dogs (Henry) **4**:112

The Wagon Race (Heine) **18**:149

Wagstaffe the Wind-Up Boy (Needle) **43**:142

Wag-Tail Bess (Flack) **28**:122

Wait for William (Flack) **28**:124

Wait till the Moon Is Full (Brown) **10**:57

Waiting for Anya (Morpurgo) **51**:131

Waiting for the Rain: A Novel of South Africa (Gordon) **27**:91

The Waiting Game (Bunting) **28**:52

Waiting to Waltz: A Childhood (Rylant) **15**:169

Wake Up and Goodnight (Zolotow) **2**:237

Wake Up, City! (Tresselt) **30**:206

Wake Up, Farm! (Tresselt) **30**:205

Walk a Mile and Get Nowhere (Southall) **2**:157

Walk Home Tired, Billy Jenkins (Thomas) **8**:213

A Walk in the Park (Browne) **19**:62

Walk, Rabbit, Walk (McNaughton) **54**:49

Walk Together Children: Black American Spirituals (Bryan) **18**:33

Walk Two Moons (Creech) **42**:41

Walk with Your Eyes (Brown) **12**:107

Walker, the Witch, and the Striped Flying Saucer (Stevenson) **17**:152

The Walking Stones (Hunter) **25**:78

The Walking Stones (Hunter)
See *The Bodach*

Walking through the Dark (Naylor) **17**:51

Walking Up a Rainbow: Being the True Version of the Long and Hazardous Journey of Susan D. Carlisle, Mrs Myrtle Dessery, Drover Bert Pettit, and Cowboy Clay Carmer and Others (Taylor) **30**:193

The Wall (Bunting) **28**:64

Wall Street: The Story of the Stock Exchange (Sterling) **1**:182

Walls: Defenses throughout History (Giblin) **29**:88

Walter, the Lazy Mouse (Flack) **28**:126

The Wanderers (Coatsworth) **2**:63

Wandering Minstrels We: The Story of Gilbert and Sullivan (Lavine) **35**:145

The War and Freddy (Hamley) **47**:63

War and Peas (Foreman) **32**:88

The War and the Protest: Viet Nam (Haskins) **3**:68

War Boy: A Country Childhood (Foreman) **32**:102

War Dog (Treece) **2**:190

War Horse (Morpurgo) **51**:119

The War of Jenkins' Ear (Morpurgo) **51**:136

The War on Villa Street (Mazer) **16**:130

The War on William Street (Ottley) **16**:187

The War with Mr. Wizzle (Korman) **25**:107

War with Old Mouldy! (Ure) **34**:184

The Warding of Witch World (Norton) **50**:163

'Ware Hawk (Norton) **50**:162

Warlock at the Wheel and Other Stories (Jones) **23**:195

The Warlock of Westfall (Fisher) **18**:125

The Warnings (Buffie) **39**:25

The Warrior and the Wise Man (Wisniewski) **51**:191

Warrior Scarlet (Sutcliff) **1**:191; **37**:153

Wart, Son of Toad (Carter) **22**:18

A War-Time Handbook for Young Americans (Leaf) **25**:126

A Was an Angler (Domanska) **40**:54

Washington, D. C.: The Nation's Capital (Epstein and Epstein) **26**:57

The Washington Picture Book (Lenski) **26**:100

Wasteground Circus (Keeping) **34**:101

The Watch House (Westall) **13**:252

Watch Out! A Giant! (Carle) **10**:82

Watch Out for the Chicken Feet in Your Soup (dePaola) **4**:56

Watch Out for the Giant-Killers! (McNaughton) **54**:60

The Watchbirds (Leaf) **25**:125

The Watcher in the Garden (Phipson) **5**:186

The Watcher in the Mist (St. John) **46**:117

The Watchers (Curry) **31**:79

Watchers in the Wild: The New Science of Ethology (Cohen) **3**:43
The Watchers of the Trails: A Book of Animal Life (Roberts) **33**:193
Watching Foxes (Arnosky) **15**:8
Water (Graham) **31**:95
The Water Flowers (Gorey) **36**:103
Water for the World (Branley) **13**:47
Water Girl (Thomas) **19**:221
The Water Horse (King-Smith) **40**:161
Water Music: Poems for Children (Yolen) **44**:208
The Water of Life (Williams) **8**:238
Water on Your Street (Simon) **9**:209
Water Plants (Pringle) **4**:179
Water since the World Began (Lavine) **35**:149
Water to Burn (Epstein and Epstein) **26**:44
Watership Down (Adams) **20**:10-32
Waterslain and Other Poems (Crossley-Holland) **47**:45
Watersmeet (Garden) **51**:71
The Watertower (Crew) **42**:59
A Watery Grave (Corcoran) **50**:30
Watson, the Smartest Dog in the U.S.A. (Kuskin) **4**:139
The Wave (Strasser) **11**:248
A Wave in Her Pocket: Stories from Trinidad (Pinkney) **54**:135
The Wave of the Sea-Wolf (Wisniewski) **51**:198
Waves (Zim) **2**:232
Waving: A Counting Book (Sis) **45**:160
The Way Home (Phipson) **5**:182
The Way Mothers Are (Schlein) **41**:185
The Way of Danger: The Story of Theseus (Serraillier) **2**:143
The Way of the Grizzly (Patent) **19**:164
The Way of the Storyteller (Sawyer) **36**:157
A Way Out of No Way: Writings About Growing Up Black in America (Woodson) **49**:207
The Way over Windle (Allan) **43**:14
The Way Things Are and Other Poems (Livingston) **7**:171
The Way to Sattin Shore (Pearce) **9**:158
Wayside School Is Falling Down (Sacher) **28**:203
We Alcotts: The Life of Louisa May Alcott as Seen Through the Eyes of 'Marmee' (Fisher) **49**:49
We Are Best Friends (Aliki) **9**:29
We Are Mesquakie, We Are One (Irwin) **40**:108
We Can't Sleep (Stevenson) **17**:159
We Danced in Bloomsbury Square (Estoril) **43**:16
We Dickensons: The Life of Emily Dickenson as Seen Through the Eyes of Her Brother Austin (Fisher) **49**:42
We Didn't Mean to Go to Sea (Ransome) **8**:178
We Have Tomorrow (Bontemps) **6**:80
We Hide, You Seek (Aruego) **5**:30
We Interrupt This Semester for an Important Bulletin (Conford) **10**:96
We Live by the River (Lenski) **26**:119
We Live in the Country (Lenski) **26**:121
We Live in the North (Lenski) **26**:122
We Live in the South (Lenski) **26**:116
We Lived in Drumfyvie (Sutcliff) **37**:165
We Love Them (Waddell) **31**:196
We Read: A to Z (Crews) **7**:55
We Went Looking (Fisher) **49**:49
Weasels, Otters, Skunks, and Their Families (Patent) **19**:147
Weather (Pienkowski) **6**:230
The Weather Changes Man (Bova) **3**:36
The Weather Sky (McMillan) **47**:177
The Weathermonger (Dickinson) **29**:37
The Weaver's Gift (Lasky) **11**:115

Web of Traitors: An Adventure Story of Ancient Athens (Trease) **42**:182
Der Wecker (Heine) **18**:149
The Wedding Ghost (Garfield) **21**:120
The Wedding Ghost (Keeping) **34**:107
The Wednesday Surprise (Bunting) **28**:63
Wee Gillis (Leaf) **25**:124
A Weed Is a Flower: The Life of George Washington Carver (Aliki) **9**:18
Weekend (Pike) **29**:171
A Weekend with Wendell (Henkes) **23**:127
Weetzie Bat (Block) **33**:30
Weight and Weightlessness (Branley) **13**:38
Weird and Wacky Inventions (Murphy) **53**:100
The Weird Disappearance of Jordan Hall (Gaberman) **33**:15
The Weirdo (Taylor) **30**:196
The Weirdstone: A Tale of Aderley (Garner) **20**:100
The Weirdstone of Brisingamen: A Tale of Aderley (Garner) **20**:100
Welcome Home! (Bemelmans) **6**:75
Welcome Is a Wonderful Word (Fujikawa) **25**:40
Welcome to the Green House (Yolen) **44**:199
Welcome, Twins (Khalsa) **30**:144
The Well (Kemp) **29**:119
The Well-Mannered Balloon (Willard) **5**:246
The Well-Wishers (Eager) **43**:88
We're Going on a Bear Hunt (Rosen) **45**:138
Het wereldje van Beer Ligthart (Haar) **15**:116
The Werewolf Family (Gantos) **18**:142
Werewolves (Garden) **51**:65
West to a Land of Plenty: The Diary of Teresa Angelino Viscardi (Murphy) **53**:117
West with the White Chiefs (Harris) **43**:78
Western Wind (Fox) **44**:76
The Westing Game (Raskin) **12**:225
Westmark (Alexander) **5**:24
Westward to Vinland (Treece) **2**:190
A Wet and Sandy Day (Ryder) **37**:85
Whales: Giants of the Deep (Patent) **19**:160
Whales, the Nomads of the Sea (Sattler) **24**:221
Whalesinger (Katz) **45**:36
What a Fine Day For... (Krauss) **42**:128
What a Good Lunch! Eating (Watanabe) **8**:216
What about Grandma? (Irwin) **40**:110
What Alvin Wanted (Keller) **45**:53
What Am I? Looking Through Shapes at Apples and Grapes (Leo and Diane Dillon) **44**:48
What Bounces? (Duke) **51**:47
What Can You Do with a Pocket? (Merriam) **14**:194
What Can You Do with a Word? (Williams) **8**:227
What Color Is Love? (Anglund) **1**:21
What Did You Bring Me? (Kuskin) **4**:141
What Did You Leave Behind? (Tresselt) **30**:215
What Do I Do Now? Talking about Teenage Pregnancy (Kuklin) **51**:106
What Do People Do All Day? (Scarry) **41**:162
What Do You Call a Dumb Bunny? And Other Rabbit Riddles, Games, Jokes, and Cartoons (Brown) **29**:10
What Do You Do When Your Mouth Won't Open? (Pfeffer) **11**:201
What Do You See? (Domanska) **40**:44
What Do You Think? An Introduction to Public Opinion: How It Forms, Functions, and Affects Our Lives (Schwartz) **3**:191
What Do You Want to Know about Guppies? (Simon) **9**:211
What Does It Do and How Does It Work? (Hoban) **3**:83
What Happened at Rita's Party (Breinburg) **31**:68
What Happened in Marston (Garden) **51**:64

What Happens Next? (Domanska) **40**:51
What Happens to a Hamburger (Showers) **6**:245
What Holds It Together (Weiss) **4**:228
What I Did for Roman (Conrad) **18**:88
What I Did Last Summer (Prelutsky) **13**:172
What I Really Think of You (Kerr) **29**:152
What I'd Like to Be (Munari) **9**:125
What If? (Minarik) **33**:127
What If They Saw Me Now? (Ure) **34**:172
What Is a Color? (Provensen and Provensen) **11**:209
What Is a Man? (Krahn) **3**:106
What Is It? (Hoban) **13**:109
What Is Right for Tulip (Duvoisin) **23**:104
What It's All About (Klein) **2**:101
What Jim Knew (Hoberman) **22**:109
What Made You You? (Bendick) **5**:44
What Makes a Boat Float? (Corbett) **1**:47
What Makes a Light Go On? (Corbett) **1**:48
What Makes a Plane Fly? (Corbett) **1**:48
What Makes Day and Night (Branley) **13**:29
What Makes Me Feel This Way? Growing Up with Human Emotions (LeShan) **6**:188
What Makes the Sun Shine? (Asimov) **12**:46
What Next, Baby Bear! (Murphy) **39**:172
What Shall We Do with the Land? (Pringle) **4**:186
What the Dickens! (Curry) **31**:88
What the Gulls Were Singing (Naylor) **17**:49
What the Moon Is Like (Branley) **13**:31
What the Moon Saw (Wildsmith) **52**:183
What the Neighbours Did and Other Stories (Pearce) **9**:154
What Time is it Around the World (Baumann) **35**:55
What to Do about Molly (Flack) **28**:125
What to Do: Everyday Guides for Everyone (Bendick) **5**:41
What Would a Guinea Pig Do? (Duke) **51**:48
What You Don't Know Can Kill You (Gaberman) **33**:18
Whatever Happened to Beverly Bigler's Brithday? (Williams) **48**:197
Whatever Next! (Murphy) **39**:172
Whatever Words You Want to Hear (Pfeffer) **11**:198
What's Behind the Word (Epstein and Epstein) **26**:67
What's Best for You (Gaberman) **33**:9
What's for Lunch? (Carle) **10**:85
What's for Lunch? The Eating Habits of Seashore Creatures (Epstein and Epstein) **26**:70
What's Fun Without a Friend (Iwasaki) **18**:155
What's Going to Happen to Me? When Parents Separate or Divorce (LeShan) **6**:190
What's Happening to our Weather? (Cohen) **43**:39
What's Hatching Out of That Egg? (Lauber) **16**:119
What's in Fox's Sack? (Galdone) **16**:104
What's So Funny, Ketu? A Nuer Tale (Aardema) **17**:6
What's the Big Idea, Ben Franklin? (Fritz) **14**:113
What's the Matter with Carruthers? A Bedtime Story (Marshall) **21**:168
What's Under My Bed? (Stevenson) **17**:160
What's Wrong with Being a Skunk? (Schlein) **41**:185
Wheat: The Golden Harvest (Patent) **19**:165
Wheel on the Chimney (Brown) **10**:64
The Wheel on the School (DeJong) **1**:61
Wheels (Graham) **31**:95
Wheels: A Pictorial History (Tunis) **2**:194
The Wheels on the Bus (Kovalski) **34**:112
When Birds Could Talk and Bats Could Sing: The Adventures of Bruh Sparrow, Sis Wren, and Their Friends (Moser) **49**:191

Title Index

When Cats Dream (Pilkey) **48**:103
When Clay Sings (Baylor) **3**:17
When Dad Felt Bad (Causley) **30**:39
When Did You Last Wash Your Feet? (Rosen) **45**:135
When Everyone Was Fast Asleep (dePaola) **4**:57
When Francie Was Sick (Keller) **45**:48
When I Am Old with You (Johnson) **33**:95
When I Dance: Poems (Berry) **22**:10
When I Grow Up (Lenski) **26**:122
When I Have a Little Girl (Zolotow) **2**:238
When I Have a Son (Zolotow) **2**:238
When I Left My Village (Pinkney) **54**:146
When I See My Dentist (Kuklin) **51**:101
When I See My Doctor (Kuklin) **51**:101
When I Walk I Change the Earth (Krauss) **42**:130
When I Was a Boy (Kaestner) **4**:126
When I Was a Little Boy (Kaestner) **4**:126
When I Was Nine (Stevenson) **17**:165
When I Was Young in the Mountains (Rylant) **15**:168
When I'm Big (Bruna) **7**:52
When It Comes to Bugs (Fisher) **49**:59
When No One Was Looking (Wells) **16**:211
When She Hollers (Bone) **48**:181
When Shlemiel Went to Warsaw, and Other Stories (Singer) **1**:176
When Someone You Know Is Gay (Cohen) **43**:51
When the City Stopped (Phipson) **5**:185
When the Phone Rang (Mazer) **16**:132
When the Pie Was Opened (Little) **4**:148
When the Rattlesnake Sounds (Childress) **14**:92
When the Siren Wailed (Streatfeild) **17**:199
When the Sirens Wailed (Streatfeild) **17**:199
When the Tide Goes Far Out (Milne and Milne) **22**:121
When the Water Closes over My Head (Napoli) **51**:158
When the Wind Blew (Brown) **10**:47
When the Wind Blows (Briggs) **10**:30
When the Wind Changed (Park) **51**:177
When the Wind Stops (Zolotow) **2**:238
When the Woods Hum (Ryder) **37**:96
When Thunders Spoke (Sneve) **2**:145
When We First Met (Mazer) **23**:228
When We Went to the Park (Hughes) **15**:131
When We Were Very Young (Milne) **26**:126
When Will the World Be Mine? (Schlein) **41**:176
When Willard Met Babe Ruth (Moser) **49**:192
When Winter Comes (Freedman) **20**:81
When You Were a Baby (Jonas) **12**:172
Where Are You, Ernest and Celestine? (Vincent) **13**:221
Where Butterflies Grow (Ryder) **37**:94
Where Can It Be? (Jonas) **12**:178
Where Do You Think You're Going, Christopher Columbus? (Fritz) **14**:115
Where Does Everyone Go? (Fisher) **49**:37
Where Does the Day Go? (Myers) **4**:155
Where Does the Garbage Go? (Showers) **6**:245
Where Does the Sun Go at Night? (Ginsburg) **45**:15
Where Does the Trail Lead? (Pinkney) **54**:136
Where Have You Been? (Brown) **10**:61
Where Is Everybody? (Charlip) **8**:26
Where Is It? (Hoban) **13**:103
Where Is My Friend? (Pfister) **42**:133
Where Is My Friend? A Word Concept Book (Betsy and Giulio Maestro) **45**:66
Where is Sarah? (Graham) **31**:92
Where the Bald Eagles Gather (Patent) **19**:159
Where the Forest Meets the Sea (Baker) **28**:21

Where the Lilies Bloom (Cleaver and Cleaver) **6**:103
Where the River Begins (Locker) **14**:157
Where the Sidewalk Ends (Silverstein) **5**:210
Where the Wild Geese Go (Pierce) **20**:184
Where the Wild Things Are (Sendak) **1**:172; **17**:112
Where the Winds Never Blew and the Cocks Never Crew (Colum) **36**:44
Where There's a Will, There's a Wag (Singer) **48**:130
Where Was Patrick Henry on the 29th of May? (Fritz) **2**:81
Where Wild Willie (Adoff) **7**:34
Where'd You Get the Gun, Bill? (Gaberman) **33**:17
Where's My Baby? (Rey) **5**:195
Where's My Daddy? (Watanabe) **8**:217
Where's Spot? (Hill) **13**:91
Where's the Baby? (Hutchins) **20**:154
Where's Waldo? (Handford) **22**:73
Where's Wally (Handford) **22**:73
Where's Wally Now? (Handford) **22**:74
Wherever Home Begins: 100 Contemporary Poems (Janeczko) **47**:116
Which Horse Is William? (Kuskin) **4**:136
Which Way Freedom? (Hansen) **21**:151
While I Sleep (Calhoun) **42**:33
The Whingdingdilly (Peet) **12**:199
The Whipping Boy (Fleischman) **15**:112
The Whipping Boy (Sis) **45**:159
Whiskers, Once and Always (Orgel) **48**:89
The Whisky Rebellion, 1794: Revolt in Western Pennsylvania Threatens American Unity (Knight) **38**:108
A Whisper of Lace (Clarke) **28**:87
Whisper of the Cat (St. John) **46**:121
The Whispering Knights (Lively) **7**:152
The Whispering Mountain (Aiken) **1**:8
Whispers and Other Poems (Livingston) **7**:167
Whispers from the Dead (Nixon) **24**:153
Whistle for the Train (Brown) **10**:66
Whistle for Willie (Keats) **1**:118; **35**:130
The White Archer: An Eskimo Legend (Houston) **3**:87
White Bear, Ice Bear (Ryder) **37**:91
White Boots (Streatfeild) **17**:191
White Boots (Streatfeild)
  See *Skating Shoes*
The White Cat: An Old French Fairy Tale (San Souci) **43**:185
The White Dragon (McCaffrey) **49**:143
The White Elephant (Clarke) **28**:73
The White Goose (Tudor) **13**:192
The White Horse Gang (Bawden) **2**:14; **51**:14
The White Horse of Zennor: and Other Stories from Below the Eagle's Nest (Morpurgo) **51**:120
The White Marble (Zolotow) **2**:239
The White Mountains (Christopher) **2**:43
The White Mountains Trilogy (Christopher) **2**:43
White Peak Farm (Doherty) **21**:56
A White Romance (Hamilton) **40**:74
The White Room (Coatsworth) **2**:64
The White Sea Horse (Cresswell) **18**:98
White Serpent Castle (Namioka) **48**:62
The White Shadow (Guillot) **22**:62
White Snow, Bright Snow (Duvoisin) **23**:92
White Snow, Bright Snow (Tresselt) **30**:201
The White Sparrow (Colum) **36**:40
The White Stag (Seredy) **10**:173
White Stallion of Lipizza (Henry) **4**:114
The White Stone in the Castle Wall (Oberman) **54**:77
White Witch of Kynance (Calhoun) **42**:16

Whizz! (Domanska) **40**:44
Whizz! (Lear) **1**:128
Who Am I Anyway? (Corcoran) **50**:33
Who are the Handicapped? (Haskins) **39**:34
Who Calls from Afar? (Brinsmead) **47**:11
Who Cares? I Do (Leaf) **25**:135
Who Discovered America? Settlers and Explorers of the New World Before the Time of Columbus (Lauber) **16**:115
Who Drew on the Baby's Head (Rosen) **45**:143
Who Got Rid of Angus Flint? (Jones) **23**:188
Who Has a Secret (McGovern) **50**:110
Who Has the Lucky-Duck in Class 4-B? (Gaberman) **33**:12
Who I Am (Lester) **2**:115
Who Is Bugs Potter? (Korman) **25**:105
Who is Frances Rain? (Buffie) **39**:15
Who Killed Mr. Chippendale? A Mystery in Poems (Glenn) **51**:91
Who Look at Me (Jordan) **10**:115
Who Needs Holes? (Epstein and Epstein) **26**:62
Who Owns the Moon? (Levitin) **53**:58
Who Put That Hair in My Toothbrush? (Spinelli) **26**:202
Who Really Killed Cock Robin? (George) **1**:94
Who, Said Sue, Said Whoo? (Raskin) **1**:157
Who Sank the Boat? (Allen) **44**:6
Who Says You Can't? (Epstein and Epstein) **26**:61
Who Stole the Pie? (McNaughton) **54**:56
Who Stole the Wizard of Oz? (Avi) **24**:9
Who Will Comfort Toffle? (Jansson) **2**:95
Whodunnit? (Cresswell) **18**:112
The Whole World of Hands (Berger) **32**:27
Whooping Crane (McClung) **11**:181
Whoppers: Tall Tales and Other Lies (Schwartz) **3**:192
Who's a Clever Baby Then? (McKee) **38**:178
Who's Been Sleeping in My Porridge?: A Book of Silly Poems and Pictures (McNaughton) **54**:59
Who's Hu? (Namioka) **48**:64
Who's in Rabbit's House? A Masai Tale (Aardema) **17**:5
Who's in Rabbit's House? A Masai Tale (Leo and Diane Dillon) **44**:32
Who's in the Egg? (Provensen and Provensen) **11**:210
Who's Out There? The Search for Extraterrestrial Life (Aylesworth) **6**:51
Who's Seen the Scissors? (Krahn) **3**:106
Who's That Banging On the Ceiling?: A Multi-story Story (McNaughton) **54**:62
Who's That Stepping on Plymouth Rock (Fritz) **2**:82
Who's There? Open the Door! (Munari) **9**:124
Whose Furry Nose? Australian Animals You'd Like to Meet (Drescher) **20**:60
Whose Scaly Tail? African Animals You'd Like to Meet (Drescher) **20**:60
Whose Town? (Graham) **10**:107
Whose Turtle? (Orgel) **48**:77
Why? A Books of Reasons (Adler) **27**:15
Why Can't I? (Bendick) **5**:43
Why Can't I Be William? (Conford) **10**:90
Why Don't You Get a Horse, Sam Adams? (Fritz) **2**:82
Why I Cough, Sneeze, Shiver, Hiccup, and Yawn (Berger) **32**:29
Why It's a Holiday (McGovern) **50**:110
Why Me? (Conford) **10**:100
Why Mosquitoes Buzz in People's Ears: A West African Tale (Aardema) **17**:4

Why Mosquitoes Buzz in People's Ears: A West African Tale (Leo and Diane Dillon) **44**:25
Why Noah Chose the Dove (Singer) **1**:176
Why So Much Noise? (Domanska) **40**:37
Why the Sun and Moon Live in the Sky (Daly) **41**:63
Why the Tides Ebb and Flow (Brown) **29**:6
Why the Whales Came (Morpurgo) **51**:123
Why Things Change: The Story of Evolution (Bendick) **5**:46
The Whys and Wherefores of Littabelle Lee (Cleaver and Cleaver) **6**:108
The Wicked City (Singer) **1**:176
The Wicked Enchantment (Benary-Isbert) **12**:74
The Wicked One (Hunter) **25**:86
The Wicked Tricks of Till Owlyglass (Rosen) **45**:139
The Wicked Tricks of Tyl Uilenspiegel (Williams) **8**:236
Wide Awake and Other Poems (Livingston) **7**:167
The Wider Heart (St. John) **46**:98
Wiggle to the Laundromat (Lee) **3**:116
The Wigmakers (Fisher) **18**:122
Wigwam in the City (Smucker) **10**:189
The Wild (Graham) **31**:96
Wild and Woolly Mammoths (Aliki) **9**:25
The Wild Angel (Spykman) **35**:218
The Wild Baby (Lindgren) **20**:156
The Wild Baby Gets a Puppy (Lindgren) **20**:158
Wild Baby Goes to Sea (Lindgren) **20**:157
The Wild Baby's Boat Trip (Lindgren) **20**:157
The Wild Baby's Dog (Lindgren) **20**:158
Wild Cat (Peck) **45**:105
The Wild Christmas Reindeer (Brett) **27**:43
Wild Foods: A Beginner's Guide to Identifying, Harvesting, and Cooking Safe and Tasty Plants from the Outdoors (Pringle) **4**:183
The Wild Horses (Bunting) **28**:44
The Wild Hunt (Yolen) **44**:206
The Wild Hunt of Hagworthy (Lively) **7**:153
The Wild Hunt of the Ghost Hounds (Lively) **7**:153
Wild in the World (Donovan) **3**:54
Wild Jack (Christopher) **2**:43
The Wild Little House (Dillon) **26**:21
Wild Pitch (Christopher) **33**:55
Wild Robin (Jeffers) **30**:131
The Wild Swans (Jeffers) **30**:135
The Wild Washerwomen: A New Folk Tale (Blake) **31**:22
The Wild Washerwomen: A New Folk Tale (Yeoman) **46**:179
The Wild White Stallion (Guillot) **22**:65
Wild Wild Sunflower Child Anna (Pinkney) **43**:161
Wild Wood (Needle) **43**:135
Wildcat under Glass (Zei) **6**:260
The Wildest Horse Race in the World (Henry) **4**:113
Wildfire (Clark) **30**:59
The Wildman (Crossley-Holland) **47**:34
The Wildman (Keeping) **34**:102
Wiley and the Hairy Man (Pinkney) **54**:145
Wiley and the Hairy Man: Adapted from an American Folktale (Bang) **8**:19
Wilfred the Rat (Stevenson) **17**:153
Wilfred's Wolf (Nimmo) **44**:154
Wilfrid Gordon McDonald Partridge (Fox) **23**:114
Wilkie's World (Hurd and Hurd) **49**:128
Wilkin's Tooth (Witch's Business) (Jones) **23**:182
Will It Rain? (Keller) **45**:47
Will You Be My Friend (Iwasaki) **18**:154
Will You Be My Posslq? (Bunting) **28**:61
Will You Please Feed Our Cat? (Stevenson) **17**:167
Will You Sign Here, John Hancock? (Fritz) **14**:112

Will You Take Me to Town on Strawberry Day? (Singer) **48**:122
Willaby (Isadora) **7**:103
William and His Kitten (Flack) **28**:127
William and Mary: A Story (Farmer) **8**:85
William and the Good Old Days (Greenfield) **38**:95
William Crawford Gorgas: Tropic Fever Fighter (Epstein and Epstein) **26**:49
William in Love (Ure) **34**:190
William Tell (Bawden) **51**:31
William's Doll (Zolotow) **2**:239
Willie Bea and the Time the Martians Landed (Hamilton) **11**:90
Willie Blows a Mean Horn (Thomas) **8**:214
Willie's Adventures: Three Stories (Brown) **10**:63
Willie's Farm (Hurd and Hurd) **49**:121
Willie's Fire-Engine (Keeping) **34**:105
Willie's Not the Hugging Kind (Cummings) **48**:50
Willie's Walk to Grandmama (Brown) **10**:52
Will's Quill (Freeman) **30**:79
Willy and His Wheel Wagon (Gibbons) **8**:88
Willy Is My Brother (Parish) **22**:155
Willy Nilly (Gay) **27**:89
Willy Nilly: A Children's Story for Narrator and Orchestra (Flack) **28**:125
Willy the Champ (Browne) **19**:69
Willy the Wimp (Browne) **19**:68
Willy's Raiders (Gantos) **18**:142
Wilma Unlimited: How Wilma Rudolph Became the World's Fastest Woman (Krull) **44**:112
Wilson's World (Hurd and Hurd) **49**:128
The Wind and Peter (Tresselt) **30**:202
The Wind between the Stars (Mahy) **7**:184
The Wind Blew (Hutchins) **20**:147
The Wind Eye (Westall) **13**:252
The Wind Has Wings: Poems from Canada (Cleaver) **13**:64
A Wind in the Door (L'Engle) **1**:132; **14**:149
The Wind in the Willows (Grahame) **5**:128
The Wind of Chance (Guillot) **22**:57
The Windmill at Magpie Creek (Mattingley) **24**:122
Window (Baker) **28**:22
Window on the Wind (Scott) **20**:199
Window Wishing (Caines) **24**:63
The Winds of Time (Corcoran) **50**:18
The Winds That Come from Far Away, and Other Poems (Minarik) **33**:126
The Windswept City: A Novel of the Trojan War (Treece) **2**:191
The Wing on a Flea: A Book about Shapes (Emberley) **5**:90
Wing T Fullback (Christopher) **33**:38
The Winged Colt of Casa Mia (Byars) **1**:37
Wingman (Pinkwater) **4**:163
Wingman on Ice (Christopher) **33**:40
Wings: A Tale of Two Chickens (Marshall) **21**:181
Wings for Icarus (Baumann) **35**:56
Wings for Per (d'Aulaire and d'Aulaire) **21**:48
Wings in the Woods (McClung) **11**:178
The Wings of a Falcon (Voigt) **48**:179
Winnie Mandela: Life of Struggle (Haskins) **39**:55
Winnie Mandela: The Soul of South Africa (Meltzer) **13**:151
Winnie-the-Pooh (Milne) **26**:126
Winning (Brancato) **32**:70
Winston Churchill: Lion of Britain (Epstein and Epstein) **26**:63
Winston, Newton, Elton, and Ed (Stevenson) **17**:155
Winter (McNaughton) **54**:55
Winter Cottage (Brink) **30**:16

Winter Holiday (Ransome) **8**:175
The Winter Noisy Book (Brown) **10**:56
The Winter of the Birds (Cresswell) **18**:107
The Winter Room (Paulsen) **54**:96
Winter Story (Barklem) **31**:2
Winter Tales from Poland (Wojciechowska) **1**:200
Winter Whale (Ryder) **37**:98
The Winter Wren (Cole) **18**:82
Winterbound (Bianco) **19**:55
Winterkill (Paulsen) **19**:169
Winter's Coming (Bunting) **28**:46
Winter's Tales (Foreman) **32**:91
Winterthing (Aiken) **1**:8
Wintle's Wonders (Dancing Shoes) (Streatfeild) **17**:193
Wiplala (Schmidt) **22**:221
Wir Pfeifen auf den Gurkenkönig (Noestlinger) **12**:184
The Wise Fool (Galdone) **16**:93
The Wise Men on the Mountain (Dillon) **26**:29
A Wise Monkey Tale (Betsy and Giulio Maestro) **45**:65
The Wish Card Ran Out! (Stevenson) **17**:157
Wish on a Unicorn (Hesse) **54**:33
The Wish Workers (Aliki) **9**:17
The Wishing Pool (Leaf) **25**:134
The Wishing Star (St. John) **46**:98
Witch (Pike) **29**:174
Witch Baby (Block) **33**:31
The Witch Family (Estes) **2**:76
The Witch Herself (Naylor) **17**:54
The Witch in the Cherry Tree (Mahy) **7**:182
The Witch of Blackbird Pond (Speare) **8**:205
The Witch of Hissing Hill (Calhoun) **42**:9
Witch Water (Naylor) **17**:52
Witch Week (Jones) **23**:192
The Witch Who Lost Her Shadow (Calhoun) **42**:26
The Witch Who Wasn't (Yolen) **4**:256
Witchcraft, Mysticism, and Magic in the Black World (Haskins) **3**:69
Witchery Hill (Katz) **45**:32
Witches (Blumberg) **21**:25
The Witches (Dahl) **7**:83
Witches (Garden) **51**:65
The Witches and the Singing Mice: A Celtic Tale (Nimmo) **44**:150
Witches Four (Brown) **29**:6
The Witches of Worm (Snyder) **31**:159
The Witch-Finder (Rayner) **41**:120
The Witch's Brat (Sutcliff) **1**:191; **37**:162
Witch's Business (Jones) **23**:182
Witch's Business (Jones)
    See *Wilkin's Tooth*
The Witch's Daughter (Bawden) **2**:15; **51**:16
The Witch's Pig: A Cornish Folktale (Calhoun) **42**:23
Witch's Sister (Naylor) **17**:51
The Witch's Tears (Nimmo) **44**:155
Witcracks: Jokes and Jests from American Folklore (Schwartz) **3**:192
With Love, at Christmas (Fox) **23**:116
With You and Without You (Martin) **32**:201
Wizard Crystal (Pinkwater) **4**:162
The Wizard in the Tree (Alexander) **1**:18; **5**:23
The Wizard in the Woods (Ure) **34**:189
Wizard in Wonderland (Ure) **34**:192
The Wizard Islands (Yolen) **4**:260
A Wizard of Earthsea (Le Guin) **3**:124; **28**:144-88
The Wizard of Op (Emberley) **5**:99
The Wizard of Oz (Baum) **15**:42
The Wizard of Washington Square (Yolen) **4**:258
Wizard's Hall (Yolen) **44**:193

Wobble Pop (Burningham) **9**:51

Wobble, the Witch Cat (Calhoun) **42**:6

Woe Is Moe (Stanley) **46**:154

Wolf (Cross) **28**:96

Wolf at the Door (Corcoran) **50**:41

Wolf by the Ears (Rinaldi) **46**:82

Wolf Rider: A Tale of Terror (Avi) **24**:12

Wolf Run: A Caribou Eskimo Tale (Houston) **3**:88

The Wolves of Aam (Curry) **31**:83

The Wolves of Willoughby Chase (Aiken) **1**:8

The Woman in Your Life (Corcoran) **50**:32

The Woman Who Loved Reindeer (Pierce) **20**:184

The Wonder City: A Picture Book of New York (Lenski) **26**:99

Wonder Kid Meets the Evil Lunch Snatcher (Duncan) **29**:79

Wonder Wheels (Hopkins) **44**:90

Wonder-Fish from the Sea (Tresselt) **30**:213

The Wonderful Adventures of Nils (Lagerlof) **7**:110

The Wonderful Dragon of Timlin (dePaola) **4**:53

The Wonderful Farm (Ayme) **25**:1

The Wonderful Flight to the Mushroom Planet (Cameron) **1**:42

Wonderful Story Book (Brown) **10**:56

The Wonderful Story of Henry Sugar and Six More (Dahl) **7**:75

The Wonderful Wizard of Oz (Baum) **15**:42

The Wonderful Wizard of Oz (Denslow) **15**:100

Wonders of Badgers (Lavine) **35**:169

Wonders of Camels (Lavine) **35**:159

Wonders of Coyotes (Lavine) **35**:168

Wonders of Donkeys (Lavine) **35**:158

Wonders of Draft Horses (Lavine) **35**:165

Wonders of Flightless Birds (Lavine) **35**:162

Wonders of Foxes (Lavine) **35**:170

Wonders of Giraffes (Lavine) **35**:170

Wonders of Goats (Lavine) **35**:160

Wonders of Herbs (Lavine) **35**:157

Wonders of Hippos (Lavine) **35**:166

Wonders of Hummingbirds (Simon) **39**:183

Wonders of Marsupials (Lavine) **35**:159

Wonders of Mice (Lavine) **35**:161

Wonders of Mules (Lavine) **35**:164

Wonders of Peacocks (Lavine) **35**:163

The Wonders of Physics: An Introduction to the Physical World (Adler) **27**:20

Wonders of Pigs (Lavine) **35**:162

Wonders of Ponies (Lavine) **35**:161

Wonders of Rhinos (Lavine) **35**:164

Wonders of Sheep (Lavine) **35**:165

Wonders of Speech (Silverstein and Silverstein) **25**:224

Wonders of Terrariums (Lavine) **35**:158

Wonders of the Ant Hill (Lavine) **35**:147

Wonders of the Aquarium (Lavine) **35**:146

Wonders of the Bat World (Lavine) **35**:151

Wonders of the Beetle World (Lavine) **35**:148

Wonders of the Bison World (Lavine) **35**:156

Wonders of the Butterfly World (Simon) **39**:183

Wonders of the Cactus World (Lavine) **35**:154

Wonders of the Eagle World (Lavine) **35**:154

Wonders of the Fly World (Lavine) **35**:151

Wonders of the Hawk World (Lavine) **35**:152

Wonders of the Hive (Lavine) **35**:147

Wonders of the Owl World (Lavine) **35**:152

Wonders of the Spider World (Lavine) **35**:150

Wonders of the World of Horses (Lavine) **35**:152

Wonders of Tigers (Lavine) **35**:172

Wonders of Turkeys (Lavine) **35**:167

Wonders of Woodchucks (Lavine) **35**:166

Won't Know Till I Get There (Myers) **16**:139

Won't Somebody Play with Me? (Kellogg) **6**:171

The Wood Street Group (Allan) **43**:18

The Wood Street Rivals (Allan) **43**:21

The Wood Street Secret (Allan) **43**:18

Wooden Ship (Adkins) **7**:23

Woodsedge and Other Tales (Bedard) **35**:59

Woodsong (Paulsen) **54**:98

A Word about Horses (Ottley) **16**:188

A Word from Our Sponsor: Or, My Friend Alfred (Gaberman) **33**:4

A Word or Two with You: New Rhymes for Young Readers (Merriam) **14**:201

Word to Caesar (Trease) **42**:183

Wordhoard: Anglo-Saxon Stories (Crossley-Holland) **47**:26

Wordhoard: Anglo-Saxon Stories (Walsh) **2**:201

Words by Heart (Sebestyen) **17**:86

Words from History (Asimov) **12**:43

Words from the Exodus (Asimov) **12**:37

Words from the Myths (Asimov) **12**:35

Words in Genesis (Asimov) **12**:36

Words of Science, and the History behind Them (Asimov) **12**:33

Words on the Map (Asimov) **12**:36

Workin' for Peanuts (Strasser) **11**:250

Working (Oxenbury) **22**:141

Working with Cardboard and Paper (Weiss) **4**:229

Worksong (Paulsen) **54**:121

A World in a Drop of Water (Silverstein and Silverstein) **25**:201

The World in the Candy Egg (Tresselt) **30**:209

The World is Not Flat (Hurd) **49**:114

The World is Round (Hurd) **49**:114

The World of Ben Lighthart (Haar) **15**:116

The World of Bionics (Silverstein and Silverstein) **25**:218

The World of Captain John Smith, 1580-1631 (Foster) **7**:98

The World of Christopher Robin (Milne) **1**:143

The World of Columbus and Sons (Foster) **7**:98

The World of Dance (Berger) **32**:22

World of Our Fathers: The Jews of Eastern Europe (Meltzer) **13**:133

A World of Poetry (Rosen) **45**:142

The World of Pooh (Milne) **1**:143

World of the Brain (Silverstein and Silverstein) **25**:210

The World of the Pharaohs (Baumann) **35**:43

The World of UFOs (Cohen) **43**:37

The World of William Penn (Foster) **7**:100

The World of Worms (Patent) **19**:153

World on a String: The Story of Kites (Yolen) **4**:258

World Problems (Gordon) **27**:90

World Song (Clark) **16**:81

World War Won (Pilkey) **48**:100

Worlds Apart (Murphy) **39**:174

The World's Best Karlson (Lindgren) **39**:159

World's End Was Home (Chauncy) **6**:89

The World's Greatest Freak Show (Raskin) **1**:157

The World's Most Famous Ghosts (Cohen) **43**:38

Worm Weather (Mattingley) **24**:123

The Worms of Kukumlina (Pinkwater) **4**:171

A Worm's Tale (Lindgren) **20**:158

Worse than Rotten, Ralph (Gantos) **18**:141

Worse than Willy! (Stevenson) **17**:161

The Worst Person in the World (Stevenson) **17**:154

The Worst Person in the World at Crab Beach (Stevenson) **17**:168

The Worst Witch (Murphy) **39**:168

The Worst Witch All at Sea (Murphy) **39**:179

The Worst Witch Strikes Again (Murphy) **39**:168

Would You Rather... (Burningham) **9**:49

Wouldn't You Like to Know (Rosen) **45**:129

Wraiths of Time (Norton) **50**:159

The Wreck of the Wild Wave (Hurd) **49**:116

The Wreck of the Zanzibar (Morpurgo) **51**:144

The Wreck of the Zephyr (Van Allsburg) **13**:207

A Wrinkle in Time (L'Engle) **1**:133; **14**:142

The Writing Bug (Hopkins) **44**:98

The Writing on the Wall (Reid Banks) **24**:195

The Wrong Number (Stine) **37**:112

The Wuggie Norple Story (Pinkwater) **4**:170

Wulf (Crossley-Holland) **47**:47

The Wump World (Peet) **12**:200

The X Factor (Norton) **50**:143

Yang the Third and Her Impossible Family (Namioka) **48**:67

Yang the Youngest and His Terrible Ear (Namioka) **48**:65

The Yangtze River (Rau) **8**:186

The Year at Maple Hill Farm (Provensen and Provensen) **11**:213

The Year Mom Won the Pennant (Christopher) **33**:43

Year of Columbus, 1492 (Foster) **7**:99

Year of Impossible Goodbyes (Choi) **53**:42

Year of Independence, 1776 (Foster) **7**:99

A Year of Japanese Festivals (Epstein and Epstein) **26**:65

The Year of Jubilo (Sawyer) **36**:155

Year of Lincoln, 1861 (Foster) **7**:100

The Year of Sweet Senior Insanity (Levitin) **53**:64

The Year of the Christmas Dragon (Sawyer) **36**:163

The Year of the Currawong (Spence) **26**:192

The Year of the Gopher (Naylor) **17**:61

The Year of the Horseless Carriage, 1801 (Foster) **7**:101

The Year of the Lucy (McCaffrey) **49**:147

The Year of the Panda (Schlein) **41**:195

Year of the Pilgrims, 1620 (Foster) **7**:99

Year Walk (Clark) **16**:84

Yeck Eck (Ness) **6**:208

Yeh-Shen: A Cinderella Story from China (Young) **27**:219

Yellow and Pink (Steig) **15**:198

The Yellow Auto Named Ferdinand (Janosch) **26**:76

Yellow Bird and Me (Hansen) **21**:151

Yellow Butter, Purple Jelly, Red Jam, Black Bread: Poems (Hoberman) **22**:113

The Yellow Shop (Field) **21**:75

The Yellow Umbrella (Drescher) **20**:62

Yertle the Turtle and Other Stories (Dr. Seuss) **1**:88

Yesterday's Child (Levitin) **53**:77

Yesterday's Island (Bunting) **28**:49

Yobgorgle: Mystery Monster of Lake Ontario (Pinkwater) **4**:170

Yossel Zissel and the Wisdom of Chelm (Schwartz) **25**:193

You Are the General (Aaseng) **54**:19

You Are the General II: 1800-1899 (Aaseng) **54**:23

You Are the Juror (Aaseng) **54**:25

You Are the President (Aaseng) **54**:20

You Are the Senator (Aaseng) **54**:24

You Bet Your Britches, Claude (Nixon) **24**:154

You Can Pick Me Up at Peggy's Cove (Doyle) **22**:30

You Can't Catch Me! (Rosen) **45**:130

You Can't Make a Move without Your Muscles (Showers) **6**:248

You Can't Pet a Possum (Bontemps) **6**:79

You Have to Draw the Line Somewhere (Harris) **24**:77

You Just Don't Listen! (McBratney) **44**:124

You Know Who (Ciardi) **19**:78

You Lucky Duck! (McCully) **46**:62

You Never Can Tell (Conford) **10**:100

You Never Knew Her as I Did! (Hunter) **25**:87

You Put Up with Me, I'll Put Up with You (Corcoran) **50**:34
You Read to Me, I'll Read to You (Ciardi) **19**:77
You Tell Me (Rosen) **45**:130
You Two (Ure) **34**:176
You Win Some, You Lose Some (Ure) **34**:176
You'll Soon Grow into Them, Titch (Hutchins) **20**:152
The Young Ardizzone: An Autobiographical Fragment (Ardizzone) **3**:8
Young Booker: Booker T. Washington's Early Days (Bontemps) **6**:84
Young Faces in Fashion (Epstein and Epstein) **26**:53
Young Ghosts (Cohen) **43**:38
Young Jim: The Early Years of James Weldon Johnson (Tarry) **26**:215
Young Joe (Ormerod) **20**:179
Young Kangaroo (Brown) **10**:65
The Young Landlords (Myers) **4**:159
Young Man from the Piedmont: The Youth of Thomas Jefferson (Wibberley) **3**:232
Young Man in a Hurry: The Story of Cyrus W. Field (Latham) **50**:101
The Young Man of Cury and Other Poems (Causley) **30**:44
Young Martin's Promise (Myers) **35**:203
A Young Patriot: The American Revolution as Experienced by One Boy (Murphy) **53**:116
Young Paul Revere's Boston (Epstein and Epstein) **26**:61
The Young Performing Horse (Yeoman) **46**:178
A Young Person's Guide to Ballet (Streatfeild) **17**:199
Young Poet's Primer (Brooks) **27**:44-56
The Young Unicorns (L'Engle) **1**:134
The Young United States: 1783 to 1830 (Tunis) **2**:195
Your Body and How It Works (Lauber) **16**:114
Your Body's Defenses (Knight) **38**:116
Your Brain and How It Works (Zim) **2**:232
Your First Garden Book (Brown) **29**:7
Your Heart and How It Works (Zim) **2**:233
Your Immune System (Nourse) **33**:143
Your Insides (Cole) **40**:31
Your Mother Was a Neanderthal (Smith) **47**:206
Your Move, J.P.! (Lowry) **46**:41
Your New Potty (Cole) **40**:27
Your Skin and Mine (Showers) **6**:242
Your Stomach and Digestive Tract (Zim) **2**:233
You're Allegro Dead (Corcoran) **50**:29
You're Only Old Once! (Dr. Seuss) **53**:136
You're the Scaredy-Cat (Mayer) **11**:169
You're Thinking about Doughnuts (Rosen) **45**:137
Yours Turly, Shirley (Martin) **32**:204
The You-Two (Ure) **34**:176
Yuck! (Stevenson) **17**:162
Yum Yum (Ahlberg and Ahlberg) **18**:9
Yum, Yum (Dorros) **42**:66
Yummers (Marshall) **21**:68
Yummers Too: The Second Course (Marshall) **21**:181
Yunmi and Halmoni's Trip (Choi) **53**:50
Z for Zachariah (O'Brien) **2**:129
Zamani Goes to Market (Feelings and Feelings) **5**:105
Zampano's Performing Bear (Janosch) **26**:77
Zanu (Matas) **52**:78
Zaza's Big Break (McCully) **46**:64
The Zebra Wall (Henkes) **23**:129
Zebra's Hiccups (McKee) **38**:180
Zebulon Pike, Soldier and Explorer (Wibberley) **3**:233

Zed (Harris) **30**:122
Zed and the Monsters (Parish) **22**:164
Zeee (Enright) **4**:77
Zeely (Hamilton) **1**:106
Zel (Napoli) **51**:161
Zella, Zack, and Zodiac (Peet) **12**:208
Zeralda's Ogre (Ungerer) **3**:204
The Zero Stone (Norton) **50**:146
Zesty (McBratney) **44**:120
Zia (O'Dell) **16**:171
Zlateh the Goat and Other Stories (Singer) **1**:177
Zoo (McNaughton) **54**:55
Zoo Doings: Animal Poems (Prelutsky) **13**:171
A Zoo for Mister Muster (Lobel) **5**:163
The Zoo in My Garden (Nakatani) **30**:159
Zoo, Where Are You? (McGovern) **50**:111
Zoom at Sea (Wynne-Jones) **21**:229
Zoom Away (Wynne-Jones) **21**:229
Zozo (Rey) **5**:193
Zozo Flies a Kite (Rey and Rey) **5**:198
Zozo Gets a Medal (Rey) **5**:198
Zozo Goes to the Hospital (Rey and Rey) **5**:199
Zozo Learns the Alphabet (Rey) **5**:199
Zozo Rides a Bike (Rey) **5**:196
Zozo Takes a Job (Rey) **5**:196
The Zucchini Warriors (Korman) **25**:111

Title Index

ISBN 0-7876-2082-3

90000